T0140232

Lecture Notes in Artificial Intelligence 13013

Subseries of Lecture Notes in Computer Science

Series Editors

Randy Goebel
University of Alberta, Edmonton, Canada

Yuzuru Tanaka
Hokkaido University, Sapporo, Japan

Wolfgang Wahlster
DFKI and Saarland University, Saarbrücken, Germany

Founding Editor

Jörg Siekmann
DFKI and Saarland University, Saarbrücken, Germany

More information about this subseries at http://www.springer.com/series/1244

Xin-Jun Liu · Zhenguo Nie · Jingjun Yu ·
Fugui Xie · Rui Song (Eds.)

Intelligent Robotics and Applications

14th International Conference, ICIRA 2021
Yantai, China, October 22–25, 2021
Proceedings, Part I

 Springer

Editors
Xin-Jun Liu
Tsinghua University
Beijing, China

Zhenguo Nie
Tsinghua University
Beijing, China

Jingjun Yu
Beihang University
Beijing, China

Fugui Xie
Tsinghua University
Beijing, China

Rui Song
Shandong University
Shandong, China

ISSN 0302-9743   ISSN 1611-3349 (electronic)
Lecture Notes in Artificial Intelligence
ISBN 978-3-030-89094-0   ISBN 978-3-030-89095-7 (eBook)
https://doi.org/10.1007/978-3-030-89095-7

LNCS Sublibrary: SL7 – Artificial Intelligence

This Springer imprint is published by the registered company Springer Nature Switzerland AG
The registered company address is: Gewerbestrasse 11, 6330 Cham, Switzerland

Preface

With the theme "Make Robots Infinitely Possible", the 14th International Conference on Intelligent Robotics and Applications (ICIRA 2021) was held in Yantai, China, during October 22–25, 2021, and designed to encourage advancement in the field of robotics, automation, mechatronics, and applications. The ICIRA series aims to promote top-level research and globalize quality research in general, making discussions and presentations more internationally competitive and focusing on the latest outstanding achievements, future trends, and demands.

ICIRA 2021 was organized by Tsinghua University, co-organized by Beihang University, Shandong University, YEDA, Yantai University, and IFToMM China-Beijing, undertaken by the Tsingke+ Research Institute, and technically co-sponsored by Springer. On this occasion, three distinguished plenary speakers and 10 keynote speakers delivered their outstanding research works in various fields of robotics. Participants gave a total of 186 oral presentations and 115 poster presentations, enjoying this excellent opportunity to share their latest research findings.

The ICIRA 2021 proceedings cover over 17 research topics, with a total of 299 papers selected for publication in four volumes of Springer's Lecture Note in Artificial Intelligence. Here we would like to express our sincere appreciation to all the authors, participants, and distinguished plenary and keynote speakers. Special thanks are also extended to all members of the Organizing Committee, all reviewers for peer review, all staff of the conference affairs group, and all volunteers for their diligent work.

October 2021

Xin-Jun Liu
Zhenguo Nie
Jingjun Yu
Fugui Xie
Rui Song

Organization

Honorary Chair

Youlun Xiong   Huazhong University of Science and Technology, China

General Chair

Xin-Jun Liu   Tsinghua University, China

General Co-chairs

Rui Song	Shandong University, China
Zengguang Hou	Institute of Automation, CAS, China
Qinchuan Li	Zhejiang Sci-Tech University, China
Qinning Wang	Peking University, China
Huichan Zhao	Tsinghua University, China
Jangmyung Lee	Pusan National University, South Korea

Program Chair

Jingjun Yu   Beihang University, China

Program Co-chairs

Xin Ma	Shandong University, China
Fugui Xie	Tsinghua University, China
Wenguang Yang	Yantai University, China
Bo Tao	Huazhong University of Science and Technology, China
Xuguang Lan	Xi'an Jiatong University, China
Naoyuki Kubota	Tokyo Metropolitan University, Japan
Ling Zhao	Yantai YEDA, China

Publication Chair

Zhenguo Nie   Tsinghua University, China

Award Chair

Limin Zhu   Shanghai Jiao Tong University, China

Advisory Committee

Jorge Angeles	McGill University, Canada
Jianda Han	Shenyang Institute of Automation, CAS, China
Guobiao Wang	National Natural Science Foundation of China, China
Tamio Arai	University of Tokyo, Japan
Qiang Huang	Beijing Institute of Technology, China
Tianmiao Wang	Beihang University, China
Hegao Cai	Harbin Institute of Technology, China
Oussama Khatib	Stanford University, USA
Tianran Wang	Shenyang Institute of Automation, CAS, China
Tianyou Chai	Northeastern University, China
Yinan Lai	National Natural Science Foundation of China, China
Yuechao Wang	Shenyang Institute of Automation, CAS, China
Jie Chen	Tianjin University, China
Jangmyung Lee	Pusan National University, South Korea
Bogdan M. Wilamowski	Auburn University, USA
Jiansheng Dai	King's College London, UK
Zhongqin Lin	Shanghai Jiao Tong University, China
Ming Xie	Nanyang Technical University, Singapore
Zongquan Deng	Harbin Institute of Technology, China
Hong Liu	Harbin Institute of Technology, China
Yangsheng Xu	The Chinese University of Hong Kong, China
Han Ding	Huazhong University of Science and Technology, China
Honghai Liu	Harbin Institute of Technology, China
Huayong Yang	Zhejiang University, China
Xilun Ding	Beihang University, China
Shugen Ma	Ritsumeikan University, Japan
Jie Zhao	Harbin Institute of Technology, China
Baoyan Duan	Xidian University, China
Daokui Qu	SIASUN, China
Nanning Zheng	Xi'an Jiatong University, China
Xisheng Feng	Shenyang Institute of Automation, CAS, China
Min Tan	Institute of Automation, CAS, China
Xiangyang Zhu	Shanghai Jiao Tong University, China
Toshio Fukuda	Nagoya University, Japan
Kevin Warwick	Coventry University, UK

Contents – Part I

Sensors, Actuators, and Controllers for Soft and Hybrid Robots

Human-Centered Wearable Robotics

Hybrid System Modeling and Human-Machine Interface

Robotic Dexterous Manipulation

A Spatial Layout Method of Robots Relative to Operating Space Based on Its Flexible Workspace Simulation

Jianhua Wang[1,2], Longfei Li[1,2], Zhifeng Liu[1,2(✉)], Jingjing Xu[1,3], Congbin Yang[1,3], and Qiang Cheng[1,3]

[1] Institute of Advanced Manufacturing and Intelligent Technology, Beijing University of Technology, Beijing, China
lzf@bjut.edu.cn
[2] Beijing Key Laboratory of Advanced Manufacturing Technology, Beijing University of Technology, Beijing, China
[3] Mechanical Industry Key Laboratory of Heavy Machine Tool Digital Design and Testing, Beijing University of Technology, Beijing, China

Abstract. In modern work units, industrial robots have been widely utilized to perform various operations, like welding, assembly and carrying etc. Facing a fixed operating space, how to determine the initial standing pose of the robot has been a significant problem for real applications, which will largely affect the robotic flexibility to arrive operating targets. For this problem, this work presented a spatial layout method of the robot relative to the known operating space through the workspace simulation of the robot based on screw theory and Monte Carlo method. In this method, the feature of the robotic workspace is analyzed based on the simulation, based on which the workspace volume is modeled and optimized considering the size of the operating tool. During the layout, layout variables, including translation distances in three axial directions and the rotational angle about the z axis of the robotic origin base frame, are modeled relative to the known operating space. The effectiveness of the proposed method is validated using a simulation example. Results show that the flexible workspace of the robot can better contain the known operating space after the adjustment of the robotic standing pose. This method will provide an important theoretical foundation for the real layout of work units.

Keywords: Spatial layout · Workspace simulation · Monte Carlo method · Robotic flexibility · Work unit

1 Introduction

With the development of industrial automation, robots have been widely applied to transform the traditional work units into automatic production line in the industry filed, which leads to a problem about how to determine the initial standing pose of the robot according to its tasks. In most units, the equipment or working platform interacted with

© Springer Nature Switzerland AG 2021
X.-J. Liu et al. (Eds.): ICIRA 2021, LNAI 13013, pp. 3–13, 2021.
https://doi.org/10.1007/978-3-030-89095-7_1

the robot is inconvenient to move, such as CNC machine tool, it will be a significant work to guarantee the robotic flexibility to get operating points through the standing pose adjustment of the robot. It is significant to propose an efficient spatial layout method for industrial robots. Relate existing works include the analysis of the robotic workspace, which is an important foundation for the solution of the proposed problem, as well as the layout of the robot using theoretical methods.

Some researchers introduced the traditional Monte Carlo method to determine the distribution of spatial points reached by the robot, but this method has low precision on obtaining points located at the boundary. Xu et al. [1] proposed a modified method to more precisely describe each region by setting an accuracy threshold in the process of expansion based on the normal distribution. Other scholars [2] tried to plot and compute the robotic workspace through tracing the motion trajectory of the end effector based on simulation, which improved the execution efficiency of the solution. The Monte Carlo method has been widely used to analyze the robotic workspace by generating point clouds that the robotic end effector can reach in the task space.

Except for the robotic workspace solution, researchers also focused on the analysis of the robotic flexibility. The robotic flexibility plays an important guiding role in the research of robot selection, scale synthesis, trajectory planning and obstacle avoidance [3]. Gotlih [4] described the operability of discrete points of the workspace based on the velocity anisotropy at each point. Jian [5] and Ma [6] analyzed the flexible workspace based on the concept of service sphere, based on which the machining path of the robot can be selected.

For the layout of the robot, almost existing studies are all presented based on optimizations with single or multiple objectives [7–10]. For example, Aly et al. [7] optimized the standing pose of the robot relative to the machine using genetic algorithm based on the calculation of the workspace. Zhuo [8] used a modified particle swarm optimization algorithm to optimize the robotic cellular layout by taking improving work efficiency as the evaluation objective.

In summary, methods based on optimization can better solve the robotic layout, but have lower efficiency due to iterations during the optimization. To overcome this drawback, a novel layout method is proposed based on screw theory and Monte Carlo method through workspace simulation, for which the layout problem is not converted into an iterative optimization problem but is simplified as a simple matrix transformation problem of two poses, which are utilized to describe the robotic workspace and its task space, respectively.

2   Kinematics Analysis Based on Screw Theory

In this work the screw theory is used to obtain inverse kinematics (IK) solutions of the robot to improve the whole execution efficiency of the proposed layout method. And three Paden-Kahan sub-problems [11] can provide the solution method based on screw method. The forward kinematics (FK) of the robot is the mapping from angular displacements in joint space to the end-effector pose in workspace. With the known angles $\theta_i (1 \leq i \leq 6)$, the FK can be expressed as follows,

$$\mathbf{g}_{st}(\theta) = \exp(\hat{\xi}_1\theta_1) \exp(\hat{\xi}_2\theta_2) \cdots \exp(\hat{\xi}_6\theta_6)\mathbf{g}_{st}(0) \tag{1}$$

Where $\mathbf{g}_{st}(\theta)$ and $\mathbf{g}_{st}(0)$ means the robotic target pose and initial pose, respectively, $\hat{\xi}$ means the twist coordinate.

The IK of the robot aims to work out angular displacements of joints when the robotic target pose is given. Using the idea of Paden-Kahan sub-problem, the complex motion is decomposed into several simple motions for the step-by-step solution [12, 13], and the six joint angles are obtained. According to the literature [14], the inverse solution in joint space under a fixed Cartesian pose of the end effector might have two, four and eight groups of solutions (Fig. 1).

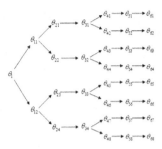

Fig. 1. Possible solution sets of the robotic kinematics

3   Workspace Optimization and Layout of the Six-DOFs Robot

3.1   Workspace Optimization of the Six-DOFs Robot

Due to the large size of the real end-effector, it can more easily collide with the workspace and mechanical arms of the robotic body during the motion process [15], which means that the end-effector size cannot be ignored as calculating its workspace. Based on angular ranges of all robotic joints, the Monte Carlo method is used to generate N groups of angular values for each joint randomly as follows,

$$\theta_i = \theta_{i\,\min} + (\theta_{i\,\max} - \theta_{i\,\min})x_j \tag{2}$$

where θ_i denotes random joint angles, $\theta_{i\,\min}$ and $\theta_{i\,\max}$ denote the minimum and maximum of joint angles, respectively. $x_j \in [0, 1]$ [0,1] is a random number. The algorithm of the numerical simulation based on Monte Carlo method is shown in the following table.

Algorithm: the numerical simulation based on Monte Carlo method
1. Input l_i and θ_i
2. Calculate θ via Eq. (2)
3. Calculate forward space of robot via Eq. (1)
4. Calculate num via IK
5. Judge whether reach maximum N
6. Output the cloud pictures

Note: where l_i denotes the dimension parameters for robot model.

When the robotic end pose is given, the number of effective IK solutions under this pose is studied to evaluate the robotic kinematic flexibility [16]. However, considering the limitation of the robotic structure, some IK solutions are invalid for the real robotic operation, which means that they must be eliminated when the robotic kinematic flexibility is evaluated. The number of exact IK solutions can be taken to represent the robotic kinematic flexibility of reaching one certain target pose, and the robotic kinematic flexibility is divided into two levels: the high level that there exist eight IK solutions, and the low level with four IK solutions. To improve the kinematic dexterity of the real robotic motion, the workspace with the high level of flexibility is considered to determine the layout of the robot relative to operation targets.

Based on point clouds obtained the above simulation, the workspace of the 6 DOFs robot is irregular but more approximate to an annular ellipsoid. In order to describe it conveniently, the robotic workspace can be enveloped using an ellipsoid called space 2, when only considering reachable poses of the real end effector with the high level of flexibility. However, the actual robotic workspace should remove the area composed of collision points for safety reasons. According to the geometric feature of the robotic base, it can be enveloped by an ellipsoid at the robotic base, which is called space 1 in the following. Finally, the real robotic workspace can be similarly described using an annular ellipsoid.

To consider the influence of the size of the real end effector, in this work the robotic workspace can be maximized by taking the size of the operating device as the variable, and the requirement of the device's structure as the optimization constraint. To represent the size of the robotic workspace, its boundary points are extracted by the method of reduction dimensions. Also, since the internal hollow is a fixed 3D region, the optimization objective only considers the volume size V of the ellipsoid enveloped by space 2 during the optimization. The detailed calculation steps of the volume based on the idea of the finite element analysis are as follows:

(1) To simplify the calculation of the volume V, the ellipsoid is firstly divided into k layers along z axis of the robotic base coordinate system. The height of each layer is determined by $h = (Z_{max} - Z_{min})/k$, where Z_{max} and Z_{min} denote the maximum and minimum values in z axis of the workspace. Also, the body is divided into m columns in y axis. The size of each column is determined by $\varepsilon = (Y_{max} - Y_{min})/m$.

(2) Based on the above division, boundary points of each row can be located by searching for the maximum and minimum values of x coordinates of all spatial points located on each row. Using this method, all boundary points located on the ellipsoidal workspace can be obtained finally.

Through the above steps, the workspace is described using series of spatial points located on the ellipsoidal surface, so that the equation of the boundary surface can be expressed using the parametric equation of the ellipsoid, $\frac{(x-x_0)^2}{a^2} + \frac{(y-y_0)^2}{b^2} + \frac{(z-z_0)^2}{c^2} = 1$, wherein parameters can be determined by the least square method. In this method, parameters can be determined by minimizing with the value of the objective f defined by follows,

$$f = \sum \left| \sqrt{\frac{(x_i - x_0)^2}{a^2} + \frac{(y_i - y_0)^2}{b^2} + \frac{(z_i - z_0)^2}{c^2}} - 1 \right| \tag{3}$$

Then based on the fitted equation of the boundary, the volume of the workspace can be calculated. Finally, the robotic workspace can be obtained by maximizing the value of the volume V through searching for the optimal size X of the real end effector, considering bounds of the size X_{min}, X_{max} determined by the real requirement of the robotic structure.

3.2 Layout of the Six-DOFs Robot

The operating workspace of the robot can be described by a spatial cuboid with sizes determined by the working platform or the collaborative machine of the robot, and herein it is defined by the space 3. For the ease of determining the layout of the robot relative to the operating space, the robotic workspace is divided into two parts using the yoz coordinate plane of the robotic base coordinate system, which are named by subspace R-1 and R-2, respectively. In real settings, we mostly want the operating space is located at the forward area of the robot, which can reduce the energy assumption as well as speedup the working efficiency due to the shortened motion path. Therefore, in this work the mathematical problem of the robotic layout is how to make the subspace R-1 and the operating space 3. Moreover, in practical applications, the robot can be re-located with translation motions along three coordinated directions of the world coordinate system and the rotation motion around z axis. Therefore, in this section motion variables including the translation displacements x, y, z and the rotating angle α are modeled to solve this problem (Fig. 2).

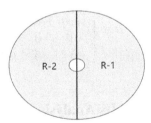

Fig. 2. $z = 0$ plane on space 2.

To model these variables, the origin robotic base coordinate system is firstly taken as the world coordinate system. For the proposed problem, the unknowns are calculated based on the given robotic parameters, as well as locations of spaces R-1 and 3 in the world coordinate system. In the modeling, two frames are established for two spaces to represent their relative pose as shown in Fig. 3. For the coordinate system of the space R-1, three unit directional vectors V_{21}, V_{22}, V_{23} of the coordinate system for the space

2 have the same directions with three coordinate axes of the robotic base coordinate system, respectively. And the location of its center can be determined by follows,

$$x_c = \frac{\sum V_i x_i}{V}, \quad y_c = \frac{\sum V_i y_i}{V}, \quad z_c = \frac{\sum V_i z_i}{V} \tag{4}$$

Where x_c, y_c, z_c means the central location coordinate of the space 2.

The coordinate system of the space 3 is built at the center of the spatial cuboid. And its unit directional vectors V_{31}, V_{32}, V_{33} are defined based on the desired pose of the coordinate system of the space 2, under which pose the robotic workspace can better envelop the operating space.

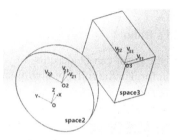

Fig. 3. The definitions of space 2 and 3. O_2 and O_3 are the coordinate vectors of the origin of the coordinate system of space 2 and 3 relative to the world coordinate system respectively.

Based on two frames, poses of spaces 2 and 3 can be expressed by matrices $A = \begin{bmatrix} V_{21} & V_{22} & V_{23} & O2 \\ 0 & 0 & 0 & 1 \end{bmatrix}$ and $B = \begin{bmatrix} V_{31} & V_{32} & V_{33} & O3 \\ 0 & 0 & 0 & 1 \end{bmatrix}$, respectively. Then the motion variables of the robotic pose adjustment can be solved through the calculation of the conversion matrix from the matrix A to B as follows,

$$X = A^{-1}B = \begin{bmatrix} \cos\theta & -\sin\theta & 0 & x \\ \sin\theta & \cos\theta & 0 & y \\ 0 & 0 & 1 & z \\ 0 & 0 & 0 & 1 \end{bmatrix} \tag{5}$$

4   Simulation Example and Its Analysis

The 6-DOFs robot (KUKA KR16) with the bolt-tightening device mounted at its end effector is taken as the research object, as shown in Fig. 4. Firstly, the robotic workspace is obtained using the simulation based on Monte Carlo method. In this simulation, the initial pose of the robotic real end effector is given by follows,

$$g_{st}(0) = \begin{bmatrix} 1 & 0 & 0 & 815+d \\ 0 & 1 & 0 & 0 \\ 0 & 0 & 1 & 1450-L \\ 0 & 0 & 0 & 1 \end{bmatrix} \tag{6}$$

wherein d and L denote the width and length of the bolt tightening device, which determine its size and affect the volume of the robotic workspace, since L can be adjusted according to the length of the motor used to tighten the bolt, but d has very small allowable range due to the limitation of the thickness of the connecting plate due to the robotic rated load, in the following, the robotic workspace will be optimized by taking the value of L as the variable.

Fig. 4. 3D model of the six-DOFs robot with the bolt tightening device

Figure 5 shows the cloud pictures of the robotic workspace under the case that, $d = 0$, as well as projections of the workspace on coordinate planes xoy, xoz and yoz of the base frame. In these cloud pictures, locations of the end effector corresponding to 8 and 4 groups of exact inverse solutions are drawn by blue points and red points, respectively. As introduced in the above, the workspace formed by blue points has the higher degree of the robotic kinematic flexibility.

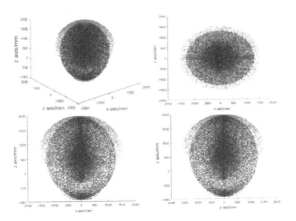

Fig. 5. Robotic workspace

From Fig. 5, we can conclude that spatial blue points are densely distributed surrounding the robotic base and formed an ellipsoidal space, but red points are scattered and mostly concentrated at the upper edge region of the ellipsoidal space. Therefore, the ellipsoidal space with higher flexibility of the robot is considered in the layout of the robot relative to the operating space, due to the irregular distribution feature of red spatial points, which will lead to the difficulty of the volume calculation of the robotic workspace. Moreover, ranges in three coordinate directions are (-1200,1200), (-1200,1200) and (-900,1800), respectively.

Then, based on the volume calculation of the workspace as presented in Sect. 3.1, the workspace is optimized considering the size of the bolt-tightening device. With the requirement of the structure, the allowable range of L is taken by $300 \leq L \leq 500$ mm. Figure 6 shows the relation between the volume V and the size L, which indicates that the volume increases with the change of the size in general, but has small falling fluctuations during the increase, and the largest falling value reaches to 0.68 m^3. From this relation, we can conclude that the maximum value of the volume is 18.74 m^3 when the size is taken by 488 mm.

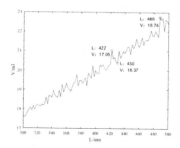

Fig. 6. Relation between the volume V and the size L

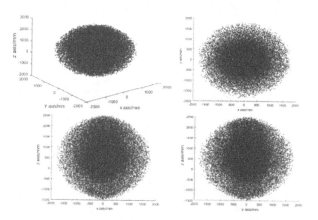

Fig. 7. The bolt-tightening robotic flexible workspace

Cloud pictures of the ellipsoidal workspace are given in Fig. 7, wherein ranges in three coordinate directions are (-1600,1600), (-1600,1600) and (-1300,2300), respectively. The fitted equation of the ellipsoidal surface of the workspace can be expressed by $\frac{x^2}{1580^2} + \frac{y^2}{1580^2} + \frac{(z-477.5)^2}{1792^2} = 1$. Also, considering the robotic base, the space around the base is expressed by a sphere with the radius 300 mm, which can better envelop the base structure. Then using Eq. (5), the center of the frame of the robotic workspace can be calculated as (535.9,0,500). Therefore, the matrix A can be obtained as $\begin{bmatrix} 1 & 0 & 0 & 535.9 \\ 0 & 1 & 0 & 0 \\ 0 & 0 & 1 & 500 \\ 0 & 0 & 0 & 1 \end{bmatrix}$.

To simulate the layout of the robot relative to the operating space, the matrix B for the space 3 is taken by $\begin{bmatrix} 0.866 & -0.5 & 0 & 1200 \\ 0.5 & 0.866 & 0 & -450 \\ 0 & 0 & 1 & 800 \\ 0 & 0 & 0 & 1 \end{bmatrix}$.

Using Eq. (5), the conversion matrix between two frames can be computed as $X = \begin{bmatrix} 0.866 & -0.5 & 0 & 551.5392 \\ 0.5 & 0.866 & 0 & -824.4 \\ 0 & 0 & 1 & 300 \\ 0 & 0 & 0 & 1 \end{bmatrix}$, from which translation displacements in three axial directions and the rotational angle about the z axis can be determined. To further validate the effectiveness for the proposed method, the simulation based on the result is performed in software PQArt. In this simulation, the robot initially stands under the origin pose, and the operating space is represented by a box with the pose determined by the real environment. According to the calculated conversion matrix X, the robotic pose is adjusted by the calibration function in PQArt software. After the adjustment of the robotic pose, the ellipsoidal space can completely contain the operating space, as shown in Fig. 8, which indicates that based on the proposed method, the robotic end effector can flexibly reach to all spatial points within the operating space.

Before the movement   After the movement

Fig. 8. Relative poses between the robot and the operating space before and after the movement

In previous methods, the DH conversion is always used to describe the robotic motion and do the layout optimization. In order to validate the efficiency, execution times of the screw-based method (the proposed method) under different refinement sizes are compared with that based on DH-conversion-based method (the previous method). And in the simulation, the same group of experiments were run for many times and the average value was calculated. After each operation, all variables and random numbers were cleared and regenerated. Under the different numbers of random points, the running time data of the two methods are shown in Table 1. The computer environment of this experiment is: CPU (dual-core 1.80 GHz), RAM (4.0GB), and Windows 10.

The comparison of the operation time based on the two methods is completed to show the advantage of the modified method, which is shown in Table 1. As the number of random points increases, the value of p/m also increases, indicating that the modified method has more obvious advantages.

Table 1. The running time data of the two methods.

number	10000		20000		50000		100000	
method	P	M	P	M	P	M	P	M
1	21.065	0.824	40.726	1.383	103.023	2.919	200.718	5.761
2	20.891	0.912	40.697	1.367	103.604	2.757	201.213	5.541
3	21.437	0.841	40.44	1.427	101.873	3.168	203.192	5.774
4	20.571	0.754	40.21	1.325	102.75	3.049	202.547	5.514
5	20.998	0.797	41.426	1.365	101.339	2.821	204.112	5.553
average	20.992	0.826	40.670	1.373	102.518	2.943	202.356	5.629
P/M	25.415		29.621		34.835		35.949	

Note: P = previous method, M = modified method

5 Conclusion and Future Work

In this work, the layout method of the robot relative to the operating space is presented through the robotic workspace simulation based on screw theory and Monte Carlo method. In the simulation, the volume of the workspace is modelled and maximized considering the size of the real end effector. During the layout, translation displacements in three axial directions and the rotational angle about the z axis of the origin base frame are finally modelled to guarantee the robotic kinematic flexibility on end-effector targets within the operating space. From the simulation example, we can conclude that the workspace volume largely increases with the larger size of real end effector in general, but there still exist many small fluctuations, and the robotic layout relative the known operating space can be obtained based on the proposed method considering the robotic motion flexibility in real applications. Simulation results indicate that in real applications the structure of the operating tool needs to be well designed to obtain a larger robotic workspace, and the operating standing pose of the robot needs to be well adjusted according to the working environment, which can finally improve the robotic dexterity and help the operating path planning of the robot with high efficiency and low energy consumption.

Actually, environmental obstacles will largely reduce the real workspace of the robot, and finally affect the layout of the work unit. In the future work, we will further study the robotic layout relative to the operating space considering the influence of obstacles existed in the working environment.

Acknowledgement. This work was supported by National Natural Science Foundation of China (51805012); National Science and Technology Major Project (2018ZX04032002); Beijing Postdoctoral Foundation Class A of China(No. Q6001211202101 and No. 6001211202102); Beijing Nova Programme Interdisciplinary Cooperation Project (Z191100001119010).

References

1. Xu, Z.B., et al.: Improvement of Monte Carlo method for robot workspace solution and volume calculation. Opt. Precis. Eng. **26**(11), 2703–2713 (2018)
2. Zhao, Y., et al.: A method for solving robot workspace based on Matlab. Mech. Sci. Technol. Aerosp. Eng. **28**(12), 1657–1661 (2009)
3. Wagner, M., et al.: Reachability analysis for cooperative processing with industrial robots. In: 2017 22nd IEEE International Conference on Emerging Technologies and Factory Automation (ETFA), Limassol, pp. 1–6 (2017)
4. Gotlih, K., et al.: Velocity anisotropy of an industrial robot. Robot. Comput. Integr. Manuf. **27**(1), 205–211 (2011)
5. Jian, Y.Y.: Working space and dexterity analysis and application for 6-DOF industrial robots. Ph.D. thesis, Huazhong University of Science and Technology (2015)
6. Ma, R.R., Zhang, H.H.: The analysis and research on dexterity of 6R type arc welding robot based on flexibility. J. Changchun Univ. Sci. Technol. (Nat. Sci. Edn.). **37**(05), 64–68 (2014)
7. Aly, M.F., Abbas, A.T., Megahed, S.M.: Robot workspace estimation and base placement optimisation techniques for the conversion of conventional work cells into autonomous flexible manufacturing systems. Int. J. Comput. Integr. Manuf. **23**(12), 1133–1148 (2010)
8. Zhuo H.L..: The optimization of robotic cellular layout by the improved practical swarm optimization algorithm. Ph.D. thesis, Huazhong University of Science and Technology (2017)
9. Kats, V., Lei, L., Levner, E.: Minimizing the cycle time of multiple-product processing networks with a fixed operation sequence, setups, and time-window constraints. Eur. J. Oper. Res. **187**(3), 1196–1211 (2008)
10. Alim, A.M., et al.: Robot workcell layout optimization using firefly algorithm. In: Swarm Evolutionary and Memetic Computing, pp. 188–200 (2015)
11. Xu, J.J., et al.: Models for three new screwbased IK sub-problems using geometric descriptions and their applications. Appl. Math. Model. **67**(1), 399–412 (2018)
12. Sariyildiz, E.: A new formulation method for solving kinematic problems of multiarm robot systems using quaternion algebra in the screw theory framework. Turk. J. Electr. Eng. Comput. Sci. **20**(4), 607–628 (2012)
13. Chen, Q., et al.: Improved inverse kinematics algorithm using screw theory for a six-DOF robot manipulator. Int. J. Adv. Robot. Syst. **12**(10), 140 (2015)
14. He, J.W., Ping, X.L., Li, Z.Y., Jiang, Y.: Research and application of the solving method for robotic workspace. J. Mech. Transm. **39**(10), 68–71 (2015)
15. Fu, B., et al.: The solution of robot manipulator's collision free workspace based on Monte Carlo method. Mod. Mach. Tool Autom. Manuf. Techn. **2**(2), 16–19 (2016)
16. Bi, Z.M.: Analysis and synthesis of robotic posture space. Mech. Sci. Technol. **15**(1), 11–16 (1996)

Hand Posture Reconstruction Through Task-Dependent Hand Synergies

Bingchen Liu, Li Jiang, and Shaowei Fan[(✉)]

State Key Laboratory of Robotics and System, Harbin Institute of Technology, Harbin 150080,
China
fansw@hit.edu.cn

Abstract. Currently, the propose of postural synergies theory has made great
contribution to analysis of human hand function. However, most studies ignored
the hand synergy patterns varying in different kinds of grasping tasks. Therefore,
a set of task-dependent hand synergies was proposed in this paper. Firstly, a functional hand movement dataset was established, and "The GRASP Taxonomy"
proposed by Thomas Feix was chosen as the experimental paradigm. Then, in
order to extract specific coordination strategy in similar tasks, these 33 kinds of
grasp types were clustered into six groups. Next, Principal Components Analysis
(PCA) was separately applied on each cluster of tasks instead of the whole dataset
to get task-dependent hand synergies. Finally, the postural reconstruction error
was used as evaluation indicator for comparing the accuracy of synergy model
proposed in this paper and previous invariant synergy model. The results showed
that the mean joint reconstruction error in this improved model has been reduced
by 63.98% using the same number of hand synergies, verifying the necessity of
adjusting synergy strategy according to task requirement.

Keywords: Grasp taxonomy · Cluster analysis · Hand synergy · Principal
Component Analysis · Rehabilitation

1 Introduction

The human hand plays a crucial role in performing activities of daily living. Although
the hand contains 19 articulations, 31 muscles and more than 23 degrees of freedom
(DOFs), it can still complete grasping tasks and dexterous manipulation of diverse
objects with ease [1]. Analyzing hand movement function is of great significance in
several fields like rehabilitation, prosthetics and robotics [2]. For better understanding
the autonomous grasping ability of the hand, researchers attempted to describe it from
hierarchical taxonomy on task level and motor control principle on neural level.

Organizing various grasping tasks into a hierarchical taxonomy can help us understand how our hands interact with different objects more clearly. In 1956, Napier et al.
initially divided the grasping behavior into power grasp and precision grasp tasks [3], and
this conclusion has influenced most of afterwards research. On this basis, Cutkosky et al.
proposed several analytic grasp measures like manipulability, isotropy, compliance and

© Springer Nature Switzerland AG 2021
X.-J. Liu et al. (Eds.): ICIRA 2021, LNAI 13013, pp. 14–24, 2021.
https://doi.org/10.1007/978-3-030-89095-7_2

other parameters, then organized 16 extended kinds of grasp patterns into a hierarchical tree according to these measures [4]. Focusing on dexterous manipulation, Bullock et al. gave a common hand-centric and motion-centric manipulation classification, and in their study a certain complex task was decomposed into simpler stages [5]. More recently, Feix et al. generated a comprehensive human grasp taxonomy including 33 unique prehensile grasp types, while considering grasp types, opposition types, virtual fingers and so on [6].

At the same time, researchers attempted to clarify the principal control patterns on the neural mechanisms of kinesiology. It is generally acknowledged that the brain relies on kinematic synergy to cope with the abundancy of the degrees of freedom (DoFs) and simplify the motion generation [7]. While, the postural synergies in hand kinematics was first proposed by Santello et al. in 1998 [8]. They recorded 15 joint angles while performing virtual grasping, and applied Principal Components Analysis (PCA) on analysis of joint collaborative properties. The result showed that two main principal components (hand synergies) could already account for more than 80% of the overall variation. In order to get more accurate postural synergies, researchers further expanded the sample size of database and increased the complexity of the experimental paradigm [9]. Néstor et al. established the largest publicly available dataset including hand kinematic data of 77 subjects, performing up to 20 hand grasps. Twelve synergies were extracted by them and the first three synergies were used as primary synergies, while remaining ones targeted on finer movements [10]. Besides, in order to increase the adaptability for various task, the different relative positions between human hand and objects were also considered in experimental paradigm design [11]. Bicchi et al. combined the movement synergies with the flexibility properties of human hand, then proposed a soft synergies theory [12].

Although many breakthroughs have been made in analysis of hand movement function, some fundamental questions remain open. On one hand, the grasp taxonomy is obtained by finding the largest set of distinct grasps from observing pictures or videos by experience, so the classification result was subjective [13]. On the other hand, some recent studies showed that the central nervous system (CNS) generates muscular activity or hand movement through specific synergy patterns for certain task [14], but most research did not consider the variety of synergy patterns in different tasks. Therefore, combing grasp taxonomy and hand synergy theory can overcome these limitations. The benchmark of task similarity provides a quantitative basis for grasp taxonomy, while grasp taxonomy provides task requirements for extracting specific hand synergies.

In this paper, a set of task-dependent hand synergies was proposed, giving a comprehensive and quantitative description on hand movement function. Experimental paradigm was designed according to "The GRASP Taxonomy" proposed by Thomas Feix [7], movement of 5 right-handed healthy participants while performing 33 grasp movements were recorded. Then, in order to obtain the hand synergies for specific tasks, these 33 types of grasp movements were clustered into 6 groups according to their similarity through hierarchical cluster analysis, thus the hand synergies were extracted from specific tasks instead of the whole dataset. Finally, to verify the feasibility of this model, posture reconstruction accuracy through these task-dependent synergies and former invariant hand synergies was compared. The results showed that the mean joint reconstruction error had been greatly reduced.

2 Experiment Description

2.1 Participants

Five healthy subjects (22 ~ 28 years old, 4 men and 1 woman, among which all right-handed) volunteered to participate in this experiment. All participants were in good health and reported no history of neurological or motor disorders. This study analyzed on dexterity of human hand in healthy subjects and the experimental procedure was approved by the "institutional review board (IRB)" of Harbin Institute of Technology, Harbin, P. R. China. Before the experiment, all subjects provided informed consent, including the purpose and time required the whole experiment and the experimental procedure in detail. All participants signed the informed consent after they agree to the voluntary participation request.

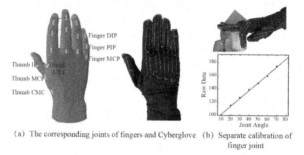

(a) The corresponding joints of fingers and Cyberglove   (b) Separate calibration of finger joint

Fig. 1. The joints measured in this study and the calibration method of sensors in CyberGlove

2.2 Apparatus and Experimental Procedure

In order to record human hand movement data and evaluate the postural reconstruction accuracy with hand synergies, a recording and reconstruction system of hand grasping postures was established. The system was consisted of three modules: human hand posture data acquisition device, data processing software, and human hand synergies extraction and posture reconstruction interface. In this study, CyberGlove III (Cyber Glove Systems LLC, USA) was used to record the finger joint values during the experiment at a resolution of $< 1°$ and sampled at 100 Hz. Then, the raw joint angle data would be calibrated and filtered on a self-developed C+ + software. Finally, the hand synergies model is obtained by multivariate analysis packages in R studio.

The hand kinematic model used in this study has been shown in Fig. 1, and a simple joint angle calibration method was applied according to [15].

In this section, the overall experimental procedure will be briefly introduced.

Subjects were shown a brief demonstration of the experimental procedure at first. Before the experiment, subjects had well practiced the 33 kinds of grasping movements to get familiar with them. Each subject was asked to perform reach-to-grasp task with proper object three times. The experimental environment and the chosen objects had been shown in the Fig. 2.

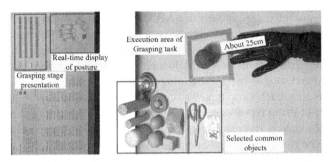

Fig. 2. Illustration of the preparation of experimental scene.

Besides, due to the hysteresis error of piezoelectric sensor, the reaction time and measurement accuracy of real angular value had been affected. In order to solve these problems, the raw output data was filtered and smoothed. Angular data were processed by a 2nd-order 2-way low-pass Butter-worth filter, while the band pass frequency was set at 60 Hz and stopband frequency was set at 200 Hz. Then, the smooth angular data are obtained from polynomial splines with terminal second-order constraints.

3   Hand Synergies Extraction

The extraction process of task-dependent hand synergies has been shown in Fig. 3, and the following statistical analyses were performed in detail:

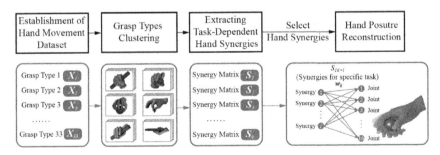

Fig. 3. The extraction process of task-dependent hand synergies.

3.1 Grasp Types Clustering

In order to give quantitative measures on grasp taxonomy and obtain hand synergies for specific tasks, 33 basic grasp types in "The Grasp Taxonomy" were clustered according to their similarity through a hierarchical cluster analysis. Since the firmly grasping posture can best reflect the intention of the task, the mean angular degrees during this phase were used in hierarchical cluster analysis.

In this study, AGglomerative NESting(AGNES) algorithm was applied and the hierarchical agglomerative clustering followed bottom-up approach. Before similarity calculation, all angular data should be normalized to [0,1] according to their range of movement. Then, pairwise distances (Mahalanobis distance) between two grasp types were calculated and used as basis of building the dendrograms.

At the beginning, each grasp type was considered as a single cluster. After that, two nearest clusters of grasp types were combined step by step according to their pairwise distances, until reaching the pre-selected number of clusters. The minimum pairwise distances between two clusters was calculated as follows

$$dist(\mathbf{x}_m, \mathbf{x}_n) = (\mathbf{x}_m - \mathbf{x}_n)^T \Sigma^{-1} (\mathbf{x}_m - \mathbf{x}_n) \tag{1}$$

$$d_{\min}(\mathbf{C}_i, \mathbf{C}_j) = \min_{\mathbf{x}_m \in \mathbf{C}_i, \mathbf{x}_n \in \mathbf{C}_J} dist(\mathbf{x}_m, \mathbf{x}_n) \tag{2}$$

In which $\mathbf{x}_m$ and $\mathbf{x}_n \in \mathbf{R}^{1 \times 16}$ represented the original grasp types vectors contain 16 dimensions joint angle data, m and n are ranging from 1 to N, where $N = 33$. Σ represented the covariance matrix of X. $\mathbf{C}_i$ and $\mathbf{C}_j$ represented the grasp type combination formed after clustering. The number of clusters should be the minimum number ensuring that no cluster contains multiple grasp types from the same subject. According to previous studies [16], the number of clusters was chosen to be 6 since further subdivision of the number of clusters may over-fit the movement data. While, further reducing the number of clusters may lead to too general results.

3.2 Task-Dependent Hand Synergies Extraction

Principal Components Analysis (PCA) is a typical dimension reduction technique derived from statistics, and it has been verified to be an effective method in extracting human kinematic synergies. The aim of PCA is to transform a large number of related variables $x_i \in \mathbf{R}^{1 \times 16}$ into few linearly uncorrelated variables $s_i \in \mathbf{R}^{1 \times l}(l < 16)$ called Principal Components (PCs), while preserving the original information as much as possible. Mathematical, PCs can be calculated as the eigenvectors of the covariance matrix of posture data

$$\Sigma = \mathbf{X}\mathbf{X}^T - \overline{\mathbf{X}\mathbf{X}} \tag{3}$$

where $\overline{\mathbf{X}}$ is the average posture matrix and the j row of $\overline{\mathbf{X}}$ is $\overline{\mathbf{x}}_{*,j} = \frac{1}{n} \sum_{i=1}^{n} x_{i,j}$.

When came to the description of hand kinematic, these vectors are typically called Postural Synergies [9]. Posture reconstruction with postural synergies is achieved by linear combination of these eigenvectors. Using the PCs corresponding to the largest l eigenvalues, a hand posture x_k can be approximated as presented in Eq. (4)

$$\tilde{\mathbf{x}}_k = \overline{\mathbf{x}} + \left[w_{k,1} \ w_{k,2} \ \cdots \ w_{k,l} \right]^T \begin{bmatrix} s_{1,1} & \cdots & s_{l,1} \\ \vdots & & \vdots \\ s_{1,16} & \cdots & s_{l,16} \end{bmatrix} \tag{4}$$

$\mathbf{w}_k = \left[w_{k,1} \ w_{k,2} \ \cdots \ w_{k,l} \right]^T$ represented the projection of original angular variables x_k to eigenvectors, then easy to get reconstruction error for any posture x_k.

$$\mathbf{x}_k^{err} = |\mathbf{x}_k - \tilde{\mathbf{x}}_k| \tag{5}$$

Different from previous studies, PCA was separately applied on specific cluster of tasks instead of the whole dataset. To evaluate the effectiveness of this method, we compared the average posture reconstruction error using task-dependent hand synergies and traditional invariant hand synergies.

4 Results and Discussion

4.1 Clustering Results of the GRASP Taxonomy

Figure 4 shows the hierarchical cluster result on 33 grasp types. Some clear similarities could be observed in each cluster:

Cluster I (named Cylinder Grasp) brings together activities #2, #3, #4, #5, #15, #16, #20, #23, #30 (small diameter, medium wrap, adducted thumb, light tool, fixed hood, lateral, writing tripod, abduction grip, palmar). This cluster contains maximum number of grasp types and grasp types in this cluster take high similarity. PIP and DIP joints have the highest mean value, and the bending amplitude of each finger are close. Besides, the inner adduction of the thumb is small, which is close to the natural relaxation position.

Cluster II (named Small Size Tripod Grasp) includes activities #7, #8, #14, #19, #25 (prismatic 3 finger, prismatic 2 finger, tripod, distal type, lateral tripod). Grasp types in this cluster both have high positive mean value for MCP and PIP joints, especially for MCP joints in thumb, index and middle finger. Besides, the thumb is adducted opposite to the palm. Most of the grasp types in this cluster are precision grasp, so only fingertips contact with the object.

Cluster III (named Large Size Tripod Grasp) includes activities #1, #11, #13, #26, #27, #28 (power, power sphere, precision sphere, sphere 4 finger, quadpod, sphere 3 finger). Grasp types in this cluster are quite similar with that in Cluster II, but the flexion of the thumb, index and middle fingers are smaller. Besides, in order to realize the envelope for larger size objects, a larger scale of palmar arch is needed, and both the digit pulp and the palm contact with the object.

Cluster IV (named Ring Pick) comprises activities #9, #24, #31, #33 (palmar pinch, tip pinch, ring, inferior pincer), in which are most precision grasp with thumb and index finger. This cluster has the highest negative mean value for palmar-thumb coordination (thumb moves outward to the palm), while the last three digits only bend naturally.

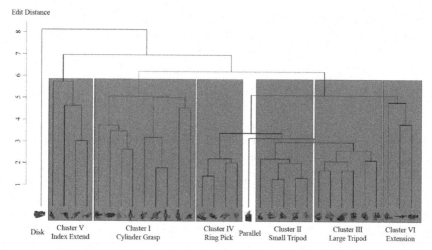

Fig. 4. The clustering results of the 33 grasp types in "The GRASP Taxonomy" proposed by Thomas Feix.

Cluster V (named Index Extension Type) includes activities #17, #21, #29, #32 (index finger extension, tripod variation, stick, ventral). The biggest difference between grasp types in this cluster and others is the high independence of index finger.

At last, Cluster VI (named Extension Grasp) combines activities #6, #12, and #18 (prismatic 4 finger, precision disk, extension type). Grasp types in this take higher mean value of MCP or DIP joints of index, middle and ring finger, and most of these tasks are precision grasp for larger size objects. While, power disk (activities #10) and parallel extension (activities #22) are not discussed here due to the large difference between these grasp and others.

4.2   Overall Dependencies Between Finger Joints

Calculation of correlation coefficient matrix Σ between finger joints is a prerequisite for extracting hand synergy patterns, and Pearson correlation coefficient between each two finger Joint A and Joint B can be presented as follow.

$$r_{JointA,JointB} = \frac{\sum_i (JointA_i - \overline{JointA})(JointB_i - \overline{JointB})}{\sqrt{\sum_i (JointA_i - \overline{JointA})^2} \sqrt{\sum_i (JointB_i - \overline{JointB})^2}} \qquad (6)$$

The full finger joint correlation matrix varying in 6 different clusters of tasks has been shown in Fig. 5. From the figure, it can be seen that the coordination relationship between finger joints varies in different clusters of tasks. The relevance of same joint (MCP/PIP&DIP) in last three fingers are quite high and relatively stable during different tasks, but the synergy strategy of thumb and index finger is optimized according to specific tasks. Following these rules, a task-dependent hand synergy patterns could be extracted, and the contribution coefficients of joints to hand synergies should be further determined in accordance with appropriate task.

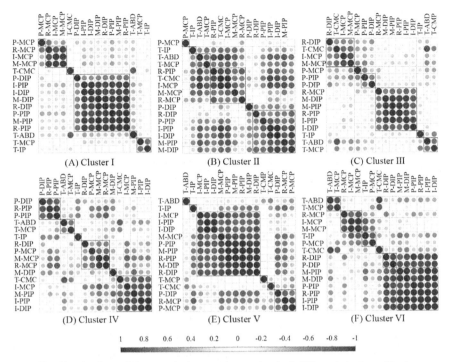

Fig. 5. The finger joint correlation matrix varying in 6 different clusters of tasks.

4.3 The Joint Contribution to Task-Dependent Hand Synergies

In Table 1, 3 sets of hand synergies respectively extracted from specific tasks have been shown, and the variance each PC accounted were also displaced (for the sake of space, only the first three hand synergies in Cluster I, II, and IV were shown as representative samples). Besides, the estimated PCs which had the biggest correlations with the original joint variables were shown in bold. The results showed that five PCs could already account for 98.44% of total variance on average, and the first three were responsible for 90.34% of the variance.

For Cylinder Grasp, the main effect of the first-order hand synergy is reverse movement of MCP and PIP joints of last four fingers. While the second-order hand synergy is responsible for bending of thumb and MCP and PIP joints of last two fingers. Besides, the third-order hand synergy could be mainly regarded as compensation for thumb, index and little finger movement. The role of hand synergies in Large Size Tripod Grasp is similar to Cylinder Grasp. The difference is that the first-order hand synergy has more obvious control effect on the thumb but less effect on the back two fingers, while the second-order hand synergy mainly actuated the movement of thumb IP joint.

In Tripod Grasp, the first-order hand synergy controls the movement of thumb MCP joint and index PIP joint. Then, the second-order hand synergy dominant the movement of thumb IP joint and middle finger MCP and PIP joint, ring finger also occurred synergistic movement due to the high correlation between ring and middle finger. Lastly, the third-order hand synergy can be seemed as compensation movement for thumb. Ring Pick has

Table 1. Correlations of the PCs with the original variables in Cluster I, II, and IV

Original variables		Estimated PCs								
		Cluster I			Cluster II			Cluster IV		
Digit	Joint	PC_1	PC_2	PC_3	PC_1	PC_2	PC_3	PC_1	PC_2	PC_3
Thumb	CMC	−0.04	0.47	**−0.64**	**0.46**	−0.05	0.39	−0.14	0.09	**−0.37**
	ABD	0.06	**−0.30**	0.07	**−0.12**	−0.01	0.10	−0.09	0.07	**0.16**
	MCP	−0.04	0.07	**−0.13**	0.01	**−0.08**	0.03	−0.19	**0.34**	0.18
	IP	−0.14	**0.38**	−0.33	−0.01	0.20	**−0.64**	−0.13	**−0.71**	0.38
Index	MCP	**−0.29**	0.10	0.20	**0.27**	−0.05	−0.06	**−0.62**	−0.23	−0.55
	PIP	0.28	0.31	**0.32**	**0.49**	0.12	0.10	**−0.42**	−0.03	0.27
	DIP	**0.23**	0.16	0.11	**0.25**	0.15	−0.11	**−0.36**	−0.10	0.14
Middle	MCP	**−0.32**	0.15	0.23	−0.18	**−0.36**	−0.13	**−0.29**	0.27	0.13
	PIP	**0.35**	0.14	0.09	0.22	**0.42**	−0.19	−0.10	0.05	**0.13**
	DIP	**0.21**	0.10	0.03	0.23	0.25	**−0.32**	−0.02	0.03	**0.14**
Ring	MCP	**−0.42**	0.26	0.19	0.19	**−0.54**	−0.32	−0.20	**0.34**	−0.13
	PIP	**0.37**	0.26	0.11	0.40	**−0.41**	−0.20	−0.11	0.28	**0.34**
	DIP	**0.18**	0.11	0.01	0.06	0.11	**−0.15**	−0.02	0.00	**−0.05**
Little	MCP	−0.29	0.33	**0.39**	0.15	**−0.22**	0.03	**−0.27**	0.03	0.22
	PIP	0.21	**0.29**	0.18	0.20	0.11	**0.28**	−0.05	**0.18**	0.11
	DIP	**0.10**	0.08	0.07	**0.05**	0.02	0.03	0.00	0.04	**0.09**
Explained variance(%)		45.69	22.58	12.95	49.22	27.32	10.78	51.89	28.96	15.62

much in common with Tripod Grasp as they were both precision grasps. PC1 responsible for the index finger movement independently, while PC2 makes the thumb, middle finger and ring finger move together.

Index Extension Type could be regarded as a differentiation of Extension Grasp, movement form of these two kinds of grasp were relatively simple and close to the average grasping posture. Using two sets of hand synergies can already reproduce the posture accurately. In first-order hand synergy, the PIP and DIP joints of last four fingers complete the envelope motion, and the second-order hand synergy is responsible for the adjustment movement of MCP and PIP (IP) joints of thumb and index finger. The difference between these two tasks is that the movement direction of some joints was different.

In fact, the effect of traditional invariant hand synergies on finger joints were most similar with the task-dependent hand synergies extracted from Cylinder Grasp. In Fig. 6, the posture reconstruction error when using 3, 4, 5 sets of hand synergies with these two methods were separately shown. Obviously, the increase in the number of hand synergies leads to the reduction of reconstruction error. Besides, it can be seen that the reconstruction error of MCP joints were on a high side, that may be because MCP joints are more important in posture adjustment. It is worth noting that the joint reconstruction error has been greatly reduced when using task-dependent hand synergies, and the reconstruction error with two sets of task-dependent hand synergies is equivalent to that of five sets of invariant hand synergies. At the same time, Fig. 6 (b) shows that the reconstruction error is relatively stable in all kinds of tasks, except slightly higher in Cluster I.

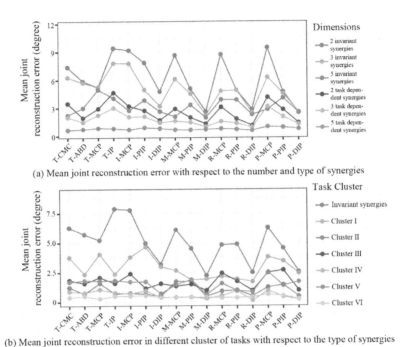

(a) Mean joint reconstruction error with respect to the number and type of synergies

(b) Mean joint reconstruction error in different cluster of tasks with respect to the type of synergies

Fig. 6. The result of mean joint reconstruction error through task-dependent hand synergies compared with traditional invariant hand synergies.

5   Conclusion

In this paper, a set of task-dependent hand synergies was proposed to give a comprehensive and quantitative description on human hand grasping function. The main contribution of this work is to distinguish the joint correlation properties and hand coordination strategies in different tasks. It also improved and refined the traditional invariant hand synergy theory. By comparison, it was found that using task-dependent hand synergies can reduce reconstruction error even with lower number of synergies. These above conclusions could inspire the mechanism and control system design of robotic hand. Through design of appropriate joint adaptive modules according to different tasks on mechanical structure and control level, the adaptability of robotic hand in varying tasks could be improved.

Acknowledgements. This work was supported in part by the China National Key Research and Development Program under Grant No. 2020YFC2007801, and in part by the National Natural Science Foundation of China under Grant No. U1813209.

References

1. Mandery, C., et al.: Unifying representations and large-scale whole-body motion databases for studying human motion. IEEE Trans. Robot. **32**(4), 796–809 (2016)
2. Chiu, H.: The use of the motion analysis system for evaluation of loss of movement in the finger. J. Hand Surg. **25-B**(2), 195–199 (2000)
3. Napier, J.R.: The prehensile movements of the human hand. J. Bone Joint Surg. **38B**(4), 902–913 (1956)
4. Cutkosky, M.R.: On grasp choice, grasp models, and the design of hands for manufacturing tasks. IEEE Trans. Robot. Autom. **5**(3), 269–279 (1989)
5. Bullock, I.M., Ma, R.R., Dollar, A.M.: A hand-centric classification of human and robot dexterous manipulation. IEEE Trans. Haptics **6**(2), 129–144 (2013)
6. Feix, T., et al.: The GRASP taxonomy of human grasp types. IEEE Trans. Hum. Mach. Syst. **46**(1), 66–77 (2016)
7. Bian, W., Tao, D., Rui, Y.: Cross-domain human action recognition. IEEE Trans. Syst. Man Cybern. B Cybern. **42**(2), 298–307 (2012)
8. Santello, M., Flanders, M., Soechting, J.F.: Postural hand synergies for tool use. J. Neurosci. **18**(23), 10105–10115 (1998)
9. Patel, V., Burns, M., Chandramouli, R., Vinjamuri, R.: Biometrics based on hand synergies and their neural representations. IEEE Access **5**, 13422–13429 (2017). https://doi.org/10.1109/ACCESS.2017.2718003
10. Jarque-Bou, N.J., Atzori, M., Müller, H.: A large calibrated database of hand movements and grasps kinematics. Sci. Data **7**(1), 1–10 (2020). https://doi.org/10.1038/s41597-019-0349-2
11. Touvet, F., Roby-Brami, A., Maier, M.A., Eskiizmirliler, S.: Grasp: combined contribution of object properties and task constraints on hand and finger posture. Exp. Brain Res. **232**(10), 3055–3067 (2014). https://doi.org/10.1007/s00221-014-3990-1
12. Bicchi, A., Gabiccini, M., Santello, M.: Modelling natural and artificial hands with synergies. Philos. Trans. Roy. Soc. B. Biol. Sci. **366**(1581), 3153–3161 (2011)
13. Starke, J., et al.: Human-inspired representation of object-specific grasps for anthropomorphic hands. Int. J. Hum. Robot. **17**(2), 205008 (2020)
14. Faria, D.R., et al.: Extracting data from human manipulation of objects towards improving autonomous robotic grasping. Robot. Auton. Syst. **60**(3), 396–410 (2012)
15. Jarrassé, N., et al.: Analysis of hand synergies in healthy subjects during bimanual manipulation of various objects. J. NeuroEng. Rehabil. **11**, 113 (2014)
16. Romero, J., et al.: Spatio-temporal modeling of grasping actions. In: IEEE International Conference on Intelligent Robots & Systems (IROS) Taipei, China, pp. 2103–2108 (2010)

Application of CG Pseudo-spectral Method to Optimal Posture Adjustment of Robot Manipulator

Qingxin Shi, Jianwu Li, Junjie Dong, Fansheng Meng, Rui Ma, Quanbin Lai, and Xingguang Duan$^{(\boxtimes)}$

Beijing Institute of Technology, Beijing 100081, China
duanstar@bit.edu.cn

Abstract. To consider the energy saving during the robot motion, optimal posture control method for a robot manipulator is proposed. The Chebyshev-Gauss (CG) Pseudo-spectral method is used to discuss the problem with the energy optimal control. The Lagrange interpolation of barycentre is adopted to approximate the state and control variables. The continuous optimal control problem can be converted to a discrete nonlinear programming (NLP) problem. And then it can be solved by Sequential Quadratic Programming (SQP) algorithm. The simulation results of optimal energy control make the robot manipulator from the initial state to the desired terminal posture successfully. The terminal angular velocity of each link is also meet the predetermined value. The control law does not exceed the preset boundary of control.

Keywords: Pseudo-spectral method · Optimal control · Robot manipulator

1 Introduction

Intelligent robots are becoming a popular techniques in the human activities, as replacing human labor with robots can provide remarkable cost savings [1]. Meanwhile, the energy consumption of the robot is a question during the practical applications of the robot. The saving of the energy consumption is of great importance in industrial production, which has aroused the research interest of many scholars. Li et al. studied the principle of the minimum, discussed time optimal control, and energy optimal control, and gave the respective indicator functions [2]. In addition, an optimal posture trajectory planning problem about the object is considered with the fixed-time energy optimal and time-energy optimal cases [3]. The Pseudo-spectral method, as a means of optimization, has been widely applied in many fields. Some results show the energy consumption is really reduced through the Pseudo-spectral method [4, 5]. The application of Pseudo-spectral method to posture adjustment of robot system is studied and discussed the feasibility [6]. In recent years, Tang proposed two improved Pseudo-spectral methods [7, 8]. The one is Chebyshev-Gauss (CG) Pseudo-spectral method which solves the optimal control problem with complex constraints and the author also has deduced the

© Springer Nature Switzerland AG 2021
X.-J. Liu et al. (Eds.): ICIRA 2021, LNAI 13013, pp. 25–35, 2021.
https://doi.org/10.1007/978-3-030-89095-7_3

corresponding karush-kuhn-tucker (KKT) condition. Another is named as multi-interval integral Gegenbauer Pseudo-spectral method, which is used to study the attitude control problem, and compared with the simulation result based on GPOPS-II software package. The advantages of solving precision and rapidity were illustrated about the novel Pseudo-spectral method. Ge et al. [9] studied an attitude maneuver problem of two rigid body system. The energy optimal control law is successfully planned based on CG Pseudo-spectral method. To the author's knowledge, it is not found the literature about applying such an optimal method on a robot manipulator system. The optimal control of robot manipulator is investigated in this paper. The energy indicator function is used to solve the optimal posture adjustment. The optimal posture trajectory, angular velocity curve, and optimal control law are then obtained by the Sequence Quadratic Program (SQP) algorithm. Numerical simulations and results are presented.

2   Problem Formulation

2.1   Dynamic Model of the Robot Manipulator

The dynamics of a n-DOF robot manipulator can be written as [10–12]

$$M(q)\ddot{q} + C(q, \dot{q})\dot{q} + D\dot{q} + G(q) = \tau \tag{1}$$

where $q, \dot{q}, \ddot{q} \in \mathbb{R}^n$ denote the generalized link position, velocity, and acceleration, respectively, $M(q) \in \mathbb{R}^{n \times n}$ represents the inertia matrix, $C(q, \dot{q}) \in \mathbb{R}^{n \times n}$ denotes the centrifugal-Coriolis matrix, $D \in \mathbb{R}^{n \times n}$ represents the matrix composed of viscous friction coefficients for each joint, $G(q) \in \mathbb{R}^n$ is the vector representing gravity force, and $\tau \in \mathbb{R}^n$ denotes the torque input. The detailed dynamics expression of robot manipulator refers to Ref. [13]. Furthermore, a Coulomb friction is also considered here.

2.2   Optimal Control

To reach the desired terminal posture of the manipulator with minimized energy consumption, the optimal control strategy is adopted to solve this problem. Without losing the general, the optimal control of posture adjustment can be written as a Bolza form:

$$\begin{cases} \min J = \Phi(x(t_0), t_0, x(t_f), t_f) + \int_{t_0}^{t_f} g(x(t), u(t), t)\mathrm{d}t \\ \text{s.t. } \mathbf{R}(t) = f(x(t), u(t), t) \quad t \in [t_0, t_f] \\ \phi(x(t_0), t_0, x(t_f), t_f) = 0 \\ C(x(t), u(t), t) \leq 0. \end{cases} \tag{2}$$

In Eq. (2), $\Phi(*)$ is the Mayer cost function, g(*) is the Lagrange cost function, $f(*)$ represents the constraint of state equation, $\phi(*)$ represents the constraints of initial boundary and terminal boundary, $C(*)$ represents the constraint of path, $x(t)$ denote the state variable, $u(t)$ denote the control variable, t0 is the initial time, and tf is the terminal time. The first function in Eq. (2) is the indicator function.

Given out the constraints of state boundary x_0 and x_f (thecx initial and terminal configurations), the pseudo-control variable $u(t)$ can be searched by the indicator function.

Next, the trajectory of spacecraft maneuvered from x_0 to x_f can be obtained. At the time of start and stop about actuation of gimbal, the angular velocity of motor should be zero. In other words, the constraints of control boundary are zero ($u_0 = u_f = 0$). So, the control variable values will not be the infinite and should have a maximum. Above all, let $||u||_\infty \leq u_{max}$.

3   CG Pseudo-spectral Method

The CG Pseudo-spectral method converts the continuous optimal control problem to a discrete problem of parameter optimization, which contains algebraic constraints in a series of conversion (namely, the NLP problem). The conversion contains the following steps.

3.1   The Affine Transformation of Time and Approximation of Variable

This method needs a new time interval that transforms the real time interval $[t_0, t_f]$ of system into the interval $\tau \in [-1, 1]$. The affine transformation can be written as

$$t = \frac{t_0 + t_f}{2} - \frac{t_0 - t_f}{2}\tau. \tag{3}$$

The approximation of control variable and the approximation of state variable consider the K CG points and $\tau_0 = -1$ as the collocation points. And the CG points can be written as follows

$$\tau_i = \cos\left[\frac{(K + 1 - i)\pi}{K + 1}\right], \ i = 1, 2, \cdots, K. \tag{4}$$

The CG points named Fejér-2 points [14]. This distribution of CG points over interval $(-1, 1)$ has an advantage. It can suppress the Runge problem which is produced during interpolation.

The state variables can be approximated using Lagrange interpolating polynomials,

$$x(\tau) \approx X(\tau) = \sum_{i=0}^{K} L_i(\tau)X(\tau_i). \tag{5}$$

The barycentric interpolation of Lagrange is adopted for improving computational efficiency and numerical stability [15],

$$L_i(\tau) = \frac{\frac{\xi_i}{\tau - \tau_i}}{\sum_{j=0}^{K} \frac{\xi_j}{\tau - \tau_j}}, \ i = 0, 1, \cdots, K \tag{6}$$

where the weight of barycentre ξ_i is written as

$$\xi_i = \frac{1}{\prod_{j=0, j \neq i}^{K} (\tau_i - \tau_j)}, \ i = 0, 1, \cdots, K. \tag{7}$$

In the denominator of Eq. (7), when calculating the $(\tau_i - \tau_j)$, the error of floating point may appear. For avoiding the problem, we adopted a method. At first, divide the initial and terminal point [15], and ξ_i' can be written as

$$\xi_i' = \frac{1}{\prod\limits_{j=0,j\neq i}^{K+1}(\tau_i - \tau_j)} = \begin{cases} \frac{(-1)^{K+1-i}}{2}, & i = 0, K+1 \\ (-1)^{K+1-i}, & i = 1, 2, \cdots, K. \end{cases} \tag{8}$$

It is easy to see that Eqs. (7) – (8) have a relationship as follows

$$\begin{aligned}\xi_i = (\tau_i - \tau_{K+1})\xi_i' &= \begin{cases} (\tau_0 - 1)\xi_0' = -2\xi_0', & i = 0 \\ \left[\cos\left[\frac{(K+1-i)\pi}{K+1}\right] - 1\right]\xi_i', & i = 1, 2, \cdots, K \end{cases} \\ &= \begin{cases} (-1)^K, & i = 0 \\ (-1)^{K-i} 2\sin^2\left[\frac{(K+1-i)\pi}{2(K+1)}\right], & i = 1, 2, \cdots, K. \end{cases} \end{aligned} \tag{9}$$

There is not existing derivative of control variable in state equation. Thus, the control variable of approximation is simple. The CG points are chose as collocation-points for keeping a consistency in the form. The Kth-order Lagrange polynomials of barycentre $\tilde{L}_i(\tau)(i = 1, \cdots, K)$ are adopted to approximate the control variables,

$$\boldsymbol{u}(\tau) \approx \boldsymbol{U}(\tau) = \sum_{i=1}^{K} \tilde{L}_i(\tau)\boldsymbol{U}(\tau_i). \tag{10}$$

For the CG Pseudo-spectral method, the global orthogonal polynomial is adopted to approximate the state variables. Hence, the time derivative of state variable can be generated from Eq. (5),

$$\dot{\boldsymbol{x}}(\tau_k) \approx \dot{\boldsymbol{X}}(\tau_k) = \sum_{i=0}^{K} \dot{L}_i(\tau_k)\boldsymbol{X}(\tau_i) \tag{11}$$

where the Lagrange polynomials of barycentre can be expressed by differential matrix $\boldsymbol{D} \in \mathbb{R}^{K \times (K+1)}$

$$D_{ki} = \dot{L}_i(\tau_k) = \begin{cases} \frac{\xi_i}{\xi_k(\tau_k - \tau_i)}, & k \neq i \\ -\sum\limits_{j=0,j\neq k}^{K} D_{kj}, & k = i \end{cases} \tag{12}$$

where $k = 1, \cdots, K$, $i = 0, \cdots, K$. Substituting Eq. (12) into the equation of dynamics generates a discrete equation as follows

$$\sum_{i=0}^{K} D_{ki}\boldsymbol{X}(\tau_i) - \frac{t_f - t_0}{2} f(\boldsymbol{X}_k, \boldsymbol{U}_k, \tau_k; t_0, t_f) = 0 \tag{13}$$

It also has the problem of floating point error in Eq. (12). As we can see, τ_i (see Eq. (6)) has triangle cosine form. So we utilize the identity of trigonometry for avoiding this phenomenon and generate Eq. (14).

$$\sum_{i=0}^{K} D_{ki}X(\tau_i) - \frac{t_f - t_0}{2}f(X_k, U_k, \tau_k; t_0, t_f) = 0 \tag{14}$$

In Eq. (7), the time interval is [–1, 1), for this, the state of approximation is not including terminal state $x(\tau_f)$. Thus, the whole dynamics equation covered [–1, 1] time interval generates

$$\int_{-1}^{1} \dot{x}(\tau)\mathrm{d}\tau = \frac{t_f - t_0}{2} \int_{-1}^{1} f(x(\tau), u(\tau), \tau)\,\mathrm{d}\tau. \tag{15}$$

The rules of Clenshaw-Curtis [16] quadrature are utilized in approximating the Eq. (15),

$$X_f = X_0 + \frac{t_f - t_0}{2} \sum_{k=1}^{K} \mu_k^{cc} f(X_k, U_k, \tau_k; t_0, t_f). \tag{16}$$

The expansion in the left side of Eq. (17) can obtain a linear term.

$$X_f = X_0 + \int_{-1}^{1} \dot{x}(\tau)\mathrm{d}\tau = X_0 + \int_{-1}^{1} \sum_{i=0}^{K} \dot{L}_i(\tau)X(\tau_i)\mathrm{d}\tau = X_0 + \sum_{i=0}^{K} X(\tau_i)\left(\int_{-1}^{1} \dot{L}_i(\tau)\mathrm{d}\tau\right)$$

$$= X_0 + \sum_{i=0}^{K} X(\tau_i)\left[\sum_{k=1}^{K} \mu_k^{cc}\dot{L}_i(\tau_k)\right] = X_0 + \sum_{i=0}^{K} X(\tau_i) \sum_{k=1}^{K} \mu_k^{cc}D_{ki} \tag{17}$$

where τ_k denotes CG point, μ_k^{cc} is the weights of Clenshaw-Curtis quadrature. And it can be acquired by utilizing Fast Fourier Transform [17]

$$\mu_k^{cc} = \begin{cases} F_{K+1}^{-1}v_k + \frac{c_k(-1)^k}{(K+1)^2 - 1}, & (K+1) \text{ is even} \\ F_{K+1}^{-1}v_k + \frac{c_k(-1)^k}{(K+1)^2}\cos(\frac{k\pi}{K+1}), & (K+1) \text{ is odd} \end{cases} \tag{18}$$

where c_k is defined by

$$c_k = \begin{cases} 1, & k = 0 \text{ or } k = K + 12, \\ 2, & \text{otherwise,} \end{cases} \tag{19}$$

and μ_k^{f2} represents the Fejér-2 quadrature weight,

$$\mu_k^{f2} = F_{K+1}^{-1}v_k \tag{20}$$

where F_{K+1}^{-1} represents the inverse Fast Fourier Transformation, and v_k is defined as follows

$$\begin{cases} v_k = \frac{2}{1-4k^2}, \quad k = 0, 1, \cdots, \left[\frac{K+1}{2}\right] - 1, \, v_{[(K+1)/2]} = \frac{K-2}{2[(K+1)/2]-1} \\ v_{K+1-k} = v_k, \quad k = 1, 2, \cdots, \left[\frac{K}{2}\right]. \end{cases} \tag{21}$$

Finally, we assume that $\mu_{K+1}^{f2} = \mu_0^{f2} = 0$ and $\mu_{K+1}^{cc} = \mu_0^{cc}$. After calculating, the real term of the Eq. (20) should be taken.

Using the rules of Clenshaw-Curtis quadrature to approximate the integral term of optimal control problem, the following equation can be yielded

$$J = \Phi(X_0, t_0, X_f, t_f) + \frac{t_f - t_0}{2} \sum_{k=1}^{K} \mu_k^{cc} g(X_k, U_k, \tau_k; t_0, t_f). \tag{22}$$

The initial state constraints, the terminal state constraints and the control, as well as the control constraints, are all set as

$$x_0 - X_0 = 0, \quad x_f - X_f = 0, \quad u_0 - U_0 = 0, \quad u_f - U_f = 0, \quad \|U\|_\infty \leq U_{max} \tag{23}$$

where X_0 is the first column of the state of approximation, X_f denotes the last column of the state of approximation, and U_0 and U_f have same meaning. In Eq. (23), U_{max} represents the maximum of control.

Then, a common NLP problem of the optimal attitude control can be written as

$$\begin{cases} \min \quad J = F(y) \\ s.t. \quad h_i(y) = 0 \quad i = 1, 2, \cdots, M \times (K+1) + 2 \times (M+N) \\ \quad\quad g_i(y) \leq 0 \quad i = 1, 2, \cdots, N \times K \end{cases} \tag{24}$$

where y denotes the design variables which including control and state variables. M is the number of state variables, and N represents the number of corresponding control variables.

3.2 Procedure of Optimization

In fact, the number of the designed variables is large because the large number of the CG points we have to choose. Firstly, it is hard to choose an initial values of surmise in the SQP algorithm for everyone. Secondly, the global optimization is not suitable for the SQP algorithm, while it only depends on what the initial values are. Thirdly, when the initial values with randomness are chosen, the SQP strategy cannot give a reasonable result, and a local optimal result may achieve. Hence, a novel strategy of optimization is presented as follows.

Calculation Method of Feasible Solution. The main idea of the feasible solution is not searching an optimal solution. Though this optimal solutions meet equality constraints and inequality constraints. This method presents a changed equality constraints as a new pseudo objective function. Thus, this new NLP does not include equality constraints. The equality constraints can be obtained from Eq. (24),

$$\begin{cases} \min J = sqrt \left(\sum_{i=1}^{M \times (K+3) + 2 \times N} h_i(\boldsymbol{y})^2 \right) \\ \text{s.t.} \quad g_i(\boldsymbol{y}) \leq 0 \quad i = 1, 2, \cdots N \times K. \end{cases} \tag{25}$$

A high accuracy of result can be calculated using Pseudo-spectral with low nodes actually. And it also has low sensitivity of initial values. In this essay, fewer nodes $K1$ is chosen. We adopt the SQP method to acquire the feasible solution.

Calculation Method of Optimal Solution. From the first step, we can obtain discrete solution, and then, let these discrete solution be the interpolating nodes applying cubic spline interpolation method. After this step, more CG points can be obtained by using the discrete time CG points into the spline interpolation function. Put another way, the initial values of K2 are generated by interpolating nodes of K1. And then, the results of optimal control can be calculated by substituting initial values of K2 into the SQP method (see Eq. (25)).

4 Simulation Results

In this section, the mathematic simulations are conducted to prove the effectiveness of CG Pseudo-spectral method. The parameters are given as follows [13].

4.1 Parameters and Objective Settings

We consider a task of short time with energy optimal strategy. The parameters were given in SI units and summarized as follows [13].

$\theta_1 = 2.351$, $\theta_2 = 0.084$, $\theta_3 = 0.102$, $\theta_4 = 38.465$, $\theta_5 = 1.825$, $\theta_6 = 2.288$, $\theta_7 = 0.175$, $\theta_8 = 7.170$ if $\dot{q}_1 > 0$ and 8.049 if $\dot{q}_1 < 0$, and $\theta_9 = 1.724$. We supposed that the initial angular velocity and terminal angular velocity of the robot manipulator were zero. Moreover, the terminal posture of the robot manipulator was not constrained, hence, the initial state of the model was $\boldsymbol{x}_0 = [0, 0, 0, 0]^T$ and the terminal state was $\boldsymbol{x}_0 = [0, 0, 0, 0]^T \boldsymbol{x}_f = [q_{t1}, q_{t2}, 0, 0]^T$. The path constraints were $|q_i| \leq 10 \text{rad/s}$, $|\tau_i| \leq 30 \text{N} \cdot \text{m}$. The initial time t_0 was set to zero, and the terminal time t_f was set to 0.5 s. The novel strategy of optimization is used during the calculation of optimization. In the step of feasible solution, 6 CG points are selected, and in the step of optimal solution, 36 CG points are selected.

4.2 Results of Three Cases

We designed three cases to validate the CG Pseudo-spectral method, and each case contained a set of target posture. These values were changed based on Ref. [13].

Case 1. In the first case, we set the terminal posture with same direction of motor rotation and the same rotation value, and the value was set as $q_{t1} = q_{t2} = \pi/6$. The simulation curves of link trajectory, motor velocity, and control torque are shown in Fig. 1-(1), respectively.

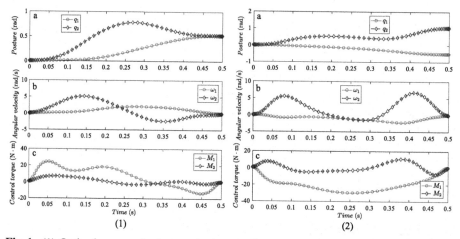

Fig. 1. (1) Optimal curves of robot manipulator in Case 1: (a) Optimal trajectory. (b) Optimal angular velocity. (c) Optimal control torque: The maximum value of control torque is 24.2 N·m at 0.04624 s, which does not exceed the boundary of minimum. (2) Optimal curves of robot manipulator in Case 2: (a) Optimal trajectory. (b) Optimal angular velocity. (c) Optimal control torque: The minimum value of control torque is –29.87 N·m at 0.2564 s, which does not exceed the boundary of minimum.

Case 2. In this case, we set the terminal posture with different direction of motor rotation and the two different rotation values, and the values were set as $q_{t1} = -\pi/6$, $q_{t2} = \pi/3$, respectively. The simulation curves of link trajectory, motor velocity, and control torque were shown in Fig. 1-(2), respectively.

Case 3. In the last case, we set the terminal posture with one original angle and another different angle, and the values were set as $q_{t1} = -\pi/6$, $q_{t2} = 0$, respectively. The simulation curves of link trajectory, motor velocity, and control torque were shown in Fig. 2, respectively.

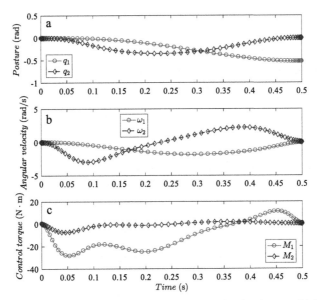

Fig. 2. Optimal curves of robot manipulator in Case 3: (a) Optimal trajectory. (b) Optimal angular velocity. (c) Optimal control torque: The minimum value of control torque is -28.29 N·m at 0.05397 s, which does not exceed the boundary of minimum.

4.3 Discussions

The simulation results demonstrate the three results all complete the predetermined tasks. The final postures and the final angular velocities are meet the terminal values in the three cases. The curves of link trajectory, angular velocity, and control torque give the smooth results without dramatic change in each case. It also shows the curves are well limited with the fixed boundaries. The computer running time of the three cases are 28.233 s, 32.752 s, and 27.369 s, respectively. These results show the feasibility of the application of optimal robot manipulator motion based on the CG Pseudo-spectral scheme. Besides, as can be clearly seen, the results of three cases are obviously different from the conventional optimal results of trapezoidal-shape trajectory [18], which is because the Pseudo-spectral is a global optimization method, and pays no attention to the control of each single motor. In case 1, the two curves of angular velocity in Fig. 3b are like the trapezoidal trajectory, and we infer the motors rotation with the same direction is a simple situation which may be simplified to a 1-DOF problem, so the curves are like the trapezoidal trajectory. Furthermore, the motor of link 2 is moving during the simulation motion in Case 3, despite the terminal posture are same to its initial posture we set, which is one of the further work about this paper.

5 Conclusions

In this paper, energy indicator function is used to solve the optimal posture adjustment control problem of robot manipulator based on CG Pseudo-spectral method. The continuous optimal control problem can be converted to the discrete problem using CG

Pseudo-spectral method. After that, it can be solved by SQP algorithm. To avoid the sensitivity of the initial values with SQP, a novel strategy of optimization from feasible solution to optimal solution is presented. The optimization results of energy indicator function makes the system from the initial state to the terminal posture. The terminal angular velocity is also meet the predetermined value. The results of optimal control can reach the desired control of zero bound, and does not exceed the predetermined bounds. The curves of link trajectory, angular velocity, and control torque give the smooth results without dramatic change in each case. Therefore, it is feasible to solve the optimal control of posture adjustment for robot based on CG Pseudo-spectral method, and the energy optimal control may have more applications in the practical problems. Last but not least, this method provides an optimal solution of robot manipulator motion in the field of industrial production, while it may not suit for dealing with the robot manipulator motion under environmental uncertainties.

Acknowledgement. This research was supported by the National Key R&D Program of China (Grant No. 2019YFB1301403) and National Natural Science Foundation of China (Grant No.62073043). (Corresponding author: Xingguang Duan).

References

1. Theodoridis, T., Hu, H.S.: Toward intelligent security robots: a survey. IEEE Trans. Syst. Man. Cy. C. **42**(6), 1219–1230 (2012)
2. Li, C.J., Ma, G.F.: Optimal Control (in Chinese). Science Press, Beijing (2011)
3. Li, S., Duan, G.R.: Parametric approach to track following control of FFSM. J. Syst. Eng. Electron. **22**, 810–815 (2011)
4. Mostaza-Prieto and P. C. E. Roberts, "Perigee attitude maneuvers of geostationary satellites during Electric orbit raising," J. Guid. Control. Dynam., 40, 1978–1989, 2017.
5. Liao, Y.X., Li, H.F., Bao, W.M.: Indirect Radau pseudospectral method for the receding horizon control problem. CHINESE J. Aeronaut. **29**, 215–227 (2016)
6. Yao, Q., Ge, X.: Optimal reorientation of a free-floating space robot subject to initial state uncertainties. J. Braz. Soc. Mech. Sci. Eng. **40**(3), 1–12 (2018). https://doi.org/10.1007/s40 430-018-1064-1
7. Tang, X.J., Wei, J.L., Kai, C.: A Chebyshev-Gauss pseudospectral method for solving optimal control problems. ACTA Automatica Sinica. **41**, 1778–1787 (2015)
8. Tang, X.J.: Numerical solution of optimal control problems using multiple-interval integral Gegenbauer pseudospectral methods. ACTA Astronaut. **121**, 63–75 (2016)
9. Ge, X., Yi, Z., Chen, L.: Optimal control of attitude for coupled-rigid-body spacecraft via Chebyshev-Gauss pseudospectral method. Appl. Math. Mech. **38**(9), 1257–1272 (2017). https://doi.org/10.1007/s10483-017-2236-8
10. Arimoto, S.: "Control theory of non-linear mechanical systems: A passivity-based and circuit-theoretic approach. Clarendon Press, Oxford, U.K. (1996)
11. Lewis, F.L., Dawson, D.M., Abdallah, C.T.: Robot manipulator control: Theory and practice. Marcel Dekker, New York (2004)
12. Sciavicco, L., Siciliano, B.: Modeling and control of robot manipulators, 2nd edn. Springer-Verlag, London, U.K. (2000)
13. Su, Y.X., Müller, P.C., Zheng, C.H.: Global asymptotic saturated pid control for robot manipulators. IEEE Trans. Contr. Syst. T. **18**(6), 1280–1288 (2010)

14. Weideman, J., Trefethen, L.: The kink phenomenon in Fejér and Clenshaw-Curtis quadrature. Numer. Math. **107**, 707–727 (2007)
15. Berrut, J.P., Trefethen, L.N.: Barycentric lagrange interpolation. Siam Rev. **46**, 501–517 (2004)
16. Costa, B., Don, W.S.: On the computation of high order pseudo-spectral derivatives. Appl. Numer. Math. **33**, 151–159 (2000)
17. Waldvogel, J.: Fast construction of the Fejér and Clenshaw-Curtis quadrature rules. BIT Numer. Math. **46**, 195–202 (2006)
18. Wang, Y.B., Zhao, Y.M., Bortoff, S.A., Ueda, K.: A real-time energy-optimal trajectory generation method for a servomotor system. IEEE Trans. Ind. Electron. **62**(2), 1175–1188 (2015)

Semi-autonomous Robotic Manipulation by Tele-Operation with Master-Slave Robots and Autonomy Based on Vision and Force Sensing

Haibin Wei, Manjia Su, and Yisheng Guan[✉]

Biomimetic and Intelligent Robotics Lab (BIRL), School of Electro-Mechanical Engineering, Guangdong University of Technology, Guangzhou, Guangdong Province, China
ysguan@gdut.edu.cn

Abstract. In the current social production activities, many operations in dangerous environments need to be completed manually. For example, on high-altitude power grids, inspection or replacement of parts; maintenance of equipment under high temperature or radiation environment, etc. The operator's physiology and psychology are under tremendous pressure and risks. Therefore, robots are needed to assist operators in their work. In this article, we propose a robot control system that combines teleoperation and autonomous motion based on vision and force sensors. In this system, the robot arm that performs the job first performs the motion control in the global environment through master-slave remote operation. When the robot arm reaches the ideal working position, it then performs local autonomous fine operations by visual processing and force feedback. In the entire operation process, teleoperation frees workers from the dangerous working environment. At the same time, the robot's autonomous operation based on vision and force improves the accuracy and efficiency of the operation. The nut-tightening operation experiment in the article verifies the feasibility of this semi-autonomous operation system.

Keywords: Semi-automation · Teleoperation · Master-slave control · Visual processing · Force sensing

1 Introduction

Robots have been used in many areas of human life, such as industry, military, medical, education, entertainment, housekeeping and social services [1]. In industrial production, robots are used by people in various tasks, especially dangerous, high-intensity or repetitive tasks. For example, the parts on the high-voltage power grid need to be repaired or replaced, and the equipment in the high temperature or dust environment

The work in this paper is supported by the Key Research and Development Program of Guangdong Province (Grant No. 2019B090915001) and the Frontier and Key Technology Innovation Special Funds of Guangdong (Grant No. 2017B050506008, 2017B090910008).

© Springer Nature Switzerland AG 2021
X.-J. Liu et al. (Eds.): ICIRA 2021, LNAI 13013, pp. 36–46, 2021.
https://doi.org/10.1007/978-3-030-89095-7_4

needs to be maintained. Taking the high-altitude power grid as an example, adjusting the anti-vibration hammer and cleaning the drain plate will involve screwing nuts [2]. Using robots to complete the screwing of nuts will greatly reduce the burden on workers, and robot operations can improve efficiency and accuracy.

In terms of power grid robots, in 2015, the Canadian Electric Power Research Institute invented a power grid robot for inspection and maintenance of high-voltage lines [3]. By controlling the two joysticks, the operator controls the robot to move on-line to realize the inspection of the power grid and the maintenance of parts, such as tightening loose nuts. Because robots need manual operations to move and perform tasks, they have high requirements on workers' skills and lack autonomous intelligence. In 2016, Meiji University in Japan developed a screw nut robot system based on master-slave remote operation for the maintenance tasks of power distribution lines [4]. Under the video monitoring of three cameras, it controls the manipulator to screw the nut through the teleoperation module. In the control interface, there will be strong feedback information to judge the contact between the wrench and the nut according to the force information. However, this system only has manual teleoperation to complete the job, without realizing the automatic control of the robot system, and the accuracy is not high. In 2017, Hunan Power Company of State Grid of China also developed a transmission line fastening bolt robot [5]. The robot can use its mobile wheel to move on the wire. When it reaches the working area, it moves the manipulator to find the bolts and nuts and perform the task of turning the nuts through the images fed back by the camera. But it does not use visual positioning and force sensing control, can not ensure the accuracy and safety of the operation. In 2019, Guangdong University of Technology used a 5-DOF modular tele-operation robot to adjust the anti-shock hammer and clean the drainage plate in the maintenance task of power grid, both using screw nuts [6]. However, because no visual and force feedback is introduced, the robot works less efficiently.

Considering the complexity of different operating environments, it is still a big challenge for the robot to fully intelligently and autonomously perform the nut twisting operation. Because this process involves robot path planning, obstacle avoidance, etc. Master-slave teleoperation mentioned in this paper can well combine human decision-making with robot [7]. Meanwhile, visual and force feedback provides the basis for autonomous movement of robot.

2 Architecture of the Semi-autonomous System

In this section, we propose the architecture of the semi-autonomous robotic system that combines teleoperation with autonomous manipulation based on vision and force sensors. The whole system includes a master robot, a slave robot for remote mainpulation, a force sensor, a camera for vison monitoring, an industrial computer and a power module. Among them, the main robot and the operation of the manipulator are modular design. In terms of structure, the main robot and manipulator are both composed of swing joints (T module) and rotary joints (I module) of the same configuration. This design ensures a clear and intuitive mapping relationship in the master-slave control. Because it requires perfect intelligence for a robot to recognize the working environment independently and make decisions to perform tasks. Master-slave control can transfer the optimal control strategy of human brain to the robot arm to deal with the complex and changeable operating environment [8]. The master-slave teleoperation can improve the decision-making ability of the system, and integrate the decision-making of human brain into the operation control, which will pave the way for the following sensor-based autonomous motion. At the same time, it is difficult to control the precise motion of the robot manually during the fine operation of teleoperation. Therefore, visual and force feedback can be used to achieve fine autonomous motion. These two control modes complement each other. Table 1 shows the comparison of the advantages and disadvantages of three different power grid robots and the semi-autonomous robots proposed in this paper in recent years.

Table 1. Comparison of several power grid robots.

Country (Robot name)	Tele-operation	Vision sensing	Force sensing	Adavantages	Disadvantages
Japan (Phase III)	Joystick control	Only video monitoring	\	Remote operation	Lack of autonomy Low accuracy
Canada (LineScout 5)	Joystick control	Only video monitoring	\	Remote operation	Lack of autonomy Low accuracy
China (Drainage plate fastening robot)	\	Only video monitoring	Only torque detection	Remote operation	Lack of autonomy Low efficiency
In this paper (Semi-autonomous robot)	Master-slave intuitive control	Autonomy based on vision	Autonomy based on force control	Teleoperation and Autonomy	Remote operation needs to be improved

In the above table, master-slave teleoperation and sensor-based autonomous movement have their own advantages and disadvantages. The semi-autonomous system architecture proposed in this section combines the advantages of the two well. The overall system architecture is shown in Fig. 1. It can be seen from the above table that in the power grid robot, the combination of teleoperation and autonomous control based on vision and force can effectively improve the efficiency and accuracy of the operation. The system of this paper will perform screw nut operation in the power grid environment to verify the feasibility of the system architecture. The camera on the electric wrench can obtain the image information of the nut. Through image processing, the mechanical arm obtains the coordinates of the center of the nut to achieve alignment. The electric wrench and the end of the mechanical arm are connected by a six-dimensional sensor. The force sensor can obtain the force in the X, Y, and Z directions and the torque around the three axes. This semi-autonomous operation system combined with remote operation can adapt to the complex power grid environment. At the same time, its autonomous control based on vision and force effectively guarantees the accuracy and efficiency of operations.

This semi-autonomous operation system can also be applied to a variety of tasks, especially those dangerous tasks that have not yet achieved the robot's fully autonomous operation. For example, for power grid parts, insert cotter pins. Teleoperation initial positioning and autonomous operation based on vision and force feedback can greatly improve the feasibility of operations.

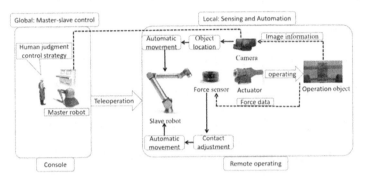

Fig. 1. System composition and architecture

3 Master-Slave Mapping for Teleopertation

The joint configurations of the master robot and the slave robot are the same, in which the encoder records the rotation angle of the master robot's joint for each rotation joint and swing joint. In the master-slave control mode, the slave robot makes the corresponding angle change according to the joint angle of the master robot. The master-slave mapping relationship is shown in Fig. 2.

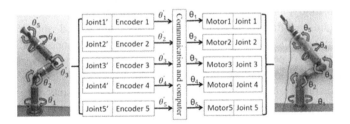

Fig. 2. Master-slave mapping

In our system, teleoperation adopts master-slave mode by two master and slave robots with the same configuration. Their kinematic mapping can be summarized as changes in scaling and configuration bias. In Cartesian space, it can be expressed by the following formula.

$$\begin{bmatrix} R_s & P_s \\ 0 & 1 \end{bmatrix} = \begin{bmatrix} K_r R_m & K_p P_m \\ 0 & 1 \end{bmatrix} + \begin{bmatrix} R_\gamma & P_\gamma \\ 0 & 1 \end{bmatrix} \tag{1}$$

Where, RS and PS represent the attitude matrix and position vector of the slave robot, respectively, Rm and Pm represent the attitude matrix and position vector of the master robot, Ry and Py represent the attitude offset matrix and position offset vector of the master robot after scaling, Kr and Kp represent the posture conversion coefficient matrix and position ratio coefficient matrix of the master robot mapped to the slave robot.

The pose information needs to be converted into the rotation angle of each joint of the robot to realize the specific movement. Therefore, in the joint space, the master-slave mapping relationship can be expressed as: θm = θS. θm and θS respectively represent the joint rotation angle of the master robot and the slave robot.

In this design, the displacement of each joint of the master robot can be directly used to control the movement of each joint of the slave robot. Therefore, this mapping of master-slave control is intuitive and simple, and can simultaneously ensure the isomorphism of master-slave dual ends in joint space and Cartesian space at any moment, with high position transparency and strong operability of tasks. For the details of the modular master-slave tele-operation, refer to [6].

4 Identification and Location of Screw Nut by Vision

In this section, the feasibility of the system will be verified by screwing nuts. When the robot needs to screw the nut autonomously, the first thing to do is to identify the center position of the nut. After obtaining the coordinate of the center point of the nut, according to the relationship between the coordinate of the center point and the robot base mark, the robot can obtain the corresponding position information under the base mark system, solve the rotation Angle of each joint through the inverse kinematics of the robot, and then complete the centering operation of the electric wrench and the center of the nut through the autonomous movement. In this process, the nut image should be gray processed firstly, and then the non-edge points of the image should be filtered by linear filter. Then, the gradient amplitude and direction are solved, and all the gradient amplitude except for the maximum value in the gradient direction were reduced to 0, and the non-edge pixel points were removed. The maximum inter-class variance method was used to select the optimal threshold value of the circular hole, and the pixel points outside the threshold value were removed, and then the pixel points at the edge of the circular hole were connected. Finally, Hough circle transformation is carried out on the edge pixels of the extracted circular hole to output the coordinates of the center of the circle.

The nut center detection and positioning figure obtained by using the improved Hough circle transformation algorithm is shown in Fig. 3. Where in (a) is the grayscale image, (b) is the image after Gaussian filtering, (c) is the edge connection image of the circular hole detected by the edge detection algorithm, and (d) is the location image of the center of the nut transformed by Hough circle.

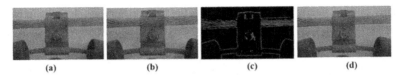

Fig. 3. Nut center positioning

The center coordinates obtained above are the coordinates of the center of the circle in pixel coordinate system. Then the world coordinates of the center of the nut can be obtained by means of multi-view geometry. A hand-eye calibration experiment was performed on the camera mounted on the electric wrench to find the internal and external parameters of the camera, in which the external parameters are the transformation matrix between the camera coordinate system and the TCP coordinate system of the electric wrench. The imaging relationship between the camera and the object in this system is shown in Fig. 4. Respectively, 0-XcYcZc represents the camera coordinate system, 0-xy represents the image plane coordinate system, and 0-uv represents the pixel coordinate system.

Fig. 4. Relationship of coordinate systems

When solving the spatial position of the center point of the nut through triangulation, the electric wrench takes pictures of the nut at two different positions, and the pixel coordinate of the center of the nut can be obtained through the nut center recognition algorithm. Then the three-dimensional space coordinates of the nut center were obtained through two camera postures and the coordinates of the center of the nut. When the camera takes pictures, coordinate mapping is obtained as shown in Fig. 5.

Fig. 5. The mapping point of the nut center at different positions

The following formula represents the transformation relationship between the nut in pixel coordinates and the world coordinate system. M1 is determined by the external parameters of the camera, and here represents the transformation relationship between the camera coordinate system and the robot's TCP coordinate system, which is represented by a rotation matrix and a translation vector. The transformation relationship between the camera coordinate system and the TCP coordinate system can be obtained through the hand-eye calibration experiment [9, 10]. M2 is determined by the internal parameters of the camera, the focal length, the size of each pixel, and the coordinates of the center pixel.

$$\lambda \begin{bmatrix} u \\ v \\ 1 \end{bmatrix} = \begin{bmatrix} \alpha_x & 0 & u_0 & 0 \\ 0 & \alpha_y & v_0 & 0 \\ 0 & 0 & 1 & 0 \end{bmatrix} \begin{bmatrix} R & T \\ 0 & 1 \end{bmatrix} \begin{bmatrix} x_w \\ y_w \\ z_w \\ 1 \end{bmatrix} = M_2 M_1 \begin{bmatrix} x_w \\ y_w \\ z_w \\ 1 \end{bmatrix} \tag{2}$$

The above formula can be transformed as follows: u represents the pixel coordinates of the center of the circle, the inner and outer parameters are represented by the matrix P, X represents the world coordinates of the center of the circle, where u^ represents the antisymmetric matrix of u.

$$\lambda u = PX \tag{3}$$

$$\hat{u}PX = 0 \tag{4}$$

And the following equations can be obtained from two different sets of equations to solve the world coordinates of the centerf the nut circle. The robot can be aligned with the center of the nut according to this coordinate [11].

$$\begin{bmatrix} v_1 P^{\frac{1}{3}} - P^{\frac{1}{2}} \\ P^{\frac{1}{1}} - u_1 P^{\frac{1}{3}} \\ v_2 P^{\frac{2}{3}} - P^{\frac{2}{2}} \\ P^{\frac{2}{1}} - v_2 P^{\frac{2}{3}} \end{bmatrix} X = 0 \tag{5}$$

5 Fitting Screw Nut Based on Force Sensing

In the previous section, image processing was used to find the center of the nut to achieve the alignment of the electric wrench and the center of the nut. After completing the alignment operation, the electric wrench should be controlled by the robot to complete the steps of fitting the nut sleeve. Because in this process, the electric wrench needs to contact and interact with the nut, which will generate contact force. In order to improve the probability of successful assembly of the sleeve, the robot needs to realize the smooth assembly of the sleeve and the nut on the electric wrench through autonomous movement according to the feedback information of the six-dimensional sensor and the set robot control strategy.

The assembly process of socket and nut of electric spanner can be divided into approach stage, contact stage, adjustment stage and complete assembly stage. In the

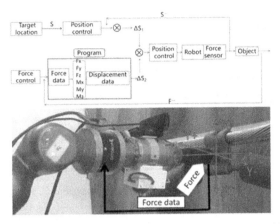

Fig. 6. Force position hybrid control strategy for sleeve assembly nut

contact stage, the contact between the sleeve and the nut can be judged according to the force information of the force sensor.

In this paper, a hybrid control strategy of force and position is used to perform the operation of nut assembly sleeve. As shown in Fig. 6, in the control strategy framework, S represents the target position. First, input a target position to the robot, and S- represents the position information feedback value. The robot continues to move according to the difference $\Delta S1$ between the position target value and the feedback value. Due to the existence of assembly errors, positioning errors and other factors, the target position S is not an ideal assembly position. When the robot approaches the target position, a contact force is generated with the nut. F- represents the force feedback data. According to the force information, the displacement of the end effector $\Delta S2$ is calculated, and then the displacement of the end effector is determined by $\Delta S1$ and $\Delta S2$. In the entire control framework of mixed force and position, the position information mainly controls the displacement of the end effector in the Z direction, and the force information adjusts the position of the end effector on the XY plane.

6   Implementation and Experiments

In order to further verify the feasibility of the semi-autonomous nut screwing robot system based on vision and force sense proposed above, this part builds the hardware and software experimental platform on the basis of the above research, and carries out experimental verification of nut screwing operation. The whole experimental platform mainly includes the hardware system and control system of the master-slave robot, the visual monitoring module and the image processing module, the force sensor and the electric wrench of the nut. The hardware system of the master-slave robot is a self-designed 5-DOF modular manipulator with the same configuration. In terms of control, the communication mode of USB to CAN is adopted. The upper computer sends instructions to the Copley drive board to control the movement of the Maxon motor, so as to realize the movement of the robot. Figure 7 shows the layout of the entire experimental system.

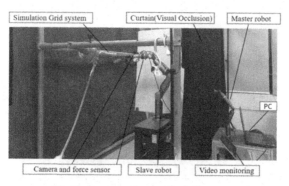

Fig. 7. Layout of experimental system

The whole system is divided into control part and execution part. The system is set up in the simulated environment of high-voltage power grid operation, through the semi-autonomous telecontrol control robot to perform nut operation. The control part and the executive part are separated by a curtain to form a visual barrier, which well simulates the remote operation when the nut is screwed.

In this experiment, the operator through the first video monitoring observation grid work environment, at the end of the mechanical arm through teleoperation control electric wrench to move to the operation of the ideal location, again through the camera on the electric wrench through image processing, get the nut, and the world coordinate of the center of the circle of independent complete electric wrench and nut center alignment, finally in the force sensor auxiliary control strategy, Automatically complete the assembly of sleeve and nut, and tighten or loosen. The experimental process is depicted in Fig. 8 (a). And in Fig. 8 (b), it shows the process of force sensing information and self-adjusting assembly of the manipulator arm when the manipulator arm autonomically controls the electric wrench to assemble the nut.

In the whole system, the robot is in the simulated high voltage line grid environment, performing nut operation. Because in practical application, the power grid is high in the air, and the environment of the power grid is dangerous. Operators operating in close proximity can be very dangerous. The purpose of the robot is to liberate the operator. The middle curtain forms a visual barrier. In this way, the situation of remote operation is well simulated, and to a certain extent, it is verified that the addition of visual feedback and force feedback in this system improves the feasibility of robot nut twisting. At the same time, due to the complexity and uncertainty of the operation environment, master-slave teleoperation can well transfer the decision-making of human brain to the robot. In the second half of the robot, the sensor-based autonomous movement ensures the accuracy of the operation. In this semi-autonomous control logic, teleoperation and autonomous motion are complementary.

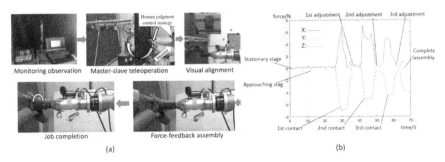

Fig. 8. Experimental process

7 Conclusion

In this paper, a semi-autonomous screw nut operation robot system was proposed based on the master-slave teleoperation and robot autonomous movement. In this process, visual positioning based on image processing and assembly control based on force feedback were developed. The main work and research results of this paper are summarized as follows:

Aiming at the dangerous high-altitude power grid operation, a portable modular master-slave teleoperation control robot system is proposed. Teleoperation can make workers break away from the dangerous environment and greatly reduce the physiological and psychological burden on workers. At the same time, teleoperation can directly map the thinking and decision-making of human to the slave robot, which can cope with the complex and changeable working environment.

The visual positioning system and force feedback system are introduced to the system of the robot vision positioning system and force feedback system, on the one hand, such robots semi-autonomous movement, however, to a certain extent, improve the precision and efficiency of operation, on the other hand, the addition of force feedback, robot has a length of awareness, to ensure the safety in the process of operation.

The semi-autonomous nut twisting robot system proposed in this paper can be applied to many scenes in modern industrial production, especially to dangerous environment, which has great practical significance. But in this paper, the deficiency is that, when looking for the ideal operation position of the electric wrench through teleoperation, the current stage is to move the electric wrench to a position perpendicular to the plane where the nut is located through the set monitoring camera. That is, the axis of the electric wrench needs to be parallel to the central axis of the nut. As shown in Fig. 9, the figure describes the spatial position relationship between the electric spanner and the central axis of the nut during teleoperation. In future work, it is necessary to introduce attitude estimation or laser sensor methods to replace the terminal attitude adjustment of remote operation and improve intelligence.

Not parallel   Parallel

Fig. 9. Teleoperation to adjust position

References

1. Heyer, C.: Human-robot interaction and future industrial robotics applications. In: IEEE/RSJ International Conference on Intelligent Robots and Systems, pp. 4749–4754 (2010)
2. Tani, E., Yamada, H., Kato, R., et al.: Development of the tightening nut task skill using a power distribution line maintenance experimental robot. In: IEEE/SICE International Symposium on System Integration (SII), pp. 558–563 (2015)
3. Nicolas, P., Richard, P., Montambault, S.: LineScout technology opens the way to robotic inspection and maintenance of high-voltage power lines. IEEE Power Energy Technol. Syst. J. **21**, 1–11 (2015)
4. Yamashita, K., Kato, Y., Kurabe, K., et al.: Remote operation of a robot for maintaining electric power distribution system using a joystick and a master arm as a human robot interface medium. In: IEEE International Symposium on Micro-NanoMechatronics and Human Science (MHS), pp. 1–7 (2016)
5. Li, W.: Development of on-line fastening bolt robot for transmission line, high voltage appliances (2017), 53, 07, 147-152-158
6. Zhong, Y., Fu, Z., Su, M., et al.: Development of a robot system performing maintenance tasks on high-voltage power transmission lines. In: IEEE International Conference on Robotics and Biomimetics (ROBIO), pp. 1344–1349 (2019)
7. Feng, F., Yang, H., Tang, L.: Bilateral force feedback teleoperation dual-arm mobile robot system for nuclear facility decommissioning. Robot. Appl. **04**, 13–18 (2020)
8. Zhang, T., Chen, Z., Wang, X., Liang, B.: Summary and prospect of key technologies of space robot teleoperation. Space Control Technol. Appl. **40**(06), 1–9, 30 (2014)
9. Zhang, Y., Qiu, Z., Zhang, X.: Calibration method for hand-eye system with rotation and translation couplings. Appl. Opt. **58**(20), 5375–5387 (2019)
10. Li, W., Xie, H., Zhang, G., et al.: Hand-eye calibration in visually-guided robot grinding. IEEE Trans. Cybern. **46**(11), 2634–2642 (2015)
11. Chen, J., Wu, D., Song, P., Deng, F., He, Y., Pang, S.: Multi-view triangulation: systematic comparison and an improved method. IEEE Access **8**, 21017–21027 (2020)

Adaptive Grasping Strategy of Dexterous Hand Based on T-test

Yanjiang Huang[1,2], Jiepeng Liu[1,2], Haonan Wang[1,2], and Xianmin Zhang[1,2(✉)]

[1] School of Mechanical and Automotive Engineering, South China University of Technology, Guangzhou 510640, China
zhangxm@scut.edu.cn
[2] Guangdong Provincial Key Laboratory of Precision Equipment and Manufacturing Technology, South China University of Technology, Guangzhou 510640, China

Abstract. Tactile is an important feeling of human beings. When people grasp objects, they will determine the grasping force according to the properties of the objects. Through tactile, they can sense the slipping of objects and adjust the force to grasp objects stably. Tactile sensing is also an important way for robots to interact with the external environment. In this paper, the tactile sensor is applied to the grasp of dexterous hand, and a slip detection algorithm based on t-test is proposed. The algorithm is used to design the adaptive grasping strategy of dexterous hand, which ensures that the dexterous hand can grasp with the force without damaging the object, and react after detecting the slippage in the process of grasping, so as to avoid the object falling. Finally, through the experiments of grasping objects with different characteristics, the results show that the proposed method can grasp different objects stably and safely, has good adaptability, and can be applied in different scenes.

Keywords: Adaptive grasping · Slip detection · T-test · Tactile · Dexterous hand grasping

1 Introduction

Human hand is the result of natural evolution, which helps human use various tools and complete different complex manipulations. Human beings can recognize many characteristics of objects to be touched: roughness, shape, size, weight, hardness and humidity. Based on these characteristics, human hand can adjust the force of each finger when grasping objects [1]. Tactile perception is also an important way for robot to interact with the environment. Tactile signals provide the robot with the information of the objects in its environment and the interaction with these objects [2]. There are many researches on using tactile sensor to grasp. The control system of human is simulated by tactile sensor and hand-held accelerometer [3]; The feedback of the three-axis tactile sensor is used to adjust the grasping force of the finger to achieve adaptive grasping [4]; In order to improve the robustness of grasping, an algorithm based on tactile is proposed in [5]; In order to ensure the grasping stability of multi fingered robot arm, [6] proposed

© Springer Nature Switzerland AG 2021
X.-J. Liu et al. (Eds.): ICIRA 2021, LNAI 13013, pp. 47–55, 2021.
https://doi.org/10.1007/978-3-030-89095-7_5

a tactile sensor system for measuring normal force and shear force distribution using tunnel effect.

Slipping sense is a sense based on tactile. In [7], the physical phenomena of slipping and the physiological basis of human slipping sense are briefly analyzed, and slipping is defined as a continuous process; A slip detector is designed for the gripper, and it is used to detect the slip in the process of grasping [8]; For different tactile sensors, different slip detection methods and grasping force control strategies are proposed [9–14], and the machine learning methods such as k-nearest neighbor and SVM are used to classify slip cases [13, 14]. Many slip detection methods use special slip detector or tri-axial force sensor, but there is little research on the correlation between slip and normal force.

Our main works are as follows:

1) Slip detection algorithm based on t-test: we propose a slip detection algorithm, which can quickly and accurately determine whether slip occurs in the motion process after grasping, and the tactile sensor only needs one-dimensional pressure sensor, without tri-axial force sensor or special slip detector;

2) Adaptive grasping strategy: based on the slip detection algorithm of 1), we design an adaptive grasping strategy, which uses a small initial force to grasp and react after the slip occurs to ensure the stability of the grasping process;

3) Experimental verification: for the adaptive grasping strategy designed in 2), we grasp and move objects with different characteristics to evaluate the stability of the adaptive grasping strategy and the degree of damage to objects.

The remainder of the paper is organized in this manner. Section 2 introduces the hardware setup. Section 3 describes the proposed method. Section 4 conducts experiments to verify the feasibility of the grasping strategy, while Sect. 5 reports the conclusion.

2 Hardware Setup

In our experiment, the hardware configuration consist of a UR5 robot arm, a Robotiq 2f-85 gripper, and two TakkTile tactile sensor arrays (see Fig. 1). All of them can communicate with the computer equipped with ROS. The UR5 robot arm controlled by MoveIt!. The maximum grasping width of the gripper is 85 mm originally. Due to the sensor array, the actual grasping width is 75 mm. The Robotiq gripper can grasp the object adaptively. The principle is that when the object is grasped, the gripper is subject to the reaction force of the object, the torque of the motor increases, and the current increases. When the current reaches threshold, the closing action stops. However, the result of grasping is very poor for the deformable and fragile objects. Takktile tactile sensor array (see Fig. 2), can measure the normal force and output dimensionless value, and the output frequency is 60 Hz. Each point of tactile sensor array is an air pressure gauge covered by rubber. The air pressure gauge will output different values when different pressures are applied to the rubber.

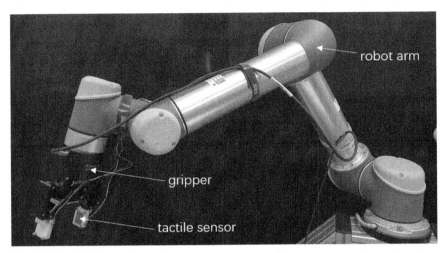

Fig. 1. Hardware configuration, including UR5 robot arm, Robotiq 2f-85 gripper and TakkTile tactile sensor array.

Fig. 2. Tactile sensor array for single finger.

3   Method

This section introduces the proposed method, which is mainly composed of two parts: slip detection algorithm based on t-test and adaptive grasping strategy based on slip detection algorithm.

3.1   Slip Detection Algorithm Based on T-test

The initial slippage produces small vibrations at the contact surface between the fingertip and the object [7]. In humans, slipping sense is mainly based on vibration detection. At the beginning of slip, the pressure signal measured theoretically is irregular and disordered, and the mean value and difference of pressure are very different; when there is no slipping, the pressure value remains unchanged or changes in the same way, that is, there is no obvious difference between the mean value and difference of pressure.

Paired sample t-test is used to analyze the difference comparison relationship between paired quantitative data, and judge whether a hypothesis is tenable according to the difference between the mean values of the same group of samples in different scenes.

$$t = \frac{\overline{d} - \mu_0}{s_d / \sqrt{n}} \tag{1}$$

$\overline{d}$ is the average of the difference between paired samples, s_d is the standard deviation of the difference between paired samples, and n is the number of paired samples. After the t value is calculated, the p value is confirmed by querying the corresponding cut-off table, and compared with the significance level α. There was no significant difference between the two samples when p is greater than α.

Through the above analysis, we can use t-test to detect the occurrence of slip. Algorithm 1 is the pseudo code of the proposed algorithm. We set the significance level α = 0.05, and then through t-test of the pressure values F_{pre} and F_{sub} in two consecutive times before and after each tactile point, we get the test statistic t and the corresponding cut-off value p. We take the smallest p obtained by t-test of 12 tactile points and compare it with α. When p is greater than α, there is no statistical difference in the pressure values before and after receiving, that is, there is no slip, and print 0, otherwise, it means slip, print 1. Then update the F_{pre} and F_{sub} to continue the detection at the next time.

Algorithm 1: Slip Detection Algorithm.
Require: $F_{pre}[i]$ is the force value of the i-th sensor for 5 consecutive times previously and the length is 5, $F_{sub}[i]$ is the force value of the i-th sensor for 5 consecutive times subsequently, $F_{now}[i]$ is the force value of the i-th sensor for 5 consecutive times now, α is the significance level, p_{min} is the minimum threshold, k is the tactile array length.

```
1:  α ← 0.05
2:  while the program did not stop do
3:      p_min ← 1
4:      k ← 0
5:      F_now ← pressure array of the tactile sensors now
6:      F_pre ← F_sub
7:      F_sub ← F_now
8:      while k < 12 do
9:          t, p ← t-test(F_pre[k], F_sub[k])
10:         if p < p_min then
11:             p_min ← p
12:         k ← k+1
13:     if p_min < α then
14:         print 1
15:     else
16:         print 0
```

3.2 Adaptive Grasping Strategy

When two fingers hold an object of mass M. The analysis is limited to the vertical direction, and the stable grasp requires adjusting the compression forces so that $F_{t1} + F_{t2} = Ma$ (see Fig. 3). Of course, according to Coulomb friction model, $F_{tk} \leq \mu_s F_{nk}$ ($k = 1, 2$), where μ_s is the (static) friction coefficient. Adjusting the normal component of the grasp force (F_n) to the minimum effective value is the simplest strategy to prevent object slipping [7]. Our strategy is to apply a very small force on the object first to avoid damaging the object, and then increase the force of the gripper when slippage occurs to avoid the slipping of the object and achieve adaptive grasping.

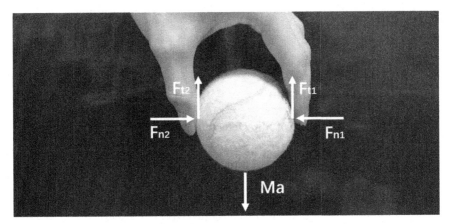

Fig. 3. Grasping forces during weight lifting.

Algorithm 2 is the pseudo code of the adaptive grasping strategy algorithm. When the SRSS of left finger sensor array is less than 0.15N or the SRSS of right finger sensor array is less than 0.15N, we think the object is not grasped, p increases, and the gripper continues to close, otherwise, we think the object is grasped. The robot arm starts to move the object. In this process, algorithm 1 is used to detect slip continuously. When the slip occurs, the gripper closes slightly until the end of the robot arm movement and the object is put down.

Algorithm 2: Adaptive grasping strategy.

Require: F is the pressure value array of sensor array, length is 12, index 0-5 is the pressure values of left finger, index 6-11 is the pressure values of right finger, F_{thr} is the pressure threshold, p is the closing value of gripper, from 0 to 255, 255 is the fully closed value.

1: $F_{thr} \leftarrow 0.15$
2: $F \leftarrow$ all zero array
3: $p \leftarrow 0$
4: **while** $\sqrt{\sum_0^5 \boxed{?}[\boxed{?}]^2} < F_{thr}$ **or** $\sqrt{\sum_6^{11} \boxed{?}[\boxed{?}]^2} < F_{thr}$ **do**
5:    $p \leftarrow p+1$
6:    $F \leftarrow F_{now}$
7: **while** the moving process of robot arm with object is not finished **do**
8:    **if** Slip occurs **then**
9:        $p \leftarrow p+2$

4 Experimental Evaluation

4.1 Experimental Evaluation of Slip Detection Algorithm

In order to evaluate the slip detection algorithm, we let the gripper gently grasp the 3D printed block, and then artificially apply a downward force (see Fig. 4 (a)), so that the block and the gripper fingers slip. The pressure curve shows chaotic fluctuations (see Fig. 4 (b)). The curve of slip changes to 1 (see Fig. 4 (c)), indicating that the slip is detected. Experiments show that our slip detection algorithm is sensitive.

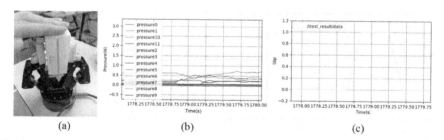

(a)   (b)   (c)

Fig. 4. Experiment of slip detection algorithm. (a) Slip is caused by artificial force. (b) The pressure curve of the sensor array. (c)The curve of slip detection.

4.2 Experimental Evaluation of Adaptive Grasping Strategy

We selected sponge, doll, bread, chips, jelly and banana as the grasped object (see Fig. 5 (a)). In order to compare the results of our adaptive grasping strategy and Robotiq self-contained method, we selected sponge and doll two kinds of objects which are not easy to damage but easy to deform for the grasp comparison experiment. After the object is grasped, the robot arm carries gripper moves 0.2 m along the positive direction of z-axis, and then moves 0.2 m along the negative direction of z-axis to return to the origin, and then moves the same along the x-axis and y-axis (The joint speed and acceleration of UR5 are set to the maximum value, that is, it moves at the fastest speed). Because the adaptive grasping strategy will detect slip and increase the grasp force during the movement, we compare the results of the grasp after the movement. The method of Robotiq is that the deformation of sponges and dolls is very large, while the deformation of sponges and dolls grasped by adaptive grasping strategy is very small (see Fig. 5 (c)).

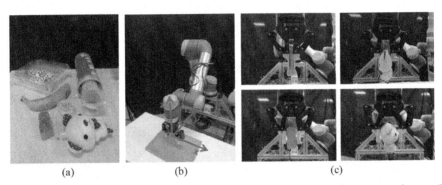

(a)   (b)   (c)

Fig. 5. Grasp comparison experiment. (a) The object to be grasped in the experiment. (b) Schematic diagram of the coordinate system at the end of the gripper. (c) Comparison between the results of our grasping strategy and that of the Robotiq self-contained method. The above figure is the result of the Robotiq self-contained method, and the below figure is the result of our strategy.

In order to further evaluate the adaptive grasping strategy, we test the grasping of four representative foods, which are easily damaged bananas, easily deformed bread, smooth jelly and fragile chips (to prevent contamination of the tactile sensors, we attach a layer of preservative film to the food). Each object is grasped ten times, and the process is also moving with the robot arm after grasping.

The experimental results show that the adaptive grasping strategy has good adaptability to deformable and fragile objects, but the adaptability to smooth objects is general (see Table 1), similar to human beings, and it is difficult to grasp smooth objects from the side; In addition, the adaptive grasping strategy can protect the integrity of the object very well (see Fig. 6).

Table 1. Grasping success rate of four objects.

Object type	Banana	Bread	Jelly	Chip
Grasping success rate	9/10	9/10	7/10	10/10

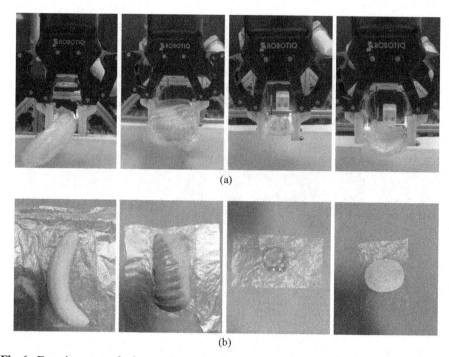

Fig. 6. Experiments to further evaluate the adaptive grasping strategy. (a)Grasp the object successfully. (b)The objects keep good integrity after adaptive grasp.

5   Conclusion

In this paper, we analyze the generation of human slipping sense and design a slip detection algorithm combined with t-test. Based on the proposed algorithm, we design an adaptive grasping strategy of dexterous hand, which simulates the behavior of human grasping objects, applies a small force first, and adjusts the grasping force through slip detection. The experiment result show that the slip detection algorithm is sensitive and the adaptive grasping strategy is effective. For deformable, damaged and fragile objects, the adaptive grasping strategy can guarantee the original shape of objects. However, the grasping effect is general for smooth objects, which is close to the performance of human grasping this kind of objects.

Acknowledgment. This work was supported in part by the National Natural Science Foundation of China under Grant 52075178, in part by the Dongguan Postgraduate Joint Training (Practice) Workstation Project under Grant 2019707122025, in part by Guangdong Basic and Applied Basic Research Foundation under Grant 2019A1515011154; in part by the Scientific and Technological Project of Guangzhou under Grant 202002030233.

References

1. Romeo, R.A.: Methods and sensors for slip detection in robotics: a survey. IEEE Access **8**, 73027–73050 (2020)
2. Li, Q.: A review of tactile information: perception and action through touch. IEEE Trans. Robot. **36**(6), 1619–1634 (2020)
3. Romano, J.M.: Human-inspired robotic grasp control with tactile sensing. IEEE Trans. Robot. **27**(6), 1067–1079 (2011)
4. Zhang, T.: Fingertip three-axis tactile sensor for multifingered grasping. IEEE/ASME Trans. Mechatron. **20**(4), 1875–1885 (2015)
5. Kim, W.D., Kim, J.: Tactile event based grasping algorithm using memorized triggers and mechanoreceptive sensors. In: IEEE/RSJ International Conference on Intelligent Robots and Systems (IROS), Las Vegas, Nevada, pp. 10438–10443 (2020)
6. Zhang, T., Fan, S.: Multifingered robot hand dynamic grasping control based on fingertip three-axis tactile sensor feedback. In: Proceeding of the 11th World Congress on Intelligent Control and Automation, Shenyang, China, pp. 3321–3326 (2014)
7. Francomano, M.T.: Artificial sense of slip—a review. IEEE Sens. J. **13**(7), 2489–2498 (2013)
8. Venter, J., Mazid, A.M.: Tactile sensor based intelligent grasping system. In: IEEE International Conference on Mechatronics (ICM), Churchill, Victoria, pp. 303–308 (2017)
9. Gunji, D.: Grasping force control of multi-fingered robot hand based on slip detection using tactile sensor. In: IEEE International Conference on Robotics and Automation, Pasadena, California, pp. 2605–2610 (2008)
10. Stachowsky, M.: A slip detection and correction strategy for precision robot grasping. IEEE/ASME Trans. Mechatron. **21**(5), 2214–2226 (2016)
11. Yussof, H., Wada, J.: A new control algorithm based on tactile and slippage sensation for robotic hand. In: World Automation Congress, Kobe, Japan, pp. 1–6 (2010)
12. Dzitac, P., Mazid, A.M.: Friction-based slip detection in robotic grasping. In: IECON 41st Annual Conference of the IEEE Industrial Electronics Society, Yokohama, Japan, pp. 004871–004874 (2015)
13. Goeger, D., Ecker, N.: Tactile sensor and algorithm to detect slip in robot grasping processes. In: IEEE International Conference on Robotics and Biomimetics 2008, Bangkok, Thailand, pp. 1480–1485 (2009)
14. James, J.W.: Slip detection for grasp stabilization with a multifingered tactile robot hand. IEEE Trans. Robot. **37**(2), 506–519 (2021)

Reinforcement Learning Strategy Based on Multimodal Representations for High-Precision Assembly Tasks

Ajian Li, Ruikai Liu, Xiansheng Yang, and Yunjiang Lou[✉]

Harbin Institute of Technology Shenzhen, Shenzhen, China
louyj@hit.edu.cn

Abstract. Robotic peg-in-hole task has always attracted researchers' attention. With the development of real-time sensors and machine learning algorithms, collaborative robots are now having potential to insert tiny and delicate components of digital products. Due to grasping error, the absolute position of the peg would not be calculated directly by forward kinematics, but through high-resolution sensors. However, for each single modality, such as RGB-D image and proprioception, has its own limitation during the insertion process. Camera cannot provide accurate information when the peg is closed to the target, while force/torque sensor is entirely blind before contact status begin. This paper used multimodal fusion method to utilize all the valuable information from multiple sensors. Representation cores from multimodal data were trained to forecast relative position between the peg and hole. Reinforcement learning network was then able to use the relative position to generate appropriate action of the robot. This paper verified the above algorithms through USB-C insertion experiments in ROS-Gazebo simulation.

Keywords: Robotic assembly · Peg-in-hole · Multimodal representation · Reinforcement learning

1 Introduction

At the end of the mobile-phone assembly line, batches of phones need to be inserted with USB cables, for purpose of system installation and function test. At present, most of the insertion tasks are accomplished by human workers, due to the small clearance and fragile structure. For most of the robotic assembly tasks in industry, workers always use guiding mode or basic position controller to directly lead the end-effector towards target position. This control method relies heavily on positioning accuracy, and could not be robust on unexpected obstacles. To make the assembly process more intelligent, sensors feedback could be used properly. During the past researches, modalities like RGB images [1] and force/torque data [2, 3] were frequently chosen to give the robot abilities to see and feel the external environment. In particular, several more accurate and intuitive ones were appended, such as tactile arrays and proprioception [4], which could provide more information to the controller.

© Springer Nature Switzerland AG 2021
X.-J. Liu et al. (Eds.): ICIRA 2021, LNAI 13013, pp. 56–66, 2021.
https://doi.org/10.1007/978-3-030-89095-7_6

However, RGB images will turn blurry when the end-effector of the robot is extremely close to the target port, for the reason of shelter and low illumination. Force/torque data is even null before contact begins, and force sensation is too localized for the robot to perceive relative positions. Multimodal fusion has always been a popular topic in natural language processing (NLP), aiming to establish relationship among common modalities like sound, words, pictures, etc. In the area of robotics, multiple modalities cooperation is also warm-welcomed. Liang et al. [5] fused vision and proprioception to teach the robot to understand human motion behavior. Xue et al. [6] fused vision and haptics to train the robot to grasp an object stably. For peg-in-hole task, Song et al. [7] proposed an assembly strategy for complex-shaped parts, based on visually-obtained CAD model and force/torque feedback. However, shape of the peg is considered to be known as precondition. Lee et al. [8] took RGB-D images, force/torque data and proprioception features as input of multimodal representation network, but the fusion method could still be optimized, for data from different modalities have different physical meanings. The clearance between the peg and the hole in the article is also too large to be used in industry. From daily life, human can insert a charging cable into mobile phone smoothly, only depending on vision and force feedback. Therefore, we used autoencoder as multimodal fusion method in this article, in order to train the robot to perceive environmental events and complete the USB-C insertion task.

Reinforcement learning is a typical method for an agent to learn from attempts. Unlike supervised learning, the agent get reward not from manual labeling, but from experimental feedback. Wang et al. [9] successfully trained an UR robot to plug in optical fiber using actor-critic method. Nevertheless, the learning process is tedious and inefficient. Scherzinger et al. [10] used an LSTM-based neural network to present robotic learning from human demonstration, which is able to help non-experts program force-sensitive assembly tasks on robots.

To guarantee that the representation core from the encoder contains as many valuable messages as possible, a neural network was built to forecast real-time relative position between the peg and the hole. The well-trained relative position predictions would then become input of a self-supervised reinforcement learning network, producing a 6-dimensional action array, which corresponds to x-y-z-R-P-Y motion of the end-effector. Due to rich contact-and-groping events during experiments, an impedance controller [11] was used to avoid the robot from being destroyed.

The main contributions of this article are listed as follows:

1) An autoencoder-based multimodal network which combined RGB-D images and force/torque data of the end-effector.
2) A NAF-based self-supervised learning network which produced proper 6-d action for the end-effector of the robot.
3) Demonstration of the robotic USB-C insertion task respectively using vision and force/torque data.
4) The path planning in Cartesian space combined with joint impedance control ensures flexible contact and response speed at the same time.

The rest of this paper is organized as follows. In Sect. 2, we will give all the theories and methods about this article. Section 3 describes the whole environment and experiments, with the results following behind. In Sect. 4, we will summarize the article and plan our future work.

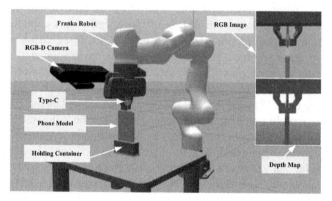

Fig. 1. Simulation environment.

2 Learning Strategy Based on Multimodal Fusion

The target of this paper is using proposed strategy to solve the task of robotic precision assembly. We use sensor information from multiple sources, and then fuse them to a vector that characterizes the position and posture information of the robot's end-effector. In order to make the sampled data more representative, we use the learning process of reinforcement learning for data collection. The dimensions of different modalities are reduced by encoding, and then be fused into a pose estimation vector as strategy input.

We model the assembly process as a potential functional relationship between the reward (R), present state (S), next state (S$'$), and action (A), namely (S, A) → R, (S, A) → S$'$. After continuous training, the strategy is more stable and long-term optimal, which means looking for the optimal action in different states and maximize the expectation. We use artificial neural network to express the potential functional relationship between reward, next state and action. Convolutional neural networks have great advantages in high-dimensional data dimensionality reduction, especially in image data processing. The multi-source sensor data used by our proposed method includes RGB data, depth data, as well as force/torque, position, and posture of the end-effector of the robotic arm. We only focus on the final stage of the assembly task, that is, the hole searching and inserting after the assembly parts are moved near the hole, so what we need to do is precision assembly in a small area. In order to avoid making the network too deep, we divide the steps into two parts instead of directly using the state as input to estimate the pose. Therefore, the policy can be divided into four parts, including latent representation, supervised prediction, policy learning and control method, as shown in Fig. 2.

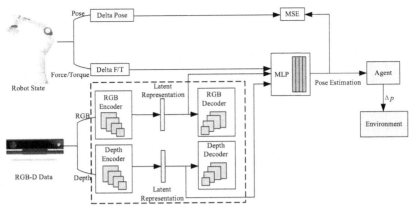

Fig. 2. System framework of neural network combining self-supervised learning and supervised learning. The network takes four different types of sensor information as input: RGB, depth, force/torque, and end-effector position/orientation. RGB and depth are each encoded into 32-dimensional vectors using self-supervised learning, and then combined with the force/torque, encoded to the end-effector position and orientation using supervised learning, which is a 6-d vector. The encoded vector is used as policy input. (Color figure online)

2.1 Latent Representation

The input of model includes three modalities: RGB, depth and force/torque. The size of RGB data is (256, 256, 3), depth data is (256, 256), and force/torque data is (6, 1). Due to the huge difference in data dimensions and data volume, and in order to fully reflect the importance of each modality, we cannot use them as a strategy input directly, which is not conducive for learning. For RGB, a self-supervised learning method is adopted. A 4-layer convolutional neural network is used to encode the RGB into a potential 32-dimensional vector, and then a 4-layer deconvolution neural network is used to decode the potential vector to a same dimension output as the input data. For the encoding part, kernel size of convolution layer is 3, both stride and padding are 1. Kernel size and stride of pooling layer are 2. For the decoding network, kernel size of deconvolution layer is 3, stride is 2, and padding is 1.

For depth network, we use a structure similar to RGB, except changing its size from (256, 256) to (256, 256, 1). Similar to RGB network, the latent representation of the depth network is also a vector with length 32. The optimization goals are Mean Squared Error (MSE) between the input and output. If the MSE is small enough, the low-dimensional latent representation vector generated in the middle of the network can represent the original high-dimensional data.

2.2 Pose Estimation Based on Supervised Learning

Supervised learning is used for position and posture estimation. In addition to RGB and depth, it also includes the force/torque data at the end of the robot arm. These are mapped to the assembly pose relative to the hole. Once the RGB and depth self-supervised networks are well trained, their parameters will remain unchanged. The latent representation is used to replace the original RGB-D data as the input state. Combined with force/torque, the state is spliced to a 70-d vector, which is used as the input for supervised learning. In order to make the output of the supervised learning network represent position and posture of the peg relative to the hole, the output dimension of the supervised learning network is 6, and the optimization goal of the supervised learning network is the least MSE of the output and the relative pose.

Considering that the assembly task is moving in a small area, the unit of the translation direction (x, y, z) of the collected data is millimeter, and the unit of the rotation direction (R, P, Y) is degree in order to make the data distinguishable. The data collected are consistent in the order of magnitude, which is good for setting the loss function. Similar to self-monitoring, when the loss is small enough, the low dimensional output can approximately represent the high dimensional input data.

2.3 Policy Learning

Reinforcement learning algorithm is a good method for policy decision. Different from deep learning, reinforcement learning dynamically updates the network parameters through reinforcement information of environmental feedback, so as to select the appropriate decision in different states. The state space is a six-dimensional vector encoded by RGB, depth and F/T data. The action space is composed of translational momentum x, y, z and rotations R, P, Y, that is, the output action is a six-dimensional vector of $(\Delta x, \Delta y, \Delta z, \Delta R, \Delta P, \Delta Y)$. This motion increment method is suitable for motion in Cartesian task space. Considering the continuous state space, action space also needs to be continuous. In order to solve the continuous control problem in reinforcement learning, Gu et al. [12] proposed the NAF algorithm, which is what we use as policy in this paper.

2.4 Controller

In order to meet the motion control requirements of the experiment, it is necessary to limit the output action. We expect the assembly process to be flexible as human assembly process. Impedance control is a flexible control method, which can ensure that the parts will not be damaged due to excessive assembly force in the assembly process. The assembly task is covered by translation and rotation of parts in Cartesian space, in which rotation is represented by Euler angle.

Impedance control in Cartesian task space can be modeled as a Mass-Spring-Damper model, which is expressed as.

$$M\ddot{x} + B\dot{x} + Kx = F_d - F_{ext}, \tag{1}$$

where F_{ext} is applied force, F_d is desired force, M is mass of the controlled object, B is damping coefficient, K is stiffness of the spring, x, $\dot{x}$ and $\ddot{x}$ are position, velocity and acceleration of the mass relative to the origin respectively. Let $F = F_d - F_{ext}$, then $F = (Ms^2 + Bs + K)x$, and the desired action can be converted into desired output force. When arriving to the desired position, the desired force F is 0. In other words, when the force reaches the desired value, the movement will stop to ensure that the force does not exceed the threshold, which meets the requirements of compliance and ensuring the safety of the assembly process. Control of the robot is different from the Mass-Spring-Damping system, and the issues are more complicated. Consider a single-arm robot with seven degrees of freedom. Assume that the forward kinematics of the robot is $x = T(\theta)\theta$, and the differential equation is $\dot{x} = J(q)\dot{\theta}$, in which q is the 7×1 joint position, and $J(q)$ is the 6×7 Jacobian matrix when the joint position is q. The torque of joints should be $\tau = J^{T}(q)F$, then the desired position and posture are changed into output torque.

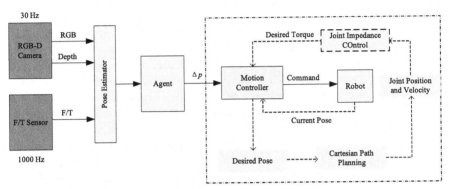

Fig. 3. Motion control framework. Combined the robot's end-effector position, orientation and policy output to get the desired pose, then get the joint position and velocity through Cartesian path planning. Use joint impedance control to get the desired output torque.

However, when the output action is relatively small, the robot will move slowly, which decreases the efficiency of assembly task. We try to raise the responding speed by adjusting P and D parameters of the impedance controller but it not works, turns unstable. Considering the fast response of position control in Cartesian space, we propose a method which combines both Cartesian path planning and joint impedance controller. The idea is to calculate joint position and velocity from the start point to the target position by Cartesian space motion planning, and then use impedance controller in joint space to control the motion of the robot. The method uses Cartesian path planning method, which is suitable for operation tasks in Cartesian space. A series of planned waypoints are used as the input of joint impedance controller, which not only guarantees the responding speed, but also makes the control process flexible. Figure 3 shows the whole motion control process of the robot.

3 Simulation and Results Analysis

Our method is designed specifically for precision assembly, and of course it is not limited into precision assembly. As a classic assembly task, although many people have explored it, the peg-in-hole problem has not been completely solved. We will verify the policy in the peg-in-hole task.

3.1 Simulation Environment

Simulation experiment is implemented in ROS. Gazebo is integrated into ROS and used as a physical simulation environment for the experiment. There are many types of sensors in Gazebo, including RGB-D cameras and joint force/torque sensors required for experiment, which provide RGB, depth and force/torque feedback respectively. Moveit is also integrated in ROS, which can provide Cartesian path planning for simulation and return the joint position and joint velocity required for joint impedance control. The simulation experiment uses a Franka robot with seven degrees of freedom as the assembly robot. The robot is controlled in real time with a control frequency of 1000 Hz. Franka-Ros-Interface can provide interfaces required by simulation and real robots.

The frequency of force feedback is 1000 Hz, which provides force/torque feedback information at the end of the robotic arm. The frequency of the camera is 30 Hz, and the camera provides RGB and depth data feedback at the same time. The assembly objects in the simulation environment are USB-C data cable connectors and model mobile phones, which are assembled with a fit clearance of <0.1 mm. Figure 1 shows the simulation environment. The resolution of the camera is 1920×1080, but we only collect the image information near the assembly space, that is, crop the area of (256, 256) size including the assembly point. There are three advantages to that. The first one is to save the storage space required to collect data. The second is to reduce the width and depth of the encoding network. The last is to save running memory, because we usually load all the data into the memory.

3.2 Design of Reward Function

Our algorithm does not divide the assembly task into hole searching and inserting, but treats it as a process. Therefore, there is no need to design two networks for searching hole and inserting respectively. We encourage downward movement, and also encourage movement towards the position and posture of the hole. We only move in a small area, so the reward design needs to punish the behavior beyond the area.

We define the grasping error as the random initial pose error of the end-effector of the robot relative to the hole and record the pose as P_h when the assembly successfully, in which

$$P_h = \left[x_h, y_h, z_h, R_h, P_h, Y_h \right]. \tag{2}$$

Pose before moving is

$$P_{\text{prime}} = \left[x_0, y_0, z_0, R_0, P_0, Y_0 \right]. \tag{3}$$

Pose after moving is

$$P_{\text{current}} = \left[x_1, y_1, z_1, R_1, P_1, Y_1 \right]. \tag{4}$$

Displacement in z direction before and after the movement is $\Delta z = z_0 - z_1$. Change in distance from the center plane of the hole is

$$\Delta xy = |(x_1, y_1) - (x_h, y_h)| - |(x_0, y_0) - (x_h, y_h)|. \tag{5}$$

Change in rotation is

$$\Delta RPY = |(R_1, P_1, Y_1) - (R_h, P_h, Y_h)| - |(R_0, P_0, Y_0) - (R_h, P_h, Y_h)|. \tag{6}$$

As a condition for judging whether the movement exceeds the threshold, the current absolute position error is defined as

$$\Delta_{xy} = |(x_1, y_1) - (x_h, y_h)|. \tag{7}$$

Absolute angle error is

$$\Delta_{RPY} = |(R_1, P_1, Y_1) - (R_h, P_h, Y_h)|. \tag{8}$$

Absolute assembly depth is $\Delta z_{deep} = z_h - z_1$. The unit of distance is millimet. The design of reward function is as follows:

$$R = \begin{cases} -1 & f > F_{th} \text{ or } \Delta_{xy} > Error_{xy} \text{ or } \Delta_{RPY} > Error_{RPY} \\ 1, & z_1 \leq z_h \\ -\Delta z - \Delta xy - \Delta RPY, & \text{other} \end{cases}. \tag{9}$$

3.3 Implementation Details

To train self-supervised learning and supervised learning network, we collect dataset with size 5000. The random error of position is 3mm and orientation is 5 degree when collecting data. We use NAF algorithm to collect data. The input state is relative position and orientation between the USB-C plug and the mobile phone. The assembly clearance is less than 0.1 mm. The models have been trained for 300 episodes on a Nvidia 1660 before policy learning. The training details can be found in Appendix.

3.4 Results

Encoding by Self-supervised Learning: Latent representation includes RGB images and depth maps. RGB data contains three channels and each channel is input data with size (256, 256). The RGB data is normalized and then input into the network for training. There is only one channel for depth data, and the size is same to RGB network. Both networks contain a four-layer convolutional network and a four-layer deconvolutional network. The output of encoding network is tiled and then reduced to 32 dimensions by two multi-layer perceptron (MLP) as potential feature vectors. The ratio of the test dataset is 0.1, and the loss curve of self-supervised learning is shown in Fig. 4.

The loss function is defined as the Mean Square Error of the normalized input and output data. After training, the RGB and depth test dataset loss is less than $4.5e{-}05$ and $1.7e{-}04$, respectively.

Pose Estimation by Supervised Learning: After self-supervised learning, training the pose estimation based supervised learning. RGB and depth are input to the trained model, and 32-dimensional vector outputs as input data of supervised learning. The loss curve

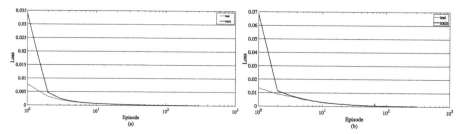

Fig. 4. Loss of self-supervised learning training. (a) shows the RGB image encoder loss, and (b) is the depth map encoder loss.

of pose estimation is shown in Fig. 5. Let (x, y, z, R, P, Y) be $(X_1, X_2, X_3, X_4, X_5, X_6)$, then the loss equation of pose estimation can be expressed as

$$Loss = \frac{1}{n} \sum_{i=1}^{n} (X_i - Y_i)^2, \tag{10}$$

where Y_i is the element of output. Pose estimation is trained with 300 episodes.

Policy Learning: The policy network using to make decision consists of four layers of MLP, and each of which is 128 in width. The encoder encodes the RGB, depth, and F/T data obtained in real time as the input of reinforcement learning. Details of reinforcement learning is shown in Appendix. The policy network has been trained for 200 episodes. Figure 6 is the curve of the reward during the training process.

Models (Type-C plug and phone) used in the experiments are modeled strictly based on the actual size. Them are even interference fit in practice sometimes. We compare the output of the strategy in three different combinations. Figure 6 shows the learning results of policy. With only force/torque, the strategy learning has not been successful at all.

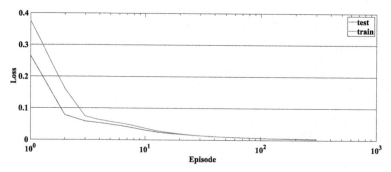

Fig. 5. MSE of pose estimation. The loss of trained data less than 0.003, and the loss of test dataset less than 0.004 after training.

With only vision, the training has achieved some success, but it is not stable. It may be due to visual occlusion that the information provided by vision in a small area is not enough to clearly represent the pose information. Finally, we combine force and vision, and the training achieves a good result. It can be seen from the figure that after step 120, and the result of simulation shows its stable performance. The result shows that the combination of multi-modals is easier to obtain a stable strategy, and demonstrates the effectiveness of the framework we proposed.

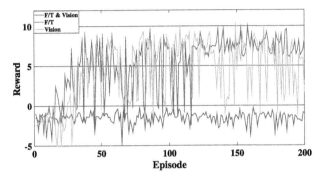

Fig. 6. Return reward for each step in the training process.

4   Conclusions

We propose a system framework that combines multiple sensor data for strategy learning. The framework uses RGB image, depth map and force/torque to estimate the relative pose of the parts. The framework can be divided into two parts: pose estimation and strategy learning. Pose estimation includes autoencoder with self-supervised learning and encoder with supervised learning. Latent features are fused with the force/torque to estimate the pose in current state. In order to overcome the excessive assembly force in the assembly process, we use impedance control, combined with Cartesian path planning and joint impedance control. This method also solved slow responding speed problem of impedance control. The simulation experiment results show that the proposed framework is effective.

In the future, we will focus on the contact force information in the assembly process. For precision assembly, when the assembly process reaches the blind spot of visual guidance, contact forces can provide richer information than vision. Therefore, we will change the weights of different modalities in assembly process, and compare the effects under different weights.

Acknowledgment. This work was supported partially by the NSFC-Shenzhen Robotics Basic Research Center Program (No. U1713202) and partially by the Shenzhen Science and Technology Program (No. JSGG20191129114035610).

References

1. Sahin, C., Kim, T.-K.: Recovering 6D object pose: a review and multi-modal analysis. In: Leal-Taixé, L., Roth, S. (eds.) Computer Vision – ECCV 2018 Workshops. LNCS, vol. 11134, pp. 15–31. Springer, Cham (2019). https://doi.org/10.1007/978-3-030-11024-6_2

2. Kapusta, A., Park, D., Kemp, C.C.: Task-centric selection of robot and environment initial configurations for assistive tasks. In: IEEE International Conference on Intelligent Robots and Systems (IROS), pp. 1480–1487 (2015)

3. Rozo, L., Bruno, D., Calinon, S., Caldwell, D.G.: Learning optimal controllers in human-robot cooperative transportation tasks with position and force constraints. In: IEEE International Conference on Intelligent Robots and Systems (IROS), pp. 1024–1030 (2015)

4. Bartolozzi, C., Natale, L., Nori, F., Metta, G.: Robots with a sense of touch. Nat. Mater. **15**(9), 921–925 (2016)

5. Liang, P., Ge, L., Liu, Y., Zhao, L., Li, R., Ke, W.: An augmented discrete-time approach for human-robot collaboration. Discret. Dyn. Nat. Soc. (2016)

6. Xue, T., et al.: bayesian grasp: robotic visual stable grasp based on prior tactile knowledge (2019). http://arxiv.org/abs/1905.12920

7. Song, H.C., Kim, Y.L., Song, J.B.: Automated guidance of peg-in-hole assembly tasks for complex-shaped parts. In: IEEE International Conference on Intelligent Robots and Systems (IROS), pp. 4517–4522 (2014)

8. Lee, M.A., et al.: Making sense of vision and touch: learning multimodal representations for contact-rich tasks. IEEE Trans. Robot. **36**(3), 582–596 (2019)

9. Wang, Z., Yang, X., Hu, H., Lou, Y.: Actor-critic method-based search strategy for high precision peg-in-hole tasks. In: 2019 IEEE International Conference on Real-Time Computing and Robotics (RCAR), pp. 458–463 (2019)

10. Scherzinger, S., Roennau, A., Dillmann, R.: Contact skill imitation learning for robot-independent assembly programming. In: IEEE International Conference on Intelligent Robots and Systems (IROS), pp. 4309–4316 (2019)

11. Sidhik, S.: panda_simulator: Gazebo simulator for Franka Emika Panda robot supporting sim-to-real code transfer. Zenodo (2020)

12. Gu, S., Lillicrap, T., Sutskever, I., Levine, S.: Continuous deep q-learning with model-based acceleration. In: 33rd International Conference on Machine Learning (ICML), vol. 6, pp. 4135–4148 (2016). http://arxiv.org/abs/1603.00748

A Scalable Resource Management Architecture for Industrial Fog Robots

Xiang Xu, Ziqi Chai, Zhenhua Xiong[⊠], and Jianhua Wu

State Key Laboratory of Mechanical System and Vibration, School of Mechanical Engineering,
Shanghai Jiao Tong University, Shanghai 200240, China
mexiong@sjtu.edu.cn

Abstract. Smart factories call for a new system architecture to control massive industrial robots and sensors. Right after the concept of Cloud Robotics, Fog Robotics provide an appropriate architecture for this type of control system because of its low latency. Based on Fog Robotics, aiming at scalable resource management, we propose a Kubernetes-based microservice architecture for smart factories, including Terminal, Fog, and Cloud Layer. Kubernetes is utilized to settle the resource management of the architecture. Considering smart factory applications, we describe functions for each layer. To be specific, the warehouse scenario is studied for launching the architecture in reality. The requirements and difficulties are analyzed and settled by utilizing Robot Operating System (ROS) and microservices. ROS is used to provide the interfaces of robots and data. Warehouse tasks are separated into different microservices to develop and update conveniently. A case study in warehouses is provided, which considers the standardization, industrial requirements, and microservices. Based on path planning microservices and ROS, experiments are conducted to evaluate the performance while expanding the architecture. The results demonstrate the feasibility of launching the architecture in real applications.

Keywords: Kubernetes · Microservice · Warehouse · Fog Robotics

1 Introduction

Driven by the Industry 4.0 and other smart manufacturing strategies, the automation degree is the most important bottleneck to break [1]. The robots, especially the Automatic Mobile Robot (AMR), are responsible for the flexible manufacturing for small batch and personalized yielding. In 2010, J. Kuffer proposed the "Cloud Robotics (CR)" concept, integrating the resources distributed geographically into the cloud platform [2]. Inspired by the CR concept, many organizations achieved the CR platform development to share knowledge and experiences among heterogeneous robots, e.g., the RoboEarth [3], Rapyuta [4].

Though the platform gives the robots the chance to improve continuously by the AI algorithms, it suffers from network limitations due to the increasing robot number under cloud services. To break the limits, S. Gudi proposed the "Fog Robotics (FR)" architecture [5, 6], which is the combination of CR and Fog Computing or Edge Computing. By

X.-J. Liu et al. (Eds.): ICIRA 2021, LNAI 13013, pp. 67–77, 2021.
https://doi.org/10.1007/978-3-030-89095-7_7

adding the local Fog Robot Server (FRS), some tasks could be offloaded from the cloud to the local Fog Node (FN) to gain lower latency and save bandwidth of transferring the data [7, 8]. Even for the lowest latency, the concept "Dew Robotics" was proposed based on Dew Computing [9].

Applying the FR concept to factories, the control system needs to control different kinds of sensors besides robots. In [10], fog computing was used to preprocess the data produced by the Industrial Internet of Things (IIoT) and transport them into the cloud platform. The fog layer plays the role of gateway and route between the cloud and the devices. Further, the intelligent industrial services were optimized and divided into fog and cloud layers in [11], which gives the fog layer more capability. A smart factory scenario was considered in [12], while the attention was paid to the allocation schedule rather than the architecture. In spite of these advancements, there are still a lot of challenges in employing the concept to factories mentioned in [13, 14].

For real factory applications, the architecture itself is not enough to undertake the requirements, including integrate the resources in various kinds of computers, handle the concurrent data or requests, keep services highly available, and standardize the data from the system. With the help of ROS or Programmable Logic Controllers (PLC), the system could control heterogeneous devices and standardize the data form. Besides virtualization, containerization is also a technology to isolate resources uniformly among different computers. In [15], a demo was carried out to realize the target recognition and single robotic arm control under ROS in Docker, which is the most popular container. Though the resource isolation is settled, resource management still needs to be solved. Kubernetes, as the manager and orchestration tools, settles the resource isolation and management. In [16], Kubernetes was launched to orchestrate the containers to control the whole factory. However, the Fog Layer function is like a gateway to compress raw data. The applications in Fog Node are multi-threads, whose resources are in waste when the data number is small. T. Goldschmidt proposed a container-based architecture to achieve flexible control for PLC to standardize the data without using ROS [17].

Recently, microservice, as a new Service-Oriented Architecture (SOA) framework, can separate applications into fine-grained parts to develop and update conveniently. In [18], the authors provided a solution based on the microservice for the fog-cloud industrial network, but they paid more attention to the system scheduling strategy rather than industrial applications. Microservices could make full use of the resources integrated by Kubernetes.

Combining the microservice with Kubernetes is an efficient method to control the factory globally, which can take advantage of both sides. In [19], a Kubernetes-based microservice architecture was put forward for the cloud platform, which costs less task execution time than traditional architectures. The same concept of the CR was shown in [20]. However, the communication limititations are not nononegligible. Furthermore, for the FR, only in [21], the authors came up with the microservices framework based on Kubernetes. However, the cluster is too large to control and deploy for factories.

Based on the FR concept, the Kubernetes-based microservice architecture is proposed for the smart factory in this paper, which considers more on the scalable resource management. The remainder of this paper is organized as follows. In Sect. 2, the new architecture is proposed for smart factories, including the software solution. A warehouse case is studied in Sect. 3, which also includes the difficulties and solutions. Experiments are conducted in Sect. 4 to evaluate the architecture. In Sect. 5, the paper is concluded.

2 Architecture

Following the development from distributed computing to Cloud-Edge computing through Cloud computing, the control system could give commands to more robots. With the tendency of IoT, the sensors could connect to the Ethernet directly, causing massive data produced in real-time. For flexible manufacturing, the control system is responsible for the assembly line and the optimization of processes. As the architecture, it is responsible to manage whole resources.

2.1 Resource Management

Because the capabilities of computers are different, it is difficult to control all the resources globally, which leads to resource integration and management. Compared to virtualization for Cloud Computing, containerization encapsulates each processor into containers, avoiding launching the Operating System (OS) on the original one. Containers provide a more concise solution to execute the applications or codes by utilizing the system resource directly. Meanwhile, it is convenient to pack the codes and dependencies to transfer as a unit called image. Though the resource isolation degree is not as high as virtualization, containerization could afford the tasks. Docker is selected for the architecture among several most popular containers because of its open-source and high community activity.

No matter in the cloud or FN, resources could be integrated and isolated by Docker. Dealing with many containers, Kubernetes is a platform to orchestrate them by the master node. By Kubernetes, managers could handle the Pods to execute images as the minimum unit to control. Conveniently, the platform maintains states of all pods. For high availability, Kubernetes could combine the Linux Virtual Server (LVS) to switch master nodes seamlessly. Compared to OpenStack, the resource consumption of Kubernetes is less, which is the container-native platform. With the ingress, Kubernetes could process concurrent requests to some extent.

2.2 The Architecture

As for smart factories, the architecture based on the Kubernetes, Docker, and Microservice is not specific to achieve. In the section, we propose a new architecture as shown in Fig. 1.

As the common cloud-fog architecture, there are three layers, including Terminal, Fog, and Cloud Layer. The difference is focusing on the Fog Layer. First, we give the Fog Layer more computing and storage capabilities to make decisions rather than transporting the data as a gateway. Then, each FN is placed in a workshop to bear its unique process, as a Kubernetes Cluster. As shown in the figure, the Terminal Layer comprises devices and their driver microservices as the product base. The FNs are responsible for each craft, including process the raw data, executing the technology, and controlling the devices to collaborate. The cloud Layer contains microservices for Data Mining to optimize crafts and predict the factory state.

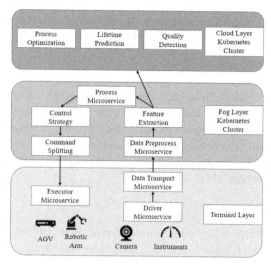

Fig. 1. The scalable resource management architecture for smart factories. Each box stands for a kind of microservices in the flowchart. The arrows show the flow of data.

3   Case Study

Warehouses, as the common part of all factories, are also influenced by the automation trend. There are usually many AGVs to get and deliver goods. As a concrete workshop in the factory, the warehouse is under the management of the FN rather than the Cloud platform, referring to the architecture proposed above. Meanwhile, the AGV number occupies the majority of the factory, bringing out a great challenge for control in real-time. Because of the mobility of AGVs, the control precision requirement is high, and the latency is required to be very short.

3.1   Difficulties

The workflow of warehouses could be divided into four parts, including simultaneous localization and mapping (SLAM), path planning, state observation, and goods transportation. By SLAM algorithms, AGVs can percept the environment and navigate around the warehouse. As the core function, goods transportation helps the AGV recognize the types of goods and points out the delivery place by querying the database. With the input of starting point and destination coordinates, the path planning algorithm computes paths for AGVs. The state observation is used to avoid collisions between AGVs. Though many organizations have achieved automatic warehouses, the AGVs usually follow fixed paths rather than entirely flexible paths. The difficulties are sorted out to be in three dimensions, namely microservices allocation, industrial requirements, and standardization.

Standardization

Standardization contains two aspects, including devices and data. As for terminals, there are massive heterogeneous robots and sensors required for the Ethernet. The FN needs to support various drivers for devices from different manufacturers. On the other hand, data are full of the whole control system, which needs to be formalized, including commands and intermediate data. Based on the standard, the interfaces of microservices could develop uniformly.

Industrial Requirements
Once an error occurred in the system, the repairment damages profits and causes maintenance costs. In industry, the applications need to keep high stable and available 24 h a day, as the advantages of automation. The number of microservices is too large to observe each status artificially, which can be solved with Kubernetes. Also, as described in Sect. 2, the high stable could be settled through LVS to avoid single-point failure. It is inevitable the scale of the warehouse needs to adjust dynamically depending on the needs, which means the architecture could extend conveniently under the same performance nearly.

Microservices Allocation
Microservice is a variant from the SOA, taking apart the application. Dividing the applications into fine-grained codes, the difficulty of development and upgrading is lower than before. Because of the algorithm complexity of different application parts, managers change the number of elements to gain the best performance and cost the smallest resource. Microservice architecture gives flexibility to the applications, calling for the fine-grained OS. So, the combination of Microservice, Kubernetes, and Docker is the appropriate solution for the cloud and FNs.

Because the computational complexity and resource consumption are different among microservices, managers adjust microservice numbers to gain the best control performance. Meanwhile, the same kind of microservices could be reused for various applications. Compared to the traditional control system, microservices face requests from AGVs rather than the specified AGV as a service provider. So, how to divide the applications of warehouses into microservices is a crucial difficulty to settle.

3.2 The Proposed Solution

ROS supports a wide range of robot types and sensors as the most popular operating system. ROS plays the role of interfaces in data transportation. With more hardware manufacturers supporting ROS, the platform would be universal if the architecture could utilize ROS.

Whether in Cloud or Fog, the requests can be classified into two kinds, including outside and inside. The inside means the sensors and robots are in the cluster. With the network provided by Kubernetes, ROS could be set up in the cluster, as shown in Fig. 2(a). Due to the communication mechanism of ROS, the master and nodes should be in the same LAN(Local Area Network), which causes the quantitative restriction devices accessed to the network. Quite the opposite, requests mainly come from the outside of the cluster and it is hard to access the same ROS. Under the circumstance, the cluster is a service provider to handle massive requests, just like the Web Servers. Each master of

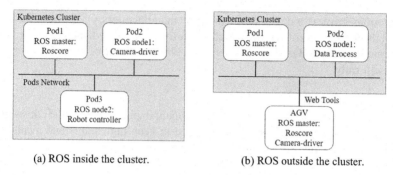

(a) ROS inside the cluster.   (b) ROS outside the cluster.

Fig. 2. The solution to apply ROS into the architecture.

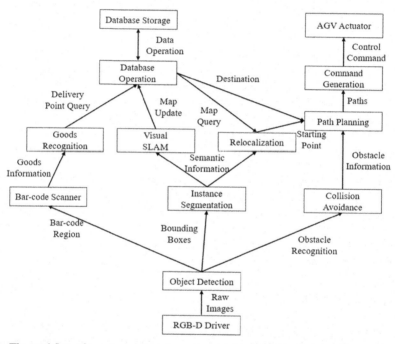

Fig. 3. The workflow of warehouses based on microservice. Each block represents a microservice for the system.

ROS could run on each AGV, and sends the requests to the server with the help of Web Tools, as shown in Fig. 2(b).

Workflow

According to the coupling degree, four parts of warehouses are divided into microservices shown in Fig. 3. We chose the Semantic SLAM for the example. Because the semantic information depends on the object detection results, the object detection microservice is independent, convenient to reuse by other parts. Like the database operation, the object detection microservice could be used for the whole system, as an advantage of microservices.

From capturing the raw image to control the AGV, the whole system is taken apart into microservices. Many microservices could be reused, calling for the interfaces of ROS. The data flow and information are shown in Fig. 3. Combining the microservice workflow and ROS mentioned above, a concrete architecture has been elaborated.

4   Evaluation

4.1   Simulation Environment

To launch the architecture still needs to evaluate the network performance. Because of possible large amounts of concurrency numbers in factories, we selected the path planning algorithm to assess the feasibility and scalability of the architecture.

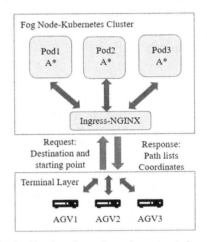

Fig. 4. The data flow of warehouse experiments.

We simplified the data interaction between the AGVs and the fog node, as shown in Fig. 4. AGVs post the start-point and destination coordinates and request the path planning services utilizing ROS Web Tools. Once the fog node receives the request, it executes the algorithm and returns the coordinates as the path lists. As for setting up the Kubernetes cluster, a Container Network Interface (CNI) named flannel and an ingress interface called ingress-Nginx are placed to ensure the network connections. Established by usage, there is one container in a pod, which is the minimum dispatch unit.

Concreted to the experiment, we concentrate on the architecture of fog nodes rather than the cloud platform for industrial warehouses. The fog node comprises three local computers in the laboratory, whose hardware configuration is shown in Table 1. The A* path planning algorithm is encapsulated to an interface to handle the requests from AGVs and return the result paths. The size of the experiment raster map is 1000 by 1000, which could cover a large number of warehouse sizes in the real world. We do not take

Table 1. The hardware configuration of localhosts

	CPU Model	CPU cores number	Processors number
Master	Intel Core I5-8400	6	12
Node1	AMD R9-3900x	12	24
Node2	Intel Core I7-6700K	4	8

the collision avoidance into consideration in this case. The frequency for requesting of the AGV is set to be 2 Hz.

The QoS (Quality of Service) of the fog node is evaluated by the average latency times, standing for the waiting times from submitting requests to receiving the path coordinates of each AGV. The QPS (Queries Per Second) parameter stands for the requests received within one second. The concurrency means the requests arrived at the same time. The concurrency number refers to the concurrency number for each pod (planner) rather than for the system. The requests from AGVs are simulated by software to control the post time conveniently.

4.2 Single Pod

Each pod contains one container, which is at the A* microservice level. Firstly, a single pod performance experiment is executed for the basic data as a reference, whose result is shown in Table 2.

Table 2. The performance of single microservice

Concurrency number	QPS	Robot number	Average latency time (s)
1	2	1	0.1484
1	8	4	0.1435
4	8	4	0.8385
8	8	4	1.7089

If the concurrency number is 1, the A* microservice could bear eight requests per second. However, the microservice is a single-threaded program that can not process several requests simultaneously. If the concurrency number is no longer one, though the QPS is still 8, the requests will block at the service entrance. So, following the increase of concurrency numbers, the QoS becomes worse than before. That is, the concurrency number is a more important parameter for the average latency time compared to the QPS. In reality, the requests from robots or AGVs are random among the same second because of the network fluctuation and their clocks. It is vital to evaluate the architecture under high pressure and concurrent to guarantee the stability of the services. Hence, we considered the requests from AGVs arrived concurrently. Further experiments are taken as below.

4.3 Architecture Evaluation

Since the concurrency number has a more important influence than QPS, it is necessary to be the key variable to evaluate the performance under pressure. The concurrency number equal to one is abandoned. The pod number increasing is to simulate the extension of microservices because of the resource expansion and increasing robot numbers. Different concurrency numbers represent various pressure degrees for fog nodes. Through testing, we get the average latency times, as shown in Fig. 5.

From the hardware configuration, there are 44 processors provide for pods. Besides the pods for the APIServer, the etcd, and the scheduler required by the Kubernetes system, nearly 30 containers could be available for microservices in the fog node. The average latency times increase slowly following the increasing pod number under the same concurrency number. Because the ingress applied is not so efficient for the task allocation, the growing trend is reasonable. If the number of pods is less than 30, the fog node could afford the resource consumption completely. The wave of times changes in a smaller range because of network jitter.

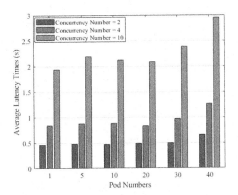

Fig. 5. The influence of increasing pod numbers for average latency times. The concurrency number is for the single pod (planner). The robot numbers could calculate by pod numbers multiple concurrency numbers. The pod number refers to the number of A* microservice.

Compared to the single-pod result, the average latency time is nearly the same, which means the QoS level remains though the robot number is increasing. It demonstrates the high scalability of the architecture. Limited to the A* algorithm, each pod costs more time for data processing than data I/O and transportation. Up to 30 pods, the fog node could bear more than 60 robots to plan paths within 0.5s. Even the number of pods exceeds 30, the architecture could also handle these requests for a slower time. Contacted to the architecture above, the software could provide the services for robots in a workshop as a fog node.

5 Conclusion

This paper proposes an architecture based on Kubernetes and microservices to control multi-robots, launching the FR concept into factories. We distribute each Fog Node to control the specified workshop, while the Cloud Platform is responsible for the whole factory. Furthermore, the warehouse scenario is studied to absorb the architecture. To overcome difficulties from standardization, industrial requirements, and microservice division, we set up ROS in the cluster as the interface provider. We divide the tasks into different microservices to improve the reuse rate of microservice. The workflow of microservices is given to describe the data flow of the control system. Through the experiments carried out, we demonstrate the scalability and feasibility of the system in high concurrency. In summary, the architecture is an efficient solution for factories utilizing the FR concept. But the whole system still needs to explore in the future.

Acknowledgement. This work is jointly supported by National Natural Science Foundation of China (U1813224), National Key R&D program of China (2019YFB1310801) and Ministry of Education China Mobile Research Fund Project (CMHQ-JS-201900003).

References

1. Javaid, M., Haleem, A., Vaishya, R., Bahl, S., Suman, R., Vaish, A.: Industry 4.0 technologies and their applications in fighting COVID-19 pandemic. Diabetes Metab. Syndr.: Clin. Res. Rev. **14**(4), 419–422 (2020)
2. Kuffner, J.: Cloud-enabled humanoid robots. In: 2010 10th IEEE-RAS International Conference on Humanoid Robots (Humanoids), pp. 519–526. IEEE, Nashville (2010)
3. Waibel, M., et al.: Roboearth. IEEE Robot. Autom. Mag. **18**(2), 69–82 (2011)
4. Mohanarajah, G., Hunziker, D., D'Andrea, R., Waibel, M.: Rapyuta: a cloud robotics platform. IEEE Trans. Autom. Sci. Eng. **12**(2), 481–493 (2014)
5. Gudi, S.C.: Fog robotics: an introduction. In: IEEE/RSJ International Conference on Intelligent Robots and Systems. IEEE, Vancouver (2017)
6. Gudi, S.L.K.C., Ojha, S., Johnston, B., Clark, J., Williams, M.A.: Fog robotics for efficient, fluent and robust human-robot interaction. In: 2018 IEEE 17th International Symposium on Network Computing and Applications, pp. 1–5. IEEE, Cambridge (2018)
7. Hu, L., Miao, Y., Wu, G., Hassan, M.M., Humar, I.: iRobot-Factory: an intelligent robot factory based on cognitive manufacturing and edge computing. Futur. Gener. Comput. Syst. **90**(10), 569–577 (2019)
8. Chen, Y., Feng, Q., Shi, W.: An industrial robot system based on edge computing: an early experience. In: Proceedings of USENIX Workshop on Hot Topics in Edge Computing. USENIX Association, Boston (2018)
9. Botta, A., Gallo, L., Ventre, G.: Cloud, fog, and dew robotics: architectures for next generation applications. In: 2019 7th IEEE International Conference on Mobile Cloud Computing, Services, and Engineering, pp. 16–23. IEEE, Newark (2019)
10. Aazam, M., Zeadally, S., Harras, K.A.: Deploying fog computing in industrial Internet of Things and industry 4.0. IEEE Trans. Industr. Inf. **14**(10), 4674–4682 (2018)
11. Lager, A., Papadopoulos, A., Nolte, T.: IoT and fog analytics for industrial robot applications. In: 2020 25th IEEE International Conference on Emerging Technologies and Factory Automation, vol. 1, pp. 1297–1300. IEEE, Vienna (2020)

12. Yang, Y., Luo, X., Chu, X., Zhou, M.T.: Fog-enabled multi-robot system. In: Fog-Enabled Intelligent IoT Systems, pp. 99–131. Springer, Cham (2020). https://doi.org/10.1007/978-3-030-23185-9_4
13. Shaik, M.S., et al.: Enabling fog-based industrial robotics systems. In: 2020 25th IEEE International Conference on Emerging Technologies and Factory Automation, vol. 1, pp. 61–68. IEEE, Vienna (2020)
14. Shaik, M.S., et al.: Fog-based industrial robotic system: applications and challenges
15. Galambos, P.: Cloud, fog, and mist computing: advanced robot applications. IEEE Syst. Man Cybern. Mag. **6**(1), 41–45 (2020)
16. Omar, A., Imen, B., M'hammed, S., Bouziane, B., David, B.: Deployment of fog computing platform for cyber physical production system based on docker technology. In: 2019 International Conference on Applied Automation and Industrial Diagnostics, vol. 1, pp. 1–6. IEEE, Elazig (2019)
17. Goldschmidt, T., Hauck-Stattelmann, S., Malakuti, S., Grüner, S.: Container-based architecture for flexible industrial control applications. J. Syst. Archit. **84**, 28–36 (2018)
18. Khoso, F.H., Lakhan, A., Arain, A.A., Soomro, M.A., Nizamani, S.Z., Kanwar, K.: A microservice-based system for industrial Internet of Things in fog-cloud assisted network. Eng. Technol. Appl. Sci. Res. **11**(2), 7029–7032 (2021)
19. Yin, Z., Liu, J., Chen, B., Chen, C.: A Delivery robot cloud platform based on microservice. J. Robot. **2021**, 1–10 (2021)
20. Xu, B., Bian, J.: A cloud robotic application platform design based on the microservices architecture. In: 2020 International Conference on Control, Robotics and Intelligent System, pp. 13–18. ACM, Xiamen (2020)
21. Wang, R., et al.: Cloud-edge collaborative industrial robotic intelligent service platform. In: 2020 IEEE International Conference on Joint Cloud Computing, pp. 71–77. IEEE, Oxford (2020)

Robot Predictive Maintenance Method Based on Program-Position Cycle

Dongdong Guo[1,2], Yan Zhang[1(✉)], and Xiangqun Chen[2]

[1] Beijing Benz Automotive Co., Ltd., Beijing 100176, People's Republic of China
Zhangyan4@bbac.com.cn
[2] Peking University School of Software and Microelectronics, Beijing 102600,
People's Republic of China

Abstract. A condition monitoring method of industrial robot based on program-position cycle is proposed to serve predictive maintenance. In this method, actual working conditions in factory is taken as the background. The data is processed according to the robot program-position cycle: the sequence of the robot position in each program is used as the periodic index, to avoid program-time cycle differences due to waiting signals. Data is processed in path segments of each robot motion command instead of each position point to reduce the amount of calculations. Take the axis current monitoring as an example, a reference range of current of each axis in each path section is constructed with the suitable percentile form historical data under normal working conditions. The change of the current relative to the reference range is recognized, and the proportion of data exceeding the range is calculated, and an alarm is issued accordingly. No extra sensor or extra testing time is needed in this method. The validity of the algorithm is verified by failure cases in factory conditions. The verification results show that the method can serve predictive maintenance for a variety of mechanical failures. This paper exemplifies the data verification of balancing cylinder problems, and path accuracy problem due to worn of spline shaft. A change in the mechanical condition is identified days before the failure occurs.

Keywords: Industrial robot · Condition monitoring · Predictive maintenance · Intelligent manufacturing · Data-driven

1 Introduction

In automated factories, industrial robots are widely used. It is of far-reaching significance to conduct predictive maintenance research on robots based on big data. Take Beijing Benz Automobile Factory as an example. By the year 2020, the number of robots in use has reached 3,000. The maintenance tasks are heavy, especially the mechanical maintenance of robots: 1. The daily maintenance workload is large, and it is difficult to maintain timely. It is difficult to accurately quantify and measure the risk of each robot due to overdue maintenance tasks. Using big data to achieve precise maintenance of equipment will produce huge economic benefits for enterprises. 2. The solving of

© Springer Nature Switzerland AG 2021
X.-J. Liu et al. (Eds.): ICIRA 2021, LNAI 13013, pp. 78–88, 2021.
https://doi.org/10.1007/978-3-030-89095-7_8

mechanical system failure requires special equipment, which takes a long time and causes the a long time break down, which affects the completion of production tasks and causes huge losses. Realizing intelligent predictive maintenance, accurately predicting potential equipment problems, making timely adjustments and processing, avoiding the occurrence of downtime and the consumption of spare parts, will be of great significance to the enterprise.

At present, the condition monitoring and prediction of robot mechanical problems are in the laboratory research stage. Riccardo Pinto [1] et al. took Comau robot's spot welding pipeline package fault as an example, and selected characteristic variables based on experience to perform data-driven fault diagnosis. Shows a certain potential for predictive maintenance based on data-driven. Wang Jiugen and others [2, 3] made related research on the fault diagnosis of the RV reducer of the robot component, respectively using the residual network algorithm and a convolutional neural network under noise interference to make Fault Diagnosis. The research are mostly for a single mechanical component. The data equipment and operating environment obtained in the laboratory are relatively single, and even the same failure equipment and the same degree of failure are used for each failure mode. This prerequisite is difficult to meet in actual diagnosis situations, and what can actually be used to train a diagnosis model is usually historical data collected from the same type of equipment or different working conditions [2–11]. The actual operating conditions of the robot are relatively complicated. The speed and load of each axis will be affected by the robot's motion trajectory, motion speed, acceleration, working conditions, and the load of the tools carried by the robot. The range of changes is large, and the actual working conditions are difficult to simulate in the laboratory. In addition, at present, data-driven fault diagnosis using vibration signals as characteristic variables is common [2, 3, 12–14]. In the actual operating conditions of the robot, it is necessary to add sensors to collect the vibration signals of various mechanical components, which is difficult to operate and high cost. In addition, the complex working environment will generate a lot of noise, which will interfere with the extraction and further application of the signal. At present, there is no mature application in the field of industrial robots.

In this paper, taking the robot working conditions in factory as the background, using robot running data from its controller (no extra sensor is needed), a method for monitoring the general mechanical state of the robot based on the program-position cycle is proposed.

2   Condition Monitoring Method Based on Robot Program-Position Cycle

2.1   Data Background

The condition monitoring method proposed in the article uses the process data of the robot running under working conditions. Take Beijing Benz as an example, who use KUKA robot. KUKA robot can use MQTT protocol to send process data outwards. In order to ensure a reasonable memory usage rate, the process data sending frequency is 0.5 Hz, that is, every 2 s. Real-time process data, the data content can be set by yourself, such as time stamp, robot number, robot axis torque, current, following error, speed, base frame or tool coordinate system, current robot position, current location Program and command line, etc. These data are received by the server and stored in the data lake for recall and processing. The data obtained in this way has insufficient regularity and discontinuity. Even if continuous data acquisition is achieved, the key parameters are affected by factors such as the robot's motion trajectory, motion speed, acceleration, working conditions, and the tool load carried by the robot. The range of changes is large and lacks regularity. It is necessary to find the periodicity and compare the difference between the monitoring data and the historical normal working data of the same robot.

2.2 Exploration of Periodic Laws

The robot's work operation is based on the program. The work tasks and robot working condition in same program are almost the same. So, first observe the data from the perspective of program-time cycle. As shown in Fig. 1 is the collected current data of each axis of a robot. The sampling period is 20 ms, and the program where the robot is located during data collection is marked with color in the figure. It can be seen from the figure that there is a certain law for observing data from the program-time cycle perspective. However, the period of the same program is inconsistent due to the influence of the signal waiting time in the program, such as interference zone signals. In addition, the data-sampling period under actual working conditions is 2 s, and the data is discrete, which adds difficulty to the periodic regularity of data extraction and data clean.

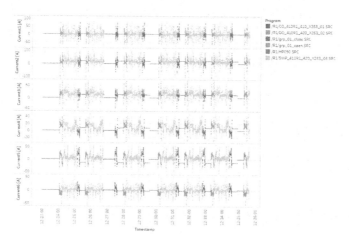

Fig. 1. Current-time scatter plot, colored by its program

In order to solve this problem, this paper proposes to analyze data based on the robot program-position cycle. Excluding the signal waiting time, there is a one-to-one correspondence between the robot's program-time cycle and the robot's program-path position cycle. Therefore, the sequence of the robot position in each program is used as the periodic index to design algorithm, to avoid program time cycle differences due to waiting signals.

Using discrete data can obtain complete cycle data under the superposition of multiple cycles. Figure 2 is the robot tool center point (TCP) position scatter plot of 80 working hours. Data collected every 2 s. Discrete position scatters make up a complete working path under multiple cycles. (The discontinue part is due to the changes of tool or base coordinate system).

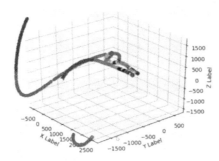

Fig. 2. Scatter plot of robot TCP position of multiple cycles.

2.3 Process of the Predictive Maintenance Method

The algorithm is divided into four major steps: 1) Data collection and cleaning; 2) Feature selection and extraction; 3) Monitoring model construction; 4) Condition monitoring process realization. 5) Predictive maintenance realization. Figure 3 is the basic process of the predictive maintenance method.

Data Cleaning
To identify the change of the characteristic variables related to the mechanical problems of the robot with respect to its historical state, it is necessary to ensure the consistency of the operating conditions of the robot. Therefore, the data is collected in the certain condition: normal automation operation mode, no error is reported, and the program is not in waiting mode.

Feature Selection
In industrial production, it usually takes a period of time(days or even month) for the mechanical failure completely. If the change of the mechanical state is recognized and manual intervention is performed during this period, the loss caused by the failure of the production line can be prevented, thereby achieving predictive maintenance.

Common robot mechanical failures include abnormal noise, axis torque out-of-tolerance alarms or robot position accuracy deviation caused by mechanical component failure. Table 1 is the Failure modes and effect analysis of core mechanical components of industrial robot. Some failures will cause increase in the torque of the relevant axis movement, such as bearing wear, balance cylinder failure, gear wear, etc. Robot position accuracy deviation will eventually crash and stop, such as: the aging of the transmission belt, the spline wear of the transmission rod, etc., such problems cause motion interference, which causes the torque of each axis at the interference point to change. The change of the drive current data of each axis is similar to the change trend of the torque, and there is no need to install sensors and can be directly obtained from the robot controller. Therefore, the drive current of each axis is selected as the key feature variable.

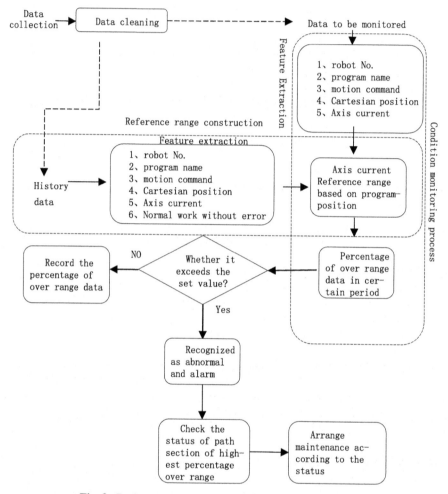

Fig. 3. Basic process of the predictive maintenance method

To design an algorithm based on program-position cycle. Program name and position information are needed as Features. Robot program path is composed of motion command path segments, and each motion path is composed of the robot's motion position points. To better deal with the position data, motion command and Cartesian coordinate position are taken as the feature variable.

Therefore, feature variable: the robot No, program name, motion command, Cartesian position, Axis current.

Table 1. Failure modes and effect analysis of core mechanical components of industrial robot

Core mechanical components	Failure modes	Failure affect	Break down event
Balance cylinder	Hydraulic failure	Safety risk	Robot fall down
	Bearing wear	Torque increase	Robot error
Reducer	Gear wear	Motion accuracy decrease	Interference, collision
	Connecting bolt broken		
	Impurities in gear box oil	Torque increase	Robot error
Bearing	Wear	Torque increase	Robot error
Connecting rod	Wear	Motion accuracy decrease	Interference, collision
Belt	Wear	Motion accuracy decrease	Interference, collision

Construction of the Condition Monitoring Model

Processing historical normal working data to make reference interval. In the actual operation process, thousands of robot need to be monitored, therefore reduce the calculations as much as possible is needed. Calculate the reference interval with path section instead of with path position point is needed. The finer the path segment divided, the more sensitive the monitoring, but at the same time, the more data is needed, it needs to be balanced according to actual needs. Use the motion command path as the path section is the most convenient way. That is group the history normal working data according to the program number - motion command line to calculate the reasonable reference range. The range will be stored in the data structure shown in Fig. 4 for monitoring operations to call.

In the actual operation process, the data of each axis of the robot may contain abnormal points, as show in Fig. 5. In the process of data processing to make the reasonable reference range, percentile P and percentile 100-P is used as the lower and upper limits of the reference range, and then enlarge it with tolerance t, according to robot normal working condition. See the formula 1, 2.

$$Reference\ Range\ n_{\max} = P_{100-p} + t \tag{1}$$

$$Reference\ Range\ n_{\min} = P_p - t \tag{2}$$

Realization of the Condition Monitoring Process and Predictive Maintenance

Find the current reference range of each axis according to the robot number, the program name, the movement comment of the data to be measured. Compare it with the corresponding current data of each axis, and counts the out-of-tolerance ratio j. When the ratio is greater than a certain set value i, it prompts that some abnormal event happened

Key:

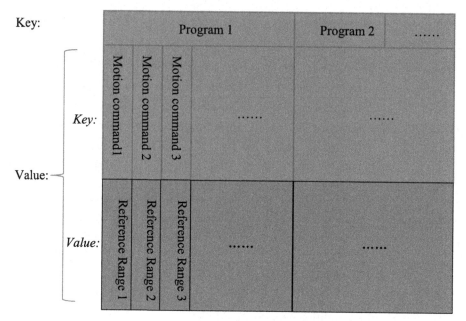

Fig. 4. Data structure of reference range

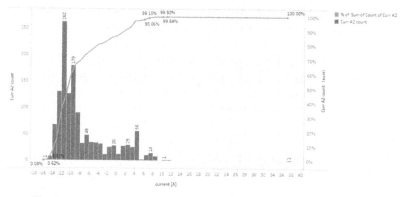

Fig. 5. Distribution of current points in a motion command path section

and make an alarm. Check the status of path section of highest percentage over range, and then inspect the mechanical structure related to the axis, and handles it according to the inspection result.

3 Verification of Monitoring Methods Under Factory Conditions

In the following verification process, the parameters are set as follows: $P = 1, t = 0.5$A, $i = 1\%$.

3.1 The Robot Balancing Cylinder Problem Case

Background: At August 5, 2020, a robot balance cylinder was found to have abnormal noise in the factory. By temporarily adding lubricating grease to the balance cylinder bearings, the abnormal noise disappeared.

Algorithm verification: Collect historical data from April 10 to May 10 to make a reference range. Perform monitoring calculations of the six axis current from June 22 to August 6. The results are shown in Table 2, Axis 1 and Axis 2 over range percentage increased significantly in July, and decreased after adding grease.

Table 2. Overrun percentage of reference range

Value	Date					
	6.22–6.25	7.7–7.10	7.14–7.17	7.20–7.23	8.3–8.5	8.5 (after add grease)
Current A1	0.56%	0.49%	0.60%	2.87%	3.05%	0.72%
Current A2	0.71%	0.64%	1.40%	2.14%	2.50%	1.09%
Current A3	0.38%	0.40%	0.88%	0.39%	0.97%	0.51%
Current A4	0.22%	0.32%	0.82%	0.34%	0.87%	0.46%
Current A5	0.33%	0.48%	0.81%	0.25%	0.99%	0.68%
Current A6	0.33%	0.60%	0.64%	0.66%	0.70%	0.52%

Figure 6 is a data graph of a path segment with the highest percentage of over range. Between the bottom line and the upper line is the reference range of this path section, and the curve is the current of the A2 axis of the data to be monitored, Unit A.

From Fig. 6(a), it shows that the current began to frequently exceeded the reference range on July 20th. From Fig. 6(b), it can be seen that on August 5th, after the lubricating oil is applied, the current barely return into the reference range.

3.2 Shaft Spline Ware Case

Failure background: On November 8, 2020, the pick-and-place robot on the production line scratched with the part fixture. The reason is that the 4-axis transmission connecting rod spline was severely worn. Wear part as shown in Fig. 7.

Algorithm verification: Collect historical data from July 1 to July 31 to create reference intervals. Monitoring the data after August. It shows that the proportion of the robot's 4-axis drive current exceeding the reference range has been on the rise since October, as shown in Fig. 8. In addition, there are also obvious abnormal out-of-range of the robot's 1, 2, and 6-axis, and the abnormal out-of-range of these axes is mainly at part loading position.

Figure 9 shows the status of the 4-axis current at the part loading position. The figure shows that most of the monitored current values are 0 or exceed the reference range, which due to the severe wear of the transmission spline. Due to the deterioration of position accuracy, the interference torque with the fixture increases and exceeds the

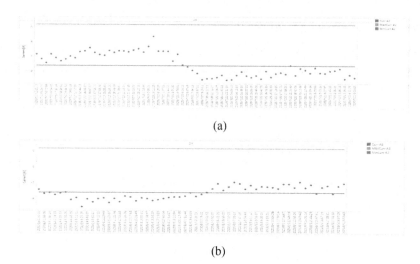

(a)

(b)

Fig. 6. Axis-2 current monitoring graph of the typical path section of the balance cylinder case

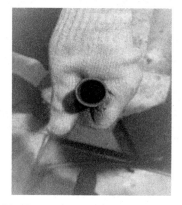

Fig. 7. Worn spline of connecting rod

reference range. Sometimes, robot cannot get part position ok signal and waiting for the signal, at this time, the 4-axis current value are 0.

In cases above, the abnormality can be monitored more than 10 days before the downtime, and timely intervention can prevent the break down.

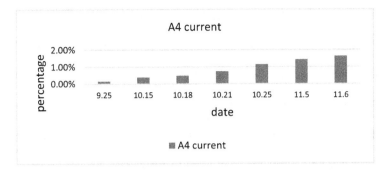

Fig. 8. Axis4 current monitoring over-range ratio of the Balance cylinder case

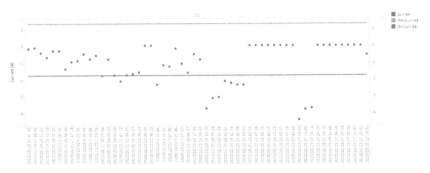

Fig. 9. Axis4 current monitoring graph of the load part position

4 Conclusion

The thesis puts forward a method of industrial robot condition monitoring based on program-position cycle to serve for predictive maintenance. This method studies under factory working conditions, can avoid program-time cycle differences due to waiting signals and can regularize the discontinues data. Take current monitoring as an example. The current changes of each axis of the robot relative to its history are identified in each cycle. The percentage of over reference range is recorded and alarm accordingly.

The verification results show that the method can identify the abnormality of the mechanical state (path accuracy problem, torque change due to mechanical wear) and give an early warning at least a few days before malfunctions happen of mechanical components. This method has high practical application value for predictive maintenance of factories.

In addition, the condition monitoring method proposed in the article provides a new effective perspective for the development of fault diagnosis algorithms and the search for characteristic values: program-position cycle.

References

1. Pinto, R., Cerquitelli, T.: Robot fault detection and remaining life estimation for predictive maintenance. Procedia Comput. Sci. **151**, 709–716 (2019)

2. Wang, J., Liangliang, K.E.: Fault diagnosis for RV reducer based on residual network. J. Mech. Eng. **55**(3), 73–80 (2019)
3. Peng, P., Liangliang, K.E., Wang, J.: Fault diagnosis of RV reducer with noise interference. J. Mech. Eng. **56**(1), 30–36 (2020)
4. Zheng, H., Wang, R., Yang, Y., et al.: An empirical analysis about the generalization performance of data-driven fault diagnosis methods. J. Mech. Eng. **56**(9), 102–117 (2020)
5. Biet, M.: Rotor faults diagnosis using feature selection and nearest neighbors rule : application to a turbo generator. IEEE Trans. Industr. Electron. **60**(9), 4063–4073 (2013)
6. Illias, H.A., Chai, X.R., Abu Bakar, A.H.: Hybrid modified evolutionary particle swarm optimisation-time varying acceleration coefficient-artificial neural network for power transformer fault diagnosis. Measurement **90**, 94–102 (2016)
7. Zhang, X., Chen, W., Wang, B., et al.: Intelligent fault diagnosis of rotating machinery using support vector machine with ant colony algorithm for synchronous feature selection and parameter optimization. Neurocomputing **167**, 260–279 (2015)
8. Lei, Y., Jia, F., Lin, J., et al.: An intelligent fault diagnosis method using unsupervised feature learning towards mechanical big data. IEEE Trans. Industr. Electron. **63**(5), 3137–3147 (2016)
9. Li, Y., Yang, Y., Wang, X., et al.: Early fault diagnosis of rolling bearings based on hierarchical symbol dynamic entropy and binary tree support vector machine. J. Sound Vib. **428**, 72–86 (2018)
10. Zhao, R., Wang, D., Yan, R., et al.: Machine health monitoring using local geature-based gated recurrent unit networks. IEEE Trans. Industr. Electron. **65**(2), 1539–1548 (2018)
11. Shao, H., Jiang, H., Lin, Y., et al.: A novel method for intelligent fault diagnosis of rolling bearings using ensemble deep auto-encoders. Mech. Syst. Sig. Process. **102**, 278–297 (2018)
12. Wang, X., Hong, Y., Qiu, D.: Fault diagnosis and mechanism study of water-film whirl in vertical reactor coolant pumps. J. Mech. Eng. **56**(11), 89–95 (2020)
13. Liu, D., Cheng, W., Wan, G.: Bearing fault diagnosis based on fault characteristic trend template. J. Mech. Eng. **53**(9), 83–91 (2017)
14. Zheng, J., Pan, H., Cheng, J., et al.: Adaptive empirical fourier decomposition based mechanical fault diagnosis method. J. Mech. Eng. **56**(9), 125–136 (2020)

Design of Manipulator Control System Based on Leap Motion

Yudong Ma[1] , Qingdang Li[1,2] , Mingyue Zhang[2]([⊠]) , and Zhen Sun[3]

[1] College of Automation and Electronic Engineering, Qingdao University of Science and
Technology, Qingdao 266061, China
lqd@qust.edu.cn
[2] College of Sino-German Science and Technology, Qingdao University of Science and
Technology, Qingdao 266061, China
[3] College of Information Science and Technology, Qingdao University of Science and
Technology, Qingdao 266061, China
sunzhen@qust.edu.cn

Abstract. Fixed program control and handle control are two main methods to
control manipulators. However, these control methods have many problems such
as inflexibility and non-intuition. To solve these problems, this paper proposes
a gesture-based manipulator control scheme, which realizes that the manipulator operator can directly control the movement of the manipulator through the
movement of their own hands. Firstly, the principle of the system is explained. A
five-degree-of-freedom manipulator model is established through Unity3d engine.
The communication among Leap Motion, manipulator model and actual manipulator is established. Secondly, the logical structure of the system is established,
and the UI interface and parameters of the control system interface are completed.
Besides, a filtering method combining percentile filtering and Gaussian filtering
is proposed to improve the target point jitter problem of the manipulator. Finally,
the feasibility of the method is verified by experiments. The final experimental
results show that the entire manipulator control system can run smoothly on the
planned trajectory, and the jitter problem of the manipulator target point has also
been greatly improved. Thus, the improved filtering effect is obviously better than
no filtering and only Gaussian filtering in terms of volatility and discreteness. It
can be seen that the control method simplifies the operation process and enhances
the intuitive experience of the operator.

Keywords: Leap Motion · Manipulator · Percentile filtering · Gaussian
filtering · Unity3D

1 Introduction

The control method of the manipulator has always been a hot topic of discussion in the
industry. Youshaa Murhij and others tried to use virtual reality equipment to control the
manipulator [1]. Compared with the traditional control method, this control method has
been greatly improved. The operator can control the manipulator immersive. However,

© Springer Nature Switzerland AG 2021
X.-J. Liu et al. (Eds.): ICIRA 2021, LNAI 13013, pp. 89–99, 2021.
https://doi.org/10.1007/978-3-030-89095-7_9

this control method uses a control handle, and the operator does not really free his hands. The buttons of the control handle are limited and their functions are relatively single. Some scholars try to recognize the control commands of manipulators through neural networks [2]. The advantage of this control method is that the control information can be captured only by using an ordinary monocular camera. However, the recognition accuracy of the model trained by the neural network is not high, sometimes the model cannot recognize the position of the hand, causing the operating system to malfunction. Some scholars try to control the manipulator through Kinect [3], but the accuracy of Kinect is not very high, and the control accuracy of the manipulator can only reach the centimeter level. Kinect's recognition range is the entire human body, but at most it can only recognize human hands [4], which cannot recognize fingers. This is also a waste of Kinect performance. However, Leap Motion can recognize subtle movements of fingers and joints.

To this end, this paper designs a new set of robotic arm control system. First, a five-degree-of-freedom manipulator model was established in the Unity3D game engine to simulate various actions of the real manipulator. The operator can also monitor the real manipulator by viewing the posture of the manipulator model. And then, LeapMotion's software development kit was imported [5], which provides some hand models and various Leap Motion program interfaces to facilitate future development work. The key to the whole system is to map the position of the center point of the palm surface captured by the Leap Motion sensor to the end target point of the five-degree-of-freedom manipulator. Then the coordinates and pitch angle obtained by Leap Motion are filtered and input to the end of the manipulator. Compared with the immersive industrial robotic arm control system of Youshaa Murhij et al. [7], this system avoids redundant external equipment, and in terms of filtering, this article not only provides a variety of filtering operation methods, but also focuses on common jitter and local A targeted filtering algorithm is provided for scenes with strong jitter. System Principle

1.1 Manipulator Introduction

The main hardware of this system includes Leap Motion sensor and five-degree-of-freedom manipulator. The outline drawing of the manipulator is shown in Fig. 1. The manipulator is driven by an AX-12A type servo. The communication module uses a USB2HDXL half-duplex TTL serial port. As for communication, the five dynamixel servos are controlled by the binary command packet sent by the controller. The servo systems will also transmit status packets for real-time status feedback. Since the five servo systems are connected by a bus, each group of data will have its own ID. The ID is used to distinguish which servo system sends or receives.

The Leap Motion is a vision-based somatosensory sensor, it can recognize the semantics of the operator's hand to control the PC. In addition, its recognition accuracy can reach 0.01 mm, and it has 215 frames per second output. It has APIs in multiple languages and can obtain key information such as hand position, deflection angle, and movement speed. Its recognition range is about a 40 cm cone on its front. The appearance of Leap Motion is shown in Fig. 2.

Fig. 1. Outline drawing of the five-degree-of-freedom manipulator.

Fig. 2. Leap Motion outline drawing.

1.2 The Principle of Leap Motion and Filter

Leap Motion uses the stereo vision principle of the binocular camera to locate the 3D coordinates. When the operator's hand appears in its working area, the two cameras simultaneously capture the target, and calculate the target's depth information based on the target's parallax. The imaging principle of the binocular camera is shown in Fig. 3. Where u_R is the detection target, b is the distance between the centers of the apertures of the two cameras, u_L is the distance between the center of the left aperture and the left imaging point, u_R is the distance between the center of the right aperture and the right imaging point, and z is the distance between the target and the center of the aperture, f is the focal length, and the length of the parallax is d = $u_L + u_R$. The y-axis is perpendicular to the x-axis and the z-axis. Let the point on the y-axis of the camera on the left be y_L, and the point on the y-axis of the camera on the right as y_R.

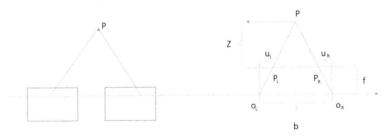

Fig. 3. Schematic diagram of the binocular recognition principle.

Then calculate the x,y and z values of point p. According to the criterion of similar triangles, Eq. (1) can be listed. Eq. (2) can be derived from Eq. (1). This results in the depth value z, and the values of x and y. In this way, the binocular camera can be used to obtain the depth data of the object being photographed.

$$\begin{cases} b - u_L - u_R)/b = (z - f)/z \\ z/f = (b - x)/(b - u_R) \\ z/f = y/y_L = y/y_R \end{cases} \tag{1}$$

$$\begin{cases} z = fb/(u_L + u_R) = fb/d \\ x = zu_L/f = (b - zx_R)/f \\ y = zy_L/f = zy_R/f \end{cases} \tag{2}$$

This article uses Gaussian filtering to process the target points of the manipulator. Gaussian filtering is shown in the Eq. (3).The value of μ is generally set to zero, which represents the position of the center point.σ represents the degree of dispersion of the data. The larger the value of σ, the better the denoising effect of Gaussian filtering, and vice versa. In this paper σ is set as 1.5. The image of the one-dimensional Gaussian function is shown in Fig. 4. Gaussian filtering is a linear smoothing filter, which is suitable for eliminating Gaussian noise and is widely used in the noise reduction process of digital signal processing. Gaussian filtering is the process of weighted averaging the values of the entire sequence. The value of each point is obtained by weighted averaging of itself and other values in the neighborhood. The specific operation of Gaussian filtering is to use a model (or convolution, mask) to scan each value in the sequence, and use the weighted average of the values in the neighborhood determined by the model to replace the value of the center point of the model. This paper uses a fifth-order Gaussian model, and the sum of each weight value is equal to 1. The Gaussian model is shown in Fig. 5.Each point of the robot coordinate value is brought into the last shift of Gaussian for weighting, and then the coordinate value after Gaussian filtering can be obtained.

$$f(x) = \frac{1}{\sigma\sqrt{2\pi}} e^{-(x-\mu)^2/2\sigma^2} \tag{3}$$

Gaussian filtering is not obvious for data processing with large differences at a specific time point. In order to enable the manipulator to automatically ignore the error value when encountering a jitter with a large difference, a processing method of combining percentile morphological filtering and Gaussian filtering is introduced. The percentile filter value in this article is set as 50%. The advantage of Gaussian filtering after percentile filtering is that it can filter out individual values that locally deviate from the overall coordinate value, so that values with large differences are prevented from participating in the process of Gaussian filtering. The percentile filtering formula is shown in Eq. (4).

$$X_{3desired} = X_{50\%} \tag{4}$$

Among them: $X_{3desired}$ is the filtered value of X_3 in $X_1,X_2,X_3,X_4,X_5.X_{50\%}$ is the median value among X_1,X_2,X_3, X_4 and X_5.

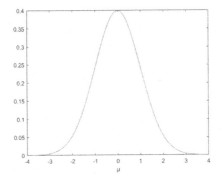

Fig. 4. Gaussian function two-dimensional graph.

$$0.186 \mid 0.361 \mid 0.453 \mid 0.361 \mid 0.186$$

Fig. 5. Fifth-order Gaussian model.

This paper uses the range method, standard deviation, and percentage measurement method to measure the volatility and dispersion of data. The formulas of the range method, standard deviation, and percentage measurement method are as follows Eqs. (5), (6) and (7).

$$A = X_{max} - X_{\min} \tag{5}$$

$$\sigma = \sqrt{\frac{1}{N} \sum_{i=1}^{N} (x_i - \mu)^2} \tag{6}$$

$$B = 100 * \frac{(X_{max} - X_{\min})}{(X_{avg} + 100)} \tag{7}$$

2 System Structure and Main Program

2.1 System Construction

In order to realize the real-time simulation of the manipulator's pose, the manipulator is modeled. The hand model can be imported from the official model established by Leap Motion. In this way, the virtual console is established. Next, Leap Motion is connected to the computer through the USB interface, and then the computer is connected to the robotic arm. Leap Motion transfers the collected data to Unity3D for processing and monitoring. The manipulator model follows the Operator's hand movement in Unity3D, and Unity3D transmits the information of the respective degree deflection angle to the real manipulator to drive its movement. The overall architecture of the system is shown in Fig. 6.

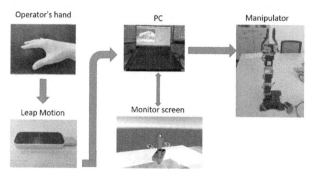

Fig. 6. Overall architecture of the system.

2.2 Manipulator Communication and Control

According to the communication protocol of the steering gear, this paper need to define important information such as the steering gear rotation range, rotation speed, target value, feedback value, data length, baud rate, and port number. Here we set the baud rate to 1000000Bd, the data length of the target value and feedback value information is two bytes, the steering gear rotation range is 200–300, the unit precision is 0.29°, and the corresponding angle is 58°–87°.

2.3 Data Control

As shown in Fig. 7, first the whole system is running. The operator moves the arm within the recognition range of Leap Motion. The position and direction information of the hand collected by the sensor is processed by a filtering algorithm combining percentile filtering and Gaussian filtering. Then it is transmitted to Unity3D for processing to obtain the target point position and direction information of the robot arm, and then the deflection angle of each degree of freedom is obtained through the FABRIK inverse kinematics algorithm, and finally the obtained angle deflection information is transmitted to the real manipulator through the serial port to complete the manipulator actions.

2.4 UI and Monitoring Screen

In order to improve the operator's control experience, this paper designs the system's human-computer interaction interface, including functions such as "real-time control", "record path", "storage path" and "load path". After the operator connects the entire hardware system, he first needs to turn on the "real-time control", and the Unity3D engine will establish communication with the steering gear and send control data to the steering gear in real time. If the path needs to be recorded, first click "Record Path", then control the manipulator to perform the required actions, and next click "Save Path" to save, multiple paths can be saved at the same time, if the saved path needs to be repeated, click "Load Path". After that, the manipulator will move along the stored path to complete the target action.

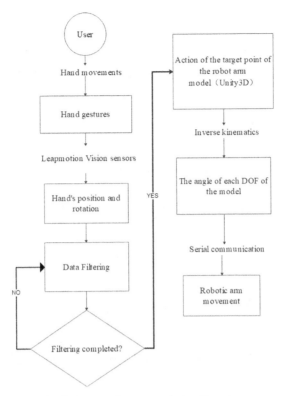

Fig. 7. System data transmission flow chart.

3   Filtering Data from Leap Motion

First the whole system is opened, so that the end of the manipulator moves with the center of the palm. Move the target point of the manipulator along the y axis of the manipulator coordinate system, try to keep the x-axis of the manipulator target point at the zero coordinate position of the entire manipulator coordinate system, and artificially increase a little jitter interference. The original motion trajectory of the target point of the manipulator during the manipulator test is recorded, perform Gaussian filtering on the motion trajectory of the target point of the manipulator and re-input it into the manipulator, then the trajectory of the target point is re-recorded. Then the original target point motion trajectory is filtered by a combination of percentile filtering and Gaussian filtering, and then the target point motion trajectory is recorded. In this way, three manipulator target points movement trajectories are obtained, which are the original trajectory of the manipulator target point; the trajectory of the manipulator target point after Gaussian filtering; the trajectory of the manipulator target point after percentile filtering and Gaussian filtering. Use the same method to keep the end of the manipulator moving along the x-axis and the y-axis at the zero coordinate. After moving the x-axis along the z-axis to maintain the zero coordinate, record the two groups of manipulators on the y-axis and z-axis without filtering, Gaussian filtering, and 100 the trajectory after quantile filtering and Gaussian filtering. Here, taking the collected x-axis coordinate trajectory as an example, the original x-axis coordinate trajectory is shown in Fig. 8. It can be seen that the jitter of the target point of the manipulator in the x-axis direction is very obvious, and the value of the x-axis deviates from the zero point very seriously at some artificial jitter points.

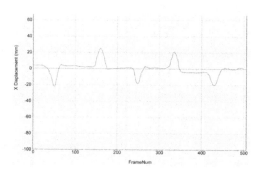

Fig. 8. The unfiltered wave x-coordinate curve of the target point of the manipulator.

Subsequently, this data is processed by Gaussian filtering, and Gaussian filtering is shown in the formula Eq. (3).The trajectory obtained after Gaussian filtering is shown in Fig. 9. It can be seen that the jitter effect has been significantly improved after processing.

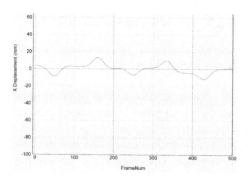

Fig.9. The x-coordinate curve of the target point of the manipulator after Gaussian filtering.

Then the original trajectory is processed by a combination of Gaussian filtering and percentile filtering. The trajectory obtained after processing is shown in Fig. 10.

Then, the values of the x-coordinates, y-coordinates, and z-coordinates of the three sets of data obtained are sampled equidistantly, and 31 sets of sample data are taken.

The range method, standard deviation, and percentage measurement method are used to measure the volatility and dispersion indicators obtained by the data as shown in Fig. 11.

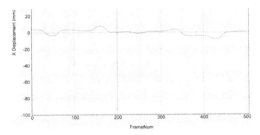

Fig. 10. The x-coordinate curve of the target point of the manipulator after Gaussian filtering and percentile filtering combined with filtering.

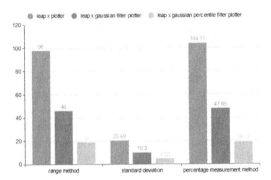

Fig.11. Comparison chart of volatility and dispersion indicators.

4   Experimental verification

In order to test the feasibility of real-time control, this paper designs a human-computer interaction experiment [16]. The goal of the experiment is to imitate cargo handling tasks in industrial production scenarios. The task of the operator is to control the real robot arm to pick up the goods from the X area, and then slowly move to Y in the air. At this time, due to the natural shaking of the operator's hand, it is easy to make the goods picked by the robot run uneven At this time, the filtering method combining Gaussian filtering and percentile filtering should be turned on to ensure the smooth operation of the entire system. After reaching Y, the gripper of the manipulator is released to complete the task of cargo handling. The Fig. 12 shows the monitoring screen and real screen of cargo handling. In the process of cargo handling, the system runs smoothly and the task is successfully completed.

Fig.12. Transporting the experimental console and monitoring screen.

5   Conclusion

After experimental verification, the entire system runs smoothly. Compared with the traditional control method, it provides a more intuitive operation experience. In the process of improving the anti-shake of the manipulator, whether it is from the range method, standard deviation or percentage measurement method to verify, the volatility and dispersion indicators of the end of the manipulator are better than the original data. And after a combination of percentile filtering and Gaussian filtering, its volatility and dispersion index are better than just Gaussian filtering. From the trajectory curve of the end coordinates of the manipulator, it can also be seen that the processing method combined with percentile filtering and Gaussian filtering has a significant improvement effect on the coordinates that deviate from the target value. In general, this system can meet the needs of more immersive and stable control.

References

1. Murhij, Y., Serebrenny, V.: An application to simulate and control industrial robot in virtual reality environment integrated with IR stereo camera sensor. IFAC PapersOnLine. **52**(25), 203–207 (2019). https://doi.org/10.1016/j.ifacol.2019.12.473
2. Horton, B.K., et al.: Game-engine-assisted research platform for scientific computing (GEARS) in virtual reality. SoftwareX 9 (2019). https://doi.org/10.1016/j.softx.2019.01.009
3. Haiyang, J., et al.: Multi-leap motion sensor based demonstration for robotic refine tabletop object manipulation task. CAAI Trans. Intell. Technol. 1(1) (2016). https://doi.org/10.1016/j.trit.2016.03.010
4. Nama, T., et al.: Designing a humanoid robot integrated Exer-Learning-Interaction (ELI). Procedia Comput. Sci. 167 (2020). https://doi.org/10.1016/j.procs.2020.03.363
5. Lee, B., et al.: Designing canonical form of finger motion grammar in leap motion contents. In: Proceedings of 2016 International Conference on Mechatronics, Control and Automation Engineering (MCAE2016), pp. 59–61 (2016)
6. Hernandez, V., et al.: Convolutional and recurrent neural network for human activity recognition: application on American sign language. PloS ONE 15(2) (2020). https://doi.org/10.1371/journal.pone.0228869
7. Gomez-Donoso, F., et al.: Accurate and efficient 3D hand pose regression for robot hand teleoperation using a monocular RGB camera. Expert Syst. Appl. 136 (2019). https://doi.org/10.1016/j.eswa.2019.06.055
8. Li, J., et al.: A two-sided collaborative transparent display supporting workspace awareness. Int. J. Hum.-Comput. Stud. 101 (2017). https://doi.org/10.1016/j.ijhcs.2017.01.003

9. Li, C., et al.: An augmented reality based human-robot interaction interface using Kalman filter sensor fusion. Sensors 19(20) (2019). https://doi.org/10.3390/s19204586

10. Covarrubias, M., et al.: A hand gestural interaction system for handling a desktop haptic strip for shape rendering. Sens. Actuators: A. Phys. 233 (2015). https://doi.org/10.1016/j.sna.2015.07.024

11. Menegozzo, G., et al.: Automatic process modeling with time delay neural network based on low-level data. Procedia Manuf. 38 (2019). https://doi.org/10.1016/j.promfg.2020.01.017

12. Alban, V., et al.: Python based internet tools in control education. IFAC PapersOnLine 48(29) (2015). https://doi.org/10.1016/j.ifacol.2015.11.211

13. Figueiredo, F., et al.: A comparative evaluation of direct hand and wand interactions on consumer devices. Comput. Graph. 77 (2018). https://doi.org/10.1016/j.cag.2018.10.006

14. Hou, W., et al.: A fuzzy interaction scheme of mid-air gesture elicitation. J. Vis. Commun. Image Represent. 64 (2019). https://doi.org/10.1016/j.jvcir.2019.102637

15. Guanglong, D., et al.: Human-manipulator interface using particle filter. Sci. World J. 2014 (2014). https://doi.org/10.1155/2014/692165

16. Santos, M.E.C., Taketomi, T., Sandor, C., Polvi, J., Yamamoto, G., Kato, H.: A usability scale for handheld augmented reality. In: Proceedings of the Twentieth ACM Symposium on Virtual Reality Software and Technology, pp. 167–76. ACM (2014)

17. Yang, C., Zeng, C., Liang, P., Li, Z., Li, R., Su, C.Y.: Interface design of a physical humanrobot interaction system for human impedance adaptive skill transfer. IEEE Trans. Autom. Sci. Eng. 15, 329–340 (2018)

18. Dang, T.L.: Level Designing in Game Engine. Helsinki Metropolia University of Applied Sciences (2017)

19. Guna, J., et al.: An analysis of the precision and reliability of the leap motion sensor and its suitability for static and dynamic tracking. Sensors 14(2) (2014). https://doi.org/10.3390/s140203702

20. Anna-Lisa, V., et al.: Robots show us how to teach them: feedback from robots shapes tutoring behavior during action learning. PLoS ONE 9(3) (2014). https://doi.org/10.1371/journal.pone.0091349

Contouring Errors and Feedrate Fluctuation of Serial Industrial Robot in Complex Toolpath with Different Controller

Deng Kenan, Gao Dong, Ma Shoudong, and Lu Yong[⊠]

Harbin Institute of Technology, Harbin, China
luyong@hit.edu.cn

Abstract. In order to compare the dynamic performance of CNC controller and robot controller for serial industrial robot. In this paper, the contouring errors and velocity of the industrial robot under different controllers are analyzed. Firstly, a method for measuring the trajectory error of the milling robot based on a laser tracker is proposed. Then, a series of experiments of the KUKA KR160 robot with KRL kernel and CNC kernel are implemented to analyze the dynamic performance of complex trajectory, considering different feedrate, smoothing methods, and parameter setting. Experimental results show that the KRL kernel with appropriate parameters can achieve the same trajectory accuracy and feedrate response as CNC kernel.

Keywords: Contouring errors · Feedrate · Controller · Industrial robot

1 Introduction

Industrial robots are recently used for machining applications like grinding, polishing, and milling due to their advantage of the large workspace, flexibility, and low cost. However, traditional industrial robots are usually designed to achieve precise point movement and repeatable tasks, while the trajectory accuracy and absolute positioning accuracy are less accurate [1, 2]. Because of their series structure and low joint stiffness, the industrial robot is prone to vibration and large deformation in the process of complex curved surface machining.

Compared to industrial robots controller, CNC controller have advantages in operability, continuous-path performance, and functionality. A CNC controller kernel was integrated on the KUKA KR C4 controller and operated through a CNC-specific user interface [3]. Wen [4] and Susemihl [5] use Siemens 840D CNC controller to control mobile robots for large component machining. Xie and Liu [6–9] proposed integrated methods combining elasto-geometrical error calibration, continuity toolpath smoothing, and real-time tracking errors compensation for improving machining precision, which was tested in a mobile parallel robot with ISG CNC kernel. However, compared with the robot controller, the CNC controller requires additional system software of robotic machining system, which increases the cost, so the robot controller is still a standard

© Springer Nature Switzerland AG 2021
X.-J. Liu et al. (Eds.): ICIRA 2021, LNAI 13013, pp. 100–108, 2021.
https://doi.org/10.1007/978-3-030-89095-7_10

control method in many small and medium enterprises (SME). So it is necessary to compare the robot trajectory performance under the CNC controller and the robot controller to provide more choices for enterprises.

NC programs, programmed offline using a CAD/CAM system, is consisted of linear toolpath segments. CNC controller and robot controller have different toolpath smoothing algorithms to improve continuity, influencing robot trajectory accuracy and dynamic performance. Adel [10] proposed a cartesian space motion planning strategy to suppress vibration. Tunc [11] analyzed the influence of trajectory approximation method accuracy setting option on hexapod robot path contouring accuracy and feedrate. Wu [12, 13] researched the dynamic performance of the CNC kernel and KRL kernel of the KUKA robot in line path and corner path, which consider high/low running speeds and acceleration. Found that dynamic performance and trajectory accuracy of CNC kernel was better at high running speeds. However, the running speeds of the machining process are generally low, and the CNC controller provides alternative toolpath smoothing methods that need to be tested using complex curved paths.

In summary, these methods above ignoring comparing the positioning trajectory errors between CNC controller and robot controller for complex trajectory, and does not analyze the parameter settings that affect the dynamic performance of the robot controller. This paper compares the robot motion accuracy and velocity performance under different control kernels with several parameters. First, propose a method to calculate path errors of the industrial robot based on laser tracker dynamic measurement, which exactly matches the data from the measured values of the laser tracker coordinate system to the programmed points values of the workpiece coordinate system. Then, the constant load running experiments of complex toolpath in cartesian space are designed based on the KRL kernel and CNC kernel of the KUKA robot. Finally, the influence of different velocities and approximate parameters on the trajectory errors and velocity stable is studied.

2   Toolpath Contouring Errors of Industrial Robot

For identifying toolpath contouring errors of industrial robots with a laser tracker, exactly match the coordinates data from programmed points with measurement data of laser tracker is required. CAD/CAM software is usually used to generate a cutter location file containing many discrete tool position vectors and orientation vectors and then generate the processing program in the workpiece coordinate after post-processing according to the robot characteristics and the control system language.

P_{code}^{rb} is the position of the programming point in the robot base coordinate system and is defined as follows

$$P_{code}^{rb} = T_{wp}^{rb} T_{tool}^{wp} T_{fl}^{tool} P_{code}^{fl} \tag{1}$$

Where T_{wp}^{rb} is the homogeneous transformation matrix between robot base coordinate system and workpiece coordinate system, T_{tool}^{wp} is the homogeneous transformation matrix between workpiece coordinate system and robot tool coordinate system, T_{tool}^{fl} is the homogeneous transformation matrix between robot flange coordinate system and tool coordinate system, P^{fl}_{code} is the position of the programming point in the robot flange coordinate system (Fig. 1).

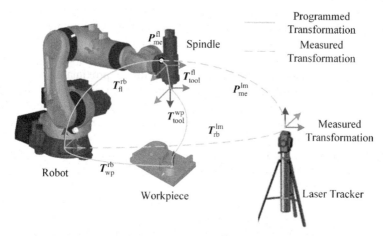

Fig. 1. Transformations for robot milling system

In order to improve the prediction accuracy of contour error, the isoparametric linear method is used to interpolate the parameter points. For the interpolation points between $P^{fl}_{code\_i}$ and $P^{fl}_{code\_i+1}$

$$P^{fl}_{code\_i,k} = \frac{\left(P^{fl}_{code\_i+1} - P^{fl}_{code\_i}\right)}{\text{floor}\left(\left\|P^{fl}_{code\_i}\overrightarrow{P^{fl}_{code\_i+1}}\right\|/d\right)} + P^{fl}_{code\_i},$$
$$k = 1 \cdots \text{floor}\left(\left\|P^{fl}_{code\_i}\overrightarrow{P^{fl}_{code\_i+1}}\right\|/d\right) \tag{2}$$

Where d is the minimum distance of two control points. After interpolation, the number of program points is changed from n to n_{in}.

The position of the auxiliary measurement points in the robot base coordinate system is expressed as follows

$$P^{rb}_{me} = T^{rb}_{lm}P^{lm}_{me} \tag{3}$$

Where T^{rb}_{lm} is the transformation matrix representing the pose of the laser tracker coordinate system with respect to robot base coordinate system, P^{lm}_{me} is the position of the auxiliary measurement point in the robot flange coordinate system.

The orthogonal distance between the measuring point and the closest linear toolpath segments of the program and the distance between the measuring point and the closest reference point of the program, where the minimum value is taken as the contour error [14].

The position vector $\hat{r}_{p\_j}$ from the closest programmed point to the measuring point is

$$\hat{r}_{p\_j} = P^{rb}_{code\_t}\overrightarrow{P^{rb}_{me\_j}}, t = 1, \cdots n_{in}; j = 1, 2 \cdots m \tag{4}$$

The normalized toolpath segment vectors of programmed code are defined as

$$\hat{r}_t = \frac{\overline{P^{rb}_{code\_t-1} P^{rb}_{code\_t}}}{\left\| P^{rb}_{code\_t-1} P^{rb}_{code\_t} \right\|} \tag{5}$$

$$\hat{r}_{t+1} = \frac{\overline{P^{rb}_{code\_t} P^{rb}_{code\_t+1}}}{\left\| P^{rb}_{code\_t} P^{rb}_{code\_t+1} \right\|} \tag{6}$$

Where $P^{rb}_{code\_t}, P^{rb}_{code\_t+1}$ and $P^{rb}_{code\_t+1}$ are three adjacent programmed points.

The orthogonal distance ε_{c1} between the measuring point and the closest linear toolpath segments of the program is defined as

$$\varepsilon_{c1} = \left\| \hat{r}_{p_j} - \frac{(\hat{r}_{p_j} \cdot \hat{r}_t)}{\|\hat{r}_t\|^2} \hat{r}_t \right\| \tag{7}$$

Moreover, the contour error is estimated as follows

$$\varepsilon_c = \min(\varepsilon_{c1}, \|\hat{r}_{p_j}\|) \tag{8}$$

3   Experiment and Discussion

In order to compare the two different control systems, a 5-axis complex curve toolpath is planned to analyze the performance of a KUKA robot under the two controllers, and a laser tracker is used to measure the toolpath contouring accuracy and feed speed. In order to avoid the influence of cutting force on the contour accuracy of the industrial robot, the measurements are performed under no-machining operational conditions.

The experiment setup is shown in Fig. 2. Within the KUKA robot milling system (KR 160 R1578), an electric spindle is installed at the robot's flange. The robot milling system's total weight is about 698 kg, and the maximum robot load is 160 kg. The position repetition accuracy can reach ±0.06 mm, and the maximum can reach 1578 mm. The CNC kernel and KRL kernel have been completely integrated into a KR C4 control system.

The CNC kernel can run NC programs directly on the KR C4 controller, and preload 150 path points to achieve more precise and efficient trajectory planning. Several path smoothing methods are provided to rounding and smoothing a programmed curve within specific tolerances, such as Contour Mode, B-Spline Method, Filter programming, Akima spline, and PSC functions. The KRL kernel implements the NC program of many short linear blocks through the LIN instruction and trajectory approximation function. The kernel only preloads five path points, which limits the robot's contour tracking performance.

The API T3 laser tracker has been used to determine the reference and the dynamic measurement of the trajectories at a sampling frequency of 100 Hz, and its accuracy is better than 0.025 mm. The laser tracker tracks the robot's movement by identifying a target ball glued to the side of the motorized spindle. Before the experiment, the actual position of the auxiliary measuring point in the robot flange coordinate system was calibrated using the reference method [5, 15]. In order to determine the influence of approximation contour method parameter settings on the densely discretized toolpath, robot Sensor Interface (RSI) is used to record the command angles and measured angles of the robot joints when using the KRL kernel. RSI is an official software provided by KUKA company, which can read the robot system parameters in a cycle of 4 ms or 12 ms.

Table 1. Parameters in toolpath program

Type	Type of contouring	Parameters of contouring	Feedrate (mm/min)	Acceleration
KRL	Approximation mode	0.05 mm, 0.5 mm	1500, 3000	100%
CNC	B-spline	0.05 mm, 0.1°	1500, 3000	100%

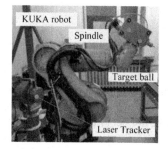

Fig. 2. Robot milling system   **Fig. 3.** S-shaped toolpath of base coordinate

According to G code and KRL language specification, the linear segments toolpath of the 5-axis S-shaped part [6] generated by NX is converted into an executive program of different controllers. As shown in Fig. 3, the toolpath length is 516.04 mm that contains 822 path points, the maximum interval of path points is 4.3 mm, the minimum interval is 0.071 mm, and the trajectory error tolerance is 0.05 mm.

As shown in Fig. 4, the B-spline method was used for the CNC kernel in the experiments, which needs to be determined maximum deviation (PATH_DEV) of B spline from the programmed path and maximum deviation of tracking axes (TRACK_DEV). KRL kernel adopts trajectory approximation contour method that defines the &APO.CDIS value in the program to determine the distance from the starting point to the corner point of the trajectory approach, and the trajectory approach to the endpoint depends on the speed set by the program (Fig. 5). Two values are set to see if the $APO.CDIS has an impact on the industrial robot dynamic performance. The velocity and acceleration weighting are set the same value to compare the two control systems (Table 1).

Figure 6 shows the robot's S-shaped toolpath contouring errors are similar at different experimental conditions, which are measured by laser tracker. Moreover, the feedrate

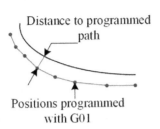

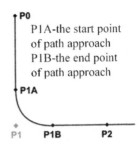

Fig. 4. Parameters of B-spline method of contour the CNC kernel

Fig. 5. Parameters of approximation method of the KRL kernel

commonly used in machining does not affect the toolpath contouring accuracy, which is different from [12]. Figure 7 shows the trajectory errors calculated by joint tracking errors and forward kinematics of the robot. It was found out that the cartesian tracking errors of the robot are below 0.05 mm under different parameters; however, the contouring errors are between 0.5–1.5 mm that measured by the laser tracker.

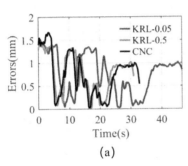

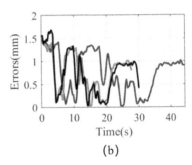

Fig. 6. Contouring errors is measured by laser tracker. (a) V = 1500 mm/min and (b) V = 3000 mm/min

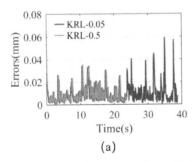

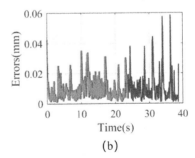

Fig. 7. Tracking errors is calculated by RSI. (a) V = 1500 mm/min and (b) V = 3000 mm/min

Table 2 lists the maximum error, mean errors, and standard variance. The contouring errors of the CNC kernel are not smaller than the KRL kernel based on the programmed velocities of 1500 mm/min and 3000 mm/min.

Table 2. Errors of s-shaped toolpath

Feedrate (mm/min)	Type	Maximum error(mm)	Mean error(mm)	Standard variance(mm)
1500	CNC	1.670	0.753	0.460
3000	CNC	1.685	0.752	0.454
1500	KRL(0.5)	1.486	0.787	0.417
3000	KRL(0.5)	1.449	0.763	0.421
1500	KRL(0.05)	1.518	0.773	0.431
3000	KRL(0.05)	1.481	0.766	0.432

According to Fig. 8, the running time of the CNC kernel is similar to that of the KRL kernel (APO_DIS = 0.5 mm), while the running time of the KRL kernel (APO_DIS = 0.05 mm) is longer. However, it isn't easy to reach the set value of 3000 mm/min in either controller with different parameters. Moreover, when the feedrate curve of the CNC kernel is around 15.36 s (programmed feedrate at 1500 mm/min) and 13.33 s (programmed feedrate at 1500 mm/min), the velocity of the industrial robot drops rapidly, however the velocity with the KRL kernel reduced by a smaller range. The contouring errors of the two controllers are both large.

Table 3 indicates that, at the same programmed feedrate, the minimum feedrate of the CNC kernel and KRL kernel (APO_DIS = 0.5 mm) is close, which is different from the value of the KRL kernel (APO_DIS = 0.05 mm). At different programmed feedrates, the minimum feedrate of the same kernel and parameters is close. Regardless of which controller, the measured minimum feedrate is too low compared to the programmed feedrate, which means that the serial industrial robot is difficult to use in high-speed machining of complex features. Compared with the figure and figure, the feedrate and contour error have a similar trend of change, and the feedrate mutation caused a significant path error.

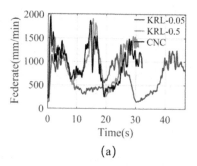
(a)

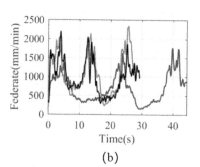
(b)

Fig. 8. Feedrate is measured using laser tracker (a) V = 1500 mm/min and (b) V = 3000 mm/min

The velocity is calculated by RSI measurement data (Fig. 9). It can be seen that the variation of the feedrate is close to the measurement result of the laser tracker. In the

Table 3. Minimum feedrate of s-shaped toolpath(mm/min)

Instruction feedrate	CNC kernel	KRL kernel(0.5 mm)	KRL kernel(0.05 mm)
1500	255.15	253.21	167.57
3000	294.373	240.338	157.345

process of running, the robot's velocity cannot exceed the design value and the velocity calculation errors of the laser tracker caused by the dynamic measurement errors.

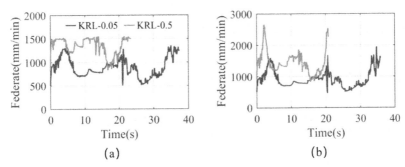

(a)   (b)

Fig. 9. Feedrate is measured using RSI. (a) V = 1500 mm/min and (b) V = 3000 mm/min

4   Conclusion

This paper focused on comparing the effectiveness of the CNC kernel and KRL kernel in reducing contouring errors and maintaining velocity constant when executing complex curves. The results suggest that different controller and parameters setting dose not affect the contour accuracy of the dense discrete toolpath, but significantly affect the dynamic feedrate response. The minimum feedrate is too low compared with the designed feedrate, making it difficult for the serial industrial robot to be used for high-speed machining of complex features.The CNC kernel provides more toolpath smoothing algorithms when there are many short linear blocks, however using the appropriate APO_DIS value can obtain the same feedrate response and contouring errors as the CNC kernel, which helps the user to select the controller and parameters setting.

Acknowledgement. This work was supported by the National Key R&D Program of China under Grant 2018YFB1306800.

References

1. Verl, A., Valente, A., Melkote, S., et al.: Robots in machining. CIRP Ann. **68**(2), 799–822 (2019)

2. Tao, B., Zhao, X.W., Ding, H.: Mobile-robotic machining for large complex components: A review study. Sci. China Technol. Sci. **62**(8), 1388–1400 (2019)
3. KUKA Roboter GmbH (https://www.isg-stuttgart.de/kernel-html5/en-GB/index.html#474 914443)
4. Wen, K., Zhang, J.B., Yue, Y., et al.: Method for improving accuracy of NC-driven mobile milling robot. J. Mech. Eng. **57**(05), 72–80 (2021)
5. Susemihl, H., Brillinger, C., Stürmer, S.P., et al.: Referencing strategies for high accuracy machining of large aircraft components with mobile robotic systems. SAE Technical Paper (2017)
6. Xie, Z., Xie, F., Liu, X.J., et al.: Tracking error prediction informed motion control of a parallel machine tool for high-performance machining. Int. J. Mach. Tools Manuf. **164**, 103714 (2021)
7. Mei, B., Xie, F., Liu, X.J., et al.: Elasto-geometrical error modeling and compensation of a five-axis parallel machining robot. Precis. Eng. **69**, 48–61 (2021)
8. Xie, Z., Xie, F., Liu, X.J., et al.: Global G3 continuity toolpath smoothing for a 5-DoF machining robot with parallel kinematics. Robot. Comput.-Integrat. Manuf. **67**, 102018 (2021)
9. Luo, X., Xie, F., Liu, X.J., et al.: Kinematic calibration of a 5-axis parallel machining robot based on dimensionless error mapping matrix. Robot. Comput.-Integrat. Manuf. **70**, 102115 (2021)
10. Olabi, A., Béarée, R., Gibaru, O., et al.: Feedrate planning for machining with industrial six-axis robots. Control. Eng. Pract. **18**(5), 471–482 (2010)
11. Wu, K., Krewet, C., Bickendorf, J., et al.: Dynamic performance of industrial robot with CNC controller. Int. J. Adv. Manuf. Technol. **90**(5–8), 2389–2395 (2017)
12. Wu, K., Krewet, C., Kuhlenkötter, B.: Dynamic performance of industrial robot in corner path with CNC controller. Robot. Comput.-Integrat. Manuf. **54**, 156–161 (2018)
13. Tunca, L.T., Sapmaza, O.F.: Challenges for industrial robots towards milling applications. Dynamics **2**, 4 (2017)
14. Erkorkmaz, K., Yeung, C.-H., Altintas, Y.: Virtual CNC system. Part II. High speed contouring application. Int. J. Mach. Tools Manuf. **46**(10), 1124–1138 (2006). https://doi.org/10.1016/j.ijmachtools.2005.08.001
15. Klimchik, A., Furet, B., Caro, S., et al.: Identification of the manipulator stiffness model parameters in industrial environment. Mech. Mach. Theory **90**, 1–22 (2015)

Research on a New Flexible Tactile Sensor for Detecting Vertical and Sliding Tactile Signals

Rui Zhang, Zina Zhu$^{(\boxtimes)}$, Guohua Cui, and Peixing Li

Institute of Intelligent Cooperative Robot Application Technology, Shanghai University of Engineering Science, Shanghai 201620, China

Abstract. In this paper, a new type of flexible tactile sensor is designed based on the coupling principle of eddy current and piezoelectric effect. The tactile sensor is simple in structure and has the characteristics of flexibility. The contact surface of tactile sensor is designed as corrugation by imitating the physiological skin structure of human body. COMSOL Multiphysics is used to simulate and analyze the electromechanical response characteristics, dynamic force, transient force, and different direction tactile signals of the sensor. It can be obtained that the sensor has a large response range, high sensitivity and is suitable for the measurement of dynamic force. Vertical and sliding tactile signals have obvious characteristic differences so that the mechanical force can be detected by the output voltage signal of the sensor.

Keywords: Tactile sensor · Flexibility · Dynamic force · Transient force

1 Introduction

Tactile sense is an important perception for human to perceive the external environment, which can provide a variety of contact information, such as texture, temperature, humidity, sliding and other sensory information. Tactile sensors based on human's touch can be applied to mechanical grasp, medical rehabilitation and other fields [1, 2], enabling them to have human perception ability and make a series of judgments on the contact information of the outside world. For tactile sensors, high sensitivity and large response range are important indicators to measure their performance, while the relationship between the them is a trade-off. Currently, the common principles of tactile sensors can be divided into piezoelectric, eddy current, resistance and capacitance. Most tactile sensors are only based on one principle, which cannot consider the sensitivity and response range at the same time. Therefore, a novel tactile sensor is proposed in this paper, which takes advantage of the large response range of eddy current principle [3–5] and the high sensitivity which caused by the thin film piezoelectric characteristics of polyvinylidene fluoride (PVDF) [6, 7]. In addition, in order to avoid causing damage or leaving traces on the

National Natural Science Foundation of China (Grant No. 51775165).

R. Zhang (1995)---Research direction: Flexible tactile sensor.

Z. Zhu (1987)---Research direction: Magnetic coupling drive, mechanism optimi-zation design.

X.-J. Liu et al. (Eds.): ICIRA 2021, LNAI 13013, pp. 109–116, 2021.
https://doi.org/10.1007/978-3-030-89095-7_11

target when the tactile sensor is used in the work, the characteristic of flexibility should also be taken into account.

In this paper, based on the principle of eddy current and piezoelectric effect, a corrugation flexible tactile sensor is designed to imitate the physiological skin structure of human body. By using the analysis module of coupling multiple physical fields in COMSOL Multiphysics, the finite element simulation analysis of the designed tactile sensor is carried out, and the relevant performance parameters are obtained to show that this kind of tactile sensor can be used to detect the tactile signals.

2 The Working Principle of the Flexible Tactile Sensor

The proposed flexible tactile sensor is based on the coupling principle of eddy current and piezoelectric effect. The principle of eddy current is based on Faraday's law of electromagnetic induction [8]. As shown in Fig. 1, the tactile sensor structure includes a thin metal layer, four PVDF films, an excitation coil and a flexible substrate. The working principle of the flexible tactile sensor is shown in Fig. 2. When the materials and dimensions of the coil and the metal plate in the tactile sensor is determined, a sinusoidal alternating current is applied into the coil. The output voltage of the coil caused will change by the distance change between the coil and the metal layer, that is, the induced voltage is a single-valued function of the distance d. PVDF is a kind of organic polymer piezoelectric material. This material not only has good flexibility and fatigue resistance, but also has the characteristic of high sensitivity of force-electric conversion. When the piezoelectric film made of PVDF is subjected to external force, and the mechanical deformation occurs, so that he upper and lower surfaces of the film will produce the same size and opposite polarity of charge, forming a potential difference, which is known as the positive piezoelectric effect. When the two principles are applied to a tactile sensor at the same time, the charge generated on the surface of the PVDF piezoelectric film will change the internal magnetic field of the tactile sensor, and then affect the inductive voltage output of the coil. By detecting the value of the induced voltage, the information of the applied force is judged, and then the touch operation can be perceived.

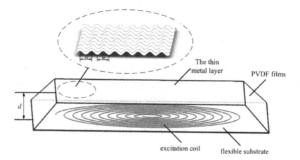

Fig. 1. The new flexible tactile sensor structure

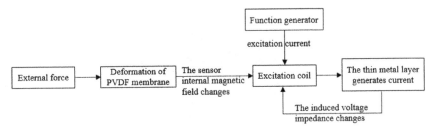

Fig. 2. Working principle diagram of the flexible tactile sensor

3 The Finite Element Analysis of the Flexible Tactile Sensor

Considering the interaction of eddy current field and electric field in the designed the flexible tactile sensor, we carried out analysis of eddy current and piezoelectric in COMSOL Multiphysics coupling, by using structural mechanics analysis module and magnetic field analysis module. Piezoelectric coupling can be used form of either stress-charge or strain-charge, and the stress-charge form is chosen in this paper.

3.1 Model Building

Firstly, the flexible tactile sensor was modelled SolidWorks. Based on the human physiological skin structure, the both surfaces of the thin metal layer are designed to be corrugated, with a side length of 4000 μm and a thickness of 200 μm, and the space of corrugation is 100 μm, as shown in Fig. 1. The thickness of the PVDF piezoelectric films is 200 μm, the height is 500 μm. The shape of PVDF piezoelectric films is trapezoidal, and its top and bottom side lengths are 4000 μm and 5000 μm respectively. The side length of the flexible substrate is 5000 μm and the thickness 200 μm. The number of turns of the coil $N = 10$ and the pitch is 185 μm.

3.2 Material Parameter Setting

The material of PVDF piezoelectric film is set as a density of 1.78 g/cm^3, a relative permittivity of 11, a piezoelectric strain constant of 28 pC/N, a Poisson's ratio of 0.29 and a modulus of elasticity of 1.6 GPa. The material of both the thin metal layer and the coil is set as copper, where the relative permeability and relative permittivity are 1 and the conductivity is 5.998×10^7 S/m.

3.3 Mesh Division

As shown in the Fig. 3, the excitation coil is meshed by the mapping method and the rest is meshed by the free division method to improve the simulation speed and ensuring the simulation accuracy.

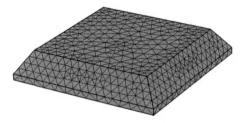

Fig. 3. Meshing model

4 Performance Analysis of the Flexible Tactile Sensor

Based on the property of PVDF piezoelectric film, it can be considered as an idealized capacitor in the stressed state, and the strain response of the PVDF film is considered as a weighted algebraic sum of the transverse and longitudinal strain effects. When the PVDF piezoelectric film is subjected to an external force, the output charge of per unit area can be expressed as,

$$Q = d_{31}T_1 + d_{31}T_2 \tag{1}$$

where d_{31} is the piezoelectric strain constant $(i = 1, 2)$ is the strain.

As shown in Fig. 4, when the vertical force of 20 kPa is applied to the sensor, the deformation of PVDF films is smaller, the deformation of the metal thin layer is more obvious.

Fig. 4. Deformation of stress diagram

4.1 Force- Electrical Response Analysis

The output voltage signal was obtained under high frequency sampling by applying a growing pressure to the sensor is shown in Fig. 5. After linear fitting of the output voltage data, it can be seen that the pressure applied to the sensor has a good linear relationship with the output voltage, and the force-electric response of the fitted straight line is calculated 0.0083 V/KPa, with a good force-electric response characteristic.

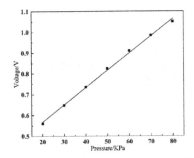

Fig. 5. Force- electrical response analysis

4.2 Dynamic Force Measurement Analysis

The pressure applied to the metal thin layer surface of the sensor is stepped increasing, and the pressure is applied for 1s and then removed. The voltage output curve is shown in Fig. 6(a), (b), (c) and (d) are correspond to the pressure magnitude of 20 kPa, 40 kPa, 60 kPa and 80 kPa respectively. The maximum values of the output voltage signals obtained are 0.56 V, 0.736 V, 0.91 V,1.05 V. The curves in the graph show that the PVDF film accumulates charge during the force is applied, and the charge is released when the force is removed, which changes the internal magnetic field of the sensor, thus changing the output voltage of the excitation coil. The whole process of charge accumulation and release takes about 2.8 s, and it can be included that the charge of the designed sensor changes as the force state changes, which cause the change of output voltage, and the response time is short, indicating it is sensitive to dynamic force. So the sensor is suitable for tactile analysis.

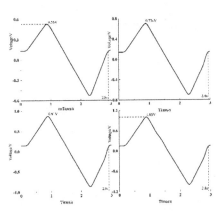

Fig. 6. Dynamic force analysis

4.3 Transient Analysis

In addition, a transient analysis of the flexible tactile sensor was carried out for detecting vertical and sliding forces.

A vertical force of 10 N is applied to the thin metal layer of the sensor, and the detected output voltage curve as shown in Fig. 7(a). The maximum output signal amplitude is 4.97 V. After 2.2 s, the 10N force is removed and the PVDF film begins to release its charge, and the minimum output signal amplitude is −5.58 V.

Next a sliding force of 10 N is applied to the sensor, as shown in Fig. 7(b). When the sliding force is applied, the projection area of the thin metal layer on the excitation coil decrease, and it causes the change of internal magnetic field of sensor. Compared with Fig. 7(a), the frequency of output voltage changes is higher, but the voltage value is smaller. The maximum amplitude of 0.397 V at 1.9 s. So, the form and value of tactile signals can be distinguished by the change of output voltage waveform.

As shown in Fig. 7(c), a sliding force of 10 N is applied to the sensor and then a vertical force of 3 N for a cyclical period of 5 s is applied from the moment of 1.6 s. When the vertical force is applied, the output voltage value and the curve fluctuation range increase, and the maximum amplitude of the output voltage reaches up to 1.92 V. When the vertical force is removed, the output voltage value and the curve fluctuation range return to the original output state.

By analyzing the simulation results above, it can be seen that the deformation of PVDF film is different when the force value and direction change, the distance between metal thin layer and excitation coil decrease and the projection area are also decrease, which cause the output curves of output voltage have obvious differences. Tactile signals can be distinguished according to the output voltage amplitude and curve fluctuation. So, the tactile sensor can detect the vertical and sliding force.

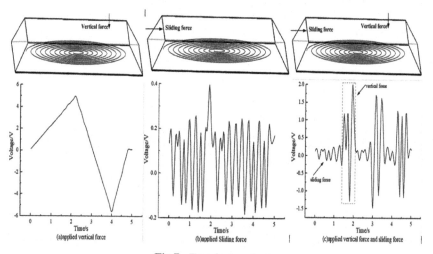

Fig.7. Transient analysis

5 Conclusions

For tactile sensors, large response range and high sensitivity are two important indexes, and the relationship between them is changing. The tactile sensor proposed in this paper is based on eddy current and the PVDF piezoelectric effect principle by imitating the physiological skin structure of human body. The PVDF Piezoelectric tactile sensor has high sensitivity and good stability. The eddy current tactile sensor has wide dynamic response range and linear output. Compared with the traditional tactile sensor based on one of the principles, the proposed sensor has both large response range and high sensitivity, and it also has a wider application range. In addition, the overall size of the proposed tactile sensor is small, so it can be applied to complex curved surfaces by using flexible materials. The amount of charge generated on the surface of PVDF film varies with the direction of external force, which can realize three-dimensional force detection. Through simulation and analysis of the force-electrical response characteristics, dynamic force and transient force of the sensor, it shows that the sensor has a large response range and a high sensitivity, which is suitable for dynamic force detection. In addition, it also can detect vertical and sliding tactile signals, so that the value and direction of mechanical force can be judged.

Acknowledgement. This paper was funded by the National Natural Science Foundation of China (Grant No.51775165).

References

1. Kim, D.-H., Ghaffari, R., Nanshu, L., Rogers, J.A.: Flexible and stretchable electronics for biointegrated devices. Ann. Rev. Biomed. Eng. **14**(1), 113–128 (2012). https://doi.org/10.1146/annurev-bioeng-071811-150018
2. Nathan, A., et al.: Flexible electronics: the next ubiquitous platform. Proc. IEEE **100**(Special Centennial Issue), 1486–1517 (2012). https://doi.org/10.1109/JPROC.2012.2190168
3. Wang, H., Kow, J., de Boer, G., et al.: A Low-cost, High-Performance, Soft Tri-axis Tactile Sensor based on Eddy-Current Effect. IEEE Sensors, pp. 1–3 (2017)
4. Kawasetus, T., Horii, T., Ishihara, H., et al.: Flexible tri-axis tactile sensor using spiral inductor and magnetorheological elastomer. IEEE Sens. J. **18**(14), 5834–5841 (2018)
5. Youssefian, S., Rahbar, N., Torres-Jara, E.: Contact behavior of soft spherical tactile sensors. IEEE Sens. J. **14**(5), 1435–1442 (2014)
6. Xin, Y., Tian, H., Jiang, Q., et al.: PVDF based sliding contact recognition system for piezoelectric thin film based on LabVIEW. Piezoelect. Acousto-optic **37**(5), 793–795 (2015)
7. Zhelang, T.: piezoelectric ceramic material. Translated by Chen junyan, pp. 7–12. Science press, Beijing (1982)
8. Chao-ming, S., Yan-lin, X., Bao, L.: Analysis of validation of numerical calculation of electromagnetic field in eddy current testing using finite element method. Nondestruc. Exam. **28**(11), 561–564 (2006)
9. Jung, Y., Lee, D.-G., Park, J., et al.: Piezoresistive tactile sensor discriminating multidirectional forces. Sensors. **15**, 25463–25473 (2015)
10. Xianhe, D., Kuribayashi, K., Hashida, T.: Development of a new type tactile sensor using micro electromagnetic coil for human robot. MHS2000. In: Proceedings od 2000 International Symposium on Micromechatronics and Human Science, pp. 181–187 (2000)
11. Tiwana, M.I., Redmond, S.J., Lovell, N.H.: A review of tactile sensing technologies with applications in biomedical engineering. Sens. Actuat. A **179**(3), 17–31 (2012)
12. Khan, S., Tinku, S., Lorenzelli, L., et al.: Flexible tactile sensors using screen-printed (PVDF-TrFE) and MWCNT /PDMS composites. IEEE Sens. J. **15**(6), 3146–3155 (2015)

13. Drossel, W.G., Bucht, A., Hochmuth, C., et al.: High performance of machining processes by applying a daptronic systems. Procedia Cirp **14**, 500–505 (2014)
14. Wang, Y., Li, B.: The main technology of flexible tactile sensor. Sensor Microsyst. **31**(12), 1–4 (2012)

Sensors, Actuators, and Controllers
for Soft and Hybrid Robots

Analysis of Kinematic Parameter Identification Method Based on Genetic Algorithm

Jing Yang, Lingyan Jin, Zejie Han, Deming Zhao, and Ming Hu[✉]

Faculty of Mechanical Engineering and Automation, Zhejiang Sci-Tech University, Hangzhou 310018, China
huming@zstu.edu.cn

Abstract. For the kinematic parameters calibration of manipulator, different identification methods affect the final calibration results. Comprehensive range error model, the author of this paper, relative distance error model, comprehensive posture error model and relative posture error model of four kinds of error identification model, combined with multiple population genetic algorithm analysis of different methods of parameter identification results, and finally the effect of mechanical arm end position error, and starting from the actual measurement error, to bring the end of the error posture as identification data set, get different adaptive identification method of error, for actual kinematic parameters provide different selection of recognition method based on calibration.

Keywords: Kinematic parameters · Identification error · Optimization index · Pose error · Genetic algorithm

1 Introduction

Absolute position accuracy is a key indicator to measure the motion performance of robots, which is generally expressed as the difference between the measured pose of the robot end and the theoretical pose. The main factors affecting the absolute positioning accuracy are kinematic parameter error and dynamic parameter error, of which the former accounts for about 80% [1]. Therefore, improving the calibration accuracy of robot kinematic parameters plays an important role in improving its kinematic accuracy.

The calibration of kinematic parameters generally has four steps: error modeling, end pose measurement, parameter identification and error compensation [2]. There are two kinds of robot kinematics calibration methods: circle method and kinematics loop method [3]. Among them, the compensation effect of kinematic loop method is obvious, which is not easily affected by external human factors and is widely used. In the identification process, the selection of kinematic model parameters and error model will directly affect the identification and compensation results. NGUYEN H [4] and HE R [5] solved the geometric relationship between joints and links under the DH model of the robot by calibration and established the kinematics equation of the robot. Based on the screw theory and the position error model, Gao Wenbin et al. [6] proposed the kinematic parameter calibration method of 5-DOF manipulator in the form of exponential product.

© Springer Nature Switzerland AG 2021
X.-J. Liu et al. (Eds.): ICIRA 2021, LNAI 13013, pp. 119–128, 2021.
https://doi.org/10.1007/978-3-030-89095-7_12

Lu Yi et al. [7] established calibration equation to identify structural parameter error by imposing physical constraints on the end of industrial robots, and proposed a structural parameter calibration method based on closed size chain. Zhuang et al. [8] used CPC model and MCPC model to calibrate the kinematic parameters of the robot. Model-free method is a method to directly fit the relationship between the input joint angle and the end pose of the manipulator by some means. The methods include least square method [9, 10], genetic algorithm [11] and artificial neural network [12, 13]. For example, Hage et al. [14] established the manipulator workspace by installing a contact probe on the end effector of the manipulator, and fixedly placed a cube with high machining accuracy to obtain the corresponding constraint equation to solve the geometric parameters through contact. Meggiolaro M et al. [15] fixed and installed a spherical joint in the working space of the manipulator, and constructed the functional relationship between the measured position coordinate, the theoretical position coordinate and the parameter error. Finally, the parameter error was fitted by the least square method. In the parameter identification method. References [16, 17] introduced the distance error into DH model, MDH model, DH/MDH model and additive exponential product model, and identified the kinematic parameters of the robot. However, the research does not consider the influence of error model on identification results for robots with different configurations.

In this paper, four error identification models of integrated position error, relative position error, integrated pose error and relative pose error are established. The kinematic loop method combined with multi-population genetic algorithm is used to identify the parameters. The ideal pose data set and the pose data set with error are used to analyze the influence of different error models on the final parameter identification results and the pose error of the end of the manipulator.

2   Forward Kinematics Model and Verification of UR10

The UR10 robot consists of six rotational joints. The first three joints of the manipulator mainly control the end position, and the last three joints mainly control the end orientation. The structure is shown in Fig. 1. According to the DH kinematic modeling method, the kinematic coordinate system of the robot is established, and the kinematic parameters of the robot are obtained, as shown in Table 1.

According to the DH kinematics modeling method, the transformation relationship between the adjacent link coordinate system of the manipulator is shown in formula (1).

$$T_i = \begin{bmatrix} c\theta_i & -s\theta_i c\alpha_{i-1} & s\theta_i s\alpha_{i-1} & a_{i-1}c\theta_i \\ s\theta_i & c\theta_i c\alpha_{i-1} & -c\theta_i s\alpha_{i-1} & a_{i-1}s\theta_i \\ 0 & s\alpha_{i-1} & c\alpha_{i-1} & d_i \\ 0 & 0 & 0 & 1 \end{bmatrix} \tag{1}$$

Among them, c represents $\textit{cos}$ and s represents $\textit{sin}$.

The pose transformation moment of the robot end tool coordinate system relative to the base coordinate system is shown in Eq. (2).

$$\begin{matrix} 0 \\ 6 \end{matrix} T = T_1 \cdot T_2 \cdot T_3 \cdot T_4 \cdot T_5 \cdot T_6 = \begin{bmatrix} n_x & o_x & a_x & p_x \\ n_y & o_y & a_y & p_y \\ n_z & o_z & a_z & p_z \\ 0 & 0 & 0 & 1 \end{bmatrix} \tag{2}$$

The position parameter is the position parameter in formula (2), and the orientation angle can be solved by RPY analytic attitude matrix method.

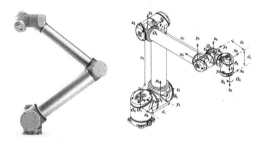

Fig. 1. Structure and kinematics coordinate system of UR10 robot

Table 1. DH parameters of UR10 robot kinematics

Joint	a_i/mm	a_i/rad	d_i/mm	θ_i/rad
1	0	$\pi/2$	127.3	θ_i
2	-612	0	0	θ_2
3	-572.3	0	0	θ_3
4	0	$\pi/2$	163.9	θ_4
5	0	$-\pi/2$	115.7	θ_5
6	0	0	92.2	θ_6

The mechanism model of UR manipulator is built by MATLAB-simmechanics, and the simulation verification program is shown in Fig. 2. By giving the same input to the mechanism model and the theoretical model, and comparing the end pose output errors of the two models, we can prove the correctness of the established robot kinematics model.

3 Parameter Identification Method of Kinematic Model

3.1 Introduction of Identification Method

When calibrating the kinematic parameters of the manipulator, the ball bar, laser tracker and physical constraints are often used to measure the pose of the end of the manipulator,

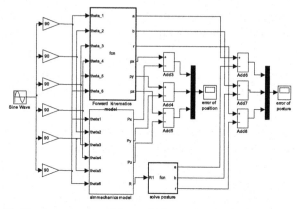

Fig. 2. Verification program of forward kinematics simulation of manipulator

and the parameters are identified with the specific error model. In the process of robot kinematic parameter identification, the most critical step is to establish an appropriate error model.

In order to analyze the influence of different error models on the accuracy of kinematic parameter identification, we select position error and full pose error, and combines two different evaluation indexes to establish four error models, namely, relative position error model DH-PP (ϕ_1), comprehensive position error model DH-PS (ϕ_2), relative pose error model DH-PP (ϕ_3) and comprehensive pose error model DH-PPS (ϕ_4), as shown in formula (3)–(6). Among them, $P_T = \begin{bmatrix} p_x^T & p_y^T & p_z^T & \alpha^T & \beta^T & r^T \end{bmatrix}$ is the pose parameters of the robot end obtained by the theoretical modeling of the kinematics model, and $P_E = \begin{bmatrix} p_x^E & p_y^E & p_z^E & \alpha^E & \beta^E & r^E \end{bmatrix}$ is the pose parameters of the end obtained by the simulation. For error models ϕ_1 and ϕ_3, when measuring the identification data groups, the data of zero position are manually removed.

$$\phi_1 = \left| \frac{P_x^E - P_x^T}{P_x^E} \right| + \left| \frac{P_y^E - P_y^T}{P_y^E} \right| + \left| \frac{P_z^E - P_z^T}{P_z^E} \right| \tag{3}$$

$$\phi_2 = \sqrt{(P_x^E - P_x^T)^2 + (P_y^E - P_y^T)^2 + (P_z^E - P_z^T)^2} \tag{4}$$

$$\phi_3 = \left| \frac{P_x^E - P_x^T}{P_x^E} \right| + \left| \frac{P_y^E - P_y^T}{P_y^E} \right| + \left| \frac{P_z^E - P_z^T}{P_z^E} \right| + \left| \frac{\alpha^E - \alpha^T}{\alpha^E} \right| + \left| \frac{\beta^E - \beta^T}{\beta^E} \right| + \left| \frac{\gamma^E - \gamma^T}{\gamma^E} \right| \tag{5}$$

$$\phi_4 = \sqrt{(P_x^E - P_x^T)^2 + (P_y^E - P_y^T)^2 + (P_z^E - P_z^T)^2 + (\alpha^E - \alpha^T)^2 + (\beta^E - \beta^T)^2 + (\gamma^E - \gamma^T)^2} \tag{6}$$

The identification data set and its optimization objective function required for the identification of four error models using multi-population genetic algorithm are shown in Table 2. After the kinematic parameter identification is completed, the pose data of another group are used to analyze and evaluate the identification effect of the model.

Table 2. Identification dataset and optimization objective function of four methods

Error model	Identification data sets	Optimization object
DH-PP	$[P_xP_yP_z]$	Φ_1
DH-PS	$[P_xP_yP_z]$	Φ_2
DH-PPP	$[P_xP_yP_z\alpha\ \beta\ r]$	Φ_3
DH-PPS	$[P_xP_yP_z\alpha\ \beta\ r]$	Φ_4

3.2 Parameter Identification Based on Multi-population Genetic Algorithm

Multi-population genetic algorithm is a global search optimization method. The program flow of the whole optimization process is shown in Fig. 3. The main processes are as follows:

Step 1: In the initialization phase, N initial populations ($N = 20$) are randomly generated within the parameter range of design variables to be identified.

Step 2: After initialization, the double-space index of each group corresponding to each design variable parameter is calculated as the fitness value of the corresponding individual. In the optimization process of this paper, the optimization process is to solve the minimum index in the design variable space, as shown in Eq. (7).

$$\Phi = \min(\phi) \tag{7}$$

Step 3: According to the size of individual fitness in the current population, the best individual in the current population migrates to the target population, and the low fitness individuals in the target population are eliminated. At the same time, according to the fitness, the best individual of each group is stored in the elite population by artificial selection operator.

Step 4: Select the best individuals in the elite population to compare with the best individuals selected in the previous generation. If the two are the same, then the best individual preserving algebra gen = gen + 1; Otherwise, gen = 0, and save the best individual for this selection instead of the global best individual. Compare the optimal individual retention algebra gen with the maximum conservative algebra MAXGEN. If gen > MAXGEN, the recognition process terminates. In this case, the optimal individual is the optimal solution of design variable optimization; Otherwise, the next step will continue.

Step 5: Select, cross and mutate individuals in each group to generate the next generation population, and then repeat step 2 for a new round of optimization. Wheel selection, real number crossover and random variation were used for genetic operation.

4 Comparison of Four Identification Models

4.1 Evaluation and Analysis of Identification Accuracy Under Ideal Conditions

Based on the DH parameters of the nominal UR manipulator and the forward kinematics model of the robot, 200 groups of joint angles θ and the end pose ($px, py, pz, \alpha, \beta, r$) of

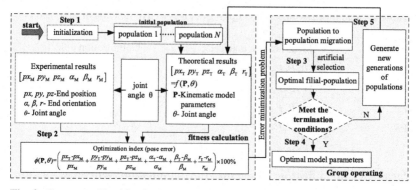

Fig. 3. Parameter identification process based on multi-population genetic algorithm

the manipulator with zero removal can be randomly generated by MATLAB software programming. Among them, 100 groups of data are used for multi-population genetic algorithm (MGPA) to identify DH parameters, and the remaining 100 groups of data are used to analyze and evaluate the identification results.

In this paper, nine parameters that need to be identified are size parameters (a_2, a_3, d_1, d_4, d_5, d_6) and angle parameters (α_1, α_4, α_5), and the remaining parameters are zero. The kinematic parameter identification results for the four error models are shown in Table 3.

The DH parameters identified by different error models under ideal conditions are brought into the joint angle θ of another 100 groups of data to obtain the position and attitude of the end of the identified manipulator. Compared with the theoretical position and attitude of the end, the position error and attitude error of the end are obtained, as shown in Fig. 4.

4.2 Identification Accuracy and Anti-interference Ability Analysis Under Ideal Conditions

When evaluating the comprehensive performance of an error identification model, we should not only consider its own identification accuracy, but also consider its anti-interference ability. On the basis of ideal conditions, the random error of 0–0.05 mm is added to the position parameters (px, py, pz) of the identification data set, and the random error of 0–0.05° is added to the orientation parameters (α, β, r). Then it is used for parameter identification of four error models, and the identification accuracy and anti-interference ability are analyzed. The DH parameter identification results are shown in Table 4. The end pose errors of the four error models under error conditions are compared, as shown in Fig. 5.

We can find that the error of DH-PPS and DH-PPP is very small compared with the nominal DH parameter, and the error of each kinematic parameter is less than 1‰. The identification error of the two models for attitude angle is almost zero, and the identification accuracy is very high. However, the position error of DH-PPS is smaller than that of DH-PPP, and DH-PPS has stronger anti-interference ability under error conditions. DH-PS and DH-PP have only three parameters (d_5, d_6, α_5) error of more

Table 3. Comparison of four error model identification results

Nominal DH parameter		DH-PP identification value	DH-PS identification value	DH-PPP identification value	DH-PPS identification value
d_1	0.1273	0.1273	0.1273	0.1273	0.1273
d_4	0.1639	0.1639	0.1639	0.1639	0.1639
d_5	0.1157	0.05954 (−48.5%)	0.11832 (2.3%)	0.1157	0.1157
d_6	0.0922	0.10796 (17.1%)	0.09223 (0.04%)	0.09219 (−0.02%)	0.0922
a_2	−0.612	−0.612	−0.612	−0.61199 (−0.01%)	−0.612
a_3	−0.5723	−0.5723	−0.5723	−0.57229 (0.01%)	−0.5723
α_1	1.5708	1.5708	1.5708	1.5708	1.5708
α_4	1.5708	1.5708	1.5708	1.5708	1.5708
α_5	−1.5708	−1.0237 (−34.8%)	−1.5992 (1.8%)	−1.5708	−1.5708

Note: The error percentage of error parameters is marked in the table. The size parameter unit is m and the angle parameter unit is rad.

Table 4. Comparison of the results of parameter identification methods under error conditions

Nominal DH parameter		DH-PP	DH-PS	DH-PPP	DH-PPS
d_1	0.1273	0.12777	0.12772	0.12778	0.12772
d_4	0.1639	0.16414	0.16386	0.16398	0.16386
d_5	0.1157	0.09591 (−17.1%)	0.05871 (−49.26%)	0.11553	0.11564
d_6	0.0922	0.09433 (2.31%)	0.10834 (17.51%)	0.09226	0.09218
a_2	−0.612	−0.61197	−0.61198	−0.61193	−0.61198
a_3	−0.5723	−0.57208	−0.57236	−0.57207	−0.57236
α_1	1.5708	1.5706	1.5708	1.5708	1.5708
α_4	1.5708	1.5724	1.5708	1.5708	1.5708
α_5	−1.5708	−1.3611 (−13.3%)	−1.0175 (−35.22%)	−1.5708	−1.5708

Note: The error percentage of the parameters with error more than 1% is marked in the table. The size parameter unit is m, and the angle parameter unit is rad.

than one percent relative to the nominal DH parameter, which are −49.26%, 17.81%, −35.22% and −17.11%, 2.31%, −13.35%, respectively. It is easy to find that DH-PS has large error for size parameters, and large error for DH-PP angle parameters. Combined with Fig. 5, the position error of DH-PP is smaller, and the orientation error of DH-PS is smaller, that is, DH-PP and DH-PS have stronger anti-interference ability when identifying position parameters and attitude angle parameters, respectively.

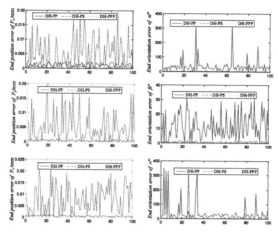

Fig. 4. Comparison of parameter identification errors under ideal conditions

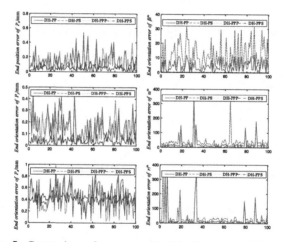

Fig. 5. Comparison of parameter identification errors with errors

4.3 Identification Accuracy and Anti-interference Ability Analysis Under Error Conditions

The identification of the four error models under ideal conditions and with errors can be seen in Table 5. We can find that:

DH-PPS is an ideal kinematics parameter error identification model because of its high identification accuracy, small orientation error and excellent anti-error interference ability. At the same time, DH-PPP parameter identification accuracy is high, the identification error of orientation parameters are small, the position error is "medium", the error anti-jamming ability is "good", is an ideal error identification model.

The parameter identification accuracy and attitude error of DH-PS are both "medium", the position error is small, and the error capacity of resisting disturbance is "poor". Therefore, it can be used to identify only the kinematics dimension parameters, and the identification effect is acceptable without the orientation angle measurement. The parameter identification accuracy and position error of DH-PP are "medium", the orientation error is large, and the error anti-jamming ability is "poor", so it is not recommended to use this model for parameter identification.

Table 5. Evaluation table of the identification ability of four error models

Error model	Accuracy of parameter identification	Position error	Orientation error	Capacity of resisting disturbance
DH-PP	Medium	Medium	Big	Poor
DH-PS	Medium	Medium	Medium	Poor
DH-PPP	High	Medium	High	Good
DH-PPS	Excellent	Small	Small	Excellent

5 Conclusions

Aiming at the calibration of the kinematics parameters of the manipulator, four different error identification models were proposed in this paper. Combined with multi-population genetic algorithm, the influences of the four models on the final parameter identification results and the pose error of the manipulator end under ideal conditions and with errors were analyzed. Through theoretical simulation identification, the following conclusions could be drawn:

(1) The comprehensive pose error model and the relative pose error model have high identification accuracy for the kinematics parameters themselves, and the identification errors of the attitude and position are not large, and the anti-error ability is acceptable. When all the kinematics parameters need to be identified, they are the ideal error models.

(2) The comprehensive position error model and the relative position error model have poor anti-error ability for the identification of the kinematic orientation angle, so they are not suitable for the identification of the kinematic orientation angle parameters.

(3) In the identification with error conditions, the position error of the comprehensive position error model is the smallest, and the attitude angle does not need to be considered and measured by this model. Therefore, if only the kinematic dimension parameters are identified, this model can be adopted, and better identification effect can be obtained with less energy.

(4) When applying the relative position error model and the relative pose error model, it is necessary to avoid the end pose being close to the origin of coordinates during data collection to avoid the defects of the model itself.

(5) Orientation angle is very sensitive to error interference. In this paper, only the error of 0.05° is considered, but the orientation error after identification is all about 5°, and the error amplification is nearly 100 times. Therefore, if orientation angle parameters are to be identified, attention should be paid to selecting high-precision orientation angle measuring instrument or measurement method.

References

1. Lim, H.K., Kim, D.H., Kim, S.R., et al.: A practical approach to enhance positioning accuracy for industrial robots. In: ICCAS-SICE 2009. IEEE (2009)
2. Zhang, X., Zheng, Z., Qi, Y.: Parameter identification and calibration of D-H model for 6-DOF series robot. Robot **38**(03), 360–370 (2016)
3. Nubiola, A., Bonev, I.A.: Absolute calibration of an ABB IRB 1600 robot using a laser tracker. Robot. Comput. Integr. Manuf. **29**(1), 236–245 (2013). https://doi.org/10.1016/j.rcim.2012.06.004
4. Nguyen, H., Zhou, J., Kang, H., et al.: A calibration method for enhancing robot accuracy through integration of an extended Kalman filter algorithm and an artificial neural network. Neurocomputing **151**, 996–1005 (2015)
5. He, R., Zhao, Y., Yang, S., et al.: Kinematic-parameter identification for serial-robot calibration based on POE formula. IEEE Trans. Rob. **26**(3), 411–423 (2010)
6. Wenbin, G.A.O., Hongguang, W.A.N.G., Yong, J.I.A.N.G., Xin'an, P.A.N.: Kinematic calibration method of robots based on distance error. Robot **35**(5), 600 (2013). https://doi.org/10.3724/SP.J.1218.2013.00600
7. Lu, Y., Yu, L., Guo, B.: Structural parameter calibration of industrial robot based on closed dimension chain. Chin. J. Sci. Instrum. **39**(2), 38–46 (2018)
8. Zhuang, H., Roth, Z.S., Hamno, F.: A complete and parametrically continuous kinematic model for robot manipulators. IEEE Trans. Robot. Autom. **8**(4), 451–463 (2002)
9. Yang, L., Qin, X., Cai, J., et al.: Research on positioning accuracy calibration technology of industrial robot. Control Eng. **20**(4), 785–788 (2013)
10. Gong, X., Shen, J., Tian, W., et al.: Absolute positioning error model and compensation algorithm for industrial robot. J. Nanjing Univ. Aeronaut. Astronaut. **44**(S), 60–64 (2012)
11. Dolinsky, J.U., Jenkinson, I.D., Colquhoun, G.J., et al.: Application of genetic programming to the calibration of industrial robots. Comput. Ind. **58**(3), 255–264 (2007)
12. Jang, J.H., Kim, S.H., et al.: Calibration of geometric and nongeometric errors of an industrial robot. Robotics **19**(3), 305–701 (2001)
13. Bai, Y., Zhuang, H.: Modeless robots calibration in 3D workspace with an on-line fuzzy interpolation technique. In: Proceedings of IEEE International Conference on Man and Cybernetics, Washington, pp. 5233–5239. IEEE (2004)
14. Hage, H., Bidaud, P., Jardin, N.: Practical consideration on the identification of the kinematic parameters of the Staubli TX90 robot. In: Mechanism and Machine Science, Guanajuato, pp. 1–8 (2011)
15. Meggiolaro, M., Scriffignano, G., Dubowsky S.: Manipulator calibration using a single end-point contact constraint. In: Proceedings of ASME Design Engineering Technical Conference, pp. 1–9 (2000)
16. Wang, Z., Xu, H., Chen, G., et al.: A distance error based industrial robot kinematic calibration method. Ind. Robot. **41**(5), 439–446 (2014)
17. Hu, S., Zhang, M., Zhou, C., et al.: A novel self-calibration method with POE-based model and distance error measurement for serial manipulators. J. Mech. Sci. Technol. **31**(10), 4911–4923 (2017)

Design and Analysis
of a Muti-Degree-of-Freedom Dexterous
Gripper with Variable Stiffness

Pan Zhou[1], Jiantao Yao[1,2(✉)], Xuanhao Zhang[1], and Yongsheng Zhao[1,2]

[1] Hebei Provincial Key Laboratory of Parallel Robot and Mechatronic System,
Yanshan University, Qinhuangda 066004, China
jtyao@ysu.edu.cn
[2] Key Laboratory of Advanced Forging & Stamping Technology and Science, (Yanshan
University), Ministry of Education of China, Qinhuangda 066004, China

Abstract. Variable stiffness is the focus and difficulty in the research of soft robotics technology, and the variable stiffness of the multi-degree-of-freedom (MDOF) soft structure is more challenging. Inspired by the transverse and longitudinal muscle structure of octopus arms, using parallel and spiral pneumatic artificial muscles (PAMs) to imitate the transverse and longitudinal muscle structure respectively, and then the MDOF movement and variable stiffness function of a soft finger can be realized by the mutual coupling of PAMs. Based on the rigid-flexible-soft design strategy, a rigid frame is embedded in the spiral PAM, which improves the regularity and stability of the finger module movement, and provides a good hardware foundation for simplifying theoretical model. A dexterous gripper is designed based on the MDOF variable stiffness finger module, which has four grasping modes, such as non-parallel bending inward, non-parallel bending outward, parallel bending inward, and parallel bending outward. Then the kinematics model of the soft finger is established based on the assumption of constant curvature and its workspace is solved. The MDOF variable stiffness performance of the finger module is experimentally analyzed, and a multi-target grasping experiment is carried out. It is proved that the dexterous gripper has good adaptability and flexibility, and experimental results show that the load capacity of the soft gripper can be improved by this variable stiffness method. This research provides a theoretical and technical reference for the development of MODF soft structures with variable stiffness.

Keywords: Soft robot · Variable stiffness · Pneumatic artificial muscle · Dexterous gripper

1 Introduction

Soft robots composed of flexible and soft materials can change their shape in a wide range and realize soft interaction with their surrounding environment under the premise of ensuring their own working ability, which play an important role in the frontier

© Springer Nature Switzerland AG 2021
X.-J. Liu et al. (Eds.): ICIRA 2021, LNAI 13013, pp. 129–139, 2021.
https://doi.org/10.1007/978-3-030-89095-7_13

research of robots [1–3]. With the deep development of soft robotics, various complex soft structures are created to meet the increasingly complex operation requirements. Among them, soft grippers have been well developed with their excellent performance and wide application. Soft grippers make full use of the flexibility of various soft materials (such as rubber, polymers, smart materials, multifunctional materials, etc.), having high flexibility and good man-machine.

With the in-depth development of soft robot technology, a variety of new soft grippers have been created to meet the increasingly complex operation requirements. Drotman et al. [4] designed pneumatic actuators with bellows by 3D printing technology. Calisti et al. [5–7] designed a soft gripper based on line-driven bionic octopus tentacles, which can grasp objects by producing a curling motion. Walker et al. [8–10] have made a soft manipulator imitating elephant trunk by using pneumatic artificial muscle, which can grasp objects of various shapes. Hao et al. [11] developed a soft manipulator based on the design principle of fold layers, and it can be applied to actual production. Wang et al. [12] have embed reinforcing fibers in pneumatic soft actuators to improve their stability and movement accuracy.

These soft grippers have excellent flexibility, high environmental adaptability and human-machine interaction safety, while soft structures cannot provide the grasping stability provided by rigid structures. The establishment of variable stiffness mechanisms is an ideal solution to reconcile the flexibility and stability requirements of soft grippers. In recent years, many domestic and foreign researchers have launched research on variable stiffness soft grippers. Variable stiffness methods mainly include particle jamming [13, 14], layer jamming [15], kinematic coupling [16, 17], and stiffness controlled materials [18]. Variable stiffness is the focus and difficulty in the research of soft grippers, and the variable stiffness of the multi-degree-of-freedom (MDOF) soft structure is more challenging.

This work is dedicated to studying MDOF variable stiffness dexterous grippers. Inspired by the transverse and longitudinal muscle structure of octopus arms, using parallel and spiral pneumatic artificial muscles (PAMs) to imitate the transverse and longitudinal muscle structure respectively, and then the MDOF movement and variable stiffness function of a soft finger module can be realized by the mutual coupling of PAMs. Based on the rigid-flexible-soft design strategy, a rigid frame is embedded in the spiral pneumatic artificial muscle, which improves the regularity and stability of the finger module movement, and provides a good hardware foundation for simplifying theoretical model. A dexterous gripper is designed based on the MDOF variable stiffness finger module, which has four grasping modes, such as centripetal bending, bending outward, centripetal parallel bending and parallel bending outward mode. Then the kinematics model of the soft finger is established based on the assumption of constant curvature and its workspace is solved. The MDOF variable stiffness performance of the finger module is experimentally analyzed, and a multi-target grasping experiment is carried out. It is proved that the dexterous gripper has good adaptability and flexibility, and experimental results show that the load capacity of the soft gripper can be improved by this variable stiffness method. And the further research and application of the soft gripper have been discussed.

2 Inspiration and Design

The goal of biological inspiration is to understand the principles underlying the behavior of animals and humans and transfer them to the development of robots [2]. Nowadays, the biological inspiration is a common method for developing new soft robots. Inspired by the motion principle of octopus arms, various types of soft robots, such as continuous robots and soft grippers, have been created successively [19, 20]. It's worth noting that octopus arms show good variable stiffness characteristics when gripping objects, which is due to their special muscle tissues composed of a large number of longitudinal muscles, transverse muscles and oblique muscles [21] (Fig. 1(a)).

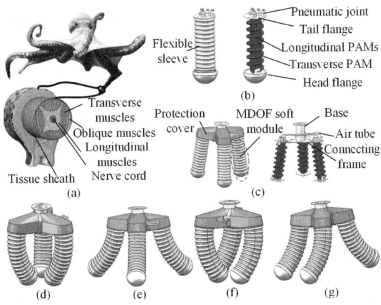

Fig. 1. (a) Schematics of the muscle composition of octopus arms. (b) Three-dimensional model of the MDOF soft module. (c) Three-dimensional model of the soft dexterous gripper. Schematic diagram of grasping mode of the soft dexterous gripper: Non-parallel bending inward (d), non-parallel bending outward (e), parallel bending inward (f), and parallel bending outward (g).

Inspired by octopus arms, we used three longitudinally arranged PAMs to imitate the longitudinal muscles and a spirally arranged PAM to imitate the transverse muscles and oblique muscles, and then formed a soft finger with variable stiffness, as shown in Fig. 1(b). The longitudinal PAMs were evenly distributed and their both ends were fixed with a tail flange and a head flange respectively. The spiral PAM was wound around the outside of the longitudinal PAMs, and its both ends were also fixed by the tail flange and the head flange. A flexible sleeve was arranged on the outer side of the soft finger to protect its internal PAMs and grasped objects. Further, we used three such soft fingers to design a soft MDOF dexterous gripper with variable stiffness, as shown in Fig. 1(c). Three soft fingers were mounted on the connecting frame connected with the base. A protection cover was mounted on the connecting frame, which is used to cover tubes, prevent the collision of external objects and dust falling in. The grasping part of the soft dexterous gripper is made of soft material, and thus it can provide certain protection for grasped objects, which can be used for grasping fragile objects.

The soft finger can achieve bending in any direction by pressurizing the longitudinal PAMs, so that the soft dexterous gripper' fingers can flexibly change their grasping postures, enabling the gripper to grasp in multiple modes, such as non-parallel bending inward (Fig. 1(d)), non-parallel bending outward (Fig. 1(e)), parallel bending inward (Fig. 1(f)), and parallel bending outward (Fig. 1(g)). The multiple gripping modes of the gripper enable it to be suitable for a wider variety of targets. For example, it can not only grasp solid objects by bending inward, but also various ring-shaped objects by bending outward. At the same time, when the spiral PAM is pressurized, the stiffness of the gripper increases, and thus it can grip objects more stably and can grip heavier objects.

3 Modeling

3.1 Forward Kinematics

The forward kinematics of the soft finger mainly solves the relationship between its space and the lengths of PAMs. The end position of the finger is mainly controlled by the three longitudinal PAMs. Thus, we can neglect the effect of the spiral PAM, and use the lengths of the three longitudinal PAMs to define the space of the soft finger. According to the structural characteristics of the soft finger, we get a space bending diagram of its ideal model as shown in Fig. 2. When the three longitudinal PAMs are pressurized with different pressures, the soft finger can achieve contraction and bending in the space, and its bending shape is approximately a circular arc. The space q of the finger can be represented by the lengths of the three longitudinal PAMs S_i as follows:

$$q = \begin{bmatrix} S_1 & S_2 & S_3 \end{bmatrix}^T \tag{1}$$

The position of the MDOF soft finger can be defined based on its centerline relative to each of the three longitudinal PAMs as:

$$S(q) = (S_1 + S_2 + S_3)/3 \tag{2}$$

$$\phi(q) = \arctan\left(\frac{\sqrt{3}(S_3 + S_2 - 2S_1)}{3(S_2 - S_3)}\right) \tag{3}$$

$$k(q) = \frac{2\sqrt{S_1^2 + S_2^2 + S_3^2 - S_1 S_2 - S_2 S_3 - S_1 S_3}}{d(S_1 + S_2 + S_3)} \tag{4}$$

$$\theta(q) = S(q)k(q) \tag{5}$$

where S is the centerline length of the soft finger, and d is the distance between the centerline of the soft finger and a longitudinal PAM, k is the curvature of the soft finger,

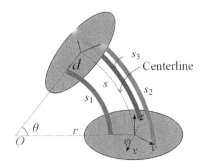

Fig. 2. The space bending diagram of ideal model of the MDOF soft finger.

θ is the central angle corresponding to the centerline length S, and φ is the angle of the soft finger in the xy plane.

The configuration space of the soft finger is then mapped to its task space. This space represents the Cartesian coordinates of the distal end of the MDOF soft finger

$$l = 2r \, \sin(\frac{\theta}{2}) \tag{6}$$

$$x = l \sin (\frac{\theta}{2}) \cos(\phi) \tag{7}$$

$$y = l \, \sin(\frac{\theta}{2}) \sin(\phi) \tag{8}$$

$$z = l \, \cos(\frac{\theta}{2}) \tag{9}$$

where l is the chord length of the finger, r is the radius of the finger ($r = 1/k$), and x, y, and z are the x-coordinate, y-coordinate, and z-coordinate at the tip of the finger, respectively.

3.2 Inverse Kinematics

The inverse kinematics can be used to find the lengths of PAMs associated with a desired tip position of the finger. The inverse kinematics of the soft finger can be resolved by relating the individual lengths of the PAMs to the centerline of the soft finger as:

$$\phi(q) = tan^{-1}\left(\frac{y}{x}\right) \tag{10}$$

$$k = \frac{2\sqrt{x^2 + y^2}}{x^2 + y^2 + z^2} \tag{11}$$

$$\theta = \begin{cases} \cos^{-1}(1 - k\sqrt{x^2 + y^2}), & \text{if } z > 0 \\ 2\pi - \cos^{-1}(1 - k\sqrt{x^2 + y^2}), & \text{if } z \leq 0 \end{cases} \tag{12}$$

$$S = \frac{\theta}{k} \tag{13}$$

The lengths of each individual PAM are then mapped to the position of the soft finger in 3-D space

$$S_i = S - \theta d \cos\left(\frac{2\pi}{3}(i-1) + \frac{\pi}{2} - \phi\right) \tag{14}$$

3.3 Mathematical Model Simulation Analysis

Based on the kinematics model of the soft finger established above, we used MATLAB software to perform the mathematical model simulation analysis of the soft gripper. Simulating the spatial motion of the three soft fingers, their connecting frame was replaced by a circular plane. And the three soft fingers were circumferentially,

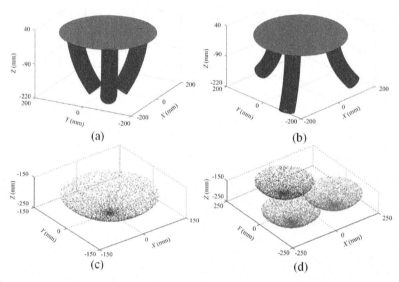

Fig. 3. (a) The simulation analysis of the three soft fingers when they simultaneously bend inward. (b) The simulation analysis of the three soft fingers when they simultaneously bend outward. (c) The workspace of the soft finger. (d) The workspace of the three soft fingers.

evenly fixed on the circular plane. Setting the center arc length $S_0 = 250$ mm and the curvature of the arc $k = 0.003$ for each soft finger. The three soft fingers simultaneously bend inward, as shown in Fig. 3(a). Then setting center arc length $S_0 = 250$ mm and the curvature of the arc $k = -0.003$. The three MDOF modules simultaneously bent outward, as shown in Fig. 3(b). By using MATLAB software to mathematically simulate the kinematics model of the soft finger, the visualization of the shape of the soft dexterous gripper was realized.

The workspace of the soft finger was simulated according to the equations obtained in mathematical modeling by using MATLAB software. First, setting the working boundary conditions of the soft finger and simulating its workspace. The deflection angle φ of the soft finger around the z-axis is 0 to 360°. And the maximum curvature k corresponding to its curved arc is 0.005. Then we got its working space, as shown in Fig. 3(c). It can be seen from the Fig. 3(c) that the soft finger can realize bending motion at any angle in the space and its flexibility is strong.

The working space of the three soft fingers is shown in Fig. 3(d). It can be seen from Fig. 3(d) that the end position points of the three soft fingers have some overlapping parts in the center of their working space. That is, when the three soft fingers move in space, they will interfere with each other in certain motion states. Therefore, when building the control system of the soft dexterous gripper, it is necessary to set the boundary conditions according to the actual situation and control the input gas pressure of each actuator to avoid the interference of the three soft fingers during the movement.

4 The MDOF Variable Stiffness Performance Analysis

The performance test system of the soft finger mainly includes an industrial robot, a pneumatic control box, an attitude sensor and a fixture. The internal air pressure of PAMs was controlled by electric proportional valves. The attitude sensor was installed at the end of the soft finger to measure its bending angle. The MDOF variable stiffness performance of the soft finger is studied from four aspects: the air pressure of the parallel and spiral PAMs, the load weight and bending angle of the soft finger.

When the spiral PAM was not pressurized, the relationship curve between the bending angle of the soft finger and the air pressure of a single longitudinal PAM under different loads was fitted by MATLAB software, as shown in Fig. 4(a). It is shown that the bending angle of the soft finger becomes larger as the pressure in the longitudinal PAM increases under the same load weight, showing a non-linear proportional relationship. When the soft finger produces the same bending angle, the air pressure required for the longitudinal PAM increases with the increase of the load. Therefore, the soft gripper can grasp objects by the MDOF bending of the three soft fingers, meanwhile as the weight of the grasped object increases, the air pressure of the parallel PAMs needs to be increased to achieve a good grasping.

When the spiral PAM was pressurized with 0.04 MPa and 0.07 MPa respectively, the curves of relationship between the bending angle of the soft finger and the air pressure of the single longitudinal PAM under different loads are shown in Figs. 4(b) and 4(c). Comparing the data in Figs. 4(a),4(b), and 4(c), it is found that as the pressure of the spiral PAM increases, the bending angle of the soft finger will decrease under the same load weight and the same pressure of the longitudinal PAM. This means that the soft finger's ability to resist bending deformation is improved and its overall stiffness is enhanced. Therefore, the variable stiffness characteristics of the soft gripper can be achieved by changing the internal air pressure of the spiral PAM. Moreover, the increasing trend of stiffness is different under different loads.

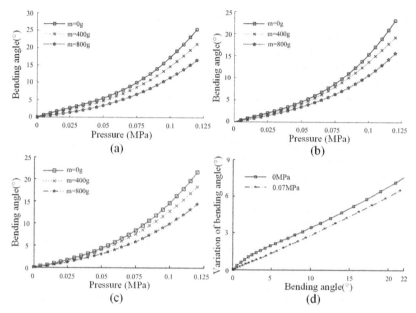

Fig. 4. (a) The relationship between the bending angle of the soft finger and the internal pressure of a single longitudinal PAM when the spiral PAM was unpressurized. The relationship between the bending angle of the soft finger and the internal pressure of a single longitudinal PAM when the spiral PAM was pressurized with 0.04MPa (b) and 0.07 MPa (c), respectively. In Figs. (a) - (c), m is the mass of the weight hanging from the tip of the soft finger. (d) The variation of bending angle of the soft finger at different bending angles after increasing the load from 0 g to 800 g when the spiral PAM was unpressurized and pressurized with 0.07 MPa, respectively.

In order to further verify the variable stiffness characteristics of the soft gripper, the bending angle changes of the soft finger at different bending angle as the load was increased from 0 g to 800 g were measured when the spiral PAM was unpressurized and pressurized with 0.07 MPa, respectively, verifying the influence of the spiral PAM pressure on the stiffness of the soft finger under different loads, as shown in Fig. 5(d). It was shown that the variation of bending angle of the soft finger when the spiral PAM was pressurized with 0.07 MPa was smaller than that when the spiral PAM was unpressurized, and as the load increases, the difference increases. It shows that the stiffness of the soft finger increases with the increase of the pressure of the spiral PAM. Moreover, as the load of the soft finger is greater, the increase in the spiral PAM pressure will increase the stiffness of the soft finger more significantly.

Therefore, the MDOF movements of the soft finger can be realized by controlling the air pressure of the three parallel PAMs, and meanwhile its variable stiffness can be achieved by changing the air pressure of the spiral PAM. The MDOF variable stiffness function of the soft dexterous gripper when it grips objects can be realized by simultaneously controlling the pressure in the parallel PAMs and spiral PAM of the three parallel soft fingers.

5   Multiple Objects Gripping

The MDOF characteristic of the soft dexterous gripper enables it to better adapt to the shape of objects. We have carried out gripping experiments on multiple objects, as shown in Fig. 5. It can be seen that the soft dexterous gripper can steadily grasp objects having various shapes and materials, such as a spherical wooden block, a plush toy with irregular shape, a bag of snacks, a sneaker, a short cylindrical plastic bucket, a cuboid plastic bucket, a pineapple, a long cylinder thermos cup, an electric drill, a bucket of laundry liquid, and a cuboid carton.

In order to further verify the variable stiffness characteristic of the soft dexterous gripper, its maximum load weight was tested when the spiral PAM was unpressurized and pressurized with 0.07 MPa at the 20° bending angle of the soft fingers, as shown in Fig. 5(l). The maximum load weight of the dexterous gripper was 2.7 kg when the spiral PAM was pressurized with 0.07 MPa at the 20° bending angle of the soft fingers, and the maximum load weight of the dexterous gripper was 2.4 kg when the spiral PAM was unpressurized. It can be seen that the load capacity of the dexterous gripper becomes larger as the air pressure inside the spiral PAM increases under the same bending angle of the soft finger, and its stiffness also increases.

Fig. 5. The multiple objects gripping experiments of the soft dexterous gripper: (a) a spherical wooden block, (b) a plush toy with irregular shape, (c) a bag of snacks, (d) a sneaker, (e) a short cylindrical plastic bucket, (f) a cuboid plastic bucket, (g) a pineapple, (h) a long cylinder thermos cup, (i) an electric drill, (j) a bucket of laundry liquid, (k) a cuboid carton, and (l) the maximum load weight of the dexterous gripper when the spiral PAM was pressurized with 0.07 MPa at the 20° bending angle of the soft fingers.

6   Conclusion

Based on the MDOF coupling variable stiffness method, this paper proposed a bioin-spired MDOF module with variable stiffness for soft dexterous grippers. The research results are as follows:

(1)   The proposed soft dexterous gripper has four grasping modes: centripetal bending, bending outward, centripetal parallel bending and parallel bending outward mode,

which improves its ability to work in unstructured environments and grasp non-cooperative targets. The rigid-flexible-soft design strategy is adopted to improve the regularity and stability of the finger module movement and provide a good hardware foundation for its theoretical modeling.

(2) The kinematics model of the soft finger is established based on the assumption of constant curvature and its working space is solved, which provides a theoretical basis for the control of the soft dexterous gripper.

(3) The experimental results show that the soft finger can achieve MDOF bending movement by controlling the air pressure of the parallel PAMs, and increasing the air pressure of the spiral PAM can increase the stiffness of the soft finger. It is experimentally proved that the soft gripper has good adaptability and flexibility, and this coupling variable stiffness method can improve its load capacity.

The Future work will focus on studying new bionic structures having MDOF variable stiffness, and will further improve the variable stiffness characteristics and load capacity of MDOF soft structures.

References

1. Lee, C., et al.: Soft robot review. Int. J. Control Autom. Syst. **15**(1), 3–15 (2016). https://doi.org/10.1007/s12555-016-0462-3
2. Pfeifer, R., Lungarella, M., Iida, F.: The challenges ahead for bio-inspired soft robotics. Commun. ACM **55**(11), 76–87 (2012)
3. Rus, D., Tolley, M.T.: Design, fabrication and control of soft robots. Nature **521**(7553), 467–475 (2015)
4. Drotman, D., Ishida, M., Jadhav, S., Tolley, M.T.: Application-driven design of soft, 3D printed, pneumatic actuators with bellows. IEEE/ASME Trans. Mechatron. **24**(1), 78–87 (2018)
5. Calisti, M., Giorelli, M., Levy, G., et al.: An octopus-bioinspired solution to movement and manipulation for soft robots. Bioinspir. Biomim. **6**(3), 2–12 (2011)
6. Calisti, M., Arienti, A., Giannaccini, M.E., et al.: Study and fabrication of bioinspired Octopus arm mockups tested on a multipurpose platform. In: IEEE Ras & Embs International Conference on Biomedical Robotics & Biomechatronics 2010, pp. 461–466. IEEE, Tokyo, (2010). https://doi.org/10.1109/BIOROB.2010.5625959
7. Guglielmino, E., Tsagarakis, N., Caldwell, D.G.: An octopus anatomy-inspired robotic arm. In: International Conference on Intelligent Robots & Systems 2010, pp. 3091–3096. IEEE, Taipei (2010). https://doi.org/10.1109/IROS.2010.5650361
8. Walker, I.D., Kier, W.M., Rahn, C.D., et al.: Continuum robot arms inspired by cephalopods. In: Proceedings of SPIE-The International Society for Optical Engineering 2005, vol. 5804, pp. 303–314. SPIE, USA (2005)
9. Jones, B.A., Walker, I.D.: Three-dimensional modeling and display of continuum robots. In: International Conference on Intelligent Robots and Systems 2006, pp. 5872–5877. IEEE, Beijing (2006). https://doi.org/10.1109/IROS.2006.282464.
10. Giri, N., Walker, I.: Continuum robots and underactuated grasping. Mech. Sci. **2**(1), 51–58 (2011)
11. Hao Y, Gong Z, Xie Z, et al.: Universal soft pneumatic robotic gripper with variable effective length. In: Proceedings of the 35th Chinese Control Conference 2016, pp. 6109–6114. IEEE, Chengdu (2016). https://doi.org/10.1109/ChiCC.2016.7554316

12. Wang, Z., Polygerinos, P., Overvelde, J.T.B., et al.: Interaction forces of soft fiber reinforced bending actuators. IEEE/ASME Trans. Mechatron. **22**(2), 717–727 (2017)
13. Jiang, P., Yang, Y.D., Chen, M.Z.Q., et al.: A variable stiffness gripper based on differential drive particle jamming. Bioinspiration Biomimetics **14**(3), 036009 (2019)
14. Jiang, A., Ranzani, T., Gerboni, G., et al.: Robotic granular jamming: does the membrane matter? Soft Rob. **1**(3), 192–201 (2014)
15. Bamotra, A., Walia, P., Prituja, A.V., et al.: Layer-jamming suction grippers with variable stiffness. J. Mech. Robot. **11**(3), 035003 (2019)
16. Hassanin, A.F., Samis, N.M., Theo, T., et al.: The design and mathematical model of a novel variable stiffness extensor-contractor pneumatic artificial muscle. Soft Rob. **5**(5), 576–591 (2018)
17. Yoshida, S., Morimoto, Y., Zheng, L.Y., et al.: Multipoint bending and shape retention of a pneumatic bending actuator by a variable stiffness endoskeleton. Soft Rob. **5**(6), 718–725 (2018)
18. Zhang, Y.F., Zhang, N.B., Hingorani, H., et al.: Fast-response, stiffness-tunable soft actuator by hybrid multimaterial 3D printing. Adv. Funct. Mater **29**(15), 1806698 (2019)
19. Xie, Z.X., Domel, A.G., An, N., et al.: Octopus arm-inspired tapered soft actuators with suckers for improved grasping. Soft Rob. **7**(5), 639–648 (2020)
20. Laschi, C., Cianchetti, M., Mazzolai, B., et al.: Soft robot arm inspired by the octopus. Adv. Robot. **26**(7), 709–727 (2012)
21. Trivedi, D., Rahn, C.D., Kier, W.M., et al.: Soft robotics: biological inspiration, state of the art, and future research. Appl. Bionics Biomech. **5**(3), 99–117 (2008)

Design of an Antagonistic Variable Stiffness Finger for Interactions and Its Analysis

Handong Hu, Yiwei Liu[(✉)], Zongwu Xie, Hong Liu, and Jianfeng Yao

State Key Laboratory of Robotics and System, Harbin Institute of Technology, West Dazhi Street, Harbin 150001, China
lyw@hit.edu.cn

Abstract. The principle of mechanical passive compliance is widely used in interactive robots to ensure the safety of robot interaction. Rigid dexterous hands are inclined to be damaged by physical collisions in unpredictable situations such as unstructured environments or operational errors. As robots are required to manipulate in unpredictable unstructured environments, it is urgent to develop a robust dexterous hand which can guarantee their own safety in the process of interaction. According to the passive compliance principle of mechanical system, a design of flexible joint finger with variable stiffness is proposed in this paper. The main goal is to achieve the robustness of the multi-fingered hands against physical impacts. The maximum fingertip force of the finger reaches 30N. Hammer knocking test proves that it has good resistance to physical impact.

Keywords: Dexterous hand · Finger design · Variable stiffness actuation · Antagonistic

1 Introduction

With the increasing demand of robot interaction tasks, robots with rigid grippers cannot satisfy the flexible and varied demands of unstructured environment, multi-functional requirements and other challenges [1]. As a consequence, multi fingered robot hand became an efficient solution for precise manipulation or grasp, which attracts much attention from NASA [2], DLR [3], Stanford University [4], University of Tokyo [5], HIT [6], and other institutions. In addition, in recent years, Shadow hand [7], Schunk hand [8] and other commercialized dexterous hands are manufactured with flexible functional characters and show illustrious performance. However, multi fingered hands are fragile to physical collision when they are exposed to an unstructured environment, and the energy generated by impact and vibration will damage the hardware systems. Therefore, passive compliance principle is proposed and widely used to solve the issues of robot interaction security [9]. DLR proposes a VSA (variable stiffness actuator) based on tendon mechanism, which is applied to actuate the fingers of the Awiwi hand [10]. The finger is intact in the slightest way after being physically impacted by a hammer. However, the mechanical system of the hand is too complex, which makes manufacturing and maintenance difficult and costly Ishikawa team proposed a magnet linkage hand, in

© Springer Nature Switzerland AG 2021
X.-J. Liu et al. (Eds.): ICIRA 2021, LNAI 13013, pp. 140–148, 2021.
https://doi.org/10.1007/978-3-030-89095-7_14

which the traditional stiff couplers are replaced by the magnetic couplers in joint transmission chains [11]. When the finger is impacted physically, the coupling of magnetic field of the magnet linkage ruptured fleetingly without any structural damage. Due to the limited load of the magnetic coupling, the dexterous hand can only grasp small weight objects. Based on the principle of passive compliance of mechanical system and considering the complexity and performance of mechanical system (fingertip force, weight, accuracy and cost, etc.), this paper proposes a variable stiffness joint finger. The main goal is to achieve robustness of the dexterous hand against physical impacts. In Sect. 2, the implementation of the antagonism variable stiffness actuation principle in the finger will be introduced. Section 3 will carry out kinematic and dynamic modeling respectively. Section 4 will establish the finger position controller according to the dynamic model. Finally, the finger position control experiment and impact resistance test will be carried out.

2   Finger Mechanical Design

Dexterous hands are not only able to perform anthropopathic grasping and manipulation, but also provide high robustness and dynamic response during the interaction. The anti-impact ability of the finger is crucial to improve the robustness of the entire hand. Therefore, in this section, a novel compact and flexible finger based on the principle of variable stiffness is presented.

2.1   Antagonistic Variable Stiffness Finger Mechanism

VSA is a redundant actuator which uses two actuators to drive only one DOF joint. Since the integration of a large number of actuators in the dexterous hand will increase its weight, volume and system complexity which is inappropriate. Furthermore, the primary motivation for the development of variable stiffness actuators is to protect finger hardware from damage when subjected to unexpected impacts. Therefore, a compromise method is adopted, that is, part of the joint freedom needs to be sacrificed when the stiffness is adjusted.

Based on the above considerations, an antagonistic variable stiffness finger mechanism is developed, which realizes not only the mechanical compliance of the finger but also achieves its stiff variation. The finger joint stiffness can be adjusted through the antagonism between two CAUs (compliant actuator unit), and its mechanism can be switched to series elastic actuated finger mechanism. In order to facilitate integration and analysis, the finger mechanism is principally divided into three modules: two CAUs and finger joint differential mechanism. Both two identical CAUs mainly composed of harmonic gear, circular spline pivot, two linear springs and slider guides. harmonic gear Choosing harmonic gears is on account of achieving very high transmission ratio in very small mass and volume. The circular spline is mounted movably on the base with revolute ability. When the flexspline is subjected to an external load, the circular spline is going to rotate relative to the base under the drive of the load, as shown in Fig. 7(a); The pivot of the wheel rotation arm will move linearly relative to the CS pivot, which results in a variation in the effective arm of force supporting the CS, as shown in Fig. 7(b). This mechanism achieves the non-linear stiffness of the CAU. The finger joint differential mechanism is composed of input bevel gear 1, input bevel gear 2, output bevel gear and near knuckle. The driving forces of the two CAUs are respectively transmitted to the two input bevel gears by the timing belt. The input bevel gear 1 and the input bevel gear 2 are used as two sun gears, the output bevel gear is a planet gear, and the proximal phalanx is regard as a planet pivot, and the four constitute a differential mechanism. The movement of the output bevel gear is transmitted to the distal phalanx through another pair of bevel gears (Fig. 1).

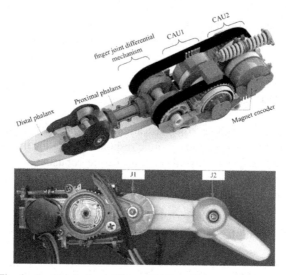

Fig. 1. Sectional view of finger CAD model and its prototype.

2.2 Compliant Actuation Unit

The CAU is mainly composed of brushless motor, harmonic gear and nonlinear elastic mechanism, as shown in Fig. 2(a). Each CAU is equipped with two absolute position magnetic encoders with 14-bit accuracy to measure the angular position of the motor rotor and the angular position of the output shaft respectively. The nonlinear elastic mechanism primely plays two roles in the CAU: storing kinetic energy as potential energy; as a flexible connection between the actuator and the base which directly transmits the external load. The stiffness of a nonlinear elastic mechanism is variable, which is related to the deformation of the elastic element. The stiffness can be changed by changing the preload of the elastic element. However, the stiffness of a linear elastic mechanism is constant, which is immutable. The stiffness variation characteristics of nonlinear elastic mechanism are determined by its structure and the characteristics of its elastic elements, which is shown in Fig. 2(b).

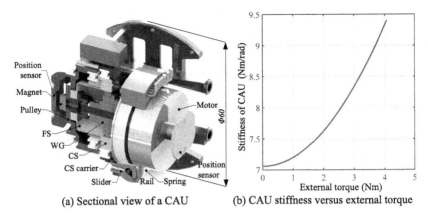

(a) Sectional view of a CAU   (b) CAU stiffness versus external torque

Fig. 2. Compliant actuation unit (CAU).

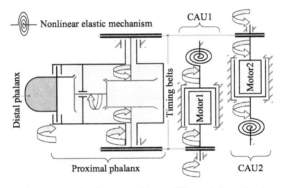

Fig. 3. Schematic diagram of joint differential mechanism.

2.3   Joint Differential Mechanism

In order to realize antagonistic variable stiffness function, two CAUs need to form antagonistic configuration. In Fig. 3, a gear differential mechanism is presented, which not only realizes the differential of finger joint, but also couples the torque of two CAUs to achieve antagonistic confrontation under certain conditions. When the finger joint moves in normal mode, the two CAUs perform in the identical way of SEA. The springs in CAU make each finger joint possess mechanical flexibility. When either of the two finger joints is blocked, the driving torques of the two CAUs will squeeze each other and the preloads of two CAU's nonlinear elastic mechanisms will be varied, ultimately, resulting in a change in stiffness of the two finger joints. In fact, the implementation of the differential mechanism not only realizes the contraction between CAUs, but also improves the maximum fingertip force compared with the series joint mechanism.

3 Kinematics and Dynamics Modeling

3.1 Finger Kinematics

Finger kinematics describes the relationship between the motions in operating space and motions in actuation space, mainly including finger link kinematics and joint kinematics. Finger linkage kinematics illustrates the motion mapping between Cartesian space and joint space. Joint kinematics illustrates the kinematic mapping between joint space and actuator space.

The Denavit-Hartenberg model of the finger is presented in Fig. 4(a) and the fingertip workspace is shown in Fig. 4(b).

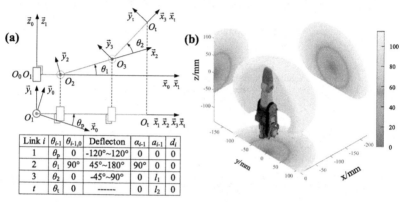

Link i	θ_{i-1}	$\theta_{i-1,0}$	Deflection	α_{i-1}	a_{i-1}	d_i
1	θ_p	0	-120°~120°	0	0	0
2	θ_1	90°	45°~180°	90°	0	0
3	θ_2	0	-45°~90°	0	l_1	0
t	θ_t	0	------	0	l_2	0

Fig. 4. Kinematics model and workspace. (a) Finger Denavit-Hartenberg model. (b) Fingertip workspace.

The joint differential mechanism couples the motion of two output shafts of CAU to synthesize the motion of two finger joints. The homogeneous transformation matrix from the actuation space to the fingertip space can be obtained as follows:

$$
{}^{CAU}_{t}T = \begin{bmatrix} c\theta_p c\psi & -c\theta_p s\psi & s\theta_p & pc\theta_p + l_2 c\theta_p c\gamma + l_1 c\theta_p c\beta \\ s\theta_p s\psi & -s\theta_p s\psi & -c\theta_p & ps\theta_p + l_2 s\theta_p c\gamma + l_1 s\theta_p c\beta \\ s\psi & c\psi & 0 & l_2 s\gamma + l_1 s\beta \\ 0 & 0 & 0 & 1 \end{bmatrix} \tag{1}
$$

For the sake of brevity, the conventions are $s_\zeta = \sin(\zeta)$ and $c_\zeta = \cos(\zeta)$, in which $\zeta = \psi$, γ or β. In Eq. (1), i_a and i_b are the transmission ratios of synchronous belt and differential gear respectively, q_1 and q_2 re the angular positions of CAU1 output shaft and CAU2 output shaft respectively, $\psi = 0.5 i_a^{-1} i_b^{-1}[(i_a + 1)q_1 + (1-i_b)q_2] + \theta_t$, $\gamma = \psi - \theta_t$, and $\beta = 0.5 i_a^{-1}(q_1 - q_2)$.

3.2 Dynamics Modeling

Using Newton-Euler method, the closed form of dynamic equation of finger link is obtained, and its state space equation is as follows:

$$\begin{bmatrix} \tau_1 \\ \tau_2 \end{bmatrix} = \mathbf{M}_L(\Theta)\ddot{\Theta} + \mathbf{V}_L(\Theta, \dot{\Theta}) + \mathbf{G}(\Theta) + \begin{bmatrix} \tau_{\text{ext1}} \\ \tau_{\text{ext2}} \end{bmatrix} = \begin{bmatrix} i_a & -i_a \\ i_a i_b & i_a i_b \end{bmatrix} \cdot \begin{bmatrix} \tau_{\text{CAU1}} \\ \tau_{\text{CAU2}} \end{bmatrix} \tag{2}$$

In Eq. (2), $\mathbf{M}_L(\Theta)$ is the mass matrix of finger links, $\mathbf{V}_L(\Theta, \dot{\Theta})$ is the vector of centrifugal forces and Coriolis forces and $\mathbf{G}(\Theta)$ is the gravity vector. τ_{CAU1} and τ_{CAU2} are the output torques of CAU1 and CAU2 respectively.

Although the flexibility of the flexspline in harmonic gear and the flexibility of the timing belt have a certain level of flexibility, they are negligible compared with the flexibility of the non-linear elastic mechanism in CAU.

For the i-th ($I = 1,2$) CAU, since the non-linear elastic mechanism acts as a support, the torque of the CS and the output torque of CAU are equivalent to the force-reaction relationship, then the output torque of i-th CAU is

$$\tau_{\text{CAU}i}(q_i, \theta_{Mi}) = 2K_s R^2 \tan(\theta_{Mi} - q_i) \tag{3}$$

In Eq. (2), θ_{Mi} is the moderative motor angular position, $\theta_{Mi} = \theta_{mi}/N$, N is the deceleration ratio of the harmonic gear, $N = -100$, θ_{mi} is the motor angular position and K_s is the stiffness coefficient of the linear springs.

According to Eq. (2) and Eq. (3), the motor side dynamic equation is obtained as

$$\begin{bmatrix} \tau_{M1} \\ \tau_{M2} \end{bmatrix} = \begin{bmatrix} J_{M1}\ddot{\theta}_{M1} + \mu_1 \text{sgn}(\dot{\theta}_{M1}) + \nu_1\dot{\theta}_{M1} - \tau_{\text{CAU1}} \\ J_{M2}\ddot{\theta}_{M2} + \mu_2 \text{sgn}(\dot{\theta}_{M2}) + \nu_2\dot{\theta}_{M2} - \tau_{\text{CAU2}} \end{bmatrix} \tag{4}$$

where τ_{M1} and τ_{M2} are the torques of the two motors respectively, μ_1 and μ_2 are the Coulomb friction coefficients respectively, ν_1 and ν_2 are the sliding friction coefficients respectively, J_{M1} and J_{M2} are the rotational inertias of the two motors respectively.

4 Motion Control and Simulations

A PD controller with good stability and rapidity is adopted in the finger motion control system. The control law of the controller is:

$$\begin{bmatrix} u_1 \\ u_2 \end{bmatrix} = \begin{bmatrix} K_{p1} & 0 \\ 0 & K_{p2} \end{bmatrix} \left(\mathbf{T}_K^{-1} \begin{bmatrix} \theta_{1,\text{des}} \\ \theta_{2,\text{des}} \end{bmatrix} - \begin{bmatrix} q_1 \\ q_2 \end{bmatrix} \right) + \begin{bmatrix} K_{d1} & 0 \\ 0 & K_{d2} \end{bmatrix} \left(\mathbf{T}_K^{-1} \begin{bmatrix} \dot{\theta}_{1,\text{des}} \\ \dot{\theta}_{2,\text{des}} \end{bmatrix} - \begin{bmatrix} \dot{q}_1 \\ \dot{q}_2 \end{bmatrix} \right)$$
$$\mathbf{T}_K = \begin{bmatrix} (2i_a)^{-1} & -(2i_a)^{-1} \\ (2i_a i_b)^{-1} & (2i_a i_b)^{-1} \end{bmatrix} \tag{5}$$

In Eq. (5), $\theta_{1,\text{des}}$ and $\theta_{2,\text{des}}$ are the desired angular positions of the finger joints respectively, $\dot{\theta}_{1,\text{des}}$ and $\dot{\theta}_{2,\text{des}}$ are the desired angular velocity of the finger joints respectively. K_{p1} and K_{d1} are the proportional gain and differential gain of motor 1 respectively, K_{p2} and K_{d2} are the proportional gain and differential gain of motor 2 respectively, and $\mathbf{T}_K$ is the forward joint differential kinematics transform matrix.

For the finger joint position controller, a PD controller with $K_{P1} = K_{P2} = -2.5$ and $K_{D1} = K_{D2} = -0.1$ is adopted, as shown in Fig. 6. In the finger joint space, a quintic polynomial programming algorithm is used to plan the motion of two finger joints from $0°$ to $30°$. To observe the performance of the controller under the condition of no load and load. The starting torque of finger motor is 263 mNm, and the position of output shaft and motor of each CAU is measured and fed back by magnetic encoder (Fig. 5).

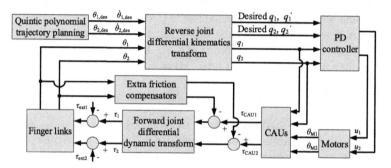

Fig. 5. Block diagram of finger position control system.

(1) No-load test: in Fig. 6, the positions of J1 and J2 tend to be stable at 8s, the maximum position hysteresis of J1 reaches 7%, and the maximum position hysteresis of J2 reaches 6.3%;

(2) Load test: applying step load of 0.4Nm and 0.2Nm to J1 and J2 respectively at 2s, which causes sudden change of system position and torque, but finally stabilizes at 7s, as shown in Fig. 6 and Fig. 7. During this process, the maximum position hysteresis of J1 reaches 11.3% and the maximum position hysteresis of J2 reaches 11.0%.

By comparing the two tests, it can be seen that the position overshoot of the loaded system is less than that of the unloaded system. However, the position hysteresis of the loaded system is larger than that of the unloaded system. In fact, as the load increases, the amount of hysteresis in the joint position increases, which is caused by the flexibility of the system. In addition, the loaded system tends to stabilize earlier than the no-load system.

The maximum fingertip force reaches to 30N. In finger strength experiments, the finger can easily lift a weight of 3 kg hanging at the fingertip. Next, a 2.5 kg hammer be used to quickly hit the fingertip without any damage to the finger, as shown in Fig. 8.

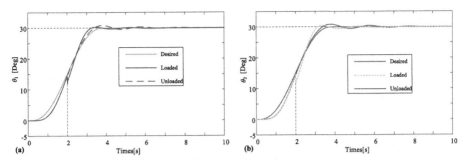

Fig. 6. Control effect under the PD controller with $K_{P1} = K_{P2} = -2.5$ and $K_{D1} = K_{D2} = -0.1$. (a) Control performances of Joint 1 under loading and unloading. (b) Control performances of Joint 2 under loading and unloading.

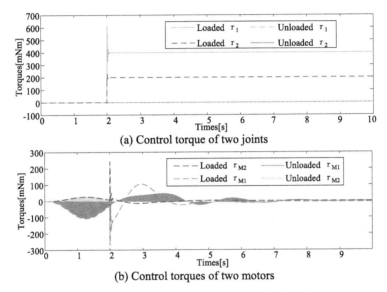

(a) Control torque of two joints

(b) Control torques of two motors

Fig. 7. Forces of the system before and after loading.

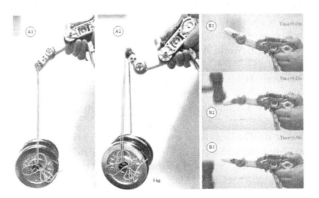

Fig. 8. Loading experiments and collision tests.

5 Conclusions

Based on the principle of passive compliance of mechanical system and the characteristics of dexterous finger, an antagonistic variable stiffness finger mechanism is presented in this paper and its prototype has been developed. The main goal is to achieve robustness of dexterous hands against physical impacts. In addition, the finger has the following characteristics: adjust the mechanical stiffness according to different task requirements; and enhance the dynamic performance of finger movement by storing energy. In the course of establishing the kinematics and dynamic model of the finger, it is found that the finger drive is highly coupled. Because of the flexibility of the finger, a PD controller is used to control the position of the finger joint. The simulation results show that the controller has certain stability and rapidity.

Acknowledgments. This work is supported by the National Key R&D Program of China(Grant No. 2017YFB1300400)and the Major Research plan of the National Natural Science Foundation of China (Grant No. 91848202).

References

1. Rebollo, D.R.R., Ponce, P., Molina, A.: From 3 fingers to 5 fingers dexterous hands. Adv. Robot. **31**, 1051–1070 (2017)
2. Bridgwater, L.B., et al.: The robonaut 2 hand - designed to do work with tools. In: 2012 IEEE International Conference on Robotics and Automation, Saint Paul, MN, USA, pp. 3425–3430. IEEE (2012)
3. Hirzinger, G.: Advances in robotics: the DLR experience. Int. J. Robot. Res. **18**(11), 1064–1087 (1999)
4. Hemami, H.: Robot hands and the mechanics of manipulation (T. Mason and J.K. Salisbury, Jr. (Cambridge, MA: M.I.T., 1985) [Book Reviews]. IEEE Trans. Automat. Contr. **31**(9), 879–880 (1986)
5. Kawasaki, H.: Mechanism design of anthropomorphic robot hand: gifu hand I. J. Robot. Mechatron. **11**(4), 269–273 (1999)
6. Liu, H., Meusel, P., Seitz, N., Willberg, B., Hirzinger, G., Jin, M.H., et al.: The modular multisensory dlr-hit-hand. Mech. Mach. Theory **42**(5), 612–625 (2007)
7. Wolf, S., Hirzinger, G.: A new variable stiffness design: matching requirements of the next robot generation. In: 2008 IEEE International Conference on Robotics and Automation, Pasadena, CA, USA, pp. 1741–1746. IEEE (2008)
8. Shadow Robot Company: Developments in dexterous hands for advanced applications. In: Proceedings of the IEEE World Automation Congress, Seville, Spain, pp. 123–128. IEEE (2004)
9. Ruehl, S.W., Parlitz, C., Heppner, G., Hermann, A., Roennau, A., Dillmann, R.: Experimental evaluation of the schunk 5-Finger gripping hand for grasping tasks. In: 2014 IEEE International Conference on Robotics and Biomimetics, Bali, Indonesia, pp. 2465–2470. IEEE (2014)
10. Grebenstein, M., et al.: The DLR hand arm system. In: 2011 IEEE International Conference on Robotics and Automation, Shanghai, China, pp. 3175–3182. IEEE (2011)
11. Koyama, K., Shimojo, M., Senoo, T., Ishikawa, M.: Development and application of low-friction, compact size actuator "MagLinkage". In: The Proceedings of JSME Annual Conference on Robotics and Mechatronics 2P1-H02 (2019)

Directivity Analysis of Ultrasonic Array in Directional Sound System

Zhao Peng, Zhili Long$^{(\boxtimes)}$, and Zhexuan Ma

Harbin Institute of Technology, ShenZhen, China
longzhili@hit.edu.cn

Abstract. Sound wave, as an important component in daily life, has the characteristic of 360° propagation, which is difficult to propagate in a fixed area, resulting in noise pollution and other problems. Directional sound system can deal with the problem. It modulates the low-frequency signal linearly to the ultrasonic signal, transmits the signal to the air through ultrasonic array, and demodulates itself in the air. Due to the narrow beam of the ultrasonic wave, directional propagation of the sound is realized. For this technology, directivity is an important parameter, which is related to the characteristics and scale of the ultrasonic array. The existing micro array research mostly uses simulation to explore its directivity law but lacks corresponding experiments. In this paper, the PZT transducer is used to build a directivity test platform for experimental exploration. The experimental results show that 8 × 8 array is an optimal choice for plane parallel arrangement, and the 3D concave array is proved to be applicable in directional sound system.

Keywords: Directional sound system · Piezoceramic transducer · Ultrasonic array · Directivity

1 Introduction

Directional sound system (DSS) [1] is an innovative technology to propagate sound in specific area. It depends on the narrow beam of ultrasonic signals and nonlinear self-demodulation in air. Compared with the traditional sound, it has the advantages of fantastic directivity and long propagation distance, which is widely used in security systems, digital entertainment, advertising, restaurants, military and other scenes [2]. DSS involves many key technologies, such as parametric array modeling [3], signal modulation [4–6], hardware and software circuit design, ultrasonic array design, impedance matching, filtering [7] and so on, among which directivity [8] decided by the array is crucial to the effect of DSS. Yoneyama [9] et al. used 547 piezoelectric ultrasonic transducers to form a planar hexagonal array in DSS. Then T. Kamakura [10] et al. increased the number of ultrasonic transducers to 1410, using 28 kHz dual piezoelectric chip transducer to improve the electroacoustic conversion efficiency. Dr. Pompei [11] proposed that the use of large transducer array can effectively suppress the grating lobe and enhance the directivity. Holosonics, founded by Pompei, developed a transducer technology based on moving film. This technology has high fidelity and wide bandwidth,

© Springer Nature Switzerland AG 2021
X.-J. Liu et al. (Eds.): ICIRA 2021, LNAI 13013, pp. 149–157, 2021.
https://doi.org/10.1007/978-3-030-89095-7_15

which is one of the indispensable technologies of audio spotlight. The ultrasonic array design is a significant factor. Many studies have been carried out to explore the influence of array size, arrangement as well as materials on the directivity of DSS. However, due to the limitation of research conditions and technology, most of DSS research is based on the traditional micro PZT ultrasonic array, the size and arrangement of the array are determined by the directivity formula, which lacks the actual experimental verification. In consequence, we use simulation and experiment to explore the directivity law of micro planar parallel array. At the same time, we design and manufacture the 3D concave array according to the phased array, and its directivity gets the preliminary validation in DSS. This provides practical data reference for the array design of DSS in micro scale, and proposes further exploration for the 3D array application in DSS.

2   Simulation

2.1   Relationship Between Directivity of the Ultrasonic Array and DSS

DDS is based on the theory of acoustic parametric array and includes main technologies such as signal modulation processing, array directivity, and circuit design. The parametric array in air provides the theoretical basis for DSS so that the highly directional audible sound can be reproduced through modulation and self-demodulation. Signal modulation processing provides an implementation method for modulating the audible signal to the ultrasonic signal. Circuit design is the physical realization carrier of the whole system, and its impedance design and module selection affect the performance of DSS. The audible signal modulated to ultrasonic frequency band is emitted into the air through the ultrasonic array. And due to nonlinear propagation effect, the modulated signal self-demodulates in the air and eventually reproduces the audible sound with high directivity. The characteristics of ultrasonic transducer, the scale and shape of the ultrasonic array will influence the directivity of the emitted sound waves.

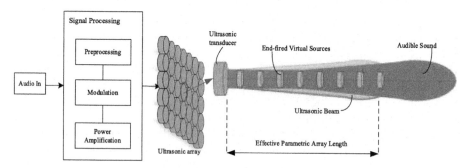

Fig. 1. Overall composition framework of DSS

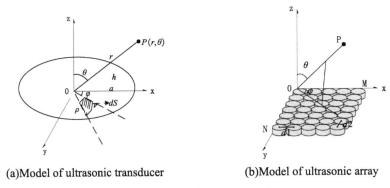

(a)Model of ultrasonic transducer   (b)Model of ultrasonic array

Fig. 2. Directivity model of ultrasonic transducer and array

2.2 Model of the Ultrasonic Transducer and Array

In DDS, the theoretical model of the transducer can be regarded as the circular piston radiator on the rigid baffle. The directivity function is:

$$D(\alpha) = \left| \frac{2J_1(ka \sin \alpha)}{ka \sin \alpha} \right| \tag{1}$$

Where J_1 is the first order Bessel function, k is the wave number, $k = 2\pi f/c$, c is the sound velocity in the medium.

The array model is constructed as shown in Fig. 1 (b). It is composed of M × N ultrasonic transducers. The distance between two transducers in x-axis is d_1, d_2 in y-axis. P is a casual point in the space, the angle between OP and z-axis is θ, the angle between the projection of OP in xoy plane and x-axis is φ, then the directivity function of the array can be expressed as (Fig. 2):

$$D(\varphi, \theta) = \frac{\sin\left(\frac{kMd1}{2} \cos \varphi \sin \theta\right) \sin\left(\frac{kNd2}{2} \sin \varphi \sin \theta\right)}{M \sin\left(\frac{kd1}{2} \cos \varphi \sin \theta\right) N \sin\left(\frac{kd2}{2} \sin \varphi \sin \theta\right)} \tag{2}$$

According to the formula (2), the directivity of the array with certain parameters is only related to the pitch angle φ and θ determined by the position of point P. The projections in xyz axis are calculated through the angle respectively and the three-dimensional directivity of the array is revealed in the 3D coordinate grid.

2.3 Directional Simulation

According to the formula (1), the directivity of the transducer is related to the frequency. The directivity function value of the low-frequency signal remains at about 1, indicating that the low-frequency signal does not have the characteristics of directivity. And according to the directivity function curves of the signals at 2 kHz, 20 kHz, 40 kHz, and 80 kHz as shown in Fig. 3, with the increase of frequency, the main lobe of the sound beam becomes sharper, the side lobes are suppressed, and the directivity improves. According to the formula (2) of ultrasonic array, the three-dimensional directivity diagram of square array with different sizes are shown in Fig. 4 (a)–(d). With the increase of the array size, the main lobe narrows, and the directional intensity improves. At the same time, the inhibition of grating lobe and side lobe is more obvious. The projections of the three-dimensional directivity in *xoz* plane of different array are shown in Fig. 4 (e)–(h). Though the number of the array is same, they have different directivity performance under different array arrangement.

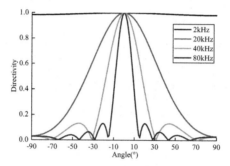

Fig. 3. Directivity function curves of ultrasonic transducer at different frequencies

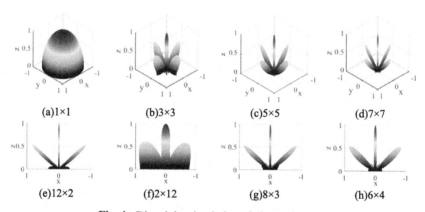

Fig. 4. Directivity simulation of ultrasonic array

3   Experiments

3.1   Directional Experimental Platform

In the actual application process, considering the inherent characteristics such as the resonance frequency of the PZT, the carrier frequency of the DSS is selected as 40 kHz. The final input signal of the ultrasonic array is the audible signal modulated to the

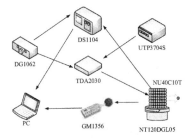
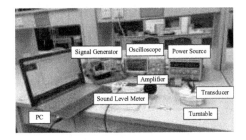

Fig. 5. Principle diagram and material diagram of directional experimental platform

ultrasonic wave. Therefore, a 40 kHz sine signal is utilized during the basic directivity test. The experimental platform shown in Fig. 5 is constructed to test the directivity of the transducer and array. DG1062 signal generator is used to generate the input signal. In order to drive the array conveniently, the standard sinusoidal signal is used as the actual output of DG1602. The signal generator is adjusted to generate signals with different frequencies, amplitudes and offsets, which are fed into TDA2030. The power amplifier is a single-ended input amplifier for low frequency to amplify the corresponding voltage and current to drive the ultrasonic transducer or array. UTP3704S DC power supply provides ± 3 V to ± 22 V working voltage for TDA2030. In an infinite plane space, a single transducer can be approximately regarded as a point sound source. Therefore, the directivity of the single transducer is explored based on the point sound source. The transducer or array is fixed over the NT120DGL05 bidirectional controllable speed control turntable, so that the transducer or array centroid is aligned to the center of the turntable, and 360° rotation is carried out under the driving of the turntable. GM1356 sound level meter probe has the same height as the center of the ultrasonic transducer or array. The waveform is monitored by the oscilloscope. The data collected by the sound level meter and the waveform of the oscilloscope is analyzed on PC. The key parameters in the experiment are in Table 1.

Table 1. Key parameters in directional experimental platform.

Parameter	Type or Value
Power amplifier supply voltage	21 V
Voltage and frequency of the Signal	810 mV, 40 kHz
Type of the transducer	NU40C10T
Horizontal distance between sound level meter and array center	20 cm

3.2 Design for the Three-Dimensional Array and Construction of DSS

The three-dimensional array, different from the existing two-dimensional plane array, is proposed and designed in solidworks. In order to obtain a better performance in sound pressure, the array is arranged in spherical form, and the physical object is made by 3D printing technology. The 3D concave array is shown in Fig. 6.

Fig. 6. Model and physical object of the 3D concave array

DSS is built by analog circuits, and the whole directivity test system is constructed as shown in Fig. 7.

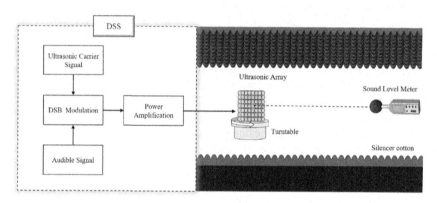

Fig. 7. Directivity test system of DDS

3.3 Experimental Data

Figure 8 shows the sound pressure level (SPL) curve of the single transducer within the range of 2π. With the increase of the frequency, the SPL will be significantly improved. The SPL of the transducer in the positive and negative half-cycles is not the same, which reflects the existence of sound field on the back of the transducer [12]. And the back sound field intensity is obviously weaker than that generated by the vibration positive spindle. Figure 9 shows the directivity curve in the range $[0, \pi]$. Compared with the directivity simulation in Sect. 2.3, although it still meets the characteristic that high frequency accompanies with intensive directivity, its high-frequency directivity is not prominent, and the transducer is not powerful to provide high-directional ultrasound. It needs to be expanded to the transducer array.

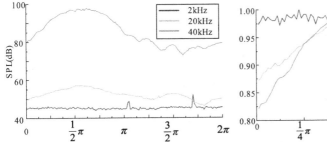

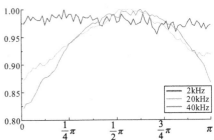

Fig. 8. SPL curves of single transducer

Fig. 9. Directional curve of single transducer

Figure 10 shows the SPL curves of square arrays with different sizes. It can be seen from the curves that the array arrangement can significantly improve the acoustic energy compared with the single transducer. SPL, energy, directivity is positively correlated with the array size. Along the test direction, the number of the transducers is the same as the peaks, and the distribution is basically symmetrical. Figure 11 is the SPL curves of the same rectangular array under different arrangements. For the same array, the sound pressure energy distribution is basically the same, but due to the different transducer arrangement along the test direction, the number and the form of sidelobes are not the same. 12×2 array obviously has more sidelobes than 2×12 array.

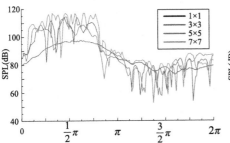

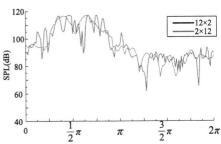

Fig. 10. SPL curves of different square array

Fig. 11. Different arrangement of the same array

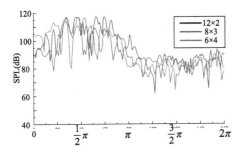

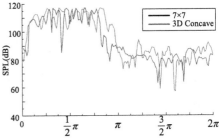

Fig. 12. SPL curves with the same number

Fig. 13. 3D and 2D array

Figure 12 is the SPL curves of rectangular array with the same number of transducers and different arrangements. There is little difference in the maximum SPL. In terms of the directivity, we can increase the number of the transducers along the test direction to suppress the sidelobes. Different from the strong directivity of the simulation results, the directivity range of the actual sound pressure is 0.4–1, but the directivity law of the array is consistent with the basic law of the conclusion of directional simulation. Figure 13 is the SPL curve between the three-dimensional array of 45 transducers and the two-dimensional array of 49 transducers. Although the number of transducers is relatively small for the three-dimensional array, the sound pressure performance of it is better and the directivity is pretty similar. It can be considered to apply the 3D concave array to DSS. The SPL curves based on DSS of three different shaped arrays are shown in Fig. 14. The sound pressure amplitude of the 8 × 8 array is slightly lower than that of the 7 × 7 array, but is smoother with fewer sidelobes. So, the audio effect of 8 × 8 array is relatively better. The 3D array also shows directional effects obviously.

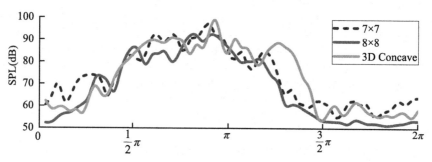

Fig. 14. SPL curves measured in DSS

4   Conclusion

In this paper, the directivity, one of the key technologies in DSS is studied. According to the basic law of the ultrasonic transducer and array obtained by simulation, the experimental platforms for exploring the directivity are designed and built. By making micro arrays of different sizes to experiment, the following conclusions are obtained:

(1) The SPL curve is drawn from the sound pressure data. The directivity is positively correlated with the sound pressure. Therefore, the SPL curve can be used to approximately replace the directivity curve to analyze the directivity.
(2) Directivity of the array is significantly better than that of the single transducer, and improved with the increase of array size.

(3) With the increasing number of transducers along the test direction, the number of side lobes increases, the sound pressure effect is not obvious, but requires more energy. At the same time, in order to obtain a more uniform sound field, we are more inclined to choose a geometrically symmetrical array arrangement.

In summary, 8×8 array is an optimal arrangement to compose the plane parallel array by the piezoelectric ceramic transducers. At the same time, we present an idea of applying 3D concave array to DSS and verify its feasibility. However, we have only initially verified that the 3D array can be applied in DSS. The critical factors of the 3D array such as sound field model, arrangement and radian will be further explored.

References

1. Alunno, M., Botero, A.Y.: Directional landscapes: using parametric loudspeakers for sound reproduction in art. J. New Music Res. **46**(2), 201–211 (2017)
2. Gan, W.-S.: Audio projection: directional sound and its application in immersive communication. IEEE Signal Process. Mag. **28**(1), 43–57 (2011)
3. Gan, W.S., Yang, J., Kamakura, T.: A review of parametric acoustic array in air. Appl. Acoust. **73**(12), 1211–1219 (2012)
4. Nakayama, M., Nishiura, T.: Synchronized amplitude-and-frequency modulation for a parametric loudspeaker. In: 2017 Asia-Pacific Signal and Information Processing Association Annual Summit and Conference (APSIPA ASC 2017), Kuala Lumpur, Malaysia, pp. 130–135 (2017)
5. Ji, P.F., Yang, J.: An experimental investigation about parameters' effects on spurious sound in parametric loudspeaker. Appl. Acoust. **148**, 67–74 (2019)
6. Farias, F., Abdulla, W.: A method for selecting a proper modulation technique for the parametric acoustic array. J. Phys. Conf. Ser. **1075**, 012035 (2018)
7. Rakov, D.S., Rakov, A.S., Kudryavtsev, A.N., et al.: A study of directional patterns of ultrasonic parametric array. Arch. Acoust. **44**(2), 301–307 (2019)
8. Zhang, F.D., Xu, L.M., Chen, M.: The design of beam-forming for broadband beam-steerable parametric array. In: IEEE International Conference on Mechatronics and Automation (ICMA), Chengdu, China, pp. 1580–1585 (2012)
9. Yoneyama, M., Fujimoto, J., Kawamo, Y., et al.: The audio spotlight: an application of nonlinear interaction of sound waves to a new type of loudspeaker design. J. Acoust. Soc. Am. **73**(5), 1532–1536 (1983)
10. Aoki, K., Kamakura, T., Kumamoto, Y.: Parametric loudspeaker-characteristics of acoustic field and suitable modulation of carrier ultrasound. Electron. Commun. Jpn. Pt. III Fundam. Electron. Sci. **74**(9), 76–82 (1991)
11. Pompei, F.J., Wooh, S.C.: Phased array element shapes for suppressing grating lobes. J. Acoust. Soc. Am. **111**(5), 2040–2048 (2002)
12. Zhong, J.X., Wang, S.P., Kirby, R., et al.: Reflection of audio sounds generated by a parametric array loudspeaker. J. Acoust. Soc. Am. **148**(4), 2327–2336 (2020)

Design of Space Manipulator Trajectory Optimization Algorithm Based on Optimal Capture

Liang Changchun[✉], Xin Pengfei, Pan Dong, and Wang Rui

Beijing Key Laboratory of Intelligent Space Robotic System Technology and Applications, Beijing Institute of Spacecraft System Engineering, Beijing 100094, China

Abstract. With the diversification and complexity of space manipulator on-orbit tasks, it is an inevitable trend to realize on-orbit capture and assembly. In this paper, the relevant technologies involved in the acquisition process of the space station manipulator to the hovering target are studied. The corresponding acquisition control strategy and algorithm are designed, and the development of the acquisition control system of the hovering vehicle of the space manipulator is carried out, and the simulation verification is carried out. The results show that the trajectory planning algorithm based on optimal capture is effective to reduce the end pose disturbance and base pose disturbance. It is of great significance to improve the ability of mission completion.

Keywords: Space manipulator · Optical capture · Trajectory optimization

1 Overview

With the continuous expansion of space missions, on-orbit supply, component assembly, fault maintenance and other on orbit service technologies are gradually concerned by all countries. The United States, Japan, Canada and other space powers, as well as the European Space Agency and other international space agencies have carried out relevant research projects, trying to get rid of the constraints of limited carrying capacity on the construction of large space facilities by developing the above technologies, and to enhance the spacecraft's on orbit self-supporting ability and extend the spacecraft's on orbit life. China will launch the core module of the manned space station around 2021 and complete the construction of the space station around 2023. In the construction process of space station, a large number of spacecraft docking and transposition and other complex tasks are involved. Because the spacecraft has a large mass and the space environment is extremely harsh, it is difficult to complete the extravehicular operation by astronauts alone. We must rely on the various equipment and devices carried by the spacecraft, realize the docking and assembly of the spacecraft autonomously or semi autonomously through on orbit assembly and other technologies, so as to realize the construction and maintenance of the space station.

Based on this background, this paper studies the relevant technologies involved in the acquisition process of the space manipulator to the hovering target, and designs the corresponding acquisition control strategy and algorithm.

© Springer Nature Switzerland AG 2021
X.-J. Liu et al. (Eds.): ICIRA 2021, LNAI 13013, pp. 158–169, 2021.
https://doi.org/10.1007/978-3-030-89095-7_16

2   Capture Process Analysis

In the tracking phase of target acquisition, the end effector of the manipulator can app-roach the hovering target with different trajectories, and the target configuration of the manipulator has a variety of choices. Therefore, by selecting the appropriate trajectory of the manipulator, the impact of contact collision on the space station and hovering target can be reduced, and the acquisition process can be optimized(Fig. 1).

The capture diagram of hovering vehicle with space manipulator is shown in Fig. 2. Among them, Σ_{Cb} represents the geometric coordinate system of the core module body and defines it as the inertial system of the system; Σ_{Cr} is the root coordinate system of the space manipulator; Σ_{Ce} represents the coordinate system of the end tool of the space manipulator; Σ_{Cd} is the docking coordinate system of the core module; Σ_{Tb} is the geometric coordinate system of the aircraft body; Σ_{Tg} is the target adapter coordinate system of the visiting aircraft; Σ_{Td} is the docking coordinate system of the visiting aircraft.

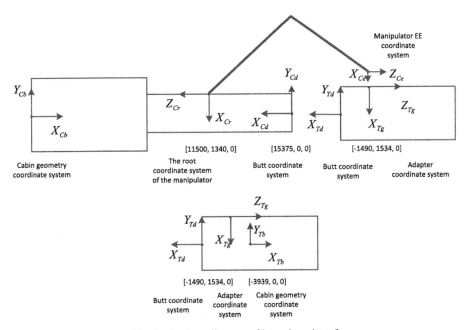

Fig. 1. Capture diagram of hovering aircraft

Combined with the concept of capture box, the constraint conditions are shown in the figure below.

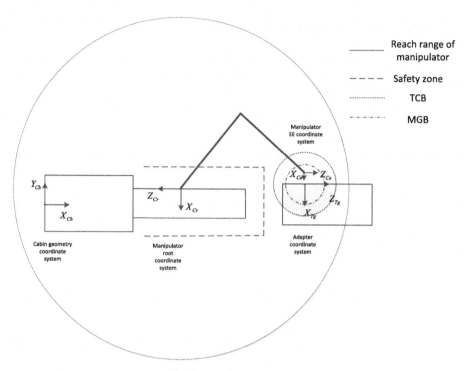

Fig. 2. Capture constraints

3 Trajectory Planning Algorithm Design of Manipulator Based on Optimal Capture

This chapter aims at the optimal capture, focusing on the first contact collision between the end effector of the manipulator and the visiting aircraft, and planning the trajectory of the space manipulator before capture. Firstly, the influence factors of flexible wire rope capturing contact force are analyzed from two levels of contact velocity and contact position. Then, the optimization objective function is established to minimize the disturbance of the end pose of the space manipulator and the disturbance of the base pose, and the configuration of the manipulator before capturing is optimized. Finally, combined with the path planning algorithm, the motion planning of the manipulator from the initial configuration to the optimal capture configuration is realized.

The optimization strategy of space manipulator before snare rope capture is mainly aimed at the first contact between space manipulator and target load. In the space microgravity environment, the first contact collision between the space manipulator and the target load faces two risks: if the contact collision force is too large, the target load and the space manipulator may be damaged; if the disturbance caused by the contact collision is too large, the system may be unstable and the target load may escape. In order to improve the reliability and safety of the snare type rope capture operation of space manipulator, the following two-step optimization strategy is proposed.

Step 1: adjust the attitude of the capture device at the end of the space manipulator so that the capture plane formed by three flexible wire ropes is perpendicular to the axis of the target load capture rod, so that the contact impact force between the target load and the flexible wire rope is located in the plane, which can greatly reduce the possibility of the target load escaping; then, rotate the capture device to adjust the connection between the target load and the flexible wire rope The contact position can reduce the peak value of force in the process of contact collision;

Step 2: keep the position and pose of the end capture unchanged, adjust the capture configuration of the space manipulator to reduce the disturbance caused by contact impact on the end or base of the space manipulator, which can reduce the possibility of target load escape caused by excessive disturbance.

3.1 Analysis of Factors Influencing the Capture Contact Force of Flexible Wire Rope

During the capture operation of space manipulator, due to the residual velocity and sensor error, the impact force between space manipulator and target load is inevitable. Compared with the traditional rigid claw capture device, the rigid flexible coupling capture device can greatly reduce the peak value of contact force, and greatly reduce the damage of space manipulator and target load caused by contact collision. However, in the future, the tasks of space manipulator applications will be more refined and complex. Therefore, any operation task needs to be more refined and comprehensive optimization. When the space manipulator captures the flexible wire rope, different contact speeds will produce different contact and collision forces (Fig. 3), and at the same speed, the contact between the target load and different nodes of the flexible wire rope will also produce different contact and collision forces (Fig. 4).

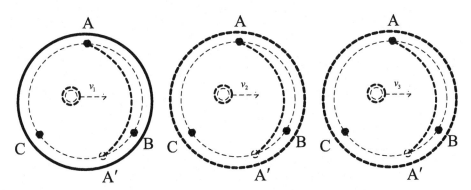

Fig. 3. The catching rod contacts with the flexible wire rope at different speeds

The Catching Rod Contacts With the Flexible Wire Rope at Different Speeds.

In order to ensure the safety and reliability of space rope capture, a very low capture speed is usually used to capture the target. The expression of the contact force between

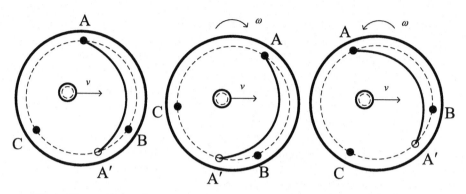

Fig. 4. The catching rod contacts with the flexible wire rope at different contact points

the capture rod and the flexible wire rope can be approximated by polynomial as follows:

$$F_c = f(\delta) + g(d_{se}) + h(\delta, d_{se}) \tag{1}$$

Since only the initial collision time is studied to ensure that the target load will not be "bounced" or damaged after the initial contact, d_{se} is a constant in the above formula. In addition, in order to ensure the large tolerance of the capture area of the capture ring, it is not realistic to arbitrarily adjust d_{se}. Therefore, the above formula can be simplified as a polynomial only concerning the compression δ, as follows:

$$F_c = \tilde{f}(\delta) \tag{2}$$

From the above formula, it can be concluded that:

$$0 = \tilde{f}(\delta) + m_t \ddot{\delta} \rightarrow \frac{d\dot{\delta}}{d\delta} = \frac{\ddot{\delta}}{\dot{\delta}} = \frac{-\tilde{f}(\delta)}{m_t \dot{\delta}} \rightarrow m_t \dot{\delta} d\dot{\delta} = -\tilde{f}(\delta) d\delta \tag{3}$$

By integrating the two sides of the above formula from the initial contact to the maximum compression, we can get the following results:

$$\int_{\dot{\delta}^{(-)}}^{0} m_t \dot{\delta} d\dot{\delta} = -\int_{0}^{\delta_{max}} \tilde{f}(\delta) d\delta \rightarrow \hat{f}(\delta_{max}) = \frac{m_t}{2}\left(\dot{\delta}^{(-)}\right)^2 + \hat{f}(0) \tag{4}$$

Among them, $\dot{\delta}^{(-)}$ is the initial relative velocity of the contact point along the collision direction, δ_{max} is the maximum compression, $\hat{f}(\delta_{max})$ is the integral function of polynomial function $\tilde{f}(\delta)$. The stiffness of virtual spring is not a constant, it increases with the increase of embedded depth. There are two meanings in this sentence, 1) $f(\delta) \in [0, +\infty)$; 2) $f(\delta)$ increases with the increase of δ, which is a monotone increasing function. Based on the above conclusions, the integral function $\tilde{f}(\delta)$ also increases with the increase of δ in the range of $\delta \in [0, +\infty)$. The corresponding formula of increase and decrease can be obtained as follows:

$$\dot{\delta}^{(-)} \uparrow \rightarrow \hat{f}(\delta_{max}) \uparrow \rightarrow \delta_{max} \uparrow \rightarrow \tilde{f}(\delta_{max}) \uparrow \tag{5}$$

That is to say, the increase of relative velocity at the initial time will make the peak value of impact contact force larger. The impact impulse is as follows:

$$P = \int_{t^{(-)}}^{t^{(+)}} f(t)dt = m_t \Delta \dot{\delta} \approx \frac{m_t m_e}{m_t + m_e}(1 + \tilde{c}_r)\dot{\delta}^{(-)} \qquad (6)$$

Where, $\tilde{c}_r$ is the equivalent coefficient of restitution at the contact point between the capture rod and the flexible wire rope, and the impact pulse is directly proportional to the initial impact velocity, so the impact impulse will also increase with the increase of the relative velocity in the impact direction at the initial time. Therefore, from the perspective of safety and success rate of space manipulator in orbit capture, the relative speed of capture should be controlled in a low range.

The Catching Rod Contacts With the Flexible Wire Rope at Different Positions.
Under the condition of constant initial contact velocity, different contact forces will be produced when the capture rod collides with the flexible wire rope at different positions. The relationship between the collision force, compression and the distance between the end and the head can be simulated by high-order polynomial. Since the whole flexible wire rope is divided into 50 sections and 51 nodes are symmetrical with respect to node 26, the contact and collision characteristics of nodes 2–25 are the same as those of nodes 50–27, and only the contact and collision relations of nodes 2–26 are listed here. Assuming that the initial velocity is 0.05m/s, the distance between the starting point and the ending point at the initial time is $d_{se} = 0.91$m, The peak force of the capture rod after colliding with each node is shown in Fig. 5.

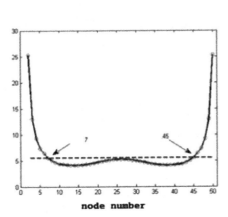

Fig. 5. Peak value of contact impact force at different nodes

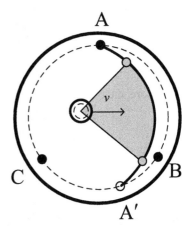

Fig. 6. Contact safety area between capture rod and flexible wire rope

The maximum force is 25.36N at node 2 and node 50, and the minimum force is 4.08N at node 14 and node 40. It can be seen from the figure that the contact collision between the capture rod and the flexible wire rope will produce a larger force at both ends of the flexible wire rope, and the collision force in the middle is not different and relatively small. Therefore, setting the contact collision from node 7 to node 45 is considered as a better choice, and the maximum force in this section is 5.53N. The capture "safe area" of the capture rod and the flexible wire rope is shown in Fig. 6.

3.2 Snare Type Rope Catcher

Establishment of Optimal Objective Function for SNARE Type Rope Capture.
In the last section, we design a safe capture area of SNARE capture to ensure that the contact impact force is small. Next, we study how to reduce the damage to the space manipulator by the contact impact force. Because the performance characteristics of different space manipulators are different, and the task requirements are different for different tasks, the following design objective function takes the minimum pose disturbance of the end of the space manipulator as the typical task.

The end pose maintenance of space manipulator is very important for the capture operation task. For the snare type rope capture, if the capture rod first contacts with the flexible wire rope, the disturbance at the end of the manipulator is large, it may cause the capture rod to deviate from the safe capture area, or even escape. During the capture operation of space manipulator, its terminal inertial characteristics can be expressed as an ellipsoid.

$$m_e = \frac{1}{u^T \hat{H}_v^{-1} u}, \; l_e = \frac{1}{z^T \hat{H}_\omega^{-1} z} \tag{7}$$

In the case of a certain impact force at the end, it can be seen from formula (8) that the greater the mass of the space manipulator in the collision direction, the smaller the linear velocity disturbance caused. Similarly, the greater the inertia in the rotation direction, the smaller the angular velocity disturbance caused.

$$P = m_e \delta v_e, \; M = I_e \delta \omega_e \tag{8}$$

Therefore, the objective function is set as follows:

$$g_e = \chi_1 g_{em} + \chi_2 g_{ei} \tag{9}$$

Where χ_1, χ_2 is the weight coefficient, $g_{em} = u^T \hat{H}_v^{-1} u$, $g_{ei} = z^T \hat{H}_\omega^{-1} z$. Because the mass and inertia characteristics of the end of the space manipulator are two completely independent variables, the maximum mass in the U direction is likely to lead to the minimum inertia in the Z direction in an optimal configuration, that is to say, it is likely that the optimization objectives are contrary, leading to the unsatisfactory optimization results. Therefore, in the process of optimization, we need to focus on the optimization according to the specific task, if the influence of the end position accuracy of the space manipulator is more important, $\chi_1 > \chi_2$ need to set, Even χ_2 can be set to 0 and vice versa.

Optimization of the Configuration of the Snare Type Rope Capture Manipulator.
By using the null space term of space manipulator to optimize the configuration, the

configuration can be adjusted by the self-motion of null space joint without affecting the pose accuracy of the end. Firstly, the relationship between the joint velocity and the end velocity of the space manipulator is obtained.

$$\dot{x}_e = J_f \dot{\theta} \tag{10}$$

$$\dot{\theta} = J_f^\dagger \dot{x}_e + (E - J_f^\dagger J_f) k \varepsilon \tag{11}$$

Among them, ε is any vector in the joint null space. In the joint null space, the additional task can be optimized without affecting the main task. Based on the defined objective function, gradient projection method is used to determine $\dot{\varepsilon}$ to increase or decrease the objective function. At the same time, it should be noted that there is joint limit in the practical application of space manipulator, so the constraint joint angle limit should be added in the optimization process.

The designed joint angle limit function is as follows:

$$h_j = \rho \sum_{i=1}^{n} \frac{(\theta_{i\,max} - \theta_{i\,min})^2}{(\theta_{i\,max} - \theta_i)(\theta_i - \theta_{i\,min})} \tag{12}$$

Among them, $\theta_{i\,max}$, $\theta_{i\,min}$ are the upper and lower limit of joint angle. When the joint angles are close to the middle of the joint limit range $\frac{\theta_{i\,max} + \theta_{i\,min}}{2}$, h_j get the minimum $4n\rho$, When the joint angle approaches its limit value, h will approach infinity. As shown in Fig. 7.

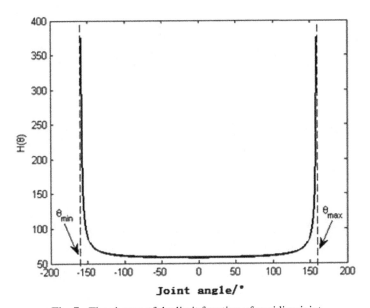

Fig. 7. The change of the limit function of avoiding joint

4 Simulation Verification

The initial pose of the end of the space manipulator is assumed to be [7m, 0m, 3m, −1.0rad, −0.5rad, −2.0rad]. The initial joint angle and base attitude Euler angle are [−1.69, −1.75, −2.60, 1.78, −0.46, −0.33, −1.93](rad) and [−6.57, 1.41, 3.80] × 10^{-4}(rad) respectively. At the initial time, the equivalent mass and inertia of the end of the space manipulator in the direction of contact force [0.93, 0.37, 0] and moment [0, 0, 1] are m_e= 58.82kg and I_e= 20.75kg · m^2 respectively.

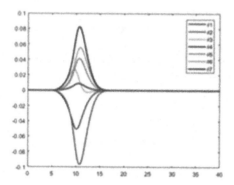

Fig. 8. Minimization of joint angular velocity variation by end perturbation

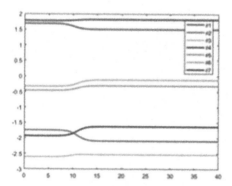

Fig. 9. Minimizing joint angle variation with end perturbation

Set the weight coefficient as χ_1=60, χ_2= 20, During the optimization process, the angular velocity of each joint of the manipulator changes as shown in Fig. 8. It can be seen from the figure that in the whole optimization process, each joint runs smoothly, and the optimization process ends in about 18 s. At this time, the optimal capture configuration of the space manipulator is reached. The changes of each joint angle are shown in Fig. 9, and the changes of base angular velocity and attitude are shown in Fig. 10 and Fig. 11 respectively.

Through the above optimization process, the optimal joint angle and Euler angle of   the   base   attitude   of   the   space

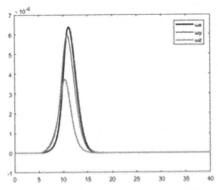 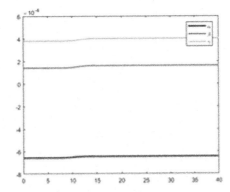

Fig. 10. Variation diagram of angular velocity of base for minimizing terminal disturbance   **Fig. 11.** Minimization of Euler angle variation of base by end perturbation

manipulator   are $[1.50, -2.10, -2.53, 1.82, -0.31, -0.12, -1.63]$(rad)   and $[-6.45, 1.63, 4.01] \times 10^{-4}$ (rad), respectively. The changes of objective function values are shown in Fig. 12. In the whole optimization process, the value of g_{em} decreases from 1.705×10^{-2} to 1.464×10^{-2}. This means that the end equivalent mass of space manipulator increases from 58.65 kg to 68.31 kg, with an increase of 16.47%; In this task, the direction of the rotating torque is in the same direction as the axis of the rotating joint at the end of the manipulator, which means that as long as the attitude of the end remains unchanged, the effective moment of inertia at the end of the space manipulator is almost all contributed by the end effector, so in this case, the effective moment of inertia at the end is not affected It has obvious optimization effect. The final end capture pose of space manipulator is[6.99 m, 0.01 m, 3.00 m, −1.00 rad, −0.50 rad, −2.00 rad]. In order to change the configuration of the space manipulator during the optimization process, the red mark is the optimal configuration of the capture mission (Fig. 13).

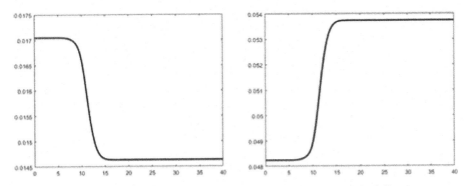

Fig. 12. Changes of g_{em} and g_{im} in the process of minimizing terminal disturbance

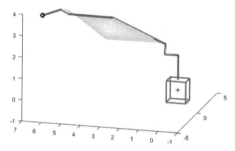

Fig. 13. Change of manipulator configuration with minimum end disturbance

The comparison results of the collision disturbance before and after optimization are as follows. It can be seen that the linear velocity disturbance at the end of the space manipulator is significantly reduced after the optimization of the configuration before capture.

$$\delta v_e = \begin{bmatrix} 1.47, 0.59, -2.81 \times 10^{-6} \end{bmatrix} \times 10^{-2} \text{ m/s},$$
$$\delta v'_e = \begin{bmatrix} 1.26, 0.50, 2.41 \times 10^{-6} \end{bmatrix} \times 10^{-2} \text{ m/s},$$
$$\delta \omega_e = \begin{bmatrix} -1.64 \times 10^{-7}, 4.06 \times 10^{-7}, -1 \times 10^{-3} \end{bmatrix} \text{ rad/s},$$
$$\delta \omega'_e = \begin{bmatrix} -1.83 \times 10^{-7}, 4.53 \times 10^{-7}, -1.1 \times 10^{-3} \end{bmatrix} \text{ rad/s}.$$

5 Summary

The trajectory planning algorithm of manipulator based on optimal capture is based on the linear path planning. After the end of the manipulator reaches the predetermined capture area, the attitude of the capture device and the capture configuration of the manipulator are optimized to minimize the pose disturbance of the end of the space manipulator and the attitude disturbance of the base. The negative impact of collision on the manipulator system is reduced by pre collision optimization, which is called by hover capture process.

Aiming at the optimal capture, this paper focuses on the first contact collision between the end effector of the manipulator and the visiting aircraft, and plans the trajectory of the space manipulator before capture. Firstly, the influence factors of flexible wire rope capturing contact force are analyzed from two levels of contact velocity and contact position, and the relationship between contact velocity, contact position and contact impact force is obtained. Then, the optimization objective function is established by minimizing the disturbance of the end pose of the space manipulator and the disturbance of the base pose, and the zero space term of the space manipulator is used to optimize the configuration of the manipulator before capturing The optimal capture configuration was obtained by optimization. Finally, combined with the path planning algorithm, the motion planning of the manipulator from the initial configuration to the optimal capture configuration is realized.

References

1. Zimpfer, D., Spehar, P.: STS-71 shuttle/MIR GNC mission overview. Adv. Astronaut. Sci. **93**, 441–460 (1996)
2. Hirzinger, G., Brunner, B., Dietrich, J., et al.: Sensor-based space robotics-rotex and its telerobotic features. IEEE Trans. Robot. Autom. **9**(5), 649–663 (1993)
3. Hirzinger, G., Landzettel, K., Brunner, B., et al.: DLR's robotics technologies for on-orbit servicing. Adv. Robot. **18**(2), 139–174 (2004)
4. Landzettel, K., Albu-Schaffer, A., Preusche, C., et al.: Robotic on-orbit servicing – DLR's experience and perspective. In: Proceedings IEEE/RSJ International Conference on Intelligent Robots and Systems, Beijing, China, pp. 4587–4594 (2006)
5. Yoshida, K.: Engineering test satellite VII flight experiments for space robot dynamics and control: theories on laboratory test beds ten years ago, now in orbit. Int. J. Rob. Res. **22**(5), 321–335 (2003)
6. Robert, G., Beck, J.R.: On the design and development of the space station. In: 42nd Congress of the International Astronautical Federation, pp. 5–11 (1991)
7. Michael, E., Laurenzio, D.A.: Control system architecture of the mobile servicing system. 42nd Congress of the International Astronautical Federation, pp. 1–7 (1991)

Fall Detection and Protection System Based on Characteristic Areas Algorithm

Jun Du[1], Jingyi Shi[1], Xiaodong Wei[2], Ying Xu[2], and Diansheng Chen[2(✉)]

[1] Institute of Robotics, School of Mechanical Engineering and Automation, Beihang University, Beijing 100191, China
junnydu@buaa.edu.cn
[2] Beijing Advanced Innovation Center for Biomedical Engineering, Beihang University, Beijing 100191, China
chends@buaa.edu.cn

Abstract. Hip fracture caused by falls and its complications is one of the greatest threats to disability and death of the elderly. To reduce physical damage from falls in the elderly, the current solution to achieve effective protection is detecting fall trends and turning on protective devices. However, the existing products have the problems of low accuracy and poor real-time. In this paper, a high accuracy and high real-time human fall detection and protection system based on characteristic areas algorithm is designed, which can detect the trend of falls within 400 ms after the human body begins to fall and is filled with the airbag in the 400 ms later, realizing effective protection of the human hip. The system got 95.33% accuracy, with an average airbag opening time of 70 ms.

Keywords: Fall detection · Fall protection · Characteristic areas · Airbag devices

1 Introduction

According to the WHO, the global rate of falls among the elderly has increased from 28% to 42%. In China, falls are an important inflection point for the elderly's disability and the first cause of death from injury [1]. In the event of a serious fall, the consequences of no one helping or slow relief are very serious. In view of the harm of falls to the elderly, it is important to study the fall detection and protection system to protect the elderly who are prone to falls and directly reduce the harm caused by falls.

Falling is a sudden, involuntary change in the body's posture that causes the body to fall to the ground or lower plane. The falling process is generally composed of the state of daily activity, the weightless state dumped to the ground, the impact state on landing, and the brief stationary state after landing, as shown in Fig. 1, and these four states usually occur in sequence over a period of time.

For fall detection, most scholars focus on the study of weight loss status and impact status, because it contains key information about the body's fall behavior. Fall detection methods based on inertial sensors are mainly divided into three categories: threshold method [2–5], machine learning method [6–11], and deep learning method [12–18].

© Springer Nature Switzerland AG 2021
X.-J. Liu et al. (Eds.): ICIRA 2021, LNAI 13013, pp. 170–178, 2021.
https://doi.org/10.1007/978-3-030-89095-7_17

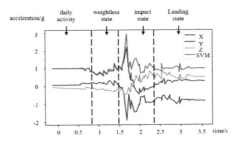

Fig. 1. The process of human falls

Widely used in wearable devices, IMU inertial sensors have the advantages of small size, low cost and simple connection. Therefore, fall detection based on inertial sensors is the most widely used scheme in the field of fall detection currently. For fall protection, accurate detection is required before the human body lands so that subsequent corresponding protective measures can be triggered. So how to detect a fall is one of the difficulties when there is no obvious fall characteristic before impact with the ground. According to the triggering principle of the airbag, it can be roughly divided into explosive [19] and mechanical inflatable protection devices [20]. The fall protection device needs to have the characteristics of high real-time so the design of a quick-response trigger mechanism is also one of the difficulties.

In view of these problems, this paper designs a human fall detection and protection system of high accuracy and high real-time. A fall trend detection algorithm based on characteristic areas is applied to detect falls from daily activities. The trigger device of air valve type cylinder based on steering gear reacts quickly, and the airbag of TPU composite cloth can realize effective protection. In addition, the experiments of fall detection, airbag inflating and fall protection were carried out, verifying the effectiveness of the system for the protection of the elderly.

2   Overall Design of the Fall Detection and Protection System

Depending on the function and performance requirements of fall detection and protection, the system can be divided into two parts, the fall detection subsystem and the protection airbag subsystem (see Fig. 2).

The fall detection subsystem includes data acquisition module, data analysis and processing module, control module, and alarm module. Through the high-precision detection algorithm before fall, the data analysis and processing module receives motion data and detects the fall trend in real-time, controlling the trigger of the fall protective airbag subsystem. The protection airbag subsystem consists of a trigger module and a protection module. When it receives a trigger signal from the control module, the trigger module responds quickly and opens the protection module to provide effective protection for the human hip.

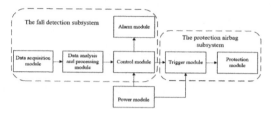

Fig. 2. Overall design for fall detection and protection systems

3 Study of Fall Detection Algorithm

In the field of image classification, some researchers have proposed a Class Activation Mapping method, which can visualize the feature regions in the original data that contribute to the classification. It can be seen that which part of the data features convolution neural network focuses on to complete the classification, providing the basis for detecting the classification of different samples by the model. In this paper, by combining class activation mapping methods with the convolutional neural network, the traditional convolutional neural network model is modified and the network model is shown in Fig. 3. Through class activation mapping method, the important contribution area used for the classification of fall time series data is analyzed. The data characteristics of this area are further summarized, and the fall detection algorithm suitable for wearable fall detection protection equipment is designed.

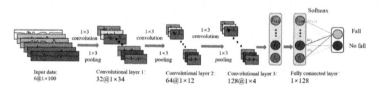

Fig. 3. Convolutional neural network model

Figure 4 shows the core network structure for implementing the class activation mapping method, which establishes the mapping relationship from the feature map to the category. For the input inertial sensor time series, $S_k(x)$ represents the output sequence on the k channel of the last reel layer, and x represents the position on the sequence at this time. The output of channel k in the global average pooling layer can be expressed as $f_k = \sum_x S_k(x)$. ω_k^c represents the weight of channel characteristic k to different category c, and the scores obtained by all feature charts on each channel c can be represented as g_c, as shown in (1)

$$g_c = \sum_k \omega_k^c \sum_x S_k(x) = \sum_k \sum_x \omega_k^c S_k(x) \tag{1}$$

Therefore, the class activation mapping from the sequence to each category c can be established, which is defined as M_c as shown in (2). M_c directly represents the importance of x position in the time series to the sequence being classified as c, that is, the linear weighted value of all channel features at the x position.

$$M_c = \sum_{k} \omega_k^c S_k(x)$$ (2)

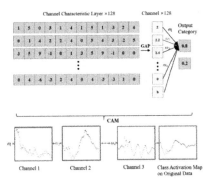

Fig. 4. Class activation mapping method principle based on global average pooling

Figure 5 shows the visualization results of class activation mapping for three samples in the MobiAct dataset. The yellow area corresponds to the important feature area that correctly classifies the sample, that is, CNN focuses on the data feature changes in this area. For example, as shown in Fig. 5(a), the data for a period of time when there is a tendency to fall and the data for a period of time during the fall play an important role in the correct classification of the sample. Similar areas also exist in the fall data we collected.

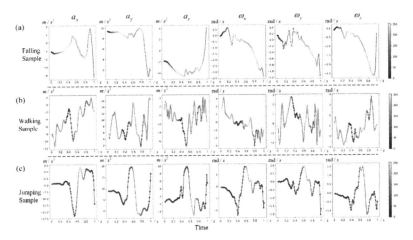

Fig. 5. Visualized class activation mapping

By analyzing the statistical characteristics of these areas, it is possible to construct an embedded fall detection algorithm for wearable fall detection and protection equipment. The algorithm flow is shown in Fig. 6.

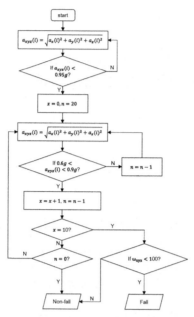

Fig. 6. Flow chart of the fall detection algorithm based on feature region threshold method

The algorithm was tested on the experimental dataset and MobiAct dataset. MobiAct is a publicly available dataset which includes data from a smartphone when participants are performing different types of activities and a range of falls. The test results are shown in Table 1. The accuracy of the final algorithm is 95.33%, the sensitivity is 94.04%, and the specificity is 97.17%.

Table 1. The results of the characteristic areas algorithm for fall detection

	Detected as fall behavior	Detected as routine behavior
Fall behavior	142	9
Routine behavior	3	103

Some research were carried out recently with state-of-the-art accuracy. But all of them are not suitable for embedded devices in an offline environment. Tao Xu et al. [20] presents a fusion fall detection algorithm combining threshold-based method and convolutional neural network. Suspected fall event are transmitted from wearable device to the server for processing, achieving high accuracy (97.46%). Hassan et al.[21] proposed a framework achieved 96.75% accuracy. Real-time data retrieved from an accelerometer sensor on a smartphone are processed and analyzed by an online fall detection system running on the smartphone itself. The comparison of performance is shown in Table 2.

Table 2. Comparison with other algorithms

	Tao Xu et al.	Hassan et al.	Our algorithm
Accuracy	97.46	96.75	95.55
Sensitivity	98.04	98.00	94.52
Specificity	96.91	96.00	96.52
Environment	Online	Online	Offline

4 System Integration and Experimental Validation

The overall hardware system of the fall detection and protection system is shown in Fig. 7. By placing the overall hardware in the wearable waist bag and using Velcro to bond, the overall system can be worn on the body.

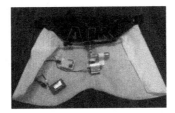

Fig. 7. The overall hardware system for fall detection and protection systems

4.1 Fall Detection Experiment

The experiment was completed by four healthy students from Beihang University (3 men and 1 woman with an average age of 24 years, an average height of 172.3 cm and an average weight of 65 kg). The experimenters performed daily actions and simulated falling actions. The experimental results are shown in Table 3. There were 80 simulated falls and 100 daily movements in the experiment of which 4 were missed and 4 falsely reported. The accuracy of the final fall detection test result was 95.56%, the sensitivity was 95%, and the specificity was 96%.

Table 3. Results of fall detection experiments

The type of action		Total number	Number of alarms	Accuracy (%)
Falling action	Fall back	20	19	95
	Fall forward	20	17	85
	Fall left	20	20	100
	Fall right	20	20	100
Daily movements	Walk	20	0	100
	Running	20	0	100
	Jump	20	0	100
	Stand up	20	3	85
	Sit down	20	1	95

4.2 Airbag Inflating Experiment

To test the time when the airbag is full of gas, a 60-frame camera is used to capture the inflation process. The steering engineer is directly triggered by STM32. The video records the time from pressing the key to triggering the steering gear as the opening time of the airbag, and the time from pressing the key to filling the airbag as the inflation time of the airbag. The results are repeated 10 times to take the average value. Finally, the opening time of the airbag is 70 ms, and the average inflation time is 383 ms. The test record is shown in Table 4.

Table 4. Airbag opening and inflation time data record

Number	1	2	3	4	5	6	7	8	9
Opening time/ms	66.7	66.7	66.7	66.7	100	66.7	66.7	66.7	66.7
Inflation time/ms	400	366.7	333.3	400	433.3	366.7	366.7	400	400

4.3 The Whole Experiment

A 60-frame camera was used to capture the whole process of human fall. Figure 8 shows the protection process of an overall airbag for a backward fall. Through analysis, the fall trend is detected 0.3 s after the fall starts, and the airbag opens in 0.4 s. The airbag is basically full in 0.7 s, which is 0.1 s ahead of the contact between the hip and the air cushion bed. And the whole airbag inflation is achieved in 0.9 s, achieving real-time protection of the fallen person.

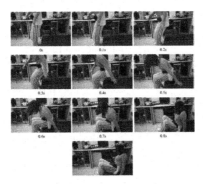

Fig. 8. The protective process of the overall airbag of a human body's rear fall

5 Conclusion

Hip fracture and its complications caused by falls are one of the biggest threats to disability and death of the elderly. In this paper, a high accuracy and real-time human fall detection and protection system is proposed for the elderly. By integrating class activation mapping method with CNN, the original fall data show their importance in fall detection, making it's possible to form a special threshold method with high accuracy in embedded devices. Further, combined with the design of wearable protective airbag and trigger mechanism, a prototype of fall detection and protection system for the elderly is developed, realizing high accuracy fall detection and high real-time fall protection. The system developed in this paper explores the development trend of fall detection and protection with high accuracy and high real-time, which lays a foundation for future production.

Acknowledgment. This research was funded by the National Key R&D Program of China (2018YFB1307002) and Beijing Municipal Science and Technology Project (Z191100004419008).

References

1. Jiang, J., Long, J., Ling, W., et al.: Incidence of fall-related injury among old people in mainland China. Arch. Gerontol. Geriatr. **61**(2), 131–139 (2015)
2. Hu, L.: Fall detection algorithms based on wearable device: a review. J. Zhejiang Univ. (Eng. Sci.) **52**(9), 1717–1728 (2018)
3. Ahn, S., Shin, I., Kim, Y.: Pre-impact fall detection using an inertial sensor unit. J. Foot Ankle Res. **7**(1), A124 (2014)
4. Lee, J.K., Robinovitch, S.N., Park, E.J.: Inertial sensing-based pre-impact detection of falls involving near-fall scenarios. IEEE Trans. Neural Syst. Rehabil. Eng. **23**(2), 258–266 (2015)
5. Otanasap, N.: Pre-impact fall detection based on wearable device using dynamic threshold model. In: 17th International Conference on Parallel and Distributed Computing, Applications and Technologies (PDCAT), pp. 362–365. IEEE Computer Society (2016)

6. Aziz, O., Russell, C.M., Park, E.J., et al.: The effect of window size and lead time on pre-impact fall detection accuracy using support vector machine analysis of waist mounted inertial sensor data. In: Proceedings of International Conference on Engineering in Medicine and Biology Society, pp. 30–33. IEEE, Chicago (2014)

7. Diep, N.N., Pham, C., Phuong, T.M.: A classifier-based approach to real-time fall detection using low-cost wearable sensors. In: Proceedings of the Fifth Symposium on Information and Communication Technology, pp. 14–20. IEEE, Hanoi (2014)

8. Er, J.K., Ang, W.T.: Evaluation of single HMM as a pre-impact fall detector based on different input signals. In: 2018 IEEE Region Ten Symposium (Tensymp), Sydney, Australia, pp. 207–212 (2018)

9. Jian, H., Chen, H.: A portable fall detection and alerting system based on k-NN algorithm and remote medicine. Communications **12**(4), 23–31 (2015)

10. Khan, S.S., Karg, M.E., Kulić, D., Hoey, J.: X-factor HMMs for detecting falls in the absence of fall-specific training data. In: Pecchia, L., Chen, L.L., Nugent, C., Bravo, J. (eds.) IWAAL 2014. LNCS, vol. 8868, pp. 1–9. Springer, Cham (2014). https://doi.org/10.1007/978-3-319-13105-4_1

11. Nukala, B.T., Shibuya, N., Rodriguez, A.I., et al.: A real-time robust fall detection system using a wireless gait analysis sensor and an artificial neural network. In: Proceedings of International Conference on Healthcare Innovation, pp. 219–222. IEEE, Seattle (2014)

12. Fakhrulddin, A.H., Fei, X., Li, H.: Convolutional neural networks (CNN) based human fall detection on body sensor networks (BSN) sensor data. In: 4th International Conference on Systems and Informatics (ICSAI), Hangzhou, pp. 1461–1465 (2017)

13. Münzner, S., Schmidt, P., Reiss, A., et al.: CNN-based sensor fusion techniques for multimodal human activity recognition. In: Proceedings of the 2017 ACM International Symposium on Wearable Computers, pp. 158–165 (2017)

14. Shi, G., Chan, C.S., Luo, Y., et al.: Development of a human airbag system for falling protection using MEMS motion sensing technology. In: IEEE/RSJ International Conference on Intelligent Robots and Systems, pp. 4405–4410. IEEE (2006)

15. Toshiyo, T., Masaki, S., Takumi, Y.: A wearable airbag to prevent fall injuries. IEEE Trans. Inf. Technol. Biomed. **13**(6), 910–914 (2009)

16. Toshiyo, T., Takumi, Y., Masaki, S.: A preliminary study to demonstrate the use of an air bag device to prevent fall-related injuries. In: Proceedings of the 29th Annual International Conference of the IEEE EMBS Cité Internationale, Lyon, France, pp. 23–26. IEEE (2007)

17. Yilun, L., Guangyi, S., Josh, L., et al.: Towards a human airbag system using μIMU with SVM training for falling-motion recognition. In: IEEE International Conference on Robotics and Biomimetics (IEEE ROBIO), Hong Kong. IEEE (2009)

18. Zeng, M., Nguyen, L.T., Yu, B., et al.: Convolutional neural networks for human activity recognition using mobile sensors. In: Sixth International Conference on Mobile Computing, Applications and Services (MobiCASE 2014), pp.197–205. IEEE (2014)

19. Zhong, Z., Chen, F., Zhai, Q., et al.: A real-time pre-impact fall detection and protection system. In: IEEE/ASME International Conference on Advanced Intelligent Mechatronics (AIM), pp. 1039–1044. IEEE (2018)

20. Guangyi, S., Cheung-Shing, C., Guanglie, Z.: Towards a mobile airbag system using MEMS Sensors and embedded intelligence. In: IEEE International Conference on Robotics and Biomimetics (ROBIO), Sanya, China, pp. 634–639. IEEE (2007)

21. Xu, T., Se, H., Liu, J.: A fusion fall detection algorithm combining threshold-based method and convolutional neural network. Microprocess. Microsyst. **82**, 103828 (2021)

22. Hassan, M.M., et al.: A smartphone-enabled fall detection framework for elderly people in connected home healthcare. IEEE Netw. **33**(6), 58–63 (2019)

Design of Flexure Hinges Using Geometrically Nonlinear Topology Optimization

Benliang Zhu, Yuanrong He, Fahua Qu, Jintao Chen, Rixin Wang[(⊠)], Hai Li, and Xianmin Zhang

Guangdong Key Laboratory of Precision Equipment and Manufacturing Technology, South China University of Technology, Guangzhou 510642, China
wangrixin@scut.edu.cn

Abstract. Topology optimization has been employed for the configurational design of flexure hinges under linear assumption in recent years. This paper presents a method for the design of flexure hinges with large displacements in which the nonlinear topology optimization is adopted. An optimization model is developed based on the spring model. The objective function is formulated by minimizing the stiffness in the desired direction. A rotational index is proposed and serves as one of the constraints for accomplishing the high precision revolute requirement. A symmetry constraint is employed to improve the practicability of the optimized results. A minimal length scale control technique is adopted to avoid point flexure issue. Several numerical results are performed to demonstrate the effectiveness of the proposed method.

Keywords: Compliant mechanisms · Flexure hinges · Topology optimization · Geometrical nonlinearity

1 Introduction

The flexure hinge has been widely utilized in compliant mechanisms. It refers to a thin member that can provide rotational movement between two rigid members. Because no assembly is required, the flexible hinge is particularly suitable for use where high-precision motion is required [6,17]. For example, the flexure hinge has been one of the key components of the compliant mechanism-based precision positioning stages which have been widely utilized for micro/nano-manipulation [13].

The first attempt at designing flexure hinges can be dated back to 1965 when the right circular flexure hinge was designed by Paros and Weisbord [19]. Since then, various new flexure hinges with different configurations have been proposed, such as V-shaped, corner-filleted, leaf-based and polynomial flexure hinges [20]. These hinges more or less can be regarded as a variant of the right circular flexure hinge. This is because their configuration can be altered through

© Springer Nature Switzerland AG 2021
X.-J. Liu et al. (Eds.): ICIRA 2021, LNAI 13013, pp. 179–189, 2021.
https://doi.org/10.1007/978-3-030-89095-7_18

profile shape variation of the right circular shape. For this reason, the systemic method for designing flexure hinges with new configurations needs to be further investigated. To design flexure hinges, systematic methods are preferable since it can develop entirely new configurations or at least can improve the functionality of the existing designs.

The screw theory-based methods have been developed for the design of compound-type flexure hinges. This method can be seen as a combination of freedom and constraint topology (FACT) [5] and screw theory in which a mapping from a geometric concept to physical entity is utilized by combining with equivalent compliance mapping and building blocks. This method is a systematic type synthesis approach that is developed for designing multiple degrees of freedom (DOF) flexure hinges. However, the fundamental elements of such design hinges still are the aforementioned flexure hinges with different notch profiles.

Over the past few years, topology optimization has been adapted to the design of flexure hinges and has shown a great promise. Topology optimization is a systematic approach that can determine the best material distribution in a given design domain [1]. It has been a popular and powerful tool to the design of stiffness structures, compliant mechanisms, etc. [4, 24].

The first attempts of using topology optimization to the design of flexure hinges can be found in [16] and [22]. In [16], a kinetoelastic formulation was developed instead of using the traditional spring model for modeling the compliant mechanism design problems. This formulation was applied to the design of the flexure translational hinges. Recently, Li and Zhu [7] used the same idea to design of rotational flexure hinge based on the level set method.

In [22], a generalized spring model was developed along with a new optimization formulation. The method was used for the design of both translational and rotational flexure hinges. Following the idea proposed in [22], several papers have been published by considering different design cases. For example, Liu et al. [10] incorporated the stress constraint into the design model to eliminate the thin part of the obtained flexure hinge to improve its manufacturability. They also proposed a new formulation to develop flexure hinges with desired performance [9]. A shortcoming of the aforementioned methods is that the obtained flexure hinges are asymmetric which will bring additional difficulties for real-world applications. To overcome this shortcoming, Zhu et al. [23] proposed a new formulation by considering a geometrically symmetric constraint. Pinskier et al. [11] proposed a method for the design of flexure hinges by considering the trade-off between rotational range and accuracy. Qiu et al. [12] proposed a single-axis multicavity flexure hinge (MCFH) by using the three-dimensional continuum topology optimization method. The hinge contains symmetric cycloidal notches and multiple cavities.

Despite all the above attempts, one has to admit that it is still in the initial stage of using topology optimization to the design of flexure hinges with different configurations. For example, almost all the conducted studies of this area are using linear assumption. However, it has been well demonstrated that for topology optimization of compliant mechanisms, nonlinearity is essential. Therefore, using nonlinear topology optimization methods to design large-displacement flexure hinges remains to be further investigated, which is the main topic of this study.

2   Problem Formulation

Figure 1(a) shows the design space utilized to illustrate the design problem. The left side of the design space is fixed, whilst the middle of the right side is subject to a vertical load F. The right 20% of the whole design space is set as solid to limit bending at the output side. The left 80% is the square design domain with a length of l. A spring k is attached to the output port A which can ensure the design problem well-posed, meanwhile limiting the upper rotational angle of the hinge.

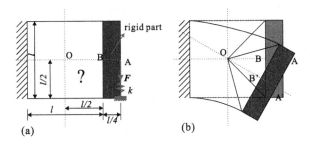

Fig. 1. (a) The considered design domain for flexure hinges, and (b) the accuracy requirement.

For the design of a flexure hinge, a finite rotation around point O will be the first requirement. This can be achieved by maximizing the vertical displacement Θ_y of point A due to load F, and this can be seen as the functional requirement of the flexure hinge.

In addition, the flexure hinge also needs to fulfill the rotational accuracy, which means that the rotational center has to be O. To achieve this, one of the most commonly used constraints is to limit η with a very small upper bound η^*

$$\eta = \frac{1}{2}\left(\frac{\Theta_y}{\theta_y} - \frac{3}{2}\right)^2 \leq \eta^* \tag{1}$$

where θ_y is the displacement of point B along axis y cause by force F. In this study, η^* is set to 0.001. To do so, the line determined by points A' and B' can be ensured to cross the geometrical center O (Fig. 1(b)).

Therefore, for topology optimization of flexure hinges, the optimization model can be expressed as

$$\min : \quad J = -\Theta_y \tag{2}$$
$$\text{s.t.} : \quad V \leq V^* \tag{3}$$
$$\eta \leq \eta^* \tag{4}$$
$$\mathbf{r} = 0 \tag{5}$$

where V^* is the upper bound on material volume V. $\mathbf{r}$ is the residual in obtaining the structural response. For large displacement flexure hinges, $\mathbf{r} = 0$ needs to be solved using an iterative procedure [8].

3   Geometrically Nonlinear Topology Optimization

3.1   The SIMP-based Finite Element Analysis

In order to solve the topology optimization problem, the power law approach is employed. In this approach, the key idea is to discretize the design domain using finite elements. The material property of each finite element is controlled. The corresponding material property will approach zero if the material in some specific area needs to be removed [1]. In this paper, the SIMP approach is employed. The controlled material property is the penalized stiffness model. Suppose that E_0 represents the stiffness of a used isotropic material and the design variable is the element density $\rho_e \in [0, 1]$. The relationship between them can be expressed as [14]

$$E_e = E(\rho_e) = E_{\min} + \rho_e^p (E_0 - E_{\min}) \tag{6}$$

where $E_{\min} > 0$ is the stiffness of the void material to prevent singularity ($E_{\min} = 10^{-9} E_0$), and $p > 1$ is the penalty and is set to 3.

Using the SIMP method, the optimization model for the design of flexure hinges can be further expressed as

$$\min_{\rho} : \quad J = -\Theta_y(\boldsymbol{\rho}) \tag{7}$$
$$\text{s.t.} : \quad \sum_{e=1}^{N} v_e \rho_e \leq V^* \tag{8}$$
$$\eta(\boldsymbol{\rho}) \leq \eta^* \tag{9}$$
$$\mathbf{r}(\boldsymbol{\rho}) = 0 \tag{10}$$

where v_e is the element material volume, and $\boldsymbol{\rho} = [\rho_1, \ \rho_2, ...\rho_e, ...\rho_N]^T$.

In nonlinear topology optimization problem, an iterative procedure is necessary to find the equilibrium. In this study, the flexure hinges are assumed to undergo large displacements. However, we assume that the strains remain small. Therefore, for the strain calculation, the second-order terms must be considered while the material behaviour remains linear. Therefore, with respect to the initial coordinates of the body ^0x, the Green-Lagrange strain measure can be defined as follows

$$\varepsilon_{ij} = \frac{1}{2}\left(\frac{\partial u_i}{\partial^0 x_j} + \frac{\partial u_j}{\partial^0 x_i} + \frac{\partial u_k}{\partial^0 x_i}\frac{\partial u_k}{\partial^0 x_j}\right) \tag{11}$$

where u is the displacement at a point in the structure. The elastic constitutive relation is expressed as

$$S_{ij}(u) = E_{ijkl}\varepsilon_{ij}(u) \tag{12}$$

where E_{ijkl} is the constitutive tensor. The residual is defined as the error between external force $\mathbf{F}$ and internal nodal force as

$$\mathbf{r(u)} = \mathbf{F} - \int_\Omega \mathbf{B}^T(\mathbf{u})\mathbf{S}d\Omega \tag{13}$$

where $\mathbf{S}$ is the internal stress vector, $\mathbf{u}$ is displacement vector which will be obtained when $\mathbf{r}$ is equal to the zero vector. The relationship between a change in displacement $d\mathbf{u}$ and a change in strain can be defined as

$$d\varepsilon = \mathbf{B(u)}d\mathbf{u} \tag{14}$$

where $\mathbf{B}$ is the transform matrix. The equilibrium (13) can be solved by using the Newton-Raphson iteration method. The tangent stiffness matrix can be defined using

$$\mathbf{K}_T = \frac{d\mathbf{r}}{d\mathbf{u}} \tag{15}$$

3.2 Sensitivity Analysis

Design sensitivities are essential for obtaining the optimized results by using gradient-based methods. The derivative of J in (7) with respect to the design variable ρ_e can be written as

$$\frac{\partial J}{\partial \rho_e} = -\frac{\partial \Theta_y}{\partial \rho_e} = -\frac{\partial}{\partial \rho_e}\left(\mathbf{l}^T\mathbf{u}\right) \tag{16}$$

where $\mathbf{l}$ is a vector of all zeros except for the output position A, where its value is one. Therefore, we have

$$\frac{\partial J}{\partial \rho_e} = -\mathbf{l}^T\frac{\partial \mathbf{u}}{\partial \rho_e} \tag{17}$$

In order to determine $\frac{\partial \mathbf{u}}{\partial \rho_e}$, we introduce a random vector $\boldsymbol{\lambda}$ and assume the equilibrium has been obtained, i.e., $\mathbf{r} = 0$. Then

$$\Theta_y = \mathbf{l}^T\mathbf{u} + \boldsymbol{\lambda}^T\mathbf{r} \tag{18}$$

and this equation is satisfied since $\boldsymbol{\lambda}^T\mathbf{r}$ equals 0. Since $\mathbf{r}$ is the function of both $\mathbf{u}$ and ρ_e, using the chain role we have

$$\frac{\partial \Theta_y}{\partial \rho_e} = \mathbf{l}^T\frac{\partial \mathbf{u}}{\partial \rho_e} + \boldsymbol{\lambda}^T\frac{\partial \mathbf{r}}{\partial \rho_e} + \boldsymbol{\lambda}^T\frac{\partial \mathbf{r}}{\partial \mathbf{u}}\frac{\partial \mathbf{u}}{\partial \rho_e} \tag{19}$$

Using Eq. (15), Eq. (19) can be further expressed as

$$\frac{\partial \Theta_y}{\partial \rho_e} = \left(1^T + \boldsymbol{\lambda}^T \mathbf{K}_T\right) \frac{\partial \mathbf{u}}{\partial \rho_e} + \boldsymbol{\lambda}^T \frac{\partial \mathbf{r}}{\partial \rho_e} \tag{20}$$

Since $\boldsymbol{\lambda}$ can be freely chosen, in order to eliminate the unknown term $\frac{\partial \mathbf{u}}{\partial \rho_e}$ we can simply let $1^T + \boldsymbol{\lambda}^T \mathbf{K}_T$ be 0, which means $\boldsymbol{\lambda}$ is obtained by solving

$$\mathbf{K}_T^T \boldsymbol{\lambda} = -1 \tag{21}$$

which leads to

$$\frac{\partial J}{\partial \rho_e} = -\boldsymbol{\lambda}^T \frac{\partial \mathbf{r}}{\partial \rho_e} \tag{22}$$

The sensitivity of the material volume V with respect to the design variable ρ_e can be obtained quite straightforward

$$\frac{\partial V}{\partial \rho_e} = \frac{\partial}{\partial \rho_e} \left(\sum_{e=1}^{N} v_e \rho_e \right) = v_e \tag{23}$$

The sensitivity of rotational accuracy constraint η with respect to ρ_e can be expressed as

$$\frac{\partial \eta}{\partial \rho_e} = \frac{1}{\theta_y^2} \left(\frac{\Theta_y}{\theta_y} - \frac{3}{2} \right) \left(\theta_y \frac{\partial \Theta_y}{\partial \rho_e} - \Theta_y \frac{\partial \theta_y}{\partial \rho_e} \right) \tag{24}$$

The only unknown term in this equation is $\frac{\partial \theta_y}{\partial \rho_e}$. Similar to the process of solving $\frac{\partial \Theta_y}{\partial \rho_e}$, we can simply obtain the sensitivity of θ_y with respect to ρ_e as

$$\frac{\partial \theta_y}{\partial \rho_e} = \boldsymbol{\chi}^T \frac{\partial \mathbf{r}}{\partial \rho_e} \tag{25}$$

where $\boldsymbol{\chi}$ is obtained by solving

$$\mathbf{K}_T^T \boldsymbol{\chi} = -\boldsymbol{\psi} \tag{26}$$

where $\boldsymbol{\psi}$ is a vector of all zeros except for the position B.

Solving Eqs. (21) and (26) for the adjoint loads is relatively easy because the tangent stiffness matrix $\mathbf{K}_T$ has been found during the equilibrium iterations.

4   Numerical Implementations

The implementation of the topology optimization problem is straight forward. However, several numerical problems need to be considered during the solution of the problem which are briefly discussed in the following. First, to avoid convergence difficulties, a hybrid interpolation scheme is employed [15]. The key idea is to model the low-density elements using linear assumption whilst the high-density elements use nonlinear assumption. The constitutive equation is chosen to be the St. Venant-Kirchhoff model. The elastic energy density is modeled as

[3,15]. Second, the mechanism deformation is nearly entirely taking place in such hinges which leads to a stress concentration problem. In this study, we use the geometric constraints in a filtering-threshold topology optimization scheme [21] to eliminate *de facto* hinges. In addition, to avoid asymmetry in results, we adopt the symmetrical constraint proposed in [23]. The underlying idea is to reset the densities inside the design domain based on the densities in the reference domain using a flip mapping (Fig. 2).

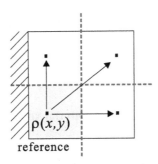

Fig. 2. The reference domain for achieving a symmetrical design.

5   Results and Discussions

In this section, the numerical results of flexure hinges using the nonlinear topology optimization are presented. The material for constructing the hinge is a flexible filament (thermoplastic polyurethanes made by Guangdong Shunde Youxian 3D technology Co. LTD.). Its material properties are Young's modulus for solid material E_0 is 38 Mpa and Poisson's ratio v is 0.45. The input load F is set to 10N. The attached spring stiffness is 100 N/m. We use 80×80 bilinear quadrilateral elements to discretize the design domain and 20×80 for the rigid part. The size of each element is 0.5×0.5 mm. The thickness of the design space is set to 10 mm.

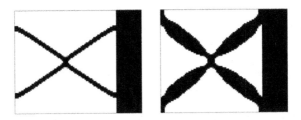

Fig. 3. Topology optimized flexure hinges with material volume fraction of 0.1 (left) and 0.3 (right).

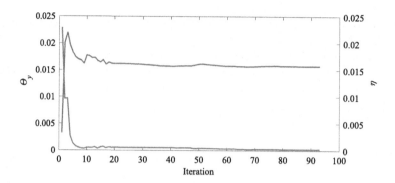

Fig. 4. Convergence histories of Θ_y and η with the design case of material volume usage 30%.

We first examine the impact of the material volume constraint on the topology optimized flexure hinges. Two design cases are considered in which the values of the maximum material usage corresponded to 10% and 30% of the design domain (the rigid part is excluded). The final designs are shown in Fig. 3. One can see that both designs have configurations similar to the cross wheel flexure hinge although the shape and size are significantly different. These results indicate that changing the maximum material usage does not affect the topology of the final design. For the design case of Fig. 3(b), the convergence histories of Θ_y and the rotational accuracy index η are shown in Fig. 4. It takes 93 iterations to converge to an optimized topology.

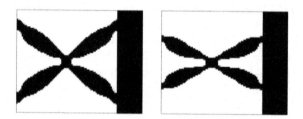

Fig. 5. Topology optimized flexure hinges with different attached spring stiffness: (a) $k = 200\,\mathrm{N/m}$, and (b) $k = 500\,\mathrm{N/m}$.

We further investigate the effects of the attached spring k on the topology results of flexure hinges. Two cases are analyzed in which the spring stiffness k is set to 200 N/m and 500 N/m. All other parameters are set to the same as those given in the design case of $k = 100\,\mathrm{N/m}$. The corresponding topology results of the two studied cases are shown in Fig. 5. The corresponding strain energy distributions are shown in Fig. 6. It can be seen that the outcome of the optimization process can be affected by the attached spring stiffness. With the increase of spring stiffness, the optimized shape shrinks along the longitudinal

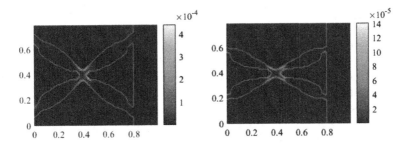

Fig. 6. The corresponding strain energy distributions of the flexure hinges shown in Fig. 5.

axis. When spring stiffness is large enough, the upper and lower parts will be merged together and thereby become a leaf-type flexure hinge, which has been demonstrated in [22].

Finally, we examine the proposed method for the design of flexure hinges with embedded components. These components can be actuators or sensors that can be used for detecting the stress or strain situation when the flexure hinge is under deformation [18]. The embedded components often have significant influence on the topology optimized design. To demonstrate this, a typical design case is shown in Fig. 7 in which two fixed rigid parts are used to simulate the embedded components. All the design parameters remain the same with the design case in Fig. 3(b). For this design case, the optimization process runs for 130 iterations. Several intermediate and the final topologies of the optimized flexure hinge are shown in Fig. 7. One can see that, during the first 30 iterations, remarkable shape and topological changes occur. The topology remains unchange for the last 100 iterations, although slightly geometrical adjustments still can be seen to approach the optimal region.

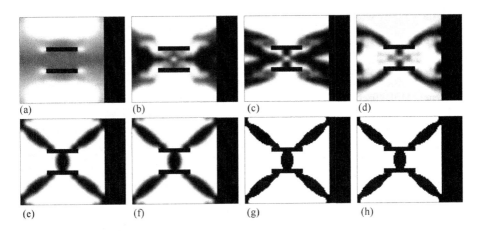

Fig. 7. Topology optimized flexure hinges with embedded components: (a) step 1, (b) step 3, (c) step 6, (d) step 10, (e) step 20, (f) step 40, (g) step 80, (h) step 130 (final).

6   Conclusions

In this work, we presented a method for nonlinear topology optimization of flexure hinges. An optimization model was developed by using the spring model and a rotational accuracy constraint. In order to improve the practicability of the optimized results, a minimal length scale control technique and a geometrical symmetry constraint were utilized. Numerical results are presented to demonstrate the effectiveness of the proposed method. The obtained results revealed that the consideration of nonlinearity will significantly affect the outcome of the optimization process when compared with the results obtained by only using the linear assumption. This indicates that it is extremely important to use large displacement theory in flexure hinge design to obtain better designs that achieve higher performance.

Acknowledgements. This research was supported by the National Natural Science Foundation of China (Grant Nos. 51975216, 52035013), the Guangdong Basic and Applied Basic Research Foundation (Grant No. 2021B1515020053), and the Fundamental Research Funds for the Central Universities.

References

1. Bendsoe, M.P.: Topology Optimization: Theory, Methods, and Applications, 2nd edn. Springer, Heidelberg (2004). https://doi.org/10.1007/978-3-662-05086-6
2. Chen, Q., Zhang, X., Zhang, H., Zhu, B., Chen, B.: Topology optimization of bistable mechanisms with maximized differences between switching forces in forward and backward direction. Mech. Mach. Theor. **139**, 131–143 (2019)
3. Chen, Q., Zhang, X., Zhu, B.: Design of buckling-induced mechanical metamaterials for energy absorption using topology optimization. Struct. Multidiscip. Optim. **58**(4), 1395–1410 (2018)
4. Christiansen, R.E., Wang, F., Sigmund, O.: Topological insulators by topology optimization. Phys. Rev. Lett. **122**(23), 234502 (2019)
5. Hopkins, J.B., Culpepper, M.L.: Synthesis of multi-degree of freedom, parallel flexure system concepts via freedom and constraint topology (fact)-part i: principles. Precis. Eng. **34**(2), 259–270 (2010)
6. Howell, L.L.: Compliant Mechanisms. Wiley, Hoboken (2001)
7. Li, L., Zhu, X.: Design of compliant revolute joints based on mechanism stiffness matrix through topology optimization using a parameterization level set method. Struct. Multidiscip. Optim. **60**(4), 1475–1489 (2019)
8. Liu, L., Xing, J., Yang, Q., Luo, Y.: Design of large-displacement compliant mechanisms by topology optimization incorporating modified additive hyperelasticity technique. Math. Probl. Eng. **2017**, 11 (2017)
9. Liu, M., Zhang, X., Fatikow, S.: Design and analysis of a multi-notched flexure hinge for compliant mechanisms. Precis. Eng. **48**, 292–304 (2017)
10. Liu, M., Zhang, X., Fatikow, S.: Design of flexure hinges based on stress-constrained topology optimization. Proc. Inst. Mech. Eng. C J. Mech. Eng. Sci. **231**(24), 4635–4645 (2017)
11. Pinskier, J., Shirinzadeh, B., Ghafarian, M., Das, T.K., Al-Jodah, A., Nowell, R.: Topology optimization of stiffness constrained flexure-hinges for precision and range maximization. Mech. Mach. Theor. **150**, 103874 (2020)

12. Qiu, L., Yue, X., Xie, Z.: Design and analysis of multicavity flexure hinge (MCFH) based on three-dimensional continuum topology optimization. Mech. Mach. Theor. **139**, 21–33 (2019)
13. Shi, C., et al.: Recent advances in nanorobotic manipulation inside scanning electron microscopes. Microsyst. Nanoeng. **2**(1), 1–16 (2016)
14. Sigmund, O.: Morphology-based black and white filters for topology optimization. Struct. Multidiscip. Optim. **33**(4–5), 401–424 (2007)
15. Wang, F., Lazarov, B.S., Sigmund, O., Jensen, J.S.: Interpolation scheme for fictitious domain techniques and topology optimization of finite strain elastic problems. Comput. Meth. Appl. Mech. Eng. **276**, 453–472 (2014)
16. Wang, M.Y.: A kinetoelastic formulation of compliant mechanism optimization. J. Mech. Robot. **1**(2), 021011 (2009)
17. Wang, R., Zhang, X.: Parameters optimization and experiment of a planar parallel 3-DOF nanopositioning system. IEEE Trans. Ind. Electron. **65**, 2388–2397 (2018)
18. Wang, Y., Luo, Z., Zhang, X., Kang, Z.: Topological design of compliant smart structures with embedded movable actuators. Smart Mater. Struct. **23**(4), 045024 (2014)
19. Weisbord, L., Paros, J.: How to design flexure hinges. Mach. Des. **27**(3), 151–157 (1965)
20. Yong, Y.K., Lu, T.F., Handley, D.C.: Review of circular flexure hinge design equations and derivation of empirical formulations. Precis. Eng. **32**(2), 63–70 (2008)
21. Zhou, M., Lazarov, B.S., Wang, F., Sigmund, O.: Minimum length scale in topology optimization by geometric constraints. Comput. Meth. Appl. Mech. Eng. **293**, 266–282 (2015)
22. Zhu, B., Zhang, X., Fatikow, S.: Design of single-axis flexure hinges using continuum topology optimization method. Sci. Chin. Technol. Sci. **57**(3), 560–567 (2014)
23. Zhu, B., Zhang, X., Liu, M., Chen, Q., Li, H.: Topological and shape optimization of flexure hinges for designing compliant mechanisms using the level set method. Chin. J. Mech. Eng. **32**(1), 13 (2019)
24. Zhi, B., et al.: Design of compliant mechanisms using continuum topology optimization: a review. Mech. Mach. Theor. **143**, 103622 (2020)

Fully Compliant Electroactive Bistable Actuator Utilizing Twisting and Coiled Artificial Muscle

Lei Jiang[1,2,3], Yakun Zhang[1,2,3], Wentao Ma[1,2,3], Guimin Chen[1,2,3], and Bo Li[1,2,3(✉)]

[1] State Key Lab of Manufacturing System Engineering, Xi'an 710049, China
[2] Shaanxi Key Lab of Intelligent Robots, Xi'an 710049, China
[3] School of Mechanical Engineering, Xi'an Jiaotong University, Xi'an 710049, China
liboxjtu@xjtu.edu.cn

Abstract. Soft actuators are essential components for soft robots. In this paper, a new fully compliant electroactive bistable actuator is developed based on minimum energy structures and the angle amplification mechanism, and it is coupled with the electroactive artificial muscle (Twisting & Coiled Polymer Fiber, TCPF) for electrical activation. Two TCPFs are arranged antagonistically to realize bistable snapping in the actuator that is capable of good discrete deformation stability. The experimental results verify the design purpose and repeatable actuation positioning is attained in the bistable snapping process. This actuator offers a potential advantage for soft robots of binary motion.

Keywords: Bistable actuator · Compliant mechanism · Twisting & coiled polymer fiber

1 Introduction

Soft robots have advantages of large deformations and safe human-computer interaction [1–3]. In recent years, researchers have developed a variety of soft actuators, namely artificial muscles, for soft robots, including shape memory alloys (SMA) [4–7], dielectric elastomer actuators (DEA) [8–11], pneumatic artificial muscles [12, 13], and ionic polymer-metal composite (IPMC) [14, 15]. These types of artificial muscles have their own characteristics. Shape memory alloy has fast deformation speed and larger output force, but its deformation is small (generally 4%–5%), and the hysteresis effect is obvious. The force generated by the dielectric elastomer actuator is low, while the drive voltage is as large as kV level. Pneumatic muscles can produce large and fast deformations and driving forces, but the demand for additional devices such as pumps, valves, and pipes makes the entire system bulky and heavy. Ion polymer-metal composite materials have light weight, flexible body, and low power consumption, but they need to be maintained in a moisturized working state that limits the application environment. It is, therefore, developing new artificial muscles with both large deformation and large output force is an essential issue for advancing soft robots.

TCPF is a new artificial muscle that can contract with an increasing temperature. It produces strain up to 49%, with a load-bearing capacity reaching 100 times that in

X.-J. Liu et al. (Eds.): ICIRA 2021, LNAI 13013, pp. 190–196, 2021.
https://doi.org/10.1007/978-3-030-89095-7_19

human muscles of the same weight, as well as a high energy density (5.3 kw/kg). In addition, it also has the advantages of small size, low cost, long service life, and high repeatability [16–23]. Therefore, in this paper, a new compliant actuator is proposed by coupling the TCPF artificial muscles and a compliant bistable mechanism. This actuator is capable of snapping between two stable states subject to voltage activation, and the snapping is repeatable and reversible.

2   The Design and Fabrication of the Actuator

Figure 1 shows the fabrication process of TCPF. We used a nylon fishing line (#6 Transparent strand, Φ0.38 mm, NORTH VIKINGS) to fabricate TCPF. One end of the fishing line was tied to the motion, and the other was connected to the slider on the slide trail. The other end of the slider was connected with a weight (200 g) to provide tensile force to prevent fishing line from winding during the following twisting and coiling. At the onset of the fishing line to coil, a silver-plated line (140D SANMAU) was placed in parallel with the twisted nylon fishing line. Then the two materials were coiled together. When the line was completely coiled, we switched the mass to 750 g and preheated the fishing line with a hot air gun (150 °C) to fix the coiled state. The preheated fishing line was tied on the frame and put into the oven for 25 min for further heat treatment (145 °C).

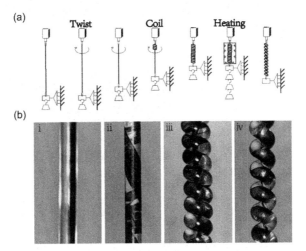

Fig. 1. The material and fabrication of TCPF. (a) The fabrication process of TCPF. (b) (i) The nylon fishing line after twisted. (ii) Intertwine the nylon fishing line and the silver-plated line. (iii) TCPF before heat treatment. (iv) TCPF after heat treatment.

The schematic diagram of the actuator is shown in Fig. 2(a). The actuator includes a rigid frame (PMMA), a flexible frame (PET), a film (VHB), TCPF, some shims (PMMA), and constrained fibers (PMMA). We coupled the rigid frame and the flexible frame together to form two compliant beams: compliant beam 1 and compliant beam 2. As the pre-stretched film (4 by 4) is bonded to the flexible elastic frame, the restoring force of the film bends the elastic frame which self-maintains in a minimum energy state. Because the frame is a hollow structure, the force of the film on the frame can be selected in two directions, that is, the flexible frame can be bent into two directions. Finally, the actuator reaches two stable states, which are symmetric (Fig. 2(b)). We tied the TCPF on both sides of the compliant beam 2 after stretching (pre-stretch level of 1.15). Under the action of the film, the compliant beam 1 amplifies the bending from beam 2 caused by the TCPF actuation (Fig. 2(c)) which will be explained in the following actuation principles.

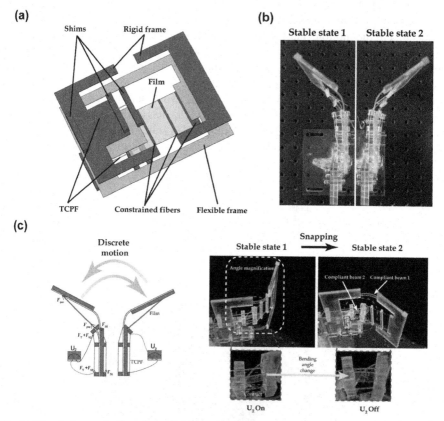

Fig. 2. The design and actuation principle of the actuator. (a) The actuator structure. (b) The two stable states of the actuator as the flexural bending motion terminates. (c) The principle of discrete motion. F_{S1} and F_{S2} are the elastic force of two TCPFs by pre-stretching, F_T is the actuation force of TCPF by voltage, F_{pre} is the force of the film by pre-stretching.

Subject to a voltage, the TCPF is heated and then contracts, offering a force output as an artificial muscle and acts on the compliant beam 2. Taking the actuator rested in stable state 1 as an example, the deployment in beam 2 is then amplified via the expanding of film to beam 1 which further deploys as a result of an unbalanced force. When the actuator is fully deployed and flattened, the voltage on TCPF is cut off. So that the force of TCPF vanished and the film contracts which leads to a quick bending in beam 1 and the actuator snaps to stable state 2. The process is reversible for snapping from stable 2 to 1 by switching the voltage on the other side of TCPF.

3   Performance Characterization of Actuation

The deformation stability of the mechanism is closely related to the performance of TCPF. The tensile test was conducted to study the cycle behaviors of TCPF (Fig. 3(a)). The stress-strain curves basically overlap in repeated cycles, which proves that TCPF has good repeatability, and enables the actuator good cycle stability. However, due to the viscoelasticity of the fishing line, a little residual strain is observed when the stress returns to zero. Therefore, pre-stretch is applied to the TCPF, to suppress the viscoelasticity as well as to improve the thermal shrinkage displacement.

TCPF is driven by electric heating. As the voltage increases, the heat generated by silver-plated textile wire raises the temperature in the fishing line and accelerates the contraction of TCPF. As the voltage continues to increase, the silver-plated textile wire blew and the TCPF breaks. Therefore, the thermal contraction force of TCPF under different voltages was characterized to find the appropriate voltage. There is an exponential increase trend between voltage and heat shrinkage force. When the voltage is below 5 V, the increase of heat shrinkage force is not obvious (related to the heat dissipation coefficient of the TCPF). When the voltage exceeds 9 V, the heat shrinkage force increases significantly.

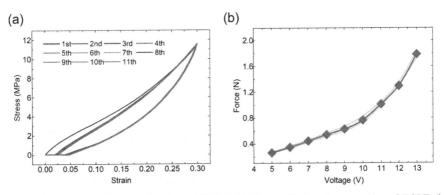

Fig. 3. Performance characterization of TCPF. (a) The cyclic tensile properties of TCPF. (b) Relationship between thermal contraction force of TCPF and the voltage.

To characterize the bistable actuation, a discrete motion between the two stable states is measured when the two TCPF artificial muscles are alternatively actuated. An electrical voltage of 11 V and a current of 0.12 A were applied on TCPF for actuation and powered off when the actuator was fully deployed to induce a consequently snap towards the other stable state. With the same actuation and control strategy on TCPF of the other side, the actuator snaps back, completing one actuation period. The red and green block on the actuator was identified by machine vision, and the bending angle of the actuator was obtained. The cycles of the actuation are recorded in Fig. 4(a).

During the binary snapping motion, the actuator self-stabilizes after a short period of damping as a result of structural compliance. Thus the peak and stable positions (+ and − for each side) are marked to characterize the damping time in Fig. 4(b). In Fig. 4(c), even after 9 cycles, the actuator is able to main its accuracy in deflection displacement. In an actuation period, five boundary positions are highlighted as the stable position for the discreet motion limits and equilibrium unstable position during the snapping, in Fig. 4(d).

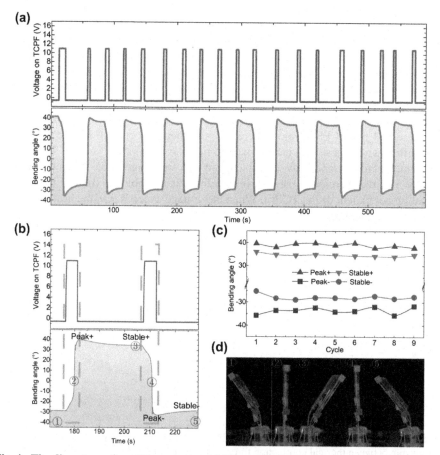

Fig. 4. The discrete motion of the actuator. (a) The cyclic of actuation voltage and the bending angle. (b) In one actuation cycle, 4 critical positions were denoted, two stable states (stable− and stable+) and two peak states (peal+ and peak−), to characterize the process when the actuator reaching the two binary positions. In addition, 5 boundary positions were recorded as well, corresponding to the onset of voltage on/off and the full deployment. (c) The collection of the 4 critical positions in the cycles binary snapping. (d) The recording of the critical positions. (Color figure online)

4 Conclusion

In summary, a fully compliant bistable actuator based on the minimum potential energy mechanism and the angle amplification mechanism was designed and actuated by TCPF. Due to the good repeatability of TCPF, we have achieved high repeatability when the actuator snapping between the two stable states. This study offers a new actuator candidate for soft robots when accurate actuation is required.

References

1. Trivedi, D., Rahn, C.D., Kier, W.M., Walker, I.D.: Soft robotics: biological inspiration, state of the art, and future research. Appl. Bionics Biomech. **5**, 99–117 (2008)
2. Gu, G.Y., Zhu, J., Zhu, L.M., Zhu, X.: A survey on dielectric elastomer actuators for soft robots. Bioinspir. Biomim. **12**, 011003 (2017)
3. Lee, C., et al.: Soft robot review. Int. J. Control Autom. Syst. **15**(1), 3–15 (2016). https://doi.org/10.1007/s12555-016-0462-3
4. Jani, J.M., Leary, M., Subic, A., Gibson, M.A.: A review of shape memory alloy research, applications and opportunities. Mater. Des. **1980–2015**(56), 1078–1113 (2014)
5. Cui, Y.S., et al.: Takeuchi, combinatorial search of thermoelastic shape-memory alloys with extremely small hysteresis width. Nat. Mater. **5**, 286–290 (2006)
6. Seelecke, S., Müller, I.: Shape memory alloy actuators in smart structures: Modeling and simulation. Appl. Mech. Rev. **57**, 23–46 (2004)
7. Zhao, P., Chen, H., Li, B., Tian, H., Lai, D., Gao, Y.: Stretchable electrochromic devices enabled via shape memory alloy composites (SMAC) for dynamic camouflage. Opt. Mater. **94**, 378–386 (2019)
8. Gu, G., Zou, J., Zhao, R., Zhao, X., Zhu, X.: Soft wall-climbing robots. Sci. Robot. **3**, eaat2874 (2018)
9. Li, T., et al.: Fast-moving soft electronic fish. Sci. Adv. **3**, e1602045 (2017)
10. Tang, C., Li, B., Fang, H., Li, Z., Chen, H.: A speedy, amphibian, robotic cube: resonance actuation by a dielectric elastomer. Sens. Actuators A **270**, 1–7 (2018)
11. Li, B., Cai, Y., Jiang, L., Liu, L., Zhao, Z., Chen, G.: A flexible morphing wing by soft wing skin actuation utilizing dielectric elastomer: experiments and electro-aerodynamic model. Smart Mater. Struct. **29**, 015031 (2020)
12. Tang, Y., et al.: Leveraging elastic instabilities for amplified performance: spine-inspired high-speed and high-force soft robots. Sci. Adv. **6**, eaaz6912 (2020)
13. Rothemund, P., et al.: A soft, bistable valve for autonomous control of soft actuators. Sci. Robot. **3**, eaar7986 (2018)
14. Bhandari, B., Lee, G.-Y., Ahn, S.-H.: A review on IPMC material as actuators and sensors: fabrications, characteristics and applications. Int. J. Precis. Eng. Manuf. **13**, 141–163 (2012)
15. Fang, B.-K., Ju, M.-S., Lin, C.-C.K.: A new approach to develop ionic polymer–metal composites (IPMC) actuator: fabrication and control for active catheter systems. Sens. Actuators A **137**, 321–329 (2007)
16. Ding, H., Yang, X., Zheng, N., Li, M., Lai, Y., Wu, H.: Tri-Co Robot: a Chinese robotic research initiative for enhanced robot interaction capabilities. Natl. Sci. Rev. **5**, 799–801 (2018)
17. Yang, Y., Tse, Y.A., Zhang, Y., Kan, Z., Wang, M.Y.: Paper Presented at the 2019 2nd IEEE International Conference on Soft Robotics (RoboSoft) (2019)
18. Wu, L., Chauhan, I., Tadesse, Y.: A novel soft actuator for the musculoskeletal system. Adv. Mater. Technol. **3**, 1700359 (2018)

19. Wu, L., de Andrade, M.J., Saharan, L.K., Rome, R.S., Baughman, R.H., Tadesse, Y.: Compact and low-cost humanoid hand powered by nylon artificial muscles. Bioinspir. Biomim. **12**, 026004 (2017)

20. Tang, X., Li, K., Liu, Y., Zhao, J.: Coiled conductive polymer fiber used in soft manipulator as sensor. IEEE Sens. J. **18**, 6123–6129 (2018)

21. Hiraoka, M., et al.: Power-efficient low-temperature woven coiled fibre actuator for wearable applications. Sci. Rep. **6**, 36358 (2016)

22. Tang, X., Li, K., Liu, Y., Zhou, D., Zhao, J.: A general soft robot module driven by twisted and coiled actuators. Smart Mater. Struct. **28**, 035019 (2019)

23. Zhao, P., Xu, B., Zhang, Y., Li, B., Chen, H.: Study on the twisted and coiled polymer actuator with strain self-sensing ability. ACS Appl. Mater. Interfaces **12**, 15716–15725 (2020)

Design and Performance Analysis of Artificial Muscle Driven by Vacuum with Large Contract Ratio and Large Load

Yu He[1,2], Lianli Zhu[2(✉)], Yiping Shen[1], and Songlai Wang[1]

[1] Hunan Province Key Laboratory of Health Maintenance of Mechanical Equipment, Hunan University of Science and Technology, Xiangtan 411201, Hunan, China
[2] Research Center of China Coast Guard, China Coast Guard Academy, Ningbo 315801, Zhejiang, China
zhulianli@126.com

Abstract. Artificial muscle is one of the most promising research orientations in the field of soft robots. Currently, the low contraction ratio and weak loading capacity of common artificial muscles are obstacles that shall be removed in case that artificial muscles are employed in many fields. In this paper, a large contraction-ratio-and-load vacuum-powered artificial muscle (LC-VAM) was proposed. The structure was constructed by a single-sided enclosed cavity with a skeleton steel ring inside, the power was provided by negative pressure contraction, and the control was realized by adjusting the pressure regulating valve to generate contraction and release. Besides, the impacts of such variable factors as the negative pressure value, steel ring diameter and contraction ratio on the performance of artificial muscles were explored. As per the principle of conservation of energy, a quasi-static analysis model of artificial muscles was established for the physical performance test and analysis experiments. The results show that the load capacity of artificial muscles is 312.1 N, the dead weight is only 81 g, and the maximum contraction ratio can reach up to 86% when the steel ring diameter is 65 mm. The analysis results will provide reference for the design of artificial muscles with large contraction ratio.

Keywords: Large contraction ratio · Large load · Vacuum-powered · Artificial muscle

1 Introduction

In nature, mammals, reptiles, birds, insects, fish and other creatures all rely on muscles to complete a series of movements, such as climbing, running, jumping, flying and swimming. Currently, most of the "muscles" in the field of robot technology are characterized by rigid structures, which is dramatically different from biological muscles[1]. Due to the fact that biological muscles are considered to be one of the best actuators available[2],

---

Y. He and L. Zhu—Contributed equally to this work.

© Springer Nature Switzerland AG 2021
X.-J. Liu et al. (Eds.): ICIRA 2021, LNAI 13013, pp. 197–207, 2021.
https://doi.org/10.1007/978-3-030-89095-7_20

many scholars dedicate themselves to the research and development of artificial muscles that possess functions comparable to biological muscles.

With the advancement of science and technology, various intelligent materials have been employed to manufacture artificial muscles, such as shape memory alloy (SMA), shape memory polymer (SMP), electroactive polymer (EAP), dielectric elastomer (DE) and common fluid artificial muscles. The internal lattice structure of SMA/SMP will change during the heating process, and as a result, their shapes will be changed. It has a high energy density (the energy density of nitinol is as high as 50 W/g) and load stress (200 MPa) [3]. Yahara S [4] utilizes SMP to change the fiber angle, and designs an artificial muscle with variable contraction ratio. However, SMA has limited strain (<8%) [5] and a low response frequency, mainly due to the long and strongly hysteresis of the heat exchange process [6, 7] and the sharp changes around the phase change temperature (Tg), which are difficult to control [8]. EAP can produce various motion forms, such as contraction, bending, tightening or expansion under the action of external electric field. DE is a typical EAP material. SRI International firstly publishes the research results of dielectric elastomer actuator (DEA) in 2000 [9], which possesses the potential to prepare artificial muscles owing to its high strain and high stress. In recent years, flying soft robots and deep-sea roaming robots driven by DE artificial muscles have been published in *Nature* [10, 11]. However, DEA often requires a higher voltage (10–100V/um) and an obvious hysteresis [12].

There are two categories of fluid-driven artificial muscles, namely pneumatic and hydraulic ones, which can realize deformation by the force of fluid pressure in the cavity on the elastic wall [13, 14] The earliest pneumatic artificial muscle can be traced back to the 1960s, and McKibben pneumatic muscle is designed by American doctors [15] up to now, it is also the most common pneumatic artificial muscles. Lei Qin [16] designs a multi-purpose crawling robot using artificial muscles and electrostatic actuators. FESTO AG & Co. KG designs a continuum mechanical arm with pneumatic artificial muscles. Meanwhile, pneumatic artificial muscles are also widely employed in rescue, pipeline and collection robots [17–19], flexible gripping devices [20], and the field of medical rehabilitation [21]. At present, most pneumatic artificial muscles are driven by positive pressure. The pressure in the working process may be too high (4 Mpa), which induces a danger of explosion leakage, the insufficiently quick and stable response, the obvious hysteresis and other defects. In response to these situations, Dian Yang [22] designs a kind of hollow structure artificial muscles driven by negative pressure with silicone material, which can produce 45% axial contraction and a load capacity up to 61 N. Shuguang Li [23] designs a fluid-driven origami artificial muscle, which can achieve multi-axis motion, including contraction, bending and torsion, with the contraction ratio up to 50% and stress of 285 kPa. Jin-Gyu Lee [5] proposes a vacuum pneumatic artificial muscle linear driver based on the origami technology, which can produce 90% contraction ratio in the active length of the driver and a load capacity of 400 N. Zhongdong Jiao [24] proposes a vacuum dynamic pneumatic artificial muscle, which can achieve a contraction ratio up to 87.5% and a load capacity of 90 N, and can also realize twisting action.

Compared with other artificial muscles, artificial muscles driven by negative pressure have the advantages of contraction ratio, high safety and large load capacity. In this paper, a large contraction-ratio-and-load vacuum-powered artificial muscle (LC-VAM) has been proposed, with the maximum contraction ratio being 86%, the lifting force reaching 312.1 N, and the dead weight being only 81 g, which has a large output ratio. By exploring the impacts of negative pressure value, steel ring diameter and contraction ratio on the load capacity, the quasi-static analysis model of artificial muscles has been established, the prototype has been manufactured and subject to the performance test and analysis, which would provide a reference for future work.

2 Structure and Preparation of Artificial Muscles

The artificial muscle has a simple structure and is easy to be manufactured. A structural schematic diagram is plotted by a three-dimensional modeling software, as shown in Fig. 1. The artificial muscle is composed of a protective cloth with an outer layer of rubbers, an inner skeleton steel ring and two 3D-printing sealing blocks. Two sealing grooves are arranged on the circumference of the sealing blocks, in which the center of the sealing block A is provided with a through hole to connect an air pipe that is externally connected with a vacuum pump, and the sealing block B is provided with a U-shaped hole, which is passed by a pulling rope and is connected with the load. There is a small elastic deformation coefficient and high tensile strength for the protective cloth with an outer layer of rubbers, which can provide greater safety in the process of load lifting and sealing function at the same time. Uniformly spaced several supporting reinforcing steel rings form an internal skeleton to prevent radial contraction during the contraction of the negative pressure. The wire diameter and spacing of steel rings are the main parameters affecting the maximum contraction ratio. The 3D-printing sealing blocks have a sealing function, and the sealing blocks (A and B) are connected with a vacuum pump and a load, respectively.

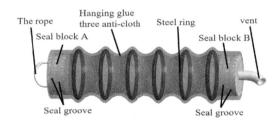

Fig. 1. Schematic diagram of 3D model of artificial muscle.

In the manufacturing process (Fig. 2), a rectangular cloth (Fig. 2a) is cut first, and then rolled into a drum by closing the cavity unilaterally for the heat sealing of the edge on the heat-sealing machine to form a cylindrical sleeve (Fig. 2b, c). The value of 4–5 mm is most suitable for the heat sealing bandwidth. The area of heat sealing bandwidth would destroy the flexibility of the cloth and harden the local material, which is not conducive to contract. The diameter of the formed sleeve is slightly smaller than that of the steel ring. The steel rings are plugged into the sleeve with the small elastic deformation property of the cloth, and they are evenly spaced free from connection (Fig. 2d–f). Both ends of the artificial muscle are respectively stuffed into 3D-printing sealing blocks A and B, with one end connected to a load through thread and the other end externally connected to a negative pressure source, which is sealed and connected with the outer cloth by wire sealing and binding (Fig. 2h). Due to the fact that negative-pressure drive reduces the requirement of air tightness, the effectiveness of this sealing method has been confirmed in later experiments (the maximum negative pressure value can reach 93 kPa).

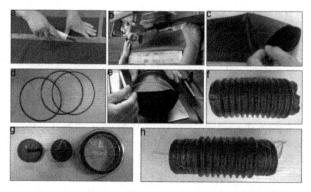

Fig. 2. Artificial muscle manufacturing process. (a) Cutting cloth; (b) Thermosetting cloth; (c) Making into a cylindrical sleeve; (d) The steel ring; (e) Built-in steel rings; (f) Making an external cavity; (g) Sealing block A and B, PE line; (h) Artificial muscle samples.

LC-VAM with steel ring diameters of 35, 45, 55 and 65 mm are manufactured respectively. There are 9 reinforced steel rings in the center. The initial distance between each two adjacent steel rings is 12 mm. The wire diameter of the selected steel ring is 1.3 mm, the thickness of the protective cloth with an outer layer of rubbers is 0.3 mm, and the overall length of the artificial muscle is about 110 mm. Besides, the weight of LC-VAM with a steel ring diameter of 65 mm is only 81 g.

3   Theoretical Modeling

The lifting performance of LC-VAM under different parameters is analyzed, and the analysis model is established, with the following assumptions proposed: (1) Due to the fact that there is a relative small elastic coefficient and large flexibility of the protective cloth with an outer layer of rubbers that forms the outer cavity, it can be assumed that the cloth has zero bending stiffness and non-expansibility; (2) In the initial state, the cloth shape between the two adjacent steel rings is a small arc that is concave inward, whose radian can be neglected on account of the small value, and therefore it can be assumed that there is a cylinder between the two adjacent steel rings in the initial state; (3) The elastic potential energy is not stored during the contracting process of the cloth.

Based on the above three assumptions and the principle of conservation of energy, it can be deduced that the external input work and the internal output work are equal:

$$-Fdl = PdV \tag{1}$$

where F represents the lifting force, dL represents a small displacement, P represents the negative pressure value inside LC-VAM, and dV represents a small change in volume.

The center angle θ of the long half axis of the elliptical arc is introduced (Fig. 3). When the LC-VAM contracts from the initial state in Fig. 3 (a) to the intermediate state in Fig. 3 (c), the center angle θ increases from 0 to $\pi/2$. With the further increase of the contraction ratio to the maximum contraction ratio (Fig. 3 (d)), the center angle θ would gradually decrease from $\pi/2$ to 0. With the increase of contraction ratio, the arc curve would change from elliptical arc to circular arc (the intermediate state), and then from circular arc to elliptical arc, where a transformation would occur between long and short axes, and the function is piecewise function.

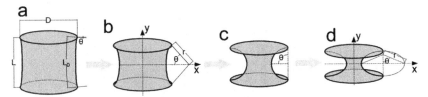

Fig. 3. Schematic diagram of the contracting process. (a) the initial state ($\theta \approx 0$); (b) the state of a small contraction ratio ($\theta \in (0, \pi/2)$); (c) the intermediate state ($\theta = \pi/2$); (d) the state of large contraction ratio ($\theta \in (0, \pi/2)$).

In the process of measurement, the central angle cannot be displayed intuitively, and it is difficult to judge the change of angle θ. The contraction ratio η is introduced here:

$$\eta = \frac{L_0 - L}{L_0} = 1 - \frac{\sin \theta}{\theta} \tag{2}$$

L_0 represents the initial length between two adjacent steel rings of LC-VAM, and L represents the real-time length between two adjacent steel rings.

As per the geometric relationship in Fig. 3(b) and Fig. 3(d), it can be obtained:

$$L_0 = 2\theta r \tag{3}$$

$$L = \begin{array}{ll} L_0 \sin \theta/\theta & \eta < 36.3\% \\ L_0(1 - \cos\theta)/\theta & \eta \geq 36.3\% \end{array} \tag{4}$$

$$b = \begin{array}{ll} L_0(1 - \cos\theta)/2\theta & \eta < 36.3\% \\ L_0 \sin \theta/\theta & \eta \geq 36.3\% \end{array} \tag{5}$$

The lifting force can be calculated as:

$$F(\theta) = -2P(\frac{\pi D^2}{8} + \frac{\pi b^2}{3} - \frac{\pi^2 bD}{8} + \frac{\frac{2}{3}\pi L b \dot{b} - \frac{\pi}{8} D L \dot{b}}{\dot{L}}) \tag{6}$$

where $\dot{L}$ represents the first derivative of the real-time spacing $L(\theta)$ to θ, while $\dot{b}$ represents the first derivative of the short half-axis $b(\theta)$ to θ.

4 Performance Testing and Result Analysis

In the experiment, the contraction and release of artificial muscles are realized by adjusting the pressure regulating valve, and the test platform is established as shown in Fig. 4. It is composed of a vacuum pump with a maximum negative pressure of 0.98 bar, a dynamometer with a measuring range of 500 N and an accuracy of 0.1%, a vise, a bracket, a switch, an air pipe and an artificial muscle prototype. The threading-sealing end of artificial muscle is connected to the tension meter, and the other end is fixed on the vise. Various performances of LC-VAM would be tested, including the impacts of such variable factors as different negative pressures, diameters and contraction ratios on lifting force performance.

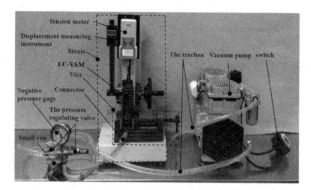

Fig. 4. Artificial muscle physical test platform.

The maximum lifting force test of LC-VAM under different negative pressures with steel ring diameters of 35 mm, 45 mm, 55 mm and 65 mm would be carried out, with the results shown in Fig. 5, which indicates that the maximum lifting force of artificial muscle is proportional to the negative pressure value; Under the same negative pressure, with the decrease of the distance between adjacent steel rings (an increase in the contraction ratio), the maximum lifting force would gradually decrease. Under the condition that the distance between the steel rings is 10 mm and the negative pressure value is 0.9 kPa, the maximum lifting force of the contraction driver with a diameter of 65 mm is 312.1 N.

The impact of the steel ring diameter of artificial muscles on the lifting force performance is explored, with the results shown in Figs. 6a–d. The points in the figure represent the actual measurement results, while the dotted lines represent the theoretical calculation values. The experimental results show that the larger the diameter of the steel ring, the greater the lifting force, which presents a quadratic function increasing relationship. By comparison, it can be found that the error between the experimental measurement results and the theoretical analysis values is very small, and the error is only 5.5% when the negative pressure is 90 kPa and the real-time spacing is 2 mm. When the negative pressure value is relatively small, the error is relatively large. When the diameter of the steel ring is 65 mm and the negative pressure is 30 kPa, the maximum error is about 25%, which may be caused by that the negative pressure value is too small, thus inducing that the LC-VAM lifting force becomes small and the real-time spacing is

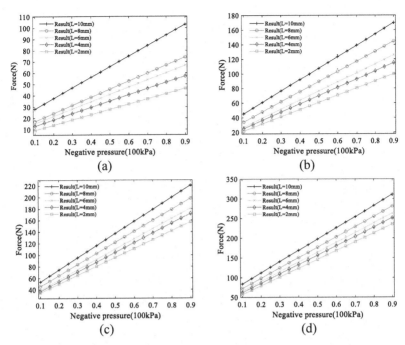

Fig. 5. Maximum lifting force under different negative pressures. (a)–(d) represent the functional relationship between the negative pressure value and the vertical lifting force at different intervals with steel ring diameters of 35 mm, 45 mm, 55 mm and 65 mm.

slightly larger than the set spacing (2, 4, 6 and 8 mm). For that reason, there would be a large measurement result under low negative pressure. Here, the functional relationship curve shown in Fig. 6e is plotted with the contraction ratio as abscissa and the lifting force as ordinate. The actual measurement value in the figure is consistent with the theoretical value curve, and the black vertical straight line represents the segmented line ($\eta = 36.3\%$). With the increase of the contraction ratio, the lifting force of the artificial muscle would gradually decrease, with the decreasing amplitude getting smaller.

The performance of LC-VAM has been tested through the above experiments, showing high load capacity and large contraction ratio. In an attempt to show the performance of artificial muscle more intuitively, the physical lift test would be carried out. The experimental platform as shown in Fig. 7 is set up. As shown in Fig. 7(a), the vacuum pump is not started, the artificial muscle is naturally vertical with a diameter of 65 mm, the upper part is fixed with a vise, and the lower part is connected with a bucket of mineral water with a capacity of 17 L and a dead weight of about 17 kg. When the vacuum pump is started, the water in the bucket is lifted quickly (<2s), which shows not only a faster response speed, but also the performance of large load and large contraction ratio (Fig. 7b).

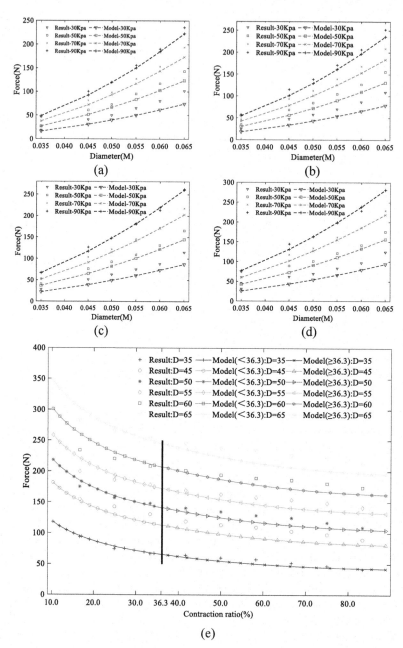

Fig. 6. Maximum tensile force of LC-VAM actuator under different diameters and different contraction ratios (a)–(d) represent the lifting forces at the real-time spacing of 2, 4, 6, and 8 mm under the same negative pressure and different diameters, respectively; (e) The lifting force of the artificial muscle at different contraction ratios

          (a)   (b)

Fig. 7. Physical lifting test. (a) Before the drive of negative pressure; (b) After the drive of negative pressure.

In an attempt to better evaluate the contraction ratio and load level of the proposed artificial muscle, the literature on the artificial muscles driven by negative pressure has been investigated, with the results shown in Table 1. By comparison, it can be seen that the proposed artificial muscles have the performance of large contraction ratio and large load at the same time, this means that LC-VAM will play an important role in the field of future robotics, such as soft robots, wearable robots, and medical rehabilitation. Due to its advantages of light weight, large shrinkage rate, high safety and large load, it can also be applied in muscle rehabilitation resistance training device, exoskeleton power system, flexible grip device and low-cost robot through simple structural design.

Table 1. Performance parameters of artificial muscles driven by negative pressure

No	Name of artificial muscle	Dimension (mm)	Weight (g)	Load Force (N/kPa)	Contraction ratio
1	VAMPs[22]	34*28*46.5	-	61N/65 kPa	45%
2	FOAMs[23]	45.5*15.5*130	43	201N/285 kPa	50%
3	OV-PAM[5]	150*150*96	160	400N/41 kPa	90%
4	V-SPTA[24]	30*40*20	19	90N/56 kPa	88%
5	LC-VAM	∅65*110	81	312N/94 kPa	86%

5 Conclusions

In this paper, the design and manufacture of the cavity are completed by the construction method of a single-sided enclosed cavity with a skeleton steel ring inside, and an artificial muscle with large contraction ratio and large load is prepared by combining with the 3D-printing sealing blocks. A quasi-static analysis model of artificial muscle is established for the physical performance test and analysis experiments via exploring the impact of such variable factors as the negative pressure value, steel ring diameter and contraction ratio on the performance of artificial muscles. The results show that the load capacity of LC-VAM is 312.1 N, the weight of the artificial muscle is 81 g, and the maximum contraction ratio is as high as 86%, when the diameter of steel ring is 65 mm. The lifting force would increase with the increase of negative pressure value, which is a quadratic function increasing relationship with the diameter of the steel ring, and is inversely proportional to the contraction ratio.

In the future, an investigation would be conducted on the impact of LC-VAM cloth on its performance, namely the impacts of the thickness, tensile coefficient and strength of the material on the overall performance of the actuator, which will conduce to a further improvement in the actuator's lifting performance. Besides, the application of artificial muscles in flexible gripping operations, rapid response control and strategy development will also be taken into account.

Acknowledgment. This work of the paper was partially supported by The National Key Research and Development Program of China (grant number 2017YFC0821206), the Research Plan of Ministry of State Security of China (grant number 2017JSYJC09), the Natural Science Foundation of Ningbo (grant number 2018A610072).

References

1. Ricotti, L., et al.: Biohybrid actuators for robotics: a review of devices actuated by living cells. Sci. Robot. **2**(12), eaaq0495 (2017)
2. Gonzalez, M.A., Walter, W.W.: An investigation of electrochemomechanical actuation of conductive polyacrylonitrile (pan) nanofiber composites. Electroact. Polym. Actuators Devices **9056**(4), 1–11 (2014)
3. Rodrigue, H., Wang, W., Han, M.W., Kim, T., Ahn, S.H.: An overview of shape memory alloy-coupled actuators and robots. Soft Robot. **4**(1), 3–15 (2017)
4. Yahara, S., Wakimoto, S., Kanda, T., Matsushita, K.: Mckibben artificial muscle realizing variable contraction characteristics using helical shape-memory polymer fibers. Sens. Actuators A **295**, 637–642 (2019)
5. Lee, J.G., Rodrigue, H.: Origami-based vacuum pneumatic artificial muscles with large contraction ratios. Soft Rob. **6**(1), 109–117 (2019)
6. Simone, F., Rizzello, G., Seelecke, S.: Metal muscles and nerves - a self-sensing sma-actuated hand concept. Smart Mater. Struct. **26**(9), 095007 (2017)
7. Mertmann, M., Vergani, G.: Design and application of shape memory actuators. Eur. Phys. J. Spec. Top. **158**(1), 221–230 (2008)
8. Yang, Y., Li, Y., Chen, Y.: Principles and methods for stiffness modulation in soft robot design and development. Bio-Des. Manuf. **1**(1), 14–25 (2018). https://doi.org/10.1007/s42242-018-0001-6
9. Pelrine, R., Kornbluh, R., Pei, Q., Joseph, J.: High-speed electrically actuated elastomers with strain greater than 100%. Science **287**(5454), 836–839 (2000)
10. Chen, Y., et al.: Controlled flight of a microrobot powered by soft artificial muscles. Nature **575**(7782), 324 (2019)
11. Li, G., et al.: Self-powered soft robot in the mariana trench. Nature **591**(7848), 66–71 (2021)
12. Anderson, I.A., Gisby, T.A., Mckay, T.G., O'Brien, B.M., Calius, E.P.: Multi-functional dielectric elastomer artificial muscles for soft and smart machines. J. Appl. Phys. **112**(4), 041101 (2012)

13. Ge, L., et al.: Design, modeling, and evaluation of fabric-based pneumatic actuators for soft wearable assistive gloves. Soft Robot. **7**(5), 583–596 (2020)
14. Han, K., Nam-Ho, K., Dongjun, S.: A novel soft pneumatic artificial muscle with high-contraction ratio. Soft Rob. **5**(5), 554–566 (2018)
15. Chou, C.P., Hannaford, B.: Measurement and modeling of mckibben pneumatic artificial muscles. IEEE Trans. Autom. Sci. Eng. **12**(1), 90–103 (1996)
16. Qin, L., Liang, X., Huang, H., Chui, C.K., Yeow, R.C., Zhu, J.: A versatile soft crawling robot with rapid locomotion. Soft Robot. **6**(4), 455–467 (2019)
17. Wang, X., Tian, M., Chen, J., Xiang, L., Yu, X.: A rigid and soft combined robot that is designed to be used in confined spaces. Robot Intell. Technol. Appl. **4**(447), 461–468 (2017)
18. Kurumaya, S., et al.: A modular soft robotic wrist for underwater manipulation. Soft Rob. **5**(4), 399–409 (2018)
19. Calderon, A.A., Ugalde, J.C., Zagal, J.C., Perez-Arancibia, N.O.: Design, fabrication and control of a multi-material-multi-actuator soft robot inspired by burrowing worms. In: 2016 IEEE International Conference on Robotics and Biomimetics, Qing Dao, China, pp. 31–38 (2016)
20. Deimel, R., Brock, O.: A novel type of compliant and underactuated robotic hand for dexterous grasping. Int. J. Robot. Res. **35**(1–3), 161–185 (2015)
21. Park, Y., Chen, B., Majidi, C., Wood, R.J., Nagpal, R., Goldfield, E.: Active modular elastomer sleeve for soft wearable assistance robots. In: 2012 IEEE/RSJ International Conference on Intelligent Robots & Systems, Algarve, Portugal, pp. 1595–1602 (2012)
22. Yang, D., et al.: Buckling pneumatic linear actuators inspired by muscle. Adv. Mater. Technol. **1**(3), 1600055 (2016)
23. Li, S., Vogt, D.M., Rus, D., Wood, R.J.: Fluid-driven origami-inspired artificial muscles. Proc. Natl. Acad. Sci. USA **114**(50), 13132–13137 (2017)
24. Jiao, Z., Ji, C., Zou, J., Yang, H., Pan, M.: Vacuum-powered soft pneumatic twisting actuators to empower new capabilities for soft robots. Adv. Mater. Technol. **4**(1), 1800429 (2019)

Parameter Adaptive Multi-robot Formation Based on Fuzzy Theory

Fangfang Zhang⑩, Wenli Zhang⑩, Bo Chen⑩, Haijing Wang⑩,
and Yanhong Liu$^{(\boxtimes)}$⑩

Zhengzhou University, Zhengzhou 450001, China
{zhangfangfang,liuyh}@zzu.edu.cn

Abstract. To solve the problem of complex parameter adjustment and low formation efficiency in traditional leader-follower method, the formation control law is improved, and a parameter adaptive multi-robot formation method based on fuzzy theory is proposed in this paper. Firstly, the kinematics model of the robot is established by introducing the virtual leader, the formation problem of multi-robots is transformed into the tracking control problem between robots. Then the tracking control law is designed, and it is theoretically proved that the designed control law can make the robot complete formation. Moreover, Using fuzzy control theory, a fuzzy controller is designed according to the pose errors between robots, and the parameters in the control law are burred so that the parameters can be adjusted adaptively. Finally, simulations are provided to verify the efficacy and superiority of the method.

Keywords: Tracking control · Parameter adaptation · Fuzzy control · Multi-robot formation

1 Introduction

With the advancement of society and the development of science and technology, the application of robots have been increasingly employed in research and actual environment, such as disaster relief [1], cargo handling [2], area search [3], etc. The development of robots is divided into single-robot systems and multi-robot systems according to the application scenarios and number of robots. Compared to the single robot, the multi-robot system [4] has the advantages in terms of parallelism, work efficiency, and robustness. And the research of multi-robot formation [5] is an important direction in the multi-robot systems.

At present, the leader-forllower method [6] is a widely used method in the research of multi-robot formation, but the leader-follower method mainly relies on the leader, many researchers improved the traditional leader-follower method or proposed some new research methods for multi-robot formation. In [7], the

Supported by the National Natural Science Foundation of China (61603345, 61703372, 61773351), Outstanding Foreign Scientist Support Project in Henan Province (GZS2019008), Young Talent Lift Project in Henan Province (2020hytp006).

© Springer Nature Switzerland AG 2021
X.-J. Liu et al. (Eds.): ICIRA 2021, LNAI 13013, pp. 208–218, 2021.
https://doi.org/10.1007/978-3-030-89095-7_21

multi-robot formation problem was transformed into a path tracking problem by introducing a virtual leader, and a finite-time consistent algorithm with input constraints using graph theory was constructed. In [8], a leader-follower formation control law was designed by using backstepping method and consistency theory. In [9] a measurement sensor was added to the follower, so that the leader does not need to publish its own speed information, and the follower can track the leader to complete the formation. In [10] a new pose controller was constructed in the traditional leader-follower method for multi-robot formation research. The iterative learning was introduced into the leader-follower method, and a multi-robot formation algorithm was proposed in [11], this method can be applied to any initial position. While many new methods or new formation control laws have been designed based on the leader-follow method, one common problem in most studies is the parameter adjustment of the controller. In [12] a measurement sensor was added to the follower, so that the leader does not need to publish its own speed information, and the follower can track the leader to complete the formation.

To solve the complex problem of parameter adjustment and improve the formation efficiency, fuzzy theory was introduced in this paper. Based on the above research, this paper considered the improvement of the control law to improve the efficiency of the formation, and the fuzzy theory [13] is used to fuzzify the adjustment parameters, so that the parameters can be adjusted adaptively, the robot can complete formations with any shape in any initial position.

The sections of this article are arranged as follows. Section 2 introduces the formation structure model of the robot; Sect. 3 improves the control law; Sect. 4 designs a fuzzy tracking controller; Sect. 5 conducts simulation experiments and analyzes the results; Sect. 6 summarizes the article.

2   Introduction to the Formation Model of Robots

The robot used in this paper is a three-wheel differential ground mobile robot. The kinematics model function of the robot is shown as Eq. 1, which corresponds to the virtual leader in Fig. 1:

$$
\begin{cases}
\dot{x}_i = v_i \cos\theta_i \\
\dot{y}_i = v_i \sin\theta_i \\
\dot{\theta}_i = \omega_i
\end{cases}
\tag{1}
$$

where (x_i, y_i) is the position coordinate of robot; θ_i represents the direction angle of the robot; v_i and ω_i represent the linear velocity and angular velocity of the robot respectively.

The multi-robot formation problem is transformed into the tracking control problem between robots by introducing the virtual leader in this paper. Each follower robot corresponds to a virtual leader. The follower in the formation only need to track the motion trajectory of their own virtual leader. The formation control model is shown in Fig. 1.

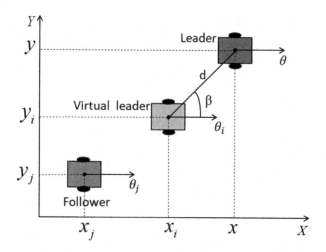

Fig. 1. Robot formation model.

In Fig. 1, the pose of the leader is $P = (x, y, \theta)$, the pose of the virtual leader is $P_i = (x_i, y_i, \theta_i)$, and the pose of the follower is $P_j = (x_j, y_j, \theta_j)$. In which, θ, θ_i, θ_j represent the heading angle of the robot, respectively. In order to ensure that the robots move in the same direction during the formation, the heading angle of the virtual navigator θ_i is the same as the heading angle of the navigator θ; β represents the position angle between the virtual leader and the leader, which is set according to the formation; d is the formation length. The actual pose of the following robot can be obtained from the kinematics equation of the robot. The pose equation of the virtual navigator can be obtained from Fig. 1:

$$\begin{cases} x_i = x - d\cos(\theta + \beta) \\ y_i = y - d\sin(\theta + \beta) \\ \theta_i = \theta \end{cases} \tag{2}$$

The world coordinate system where the robot is located is transformed to the on-board coordinate system through the coordinate transformation process of Eq. (3) to obtain the pose error of the follower.

$$P_e = \begin{bmatrix} x_e \\ y_e \\ \theta_e \end{bmatrix} = \begin{bmatrix} \cos\theta_j & \sin\theta_j & 0 \\ -\sin\theta_j & \cos\theta_j & 0 \\ 0 & 0 & 1 \end{bmatrix} \begin{bmatrix} x_i - x_j \\ y_i - y_j \\ \theta_i - \theta_j \end{bmatrix} \tag{3}$$

where x_e, y_e, θ_e represent the pose error between the virtual leader and the follower after the orthogonal transformation.

Equation (3) is differentiated and simplified to obtain Eq. (4).

$$\begin{cases} \dot{x}_e = y_e\omega_j - v_j + v_i\cos\theta_e \\ \dot{y}_e = -x_e\omega_j + v_i\sin\theta_i \\ \dot{\theta}_e = \omega_i - \omega_j \end{cases} \tag{4}$$

where v_i and v_j represent the linear velocity of the virtual leader and the follower respectively; ω_i and ω_j represent the angular velocity of the virtual leader and the follower respectively.

3   Design and Analysis of Control Law

At present, a classic control law proposed by Kanayama [14] of the University of California in the United States in 1990 is commonly used in robot tracking problems and path planning problems.

$$\begin{bmatrix} v \\ \omega \end{bmatrix} = \begin{bmatrix} v_r\cos\theta_e + k_1 x_e \\ \omega_r + v_r(k_2 y_e + k_3\sin\theta_e) \end{bmatrix} \tag{5}$$

It can be seen from the control law (5) that the adjustment of the linear velocity of robots is mainly based on the lateral distance error and the angle error, and the adjustment of the angular velocity is mainly based on the longitudinal distance error and the angle error. Experiments show that only the lateral distance error and the angle error are used to adjust the linear velocity when the longitudinal distance error is greater than the lateral distance error, although the formation can be completed, the formation efficiency is low. Therefore, the influence of the longitudinal distance error is considered in the linear speed adjustment in this article.

However, the addition of the longitudinal distance error not only consider the impact of its size on the linear velocity, but also consider the effect of its sign. As shown in Fig. 2, the positions of the virtual leader and the follower are shown in the figure. We assumed that the ideal positions corresponding to the follower 1 and follower 2 are the position of the virtual leader. The direction of the arrow indicates the direction of movement of the robot.

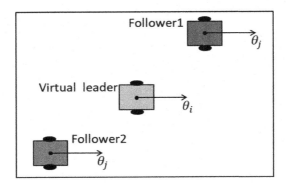

Fig. 2. The effect of the error on linear velocity.

By analyzing Fig. 2, the lateral distance error of the follower 1 in the figure shows that the follower is ahead of the expected position and needs to be decelerated; longitudinal distance error shows that there is still some distance from the desired position and needs to be accelerated. The lateral distance error at the follower 2 indicates that the follower is behind the expected position and needs to be accelerated; longitudinal distance error still shows that there is some distance from the desired position and needs to be accelerated. After analysis, the direction of the linear velocity of the robot is only related to the sign of the lateral distance error, but the size of the linear velocity is related to both the lateral distance error and the longitudinal distance error. Therefore, the following control law is considered in this article.

$$V = \begin{cases} v_j = v_i \cos \theta_e + k_x x_e + k_d sign(x_e)|y_e| \\ \omega_j = \omega_i + v_i(k_y y_e + k_\theta \sin \theta_e) \end{cases} \tag{6}$$

where the sign function is Eq. (7).

$$sign(x_e) = \begin{cases} -1, x_e < 0; \\ 1, x_e \geq 0. \end{cases} \tag{7}$$

where v_i and ω_i represent the ideal linear velocity and angular velocity of the robot, respectively; v_j and ω_j represent the actual linear velocity and angular velocity of the robot, respectively; x_e, y_e and θ_e represent the lateral distance error, longitudinal distance error and heading angle error of the robot, respectively.

In order to verify the stability of the improved control law (Eq. 6), Lyapunov stability theory is used in this paper.

Theorem 1. *Assuming $v_i > 0$, $k_x > 0$, $k_y > 0$, $k_\theta > 0$ and $k_d > 0$ in the control law (6), then $P_e = [x_e, y_e, \theta_e]^T = 0$ is a stable equilibrium point of the system. And the heading angle of robots is specified $(-\pi < \theta < \pi)$.*

Proof. Substituting Eq. (6) into Eq. (4), Eq. (8) can be obtained:

$$\begin{cases} \dot{x}_e = y_e \omega_j - v_j + v_i \cos \theta_e = y_e \omega_j - k_x x_e - sign(x_e)k_d|y_e| \\ \dot{y}_e = -x_e \omega_j + v_i \sin \theta_i \\ \dot{\theta}_e = \omega_i - \omega_j = -k_y v_i y_e - k_\theta v_i \sin \theta_e \end{cases} \tag{8}$$

The Lyapunov function is constructed:

$$V = \frac{1}{2}(x_e^2 + y_e^2) + \frac{1 - \cos \theta_e}{k_y} \tag{9}$$

In Eq. (9), it is obvious that $V \geq 0$, and $V = 0$ if and only if $x_e = 0$, $y_e = 0$ and $\theta_e = 0$, the derivative of Eq. (9) is obtained:

$$\dot{V} = x_e \dot{x}_e + y_e \dot{y}_e + \frac{\sin \theta_e}{k_y} \dot{\theta}_e \tag{10}$$

Substitute formula (8) into formula (10) to obtain formula (11):

$$\dot{V} = -k_x x_e^2 - sign x_e x_e k_d|y_e| - \frac{k_\theta}{k_y} v_i \sin \theta_e^2 \tag{11}$$

It can be seen from Eq. (11) that when $k_x > 0$, $k_y > 0$, $k_\theta > 0$ and v_i is non-negative, $\dot{V} < 0$, V is a Lyapunov function and $P_e = 0$ is a stable equilibrium point according to the Lyapunov stability criterion, and the theorem is proved. And the control law (6) can make the robot's pose error converge to zero according to the Eq. (3).

Thus, it can be shown that when the hypothesis holds, the control law of Eq. (6) can complete formation, but the value of the parameters in the control law (6) will affect the formation. To make the robot in the formation can find the most appropriate parameters and simplify the complexity of parameter adjustment. A fuzzy tracking controller is designed in this paper, so that some parameters can be adjusted adaptively according to different conditions.

4 Fuzzy Tracking Controller Design

The design principle of the fuzzy tracking controller is to fuzzy the parameters by using the pose error between the follower and the virtual leader. The schematic diagram of the fuzzy tracking controller is shown in Fig. 3.

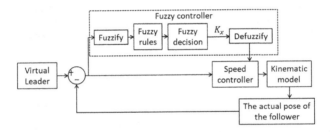

Fig. 3. Schematic diagram of fuzzy tracking controller.

To improve formation efficiency and reduce parameters overadjustment, this paper only fuzzify the parameter k_x that have great influence on formation. Because the angle change is more sensitive, the parameters of adjusting angular velocity is not blurred. And longitudinal distance error is bigger than lateral distance error when need to introduce k_d, the adjustment principle is the same as k_x, both of which are used to adjust the linear velocity. To prevent improper volatile and over adjustment, the parameter k_d is specified below (Eq. 12):

$$\begin{cases} k_d = 0, |y_e| < 2|x_e| \\ k_d > 1, |y_e| \geq 2|x_e| \end{cases} \tag{12}$$

The input of the fuzzy controller is the lateral distance error x_e, and the corresponding output is the value of the parameter k_x. According to the sensitivity and deviation, the simple triangle membership function f is used for the input and output.

$$f(x, a, b, c) = \begin{cases} 0, x \leq a \\ \frac{x-a}{b-a}, a \leq x \leq b \\ \frac{c-x}{c-b}, b \leq x \leq c \\ 0, x \geq c \end{cases} \tag{13}$$

where the parameters a and c determine the "foot" of the triangle, and the parameter b determines the "peak" of the triangle. The determination of the three parameters a, b and c is based on the corresponding domain of the input and output fuzzy subsets, as shown in Fig. 4. The defuzzification method selected the barycenter method (Eq. 14).

$$z_0 = \frac{\sum_{i=0}^{n} \mu_c(z_i) \cdot z_i}{\sum_{i=0}^{n} \mu_c(z_i)} \tag{14}$$

where z_0 is the exact value of the output of the fuzzy controller after the fuzzification; z_i is the value in the domain of fuzzy control quantity; $\mu_c(z_i)$ is the membership value of z_i.

By experimental analysis, the value entered in this paper is $[-30, 30]$, seven fuzzy subsets are taken, which are negative large (NB), negative medium (NM), negative small (NS), zero (ZO), positive small (PS), middle (PM) and positive large (PB) respectively; the value of output is $(0, 4]$, take four fuzzy subsets, which are zero (Z), small (S), medium (M) and large (B) respectively. And designs the k_x fuzzy rule as shown in Table 1.

Table 1. k_x fuzzy rule table.

x_e	NB	NM	NS	ZO	PS	PM	PB
k_x	B	M	S	Z	S	M	B

5　Experiments

In this paper, the robot is studied as a particle whose size can be ignored. The designed control law and fuzzy tracking controller are simulated and verified on the Matlab simulation platform. In the experiments, three robots are used to conduct formation simulation experiments. L represents the leader, F1; F11, F2 and F21 all represent the follower; VL1 and VL2 represent the virtual leader. The initial speed of the all robots is 0, and both the leader and the virtual leader in the formation move in a uniform straight line at a speed of 2 m/s. To prevent the sudden acceleration and deceleration of the follower, the maximum linear velocity of the followers is set at 6m/s.

5.1　Contrast Test of Control Law

In order to verify the superiority of the improved control law, a comparative experiment was conducted between the improved control law and the classical control law. At the initial time, one of the follower is the lateral distance error is larger than the longitudinal distance error; the other one is the vertical distance error is greater than 2 times the lateral distance error. The initial positions of L, F1, F11, F2, and F21 are (5,18), (1,15), (1,15), (2,26), and (2,26), respectively. In which, F1 and F2 are completed under the improved control law; F11 and F21 are completed under the original control law. The values of adjustment parameter are $k_x = 1$, $k_y = 0.9$, $k_\theta = 0.8$, $k_d = 3$, the formation length $d = 2$, the heading angle between the virtual leader and the leader is $\theta = \theta_i = 0$, and the position angle between the follower and the virtual leader is $\beta = \pi/3$. The trajectories of robot formation under the action of the two control laws are shown in Fig. 4, and the error curves of robot pose are shown in Fig. 5.

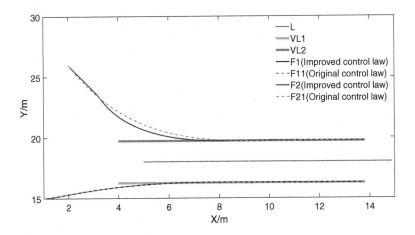

Fig. 4. Robot motion trajectory diagram.

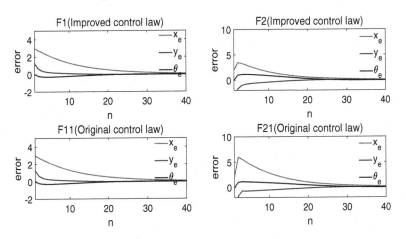

Fig. 5. Pose error curve of robot.

Figure 4 and Fig. 5 show that the improved control law of the follower 1 has little influence on the formation effect, but the improved control law of the follower 2 has higher efficiency and smaller overshoot.

The performance index of error evaluation was selected as follows: the average value of the pose error. The formation efficiency evaluation performance index is selected as: the number of iterations n when the formation is completed. The corresponding values of each evaluation index of the follower 2 under the action of the original control law and the improved control law are shown in Table 2.

Table 2. Evaluation index value.

	$\overline{x_e}/m$	$\overline{y_e}/m$	$\overline{\theta_e}/°$	n/s
Classical control law	0.4749	0.0858	0.1302	37
Improved control law	0.2836	0.0688	0.1075	26

The experimental results in Table 2 show that when the longitudinal distance error of robots in the multi-robot formation system is greater than 2 times the lateral distance error, the improved control law can reduce overshot and improve the formation speed.

5.2 Fuzzy Control Formation Experiment

In order to verify the superiority of fuzzy control over fixed parameters, this experiment moves F2 under the action of $k_x = 0.1$, $k_x = 4$ and fuzzification of k_x, respectively. Other experimental parameters of the formation are all the same as 5.1. The robot's motion trajectory is shown in Fig. 6.

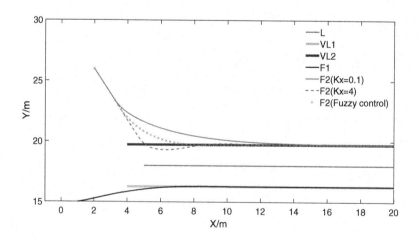

Fig. 6. Robot motion trajectory diagram.

Figure 6 shows that the value of parameters has a great influence on the formation effect. With smaller parameters, the formation speed is slower, while with larger parameters, the formation speed is faster but overshoot is larger, so the formation is easy to be unstable. By contrast, better formation effect can be obtained after the parameter is blurred. As the change of parameter k_x affects the change of robot linear velocity, the velocity change curves of fixed parameters and fuzzy control are shown in Fig. 7.

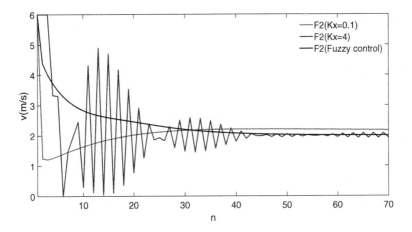

Fig. 7. Robot linear velocity curve.

As can be seen from the linear velocity change curve in Fig. 7, when the parameter is small, the linear velocity is adjusted slowly and it is difficult to converge to the ideal velocity; and large vibration is easy to occur when the parameter is too large, which also makes it difficult to converge to the ideal velocity. Compared with the fixed parameters, the linear velocity of the robot in the fuzzy control formation can be adjusted quickly and finally converges to the ideal velocity, and the curve is smooth without vibration. Therefore, parameter adaptation is very important in formation research of multi-robot system.

6   Conclusion

The formation problem of multi-robot is studied in this paper. In the classical control law, the influence of longitudinal distance error is added into the adjustment of linear velocity, and the improved control law can improve the convergence speed when the longitudinal distance error is greater than the transverse distance error. A fuzzy controller is designed to solve the complex parameter tuning problem, so that the parameters can change adaptively according to different conditions, the formation efficiency can be improved, the overshoot can be reduced, and the formation method can be simplified. Finally, the simulation results show the feasibility and superiority of the proposed algorithm.

References

1. Liu, Y., Nejat, G.: Multirobot cooperative learning for semiautonomous control in urban search and rescure applications. J. Field Robotics **33**(4), 512–536 (2016)
2. Alonso-Mora, J., Baker, S., Rus, D.: Multi-robot formation control and object transport in dynamic environments via constrained optimization. Int. J. Robot. Res. **36**(9), 1000–1021 (2017)
3. Baranzadeh, A., Savkin, A.V.: A distributed control algorithm for area search by a multi-robots team. Robotica **35**(6), 1452–1472 (2017)
4. Bohren, J., Rusu, R.B., Jones, E.G., et al.: Towards autonomous robotic butlers: lessons learned with the PR2. In: 2011 IEEE International Conference on Robotics and Automation, pp. 5568–5575. IEEE, Shanghai (2011)
5. Yongnan, J., Qing, L.: Research progress on formation control of multi-robot. J. Eng. Sci. **40**(8), 893–900 (2018)
6. Shuai, W., Lelai, Z., Yinbin, L., et al.: Research on formation navigation and following methods of multi-mobile robots. Unmanned Syst. Technol. **2**(5), 1–8 (2019)
7. Yujiao, S., Hongyong, Y., Meiyan, Y.: Research on finite time consistent control of multi-robot system based on leader-follower. Complex Syst. Complexity Sci. **17**(4), 66–72 (2020)
8. Xian, Z.: Research on Formation Control of Multi-mobile Robots Based on the Leader-Follower Method. Dalian Maritime University, Liaoning (2017)
9. Yuerui, Z.: Design and Implementation of Wheeled Robot Formation System in Unknown Environment. University of Electronic Science and Technology of China, Chendu (2020)
10. Min Y. X, Cao K. C, Sheng H.: Formation tracking control of multiple quadrotors based on backstepping. In: 34th Control Conference IEEE, pp. 4424–4430. IEEE, Hangzhou (2015)
11. Rui, H., Xuhui, B.: The robot at any initial position leads the following iterative learning formation. Comput. Eng. Appl. **56**(20), 226–231 (2020)
12. Chen, J., Li, J., Zhang, R., et al.: Distributed fuzzy consensus of uncertain topology structure multi-agent systems with nonidentical partially unknown control directions. Appl. Math. Comput. **362**, 1–16 (2019)
13. Jinkun, L., Author, T.: Advanced pid Control and MATLAB Simulation, 4th edn. Electronic Industry Press, Beijing (2016)
14. Kanayama Y, Kimura Y, Miyazaki F.: A stable tracking control method for an autonomous mobile robot. In: Proceeding of the 1990 IEEE International Conference on Robotics and Automation, pp. 384–389. IEEE, Cincinnati (1990)

Design and Experiment of Super Redundant Continuous Arm Driven by Pneumatic Muscle

Zhiwei Qiu, Jinfeng Zhao, Changqu Wu, Wenbiao Wang, Manrong Wang, and Guanjun Bao$^{(\boxtimes)}$

Zhejiang University of Technology, Hangzhou, China
gjbao@zjut.edu.cn

Abstract. Based on the traditional wire-driven continuous arm structure, a super redundant continuous arm is designed by using pneumatic artificial muscle drive instead of traditional wire drive. The continuous arm is composed of a splicing super redundant joint module in series, each module is driven by four pneumatic artificial muscles. Each pneumatic muscle is pre-lifted during installation, and the universal bending joint in the drive module supports and bends. Due to the pre-stretching of four pneumatic muscles, the single joint can achieve initial steady state in the initial state, so that the super redundant joint obtains an initial stiffness.

Keywords: Super redundant · Pneumatic muscle · Continuous arm

1 Introduction

In recent years, with the rapid development of bionic technology, continuous robots have attracted more and more attention. The continuous robot is a new type of bionic robot which is like an image nose, octopus whiskers and other soft organisms [1], without any discrete joints and rigid links [2]. Continuous robot has a strong structural flexibility and environmental adaptability, without the demand to equip with complex sensing systems. Continuous robot can be flexible to change their shape and adapt to a variety of narrow workspace and unstructured environment, it can execute grabbing, exploring and other actions in these environments [3, 4].

Structurally, continuous robots can be roughly divided into the following types: rigid continuous robot, flexible continuous robot and soft continuous robot. rigid continuum robot such as the Rope-driven robot with multi-rigid series joints designed by Simaan et al. [5, 6]. The robot has five degrees of freedom and consists of two curved joints. The end of the second section is equipped with a clamping device. The robot is composed of a central super-elastic NiTi alloy tube and a supporting disc which evenly distributed on the alloy tube. The small NiTi alloy tube is fixed around the supporting disc to realize the control of the robot. The end gripper is controlled by the alloy wire which is installed in the central super-elastic alloy tube. It can adapt to a variety of narrow, complex workspace, with high control accuracy. Flexible continuous robot is like the multi-flexible joint series pneumatic drive continuous arm designed by Hao Jiang [7, 8] of China University of Science and Technology. This continuous arm is similar to

© Springer Nature Switzerland AG 2021
X.-J. Liu et al. (Eds.): ICIRA 2021, LNAI 13013, pp. 219–231, 2021.
https://doi.org/10.1007/978-3-030-89095-7_22

a honeycomb structure, and each honeycomb can be controlled by independent inflation. After inflation, the honeycomb expands. And the robot moves by changing the air
pressure. The continuous arm responds rapidly and has high safety. However, with the
increase of air pressure, the increase of cavity volume leads to the non-linear change
of air pressure with time. It is difficult to achieve real-time and accurate control of the
continuous arm in the operation process. Software continuity robot, such as the octopus
arm designed by CECILIA [9, 10], The drive cable is uniformly distributed in the inner
cavity of the continuous arm along the arm axis, and the motion of the continuous arm
is controlled by pulling the cable drive. The control of the continuous arm is relatively
simple, and the driving force can be transmitted remotely to ensure that the rotational
inertia of the manipulator is small [11].

From the view of interaction with human beings, flexible continuous robot and
soft continuous robot can improve the safety performance of application because of its
structure of full flexible joint series or full flexible structure in the process of interaction
with human beings. Due to the flexibility of its own material, flexible continuous arms
and soft continuous arms have the following disadvantages: difficult attitude estimation
and unable to maintain their own attitude stability. Although rigid continuous robot has a
certain compliance type, but its own rigid materials in the contact process will inevitably
produce rigid collision. Its advantage is that it can achieve stable attitude estimation and
accurate motion control, with larger terminal load capacity.

In this paper, super redundant joints driven by pneumatic muscle (PAM) [14, 15]
combine the advantages of rigid arm and soft arm. The super-redundant continuous
arm is mainly composed of four parts: universal joint module, super-redundant joint
module, sensor module and the head-caudal skeleton module. The skeleton can reach a
certain angle of bending by changing the air pressure into the pneumatic muscle. With
the actuator based on pneumatic muscle drive, fast and accurate control can be carried
out to achieve bending control on six degrees of freedom. The continuous arm has good
structural strength and high load capacity at the end. Different from the ordinary rigid
structure, the continuous arm is installed by the combination of rigid skeleton and flexible
drive, which reduces the problem of rigid collision in the process of operation control.
At the same time, it can solve the problems of self-stability, motion control and attitude
acquisition in soft arm.

The structure of this paper is as follows. The second part introduces the structural
design of super redundant joint and the design of super redundant continuous arm. The
third part introduces the bending test, terminal load test and angle sensing experiment
of super-redundant continuous arm.

2 Structure Design of Super Redundant Continuous Arm

2.1 Design of Super-Redundant Joints

As shown in Fig. 1(a), it is a super redundant joint structure, which is composed of
skeleton structure, pneumatic muscle drive module, universal joint and joint locking
parts. Universal joint and skeleton structure are locked by joint locking parts. The hook
structure is installed on the joint locking parts and the skeleton. The pneumatic muscle-
driven joint is fixed in the four directions of the super redundant joints through the

hook(one) on the joint locking parts and the hook(two) on the universal joint. Each pneumatic muscle drive module has an inlet hole to provide input pressure.

Figure 1(c) is the geometry model of super redundant joints. The cylinder structure in four directions is pneumatic muscle drive module. $A_1A_2A_3A_4$ is fixed base and $B_1B_2B_3B_4$ is mobile platform. Two pneumatic muscles separated by 180° form a pair of directional control pneumatic muscles. For example, the A_1B_1 connecting rod and the A_3B_3 connecting rod are installed with a pair of directional control pneumatic muscles. The length of A_1B_1 will increase when the pneumatic muscle on the A_1B_1 side is stretched. When the length of A_1B_1 increases, the joint is affected by the middle universal joint and will rotate in the direction of A_3B_3, and the pneumatic muscle on the A_3B_3 and A_3B_3 sides will be shortened accordingly. By controlling two pairs of pneumatic muscles on the super redundant joint, the joint can be controlled to bend at any angle.

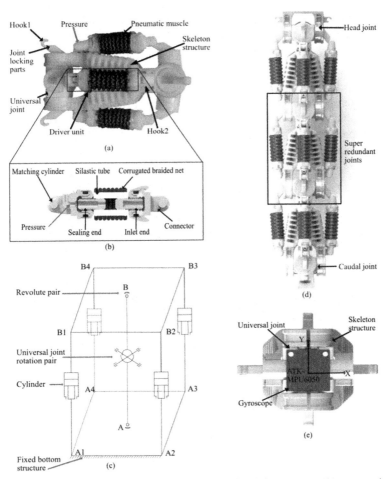

Fig. 1. The structure of continuous arm. (a) super redundant joint structure (b) pneumatic muscle drive module (c) geometry model of super redundant joints (d) continuous arm (e) installation position of the sensor.

The redundant actuation increases the stiffness and avoids kinematic singularities [16, 17]. This can help the arm obtain satisfactory dynamic performances in all directions [18].

As shown in Fig. 1(b), it is a pneumatic muscle drive module, which is mainly composed of corrugated braided net, silicone tube and the connection part of both ends. The connection part is divided into inlet end and sealing end. The inlet end is opened with a pressure input hole. The intake end and sealing end are plugged inside the silicone tube, and then connected with the connector by screw thread matching, which can ensure the air tightness of the silicone tube to a certain extent. The end of the connector is connected by a matching cylinder.

Particular attention should be paid to the fact that the pneumatic muscle drive module is installed with a pre-stretching process, which can be seen by comparing the density of the corrugated braided net in Fig. 1(a) and Fig. 1(b). In Fig. 1(b), the pneumatic muscle module is not pre-stretched, and the arrangement of corrugated braided net is very compact. While the pneumatic muscle in Fig. 1(a) is pre-stretched. The benefits of pre-stretching can provide an initial steady state for the continuous arm, which can also maintain its own stability under certain external forces. Then, this pre-stretching treatment can increase the torque of super-redundant joints when they rotate. When the pneumatic muscle at one end is inflated and stretched, the hook drives the universal joint to rotate to the pneumatic muscle at the other end. At the other end, due to the pre-stretching treatment of the pneumatic muscle, there is a recovery force in the pneumatic muscle after pre-stretching treatment, which will help to rotate and make the rotation process more compliant.

2.2 Structure Design of Continuous Arm

Figure 1(e) shows the installation position of the sensor. The sensor used in this paper is mpu6050 gyroscope, which is fixed by installing the gyroscope on the universal joint. When operating the continuous arm, the gyroscope can detect the angle changes of the *x-axis* and *y-axis* on the universal joint, and the angle information of each joint can be measured by the gyroscope installed on each super redundant joint.

Figuer 1(d) shows the overall image of the continuous arm. The continuous arm is composed of three super redundant joints and two head-caudal joints. The super redundant joints are connected through the universal joint and the joint locking parts. Two super redundant joints can be connected by four joint locking parts and one universal joint structure. Super redundant joint and head-caudal joint are also connected through universal joint and joint locking parts. The head-caudal joints of the continuous arm can be used to fix their own posture, mount the end load, and expand other equipment in the actual operation.

3 Kinematics Modeling of Super Redundant Joint

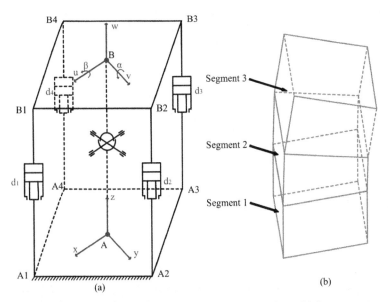

Fig. 2. Geometry and kinematics (a) single segment (b) multiple segments

3.1 Single Segment

The kinematics model of the super redundant continuous arm is similar to that of Kang et al in [18–21]. Referring to the modeling method of Kang et al, the kinematics model of the super redundant joint is shown in Fig. 2(a). Two Cartesian coordinate systems $B(u, v, w)$ and $A(x, y, z)$ are attached to the mobile platform and fixed base respectively. Origin B is the center of mass of the mobile platform, while origin A is the centroid of the fixed base. α and β are rotation angles around v and u respectively. The length of each pneumatic muscle is identified by the position vector d_i. d_i is then obtained by

$$d_i = p + b_i - a_i \tag{1}$$

where $p = \overline{AB} = \begin{bmatrix} 0 & 0 & h \end{bmatrix}^T$ is the displacement vector from A to B, $b_i = \overline{BB_i}$ is the position vector of B_i, $a_i = \overline{AA_i}$ is the position vector of A_i. All of these vectors are expressed in the fixed frame A.

Through two Euler angles α and β. The direction of the mobile platform can be determined:

$$^{A}R_B = \begin{pmatrix} \cos\alpha & \sin\alpha\sin\beta & \sin\alpha\cos\beta \\ 0 & \cos\beta & -\sin\beta \\ -\sin\alpha & \cos\alpha\sin\beta & \cos\alpha\cos\beta \end{pmatrix} \tag{2}$$

Thus,

$$b_i = {}^A R_B{}^B b_i \tag{3}$$

Where ${}^B b_i$ is the position vector of B_i expressed in frame B.
Substituting Eq. (3) into Eq. (1) yields:

$$d_i = p + {}^A R_B{}^B b_i - a_i \tag{4}$$

The length of pneumatic muscle can be calculated by dot product of d_i:

$$L_i = (p + {}^A R_B{}^B b_i - a_i)^T \bullet (p + {}^A R_B{}^B b_i - a_i) \tag{5}$$

where the length L_i is in a range, $L_i \in (L_0 - \Delta L_1, L_0 + \Delta L_2)$, L_0 is the initial length of the pneumatic muscle, ΔL_1 is the limit contraction of pneumatic muscle, ΔL_2 is the ultimate elongation of pneumatic muscle.

3.2 Multi-segments

In this paper, three segments are connected in series to form a super redundant continuous arm, as shown in Fig. 2(b).

A homogeneous transformation matrix ${}^{j-1} T_j (j = 1, 2, \dots n)$ can be defined to relate the coordinate systems of $j-1$ and j planes where n is the total number of the segments. The matrix contains both rotational and translational terms.

$$^{j-1} T_j = \begin{bmatrix} {}^{j-1} R_j & {}^{j-1} p_j \\ 0 & 1 \end{bmatrix} \tag{6}$$

$$^0 T_n = {}^0 T_1 {}^1 T_2 \cdots {}^{n-1} T_n \tag{7}$$

3.3 Motion Space Simulation

The D-H coordinate system is established based on the geometric model of super redundant joint, and the limit position of the joint in space is calculated by D-H method. The parameters of each joint and connecting rod are listed:

In Table 1, θ is the angle between the two normal lines on the joint shaft; α is the deflection angle of the bar i; d_i is the normal distance between joints; a_i is the length of the bar.

Table 1. D-H parameter table.

Number	Joint variable		
	αi (rad)	d_i (mm)	a_i (mm)
1	$\pi/2$	0	0
2	$\pi/2$	0	0
3	$\pi/2$	0	0
4	$\pi/2$	0	0
5	$\pi/2$	0	0
6	$\pi/2$	0	0

According to the D-H transformation matrix:

$$^{i-1}A_i = R_{z,\theta} T_{z,d} T_{x,a} R_{x,\alpha}$$

$$= \begin{bmatrix} \cos\theta_i & -\sin\theta_i & 0 & 0 \\ \sin\theta_i & \cos\theta_i & 0 & 0 \\ 0 & 0 & 1 & 0 \\ 0 & 0 & 0 & 1 \end{bmatrix} \begin{bmatrix} 1 & 0 & 0 & 0 \\ 0 & 1 & 0 & 0 \\ 0 & 0 & 1 & d_i \\ 0 & 0 & 0 & 1 \end{bmatrix}$$

$$\begin{bmatrix} 1 & 0 & 0 & a_i \\ 0 & 1 & 0 & 0 \\ 0 & 0 & 1 & 0 \\ 0 & 0 & 0 & 1 \end{bmatrix} \begin{bmatrix} 1 & 0 & 0 & 0 \\ 0 & \cos\alpha_i & -\sin\alpha_i & 0 \\ 0 & \sin\alpha_i & \cos\alpha_i & 0 \\ 0 & 0 & 0 & 1 \end{bmatrix} \qquad (8)$$

$$= \begin{bmatrix} \cos\theta_i & -\cos\alpha_i\sin\theta_i & \sin\alpha_i\sin\theta_i & a_i\cos\theta_i \\ \sin\theta_i & \cos\alpha_i\cos\theta_i & -\sin\alpha_i\cos\theta_i & a_i\sin\theta_i \\ 0 & \sin\alpha_i & \cos\alpha_i & d_i \\ 0 & 0 & 0 & 1 \end{bmatrix}$$

where: i for the calculation of the connecting rod number, R for the rotation matrix, T for the translation matrix.

Finally, through the simulation software, the bending curve and the point cloud of the end position of the continuous arm in all directions are drawn, as shown in Fig. 3(a) and (b).

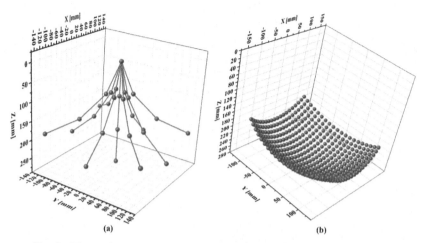

(a)   (b)

Fig. 3. Kinematic modeling figure (a) bending curve (b) motion point cloud.

4   Experimental Verification

4.1   Bending and Loading Experiments

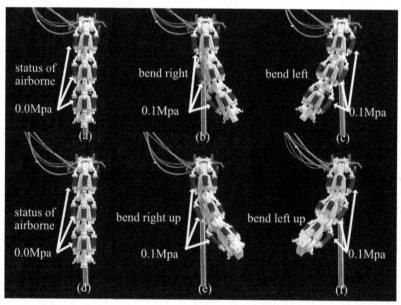

Fig. 4. Bending test experiment (a) and (d) original status (b) bend right (c) bend left (e) bend right up (f) bend left up.

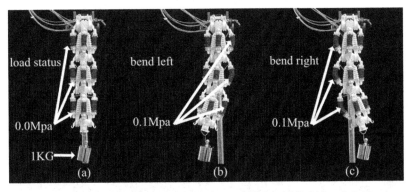

Fig. 5. End load experiment (a) load status (b) bend left (c) bend right.

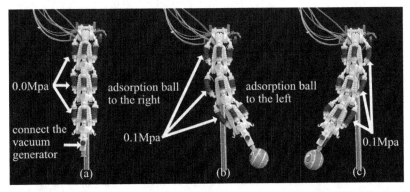

Fig. 6. Grab experiment (a) original status (b) adsorption ball to the right (c) adsorption ball to the left.

Figure 4 shows the bending test experiment of super-redundant continuous arm. Before the experiment, the head joint of the continuous arm is fixed on the base. Figure 4(a) and (d) are the original status of the continuous arm without air pressure. By changing the air pressure into the three pneumatic muscle drive modules of the continuous arm, the continuous arm will deflect to different directions, as shown in Fig. 4. Experiments show that the continuous arm can complete the bending movement in all directions.

Figure 5 shows the load test experiment of the end of the continuous arm. In the experiment, a weight is mounted on the caudal joint of the rigid-soft fusion continuous arm, and the weight used is 1 KG. Figure 5(a) is the original state of the continuous arm under hanging load. Figure 5(b) and (c) are the left and right bending movements of the continuous arm under hanging load. Compared with Fig. 4, it can be found that the continuous arm still has a certain bending ability under the condition of hanging load, which can drive the weights to bend together. The continuous arm has good structural strength and terminal load capacity, and can withstand heavy weight.

Figure 6 shows the experiment of continuous arm grasping the ball. In the experiment, a vacuum generator is installed on the caudal joint of the continuous arm. The vacuum generator provides a suction effect. When the continuous arm is bent and raised to a certain angle, the ball placed next to it can be sucked. Figure 6(b) and (c) are the movements of the continuous arm grasping the ball in both directions. By comparing Fig. 4, it shows that the installation of the vacuum generator does not affect the movement of the continuous arm, and the continuous arm has high scalability.

4.2 Sensing Test Experiments

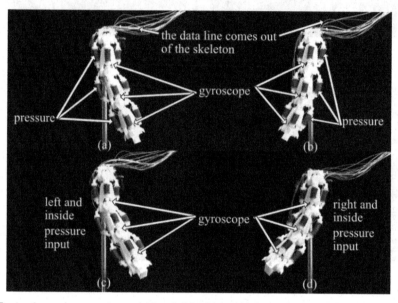

Fig. 7. Angle sensing experiment (a) bend right (b) bend left (c) bend right up (d) bend left up.

The angle sensing experiment of the continuous arm is shown in Fig. 7. In the experiment, the angle changes of three gyroscopes during the bending and lifting of the continuous arm are measured. Three gyroscopes are installed on the universal joint from top to bottom. Figure 8(a) and (b) is the image of sensor deflection angle changing with the input pressure measured in the left and right bending experiment of continuous arm. Sensor 1 is the first gyroscope from top to bottom, sensor 2 is the gyroscope installed in the middle, and sensor 3 is the gyroscope installed in the bottom. Figure 8(c), (d) and (e) is the angle data measured in the continuous arm lifting experiment. Figure 8(e) is the change image of the pitch angle of the three sensors with the input pressure. Figure 8(c) and (d) are the change of the deflection angle measured in the bending right up experiment and bending left up experiment, respectively. According to the deflection angle and pitch angle of each sensor, the attitude of the continuous arm can be effectively inferred. Combined with the installation position of the head frame, the spatial position of the continuous arm can be inferred.

Finally, the hysteresis experiment of super redundant joint during inflation and deflation is done, as shown in Fig. 8(f). During inflation, the slope signal of 0 MPa to 0.1 MPa

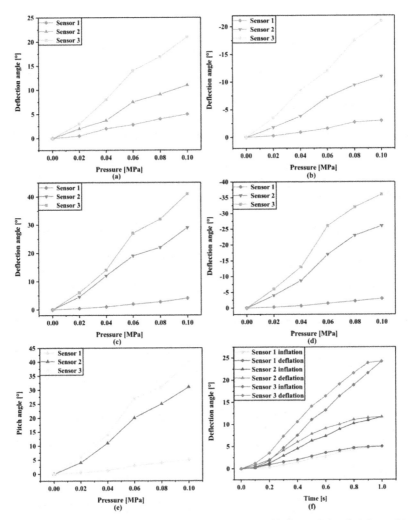

Fig. 8. Sensor angle data (a) bend left (b) bend right (c) bend left up (d) bend right up (e) bend up (f) hysteresis experiment.

is input within one second to measure the angle information of the sensors on the three super redundant joints. Then the angle change of super redundant joints can be obtained. During deflation, the slope signal of 0.1 MPa to 0 MPa was input within one second to measure the angle change of super redundant joints. It can be seen from the figure that the hysteresis from the first super redundant joint to the third super redundant joint increases gradually. The hysteresis phenomenon is caused by the friction between the corrugated braided net and the silastic tube, as well as the expansion and deformation of the silastic tube. Hysteresis will cause periodic relaxation of silastic tube in the process of inflation and deflation, and make the angle change of super redundant joint present certain nonlinear and time-varying.

5 Conclusion

This paper mainly introduces a super redundant continuous arm structure driven by pneumatic muscle, a sensor module is added to the skeleton to control the attitude of the continuous arm. And test the bending ability, load capacity and scalability of the continuous arm by experiments. During the experiment, it was found that the bending amplitude of the head joint of the continuous arm in the suspension state was small, and the bending amplitude gradually increased from the head joint to the tail joint. This paper speculates that this problem is caused by the overall gravity of the continuous arm. In order to avoid this problem, the continuous arm can be installed on the horizontal operating table for operation. Then, for the drive unit of the continuous arm, the design of the pneumatic muscle drive module can be further improved. The existing structure is very dependent on the coordination of the two ends of the cylinder and the hook, but this kind of coordination will affect the motion of the continuous arm to a certain extent. These problems need to be further improved and optimized.

Appendix

*This work is financially supported by the National Natural Science Foundation of China (Grant No. U2013212), the Opening Project of Guangdong Provincial Key Lab of Robotics, and the Fundamental Research Funds for the Provincial Universities of Zhejiang (Grand No. RF-C2019004).

F. A. Key Laboratory of Special Purpose Equipment and Advanced Processing Technology, Ministry of Education, Zhejiang University of Technology, China.

S. B. Beijing Institute of Spacecraft Environment Engineering, China Academy of Space Technology, Beijing, 100094, China.

References

1. Haegele, M., Maufroy, C., Kraus, W., et al.: Soft Robotics. Springer, Heidelberg (2015). https://doi.org/10.1007/978-3-662-44506-8
2. Laschi, C., Mazzolai, B., Mattoli, V., et al.: Design of a biomimetic robotic octopus arm. Bioinspir. Biomim. **4**(1), 015006 (2009)
3. Cianchetti, M., Calisti, M., Margheri, L., et al.: Bioinspired locomotion and grasping in water: the soft eight-arm OCTOPUS robot. Bioinspir. Biomim. **10**(3), 035003 (2015)
4. Defi, C.M., Menciassi, A.: A soft multimodule manipulator with variable stiffness for minimally invasive surgery. Bioinspir. Biomim. **12**(5), 056008 (2017)
5. Simaan, N.: Snake-like units using flexible backbones and actuation redundancy for enhanced miniaturization. In: IEEE International Conference on Robotics and Automation, Piscataway, NJ, USA, pp. 3012–3017. IEEE (2005)
6. Xu, K., Simaan, N.: An investigation of the intrinsic force sensing capabilities of continuum robots. IEEE Trans. Rob. **24**(3), 576–587 (2008)
7. Jiang, H., Liu, X., Chen, X., et al.: Design and simulation analysis of a soft manipulator based on honeycomb pneumatic networks. In: IEEE International Conference on Robotics and Biomimetics, pp. 350–356. IEEE (2017)

8. Jiang, H., Wang, Z., Liu, X., et al.: A two-level approach for solving the inverse kinematics of an extensible soft arm considering viscoelastic behavior. In: IEEE International Conference on Robotics and Automation (ICRA), pp. 6127–6133. IEEE (2017)
9. Renda, F., Cianchetti, M., Giorelli, M., et al.: A 3D steady-state model of a tendon-driven continuum soft manipulator inspired by the octopus arm. Bioinspir. Biomim. **7**(2), 025006 (2012)
10. Renda, F., Giorelli, M., Calisti, M., et al.: Dynamic model of a multibending soft robot arm driven by cables. IEEE Trans. Rob. **30**(5), 1109–1122 (2014)
11. Camarillo, D.B., Milne, C.F., Carlson, C.R., et al.: Mechanics modeling of tendon-driven continuum manipulators. IEEE Trans. Rob. **24**(6), 1262–1273 (2008)
12. Bao, G., Fang, H., Chen, L., et al.: Soft robotics: academic insights and perspectives through bibliometric analysis. Soft Rob. **5**(3), 229–241 (2018)
13. Majidi, C.: Soft robotics: a perspective-current trends and prospects for the future. Soft Rob. **1**(1), 5–11 (2014)
14. Schulte, H.F.: The characteristic of the McKibben artificial muscle. Appl. External Power Prosthet. Orthot. 94–115 (1962)
15. Chou, C.P., Hannaford, B.: Measurement and modeling of McKibben pneumatic artificial muscles. Robot. Autom. IEEE Trans. **12**(1), 90–102 (1992)
16. Merlet, J.P.: Parallel Robots. Springer, Dordrecht (2006). https://doi.org/10.1007/1-4020-4133-0
17. Tsai, L.W.: Robot Analysis: The Mechanism of Serial and Parallel Manipulators. Wiley-Interscience (1999)
18. Kang, R., Kazakidi, A., Guglielmino, E., Branson, D.T., Tsakiris, D.P., Ekaterinaris, J.A. et al.: Dynamic model of a hyper-redundant, octopus-like manipulator for underwater applications. In: Paper Presented at 2011 IEEE/RSJ International Conference on Intelligent Robots and Systems: Celebrating 50 Years of Robotics, IROS'11, San Francisco, CA, USA (2011). https://doi.org/10.1109/IROS.2011.6094468.
19. Kang, R., Branson, D.T., Guglielmino, E., Caldwell, D.G.: Dynamic modeling and control of an octopus inspired multiple continuum arm robot. Comput. Math. Appl. **64**(5), 1004–1016 (2012). https://doi.org/10.1016/j.camwa.2012.03.018
20. Kang, R., Branson, D.T., Zheng, T., Guglielmino, E., Caldwell, D.G.: Design, modeling and control of a pneumatically actuated manipulator inspired by biological continuum structures. Bioinspir. Biomim. **8**(3), 036008 (2013). https://doi.org/10.1088/1748-3182/8/3/036008. Epub 2013 Jul 15. PMID: 23851387
21. Nakajima, K., Hauser, H., Kang, R., Guglielmino, E., Caldwell, D.G., Pfeifer, R.: A soft body as a reservoir: case studies in a dynamic model of octopus-inspired soft robotic arm. Front. Comput. Neurosci. **7**, 91 (2013). https://doi.org/10.3389/fncom.2013.00091

Testing Method and Experiment of Magnetic Flux Leakage of Spiral Rising Steel Wire Rope

Jialei Lu[1,2] , Kaiwei Ma[1,2] , Wei Shi[1,2] , and Fengyu Xu[1,2(✉)]

[1] College of Automation and College of Artificial Intelligence, Nanjing University of Posts and Telecommunications, Nanjing 210023, China
[2] Jiangsu Engineering Lab for IOT Intelligent Robots (IOT Robot), Nanjing 210023, China

Abstract. In view of the magnetic flux leakage detection of cable wire broken defects, the magnetic flux leakage magnetic circuit is analyzed firstly, and the calculation formula of magnetic induction intensity and the sufficient excitation condition of the wire rope are obtained. Ansoft Maxwell software was used to carry out the finite element simulation analysis of the axial leakage magnetic field of the wire rope to verify the theoretical analysis results of the magnetic circuit model. Secondly, the modularized cable excitation detection device is designed. The filtering effects of Chebyshev digital filter and Fourier transform are compared. Finally, the magnetic detection under the spiral motion and the magnetic detection under the vertical motion are compared through experimental research.

Keywords: Wire rope · Magnetic detection · Spiral rising · Experiment

As a cable system, cable-stayed bridge has a greater span capacity than beam bridge, which is the most important choice for long-span bridge construction. As one of the main stress components of cable-stayed bridge, the running state of cable is closely related to the running state of bridge. Therefore, it is necessary to carry out regular inspection and maintenance on the cable of the cable-stayed bridge to ensure the safe operation of the bridge. Therefore, it is of great practical significance to study the nondestructive testing method of cable [1].

There are a variety of nondestructive testing methods for stay cables, and the main nondestructive testing methods applicable to stay cables include: magnetic testing method [2, 3], optical testing method [4, 5], ultrasonic testing method [6], acoustic emission testing method [7], ray testing method [8] and eddy current testing method [9]. Raišutis al. [10] studied the propagation of UGW along a multi-wire rope with polymer cores through semi-analytical finite element modeling and experimental verification, and calculated the dispersion curve. Zhang et al. [11] improved the traditional ultrasonic testing method and designed a magneto strictive guided wave nondestructive testing method under the excitation of multi-frequency pulse signals, which improved the signal-to-noise ratio and detection distance. Hirata et al. [12] invented a new X-ray photography device for fatigue defect detection of steel wire rope, and successfully tested the fatigue defect of steel wire rope. Li et al. [13] used acoustic emission method to detect the stress corrosion process of bridge cable steel wire, and obtained the damage evolution process of bridge cable stress corrosion. However, when using ultrasonic guided wave

© Springer Nature Switzerland AG 2021
X.-J. Liu et al. (Eds.): ICIRA 2021, LNAI 13013, pp. 232–240, 2021.
https://doi.org/10.1007/978-3-030-89095-7_23

detection, each steel wire will produce reflection, cannot reflect the situation of damaged steel wire in detail; The equipment based on ray method has high maintenance cost and cannot be tested continuously for a long time. Acoustic emission method is expensive and can only be used in the static load part; Eddy current methods, which produce a skin effect, are commonly used to detect surface defects.

At present, the most effective nondestructive testing method for wire rope is still the magnetic flux leakage testing method [14]. As one of the most widely used nondestructive testing methods, the research on magnetic flux leakage testing methods, especially the research on magnetic flux leakage testing of mine wire rope, has been developed very mature. Both local defects (LF) and cross-sectional area loss defects (LMA) of wire ropes can cause changes in magnetic fields, forming leakage magnetic fields that can be detected by magnetic sensitive elements [3, 15]. In recent years, with the development of nondestructive testing methods and technologies of wire rope, various magnetic leakage testing methods emerge endlessly, which can be divided into electromagnetic type and permanent magnet type according to different excitation modes. The electromagnetic type uses the coil to excite the cable, and the excitation intensity can be adjusted. Yan et al. [16] proposed the electromagnetic nondestructive testing method with simplified magnetic circuit, which realized the defect detection of wire rope in the environment of electromagnetic interference. Sun et al. [17] proposed a method of open excitation for C-type coil, which solved the problem of inconvenient installation during the use of magnetization device. Permanent magnet type is used to excite the cable with strong exciting effect and relatively small size.

To sum up, there are a variety of methods suitable for the nondestructive testing of wire rope broken wire, but the most suitable method for the magnetic flux leakage testing of wire rope is still the magnetic flux leakage testing method. AC excitation is easy to produce eddy current and lead to skin effect. DC excitation can control the excitation intensity by current, but the equipment is large and the coil will overheat and other problems. Permanent magnet excitation has the advantages of simple structure, small volume and high excitation intensity.

1   Analysis of Magnetic Flux Leakage Detection Principle of Cable Broken Wire

The principle of magnetic flux leakage detection is shown in Fig. 1. The excitation loop is composed of permanent magnets, keeper, air gaps and steel wires. Wire rope is generally made of carbon steel with good magnetic conductivity. To axial excitation of wire rope, the rope after saturated excitation, zero defect of steel wire rope of internal magnetic induction intensity B remain stable, the lines of magnetic force is uniformly distributed within the steel wire rope, and the defects such as broken wire sharply lower permeability, the lines of magnetic force is from the steel wire rope defects show that overflow, thus formed in wire rope that air leakage magnetic field. The intensity and distribution of the leakage magnetic field formed at the defect are determined by the excitation intensity, the shape and size of the defect. When the excitation intensity is constant, the defect attributes can be inferred according to the leakage magnetic field, the above leakage magnetic field signals can be obtained by Hall effect sensor, and the width, depth and other characteristics of the corresponding defect can be extracted [18].

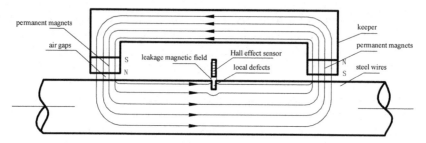

Fig. 1. Testing principle of magnetic flux leakage method

2 Finite Element Simulation Study on Magnetic Flux Leakage Detection of Wire Rope

The Maxwell finite element simulation software was used to conduct 2D/3D simulation research on the magnetic flux leakage detection of wire rope. The 3D model of magnetic flux leakage detection was shown in Fig. 2. The steel wire material adopted the B-H curve of ordinary carbon steel. The disease is set to a 5 mm wide rectangular groove defect; The permanent magnet body length is 30 mm, the thickness is 10mm, the material is N42NdFeB strong magnetic material, and its coercivity is 968000 A/m. The armature is made of 3 mm common carbon steel. Because the hall sensor only detects the magnetic induction passing through the sensor axially, the model can be simplified as a 2D model for simulation in order to simplify the calculation. Maxwell2D is used to simulate the magnetic flux leakage detection under static conditions, and the results are shown in Fig. 3. For the transient simulation under rotation, the excitation device is set to rotate clockwise around the wire rope with a speed of 60 rpm. The curve of magnetic induction intensity at a point 5mm above the defect changing with time is shown in Fig. 4.

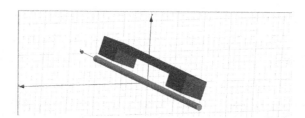

Fig. 2. 3D model of magnetic flux leakage detection

According to the 2D simulation results, the distribution of magnetic force lines in the defects of the wire rope is no longer uniform, but overflows the surface of the wire rope, forming obvious leakage of magnetic field in the air. The magnetic induction intensity is the strongest at the center of the defect and gradually decreases from the center to both sides in the axial direction. In the 3D transient simulation, at the initial position, the leakage magnetic field generated above the defect is relatively strong. With the rotation of the permanent magnet, the magnetic induction intensity decreases continuously, and

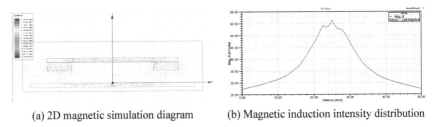

(a) 2D magnetic simulation diagram   (b) Magnetic induction intensity distribution

Fig. 3. 2D simulation results of magnetic flux leakage detection

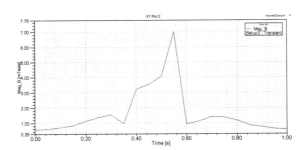

Fig. 4. Distribution of magnetic induction intensity over the defect during exciter rotation

the magnetic induction intensity is the minimum when the permanent magnet is turned to the opposite side of the wire rope, and then increases continuously with the rotation of the permanent magnet. However, it is also observed that in the simulation experiment, the permanent magnet motion is set to rotate around the wire rope once. When the time runs to half, the defect should appear directly below the exciter. However, in the simulation results, the peak value of the magnetic flux leakage signal is shifted to the direction of rotation, resulting in the lag of the magnetic flux leakage signal.

3 Preparation and Experiment

3.1 Magnetic Flux Leakage Testing Experiment

According to the actual cable structure, 24 wire ropes bundled with 6 strands of each wire were selected to fill the PVC pipe with a diameter of 50 mm to simulate cable of cable-stayed bridge, and the number of 5 artificial broken wire defects and 3 artificial broken wire defects with a width of 3 mm were set on the wire rope to simulate the broken wire damage of the wire rope (Fig. 5).

The experimental system consists of a modular excitation detection device, a signal acquisition card, a broken wire simulation device and a PC unit, as shown in Fig. 6. In the experiment, after the wire rope is fully excited by the excitation device, the excitation device is first moved along the axial direction of the wire rope, and the detected data is transmitted to the PC. Figure 7 shows the positive data of the damage site detected by Hall element. It can be clearly observed that the voltage signal at the broken wire produces a large fluctuation, and the fluctuation range increases with the increase of the number of broken wires.

Fig. 5. Simulations of broken wire damage

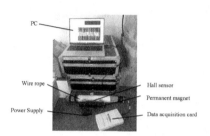

Fig. 6. Laboratory equipment

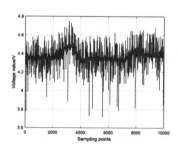

Fig. 7. Original collected data

3.2 MFL Signal Processing Method

The diamagnetic signals detected belong to low frequency weak signals and are easily interfered by external electromagnetic fields. In addition, error of data acquisition card, vibration of detection device and communication error will cause detected MFL damage signals, noise signals and data bad points. Therefore, it is of great significance to eliminate the data bad points, extract effective signals and eliminate the influence of high frequency noise for the quantitative identification of wire rope damage. The process of data processing is shown in Fig. 8.

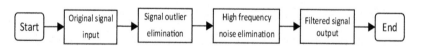

Fig. 8. MFL signal processing flow

3.3 Chebyshev Digital Filtering

The frequency response curve of Chebyshev filter is the filter with the smallest error between the frequency response curve and the ideal filter. Decay rapidly in the transition zone, but there is fluctuation, not flat.

Chebyshev filter is divided into type I Chebyshev filter and type II Chebyshev filter according to the frequency response curve which fluctuates in the pass band and stop band respectively.

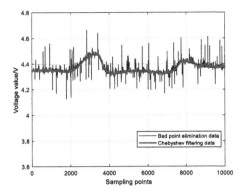

Fig. 9. Chebyshev filtering data

Chebyshev filtering results are shown in Fig. 9.

Through the data after Chebyshev digital filtering, the noise signal is obviously reduced, and the magnetic flux leakage signal has been basically extracted. However, the processed signal still contains a lot of low-frequency noise, which causes some difficulties in the quantitative identification of the broken wire damage of the wire rope.

3.4 Processing of Cable Magnetic Flux Leakage Signal Based on Fourier Transform

The magnetic flux leakage signal is a low frequency signal, and the noise signal that needs to be filtered is a high frequency signal. Fourier transform can be used to extract the frequency domain information of the data. For a one-dimensional signal x(t), its continuous Fourier transform is.

$$X(jw) = \int_{-\infty}^{\infty} x(t)e^{-jwt}dt \tag{1}$$

The inverse Fourier transform is.

$$x(t) = \frac{1}{2\pi} \int_{-\infty}^{\infty} X(jw)(t)e^{jwt}dt \tag{2}$$

By setting the threshold value of frequency, the frequency higher than the threshold value is eliminated, and then the inverse Fourier transform of the signal is carried out to realize the filtering processing of the signal. The cut-off frequency is generally chosen as one fifth of the sampling frequency. The signal processed by Fourier transform is shown in Fig. 10.

Through Fourier transform filtered data, the noise in the signal is eliminated, and the amplitude of the signal is retained, which can completely reflect the change of the magnetic flux leakage signal, and the filtering effect is good.

3.5 Contrastive Analysis of Axial Motion and Rotary Motion of Exciter

In the existing experiments, the movement of Hall sensor is all the axial movement parallel to the magnetic induction line to detect the broken wire damage of the wire rope,

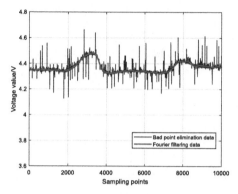

Fig. 10. Fourier transform filtered data

and the magnetic flux leakage detection experiment of the rotating climbing wire rope has not been carried out. It is of great significance to analyze the difference between the detection of rotating climbing cable and that of vertical climbing along the axial direction. To solve this problem, the experiment was carried out again, and the comparison of the two groups of data results after the proposed bad points and the noise reduction is shown in Fig. 11.

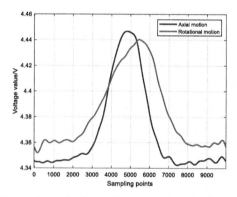

Fig. 11. Comparison of axial motion and helical motion MFL signals

Combined with the simulation and experimental results: the designed cable broken wire detection device can effectively detect the artificial damage with 5 broken wires, and the peak value of magnetic flux leakage signal in axial vertical climbing detection is 4.448 V, and the peak value of magnetic flux leakage signal in rotary climbing detection is 4.441 V. The peak value of the signal detected in the rotary climb is slightly lower than that detected in the vertical climb along the axial direction. And the signal generated by the rotation and climbing detection presents the state of offset in the direction of the rotation motion.

4   Conclusion

In this paper, the Maxwell2D/3D finite element simulation software is used to verify the analysis results. Based on the analysis of magnetic circuit of wire rope magnetic flux leakage, a set of modularized measuring device for wire rope magnetic flux leakage is designed. The experimental results show that the modularized magnetic flux leakage detection device can effectively detect the magnetic flux leakage signal generated by the wire rope at the broken wire. Chebyshev filter and Fourier transform are used to de-noise the data. The data after Fourier transform filtering effectively eliminated the interference of noise signal and did not weaken the amplitude of magnetic flux leakage signal, so it has a good filtering effect. In the comparison experiment and simulation study of the axial moving exciter and rotating moving exciter, it is found that the peak value of the axial moving detection structure is directly above the damage location, while the peak value of the magnetic flux leakage signal detected by rotating moving exciter will lag slightly, and the filtered peak value of the measured signal is 4.448 V and 4.441 V, respectively. The signal peak value detected by rotating motion is 0.007 V lower than that detected by axial motion.

Acknowledgments. This project is supported by the National Natural Science Foundation of China (51775284), the Primary Research & Development Plan of Jiangsu Province (BE2018734), the Natural Science Foundation of Jiangsu Province (BK20201379), and Six Talent Peaks Project in Jiangsu Province (JY-081).

References

1. Xu, F., Wang, X., Wu, H.: Inspection method of cable-stayed bridge using magnetic flux leakage detection: principle, sensor design, and signal processing. J. Mech. Sci. Technol. **26**(3), 661–669 (2012)
2. Jiang, F., Liu, S.L., Xiao, S.G.: Quantitative estimation of rectangular surface crack based on the 2-D modeling of surface magnetic field with long straight rectangular wire. IEEE Trans. Magn. **54**(5), 1–12 (2018)
3. Tian, J., Zhou, J., Wang, H., et al.: Literature review of research on the technology of wire rope nondestructive inspection in china and abroad. MATEC Web Conf. EDP Sci. **22**, 03025 (2015)
4. Zhou, P., Zhou, G., He, Z., et al.: A novel texture-based damage detection method for wire ropes. Measurement **148**, 106954 (2019)
5. Yaman, O., Karakose, M.: Auto correlation based elevator rope monitoring and fault detection approach with image processing. In: 2017 International Artificial Intelligence and Data Processing Symposium (IDAP), pp. 1–5. IEEE (2017)
6. Raisutis, R., Kazys, R., Mazeika, L., Samaitis, V., Zukauskas, E.: Propagation of ultrasonic guided waves in composite multi-wire ropes. Materials **9**(6), 451–466 (2016)
7. Zejli, H., et al.: Detection of the presence of broken wires in cables by acoustic emission inspection. J. Bridg. Eng. **17**(6), 921–927 (2012)
8. Peng, P.-C., Wang, C.-Y.: Use of gamma rays in the inspection of steel wire ropes in suspension bridges. NDT E Int. **75**, 80–86 (2015)
9. Wu, J., Sun, Y., Feng, B., et al.: The effect of motion-induced eddy current on circumferential magnetization in MFL testing for a steel pipe. IEEE Trans. Magn. **53**(7), 1–6 (2017)

10. Kažys, R., Žukauskas, E., Mažeika, L., et al.: Propagation of ultrasonic shear horizontal waves in rectangular waveguides. Int. J. Struct. Stab. Dyn. **16**(08), 1550041 (2016)

11. Zhang, D., Zhou, Z., Sun, J.: A Magnetostrictive guided-wave nondestructive testing method with multifrequency excitation pulse signal. IEEE Trans. Instrum. Meas. **63**(12), 3058–3066 (2014)

12. Hirata, G., Kawano, M.: X-ray photographing device: U.S. Patent 10,433,801[P]. 2019-10-8

13. Li, D., Yang, W., Zhang, W.: Cluster analysis of stress corrosion mechanisms for steel wires used in bridge cables through acoustic emission particle swarm optimization. Ultrasonics **77**, 22–31 (2017)

14. Liu, S., Sun, Y., Jiang, X., Kang, Y.: A review of wire rope detection methods, sensors and signal processing techniques. J. Nondestr. Eval. **39**(4), 1–18 (2020). https://doi.org/10.1007/s10921-020-00732-y

15. Zhou, P., Zhou, G., Zhu, Z., He, Z., Ding, X., Tang, C.: A review of non-destructive damage detection methods for steel wire ropes. Appl. Sci. **9**(13), 2771 (2019). https://doi.org/10.3390/app9132771

16. Yan, X., Zhang, D., Pan, S., et al.: Online nondestructive testing for fine steel wire rope in electromagnetic interference environment. NDT E Int. **92**, 75–81 (2017)

17. Sun, Y., Liu, S., He, L., et al.: A new detection sensor for wire rope based on open magnetization method. Mater. Eval. **75**(4), 501–509 (2017)

18. Zhang, J., Tan, X., Zheng, P.: Non-destructive detection of wire rope discontinuities from residual magnetic field images using the Hilbert-Huang transform and compressed sensing. Sensors **17**(3), 608 (2017)

Hysteresis Modeling and Compensation Control of Soft Gripper

Zhou Yi[1,2] , Kaiwei Ma[1,2] , Yang Sen[1,2] , and Fengyu Xu[1,2(✉)]

[1] College of Automation and College of Artificial Intelligence, Nanjing University of Posts and Telecommunications, Nanjing 210023, China
[2] Jiangsu Engineering Lab for IOT Intelligent Robots (IOT Robot), Nanjing 210023, China

Abstract. In order to make full use of the soft robot's characteristics of flexibility and flexibility, combined with the hysteresis model, the air pressure-position hysteresis phenomenon in the soft actuator is studied, and the hysteresis compensation control method of the soft actuator is proposed. First, on the basis of the classic Prandtl-Ishlinskii (PI) model, an improved PI model and a mathematical calculation method for parameter identification are proposed; Secondly, the physical structure of the soft actuator is described, and the hysteresis data is obtained through experimental measurement; Finally, the two models used are simulated and analyzed, as well as the experimental verification of the entire system.

Keywords: Soft gripper · Hysteresis compensation · Prandtl-Ishlinskii model

1 Introduction

Soft actuator has the advantages of high flexibility, adaptability, safety, etc., and has broad application prospects in the fields of rehabilitation, detection, rescue, etc. [1, 2]. However, due to the inherent hysteresis and other characteristics, it brings trouble to the control of the soft actuator.

In order to improve the control accuracy and anti-interference ability of the soft actuator, experts and scholars propose different control methods, which are mainly divided into (1) methods based on control theory and (2) control strategies based on hysteresis compensation.

There are many cases at home and abroad that are based on mature control theory to study soft robots. For example, the soft robot designed by Bartlett et al. [3] can complete unfettered jumps through the controller. Costa et al. [4–7] used a closed-loop control method to control the trajectory and force of the soft robot to achieve the purpose of assisting rehabilitation therapy. Xu et al. [8] carried out kinematics and dynamics modeling analysis on the proposed software robot based on the blocking variable stiffness mechanism to achieve high-stability control. In addition, there are some examples of intelligent control. For example, Zheng et al. designed a controller based on neural network. Massari et al. [10–12] established a force-deformation model of soft robot based on machine learning method.

© Springer Nature Switzerland AG 2021
X.-J. Liu et al. (Eds.): ICIRA 2021, LNAI 13013, pp. 241–252, 2021.
https://doi.org/10.1007/978-3-030-89095-7_24

It is a common method to describe the hysteresis phenomenon with hysteresis model. Common hysteresis models include Prandtl–Ishlinskii model, Bouc–Wen model and Maxwell model. Zhang et al. [13–15] used the Prandtl-Ishlinskii model as feedforward compensation, and combined the closed-loop control strategy to control the soft robot. Minh [16, 17] and others used Maxwell to model the pressure/length lag of a single artificial muscle, and the obtained model was used as a cascade position control scheme to improve the robustness of the system.

In conclusion, although researchers have proposed many effective control strategies for soft robots, the hysteresis compensation control methods for soft robots are still based on the classical hysteresis model, and the research on the asymmetric hysteresis phenomenon of pneumatic artificial muscles is still immature. Aiming at the hysteresis phenomenon in the soft gripper actuator, this paper combines the inverse hysteresis compensation and closed-loop control methods to control the position of the proposed soft gripper with higher precision.

2 Hysteresis Model

Establishing an accurate and effective hysteresis model can improve the control accuracy and dynamic characteristics of the whole system. This section analyzes the principle of prandtl-Ishlinskii (PI) model and proposes an improved PI model to describe asymmetric hysteresis.

2.1 Classic PI Model

The PI model is based on the Play operator or the Stop operator, and a hysteresis model is obtained through a series of operators with a weighted superposition. In this paper, the Play operator is used as the basic hysteresis unit of the PI model, as shown in formula (1). Divide the input $u(t)$ into N intervals, $u(t)$ is monotonously continuous in each interval $[t_i, t_{i+1}](i = 0, 1, 2, \cdots N - 1)$, where $y(t)$ is the output of the operator, and r is the threshold of the operator. As shown in Fig. 1, it is the Play operator with the threshold r of 0.1 and 0.3 respectively.

$$y(t) = P_r[u, y_{-1}](t)$$
$$= F_r(u(t), P_r[u, y_0](t_i)), \quad t_i < t < t_{i+1}, 0 \leq i < N, i = 0, 1, 2, \cdots \quad (1)$$

The PI model is a weighted superposition of PI operators, and the expression is shown in formula 2. Where $\vec{w} = [w_0, w_1, w_2, \cdots, w_n]$, is the weight vector of the PI operator. $\vec{P}_r[u, y_{-1}](t)$ is the Play operator vector, as shown in formula 3, the threshold vector is $\vec{r} = [r_0, r_1, \cdots, r_n]$.

$$f(t) = \vec{w} \cdot \vec{P}_r[u, \vec{y}_{-1}](t)$$
$$= \sum_{i=0}^{n} w_i P_{ri}[u, y_{-1}](t), \quad i = 0, 1, \cdots, n \quad (2)$$

$$\vec{P}_r[u, y_{-1}](t) = [P_{r0}[u, y_{-1}](t), P_{r1}[u, y_{-1}](t) \cdots P_{rn}[u, y_{-1}](t)]^T \quad (3)$$

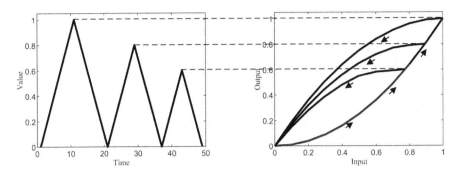

Fig. 1. The phenomenon of hysteresis

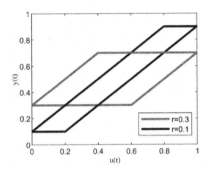

Fig. 2. PI operators with thresholds of 0.1 and 0.3

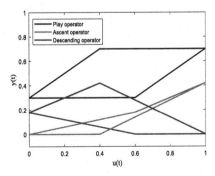

Fig. 3. The threshold value of 0.3 PI operator, up operator, down operator

2.2 Improved PI Model

Since the PI operator is symmetrical along the center, the PI model superimposed by the PI operator can only describe the hysteresis of the center symmetry. The hysteresis in the soft actuator is non-centrosymmetric. Therefore, an improved Play operator is proposed. The improved Play operator is composed of an ascending operator and a descending operator. The ascending operator is defined as shown in formula 4, where $\beta_a(t) = u(t) + r - y(t)$. The descent operator is defined as shown in formula 5, where $\beta_d(t) = y(t) - u(t) + r$. As shown in Fig. 3, when r is 0.3, PI operator, ascending operator and descending operator. Through comparison, it can be seen that the ascending operator and descending operator have asymmetric structures, and the two types of operators can describe the asymmetric hysteresis structure through weighted superposition.

$$c(t) = A_r[u, c_{-1}](t) = \beta_a(t) \cdot P_r[u, y_{-1}](t) \tag{4}$$

$$c(t) = D_r[u, c_{-1}](t) = \beta_d(t) \cdot P_r[u, y_{-1}](t) \tag{5}$$

The hysteresis model composed of the weighted superposition of the ascending operator and the descending operator is an improved PI model, as shown in formula 6. The improved PI model is composed of n ascending operators, n descending operators and a PI operator with a threshold value of r0. Among them, w_0 is the weight of the PI operator with threshold r0, w_{ai} and w_{di} are the weight of i ascending operator $A_{ri}[u, c_{-1}](t)$ and the i descending operator $D_{ri}[u, c_{-1}](t)$.

$$f(t) = w_0 \cdot P_{r0}[u, y_{-1}](t) + \sum_{i=1}^{n} w_{ai} \cdot A_{ri}[u, c_{-1}](t) + \sum_{i=1}^{n} w_{di} \cdot D_{ri}[u, c_{-1}](t)$$
$$i = 1, 2, \cdots n \tag{6}$$

2.3 Parameter Calculation and Inverse Hysteresis Model

The parameter identification of the PI model is to solve the value of w in formula 2 and formula 6. The general method of solving the weight parameter is the minimum variance method. This paper proposes a numerical calculation method. First, the pressure and response input by the soft actuator are normalized to the interval [0, 1] using formula 7 and formula 8, and the hysteresis curve with input and output in the range of [0, 1] is obtained. Among them, u_{min} and u_{max} are the minimum and maximum values of the input pressure, θ_{min} and θ_{max} are the minimum and max values of the output angle, and $u(t)$ and $\theta(t)$ are the input and output measured values.

$$u_T(t) = (u(t) - u_{min})/(u_{max} - u_{min}) \tag{7}$$

$$f_T(t) = (\theta(t) - \theta_{min})/(\theta_{Max} - \theta_{min}) \tag{8}$$

Classic PI Model Parameter Calculation. In the normalized hysteresis curve, the point when a Play operator with a threshold of r_i enters the rising or falling phase from the holding phase is called the boundary point. When the input of the operator rises, the abscissa of the boundary point is $u_j = 2r_i$, when the operator descends, the abscissa of the dividing point is $u_j = 1 - 2r_i$. And it can also be obtained that for the play operator with threshold $r_k \leq r_i$, $k = 0, 1, \cdots i$, the output at the demarcation point (u_j, f_j) is as shown in formula 9, for the threshold $r_l > r_i, l = i + 1, i + 2, \cdots n$, The output of the play operator at the demarcation point (u_j, f_j) is shown in Eq. 10.

As shown in the threshold vector $\vec{r}$, if $n + 1$ Play operators with different thresholds are set, there are $2n$ dividing points in the normalized hysteresis curve, and the dividing points $(0, 0)$ And $(1, 1)$. Due to the symmetry of the PI model, it only needs to identify the weight vector $\vec{w}$ for $n + 1$ dividing points of the ascending or descending segment.

$$y_k = u_j - r_k, \quad k = 0, 1, 2 \cdots i - 1 \tag{9}$$

$$v_l = r_l, \quad l = i + 1, i + 2, \cdots, n \tag{10}$$

Substituting formulas (9) and (10) into (2), formula (11) is obtained as the output curve of the PI model.

$$f(t) = \sum_{k=0}^{i-1} w_k \cdot (u_j - r_k) + \sum_{i=i}^{n} w_l \cdot r_l, \quad i = 1, 2, \cdots n, \quad j = 1, 2, \cdots n + 1 \tag{11}$$

Because the demarcation points (u_j, f_j) are on the hysteresis curve, substituting each hysteresis point into Eq. 11 can get the equations shown in Eq. 12. There are $n + 1$ equations, and $n + 1$ unknowns can be solved as $[w_0, w_1, \cdots, w_n]$.

$$\begin{cases} 0 = 0 + \sum_{i=1}^{n} w_l \cdot r_l \\ f_2 = \sum_{k=0}^{i-1} w_k (u_2 - r_k) + \sum_{l=i}^{n} w_l \cdot r_l \\ \quad \vdots \\ f_n = \sum_{k=0}^{i-1} w_k \cdot (u_n - r_k) + \sum_{l=i}^{n} w_l \cdot r_l \\ 1 = \sum_{k=0}^{i-1} w_k \cdot (1 - r_k) + 0.5 w_n \end{cases} \tag{12}$$

Improve PI Model Parameter Calculation. For the improved PI model, in the ascending stage, the Play operator with the threshold $r_0 = 0$, the output at the demarcation point (u_j, f_j) is as shown in Eq. 13:

$$P_{r0}[u_j, y_{-1}](t) = u_j \tag{13}$$

The output of the rising operator and the falling operator with the operator threshold value $0 < r_k < r_i$ are shown in formulas 14 and 15, respectively, and the output of the rising operator and the falling operator with the operator threshold value $r_l \geq r_i$ are show in formulas 16 and 17 respectively.

$$v_k = 2r_k \cdot (u_j - r_k), \quad k = 1, 2, \cdots, i - 1 \tag{14}$$

$$v_k = 0, \quad k = 1, 2, \cdots, i - 1 \tag{15}$$

$$v_l = u_j \cdot r_l, \quad l = i, i+1, \cdots, n \tag{16}$$

$$v_l = (2r_l - u_j) \cdot r_l, \quad l = i, i+1, \cdots, n \tag{17}$$

Substituting formulas 13, 14, 15, 16, and 17 into formula 6, the output of the improved PI model at the demarcation point of the rising section is shown in formula 18.

$$f_j = w_0 \cdot u_j + \sum_{k=1}^{i-1} 2w_{ak} \cdot r_k \cdot (u_j - r_k)$$
$$+ \sum_{l=i}^{n-1} w_{al} \cdot u_j \cdot r_l + \sum_{l=i}^{n-1} w_{dl} \cdot (2r_l - u_j) \cdot r_l + 0.5w_n \tag{18}$$

In the falling segment, the Play operator with the threshold $r_0 = 0$, the output at the demarcation point (u_j, f_j) is shown in Eq. 19

$$P_{r0}[u_j, y_{-1}](t) = u_j \tag{19}$$

The output of the rising operator and the falling operator with the operator threshold value $0 < r_k < r_i$ are shown in formulas 20 and 21, respectively, and the output of the rising operator and the falling operator with the operator threshold value $r_l \geq r_i$ are respectively formulas 22 and 23 Shown.

$$v_k = 0, \quad k = 1, 2, \cdots, i-1 \tag{20}$$

$$v_k = 2r_k(u_j + r_k), \quad k = 1, 2, \cdots, i-1 \tag{21}$$

$$v_l = (u_j - 1 + 2r_l)(1 - r_l), \quad l = i, i+1, \cdots, n \tag{22}$$

$$v_l = (1 - u_j)(1 - r_l), \quad l = i, i+1, \cdots, n \tag{23}$$

Substituting formulas 19, 20, 21, 22, and 23 into formula 6, the output of the improved PI model at the demarcation point of the descending segment is shown in formula 24:

$$f_j = w_0 u_j + \sum_{l=i}^{n-1} w_{al}(u_j - 1 + 2r_l)(1 - r_l) + \sum_{k=1}^{i-1} 2w_{dk} r_k(u_j + r_k)$$
$$+ \sum_{l=i}^{n-1} w_{dl}(1 - u_j)(1 - r_l) + 0.5w_n \tag{24}$$

Expanding and merging formulas 18 and 24, the equation system is shown in formula 25, which contains $2n$ equations, which can solve $2n$ unknown weight parameters $w_0, w_n, \overrightarrow{w_a}, \overrightarrow{w_d}$.

$$
\begin{cases}
f_1 = w_0 u_1 + \sum_{k=1}^{i-1} 2w_{ak} r_k(u_1 - r_k) + \sum_{l=i}^{n-1} w_{al} u_1 r_l + \sum_{l=i}^{n-1} w_{dl}(2r_l - u_1)r_l + 0.5w_n \\
\quad \vdots \\
f_n = w_0 u_n + \sum_{k=1}^{i-1} 2w_{ak} r_k(u_n - r_k) + \sum_{l=i}^{n-1} w_{al} u_n r_l + \sum_{l=i}^{n-1} w_{dl}(2r_l - u_n)r_l + 0.5w_n \\
f_{n+1} = w_0 u_{n+1} + \sum_{l=i}^{n-1} w_{al}(u_{n+1} - 1 + 2r_l)(1 - r_l) + \sum_{k=1}^{i-1} 2w_{dk} r_k(u_{n+1} + r_k) \\
\quad + \sum_{l=1}^{n-1} w_{dl}(1 - u_{n+1})(1 - r_l) + 0.5w_n \\
\quad \vdots \\
f_{2n} = w_0 u_{2n} + \sum_{l=i}^{n-1} w_{al}(u_{2n} - 1 + 2r_l)(1 - r_l) + \sum_{k=1}^{i-1} 2w_{dk} r_k(u_{2n} + r_k) \\
\quad + \sum_{l=1}^{n-1} w_{dl}(1 - u_{2n})(1 - r_l) + 0.5w_n
\end{cases} \tag{25}
$$

PI inverse Hysteresis Model. For the PI model, after the weight parameters are calculated, the PI inverse hysteresis model can be easily obtained through the parameters. The inverse of the PI model is still the PI model, and only the threshold r_i and the weight parameter w_i are changed on the basis of the PI model. The parameter calculation of the inverse hysteresis model is shown in formula 26.

$$
\begin{aligned}
w_0' &= \frac{1}{w_0} \\
w_i' &= \frac{-w_i}{\left(\sum_{j=0}^{i} w_j\right) \cdot \left(\sum_{j=0}^{i-1} w_j\right)}, i = 1, 2, \cdots, n-1 \\
r_i' &= \sum_{j=0}^{i} w_j(r_i - r_j), i = 1, 2, \cdots, n-1
\end{aligned}
\tag{26}
$$

3 The Preparation of the Soft Gripper and the Hysteresis

This section describes the structure and physical parameters of the soft actuator used, makes a simple analysis of the cause of the hysteresis, and obtains the hysteresis curve of the soft actuator through experiments.

3.1 Soft Actuator

The driver adopts the Pneu-net driver mode, as shown in Fig. 1. The whole driver includes the top strain layer, constraint layer and bottom layer. The non-woven fabric is embedded in the constraint layer to limit the ductility, and the semicircle in the bottom layer has small stripes on the cloth, which increases the friction force with the contact object. When the gas is inflated, the gas chamber of the strain layer expands and bends due to the constraint of the limiting layer; when the gas is deflated, the gas chamber of the strain layer contracts and returns to its original state (Fig. 4).

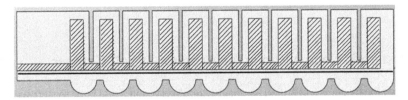

Fig. 4. The overall structure

3.2 Hysteresis in the Actuator

There are many reasons for the hysteresis phenomenon. For the soft actuator proposed in this paper, the embedded constraining layer, the friction between the air chambers, and the manufacturing materials can all cause the hysteresis phenomenon. In order to perform hysteresis compensation control on the hysteresis in the soft actuator, the hysteresis must be observed first. The design input air pressure range is [0 kPa, 50 kPa], and the measurement is performed every 5 kp during the input rising and falling stages. The measured results are shown in Fig. 6 during the input rising and falling stag. It can be seen from Fig. 6 that there is a serious asymmetric hysteresis in the soft actuator.

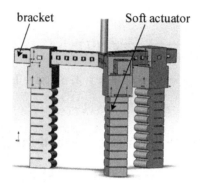

Fig. 5. Soft gripper structure drawing

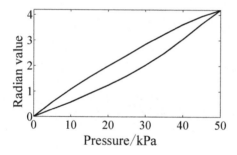

Fig. 6. Soft gripper actuator hysteresis

4 Hysteresis Compensation for Actuator of Soft Gripper

In view of the hysteresis of soft gripper actuator observed in Sect. 3, the hysteresis model and parameter identification method proposed in Sect. 2 are adopted. Using the obtained data, the correctness of the weight parameters is verified.

4.1 PI Model Weight Parameter Calculation

The hysteresis curve obtained by measurement, using the method of calculating the weight parameter in Sect. 2.3, takes $r = 0, 0.05, 0.1, \cdots, 0.5$. The weight parameters of the improved PI model are shown in Table 1.

Table 1. Weight parameters of improved PI model

i	w_{ai}	w_{di}	i	w_{ai}	w_{di}
0	0.7531	0.7531	6	0.2500	0.1667
1	−0.5240	−0.3094	7	0.3601	0.2351
2	0.6042	0.6458	8	0.1042	0.1042
3	−0.0208	0.0208	9	−0.2948	0.0031
4	0.2083	0.2083	10	−0.3440	−0.3440
5	0.3333	0.1667			

4.2 PI Hysteresis Model Simulation

In order to verify the correctness of the weight parameters, Eqs. 2 and 6 are used to verify the measured hysteresis curve, and Eqs. 7 and 8 are used to normalize the obtained data. The results are shown in Fig. 7. Figure 7a is the hysteresis curve of the classic PI model. It can be seen that the classic PI model is centrosymmetric. The verification result of the improved PI model is shown in Fig. 7b. It can be seen from the figure that the improved PI model only has a small error at the connection of the rising and falling stages of the hysteresis loop.

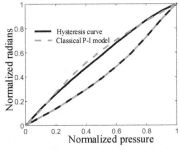
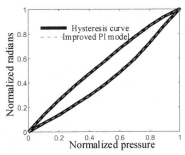

(a) The fitting renderings of the classic PI model

(b) Improved PI model fitting effect diagram

Fig. 7. Fit the graph

4.3 Tracking Control Simulation

In order to verify the validity of the inverse lag model feedforward compensation, the trajectory tracking simulation experiment of the system is carried out. The result is shown in Fig. 8. It can be seen that the tracking curve eliminates certain error at the peak value of the input curve and has better tracking effect at other positions.

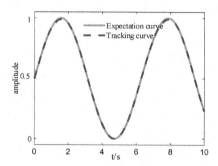

Fig. 8. PI model tracking curve

4.4 Soft Actuator Control Experiment

The improved inverse PI model is used as feedforward compensation and PID controller is added as feedback control to make the system have better dynamic characteristics. The general block diagram is shown in Fig. 9.

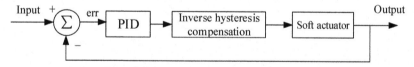

Fig. 9. Overall control block diagram of software grip actuator

The designed hysteresis compensation controller is used to control the soft gripper of Fig. 5 to grasp objects of different shapes and masses to test the performance of the soft gripper after the hysteresis compensation. Figure 10a shows the control board and Fig. 10b shows the soft gripper experiment diagram. Experiments have proved that the designed soft gripper can stably grasp objects with a diameter of 20.0 cm and a mass of less than 480 g after hysteresis compensation, with a success rate of 99.5%, which is compared with the soft gripper without hysteresis compensation. The success rate of fetching has increased significantly.

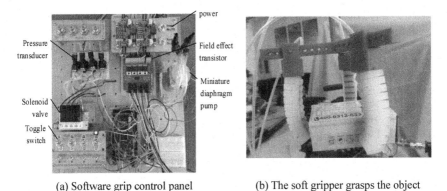

(a) Software grip control panel   (b) The soft gripper grasps the object

Fig. 10. Software grip grasping experiment

5 Conclusion

This paper proposes a hysteresis compensation control method between the air pressure and position of the software drive; Aimed at the asymmetric hysteresis phenomenon in the soft actuator, two kinds of hysteresis models, PI and improved PI, were used to model the soft actuator, and the comparison analysis was carried out. After improvement, the modeling accuracy of PI model is higher than that of traditional PI model; A mathematical method for the calculation of the weight parameters of the PI model is used to avoid the accidental factors in the process of using software to identify parameters; The prototype of the soft actuator is made, and the control grab experiment is carried out, The results show that the soft gripper actuator after hysteresis compensation can stably grasp irregularly shaped items, and the whole has strong stability.

Acknowledgment. This research is supported by National Natural Science Foundation of China (51775284), Primary Research & Developement Plan of Jiangsu Province (BE2018734), Joint Research Fund for Overseas Chinese, Hong Kong and Macao Young Scholars (61728302)and Postgraduate Research &Practice Innovation Program of Jiangsu Province (SJCX20_0253).

References

1. Lee, C., et al.: Soft robot review. Int. J. Control Autom. Syst. **15**(1), 3–15 (2016). https://doi.org/10.1007/s12555-016-0462-3
2. Polygerinos, P., Correll, N., Morin, S.A., et al.: Soft robotics: review of fluid-driven intrinsically soft devices; manufacturing, sensing, control, and applications in human-robot interaction. Adv. Eng. Mater. **19**(12), 1700016 (2017)
3. Bartlett, N.W., Tolley, M.T., Overvelde, J.T.B., et al.: A 3D-printed, functionally graded soft robot powered by combustion. Science **349**(6244), 161–165 (2015)
4. Cortez-Vega, R., Chairez, I., Feliu-Batlle, V.: Multi-link endoscopic manipulator robot actuated by shape memory alloys spring actuators controlled by a sliding mode. ISA Trans. (2020)
5. Costa, N., Caldwell, D.G.: Control of a biomimetic "soft-actuated" 10DoF lower body exoskeleton. IEEE (2006)

6. Skorina, E.H., Luo, M., Tao, W., et al.: Adapting to flexibility: model reference adaptive control of soft bending actuators. IEEE Robot. Autom. Lett. **2**(2), 964–970 (2017)

7. Gerboni, G., Diodato, A., Ciuti, G., et al.: Feedback control of soft robot actuators via commercial flex bend sensors. IEEE/ASME Trans. Mechatron. **22**(4), 1881–1888 (2017)

8. Xu, F., Jiang, Q., et al.: Design and testing of a soft robot with variable stiffness based on jamming principles. J. Mech. Eng. **56**(23), 67–77 (2020)

9. Zheng, G., Zhou, Y., Ju, M.: Robust control of a silicone soft robot using neural networks. ISA Trans. **100**, 38–45 (2020)

10. Thuruthel, T.G., et al., Soft robot perception using embedded soft sensors and recurrent neural networks. Sci. Robot. **4**(26) (2019)

11. Massari, L., et al.: A Machine-learning-based approach to solve both contact location and force in soft material tactile sensors. Soft Robot. **7**(4), 409–420 (2020)

12. Reinhart, R., Shareef, Z., Steil, J.: Hybrid analytical and data-driven modeling for feed-forward robot control. Sensors **17**(2), 311 (2017). https://doi.org/10.3390/s17020311

13. Zhang, Y., Gao, J., Yang, H., Hao, L.: A novel hysteresis modelling method with improved generalization capability for pneumatic artificial muscles. Smart Mater. Struct. **28**(10), 105014 (2019). https://doi.org/10.1088/1361-665X/ab3770

14. Abbasi, P., Nekoui, M., Zareinejad, M., Abbasi, P., Azhang, Z.: Position and force control of a soft pneumatic actuator. Soft Robot. **7**(5), 550–563 (2020). https://doi.org/10.1089/soro.2019.0065

15. Zakerzadeh, M.R., Sayyaadi, H.: Precise position of shape memory alloy actuator using inverse hysteresis model and model reference adaptive control system. Mechatron. (Oxford) **23**(8), 1150–1162 (2013)

16. Vo-Minh, T., Tjahjowidodo, T., Ramon, H., Van Brussel, H.: A new approach to modeling hysteresis in a pneumatic artificial muscle using the Maxwell-slip model. IEEE/ASME Trans. Mechatron. **16**(1), 177–186 (2011). https://doi.org/10.1109/TMECH.2009.2038373

17. Lin, C., et al.: Hysteresis modeling and tracking control for a dual pneumatic artificial muscle system using Prandtl-Ishlinskii model. Mechatron. (Oxford) **28**, 35–45 (2015)

Theoretical Analysis of a Novel Force Sensor Based on Optical Fibers Used for Semicircular Flexure Beam Unit

Haoyan Zang, Xianmin Zhang$^{(\boxtimes)}$, and Hongchuan Zhang

South China University of Technology, Guangzhou 510640, China
zhangxm@scut.edu.cn

Abstract. In the field of mechanism design, the compliant mechanisms have attracted more and more attention for the unique advantage including no need for assembling, no need for lubrication, no backlash and friction as well as easy fabrication than conventional rigid mechanisms. The periodically corrugated flexure beam units can provide a larger turn angle under the same force, so it is well suited to be designed as a revolute pair. In this paper, the relationship between external force, unit deformation and end point displacement is discussed according to the stiffness matrix method. The structural stress distribution is later discussed by the finite element method (FEM). After the mechanism analysis, a novel force sensor based on optical fibers is designed to detect the mechanical properties of the flexure units. The sensing principle is based on the intensity modulation of curved fibers that the power loss is directly related to the curvature change of a curved fiber. The mechanical-optical mapping relation is established to give the working principle of the sensor. The result shows that this newly designed force sensor has high accuracy and is suitable for the proposed structure.

Keywords: Compliant mechanisms · Optical fiber sensor · Fiber bending loss

1 Introduction

With the development of mechanism theory, conventional mechanisms struggle to overcome existing problems, but the shortcomings such as backlash, friction, and wear still exist. By contrast, compliant mechanisms can overcome these problems. They can be built in one piece, the weight can be reduced and wear, clearance, friction, noise as well as the need for lubrication can be eliminated [1, 2]. Besides, with the growth of computers, complex systems can be solved easily by using numerical methods, paving the way for studying and utilizing flexible structures [3]. Theoretically, the compliant mechanism should be made by a monolithic piece of material, and work according to the deflection of the flexible parts inside their elastic domains [4]. So the compliant mechanism can be used for many occasions including high precision manipulation stages, instruments for minimally invasive surgery, and Micro-Electromechanical Systems/Nano Electromechanical Systems (MEMS/NEMS) [5]. As for the flexure hinges, they can transmit motion between rigid members and work as revolute pairs, enabling

© Springer Nature Switzerland AG 2021
X.-J. Liu et al. (Eds.): ICIRA 2021, LNAI 13013, pp. 253–262, 2021.
https://doi.org/10.1007/978-3-030-89095-7_25

the relative rotation of two rigid parts [6]. While the periodically corrugated flexure beam units with circular contour have higher load performance and a large rotation range compared with other compliant mechanisms [7] so the flexure beam unit structure is more suitable to be used in the design process of micro-grippers. The external force applied on the flexure is small for the periodically corrugated flexure beam units with circular contour, so the force sensor used under this situation needs to have high sensitivity.

Typically, micro-force sensors are based on electrical theories, including piezoresistive [8], piezoelectric [9], electrothermal [10], and capacitive principle [11]. However, the appearance of sensors based on optical fibers has received increased attention as they present an alternative to conventional electrical sensing. As a novel work principle of the sensor, optical fiber-based sensors have brought great advantage and are used for design more and more recently. The optical fiber-based sensing principle can be divided into four types, that is intensity modulation type [12, 13], phase modulation type [14], wavelength modulation type [15], and polarization modulation type. The intensity modulation type sensors always utilize the loss during fiber curving to realize curvature change monitor. The phase modulation type sensors take advantages of the Fabry-Perot cavity by cavity length change monitoring to realize the detection of correlation quantities. As for the wavelength modulation type sensors, fiber Bragg gratings are the key elements by wavelength shift of the peak of the output spectrum acted by photo-elastic effect. Generally speaking, the structure of intensity modulation sensors is the simplest, and the fiber propagation loss is sensitive to the curvature change under a particular range.

In this paper, an optical fiber force sensor based on the principle of intensity modulation is designed to be used for the compliant mechanisms. According to the working principle of the intensity modulation optical fiber sensors based on the curvature loss of fibers, a novel sensor configuration is proposed to work under the particular range of the fiber sensor. Finally, the working principle of this novel sensor is analyzed and the sensing model is established. Besides, the feasibility of the sensor design is verified by the results of finite element analysis.

2   Optical Fiber Sensing Model Based on Bending Losses

The working principle of an optical fiber is that the light beam can be constrained inside the core of the fiber. As Maxwell's equations are a set of partial differential equations, the concept of mode is put forward to solve the equations. To be specific, the mode is a state that the electromagnetic waves propagate steadily inside the fiber core, and there is only one mode inside the single mode fiber. The optical fiber utilizing curvature loss is based on such a theory that, the conditions for mode propagation have changed as a result of bending of the propagation path. Correspondingly, the modes change and can even act with other radiation modes.

2.1   Classification of Bending Losses

The bending losses can be classified into two types, that is pure bending loss and transition loss. In the unbent fiber, the transverse mode propagates along the fiber axis and is distributed symmetrically. After the curvature, the wave is offset to one side, making the phase velocity of a part of the wave exceed the specified value and radiate away from the core. This is the pure bending loss, and is tightly related to the radius of the curvature. The mode distribution of straight single mode fiber and that of bent fiber with the curvature radius of 4mm are shown in Fig. 1 and Fig. 2 gives the simulation result of part of the bent fiber.

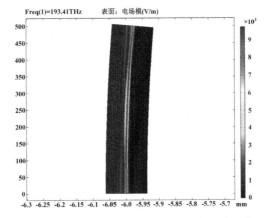

Fig. 1. The mode pattern of optical fiber under different curvature radius.

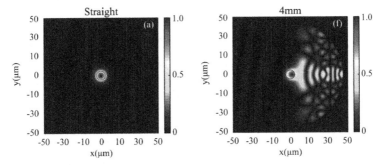

Fig. 2. The simulation result of light propagation of the bent fiber.

The formulation of pure bending loss is shown below [16].

$$\alpha_b = \int_0^L \frac{C(U,W)}{\sqrt{|R(z)|}} e^{-D(U,W)|R(z)|} dz = L \frac{C(U,W)}{|R(z)|} e^{-D(U,W)|R(z)|} \tag{1}$$

And among the above formulation, those unknown variables are defined as below. Variables U, W, and V are respectively the normalized transverse propagation constant, normalized transverse decay constant, and normalized operating frequency.

$$C(U,W) = \frac{1}{2} \left(\frac{\pi}{aW^3}\right)^{\frac{1}{2}} \left[\frac{U}{VK_1(W)}\right]^2 \tag{2}$$

$$D(U, W) = \frac{4\Delta W^3}{3aV^2} \tag{3}$$

$$U^2 = (kn_1a)^2 - (\beta_0a)^2 \tag{4}$$

$$W^2 = (\beta_0a)^2 - (kn_2a)^2 \tag{5}$$

$$V^2 = U^2 + W^2 = (ka)^2 \left(n_1^2 - n_2^2\right) \tag{6}$$

The transition loss always takes place at the junction of the straight part and bent part, and is defined as the power loss of part of the guided mode that is coupled with the radiation modes in the fiber cladding. The transition region of the bent fiber is very short, so this part of the loss is not related to the total curvature length. The result of transition loss is expressed as [17]

$$P_r = 2\frac{L}{a}A(U, W) \int_{-kn_2a}^{kn_2a} B(X)F^2(L, X)dX \tag{7}$$

with

$$A(U, W) = \left[\frac{4V^2WJ_0}{\sqrt{2\Delta}\pi J_1(U)}\right]^2 \tag{8}$$

$$B(X) = \frac{|X|(X_0^2 - X^2)^{-4}J_1^2(S)}{\left|SJ_0(S)H_1^1(Q) - QJ_1(S)H_0^1(Q)\right|^2} \tag{9}$$

$$F^2(L, X) = 2\left(\frac{a}{L}\right)\left(\frac{a}{R}\right)^2 \frac{\{1 - \cos[(X - X_0)L/a]\}}{(X - X_0)^2} \tag{10}$$

where β and β_0 are the propagation constants of radiation mode and guided mode, $J_n(x)$ and $H_n^1(x)$ are the first kind of Bessel function and Hankel function, and $X = \beta a$, $X_0 = \beta_0a$, $S^2 = (kn_1a)^2 - X^2$, $Q^2 = (kn_2a)^2 - X^2$.

The transition loss value is calculated as below.

$$\alpha_t = -10\log_{10}(1 - P_r) \tag{11}$$

2.2 Total Loss

According to the forward analysis, the loss is directly related to the curvature radius. The sum of pure bending loss, transition loss of the curvature radius less than 10 mm are calculated in the following table, of which the bending length is that of two circles under the corresponding radius.

It can be obtained from Table 1 that the total loss has a negative correlation to the curvature radius. And the best work range is in the range of 5 to 7 mm. When the radius is above this interval, the loss changes a little; while less than that, the loss gets rather large that the output is close to zero.

Table 1. Total loss of the fiber with different curvature radius.

Number	Curvature radius	Loss
1	4 mm	23.05 dB
2	5 mm	14.11 dB
3	6 mm	8.47 dB
4	7 mm	5.02 dB
5	8 mm	2.94 dB

3   Design of the Optical Fiber-Based Sensor Configuration

The optical fiber sensor utilizing bending loss is strongly related to the curvature radius. The loss value is the function of both radius and length and is an integral function of the length. It is better to utilize the semicircular compliant beam element as the sensor configuration to realize force sensing for the following reasons. First, this mechanism is well suited for the bending loss sensing methods; besides, it has small deformation together with large displacement, and is sensitive to micro forces; last but not least, this mechanism has wide applications and can be integrated for the design of precision position stages and micro grippers (Fig. 3).

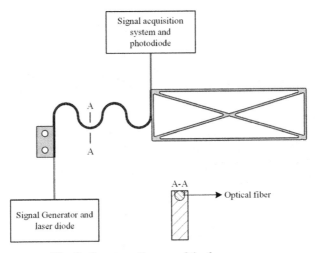

Fig. 3. Structure diagram of the force sensor.

The above analysis gives out the basic work principle of the fiber bending sensing method as well as the best work range. Based on this result, a corresponding sensor structure is designed as below.

In this sensor, the fiber is fixed on the top of a semicircular flexure beam units with 4 parts, taking the existed groove as the displacement constraint for the optical fiber. The rectangular frame with cross beams inside is designed to increase the length from external force to the semicircular units. Under this circumstance, the external force applied on the end of the rectangular frame can be considered as the pure bending moment. Thus, the deformation of the semicircular units is uniform. In addition, the structure with green parts in the above figure is the FC/APC fiber splice to connect the light path. The detailed optical connection equipment is shown in the figure below. The direction of the arrow represents the direction of signal transmission from the source to the receiver (Fig. 4).

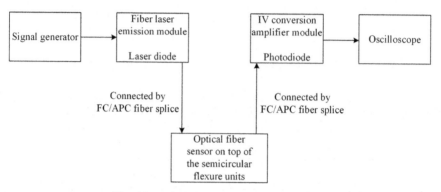

Fig. 4. Block diagram of the sensing device.

The flexure units deform under external force. The mechanical properties, that is the relationship between external force, deformation of flexure units, as well as endpoint displacement, are going to be analyzed in the next section.

4   Analysis and Verification of the Novel Optical Fiber Sensor

To get the working characteristic of the designed sensor, mechanical analysis is necessary. In this section, mechanical properties are analyzed in two ways. One is the stiffness matrix method, by calculating the stiffness matrix to establish the input-output relationship of the entire system. Another way is the FEM, by dividing the structure into a finite number of units and calculate the approximate function for each cell to obtain the total reaction of the structure.

4.1   Stiffness Matrix Method for the Mechanical Analysis

With the stiffness matrix formula of a semicircular flexure beam hinge obtained by Mohr's integral method [18],

$$
\begin{bmatrix} \sigma_x \\ \sigma_y \\ \theta_z \end{bmatrix} = \begin{bmatrix} \frac{3\pi R^3}{2EI_z} & \frac{-2R^3}{EI_z} & \frac{-\pi R^2}{EI_z} \\ \frac{-2R^3}{EI_z} & \frac{\pi R^3}{2EI_z} & \frac{2R^2}{EI_z} \\ \frac{-\pi R^2}{EI_z} & \frac{2R^2}{EI_z} & \frac{\pi R}{EI_z} \end{bmatrix} \cdot \begin{bmatrix} F_x \\ F_y \\ M_z \end{bmatrix}
\tag{12}
$$

the relation of angle θ_z and moment M_z is

$$\theta_z = \frac{\pi R}{EI_z} \cdot M_z \tag{13}$$

and the enlarged deformation diagram is shown in Fig. 5.

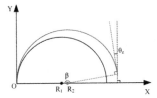

Fig. 5. Enlarged deformation diagram of a semicircular flexure beam unit.

As the total arc length keeps constant, here gives

$$(\pi - \theta_z)R_2 = \pi R_1 \tag{14}$$

the change of radius is

$$\Delta R = \frac{\theta_z}{\pi - \theta_z}R \tag{15}$$

substitute Eq. (13) into it, the result can be simplified as

$$\Delta R = \frac{R^2}{EI_z}M_z \tag{16}$$

From this result, the radius change has a linear relation with the pure moment.

4.2 Finite Element Method for the Simulation Verification

Usually, the FEM has a higher result. By fitting 100 data points calculated under the moment ranged from 0.1 N·mm to 10 N·mm of the simulation result acquired by the FEM, the fitting result is given as,

$$M_z = 1091\theta_z + 0.0001175 \tag{17}$$

$$D = 476.6\theta_z - 0.009177 \tag{18}$$

where M_z is the pure moment applied on the structure with the unit of N·mm and D is the longitudinal displacement of the end point of the rectangular frame with the unit of mm, with the material being spring steel. The thickness of the total structure is 3 mm, the beam width is 0.8 mm and the initial radius of the semicircle is 6 mm.

However, it is difficult to apply a pure bending moment to the structure. In this sensor, the rectangular frame is designed to make the applied external force can be equivalent to the pure bending moment as far as possible. The contrast diagram of stress profiles under the action of external force as well as the pure moment is shown in Fig. 6. The value of external force and the pure moment is respectively 100 mN as well as 10 N·mm, while the length of the rectangular frame is about 80 mm, which indicates that the two external loads have the roughly approximate effect.

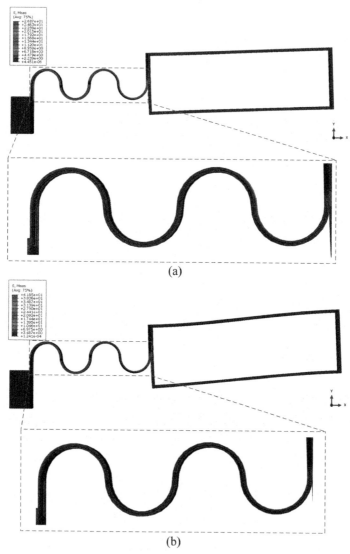

Fig. 6. Contrast diagram of stress profiles under the action of external force as well as the pure moment. (a) under the pure moment; (b) under the external force.

From the detailed figure, the stress is distributed uniformly for the structure under a pure moment. Besides, the same structure under the external force with roughly approximate value also has a uniform stress distribution when ignoring some subtle differences. Thus, it can be assumed that this structure under external force has the same effect as that under the pure moment, which greatly simplifies the analysis process.

4.3 Experiment Verification of the Force Sensor

To verify the property of the designed force sensor, an experiment is made. The end of the beam is applied with force along Y-axis and the given force is also detected by a commercial force sensor. Table 2 shows the experiment result.

Table 2. The tested value of the force sensor.

Number	Value of commercial force sensor	Output peak-to-peak voltage
1	18 mN	168.7 mV
2	31 mN	167.1 mV
3	43 mN	166.2 mV
4	53 mN	166.5 mV
5	70 mN	165.7 Mv
6	77 mN	165.0 mV
7	91 mN	164.2 mV
8	102 mN	163.7 mV
9	116 mN	162.0 mV
10	144 mN	161.9 mV

5 Conclusion

In this paper, a novel force sensor is designed based on the principle of optical fiber bending loss. As the fiber bending loss is directly related to the bending radius, the optical fiber is combined with the semicircular flexure beam units, utilizing the unit radius change caused by deformation to realize force sensing. The theoretical models are built to analyze the feasibility of the sensor and all in all, the sensor has a high sensitivity.

Acknowledgments. This work is supported by the National Natural Science Foundation of China (Grant No. 51820105007).

References

1. Pavlović, N.T., Pavlović, N.D.: Compliant mechanism design for realizing of axial link translation. Mech. Mach. Theor. **44**(5), 1082–1091 (2009)
2. Liu, M., Zhang, X., Fatikow, S.: Design and analysis of a high-accuracy flexure hinge. Rev. Sci. Instr. **87**(5), 055106 (2016)
3. Zhu, B., Zhang, X., Zhang, H., et al.: Design of compliant mechanisms using continuum topology optimization: a review. Mech. Mach. Theor. **143**, 103622 (2020)
4. Wang, P., Xu, Q.: Design of a flexure-based constant-force XY precision positioning stage. Mech. Mach. Theor. **108**, 1–13 (2017)
5. Wang, N., Liang, X., Zhang, X.: Stiffness analysis of corrugated flexure beam used in compliant mechanisms. Chin. J. Mech. Eng. **28**(4), 776–784 (2015)
6. Lobontiu, N., Cullin, M., Ali, M., et al.: A generalized analytical compliance model for transversely symmetric three-segment flexure hinges. Rev. Sci. Instrum. **82**(10), 105116 (2011)
7. Wang, N., Liang, X., Zhang, X.: Pseudo-rigid-body model for corrugated cantilever beam used in compliant mechanisms. Chin. J. Mech. Eng. **27**(1), 122–129 (2014)
8. Majstrzyk, W., Ahmad, A., Ivanov, T., et al.: Thermomechanically and electromagnetically actuated piezoresistive cantilevers for fast-scanning probe microscopy investigations. Sens. Actuators A **276**, 237–245 (2018)
9. Korayem, A.H., Korayem, M.H.: The effect of surface roughness on the vibration behavior of AFM piezoelectric MC in the vicinity of sample surface in air environment based on MCS theory. Precis. Eng. **47**, 212–222 (2017)
10. Yang, S., Xu, Q.: Design of a microelectromechanical systems microgripper with integrated electrothermal actuator and force sensor. Int. J. Adv. Rob. Syst. **13**(5), 1729881416663375 (2016)
11. Kim, K., Liu, X., Zhang, Y., et al.: Nanonewton force-controlled manipulation of biological cells using a monolithic MEMS microgripper with two-axis force feedback. J. Micromech. Microeng. **18**(5), 055013 (2008)
12. Zhao, H., O'Brien, K., Li, S., Shepherd, R.F.: Optoelectronically innervated soft prosthetic hand via stretchable optical waveguides. Sci. Robot. **1**(1), eaai7529 (2016). https://doi.org/10.1126/scirobotics.aai7529
13. Bai, H., Li, S., Barreiros, J., et al.: Stretchable distributed fiber-optic sensors. Science **370**(6518), 848–852 (2020)
14. Thondagere, C., Kaushalram, A., Srinivas, T., et al.: Mathematical modeling of optical MEMS differential pressure sensor using waveguide Bragg gratings embedded in Mach Zehnder interferometer. J. Optics **20**(8), 085802 (2018)
15. Li, R., Chen, Y., Tan, Y., et al.: Sensitivity enhancement of FBG-based strain sensor. Sensors **18**(5), 1607 (2018)
16. Gambling, W.A., Matsumura, H., Ragdale, C.M., et al.: Measurement of radiation loss in curved single-mode fibres. IEE J. Microwaves Optics Acoust. **2**(4), 134–140 (1978)
17. Zhu, Z., Brown, T.G.: Full-vectorial finite-difference analysis of microstructured optical fibers. Opt. Express **10**(17), 853–864 (2002)
18. Wang, N., Zhang, Z., Zhang, X., et al.: Optimization of a 2-DOF micro-positioning stage using corrugated flexure units. Mech. Mach. Theor. **121**, 683–696 (2018)

A New Method for Bearing Steel Ball Surface Detection with Eddy Current Sensor

Haixia Wang[1], Honghao Liu[2], Huayu Zhang[2(✉)], and Longyu Ma[2]

[1] College of Electrical Engineering and Automation, Shandong University of Science and Technology, Qingdao 266590, China
[2] College of Mechanical and Electronic Engineering, Shandong University of Science and Technology, Qingdao 266590, China
zhanghuayu@sdust.edu.cn

Abstract. As the main part of the bearing, the steel ball has a vital impact on the accuracy, running performance and service life of the bearing. Therefore, the bearing steel ball must be fully tested for the surface quality of the steel ball before leaving the factory. In this study, the one-dimensional guide-way unfolding mechanism is used to realize the complete unfolding of steel ball surface, and the eddy current sensor is used to detect the surface quality of the steel ball. Empirical mode decomposition (EMD) algorithm was used to eliminate the trend term of detection signal. Three kinds of bearing steel balls with natural defects were tested to compare with the good ones. results show that the detection system can effectively distinguish between qualified and defective steel balls.

Keywords: Steel ball · Unfolding mechanism · Defects · Eddy current · EMD

1 Introduction

Steel balls are widely used as bearing components and independent rolling elements. The quality and performance of the bearing will be greatly affected by the defected steel ball, which may lead to major safety accidents [1]. Therefore, before the bearing steel ball leaves the factory, the quality of the steel ball must be fully inspected to meet the reliability requirements of the whole mechanical system.

The traditional manual detection method is still widely used in current industrial practice [2]. The degree of automation of this method is low, which is easy to cause missed detection. Therefore, many scholars have carried out research on the steel ball detection in order to develop a fast and robust system to detect the defects on bearing steel balls. For example, capacitance sensor [3], optical fiber sensor [4], vision sensor [2, 5–7] and eddy current sensor [8–10] are used for testing the surface quality of steel ball.

Based on the comprehensive comparison of the above four detection technology (sensor), we used eddy current detection technology (sensor) to carry out the research on the on-line detection of steel ball defects.

© Springer Nature Switzerland AG 2021
X.-J. Liu et al. (Eds.): ICIRA 2021, LNAI 13013, pp. 263–274, 2021.
https://doi.org/10.1007/978-3-030-89095-7_26

The surface of steel ball is a special curved surface, which cannot be completely expanded into a plane. In the process of steel ball detection, to ensure that the steel ball is completely detected, it is necessary for the unfolding mechanism acting on the surface of the steel ball to fully unfold the steel ball, so that the surface of the steel ball can pass 100% of the detection area of the detection sensor. unfolding mechanism include disk type unfolding mechanism [2, 11], guide rail type unfolding mechanism [5–7] and wheel type unfolding mechanism [8].

One-dimensional guide-way unfolding mechanism was designed in this paper to simplify steel ball driving mechanism from two-dimensional relative motion to one-dimensional pure rolling. The steel ball quality is judge with change of the voltage amplitude output by eddy current sensor. Detection signal was processed by empirical mode decomposition (EMD) algorithm to meet the test requirements. At last the validity of the proposed detection method is verified by experiment.

2 Steel Ball Surface Unfolding Mechanism

The entire steel ball surface unfolding mechanism consists of coil fixing plate, driven wheel, coil winding skeleton and friction plate, as shown in Fig. 1.

The trapezoidal screw slide drives the friction plate to move back and forth. In order to ensure that the friction plate moves the same distance to the left and right, the friction plate will approach the capacitive proximity switch when the unfolding mechanism works, and the moving speed and distance of the friction plate are controlled by the stepper motor controller in Fig. 5. The angle between the unfolding mechanism and the worktable is θ as shown in Fig. 1. Steel ball is compressed on the driven wheel by its own gravity to ensure fixed lift-off distance between the detection coil and the steel ball. Since the eddy current sensor is sensitive to the lift-off distance, it is necessary to control the lift-off distance during the detection. Therefore, the groove on the friction plate and the steel ball form a motion constraint through point contact to prevent the ball from moving randomly.

Point A and point D on the friction plate are the position of steel ball outlet, the detection starting point of eddy current sensor is point B and point C, and the length l between B and C is the effective detection distance of steel ball. When the friction plate moves to the left, the steel ball rotates clockwise and passes through point B to point C on the friction plate in a pure rolling way. Similarly, when the friction plate moves to the right, the steel ball rotates counterclockwise and passes through point C to point B on the friction plate in a pure rolling way. The length l between BC is greater than the circumference C of the steel ball, that is: $l > C = \pi D$, D is the diameter of the steel ball, to ensure that the surface of the steel ball is completely unfolded on the friction plate. The relationship between the process of steel ball surface unfolding, detection and ball outlet and the movement position of each point (A, B, C, D) on the friction plate is shown in Table 1.

The eddy current sensor is easy to be affected by the surrounding metal conductor during the steel ball detection, so the coil fixing plate and friction plate in the unfolding mechanism are processed by PVC rigid plastic plate. The coil winding skeleton is made of SOMOS 8000 resin (Netherlands DSM Somos Company) by 3D printing.

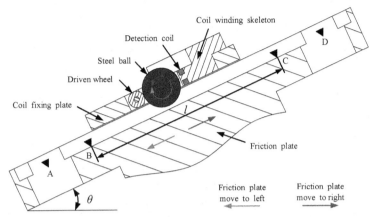

Fig.1. The one-dimensional guide-way unfolding mechanism on the surface of the steel ball. (a) Top view of the steel ball surface unfolding mechanism. (b) Half-section view of the core part of the unfolding mechanism.

Table 1. Steel ball surface unfolding, detection and ball out position.

Friction plate moves to the left		Friction plate moves to the right	
B	Steel ball entering position	C	Steel ball entering position
B → C	Surface unfolding and detection area of steel ball	C → B	Surface unfolding and detection area of steel ball
D → Ball outlet 2 → Ball outlet 3	Process of ball rolling out mechanism	A → Ball outlet 1 → Ball outlet 3	Process of ball rolling out mechanism

3 The Eddy Current Sensor

3.1 Basic Principles of Steel Ball Eddy Current Detection

Sine wave current of constant frequency f passes through the detection coil, an alternating main magnetic field will be generated around the detection coil. As the steel ball to be detected enters into the alternating main magnetic field, eddy current will be induced on the surface of the steel ball. According to Lenz's law, induced eddy current will also produce corresponding secondary alternating magnetic field, whose direction is opposite to the main magnetic field. Obviously, when surface quality defects such as cracks and scratches appear on the steel ball, the secondary alternating magnetic field changes in distribution and strength. The voltage change of the detection coil can be described by the formula [12, 13]:

$$U = F(\sigma, \mu, x, f) \tag{1}$$

In the steel ball detection, the lift-off distance x between the detection coil and the steel ball remains the same. The detection coil inputs a sine wave current of constant frequency f. If there are defects on the surface of the steel ball during the detection, the conductivity σ and permeability μ of the steel ball will change. Therefore, by detecting the change in the voltage amplitude across the coil, we can judge whether the steel ball is in defect or not.

3.2 Coil Design and Finite Element Analysis

The detection coil is an important part of the eddy current sensor, and its design parameters have a direct impact on the performance (linearity, sensitivity, and measurement range) of the eddy current sensor. In this paper, the winding of the detection coil adopts the scheme designed by reference [8]. In order to cooperate with the one-dimensional guide-way unfolding mechanism to detect the surface quality of the steel ball, the coil winding skeleton of the detection coil was redesigned. The coil winding skeleton of the detection coil is shown in Fig. 2.

The eddy current density of steel ball with micro defects was simulated by the finite element method. The parameters of the sensor detection coil are shown in Table 2, and the result of finite element analysis is shown in Fig. 3.

Figure 3(a) is the meshing diagram of the steel ball, coil and boundary during the finite element analysis. Figure 3(b) is a half cross-sectional view, and the defect width on the steel ball is 0.05 mm in the finite element analysis. At the same excitation frequency and lift-off distance, the eddy current density distribution cloud diagram of qualified steel ball surface is shown in Fig. 3(c). A semi-circular arc perpendicular to the defect is drawn on the surface of the steel ball, and its position is shown in Figs. 3(c) and (d). As the surface defect of the steel ball is perpendicular to the semi-circular arc, the eddy current density distribution cloud diagram of the surface of the defective steel ball is shown in Fig. 3(d), the red rectangular frame in Fig. 3(d) is the location of the steel ball defect. Figure 3(e) is an eddy current density line graph of the arc of qualified steel ball and defective steel ball. In Fig. 3(e), the overall trend of eddy current density on the

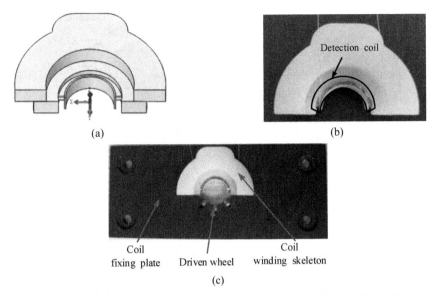

(a)   (b)

Coil   Coil
fixing plate   Driven wheel   winding skeleton

(c)

Fig.2. The winding skeleton of the detection coil and the coil fixing plate. (a) Three-dimensional model of the coil winding skeleton. (b) The physical picture of coil winding skeleton. (c) The physical pictures of coil winding skeleton and coil fixing plate.

Table 2. Parameters of sensor detection coil.

Parameters	Unit	Value
Coil inside radius	mm	4.072
Coil outside radius	mm	4.872
Distance between sensor coil and steel ball (x)	mm	0.50
Enameled wire diameter	mm	0.06
Total coil width (A)	mm	3.00
Coil side width (B)	mm	1.00
Steel ball diameter	mm	7.144
Steel ball material	–	GCr15

surface of qualified and defective steel ball is basically the same. The difference in local eddy current density reflects the effect of defect on the surface eddy current density of the steel ball. At the surface defect of the steel ball perpendicular to the semi-circular arc, the eddy current density of the steel ball at the defect position is zero, which can also reflect the width of the defect.

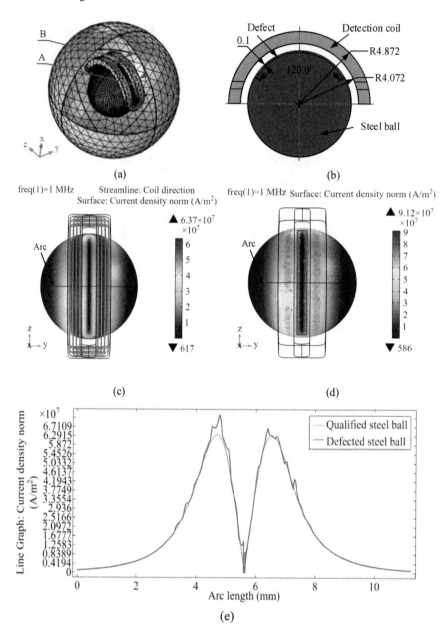

Fig. 3. (a) Meshing diagram during finite element analysis. (b) A half cross-sectional view of the defect on the steel ball and the coil. (c) Eddy current density cloud diagram and coil patterns on the surface of qualified steel balls. (d) Eddy current density cloud diagram when the surface defect of the steel ball is perpendicular to semi-circular arc. (e) Surface eddy current density line graph of qualified and defective steel ball on the semi-circular arc.

4 Experiment

The experimental device is shown in Fig. 4. Steel ball falls into the detection hole in turn. The surface quality information of the steel ball is collected and identified by the detection coil. With the data acquisition and control module USB-4711A (Advantech board, Advantech Co., Ltd., Taipei, Taiwan), the analog voltage signal of sensor output can be convert to digital quantity real time, and the digital voltage signal is transmitted to the computer for processing. Then the tested steel ball is defective or not can be determined by the voltage amplitude compare with qualified steel ball.

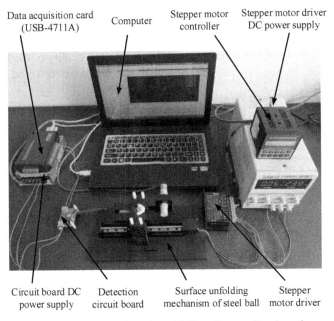

Fig. 4. The experimental device of steel ball surface quality detection system.

Qualified steel balls and steel balls with typical defects were collected from the steel ball manufacturer for testing. Figure 5 is physical picture of qualified steel ball and defective steel ball under an electron microscope. 1# is a qualified steel ball; 2# is a defective steel ball with a crack width about 0.12 mm and depth of 0.5 mm; 3# is a defective steel ball with a crack width about 0.05 mm and depth 0.1 mm; 4# is a defective steel ball with a crack width about 0.06 mm and depth 0.9 mm.

The pitch of the screw rod of the trapezoidal screw slide is 1 mm, and the slider moves 1 mm when the step motor rotates for one circle. During the experiment, the stepper motor rotates 2 circles per second, and the moving speed of the slider is 2 mm/s. The friction plate and the slider are fixed together by bolts. Therefore, the moving speed of the friction plate is 2 mm/s.

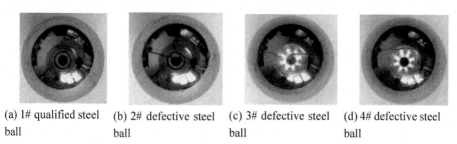

(a) 1# qualified steel
ball

(b) 2# defective steel
ball

(c) 3# defective steel
ball

(d) 4# defective steel
ball

Fig. 5. The samples of qualified and defective steel balls.

In this test, When the friction plate is moved to the left, the voltage signals of the surface quality of the four types of steel balls 1#, 2#, 3#, and 4# are collected, as show in Fig. 6. Figure 7 shows the voltage signals of the surface quality of the four types of steel balls 1#, 2#, 3#, and 4# when the friction plate is moved to the right.

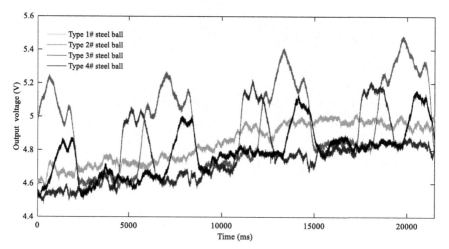

Fig. 6. The voltage signals of the surface quality of the four types of steel balls 1#, 2#, 3#, and 4# collected when the friction plate moves to the left.

In order to make the steel ball close to the driven wheel in Fig. 2(c).the steel ball surface unfolding mechanism in Fig. 4 and the work table maintained at about $\theta = 25°$. From Fig. 6 and Fig. 7, we can draw the conclusion that:

(1) The output voltage of 1# type qualified steel ball is stable within a range. The output voltage of 2# type steel ball in Fig. 6 and Fig. 7 has the most obvious voltage abrupt change at the defect. The output voltage of the 3# and 4# type steel balls at the defect is smaller than that of the 2# type steel ball.

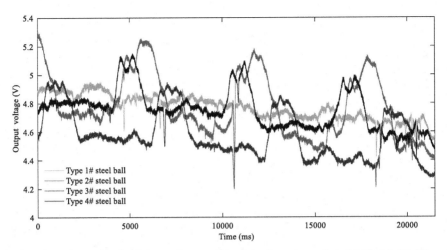

Fig. 7. The voltage signals of the surface quality of the four types of steel balls 1#, 2#, 3#, and 4# collected when the friction plate moves to the right.

(2) Since the moving speed of the friction plate is 2 mm/s, it takes about 11.22 s for a steel ball with a diameter of 7.144 mm to make one revolution. Compare the change of the output voltage before and after the time of 11.22 s in Fig. 6 and Fig. 7. For the same type of steel ball where the voltage value abruptly changes, the change in voltage amplitude is consistent.

5   Determination of the Threshold Value

Because the assembly error of the unfolding mechanism, the detection signal deviate from the baseline and a trend term during the pure rolling unfolding as shown in Fig. 6 and Fig. 7. The appearance of the trend term will not be conducive to the determination of the threshold value. As shown in Fig. 7, the peak value of the voltage signal of 3# defective steel ball and the voltage signal of 1# qualified steel ball approximately coincide, and it is difficult to distinguish between the 3# defective steel ball and the 1# qualified steel ball. In order to eliminate the impact of trend items in detection signal, which can gradually decompose the wave model of different scales hidden in the voltage signal through sifting. EMD is direct and adaptive in the whole sifting process. The basis function is directly generated from the signal itself, and different signals will generate different basis functions. The EMD method decomposes the signal according to the information of the signal itself, and the intrinsic mode functions (IMF) component obtained is limited, and each IMF component represents the real information contained in the signal. The EMD formula is as follows [14]:

$$x(t) = \sum_{i=1}^{n} imf_i(t) + r_n(t) \tag{2}$$

Where imfi (t) is the i*th* IMF obtained by the decomposition, and $rn(t)$ is the residual signal component of the n IMF obtained by the decomposition and sifting. The intrinsic mode function (IMF) is a function that satisfies two conditions [15]: (1) in the whole data set, the number of extreme and the number of zero crossings must either equal or differ at most by one. (2) The local mean value calculated from the upper and lower envelope determined by the extreme value is zero.

According to the above two conditions, the instantaneous average in the signal is removed, and finally it stops according to a certain error criterion to obtain an IMF. After repeated cycles, no more IMF can be resolved. The final component is the residual component, and the EMD decomposition ends [16].

The EMD is used to process the collected trend term voltage signal to obtain Fig. 8 and Fig. 9. It can be seen that the maximum voltage output value of the 1# steel ball is about 0.10 V, and the maximum voltage output values of the 2#, 3#, and 4# steel balls are about 0.47 V, 0.40 V, and 0.33 V, respectively. Therefore, there is a difference between 1# qualified steel ball and 2#, 3#, 4# defective steel ball. In order to realize the automatic detection of steel ball, a threshold must be set for the same batch of steel balls. If the detection value is greater than the threshold value, it indicates that the tested steel ball is unqualified. Set the threshold value of the steel ball to 0.15 V.

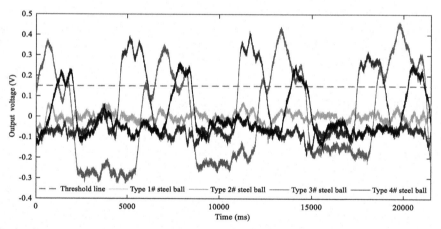

Fig. 8. The voltage signals of the surface quality of the four types of steel balls 1#, 2#, 3#, and 4# collected when the friction plate moves to the left after EMD processing.

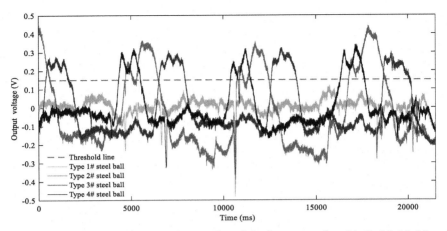

Fig. 9. The voltage signals of the surface quality of the four types of steel balls 1#, 2#, 3#, and 4# collected when the friction plate moves to the right after EMD processing.

6   Conclusion

In this paper, a one-dimensional guide-way unfolding mechanism is designed to realize the full unfolding of the steel ball surface. The steel ball is simplified from the traditional two-dimensional unfolding method to one-dimensional pure rolling, which makes the unfolding mechanism have the advantages of simple structure and convenient processing, reducing installation difficulty of debugging. By analyzing the voltage signal acquisition from the 1#, 2#, 3#, and 4# steel balls, the eddy current sensor can distinguish the surface quality of these four types of steel balls and verify the feasibility of the proposed detection system.

Acknowledgments. This work is supported by National Natural Science Foundation of China (62073199), Key Laboratory for Robot & Intelligent Technology of Shandong Province (Shandong University of Science and Technology). The authors are grateful to the reviewers who helped us improve the paper through many pertinent comments and suggestions.

References

1. Ng, T.W.: Optical inspection of ball bearing defects. Meas. Sci. Technol. **18**(9), N73–N76 (2007)
2. Chen, Y.-J., Tsai, J.-C., Hsu, Y.-C.: A real-time surface inspection system for precision steel balls based on machine vision. Meas. Sci. Technol. **27**(7), 074010 (2016)
3. Kakimoto, A.: Detection of surface defects on steel ball bearings in production process using a capacitive sensor. Measurement **17**, 51–57 (1996)
4. Li, G., Zhou, S., Ma, L., Wang, Y.: Research on dual wavelength coaxial optical fiber sensor for detecting steel ball surface defects. Measurement **133**, 310–319 (2019)
5. Lin, L., Zhong, W., Fangying, P., et al.: Sphere surface unfolding method with two image sensors. Chin. J. Sci. Instrum. **33**(7), 1641–1646 (2012). (in Chinese)

6. Wang, Z., Xing, Q., Fu, L., Sun, H.: Realtime vision-based surface defect inspection of steel balls. Trans. Tianji Univ. **21**(1), 76–82 (2015)
7. Do, Y., Lee, S., Kim, Y.: Vision-based surface defect inspection of metal balls. Measur. Sci. Technol. **22**(10), 107001 (2011). https://doi.org/10.1088/0957-0233/22/10/107001
8. Zhang, H., Zhong, M., Xie, F., Cao, M.: Application of a saddle-type Eddy current sensor in steel ball surface-defect inspection. Sensors **17**(12), 2814 (2017). https://doi.org/10.3390/s17122814
9. Zhang, H., Xie, F., Cao, M., Zhong, M.: A steel ball surface quality inspection method based on a circumferential Eddy current array sensor. Sensors **17**(7), 1536 (2017). https://doi.org/10.3390/s17071536
10. Zhang, H., Ma, L., Xie, F.: A method of steel ball surface quality inspection based on flexible arrayed eddy current sensor. Measurement **144**, 192–202 (2019). https://doi.org/10.1016/j.measurement.2019.05.056
11. Zhao, Y.L., Che, W.B., Zhou, K., et al.: Design of deployment mechanism of steel ball and surface defects recognition. Appl. Mech. Mater. **274**, 245–248 (2013)
12. Yu, R., Sun, H., Geng, J.: Research on quality inspection and sorting on-line system for bearing steel ball. In: 7th International Conference on Mechanical and Electronics Engineering (2015)
13. Tian, G.Y., Zhao, Z.X., Baines, R.W.: The research of inhomogeneity in eddy current sensors. Sens. Actuators A (Phys.) **69**(2), 148–151 (1998)
14. Kim, D., Hee-Seok, O.: EMD: a package for empirical mode decomposition and Hilbert spectrum. R J. **1**(1), 40 (2009). https://doi.org/10.32614/RJ-2009-002
15. Huang, N.E., et al.: The empirical mode decomposition and the Hilbert spectrum for nonlinear and non-stationary time series analysis. Proc. R. Soc. Lond. Ser. A Math. Phys. Eng. Sci. **454**(1971), 903–995 (1998). https://doi.org/10.1098/rspa.1998.0193
16. Wang, G., Chen, X.-Y., Qiao, F.-L., Zhaohua, W., Huang, N.: On intrinsic mode function. Adv. Adapt. Data Anal. **2**(3), 277–293 (2010)

Variable Stiffness Actuator Structure for Robot

Chuanyi Cui[1,2] 📷, Kai Guo[1,2(✉)] 📷, and Jie Sun[1,2]

[1] Key Laboratory of High-Efficiency and Clean Mechanical Manufacture, National Demonstration Center for Experimental Mechanical Engineering Education, School of Mechanical Engineering, Shandong University, Ji'nan 250061, People's Republic of China
kaiguo@sdu.edu.cn

[2] Research Center for Aeronautical Component Manufacturing Technology and Equipment, Shandong University, Ji'nan 250061, People's Republic of China

Abstract. Based on the idea of regulating the variation on stiffness by controlling the number of springs involved in the work, this paper designs a kind of variable stiffness actuator (VSA) which can be applied to the field of robot. The variable stiffness structure takes the spiral tensile spring as the elastic element, and the number of springs Participating in the work is controlled by the push-pull electromagnet. It has the accurate positive and negative 32 kinds of stiffness adjustment values. The structure model was established by using SolidWorks. MATLAB analysis was used to optimize the design of the structure and conduct mechanical and structural stiffness analysis, and the angle range and stiffness range of the actuator were obtained, which had showed a uniform characteristic of distribution of adjustable stiffness values in stiffness range interval. The conclusion is that the VSA has the advantages of real-time and accurate change of stiffness, wide variation range of stiffness and wide adjustment range of angle.

Keywords: Variable stiffness · Actuator · Robot

1 Introduction

Research for VSA has received wide-spread attention [1]. People study the design of VSA because it can minimize the impact on excessive force, realize human-machine interaction safely [2]. Researchers further hope that energy can be stored as intending in the elastic element and release to achieve the goal of saving energy. Currently, various VSA structures are designed, such as Series Elastic Actuators (SEAs) [3–6], Parallel Elastic Actuators (PEAs) [7] and serial-parallel elastic actuator (SPEA) [8, 9]. Sugar developed an actuator based on the principle of balance control stiffness [10], in which a linear spring was connected to the rigid actuator in series, and the force or stiffness required was controlled by changing the balance position of the spring. This design realizes a wide range of stiffness adjustment, but the complex transmission mechanism would lead to excessive volume and weight, which is unfavorable to the robot that needs flexible movement. Migliore et al. studied a device based on the principle of antagonistic control of stiffness [11]. Such a structure requires two series or parallel actuators with elastic elements to work against each other to control the position and

© Springer Nature Switzerland AG 2021
X.-J. Liu et al. (Eds.): ICIRA 2021, LNAI 13013, pp. 275–283, 2021.
https://doi.org/10.1007/978-3-030-89095-7_27

stiffness at the same time [12, 13]. The output position is usually controlled by the differential motion of two actuators in the same direction and opposite direction to meet its compliance adjustment [14–16]. However, this setting has obvious limitations, including high energy consumption caused by complex coupling control and continuous control. The controlling method of stiffness of Jack spring structure adopted by Hollander et al. was to increase or decrease the number of effective spring coils by rotating the spring coil, thus changing the effective stiffness of the structure [17]. This structure can easily change the stiffness presupposition. But its narrow stiffness adjustment range is a significant limitation. Y. Xu et al. developed a new VSA with S-shaped Springs [18–20], their new VSA has excellent performance. They could change the stiffness by adjusting the amount and the angle of the S-shaped Springs, but they did not concern the fatigue of the springs designed. Wolf et al. from the German Aerospace Center developed VS-Joint [21], which can change the vertical position of the slider on the spring base by driving the spindle rotation of a small motor, so as to realize the adjustment of the stiffness. There is another way like the actuator with adjustable stiffness (AwAS) [22], a pseudo-linear variable-ratio lever variable-stiffness actuator (PLVL-VSA) [23], or the serial variable stiffness actuator II (SVSA-II) [24], which regulates the stiffness by change the transmission ratio between the output and elastic element. These studies have many applications for the interaction between robots and the environment, such as exoskeleton [22], rehabilitation robots [23], hopping robots [24].

Although the current VSAs have achieved suitable performance, they still face a common fundamental limitation, namely the fixed spring constant of the elastic element. The performance of traditional VSA is largely dependent on the spring constant. Yu Haoyong from the National University of Singapore mentioned in his paper [25] that soft springs can produce high-fidelity force control with low output impedance and reduced static friction, but it also limits the allowable force range and force control bandwidth of the system when it is subjected to a strong force. Hard springs, on the other hand, can increase the bandwidth of a force but reduce its fidelity. In order to achieve the desired output force/torque, most traditional VSAs are designed with very stiff springs, resulting in poor force control, low fixed compliance, poor reverse drive capability, and heavy systems.

In this paper, the motor is no longer simply used to control the change of a single or single kind of elastic element. A control method is used to design a VSA, which controls the exact change of stiffness by controlling the number of elastic elements involved in the work. The structure of this paper is as follows. Section 2 describes the structure design of the VSA, including principal designed parameters and working principle of important structures, and the establishing of the model with SolidWorks. Section 3 introduces the mechanical calculation and MATLAB simulation with analysis. Section 4 presents the stiffness analysis of the VSA, using MATLAB to get its angle range and stiffness adjustment range. Finally, the conclusions are shown in Sect. 5.

2 Structure Design

The VSA structure designed in this paper is mainly composed of movable rod, tensile spring, mesh chip, fluted disc, electromagnet, output disc and reset spring, as shown in

Fig. 1 below. When the VSA structure works, the current is input into the electromagnet, the electromagnet pushes the movable rod, so that the mesh chip fixed on the movable rod is embedded in the fluted disc, which is connected with input shaft. Then the fluted disc drives the movable rod to rotate, so that the corresponding tensile spring participates in the work to change the overall stiffness of the VSA, and to transfer the input shaft torque to the output disc; When the current stops input, the core of electromagnet moves back, then the movable rod is pushed back by the reset spring, the mesh chip is separated from the fluted disc, and the corresponding tensile spring disengages.

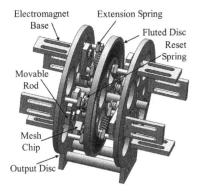

Fig. 1. VSA structure modeled by SolidWorks.

2.1 Principal Designed Parameters

Four kinds of tensile springs of SUS304-WPB materials with different stiffness were selected as elastic components, and their properties are shown in Table 1 below. The selection of springs designed in this paper is limited to prototype production in order to demonstrate the performance of VSA structures.

Table 1. Parameters pf SUS304-WPB spring with 4 different stiffnesses

Number	D (mm)	D (mm)	L (mm)	N	G (kgf * mm^{-2})	ki(g * mm^{-1})
1	0.5	5	15	10	7000	75.02
2	0.4	4	15	10	7000	60.01
3	0.3	4	15	10	7000	17.49
4	0.3	3	15	10	7000	45.01

Inside the Table 1, the stiffness (spring constant) is expressed as ki (i = 1, 2, 3, 4). Spring stiffness calculation formula (unit: kgf/mm): $k = (G * d^4)/(8 * Dm^3 * Nc)$; G: Rigidity modulus of wire rod;

L: Length;
d: Wire diameter;
D: Outside diameter;
Dm: Medium diameter = Outer diameter - Wire diameter;
N: Total number of coils;
Nc: Valid number of coils = total number of coils - 2;

2.2 Structure Design of VSA

The idea of the VSA structure is that the driving stiffness can be adjusted at any time. Through the work of each part and the division of mutual cooperation, the VSA structure designed in this paper can be divided into rod-spring structure, chip-disc structure and electromagnet propulsion structure.

Rod-Spring Structure. The 4 movable rods are connected with the output disc, conducting single directional rotating motion on the output disc. An end of the spring is fixed with the movable rod, and the other end is fixed on the output disc. The structure of the rod-spring is shown in Fig. 2 as follows.

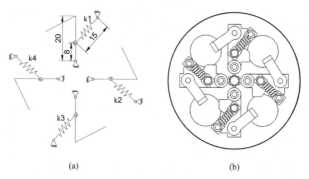

(a)   (b)

Fig. 2. The (a) is the Schematic diagram of rod-spring; (b) is the SolidWorks simulation model.

Chip-Disc Structure. The mesh chips are fixed on the movable rod to support the connection or disconnection between the rod-spring structure and the fluted disc. The fluted disc is connected with the torque input shaft, and the front and back of the fluted disc is respectively provided with a ring of fluted grooves for inserting the mesh chips.

Electromagnet Propulsion Structure. Electromagnet propulsion structure of the design of this paper is equivalent to the role of "switch". When the rated current signal is input into the electromagnet, the electromagnet will push the movable rod; When there is no current signal input to the electromagnet, the rod-spring structure will be reset. The structural schematic diagram is shown in Fig. 3.

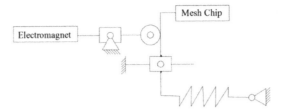

Fig. 3. Schematic diagram of the Electromagnet propulsion structure.

3 Mechanical Analysis

Tensile spring and movable rod connection diagram is shown in Fig. 4. Below. It has presented that when the springs participate in the work, they will transform the pull force into the moment. So every spring need to transform its stiffness ki, which is related to their own force and displacement, into stiffness Ki, which is related to torque and angle. The value of Ki is the stiffness spring of ki provides for VSA. The purpose of the mechanical analysis is to obtain the stiffness Ki of the VSA provided by the four kinds of tensile springs after they respectively participate in the work through mechanical and geometric calculation.

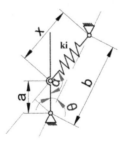

Fig. 4. Schematic diagram of connection between tension spring and movable rod.

When the movable rod is upright, x is original length of the spring, a is the distance between the connection point of the movable, from the law of cosines

$$x^2 = a^2 + b^2 - 2ab \cdot \cos\theta \tag{1}$$

The b is the distance between the connecting point of the movable rod on the output disc and the fixed end of the spring on the output disc.

According to Hooke's Law, there is a spring tension force

$$F_i = k_i \Delta x \tag{2}$$

According to the law of cosines

$$x = \sqrt{a^2 + b^2 - 2ab \cdot \cos\theta} \tag{3}$$

According to the law of sine

$$\frac{b}{sin\alpha} = \frac{x}{sin\theta} \tag{4}$$

$$sin\alpha = \frac{b \cdot sin\theta}{x} \tag{5}$$

The moment provided by the spring tension to the VSA is

$$M_i = a \cdot sin\alpha \cdot k_i \Delta x \tag{6}$$

$$M_i = \frac{k_i ab \cdot sin\theta}{x} \cdot \Delta x \tag{7}$$

Plug (3) into, then get

$$\Delta x = \sqrt{a^2 + b^2 - 2ab \cdot cos\theta} - \sqrt{a^2 + b^2 - 2ab \cdot cos\theta_0} \tag{8}$$

$$M_i = k_i ab \cdot sin\theta \cdot (1 - \frac{\sqrt{a^2 + b^2 - 2ab \cdot cos\theta_0}}{\sqrt{a^2 + b^2 - 2ab \cdot cos\theta}}) \tag{9}$$

The unit of moment M is g * mm.

From MATLAB simulation, the curve of the moment M on $\pi/6$–$\pi/2$ is shown below as Fig. 5.

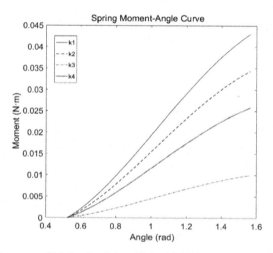

Fig. 5. The curve of M-Angle of 4 springs with different stiffness on $\pi/6$–$\pi/2$

It can be seen that the Moment-Angle curve has a good linearity. If the relationship between moment and angle is set as a linear one, there is

$$M_i = K_i\theta + C_i \tag{10}$$

Where, K_i is the stiffness of spring i converted into the overall stiffness of VSA, that is, the stiffness spring i can provide for the VSA, and the unit is $N \cdot m \cdot rad^{-1}$. Since the angle starts at $\pi/6$, the constant C_i can be abandoned, then (10) becomes

$$M_i = K_i\theta \tag{11}$$

Divide 0–$\pi/3$ into 9 equal parts, take 10 points (Fig. 6).

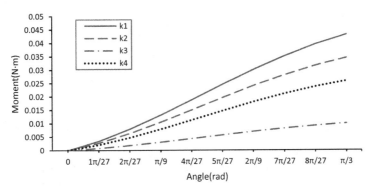

Fig. 6. The 9 bisected line chart of M-Angle of 4 springs with different stiffness on $\pi/6$–$\pi/2$

It can be seen from the above formula (9), spring stiffness of ki is directly proportional to the relationship of the moment Mi, so the single spring stiffness ki is also directly proportional to the relationship of its corresponding conversion Ki for. So, in the design of elastic element, this nature will be greatly convenient when users choose the spring stiffness and do the simulation calculation to obtain the desired adjustable stiffness value.

4 Stiffness Analysis

The stiffness of the VSA has two situations: clockwise and counterclockwise (positive and negative). In both cases, the adjustable stiffness is equal in size but opposite in direction. Therefore, the VSA designed has 16 different combined stiffnesses in each direction obtained by MATLAB simulation calculation.

5 Conclusion

Based on the concept of controlling the variation on stiffness by changing the number of elastic elements involved in the work, this paper designed a variable stiffness actuator which can be applied to the field of robot. A prototype was modeled on SolidWorks and its mechanical properties and stiffness were analyzed and simulated by using MATLAB. The VSA has the advantages of real-time and accurate change of stiffness, wide variation range of stiffness and wide adjustment range of angle. Due to the limitation of elastic elements, the VSA structure and control still has room for improvement, and the stiffness data can be further optimized. In the future, prototype will be made, and further experiments will be conducted on the control aspect based on this paper, and more data will be collected for optimization.

Although VSAs have many advantages, they still have many limitations, such as the need for more complex control algorithms. Researchers have made some progress in areas of adaptive tracking control [26, 27], neural networks [28], friction compensation [29] and other control algorithms, as well as dynamic joint stiffness identification and appropriate posture selection [30]. Therefore, structural design that can simplify the control algorithm and obtain more accurate control of velocity, force and position is also a direction of future work.

References

1. Zacharaki, A., Kostavelis, I., Gasteratos, A., Dokas, I.M.: Safety bounds in human robot interaction: a survey. Saf. Sci. **127**, 104667 (2020)
2. Ham, R.V., Sugar, T.G., Vanderborght, B., Hollander, K.W., Lefeber, D.: Compliant actuator designs. IEEE Robot. Autom. Mag. **16**(3), 81–94 (2009)
3. Vanderborght, B., Albuschaeffer, A., Bicchi, A., Burdet, E., Caldwell, D.G., et al.: Variable impedance actuators: a review. Robot. Auton. Syst. **61**(12), 1601–1614 (2013)
4. Yu, N., Zou, W., Sun, Y.: Passivity guaranteed stiffness control with multiple frequency band specifications for a cable-driven series elastic actuator. Mech. Syst. Signal Process. **117**, 709–722 (2019)
5. Sun, L., Li, M., Wang, M., Yin, W., Sun, N., Liu, J.: Continuous finite-time output torque control approach for series elastic actuator. Mech. Syst. Signal Process. **139**, 105853 (2020)
6. Chen, B., Zi, B., Wang, Z., Qin, L., Liao, W.H.: Knee exoskeletons for gait rehabilitation and human performance augmentation: a state-of-the-art. Mech. Mach. Theory **134**, 499–511 (2019)
7. Plooij, M., Wisse, M., Vallery, H.: Reducing the energy consumption of robots using the bidirectional clutched parallel elastic actuator. IEEE Trans. Robot. **32**(6), 1512–1523 (2016)
8. Mathijssen, G., Furnemont, R., Brackx, B., Van Ham, R., Lefeber, D., Vanderborght, B.: Design of a novel intermittent self-closing mechanism for a MACCEPA-based Series-Parallel Elastic Actuator (SPEA). In: Proceedings of IEEE/RSJ International Conference on Intelligent Robots and Systems, pp. 2809–2814 (2014)
9. Beyl, P., Van Damme, M., Van Ham, R., Vanderborght, B.: Pleated pneumatic artificial muscle-based actuator system as a torque source for compliant lower limb exoskeletons. IEEE/ASME Trans. Mechatron. **19**(3), 1046–1056 (2014)
10. Hollander, K.W., Ilg, R., Sugar, T.G., Herring, D.: "An efficient robotic tendon for gait assistance. J. Biomech. Eng. **128**(5), 788–791 (2006)
11. Migliore, S.A., Brown, E.A.: Biologically inspired joint stiffness control. In: Proceedings of IEEE International Conference on Robotics and Automation (ICRA 2005), pp. 4519–4524 (2005)
12. Wolf, S., et al.: Variable stiffness actuators: review on design and components. IEEE/ASME Trans. Mechatron. **21**(5), 2418–2430 (2016)
13. Tagliamonte, N.L., Sergi, F., Accoto, D., Carpino, G., Guglielmelli, E.: Double actuation architectures for rendering variable impedance in compliant robots: a review. Mechatronics **22**(8), 1187–1203 (2012)
14. Lemerle, S., Grioli, G., Bicchi, A., Catalano, M.G.: A variable stiffness elbow joint for upper limb prosthesis. In: Proceedings of IEEE/RSJ International Conference on Intelligent Robots and Systems, pp. 7327–7334 (2019)

15. Liu, Y., Liu, X., Yuan, Z., Liu, J.: Design and analysis of spring parallel variable stiffness actuator based on antagonistic principle. Mech. Mach. Theory **140**, 44–58 (2019)
16. Bilancia, P., Berselli, G., Palli, G.: Virtual and physical prototyping of a beam-based variable stiffness actuator for safe human-machine interaction. Robot. Comput. Integr. Manuf. **65**, 101886 (2020)
17. Hollander, K., Sugar, T., Herring, D.: Adjustable robotic tendon using a 'jack spring'. In: Proceedings of 9th International Conference on Rehabilitation Robotics (ICORR 2005), pp. 113–118 (2005)
18. Xu, Y., Guo, K., Sun, J., Li, J.: Design, modeling and control of a reconfigurable variable stiffness actuator. Mech. Syst. Signal Process. **160**, 107883 (2021)
19. Xu, Y., Guo, K., Sun, J., Li, J.: Design and analysis of a linear digital variable stiffness actuator. IEEE Access **9**, 13992–14004 (2021)
20. Xu, Y., Guo, K., Li, J., Li, Y.: A novel rotational actuator with variable stiffness using S-shaped springs. IEEE/ASME Trans. Mechatron. **26**(4), 2249–2260 (2020)
21. Wolf, S., Hirzinger, G.: A new variable stiffness design: matching requirements of the next robot generation. Accepted at ICRA 2008: IEEE International Conference on Robotics and Automation (ICRA2008) (2008)
22. Chen, G., Qi, P., Guo, Z., Yu, H.: Mechanical design and evaluation of a compact portable knee-ankle-foot robot for gait rehabilitation. Mech. Mach. Theory **103**, 51–64 (2016)
23. Li, X., Liu, Y., Yu, H.: Iterative learning impedance control for rehabilitation robots driven by series elastic actuators. Automatica **90**(90), 1–7 (2018)
24. Haldane, D.W., Plecnik, M.M., Yim, J.K., Fearing, R.S.: Robotic vertical jumping agility via series-elastic power modulation. Sci. Robot. **1**(1), eaag2048 (2016)
25. Yu, H., Huang, S., Chen, G., Thakor, N.: Control design of a novel compliant actuator for rehabilitation robots. Mechatronics **23**(8), 1072–1083 (2013)
26. Guo, K., Li, M., Shi, W., Pan, Y., et al.: Adaptive tracking control of hydraulic systems with improved parameter convergence. IEEE Trans. Ind. Electron., 1 (2021). https://doi.org/10.1109/TIE.2021.3101006
27. Guo, K., Pan, Y., Zheng, D., Yu, H., et al.: Composite learning control of robotic systems: a least squares modulated approach. Automatica **111**, 108612 (2020)
28. Guo, K., Zheng, D., Li, J.: Optimal bounded ellipsoid identification with deterministic and bounded learning gains: design and application to Euler-Lagrange Systems. IEEE Trans. Cybern., 1–14 (2021). https://doi.org/10.1109/TCYB.2021.3066639
29. Guo, K., Pan, Y., Yu, H.: Composite learning robot control with friction compensation: a neural network-based approach. IEEE Trans. Ind. Electron. **66**(10), 7841–7851 (2019)
30. Zhang, Y., Guo, K., Sun, J., Sun, Y., et al.: Method of postures selection for industrial robot joint stiffness identification. IEEE Access **9**, 1–10 (2021)

The FBP Gripper: Pin-Array Self-adaptive Gripper Based on Fluid-Driven Bellow Piston Mechanism

Zeming Li and Wenzeng Zhang[(✉)]

Department of Mechanical Engineering, Tsinghua University, Beijing 100084, China

Abstract. To overcome the shortcomings of pin-array gripper that have uneven grasping force, this paper proposes a design of a pin-array self-adaptive gripper based on fluid-driven bellow piston mechanism. The gripper could obtain multi-point contact through the array of multiple-slice-bellow piston when grasping, adapts to objects of different shapes and sizes by the passive sliding of slide pipes on the guide rods, so as to achieve self-adaptive characteristics. The quick and stable grasping of the object is achieved by the pushing force of the bellow piston modules that driven by the fluid pressure. The bellow piston modules give a large grasping force and the connected fluid guaranteed the automatic coordination and balance of the grasping force of multiple sliding rods on the object. The sensing and control requirements are relatively low, the control is easy, and the grasping force exerted on the object is evenly distributed. The device is suitable for all kinds of occasions that need to grab objects of different shapes and sizes.

Keywords: Universal gripper · Self-adaptive grasping · Fluidic actuator

1 Introduction

Robotic gripper, as one of the executive terminations between the robot system and the environment, plays an important role as they guarantee the stable manipulation of the object in most robot applications, thus has long been researched. As a perfect example, human hands can easily grasp objects of different sizes and shapes with high adaptabilities, humanoid robot hand is an important trend for robotic hands. In the decades of research on gripper (robot hand), researchers have a lot of analysis results show that the core function of human hand is the adaptive grasping, which need either large number of degrees of freedom [1] and sensors [2–4] (dexterous hand) or com-plex underactuated mechanism (underactuated hand [5–8]), their complicated structures and control strategies make it hard to develop.

In order to achieve the adaptive grasping that does not have to use multi-finger or multi-joint humanoid hand structure, many new designs of robotic gripper with adaptive grasping effect were researched (universal gripper) [9–14]. In the field of universal gripper, Peter et al. [15] developed an early adaptive hand with two groups of sliding arrays, the structure and gripper strategy is shown in Fig. 1, during the grasping, two groups of sliding arrays firstly slide up and down to adapt to the shape of the object under

© Springer Nature Switzerland AG 2021
X.-J. Liu et al. (Eds.): ICIRA 2021, LNAI 13013, pp. 284–292, 2021.
https://doi.org/10.1007/978-3-030-89095-7_28

the extrusion of the object, and then grasp the object by pushing the two groups of slider rods from both sides to the center. The shortcoming is that the gripper cannot grasp the strip object that lies along the direction that the sliding arrays moving, and the grasping force is small and unstable when the grasping object is smaller than the boundary of one group and cannot contact the two groups of sliding arrays at the same time.

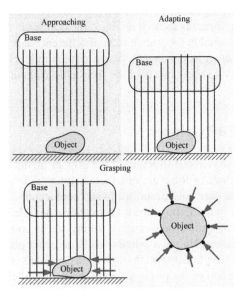

Fig. 1. Schematic illustration of the structure and grasping strategy of pin-array gripper.

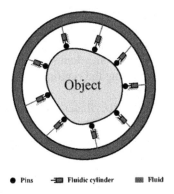

Fig. 2. Schematic illustration of the core design of the fluid-driven pin-array gripper.

Based on the basic design of the pin-array structure, Hong et al. [12] designed a pin-array universal gripper with a group of pin array that have the ability of omnidirectional gathering from their roots, called CTSA gripper, can grasp objects in different directions. It has following disadvantages: the gripper cannot have a relatively close grasping force for each pin that contact with the object when grasping the periphery of the pins was tied by the tendon rope and produce grasping force, but the inner pins are not directly contact with the tendon rope and there is no grasping force produced on them, which lead to an uneven grasping force of the object, affect its application.

In order to overcome the shortcoming of the uneven grasping force of pin-array universal gripper, this paper designs a self-adaptive gripper (or robot hand) based on bellow piston mechanism. The core design scheme is take fluid pressure as the power to drive the movement of the pin arrays, utilizing the equal pressure in the steady fluid to coordinate the grasping force, as showed in Fig. 2, the designed gripper has the effect of universal grasping and suitable for grab objects of different shape, size, have the ability to get more contact when grasping objects, can achieve parallel clamping fetching, thus suitable for fetching level sheet objects of the worktable without complex sensing and control requirements.

2   Design of the FBP Gripper

As is shown in Fig. 3, the overall structure of the gripper including a base module and nine sliding modules, three of those are distributed along the inner circle and other six are distributed along the outer circle, uniformly and homocentric. Every sliding module is consisting of a guide rod, a sliding tube that cover by a flexible film and a spring. The sliding tube is fixed to the guide rod through a sliding-sleeve coupler and connected by the spring. The base is consisting of a cylinder shell, an upper plate and a middle plate. The plates are fixed to the cylinder shell through rigid couplings and keep an appropriate distance for the installation of the primary and secondary fluid chamber. All the guide rods are parallel to each other and their freedom of motion is restricted by the through holes on the base. The three guide rods of inner circle pass through holes on the upper plate, middle plate and the cylinder shell, while the other six only pass through the holes on middle plate and cylinder shell.

The aforesaid through holes on the base (including the cylinder shell and two plates) is basically in shape of sliding chutes, of which the sliding direction for gathering from the circles to the center, restricting the freedom of motion of those inlaid guide rods down to only a translation motion along the centripetal direction of the inner and outer circle that guide rods lied on.

Inside the interval of the plates and cylinder shell there are two donut-shaped fluid chambers to drive the guide rods. The primary fluid chamber, with a slightly larger inner diameter than that of outer circle that guide rods fixed along, is fixed in the interval between the cylinder shell and middle plate through rigid coupling. The movement of the guide rods that lied on the outer circle is driven by the primary fluid chamber through six bellow piston modules that fixed on the internal round surface of primary fluid chamber. On the other hand, the secondary fluid chamber, with a slightly larger inner diameter than that of inner circle that guide rods fixed along, is fixed in the interval between the upper plate and middle plate through rigid coupling. The movement of the guide rods that lied on the inner circle is driven by the secondary fluid chamber through three bellow piston modules that fixed on the internal round surface of secondary fluid chamber.

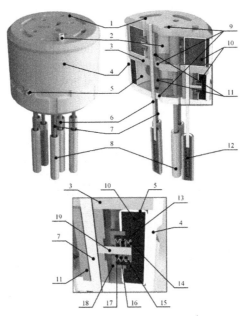

Fig. 3. The structure of the FBP gripper. 1-upper plate, 2-2nd fluid chamber, 3-middle plate, 4-cylinder shell, 5-1st fluid chamber, 6 guide rod, 7-guide rod, 8-elastic sleeve, 9-sliding chute, 10-fluid, 11-sleeve, 12-spring, 13-flexible film, 14-distal slice, 15, 16-middle slice, 17-proximal slice, 18-coupling sleeve, 19-sliding shaft.

Every bellow piston module is consisting of a distal slice, two middle slices, a proximal slice, a sliding shaft, a cylinder-shaped coupling sleeve and a flexible film. All of the slices are sliding-coupled on the sliding shaft in sequence and cover by the flexible film, among which the proximal slice is rigidly fixed on the coupling sleeve and the distal slice is rigidly fixed to the flexible film while the other side of flexible film is rigidly fixed to the proximal slice. The edges of two middle slices are also rigidly fixed to the flexible film. The sliding shaft is sliding-coupled on the axis of the coupling sleeve. The whole bellow piston module is fixed on the internal round surface of primary fluid chamber, with the side that flexible film fixed pointing to the inner surface for the primary fluid chamber and contact with the fluid directly, while the sliding shaft reverse out and contact to the corresponding guide rod. During the installation, it has to be clear that all the center lines of the sliding shaft must parallel to that of corresponding sliding chutes on the cylinder shell and middle plate. The two fluid chambers are connected to two fluid compression pumps independently, Primary pump for the primary fluid chamber, secondary pump for the secondary fluid chamber. For a single bellow piston module, the compression of the pump will lead to a differential pressure between the corresponding fluid chamber and the atmosphere, leading to a contraction potential of the flexible film toward the axes of the sliding shaft. However, such potential will be impeded by the middle slices and coupled by the sliding freedom of the slices along the sliding shaft, which will convert the shaft-axes-pointing contraction potential to the translation motion potential of the slices along the axes of the sliding shaft. This potential will give a pushing force of the distal slice of each bellow piston module toward the centripetal direction of the fluid chamber, the centripetal direction of the circle that guide rods lied. Such a force will be transmitted to the guide rod as the sliding shaft connecting the distal slice and the corresponding guide rods, giving a pushing force on the guide rod and toward the centripetal direction of the circle that guide rod lied.

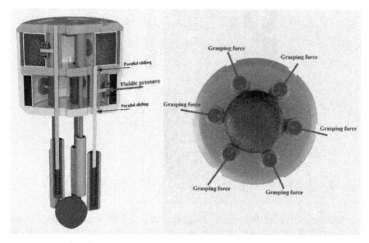

Fig. 4. Schematic illustration of the FBP gripper when grasping large-shaped object.

3 Working Principle and Analysis

3.1 Working Principle of FBP Gripper

As an example, Fig. 4 shows the working principle of the gripper. The object is placed on a horizontal work surface when grasping it. At the beginning, the gripper is driven down by the manipulator that it fixed on, and the object touches the elastic sleeves, and the elastic sleeves are pushed up to deform the corresponding springs. Since there are many slide pipes, forming an array of concentric circles. Each of the pin will adapt to the local shape and size of the outer profile of the object. The manipulator will keep moving down, letting the pins on the gripper adapting outer profile of the object until the end face of the elastic sleeve touches the work surface (the adaptive effect is obtained). At this moment, the primary and secondary fluid compression pump will inject the pressurized fluid corresponding fluid chamber, leading the contraction of the bellow piston modules, pushing the guide bar to slide horizontally. Meanwhile, the numerous elastic sleeves around the object giving the grasping force to the object. After part of the pins in contact with the object, the continuously pumping of the pumps will make more elastic sleeves contact the object and hence provide grasping force. During which the original contacted elastic sleeves are blocked by the object without further translation, the auto balance of the fluid pressure in the chamber will contribute to a final equilibrium state between all the contacted elastic sleeves that driven by same fluid chamber. Thus, the grasping of the object is realized. The grasping force is stable, and the grasping force is provided and controlled by the fluid compression pump through the fluid. The system architecture of dual fluid chamber could provide more adaptability to the gripper. For an object with large shape, the sliding modules that lied on the inner circle keep idle to passively adapt the shape of object while the sliding modules lied on the outer circle moving centripetally to provide the grasping force.

On the other hand, as shown in Fig. 5, for an object with a small shape, the sliding modules lied on the inner circle will be deployed to provide grasping force while that on outer circle keep idle. The process of releasing an object is the opposite of the above and will not be described here.

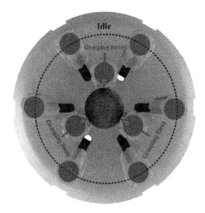

Fig. 5. Schematic illustration of the FBP gripper when grasping small-shaped object.

3.2 Working Analysis

Figure 7 shows two typical force condition of the single sliding module. The force that the end face of the elastic sleeve undergo could be expressed as:

$$F_{yi} = k\delta x_i \tag{1}$$

where k is the stiffness factor of the spring.

For the sliding module that undergo a lateral force from the object, the equation can be described based on the principle of mechanical equilibrium:

$$F_{fi} = fF_{Ni} \tag{2}$$

$$mg = \sum_{j=1}^{k} F_{Nk} \tag{3}$$

$$T_i = F_N l + F_f r \tag{4}$$

where f is the friction coefficient between the elastic sleeve and the object, m is the mass of object, g is gravitational acceleration, k is the number of sliding modules that contact with object, T is the torque provided by the slice for the guide rod.

From the above equations we can know that when grasping an object with a mass of m, the overall torque and grasping force can be expressed as:

$$M = \sum_{i=1}^{9} T_i = \sum_{i=1}^{9} (F_N l + F_f r) \tag{5}$$

$$\vec{F} = \sum_{i=1}^{9} \vec{F_N} + \sum_{i=1}^{9} \vec{F_f} \tag{6}$$

$$F = \sqrt{\left\| \sum_{i=1}^{9} F_N \right\|^2 + \left\| \sum_{i=1}^{9} F_f \right\|^2} \tag{7}$$

The relations between these parameters are showed in Fig. 6a, 6b. According to Fig. 6a, when δx increases F increases, and this indicate that the grasping force can be adjusted by change the process of the adaption between the finger and objects. When k increases F decreases, which means the elastic strength of the finger should be not too enough in order to provide the gripper suitable grasping forces. According to Fig. 6b, when k increases M decreases, which indicates the same result as Fig. 6a, when m increases M increase and it is the same as real grasping process and it indicates the model and analysis is reasonable.

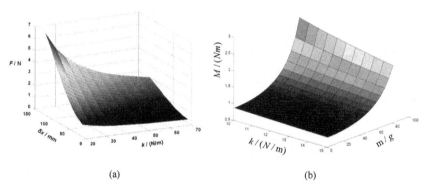

(a)   (b)

Fig. 6. The relations under different stiffness factor k of the spring. (a) The relation among F and δx under different k. (b) The relation among M and m under different k.

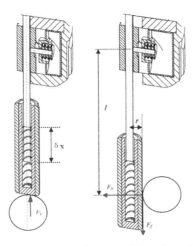

Fig. 7. Schematic illustration of the force conditions for a single sliding module

4 Conclusion

Compared with the existing design of universal gripper, the new robot gripper has the following advantages and outstanding effects.

1) The gripper could realize the universal grasping function utilizing fluid compression pump, fluid chamber and bellow piston modules.
2) The gripper obtains multi-point contact through the array of several slide modules and adapts to objects of different shapes and sizes by the passive sliding of elastic sleeves on the guide rods, so as to achieve self-adaptive characteristics.
3) During the grasping of object, the fluid chamber and the bellow piston modules assembled on it push plurality of guide rods to slide in the chute of the base, so as to realize the rapid grasping of multiple slides at the same time.
4) Because the bellow piston components could provide a large force, the connected fluid is used to obtain the automatic coordination and balance of the grasping force of multiple elastic sleeves on the object. The sensing and control requirements are relatively low, the control strategy is quite simple, and the grasping force exerted on the object is evenly distributed. The device is suitable for all kinds of occasions that need to grab objects of different shapes and sizes.

The self-adaptive gripper based on bellow piston has a general grasping effect, have the ability to adapt and grasp objects of different shapes and sizes by obtaining more contact points when grasping objects with a strong adaptability, stable grasping and uniform grasping force. Therefore, it is suitable for grasping the thin plate on the horizontal workbench and has low requirements for sensing and control. In the industrial assemble line, not only the speed of the gripper is required, but also the stability and quality of grasping. Therefore, The FBP gripper can improve the stability and convenience of the traditional industrial gripper to a certain extent.

Acknowledgement. This research was supported by National Key R&D Program of China (No. 2017YFE0113200).

References

1. Salisbury, J.K., Craig, J.J.: Articulated hands: force control and kinematic issues. Int. J. Rob. Res. **1**(4), 4–17 (1986)
2. Liu, H., et al.: The modular multisensory DLR-HIT-Hand. Mech. Mach. Theory **5**(42), 612–615 (2007)
3. Tuffield, P., Elias, H.: The Shadow robot mimics human actions. Ind. Robots **1**(30), 56–60 (2003)
4. Martin, T.B., et al.: Tactile gloves for autonomous grasping with the NASA/DARPA Robonaut. In: International Conference on Robotics and Automation (ICRA), pp. 1713–1718. IEEE, New Orleans (2004)
5. Gaiser, I., et al.: A new anthropomorphic robotic hand. In: Humanoids 2008 - 8th IEEE-RAS International Conference on Humanoid Robots, pp. 418–422. IEEE, Daejeon (2008)
6. Laliberté, T., Birglen, L., Gosselin, C.M.: Underactuation in robotic grasping hands. Mach. Intell. Rob. Control **4**(3), 1–11 (2002)
7. Demers, L.A.A., et al: Gripper having a two degree of freedom underactuated mechanical finger for encompassing and pinch grasping. U.S. Patent No. 8973958 (2015)
8. Liang, D., Song, J., Zhang, W., Sun, Z., Chen, Q.: PASA hand: a novel parallel and self-adaptive underactuated hand with gear-link mechanisms. In: Kubota, Naoyuki, Kiguchi, Kazuo, Liu, Honghai, Obo, Takenori (eds.) ICIRA 2016. LNCS (LNAI), vol. 9834, pp. 134–146. Springer, Cham (2016). https://doi.org/10.1007/978-3-319-43506-0_12
9. FESTO. Gipping Device. World Patent No. 2016146140 (2016)
10. Zhu, T., Yang, H., Zhang, W.: A spherical self-adaptive gripper with shrinking of an elastic membrane. In: International Conference on Advanced Robotics and Mechatronics (ICARM), pp. 18–20. IEEE, Macau (2016)
11. Hong, F., Zhang, W.: The development of a soft robot hand with pin-array structure. Appl. Sci. **9**(5), 1011 (2019)
12. Fu, H., Yang, H., Song, W., Zhang, W.: A novel cluster-tube self-adaptive robot hand. Robot. Biomim. **4**(1), 1–9 (2017)
13. Fu, H., Zhang, W.: Design and analysis of a parallel and self-adaptive finger with pin-array structure. In: International Conference on Advanced Robotics and Mechatronics (ICARM), pp. 708–713. IEEE, Toyonaka (2019)
14. Mo, A., Zhang, W.: A novel universal gripper based on meshed pin array. Int. J. Adv. Robot. Syst. **2**(16), 2 (2019)
15. Scott, P.B.: The 'Omnigripper': a form of robot universal gripper. Robotica **3**(3), 153–158 (1985)

Oratosquilla Oratoria-Like Amphibious Robot Based on Dielectric Elastomer

Qingzhong Li, Guoqing Yang, Fujie Yu, Yao Wang, and Yuan Chen[⊠]

Shandong University, Weihai, Shandong, China
cyzghysy@sdu.edu.cn

Abstract. A key challenge for biologically inspired Oratosquilla oratoria amphibious robots is large deformation and flexibility. We have developed a Squilla like soft robot based on dielectric elastic materials (DE). The robot is driven by high-power dielectric elastomer and uses the principle of friction difference and water resistance difference to realize amphibious multi-mode motion. The robot is 9 cm × 5 cm × 7 cm in length, width and height, and weighs 14 g. The fastest speed on land is 12.5 cm/s, and the fastest speed on water is 2.66 cm/s. The robot has high swimming efficiency and can detect the water surface. The experimental results show that the amphibious soft robot for mantis shrimp has high potential and practicability.

Keywords: Soft robot · Oratosquilla robot · Dielectric elastomer robot · Amphibious robot

1 Introduction

Many animals have multimodal movement between land and water to avoid predators and find food [1–5]. Some small creatures can use the static tension of the water surface to move or even jump on the water [6]. Some amphibians, such as frogs and turtles, can move both on land and in water [7]. This ability enables them to live in complex environments where most animals cannot survive.

The robot moving in the mixed environment is more suitable for environmental monitoring and complex space exploration [8–14]. There are many kinds of amphibious robots inspired by nature, but most of them are large in weight and volume, so they can only immerse in the water and can not move on the water [15–17]. Through surface effects such as surface tension or static electricity, the robot suspended on the surface has less resistance and greater speed than underwater [18–20]. Therefore, the amphibious robot that can move on the water surface has higher efficiency, and can explore various environments that large robots cannot enter [21, 22].

Previously inspired by water strider [23], the robot uses hydrophobic wires to support on the water surface, and can move on the water surface by using the related fluid dynamics, but the supporting legs are more difficult to move. Inspired by the water piercing beetle, the amphibious robot floats on the water surface through electric wetting to complete the water surface movement and the transition from water surface to underwater. However, the robot has poor elasticity and is easy to be damaged by external force.

© Springer Nature Switzerland AG 2021
X.-J. Liu et al. (Eds.): ICIRA 2021, LNAI 13013, pp. 293–301, 2021.
https://doi.org/10.1007/978-3-030-89095-7_29

We designed a robot based on dielectric elastomer, which can move on land, move on water, and transform between land and aquatic environment. Firstly, the soft robot is designed. Second, the circular foot is designed with the friction difference, which is used for the robot's land motion. Thirdly, we design the swimming limb and make use of the water resistance difference to make the robot move on the water. Fourthly, we further analyze the underwater finite element of the swimming limb.

2   Materials and Methods

Shrimp moves in the landing stage by a flexible gait; To swim by pulling the water with the swimming limbs and beating the body vigorously (Fig. 1). In this paper, dielectric elastomer joints were used to make abdomen, and 3D printing materials were used to make cavity and foot. The external size of the robot is 9 cm × 5 cm × 7 cm, Dielectric Elastomer(DE) (3M,VHB4910) is used as abdominal joint muscle, Polyethylene tereph-thalate (PET) is used as abdominal joint frame, PLA (3D printing) material is used as body.

The detailed manufacturing process of the soft robot is shown in Fig. 2. First, two layers of DE film (VHB4910,3M) were pre-stretched to 400% × 400%, and a layer of carbon lipid electrode was applied to the middle and both sides of the DE film, as shown in Fig. 2 (a). Secondly, the completed DE film is placed between the main frame (PET,0.188 mm) and the reinforcing tendon (PET, 0.25 mm) and pressed, as shown in Fig. 2 (b). This part is also known as the abdominal joint actuator. The completed actuator automatically bends under the action of the elastic force of the prestretched film. Then, the hollow cavity and the circular arc bottom (foot) were made by 3D printing (PLA), and the two were connected together with a wire of 1mm in diameter. After that, they were respectively connected with the large connecting plate (PET, 0.25 mm) and the small connecting plate (swimming limb, PET, 0.25 mm) for rotating pairs, as shown in Fig. 2 (c). Next, the two parts in Fig. 2 (b) and (c) were bonded together with glue to form the soft robot like mantis shrimps as shown in Fig. 2 (d). In addition, a wire with an insulating layer is connected to the high voltage positive terminal and two wires to the negative terminal (Fig. 1).

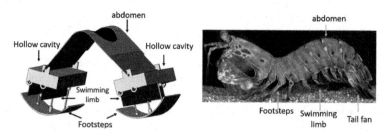

Fig. 1. The structure of the shrimp feeding robot and shrimp

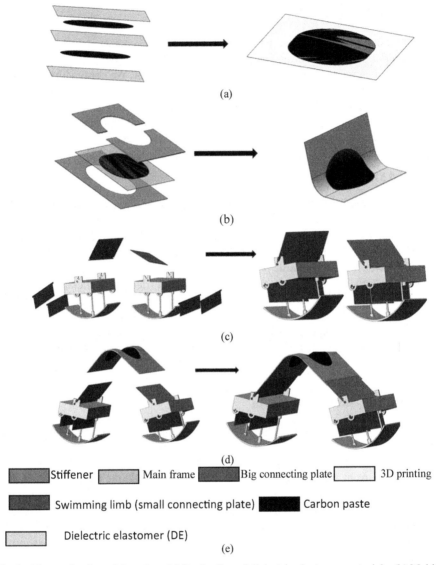

Fig. 2. The production of the robot. (a) Production of dielectric elastomer materials. (b) Making of abdominal joints. (c) The connection of the leg and the board. (d) Connection of abdominal joints and legs. (e) Different colors represent different parts of the body

3 Principle of Motion

The soft robot is composed of wired voltage source, signal generator (rigol-dg4062) and voltage amplifier (trek 10/10b-hs) to generate high voltage. During running and turning, high voltage is applied to the joint actuator of the soft robot. We apply voltage to drive the robot through power supply and external circuit. When no voltage is applied, that is, when the voltage is 0, the robot is at rest; When the cyclic voltage is applied, the robot will deform periodically (Fig. 3. a). The angle of the abdominal joint actuator remains unchanged when the power is off, and increases when the power is on (Fig. 3. b).

3.1 Land Movement

There are different friction at the touchdown position of the front and rear feet, as shown in Fig. 3. C. In the middle of the front foot, the friction coefficient is small, but in the back foot, the friction coefficient is large; The friction coefficient is larger in the middle of the back foot and smaller in the front foot. When the robot is walking on the land, when the power is off, the middle position of the front and rear foot touches the ground, the friction coefficient of the rear foot is large, and the friction coefficient of the front foot is small. At this time, the rear foot does not move when the power is on, and the front foot moves forward; When moving to the maximum position, the friction coefficient of the front foot is large, and that of the back foot is small. At this time, when the power is off, the front foot does not move, and the back foot moves forward, as shown in Figure D.

3.2 The Water-Surface Movement

In the water surface movement, the force of forward movement mainly depends on the water resistance difference of the swimming limb. As shown in Fig. 3. E, at the beginning of power on stage, the angle of the abdominal joint actuator has a tendency to expand, the front swimming limb swings backward, while the rear swimming limb remains unchanged due to the limitation of the iron wire stick, and the front resistance is less than the rear resistance; At this time, the front swimming limb remains unchanged due to the restriction of the iron wire stick, and the rear swimming limb plate swings backward, so the resistance in front is greater than that in back, and the robot moves forward.

As shown in Fig. 4, the span of the body in the power on state and the off power state is different. When the frequency is lower than 10 Hz, the robot moves and crawls in discrete motion. When the frequency is higher than 10 Hz, the robot foot moves and runs in turn. The robot moves on the acrylic board (movie 1), and the maximum speed is 12.5 cm/s (as shown in Fig. 5) when the robot is at 7kv5hz.

Floating movement on the water surface has the support function of buoyancy in the front and back cavities. Through the circulation voltage, the robot abdominal joint is circularly energized, and the swimming limb can only swing in a limited range, resulting in a poor water resistance and moving forward as a whole (movie 2). At 7kv4hz, the fastest speed is 2.66 cm/s (as shown in Fig. 5).

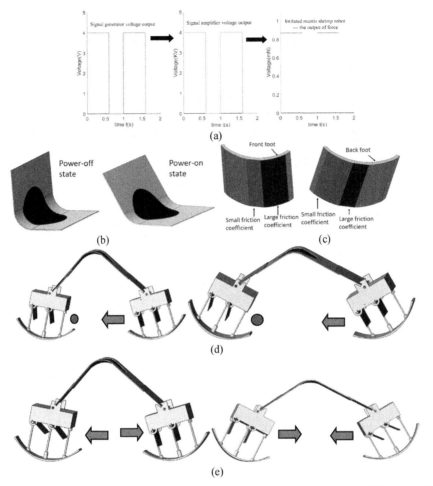

Fig. 3. Principle of robot motion. (a) Signal transmission process. (b) The state of the abdominal joints under power-off and power-on. (c) Schematic diagram of the friction position of the front and rear steps. (d) State of Oratosquilla oratoria robot walking on land. (e) State of Oratosquilla oratoria robot walking on water

4 Hydrodynamic Analysis

The viscous and incompressible Navier Stokes equations can be described by the following equations:

$$\rho\left(\frac{\partial u}{\partial t} + u \cdot \nabla u\right) = -\nabla p + \upsilon \nabla^2 u \tag{1}$$

$$\nabla \cdot u = 0$$

μ is the fluid velocity, ρ is the density, p is the pressure, υ is dynamic viscosity, using ANSYS software finite element volume method [24] (fluent module) for the first-order

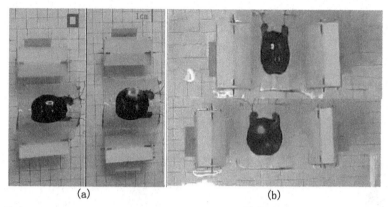

Fig. 4. Robot motion. (a) 7kv1hz land motion (stationary and moving). (b) 7kv1hz water surface motion (stationary and moving)

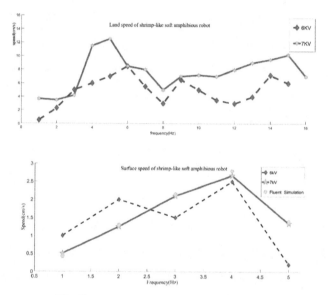

Fig. 5. Land speed and water speed of robot

time discretization and second-order space discretization of the control equation. The fluid field is calculated on an unstructured tetrahedral mesh. The robot swimming is mainly due to the swing of four swimming limbs. The second development of fluent (UDF) is carried out by measuring the swing of swimming limbs. Using define_ GRID_ The motion function simulates the rigid motion of swimming limb. 3D vorticity map and pressure cloud map can be obtained (as shown in Fig. 6 and 7).

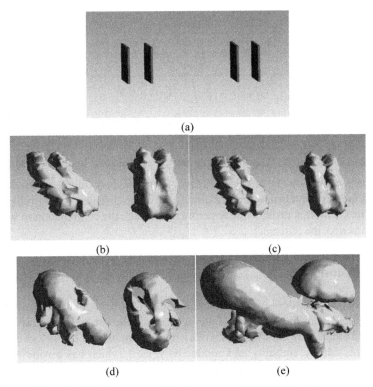

Fig. 6. 3D vorticity cloud (Robot power off/on for one cycle). (a) Before the movement. (b) 0 T. (c) 1/4 T. (d) 2/4 T. (e) 3/4 T

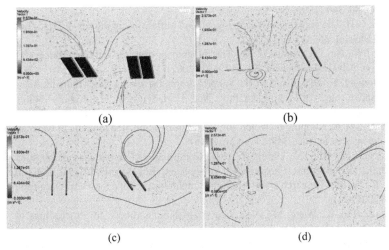

Fig. 7. Pressure and velocity nephogram (Robot power off/on for one cycle). (a) 0T. (b) 1/4T. (c) 2/4T. (d) 3/4T.

$$P_o(t) = \frac{1}{T} \int_0^T F_y(t) U dt$$

$$P_e(t) = \frac{1}{T} \int_0^T M_z(t) \dot{\theta}(t) dt \tag{2}$$

$$\eta = \frac{P_o}{P_e}$$

P_o is the output power, P_e is the input power, F_y is the force in the forward direction, M is the torque, and $\dot{\theta}$ is the angular velocity, η for efficiency. In Fig. 5, the simulation speed and the experimental speed are almost the same, because the wire has a small influence on the motion result in the experiment. Through the combination of simulation data and practice, the efficiency is 37.2%.

5 Conclusions

In conclusion, we have developed a de soft amphibious robot with high speed, high efficiency and high flexibility. The robot imitates Oratosquilla oratoria, has the ability of fast walking and efficient swimming ability of swimming limbs, and can detect underwater (temperature, salinity, turbidity and conductivity, etc.), which has a wide application prospect.

References

1. Glasheen, J., McMahon, T.: A hydrodynamic model of locomotion in the basilisk lizard. Nature **380**, 340 (1996)
2. Parker, G.H. The crawling of young loggerhead turtles toward the sea. J. Exp. Zool. A. Ecol. Genet Physiol. **36**, 322–331 (1922)
3. Bush, J.W., Hu, D.L., Prakash, M.: The integument of water-walking arthropods: form and function. Adv. Insect Physiol. **34**, 117–192 (2007)
4. van Breugel, F., Dickinson, M.H.: Superhydrophobic diving flies (Ephydra hians) and the hypersaline waters of Mono Lake. Proc. Natl Acad. Sci. USA **114**, 13483–13488 (2017)
5. Duellman, W.E., Trueb, L.: Biology of Amphibians. JHU press, Baltimore (1986)
6. Koh, J.S., et al.: Jumping on water: surface tension–dominated jumping of water striders and robotic insects. Science **349**, 517–521 (2015)
7. Rissmann, M., Kley, N., Ulrich, R., et al.: Competency of amphibians and reptiles and their potential role as reservoir hosts for rift valley fever virus. Viruses **12**(11), 1206 (2020)
8. Kai, R., Jya, B.: Research status of bionic amphibious robots: a review. Ocean Eng. **227**(8), 108862 (2021)
9. Guo, Z., Tao, L., Wang, M.: A survey on amphibious robots. In: Proceedings of the 37th China Control Conference (D) (2018)
10. Wu, Z.Y., Qi, J., Zhang, S.: Amphibious robots: a review. Appl. Mech. Mater. **494–495**, 1036–1041 (2014)
11. Zheng, L., Guo, S., Piao, Y., et al.: Collaboration and task planning of turtle-inspired multiple amphibious spherical robots. Micromachines **11**(1), 71 (2020)

12. Cocuzza, S., Doria, A., Reis, M.: Vibration-based locomotion of an amphibious robot. Appl. Sci. **11**(5), 2212 (2021)
13. Song, S., Kim, J., Kim, T., et al.: Development of biomimetic fin-type amphibious robot for precise path following missions. In: Global Oceans 2020: Singapore–US Gulf Coast, pp. 1–7 IEEE (2020)
14. Van Beek, L., den Toonder, J., Schenning, A., et al.: Analysis of liquid crystal actuation towards a light-driven amphibious soft microrobot (2021)
15. Baines, R.L., Booth, J.W., Fish, F.E., Kramer-Bottiglio, R.: Toward a bio-inspired variable-stiffness morphing limb for amphibious robot locomotion. In: 2019 2nd IEEE International Conference on Soft Robotics (RoboSoft), pp. 704–710 (2019) https://doi.org/10.1109/ROBOSOFT.2019.8722772
16. Kashem, S.B.A., Jawed, S., Ahmed, J., et al.: Design and implementation of a quadruped amphibious robot using duck feet. Robotics **8**(3), 77 (2019)
17. Kim, T., Song, Y., Song, S., et al.: Underwater walking mechanism of underwater amphibious robot using hinged multi-modal paddle. Int. J. Control Autom. Syst.1–12 (2020)
18. Li, G., Chen, X., Zhou, F., et al.: Self-powered soft robot in the Mariana trench. Nature **591**(7848), 66–71 (2021)
19. Shintake, J., Cacucciolo, V., Shea, H., Floreano, D.: Soft biomimetic fish robot made of dielectric elastomer actuators. Soft Robot. **5**(4), 466–474 (2018)
20. Chen, Y., Neel, D., Benjamin, G., et al.: Controllable water surface to underwater transition through electrowetting in a hybrid terrestrial-aquatic microrobot. Nat. Commun. **9**(1), 2495 (2018)
21. Yang, K., Liu, G., Yan, J., et al.: A water-walking robot mimicking the jumping abilities of water striders. Bioinspiration Biomimetics **11**(6), 066002 (2016)
22. Christianson, C., Cui, Y., Ishida, M., et al.: Cephalopod-inspired robot capable of cyclic jet propulsion through shape change. Bioinspiration Biomimetics **16**(1), 016014 (2020)
23. Wu, L., Lian, Z., Yang, G., et al.: Water dancer ii-a: a non-tethered telecontrollable water strider robot. Int. J. Adv. Robot. Syst. **8**(4), 39 (2011)
24. Kai, Z., Liu, J., Chen, W.: Numerical study on hydrodynamic performance of bionic caudal fin. Appl. Sci. **6**(1), 15 (2016)

Open-Loop Motion Control of a Hydraulic Soft Robotic Arm Using Deep Reinforcement Learning

Yunce Zhang[1], Tao Wang[1,3,4,5(✉)], Ning Tan[6], and Shiqiang Zhu[1,2]

[1] Ocean College, Zhejiang University, Zhoushan 316000, People's Republic of China
twang001@zju.edu.cn
[2] Zhejiang Lab, Hangzhou 310058, People's Republic of China
[3] State Key Laboratory of Fluid Power and Mechatronic Systems,
Zhejiang University, Hangzhou, People's Republic of China
[4] Engineering Research Center of Oceanic Sensing Technology and Equipment,
Ministry of Education, Zhoushan 316000, People's Republic of China
[5] Key Laboratory of Ocean Observation-Imaging Testbed of Zhejiang Province,
Zhoushan 316000, People's Republic of China
[6] School of Data and Computer Science, Sun Yat-sen University, Guangzhou 510006,
People's Republic of China

Abstract. Soft robotic arms are of great interests in recent years, but it is challenging to perform effective control due to their strongly non-linear characteristics. This work develops a model-free open-loop control method for a hydraulic soft robotic arm in spatial motion. A control policy based on reinforcement learning technique is proposed by using Deep Deterministic Policy Gradient. The kinematic model of the soft robotic arm is employed instead of physical prototype to train the control policy. A complete training framework is established through the Reinforcement Learning Toolbox and Deep Learning Toolbox in Matlab software. To make the control policy fast converge and avoid falling into local optimum, the reward is shaped by combining the position error and the action together. A series of simulations are implemented and the results verify the effectiveness of the control policy. It is also shown that the proposed control policy can achieve both of good stability and tracking performance simultaneously.

Keywords: Motion control · Reinforcement Learning · Soft robot · Hydraulic

1 Introduction

In recent years, soft robots have received extensive attention from researchers due to inherent compliance, environmental adaptability, lower inertia and safe human-machine interaction [1]. Inspired by nature and composed of low-modulus

© Springer Nature Switzerland AG 2021
X.-J. Liu et al. (Eds.): ICIRA 2021, LNAI 13013, pp. 302–312, 2021.
https://doi.org/10.1007/978-3-030-89095-7_30

materials, soft robots can deform continuously like flexible structures in biological systems [2]. Features aforementioned make soft robots have obvious advantages and promising prospect in the application of flexible grasping, surgery, rehabilitation, and bionic locomotion [3,4].

Conventional rigid robotic arms have been extensively employed in tasks such as grasping, assembling and handling. But the limited DOF and the possibility of harm to humans restrict them from working in an unstructured environment or human-machine interaction scenes [5]. Compared with the rigid robotic arms, soft robotic arms have the advantages of lightweight, flexibility and safety, so they could be used in an unstructured environment or human-machine interaction scene and perform well. With the development of the soft robotic arms, an amount of actuation methods have been applied, like hydraulic actuation [6], shape memory alloy actuation [7], pneumatic artificial muscles actuation [8], and cable-driven actuation [9]. In the aforementioned actuation technique, hydraulic actuation is widely applied and has got lots of studies due to their conformability [10]. However, modeling and controlling of the hydraulic soft robotic arms are challenging and difficult because of the strong nonlinearity between hydraulic pressure and elastic deformation [11].

Researchers have paid much effort on motion control of soft robotic arms by using both model based and model-free methods [12]. The premise of using model-based control approaches is to establish a mathematical model of the controlled object, an accurate model or a reasonably simplified model is the guarantee of the good control performance. Xie et al. develop the kinematic model of the soft robotic arm by using the piecewise constant-curvature (PCC) assumption to predict the position of its tip position [5]. Ohta et al. develop the kinematic model of the robotic arm by using DH parameters and carry out simulation and experimental results for closed-loop position control based on the kinematic model [13]. Yang et al. build a direct kinematic model from the sensor data to the deformation and an inverse kinematic model used to calculate the actuation of SMA coils base on given planned deformation [14]. In order to achieve more precise control performance, some studies pay attention to the dynamic model and achieved great progress. Renda et al. develop a dynamic model of a soft continuum robotic arm by using a rigorous geometrically exact method [15]. Tutcu et al. combine a kinematic model with a quasi-static equilibrium solution for more accurate modeling of the end effector of a soft continuum robot [16]. In addition to these, some novel methods are derived, like Chen et al. using force balance of the ending plate to build the model [17]. Tang et al. propose a model based online learning and adaptive control algorithm for the wearable soft robot [18].

For multi-segments hydraulic soft robotic arms, model-based control is difficult to achieve real-time and high accuracy without additional restrictions due to the complexity and imprecision of the mathematical model, and model-free methods offer the possibility of good control performance. Li et al. use adaptive Kalman filter to achieve path tracking for a continuum robot [19]. Melingui et al. develop two controllers based on a distal supervised learning scheme and an adaptive neural to control CBHA's kinematics and dynamics [20]. With the development of machine learning techniques, reinforcement learning has been widely used in robotic control [21], model-free reinforcement learning has obvious advantages in soft robotic arms control tasks. Ma et al. propose a reinforcement learning method based on the Deep Deterministic Policy Gradient (DDPG) algorithm to solve position control problem [22]. Shahid et al. develop a control policy parameterized by a neural network and learned using modern Proximal Policy Optimization (PPO) algorithm [23]. Satheeshbabu et al. present an open loop position control policy based on deep reinforcement learning and use Deep-Q Learning with experience replay [24]. Although some efforts have been paid on using reinforcement learning to control soft robotic arms, most of the current studies focus on planar motions, or spatial motions with less control inputs in limited environments or in small action space.

In this paper, we investigate the motion control of a double-segment hydraulic soft robotic arm, which has six control inputs and a large state-action space. To achieve open-loop motion control, a model-free control policy based on deep reinforcement learning (RL) is proposed by using Deep Deterministic Policy Gradient (DDPG) algorithm. The kinematic model [5] of the soft robotic arm is employed instead of physical prototype to train the control policy. A complete training framework is established through the Reinforcement Learning Toolbox and Deep Learning Toolbox in Matlab software. To make the control policy fast converge and avoid falling into local optimum, the reward is shaped by combining the position and the action together. A control policy with excellent performance was obtained via parameter optimization and reward function optimization. A series of simulations are implemented to evaluate the control policy, the effectiveness and good tracking performance of the control policy are verified in simulations.

The remainder of this paper is structured as follows. Section 2 describes the architecture of the system. Section 3 introduces the training framework and configurations, and show the results of simulations. Section 4 presents conclusions and future works.

2   System Description

2.1   Hydraulic Soft Robotic Arm

The studied hydraulic soft robotic arm is as shown in Fig. 1. It is totally made of soft materials and composed of an elastic cylinder, two connectors and three chambers with double-helical fiber reinforcement for each segment. Table 1 gives the key parameters of the arms. Each segment of the soft robotic arms is independent and can be quickly assembled and disassembled through the connector. In the current design, the arms can be extended to three segments, but considering the overall length of the arms and the existing experimental conditions, a two-segments arm is employed to carry out the work.

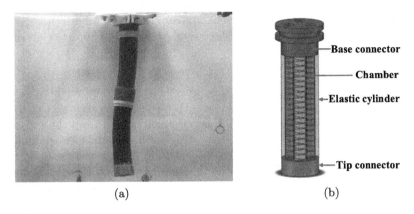

Fig. 1. (a) Two-segments hydraulic soft robotic arm prototype. (b) Schematic of the one-segment hydraulic soft robotic arm.

Table 1. Key parameters of the hydraulic soft robotic arm.

Parameters	Value
Length of elastic cylinder	140 mm
External diameter of elastic cylinder	50 mm
Height of base connector	40 mm
Height of tip connector	20 mm
External length of chamber	170 mm
Internal length of chamber	140 mm
External diameter of chamber	15 mm
Internal diameter of chamber	10 mm
The distance between the center of the chamber and the elastic cylinder	14 mm
Maximum pressure of chamber	300 kpa

2.2   Markov Decision Process Modeling

Markov Decision Process (MDP) formally defines the reinforcement learning problem, using reinforcement learning on robots requires it to be abstracted and represented as an MDP. A MDP is based on the integration of each interactive object, composed of agent and environment, and its elements include state, action and reward. The motion control task is modeled into a continuous-state, continuous-action MDP. Assuming the simplest form of representation, the RL-based motion control task of the hydraulic soft robotic arm is abstracted as follows:

State(s): State is the condition of the agent described by the environment. In the soft robotic arm motion control task, the state consists of two parts, which are the current state of the soft robotic arm and the action at the previous moment. More specifically, the current state of the soft robotic arm is error between the soft robotic arm and the target position in the direction of each coordinate axis.

Action(s): Action is the collection of actions which the agent could take, called action space. Agents based on DDPG can output continuous actions. Considering that it is difficult to establish an accuracy dynamic model from the pressure of chambers to the position of the tip of the soft robotic arm, the forward kinematic model from the length of chambers to the position of the tip of the soft robotic arm is used to train the agent in the simulation. Therefor, actions that the soft robotic arm could take is the increment of each chamber length, the upper limit and the lower limit of each increment are +1 mm and −1 mm respectively. According to the maximum pressure of the chambers, the upper bound of the length of the chambers is 200 mm. This setting can make the soft robotic arm reach the target position smoothly and quickly.

Reward(s): The reward is a quantitative indicator used to judge each action of the agent and guide the robot to complete tasks. In our task, in order to make the robotic arm move to the target position quickly and stably, the Euclidean distance between arm's tip position and target position and the action at the previous moment are used as the basis for formulating rewards. Actions that move the manipulator away from the target and are not conducive to the stability of the robot will be subject to greater penalties. On the contrary, actions that bring the robot closer to the target and approach stability will be rewarded. This can speed up the training process of the policy and contribute to the steady-state performance of the soft robotic arm. The reward structure is shown as follows:

$$
r = \begin{cases} -0.001 err_d - 0.05 \sum |a_i| - 0.0003(|err_x| + |err_y| + |err_z|), err_d > \varepsilon \\ 500 - 0.05 \sum |a_i|, err_d \leq \varepsilon \end{cases} \tag{1}
$$

where the $\varepsilon = 5\,\text{mm}$ is the target threshold, the err_d is the Euclidean distance between arm's tip position and target position, the err_x, err_y and err_z is the distance between arm's tip position and target position between the tip position of the arm and the target position on each coordinate axis. When the agent reaches the target within ε, the training episode is done. The reward is to penalize actions that are not conducive to completing the task and make the soft robotic arm reach the target position in the shortest path.

2.3   Deep Deterministic Policy Gradient Framework

DDPG is a model-free reinforcement learning method that can be extended to continuous action control [25]. We use an actor-critic framework on DDPG to make the policy stable. Convolutional neural network is used to approximate the optimal policy function μ and Q function, namely the policy network and the Q network, and the deep learning method is used to train the above neural network. DDPG needs to learn Q network while learning policy network. The implementation and training method of the Q function refers to the DQN [26]. The value iteration update of the Q function follows the Bellman equation and is defined as:

$$Q_t^\mu(s_t, a_t) = Q_t^\mu(s_t, a_t) + \alpha(r_t + \gamma \max_a Q^\mu(s_{t+1}, a) - Q_t^\mu(s_t, a_t)) \qquad (2)$$

where the s_t is the state at time step t, a_t is the action at time t, s_{t+1} is the state after taking action a_t, r_t is the reward value about a_t, α is the learning rate, and γ is the discount rate.

In the continuous action spaces training process, exploration is important to find potential better policies, so we add random noise for the action to transit the action from a deterministic process to a random process, and then sample the action from this random process and send it to the environment for execution. The above policy is called the behavior policy, which is represented by β. Ornstein-Uhlenbeck process is used to generate random noise as shown is Eq. 3.

$$\partial n = \Phi(\eta - n) + \sigma W \qquad (3)$$

where the η is the mean, the Φ is the decay rate, the σ is the variance, the W is the Wiener process. The process of training policy network is to find the optimal solution of policy network parameters, and the stochastic gradient ascent method is used to train the network. The Eq. 4 is used to judge the performance of a policy, and the optimal policy is defined by Eq. 5. The whole algorithm framework is as shown in Algorithm 1.

$$\begin{aligned} J_\beta(\mu) &= \int_S \rho^\beta(s) Q^\mu(s, a) \, ds \\ &= E_{s \sim \rho^\beta}[Q^\mu(s, a)] \end{aligned} \qquad (4)$$

where the s is the state, the ρ^β is the distribution function of the state.

$$\mu = \arg\max_\mu J(\mu) \qquad (5)$$

3 Training and Simulations

3.1 Training Setup

A high-performance computer consists of a 10900X CPU and an RTX2080Ti GPU is used to train the control policy and validate the effectiveness of policy in simulations. The policy training framework is deployed in Matlab by using Reinforcement Learning Toolbox and Deep Learning Toolbox, and trained by using a critic network and an actor network. The critic network has two hidden layers with 400 neurons and the learning rate is $1e^{-3}$. The actor network has four hidden layers with 400 neurons and the learning rate is $1e^{-4}$. The outputs of

---

Algorithm 1. DDPG framework

Input: max training episodes M, max steps of each episode T, discount factor γ, target smooth factor τ, replay buffer $\boldsymbol{R}$

Output: control policy μ

Randomly initialize critic network $Q(s, a|\theta^Q)$ and actor $\mu(s|\theta^\mu)$

Initialize target network Q' and μ' with weights $Q' \leftarrow Q$, $\mu' \leftarrow \mu$

Initialize Replay Buffer: $\boldsymbol{R}$

1: **for** episode = 1, M **do**
2:     Initialize a random process $\mathcal{N}$
3:     Receive initial observation state s_1
4:     **for** t = 1, T **do**
5:         Select action $a_t = \mu(s_t|\theta^\mu) + \mathcal{N}$ based on current policy and exploration noise
6:         Excute action a_t and observe reward r_t and new state s_{t+1}
7:         Store transition (s_t, a_t, r_t, s_{t+1}) in replay buffer $\boldsymbol{R}$
8:         Sample a random minibatch of N transition (s_i, a_i, r_i, s_{i+1}) from $\boldsymbol{R}$
9:         Set $y_i = r_i + \gamma Q'(s_{i+1}, \mu'(s_{i+1}|\theta^{\mu'})|\theta^{Q'})$
10:        Update critic network by minimizing the loss: $L = \frac{1}{N}\sum_i (y_i - Q(s_i, a_i|\theta^Q))^2$
11:        Update the actor network using the sampled policy gradient:

$$\nabla_{\theta^\mu} J \approx \frac{1}{N}\sum_i \nabla_a Q(s, a|\theta^Q)|_{s=s_i, a=\mu(s_i)} \nabla_{\theta^\mu} \mu(s|\theta^\mu)|_{s_i}$$

12:        Update the target networks:

$$\theta^{Q'} \leftarrow \tau\theta^Q + (1 - \tau)\theta^{Q'}$$
$$\theta^{\mu'} \leftarrow \tau\theta^\mu + (1 - \tau)\theta^{\mu'}$$

13:    **end for**
14: **end for**

---

the actor network are bounded between -1 and $+1$ with a tanhLayer followed a ScalingLayer. Other training parameters are set as follows, the maximum number of training episodes is set as 100000, the maximum number of steps per episode is set as 200, the discount factor is set as 0.99, the minibatch size is set as 256, the target smooth factor is set as 0.001, and the experience reply buffer is set as $1e^8$. A simulation model is built based on the kinematic model of the soft robotic arm [5] and connected with the agent in Simulink.

3.2   Position Control Results

The position control simulations and trajectory tracking simulations are implemented to validate the effectiveness and dynamic performance of the presented control policy. As for position control, we select a series of points in the workspace of the soft robotic arm as target points to test the steady-state performance of the control policy. The results are as shown in Fig. 2, the simulation step size is set to 0.01 s. The control policy transfers the soft robotic arm from the initial state to the target state with few steps, and the steady-state error is controlled within 3 mm. Simulation results revealed the effectiveness and stability of the control policy.

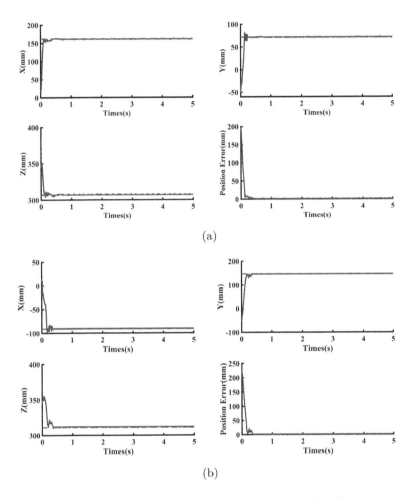

(a)

(b)

Fig. 2. (a) Position control with the target point (162, 72, 307). (b) Position control with the target point (−91, 147, 311).

3.3   Trajectory Tracking Results

The dynamic response of the control policy is the key factor that determines the dynamic performance of the system. As shown in Fig. 3, We select some trajectories according to the workspace of the soft robotic arm to verify the dynamic performance of the control policy. The soft robotic arm begins moving along the target trajectory from 50 s, the policy control soft robotic arm to quickly follow with the target trajectory, and the dynamic error is controlled within 5 mm during the whole movement. Simulation results proved the rapid dynamic response of the control policy, and the soft robotic arm based on this control policy has good tracking performance.

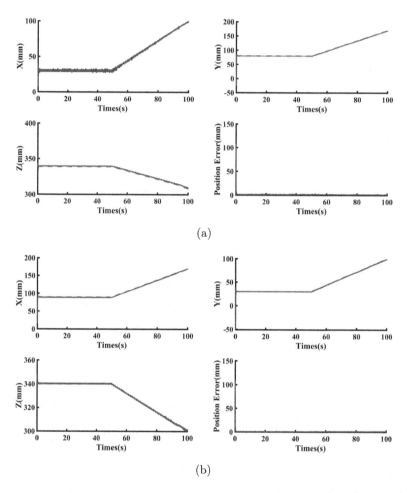

Fig. 3. (a) Trajectory tracking control with the target trajectory from the point (30, 80, 339) to the point (100, 170, 310). (b) Trajectory tracking control with the target trajectory from the point (90, 30, 340) to the point (170, 100, 300).

4   Conclusion and Future Work

Focusing on the motion control of hydraulic soft robotic arm, this paper implements the kinematic model of the soft robotic arm in simulations and develops a model-free control policy based on deep reinforcement learning. The Reinforcement Learning Toolbox and Deep Learning Toolbox are used to deploy the policy training framework, and the Deep Deterministic Policy Gradient (DDPG) algorithm is used to train the policy. The simulations experiments show the effectiveness, robustness and good dynamic performance in motion control of the proposed control policy. After experimental verification, this article is a good attempt of applying reinforcement learning to the motion control of a hydraulic soft robotic arm with highly nonlinear characteristics.

In future work, further improvement and optimization of the proposed control policy will be studied, and the policy will be deployed into the physical prototype control system.

References

1. Lee, C., et al.: Soft robot review. Int. J. Control Autom. Syst. **15**(1), 3–15 (2016). https://doi.org/10.1007/s12555-016-0462-3
2. Wang, T., Zhang, Y., Chen, Z., Zhu, S.: Parameter identification and model-based nonlinear robust control of fluidic soft bending actuators. IEEE/ASME Trans. Mech. **24**(3), 1346–1355 (2019). https://doi.org/10.1109/TMECH.2019.2909099
3. Wang, Y., et al.: A biorobotic adhesive disc for underwater hitchhiking inspired by the remora suckerfish. Sci. Robot. **2**(10) (September 2017). https://doi.org/10.1126/scirobotics.aan8072
4. Choi, C., Schwarting, W., DelPreto, J., Rus, D.: Learning object grasping for soft robot hands. IEEE Robot. Autom. Lett. **3**(3), 2370–2377 (2018). https://doi.org/10.1109/LRA.2018.2810544
5. Xie, Q., Wang, T., Yao, S., Zhu, Z., Tan, N., Zhu, S.: Design and modeling of a hydraulic soft actuator with three degrees of freedom. Smart Mater. Struct. **29**(12) (2020). https://doi.org/10.1088/1361-665X/abc26e
6. Gong, Z., et al.: A soft manipulator for efficient delicate grasping in shallow water: modeling, control, and real-world experiments. Int. J. Robot. Res. 027836492091720 (July 2020). https://doi.org/10.1177/0278364920917203
7. Laschi, C., Cianchetti, M., Mazzolai, B., Margheri, L., Follador, M., Dario, P.: Soft robot arm inspired by the octopus. Adv. Robot. **26**(7), 709–727 (2012). https://doi.org/10.1163/156855312X626343
8. Grissom, M.D., et al.: Design and experimental testing of the OctArm soft robot manipulator. In: Unmanned Systems Technology VIII, vol. 6230, p. 62301F. International Society for Optics and Photonics (May 2006). https://doi.org/10.1117/12.665321
9. Xu, F., Wang, H., Au, K.W.S., Chen, W., Miao, Y.: Underwater dynamic modeling for a cable-driven soft robot arm. IEEE/ASME Trans. Mechatron. **23**(6), 2726–2738 (2018). https://doi.org/10.1109/TMECH.2018.2872972
10. Shengda, Y., Wang, T., Zhu, S.: Research on energy consumption of fiber-reinforced fluidic soft actuators. Smart Mater. Struct. **30**(2) (2021). https://doi.org/10.1088/1361-665X/abd7e6
11. Wang, T.: A computationally efficient dynamical model of fluidic soft actuators and its experimental verification p. 8 (2019)
12. George Thuruthel, T., Ansari, Y., Falotico, E., Laschi, C.: Control strategies for soft robotic manipulators: a survey. Soft Robot. **5**(2), 149–163 (2018). https://doi.org/10.1089/soro.2017.0007

13. Ohta, P., et al.: Design of a lightweight soft robotic arm using pneumatic artificial muscles and inflatable sleeves. Soft Robot. **5**(2), 204–215 (2018). https://doi.org/10.1089/soro.2017.0044

14. Yang, H., Xu, M., Li, W., Zhang, S.: Design and implementation of a soft robotic arm driven by SMA coils. IEEE Trans. Industr. Electron. **66**(8), 6108–6116 (2019). https://doi.org/10.1109/TIE.2018.2872005

15. Renda, F., Giorelli, M., Calisti, M., Cianchetti, M., Laschi, C.: Dynamic model of a multibending soft robot arm driven by cables. IEEE Trans. Robot. **30**(5), 1109–1122 (2014). https://doi.org/10.1109/TRO.2014.2325992

16. Tutcu, C., Baydere, B.A., Talas, S.K., Samur, E.: Quasi-static modeling of a novel growing soft-continuum robot. Int. J. Robot. Res. **40**(1), 86–98 (2021). https://doi.org/10.1177/0278364919893438

17. Chen, X., Guo, Y., Duanmu, D., Zhou, J., Zhang, W., Wang, Z.: Design and modeling of an extensible soft robotic arm. IEEE Robot. Autom. Lett. **4**(4), 4208–4215 (2019). https://doi.org/10.1109/LRA.2019.2929994

18. Tang, Z.Q., Heung, H.L., Tong, K.Y., Li, Z.: Model-based online learning and adaptive control for a "human-wearable soft robot" integrated system. Int. J. Robot. Res. **40**(1), 256–276 (2021). https://doi.org/10.1177/0278364919873379

19. Li, M., Kang, R., Branson, D.T., Dai, J.S.: Model-free control for continuum robots based on an adaptive Kalman filter **23**(1), 12 (2018)

20. Melingui, A., Lakhal, O., Daachi, B., Mbede, J.B., Merzouki, R.: Adaptive neural network control of a compact bionic handling arm. IEEE/ASME Trans. Mech. **20**(6), 2862–2875 (2015). https://doi.org/10.1109/TMECH.2015.2396114

21. Wang, H., et al.: Deep reinforcement learning: a survey. Front. Inf. Technol. Electron. Eng. (1), 1–19 (2020). https://doi.org/10.1631/FITEE.1900533

22. Ma, R., et al.: Position control of an underwater biomimetic vehicle-manipulator system via reinforcement learning. In: 2020 IEEE 9th Data Driven Control and Learning Systems Conference (DDCLS), pp. 573–578 (November 2020). https://doi.org/10.1109/DDCLS49620.2020.9275206

23. Shahid, A.A., Roveda, L., Piga, D., Braghin, F.: Learning continuous control actions for robotic grasping with reinforcement learning. In: 2020 IEEE International Conference on Systems, Man, and Cybernetics (SMC), pp. 4066–4072 (October 2020). https://doi.org/10.1109/SMC42975.2020.9282951

24. Satheeshbabu, S., Uppalapati, N.K., Chowdhary, G., Krishnan, G.: Open loop position control of soft continuum arm using deep reinforcement learning. In: 2019 International Conference on Robotics and Automation (ICRA), pp. 5133–5139 (May 2019). https://doi.org/10.1109/ICRA.2019.8793653

25. Lillicrap, T.P., et al.: Continuous control with deep reinforcement learning. arXiv:1509.02971 [cs, stat] (September 2015)

26. Mnih, V., et al.: Human-level control through deep reinforcement learning. Nature **518**(7540), 529–533 (2015). https://doi.org/10.1038/nature14236

Simultaneous and Continuous Motion Estimation of Upper Limb Based on SEMG and LSTM

Zhili Ruan, Qingsong Ai, Kun Chen$^{(\boxtimes)}$, Li Ma, Quan Liu, and Wei Meng

School of Information Engineering, Wuhan University of Technology, Wuhan 430070, China
{rz1004357,qingsongai,kunchen,excellenmary,quanliu,
weimeng}@whut.edu.cn

Abstract. Continuous joint motion estimation based on surface electromyography (SEMG) signal plays an important role in human-machine interaction (HMI). Due to the requirements of several possible applications in which simultaneous control of multiple joints is needed, such as intelligent limbs and exoskeletons, simultaneous and continuous joint angle estimation of multiple joints is of great significance. In this paper, long short-term memory network (LSTM) was used to simultaneously estimate continuous elbow and wrist joint angles using time-domain features extracted from the SEMG. Nine healthy subjects participated in the experiment and their six muscle (i.e., biceps brachii (BB), triceps brachii (TB), flexor carpi radialis (FCR), extensor carpi radialis (ECR), flexor carpi ulnaris (FCU), and extensor carpi ulnaris (ECU)) SEMG signals were taken as algorithm inputs. SEMG features of each channel including mean absolute value (MAV) and root mean square (RMS) are extracted. The experimental results demonstrate that LSTM with 12 dimensional features as input presents the best estimation performance. Compared with estimation of single joint angle using genetic algorithm (GA) optimized back propagation neural network (BPNN), the average root mean square error (RMSE) for elbow and wrist were respectively reduced by 23.26% and 5.68% while the average coefficient of determination (R^2) for elbow and wrist were respectively increased by 4.90% and 2.25%. When compared with LSTM with 8-dimensional features as input, the average RMSE for elbow and wrist were respectively reduced by 29.38% and 1.88% while the average R^2 for elbow and wrist were respectively increased by 15.62% and 17.73%.

Keywords: SEMG · LSTM · Multi-joint angle estimation

1 Introduction

Stroke patients are often accompanied by irreversible central nervous damage, which will cause behavioral disorders to a certain extent [1], making it difficult for these patients to complete simple behaviors in their daily lives. Traditional passive rehabilitation method follows the model of human-machine cooperation and lacks the interaction between man and machine. Instead, an active training method combines the patient's active motion

© Springer Nature Switzerland AG 2021
X.-J. Liu et al. (Eds.): ICIRA 2021, LNAI 13013, pp. 313–324, 2021.
https://doi.org/10.1007/978-3-030-89095-7_31

intention, and the idea of human-machine collaboration [2] enhances the patient's dominance and initiative. On this basis, it can achieve the goal of ensuring the quality of rehabilitation on the premise of affecting physiological activation as little as possible [3].

Human biological signal is the sum of potentials excited by neurons carrying human movement information when they are transmitted to related tissues [4]. For effective human motion intention recognition, several bioelectric signals such as Electromyography (EMG), electrocardiography (ECG), electroocular (EOG), electroencephalography (EEG), and evoked potential/event-related potential (EP/PR) can be captured by surface electrodes [5]. Among them, EMG signals and EEG signals are mostly used to control external devices. However, it is far more difficult to implement EEG-based HMI than EMG-based HMI [5, 6], due to the very complex working mechanism of the brain. SEMG records the superposition of action potential generated by multiple motor units in time and space [4] which contains sufficient human body's movement information. The raw SEMG signals is weak and its energy mainly distributed on the frequency range of 20~500 Hz. SEMG occurs about 20~200 ms earlier than corresponding muscle contraction. However, there is a delay when using physical signals such as angle and angle velocity to express human motion intention directly. For all the characteristics above, studies have shown that SEMG signal is most suitable for HMI [6].

Forecasting continuous motion variables is the key to control robot and intelligent limb smoothly and naturally [7]. The existing continuous motion estimation methods based on SEMG are classified as either physiological models or regression models. In terms of physiological muscle model, Hill-based muscle model (HMM) is most frequently applied [4, 8]. Q. Zhang [9] et al. combined SEMG and ultrasound sonography as an input to estimate ankle dorsiflexion torque through a modified Hill-type neuromusculoskeletal model. X.Xi et al. [7] utilized a SEMG based dynamic model which contains a HMM to estimate the joint angles of the lower limbs. Physiological models can specify the estimation process at a physiological level. However, this model involves many physiological parameters, and individual differences have a great impact on the model. Compared with building a complex physiological model, a regression model directly establishes the mapping between SEMG and the physical quantities to be estimated, such as joint angles, joint speeds, and joint torques. Currently, regression model based on neural network has been widely applied and many achievements have already been made in estimating continuous joint angle. Z.Li et al. [10] proposed a time-smoothed multilayer perceptron (MLP) regression scheme for continuous knee/ankle angle estimation of multi-channel SEMG signals. It consists of a three-layer MLP regression model and a Savitzky-Golay filter. The experimental results showed that the best performance test R^2 is 0.948, and the mean square error (MSE) is 59.58. Y. Shi et al. [11] utilized a GA-BPNN and a limited amplitude filtering to estimate continuous motion of lower limb joints, the results show that the RMSE of the knee joint angles after optimization was reduced by 24% when compared to the RMSE before optimization. T. Bao et al. [12] proposed a single-stream convolutional neural network(CNN) to map SEMG signals to the wrist angle of three degrees of freedom, and the spectrum-based CNN achieved high recognition. A. M. Elbir [13] utilized radial basis function neural network (RBF) to estimate the angles of the three joints of the lower limbs simultaneously, and got results that the RMSE of hip joint is 1.0236 deg, the RMSE of knee joint is 8.0752 deg, and the RMSE of ankle joint is 11.063 deg. L. O. Suplino et al. [14] applied the nonlinear autoregressive exogenous model (NARX) to estimate the elbow joint angle trajectory, and the results proved that predicted value has a high correlation with true value, and the maximum RMSE is 7 deg. Single-joint angle prediction is easier to achieve better performance [2]. In clinical rehabilitation, the participation of joints ranging from proximal large joints to distal small joints and movement patterns from single to multi-joint movements. The elbow and wrist joints are located at each end of the upper forearm and share the same direction of freedom when performing flexion and extension movements. To our best knowledge, in the study of joint angle estimation based on SEMG, few researchers have adopted simultaneous angle estimation of elbow joint and wrist joint.

In this paper, we collected SEMG signals from six muscles of upper limb. First, correlation coefficient between each two channels is calculated. Then, two kinds of time-domain features were extracted as the input. Third, according to the correlation coefficient of each two channel, features of four channels used as input for comparison. And inspired by [13], BPNN optimized by GA is adopted to estimate the angle of a single joint angle.

2   Materials and Methods

2.1   Subjects and Data Acquisition

Nine healthy subjects participated in the experiment. TrignoTM Wireless EMG (Delsys Inc, Natick, MA, USA) was used to record SEMG signals, and the sampling rate was 2000 Hz. A Qualisys 3D motion capture and analysis system was used to record the motion of upper limb with a sampling rate of 100 Hz, and then to extract the elbow and wrist joint angles. The motion capture system consists of eight high-speed infrared cameras to capture the motion track of special material marked ball and one video camera. Additionally, synchronized data acquisition of SEMG signals and motion track can be realized through signal triggering device.

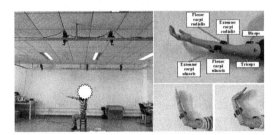

Fig. 1. Schematic diagram of experimental details.

Before experiment, the subject was sitting upright with their arms naturally relaxed. Wipe the skin surface with 75% alcohol to reduce the resistance of the skin surface and ensure good contact between skin and electrode. To determine the location of electrodes by querying SENIAM. After sticking electrode-specific disposable double-sided tape, attach the electrodes along the longitudinal direction of muscle fiber. Meanwhile, several marking balls of special material are attached to the inner forearm of upper limb to measure the angle of joints. The experimental scenario is shown in Fig. 1.

Before the movement, each subject's forearm was in a horizontal position. During the process of data collection, the subjects' elbows and wrists were simultaneously perform elbow extension and wrist extension, elbow flexion and wrist flexion. Subjects were asked to repeat the movement. Taking 20s as a group, the subjects rested for 10s between every two groups, and a total of 30 groups were collected. During the experiment, subjects were asked regularly whether they felt muscle soreness, and the rest time was extended when necessary. What's more, movement of the fingers can affect the SMG signals of the forearm muscles. Therefore, during the entire process, the subject's fingers were in a state of natural non-strength, and the fingers did not produce any movement during the experiment.

2.2 Signal Preprocessing

Chebyshev type I digital filter is adopted in our experiment to remove the noise signal, the passband is set to 20–500 Hz, meanwhile, the passband ripple and the stopband is set to 1dB and 30dB, respectively. Raw SEMG signal and filtered signal are shown in Fig. 2. Additionally, by observing the SEMG amplitude in the Fig. 2, it can be observed that the signal amplitude distributions of BB and TB are staggered. BB and TB formed a pair of active and antagonistic muscles when subjects performed elbow extension and flexion, wrist extension and flexion exercises. Similarly, FCR and ECR, FCU and ECU provide muscle support during extension and contraction, respectively. For the angle signals acquired by the motion capture system, no filtering is required and they are exported directly and used as a reference value for the angles estimated by regression model.

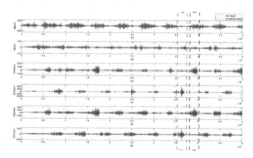

Fig. 2. Comparison of raw signal and filtered signal.

After the noise removal, 200 sampling points were further taken as the processing window to extract MAV and RMS from SEMG signals of each channel. The calculation process is shown in Eqs. (1) and (2):

$$MAV = \frac{1}{N}\sum_{i=1}^{N} |emg_i| \tag{1}$$

$$RMS = \sqrt{\sum_{i=1}^{N} emg_i^2} \tag{2}$$

where i represents the ith sampling point in a window, emg_i is SEMG signals corresponding to the sample point. A characteristic value is calculated for each window. N represents the number of sample points in a window. The length of the window we adopt contains 200 sample points, that is, N = 200. Since the sampling rate of joint angle is 100 Hz while the sampling rate of SEMG is 2000 Hz, the angle signal is averaged through a window with the size of 10 sampling points.

Six upper arm muscles were selected in our experiment; however, the forearm muscles are densely distributed. Corrcoef function in MATLAB is utilized to calculate the correlation coefficient of the MAV between each two channels to investigate whether the selected muscles were necessary. Correlations among six channels SEMG signals of one subject are detailed in Table 1.

Table 1. Correlation Coefficient of Channels

(1: biceps brachii (BB),2: triceps brachii (TB),3: flexor carpi radialis (FCR),4: extensor carpi radialis (ECR),5: extensor carpi ulnaris (ECU),6: flexor carpi ulnaris (FCU))

	1	2	3	4	5	6
1	1	0.1413	0.3395	0.1045	0.1596	0.0036
2	0.1413	1	0.0985	0.2222	0.2621	0.1072
3	0.3395	0.0985	1	0.1028	**0.4186**	0.0387
4	0.1045	0.2222	0.1028	1	**0.4163**	0.0715
5	0.1596	0.2621	**0.4186**	**0.4163**	1	0.0019
6	0.0036	0.1072	0.0387	0.0715	0.0019	1

It can be observed from the table that all the correlation coefficients among the six channels are all below 0.5. However, activation of ECU (channel5), is highly related to FCR (channel3) and ECR (channel4), whose coefficients are 0.4186 and 0.4163 respectively.

2.3 Neural Network Structures

Deep learning methods based upon neural network show obvious durability and adaptability when processing nonlinear and unstable SEMG signals [11]. In this paper, BPNN, LSTM and RBF are selected as the prediction models for multi-joint angle estimation.

Architecture of LSTM
Conventional neural networks do not have a memory function and thus lack the ability to extract information from signal sequences. LSTM is a special type of recurrent neural network (RNN). It overcomes the problems of gradient vanishing and gradient explosion

in RNN.LSTM mainly includes four important structures: cell state, forget gate, input gate, and output gate.

$$i_t = \sigma(W_{ii}x_t + b_{ii} + W_{hi}h_{(t-1)} + b_{hi}) \tag{3}$$

$$f_t = \sigma(W_{if}x_t + b_{if} + W_{hf}h_{(t-1)} + b_{hf}) \tag{4}$$

$$O_t = \sigma(W_{io}x_t + b_{io} + W_{ho}h_{(t-1)} + b_{ho}) \tag{5}$$

$$g_t = \tanh(W_{ig}x_t + b_{ig} + W_{hg}h_{(t-1)} + b_{hg}) \tag{6}$$

$$C_t = f_t \odot c_{(t-1)} + i_t \odot g_t \tag{7}$$

$$h_t = O_t \odot \tanh(c_t) \tag{8}$$

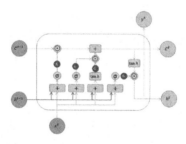

Fig. 3. Structure of a LSTM memory block.

where i_t is the input gate, f_t is the forget gate, and O_t is the output gate, σ is the logical sigmoid function, W is the weight matrix, b is the bias matrix, and $\odot$ is the scalar product. The update process of each LSTM unit is shown in Fig. 3. As shown in the Fig. 3, h^{t-1} and x^t are input to each gate structure and σ respectively represent the calculation of forget gate, input gate, and output gate. The tanh calculation is used to update the cell state.

In the experiment, 80% of collected data was used for training and 20% was used for testing, and the model was trained five times for validation. Since the movement in experiment lasted for 600s, the acquisition frequency of SEMG is 2000 Hz, and the window for extracting features including 200 samples. Thus, a total of 6000 samples were obtained, of which 4800 samples were used for training. To improve the efficiency of the training, 4800 samples were divided into 48 minibatch for batch training.

The LSTM has 12 input nodes, 10 hidden layer nodes and 2 output layer nodes, the error accuracy is 0.01 and the weights are initialized using a uniform distribution. Adaptive learning rates are used in the training process. The calculation formula is as follows, in which Lr represents learning rate, and t refers to the number of training

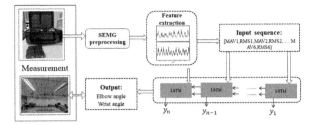

Fig. 4. LSTM-based multi-joint estimation flow.

sessions in each batch. The flow chart of multi-joint angle estimation based on LSTM is shown in Fig. 4.

$$Lr = 1/(10 + \sqrt{t}) \tag{9}$$

Architecture of BPNN
The MATLAB function feedforwardnet was utilized to create BPNN. A 12-dimensional feature vector was used as input, and two hidden layers connected contain 12 and 16 neurons, respectively. There are two neurons in the output layer, which respectively represent the angle of one degree of freedom of the elbow joint and the wrist joint. The maximum number, the training error target, and the learning rate of BPNN were set to be 1000, 1e-3, and 0.001, respectively. The activation function of the hidden layer is tansig, and the activation function of the output layer is purelin.70% of collected data was used to train the BPNN, 15% of the data was used as validation set, and 15% was used to test the model. Levenberg-Marquardt backpropagation was used as training method.

Architecture of RBF
Radical Basis Function neural network (RBF) usually contains 3 layers: input layer, middle layer, and output layer. The middle layer mainly calculates the RBF value of the Euclidean distance between the input x and the sample vector c (memory sample), and the output layer carries out a linear combination of it. The radial basis function calculation can be expressed as follows:

$$h(\|x - c_i\|) = e^{-\gamma \|x - c_i\|^2} \tag{10}$$

RBF utilizes a local activation function with the maximum response near the central point, while response which far from the central point decreases exponentially. It means each neuron corresponding to a different perceptual domain. Except for calculation rules between each layer, the network structures of RBF and BPNN are similar.

3 Experiment Results and Discussion

3.1 Experiment Results of Single Joint

Before predicting two joint angles simultaneously, a preliminary experiment is performed to predict a single joint angle. The 12-dimensional features were extracted from six muscles and BPNN was used to estimate angle of a single joint. Furthermore, GA is used to optimize the prediction effect of a single joint angle. When using the GA-optimized BPNN, the structure of the BPNN is the same as the BPNN described above. The number of evolutionary iterations, the population size, the crossover probability, and the mutation probability were set to be 20, 6, 0.3, and 0.1, respectively. Since the focus is not on GA-optimized BPNN, the specific structure will not be discussed here. The detailed results are shown in Fig. 5 and Fig. 6.

3.2 Experiment Results of Multiple Joint

BPNN, RBF, and LSTM are utilized to estimate the angles of the elbow and wrist joint simultaneously. For the three networks, inputs are all 12-dimensional time-domain feature vectors, and the outputs are all angles of elbow joint and wrist joint. In this paper, both R^2 and RMSE are selected as evaluation criteria. They can be calculated by using:

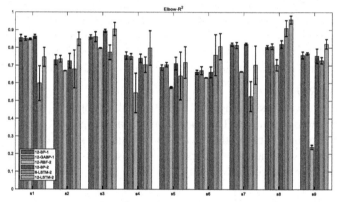

Fig. 5. Average R^2 of elbow joint angle in each subject.

$$R^2 = 1 - \frac{Var(Y^d - \widehat{Y^d})}{Var(Y^d)} \tag{11}$$

$$RMSE = \sqrt{\frac{1}{N}\sum_{i=1}^{N}(Y^d - \widehat{Y^d})^2} \tag{12}$$

where Y^d and $\widehat{Y^d}$ represent true and predicted values, respectively. In Fig. 5 and Fig. 6 12-RBF-2, 12-BP-2 and 12-LSTM-2 indicate that 12-dimensional vectors are input into RBF, BPNN and LSTM respectively. Furthermore, they were used to estimate

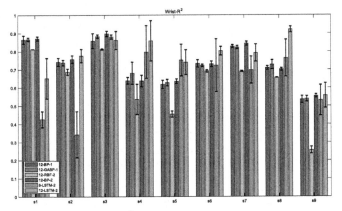

Fig. 6. Average R^2 of wrist joint angle in each subject.

the angles of the elbow and wrist joint simultaneously. It can be observed from the outcomes that the LSTM network is more dominant and can achieve higher R^2 in most case.Fig. 7, Fig. 8, and Fig. 9 presents the angle prediction curves obtained by using LSTM, BPNN, and RBF networks, respectively. From Fig. 7, it can be observed that there is a gap between the estimated angle amplitude value and the real angle amplitude value in LSTM model. Yet, the forecast curve is generally smooth. From Fig. 8 and Fig. 9, it can be found that the estimated angles of BPNN and RBF involve some high frequency components.

Specifically, in the LSTM prediction result graph, the R^2 of the elbow joint is 0.8904, the RMSE is 0.9756 deg, the R^2 of the wrist joint is 0.8783, and the RMSE is 1.0585 deg. For the BPNN prediction graph, the R^2 of the elbow joint is 0.8845, the RMSE is 1.4077 deg, the R^2 of the wrist joint is 0.7883, and the RMSE is 1.1539deg. And in the graph of RBF used as prediction model, the R^2 of the elbow joint is 0.8458, the RMSE is 1.6976 deg, the R^2 of the wrist joint is 0.8130, and the RMSE is 1.2460 deg.

3.3 Effects of Muscles Quantity

Due to the relatively high correlation coefficients between channel 3, 4, and 5, only 4 muscles are selected for comparison. They are BB, TB, FCR and ECR. According to the above experimental results, LSTM show the best performance when used as a regression model. Therefore, LSTM was used to compare the estimation results of four muscles and six muscles as input. As can be observed in Fig. 5 and Fig. 6, the estimation of 4 muscles, also known as 8-LSTM-2, is not as effective as that of 6 muscles. Compared to the method with 8-dimensional feature as input, the average RMSE of 12-dimensional feature as input decreased by 29.38% and 1.88% for the elbow and wrist joint respectively, while the average R^2 for the elbow and wrist joint improved by15.62% and 17.73% respectively.

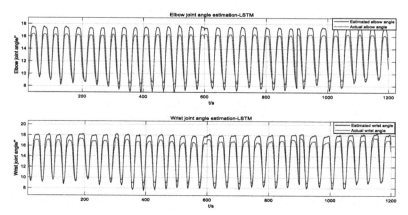

Fig. 7. Performance of LSTM in elbow and wrist joints angle estimation.

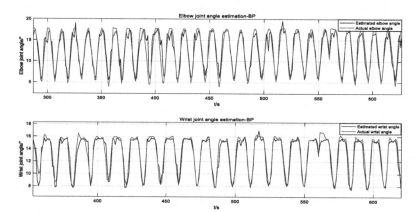

Fig. 8. Performance of BPNN in elbow and wrist joints angle estimation.

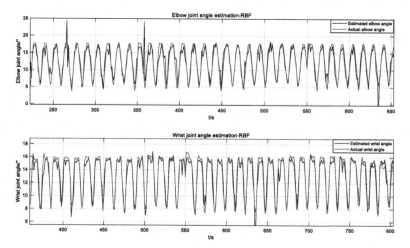

Fig. 9. Performance of RBF in elbow and wrist joints angle estimation.

4 Conclusion

This paper mainly studies the simultaneous and continuous motion estimation of elbow joint and wrist joint based on neural network. First, LSTM was selected as model for estimation, in which a 12-dimensional feature vector is utilized as input and 2-dimensional joint angles are utilized as output. In most case, LSTM can achieve higher R^2 and lower RMSE. Furthermore, it can be concluded that the estimation trajectory of LSTM needs to be improved in terms of amplitude, and the estimation trajectories of BPNN and RBF always contain some high frequency components. Second, experimental results show that simultaneous estimation of two joint angles by using LSTM performs better than single-joint angle estimation by using GA optimized BPNN. Last, there is a comparison about muscle selection. Six muscles selected in this paper has been proved to be effective and necessary. At the same time, in the part of wrist angle estimation, some subjects show better results when using fewer muscles. It shows that for different subjects, different muscle selection can be further studied. The results show that the method proposed in this paper is simple and efficient, and has good prospects for application in exoskeleton control.

References

1. Guo, S.: A Method of Evaluating Rehabilitation Stage by sEMG Signals for the Upper Limb Rehabilitation Robot. In: 2019 IEEE International Conference on Mechatronics and Automation (ICMA), pp. 1338–1343 (2019)
2. Bi, L.: A review on EMG-based motor intention prediction of continuous human upper limb motion for human-robot collaboration. Biomed. Sig. Process. Control 51, 113–127 (2019)
3. Becker, S.: Comparison of muscular activity and movement performance in robot-assisted and freely performed exercises. IEEE Trans. Neural Syst. Rehabil. Eng. 27, 43–50 (2019)
4. Ding, Q.: A Review on Researches and Applications of sEMG-based Motion Intent Recognition Methods. J. Acta Automatica Sinica 42(1), 13–25 (2016). (in Chinese)
5. Chai, Y.: A novel method based on long short term memory network and discrete-time zeroing neural algorithm for upper-limb continuous estimation using sEMG signals. Biomed. Sig. Process. Control 67, 102416 (2021)
6. Li, K.: A review of the key technologies for sEMG-based human-robot interaction systems. Biomed. Sig. Process. Control. 62, 102074 (2020)
7. Xi, X.: Simultaneous and continuous estimation of joint angles based on surface electromyography state-space model. IEEE Sens. J. 21, 8089–8099 (2021)
8. Guo, Y.: Upper limb muscle force estimation during table tennis strokes. In: 2019 IEEE 16th International Conference on Wearable and Implantable Body Sensor Networks (BSN), pp. 1–4 (2019)
9. Zhang, Q.: Prediction of ankle dorsiflexion moment by combined ultrasound sonography and electromyography. IEEE Trans. Neural Syst. Rehabil. Eng. 28, 318–327 (2020)
10. Li, Z.: A temporally smoothed MLP regression scheme for continuous knee/Ankle angles estimation by using multi-channel semg. IEEE Access 8, 47433–47444 (2020)
11. Shi, Y.: Prediction of Continuous Motion for Lower Limb Joints Based on SEMG Signal. In: 2020 IEEE International Conference on Mechatronics and Automation (ICMA), pp. 383–388 (2020)
12. Bao, T.: Surface-EMG based Wrist Kinematics Estimation using Convolutional Neural Network. In: 2019 IEEE 16th International Conference on Wearable and Implantable Body Sensor Networks (BSN), pp. 1–4 (2019)

13. Elbir, A.M.: A novel data transformation approach for DOA estimation with 3-D antenna arrays in the presence of mutual coupling. IEEE Antennas and Wirel. Propag. Lett. **16**, 2118–2121 (2017)
14. Suplino, L.O.: Elbow movement estimation based on EMG with NARX Neural Networks. In: 2020 42nd Annual International Conference of the IEEE Engineering in Medicine & Biology Society (EMBC), pp. 3767–3770 (2020)

Camera Pose Estimation Based on Plane Matching in Polarization Image

Songxin Zhou[1], Li He[1(✉)], and Ruiyin Yang[2]

[1] Department of Mechanical and Electrical Engineering,
Guangdong University of Technology, Guangzhou, China
[2] Academy of Science and Humanities, Guangdong University of Technology,
Guangzhou, China

Abstract. In visual SLAM, it is still a challenging problem to estimate camera pose in the case of low-texture, large rotation or repeated texture scenes, in which the popular feature-point-based methods may fail to work. In this paper we estimate relative pose from two consecutive frames captured by a polarization camera. Our main idea is to estimate the surface normal of a plane, which is typically texture-free and difficult for feature matching, and match planes in consecutive frames with their normals. Given the matched plane pair, we estimate camera pose accordingly. Due to the ambiguity of the zenith and azimuth angle in polarization-to-normal estimation, there are 6 possible normal values of a single plane via polarization estimation. To handle this problem, we use an IMU to initialize rotation estimation and further to eliminate normal ambiguity. We collected the testing data sets in real scenes and carried out experiments in weakly textured and richly textured scenes, with different lighting conditions. Experiments show that our method is able to provide accurate camera pose with weak textures, large rotations and repeated textures compared with the traditional visual feature methods.

Keywords: Polarimetric information · Texture-poor · Pose estimation

1 Introduction

Camera pose estimation is of great significance in visual SLAM and navigation. Accurate camera pose can effectively improve the quality of VSLAM mapping and navigation, while Epipolar Geometric Constraint is a good solution to the camera pose estimation problem in texture-rich regions. In general, at least 5 pairs of feature points are needed to accurately estimate the essential matrix, and then solve the relative pose of adjacent frames [1,2]. Even in the case of rotation, camera pose can be solved by estimating the homography matrix [3]. Other than visual feature matching, polarization matching is another solution to

R. Yang—This work was supported in part by the National Natural Science Foundation of China under Grant No. 61673125 and 61703115, in part by the Leading Talents of Guangdong Province Program under Grant No. 2016LJ06G498 and 2019QN01X761.

© Springer Nature Switzerland AG 2021
X.-J. Liu et al. (Eds.): ICIRA 2021, LNAI 13013, pp. 325–336, 2021.
https://doi.org/10.1007/978-3-030-89095-7_32

estimate camera pose. Cui *et al.* [4] used polarimetric information combined with feature points to solve the camera pose, and in return to improve the accuracy of the pose estimation. Works in [4] still require a relatively rich textured region and high matching accuracy of the feature points, and is not suitable for weak texture scenes.

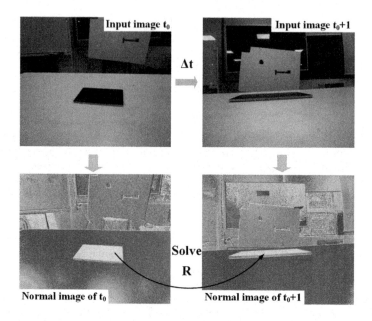

Fig. 1. Demonstration of pose estimation from polarization-based plane matching.

A polarized image contains geometric information and is robust in texture-poor environment. In recent years, many researchers have used polarimetric information for 3D reconstruction and achieved good results [5–8], but only a few works focused on camera pose estimation based on polarization. Cui *et al.* [4] first extracted feature point pairs and their normals from two polarimetric images, then optimized the refractive index, and consequently the optimal relative pose. However, this method relies on the rich texture of the environment, thus is not suitable for texture-poor scenes. In this paper, we try to use optical flow to track the plane, to estimate camera pose in a weak-textured and large-rotation scene, as shown in Fig. 1.

There are three challenges in using polarimetric information to estimate pose. Firstly, the refractive index of the object needs to be known [5] in advance to extract the surface normal from the polarimetric information. Secondly, accurate planar segmentation and data association in the weakly textured scene is still a challenge. Thirdly, the ambiguity of zenith angle and azimuth angle needs to be solved in polarized image normal estimation. In this paper, we propose our solution to overcome these challenges and get pose in texture-poor scenes.

Experiments proved that compared with the latest methods based on visual feature points, our method achieves better results.

2 Related Work

Among the standard methods for estimating camera pose, the most classic is the epipolar constraint. Only 5 pairs of well-matched points are needed to recover the camera movement between two frames. For the situation where there are more than 5 pairs of feature points, the RANSAC algorithm [9] can effectively eliminate most of the mismatches in the feature point pairs and provide a reliable input for the pose calculation, and then use the least squares method [1] to recover the camera pose. When the feature points are coplanar or the camera movement is pure rotation, the essential matrix degenerates. Then we calculate the homography matrix by using at least four pairs of feature points, and then calculate the camera pose.

About image data association, there are mainly feature point method and direct method. For the feature point method, researchers in the computer vision field have designed many stable local image features such as SIFT [10], ORB [11], etc. In the area with rich textures, it can run stably and provide a reliable pose estimation. Direct methods, alternatively, are based on the assumption of constant grey scale, which mainly include sparse optical flow and dense optical flow methods. The sparse optical flow is represented by the LK optical flow method, and it can work in some feature-missing regions.

Due to the rich geometric information contained in polarized images and the popularity of polarization sensors in recent years, many 3D reconstruction algorithms based on polarimetric information have emerged. Morel *et al.* [8] Proposed that the combination of polarimetric information and the shape-from-shading theory solved the ambiguity problem of normal estimation and restored the 3D shape at the same time. Smith *et al.* [12] combined linear polarization constraints to restore the depthless area, thereby improving the mapping effect. Cui *et al.* [13] used polarimetric information to get the normal, which can restore the depth in featureless areas. And this method is independent of illumination. Chen *et al.* [14] studied the application of phase angle in multi-view geometry. Recently, Yang *et al.* [7] have further integrated polarimetric information into SLAM systems. And Morein effectively realizes 3D real-time reconstruction in weakly textured areas based polarization [6]. These results have enriched the 3D reconstruction algorithm, while Cui [4] combined polarimetric information to obtain the relative pose. However, his algorithm relies on a good feature matching so that it is limited to texture-rich areas.

Inspired by what's mentioned above, we have implemented pose estimation in texture-poor regions by combining polarimetric information and the principle of optical flow. The refractive index depends on the material type, and since most of the texture-poor regions are made of ceramic materials in experiments, the refractive index in experimental scenes is 1.5. Generally, the normal values are similar in the same plane of the same material. However, due to the environmental noise in a real scene, the normal values of adjacent pixels may change significantly. Even the normals in the same plane can be different. We cluster the surface normal with ambiguity, making it convenient to track planes and eliminate the ambiguity. In the data association, we used the optical flow method to complete the plane tracking and matching in different images based on the polarization characteristics of planes. To obtain accurate camera poses, the RANSAC algorithm is used to optimize the planar data obtained from the segmentation. With an approximate rotation provided by a IMU, we can easily eliminate the ambiguity of the normal and estimate the relative rotation.

3   Methodology

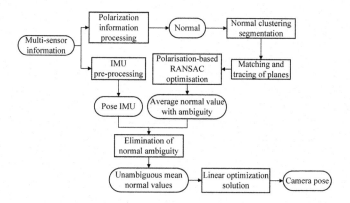

Fig. 2. System flow chart.

The flow chart of the method is shown in Fig. 2. Contents include normal estimation, planar clustering segmentation and tracking, IMU preprocessing, RANSAC optimization, normal ambiguity solution and pose solving.

3.1   Normal Estimation

From the principle of polarization, given polarization angle ϕ_{pol} and image brightness, we have

$$I\left(\phi_{pol}\right) = \frac{I_{\max} + I_{\min}}{2} + \frac{I_{\max} - I_{\min}}{2}\cos\left(2\left(\phi_{pol} - \phi\right)\right) \qquad (1)$$

Here, $I_{\max}$ and $I_{\min}$ is the maximum and minimum of the measured light intensity, ϕ represents the phase angle.

There are two kinds of reflection models in polarization analysis, namely specular and diffuse reflection model. According to the existing research [13], the $\pi-$ ambiguity of the azimuth angle α is expressed as ϕ or $\phi + \pi$ in the diffuse scene. This ambiguity is caused by (1), where both θ and $\theta+\pi$ are valid solutions to (1). For specular reflection, this azimuth angle can be expressed as $\alpha + \frac{\pi}{2}$.

Other than azimuth, we need to estimate the zenith angle β based on different reflection types. And the zenith angle is related to the degree of polarization ρ. Usually in a diffuse scene, the zenith angle is expressed as:

$$\rho = \frac{\sin \beta^2 \left(n - \frac{1}{n}\right)^2}{4 \cos \beta \sqrt{n^2 - \sin \beta^2} - \sin \beta^2 \left(n + \frac{1}{n}\right)^2 + 2n^2 + 2} \tag{2}$$

where n represents the refractive index and the zenith angle a unique solution.

Unlike the diffuse scene, the zenith angle obtained in the specular reflection has two solutions. The relationship between the zenith angle β and the degree of polarization ρ is:

$$\rho = \frac{2 \sin \beta \tan \beta \sqrt{n^2 - \sin^2 \beta}}{n^2 - 2 \sin^2 \beta + \tan^2 \beta} \tag{3}$$

When the refractive index n and polarization degree ρ are given, the zenith angle β has two values.

Given the zenith angle β and the azimuth angle α, we can express the normal in the camera coordinate system as follows:

$$n(u) = \begin{pmatrix} v_x \\ v_y \\ v_z \end{pmatrix} = \begin{pmatrix} \cos \alpha \sin \beta \\ -\sin \alpha \sin \beta \\ -\cos \beta \end{pmatrix} \tag{4}$$

For diffuse reflection, because of the ambiguity of azimuth angle α, there are two possible normals; in a specular reflection scene, there are both the ambiguity of zenith angle β and the $\pi-$ambiguity of azimuth angle α.

3.2   Surface Normal Segmentation and Matching

Generally, adjacent pixels in a plane of the same material have similar normal values and all pixels in this plane satisfy the normal Eq. (4). We perform cluster segmentation based on the difference in normal values. As shown in Fig. 3, we complete clustering of the normal planes, and select the three regions with the largest area from the segmentation results for tracking. Our main idea is to match planes via normals, and high polarization degree always leads to accurate normal estimation. So, we set a polarization degree threshold, and the area with the polarization degree higher than the threshold is used as the target area.

To track the detected planes, we use optical flow for pose estimation. Optical flow, however, is known for time consuming and not suitable for real-time applications. So, we randomly choose a few points on the targets, i.e., the planes, and tracking the selected points rather than the whole planes. a series of Gaussian-distributed pixels are generated and distributed in the target area. With the LK method, these pixels falling in the target area are tracked. If more than half of the pixels are matched, it is regarded as the same plane.

3.3   Camera Pose Estimation

This section shows the employment of polarization information to estimate the relative posture, especially the way of optimizing denoising, estimating the relative posture of the two plane pairs, and the solution of ambiguity of the zenith angle and azimuth angle.

Fig. 3. The relevant effect diagrams of the experiment. The first row represents the original image, polarization image and normal image. The second row represents the normal segmentation result, connected area image and target area pixel point generation image.

The plane fitted by the segmentation algorithm has a lot of noise points, which will affect the subsequent camera pose estimation. Therefore, before calculating the camera pose, we perform an optimization denoising on the fitted normal plane block. Based on the assumption that the normal values in the same plane block are close, we use a simple RANSAC to remove outer points. We solve the mean value of zenith angle and azimuth angle in the plane, and then process the azimuth angle of all the pixel points in the plane. Since the existence of $\pi - ambiguity$, i.e., either θ or $\theta + \pi$ is correct, we reset pixels with azimuth α 150° higher or lower than the average azimuth by $\alpha + \pi$ or $\alpha - \pi$, and then combine with the distance between the zenith angle with its average to calculate the distance of points to the model.

For each group of plane pairs (x_{p1}, x'_{p1}), we have the corresponding two groups of average normals after optimizing through the RANSAC algorithm. We express the obtained normals $(\bar{v}_{p1}, \bar{v}'_{p1})$ in the camera coordinate system. Obviously, the corresponding normals of the two frames and their relative rotation satisfy:

$$R\bar{v}_{pi} = R\bar{v}'_{pi}, \quad i = 1, 2 \tag{5}$$

Usually the rotation matrix has 3° of freedom, and can be solved with a pair of normals. However, the estimated normals in the real scene contain noise, which leads to large contingency in solving the rotation. Here we regard it as an optimization problem and use the least squares method to solve,

$$\min_{R \in SO(3)} \left\| Rv_{p1} - v'_{p1} \right\|^2 + \left\| Rv_{p2} - v'_{p2} \right\|^2 + \dots + \left\| Rv_{pn} - v'_{pn} \right\|^2 \tag{6}$$

This problem has a closed-form solution based on singular value decomposition, as shown below:

$$U \Sigma V^\top = v'_{p1} v_{p1}^\top + v'_{p2} v_{p2}^\top \tag{7}$$

Then we can get the rotation $R = U \operatorname{diag} \left(1, 1, \det \left(UV^\top\right)\right) V^\top$.

The normal ambiguity solution will be explained in the next subsection. Here, we assume that after solving the ambiguity of the zenith and azimuth angle, we can solve the relative pose transformation of any two frames of images, but we still need to understand how to solve the ambiguity. Our strategy is to find the least alignment deviation in the above formula the normal pair.

3.4 Solve the Ambiguity of Zenith Angle and Azimuth Angle

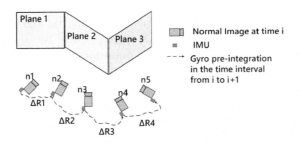

Fig. 4. Solutions to ambiguity problems.

There are 6 possibilities for the average normal of each plane, and this ambiguity is independent between images, which means that there are 36 possibilities for a set of normal pairs of two adjacent frames. If we know a rough relative rotation, we can restore the correct zenith angle and azimuth angle combination (α, β) by minimizing the alignment error of the normal line.

$$\min_{(\alpha, \beta)} \left\| Rv(\alpha, \beta) - v'(\alpha', \beta') \right\|^2 \tag{8}$$

As shown in Fig. 4, this paper uses an IMU pre-integration strategy to provide a rough rotation R^* of the system. Here we calibrate the IMU to minimize most of the noise impact, and then use the median method to integrate to obtain the relative rotation.

$$R^* = \begin{bmatrix} 1 \\ \frac{1}{2}\omega\delta t \end{bmatrix} \tag{9}$$

4   Experimental Evaluation

The experimental scene contains both specular and diffuse reflections, and we tested our algorithm under different light sources. Moreover, the effect of the RANSAC optimization algorithm on pose estimation was tested. The sensors used in the experiment include a polarization camera FLIR BFS-U3-51S5P-C, and a LPMS-B2 IMU. In the experimental, the real value is provided by the motion capture system with an localization error of 1mm. And in the scene without motion capture, the experimental accuracy is measured by artificial marking. We collected the dataset in the scenario as shown in Fig. 5, and the statistical information of the dataset is shown in Table 1.

4.1   Various Light Sources

We compared each frame in one scene with its afterwards frames within 0.4 s, resulting in a total of 4774 pose estimations in single light source and 5528 in multiple sources, both of scene 1. In scene 1, under the condition of a single light source, the average accuracy of the polarization camera pose estimation is 17.2531°, as shown in Table 2. In addition, the accuracy of our algorithm is compared with the feature point-based epipolar geometry method in the same scene. There are two popular fashions, the essential matrix and the homography matrix to calculate the pose, and in this paper we use the result with better accuracy as the final output of the feature point method.

(a) Scene 1   (b) Scene 2

Fig. 5. Experimental scenes and related renderings. (a) and (b) are the layouts of scenes 1 and 2.

Table 1. Summary table of data set statistics.

	Scene	Time(s)	Image	IMU	Mocap	Notes
Dataset 1	Scene 1	29.6	888	2962	2632	Single light source, rotational movements dominate
Dataset 2	Scene 2	44.7	1340	4467	–	Mixed scenes
Dataset 3	Scene 2	47.9	1438	4795	–	Mixed scenes
Dataset 4	Scene 2	54.4	1631	5437	–	Mixed scenes

Though the experimental scene contains weak textures, feature point method can still extract several feature points as shown in Fig. 6(b), but in the matching process, the feature-matching process cannot match the feature points in a correct way, and there are a lot of mismatches. We can see that there are 63 pairs of feature points after the two images are optimized by RANSAC, while only 9 pairs of the matched feature points are correct, and the rest are all mis-matched. This leads to large errors in camera pose estimation. As shown in Fig. 6(a), we can see that the blue area and green area are well tracked and the plane tracking is completed. As shown in Fig. 6(c) and (d), our method has better accuracy in the area of texture-poor plane, but the pose estimation of the feature point method doesn't work normally, where the maximum deviation is up to 180°.

4.2   Real Complex Scene

Usually, other than flat areas in the environment, many other areas with rich textures are also available. Therefore, we combine the polarization pose estimation and feature matching methods to solve the camera pose estimation in scenes

Table 2. Results on dataset 1

	Rmse	Mean	Median	Std	Min	Max
Ours	**20.11**	**17.25**	**15.56**	**10.33**	0.222	**40.3**
Without RANSAC	25.44	20.25	17.09	15.39	**0.2219**	167.3
Feature matching	89.6	66.28	42.24	60.33	0.34	179.9

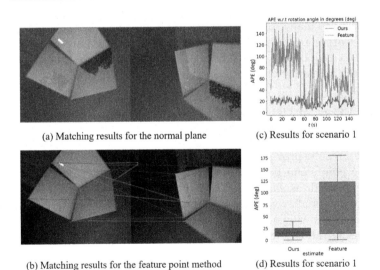

(a) Matching results for the normal plane

(c) Results for scenario 1

(b) Matching results for the feature point method

(d) Results for scenario 1

Fig. 6. The experimental results in Scene 1, Figure (a) shows the polarization-based planar matching results, Figure (b) shows the matching effect of feature point method, Figure (c) and Figure (d) show the experimental results in Scene 1.

containing both weak and rich texture areas, and improve the generality of this algorithm. Further experiments were carried out in the mixed scene 2 with weak texture and rich texture, as shown in Fig. 5(b). In scenes with less than 50 feature points and high polarization regions, we use polarization-based information to estimate camera pose. Otherwise we experiment with feature matching approach to estimate camera pose. We combined the feature point method to carry out 3 experimental evaluations. The results are shown in Table 3. We found that in the weak texture area, the feature matching has deviations, resulting in large errors. Feature points are relatively few, even if the RANSAC algorithm is used to process the feature points, the error is still large. From Fig. 7(a), it can be seen that the accuracy of polarization-based camera pose estimation is better than that of feature matching in the weakly textured region in scene 2.

Table 3. The effect in experiment scenario 2

	Rmse	Mean	Median	Std	Min	Max
Polar-featrue	**126.3**	**121.2**	**128.8**	35.48	**74.5**	160.4
Pure-feature	138.1	137.1	130.7	**16.14**	121.3	**159.2**

At this time, combining the polarization pose estimation can effectively improve the estimation accuracy. In the experiment, when most areas have obvious feature points, the effect of our algorithm is similar to the accuracy of pure feature points. When there is a weakly textured region, our algorithm has a significant improvement in accuracy over visual features. In a large part of weak texture, there are many mismatched feature points. Combining the polarization and visual feature to estimate the camera pose, the absolute cumulative error is significantly reduced, as shown in Figure. 7(a) and (b). In the normal texture area, the error accuracy of both is similar.

4.3   The Effect of Using the RANSAC Algorithm

We compared the camera pose accuracy with/without RANSAC algorithm. The experimental results proved that by using RANSAC for polishing the plane, most of the noise points can be effectively proposed, and the camera pose accuracy has been improved, as shown in Fig. 7(c) and (d). we compared each frame in one scene with its afterwards frames within 0.4 s, resulting in a total of 4774 pose estimations in single light source, the pose accuracy has been improved by 3.9° after using the RANSAC algorithm, as shown in Table 2.

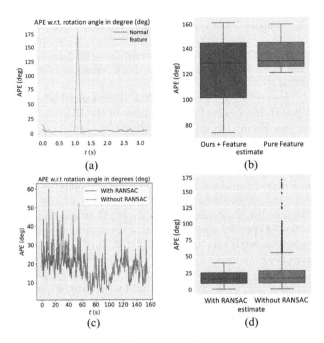

Fig. 7. Experimental effect diagram, (a) shows the pose accuracy results of our method compared with the feature point method in the weakly textured region of scene 2; (b) shows the absolute error of the pure feature point method and the polarization combined feature point method in the mixed scene; (c) and (d) show the effect before and after the RANSAC algorithm is added.

5 Conclusions

This paper proposes a camera pose estimation method based on polarization image plane matching in weak texture scenes. By using the polarization information, we calculate the normal of a plane and complete the plane matching in consequent frames. According to the matching results, We get an approximate rotation from the IMU and compare the minimum alignment error of the plane normals to resolve the normal ambiguity. And provide reliable pose estimation in weak texture scenes. Experimental results in real scenes show that, under a single light source, our algorithm can provide an accurate pose estimation that is significantly better than the feature point method.

References

1. Nistér, D.: An efficient solution to the five-point relative pose problem. IEEE Trans. Pattern Anal. Mach. Intell. **26**(6), 756–770 (2004)
2. Hartley, R., Li, H.: An efficient hidden variable approach to minimal-case camera motion estimation. IEEE Trans. Pattern Anal. Mach. Intell. **34**(12), 2303–2314 (2012)

3. Andrew, A.M.: Multiple View Geometry in Computer Vision. Kybernetes, Bristol (2001)
4. Cui, Z., Larsson, V., Pollefeys, M.: Polarimetric relative pose estimation. In: Proceedings of the IEEE/CVF International Conference on Computer Vision, pp. 2671–2680 (2019)
5. Kadambi, A., Taamazyan, V., Shi, B., Raskar, R.: Polarized 3d: High-quality depth sensing with polarization cues. In: Proceedings of the IEEE International Conference on Computer Vision, pp. 3370–3378 (2015)
6. Shakeri, M., Loo, S.Y., Zhang, H.: Polarimetric monocular dense mapping using relative deep depth prior. arXiv preprint arXiv:2102.05212 (2021)
7. Yang, L., Tan, F., Li, A., Cui, Z., Furukawa, Y., Tan, P.: Polarimetric dense monocular slam. In: Proceedings of the IEEE conference on computer vision and pattern recognition, pp. 3857–3866 (2018)
8. Morel, O., Meriaudeau, F., Stolz, C., Gorria, P.: Polarization imaging applied to 3d reconstruction of specular metallic surfaces. In: Machine Vision Applications in Industrial Inspection XIII, vol. 5679, pp. 178–186. International Society for Optics and Photonics (2005)
9. Fischler, M.A., Bolles, R.C.: Random sample consensus: a paradigm for model fitting with applications to image analysis and automated cartography. Commun. ACM **24**(6), 381–395 (1981)
10. Lowe, G.: Sift-the scale invariant feature transform. Int. J **2**(91–110), 2 (2004)
11. Rublee, E., Rabaud, V., Konolige, K., Bradski, G.: Orb: an efficient alternative to sift or surf. In: 2011 International Conference on Computer Vision, pp. 2564–2571. IEEE (2011)
12. Smith, W.A.P., Ramamoorthi, R., Tozza, S.: Linear depth estimation from an uncalibrated, monocular polarisation image. In: Leibe, B., Matas, J., Sebe, N., Welling, M. (eds.) ECCV 2016. LNCS, vol. 9912, pp. 109–125. Springer, Cham (2016). https://doi.org/10.1007/978-3-319-46484-8_7
13. Cui, Z., Gu, J., Shi, B., Tan, P., Kautz, J.: Polarimetric multi-view stereo. In: Proceedings of the IEEE Conference on Computer Vision and Pattern Recognition, pp. 1558–1567 (2017)
14. Chen, L., Zheng, Y., Subpa-Asa, A., Sato, I.: Polarimetric three-view geometry. In: Proceedings of the European Conference on Computer Vision (ECCV), pp. 20–36 (2018)

Topological and Semantic Map Generation for Mobile Robot Indoor Navigation

Yujing Chen, Jinmin Zhang, and Yunjiang Lou$^{(\boxtimes)}$

The School of Mechatronics Engineering and Automation,
Harbin Institute of Technology Shenzhen, Shenzhen, China
`louyj@hit.edu.cn`

Abstract. The current tendency in mobile robot indoor navigation is to move from the representation environment as a geometric grid map to a topological and semantic map closer to the way how humans reason. The topological and semantic map enables a robot to understand the environment. This paper presents a topological and semantic segmentation algorithm that divides a grid map into single rooms or similar meaningful semantic units with a collision-free path to connect them. First, a topological map is build based on the distance transform of the grid map. Then a semantic map is build based on the distance transform of the grid map and a circular kernel. Finally, we filter and prune the topological map by merging the nodes which represent the same room. The segmented performance of the proposed planning framework is verified on multiple maps. The experiment results show that the proposed method can accurately segment rooms and generate topological semantic maps.

Keywords: Mobile robot · Topological map · Semantic map

1 Introduction

Mobile robot navigation in an indoor environment uses a map for planning. This map is usually provided by the SLAM technologies which classically represent the environment as a two-dimension grid map, and the obstacles are represented as the occupied grid based on its geometric features [1]. The robot searches a collision-avoidance path from the starting pose to the destination based on the grid map. However, a robot that navigates a long path based on the grid map will take a long time to plan a feasible and collision-free path. This shortcoming is crucial for robot tasks, especially in the guiding or delivery tasks. On the contrary, robot navigation with a topological map shows its advantages for

This work was supported partially by the National Key Research and Development Program of China (2020YFB1313900), and partially by the Shezhen Science and Technology Program (No. JCYJ20180508152226630).

© Springer Nature Switzerland AG 2021
X.-J. Liu et al. (Eds.): ICIRA 2021, LNAI 13013, pp. 337–347, 2021.
https://doi.org/10.1007/978-3-030-89095-7_33

lightweight graph-based planning [2]. Moreover, many tasks would benefit from a high-level form of representation and reasoning such as human-robot interaction, exploration, and surveillance. It is often easier for humans to understand high-level features of the environment, such as lobbies, corridors, and rooms than to directly use the grid map. Humans can communicate places and directions to each other using lobbies' or rooms' names instead of coordinates. Thus, introducing a semantic map of the environment can improve the interaction capability of a mobile robot, such as human-robot interaction and robot-environment interaction [3].

Topological map abstracts a continuous spatial environment into graph [4] [5]. It is an intuitive way to help humans to understand the environment and provide preliminary results for further semantic labeling or topological navigation. A constructed topological map is a graph abstraction of the environment that represents the world as two types of elements, nodes, where the discrete areas are simply presented as a point to the robot, and paths, which are connections between nodes. To construct a topological map, Vachirasuk et al. [6] keep the area such as intersection, corner in corridors as a node, and the Voronoi path between nodes as edge. Oliver [7] converts the Voronoi graph into a conditional random field and then segments the environment into regions that might be rooms or corridors. According to [8], the grid map is transformed to distance map for room segmentation. In [9], the distance transform based algorithm is further extended to explore the incremental topological map building from raw sensor data. However, the topological map is constructed without any semantic labeling and only the appearance and connectivity are used.

A semantic map is constructed to give meaning to the discrete areas of the grid map. The main difference between semantic map and topological map is that the discrete areas are represented metrically or semantically. Therefore, it implies additional knowledge about the discrete area of the world and it allows the robot to infer new information [3]. It is natural to decompose an indoor environment into semantic places such as rooms or corridors to construct a semantic map. Bormann et al. [10] provide a survey and compare four room segmentation algorithms. According to [11], the semantic map is constructed by a contour-based part segmentation algorithm, which is called the DuDe segmentation algorithm. An algorithm is presented to segment the map by doing a convolution between distance transform of the grid map and then grouping pixels of the same value based on a circular kernel in [12]. However, the above algorithms do not consider constructing a collision-free topological graph that connects each semantic region for robot navigation.

To meet the requirements of fast planning and semantic reasoning for robot indoor navigation, this paper proposes a topological and semantic map construction framework (TOSE) based on the two-dimension geometric grid map. In TOSE, we first extracted the skeleton of the grid map based on its distance transformation to construct the topological graph. Each edge of the topological graph is collision-free, which can be used for robot planning. Then, we segment the grid map by doing a convolution between the distance transformation of the grid map and a circular kernel. Finally, we prune the topological graph based on the semantic map and the nodes in the same semantic region are merged. So that each node in the topological graph can represent the physical meaning of a semantic region. The contributions of this paper are as follows.

- A segmentation framework is proposed to extract regions from geometric map to construct topological and semantic map. The generated map is more suitable for the requirement of human-robot interaction for robot indoor navigation.
- A topological graph generation method is proposed. The edges of the generated topological graph are collision-free and can be used for robot navigation.
- A semantic graph generation method is proposed. The demonstrations on various map and the comparisons with the state of the art methods show the robust of the proposed semantic segmentation method.

This paper is organized as follows. Section 2 the details of the proposed segmentation framework are proposed. Section 3 is the demonstrations and comparisons. The results are summarized and our conclusions are drawn in Sect. 4.

2   Segmentation Framework

2.1   Definitions

The pipeline to generate the topological and semantic map can be found in Fig. 1. It can be divided into three phases. The first phase is to generate the topological graph of the grid map. The second phase is to segment the room of the grid map. The third phase is to prune the topological map and to associate the vertices and the room then to merge the topological map and semantic map.

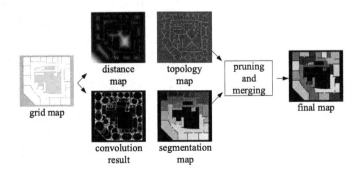

Fig. 1. Description of the proposed topological and semantic map generation framework.

2.2   Topological Map Generation

Firstly, the grid map needs to be converted to a distance map. The distance map can be generated by taking the distance to the closest obstacles. The metrics to calculate the distance can be Euclidean distance and Mahalanobis distance [13]. The main weakness of the above two metrics is that they are not accurate when there exist some clusters with different distributions in the feature space. In this work, we use the Gaussian function to generate the distance map because the Gaussian function is a more accurate similarity measure than the Euclidean distance and Mahalanobis distance. It can capture the local distribution in the feature space [13].

Distance Transformation of the Grid Map. For an occupied pixel at p_n of the grid map, where $n \in \{1, 2, 3, \cdots, N\}$ and N is the number of occupied pixel, it can be represent as a function $\delta(x - p_n)$. Thus, each pixel n in the grid map can be transformed by a convolution of $\delta(x - p_n)$ based on a Gaussian kernel G_d

$$H_n(x) = \delta(x - p_n)\dot{G}_d(x). \tag{1}$$

Then the distance map can be calculated by

$$H_a(x) = \max_{n=1}^{N} H_n(x). \tag{2}$$

We use the maximum value to be the value of each pixel in the distance map. Thus, each pixel value depends on the nearest obstacle point. An example of a distance map is shown in Fig. 2(b).

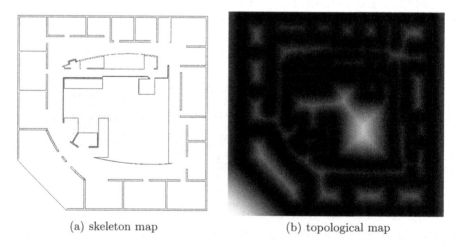

(a) skeleton map   (b) topological map

Fig. 2. An example of the generated distance map. This is lab map of Intel which comes from the database in [10]

Distance Transformation to Skeleton. As shown in Fig. 2(b), the space around the obstacles is a slope. The closer the distance, the greater the value. The path between the slope is the topological map we want to get. Thus, we use a filter to extract the paths. The Canny filter, Sobel filter, Robert filter, Prewitt filter, and Laplacian filter. We use the canny filter to extract the paths. Then we use a thinning algorithm to skeletonize the extracted paths, which is shown in Fig. 3(a).

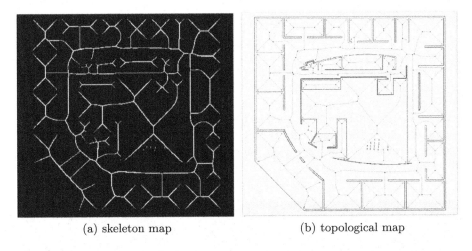

(a) skeleton map   (b) topological map

Fig. 3. An example of the generated skeleton map and the topological map.

Building the Topological Graph. The topological map can be generated based on the skeleton map. We can connect the neighboring pixels of the skeleton to generate the topological graph. For each pixel p_s of the skeleton can be assumed as a vertex, where $s \in \{1, 2, 3, \cdots, S\}$ and S is the number of the pixel of the skeleton. For each pixel p_s as the center of a 3×3 window, other pixels of the skeleton in the window can be considered as its neighbors. The pixel with more than 3 neighbors can be selected as a vertex. Finally, an example of the result topological map can be found in Fig. 3(b).

2.3   Room Segmentation

To segment the grid map, we hypothesize that the regions of the map can be recognized by looking at the design of the free space. For example, rooms or corridors are connected by doors, which are smaller than the space of rooms or corridors. Therefore, in this paper we proposed a region extraction method for room segmentation. The segmentation method has two phases, extraction of the region and detecting the door patterns, segmentation of the room based on the door.

Extraction of Region. To extract the region, we also based on the distance map of the grid map. For each pixel p_d in the distance map, we create a circular mask centered on the p_d and the radius of the circular mask is the value of the pixel, where $d \in \{1, 2, 3, \cdots, D\}$ and S is the number of the pixel of the distance map. Based on Eq. 2, each circular mask is collision-free region. Each value of the pixel in the region is set as the value of the center pixel. Once both pixel have been considered to generate the circular mask, the region have the same value are merged into a region

$$H_r(x) = \max_{d=1}^{D} H_d(x), \tag{3}$$

as shown in Fig. 4(a).

The region extraction based on a circular mask provides an over-fitting map. As shown in Fig. 4(a), ripples are introduced by the circular mask extraction. Those ripples are present in the long and narrow regions, such as corridors, and in the region of different sizes, such as the door regions. Thus, it is important to remove the ripples to merge the region at the same semantic area and to avoid creating an over-segmenting region. Moreover, the ripples that correctly divide the rooms need to be retained.

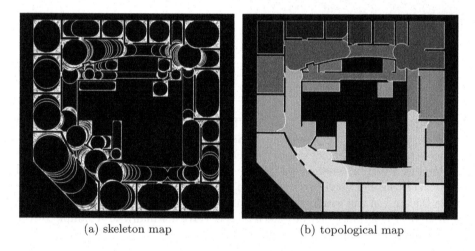

(a) skeleton map   (b) topological map

Fig. 4. (a) An example of the segmentation image based on the circular mask. The black regions are the extraction collision-free space while the white regions between the collision-free space are the ripples. (b) An example of the grey-scale segmentation map. Each region with a differently grey level is a segmented region.

Construction of Segmentation Map. A detect rule is used to check the ripples. The length of the ripple is used to determine whether a merge is needed. This determination is based on the hypothesize that the size of the door is small relative to the size of the room, so the ripple at the door to segment two room must account for less than 50% of the circumference of the circular mask. Thus, we detect each ripple and merge the region with its neighbor if this ripple's length is more than 50% of the circumference of the circular mask. Then the corresponding ripple is eliminated. The rest of the ripples are the ripple caused by the door. As shown in Fig. 4(b), the hypothesize has practical physical meaning. Based on the rest of the ripples, we find the contour of the image and then segment the regions with different semantic meanings to construct the semantic map.

2.4   Pruning and Merging the Topological Graph

After getting a topological map and a semantic map, we need to merge these two maps to generate a topological and semantic map. The meaning of this merging is to endow semantic information to the vertex of the topological graph, and also to make different semantic regions of the map have position attributes.

The enormous compactness of topological and semantic maps facilitates efficient planning when compared to the grid map, even interact with humans. Based on the map generated by our method, a robot can navigate with a human's voice command. For example, the human gives a voice command "go to the room #1 to take a cup" to the robot, then the robot can check the map by the world "room #1" to find the corresponding vertex of the "room #1" in the map and get its position. Then the robot checks the path based on the topological graph to find the global path using one of the graph search algorithms, such as Dijkstra's, A*, or dynamic programming, which is more efficient compared to the planning in the grid map. In contrast, grid map, single topological map, or single semantic map do not achieve this interaction task [14].

First, for each segmentation room, we find its central pixel. Second, for each segmentation room, we find the corresponding vertexes of the topological graph. Third, we select the vertex which is closest to the central pixel as the semantic vertex for each segmentation room. Fourth, all semantic vertexes are constructed to a semantic list. Thus, the robot can check the vertex in the semantic list to locate the room position, and check the path based on the topological graph to efficiently find the global path. The final merging topological and semantic map is shown in Fig. 5.

3   Evaluation

The algorithms run in a Laptop Intel Core i5-8250U CPU 1.60GHz with 8GB RAM with C++. The test dataset is provided in the paper [10], which including 20 maps with different sizes. We show five segmentation results of these tests, with different numbers of rooms and different structural layouts.

We evaluate the performance of the proposed framework with two indexes, the precision and recall compared with the state-of-the-art method Voronoi [10] and DuDe [11] and human labeled results. We choose this two indexes because

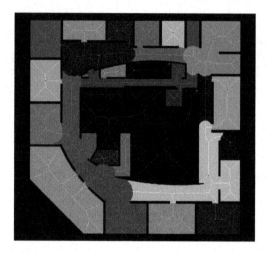

Fig. 5. An example of the topological and semantic map. The red points are the semantic vertexes and the white lines are the collision-free path. Each segmentation room is labeled with a different color.

they allow the comparison with a human labeled image. The precision and recall are

$$\text{Precision} = \frac{t_p}{t_p + f_p} = \frac{R_{\text{human}} \cap R_{\text{seg}}}{R_{\text{human}}}, \tag{4}$$

$$\text{Recall} = \frac{t_p}{t_p + f_n} = \frac{R_{\text{human}} \cap R_{\text{seg}}}{R_{\text{seg}}}, \tag{5}$$

where t_p represents the number of the pixels in both regions, the f_p represents the number of the pixels in the segmented region but not in human labeled, f_n represents the number of the pixels in the human labeled region but not in the segmented, R_{human} represents the region the human labeled and R_{seg} represents the segmented region. The results are shown in Table 1.

Quantitatively, the comparison of the proposed approach with the Voronoi method and DuDe method is summarized in Table 1. The value of recall is higher if the ground truth rooms are more contained in the found segments. The value of precision is higher if the segmented rooms are more contained in the ground truth rooms. Thus, the segmentation can fit the ground truth well if both values

Table 1. Averaged precision and recall.

Map type	Index	Voronoi	DuDe	Ours
No furniture	Recall(%)	95.0 ± 2.3	86.3 ± 9.7	95.4 ± 2.5
	precision(%)	94.8 ± 5.0	94.1 ± 3.1	95.1 ± 3.4
With furniture	Recall(%)	86.6 ± 5.2	85.8 ± 10.3	88.0 ± 4.7
	Precision(%)	94.5 ± 5.1	94.0 ± 3.2	95.5 ± 3.1

Human labeled   DuDe Segmented Algorithm   Our Segmented Algorithm

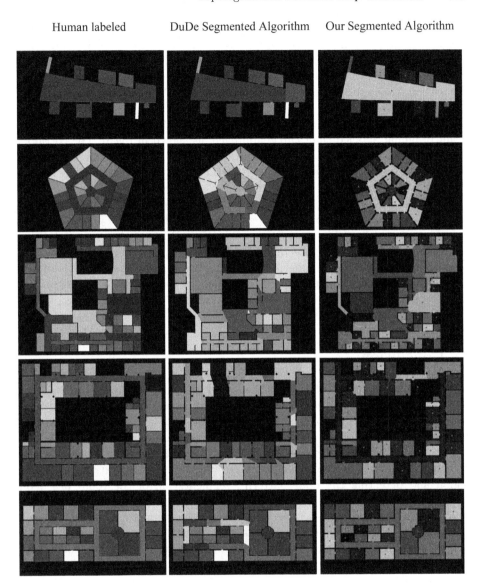

Fig. 6. The result comparisons on the datasets provided in [10]. Comparing with the DuDe approach, the results of our method are similar to the result of human labeled. The white paths are the topological path and the red vertexes are used to quickly locate the room they are in.

of recall and precision are high. If the value of recall is high when precision is low, it should be under-segmentation. In contrast, if the value of recall is low when precision is high, it should be over-segmentation. Thus, the segmentation results of the proposed approach are better than the Voronoi-based approach and DuDe approach in both scenarios with furniture and without furniture.

In addition, comparing the results between the scenarios with furniture and without furniture, the results on the scenarios without furniture are better than the scenarios with furniture. This is because the furniture will interfere with the image segmentation.

Qualitatively, the decomposition of the proposed approach is similar to the result of human labeled than DuDe approach, as shown in Fig. 6. The corridors are usually over segmented based on DuDe approach because it is based on the convexity of the regions. An "L" shaped corridor or a longer corridor are always over segmented into two or more regions.

In addition, in the proposed approach, each segmentation rooms can match with the topological map and get a position information of the grid map. This character is used to guide the robot's navigation. When each rooms is labeled with a number, the robot can quickly find the goal position of a room. The topological edges of the topological map can quickly guide the robot the find a collision avoidance path the goal. For example, the robot uses the A^* algorithm the search the global path on the topological map is more efficient than search on the grid map.

4   Conclusion

In this paper, we proposed a novel framework to generate the topological and semantic map based on the grid map. First, we generate the topological map based on the grid map with three phases, generation of a distance map based on a Gaussian function, skeleton extraction based on Canny filter, and finding the intersection point as the vertexes of the topological map. Second, we generate the semantic map based on the grid map with two phases, extraction of the region and detecting the door patterns, segmentation of the room based on the door. Third, we merge the topological map and semantic map by selecting a vertex on the topological map to represent the semantic meaning of each room. We also compare our segmentation approach with the state-of-the-art approach and human labeled result. The comparison results show the robustness and consistency of the proposed method.

References

1. Elfes, A.: Using occupancy grids for mobile robot perception and navigation. Computer **22**(6), 46–57 (1989)
2. Choset, H., Nagatani, K.: Topological simultaneous localization and mapping (slam): toward exact localization without explicit localization. IEEE Trans. Robot. Autom. **17**(2), 125–137 (2001)
3. Liu, M., Colas, F., Oth, L., Siegwart, R.: Incremental topological segmentation for semi-structured environments using discretized gvg. Auton. Robot. **38**(2), 143–160 (2015)

4. Choi, J., Choi, M., Lee, K., Chung, W.K.: Topological modeling and classification in home environment using sonar gridmap. In: Proceedings of IEEE International Conference on Robotics and Automation (ICRA), pp. 3892–3898. IEEE (2009)
5. Liu, M., Colas, F., Siegwart, R.: Regional topological segmentation based on mutual information graphs. In: Proceedings of IEEE International Conference on Robotics and Automation (ICRA), pp. 3269–3274. IEEE (2011)
6. Setalaphruk, V., Ueno, A., Kume, I., Kono, Y., Kidode, M.: Robot navigation in corridor environments using a sketch floor map. In: Proceedings of IEEE International Symposium on Computational Intelligence in Robotics and Automation. Computational Intelligence in Robotics and Automation for the New Millennium (Cat. No. 03EX694), vol. 2, pp. 552–557. IEEE (2003)
7. Wallgrün, J.O.: Hierarchical voronoi-based route graph representations for planning, spatial reasoning, and communication. In: Proceedings of the 4th International Cognitive Robotics Workshop (CogRob-2004), pp. 64–69. Citeseer (2004)
8. Diosi, A., Taylor, G., Kleeman, L.: Interactive slam using laser and advanced sonar. In: Proceedings of the 2005 IEEE International Conference on Robotics and Automation (ICRA), pp. 1103–1108. IEEE (2005)
9. Yuan, Y., Schwertfeger, S.: Incrementally building topology graphs via distance maps. In: Proceedings of IEEE International Conference on Real-time Computing and Robotics (RCAR), pp. 468–474. IEEE (2019)
10. Bormann, R., Jordan, F., Li, W., Hampp, J., Hägele, M.: Room segmentation: Survey, implementation, and analysis. In Proceedings of IEEE International Conference on Robotics and Automation (ICRA), pp. 1019–1026. IEEE (2016)
11. Fermin-Leon, L., Neira, J., Castellanos, J.A.: Incremental contour-based topological segmentation for robot exploration. In: Proceedings of IEEE International Conference on Robotics and Automation (ICRA), pp. 2554–2561. IEEE (2017)
12. Mielle, M., Magnusson, M., Lilienthal, A.J.: A method to segment maps from different modalities using free space layout maoris: map of ripples segmentation. In: Proceedings of IEEE International Conference on Robotics and Automation (ICRA), pp. 4993–4999. IEEE (2018)
13. Li, X.Q., King, I.: Gaussian mixture distance for information retrieval. In: International Joint Conference on Neural Networks. Proceedings (Cat. No. 99CH36339), IJCNN 1999, vol. 4, pp. 2544–2549. IEEE (1999)
14. Thrun, S.: Learning metric-topological maps for indoor mobile robot navigation. Artif. Intell. **99**(1), 21–71 (1998)

A Research on Bending Process Planning Based on Improved Particle Swarm Optimization

Yang Sen[1,2] (ID), Kaiwei Ma[1,2] (ID), Zhou Yi[1,2] (ID), and Fengyu Xu[1,2(✉)] (ID)

[1] College of Automation and College of Artificial Intelligence, Nanjing University of Posts and Telecommunications, Nanjing 210023, China

[2] Jiangsu Engineering Lab for IOT Intelligent Robots (IOTRobot), Nanjing 210023, China

Abstract. In order to ensure the accuracy and efficiency of sheet metal bending, a more efficient bending process planning algorithm is required. First of all, under the premise of comprehensively considering interference discrimination and efficiency guarantee, this paper establishes the fitness function of the process planning problem, and converts the process of selecting the optimal process into a problem of solving the optimal solution of the function. Then, since Particle Swarm optimization is easy to fall into the local optimal solution, an improved algorithm is proposed to solve the optimal process. Finally, the optimal bending process of sheet metal parts with different complexity is solved by experiments. The results show that the improved algorithm can calculate the optimal or nearly optimal results within a reasonable time range when there are more bending steps.

Keywords: Sheet metal · Bending process · Particle swarm optimization

1 Introduction

The sheet metal bending process is a manufacturing process that performs a series of continuous bending of sheet metal parts to generate a workpiece. The bending process planning is a key part of the process, which has an important influence on simplifying the processing process and ensuring the bending accuracy [1]. When planning the bending process, it is necessary to comprehensively consider multiple factors such as interference discrimination, workpiece positioning, production efficiency, workpiece accuracy, etc. When the number of bending steps of the workpiece is n, the number of possible processes to be analyzed is n! [2]. Although it is theoretically possible to search for the best process using the exhaustive method, it is not suitable for processes with a large number of steps due to problems such as long time-consuming and large system resource occupation [3].

In the research of bending process planning, Salem et al. [4] developed two-dimensional and three-dimensional interference detection algorithms, which reduced the complexity of process planning. Faraz et al. [5] proposed an improved branch-and-bound TSP algorithm for to calculate bending processes. Deepak et al. [6] grouped the features of the parts and determined the bending process according to different types of bending groups. Farsi [7] determined the bending operation group based on the relationship between the bending processes, and then determined the sequence of the operation

© Springer Nature Switzerland AG 2021
X.-J. Liu et al. (Eds.): ICIRA 2021, LNAI 13013, pp. 348–358, 2021.
https://doi.org/10.1007/978-3-030-89095-7_34

group using the fuzzy set theory. Although the traditional optimization algorithm has certain applicability, it also has many shortcomings, such as failing to find the global optimal solution, not suitable for discontinuous functions, etc. Since intelligent algorithms such as genetic algorithm [8, 9] and Particle Swarm optimization [10, 11] have shown excellent results in multi-objective optimization, more and more researchers have been involved in the discussion of intelligent algorithms for bending process planning. Kannan [12] adopted the elite genetic algorithm to determine the nearly optimal bending process, which solved the problem of excessive calculation amount in the case of multiple bending. Park [13] used genetic algorithm to carry out bending process planning on the basis of constructing neural network. Prasanth [2] combined the bending feasibility matrix with the best first search algorithm, and proposed a process planning algorithm superior to genetic algorithm. Using genetic algorithm to search for processes can obtain relatively excellent solutions, but because the algorithm itself is very sensitive to crossover probability and mutation probability [14], how to set appropriate parameters has become a difficult problem.

On the basis of previous research, this paper analyzes the position relationship between the sheet material and the bending machine in the bending process, and designs the appropriate bending procedure planning algorithm based on this. Section 2 introduces the issues to be considered in the bending process planning, and Sect. 3 proposes how to apply the improved Particle Swarm optimization [15] to the process planning. In Sect. 4, the above algorithm is verified experimentally, which proves the feasibility of the algorithm. Finally, in Sect. 5, all the work is summarized and future work is discussed.

2 Analysis of Sheet Metal Bending Process

2.1 Problems in Bending Process Planning

Sheet metal bending is a process of flat plate processing and forming. For a given workpiece shape, it can be decomposed into several bending steps according to the sequence of execution. Finding the best bending process is to find the best combination of all bending steps. As shown in Fig. 1a is an expanded view of a sheet metal part with 4 processing steps, which has 4 bending edges b_1, b_2, b_3, b_4 and five faces f_1, f_2, f_3, f_4, f_5. If the current bending step is b_3, the shape of the sheet metal parts before and after bending is shown in Fig. 1c. and Fig. 2d. When all the steps are completed, the final molded part of Fig. 3b. can be obtained.

During the process, various factors will affect the layout of the final bending process. It mainly contains interference collision, the number of reversals and turns, the length of horizontal movement of the workpiece, etc.

1) Interference problem: when arranging the bending process, it is necessary to first detect whether the process can avoid the occurrence of interference phenomenon. Interference mainly includes the interference of the workpiece itself and the interference between the workpiece and the mold.

2) Reverse problem: it is stipulated in this paper that if the starting edge can get the end edge by rotating the bending angle clockwise, it will be marked as positive bending, otherwise, it will be marked as negative bending. When the bending angles

before and after current bending have different relations, the number of reversals is increased by 1.

3) Turning problem: in order to facilitate the clamping of the workpiece during the bending process, it is necessary to make the center of gravity of the workpiece fall in front of the bending machine. As shown in Fig. 2 and Fig. 3, when bending, the ratio of the length $L1$ of the workpiece outside the machine tool to the total length L should be satisfied as much as possible to be greater than 0.3, that is, the front expansion coefficient $\zeta > 0.3$, if it is not satisfied, it needs to turn around.

4) Mold replacement problem: the contour of the mold has a great influence on the interference in the bending process. Standard straight dies are preferred because they carry more weight in the bending process than gooseneck upper dies. When interference occurs, try replacing the gooseneck upper die to avoid collision.

5) Accuracy problem: bending accuracy refers to the process requirements that each straight section of the sheet material needs to meet. In order to improve the final machining accuracy of the workpiece, this article divides the accuracy into three levels of High, Normal, and Close. The bending step marked High has the highest bending priority and is processed first under the premise of avoiding interference. while the bending section marked Close is the last to be bent.

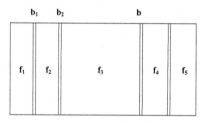

a. Plane unfolded drawing

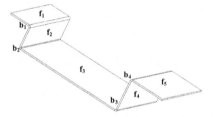

b. Final forming drawing

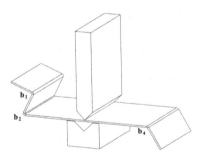

c. Before the execution of the bending work step

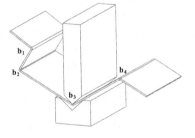

d. After the execution of the bending work step

Fig. 1. Different status of sheet metal parts

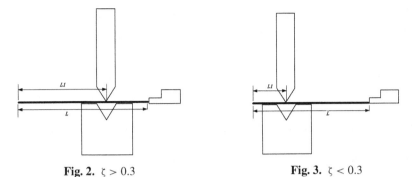

Fig. 2. $\zeta > 0.3$ **Fig. 3.** $\zeta < 0.3$

2.2 Selection of Fitness Function

Considering the interference, accuracy, efficiency and other issues in the bending process, the fitness function must clearly reflect the feasibility of the process and can clearly reflect the difference between good and bad processes. It is necessary to minimize the operation of sheet metal parts, so the lower the size of the fitness value function, the better the process. In addition, in order to prevent interference in the bending process, the fitness function needs to strictly distinguish between interference and non-interference. Therefore, the definition of fitness function in this paper is as shown in Formula 1.

$$F = \begin{cases} \frac{1}{N}(\omega_1\alpha + \omega_2\beta + \omega_3\gamma + \omega_4\frac{\eta}{L}) & g = 1 \\ 500 & g = 0 \end{cases} \tag{1}$$

Where: N represents the total number of bending processes; α, β, γ, and η represent the number of turns, the number of reversals, the number of mold changes and the length of horizontal movement of the workpiece during the bending process. ω_1, ω_2, ω_3 and ω_4 are the corresponding weights of the variables, which are assigned values of 100, 125, 175, and 150 respectively. L represents the expansion length of the workpiece, while g values 0 represents interference, and 1 represents the feasibility of the process.

3 Bending Process Planning Algorithm

3.1 Discrete Particle Swarm Optimization

Suppose that in the search space of dimension D, the Particle Swarm optimization is initialized to m particles, then the position and velocity of the i-th particle in the iterative process are respectively defined as the vector $X_i = (X_{i1}, X_{i2}, \ldots, X_{id})$ and $V_i = (V_{i1}, V_{i2}, \ldots, V_{id})$. When the algorithm is iterating, the particles update their position and velocity according to Formula 2 and Formula 3.

$$V_i(n + 1) = \omega V_i(n) + c_1 r_1(pBest - X_i(n)) + c_2 r_2(gBest - X_i(n)) \tag{2}$$

$$X_i(n + 1) = X_i(n) + V_i(n + 1) \tag{3}$$

In formulas above, $V_i(n)$ and $X_i(n)$ respectively represent the velocity and position of the ith particle in the nth iteration. ω represents the inertia weight, which is used to control the influence of the speed of the previous generation particles on the current particle speed; c_1 and c_2 represent the learning parameters, which control the self-cognition and social cognition behavior of the particles respectively. r_1 and r_2 represent two independent random numbers respectively. n represents the current iteration number of the algorithm.

Since the bending process planning problem studied in this paper is a discrete problem, it is necessary to discretize the algorithm when using the Particle Swarm optimization and redefine the operation logic. The updated particle velocity calculation formulas are as follows:

$$V_i(n+1) = \omega \otimes V_i(n) \oplus \alpha \otimes (pBest \ominus X_i(n)) \oplus \beta \otimes (gBest \ominus X_i(n)) \quad (4)$$

$$X_i(n+1) = X_i(n) \ominus V_i(n+1) \quad (5)$$

When the algorithm solves the optimal process of d bends, it initializes and generates m d-dimensional process population $\{X_1, X_2, \ldots, X_m\}$. Assume that X_o and X_p are two different processes in the process population. Now make the following definition:

Definition 1: *listEO* is the exchange sequence from X_o to X_p, such that $X_o \ominus listEO = X_p$, $X_p \ominus listEO = X_p$. In addition, *listEO* is composed of several exchange operators *EO*, and each *EO* is a set of two-dimensional vectors, representing two designated positions in the exchange process. For example, suppose $X_o = \{1,3,4,2,5\}$, $X_p = \{2,3,1,4,5\}$, then:

$$X_o \ominus \{[1, 3], [1, 4]\} = \{4, 3, 1, 2, 5\} \ominus \{[1, 4]\} = X_p \quad (6)$$

$$X_p \ominus \{[1, 3], [1, 4]\} = \{4, 3, 1, 2, 5\} \ominus \{[1, 3]\} = X_p \quad (7)$$

Definition 2: α, β and ω are three mutually independent numbers that take values in the interval $(0,1)$. From Definition 1, we can see that the calculation results of $pBest \ominus X_i(n)$ and $gBest \ominus X_i(n)$ are a set of random sequences, denoted as *listA* and *listB* respectively. And $\alpha \otimes listA$ is defined as: find the number of swap sequence in *listA* and multiply it with α, take the integer of the operation result as i_a, then the result of $\alpha \otimes listA$ is the first i_a commutative sequence of *listA*. In the same way, the calculated results of $\beta \otimes listB$ and $\omega \otimes V_i(n)$ are obtained.

Definition 3: Define operators $\oplus$ as the superposition operation between two exchange sequences, for example: exchange sequence $list1 = \{[1, 2]\}$, $list2 = \{[1\text{-}3]\}$, then it is satisfied the operation of Formula 8.

$$list1 \oplus list2 = \{[1, 2], [1, 2], [2, 3]\} \tag{8}$$

3.2 Improvement of Particle Swarm Optimization

Since PSO is easy to fall into the local optimal solution when approaching the optimal solution, which is called "premature". Therefore, this paper introduces genetic algorithm on the basis of Particle Swarm optimization to solve the problem of premature convergence.

The genetic algorithm effectively maintains the diversity of the process population due to mutation and crossover operations when it is running, and it is not easy to converge prematurely compared with the Particle Swarm optimization. Since both Particle Swarm optimization and Genetic Algorithm perform evolutionary operations on the initial population, the two algorithms can be effectively combined to make up for their own shortcomings. Therefore, this article uses two algorithms to solve the bending process:

Step1: Generate m initial bending process populations with the number of processes d, and specify the number of iterations as n,

Step2: Calculate the fitness value of each individual in the population and the average fitness value of the population,

Step3: Divide the entire population into two parts: Particle Swarm optimization population and genetic algorithm population,

Step4: Compare the fitness value of each individual with the average fitness value. If the individual fitness value is less than the average fitness value, it will be added to the genetic algorithm population, otherwise it will be added to the Particle Swarm optimization population,

Step5: Perform corresponding evolutionary algorithms on the two populations to obtain a new generation of populations,

Step6: Compare the current number of iterations with the size of n, if it is less than n, go to Step3, otherwise go to Step7,

Step7: Calculate and output the optimal process individual of this generation.

To describe the algorithm more clearly, this article writes the detailed steps as pseudo-code in Algorithm 1, where *population* is the initialized population, *fitness* array records the fitness value of each individual in the population, and *fitnessAverage* is the average of the fitness values in each generation of the population. The output of the algorithm result is the best procedure *listBest* and the best fitness function *fitnessBest*.

Algorithm 1 Improved PSO Algorithm for sequences planning of sheet metal bending
---
input: configuration parameters mentioned above
output: *listBest, fitnessBest*
1: Initialize $m, d, n, \omega, P_c, P_m, population$
2: Update *fitness* of each individual and *fitnessAverage* of *population*
3: Update *pbest* and *gbest*
4: **for** $i = 1$ to n **do**
5:   **if** *fitness(i) > fitnessAverage*
6:     *populationPSO ←population(i)*
7:   **end if**
8:   **else do**
9:     *populationGA← population(i)*
10: **end else**
11: Update *populationPSO and populationGA*
12: Update *population*
13: **end for**
14: Generate *listBest, fitnessBest*
---

4 Experiment and Simulation

In order to verify the feasibility of the above algorithm, a simulation experiment is carried out for solving the bending process with Particle Swarm optimization, genetic algorithm and hybrid algorithm. The software of bending process planning is developed with C# programming language, and its software interface is shown in Fig. 4. This software can input the related parameters of sheet metal parts by means of graphic programming, and can use algorithm to plan and calculate the bending process. Then we conducted related experiments on the experimental platform shown in Fig. 5. To verify the final feasibility of the algorithm.

The process planning of sheet metal parts with 5, 15 and 25 bending sections is carried out in the software system. The number of the initial population and the number of iterations directly affect the execution time of the algorithm. In order to facilitate the comparison, the initial population and the number of iterations are kept the same when using the three algorithms. In judging the advantages and disadvantages of the working procedure, the size of its fitness value function is observed. As mentioned above, the smaller the fitness value function is, the better the corresponding working procedure is. The experimental results are as follows:

1) 5 bending steps:

Since the number of bending segments is not large, all the algorithms can get the satisfactory procedure in a very short period of time without complicated calculation, so the size of the *population* and the number of *iterations* are set as 50. The remaining parameters are adjusted continuously through experiments. Finally, the inertia weight ω in the PSO is set as 0.8, and the learning factors α and β are set as random numbers

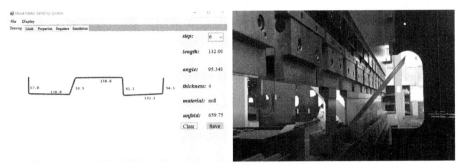

Fig. 4. 2D input interface   **Fig. 5.** Experiment platform

Table 1. Parameter table of 5 bending steps.

Iterations	Population	ω	P_c	P_m
50	50	0.8	0.8	0.01

between the interval [0,1]. In the genetic algorithm, P_c is set as 0.8 and t P_m is set as 0.01. The details are shown in Table 1.

The final execution result of the algorithm is shown in Fig. 6. All the algorithms can search for the best process within 20 evolutions. However, the improved hybrid algorithm is more efficient, and the fifth generation achieves the optimal solution.

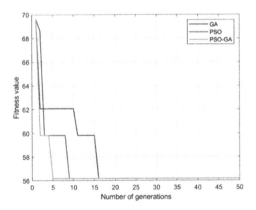

Fig. 6. Schematic diagram of 5 bending steps.

2) 15 bending steps:

In order to verify whether the improved algorithm can adapt to more complex calculation, a larger scale of 15 bending process planning is selected. As the number of bending stages increases, so does the number of potential optimal bending processes.

Therefore, the initial *populations* were set to 150 under the premise of keeping other parameters unchanged, and a total of 300 iterations were made, as shown in Table 2.

Table 2. Parameter table of 15 bending steps.

Iterations	Population	ω	P_C	P_m
300	150	0.8	0.8	0.01

As can be seen from the final effect diagram of the algorithm shown in Fig. 7., Particle Swarm optimization algorithm has fast convergence speed due to its memory property, but it is easy to fall into the local optimal solution. Compared with other algorithms, genetic algorithm has its own crossover and mutation operation, which makes the convergence process slow. Comparatively speaking, the improved hybrid algorithm is superior to the two algorithms alone in efficiency and accuracy.

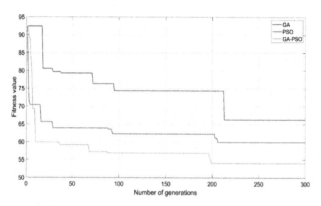

Fig. 7. Schematic diagram of 15 bending steps.

3) 25 bending steps:

When the number of bending sections reaches 25 sections, the number of viable processes is huge, as high as 25!, so the number of the initial population was increased to 200 in the experiment, and other parameters remained unchanged, as shown in Table 3.

Table 3. Parameter table of 25 bending steps.

Iterations	Population	ω	P_C	P_m
300	200	0.8	0.8	0.01

From Fig. 8, It can be seen that when the experimental scale is large, due to the influence of the crossover operator, the genetic algorithm is difficult to find the optimal solution in a short time. Therefore, the convergence rate is relatively slow. Although the particle swarm algorithm declined very quickly in the early stage, it also entered a premature state prematurely. It turns out that when the number of bending processes is large, the effect of using these two algorithms alone is not very satisfactory. However, the improved hybrid algorithm still maintains a better efficiency.

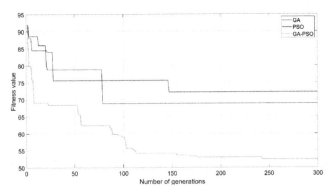

Fig. 8. Schematic diagram of 25 bending steps.

5   Conclusion

By analyzing the shape changes of sheet metal parts during the bending process, this paper establishes a fitness function to evaluate the pros and cons of a certain bending process. In order to efficiently calculate the optimal solution of the function, an intelligent bending process planning algorithm based on Particle Swarm optimization is proposed, and the crossover and mutation operators in the genetic algorithm are used to improve the algorithm, which greatly improves the convergence speed and solution accuracy of the algorithm. Through grouping experiments, we can conclude that the improved algorithm can obtain the best bending process in a reasonable time compared with the traditional algorithm. Even when the bending step is large, the algorithm can achieve good results.

Subsequent work will include improving the algorithm for calculating the position of sheet metal parts during the bending process, and improving the inertia weight and learning factor in the Particle Swarm optimization. Finally, a complete programming system for bending robots will be provided, combined with bending realization, to verify the rationality of the planning algorithm.

Acknowledgment. This research is supported by the National Natural Science Foundation of China (51775284), the Primary Research & Development Plan of Jiangsu Province (BE2018734), the Natural Science Foundation of Jiangsu Province (BK20201379), and Six Talent Peaks Project in Jiangsu Province (JY-081).

References

1. Wagner, S., Sathe, M., Schenk, O.: Optimization for process plans in sheet metal forming. Int. J. Adv. Manuf. Technol. **71**(5–8), 973–982 (2013)
2. Raj Prasanth, D., Shunmugam, M.S.: Geometry-based bend feasibility matrix for bend sequence planning of sheet metal parts. Int. J. Comput. Integr. Manuf. **33**(5), 1–16 (2020)
3. Lin, A.C., Chen, C.F.: Sequence planning and tool selection for bending processes of 2.5D sheet metals. Adv. Mech. Eng. **6**, 1–28 (2014)
4. Salem, A.A., Abdelmaguid, T.F., Wifi, A.S., Elmokadem, A.: Towards an efficient process planning of the V-bending process: an enhanced automated feature recognition system. Int. J. Adv. Manuf. Technol. **91**(9–12), 4163–4181 (2017)
5. Faraz, Z., et al.: Sheet-metal bend sequence planning subjected to process and material variations. Int. J. Adv. Manuf. Technol. **88**(1–4), 815–826 (2016)
6. Panghal, D., et al.: An automatic system for deciding bend sequence of bending parts. Adv. Mater. Process. Technol. **1**, 1–2 (2015)
7. Farsi, M.A., Arezoo, B.: Development of a new method to determine bending sequence in progressive dies. Int. J. Adv. Manuf. Technol. **43**(1), 52–60 (2009)
8. Dahmane, S.A., et al.: Determination of the optimal path of three axes robot using genetic algorithm. Int. J. Eng. Res. Africa **44**, 125–149 (2019)
9. Yao, F., et al.: Multi-mobile robots and multi-trips feeding scheduling problem in smart manufacturing system: an improved hybrid genetic algorithm. Int. J. Adv. Robot. Syst. **16**(4), (2019).
10. Peng Chen, et al.: Hybrid chaos-based particle swarm optimization-ant colony optimization algorithm with asynchronous pheromone updating strategy for path planning of landfill inspection robots. International Journal of Advanced Robotic Systems16(4), 172988141986812 (2019)
11. Tang, B., et al.: Multi-robot path planning using an improved self-adaptive particle swarm optimization. Int. J. Adv. Robot. Syst. **17**(5), 172988142093615 (2020)
12. Kannan, T.R., Shunmugam, M.S.: Planner for sheet metal components to obtain optimal bend sequence using a genetic algorithm. Int. J. Comput. Integr. Manuf. **21**(7), 790–802 (2008)
13. Park, H.S., Anh, T.V.: Optimization of bending sequence in roll forming using neural network and genetic algorithm. J. Mech. Sci. Technol. **25**(8), 2127–2136 (2011)
14. Muthiah, A., Rajkumar, R.: A comparison of artificial bee colony algorithm and genetic algorithm to minimize the makespan for job shop scheduling. Procedia Eng. **97**, 1745–1754 (2014)
15. Jordehi, A.R.: Enhanced leader PSO (ELPSO): a new PSO variant for solving global optimisation problems. Appl. Soft Comput. J. **26**, 401–417 (2014)

Rigidity Based Time-Varying Formation Tracking Control for Autonomous Underwater Vehicles with Switching Topologies

Wen Pang, Chenxia Liu, Linling Wang, and Daqi Zhu$^{(\boxtimes)}$

Shanghai Engineering Research Center of Intelligent Maritime Search & Rescue and Underwater Vehicles, Shanghai Maritime University, Haigang Avenue 1550, Shanghai 201306, China
zdq367@aliyun.com

Abstract. This paper addresses the problem of time-varying formation tracking control problem of multiply autonomous underwater vehicles (AUVs) using switching graph topologies. Different from the previous work, the states of the followers form a predefined time-varying formation while tracking the state of the leader. We introduce distance-based control laws for the multi-AUV formation, using a single-integrator agent model, the control laws are only a function of the relative distance of AUVs in an infinitesimally and minimally rigid graph, and either the desired velocity of the formation or the target's relative position to the leader and absolute velocity. Then an algorithm to design the policy with switching undirected topologies is presented, according to practical requirements, the configuration of formation can be chosen as arbitrary shape and the corresponding convergence time is allowed to be pre-estimated or preset, where the team of AUVs can translate and rotate as a virtual rigid body in 2D, so the formation size and/or geometric shape can vary in time. Thirdly, Strict stability analysis indicates that the designed formation control law can make AUVs achieve the predefined time-varying formation. Finally, a numerical simulation example with six followers and one leader is given to demonstrate that the AUVs formation control based on the backstepping control with this new structural method is stable and convergent.

Keywords: Time-varying formation control · Autonomous underwater vehicles · Lyapunov theory · Rigid graph

1 Introduction

With the development of Autonomous Underwater Vehicle (AUV) application techniques, formation control of multiple AUVs system has attracted a significant amount of research interest during the past decades [1]. Formation control of AUVs is a typical cooperative control scenario, which can coordinate a group of AUVs to collectively perform complicated tasks through achieving some prescribed formation. In contrast to

This project is supported by the National Natural Science Foundation of China (62033009, U1706224, 61873161)

© Springer Nature Switzerland AG 2021
X.-J. Liu et al. (Eds.): ICIRA 2021, LNAI 13013, pp. 359–369, 2021.
https://doi.org/10.1007/978-3-030-89095-7_35

a single AUV, multi-AUV formation represents higher efficiency and better stability for many applications [2]. Formation control can be categorized into formation acquisition and formation maneuvering based on the group reference. One of the most important part of the formation maneuvering control problem is formation tracking control, which refers to the algorithm design to coordinate a fleet of AUVs to form and maintain prescribed geometric patterns, while tracking the predesignated group reference. Due to the existence of group reference, formation tracking control has more extensive applications than formation acquisition control, such as target tracking [3, 4], search for moving targets [5], ocean mapping, suppression of enemy marine defenses, load transportation and deployment, to name just a few.

Although Multi-AUV system has unique characteristics as long as the working environments are totally different from that of aircrafts or ground mobile robots, some traditional formation control strategies have still been transplanted and modified to be applied on the underwater vehicles [6]. Various strategies and approaches have been proposed for formation control, which can be roughly categorized as centralized approach and distributed/decentralized approach from the control structure perspective [7]. In the centralized approach, a central station is used to control each AUV based on the information from the whole team. The centralized approach can be easily implemented, avoid collision and obstacle, achieve the explicit formation feedbacking and timely adjust formation shape based on the need of task, accordingly, which can achieve more flexibility and robustness in contrast to decentralized approach. While in the distributed/decentralized approach, each AUV generates its own control signal, based on local information from its neighbors communicating over networks, which can be modeled as special topology structures with cooperative and competitive interactions, hierarchical directed graph and undirected graph, fixed topology and switching topology. Compared with traditional fixed formation for a group of dynamical systems, time-varying formation can produce the following benefits: (i) covering the greater part of complex environments and (ii) collision avoidance.

On the other hand, to obtain optimal formation performance, AUVs should be able to build various formation shapes with the need of mission. There has been a little study on time-varying formation tracking problem in the past few years, especially on marine vehicles. Recently, there have been some researches on time-varying formation control for multi-AUV systems. In work [8], a robust control scheme is developed with disturbances under input saturation, but the formation size or shape remain unchanged. In contrast, the work in [9], proposes a strategy for the coordination control problem of multiple AUVs under switching communication topologies based on discrete information.

This paper is concerned with collision-free AUV formation control when the intervehicle network topology is time-varying. The proposed control law has two parts: one for converging to a desired formation (no formation structure change considered), as show in Fig. 1; the other for achieving formation shape change for collision avoidance, such as formation pass through slit. On the basis of the existing results and motivated by the aforementioned analysis, in this paper, we present a novel adaptive time-varying formation tracking control strategy for a group of UAVs. The proposed strategy can guarantee that all AUVs track the desired group reference while forming and maintaining prescribed time-varying formations. The main contributions can be summarized as follows. (i) Comparing with the existing fixed formation tracking algorithms for multi-AUV system [3, 7], we consider the time-varying formation tracking problems with quantized input. The proposed strategy can guarantee that all UAVs track the desired group reference while forming and maintaining prescribed time-varying formations with quantized input. (ii) Our research object is underwater vehicles, to the best of our knowledge, at present, time-varying formation control of underwater vehicles is seldom studied. (iii) The formation structure of any shape can be realized by topological transformation based on distance.

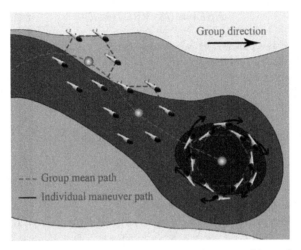

Fig. 1. Time-varying formation with scaling when tracking target without obstacle avoidance.

The structure of this paper is organized as follows. Section 2 presents some preliminaries and problem formulation. The design of the time-varying formation tracking controller and stability analysis are given in Sect. 3. Section 4 contains a simulation example to show the effectiveness of the proposed control scheme. Finally, Sect. 5 gathers concluding remarks about this work.

2 Preliminaries and Problem Description

2.1 Notations

Throughout this paper, for simplicity of notation, the superscripts "T" and "−1" stand for the matrix transposition and inverse. Let R^n, I_n, and $0_{m \times n}$ represent, respectively, the n-dimensional Euclidean space, the $n \times n$ identity matrix, and the $m \times n$ zero matrix. For a vector $x \in R^n$, $\|x\|$ signifies its standard Euclidean norm. Let $\otimes$, $diag\{...\}$ represent the Kronecker product, the diagonal matrix, respectively.

2.2 Basic Concepts on Algebraic Graph Theory

The tools from graph theory are used to describing the information exchanging among the AUVs in the formation, an undirected graph $G = (V, E, A)$ is applied. $V = \{1, 2, ..., n\}$ is the node finite set of vertices, $E \in V \times V$ represents the collection of edges such that if every vertex pair (i, j) is an element of E then so is (j, i). $(i, j) \in E$ means that AUV i can receive the information from j. $A = (a_{ij}) \in R^{n \times n}$ represents the relevant weighted adjacency matrix, if $(j, i) \in E$, $a_{ij} > 0$ and if $(j, i) \notin E$ or $i = j$, $a_{ij} = 0$. Let $l \in \{1, 2, \ldots, n(n-1)/2\}$ denotes the total number of edges in E. The set of neighbors of vertex $i \in V$ is represented by:

$$N_i(E) = \{j \in V \mid (i, j) \in E\} \tag{1}$$

A framework F is a pair (G, p), where $p = (p_1, p_2, \ldots, p_n) \in R^{2n}$ is the coordinate of all vertices. The edge function $f_G : R^2 \rightarrow R^l$ based on any arbitrary arrangement of the edges in E is given by:

$$f_G(p) = (\ldots, \|p_i - p_j\|^2, \ldots), (i, j) \in E \tag{2}$$

The rigidity matrix $R : R^{2n} \rightarrow R^{l \times 2n}$ is interpreted as:

$$R(p) = \frac{1}{2} \frac{\partial f_G(p)}{\partial p} \tag{3}$$

where we have that $\text{rank}[R(p)] \leq 2n - 3$ [10].

Lemma1 [11]: Consider frameworks $F_p = (G, p)$ and $F_q = (G, q)$. If F_p is infinitesimally rigid provided that $\Psi(F_q, F_p) = \sum_{(i,j) \in E} (\|q_i - q_j\| - \|p_i - p_j\|)^2 \leq \delta$, where δ is a sufficiently small positive constant, then F_q is also infinitesimally rigid.

Lemma2 [11]: Let $v(t) \in R^2$ and 1_n be an $n \times 1$ vector of ones, then $R(p)(1_n \otimes v(t)) = 0$.

Lemma3 [12]: If the framework $F_p = (G, p)$ is minimally and infinitesimally rigid, then the matrix $R(p)R(p)^T$ is positive definite.

2.3 Problem Description

For the multi-AUV system consisting of a fleet of n AUVs, an undirected and connected graph G is used for communication among the AUVs. Consider the single integrator dynamics [13]

$$\dot{p}_i = u_i, \; i = 1, 2, ..., n \tag{4}$$

where $p_i = (x_i, y_i) \in R^2$ is the ith AUV position with respect to an Earth-fixed coordinate frame and $u_i \in R^2$ is the (velocity-level) control input of the ith AUV, respectively.

Let the desired formation be modeled by the framework $F^*(t) = (G^*, p^*(t))$ being infinitesimally and minimally rigid, where graph $G^* = (V^*, E^*, A)$, $\dim(V^*) = m$, $\dim(E^*) = l$, and $p^* = (p_1^*, p_2^*, \ldots, p_n^*)$. Let the time-varying desired distance between the AUV i and j be defined as

$$d_{ij}(t) = \|p_i^* - p_j^*\| > 0, \; i, j \in V^* \tag{5}$$

In this paper, we deal with formation tracking control problem. It is required to design a controller to drive the AUVs from arbitrary initial conditions to track a predefined trajectory while retaining the desired geometric shape. That is, the primary control objective is to design $u_i(p_i - p_j, d_{ij}(t))$, $i = 1, 2, \ldots, n$, and $N_i(E) = \{j \in V \,|\, (i, j) \in E\}$ so that

$$\|p_i(t) - p_j(t)\| \to d_{ij}(t) \text{ as } t \to \infty \; \forall i, j \in V^* \tag{6}$$

In the formation maneuvering control problem, the secondary objective is

$$p_i(t) - v_m(t) \to 0 \text{ as } t \to \infty \tag{7}$$

where $v_m(t) \in R^2$ is the desired maneuvering velocity and it is assumed that $v_m(t)$ and $\dot{v}_m(t)$ are bounded, continuous function and they are known to all AUVs. In the target tracking problem, we choose the first AUV as the leader whose responsibility is to track the target; thus, the secondary objective is [14]:

$$p_t(t) \in \text{conv}\{p_2(t), p_3(t), \ldots, p_n(t)\} \text{ as } t \to \infty \tag{8}$$

where $p_t \in R^2$ denotes the target position and conv$\{\cdot\}$ denotes the convex hull. We assume p_t and $\dot{p}_t$ are bounded, continuous functions.

3 Control Strategy

In this section, a Lyapunov based control solution to the formation tracking problem for multiple nonholonomic AUVs is presented. The information exchange between AUVs is based on the graph, which models the interaction among the AUVs being a spanning tree. The spanning tree ensures minimum number of edges between the AUVs, which is beneficial in terms of interaction topology. The relative position of two robots can be defined as

$$\tilde{p}_{ij} = p_i - p_j, \; (i, j) \in E^* \tag{9}$$

and let $\tilde{p} = (\ldots, \tilde{p}_{ij}, \ldots) \in R^{2l}$ with the same ordering of terms as (2). The distance tracking error is given by

$$e_{ij} = \|\tilde{p}_{ij}\| - d_{ij}(t), \; (i, j) \in E^* \tag{10}$$

It follows from (10) and (8) that we can achieve the distance tracking error dynamics as

$$\dot{e}_{ij} = (\tilde{p}_{ij}^T \tilde{p}_{ij})^{-\frac{1}{2}} \tilde{p}_{ij}^T (u_i - u_j) - \dot{d}_{ij} = \frac{\tilde{p}_{ij}^T (u_i - u_j)}{e_{ij} + d_{ij}} - \dot{d}_{ij} \tag{11}$$

Let us define an auxiliary variable $z_{ij} = \|\tilde{p}_{ij}\|^2 - d_{ij}^2 = e_{ij}(\|\tilde{p}_{ij}\| + d_{ij}) = e_{ij}(e_{ij} + 2d_{ij})$, $(i, j) \in E^*$, following the backstepping control technique, with which the Lyapunov function for the first iteration is defined as [13, 15]

$$W_{ij} = \frac{1}{4} z_{ij}^2, \; (i, j) \in E^* \tag{12}$$

The Lyapunov function for all the edges can be defined as:

$$W(e) = \sum_{(i,j) \in E^*} W_{ij}(e_{ij}) \tag{13}$$

where $e = (\dots, e_{ij}, \dots) \in R^l$ is ordered as (2). The time derivative of (13) along (11) is given by

$$\dot{W} = \sum_{(i,j) \in E^*} e_{ij}(e_{ij} + 2d_{ij})[\tilde{p}_{ij}^T(u_i - u_j) - d_{ij}\dot{d}_{ij}] \tag{14}$$

It follows from (3) and (12) that (14) can be rewritten as

$$\dot{W} = z^T(R(p)v - \overline{d}) \tag{15}$$

where $v = (v_1, v_2, \dots, v_n) \in R^{2n}$ is stacked vector of control input. $z = (\dots, z_{ij}, \dots) \in R^l$, and $\overline{d} = (\dots, d_{ij}\dot{d}_{ij}, \dots) \in R^l$, $(i, j) \in E^*$. The elements in z and $\overline{d}$ are ordered in the same way as (2). The control law for the single integrator dynamics is taken as

$$u = R^+(p)(-k_v z + \overline{d}) + (1_n \otimes v_m) \tag{16}$$

where $R^+(p) = R^T(p)[R(p)R^T(p)]^{-1}$ is the Moore–Penrose pseudoinverse and $k_v > 0$ is the control gain, $v_m = [v_{m1}, v_{m2}, \dots v_{mn}] \in R^{2n}$ is the composite rigid body maneuvering velocity vector whose elements are specified by

$$v_{mi} = v_0 + w_0 \times \tilde{p}_{in}, \ i = 1, 2, \dots, n \tag{17}$$

$v_0(t) \in R^2$ denotes the desired translation velocity for the formation, $w_0(t) \in R^2$ is the desired angular velocity for the formation, and $\tilde{p}_{in}$ is the relative position between agent i and the leader AUV. Our formation tracking control protocol will consist of: a) selecting $F^*(t)$ such that $p_1^* \in \text{conv}\{p_2^*, p_3^* \dots, p_n^*\}$, b) the leader AUV tracking the moving target or predefined trajectory, and c) the follower AUVs tracking the leader while maintaining the desired formation shape. We assume the leader AUV can measure the target's relative position $p_1 - p_t$ and the absolute velocity $\dot{p}_t$, which can be achieved by onboard sensor, and can broadcast this information to the follower AUVs. Then we acquire the formation tracking control

$$u = R^+(p)(-k_v z + \overline{d}) + h \tag{18}$$

$$h = 1_n \otimes [\dot{p}_t - k_t e_t] \tag{19}$$

where $k_t > 0$ and $e_t = p_1 - p_t$, renders $e = 0$ locally exponentially stable and ensures that (6) and (8) are satisfied.

4   Simulation Result and Discussion

In this section, simulations are presented to illustrate the effectiveness of the proposed algorithms. We consider the time-varying formation tracking problem for a Multi-AUV system containing seven AUVs (one leader and six followers) with three desired formations. The finite set of desired time-varying formation $F^* = \{F_0^*, F_1^*, F_2^*\}$ is shown in Fig. 2, the local coordinate in the 2D plane is given as $F_k^* = \{p_{k1}^*, p_{k2}^*, ..., p_{k7}^*\}$, $k = 0, 1, 2$, the details of $p_{ki}^* = [x_{ki}^*, y_{ki}^*]^T$, $i = 1, 2, ..., 7$ are presented in Table 1, from which we can acquire the desired distances between all AUVs. Edge set $E = [(1, 3), (1, 4), (1, 5), (1, 6), (1, 7), (2, 3), (2, 7), (3, 4), (4, 5), (5, 6), (6, 7)]$ is defined to make the framework infinitesimally and minimally rigid. The sampling period is adopted to be 50 ms. The simulation time span is selected as 22 s. The time-varying formation $F^*(t)$ are given as follows:

$$F^*(t) = \begin{cases} F_0^* \ t \in [0, 10), \\ F_1^* \ t \in [10, 15), \\ F_2^* \ t \in [15, 22). \end{cases} \tag{20}$$

Table 1. The local coordinates.

(x_{ki}, y_{ki})	$k = 0$	$k = 1$	$k = 2k = 2$
$i = 1$	$(0, 0)$	$(0, 0)$	$(0, 0)$
$i = 2$	$(1, \sqrt{3})$	$(2, \sqrt{3}/2)$	$(2, 1/2)$
$i = 3$	$(-1, \sqrt{3})$	$(-2, \sqrt{3})$	$(0, 1/2)$
$i = 4$	$(-2, 0)$	$(-2, 0)$	$(-2, 1/2)$
$i = 5$	$(-1, -\sqrt{3})$	$(-2, -\sqrt{3})$	$(-2, -1/2)$
$i = 6$	$(1, -\sqrt{3})$	$(0, -\sqrt{3}/2)$	$(0, -1/2)$
$i = 7$	$(0, 2)$	$(2, 0)$	$(2, -1/2)$

The aim is to move the AUVs as a rigid body with desired shape to tracking a moving target with formation structure time-varying. It is assumed that $v_m(t)$ is only available to the leader AUV. The control gains in (16) and (18) are set as $k_v = 1$, $k_t = 0.5$ and the initial conditions of the agents were selected by

$$p_i(0) = p_i^* + \delta[rand(0, 1) - 0.51_2], \ i = 1, 2, ..., 7 \tag{21}$$

where $\delta = 1.5$, 1_2 is the 2×1 vector of ones, and rand(0,1) generates a random 2×1 vector whose elements are uniformly distributed on the interval $(0, 1)$.

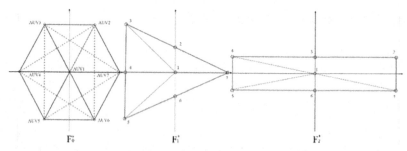

Fig. 2. The desired esired formations from left to right are F_0^*, F_1^* and F_2^* respectively. The red circle i denote the AUV i in the local coordinate and blue solid line stand for interaction between AUVs.

The simulation results are presented in Figs. 3, 4, 5, 6, 7 and 8. Figure 3 shows the trajectory of the AUVs while acquire a dynamic formation of a regular convex hexagon from random initial position, then tracking a moving target, when obstacle exist, the formation size scaling according the environment. From Fig. 4 it is clear that the distance error $e_{ij}(t)$, $i, j \in V^*$ of between any two of the seven AUVs reach to zero or constant. Figure 5 shows the control inputs of each AUV converging to $\dot{p}_t$. Figure 6 shows the trajectory of that AUVs, it follows that the AUVs can reach the desired time-varying formation and the geometric center of the system follows the leader as required. Figure 7 shows that the tracking errors $e_{ij}(t)$, $i, j \in V^*$ converge to zero or constant in finite time at each dwell time interval, which means the time-varying formations of the multi-AUV systems in the 2D plane and the tracking of the leader AUV can be achieved simultaneously, i.e., the time-varying formation tracking is accomplished. Additionally, the control inputs of each AUV in 2D space is illustrated in Fig. 8. It is clear from Figs. 3, 4, 5, 6, 7 and 8 that by using the control algorithm (16) under the aforementioned configurations, the time-varying formation tracking can be achieved for the multi-AUV system.

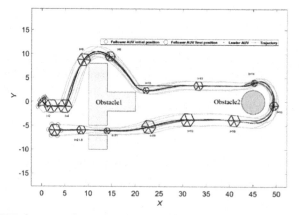

Fig. 3. Seven AUVs forms a polygon formation tracking a moving target, when under obstacles, the formation size change according to the environment.

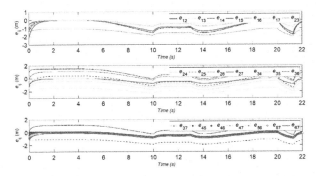

Fig. 4. Inter-AUV distance errors for $i, j \in V^*$ with formation size scaling.

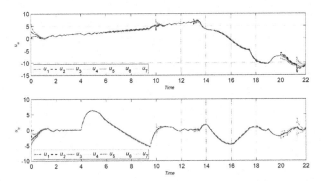

Fig. 5. Control inputs along x(top plot) and y(bottom plot) directions for $i = 1, 2, ..., 7$ with formation size scaling.

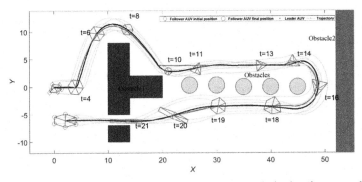

Fig. 6. Seven AUVs forms a polygon formation tracking a desired trajectory, when under obstacles, the formation size or shape will change according to the environment.

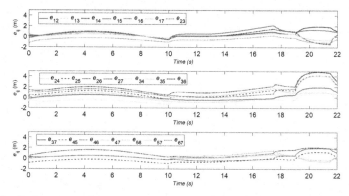

Fig. 7. Inter-agent distance errors for $i, j \in V^*$ with formation shape change.

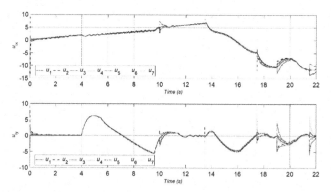

Fig. 8. Control inputs along x(top plot) and y(bottom plot) directions for $i = 1, 2, ..., 7$ with formation shape change.

5 Conclusions and Future Work

The simulation results show that a AUV formation can obtain the dynamic formation of the conventional convex hexagon from the random initial position by using the proposed method. After formation is generated, and moving targets can be tracked. In an obstacle environment, the formation size can be scaled according to the environment. In the future, we will further study double integration, or higher-order integration. And carry out experiments to further verify the feasibility of the method.

References

1. Millán, P., Orihuela, L., Jurado, I., Rubio, F.R.: Formation control of autonomous underwater vehicles subject to communication delays. IEEE Trans. Control Syst. Technol. **22**(2), 770–777 (2014)
2. Yang, Y., Xiao, Y., Li, T.: A survey of autonomous underwater vehicle formation: performance, formation control, and communication capability. IEEE Commun. Surv. Tutor. **23**(2), 815–841 (2021)

3. Li, X., Zhu, D., Chen, Y., Liu, Q.: Formation tracking and transformation control of nonholo-nomic AUVs based on improved SOM method. In: Proceedings of the 29th Chinese Control And Decision Conference (CCDC), China, pp. 500–505 (2017)

4. Li, J., Xu, Z., Zhang, H., Du, X.: Trajectory tracking control of multi-AUVs formation based on virtual leader. In: Proceedings of the IEEE International Conference on Mechatronics and Automation (ICMA), Tianjin, China, pp. 291–296 (2019)

5. Liu, W., Zheng, X., Luo, Y.: Cooperative search planning in wide area via multi-UAV formations based on distance probability. In: 2020 3rd International Conference on Unmanned Systems (ICUS), pp. 1072–1077 (2020)

6. Li, Y., Zhu, D.: Formation tracking and transformation of AUVs based on the improved particle swarm optimization algorithm. In: Proceedings of the Chinese Control and Decision Conference (CCDC), Hefei, China, pp. 3159–3162 (2020)

7. Wang, Y., He, L., Huang, C.: Adaptive time-varying formation tracking control of unmanned aerial vehicles with quantized input. ISA Trans. **85**, 76–83 (2019)

8. Li, J., Du, J., Chang, W.J.: Robust time-varying formation control for underactuated autonomous underwater vehicles with disturbances under input saturation. Ocean Eng. **179**, 180–188 (2019)

9. Hu, Z., Ma, C., Zhang, L., Halme, A.: Distributed formation control of autonomous underwater vehicles with impulsive information exchanges and disturbances under fixed and switching topologies. In: Proceedings of the IEEE 23rd International Symposium on Industrial Electronics (ISIE), Istanbul, Turkey, pp. 99–104 (2014)

10. Asimow, L., Roth, B.: The rigidity of graphs, II. J. Math. Anal. Appl. **68**(1), 171–190 (1979)

11. Cai, X., Queiroz, M.: Formation maneuvering and target interception for multi-agent systems via rigid graphs. Asian J. Control **17**(4), 1174–1186 (2015)

12. Sun, Z., Mou, S., Deghat, M., Anderson, B.: Finite time distributed distance-constrained shape stabilization and flocking control for d-dimensional undirected rigid formations. Int. J. Robust Nonlin. Control **26**(13), 2824–2844 (2016)

13. Krick, L., Broucke, M., Francis, B.: Stabilization of infinitesimally rigid formations of multi-robot networks. Intl. J. Control **83**(3), 423–439 (2009)

14. Gazi, V., Passino, K.: Swarm Stability and Optimization. Springer, New York (2011). https://doi.org/10.1007/978-3-642-18041-5

15. Dorfler, F., Francis, B.: Geometric analysis of the formation problem for autonomous robots. IEEE Trans. Autom. Control **55**(10), 2379–2384 (2010)

Field Robot Environment Sensing Technology Based on TensorRT

Bo Dai⬤, Chao Li$^{(\boxtimes)}$ ⬤, Tao Lin, Yong Wang, Dichen Gong, Xiao Ji,
and Bosong Zhu

Chengdu University of Technology, Chengdu 610059, China

Abstract. The inference speed of complex deep learning networks on embedded platforms of mobile robots is low, and it is difficult to meet actual application requirements, especially in complex environments such as the wild. This experiment out motion blur processing on the data set to improve the robustness, by using NVIDIA inference accelerator TensorRT to optimize the operation, the computational efficiency of the model is improved, and the inference acceleration of the deep learning model on the mobile quadruped robot platform is realized. The experimental results show that, on the test data set, the method achieves 91.67% mAP of 640 × 640 model on the embedded platform Nvidia Jetson Xavier NX. The reasoning speed is about 2.5 times faster than before, reaching 35 FPS, which provides support for the real-time application of mobile robot environment sensing ability in the field.

Keywords: Embedded platform · Motion blur · YOLOv5s · TensorRT · Environmental sensing

1 Introduction

With the rapid development of mobile robots, robots can be seen everywhere in all walks of life, but as the application area becomes more and more extensive, the problems they face will follow. Among them, mobile robots have an increasing demand for environmental sensing capabilities, especially in complex environments in the wild, robots have very high requirements for the real-time and accuracy of environmental perception. In addition, compared with traditional machine learning methods, deep learning has strong learning capabilities and can make better use of data sets for feature extraction, so as to effectively carry out target tracking, target orientation perception, obstacle avoidance and control judgment.

Target detection based on deep learning involves two steps [1]: In the first step, Train large amounts of tag data on the processor, the neural network learns millions of weights or parameters so that it can map the sample data to the correct response. In the second step, the newly collected data is predicted by the trained model. For automatic driving, mobile robot and other applications, inference and sensing need to be completed in real time, so it is very important to control the high throughput and response time in computing. However, the processor performance of general mobile robots is not very

© Springer Nature Switzerland AG 2021
X.-J. Liu et al. (Eds.): ICIRA 2021, LNAI 13013, pp. 370–377, 2021.
https://doi.org/10.1007/978-3-030-89095-7_36

high, and even many of them are not equipped with GPU. The reasoning speed of complex deep learning network on mobile robot platform is low, and it is difficult to meet the practical application requirements, especially in the application background of complex environment such as field.

2 Target Detection System

Target detection is to determine the position of the target in the input image and identify the category of the target in the input image. Target detection has always been the most challenging problem for mobile robots to perceive the environment in a complex environment due to the different appearance and posture of various objects, the interference of processor computing force and illumination, occlusion and other factors in the imaging process.

At present, target detection algorithms based on deep learning are mainly divided into two categories: first-stage target detection algorithms and second-stage target detection algorithms. Two-stage target detection algorithms include FAST R-CNN, Faster R-CNN, and R-FCN, etc. The first-stage target detection algorithms include: SSD, YOLOv3, YOLOv4, YOLOv5, etc. The first-stage target detection algorithm can directly predict the probability of the object category and the coordinates of its position without generating candidate regions, so as to complete target detection directly. The problem that the two-stage algorithm can not meet the real-time detection is solved [2–4].

YOLOv5, launched by Ultralytics in 2020, has the advantages of small size, fast speed and high precision, and is implemented in an ecologically mature PyTorch, with easy deployment and implementation. YOLOv5 includes YOLOv5s, YOLOv5m, YOLOv5l and YOLOv5x models. YOLOv5s image reasoning speed is up to 0.007 s, that is, it can process 140 frames per second, which meets the requirement of real-time detection of video images. Meanwhile, it has a smaller structure. The weight data file of YOLO5s version is 1/9 of that of YOLO4, and the size is 27 MB. It's network model structure still follows the overall layout of YOLOv4, which is mainly divided into four parts, namely Input, Backbone, Neck and Prediction [5].

In the original model of YOLOv5s, $GIoU$ loss was used as the bounding box loss. Compared with the original IoU, the optimization of $GIoU$ loss was to increase the penalty of erronet selection. After the training process, the detection effect of boxes with different proportions was better, and the principle was shown as follows [6]:

$$IoU = \frac{|B \cap B^{gt}|}{|B \cup B^{gt}|} \tag{1}$$

$$L_{GIoU} = 1 - IoU + \frac{|C - B \cup B^{gt}|}{|C|} \tag{2}$$

However, $GIoU$ still has the problem of unstable target box regression, and the $GIoU$ regression strategy for the non-overlapping target detection box may degenerate into the regression strategy of IoU. The main problem is that when the overlap area is 0, $GIoU$ tends to overlap the fastest way between the detection box and the target box, and then $GIoU$ punishment mechanism gradually becomes ineffective. In order to solve this problem, the loss function should consider the overlapping area, distance from the center point and aspect ratio of the predicted box and the real box, and use a *CIoU* that is more consistent with the regression mechanism, as shown in the formula:

$$L_{CIoU} = 1 - IoU + \frac{p^2(b, b^{gt})}{c^2} + av \tag{3}$$

$$v = \frac{4}{\pi^2}\left(arctan\frac{w^{gt}}{h^{gt}} - arctan\frac{w}{h}\right)^2 \tag{4}$$

$$a = \frac{v}{(1 - IoU) + v} \tag{5}$$

In the (3) loss function, the center point of the detection box and the target box is denoted by b and b^{gt}, and the Euclide distance is p. c is the slant distance of the smallest rectangle covering the detection box and the target box that is directly optimized and the speed is faster. In the (4) w^{gt} and h^{gt} are the width and height of the real box, w and h are the width and height of the prediction box. a is the parameter used to balance the proportions [7].

3 TensorRT

TensorRT is a high-performance inference optimizer from NVIDIA that provides low latency and high throughput deployment reasoning for deep learning applications. TensorRT can be used for inferred acceleration in large data centers, embedded platforms or autonomous driving platforms.

TensorRT optimization methods mainly have the following ways, the most important is the first two.

1) Layer Fusion or Tensor Fusion: When deploying model inference, TensorRT automatically parses the network computation diagram and looks for the optimized subgraph. The combined calculation diagram has fewer layers and takes up fewer CUDA(Compute Unified Device Architecture) cores, so the overall model structure (Fig. 1 on the right side)is smaller, faster, and more efficient, thus reducing reasoning delays [8].
2) Weight &Activation Precision Calibration: Data precision can be appropriately reduced during deployment reasoning, and lower data precision can reduce memory footprint and latency, as well as smaller model size.
3) Kernel auto-tuning.
4) Dynamic Tensor Memory.
5) Multi-stream Execution.

4 Data Preprocessing and Training

The experiment uses the data set of field environment images collected by lab members to train and test. It contains 9,800 samples and expands on the original data set, using

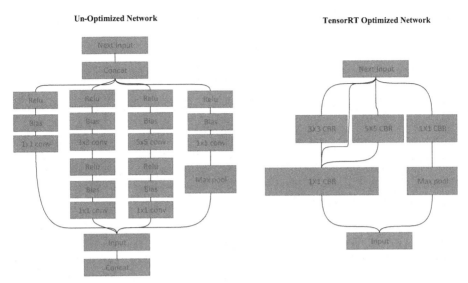

Fig. 1. Interlayer and tensor fusion (Tensorrt reduces the number of layers by combining layers horizontally or vertically (the combined structure is called CBR, meaning Convolution, Bias, and Relu layers are fused to form a single layer) Horizontal merges combine the convolution, bias, and activation layers into a single CBR structure that occupies only one CUDA core.)

both flip and rotation methods. The datasets used for training, validation, and testing included 70%, 10%, and 20% samples, respectively. The Labelimg tool is used to mark and detect the objects in the picture, including 19 categories such as people, horses, cattle, sheep, deer, etc.

As the application object is deployed on the mobile robot in the field, the mobile robot is in a complex environment with external interference and unstable movement, plus the vibration of its own movement, the ZED camera deployed by the mobile robot adopts a binocular rolling curtain camera, so collected photos can be blurry.

The fuzzy image restoration model is shown in the formula:

$$g(x, y) = h(x, y) \times f(x, y) + n(x, y) \tag{6}$$

Wherein (6), $g(x, y)$ is the observation image, $f(x, y)$ is the target image, $h(x, y)$ is the degradation function, and $n(x, y)$ is the noise function. The target is to restore $f(x, y)$ according to the observation image $g(x, y)$ and some prior or estimated information [9]. It's very difficult, and adding images to remove motion blur on mobile embedded platform will increase computing power consumption and affect real-time performance. Therefore, data enhancement was carried out on the collected samples, and 30% of the images were used for motion blur to enhance their ability to identify fuzzy targets. In addition, the motion and vibration of the mobile robot generally exist in the Z direction (the y-axis direction of the image), while the movement of the object in the environment is in the Y-direction (the x-axis direction of the image). Therefore, we create a fuzzy kernel for 30% of the data in the data set by using the fspecial function of Matlab, which convolves with the image to approximate the linear motion of the camera, the Len length is 9 pixels, and the theta values 90 and 0 are the horizontal and vertical motion angles. Figure 2, for the Raw data and motion blurred data.

Fig. 2. Raw data and motion blurred data

Based on the PyTorch deep learning network framework, parallel GPU is used for training in this paper. Firstly, the classification model based on YOLOv5s is trained on the workstation. The batch size of each training is 32, and the Stochastic Gradient descent optimization algorithm with a momentum of 0.9 is adopted. The initial learning rate is 0.001 and the weight attenuation coefficient is 0.0005. The cross entropy loss function is used to calculate the loss. The Pt model trained by PyTorch is converted into the ONNX model and then imported into TRT, which is optimized by TensorRT. NX uses the trained classification model and TensorRT to reason and accelerate the detection of categories in the picture.

5 Optimization Test and Analysis Based on Jetson NX

5.1 Experiment Platform

The field mobile robot platform adopts YoboGO full open source quadruped bionic robot dog development platform. YoboGO is a lightweight quadruped robot with high dynamic performance, equipped with advanced gait planning, leg and foot control and environment awareness technology. In this project, the NVIDIA Jetson Xavier NX development Board is mounted on the robot dog. It is connected with the UP Board controller of the robot dog through the network cable. In terms of vision, Zed camera is used to connect with NX. At the same time, ultrasonic radar and BD/GPS positioning module are deployed on the body to improve environmental sensing.

The NVIDIA Jetson Xavier NX features 384 CUDA Cores, 48 Tensor Cores, 6 ARM CPUs and 2 NVIDIA Deep Learning Accelerator engines. Accelerated computing power of up to 21 TOPS is available in the 15W 6 core to run modern neural networks in parallel and process data from multiple high-resolution sensors. Camera adopts ZED stereo camera, adopts shutter shutter, and supports CUDA. Figure 3, for the mobile robot.

The development environments shown in Table 1:

5.2 Accelerated Testing

Motion blur is added to the data set, which can handle the recognition of blurred images collected by the mobile robot in the process of movement. The detection and recognition

Fig. 3. Mobile robot(1.Yobogo quadruped robot 2. Ultrasonic radar 3. Zed camera 4. Jetson NX 5.BD /GPS positioning module)

Table 1. Development environment.

Hardware parameters	CPU: 6-core NVIDIA Carmel ARM®v8.2 64-bit CPU 6MB L2 + 4MB L3 RAM: 8G GPU: NVIDIA Volta™ GPU with 48 Tensor Cores GPU Memory: 8G CUDA Core: 384-core
Development environment	Operating System: Jetpack 4.4.1 (ubuntu 18.04) CUDA Version: 10.2.89 cuDNN Version: 8.0.0.180 TensorRT Version: 7.1.3.0 Programming Language: Python 3.8 Neural Network Framework: PyTorch 1.8.0

rate of motion blur images tested on NX is only about 10% lower than that of normal pictures. Figure 4, normal and motion blur images target detection results.

Fig. 4. Normal and motion blur images target detection results

The implementation of YOLOv5s in NX is carried out by PyTorch. In the mode of 15 W 6 core with maximum power, the GPU runs the program with full load and identifies various targets in the video stream without any object tracking. The FPS of different model image sizes with TensorRT versus without TensorRT is as Fig. 5, Use different model image size comparison, whether to use TensorRT to accelerate the comparison. When the model image size is 640 × 640, the speed of inferring a picture before acceleration is 70 ms, and the speed of inferring a picture after acceleration by TensorRT is 27 ms, which is 2.5 times higher.

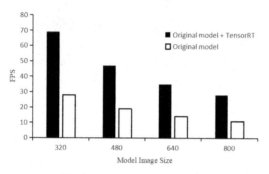

Fig. 5. Inference speed on NX

This paper uses the Pasca criterion to evaluate the model. When the intersection ratio between the ROI of the target object and the ground truth is greater than 0.3, the ROI will be marked as a positive sample by the standard. FP and FN represent false positives (false detected targets) and false positives (undetected targets), respectively. The two evaluation indexes of precision rate and recall rate can be respectively as follows:
Precision rate:

$$accurate = \frac{TP}{TP + FP} \tag{7}$$

Accuracy ratio refers to the ratio of the correct objects detected to all detected objects. Recall rate:

$$Recall = \frac{TP}{TP + FN} \tag{8}$$

The recall rate is the ratio of correctly detected targets to the total number of labeled targets.

As shown in Fig. 6, the accelerated and non-accelerated images of different image size models correspond to the mAP and recall comparisons, the mAP and recall rate accuracy varies by less than 1% with TensorRT acceleration.

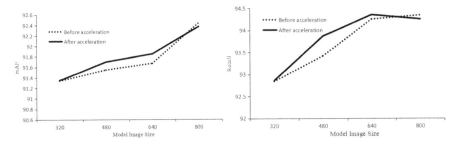

Fig. 6. Precision rated and recall rate

6   Conclusion

This paper takes the mobile robot equipped with NVIDIA Jetson NX as the research object. By building a Pytorch neural network framework on it to run YOLOv5s to perform target detection, it is found that its real-time performance is not ideal. Therefore, it is proposed to use TensorRT for reasoning optimization acceleration. First, the darknet trained model is converted into an ONNX model, and then converted into a TensorRT model, and then TensorRT is used for target detection. This method can increase the FPS by 2.5 times at 640 × 640 model without loss of accuracy. It has successfully proved that this method can make edge computing performance more excellent under the NVIDIA GPU and TensorRT acceleration, and can improve the reasoning speed while ensuring the accuracy. It can improve the environmental perception ability of mobile robots in complex environments in the wild, and provides a solution for subsequent real-time target tracking and target orientation calculation.

References

1. Du, X., Cai, Y., Wang, S., et al.: Overview of deep learning. In: 2016 31st Youth Academic Annual Conference of Chinese Association of Automation (YAC), pp. 159–164. IEEE, (2016)
2. Ruan, J.: Design and implementation of target detection algorithm based on YOLO. Beijing University of Posts and Telecommunications, Beijing (2019). (In Chinese)
3. Tan, J.: Research on an improved YOLOv3 target recognition algorithm. Huazhong University of Science and Technology, Wuhan (2018). (In Chinese)
4. Yan, H.: Research on Static Image Target Detection Based on Deep Learning. North China Electric Power University, Beijing (2019). (In Chinese)
5. Liu, Y., et al.: Research on the use of YOLOv5 object detection algorithm in mask wearing recognition. World Sci. Res. J. **6**(11), 276–284 (2020)
6. Rezatofighi, H., Tsoi, N., Gwak, J., Sadeghian, A., Reid, I., Savarese, S.: Generalized intersection over union: A metric and a loss for bounding box regression. In: The IEEE Conference on Computer Vision and Pattern Recognition (CVPR), pp. 658–666 (2019)
7. Zheng, Z., Wang, P., Liu, W., Li, J., Ye, R., Ren, D.: Distance-IoU loss: faster and better learning for bounding box regression. In: The AAAI Conference on Artificial Intelligence (2020)
8. NVIDIA. NVIDIA Deep learning SDK[DB/OL]. Accessed 27 Nov 2019, https://docs.nvidia.com/deeplearning/sdk/index.html
9. Jian, Z., Zhao, D., Gao, W.: Group-based sparse representation for image restoration. IEEE Trans. Image Process. **23**(8), 3336–3351 (2014)

The Moco-Minitaur: A Low-Cost Direct-Drive Quadruped Robot for Dynamic Locomotion

Boyang Xing[1(✉)], Yufei Liu[1], Zhirui Wang[1], Zhenjie Liang[1], Jianxin Zhao[1], Bo Su[1], and Lei Jiang[1,2]

[1] Unmanned Center, China North Vehicle Research Institute, Beijing 100072, China
11921167@zju.edu.cn

[2] College of Computer Science and Technology, Zhejiang University, Hangzhou 310027, China

Abstract. In this paper we present the Moco-Minitaur robot, a small(sub-3.5kg) 8-Dof and low-cost (sub-4500 RMB) quadruped robot for dynamic locomotion. The robot can control vertical and horizontal force and the impedance at each foot. It can perform stable drop damping, standing and dynamically trotting using the virtual model control (VMC) and impedance control (IMP) algorithm. The proposed control system makes the robot perform such a wide range of ballistic locomotion behaviors and demonstrate foot force control during impact without other sensors. In addition, the hardware and CAD structure to replicate this robot is open-source, requires only hand tools for manufacturing and assembly.

Keywords: Quadruped robot · Virtual model control (VMC) · Impedance control

1 Introduction

Quadruped robots provide a highly mobile platform to traverse difficult terrain and are ideal for accomplishing tasks in complex environment. Companies such as Boston-Dynamics, MIT and Ghost-Robotics had presented several medium sized quadruped robots like Spotmini [1], Mini Cheetah [2] and Vision-60 [3], etc. Some of them have been use in unmanned inspection and security. For quadruped robot, the parameter tuning and locomotion experiment on prototype hardware platform is very import. Although there are a lot of high fidelity simulation software, such as pybullet [4] or Webots [5], but the difference between real system and simulation is still difficult to be simulated by computer. Thus, a small and low cost quadruped robot platform for locomotion test can effectively build a bridge between simulation and real system. Moco-Minitaur is a small (sub-3.5 kg), low cost (sub-4500 RMB) 8-Dof direct-drive quadruped robot for dynamic locomotion test. This robot can control vertical and horizontal force and impedance at each foot, and performs stable drop damping, standing and trotting, meanwhile, it can

This work is supported by the National Key Research and Development Program of China (Grant No. 2019YFB1309500, GrantNo. 2019YFB1309502) and is supported by the StateAdministration of Science, Technology and Industry for NationalDefence, PRCunderGrant JCKY2019208B024.

© Springer Nature Switzerland AG 2021
X.-J. Liu et al. (Eds.): ICIRA 2021, LNAI 13013, pp. 378–389, 2021.
https://doi.org/10.1007/978-3-030-89095-7_37

sensitively estimate the touch down status without plantar sensor. This paper introduce how we design its hardware and the control algorithm used for dynamic locomotion (Fig. 1).

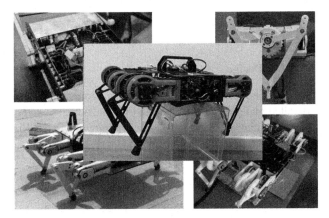

Fig. 1. Moco-Minitaur: a low-cost direct-drive quadruped robot for dynamic locomotion

The most mature way to build the low-cost quadruped robot platform is to use 8-Dof parallel legs. Many small quadruped robots use inverse kinematics algorithm to realize the locomotion control, but this method can only ensure the movement at low speed and on the flat ground. For the movement on complex terrain, the force control and impedance control is wildly used in the 12-Dof quadruped robot nowadays. However, those control method has more technical problems while constructing with 8-Dof parallel legs. For example, the X-force and Z-force of 8-Dof parallel legs are coupled, the system is under actuated thus there is no active control of lateral force, which makes it hard to control the roll attitude and rotation at the same time. At present, there are some related research contents, the MIT Super Mini Cheetah [6] can achieve the basic force balance control based on the simplified inverted pendulum model(SLIP). The Standford Doggo [7] can achieve a basic trot gait based on the inverse kinematics algorithm, which uses PD controller on brushless motor to simulate the spring to realize walking on the different terrain. The one with the most excellent ability to move in complex terrain int 8-Dof quadruped robot is the Ghost-Robotics Minitaur [8], it use the SLIP model construct the feed-forward signal and use the force feedback control to achieve better control performance in trot, bound and pace gait. Besides, there are many others 8-Dof quadruped robot design, but most of them just focuses on the design of mechanisms [9, 10].

This paper introduces the mechanisms design and the force impedance control algorithm of Moco-Minitaur. In order to solve the problem of under-actuated and control output coupling, a virtual model controller(VMC) is constructed which effectively reduce the system dimension, its virtual control output can be decomposed based on the optimal allocation algorithm and generate the expected force of each support leg. Meanwhile, a robust impedance force tracking controller(IMP) is designed, which guaranteed the 8-Dof leg can generated desired force under complex contact situations. The experiments proved this low cost robot can realize dynamic locomotion in standing and trotting. Since the total cost of Moco-Minitaur is less than 4500 RMB, and only manual tools are needed to complete the assembly, therefore it can meet the demand of low-cost platform in the future of foot robot motion control and education.

2   Method

2.1   Quadruped Robot Design

The hardware of Moco-Minitaur is open source [11]. The project includes all CAD structure documents, detailed material and assembly wiring introduction and basic software. The total cost of it is less than 4500RMB. The leg structure of Moco-Minitaur is shown in the Fig. 2, the width of the robot is 137 mm, the length is 270 mm, and its weight is less than 3.5 kg. The design of direct-drive motor and leg structure are under the premise of meeting the basic locomotion test and force control requirements of quadruped robot.

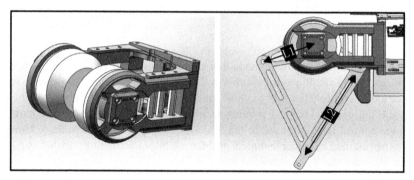

Fig. 2. The CAD structure of the Moco-Minitaur robot (L1 = 55 mm, L2 = 110 mm)

The electrical system of Moco-minitaur mainly includes a STM32 microprocessor, two motors of each leg are drove by an Odrive [12], in addition, there is a power management module to realize remote power switch. Compared with Doggo's electrical system design, Moco-minitaur use an STM32F4 microprocessor to convert the ODrive's ASIIC serial protocol to CAN bus protocol. The main CPU running the FreeRTOS operating system, and realizes the VMC control, swing trajectory planning and impedance control. The controller can calculate torque feed forward command, desired angle and joint PD parameters to each ODrive at 500 Hz, and ODrive completes the FOC control with the frequency of 10 kHz (Fig. 3).

According to the functional requirements of low-cost quadruped robot development platform, it can be seen that direct-drive or small reduction ratio can ensure precise force control, meanwhile, the robot can detect touch down collision accurately and quickly [8]. The comparison between Moco-Minitaur and other low-cost 8-Dof quadruped robot is shown in the Table 1.

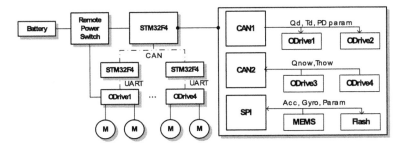

Fig. 3. Electrical diagram of Moco-Minitaur robot

Table 1. Comparison of low cost 8-Dof quadruped robot

Robot	Moco-Minitaur	Standford Doggo	Ghost Minitaur
Actuator	X5048	T-Motor MN5212	T-Motor U8
Continuous torque (Nm)	0.57	1.51	0.86
Locomotion algorithm	VMC + Impedance/Force control	Position control	SLIP + Force control
Total mass	3.5 kg	5 kg	6 kg
Total cost	4500 RMB	7000 RMB	10000 RMB

2.2 Control System Design

The locomotion control algorithm adopted by Moco-Minitaur combines force and impedance control. Basing on the virtual leg theory and decoupling theory of Marc.Raibert [13] the VMC controller and force distribution algorithm are adopted to generate appropriate desired foot force. The control logic block diagram is shown in Fig. 4. Firstly, in order to improve the rotation ability a pose command planner is designed here, which calculate the desired roll attitude and steering angular velocity

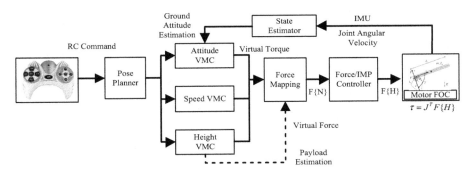

Fig. 4. VMC and IMP control diagram of diagram robot

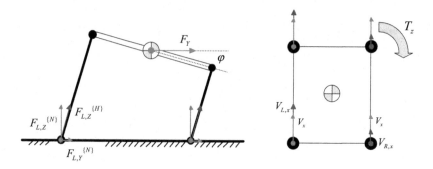

(1) Passive lateral force control   (2) Rotation differential steering model

Fig. 5. Pose command planner

according to the remote control command, thus the left and right side legs' swing end position can be get base on capture point theory; Next, the VMC controller will decouple the system as height, forward speed and attitude, and generate the virtual force and virtual torque on body; Finally, the virtual control output will be dis to the supported legs based on virtual leg and least square method, in order to track the desired force in different contact situation, a robust impedance controller is designed base on Jacobian inverse kinematics.

A. Attitude/Position/Speed Command Planner

Due to 8-Dof leg structure is under-actuated, the leg can not generate active lateral force for roll and yaw attitude movement. It is difficult to meet the physical constraints of this system for all dimension force control. Therefore, the passive lateral force can be generated by given roll attitude command as shown in Fig. 5(1). Meanwhile, the yaw rotate motion can be realized based on the differential steering model as shown in Fig. 5(2).

Figure 5(1) is the rear view of the robot, we can given the roll attitude command φ_d to generate the passive lateral force. Since the leg can only generate the active force in $\{H\}$, therefore the passive lateral force $F_{*,y}^{\{N\}}$, $F_{*,z}^{\{N\}}$, $* = L, R$ in $\{N\}$ can be calculated:

$$\begin{cases} \varphi_d = K_1 \cdot \dfrac{F_y}{2} + \varphi_{yaw}, \ -\varphi_{max} < \varphi_d < \varphi_{max} \\ \varphi_{yaw} = K_2 \cdot T_z \end{cases} \tag{1}$$

Where φ_{max} is the maximum roll attitude command, K_1, K_2 are the gain parameters, F_y is the desired lateral force in $\{N\}$, T_z is the desired rotate torque in $\{N\}$.

Figure 5(2) is the top view of the robot, since the 8-Dof leg structure can only control the yaw rotation based on forward foot force, in order to reduce this control output the differential steering model is used:

$$\begin{cases} V_{L,x} = V_{x,d} + \dfrac{\omega_{z,d} \cdot W}{2} \\ V_{R,x} = V_{x,d} - \dfrac{\omega_{z,d} \cdot W}{2} \end{cases} \tag{2}$$

Where $V_{x,d}$ is the desired forward speed, W is the width of robot, $\omega_{z,d}$ is the desired yaw rotate speed, thus the swing end position of each legs can be calculated with capture point theory:

$$p_i = p_{hip,i} + \frac{T_s}{2} V_x + \sqrt{\frac{P_z}{g}} (V_{*,x} - V_x), * = L, R \tag{3}$$

Where $p_{hip,i}$ is the hinged position of each leg in $\{B\}$, T_s is the stance time, P_z is the height of robot, V_x is the forward speed, g is acceleration of gravity.

B.   Virtual Model Controller

Based on the planner command, three PD controller are used to stable the speed, height and attitude of virtual rigid body:

$$\begin{bmatrix} F_x \\ F_y \\ F_z \end{bmatrix} = \begin{bmatrix} K_x(V_{x,d} - V_x) - D_x\dot{V}_x \\ K_y(V_{y,d} - V_y) - D_y\dot{V}_y \\ K_z(P_{z,d} - P_z) - D_z\dot{V}_z \end{bmatrix}, \begin{bmatrix} T_x \\ T_y \\ T_z \end{bmatrix} = \begin{bmatrix} K_\varphi(\varphi_d - \varphi) - D_\varphi\omega_x \\ K_\theta(\theta_d - \theta) - D_\theta\omega_y \\ K_\gamma(\gamma_d - \gamma) - D_\gamma\omega_z \end{bmatrix} \tag{4}$$

Based on the virtual torque and virtual force generated by VMC controller, the system can be decoupled. Furthermore, the virtual control output should map to the real support legs. For this goal, the Mini-Cheetha uses QP optimization [2] to obtain the optimal results. Since the Moco-Minitaur just uses low-cost microprocessor, which can not meet the real-time calculation ability of solving QP problems. Therefore, this paper uses the virtual leg theory combined with the least square solution to realize the real-time force mapping.

$$\begin{bmatrix} F_x \\ F_z \\ T_x \\ T_y \\ T_z \end{bmatrix} = \begin{bmatrix} 1 & 0 & 1 & 0 \\ 0 & 1 & 0 & 1 \\ 0 & p_{L.y} & 0 & p_{R.y} \\ p_{L.z} & -p_{L.x} & p_{R.z} & -p_{R.x} \\ p_{L.y} & 0 & -p_{R.y} & 0 \end{bmatrix} \begin{bmatrix} F_{L,x} \\ F_{L,z} \\ F_{R,x} \\ F_{R,z} \end{bmatrix} = Ax \tag{5}$$

The result of force mapping under the support of two legs is $x = (A^T A)^{-1} A^T$. For the typical 4-legged standing, we can use the virtual leg theory to calculate the LF and RH leg force $x_{LF,RH}$ based on formula (5), and RF and LH foot force $x_{RF,LH}$ too. According to the virtual leg theory, the diagonally legs can be simplified as one virtual leg, then the final leg force can be calculated by the mean value of the two virtual legs mapping results and compensate the Z-axis force output of the roll:

$$x_i = (\frac{x_{LF,RH,i}}{2} + \frac{x_{LF,RH,i}}{2})/\cos(\beta) \tag{6}$$

C. Force Impedance Controller

Firstly, the force feed-forward torque command of motor can be calculated based on the below formula:

$$\tau_f = -J^T F \tag{7}$$

However, the force feed-forward control can not guaranteed in the real robot. Taking Mini-Cheetha as an example, those medium-sized quadruped robots mainly uses WBC [2] and other dynamic optimization algorithms to realize the robust force tracking. However, this kind of algorithm requires a high-precision model of the system and require high computational power. Therefore, Moco- Minitaur uses Jacobian inverse kinematics impedance control to achieve the robust force tracking, which can reduce the amount of calculation and ensure foot force tracking accuracy.

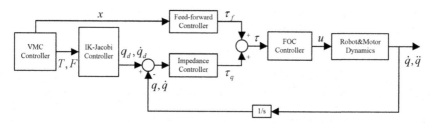

Fig. 6. Robust force impedance controller

As shown in Fig. 6, it can be seen that the final torque command sent to FOC controller consists of impedance command and force feed-forward command, so as to realize active impedance control, the control system can be construct as follows:

$$\begin{cases} f = K_q(q_d - q) + D_q(\dot{q}_d - \dot{q}) + M_q(\ddot{q}_d - \ddot{q}) \\ \tau_q = -J^T f \end{cases} \tag{8}$$

Where M_q is the kinetic coefficient, it can be eliminated in the actual closed-loop system, q_d is the desired joint angel and $\dot{q}_d$ is the desired joint angular velocity. Those joint control signal can be converted with the virtual force and torque generated by the VMC controller, and generate the expected speed of each foot as follows:

$$\begin{cases} v_{i,x} = K_{vx}(F_x + \frac{T_z}{m_i \cdot 2 \cdot W}) \\ v_{i,z} = K_{vz}(F_z + \frac{T_x}{n_i \cdot 2 \cdot W} + \frac{T_y}{l_i \cdot 2 \cdot H}) \end{cases} \tag{9}$$

$$where \begin{cases} if\ i = R\ m_i = -1, n_i = 1 \\ else\ m_i = 1, n_i = -1 \end{cases}, \begin{cases} if\ i = F\ l_i = 1 \\ else\ l_i = -1 \end{cases}$$

Where R is the right side leg and F is the front side leg. Finally, the foot movement speed can be transformed into the desired angle and angular velocity based on Jacobian inverse kinematics:

$$\begin{cases} \dot{q}_d = -J^{-1} \cdot v_{x,z} \\ q_d = \int \dot{q}_d dt, \, q_{min} < q_d < q_{max} \end{cases} \tag{10}$$

3 Experiments

In order to verify the dynamic locomotion ability of Moco-Mnitaur robot and whether the proposed control algorithm can solve the dimension reduction decoupling problem in 8-Dof leg structure. Several experiments are designed in this paper, including typical stand and trot gait, uneven ground and step terrain of 8-DOF quadruped robot. Some experiment video can be checked on https://www.bilibili.com/video/BV1pX4y1g7sa.

3.1 Damping Control During Dropping

Firstly, the drop experiment is tested. In the experiment, the robot is released from a height of 10 cm to test the effectiveness of the proposed force impedance racking controller, the drop experiment is shown as follows:

(1)   (2)   (3)   (4)

Fig. 7. Drop damping experiment

As can be seen in Fig. 7, it can be seen that the robot enters the stance force control after contact ground, the pose of robot can be stabled based on the impedance and VMC controller. The data curve of this experiment is shown as follows. As shown in this figure, the red dotted line is the expected signal and the black line is the actual value. The robot's entry force control after contact. It can be seen that the maximum Z-direction impact force is less than 10 N. After damping, the robot can resume standing (Fig. 8).

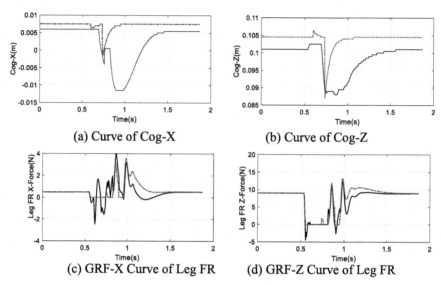

(a) Curve of Cog-X   (b) Curve of Cog-Z

(c) GRF-X Curve of Leg FR   (d) GRF-Z Curve of Leg FR

Fig. 8. Curve of drop damping experiment

3.2 Pose Control During Standing

Further experiments are designed to test the typical four legged standing gait. In the experiment, the desired attitude is tracked based on the proposed VMC and impedance controller. the experimental curve is as follows (Fig. 9):

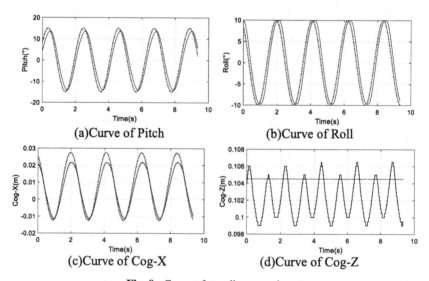

(a)Curve of Pitch   (b)Curve of Roll

(c)Curve of Cog-X   (d)Curve of Cog-Z

Fig. 9. Curve of standing experiment

3.3 Locomotion Control During Trotting

Finally, the dynamic locomotion test for uneven ground without any plantar sensor is designed. Firstly, the robot need to pass through a 1 cm obstacle (Fig. 10):

(1)   (2)   (3)   (4)

Fig. 10. Trot locomotion pass 1 cm obstacle

It can be seen from the above figure that the robot can effectively reduce the impact based on the proposed algorithm. In the process of passing through the obstacle, the body posture is stable, there is no violent fluctuation. The proposed algorithm can meet the requirements of dynamic locomotion, and further tests are carried out on a up-stair experiment:

(1)   (2)   (3)   (4)

Fig. 11. Trot locomotion up-stair experiment

As shown in Fig. 11, based on the proposed algorithm, the robot can realize a stable blind up-stair trotting, the proposed control method can realize the dynamic motion control ability in complex terrain。

In Fig. 12, the green line in the pitch axis curve is the estimated terrain angle. It can be seen that based on the proposed algorithm the robot's attitude disturbance is small when it comes to the stair. The height and forward speed can immediately recover after the disturbance. Therefore, the proposed algorithm effectively solves the under-actuated and output coupling of the 8-Dof leg structure.

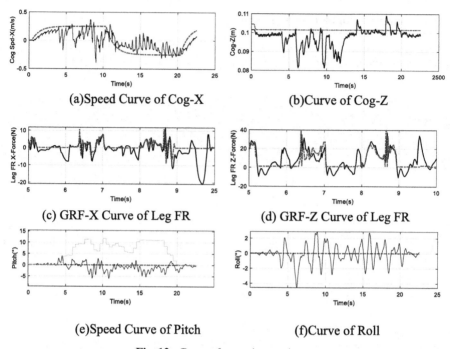

(a)Speed Curve of Cog-X

(b)Curve of Cog-Z

(c) GRF-X Curve of Leg FR

(d) GRF-Z Curve of Leg FR

(e)Speed Curve of Pitch

(f)Curve of Roll

Fig. 12. Curve of up-stair experiment

4   Conclusion

In this work we introduce Moco-Minitaur robot, a low-cost direct-drive quadruped robot for dynamic locomotion is proposed. We proposed a simple control method combine the VMC and impedance control algorithm, which can realize the dynamic locomotion in complex terrain. The proposed state-of-the-art legged robot platform can improve research and education in legged robotics by lowering the barriers to entry.

References

1. Niquille, S.C.: Regarding the pain of spotmini: or what a robot's struggle to learn reveals about the built environment. Arch. Des. **89**(1), 84–91 (2019)
2. Katz, B., Carlo, J.D., Kim, S.: Mini cheetah: a platform for pushing the limits of dynamic quadruped control. In: 2019 International Conference on Robotics and Automation (ICRA) (2019)
3. GhostRobotics. https://www.ghostrobotics.io/
4. Pybullet. https://pypi.org/project/pybullet/
5. Webots. https://www.cyberbotics.com/
6. Bosworth, W., Kim, S., Hogan, N.: The MIT super mini cheetah: A small, low-cost quadrupedal robot for dynamic locomotion. In: 2015 IEEE International Symposium on Safety, Security, and Rescue Robotics (SSRR). IEEE (2015)
7. Kau, N., Schultz, A., Ferrante, N., et al.: Stanford doggo: an open-source, quasi-direct-drive quadruped. In: 2019 International Conference on Robotics and Automation (ICRA) (2019)

8. Karlsen, R.E., Gage, D.W., Shoemaker, C.M., et al.: Gait development on Minitaur, a direct drive quadrupedal robot. In: Spie Defense + Security, p. 98370I (2016)
9. Duperret, J., Kramer, B., Koditschek, D.: Core actuation promotes self-manipulability on a direct-drive quadrupedal robot. In: Kulić, D., Nakamura, Y., Khatib, O., Venture, G. (eds.) ISER 2016. SPAR, vol. 1, pp. 147–159. Springer, Cham (2017). https://doi.org/10.1007/978-3-319-50115-4_14
10. Sha, S., Wang, J., Pan, S., et al.: Coupled drive leg of quadrupedal robot mechanism design and analysis of energy consumption. In: International Conference on Mechatronic Sciences. IEEE (2014)
11. Moco-Minitaur. https://github.com/golaced/Moco-Minitaur-LTS
12. ODrive. https://discourse.odriverobotics.com/
13. Raibert, M.H., Tello, E.R.: Legged robots that balance. IEEE Expert 1(4), 89 (1986)

Analysis of Gravitational Effects on the Dynamic Behavior of Open Loop Mechanisms with Multiple Clearance Joints

Lixin Yang, Xianmin Zhang[✉], Zhenhui Zhan, and Weijian Zhong

Guangdong Provincial Key Laboratory of Precision Equipment and Manufacturing Technology,
South China University of Technology, Guangzhou 510640, China
zhangxm@scut.edu.cn

Abstract. Joint clearance and gravitational effects are considered and their coupling effects on the dynamic performance of open loop mechanisms are modeled. A continuous dissipative Hertz contact model is applied to describe the contact phenomenon in the joint and the friction force is calculated using the modified Coulomb's friction law. The dynamic behaviors of open loop mechanisms under different combinations of clearance joints location and body masses are numerically modeled. The results show that the location of the clearance joints and the body gravity are important factors to dynamic behavior of the open loop mechanisms. The closer to the end-effector, the stronger influence on the system. The errors induced by multiple joints with clearance can be transmitted and accumulated. The component of gravity varies unevenly has an extremely strong effect the on dynamics of the open-loop topology, the farer body owns heavier weight to the end-effector, the stronger influence on the system. The results may provide a theoretical basis and technical support for the design the open loop mechanisms.

Keywords: Open loop mechanisms · Multiple clearance joints · Gravitational effects · Coupling effects

1 Introduction

Open loop mechanisms are widely used in industrial, medical, and aerospace fields, the precise modeling of these largescale open loop mechanisms continues to be a challenge especially in the complex working circumstances. As the core component of open loop mechanisms, the joint plays a crucial role in power transmission, mechanical connection, and state measurement tasks [1, 2]. Particularly, due to manufacturing error and the requirements in assembly and working processes, joint clearance is inevitable. The clearance in the articulating joint introduce nonlinearity to the open loop mechanisms, which are the main factors influence its positioning precision and motion smooth [3–6]. The micro meshing displacements are coupled with the rotation of rigid bodies and may produce unexpected effects on the dynamic behaviors of the open loop mechanisms. Especially, Joint errors in large-scale open loop mechanisms are amplified and accumulate, which results in a considerable tip positioning inaccuracy. When the journal

© Springer Nature Switzerland AG 2021
X.-J. Liu et al. (Eds.): ICIRA 2021, LNAI 13013, pp. 390–400, 2021.
https://doi.org/10.1007/978-3-030-89095-7_38

rotates through a whole clearance size and contact the bearing, it will produce collision and hence the vibration of the system. The simplification of the open loop mechanisms joint modeling and the neglect for nonlinear factors result in an irrational and unpredictable response. Therefore, it is necessary to analyze dynamic behavior for the open loop mechanisms with clearance joints.

With the increasing demand for high-precision control and the deepening of joint clearance analysis, the nonlinear modeling of clearance joint continues to be updated and improved. Typical models include:(1) continuous contact model [7, 8], assuming that the pairing element always keep contact with each other when it works; (2) two-mode model, which holds that the pairing elements exist two states [9, 10], that is, contact and free movement; (3) three-state model (Fig. 2) [11–13], which exists three phases, the contact, freedom, and collision contact. The three-state model is the most accurate one to reflect the actual motion states of mechanisms with clearance joints. Flores [14] has studied a double pendulum with one imperfect joint. The double pendulum was used as a numerical application to illustrate the spatial revolute joint clearance formulation. Selcuk Erkaya [15] focused on investigation of joint clearance effects on a welding robot manipulator with six degrees of freedom while one joint was considered as imperfect to show the effects of joint clearance on system dynamic behavior. Bai [16] presented a computational methodology for analysis of space robot manipulator systems, considering the effects of the clearances in the joint. Li [17] a dynamic simulation model of space manipulator is developed and the dynamic characteristics in the clearance joint of space manipulator are investigated. Wu and Rao [18] have focused on the optimal allocation of joint tolerances with consideration of the positional and directional errors of the robot end effector and the manufacturing cost. Zhu and Ting [19] presented a probability density function to investigate the performance uncertainty caused by the joint clearance in a robot manipulator. Bu et al. [20] have presented a novel method based on trajectory planning to avoid the detachment of joint elements of a manipulator with clearances. An improved detachment criterion for the revolute and spherical joints was proposed. The angular displacements and velocities of virtual links were approximately solved through the directions of joint forces and their time rates of the corresponding ideal mechanism.

Dynamics of multibody system with one clearance joint has been extensively studied. In reality, there often exists multiple or massive clearance joints in the multi-body manipulator. Because of its complexity, Flores [21], Bai [22], Zhang [23–25] are among the very few, who modeled multibody systems with multiple clearance joints. However, the research on the dynamics of open loop mechanisms with multiple clearance joints is still an open problem. Few work has reported the dynamical study of serial manipulators with only one clearance joint [14–20]. Moreover, many open loop mechanisms such as space manipulators are assembled on the ground while operated in the space environment, their gravity is different. Therefore, it is the key problem to be solved that the effects of clearance on the trajectories of end-effectors of open loop mechanisms under different gravity environments.

In this study, a dynamic model of open loop mechanisms with clearance joints is developed, a continuous dissipative Hertz contact model is applied to describe the contact phenomenon in the joint and the friction force is calculated using the modified Coulomb's friction law. Detailed analyses are made considering gravitational and multiple clearance joints under different situations. The results show that the clearance has an extremely strong effect the on dynamics of a space manipulator with open-loop topology because the errors induced by multiple joints with clearance can be transmitted and accumulated.

2 Model Mechanism

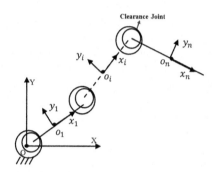

Fig. 1. The structure of the Open loop mechanism

Figure 1 Shows the typical structure of the open loop mechanism, the coordinate of the links are used as reference coordinate, for it is more convenient to describe the position and orientation of the body, correspondingly, the generalized coordinates of the system are

$$\mathbf{q} = \begin{bmatrix} x_1 \ y_1 \ \theta_1 \ \cdots \ x_i \ y_i \ \theta_i \ \cdots \ x_n \ y_n \ \theta_n \end{bmatrix}^T \tag{1}$$

Where, x_i, y_i are the position of the center of mass of body i in the generalized coordinate, θ_i is the relative angle between each local coordinate system $x_i o_i y_i$ and the global coordinate system XOY, n is the number of bodis.

3 Modeling of the Revolute Clearance Joints

As shown in Fig. 2, the centers of bearing and journal are denoted as P_i and P_j, their global coordinates are represented as

$$\mathbf{r}_k^P = \mathbf{r}_k + \mathbf{A}_k \mathbf{r}_k^{\prime P} \quad (k = i, j) \tag{2}$$

In which r_k^P is the global coordinate of point P on part k, r_k is the global coordinate of center of mass of each part, and $r_k = (x_k y_k)^T$, $\mathbf{r}_k^{\prime P}$ is the local coordinate of point P on part k, A_k is the transform matrix.

The eccentricity vector e which connects points P_i and P_j is calculated as

$$\mathbf{e} = \mathbf{r}_j^P - \mathbf{r}_i^P \tag{3}$$

The penetration depth of journal and bearing is represented as

$$\delta = e - c \tag{4}$$

Where c is the radial clearance $c = R_i - R_j$. Negative of δ means that there is no contact between the journal and the bearing.

The contact points are denoted as Q_i and Q_j, their global coordinates are represented as

$$\mathbf{r}_k^Q = \mathbf{r}_k^P + R_k \mathbf{n}(k = i, j) \tag{5}$$

where, $\mathbf{n}$ is the unit vector $\boldsymbol{e}$.

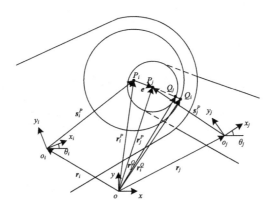

Fig. 2. Revolute joint with clearance

The relative velocity is projected onto the plane of collision and the normal plane of collision, obtaining a relative tangential velocity v_n and a relative normal velocity v_t.

$$v_n = \dot{\delta} = \left(\dot{\mathbf{r}}_j^Q - \dot{\mathbf{r}}_i^Q \right)^T \mathbf{n}$$
$$v_t = \left(\dot{\mathbf{r}}_j^Q - \dot{\mathbf{r}}_i^Q \right)^T \mathbf{t} \tag{6}$$

Where t is obtained by rotating the vector n in the counter clockwise direction by 90°.

4   Equations of Motion for the Space Manipulator

The ideal revolute joint has one relative degree of freedom, the constraint equations is,

$$\boldsymbol{\Phi}(\mathbf{q}, t) = \mathbf{0} \tag{7}$$

A revolute joint with clearance obviously does not impose kinematic constraints on the system but imposes some force constraints, it limits the journal movement within the bearing. The constraints are lost when the joint clearance is considered.

The first time derivative with respect to time of Eq. (7) provides the velocity constraint equation

$$\mathbf{\Phi_q \dot{q}} = -\mathbf{\Phi}_t \equiv \upsilon \tag{8}$$

where $\mathbf{\Phi_q}$ is the Jacobian matrix of the constraint equations, that is, $\mathbf{\Phi_q} = \partial \mathbf{\Phi}/\partial \mathbf{q}$, and similarly, $\mathbf{\Phi}_t = \partial \mathbf{\Phi}/\partial t$.

A second differentiation of Eq. (7) with respect to time leads to the acceleration constraint equations

$$\mathbf{\Phi_q \ddot{q}} = -(\mathbf{\Phi_q \dot{q}})_q \dot{q} - 2\mathbf{\Phi_{qt} \dot{q}} - \mathbf{\Phi}_{tt} \equiv \gamma \tag{9}$$

Equations (7)–(9) are the system kinematic constraint equations.

The Newton-Euler equations of the system in Cartesian coordinates are written as

$$\mathbf{M\ddot{q}} + \mathbf{\Phi_q^T} \lambda = \mathbf{g} \tag{10}$$

Where $\mathbf{M}$ is the system mass matrix, λ is the vector of Lagrange multipliers, $\mathbf{g}$ is the generalized force vector. The contact force replaces kinematic constraints when the joint clearance is taken into consideration. Then, $\mathbf{g}$ is a column vector that contains the driving torques and the equivalent forces of the contact forces of clearance joints.

Appending Eq. (10) to Eq. (19),

$$\begin{pmatrix} \mathbf{M} & \mathbf{\Phi_q^T} \\ \mathbf{\Phi_q} & \mathbf{0} \end{pmatrix} \begin{pmatrix} \ddot{q} \\ \lambda \end{pmatrix} = \begin{pmatrix} \mathbf{g} \\ \gamma \end{pmatrix} \tag{11}$$

This system of equations is solved for $\ddot{q}$ and λ. As the kinematic and velocity constraint equations are only satisfied in the first integration step, Eq. (11) represents an unstable system. The Baumgarte stabilization method is used to allow constraints to be slightly violated before corrective actions can take place, in order to force the violation to vanish [26]. The equations of motion for dynamic system utilizing Baumgarte's approach are stated in the form

$$\begin{pmatrix} \mathbf{M} & \mathbf{\Phi_q^T} \\ \mathbf{\Phi_q} & \mathbf{0} \end{pmatrix} \begin{pmatrix} \ddot{q} \\ \lambda \end{pmatrix} = \begin{pmatrix} \mathbf{g} \\ \gamma' \end{pmatrix} \tag{12}$$

Where $\gamma' = \gamma - 2\alpha \dot{\mathbf{\Phi}} - \beta^2 \mathbf{\Phi}$, and α, β are the Baumgarte parameters, which are positive constants.

5 Contact Force Models

The dynamics of a dry journal-bearing is explained by two different situations. Firstly, when the journal and bearing are not in contact with each other, there is no contact force associated to the journal-bearing. Secondly, when the contact between the two bodies occurs the contact-impact forces are modeled according to a non-linear Hertz's force law (normal force) together with the Coulomb's friction law (tangential force). These two conditions can be expressed as,

$$F = 0 \ if \ \delta < 0$$
$$F = F_n + F_t \ if \ \delta \geq 0$$

$$(13)$$

Where F_n and F_t are normal and tangential force components, respectively. A continuous contact force model, based on Herz contact law, which was proposed by Lankarani and Nikravesh [27, 28] is employed in this paper. The damping hysteretic factor was considered to account for the energy dissipation and the contact force model is expressed as

$$F_n = K\delta^n \left[1 + \frac{3(1 - c_e^2)}{4} \frac{\dot{\delta}}{\dot{\delta}^{(-)}} \right]$$

$$(14)$$

Where K is the generalized stiffness parameter, $\dot{\delta}$ is the relative penetration depth, D is the hysteresis damping coefficient and $\dot{\delta}^{(-)}$ is the relative impact velocity. The exponent n is equal to 1.5 for metallic contacts. The stiffness parameter K is given by

$$K = \frac{4}{3(\delta_i + \delta_j)} \left(\frac{R_i R_j}{R_i + R_j} \right)^{\frac{1}{2}}$$

$$(15)$$

Where the material parameters δ_k are expressed as

$$\delta_k = \left(1 - v_k^2 \right) / E_k \ (k = i, j)$$

$$(16)$$

v_k and E_k are the Poisson's coefficient and the Young's modulus associated with each body, respectively. The radius of curvature R_k is taken as positive for convex surfaces and negative for concave surfaces.

Friction forces act when contacting bodies tend to slide relative each other. These forces are tangential to the surfaces of contact and are opposite to the sliding velocity. Friction force model is expressed as [29]

$$F_t = -c_f c_d F_n \frac{\mathbf{v}_t}{|v_t|}$$

$$(17)$$

Where c_f is the friction coefficient and v_T is the relative tangential velocity. c_d is the dynamic correction coefficient and given by

$$c_d = \begin{cases} 0 \ if \ |v_t| \leq v_0 \\ \frac{|v_t| - v_0}{v_1 - v_0} \ if \ v_0 \leq |v_t| \leq v_1 \\ 1 \ if \ |v_t| \geq v_1 \end{cases}$$

$$(18)$$

Where v_0 and v_1 are given tolerances for the tangential velocity. Knowing form Eqs. (4), (6) the penetration depth and relative velocity, the normal force F_n and tangential force F_t are obtained.

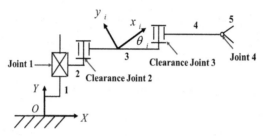

Fig. 3. The structure of the space manipulator system

Table 1. Geometric and inertia properties of Space manipulator

Bodies	Length (m)	Mass (kg)	Moment of inertia(kg*m^2)
Body 2	0.145	0.072	–
Body 3	0.245	0.412	0.009119
Body 4	0.242	0.276	0.005809
Body 5	0.058	0.035	–

Table 2. Parameters used in the dynamic simulation

	Joint 2	Joint 3
Bearing radius	10.0 mm	10.0 mm
Restitution coefficient	0.9	0.9
Young's modulus	207 GPa	207 GPa
Possion's ratio	0.3	0.3
Friction coefficient	0.05	0.05

6 Dynamic Performances of the Space Manipulator

Space manipulator, satellite solar panel as a typical example, is a open loop mechanism with a wide range of three-dimensional space motions. Therefore, a serial model of manipulator with 4 degrees of freedom is designed in this study. The end effector of the manipulator is designed to bear a load of 2.0 kg. The manipulator system structure (Fig. 3) is simplified to reduce the weight and to manufacture conveniently.

The space manipulator has four degrees of freedom while all bodies are assumed as rigid. The geometric and inertia parameters are listed in Table 1. The parameters used in the dynamic simulation are listed in Table 2. In order to discuss the influence of the clearance joints on the dynamic performance, it is assumed that joint 2 and joint 3 can move, the other joints are fixed. The driving torque applied on joint 2 is 4sin(2πt) Nm, and the torque applying on joint 3 is 2sin(2πt) Nm. Clearance analysis is divided into three cases,

Case 1: Joint 2 was considered to be imperfect, and clearance size was adjusted to 0.5 mm;

Case 2: Joint 3 was considered to be imperfect, and clearance size was adjusted to 0.5 mm;

Case 3: Both joint 2 and joint 3 were considered imperfect with the same clearance size of 0.5 mm.

In addition, the gravity has a great influence on the dynamic behavior of the open loop mechanisms with multiple clearance joints, and change the contact force. The existing research mainly analyzes the influence of clearance on the motion performance, but rarely consider the coupling relationship between the effect of multiple clearance joints and gravity. Therefore, these two factors and the coupling relationship of the open loop mechanisms are the key problem to be solved in this section, the discussion is divided into the following four conditions.

Case I: The gravities of body 3 and body 4 are m_3g and m_4g, respectively.

Case II: The gravities of body 3 and body 4 are $2*m_3g$ and m_4g, respectively.

Case III: The gravities of body 3 and body 4 are m_3g and $2*m_4g$, respectively.

Case IV: The gravities of body 3 and body 4 are $2*m_3g$ and $2*m_4g$, respectively.

The centres of the journal and the bearing were assumed to coincide before the manipulator motion started at t = 0.

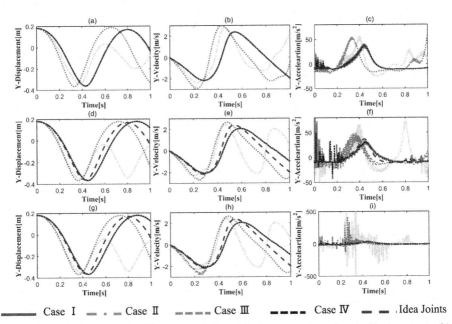

Fig. 4. Dynamic response in the revolute joint with clearance. Case 1: (a) Displacement, (b) Velocity and (c) Acceleration. Case 2: (d) Displacement, (e) Velocity and (f) Acceleration. Case 3: (h) Displacement, (i) Velocity and (j) Acceleration.

Figure 4 shows the acceleration, velocity, and position of the centre of mass of the end-effector in the Y-direction of cases 1 (a–c), 2 (d–f) and 3 (g-i) under four different gravity conditions (Case I–IV), revealing that joint clearance affected the dynamic behavior of the space manipulator bodies. When the gravity condition is Case I, in case 2 and 3, the time evolutions of the acceleration (Figs. 4f, 4i), velocity (Figs. 4e, 4h) and displacement (Figs. 4d, 4g) are significantly affected by the clearance. The acceleration is particularly affected with larger fluctuations (i.e., higher inertial forces) at the moving bodies. The nonlinear effect in case 1 is less than in case 2 and case 3. Clearance joint 2 is connected with body 2 and body 3, and body 3 is connected with body 4 at joint 3. The effect of impact force caused by the clearance on the dynamic response of end-effector is reduced by the joints and bodies behind joint 2. Contrarily in case 2, the joints behind joint 3 fixed with the body can be considered as a whole, and the effect of impact force caused by joint 3 cannot be reduced by the following joint, so the influence on displacement, velocity, and acceleration is greater. In additional, Case I displays the trend of joint clearance effect on the dynamic respond is coincident with Case IV and the effect is smaller than Case II and Case III, it is because that the gravity is equally distributed. Contrary, the gravities of body 3 and body 4 are twice in Case II and Case III, respectively, the clearance joints have obvious effect on dynamic of the open loop mechanics. Case II has more influence on Case III, Case II changed the whole motion cycle, this is because the weight of the body 3 increases lead to the inertia increases, while the end-effector is relatively light and free, due to the joint clearance effect increases on dynamic performance. Also, Fig. 4 displays the effects of joint clearance on end-effector in case 2 and case 3 are similar, indicating that the effect of joint clearance on dynamic behavior of open loop mechanism is more severe.

7 Conclusion

The gravitational effects on the dynamic behavior of the open loop mechanisms with multiple clearance joints were studied. Three difference cases about location of clearance joint and four cases about gravity effect were discussed. The trajectories indicate that multiple clearance joints and gravity are considered and their coupling effects on the dynamic performance of a serial space manipulator.

The gravitational effects on the system were be discussed by four cases (Case I - Case IV). When the gravity changes evenly, the influence of the clearance joints on the dynamic performance is consistent(Case I and Case IV). Contrary, the dynamic effect are quite sensitive to the uneven distribution of gravity (Case II and Case III), morever, Case II has more influence on Case III, Case II changed the whole motion cycle, this is because the weight of the body 3 increases lead to the inertia increases, while the end-effector is relatively light and free, due to the joint clearance effect increases on dynamic performance.

During the design process of the open loop mechanisms, important issues with respect to joint clearance should be investigated, which will influences the mechanism's dynamic performance. The joint clearance and gravitational effects proposed in this paper can provide an insight into such issues and help designers to choose proper body parameter.

Acknowledgments. This work was supported by the special funds for scientific and technological innovation and development of Guangzhou Municipal Science and Technology Bureau(202102020644), the Young Innovative Talents Program in Universities and Colleges of Guangdong Province(2020KQNCX003), the Fundamental Research Funds for the Central Universities(No.2019MS068) , the State Key Laboratory of Mechanical System and Vibration (Grant no. MSV202118) , the Foundation of Guangzhou (2019KC221) and the Dongguan Postgraduate Joint Training (Practice) Workstation Project (2019707122025).

References

1. Yang, T., Yan, S., Ma, W., Han, Z.: Joint dynamic analysis of space manipulator with planetary gear train transmission. Robotica. **34**, 1–17 (2014)
2. Liu, F.C., Hou, T.T., Qin, L., Feng, W.B.: Trajectory tracking control of space manipulator considering joint clearance and gravity. Kong Zhi Li Lun Yu Ying Yong. **32**, 665–673 (2015)
3. Zhao, Y., Bai, Z.F.: Effects of clearance on deployment of solar panels on spacecraft system. Trans. Jpn. Soc. Aeronaut. Space Sci. **53**, 291–295 (2011)
4. Zhang, L.X., Bai, Z.F., Zhao, Y., Cao, X.B.: Dynamic response of solar panel deployment on spacecraft system considering joint clearance. Acta Astronaut. **81**, 174–185 (2012)
5. Zhao, Y., Ba, Z.: Effects of clearance on deployment of solar panels on spacecraft system. Trans. Jpn. Soc. Aeronaut. Space Sci. **53**, 291–295 (2010)
6. Li, T.J., Guo, J.A., Cao, Y.Y.: Dynamic characteristics analysis of deployable space structures considering joint clearance. Acta Astronaut. **68**, 974–983 (2011)
7. Seneviratne, L.D.E.S.W.E., Fenner, D.N.: Analysis of a four-bar mechanism with a radially compliant clearance joint. Proc. Inst. Mech. Eng. C J. Mech. Eng. Sci. **210**, 215–223 (1996)
8. Furuhashi, T.M.N., Matsuura, M.: Research on dynamics of four-bar linkage with clearances at turning pairs: 1st report, general theory using continuous contact model. Bull. JSME. **21**, 518–523 (1978)
9. Dubowsky, S.G.T.N.: Dynamic interactions of link elasticity and clearance connections in planar mechanical systems. J. Eng. Ind. **2**, 652–661 (1975)
10. Wang, Y.W.Z.: Dynamic analysis of flexible mechanisms with clearances. J. Mech. Des. **118**, 592–594 (1996)
11. Flores, P.: Modeling and simulation of wear in revolute clearance joints in multibody systems. Mech Mach Theory. **44**, 1211–1222 (2009)
12. Wang, Z., Tian, Q., Hu, H., Flores, P.: Nonlinear dynamics and chaotic control of a flexible multibody system with uncertain joint clearance. Nonlinear Dyn. **86**(3), 1571–1597 (2016). https://doi.org/10.1007/s11071-016-2978-8
13. Erkaya, S., Dogan, S., Ulus, S.: Effects of joint clearance on the dynamics of a partly compliant mechanism: numerical and experimental studies. Mech Mach Theory. **88**, 125–140 (2015)
14. Flores, P., Ambrosio, J., Claro, J.C.P., Lankarani, H.M.: Spatial revolute joints with clearances for dynamic analysis of multi-body systems. Proc. Inst. Mech. Eng. Pt. K-J. Multi-Body Dyn. **220**, 257–271 (2006)
15. Erkaya, S.: Investigation of joint clearance effects on welding robot manipulators. Robot. Comput.-Integr. Manuf. **28**, 449–457 (2012)
16. Zhao, Y., Bai, Z.F.: Dynamics analysis of space robot manipulator with joint clearance. Acta Astronaut. **68**, 1147–1155 (2011)
17. Li, J., Huang, H., Yang, Y.: Modeling and simulation of joint clearance effects on space manipulator. In: 12th IEEE International Conference on Mechatronics and Automation, ICMA 2015, p. 1852--1857. Institute of Electrical and Electronics Engineers Inc. (2015)

18. Rao, S.S., Wu, A.: Optimum tolerance allocation in mechanical assemblies using an interval method. Eng. Optim. **37**, 237–257 (2005)
19. Ting, K.L., Zhu, J.M., Watkins, D.: The effects of joint clearance on position and orientation deviation of linkages and manipulators. Mech. Mach. Theory. **35**, 391–401 (2000)
20. Bu, W.H., Liu, Z.Y., Tan, J.R., Gao, S.M.: Detachment avoidance of joint elements of a robotic manipulator with clearances based on trajectory planning. Mech. Mach. Theory. **45**, 925–940 (2010)
21. Flores, P., Lankarani, H.M.: Dynamic response of multibody systems with multiple clearance joints. J. Comput. Nonlinear Dyn. **7**, 031003 (2012)
22. ZhengFeng, B., XingGui, W., Yang, Z.: Investigation on dynamic responses of manipulator with multiple clearance joints. Appl. Mech. Mater. **251**, 152–157 (2013)
23. Zhang, X., Zhang, X., Chen, Z.: Dynamic analysis of a 3-RRR parallel mechanism with multiple clearance joints. Mech. Mach. Theory. **78**, 105–115 (2014)
24. Zhang, X., Zhang, X.: A comparative study of planar 3-RRR and 4-RRR mechanisms with joint clearances. Robot. Comput.-Integr. Manuf. **40**, 24–33 (2016)
25. Zhang, X.C., Zhang, X.M.: Elastodynamics of the rigid-flexible 3-(R) under barRR mechanism using ANCF method. In: Zhang, X., Liu, H., Chen, Z., Wang, N. (eds.) Intelligent Robotics and Applications. Icira, vol. 2014, pp. 24–35. Pt Ii. Berlin, Springer-Verlag, Berlin (2014)
26. Flores, P., Machado, M., Seabra, E., da Silva, M.T.: A parametric study on the baumgarte stabilization method for forward dynamics of constrained multibody systems. J. Comput. Nonlinear Dyn. **6**, 9 (2011)
27. Lankarani, H.M., Nikravesh, P.E.: A contact force model with hysteresis damping for impact analysis of multibody systems. J Mech Des. **112**, 369–376 (1990)
28. Lankarani, H.M., Nikravesh, P.E.: Continuous contact force models for impact analysis in multibody systems. Nonlinear Dyn. **5**, 193–207 (1994)
29. Ambrósio, J.A.C.: Impact of rigid and flexible multibody systems: deformation description and contact models. Virt. Nonlinear Multibody Syst. **2**, 15–33 (2002)

Research on Intelligent Spinning Inspection Robot

Wei Wei[1,3](✉), Rougang Zhou[2], Bilu Shao[3], Yuntao Zhang[1], and Jun Wang[1]

[1] Zhejiang Institute of Water Resources and Hydropower, Hangzhou, China
weiw@zjweu.edu.cn
[2] Hangzhou Dianzi University, Hangzhou, China
[3] Hangzhou JunChen Robot Co., Ltd., Hangzhou, China

Abstract. The downstream processing industry of Chemical fiber has become the most significant foreign exchange earning industry through exportation in China's textile industry It.creatively develops the mobile robot equipped with the machine vision detection system and its data visualization service platform; aiming at the occasional abnormal situation during spinning, the inspection task is scheduled through the service platform to realize periodic and uninterrupted inspection. The actual inspection task test is to manually follow and detect three periodic tasks randomly selected from the 24-h continuous inspection tasks for 7 consecutive days. The test statistics are shown that the detection rate is about 98%, and the false detection rate is about 5%.

Keywords: Intelligent spinning inspection robot · Visual inspection system · Visualized data platform

1 Introduction

Chemical fiber products have been widely applied in traditional textile processing, aerospace, national defense and military industry, transportation, energy and environmental protection, safety protection, medical and health [1]. It is impossible for the development of chemical fiber industry to continue the growth mode of relying on quantity in the past, which shall be transformed and upgraded, and extended to such steps as R&D, design, brand, marketing and service; and the mode of production shall be transformed to be flexible, intelligent, digital, refined and green production. With the progress of computer technology, network and communication as well as related hardware and software technology, equipment manufacturing and other basic industrial technology, especially in programmatic documents like Made in China 2025, Guiding Opinions on Actively Promoting the "Internet+" Action, and Development Plan for the New Generation of Artificial Intelligence, the manufacturing technology of chemical fiber industry in China has developed from automation, digitalization and informatization to intelligence. It is feasible for chemical fiber equipment to move forward from automation equipment to intelligence through digitization and informatization [2].

The polyester filament spinning cake is formed in the way that the PET melt is extruded from the spinneret to form melt streams; after cooling and blowing, the filament

© Springer Nature Switzerland AG 2021
X.-J. Liu et al. (Eds.): ICIRA 2021, LNAI 13013, pp. 401–411, 2021.
https://doi.org/10.1007/978-3-030-89095-7_39

is formed by cluster oiling, and then the spinning cake is formed by the winding head of the winding section through the spinning shaft [3]. The filament is composed of dozens or even hundreds of fine hairlike filaments, and the filament is wound into the spinning cake at the speed of several thousand meters per minute. This process requires strict process control. Slight fluctuation of process parameters may lead to abnormal spinning, which will cause end breakage if not found and handled in time, thus reducing the product high-grade rate and then the enterprise efficiency. In the past, this problem can only be handled by manual inspection, which is not timely and even causes false inspection and missing inspection. It is considered to develop automatic inspection robots to periodically monitor the abnormal wire floating and wrong wire in the spinning process, identify the abnormal data in real time, and guide relevant staff to deal with the problem in time.

Intelligent inspection robots act as an execution platform with certain mobile sensing ability. With the help of a variety of sensors, they can detect specific states, carry out customized services, and achieve more programming operations [4]. The intelligent inspection robots based on machine vision enjoy widespread application, such as substation inspection robots [5], meter inspection robots [6] and so on. For exception identified manually by naked eyes in spinning inspection, machine vision sensors and computers can be used to simulate the visual function of human eyes, that is, to obtain and judge the environmental information through vision sensors, so as to realize the perception, recognition and understanding of the three-dimensional scene of the objective world [7]. The information display detection technology based on machine vision is significantly different from the traditional detection technology. The technology is sensitive to light conditions, and usually has to be equipped with auxiliary light source for lighting; according to the characteristics of specific detection target, the appropriate detection algorithm and targeted training are selected, and the algorithm is specific; with wide application field, it enjoys huge application market potential [8]. Characterized by high detection speed, high intelligence, and high detection accuracy, this technology can complete the detection task better than human power.

Against industry and technical background above, this paper introduces the machine vision, mobile bearer and data visualization technology, focuses on the inspection technology for spinning production, which is an important part of the chemical fiber industry.

2   Technical Proposal of Spinning Inspection Robot

During the spinning workshop production, the spinning equipment will encounter some abnormal phenomena, such as broken wire, string wire, wire hook deviation, etc. Therefore, the on-site production must be inspected manually every two hours on average. First, the harsh environment (high temperature, high humidity and high noise) on site will cause damage to the inspectors. Second, manual inspection only depends on the naked eye recognition, which may lead to problems like subjective misjudgment and fatigue identification. Third, manual inspection is time consuming, and short of record tracing.

In order to solve the exception during the production and problems with manual inspection, the method of "mobile robot + intelligent recognition visual algorithm system + visualized data platform" can be adopted for intelligent inspection robots to improve the process of on-site inspection (see Fig. 1) and the inspection effect.

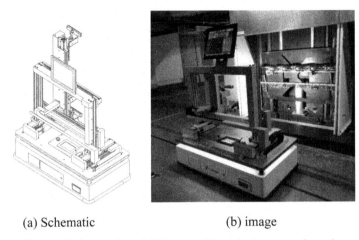

(a) Schematic   (b) image

Fig. 1. (a) Schematic and (b) image of the spinning inspection robot

2.1 Site Environment and Test Items

This spinning workshop has 2 production lines, as shown in Fig. 2(a), with the passage length of about 66 m, and the length of about 1.6 m. The production line passage has two production lines, each of which has 36 stations, and 72 stations need to be inspected. Each station is about 1.5 m long, and the station is shown in Fig. 2(b). The detection elements in the station are wire hook, oil nozzle and wire. The wire hooks and oil nozzles are arranged up and down and in a front-and-back staggered way, and they are installed one by one and relatively perpendicular to the ground, each 20.

The main content of manual detection of abnormal spinning is broken wire, string wire, wire hook (nozzle) deflection, floating impurity, etc., as shown in Fig. 3. The broken wire refers to spinning breakage, and the spinning position instantly forms floccules. The string wire means the wire on one side is dislocated to the other side, which will be in the shape of△. The wire hook (nozzle) deflection is the deflection of the angle of the hook (nozzle), and the floating impurity means there is waste wire hanging on the hook (nozzle).

2.2 Visual Inspection System Scheme

The visual inspection system mainly includes the image acquisition system and the image recognition and analysis system. The image acquisition system takes the pictures of the wire hook, the oil nozzle and the high wire as the inspection points. While ensuring the

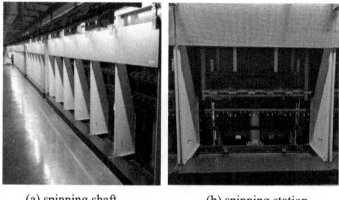

(a) spinning shaft   (b) spinning station

Fig. 2. Spinning inspection site

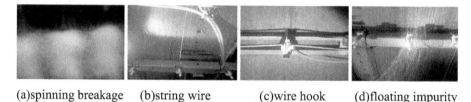

(a)spinning breakage   (b)string wire   (c)wire hook   (d)floating impurity

Fig. 3. Example of spinning faults

normal operation of the frame, we make corresponding transformation on the shooting background of the inspection station to achieve the inspection conditions, and configure the corresponding light source for optical compensation, as shown in Fig. 4. The parameters in the figure have to be adjusted according to the field situation. The image recognition and analysis system visually identify the judgment items, and the results are transmitted to the visualized data platform (see Fig. 4).

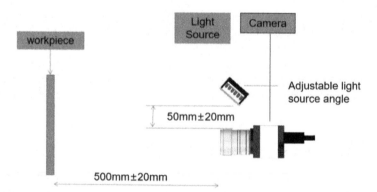

Fig. 4. Schematic diagram of camera and light source scheme

The image recognition detects the exception with different geometric measurement algorithms [9–11] according to the ROI regions of the collected image. Firstly, the gray value of the image is converted to generate the corresponding gray matrix. Secondly, the threshold value of the corresponding algorithm is set. Then, the eigenvalues of the matrix are calculated and compared with the threshold value, and the normal and abnormal detection results are provided.

The broken wire is judged by the proportion parameter of black and white pixels in the collected picture ($\geq 50\%$), as shown in Fig. 3(a). As for the string wire, the width of a section of wire is calculated to judge the consistency of the wire width. The wire width greater than 1 is regarded as abnormal string wire, as shown in Fig. 5(a). The wire hook (nozzle) deviation is judged by calculating the angle parameter ($\geq 3°$) of the wire hook (nozzle), as shown in Fig. 5(b). The floating impurity is judged by calculating the proportion parameter ($[36\%, 50\%)$) of the black-and-white pixel block on the position of the wire hook (nozzle), as shown in Fig. 5(c).

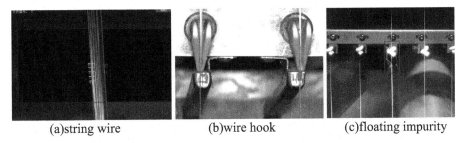

(a)string wire   (b)wire hook   (c)floating impurity

Fig. 5. Schematic diagram of abnormal spinning in visual inspection

2.3 Mobile Robot Scheme

AGV with the upper system is used for the mobile bearing machine to carry out automatic inspection. The AGV parameters are shown in Table 1. The AGV is provided with laser navigation and multiple protection such as sound and light alarm [12, 13]. Through the two-dimensional code precise positioning, the RCS system schedules the AGV mobile task, supports the specified position movement, stops and waits for 60 s when encountering obstacles to perform the avoidance function. The shovel truck has priority to pass and perform the task.

The hardware of AGV is protected by:

a. The AGV forward direction is equipped with safety laser to detect the obstacles in 180° range in the front;
b. The AGV is equipped with contact type of anti-collision touchdowns around it, which can trigger and stop moving instantaneously;
c. AGV is provided with the emergency stop button, and the emergency stop button can be pressed manually at any time to stop the car.

AGV is equipped with laser detection to avoid obstacles. The detection mechanism and safety control are as follows (the following distance can be adjusted):

a. The first gear is 1910—830 mm, the maximum speed is 600 mm/s, the deceleration distance is actual distance - 1080 mm;
b. The second gear is 830—460 mm, the maximum speed is 100 mm/s, and the deceleration distance is: actual distance - 370 mm;
c. The third gear is 460—250 mm, the maximum speed is 0 mm/s, the deceleration distance is: actual distance - 210 mm.

AGV divides the three laser detection areas into the far area, the middle area and the stop area respectively, with the former including the latter in turn. When the obstacle enters the far area and the middle area, it will slow down and but not stop. When it enters the stop area, it will slow down and stop.

Table 1. AGV parameters

Robot drive method	Differential drive
robot size (L × W × H) (mm)	940 × 650 × 300
Robot overall weight	$\leq$ 200 kg
Navigation mode	Laser + two-dimensional code
Walking mode	Forward, backward, turn
Travel speed (loaded /unloaded)	1–1.2 m/s
Navigation mode	Laser guidance
Control model	Manual/semi-automatic/fully automatic
Obstacle avoidance	Laser
Network communication mode	Support WiFi, 4G and other signal connection

2.4 Scheme of Visualized Data Platform

The visualized data platform (see Fig. 6) connects the intelligent recognition visual algorithm system and the mobile bearing robot. In case of any abnormality or fault found in the inspection, the alarm information will be sent to the workers and management personnel on site in real time, so that the on-site personnel can locate the abnormal or fault information. At the same time, the manager can check the on-site production situation remotely. The client-side display of the visualized data platform mainly includes the field operator terminal, the dedicated handheld mobile device terminal and the remote view PC terminal. According to the authority classification, the field situation can be viewed and exception recovery operation can be carried out.

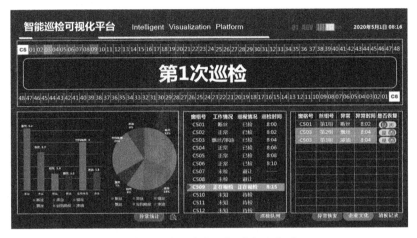

Fig. 6. Scheme of visualized data platform

2.5   Network Architecture of Robot

The spinning inspection robot conducts the communication and interaction of various information through the network. The information includes the distribution of inspection tasks, the feedback of task execution results, the display of statistical data, etc. The network connection objects involve servers, robots, switches, wireless AP, clients, monitors, etc. See Fig. 7 for the schematic diagram of network connection. The database service and RCS server are deployed in the central computer room (in this project, the server is placed in the field cabinet). The active-standby mode can be adopted for the database server and the RCS server according to the needs to improve the disaster recovery ability. AGV, the robot upper computer and other intelligent devices are connected to the network through the wireless AP to communicate with RCS. The web client and monitoring client can be of ordinary PCs, connected to the server through the switch.

As an industrial production network, AGV needs to use the frequency band exclusively, 2.4G or 5.8G band independently. At the same time, in order to ensure the uniqueness of IP address management, the MAC address binding method is adopted to manage AGV. Through AP installation, the network signal strength is greater than −55 dB, and the Ping 1500 byte packet delay is less than 100 ms; For the edge of warehouse, non-trunk channel and other non-core business areas and AGV non-cluster areas, the signal strength is recommended to be greater than −65 dB and not less than −68 dB, and the delay of the Ping 1500 byte packet is less than 200 ms.

3   Scheme Test

3.1   Test Index

This paper tests the effect and efficiency of inspection. The inspection efficiency refers to the time for the robot to inspect a production line except for avoiding obstacles. The inspection effect refers to the statistics of detection rate and false detection rate of

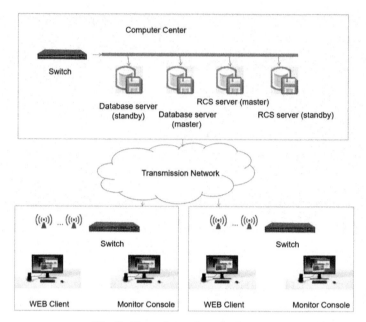

Fig. 7. Network topology deployment

spinning exception recognition. The detection rate refers to the percentage of correct detection quantity of each exception by the robot and the manual detection quantity, As shown in Eq. (1). The false detection rate refers to the percentage of the number of errors detected by the robot for each exception to the total number detected by the robot, as shown in Eqs. (2) and (3).

$$DR = RCDN/MDN \times 100\% \tag{1}$$

Here DR is Detection rate,RCDN is robot correct detection number and MDN is manual detection number

$$FDR = (TRDN - RCDN)/TRDN \tag{2}$$

$$TRDN = RCDN + RFDN \tag{3}$$

Here FDR is False detection rate, TRDN is total robot detection number and RCDN is robot false detection number.

3.2   Test Plan

A program is written in the robot, which records the start time and end time (including moving time) for the robot to reach the spinning position for inspection. By detecting 500 spinning positions, the average detection time of each spinning position is calculated, and the inspection effect is obtained, as shown in Table 2. According to Table 2, the

Table 2. Statistical table of spinning position detection time (program output)

Spinning position number	Test start time	Test end time	Test efficiency (s)
617	2020-05-10 18:05:16	2020-05-10 18:06:31	0:01:15
618	2020-05-10 18:09:51	2020-05-10 18:10:31	0:00:40
619	2020-05-10 18:16:11	2020-05-10 18:17:31	0:01:20
......	......	......	......
516	2020-05-10 19:09:15	2020-05-10 19:10:05	0:00:50
517	2020-05-10 19:11:16	2020-05-10 19:12:05	0:00:49

slowest time 40 s, the fastest time 83 s, and the average time 63 s of the inspection efficiency are calculated.

In this paper, the corresponding test plan is made for the artificial exception test and the actual inspection task, and the exception detection rate and false detection rate are recorded and calculated. The artificial exception test is first to randomly select 30 spinning positions, then artificially make each exception 5 times, and then inspect the robot designated spinning position, and the exception detection situation is recorded, as shown in Table 3. According to Eqs. (2) and (3), the detection rate is about 99%, and the false detection rate is about 3%. The actual inspection task test is to manually follow and detect three periodic tasks randomly selected from the 24-h continuous inspection tasks for 7 consecutive days. The test statistics are shown in Table 4, where the detection rate is about 98%, and the false detection rate is about 5%

Table 3. Statistical table of artificial exception test

Spinning position number	Exception type	Machine inspection (Yes/No)	Note
619	Floating impurity	Yes	
623	Wire hook	Yes	
512	String wire	No	Thin wire
......	......	......	......
532	Spinning breakage		
579	String wire	Yes	

3.3 Test Results

According to the test index given in Sect. 3.1, we conduct the inspection according to the test plan in Sect. 3.2. Actual good inspection effect is achieved, the detection rate is x, and the false detection rate is x. As shown in Fig. 8, the main reasons for false detection in the test are: (1) complicated shooting background; (2) Interference

Table 4. Actual inspection task test statistics

Day	Period	Spinning position	Machine inspection	Human inspection
1	1	501	Floating impurity	Floating impurity
1	1	543	Floating impurity/String wire	Floating impurity
1	1	562	Floating impurity	Ok
......	......	......	......	......
3	3	612	Floating impurity	Floating impurity
3	3	636	Floating impurity	Ok

of ambient light; (3) Mechanical vibration; (4) Waste wire suspending. As shown in Fig. 9, the main reasons for exception detection failures are: (1) the spinning process is a dynamic and fast winding state, which leads to the "unreal transformation" of the detection target partially; (2) Metal reflection causes excessive exposure of the image taken, which cannot be detected; (3) Because the wire is too thin, the camera cannot capture the wire and it cannot be detected.

Fig. 8. Examples of false inspection pictures

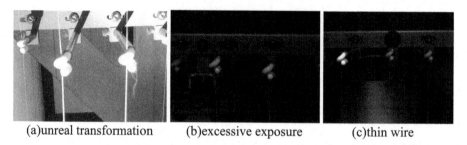

(a)unreal transformation   (b)excessive exposure   (c)thin wire

Fig. 9. Examples of undetected pictures

4   Conclusions

Based on the AGV chassis equipped with high-definition visual recognition system, the spinning inspection robot is designed to realize the periodic inspection task of the planning path; the exception detection with the help of the visual inspection system based on geometric calculation possesses the advantages of high accuracy, simple maintenance and low cost; and the network transmission mode is adopted to realize real-time data collection, statistics and feedback. Through the visual platform, the on-site operator can understand the exception situation in real time and remove the abnormal situation.

Acknowledgement. This work was supported in part by the key research and development plan of Zhejiang Province (No. 2019C01039 and No. 2021C03019) and a project of Zhejiang Provincial Department of Education (No. Y201840303).

References

1. Rong, Z., Guan, X., Yang, T.: Industry brands development report of China chemical fibers. Text. Sci. Res. (9), 14–19 (2017)
2. Wan, L.: Intelligent manufacturing development status and trend of China chemical fiber industry. China Synt. Fiber Ind. **041**(006), 36–41 (2018)
3. Yu, C., Liu, Y., Wang, Y., et al.: Application of green intelligent manufacturing in chemical fiber industry. Synth. Fiber China (8) (2020)
4. Cheng, M., Li, J.: Application of intelligent inspection robot and problem analysis. Zhongguo Gaoxin Keji **77**(17), 73–74 (2020)
5. Xie, S.: Application and Research of Intelligent Patrol Robot in 500 kV Transformer SUBSTATION. South China University of Technology, Guangzhou (2019)
6. Wei, W.: The Location and Navigation System of Substation Inspecting Robot Based on RTK GPS. Harbin Institute of Technology, Harbin (2015)
7. Guo, Z.: Research on 3D Reconstruction Technology Based on Binocular Stereo Vision. Guizhou Normal University, Guiyang (2016)
8. Bi, W.: Research on Dimension Recognition of Mechanical Parts Based on Machine Vision. Shandong University, Jinan (2006)
9. Angrisani, L., Daponte, P., Pietrosanto, A., et al.: An image-based measurement system for the characterisation of automotive gaskets. Measurement **25**(3), 169–181 (1999)
10. Lu, R.S., Li, Y.F., Yu, Q.: On-line measurement of the straightness of seamless steel pipes using machine vision technique. Sens. Actuators A **94**(1–2), 95–101 (2001)
11. Xiao, G., Li, Y., Xia, Q., et al.: Research on the on-line dimensional accuracy measurement method of conical spun work-pieces based on machine vision technology. Measurement **148**, 106881 (2019)
12. Peng, X., Luan, Y.Q., Guo, R., et al.: Research of the laser navigation system for the intelligent patrol robot. Autom. Instrument. **27**, 5–9 (2012)
13. Xu, Q., Xu, Z.-W., Du, X.-F.: Vision navigation AGV system based on QR code. Transd. Microsyst. Technol. (2019)

Liquid Metal-Enabled Soft Actuators for Untethered Manipulation

Tian-Ying Liu[1,2] (ID), Jiao Ye[1,2] (ID), Jun-Heng Fu[1,2] (ID), Dong-Dong Li[1,3] (ID),
and Jing Liu[1,2,4(✉)] (ID)

[1] Beijing Key Laboratory of Cryo-Biomedical Engineering, CAS Key Laboratory
of Cryogenics, Technical Institute of Physics and Chemistry, Chinese Academy of Sciences,
Beijing 100190, China
jliu@mail.ipc.ac.cn
[2] School of Future Technology, University of Chinese Academy of Sciences,
Beijing 100049, China
[3] School of Engineering Science, University of Chinese Academy of Sciences,
Beijing 100049, China
[4] Department of Biomedical Engineering, School of Medicine, Tsinghua University,
Beijing 100084, China

Abstract. Recently, the newly emerging soft robotics has attracted extensive interest because of its flexible actuating strategies, compatibility for various working occasions, and safe interaction with humans. Among the various strategies to actuate soft devices, the very one based on magnetic manipulation is promising as the untethered control will be beneficial for the ultimate autonomy of soft robots. Therefore, the development of magnetic responsive materials as well as proper soft structures, should be taken into consideration. The room-temperature liquid metal (LM) has recently become a promising kind of functional material due to its unique characteristics. Moreover, the superiority of LM to construct soft composites with multi-functions will expand its role in the field of soft robots. Here in this article, a kind of functional multilayer structure assisted by soft magnetic LMs was introduced, which featured magnetic responsiveness, ease of fabrication, and flexibility of usage. Based on this structure, a series of soft actuators with specific configurations were proposed and manufactured. Motions about terrestrial locomotion, jumping, and periodical flowering were fulfilled, respectively. Furthermore, two occasions about load transportation and electrical switch were performed to prove their potentials in practical use. We hope that such a magnetic LM enabled structure can have more applications in advanced soft robots in the future.

Keywords: Liquid metal · Magnetic manipulation · Soft actuator · Untethered control

1 Introduction

Since its inception, the newly emerging soft robotics has been closely coupled with bionics and materials, which possesses a variety of actuating strategies such as electrical

X.-J. Liu et al. (Eds.): ICIRA 2021, LNAI 13013, pp. 412–421, 2021.
https://doi.org/10.1007/978-3-030-89095-7_40

stimulus [1, 2], magnetism [3, 4], heating [5], lighting [6, 7], hydraulics [8, 9] and pneumatics [10]. Among these options, the magnetic manipulation is an advantageous one, where the non-contact control can unleash the device from outer lumpish facility, which will be beneficial for the goal of robotic autonomy and adaptation for different working occasions. Besides, the regulation of direction or intensity from magnetic fields can also be quite convenient and accurate, thus enabling a programmable and adjustable motion of soft robots [4]. However, the soft material capable of magnetic responsiveness is a major challenge, because most of the ferromagnetic substances obtains rigid morphology. Therefore, trying to import ferromagnetism into systems of soft material and further construct proper flexible structure for actuation, deserve more dedicated researches.

The liquid metal (LM) refers to a series of pure metals or alloys which show low melting points around room temperature. Applications related to LMs have been vastly broadened including the advanced thermal management [11, 12], soft electronics [13, 14] and biomedical treatment [15, 16]. Besides, the characteristic of easily being oxidized has enabled the LM to become an excellent substrate to construct functional soft composites, which can well reconcile different properties including flexible conductivity, adjustable fluidity and so on. For example, particles of Ni, Fe, and NdFeB have been tried to mix with LMs to build magnetic-responsive material [17–19], which played a role in dynamically conducting or healing soft circuits. Considering the robotic demands about soft materials, the LM-based responsive composites is a promising candidate and should be tried more.

Herein this study, a kind of functional actuating structure was proposed based on magnetic LMs, which featured good magnetic responsiveness, flexible shaping, and ease of manufacture. Based on this structure, a series of untethered soft actuators were fabricated with specific capacities about terrestrial locomotion and jumping. The potential of these actuators in practical applications were also proved as well. This study exhibits a strategy about fast preparation of magnetic-driven device. The LM holds great convenience for helping make magnetic soft structures, and the untethered manipulation represents an available method toward the goal of full autonomy for soft robots.

2 Materials and Basic Structure

In this chapter, the preparation of magnetic LMs was introduced, and its relevant characteristics were tested and regulated, which could help get a better understanding of this material. Afterwards, the basic manufacture of functional structure was interpreted as well.

2.1 Magnetic LM and Its Characteristics

The magnetic LM was prepared based on nonmagnetic EGaIn ($Ga_{75.5}In_{24.5}$) and magnetic NdFeB microparticles (average size of 10 μm, purity of 75%). The oxide layers of LM can play a role as adhesives to wrap other components for firm mixing. After being weighed in proper proportion, these raw materials were completely mixed by a stirrer with 500 r/min for 2 h (Fig. 1a). Finally, the magnetic paste-like composites were obtained (shown in Fig. 1b). The scanning electron micrograph (SEM) of tested samples showed that the NdFeB microparticles were evenly distributed in the EGaIn matrix (Fig. 1c). Such a distinction was quite vital for the magnetic functionality of the material, for it would influence the evenness of forces under the external stimulus. Besides, the magnetic LMs applied in our devices would not be magnetized, which could help avoid possible agglomeration due to perturbation from such an operation.

Fig. 1. Preparation of magnetic LMs. a) The schematic of technological procedure. b) The image of the silvery and paste-like material. c) SEM results of the magnetic LM.

The attaching performance, which determines the closeness between magnetic LMs and soft substrates, was evaluated at first. The adhesion of sample on a polyethylene terephthalate (PET) film (also chosen as the soft substrate in our applications) was tested with a surface tensiometer (Dataphysics DCAT21, Beijing Eastern-Dataphy Instruments Co., Ltd., China). Four kinds of samples with different contents about NdFeB in 0%, 5%, 15%, and 25% were prepared. Bars in Fig. 2a shows that the increase of solid particles could reduce the fluidity of LM for better adhesion on PET substrates. However, an excessive ratio of solid particles would obstruct the continuous phase state of LM, thus destroying the stability of composites. In our practical usage, the proportion of NdFeB was chosen as 25%. Furthermore, Fig. 2b visually described the steady adhesion of samples (25% of NdFeB) on PET with different dip angles, once again proving its good usage in more working occasions.

The magnetic responsiveness of material was directly related to the blended NdFeB particles. When in its dormant state, the random directions of magnetic moments from those tiny particles led to nonmagnetic status about the overall material [20]. However, after being approached to an external magnetic field, a magnetic force in the direction of the maximum gradient about magnetic field would be induced. To evaluate the responsiveness, a test was conducted that focused on the minimum magnetic field to activate the material. As shown in Fig. 2c, a vertically-fixed permanent magnet was assigned as the only external magnetic source. The flux density would vary related to the distance away from the surface, which could be measured by a teslameter. Samples of magnetic LMs were uniformly coated on the surface of a small piece of PET film (1.5 cm × 1.5 cm) with the same dosage (total weight of 0.26 g), while distinguished by proportion of NdFeB. The maximum distance when the film began moving to the magnet was measured. According to Fig. 2d, the sample with 25% NdFeB showed the maximum value of the actuating height at 2.2 cm (equivalently about 97 mT), while the sample with 5% NdFeB exhibited the height at 1.5 cm (equivalently about 48 mT). The results could be interpreted referring to the following equation,

$$F_{mag} = \frac{m\Delta\chi}{\rho\mu_0}(\nabla B)B \tag{1}$$

where m was the mass of NdFeB, $\Delta\chi$ was the dimensionless parameter about deviation in magnetic susceptibilities, ρ was the density of NdFeB, μ_0 was the permeability of vacuum, B was magnetic flux density and ∇B was magnetic field gradient, respectively [21]. Therefore, the amount of NdFeB mixed in would directly affect the minimum magnetic intensity for actuation. Putting all these together, we thought that the choice of 25% NdFeB was quite proper for our applications.

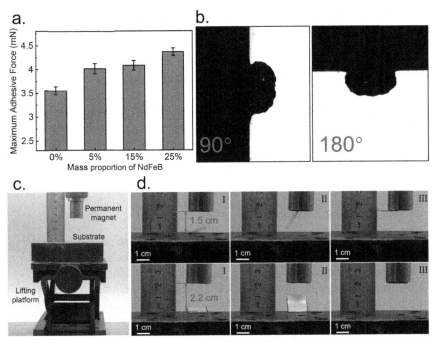

Fig. 2. Characterization about the magnetic LMs. a) A bar chart about the adhesive forces of different samples. b) Images about the test to prove the stickiness of samples, where the samples were sticked to surfaces with angles of 90° and 180°. c) Details about the testing platform for magnetic responsiveness. d) Snapshots about actual responses of different samples.

2.2 Preparation of Soft Magnetic Structure

The soft magnetic structure obtained a sandwich configuration. The bottom layer made of PET film (50 μm thick) was the actuating unit which could perform energy transmission between external stimulus and elastic deformation, finally realizing various motions. The film showed enough mechanical strength with good flexibility, so it could perform large elastic deformation with different patterns, determining the moving mode in practice.

The middle layer was coated with magnetic LMs that would respond to external magnetic field and induce force effects, ensuring untethered control. Besides, there was another more layer of packaging to protect the structure for longer use. Here we applied a kind of waterborne polyurethane (PU2834, Guangzhou Guanzhi New Material Technology Co., Ltd., China) that exhibited good toughness to adapt to frequent deformation.

Manufacture of this multilayered structure was quite easy as well. After the substrate layer of PET was prepared, magnetic LMs should be smeared uniformly on the surface of PET with a brush, the thickness of which was usually controlled within 200 μm to make a balance between responsiveness and overall weight. As for packaging, the PU2834 was first mixed with a little water with a mass ratio of 10:1, and then painted on the metal layer to form a thin liquid film. The object should be placed in ambient environment for two hours until the sealing layer was solidified. Furthermore, an annealing process would be quite efficient to help tailor its structure if the substrate layer needed a complex spatial shape.

3 Soft Actuators Based on the Functional Structure

Based on the structure introduced above, herein we exhibited two kinds of prototypes for various soft actuation. With their own configuration design, motions about terrestrial locomotion and jumping were fulfilled, respectively. Furthermore, two occasions about load transportation and electrical switch were performed to prove their potentials in practical use.

3.1 A Soft Wriggling Actuator

The soft wriggling actuator presented here obtained a concise pattern with a 50 mm-by-25 mm curved soft body made of PET, the layer of magnetic LMs being an effector. Details of manufacture was shown in Fig. 3a.

Among various strategies to drive a soft structure for locomotion, a universal principle is breaking the existing mechanical equilibrium of the system to cause a nonstationary state, and thus the device will make itself move to convert to a new stable state for stillness. Following this strategy, a modification was conducted for the "feet" of the actuator, which contacted with the ground and generated frictional forces. As shown in Fig. 3a, a small piece of plane PET film was sticked to one foot while another kept bare. Such a handling would bring obvious distinction about the frictional effect between the actuator and the ground. The area to paint magnetic LMs was symmetrically located on the body. Therefore, when an external magnetic field was applied vertically just below the coated area, the magnetic force would drag the elastic PET body to bend down and cause reciprocal movements of the two feet. Since the magnetic dragging was quite strong, the slipping distance of each foot was not obviously different from the other. However, when the magnetic field was removed and the body returned to its initial shape with elastic energy released, the distinct resistances with the ground began to play a role. The very one with stronger frictional effect would actually anchor the actuator, compelling the other one to slip back more to match up with the reverting of elastic body, and finally achieved a certain directional moving (also interpreted in Fig. 3b). To sum up, in each period of exerting and removing external magnetic field, this soft actuator would wriggle forward via periodically elongating and contracting together with the differentiated frictional effects, which was similar with the locomotion of some kinds of annelids in nature.

Figure 3c depicted the details of our soft actuator in a single moving cycle of about 0.58 s, where the applied magnetic field was about 350 mT (generated from a permanent magnet and operated manually) at the position of ground. The motion could be divided into two stages of bending down and springing back. The first three photos about stage one showed that the front edge had a tiny movement, while locomotion in stage two was more prominent due to the release of elastic energy. Compared with its initial position, the actuator finally exceeded around 0.5 cm. When such a moving became periodically repeated, the actuator exhibited a smooth and deft locomotion, which proved the availability of this mode for continuous movement of soft structures.

To show the practicability of this kind of wriggling soft actuator, a conceptual application about loading transportation was conducted. To be specific, a small weight of 2.0 g was assigned as the task load to be put on its back, while the empty weight of this actuator was only 0.26 g. As Fig. 3d showed, the actuator accomplished the whole journey of 12.4 cm in 97 s, with an average speed of 0.13 cm s^{-1}. Performances of the actuator were generally steady, and the load did not creep down either. For further applications, its load capacity could be focused on, which was directly related to the elastic energy released during its spring back, because such an energy would pay for the gravitational potential energy from the load. Besides, the initial structure must be able to bear the load, which should also be considered.

To conclude, considering the elasticity and magnetic responsiveness of the structure, we designed a moving strategy based on differentiated frictional effects that was inspired by nature. The periodically exerting of external magnetic field enabled periodical elastic deformation of the soft body, thus leading to two sliding in every cycle. Frictional differences between the front and the back finally triggered movements. The soft actuator showed good performance of continuously steady motion, and further demonstrated its practical potential in carrying loads, which was almost ten times of its weight.

3.2 A Multi-petal Soft Actuator with Multiple Functions

In this section, we proposed another new configuration of soft actuator. This prototype featured a flower-like shape owning several independent petals with magnetic LMs coated. Such a design implied the desire to realize an acting mode of stretching and shrinking, which could be further applied for grasping, jumping and some other needs. Meanwhile, an external magnetic field would be preset below the device. Since the layer of magnetic LMs was too thin to ensure a satisfying magnetization with fixed magnetic direction, the external field mainly provided a dragging effect to actuate the petal. By controlling the magnetic field, more complex combinations of manipulation could be fulfilled. Specific cases are shown in the following.

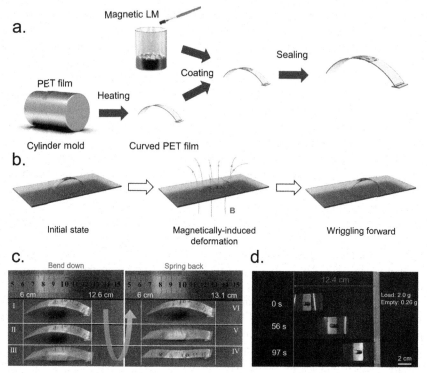

Fig. 3. A soft wriggling actuator. a) Manufacture about the actuator. b) The schematic about the moving mechanism of the actuator. c) Snapshots about the movements of the actuator. d) The test of loading transportation.

3.2.1   Jumping

Jumping is an important athletic ability for animals, which is also valuable for manual actuators in discovery and rescue. Here we demonstrated the jumping motion of the soft actuator.

Since the jumping was a kind of powerful process within rapid time, the maximum elastic energy to acquire and the period to release energy were of priority. Details about one jump about the device was shown in Fig. 4a, where the applied magnetic field was about 450 mT at the position of ground. The process could be divided into three stages. In the first step of bending, dragging from the external magnetic field would induce a maximum deformation of the actuator to gather elastic energy. Then a sudden disappearing of magnetic effect would free the actuator from restrains, so the structure would return to its original shape and convert elastic energy into kinetic energy thus letting it jump up into the air. Finally, it would drop down on the ground, and the configuration of six legs ensured enough supporting points for a stable landing.

With a further expectation about jumping forward of the actuator, we can make some more improvements. For example, the length of six legs need not be equal. If we cut the length of two adjacent petals, then the actuator will obtain an initial angle with horizonal plane. Repeating the operations above and the device will get a directional jump, which means jumping forward. The angle will be closely related to the distance it can achieve, which can also be easily regulated by the very length of two shorted adjacent petals.

3.2.2 Electrical Switch

Here we conceptually showed the application for this kind of actuator as electrical switch for flexible electronics. The shape was modified into four petals for practical needs and the coated area was enlarged as well (Fig. 4b). To demonstrate that ability, we prepared a flexible circuit painted on the paper, which was also made of the magnetic LMs with good conductivity, to light two light-emitting diodes (LEDs). The circuit was not thoroughly connected, which was just the function of the four-petal device. To be specific, it was placed around the position of disconnection.

When there was no external magnetic field, the device maintained its original state, the spanning length between two opposite petals was shorter than that of disconnection, so the circuit was still open with two LEDs off (Fig. 4c). As the magnetic field was applied (about 450 mT at the position of ground), the soft structure was dragged down to the ground and the length of two opposite ends about petals was extended, just matching the broken distance. Therefore, the circuit was switched on with two LEDs lighting (Fig. 4d).

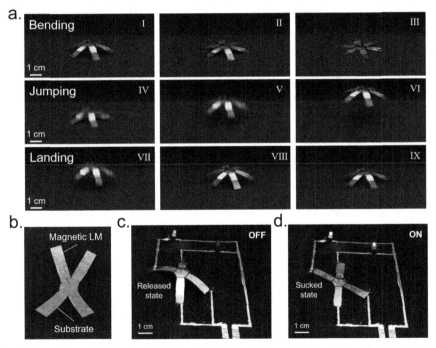

Fig. 4. A multi-petal soft actuator. a) Snapshots about the vertical jumping of the actuator. b) Image about the modified type for electrical switch. c) The off state of the circuit where the actuator maintained its original shape. d) The on state of the circuit with the connection due to the deformation of actuator.

Although the device here is only an easy demonstration, it is entirely possible to fulfill more functions with essential adjustments. For example, if the magnetic LMs painted on different pairs of petals are magnetized with specific directions, the device can realize more switching like interlocking. Besides, increasing the number of petals will also enable it to control circuits with more branches.

4 Conclusion

Human's fascination about functional soft entity to mimic natural creatures has lasted for decades. The development of smart materials as well as the innovation of soft structures, will basically determine the blooming of more advanced soft robots in the future. Here in this article, a kind of functional multilayer structure assisted by magnetic LMs was introduced, which exhibited magnetic responsiveness, ease of fabrication, and flexibility of usage. Based on this structure, a series of soft actuators with specific configurations were proposed and manufactured. Motions about terrestrial locomotion and jump were fulfilled, respectively. Furthermore, two occasions about load transportation and electrical switch were performed to prove their potentials in practical use. Further applications based on these configurations can also be broadened. Taking the jumping prototype as an example, it can be designed to grasp or release substances regularly and used in occasions of small scale like drug delivery. Moreover, such an acting mode is similar with the swing of tentacles in some kinds of aquatic mollusks, so it can be considered to perform as a propeller for soft machines in water. In a nutshell, we hope that the magnetic LM enabled actuating structures can have more applications in the future.

Acknowledgements. This work was partially supported by NSFC under Grants No. 81701850, 91748206 and 51890839, and the Frontier Project of the Chinese Academy of Sciences.

Conflict of Interest. The authors declare no conflict of interest.

References

1. Wu, Y., et al.: Insect-scale fast moving and ultrarobust soft robot. Sci. Rob. **4**(32), eaax1594 (2019)
2. Ujjaval, G., Lei, Q., Yuzhe, W., Hareesh, G., Jian, Z.: Soft robots based on dielectric elastomer actuators: a review. Smart Mater. Struct. **28**(10), 103002 (2019)
3. Hu, W., Lum, G.Z., Mastrangeli, M., Sitti, M.: Small-scale soft-bodied robot with multimodal locomotion. Nature **554**(7690), 81–85 (2018)
4. Kim, Y., Yuk, H., Zhao, R., Chester, S.A., Zhao, X.: Printing ferromagnetic domains for untethered fast-transforming soft materials. Nature **558**(7709), 274–279 (2018)
5. Miriyev, A., Stack, K., Lipson, H.: Soft material for soft actuators. Nat. Commun. **8**(1), 596 (2017)
6. Zhao, Y., et al.: Soft phototactic swimmer based on self-sustained hydrogel oscillator. Sci. Rob. **4**(33), 7112 (2019)
7. Hiraki, T., et al.: Laser pouch motors: selective and wireless activation of soft actuators by laser-powered liquid-to-gas phase change. IEEE Robot. Autom. Lett. **5**(3), 4180–4187 (2020)

8. Yuk, H., Lin, S., Ma, C., Takaffoli, M., Fang, N.X., Zhao, X.: Hydraulic hydrogel actuators and robots optically and sonically camouflaged in water. Nat. Commun. **8**, 14230 (2017)
9. Must, I., Sinibaldi, E., Mazzolai, B.: A variable-stiffness tendril-like soft robot based on reversible osmotic actuation. Nat. Commun. **10**(1), 344 (2019)
10. Wehner, M., et al.: An integrated design and fabrication strategy for entirely soft, autonomous robots. Nature **536**(7617), 451–455 (2016)
11. Yang, X.-H., Tan, S.-C., He, Z.-Z., Liu, J.: Finned heat pipe assisted low melting point metal PCM heat sink against extremely high power thermal shock. Energy Convers. Manage. **160**, 467–476 (2018)
12. Yang, X.-H., Tan, S.-C., Liu, J.: Thermal management of Li-ion battery with liquid metal. Energy Convers. Manage. **117**, 577–585 (2016)
13. Leber, A., Dong, C., Chandran, R., Das Gupta, T., Bartolomei, N., Sorin, F.: Soft and stretchable liquid metal transmission lines as distributed probes of multimodal deformations. Nat. Electron. **3**, 316–326 (2020)
14. Li, Q., Lin, J., Liu, T.-Y., Zhu, X.-Y., Yao, W.-H., Liu, J.: Gas-mediated liquid metal printing toward large-scale 2D semiconductors and ultraviolet photodetector. NPJ 2D Mater. Appl. **5**(1), 36 (2021)
15. Zhu, P., et al.: Inorganic nanoshell-stabilized liquid metal for targeted photonanomedicine in NIR-II biowindow. Nano Lett. **19**(3), 2128–2137 (2019)
16. Fan, L., et al.: Injectable and radiopaque liquid metal/calcium alginate hydrogels for endovascular embolization and tumor embolotherapy. Small **16**(2), 1903421 (2019)
17. Ma, B., Xu, C., Chi, J., Chen, J., Zhao, C., Liu, H.: A versatile approach for direct patterning of liquid metal using magnetic field. Adv. Funct. Mater. **29**(28), 1901370 (2019)
18. Guo, R., Sun, X., Yuan, B., Wang, H., Liu, J.: Magnetic liquid metal (Fe-EGaIn) based multifunctional electronics for remote self-healing materials, degradable electronics, and thermal transfer printing. Adv. Sci. (Weinh) **6**(20), 1901478 (2019)
19. Cao, L., et al.: Ferromagnetic liquid metal plasticine with transformed shape and reconfigurable polarity. Adv. Mater. **32**(17), 2000827 (2020)
20. Deng, H., Sattari, K., Xie, Y., Liao, P., Yan, Z., Lin, J.: Laser reprogramming magnetic anisotropy in soft composites for reconfigurable 3D shaping. Nat. Commun. **11**(1), 6325 (2020)
21. Chen, R., et al.: Magnetically controllable liquid metal marbles. Adv. Mater. Interfaces **6**(20), 1901057 (2019)

Design and Modeling of a Multi-joint Reinforced Soft Pneumatic Actuator

Wei-Bin Xu and Xiao-Jun Yang[✉]

School of Mechanical Engineering and Automation, Harbin Institute of Technology,
Shenzhen, China
yangxiaojun@hit.edu.cn

Abstract. In order to improve the tip force and controllability of soft pneumatic actuator (SPA), this paper presents the design principle and mathematical modeling method of a multi-joint reinforced soft pneumatic actuator (MRSPA). The MRSPA is composed of an equivalent three driven joints and a spring leaf on the bottom of the MRSPA. Through finite element analysis (FEA), the influence of different chamber distribution on the bending performance of a single joint under the same length is explored. In addition, a mathematical model is established to explore the relationship between pressure, load and bending angle of the driven joints and to estimate the curved configuration of the MRSPA. The FEA results show that the uniform chamber distribution is easier to enable the two-way bending of the SPA. The mathematical model of the MRSPA is validated by comparing the simulation results based on the mathematical model with the FEA results.

The main contribution of this paper is to establish a mathematical model to estimate the tip force and configuration of the MRSPA at the same time.

Keywords: Soft pneumatic actuator · Curved configuration · Tip force

1 Introduction

In the field of large-scale production that requires precise control and repetition, rigid robots have shown better performance. However, rigid robots perform poorly when the interactive environment is uncertain[1]. Compared with rigid robots, soft robots have lower rigidity and are mainly composed of stretchable flexible materials. In the face of uncertain working environments, soft robots have better flexibility and adaptability. When collaborating with people, soft robots also show better safety [2]. The research focus of soft robots is on the motion characteristics [3]. The movement characteristics are mainly determined by the driving method, structure and material. The driving mode of the flexible robot mainly includes pneumatic actuation [4], variable length tendon [5], shape memory alloys [6] and so on. Silicon rubber is the main material [7].

Gripping is an important application of soft robots. Soft pneumatic actuator (SPA) is the most widely used in the field of soft crawling. Early SPA can only achieve internal unidirectional bending under air pressure [8]. Hao et al. designed a variable length SPA [9]. This SPA is entirely made of elastic materials, and can be driven by air pressure

© Springer Nature Switzerland AG 2021
X.-J. Liu et al. (Eds.): ICIRA 2021, LNAI 13013, pp. 422–432, 2021.
https://doi.org/10.1007/978-3-030-89095-7_41

to achieve bidirectional in-plane bending, which enhances its grasping ability. On this basis, Hao et al. optimized the design of the SPA [10]. The influence of different geometric parameters and material combinations on the motion characteristics of soft-body actuators is explored. However, the possible influence of different chamber distributions is not considered. Yap et al. designed a SPA with greater gripping power [11]. It uses a more rigid flexible material and is prepared by 3D printing, which can output a greater gripping force. Inspired by the Venus flytrap, Wang et al. designed a bi-stable reinforced SPA [12]. By adding spring leaf in the SPA, the gripping force of the actuator is greatly increased. Although SPA has the safety and adaptability that rigid robots do not have in the field of gripping, its movement is uncertain and it is difficult to achieve precise control. Alici et al. established an analytical model to estimate the quasi-static bending displacement of SPA [13]. The model derives the relationship between the driving air pressure and the bending angle of the SPA. The relationship curve between driving air pressure and blocking force is measured through experiments. However, this model does not give the curved configuration of SPA under the action of pressure and blocking force. In addition, the above-mentioned SPA has only one degree of freedom in the plane and cannot realize segmented bending control. This limits the flexibility of SPA to a certain extent.

In this paper, a multi-joint reinforced soft pneumatic actuator (MRSPA) is designed by synthesizing the research results obtained by the predecessors. The actuator contains three bending joints, which can realize segmented bending control. By using finite element analysis (FEA) simulation, we explored the influence of the chamber distribution on the bending of the actuator. Then we choose the appropriate chamber distribution to design MRSPA. Using FEA simulation, the relationship between pressure, load and bending angle was explored. We also established a mathematical model to control the curved configuration and the tip force of the MRSPA. By comparing the calculation results of the mathematical model with the FEA results, we proved the validity of the mathematical model.

2 Design

2.1 Driven Joint Structure Design and Optimization

Combining the previous research on the SPA that can bend in both directions [10], high-strength SPA [11] and reinforced SPA [12], we designed a reinforced soft pneumatic actuator (RSPA). RSPA bends inward under pressurization and outward under depressurization. The structural dimensions of RSPA are shown in Fig. 1(a) and 1(b). s represents the distance between the inner walls of the chamber. $s = 3$ mm. t_1 represents the thickness of the chamber wall. $t_1 = 1.2$ mm. t_3 represents the total thickness of the bottom layer including the spring steel sheet. $t_3 = 1.4$ mm. l represents the total length of the driven joint. $l = 36.6$ mm. t_2 represents the thickness of the side wall of the chamber. $t_2 = 1$ mm. h_1 represents the height of the wedged top of the chamber. $h_1 = 5$ mm. h_2 represents the height of the low part of the chamber. $h_2 = 7$ mm. b and b represent the length and width of the passage. $b_1 = 2$ mm. $b_2 = 4$ mm. w_s represents the width of the bottom spring steel sheet. $w_s = 20$ mm. t_s represents the thickness of the bottom spring leaf. $t_s = 0.2$ mm. $h = 14.6$ mm. $w = 30$ mm. We design the top of the RSPA chamber as a wedge-shaped structure, which is conducive to improving the outward bending performance of the RSPA. We also add spring leaf in the middle of the bottom layer of RSPA. The material of spring leaf is 65Mn steel. The spring steel sheet can not only increase the rigidity of RSPA and enhance its load-bearing capacity, but also act as a strain-limiting layer at the bottom, limiting the elongation of RSPA during bending and deformation. RSPA uses NinjaFlex (NinjaTex, PA) material. This material has a Shore hardness of 85A, which enables RSPA to output a greater tip force.

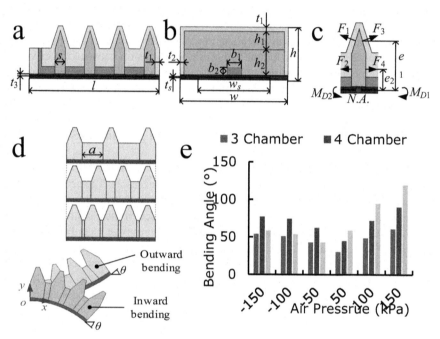

Fig. 1. Design and FEA results under different chamber distribution of the RSPA. (a) Longitudinal section of RSPA. (b) Cross-sectional view of RSPA. (c) Internal force diagram of chambers. (d) Different chamber distribution of RSPA. (e)The bending angles of the RSPA under different chamber distribution and pressure.

In order to explore the influence of different chamber distribution on the bending characteristics of RSPA, we established three RSPA models with the same length but different number of chambers. As shown in Fig. 1(d). The bending angle (θ) represents the angle between the tangent direction of arc end and the horizontal direction. a represents the distance between the outer walls of the chamber, and the distribution structure of the chamber can be adjusted by changing the value of a. In the three-chamber distribution, $a = 7.2$ mm $> s$. In the four-chamber distribution, $a = 3$ mm $= s$. In five-chamber distribution, $a = 0.9$ mm $< s$. θ is the angle between the tangent direction and the horizontal direction at the end of the bottom bending section. θ represent the bending angle of the RSPA. RSPA bends inward under pressurization and outward under depressurization.

We adjust the density of the RSPA chamber distribution by changing the space between the walls of the chamber (a).

We import the RSPA model into the FEA software ABAQUS (ABAQUS 6.14; SIMU-LIA Inc., France) for simulation. According to [11], We use the Ogden model with parameter values $N = 3, \alpha_1 = 0.508, \mu_1 = -30.921$ MPa, $\alpha_2 = 1.375, \mu_2 = 10.342$ MPa, $\alpha_3 = -0.482, \mu_3 = 26.791$ MPa. According to the simulation analysis results in Fig. 1(e), we found that the sparse chamber distribution will weaken the bidirectional bending ability of RSPA. At this time, the cavity wall spacing (s) is smaller than the cavity wall spacing (a). When s is equal to a, the chamber distribution is more uniform. RSPA obtains the best outward bending ability. When s is smaller than a, the chambers are more densely distributed. The outward bending ability of RSPA is weakened, and the inward bending ability is enhanced. According to the FEA results of the different chamber distribution, we chose the four-chamber RSPA as the joint structure, which can achieve better bending performance under both pressurization and depressurization.

2.2 Overall Structure Design of MRSPA

To imitate the grasping characteristics of human fingers, we designed a multi-joint reinforced soft pneumatic actuator (MRSPA). MRSPA contains three bending joints. Each joint can perform independent bending motions. The first joint bends outwards during grasping to increase the grasping range. The second joint and third joint bend inwards to envelope object. The materials of the top layer and bottom layer 1 and bottom layer 2 of MRSPA are all made of NinjaFlex (NinjaTex, PA) and prepared by 3D printing. The spring steel sheet is made of 65Mn steel, which is customized and processed according to the design size.

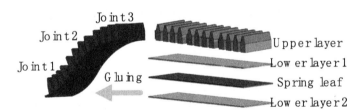

Fig. 2. Overall structure model of MRSPA

3 Modeling

3.1 Determination of Bending Rigidity

Since the RSPA is composed of different materials, the elastic modulus (E) is difficult to determine. In addition, the particularity of the structural design also makes it difficult to accurately calculate the section moment of inertia (I) of RSPA. We use an equivalent method to calculate the flexural stiffness (EI) of RSPA. According to Euler-Bernoulli principle, the bending angle of the RSPA is:

$$\theta = \frac{ML}{EI} \tag{1}$$

θ, M, L and EI are the bending angle, moment, length and bending rigidity of the RSPA. Assuming that the length (L) and bending rigidity (EI) of RSPA are constant, there is a linear function relationship between M and θ. The ratio of L to EI represents the slope. We imported the RSPA model into the FEA software ABAQUS for simulation. By fixing one end of the RSPA, a different moment (M) is applied to the other end. According to the different working conditions of RSPA, we carried out simulation analysis on RSPA inward bending and outward bending. Using the simulation results and the arc fitting program to calculate the bending angle (θ) of RSPA, we can get the linear function between M and θ. According to the slope of the linear function, we can calculate the EI of RSPA. The EI is 0.004570N·m^2 when the RSPA bends outward. The EI is 0.004731N·m^2 when bending inward.

3.2   Relationship Between Pressure and Moment

As the RSPA bending under pressurization, the bottom shape can be approximated as a circular arc. According to the research done in [13], we equate the work done by the driving air pressure of the RSPA to the work done by the driving moment. The driving moment (M_D) is equal to the pulling force multiplied by the offset between the center of pressure and the neutral axis (N.A.). As shown in the Fig. 1(c), the neutral axis is the line of intersection between the neutral layer and the interface. We assume that the neutral layer is located in the middle layer of the spring steel sheets. e_1 and e_2 represent the offset. $e_1 = 4.2$ mm. $e_2 = 6.7$ mm. As the driving air pressure is P, M_D is:

$$M_D = P \cdot [h_2 \cdot (w - 2t_2) \cdot e_1 + h_1 \cdot (w - 2t_2) \cdot e_2] \tag{2}$$

Assuming that the mechanical efficiency of the driving moment in this state is η_1, the relationship between actual moment (M) and M_D is:

$$M = \eta_1 \cdot M_D \tag{3}$$

When the RSPA is in grasping condition, it will interact with the external environment, and the RSPA will be affected by the combined action of the driving air pressure (P) and the load. The mechanical efficiency of the load moment (M_L) is 1 in the ideal state. Assuming that the mechanical efficiency of the driving moment in this state is η_2, the relationship between M, M_D, and M_L is:

$$M = \eta_2 M_D + M_L \tag{4}$$

By applying different air pressures inside the RSPA and different moments at the end, we have obtained a series of simulation results. After calculating the bending angles using the arc fitting method, we solved the corresponding values of η_1 and η_2.

3.3 Mathematic Models of MRSPA

MRSPA needs two steps to perform the grasping work. In the first step, MRSPA is deformed in the plane for the first time under driving air pressure. In the second step, MRSPA that has been deformed comes into contact with the object. The contact force and moment cause MRSPA to be second deformed in the plane. With reference to the flexible cantilever beam analysis method proposed in [14], we modeled the curved configuration of MRSPA in the first step.

Assuming that the neutral layer of MRSPA is located on the middle layer of the bottom spring steel sheet, we discretize MRSPA and establish a coordinate system on the bottom spring steel sheet, as shown in Fig. 3(a). In the first step, the curved configuration and moment of the i-th segment of MRSPA are shown in Fig. 3(b). The moment and deflection parameters of the i-th segment in the first step are normalized as

$$m_{Ii} = \frac{M_{Ii}L}{EI}, \quad l_i = \frac{L_i}{L}, \quad h_i = \frac{H_i}{L}, \quad \rho_i = \frac{R_i}{L} = \frac{1}{\alpha_i}, \quad \alpha_i = \alpha_i \tag{5}$$

M_{Ii}, L_i and H_i, represent the driven moment, the X_i-axis coordinate and the Y_i-axis coordinate at the i-th node in the first step. R_i and α_i represent the bending radius and the bending angle of the i-th segment in the first step. According to the Euler-Bernoulli principle, the derivation is as follows:

$$\frac{1}{R_i} = \frac{M_{Ii}}{EI} \Rightarrow \frac{L}{R_i} = \frac{M_{Ii}L}{EI} \Rightarrow \alpha_i = m_{Ii} \tag{6}$$

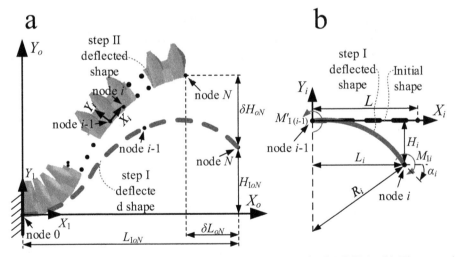

Fig. 3. Mathematical model diagram. (a) Discretization model of MRSPA. (b) The curved configuration and moment of the i-th segment in the first step.

At this time, all segments of MRSPA are arc segments, and the position of the end of the i-th segment in the coordinate system of the i-th segment can be solved according to the geometric relationship:

$$l_i = \frac{\sin \alpha_i}{\alpha_i}, \quad h_i = \frac{1 - \cos \alpha_i}{\alpha_i} \tag{7}$$

After the first step of bending deformation, the bottom sections of MRSPA are all circular arc segments. In the second step, MRSPA will come into contact with the object being grasped and generate force. As the i-th segment completed the first step of deformation, the curved configuration of each driven joint is already a circular arc segment with known curvature. According to the initial bending constraint beam modeling analysis method proposed by [15]. Discrete the i-th segment of MRSPA into N_i units of equal length and establish a corresponding coordinate system. Each unit is represented by j-th, as shown in Fig. 4. F, P and M represent the force parallel to the X-axis, the force parallel to the Y-axis and the moment. γ and λ represent the bending angle in the second step and the increment angle in the second step compared with the first step. δL and δH represent the increment on the X-axis coordination and Y-axis coordination in the second step compared with the first step N_i satisfies:

$$N_i \geq \lceil 10\alpha_i \rceil \tag{8}$$

Since each unit of the i-th segment has the same length, the deflection angle (α_{ij}) of each unit in the respective coordinate system is the same, and the projection length (L_{ij}) of each unit on the X_{ij}-axis in the respective coordinate system is the same. In order to facilitate the writing of expressions, we define:

$$\beta_i = \alpha_{ij} = \frac{\alpha_i}{N_i}, \quad L_{ei} = L_{ij} = R_i \sin \beta_i \tag{9}$$

The physical quantities in the i-th segment and the j-th unit in the i-th segment in the second step of the deformation are processed without dimension:

$$m_i = \frac{M_i L_{ei}}{EI}, \quad f_i = \frac{F_i L_{ei}^2}{EI}, \quad p_i = \frac{P_i L_{ei}^2}{EI}, \quad \delta l_i = \frac{\delta L_i}{L_{ei}}, \quad \delta h_i = \frac{\delta H_i}{L_{ei}},$$
$$l_i = \frac{L_i}{L_{ei}}, \quad h_i = \frac{H_i}{L_{ei}}, \quad x_i = l_i + \delta l_i, \quad y_i = h_i + \delta h_i, \quad \alpha_i = \alpha_i, \quad \gamma_i = \gamma_i \tag{10}$$

$$m_{ij} = \frac{M_{ij} L_{ei}}{EI}, \quad f_{ij} = \frac{F_{ij} L_{ei}^2}{EI}, \quad p_{ij} = \frac{P_{ij} L_{ei}^2}{EI}, \quad \delta l_{ij} = \frac{\delta L_{ij}}{L_{ei}}, \quad \delta h_{ij} = \frac{\delta H_{ij}}{L_{ei}}, \quad l_{ij} = \frac{L_{ij}}{L_{ei}},$$
$$h_{ij} = \frac{H_{ij}}{L_{ei}}, \quad x_{ij} = l_{ij} + \delta l_{ij}, \quad y_{ij} = h_{ij} + \delta h_{ij}, \quad \lambda_{ij} = \lambda_{ij}, \quad \beta_i = \beta_i, \quad \kappa_i = \frac{1}{R_i/L_{ei}}, \quad t_i = \frac{T_i}{L_{ei}} \tag{11}$$

T_i is the thickness of the spring steel sheet at the bottom of MRSPA. According to the i-th discretization model shown in Fig. 4(a), using geometric relations to solve the problem, there are:

$$\alpha_{ij} = (j - 1)\beta_i, \quad \gamma_{ij} = \alpha_{ij} + \sum_{k=1}^{j-1} \lambda_{ik} (k = 2, 3, ..., N_i) \tag{12}$$

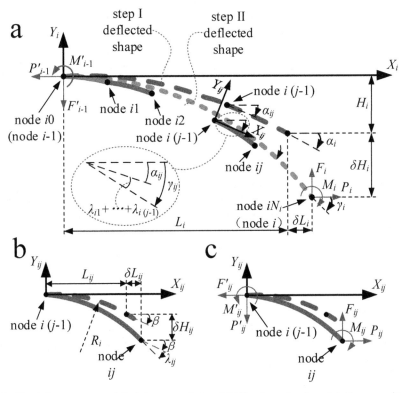

Fig. 4. The i-th segment model of the second step. (a) The discretized model diagram of the i-th segment of the second step. (b) The curved configuration of the j-th unit in the i-th segment. (c) The force of the j-th unit of the i-th segment.

Combined with the analysis of the plane large-deflection initial bending beam model, the relationship between the curved configuration and the force of the j-th element in the i-th segment can be solved, as follows:

$$
\begin{bmatrix} f_{ij} \\ m_{ij} \end{bmatrix} = \begin{bmatrix} 12 & -6 \\ -6 & 4 \end{bmatrix} \begin{bmatrix} \delta h_{ij} \\ \lambda_i \end{bmatrix} + p_{ij} \begin{bmatrix} 6/5 & -1/10 \\ -1/10 & 2/15 \end{bmatrix} \begin{bmatrix} \delta h_{ij} \\ \lambda_i \end{bmatrix}
$$
$$
+ p_{ij}^2 \begin{bmatrix} -1/700 & 1/1400 \\ 1/1400 & -11/6300 \end{bmatrix} \begin{bmatrix} \delta h_{ij} \\ \lambda_i \end{bmatrix} + p_{ij} \begin{bmatrix} \kappa_i/2 \\ \kappa_i/12 \end{bmatrix}
$$

(13)

$$
\delta l_{ij} = \frac{t_i^2 p_{ij}}{12} - \frac{\kappa_i}{2} \delta h_{ij} - \frac{\kappa_i}{12} \lambda_i - \frac{1}{2} \begin{bmatrix} \delta h_{ij} & \lambda_i \end{bmatrix} \begin{bmatrix} 6/5 & -1/10 \\ -1/10 & 2/15 \end{bmatrix} \begin{bmatrix} \delta h_{ij} \\ \lambda_i \end{bmatrix}
$$
$$
- p_i \begin{bmatrix} \delta h_{ij} & \lambda_i \end{bmatrix} \begin{bmatrix} -1/700 & 1/1400 \\ 1/1400 & -11/6300 \end{bmatrix} \begin{bmatrix} \delta h_{ij} \\ \lambda_i \end{bmatrix} + p_i \frac{\kappa_i}{360} \lambda_i + p_i \frac{\kappa_i^2}{720}
$$

(14)

The curved configuration of the end point of the i-th segment in the i-th coordinate system can be obtained by

$$
\begin{cases}
\sum_{j=1}^{N} \left[(1 + \delta l_{ij}) \cos \gamma_{ij} - (0.5\kappa_i + \delta h_{ij}) \sin \gamma_{ij}\right] = x_i \\
\sum_{j=1}^{N} \left[(1 + \delta l_{ij}) \sin \gamma_{ij} + (0.5\kappa_i + \delta h_{ij}) \cos \gamma_{ij}\right] = y_i \\
\alpha_i + \sum_{j=1}^{N} \lambda_{ij} = \gamma_i
\end{cases}
\tag{15}
$$

In order to ensure that the mathematical model has a solution, we discretize MRSPA into three segments and set the following boundary constraints: 1) Set the tip height H. 2) Set the tip force F. 3) To ensure the curved configuration smooth, we set the second and third joints to have the same bending angle. 4) To ensure the stability of grasping, we set the bending angle of the first joint is equal to the sum of the bending angles of the second joint and the third joint.

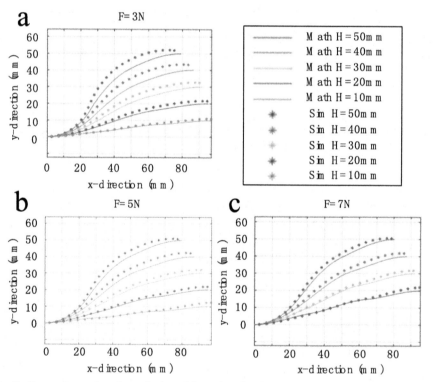

Fig. 5. Comparison of mathematical model results of and the FEA results. (a) Set the gripping force to 3N. (b) Set the gripping force to 5N. (c) Set the gripping force to 7N.

4 FEA Simulation and Analysis

According to the modeling analysis, the driving air pressure of MRSPA under specific curved configuration and specific tip force can be solved. Using ABAQUS to establish a FEA simulation model, we input the driving air pressure calculated by the mathematical model into each joint of MRSPA, and apply a contact force at the end. Set up different value of tip heights and tip forces for mathematical modeling and simulation. Select equidistant feature points on the middle layer of the bottom spring leaf of the FEA results and record their coordinates. The accuracy of the mathematical model is verified by comparing the calculation results of the mathematical model with the simulation analysis results. The comparison result is shown in Fig. 5. The end height error is less than 2 mm. On the basis of the mathematical model, we can control the position of the MRSPA and the tip force by driving air pressure.

5 Conclusion

In this article, we designed a multi-joint reinforced pneumatic actuator (MRSPA). Compared with the traditional structure of SPA, MRSPA has greater rigidity and stronger flexibility, and each joint can achieve bidirectional bending. In order to optimize the RSPA structure of each joint, we explored the influence of the different chamber distribution on the bending performance of RSPA. In addition, we also determined the flexural stiffness of RSPA and the efficiency of the driving air pressure through simulation. On this basis, we established a mathematical model of MRSPA. This model can describe the curved configuration of MRSPA under driving air pressure and load.

The research results show that uniform chamber distribution is more conducive to RSPA to achieve the best two-way bending performance. As the bending direction of RSPA different, its bending rigidity is also different. The bending rigidity of RSPA is greater when bending inward. In addition, the efficiency of the driving air pressure is affected by the bending angle of RSPA and the external load. The increase of the bending angle will reduce the efficiency of the driving air pressure. While, the effect of the external load will increase the efficiency of the driving air pressure. Using the revised mathematical model, we can better predict the curved configuration of MRSPA. The error of the end point height of the mathematical model result and the FEA result is less than 2 mm.

References

1. Shiva, A., et al.: Tendon-based stiffening for a pneumatically actuated soft manipulator. IEEE Robot. Autom. Lett. 1(2), 632–637 (2016). https://doi.org/10.1109/LRA.2016.2523120
2. Walker, J., et al.: Soft robotics: a review of recent developments of pneumatic soft actuators. Actuators 9(1) (2020). https://doi.org/10.3390/act9010003
3. Pawlowski, B., Sun, J., Xu, J., Liu, Y., Zhao, J.: Modeling of soft robots actuated by twisted-and-coiled actuators. IEEE/ASME Trans. Mechatron. 24(1), 5–15 (2019). https://doi.org/10.1109/TMECH.2018.2873014

4. Kang, R., Branson, D.T., Zheng, T., Guglielmino, E., Caldwell, D.G.: Design, modeling and control of a pneumatically actuated manipulator inspired by biological continuum structures. Bioinspiration Biomimetics **8**(3) (2013). https://doi.org/10.1088/1748-3182/8/3/036008

5. Manti, M., Hassan, T., Passetti, G., D'Elia, N., Laschi, C., Cianchetti, M.: A bioinspired soft robotic gripper for adaptable and effective grasping. Soft Robot. **2**(3), 107–116 (2015). https://doi.org/10.1089/soro.2015.0009

6. Seok, S., Onal, C.D., Cho, K.J., Wood, R.J., Rus, D., Kim, S.: Meshworm: a peristaltic soft robot with antagonistic nickel titanium coil actuators. IEEE/ASME Trans. Mechatron. **18**(5), 1485–1497 (2013). https://doi.org/10.1109/TMECH.2012.2204070

7. Elsayed, Y., Lekakou, C., Geng, T., Saaj, C.M.: Design optimisation of soft silicone pneumatic actuators using finite element analysis. In: IEEE/ASME International Conference on Advanced Intelligent Mechatronics, AIM, pp. 44–49 (2014). https://doi.org/10.1109/AIM. 2014.6878044

8. Mosadegh, B., et al.: Pneumatic networks for soft robotics that actuate rapidly. Adv. Funct. Mater. **24**(15), 2163–2170 (2014). https://doi.org/10.1002/adfm.201303288

9. Hao, Y., et al.: Universal soft pneumatic robotic gripper with variable effective length. In: Chinese Control Conference on CCC, vol. 2016-August, pp. 6109–6114 (2016). https://doi. org/10.1109/ChiCC.2016.7554316

10. Hao, Y., et al.: Modeling and experiments of a soft robotic gripper in amphibious environments. Int. J. Adv. Robot. Syst. **14**(3), 1–12 (2017). https://doi.org/10.1177/1729881417707148

11. Yap, H.K., Ng, H.Y., Yeow, C.H.: High-force soft printable pneumatics for soft robotic applications. Soft Robot. **3**(3), 144–158 (2016). https://doi.org/10.1089/soro.2016.0030

12. Zhang, N.: Ac ce d M us pt. 2D Mater. (2020). https://iopscience.iop.org/article/. https://doi. org/10.1088/2053-1583/abe778

13. Alici, G., Canty, T., Mutlu, R., Hu, W., Sencadas, V.: Modeling and experimental evaluation of bending behavior of soft pneumatic actuators made of discrete actuation chambers. Soft Robot. **5**(1), 24–35 (2018). https://doi.org/10.1089/soro.2016.0052

14. Ma, F., Chen, G.: Modeling large planar deflections of flexible beams in compliant mechanisms using chained beam-constraint-model. J. Mech. Robot. **8**(2) (2016). https://doi.org/10. 1115/1.4031028

15. Chen, G., Ma, F., Hao, G., Zhu, W.: Modeling large deflections of initially curved beams in compliant mechanisms using chained beam constraint model. J. Mech. Robot. **11**(1) (2019). https://doi.org/10.1115/1.4041585

Quartz Resonance Based Torque Sensor Design

Hao Fu[1,2], Chin-Yin Chen[2(✉)], Chongchong Wang[2], MinChiang Chao[3],
Qiang Zhou[3], Guilin Yang[2], and Yonghui Zhou[2]

[1] School of Mechanical Engineering, Southwest Jiaotong University, Chengdu 610031, China
[2] Zhejiang Key Laboratory of Robotics and Intelligent Manufacturing Equipment Technology,
Ningbo Institute of Materials Technology and Engineering, CAS, Ningbo 315201, China
chenchinyin@nimte.ac.cn
[3] TXC (Ningbo) Co., Ltd., Ningbo 315800, China

Abstract. In this paper, a design method for torque sensor based on AT-cut quartz crystal resonators is proposed. The resonance frequency of AT-cut quartz crystal has the characteristic of changing with external force. In order to study the quartz resonant torque sensor, firstly, the quartz crystal resonators are designed by the requirement of resolution and measurement range. In order to obtain a sensor with high response characteristics, the quartz crystal is mounted on a unique spoke structure, and the finite element analysis software is employed to analyze the installation position of the quartz crystal sensitive unit and the stress of the quartz crystal are determined. The quartz crystal resonator with the fundamental frequency of 25 M is selected as the sensitive unit, and the force-frequency coefficient and the limit force of the quartz crystal resonators are determined. Moreover, the pierce circuit is selected as the quartz crystal oscillation circuit, and the frequency counting pre-processing circuit is designed to realize frequency counting. Finally, the sensor is placed in the calibration device for calibration, and the static indicators of sensor range, sensitivity, linearity, hysteresis, resolution and so on are obtained.

Keywords: Torque sensor · Quartz crystal resonator

1 Introduction

In recent years, with the continuous improvement of industrial automation, the application of robots in service, military and other fields has increased. Its development trend is no longer just a single and repetitive end-execution motion but can perform more complex actions. To achieve more accurate interaction control, torque sensors play a vital role [1-3].

Research institutions and enterprises at home and abroad have conducted much research on torque sensors. Their research history has changed from the initial strain gauge type to the magneto-elastic type, photoelectric type, capacitive type and piezoelectric type. The most widely used strain gauge sensor has the advantages of mature technology. However, the disadvantages are that the accuracy is not high, the measurement speed is relatively slow, and the resolution is low. It cannot meet the current

© Springer Nature Switzerland AG 2021
X.-J. Liu et al. (Eds.): ICIRA 2021, LNAI 13013, pp. 433–443, 2021.
https://doi.org/10.1007/978-3-030-89095-7_42

increasing requirements for high precision and rapid measurement. The signal noise is relatively large [4, 15].

The quartz resonant torque sensor studied in this paper uses an AT-cut quartz crystal resonator as the sensitive unit. The quartz crystal will change in frequency when it is stressed, and the torque can be detected by detecting the frequency. Quartz crystals can generally be utilized to make high-precision detection elements [5]. The resonant torque sensor with quartz crystal as the sensor unit can obtain high accuracy, and at the same time, has the advantages of high sensitivity and inherent insensitivity to signal noise. Its digital oscillator circuit outputs extremely stable frequency signals so that the sensor has good output stability.

2 Quartz Crystal Design

This research uses AT-cut quartz crystals. AT-cut quartz crystals provide high resonant frequencies and exhibit excellent temperature stability in resonance near room temperature [3]. Silver electrodes are plated on both sides of a quartz crystals, and an oscillation circuit is added to the silver electrode, and the quartz crystals will oscillate. Mount the quartz crystals on the torque sensor. When the torque is applied, the external force is transmitted through the sensor structure and acts on the quartz crystals, causing its oscillation frequency to change in direct proportion to the external force [6, 16, 17].

$$\Delta f = S * \Delta T * \eta \tag{1}$$

Where S is the force frequency coefficient, given by formula (2), η is Power conversion efficiency, and ΔT is the applied torque. Through the sensor structure and the special installation method of the sensitive unit, the torque is finally converted into a force in a certain direction and acts on both ends of the quartz crystals.

$$S = Kf * \frac{(\frac{1.67}{t})^2}{D * n} \tag{2}$$

Where Kf is the force sensitivity coefficient, which is related to the cutting type and the force direction of the quartz crystals, t is the thickness of the quartz crystals, and D is the length and width coefficient of the quartz crystals.

Because the quartz crystals is very thin and its mechanical properties are poor, the range of the sensor is mainly determined by the quartz crystals. According to previous studies, the ultimate force of a quartz crystals depends on the buckling stress [7], and the theoretical value is expressed as Euler's critical buckling load.

$$F_{cr} = \frac{\pi^2 EI}{(\mu L)^2} \tag{3}$$

Where E is the elastic modulus 72 Gp, I is the moment of inertia of the cross section, which depends on the width and thickness of the quartz crystal, L is the unsupported length of the quartz crystal, and μ It depends on the fixing method of quartz crystal.

The frequency change range P of the sensor is determined by the limit load of the quartz crystals and the force-frequency coefficient of the quartz crystals.

$$P = F_{cr} * S \tag{4}$$

It can be seen that the range P of the sensor is related to the design of the length, width, and thickness of the quartz crystals, and the thickness of the quartz crystals directly determines the fundamental frequency of the oscillation of the quartz crystals.

Taking the above formula as a reference, three types of quartz crystals is designed and selected, the fundamental frequency are 8M, 25M, 48M, and the length and width of all quartz crystals are 3.5* 1.8 mm, which are suitable for sensors of different measuring ranges. The following Table 1 gives the theoretical force-frequency coefficients and limit forces of the three types of quartz crystals.

Table 1. Theoretical force frequency coefficient and limit force of quartz crystals

Mechanical properties	8M	25M	48M
Ultimate force (N)	80	7	1.7
Force frequency coefficient (Hz/N)	435	4340	16127

After that, specific experiments are carried out to verify the parameters such as the limit force and the force-frequency coefficient of each quartz. In the experiment, 3 quartz crystals of 8M, 25M, and 48M were selected and fixed on the press, and pressure is directly applied to the quartz crystal, and the frequency of the quartz crystal is measured in real-time with a spectrum analyzer (N9020A-503 spectrum analyzer, see Fig. 1).

As can be seen from Fig. 1, the relationship between the applied load and frequency of 8M, 25M, and 48M quartz crystals is approximately as follows:

$$ya = 510x + 8E + 06 \tag{5}$$

$$yb = 5400x + 2.5E + 07 \tag{6}$$

$$yc = 19650x + 4.8E + 07 \tag{7}$$

Therefore, the force-frequency coefficients of 8M, 25M, and 48M quartz crystals are 510 Hz/N, 5400 Hz/N, 19650 Hz/N, and the ultimate force is 86 N, 10 N, 1.5 N, respectively. The experimental results are much closed from the theoretical values (). It can be concluded that the frequency change ranges of the three quartz crystals are 45900 Hz, 54000 Hz, and 29475 Hz, respectively. Comprehensive range and force frequency coefficient, finally the 25M quartz crystals is selected as the sensitive unit for application.

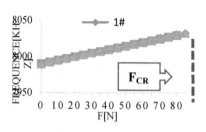

(a) 8M force-frequency curve

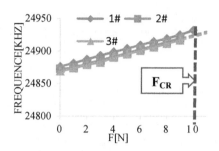

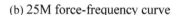

(b) 25M force-frequency curve

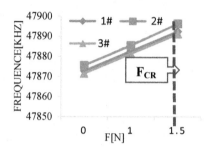

(c) 48M force-frequency curve

Fig. 1. 8M, 25M, 48M quartz crystals test data

3 Design and Analysis of Torque Sensor

Traditional strain gauge sensors mostly use a spoke design, and the strain gauge is pasted on the strain beam to detect the torque value. The design of the quartz resonant torque sensor still adopts the spoke structure design [2]. The specific structure is shown in Fig. 2(a). Compared with traditional torque strain gauge sensors, quartz resonant torque sensors do not need to use a bridge circuit for voltage output value amplification and temperature compensation [8], so there is no need to design four strains beam that is used to install 8 strain gauges, but considering the symmetry of the structure, two strain beams are designed, and support beams are set at other positions to improve the rigidity of the sensor.

Table 2. Material parameters of 7075 aluminum and quartz crystal

Material type	Young's modulus	Density	Yield strength	Poisson's ratio
7075 Aluminum	71 GP	2.81 g/cm^3	455 Mpa	0.33
Quartz crystal	72 GP	2.65 g/cm^3	–	0.16

In order to obtain the lightweight of torque sensor, 7075 aluminum alloy is selected as the material, and the specific material parameters are shown in Table 2. Through the simulation analysis of finite element analysis software, the results are shown in Fig. 2 (b). The sensitive unit is installed at the stress sensitive position on both sides of the strain beam to ensure the sensitivity of the sensitive unit during installation. When torque is applied, the sensitive unit on the same beam is subjected to tension and pressure respectively to form a differential structure [9]. At the same time, the quartz crystal forms a beam film structure with the beam to improve the force sensitivity of the quartz crystal. Opening a hole in the middle of the strain beam can further improve the sensitivity of the sensor from the structure [2].

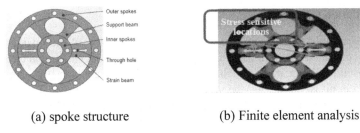

(a) spoke structure   (b) Finite element analysis

Fig. 2. Sensor spoke structure

In order to ensure that the silver-plated sensitive unit can have a longer life, it is necessary to encapsulate the quartz crystals in the structure, as shown in Fig. 3. The external force is transferred to the quartz crystals through the package body, so that the quartz crystals produces frequency changes after receiving the external force.

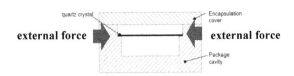

Fig. 3. Schematic diagram of sensitive unit

In order to ensure that the quartz crystal can better detect the torque/force changes, and is not interfered by other direction forces, the principal stress direction of the quartz crystals should be parallel to the quartz crystals. As Fig. 4 shown, the finite element is used to calculated the assembled sensor structure to view the force direction of the quartz crystals and the force magnitude of the quartz crystals. The principal stress direction of the quartz crystals is almost parallel to the quartz crystals, and there is almost no principal stress in other directions, and the principal stress of the quartz crystals under tension and pressure is the same.

(a) Compressed quartz crystals

average stress 95.9MP

(b) Tensile quartz crystalsp

average stress 95.7MP

Fig. 4. Quartz crystals simulation results

4   Quartz Crystal Experiment

4.1   Oscillation Circuit

In order to be able to produce a stable frequency oscillation of the quartz crystal, a reasonably designed oscillation circuit is required. The current oscillation circuit of the quartz crystal oscillator mainly includes Pierce, Colpits and Clapp [9]. Among them, the Pierce circuit is simple and the application is the most extensive. Thus, the Pierce circuit is used as the oscillator circuit. The CMOS inverting amplifier and the negative feedback resistor R3 are connected to the quartz crystal to reverse the phase of the circuit by 180°. At the same time, it is connected to the load capacitors C3 and C2 to form a three-point capacitive type. It is reversed by 180°, and finally the total circuit is reversed by 360°. Therefore, when the negative feedback gain is greater than 1, the "Barkhausen" criterion is met [11], causing oscillation. The schematic diagram of the oscillation circuit is shown in Fig. 5.

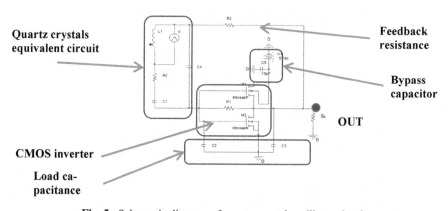

Fig. 5. Schematic diagram of quartz crystal oscillator circuit

4.2   Quartz Crystal Characteristic Test

A 250B network analyzer was used to measure the characteristics of the prepared 25 M quartz crystal. The test results are shown in Fig. 6(a). It can be seen from the figure that the phase reversal point of the quartz crystal is located between the series resonance and parallel resonance frequencies, and the phase value is less than 0, which satisfies the quartz crystal oscillation condition. At the same time, the equivalent resistance and equivalent inductance of the quartz crystal can be measured as R = 15.61Ω and L = 9 mH respectively. And use a frequency meter (KEYSIGHT 53230A) to finally confirm the oscillation frequency of the quartz crystal, and the result is shown in Fig. 6(b).

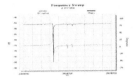   

(a) Quartz crystal characteristics   (b) oscillation frequency

Fig. 6. Quartz crystal characteristic test

Vibration Q factor is a key parameter of the resonant system. It quantitatively represents the stability of the crystal vibration system. It is defined as the ratio of stored energy to dissipated energy in a vibration period. The high Q factor of the thickness shear mode is necessary to achieve high sensitivity Conditions [3]. According to formula (8), the oscillation stability coefficient Q of 25 m quartz crystal is 90000.

$$Q = \frac{2\pi f * L}{R} \tag{8}$$

5   Sensor Signal Processing Circuit

5.1   Processing Circuit Design

The differential structure is adopted in the circuit design of the sensor to eliminate the measurement error caused by the ambient temperature and installation preload. At the same time, in signal processing, frequency mixing, amplification, shaping and other circuits are used to preprocess the frequency signal [6].

Due to the piezoelectric characteristics of the crystal, it will produce equal and opposite frequency changes (*fa* and *fb*) when it is subjected to tension (*Fa*) and pressure (*Fb*).

At the same time, the ambient temperature (*f_T*) and the pre-tightening force (*f_R*) of the sensitive unit assembly will also cause frequency changes.

$$\Delta f_1 = f_a + f_T + f_R \tag{9}$$

$$\Delta f_2 = f_b + f_T + f_R \tag{10}$$

Through the mixer circuit, the frequency change value caused only by the tension and pressure can be finally obtained.

$$\Delta f_{total} = f_0 + \Delta f_1 - f_0 - \Delta f_2 = |f_a| + |f_b| \tag{11}$$

The signal after mixing is passed through a low-pass filter to remove the residual high-frequency signal in the signal, and finally the filtered frequency is reshaped and amplified, which is convenient for frequency counting with a spectrum analyzer in the later stage, and the output frequency value Δf_{total}.

5.2 Circuit Test Verification

The designed circuit is tested. Firstly, two designed two sensitive units are selected to generate two frequency signals and input them into the processing circuit. After mixing, amplification and shaping (as shown in Fig. 7a), the final frequency measurement is carried out with an oscilloscope (mso × 3104t). As shown in Fig. 7 (b), the standard square wave is output with a peak to peak value of 3.3V. At the same time, the output stability of frequency is also very important [14]. When the circuit is placed at room temperature for two hours, the frequency output drift is shown in Fig. 8. The standard deviation DF of frequency variation is 5.9 Hz, that is, relative to f of the total frequency, DF/F = 0.006%.

(a) Sensitive unit and circuit   (b) Output waveform

Fig. 7. Processing circuit

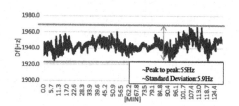

Fig. 8. Output stability   **Fig. 9.** Sensor static calibration

6 Static Calibration

Completed the installation of the sensitive unit and the main structure, place the sensor on the calibration device, (as shown in Fig. 9) connect the designed pre-processing circuit, and perform static calibration by hanging weights [12], get the relationship curve between the sensor output frequency value and the applied torque value. Finally the frequency change of the sensor is collected by the spectrum analyzer.

In the experiment, apply torque from 0–150 NM in 10 times, then unload torque from 150–0 NM in 10 times, repeat 3 times, and record the frequency change of the sensitive unit on the sensor. Since there are two strain beams and two sensitive units on each beam, a set of differential frequency data can be obtained, and two strain beams can get two sets of data. Finally, it can be calculated by a single-chip microcomputer and output the average of the two sets of data. Now only use a spectrum analyzer to test and verify the frequency data on one of the strain beams. The result is shown in Fig. 10.

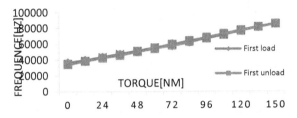

Fig. 10. Sensor static calibration test

As can be seen from Fig. 10, the relationship between the applied load and frequency of the sensor is roughly as follows:

$$Y = 350x + 30000 \tag{12}$$

Therefore, the force frequency coefficient of the sensor is about 350 Hz/NM, and the torque range is 150 NM. The total range of frequency change is 50400 Hz, so the theoretical frequency change of 1/5000 target resolution is 10 Hz, and the corresponding torque change is 0.03 NM. Converted into a weight, the weight is 4 g. Therefore, by adding a weight of 4 g to apply a 0.03 NM torque, observe whether the final frequency output reading is stable, to complete the resolution experiment, the specific experimental results are shown in Fig. 11.

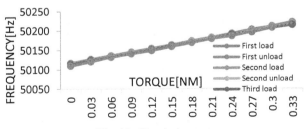

Fig. 11. Resolution test

When a 4 g weight is applied, the experimental results show that the frequency output change is stable, with good linearity, and is not much different from the theoretical value of 10 Hz, so it can reach a resolution of 1/5000. Finally, according to the national standard (JB 13359–2018), the static indicators of the torque sensor are calculated using Matlab as shown in Table 3.

Table 3. Static index of torque sensor.

Linearity	Sensitivity	Repeatability	Hysteresis	Resolution
98.14%	350 Hz/NM	98.44%	0.51%	0.02%

Finally, the designed sensors are compared with the existing commercial sensors, including TB2 and M2210A and other results are shown in Table 4. The results show that the sensor designed by us has a smaller thickness and mass, and the stiffness can reach 88000 nm/rad, the sampling frequency of the sensor can reach 2000 Hz, and the resolution is far higher than other sensors. It can be seen that the developed sensor has the same performance as commercial sensor, even the performance of resolution is far higher than that of the existing sensor.

Table 4. Parameter comparison.

Parameter	Unit	TB2	M2210A	[2]	[13]	Our application
Thickness	mm	60	7	8	20	8
Diameter	mm	112	53	74	65	80
Weight	g	700	90	75	250	89
Rigidity	NM/rad	160000	80000	-	-	88000
Torque range	Nm	100	50	30	80	150
Resolving power		1:3000	1:200	1:300	1:2700	1:5000
Sampling frequency	Hz	65	-	-	1000	2000
Linear	%FSO	99.95	99.5	99.64	98	98.14
Repeatability	%FSO	99.95	99	-	-	98.44
Hysteresis	%FSO	0.03	1.0	0.11	0.26	0.51

7 Conclusion

In this paper, a quartz resonant torque based sensor is designed. First, the fundamental frequency 25 M quartz crystal is design and selected as the sensitive unit. The force-frequency coefficient of the quartz crystals is 5400 Hz/N, and the limit force is 10 N. The sensor structure is analyzed by finite element analysis software to determine the installation position of the quartz crystals sensitive unit and the force of the quartz crystals, to ensure that the principal stress direction of the quartz crystals is parallel to the quartz crystals and the sensitivity of the sensor is structurally ensured. The Pierce circuit is selected as the oscillation circuit, and the frequency counting pre-processing circuit is designed to realize the frequency counting. The sensor is placed in the calibration device for calibration, and finally, the sensor has a range of 150 NM, a sensitivity of 350 Hz/NM, and linearity of 98.14%, hysteresis of 0.51%, repeatability of 98.44%, resolution of 0.02%.

Acknowledgements. This work was supported by grant: No.2019YFB1309904, No.174433KYSB20190036,No.U1813223,No.2019B10122,No.2018B10058,andNo.51805523.

References

1. Gai, H., Fang, X., Kai, J., et al.: Design and research of a robot joint torque sensor. Mod. Manufact. Eng. (2017)
2. Lou, Y., Wei, J., Song, S.: Design and optimization of a joint torque sensor for robot collision detection. J. IEEE Sens. J. **19**(16), 6618–6627 (2019)
3. Asakura, A., Fukuda, T., Arai, F.: Design, fabrication and characterization of compact force sensor using AT-cut quartz crystal resonators. In: IEEE/RSJ International Conference on Intelligent Robots and Systems. IEEE (2008)
4. Yang, Q., Huang, J.Y., Lu, H.F., et al.: Research on torque measurement method based on resistance strain gauge. J. Electron. World **000**(004), 213 (2014)
5. Danel, J.S., Delapierre, G.: Quartz: a material for microdevices. J. Micromech. Microeng. **1**(4), 187 (1999)
6. Zhu, H.Z., Feng, G.P.: Differential quartz resonant force sensor. J. Instrum. Technol. Sens. **000**(005), 7–9 (1999)
7. Murozaki, Y., Sakuma, S., Arai, F.: Improvement of the measurement range and temperature characteristics of a load sensor using a quartz crystal resonator with all crystal layer components. J. Sens. **17**(5) (2017)
8. Tang, Z.G.: Brief analysis of resistance strain sensor bridge measurement circuit. J. Sci. Consult. (2018)
9. Wei, X.Y., Wang, D.J., Ren, Z.M., et al.: A Probe Type High Precision Force Sensor Based on Quartz Resonator: cn110017921a (2019)
10. Zhu, Y.L., Chen, T.: PSPICE simulation of quartz crystal oscillation circuit based on CMOS inverter. J. Mod. Electron. Tech. (2012)
11. Hu, Y.X., Zhang, L.: Explore the principle and matching method of crystal oscillator circuit. J. Sci. Inf. Technol. **000**(001), 53 (2018)
12. Xu, Z.F.: Research on Joint Torque Sensor of Light Arm (2004)
13. Kim, Y.B., Kim, U., Seok, D.-Y., So, J., Lee, Y.H., Choi, H.R.: Torque sensor embedded actuator module for robotic applications. IEEE/ASME Trans. Mech. **23**(4), 1662–1672 (2018)
14. Murozaki, Y., Nogawa, K., Arai, F.: Miniaturized load sensor using quartz crystal resonator constructed through microfabrication and bonding. Robomech. J. **1**, 3 (2014)
15. Kang, J.S., Lin, P., Chen, S.F.: Calibration and application of thin quartz stress sensor. China New Technol. New Prod. **388**(06), 79–80 (2019)
16. Zhang, M.L., Wang, X.D., Yang, F.H.: Resonant MEMS Differential Pressure Sensor and its Preparation Method: cn111579147a (2020)
17. Wang, H.: A Resonant MEMS Pressure Sensor: cn110803675a (2020)

Light and Variable Stiffness Bending Actuator Bionic from Inchworm

Jie Pan, Jingjun Yu, Shengge Cao, Guoxin Li, and Xu Pei[✉]

School of Mechanical Engineering and Automation, Beihang University, Beijing 100191, China
Peixu@buaa.edu.cn

Abstract. Soft gripper is with many advantages, it can grasp and move fragile objects safely. Soft gripper has a good shape adaptive ability for grasping the irregular objects. The grippers actuated by shape memory alloy (SMA) are with the characteristics of light weight and easy control, but their bending angle is small and grasping ability is very limited. In this paper, we proposed a kind of super lightweight variable stiffness gripper based on the SMA wire, the design principle was inspired by the movement of the inchworm. Compared with the previous soft grippers, the bending theory of the gripper is novel. The gripper is with a larger bending angle, and the characteristics of light weight and simple fabrication structure. The gripper contacted the object at low stiffness and grasped at high stiffness. The experimental results indicated that the gripper could grasp the target object smoothly, and the bending angle and force can adapt to some special situations.

Keywords: Soft gripper · Adaptive · Shape memory alloy · Variable stiffness · Bionic

1 Introduction

Gripper is an indispensable end-effector of robot. At present, the research on gripper mainly includes rigid gripper and flexible gripper [1]. The soft gripper has been studied for many years and has been successfully applied in industry. In some special condition, the soft gripper has better performance than the rigid gripper [2], such as grasping fragile objects, strong adaptability to some irregular objects, safe human-computer interaction and so on. At present, the research of soft gripper can be divided into three directions [3–5], include wire-driven, pneumatic driven and smart materials driven. The wire-driven soft gripper has reliable output force and precision motion [6]. Pneumatic gripper has high grasping efficiency and no pollution to the environment [7]. Pneumatic grip has been successfully applied in industrial environment and has been commercialized [8]. However, these two driving modes have to rely on motor and air pump, resulting in large system mass and volume, which is difficult to be applied in small space or weightless space [9, 10]. Soft gripper driven by smart material, mainly including dielectric elastomer (DE) [11], SMA [12], SMP (shape memory polymer) [13], electro-rheological fluids [13] and so on. This type of grippers use the soft material as the gripper body and the

© Springer Nature Switzerland AG 2021
X.-J. Liu et al. (Eds.): ICIRA 2021, LNAI 13013, pp. 444–454, 2021.
https://doi.org/10.1007/978-3-030-89095-7_43

smart material as the actuator. The actuating mode can be selected according to the characteristics of the working environment.

Low working stiffness is the main problem of soft gripper [14]. Some researchers used DE and low temperature liquid metal to enhance the variable stiffness ability of the robot to improve the grasping ability [15]. Some scholars enlarged the bending angle of SMA driven gripper by increasing the working stroke of SMA spring [16]. Some scholars improved the output force of the gripper by mixing wire-drive and SMA drive [17, 18]. These studies further expanded the application of SMA gripper, but did not further promote the lightweight and miniaturization of this gripper. In addition, SMA wire material was with the properties of driving and resistance information feedback [19], which is more suitable for application in the field of miniature robot. However, due to the small amount of deformation of SMA wire, it is difficult to be applied in large deformation soft gripper [20]. Though the shape variable of SMA spring is large, the mass and volume is larger than SMA wire, the heat dissipation speed is slow, thus it is difficult to be used as the driving material on small volume gripper. At present, some scholars have produced drive units applied in different occasions by weaving SMA wires. However, it is noteworthy that there are few studies on the large deformation modeling of SMA wire, most of the research work are based on the beam model, and the accuracy of the model needs to be improved [21, 22].

In our earlier research, the structure, actuation and sensing of SMA wire have been studied [23]. In this study, we made a universal lightweight soft gripper driven by using the shape memory properties of the SMA wire, combining weaving technology and bionic inchworm movement, we made a variable stiffness gripper in this paper. The kinematics model of the gripper was analyzed by mathematical modeling, and the influence of pre bending angle on the gripper bending angle was obtained. The experimental results show that the actuator was with a good application ability, and has a potential application prospect in gripping and biomimetic soft robots in small space.

2   Design and Working Principle of the Actuator

In our previous study [23], the properties of the SMA wire (DYNALLOY, INC. www.dynalloy.com) was researched. The SMA wire has shape memory ability, it can shrink 4%–5% of its original length during heating by a DC power source. At present, the SMA driven actuators are mainly made of silica gel elastomer as flexible support, and this driving method has some disadvantages, such as small bending Angle, low bending efficiency and complex pouring process of silica gel.

In this paper, we designed a new type of bending actuator bionic from the crawling of inchworm, which not only takes advantage of the shrinkage effect of SMA wire, but also takes advantage of its shape memory property and variable stiffness ability during be heating. The bending and straightening of SMA wire is used to imitate the inchworm's crawling motion. We use SMA wires to replace the inchworm's longitudinal muscle fibers as the tendon of robot and control the movement by electric heating. SMA wire is with low elastic modulus (25 Gpa) at room temperature and is easy to deform under external force. When the SMA wire is heated, it will generate a phase change due to heating, the elastic modulus increases (75 Gpa), and it will return to the shape before deformation, this progress is as shown in Fig. 1.

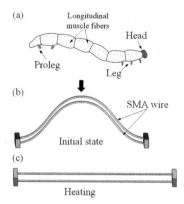

Fig. 1. The actuating process of SMA wire used of memory properties. (a) Initial state; (b) Heating.

If the bent SMA wire is constrained through the straight SMA wire to form a new structure as shown in Fig. 2(a), then with the electric heating of the bent SMA wire (the inner wire), the actuator will bend and deform due to the material memory properties of the SMA, as shown in Fig. 2(b). In order to reduce the number of wires, a whole SMA wire is woven into the inner wire, and a whole SMA wire is woven into the outer wire as shown in Fig. 2(c). It can be seen from Fig. 2 that the inner SMA wire was pre bent. When the inner SMA wire was heated, the inner SMA wire generated shape recovery deformation due to the shape memory property of the SMA wire. The inner SMA wire cannot be elongated due to the constraint of the outer SMA wire, thus it produced bending deformation to provide bending moment for the bending actuator.

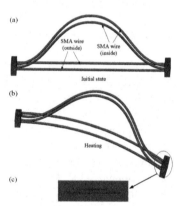

Fig. 2. Schematic diagram of the structure and drive of the bending actuator. (a) Initial state; (b) Heating; (c) Constraint plate and the arrangement of SMA wire.

As the SMA wire is pre bent and exposed, this bending actuator has larger bending angle and response rate compared with the previous research. In view of the light weight of SMA wire, it can be attached to the surface of the object and the surface of the human body without causing the movement obstruction. Therefore, the application of bending actuator can be used as a light gripper applied to the continuous robot with low load, a rehabilitation device for finger bending training, a bending joint of a miniature crawling robot and so on.

3 Analysis

The outer SMA wire of the bending actuator is arranged in straight line shape, and the inner SMA wire is arranged in a circular arc. After the inner SMA wire is heated, its shape memory property will make the arc shape revert to the straight line shape, and then generate a bending moment for the outer SMA wire, this in turn drives the bending motion of the actuator. When the power is off, the bending shape of the bending actuator is almost unchanged, but the elastic modulus of the SMA returns to the value at room temperature. In order to return the actuator to the initial state, it is only necessary to heat the outer wire. Because of the shape memory property, the outer wire returns to the straight line shape during be heating, and then the actuator returns to the initial state. Conventional beam bending models are designed for small deformations as shown in Fig. 3(a), while large angle bending of SMA wire needs to be modeled using a critical stress model of slender elastic rod as shown in Fig. 3(b).

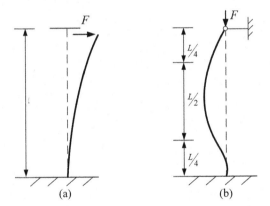

Fig. 3. Two kinds of beam bending models. (a) Conventional beam bending model; (b) Stress model of slender elastic rod.

In order to model the SMA bending actuator accurately, according to the symmetry of the SMA wire structure inside the actuator, it is simplified into 1/4 ellipse for modeling, as shown in Fig. 4.

As $1/\rho = M/EI$, $1/\rho = d\theta/ds$, $M = Fy$, then there is the force balance equation of SMA wire:

$$\frac{d\theta}{ds} + \frac{F}{EI}y = 0 \tag{1}$$

Define $k^2 = F/EI$, derivative of s in formula (1), as $dy/ds = sin\theta$, the governing equation of the SMA wire is obtained by calculation:

$$\frac{d^2y}{ds^2} + k^2 \sin\theta = 0 \tag{2}$$

According to the boundary conditions, the length expression of SMA wire is obtained as follows:

$$l = \frac{1}{2k} \int_0^a \frac{d\theta}{\sqrt{\sin^2\frac{a}{2} - \sin^2\frac{\theta}{2}}} \tag{3}$$

To simplify the integral expression in Eq. (3), $\rho = sina/2$, a is the rotation angle of the end-effector. Here define a new variable ψ, which satisfies the following equation:

$$\sin\frac{\theta}{2} = \sin\psi \sin\frac{a}{2} \tag{4}$$

Thus, the l can be calculated as:

$$l = \frac{1}{k} \int_0^{\frac{\pi}{2}} \frac{d\psi}{\sqrt{1 - \rho^2 \sin^2\psi}} \psi = \frac{1}{k}K(\psi) \tag{5}$$

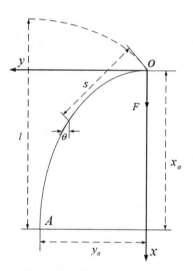

Fig. 4. Analysis of bending force of inner SMA wire.

Here, $K(\psi)$ represents the first kind of complete elliptic integral. The value of the a, θ, ρ, ψ can be ignored when the axis length of the SMA wire is relatively small, so the Eq. (6) can be simplified as:

$$l = \frac{1}{k} \int_0^{\frac{\pi}{2}} \frac{d\psi}{\sqrt{1 - \rho^2 \sin^2\psi}} \psi = \frac{\pi}{2k} \tag{6}$$

The critical load of SMA wire can be calculated as follow:

$$F_{cr} = \frac{\pi^2 EI}{(0.7l)^2} \tag{7}$$

$$\frac{F}{F_{cr}} = \frac{4K^2(\psi)}{\pi^2} \tag{8}$$

Using Eq. (7) and (8), we can calculate the expression of F.

$$F = F_{cr} \cdot \frac{4K^2(\psi)}{\pi^2} \tag{9}$$

Since $K(\psi)$ is obtained by querying the elliptical table, the axial force F can be obtained by calculating the pre bending angle a.

The deflection y_a and axial displacement equation x_a generated by the free end of the SMA wire can be calculated as:

$$x_a = \frac{2}{k} \int_0^{\frac{\pi}{2}} \sqrt{1 - \rho^2 \sin^2 \psi} \, d\psi - l = \frac{2}{k} E(\rho) - l \tag{10}$$

$$y_a = \frac{2\rho}{k} \int_0^{\frac{\pi}{2}} \sin \psi \, d\psi = \frac{2\rho}{k} \tag{11}$$

Here $E(\rho)$ represents the second type of complete elliptic integral, combined with $k^2 = F/EI$, the Eq. (10) and (11) can be expressed as:

$$x_a = \left(\frac{2E(\rho)}{K(\rho)} - 1 \right) \cdot l \tag{12}$$

$$y_a = \frac{2\rho l}{K(\rho)} \tag{13}$$

Therefore, on the premise of calculating the SMA wire rotation angle a, the values of x_a and y_a can be calculated by querying the ellipse table.

The torque M_{sma1} of SMA wire can be expressed:

$$M_{sma1} = F \cdot y_a \tag{14}$$

As shown in Fig. 5, the inner SMA wire of the actuator is constrained by the outer SMA wire, thus the torque M_{sma1} is applied on the outer SMA wire, which drives the bending actuator to bend.

$$\begin{cases} \dfrac{1}{\kappa} = \dfrac{M}{EI} \\ \kappa = \dfrac{L}{\theta} \end{cases} \tag{15}$$

From the Eq. (14) and (15), the bending angle θ of the outside SMA wire is expressed as:

$$\theta = \frac{F \cdot y_a}{EI} \tag{16}$$

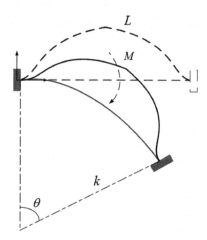

Fig. 5. Bending motion of the bending actuator.

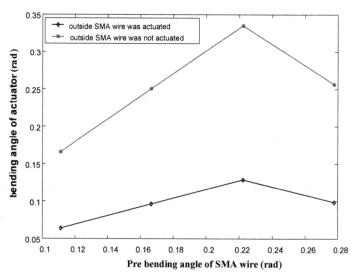

Fig. 6. The relationship between the pre bending angle of the inner SMA wire and the theoretical bending angle of the actuator.

Therefore, according to the attribute parameters of the SMA wire and the above formula, the bending angle of the bending actuator can be calculated through the initial angle of the inner SMA wire. As shown in the Fig. 6, the bending angle of the actuator decreases with the increase of the pre bending angle value. One of the reasons is that the larger the pre bending angle is, the bigger axial force generated by the SMA outer wire, thus will lead to the smaller bending deformation of the actuator. Therefore, according to the relationship between the pre bending angle of the SMA wire and the bending angle of the actuator in the Fig. 6, the value of 0.222 rad is selected as the pre bending angle of the actuator.

4   Experiment and Discuss

4.1   Bending Test

In this paper, the current value of SMA wire was 1.5 A. First, keep the initial state of the outside SMA wire in a straight line, and then apply 1.5 A current to the inside SMA wire to record the bending angle of the actuator. Then 1.5 A current was applied to the inner wire and the outer wire respectively at the same time to record the angle of the actuator.

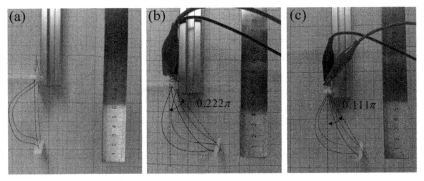

Fig. 7. Bending test of the actuator. (a) Initial attitude; (b) Heating the inner SMA wire; (c) Heating the inner and outer SMA wires at the same time.

Through the measurement in the actuator bending test, the pre bending angle of the inside SMA wire was 0.222 rad, and the theoretical value of bending angle was 0.096π when the heated the inside SMA wire only, and the theoretical value of bending angle was 0.251π when heated the inside and outside SMA wire at the same time. The corresponding actual measured values were 0.111π and 0.222π respectively, as shown in the Fig. 7. The actual measured value was close to the theoretical value, which proves the correctness of the application of the thin beam bending theory in the kinematics modeling of SMA wire.

4.2 Bending Force Test

At first, connect 1.5 A current into inside SMA wire, after the actuator was completely bent, the displacement in the X-axis direction was measured as 40 mm. Then move the force sensor (YISIDA, DS2-50N) from 10 mm to 40 mm along the x-axis direction, and recorded the values of the dynamometer under different displacements, as shown in the Fig. 8(a).

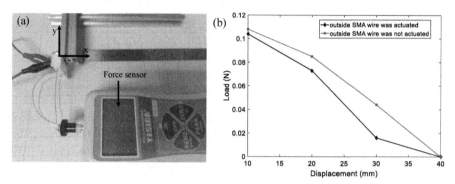

Fig. 8. Bending test of the actuator. (a) Test device diagram; (b) Bending force test under different displacement.

when heated the inside SMA wire only, the maximum force of the actuator in bending was 0.108 N and the minimum force was 0 N. While the inside and outside SMA wires were both heated at the same time, the maximum bending force of the driver was 0.104 N, and the minimum bending force was 0N. According to the data in the Fig. 8(b), when the outer SMA wire was heated, the bending force of the actuator was reduced. This phenomenon could be explained as the shape memory property of SMA actuated the SMA wire to change in a straight line during be heating, which was antagonistic to the inner SMA wire, thus reducing the bending angle of the actuator. From the Fig. 8(b), we obtained the closer the force sensor was to the initial position of the bending actuator, the larger the bending force was. Therefore, the appropriate force position should be selected reasonably according to different operation requirements.

4.3 Grasp Ability Test

The soft gripper with variable stiffness (the weight of the gripper is 0.06 N) is made by arranging the bending actuators symmetrically, as shown in the Fig. 9. Then, the common objects in daily life were grasped by the gripper to test the grasping performance, include paper cup (the weight of the cup is 0.042 N), ping-pong ball, (the weight of the ball is 0.029 N), clip (the weight of the clip is 0.0095 N). The experimental results showed that the gripper was with a certain shape adaptive ability, and it can grasp objects with larger weight than it, and it can also successfully grasp broken screws and nuts. Considering that the gripper can be designed in the direction of lightweight and miniaturization, so the gripper can be applied to industrial manipulator, continuum robot as end effector and medical rehabilitation training gloves. In the future research, we can increase the number of bending wires in series and parallel to increase the grip force.

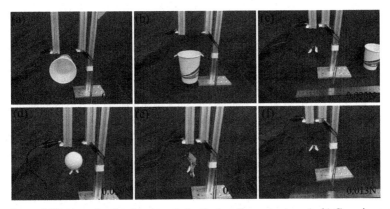

Fig. 9. Grasp ability test of soft gripper made by the bending actuators. (a–b) Grasping a cup; (c) Grasping a nut; (d) Grasping a ping-pong ball; (e) Grasping a clip; (f) Grasping a blot.

5   Conclusions

In this paper, we designed and manufactured a new bending actuator driven by SMA wires that was inspired by the movement of the inchworm. Based on the motion form of the inchworm, the soft bending actuator can bend and straighten. By pre bending the inside SMA wire, the bending angle of the actuator can be increased, which had a larger bending range than the conventional bending method based on the 4%–5% shrinkage deformation of SMA wire. The manufacturing process of the bending actuator was simple and the weight was small. The thin beam model was used to analyze the bending of the actuator, through the bending test, the results fitted to the theoretical values, which proved the effectiveness of the thin beam model. This bending actuator is light and the operation stiffness can be controlled. The overall output performance of the actuator can be increased through series and parallel connection. Because of its simple structure and light weight, it is suitable for small-scale crawling robot, end effector of continuum robot and medical rehabilitation training gloves, etc.

Acknowledgements. This work was supported in part by the National Key Research and Development Program of China (Grant No. 2019YFB1311200) and the National Natural Science Foundation of China (Grant No. U1813221).

1. References

1. Fitzgerald, S.G., Delaney, G.W., Howard, D.: A review of jamming actuation in soft robotics. Actuators **9**(4), 104 (2020)

2. Shepherd, R.F., Ilievski, F., Choi, W., et al.: Multigait soft robot. Proc. Natl. Acad. Sci. U.S.A. **108**(51), 20400–20403 (2011)

3. Camarillo, D.B., Milne, C.F., Carlson, C.R., et al.: Mechanics modeling of tendon-driven continuum manipulators. IEEE Trans. Robot. **24**(6), 1262–1273 (2008)

4. Shintake, J., Cacucciolo, V., Floreano, D., et al.: Soft robotic grippers. Adv. Mater. **30**(29), 1707035.1–1707035.33 (2018)

5. Ilievski, F., Mazzeo, A.D., Shepherd, R.F., et al.: Soft robotics for chemists† **50**(8), 1890–1895 (2011)

6. Deimel, R., Brock, O.: A novel type of compliant and underactuated robotic hand for dexterous grasping. Int. J. Robot. Res. **35**(1–3), 161–185 (2016)

7. Brown, E., Rodenberg, N., et al.: Universal robotic gripper based on the jamming of granular material. Proc. Natl. Acad. Sci. **107**(44), 18809–18814 (2010)

8. Amend, J., Cheng, N., Fakhouri, S., et al.: Soft robotics commercialization: jamming grippers from research to product. Soft Robot **3**, 213–222 (2016)

9. Nicolas Mouazé, B.L.: Deformation modeling of compliant robotic fingers grasping soft object. J. Mech. Robot. 1–17 (2020)

10. Yu, S., Lee, J., Park, B., Kim, K.: Design of a gripper system for tendon-driven telemanipulators considering semi-automatic spring mechanism and eye-in-hand camera system. J. Mech. Sci. Technol. **31**(3), 1437–1446 (2017). https://doi.org/10.1007/s12206-017-0244-8

11. Gu, G., Jiang, Z., Zhao, R., et al.: Soft wall-climbing robots. Sci. Robot. **3**(25), eaat2874 (2018)

12. Meng, L., Kang, R., Gan, D., et al.: A mechanically intelligent crawling robot driven by shape memory alloy and compliant bistable mechanism. J. Mech. Robot. **12**, 061005 (2020)

13. Leps, T., Hartzell, C., Wereley, N., et al.: Simulation of a magneto-rheological fluid based, jamming, soft gripper using the soft sphere DEM in LIGGGHTS. In: 70th Annual Meeting of the APS Division of Fluid Dynamics. American Physical Society (2017)

14. El-Atab, N., Mishra, R.B., Al-Modaf, F., et al.: Soft actuators for soft robotic applications: a review. Adv. Intell. Syst. **2**(10), 2000128 (2020)

15. Shintake, J., Schubert, B., Rosset, S., et al.: Variable stiffness actuator for soft robotics using dielectric elastomer and low-melting-point alloy. In: 2015 IEEE/RSJ International Conference on Intelligent Robots and Systems (IROS), Hamburg, Germany, pp. 1097–1102 (2015)

16. Lee, J.H., Chung, Y.S., Rodrigue, H.: Application of SMA spring tendons for improved grasping performance. Smart Mater. Struct. **28**, 035006 (2018)

17. Li, J., Sun, M., Wu, Z.: Design and fabrication of a low-cost silicone and water-based soft actuator with a high load-to-weight ratio. Soft Robot. **8**, 448–461 (2020)

18. Dong, X., Axinte, D., Palmer, D., et al.: Development of a slender continuum robotic system for on-wing inspection/repair of gas turbine engines. Robot. Comput. Integr. Manuf. **44**(4), 218–229 (2017)

19. Jin, H., Dong, E., Alici, G., et al.: A starfish robot based on soft and smart modular structure (SMS) actuated by SMA wires. Bioinspiration Biomimetics **11**(5), 056012 (2016)

20. Yan, S., Yang, T., Liu, X., et al.: Tactile feedback control for a gripper driven by SMA springs. AIP Adv. **2**(3), 032134 (2012)

21. Li, J., Harada, H.: Modeling of an SMA actuator based on the Liang and Rogers model. Int. J. Appl. Electromagnet. Mech. **43**(4), 325–335 (2013)

22. Rodrigue, H., Wang, W., Kim, D.R., et al.: Curved shape memory alloy-based soft actuators and application to soft gripper. Compos. Struct. **176**(9), 398–406 (2017)

23. Pan, J., Shi, Z.Y., Wang, T.M.: Variable-model SMA-driven spherical robot. Sci. China (Technol. Sci.) **62**, 1401–1411 (2019)

Continuous Super-Twisting Observer-Based Super-Twisting Control of Euler-Lagrange Systems

Guizhou Cao[1,2], Huige Shi[3], Xiaoke Zhang[1], Zheran Zhu[4], Yanhong Liu[2(✉)], and Hongnian Yu[2,5]

[1] State Grid Henan Electric Power Research Institute, Zhengzhou 450052, China
[2] School of Electrical Engineering, Zhengzhou University, Zhengzhou 450001, China
liuyh@zzu.edu.cn
[3] State Grid Nanyang Electric Power Supply Company, Nanyang 473000, China
[4] State Grid Jiaozuo Electric Power Supply Company, Jiaozuo 454100, China
[5] School of Engineering and the Built Environment, Edinburgh Napier University, Edinburgh, UK

Abstract. Higher-order observer-based robust controllers are commonly applied to Euler-Lagrange (EL) systems in presence of unavoidable uncertainties and unmeasurable states. However, the controllers are constructed by an assumption of differential system uncertainties, which constrains the physical applications disrupted by non-differentiable noises, such as discontinuous signals. This paper proposed a continuous observer-based sliding mode controller by utilizing the super-twisting algorithm (STA) and an integral sliding mode surface, and the condition of uncertainties is relaxed to be bounded. First, an improved STA-based observer is employed to estimate system states and adaptively compensate system uncertainties. Second, a novel integral sliding mode surface is employed to design a continuous STA-based controller for EL systems in presence of uncertainties without knowledge of upper bound in prior. The proposed controller relaxes the differential uncertainties to be bounded, achieve continuous inputs and improve system robustness. Finally, numerical simulations verify the effectiveness of the proposed controller.

Keywords: Euler-lagrange system · Sliding model control · Super-twisting algorithm · Observer-based controller

This work is supported by the National Key Research and Development Project (No. 2020YFB1313701), the National Natural Science Foundation of China (No. 61603345, 62003309), the Outstanding Foreign Scientist Support Project of Henan Province (No. GZS2019008), and Science & Technology Research Project in Henan Province of China (No. 202102210098).

© Springer Nature Switzerland AG 2021
X.-J. Liu et al. (Eds.): ICIRA 2021, LNAI 13013, pp. 455–465, 2021.
https://doi.org/10.1007/978-3-030-89095-7_44

1 Introduction

Euler–Lagrange (EL) systems can be used to describe numerous physical systems, such as electrical machines, autonomous vehicles, mobile robots, robotic manipulators, aircraft, satellites [1]. In practice, system uncertainties are unavoidable and some states may be unmeasurable, inducing that observer-based robust controllers attract lots of research interest. The sliding mode algorithm is famous for robustness, but it also tarnishes the chattering problem. Super-twisting algorithm (STA) is a chattering-free second-order sliding mode method, and it has been successfully employed in lots of applications, such as STA-based control (STC) of a doubly-fed induction generator [2], tethered space net robot [3], and state estimation of induction machines [4], pneumatic cylinder servo system [5] by using STA-based observer (STO). However, the STO-based STC under a linear sliding mode surface for EL systems with particular unmeasurable states is proved to be discontinuous [6,7].

Motivated by eliminating the chattering problem from STO-based STC, some studies represent the attitude globally and uniquely in terms of higher-order algorithms (HOA) based observer, i.e., higher-order sliding mode (HOSM) observer and extended-state-observer (ESO), to replace the STO. These observers not only estimate unavailable states but also the lumped system uncertainties of autonomous microgrids [8], coupled systems [9], aircrafts [10], Helmholtz coil system [11] and interceptors [12]. Since the continuous second term in the HOA, rather than the discontinuous second term in the STA, is compensated by the controller, the continuous of the HOA-based STC can be achieved. However, the lumped system uncertainties are estimated by third or higher-order terms in the HOA, inducing that it should be constrained as a differential term, which may be further limited by discontinuous noises generally existed in the environment.

The STA-based observer can relax the condition of differential uncertainties to be bounded. Different from existed works, the STO, rather than HOA-based observers, and integral sliding mode (ISM) surfaces are employed to construct a continuous STC in this paper. By utilizing the ISM method, the robustness of SMCs can be further improved [13]. In SMC, the system trajectory is divided into two phases: reaching phase and sliding phase [14]. On the reaching phase, system states are enforced into predefined sliding mode manifold in finite time, known as reaching time, whereas the robustness of the sliding mode controller on the reaching phase is similar to other controllers'. On the sliding phase, the SMC presents inherent robustness due to the manually designed manifold is insensitive to system uncertainties. To reduce the reaching time, an integral sliding mode algorithm is addressed to ensure system states stay on the sliding mode manifold at the initial time. To eliminate the condition of derivative uncertainties as well as improve the system robustness, an integral sliding mode surface combining into the STO-based STC is meaningful and valuable for physical applications, whereas there is still an open area to the best of authors' knowledge.

This paper is focused on designing a continuous STO-based STC for Euler-Lagrange systems by utilizing an integral sliding mode surface. The exact contributions of this paper can be summarized as

1. A novel continuous STO-based STC is proposed for EL systems, and the lumped uncertainties are relaxed to be bounded, while the unknown uncertainties are further adaptively compensated.
2. A novel integral sliding mode surface is addressed to improve the robustness of Euler-Lagrange systems.

2 Problem Statements and Preliminaries

In this section, the controlled plant is firstly given. Second, since some system states are unmeasurable, the HOSM-based SMC is restated and corresponding control problems are summarized. Finally, the control target is presented and some facilitated assumptions/lemmas are introduced.

2.1 Dynamic Model

EL systems can be formed as

$$M(q_1)\dot{q}_2 + C(q_1, q_2)q_2 + G(q_1) = u + v, \tag{1}$$

where $q_1, q_2 \in \mathbb{R}^{n \times 1}$ are position and velocity of the systems, respectively. $M(q_1) \in \mathbb{R}^{n \times n}, C(q_1, q_2) \in \mathbb{R}^{n \times n}, G(q_1) \in \mathbb{R}^{n \times 1}$ are the inertia matrix, the centripetal and Coriolis matrix and the hybrid force matrix, respectively. $u \in \mathcal{R}^{n \times 1}$ is the control input and v denotes lumped system uncertainties including external disturbance, unmodeled dynamics and parameter variations.

Based on the EL Eq. (1), the following properties are satisfied.

Property 1. [15] The inertia matrix $M(q)$ is symmetrical and positive definite, i.e.,

$$\lambda_{min}(M)I \le M(q_1) \le \lambda_{max}(M)I, \tag{2}$$

where I is an identity matrix with proper dimensions, and $\lambda_{min}, \lambda_{max}$ are the minimal and maximum eigenvalues of M, respectively.

Property 2. [16] The equation $x^T \left(\dot{M}(q_1) - 2C(q_1, q_2) \right) x = 0$ holds for each $x = [x_1, x_2, \cdots, x_n]^T$.

Property 3. [16] Since $C(q_1, q_2)$ is bounded in q_1 and linear in q_2, then

$$\begin{aligned} C(q_1, q_2)x &= C(q_1, x)q_2, \\ \|C(q_1, q_2)\| &\le K_C\|q_2\|, \end{aligned} \tag{3}$$

where K_C is a positive constant and $\|\cdot\|$ is Euclidean 2-norm.

Controlled Plant: By denoting the desired trajectory as q_d, the tracking error can be defined as $e_1 = q_1 - q_d$ and $e_2 = q_2 - \dot{q}_d$, such that the dynamic model (1) is transformed to a tracking error system

$$\begin{cases} \dot{e}_1 = e_2, \\ \dot{e}_2 = M^{-1}(q_1)\left[-C(q_1, q_2)q_2 - G(q_1) + u + v\right] - \ddot{q}_d \\ \quad = f(q_1, q_2) + u_t + d, \end{cases} \tag{4}$$

where $f(q_1, q_2) = M^{-1}(q_1)[-C(q_1, q_2)q_2 - G(q_1)] - \ddot{q}_d$, $u_t = M^{-1}u$ is the controller designed in next section, $d = M^{-1}v$ is the lumped system uncertainties.

Notation 1: For convenience, the following equations are given

$$sig^\epsilon(x) = [|x_1|^\epsilon \text{sign}(x_1), \cdots, |x_n|^\epsilon \text{sign}(x_n)]^T,$$
$$|x|^\epsilon = [|x_1|^\epsilon, |x_2|^\epsilon, \cdots, |x_n|^\epsilon]^T, \tag{5}$$

where $x_i \in R, i = 1, 2, \cdots, n$, ϵ is a positive constant, $|\cdot|$ is the absolute function and sign $(\cdot)$ is the sign function.

Notation 2: A matrix $K > 0$ represents the matrix is positive definite, and

$$\lambda_{min}(K)I \le K \le \lambda_{max}(K)I, \tag{6}$$

where $\lambda_{min}(K), \lambda_{max}(K)$ denote the minimal and maximal eigenvalues of K, respectively.

2.2   Problem Statement

Consider that the velocity $\dot{q}$ of the EL systems (1) is unavailable, then the HOSM-based observer is addressed as

$$\begin{cases} \dot{x}_1 = -k_{1d}sig^{\frac{2}{3}}(x_1 - q_1) + x_2, \\ \dot{x}_2 = -k_{2d}sig^{\frac{1}{2}}(x_1 - q_1) + u_d + f(q_1, x_2) + \ddot{q}_d, \\ \dot{x}_3 = -k_{3d}sign(x_1 - q_1), \end{cases} \tag{7}$$

in which u_d is a designed controller, and x_1, x_2, x_3 are estimations of q_1, q_2 and system uncertainties v_t, respectively.

Define estimated errors as $\tilde{x}_1 = x_1 - q_1, \tilde{x}_2 = x_2 - q_2, \tilde{x}_3 = x_3 - v$, then the estimated error dynamics can be expressed as

$$\begin{cases} \dot{\tilde{x}}_1 = -k_{1d}sig^{\frac{2}{3}}(\tilde{x}_1) + \tilde{x}_{2d}, \\ \dot{\tilde{x}}_2 = -k_{2d}sig^{\frac{1}{2}}(\tilde{x}_1) + \tilde{x}_{3d}, \\ \dot{\tilde{x}}_3 = -k_{3d}sign(\tilde{x}_1) + \dot{d}_c, \end{cases} \tag{8}$$

where $d_c = f(q_1, x_2) - f(q_1, q_2) - v$. Therefore, the estimated errors can be proved to be finite-time stable by the HOSM algorithm [17].

By employing the controller as

$$u_d = -f(q_1, x_2) - \lambda_c \hat{e}_{2c} + k_{2d}sig^{\frac{1}{2}}(\tilde{x}_1) - k_{1u}sig^{\frac{1}{2}}(s_d) - \int_0^t k_{2u}sign(s_d)d\sigma, \tag{9}$$

the derivative of linear sliding mode surface $s_d = \hat{e}_{2c} + \lambda_c e_1$ is

$$\dot{s}_d = \dot{\hat{e}}_{2c} + \lambda_c \dot{e}_1 = \dot{x}_2 - \ddot{q}_d + \lambda_c \dot{e}_1$$
$$= -k_{2d}sig^{\frac{1}{2}}(\tilde{x}_1) + u_d + f(q_1, x_2) + \lambda_c \dot{e}_1 = -k_{1u}sig^{\frac{1}{2}}(s_d) - \int_0^t k_{2u}sign(s_d)d\sigma - \lambda_c \tilde{x}_2, \tag{10}$$

where $\hat{e}_{2c} = \dot{x}_2 - \ddot{q}_d$ is an estimated tracking error. Therefore, the sliding variance s_d can be proved to be finite-time stable by employing the STA, then tracking errors asymptotically converge to zero as time tends to infinity [9].

Although the controller (9) is continuous and the sliding variance s_d is finite-time stable, the following issues are presented:

1. The lumped system uncertainty d_c is required to be derivative as presented in the observer (8).
2. The choices of gains k_{1d}, k_{2d}, k_{3d} are theoretically unresolved to guarantee finite-time stability for EL systems particular with unknown bound of d_c [18].
3. The sliding mode surface s_d is linear, whereas the system robustness can be further improved.

2.3   Preliminaries

Control Target: This paper is devoted to constructing a continuous STO-based STC for the system (4) without the requirements of differential uncertainties, such that tracking errors e_1, e_2 asymptotically tend to zero, i.e., $\lim\limits_{t \to \infty} (e_1) = 0$, $\lim\limits_{t \to \infty} (e_2) = 0$.

The achievement of the control target is facilitated by the following assumptions and lemmas.

Assumption 21. *The desired trajectory q_d is assumed to be known, bounded and twice differential, which implies $\dot{q}_d, \ddot{q}_d$ are existed and bounded, i.e., $||q_d||, ||\dot{q}_d||, ||\ddot{q}_d|| \leq K_d$, where K_d is a known positive constant.*

Assumption 22. *The external disturbance d is assumed to be bounded, yet the knowledge of the upper bound is not required.*

Lemma 1. *[6] If a continuous differentiable positive definite function: $V(t):$ $U \to \mathcal{R}$ satisfies the following condition,*

$$\dot{V}(t) \leq -cV^{\alpha}(t), \forall t \geq t_0, V(t_0) \geq 0. \tag{11}$$

where $c > 0$ is a positive constant, and t_0 is the initial time. Then for any given $t_0, V(t)$ satisfies

$$V^{1-\alpha}(t) \leq V^{1-\alpha}(t_0) - c(1-\alpha)(t-t_0), \tag{12}$$

And $V(t) \equiv 0, t_0 \leq t \leq t_1$ with t_1 given by

$$t_1 = t_0 + \frac{V^{1-\alpha}(t_0)}{c(1-\alpha)}. \tag{13}$$

Furthermore, for any real numbers $\lambda_1 > 0, \lambda_2 > 0$ and $0 < \alpha < 1$, an extended Lyapunov description of finite-time stability can be given with the form of fast terminal sliding mode as

$$V(t) + \lambda_1 V(t) + \lambda_2 V^{\alpha}(t) \leq 0. \tag{14}$$

3   Observer and Controller Design

To estimate system states, an improved STO is employed as

$$\begin{cases} \dot{\hat{q}}_1 = -k_{o1} sig^{\frac{1}{2}}(\tilde{q}_1) - k_{o2}\tilde{q}_1 + \hat{q}_2, \\ \dot{\hat{q}}_2 = -k_{o3}\text{sign}(\tilde{q}_1) - k_{o4}\tilde{q}_1 + \tau_1, \end{cases} \tag{15}$$

where $\hat{q}_1, \hat{q}_2$ are estimation on angle and velocity, respectively, $\tilde{q}_1 = \hat{q}_1 - q_1$ is defined as estimated error vector, and τ_1 is an additional controller.

Inspired by [17], the homogeneous property is used for estimating the upper bound of uncertainties and simplifying the choice of $k_{o1}, k_{o2}, k_{o3}, k_{o4}$ such that these gains share one common parameter ψ, then the following variables are used

$$k_{o1} = k_{t1}\sqrt{\psi}, k_{o2} = k_{t2}\psi, k_{o3} = k_{t3}\psi, k_{o4} = k_{t4}\psi^2, \dot{\psi} = \psi_1 |\text{sign}(\tilde{q}_1)|, \tag{16}$$

where $k_{t1}, k_{t2}, k_{t3}, k_{t4}$ are positive definite matrices, and ψ_1 is a positive constant.

Theorem 1. *Consider the system (4) with Assumptions 21 and 22. Estimated errors will converge to zero in finite time, and tracking errors will asymptotically tend to zero on the sliding mode surface, if the controller is designed as*

$$\begin{cases} u_t = M^{-1}(q_1)u, u = M(q_1)\tau_1 + G(q_1) + C(q_1, \hat{q}_2)\hat{q}_2, \\ \tau_1 = -k_s sig^{\frac{1}{2}}(S_i) - k_t \int_0^t sign(S_i)d\sigma + \ddot{q}_d - K_A\hat{e}_2 - K_B e_1, \end{cases} \tag{17}$$

with an integral sliding mode surface

$$S_i = \hat{e}_2 - \hat{e}_2(0) + \int_0^t K_A\hat{e}_2 + K_B e_1 + k_{o3}sign(\tilde{q}_1) + k_{o4}\tilde{q}_1 dt, \tag{18}$$

where $\hat{e}_2 = \hat{q}_2 - \dot{q}_d$ is an estimated tracking error, and gains of the observer (15) $k_{t1}, k_{t2}, k_{t3}, k_{t4}$ are properly selected to satisfy the following inequality

$$-9k_{t1}^2 k_{t3}^2 - 8k_{t2}k_{t3}^2 + 16k_{t2}k_{t4} > 0. \tag{19}$$

Proof. The proof is divided into three steps. First, estimated errors are proved to converge to zero in finite time. Second, system states reach the sliding mode surface in finite time, thereafter they always stay on the surface in the rest of time. Finally, system states asymptotically tend to zero on the sliding mode surface.

Step I: The estimated errors are converged to zero in finite time. Based on $\tilde{q}_1 = \hat{q}_1 - q_1, \tilde{q}_2 \triangleq \hat{q}_2 - q_2$, the observer (15) can be transformed as

$$\begin{cases} \dot{\tilde{q}}_1 = -k_{o1} sig^{\frac{1}{2}}(\tilde{q}_1) - k_{o2}\tilde{q}_1 + \tilde{q}_2, \\ \dot{\tilde{q}}_2 = -k_{o3}\text{sign}(\tilde{q}_1) - k_{o4}\tilde{q}_1 + d_o, \end{cases} \tag{20}$$

where one has

$$\begin{aligned} d_o &= \tau_1 - M^{-1}(q_1)\left[-C(q_1, q_2)q_2 - G(q_1) + u + d\right] \\ &= -M^{-1}(q_1)\left[-C(q_1, q_2)q_2 + C(q_1, q_2)\hat{q}_2 - C(q_1, q_2)\hat{q}_2 + C(q_1, \hat{q}_2)\hat{q}_2 + d\right] \\ &= -M^{-1}(q_1)\left[-2C(q_1, q_2)\hat{e}_2 + d\right], \end{aligned} \tag{21}$$

in which $\hat{e}_2 = \hat{q}_2 - \dot{q}_d$. The estimated errors are proved to be finite-time convergent in previous works [6,7], and they are omitted here for the sake of spaces.

Step II: System states is proved to reach the sliding mode surface in finite time. According to the definition of the sliding mode surface S_i, then the time derivative of S_i is expressed as

$$
\begin{aligned}
\dot{S}_i &= \hat{e}_2 + K_A\hat{e}_2 + K_B e_1 + k_{t3}\text{sign}(\tilde{q}_1) + k_{t4}\tilde{q}_1 \\
&= -k_{t3}\text{sign}(\tilde{q}_1) - k_{t4}\tilde{q}_1 + \tau_1 - \ddot{q}_d + K_A\hat{e}_2 + K_B e_1 + k_{t3}\text{sign}(\tilde{q}_1) + k_{t4}\tilde{q}_1 \\
&= -k_s sig^{\frac{1}{2}}(S_i) - k_t \int_0^t \text{sign}(S_i)d\sigma,
\end{aligned}
\tag{22}
$$

Defining an auxiliary state ξ as follows

$$
\begin{cases}
\dot{S}_i = -k_s sig^{\frac{1}{2}}(S_i) + \xi, \\
\dot{\xi} = -k_t\text{sign}(S_i),
\end{cases}
\tag{23}
$$

The finite-time stability of the STA (23) can be proved if one choses an auxiliary state as $\rho = [\rho_1, \rho_2]^T = [sig^{\frac{1}{2}}(S_i), \xi]^T$ and set the candidate Lyapunov function as

$$
V_s = \rho^T P_s \rho,
\tag{24}
$$

where P_s is a positive definite matrix

$$
P_s = \frac{1}{2}\begin{bmatrix} k_s^2 + 4k_t & -k_s \\ -k_s & 2 \end{bmatrix}.
\tag{25}
$$

The rest proof of this step can be found in previous works [19,20], and it is omitted here for brevity. According to the finite-time Lemma 1, one has $\dot{V}_s \leq 0$, thus we can see $s\dot{s} < 0, \forall s \neq 0$. System states will stay on the sliding model surface after they reach it.

Step III: On the sliding mode surface, $S_i = 0 \rightarrow \dot{S}_i = 0$, therefore, one gets,

$$
\dot{S}_i = \dot{e}_2 + K_A e_2 + K_B e_1 = 0,
\tag{26}
$$

which induces that the second-order system is asymptotically stable if K_A, K_B are Hurwitz. ∎

Remark 1. As illustrated in the proof, the estimated error system and the tracking error system are both finite-time stable, i.e., the separation principle is satisfied, which enables us to design the observer and the tracking control law separately [10,21].

Remark 2. The lumped system uncertainties d_o are not required to be derivative, and the prior knowledge of uncertainties is not required. Under the updated law (16), gains of observer are adaptively turned. It worth noting that the updated law ψ is positive except $\tilde{q} = 0$. In practice, estimated states are always disrupted by external noises, implying that $\tilde{q}$ cannot be exactly zero. Therefore, a dead layer is employed to modify the law,

$$\dot{\psi} = \begin{cases} \psi_1 \left| \text{sign}\left(\tilde{q}_1\right)\right| & \text{if} \quad |\tilde{q}_1| > \delta, \\ 0 & \text{if} \quad |\tilde{q}_1| \leq \delta, \end{cases} \tag{27}$$

where δ is a positive constant. Decreasing δ leads to higher control precision but increasing risk of controller saturation, therefore the choice of δ is a trade-off between control precision and saturation risk.

4 Simulations

As a kind of EL systems, pneumatic soft actuators presents inherent flexibility, adaptivity and safety for the unstructured environment due to soft bodies, providing state-of-art solutions for vigorous applications including high-voltage cable overhaul [22], nuclear power plant detection [23]. However, the soft bodies also hinder rigid state sensors, such as tachometers, speedometers and gyroscopes, to measure the velocity information for feedback controller implementation [24]. To tackle the unavailable velocity and unavoidable system uncertainties of soft actuators, observer-based robust controllers are preferred methods.

Recently, the generalized dynamics of pneumatic soft actuators have been addressed by exploring the Lagrangian method [25]. The dynamics of soft actuators are formed as

$$M\left(q\right)\ddot{q} + C\left(q,\dot{q}\right)\dot{q} + G_v\left(\dot{q}\right) = \tau + d_0, \tag{28}$$

where $M\left(q\right) = mL^2\left(\dfrac{1}{20} - \dfrac{q^2}{504}\right), C\left(q,\dot{q}\right) = -\dfrac{mL^2 q\dot{q}}{504}, G_v\left(q\right) = \dfrac{mgLq}{12}, \tau = k_p p$, and L, m, g are the total length, the mass and gravity coefficient, respectively. Since the pneumatic network actuator is driven by internal pressure p, the controller will be eventually converted into the pressure with an estimated coefficient k_p. It should note that the unmodeled dynamics and external disturbances are seemed as system uncertainties, which are contained in d_0.

A soft actuator is simulated with $m = 0.04\,\text{kg}, L = 0.114\,\text{m}$. The desired trajectory is set as $q_d = 0.9 + 0.8\sin(0.8t - \pi/2)(\text{rad})$, and the lumped system uncertainties are set as white noises with magnitude of $1(\text{N})$, which implies that HOSM-based controllers cannot applied to this scene. Gains of the observer and the controller are chosen after trail-in-errors, and they are $\psi_1 = 0.5, k_{t1} = 2, k_{t2} = 345, k_{t3} = 1, k_{t4} = 270, k_s = 100, k_t = 10, K_A = 18, K_B = 280$. The initial tracking error is set as $e_1 = 0.1(\text{rad})$, and the initial estimated error $\tilde{q}_1 = 0.1(\text{rad})$. Corresponding simulation results are shown in Fig. 1 and Fig. 2.

Under initial tracking errors, both angle and velocity tracking errors can asymptotically converge to zero as presented in Fig. 1, which illustrates the effectiveness of the proposed controller. Compared with angle errors, velocity errors are larger due to its more sensitive to external noises. The proposed controller has continuous inputs as illustrated in Fig. 2 and an inset.

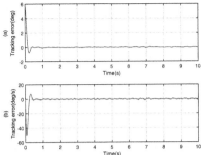

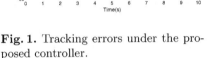

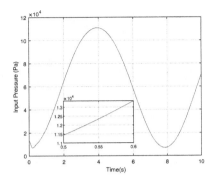

Fig. 1. Tracking errors under the proposed controller.

Fig. 2. Controlled input pressure.

5   Conclusion

This paper constructs a continuous STO-based STC for EL systems through an integral sliding mode surface. By employing the STO, rather than HOA, the condition of differential and bounded uncertainties is relaxed to be bounded, and the proposed controller is suitable for wider applications. Furthermore, the robustness of the closed-loop system is improved by integral sliding mode surface as system states stay in the surface in the beginning. Finally, the observer and controller share the same effects of gains of STA, simplifying the parameter turning process in simulations. The proposed controller will be further applied to physical systems in the future.

References

1. Roy, S., Baldi, S.: Towards structure-independent stabilization for uncertain underactuated Euler-Lagrange systems. Automatica **113**, 108775–108713 (2020)
2. Wang, J., Bo, D., Miao, Q., Li, Z., et al.: Maximum power point tracking control for a doubly fed induction generator wind energy conversion system based on multivariable adaptive supertwisting approach. Int. J. Elec. Power **124**, 106347–106399 (2021)
3. Zhao, Y., Zhang, F., Huang, P.: Capture dynamics and control of tethered space net robot for space debris capturing in unideal capture case. J. Franklin Inst. **357**(17), 12019–12036 (2020)
4. Han, L., Xu, W., Kang, P., Yuan, H.: Speed observer structure of induction machine based on sliding super-twisting and backstepping techniques. IEEE Trans. Ind. Inform. **17**(2), 1166–1175 (2021)
5. Zhao, L., Zheng, C., Wang, Y., Liu, B.: A finite-time control for a pneumatic cylinder servo system based on a super-twisting extended state observer. IEEE Trans. Syst. Man Cybern. Syst. **51**(2), 1164–1173 (2021)

6. Cao, G., Liu, Y., Jiang, Y., Zhang, F., Bian, G., Owens, D.H.: Observer-based continuous adaptive sliding mode control for soft actuators. Nonlinear Dyn. **105**(1), 371–386 (2021). https://doi.org/10.1007/s11071-021-06606-w

7. Cao, G., Xie, C., Liu, Y.: Observer-based adaptive sliding mode tracking control for soft bending actuators. In: Proceedings of the 2020 Chinese Automation Congress (CAC), pp. 5789–5794 (2020)

8. Ge, P., Dou, X., Quan, X., Hu, Q., et al.: Extended-state-observer-based distributed robust secondary voltage and frequency control for an autonomous microgrid. IEEE Trans. Sustain. Enegy **11**(1), 195–205 (2020)

9. Sadala, S.P., Patre, B.M.: Super-twisting control using higher order disturbance observer for control of SISO and MIMO coupled systems. ISA T **106**(3), 303–317 (2020)

10. Liu, J., Sun, M., Chen, Z., Sun, Q.: Super-twisting sliding mode control for aircraft at high angle of attack based on finite-time extended state observer. Nonlinear Dyn. **99**(4), 2785–2799 (2020). https://doi.org/10.1007/s11071-020-05481-1

11. Jialin, J., Lidong, Y., Li, Z.: Closed-loop control of a Helmholtz coil system for accurate actuation of magnetic microrobot swarms. IEEE Robot. Autom. Lett. **6**(2), 827–834 (2021)

12. Khankalantary, S., Sheikholeslam, F.: Robust extended state observer-based three dimensional integrated guidance and control design for interceptors with impact angle and input saturation constraints. ISA T **104**(3), 299–309 (2020)

13. Guo, Y., Huang, B., Li, A.J., Wang, C.: Integral sliding mode control for Euler-Lagrange systems with input saturation. Int. J. Robust Nonlinear Control **29**(4), 1088–1100 (2019)

14. Zhao, L., Zhang, B., Yang, H.J., Wang, Y.J.: Observer-based integral sliding mode tracking control for a pneumatic cylinder with varying loads. IEEE Trans. Syst Man Cybern. Syst. **50**(7), 2650–2658 (2020)

15. Della Santina, C., Bicchi, A., Rus, D.: On an improved state parametrization for soft robots with piecewise constant curvature and its use in model based control. IEEE Robot. Autom. Lett. **5**(2), 1001–1008 (2020)

16. Della Santina, C., Katzschmann, R.K., Bicchi, A., Rus, D.: Model-based dynamic feedback control of a planar soft robot: trajectory tracking and interaction with the environment. Int. J. Robot. Res. **1**(3), 1–24 (2020)

17. Arie, L.: Higher-order sliding modes, differentiation and output-feedback control. Int. J. Control. **76**(9–10), 924–941 (2003)

18. Zhang, K., Duan, G.: Output-feedback super-twisting control for line-of-sight angles tracking of non-cooperative target spacecraft. ISA Trans. **94**(1), 17–27 (2019)

19. Kali, Y., Saad, M., Benjelloun, K., Khairallah, C.: Super-twisting algorithm with time delay estimation for uncertain robot manipulators. Nonlinear Dyn. **93**(2), 557–569 (2018). https://doi.org/10.1007/s11071-018-4209-y

20. Perez-Ventura, U., Fridman, L.: Design of super-twisting control gains: a describing function based methodology. Automatica **99**, 175–180 (2019)

21. Li, B., Qin, K., Xiao, B., Yang, Y.: Finite-time extended state observer based fault tolerant output feedback control for attitude stabilization. ISA Trans. **91**(1), 11–20 (2019)

22. Liao, B., Zang, H., Chen, M., Wang, Y.: Soft rod-climbing robot inspired by winding locomotion of snake. Soft Robot. **7**(4), 500–511 (2020)

23. Li, Y., Ren, T., Li, Y., Liu, Q., et al.: Untethered-bioinspired quadrupedal robot based on double-chamber pre-charged pneumatic soft actuators with highly flexible trunk. Soft Robot. **8**(1), 97–108 (2021)

24. Cao, G., Huo, B., Yang, L., Zhang, F., et al.: Model-based robust tracking control without observers for soft bending actuators. IEEE Rob. Autom. Lett. **6**(3), 5175–5182 (2021)

25. Wang, T., Zhang, Y., Zhu, Y., Zhu, S.: A computationally efficient dynamical model of fluidic soft actuators and its experimental verification. Mechatronics **58**(1), 1–8 (2019)

A Continuum Robot with Twin-Pivot Structure: The Kinematics and Shape Estimation

Zheshuai Yang, Laihao Yang$^{(\boxtimes)}$, Lu Xu, Xuefeng Chen, Yanjie Guo, Jinxin Liu, and Yu Sun

Xi'an Jiaotong University, Xi'an 710049, China
{yzs12138,godfather707}@stu.xjtu.edu.cn, yanglaihao@xjtu.edu.cn

Abstract. Continuum robot, unlike conventional rigid-link robots, has numerous numbers of degrees of freedom, enabling it to be applied for confined space works, such as minimally invasive surgery, safe robot/objective interactions, and in-situ aero-engine detection. This study presented a cable-driven continuum robot with twin-pivot structure, which poses smaller diameter-length-ratio and torsion resistance ability compared with conventional single-pivot structure, as well as the kinematics and shape estimation. The kinematics model of the twin-pivot continuum robot is established based on the assumption of piecewise constant curvature, with which the mapping between driving space and operation space are presented. Finally, a prototype of continuum robot system with single section is constructed to verify the validation of the kinematics model and study the shape estimation. Based on the constructed prototype, the shape estimation of the continuum robot with different payloads is performed. The comparative results suggest that relative error is less than 5% for total length of the single section without payload, verifying the validity of the kinematics model. The comparison between the results with different payloads indicate that the increasing payload will increase the relative error.

Keywords: Continuum robot · Twin-pivot · Kinematics model · Shape estimation

1 Introduction

Continuum robots, which are inspired by the snakes and elephant trunks in nature, show incomparable flexibility and unique adaptability to confined space that conventional rigid-link robots are unable to achieve [1, 2]. Owing to these properties, continuum robots have been widely used in minimally invasive surgery [3–5], nuclear reactor maintenance [6] and rescue [7], etc. Recently, continuum robots were applied to the field of aero-engine engineering, serving as a novel solution for in-situ aero-engines repair [8–11], which has aroused extensive interests.

According to the joint structure, most continuum robots can be classified into two categories: rigid backbone continuum robot and flexible backbone continuum robot [12, 13]. The rigid backbone continuum robots were extensively investigated [11, 13, 14], and

© Springer Nature Switzerland AG 2021
X.-J. Liu et al. (Eds.): ICIRA 2021, LNAI 13013, pp. 466–475, 2021.
https://doi.org/10.1007/978-3-030-89095-7_45

some successfully commercial cases were reported by OC robotics [15] and SIASUN [16]. However, because of the large diameter and rigid backbone, the application of rigid backbone continuum robots in the confined space works is restricted [12, 17]. On the contrary, the flexible backbone enables the minimization of the size of continuum robot and poses better accessibility in confined space works. However, the length of these robots is generally shorter than the rigid backbone ones, and the payloads are limited [10]. So far, it is still a tough task to develop a flexible backbone continuum robot with smaller diameter-length-ratio and larger load carrying capacity. In this paper, the twin-pivot structure is introduced, which minimizes the size of the continuum robot and reduces the twisting angle caused by weight of the robot arm.

Apart from the structural design, it is necessary to establish a kinematics model for continuum robot. Most of the kinematics model for the rigid backbone continuum robots are based on the D-H method, while this method cannot be directly applied to the kinematics modeling of flexible backbone continuum robots since these robots have no definite joints. The kinematics model of flexible ones is generally based on the assumption of piecewise constant curvature (PCC), where each section of robotic arm is assumed to be a constant arc [1, 18, 19]. This method greatly simplifies the kinematics model. Thus, it has been widely used. However, the PCC-based kinematics model ignores the effects of loads, gravity, and friction [20, 21], which leads to lower accuracy. To improve the accuracy of modeling, a comprehensive static model that considers the effects of friction, loads, etc. is reported in [10] and [20], which has achieved great improvement in the model accuracy. However, the statics model suffers the defects of complex iteration and large computation, which makes it difficult to implement in real-time control directly. Generally speaking, the PCC-based kinematics model is still a reliable and the most used modeling method in the field of continuum robotics because of the simple principle of modeling and low computation cost with an acceptable error.

In this paper, the prototype of single section continuum robot driven by four cables is studied. The kinematics model is established based on the assumption of PCC, which maps the relationship between drive space and operation space. Furthermore, the shape estimation of the prototype with/without payload is detected by the vision system to evaluate the motion accuracy of the continuum robot and the reliability of the kinematic model.

The remainder of this paper is organized as follows. Section 2 establishes the mechanical structure and kinematics model. In Sect. 3, the experimental platform is presented, and the shape estimation of the prototype is detected by vision system. The last section summarizes the whole paper and gives the conclusions.

2 Modeling

2.1 Structure of Continuum Robot

The twin-pivot structure reported in [12] has been proven to effectively reduce the twisting angle of the continuum robot. The structure of this continuum robot with two sections is shown in Fig. 1. Each section consists of several segments which are composed of disks and NiTi rods, and is driven by four even distributed cables. As shown in Fig. 1, the four dots indicate the location of the cables which drive the 2nd section, thus, the cables of 2nd section will pass through 1st section.

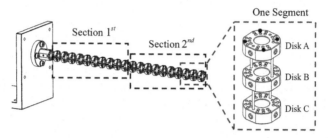

Fig. 1. The structure of the twin-pivot continuum robot.

2.2 Kinematics Model

Forward Kinematics. The purpose of the forward kinematics is to determine the tip position of the continuum robot based on the given lengths of cables. Since the continuum robot is composed of identical segment, the kinematic model is obtained, based on the analysis of a segment on which the joint coordinate system is shown in Fig. 2, and the joint parameters can be obtained from Table 1. According to these parameters, the homogeneous transformation matrix from coordinate system $\{i\}$ to $\{i+1\}$ can be written as:

$$^{i-1}_i T = \text{Rot}(x, \alpha_{i-1}) \cdot \text{Trans}(a_{i-1}, 0, 0) \cdot \text{Rot}(z, \theta_i) \cdot \text{Trans}(0, 0, d_i) \tag{1}$$

where $i = 1, 2, 3$.

The forward kinematics of the segment can be written as:

$$^0_3 T = {}^0_1 T \cdot {}^1_2 T \cdot {}^2_3 T \tag{2}$$

thus, the forward kinematics model of continuum robot can be written as:

$$T = T_1 \cdot T_2 \cdot \ldots \cdot T_N \tag{3}$$

where N is the number of sections.

Inverse Kinematics. The purpose of the inverse kinematics is to determine the lengths of cables according to the known position. As shown in Fig. 3 and Fig. 4, taking the 1st

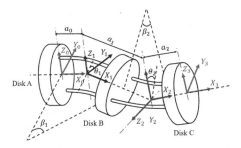

Fig. 2. The joint coordinate system of segment.

Table 1. The joint parameters.

Joint i	α_{i-1}	a_{i-1}	d_i	θ_i
1	0	$\frac{l_0}{\beta_1} \cdot \tan \frac{\beta_1}{2}$	0	$-\beta_1$
2	$\frac{\pi}{2}$	$\frac{l_0}{\beta_1} \cdot \tan \frac{\beta_1}{2} + h + \frac{l_0}{\beta_2} \cdot \tan \frac{\beta_2}{2}$	0	β_2
3	$-\frac{\pi}{2}$	$h + \frac{l_0}{\beta_2} \cdot \tan \frac{\beta_2}{2}$	0	0

section as an example, the lengths of the cables can be written as:

$$
\begin{cases}
\Delta l_{1,1} = \Delta l_{1,1}^1 = 2n_1\left[\left(\dfrac{l_0}{\beta_1} - r \cdot \cos \delta_1\right) \cdot \sin \dfrac{\beta_1}{2} + \left(\dfrac{l_0}{\beta_2} - r \cdot \sin \delta_1\right) \cdot \sin \dfrac{\beta_2}{2} - l_0\right] \\[2mm]
\Delta l_{1,2} = \Delta l_{1,2}^1 = 2n_1\left[\left(\dfrac{l_0}{\beta_1} - r \cdot \sin \delta_1\right) \cdot \sin \dfrac{\beta_1}{2} + \left(\dfrac{l_0}{\beta_2} + r \cdot \cos \delta_1\right) \cdot \sin \dfrac{\beta_2}{2} - l_0\right] \\[2mm]
\Delta l_{1,3} = \Delta l_{1,3}^1 = 2n_1\left[\left(\dfrac{l_0}{\beta_1} + r \cdot \cos \delta_1\right) \cdot \sin \dfrac{\beta_1}{2} + \left(\dfrac{l_0}{\beta_2} + r \cdot \sin \delta_1\right) \cdot \sin \dfrac{\beta_2}{2} - l_0\right] \\[2mm]
\Delta l_{1,4} = \Delta l_{1,4}^1 = 2n_1\left[\left(\dfrac{l_0}{\beta_1} + r \cdot \sin \delta_1\right) \cdot \sin \dfrac{\beta_1}{2} + \left(\dfrac{l_0}{\beta_2} - r \cdot \cos \delta_1\right) \cdot \sin \dfrac{\beta_2}{2} - l_0\right]
\end{cases}
\tag{4}
$$

where n_1 is the number of the segments in the 1st section.

The inverse kinematics model of the continuum robot can be then written as:

$$
\Delta l_{i,j} = \sum_{k=1}^{i} \Delta l_{i,j}^k
\tag{5}
$$

where $\Delta l_{i,j}^k$ is the cable length of the jth cable driving the ith section at the kth section, $i = 1, 2, \ldots, N$, and $j = 1, 2, 3, 4$.

The forward and inverse kinematics of the continuum robot can be expressed as Eq. (3) and Eq. (5), with which the mapping relationship between drive space and operation space is established.

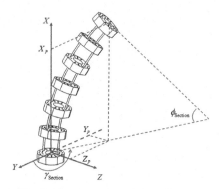

Fig. 3. Configuration of single section.

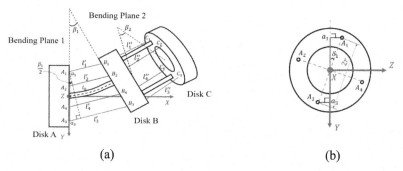

(a)   (b)

Fig. 4. (a) Configuration of segment; (b) Top view of disk A.

3   Shape Estimation

To verify the validation of the kinematics model, shape estimation is experimentally performed on a vision detection system. First of all, a prototype of single section cable-driven continuum robot is fabricated. Then the kinematic analysis and shape estimation experiments of the single section with or without payload in-plane are carried out.

3.1   Experimental Setup

As shown in Fig. 5, the experimental mainly consists of a continuum robot prototype, a vision system, pulleys, and motor units. The continuum robot prototype is fixed to an optical platform and driven by four cables which are controlled by four motor units. The pulleys are employed to change the directions of cables. In addition, the shape estimation in the xoz plane of the continuum robot could be detected by a vision system with a 5472×3648 pixel camera. By the way, the precision of the vision measuring system is 0.01 mm, which satisfies the shape estimation accuracy. It should be noted that the shape estimation is done by detecting the marked center point of each disk.

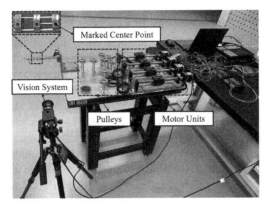

Fig. 5. The experimental platform.

As shown in Fig. 6, three continuum robot prototypes with different diameter-length-ratio (17/250, 17/200, and 17/150) are made, where each prototype contains 10 ten disks with a diameter of 17mm, and the only difference is the length of the NiTi rods. It is found that the diameter-length-ratio of 17/150 can better overcome the twist effect caused by gravity, thus, we choose this prototype (i.e. diameter-length-ratio of 17/150) for kinematics validation and shape estimation experiments.

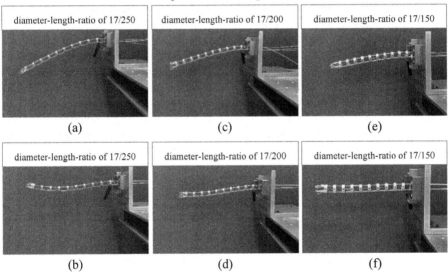

Fig. 6. (a) The prototype with diameter-length-ratio of 17/250 without cables constraint; (b) The prototype with diameter-length-ratio of 17/250 with cables constraint; (c) The prototype with diameter-length-ratio of 17/200 without cables constraint; (d) The prototype with diameter-length-ratio of 17/200 with cables constraint; (e) The prototype with diameter-length-ratio of 17/150 without cables constraint; (f) The prototype with diameter-length-ratio of 17/150 with cables constraint.

3.2 Shape Estimation of a Single Section

To evaluate the motion accuracy of the continuum robot and the reliability of the kinematic model, the shape of the single section is detected by the vision system. As shown in Fig. 7, the plane bending experiment ($\theta = 0°$ to $90°$) without payload is carried out, and the total length of the prototype is 150 mm. Another two experiments with a payload of 51.3 g and 101.3 g are conducted, where the masses of the weights are 50 g and 100 g respectively, and the mass of the cable used to fix the weights is 1.3 g. The results are shown in Fig. 8 and Fig. 9, where the experimental data are represented by blue boxes and the kinematic-model-calculated data are represented by red stars. And the top position accuracy measurement results are shown in Table 2.

As shown in Fig. 7, the single section prototype is in good agreement with the kinematic model when the bending angle is $90°$. By comparing the experimental and model-based data, the maximum error is 7.4 mm, which accounts for 4.9% of the entire length of the single section (i.e. 150 mm). In Fig. 8 and Fig. 9, due to the influence of the payload, the kinematics model is unable to accurately estimate the shape of the prototype, and the maximum errors are 14.91 mm and 23.38 mm, accounting for 9.94% and 15.59% of the entire section length.

3.3 Limitation Discussion

As shown in the comparative experimental results, to some degree, the kinematics model based on PCC can characterize the motion of the continuum robot within an acceptable error. However, since the assumption of PCC ignores the effects of gravity, payload, and friction, the simulation accuracy is limited, especially when the payload or the length of continuum robot is increased. In the coming future, the kinematic and static model which considers the mechanical characteristics of continuum robot and other methods [22, 23] will be further deduced to improve the motion accuracy and reliability. In addition, the FBG sensing-based shape reconstruction techniques will be applied to solve the kinematic modeling problems, since it is independent of the theoretical model and the shape of the continuum robot can be obtained in real-time [24].

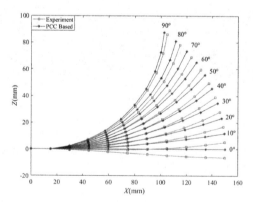

Fig. 7. A bending test without payload.

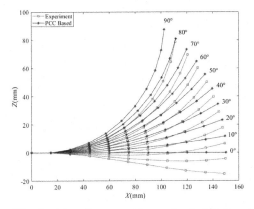

Fig. 8. A bending test with a payload of 51.3 g.

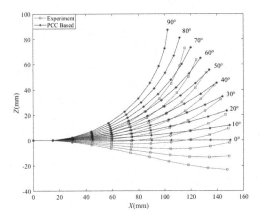

Fig. 9. A bending test with a payload of 101.3 g.

Table 2. Top accuracy measurement results

Bending angle (deg)	Desired position (mm)		Actual position without payload (mm)		Actual position with payload of 51.3 g (mm)		Actual position with payload of 101.3 g (mm)	
	X	Z	X	Z	X	Z	X	Z
0	150	0	149.78	−6.24	148.83	−14.91	147.59	−23.26
10	149.34	11.75	149.75	5.12	149.57	−4.32	149.02	−12.65
20	147.38	23.34	148.46	16.93	149.18	6.61	149.33	−1.96
30	144.16	34.61	145.95	27.99	147.60	17.84	148.44	9.23
40	139.71	45.39	142.20	38.90	144.76	29.13	146.38	20.31

(continued)

Table 2. (*continued*)

Bending angle (deg)	Desired position (mm)		Actual position without payload (mm)		Actual position with payload of 51.3 g (mm)		Actual position with payload of 101.3 g (mm)	
	X	Z	X	Z	X	Z	X	Z
50	134.13	55.55	137.21	49.53	140.68	39.82	142.72	32.36
60	127.50	64.95	131.03	59.47	135.36	50.18	137.84	43.45
70	119.91	73.47	123.45	69.04	128.59	60.40	131.75	53.74
80	111.54	81.00	114.76	78.13	120.69	69.63	124.24	63.59
90	102.47	87.47	104.80	86.17	110.08	78.84	115.36	72.98

4 Conclusions

In this paper, the kinematics model and shape estimation of the twin-pivot continuum robot are numerically and experimentally studied. First and foremost, an experimental platform consisting of a prototype, a vision system, pulleys, and motor units is presented. Then the kinematics model of prototype is established based on the assumption of PCC. Finally, the vision system is utilized to detect the shape of the continuum robot. With the estimated shape, the motion accuracy of the continuum robot and the reliability of the kinematic model are evaluated. The results suggest that the maximum error is 7.4mm, which accounts for 4.9% of the entire length of the single section. In addition, the payload tests are carried out, the comparative results indicates that the kinematics model accuracy for the cases with payload is restricted due to the limitation of PCC assumption.

The results show that the kinematic model is enabled to accurately estimate the shape of the prototype with an acceptable error, while the motion accuracy with the payload increasing. In the coming works, the payload performance of the continuum robot can be improved by optimizing the structure design and adding variable stiffness structure. In addition, a kinematics and statics model should be used to compensate the effect of the payload and the FBG sensing-based shape reconstruction techniques will be applied to solve the kinematic modeling problems.

Acknowledgements. This work is sponsored by the National Natural Science Foundation of China (Nos. 52105117, 91860127).

References

1. Webster, R.J., Jones, B.A.: Design and kinematic modeling of constant curvature continuum robots: a review. Int. J. Robot. Res. **29**(13), 1661–1683 (2010)
2. Hannan, M.W., Walker, I.D.: Kinematics and the implementation of an elephant's trunk manipulator and other continuum style robot . Robot Syst. **20**(2), 45–63 (2003)

3. Ji, D., Kang, T.H., Shim, S., et al.: Analysis of twist deformation in wire-driven continuum surgical robot. Int. J. Control Autom. Syst. **18**(1), 10–20 (2019)
4. Shin, W.H., Kwon, D.S.: Surgical robot system for single-port surgery with novel joint mechanism. IEEE Trans. Biomed. Eng. **60**(4), 937–944 (2013)
5. Camarillo, D.B., Carlson, C.R., Salisbury, J.K.: Configuration tracking for continuum manipulators with coupled tendon drive. IEEE Trans. Rob. **25**(4), 798–808 (2009)
6. Buckingham, R., Graham, A.: Nuclear snake-arm robots. Ind. Robot Int. J. **39**(1), 6–11 (2012)
7. Kamegawa, T., Yamasaki, T., Igarashi, H., et al.: Development of the snake-like rescue robot "KOHGA. In: 2004 IEEE International Conference on Robotics and Automaton on Proceedings, pp. 5081–5086. IEEE, New York (2004)
8. Dong, X., Palmer, D., Axinte, D., et al.: In-situ repair/maintenance with a continuum robotic machine tool in confined space. J. Manuf. Process. **38**, 313–318 (2019)
9. Dong, X., Axinte, D., Palmer, D., et al.: Development of a slender continuum robotic system for on-wing inspection/repair of gas turbine engines. Robot. Comput. Integr. Manuf. **44**, 218–229 (2017)
10. Wang, M., Dong, X., Ba, W., et al.: Design, modelling and validation of a novel extra slender continuum robot for in-situ inspection and repair in aeroengine. Robot. Comput.-Integr. Manuf. **67**, 102054 (2021)
11. Tang, L., Wang, J., Zheng, Y., et al.: Design of a cable-driven hyper-redundant robot with experimental validation. Int. J. Adv. Robot. Syst. **14**(5), 1–12 (2017)
12. Dong, X., Raffles, M., Cobos-Guzman, S., et al.: A novel continuum robot using twin-pivot compliant joints: design, modeling, and validation. J. Mech. Robot.-Trans. ASME **8**(2), 021010 (2016)
13. Xu, W., Liu, T., Li, Y.: Kinematics, dynamics, and control of a cable-driven hyper-redundant manipulator. IEEE/ASME Trans. Mechatron. **23**(4), 1693–1704 (2018)
14. Tang, L., Huang, J., Zhu, L., et al.: Path tracking of a cable-driven snake robot with a two-level motion planning method. IEEE/ASME Trans. Mechatron. **24**(3), 935–946 (2019)
15. Bogue, R.: Snake robots a review of research, products and applications. Ind. Robot-Int. J. **41**(3), 253–258 (2014)
16. SIASUN. http://www.siasun.hk/. Accessed 16 Apr 2021
17. Dong, X., Raffles, M., Guzman, S.C., et al.: Design and analysis of a family of snake arm robots connected by compliant joints. Mech. Mach. Theory **77**, 73–91 (2014)
18. Renda, F., Giorelli, M., Calisti, M., et al.: Dynamic model of a multibending soft robot arm driven by cables. IEEE Trans. Robot. **30**(5), 1109–1122 (2014)
19. Garriga-Casanovas, A., Rodriguez, Y., Baena, F.: Kinematics of continuum robots with constant curvature bending and extension capabilities. J. Mech. Robot. **11**(1), 011010 (2019)
20. Yuan, H., Zhou, L., Xu, W.: A comprehensive static model of cable-driven multi-section continuum robots considering friction effect. Mech. Mach. Theory **135**, 130–149 (2019)
21. Xu, K., Simaan, N.: Analytic formulation for kinematics, statics, and shape restoration of multibackbone continuum robots via elliptic integrals. J. Mech. Robot.-Trans. ASME **2**(1), 13 (2010)
22. Barrientos-Diez, J., Dong, X., Axinte, D., et al.: Real-time kinematics of continuum robots: modelling and validation. Robot. Comput.-Integr. Manuf. **67**, 12 (2021)
23. Bieze, T.M., Kruszewski, A., Carrez, B., et al.: Design, implementation, and control of a deformable manipulator robot based on a compliant spine. Int. J. Robot. Res. **39**(14), 1604–1619 (2020)
24. Shi, C., Luo, X., Qi, P., et al.: Shape sensing techniques for continuum robots in minimally invasive surgery: s survey. IEEE Trans. Biomed. Eng. **64**(8), 1665–1678 (2017)

Guaranteed Cost Formation Control for Linear Multi-agent Systems with Switching Topologies

Yaxiao Zhang[1,2(✉)], Ning Huang[3], Shiwen Tong[1,2], and Bopei Zheng[1,2]

[1] Beijing Key Laboratory of Information Service Engineering,
Beijing Union University, Beijing 100101, China
zdhtyaxiao@buu.edu.cn
[2] College of Robotics, Beijing Union University, Beijing 100027, China
[3] Beijing spacecrafts Ltd., Beijing 100094, China

Abstract. Guaranteed-cost formation problem for linear multi-agent systems with switching topologies is investigated. The guaranteed cost formation problem is transformed into a guaranteed cost control problem of an reduced-order switched systems equivalently by a linear transformation. Then, a necessary and sufficient condition for guaranteed cost formation is proposed. Moreover, based on an average dwell time scheme, a sufficient condition for the guaranteed cost formation of linear multi-agent system with switching topologies are presented in terms of linear matrix inequality techniques, and an upper bound of the guaranteed cost function is given. Finally, a numerical example is given to demonstrate the effectiveness of the theoretical results.

Keywords: Guaranteed-cost formation · Multi-agent systems · Switching topologies · Average dwell-time

1 Introduction

During the past decades, coordinations of multi-agent systems have received more attention due to its wide applications in military and civilian areas. In the multi-agent systems, formation control has already been a hotspot of research, many researchers focused on formation control problems, such as leader-follower [1], virtual structure [2], behavior-based [3], and consensus-based strategy [4], which have been well developed and applied.

However, in many practical cases, the communication topologies of multi-agent systems may be switching due to that the communication channel may

This work is supported by Beijing Municipal Science and Technology Project (KM202011417004), Special Research Projects of Beijing Union University (ZK30202002), Beijing Nova Program (Z201100006820101), Science and Technology Program of Beijing Municipal Education Commission (KM201811417001), 2021 "Star" College Students Science and Technology Innovation and Entrepreneurship Project (20211010,20212038).

X.-J. Liu et al. (Eds.): ICIRA 2021, LNAI 13013, pp. 476–486, 2021.
https://doi.org/10.1007/978-3-030-89095-7_46

fail or new channels may be created during movement. Time-varying formation control problems for multi-agent systems with switching topologies are investigate in [5] by using the common Lyapunov functional approach and algebraic Riccati equation technique. As we know, the dynamic structures of agents and the communication topology of multi-agent systems are key factors for formation. However, switching signals of communication topological are also one of the important factors of formation feasible for multi-agent systems with switching topologies. Average dwell time and dynamic dwell time scheme were presented to investigate the formation problem of linear multi-agent systems with switching communication topologies in [6,7].

Moreover, in practical applications, each agent of multi-agent systems may have limited energy supply to perform certain tasks, such as sensing, communication, and movement as well as be required to achieve some formation performance. Therefore, it is very important to realize a balance between formation performance and energy consumption, which can usually be modeled as optimal or suboptimal formation problems. To the best of our knowledge, there are few papers addressing guaranteed cost formation problems for multi-agent systems with switching topologies. Guaranteed cost formation control under fixed topology for multi-agent systems were investigated in [8,9]. Energy-constraint output formation problems for high-order linear multi-agent systems with switching topologies and the random communication silence were investigated in [10]. Guaranteed-cost consensus for multi-agent systems with switching topologies were investigated, where the topology was described by an undirected graph and the dwell time of each topology was assumed to be the same in [11–13].

Motivated by this, guaranteed cost formation control problem of high-order continuous-time linear multi-agent systems with switching communication topology is investigated in this paper. Compared with the literature mentioned above, the main contribution of the current paper is that: i) the guaranteed cost formation problem with switching topologies under directed graphs is considered; ii) the average dwell time scheme is introduced into guaranteed cost formation problem with switching topologies.

The rest of the paper is organized as follows. Section 2 shows the problem description based on graph theory. A linear transformation approach is presented in Sects. 3, sufficient condition for guaranteed-cost formation for linear multi-agent systems under switching topologies is proposed, and the upper bound of guaranteed cost are presented. Numerical results are presented in Sect. 5.

Notations: $\mathbb{R}^n$ and $\mathbb{R}^{n \times m}$ are the n-dimension real column vector and the set of $n \times m$ dimensional real matrices, respectively. Let 0 be zero number, zero vectors, or zero matrices in appropriate dimension, respectively. Let $\mathbf{1}_N$ denote an N-dimensional column vector with $\mathbf{1}_N = [1, 1, \cdots, 1]^T$. Let P^T and P^{-1} denote the transpose and the inverse matrix of P, respectively. $P^T = P > 0$ stands for matrix P is symmetric and positive definite. The notation $*$ denotes the symmetric terms of a symmetric matrix. I_N represents the identity matrix of order N, $\otimes$ is applied to denote the Kronecker product of matrices. $\lambda(\cdot)$ denotes the eigenvalue of a matrix.

2   Problem Description

Consider a linear multi-agent system (LMAS) consisting of N agents, where each agent takes the following dynamics:

$$\dot{x}_i(t) = Ax_i(t) + Bu_i(t), \ i \in \{1, \cdots, N\}, \tag{1}$$

with

$$A = \begin{bmatrix} 0 & I_n \\ 0 & 0 \end{bmatrix} \in \mathbb{R}^{2n \times 2n}, B = \begin{bmatrix} 0 \\ I_n \end{bmatrix} \in \mathbb{R}^{2n \times m},$$

where (A, B) is stabilizable. $x_i(t) \in \mathbb{R}^{2n}$ is the state variable of agent i, and $x_i(t) = [s_i^T(t), v_i^T(t)]^T$, $s_i(t) \in \mathbb{R}^n$ and $v_i(t) \in \mathbb{R}^n$ are the position state and the velocity state of agent i respectively, $u_i(t) \in \mathbb{R}^m$ is formation control protocol of agent i, which depends on agents x_i and x_j. Agent j is called a neighbor of agent i if there exists a communication channel from j to i, and $\mathcal{I} = \{1, \cdots, N\}$ is the index set of agents.

Let $N_i(t)$ denote the set of the neighbors of the agent i at time t, and $\mathcal{N}(t) = \{N_i(t), i \in \mathcal{I}\}$ is a communication configuration of the system (1) at time t. $\mathcal{N}(t)$ can be expressed by a dynamic digraph $\mathcal{G} = (\mathcal{V}, \mathcal{E}(t), W(t))$. Vertex set $\mathcal{V} = \{1, 2, \cdots, N\}$ represents the group of agents. Time-varying edge set $\mathcal{E}(t) \subseteq V \times V$ denotes the communication topology $\mathcal{N}(t)$, i.e., $(j, i) \in \mathcal{E}(t) \Leftrightarrow j \in N_i(t)$, and $W(t) = [w_{ij}] \in \mathbb{R}^{N \times N}$ is a weighted adjacency matrix.

A formation, which described by a vector $H = [h_1^T, h_2^T, \cdots, h_N^T]^T \in \mathbb{R}^{2nN}$, is a geometric pattern, it satisfies some predefined geometric constraints which is required to achieve and maintain for the LMAS (1). H represents the desired formation. In the current paper, the formation vector $h_i = [h_{is}^T, h_{iv}^T]^T$ is used to express the relative position h_{is} and the relative velocity h_{iv} of agent i respectively. It is generally known that the velocity state $v_i(t)$ are synchronous when multi-agent system (1) achieves the formation H, therefore, there is $H = [h_1^T, h_2^T, \ldots, h_N^T]^T$ with $h_i = [h_{si}^T, 0]^T \in \mathbb{R}^{2n}, i = 1, \cdots, N$.

For a desired formation H, a formation protocol is considered as follows:

$$u_i(t) = K \sum_{j \in N_i(t)} w_{ij}(t)[(x_j(t) - h_j) - (x_i(t) - h_i)], t \geq 0, \tag{2}$$

where $w_{ij}(t)$ represents the coupling strength with respect to a communication channel from j to i at time t.

Definition 1. Denote $H = [h_1^T, h_2^T, \cdots, h_N^T]^T \in \mathbb{R}^{2nN}$ be a specified formation. Linear multi-agent system(LMAS) (1) is said to achieve formation H, if there exist vector-valued functions $\xi(t) \in \mathbb{R}^{2n}$ and a control protocol (2), such that $\lim_{t \to \infty} \|x_i(t) - h_i\| = \xi(t), i \in \mathcal{I}$, and the vector-valued function $\xi(t)$ is called a formation center function.

Assume the communication topology of system (1) is time-varying. Without loss of generality, assume the communication topology of system (1) switches in a topology set, i.e.$\mathcal{N}(t) \in \{\mathcal{N}^k, k \in \mathfrak{M}\}$, $\mathcal{N}^k = \{N_i^k, i = 1, \cdots, N\}$, where $\mathfrak{M} = \{1, \cdots, M\}$ is an index set. Thus, the communication topology $\mathcal{N}(t)$ is piecewise time-invariant as the system evolves. Define a switching signal $\sigma : [0, +\infty) \to \mathfrak{M}$, which is a piecewise constant and right-continuous function of time, to describe the switching rules among the communication topologies $\{\mathcal{N}^k, k \in \mathfrak{M}\}$, i.e.$\mathcal{N}(t) = \mathcal{N}^k \Leftrightarrow \sigma(t) = k$. The switching signal specifies the index of the actived topology $\{\mathcal{N}^k, k \in \mathfrak{M}\}$ at time t.

Assume that the switching is finite in any finite time interval, and there are no jumps in the state at the switching instants. Corresponding to the switching signal $\sigma(t)$, we have the switching sequence $\{(t_0, k_0), (t_1, k_1), \cdots, (t_r, k_r), \cdots, | k_r \in \mathfrak{M}, r = 0, 1, \cdots\}$, which means that the communication topology of system (1) is $\mathcal{N}^{k_r}$ when $t \in [t_r, t_{r+1})$.

Consider the following linear quadratic cost function

$$J_C = \sum_{i=1}^{N} \int_0^\infty \{\sum_{j=1}^{N} w_{ij}(t)[(x_j(t) - h_j)$$
$$- (x_i(t) - h_i)]^T Q[(x_j(t) - h_j) - (x_i(t) - h_i)] + u_i^T(t)Ru_i(t)\}dt, \quad (3)$$

where Q and R are given symmetric positive matrices.

Definition 2. LMAS (1) is said to achieve guaranteed cost formation H via protocol (2) under the communication topologies $\{\mathcal{N}^k, k \in \mathfrak{M}\}$ with the switching signal $\sigma(t)$, if for any initial condition sequence $x(0)$, there is $\lim_{t\to\infty} \|(x_i(t) - h_i) - (x_j(t) - h_j)\| = 0, i, j \in \mathcal{I}$, and there exists a $J_C^* > 0$, such that $J_C \leq J_C^*$, J_C^* is said to be a guaranteed cost.

Definition 3. LMAS (1) with respect to the formation H is said to be guaranteed cost feasible via formation protocol (2) under the communication topologies $\{\mathcal{N}^k, k \in \mathfrak{M}\}$ with the switching signal $\sigma(t)$, if there exist control gain matrix K such that multi-agent system (1) achieves guaranteed cost formation H.

Let $x = [x_1^T \ldots x_N^T]^T \in \mathbb{R}^{2nN}$, and the dynamics of the LMAS (1) with formation protocol (2) can be described by a compact form as follows:

$$\dot{x}(t) = (I_N \otimes A)x(t) - ((L_{\sigma(t)} \otimes BK_{\sigma(t)})(x(t) - H), \quad (4)$$

where outer-coupling matrix $L_{\sigma(t)} = [l_{ij}]_{\sigma(t)} \in \mathbb{R}^{N \times N}$ is Laplacian matrix induced by the communication topology $\mathcal{N}(t) = \{N_i^{\sigma(t)}, i \in \mathcal{I}\}$, and its entries are defined by

$$l_{ij}^{\sigma(t)} = \begin{cases} \sum_{k \in N_i} w_{ik}^{\sigma(t)}, & j = i \\ -w_{ij}^{\sigma(t)}, & j \neq i, j \in N_i \\ 0, & j \notin N_i \end{cases}$$

Note that for a given protocol (2), switching signals of communication topological are one of the important factors for formation control problem of LMAS

(1) with switching topologies. Based on this, this paper mainly studies the influence of the change of communication topology on guaranteed cost formation control for continuous-time linear multi-agent systems. Based on the actual situation of the communication topology, the following case is analyzed:

Assumption 1. Communication topology $\mathcal{N}(t)$ switches among set $\{\mathcal{N}^k, k \in \mathfrak{M}\}$, and there exist a spanning tree for each communication topology in set $\{\mathcal{N}^k, k \in \mathfrak{M}^- = \{1, 2, \cdots, r\}\}$, $1 \le r < M$ meanwhile there does not exist a spanning tree for each communication topology in set $\{\mathcal{N}^k, k \in \mathfrak{M}^+\}$, as well as $\mathfrak{M} = \mathfrak{M}^- \cup \mathfrak{M}^+$.

3 Problem Transformation

In this section, guaranteed cost formation control problem for LMAS (1) with switching topologies are converted into guaranteed cost control problem of a corresponding auxiliary switched systems.

Transform system (4) by the following linear transformation [7]:

$$\bar{x}(t) = S(x(t) - H), \tag{5}$$

where

$$S = \begin{bmatrix} \tilde{S}_0 \\ 1_N^T \end{bmatrix} \otimes I_{2n}, \tilde{S}_0 = \begin{bmatrix} 1 & -1 & 0 & \cdots & 0 \\ 0 & 1 & -1 & \cdots & 0 \\ \vdots & & \ddots & \ddots & \vdots \\ 0 & \cdots & 0 & 1 & -1 \end{bmatrix}.$$

The inverse matrix of S can be worked out as follows:

$$S^{-1} = \frac{1}{N} \begin{bmatrix} N-1 & N-2 & \cdots & 1 & 1 \\ -1 & N-2 & \cdots & 1 & 1 \\ \vdots & \vdots & \ddots & \vdots & \vdots \\ -1 & -2 & \cdots & 1 & 1 \\ -1 & -2 & \cdots & -(N-1) & 1 \end{bmatrix} \otimes I_{2n} = \begin{bmatrix} \hat{S}_0 & N^{-1}1_N \end{bmatrix} \otimes I_{2n}.$$

By the linear transformation (5), system (4) is transformed into the following system:

$$\dot{\bar{x}}(t) = S[(I_N \otimes A) - L_{\sigma(t)} \otimes BK]S^{-1}\bar{x}(t) + S(I_N \otimes A)H. \tag{6}$$

Let $\bar{x} = [y^T\ z^T]^T$, where $y = [\bar{x}_1^T \ldots \bar{x}_{N-1}^T]^T$, unfold system (6) by $\bar{x} = [y^T\ z^T]^T$:

$$\dot{\bar{x}} = \begin{bmatrix} \dot{y}(t) \\ \dot{z}(t) \end{bmatrix}$$

$$= (\begin{bmatrix} \tilde{S}_0 \\ 1_N^T \end{bmatrix} \otimes I_{2n})[(I_N \otimes A) - (L_{\sigma(t)} \otimes BK)]([\hat{S}_0 \quad N^{-1}1_N] \otimes I_{2n}) \begin{bmatrix} y(t) \\ z(t) \end{bmatrix}$$

$$+ \begin{bmatrix} (\tilde{S}_0 \otimes A)H \\ (1_N^T \otimes A)H \end{bmatrix} = \begin{bmatrix} \mathfrak{A}_{11} & \mathbf{0} \\ \mathfrak{A}_{21} & A \end{bmatrix} \begin{bmatrix} y(t) \\ z(t) \end{bmatrix} + \begin{bmatrix} (\tilde{S}_0 \otimes A)H \\ (1_N^T \otimes A)H \end{bmatrix}.$$

where

$$\mathfrak{A}_{11} = I_{N-1} \otimes A - (\tilde{S}_0 L_{\sigma(t)} \hat{S}_0) \otimes BK,$$
$$\mathfrak{A}_{21} = -(1_N^T L_{\sigma(t)} \hat{S}_0) \otimes BK.$$

System (6) is equivalent to the following system:

$$\begin{cases} \dot{y}(t) = [I_{N-1} \otimes A - (\tilde{S}_0 L_{\sigma(t)} \hat{S}_0) \otimes BK]y(t) + (\tilde{S}_0 \otimes A)H, \\ \dot{z}(t) = Az(t) - (1_N^T L_{\sigma(t)} \hat{S}_0) \otimes BKy(t) + (1_N^T \otimes A)H. \end{cases}$$

Let $\bar{A} = I_{N-1} \otimes A$, $\bar{B}_{\sigma(t)} = -(\tilde{S}_0 L_{\sigma(t)} \hat{S}_0) \otimes B$, $\bar{K} = I_{N-1} \otimes K$.

According to the structure of A and H, it derived that $(\tilde{S}_0 \otimes A)H = 0$. Hence, the above equation can be expressed by

$$\begin{cases} \dot{y}(t) = (\bar{A} + \bar{B}_{\sigma(t)} \bar{K})y(t), \\ \dot{z}(t) = Az(t) - (1_N^T L_{\sigma(t)} \otimes BKy(t). \end{cases} \tag{7}$$

Obviously, there is no relationship between $y(t)$ and $z(t)$ in the first equation in system (7). Therefore, the following Lemma is obtained which transforms the formation problem with switching topologies into a asymptotic stability problem of reduced-order switched systems equivalently.

Lemma 1. LMAS (1) achieves formation H via protocol (2) under the communication topologies $\{\mathcal{N}^k, k \in \mathfrak{M}\}$ with the switching signal $\sigma(t)$ for any bounded initial states $x(0)$ if and only if switched systems

$$\dot{y}(t) = (\bar{A} + \bar{B}_{\sigma(t)} \bar{K})y(t) \tag{8}$$

is asymptotically stable.

Cost function J_C in (3) can be rewritten as follows:

$$J_C = \int_0^\infty y^T(t)\{2L_{\sigma(t)} \otimes Q + [L_{\sigma(t)}^T L_{\sigma(t)} \otimes (K^T RK)\}y(t)dt. \tag{9}$$

According Lemma 1 and Definition 2, the following theorem can be obtained:

Theorem 1. LMAS (1) achieves guaranteed cost formation H via protocol (2) under the communication topologies $\{\mathcal{N}^k, k \in \mathfrak{M}\}$ with the switching signal $\sigma(t)$ for any bounded initial states $x(0)$, if and only if switched systems (8) is asymptotically stable and there exists a $J_C^* > 0$, such that $J_C \leq J_C^*$.

4 Main Results

In this section, guaranteed-cost formation criteria is presented based on the average dwell time method. The communication topologies $\mathcal{N}(t)$ of LMAS (1) satisfies Assumption 2. Communication topology $\mathcal{N}(t)$ switches among set $\{\mathcal{N}^k, k \in \mathfrak{M}\}$, and there exist a spanning tree for each communication topology in set $\{\mathcal{N}^k, k \in \mathfrak{M}^-\}$, meanwhile there does not exist a spanning tree for each communication topology in set $\{\mathcal{N}^k, k \in \mathfrak{M}^+\}$, as well as there is $\mathfrak{M} = \mathfrak{M}^- \cup \mathfrak{M}^+$.

It follows that matrices $(\bar{A} + \bar{B}_k \bar{K}), k \in \mathfrak{M}^-$ are Hurwitz, matrices $(\bar{A} + \bar{B}_k \bar{K}), k \in \mathfrak{M}^+$ are not Hurwitz. There exist normal number $\theta_1, \dots, \theta_r, \theta_{r+1}, \cdots, \theta_M$, such that $(\bar{A} + \bar{B}_k \bar{K}) + \theta_k I, k \in \mathfrak{M}^-$ and $(\bar{A} + \bar{B}_k \bar{K}) - \theta_k I, k \in \mathfrak{M}^+$ are Hurwitz matrices. Hence, there exist positive definite symmetric matrices $T_k, k \in \mathfrak{M}$ satisfy

$$\begin{cases} (\bar{A} + \bar{B}_k \bar{K} + \theta_k I)^T M_k + M_k (\bar{A} + \bar{B}_k \bar{K} + \theta_k I) < 0, \ k \in \mathfrak{M}^-, \\ (\bar{A} + \bar{B}_k \bar{K} - \theta_k I)^T M_k + M_k (\bar{A} + \bar{B}_k \bar{K} - \theta_k I) < 0, \ k \in \mathfrak{M}^+. \end{cases} \quad (10)$$

Homogeneously, denote $\alpha_1 = \min_{k \in \mathfrak{M}} \lambda(M_k)$, $\alpha_2 = \max_{k \in \mathfrak{M}} \lambda(M_k)$, $\mu = \alpha_2 \alpha_1^{-1}$. Let $T^-(t)$ $(T^+(t))$ signify the total activation time of the LMAS (1) under topologies $\mathcal{N}^k, k \in \mathfrak{M}^-$ ($\mathcal{N}^k, k \in \mathfrak{M}^+$). Denote $\theta^- = \min_{k \in \mathfrak{M}^-} \theta_k$ and $\theta^+ = \max_{k \in \mathfrak{M}^+} \theta_k$ then for any given $\theta \in (0, \theta^-)$, choose $\theta^* \in (\theta, \theta^-)$, proposing the switching condition:

$$\inf_{t \geq 0} \frac{T^-(t)}{T^+(t)} \geq \frac{\theta^+ + \theta^*}{\theta^- - \theta^*}. \quad (11)$$

Next, we try to characterize the switching signals within the communication topologies such that the LMAS (1) achieves formation via the protocol (2). We focus on the switched linear system (8) and introduce the following definition and Lemma.

Definition 4. [14] For any $t > t_0 \geq 0$, let $N_\sigma(t_0, t)$ denote the number of switchings of the signal $\sigma(t)$ over the time interval (t_0, t). If $N_\sigma(t_0, t) \leq N_0 + (t - t_0)\tau_a^{-1}$ holds for $\tau_a > 0$ and $N_0 \geq 0$, then τ_a is called the average dwell time, and N_0 is the chatter bound of the switching signal $\sigma(t)$. Denote $S_{ave}[\tau_a, N_0]$ be the set of all switching signals $\sigma(t)$ with the average dwell time τ_a and the chatter bound N_0.

Lemma 2. [15] (Schur Complement)
For given symmetric matrix $P \in \mathbb{R}^{(m+n) \times (m+n)}$:

$$P = P^T = \begin{bmatrix} P_{11} & P_{12} \\ * & P_{22} \end{bmatrix}$$

where $P_{11} \in \mathbb{R}^{m \times m}$, $P_{22} \in \mathbb{R}^{n \times n}$. Then the following three conditions are equivalent:

(1) $P < 0$;
(2) $P_{11} < 0, P_{22} - P_{12}^T P_{11}^{-1} P_{12} < 0$;
(3) $P_{22} < 0, P_{11} - P_{12} P_{11}^{-1} P_{12}^T < 0$.

Theorem 2. Suppose Assumption 1 hold, LMAS (1) with respect to the formation H is guaranteed cost feasible via protocol (2) under the communication topologies $\{\mathcal{N}^k, k \in \mathfrak{M} = \mathfrak{M}^- \cup \mathfrak{M}^+\}$, if the following two conditions hold simultaneously:

i) There is a finite constant $\tau_a^* = \frac{\ln \mu}{2(\theta^* - \theta)}$, such that the switching signal $\sigma(t)$ satisfies switching condition (11) as well as $\sigma(t) \in S_{ave}[\tau_a, N_0]$.

ii) There exist $2n(N-1)$-dimensions matrices $X_k = X_k^T > 0$ and matrix W_k such that

$$\Phi_k = \begin{bmatrix} \phi_{11} & I & L_k \otimes K \\ * & -\frac{1}{2}(L_k \otimes Q)^{-1} & 0 \\ * & * & -R^{-1} \end{bmatrix} < 0, \tag{12}$$

where

$$\phi_{11_k} = \bar{A}X_k + \bar{B}_k W_k + (\bar{A}X_k + \bar{B}_k W_k)^T.$$

In this case, the control gain matrix in formation protocol (2) satisfies $K_k = W_k X_k^{-1}$, and guaranteed cost $J_{Ck}^* = y_0^T X_k^{-1} y_0$, $J_C^* = \max_{k \in \mathfrak{M}} J_{Ck}^*$.

5 Simulation Example

In this section, a numerical example is given to illustrate the effectiveness of the obtained theoretical results. As Theorem 2 is a special case of Theorem 3, we only present a example that satisfies Assumption 2. Consider a multi-agent systems with 4 agents and the dynamics of each agent is described by LMAS (1) with

$$A = \begin{bmatrix} 0 & 1 \\ 0 & 0 \end{bmatrix}, B = \begin{bmatrix} 0 \\ 1 \end{bmatrix}, \tag{13}$$

where $x_i(t) = [x_{i1}(t) \ x_{i2}(t)]^T$, $x_{i1}(t)$ and $x_{i2}(t)$ denote position and velocity of agent i respectively. The initial state is chosen randomly:

$$x(0) = [0 \ 50 \ 150 \ 40 \ 300 \ 30 \ 450 \ 20]^T.$$

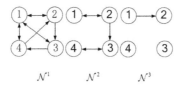

Fig. 1. Three communication topologies of LMAS (1)

Figure 1 shows the communication topologies $\mathcal{N}^1$, $\mathcal{N}^2$, $\mathcal{N}^3$, which satisfies Assumption 2, without loss of generality, let the communication topology weight is 1. One can figure out $\tau_a^* = 0.4808$ and $\frac{T^-(t)}{T^+(t)} = 3$. We choose a switching signal $\sigma(t)$ which satisfies Theorem 3 is shown in Figure Fig. 2. In the guaranteed cost function (3) we choose $Q = 0.02I_2$ and $Q = 0.04I_2$. The target formation $H = [50 \ 100 \ 150 \ 200]^T \otimes [1 \ 0]^T$.

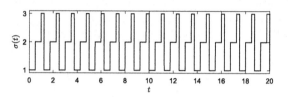

Fig. 2. A switching signal $\sigma(t)$

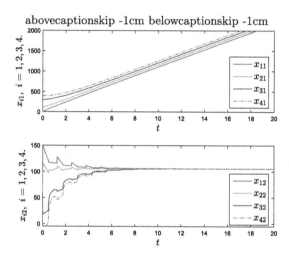

Fig. 3. Position and velocity state trajectories of LMAS (1) under topologies $\mathcal{N}^1$, $\mathcal{N}^2$, $\mathcal{N}^3$ with switching signal $\sigma(t)$

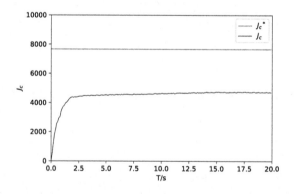

Fig. 4. Trajectory of the guaranteed cost function J_C^* and J_C^*

In Fig. 3, the state(position and velocity) trajectories of LMAS (1) are shown, One can see from Fig. 3 that the position trajectories of all agents converge with a fixed difference and the position trajectories of all agents converge to the ones. Figure 4 depicts the trajectory of the cost function J_C and J_C^*. The cost function J_C converges to a finite value less than J_C^*. The simulation results illustrate that LMAS (1) achieves guaranteed-cost formation with protocol (2) under topologies $\mathcal{N}^1$, $\mathcal{N}^2$, $\mathcal{N}^3$ with switching signal $\sigma(t)$.

6 Conclusion

The guaranteed cost formation control for multi-agent systems with switching topologies under directed graphs was investigated in this paper. By a linear transformation, the guaranteed cost formation problem for multi-agent systems were equivalently converted into guaranteed cost control problem of a reduced-order auxiliary switched systems. A sufficient condition for the guaranteed cost formation control was given based on two types of switching topologies, and an upper bound of the guaranteed cost function was determined. Finally, the effectiveness of the proposed theory has been illustrated by a 4 agents systems experiments. Further research will be conducted to design the formation protocol and optimize guaranteed cost function for formation problem of multi-agent systems with switching topologies and time-delays.

References

1. Consolini, L., Morbidi, F., Prattichizzo, D., Tosques, M.: Leader-follower formation control of nonholonomic mobile robots with input constraints. Automatica **44**(5), 1343–1349 (2008)
2. Lewis, M.A., Tan, K.H.: High precision formation control of mobile robots using virtual structures. Auton. Robots **4**(4), 387–403 (1997). https://doi.org/10.1023/A:1008814708459
3. Balch, T., Arkin, R.C.: Behavior-based formation control for multirobot teams. IEEE Trans. Robot. Autom. **14**(6), 926–939 (1998)
4. Ren, W., Sorensen, N.: Distributed coordination architecture for multi-robot formation control. Robot. Autonom. Syst. **56**(4), 324–333 (2008)
5. Zhou, Y., Dong, X., Lu, G., et al.: Time-varying formation control for unmanned aerial vehicles with switching interaction topologies. In: International Conference on Unmanned Aircraft Systems, pp. 1203–1209 (2014)
6. Zhang, Y.: Consensus of multiagent with time delays under switching topologies and the applications in formation. Beijing University of Technology, pp. 81–106 (2016)
7. Zhang, Y., Chen, Y., Qu, X.: Design of topology switching law for formation problem of linear multi-agent systems with time-varying delay. In: Proceedings of Chinese Control Conference, pp. 7115–7120 (2016)
8. Wang, Z., Liu, G., Xi, J., et al.: Guaranteed cost formation control for multi-agent systems: consensus approach. In: Proceedings of the 34th Chinese Control Conference, pp. 7309–7314 (2015)

9. Wang, L., Xi, J., Yuan, M., Liu, G.: Guaranteed-performance time-varying formation control for swarm systems subjected to communication constraints. IEEE Access **6**, 45384–45393 (2018)
10. Jin, J., Li, J., Wang, L., et al.: Energy-constraint output formation for networked systems with random communication silence and switching topologies. IEEE Access **99**, 1–12 (2021)
11. Xi, J., Yu, Y., Liu, G., et al.: Guaranteed-cost consensus for singular multi-agent systems with switching topologies. IEEE Trans. Circ. Syst. I Regular Papers **61**(5), 1531–1542 (2017)
12. Xi, J., Yang, X., Yu, Z., et al.: Leader-follower guaranteed-cost consensualization for high-order linear swarm systems with switching topologies. J. Franklin Inst. **352**(4), 1343–1363 (2015)
13. Xi, J., Fan, Z., Liu, H., et al.: Guaranteed-cost consensus for multiagent networks with Lipschitz nonlinear dynamics and switching topologies. Int. J. Robust Nonlinear Control **28**, 2841–2852 (2018)
14. Hespanha, J.P., Morse, A.S.: Stability of switched systems with average dwell-time. In: Proceeding of the 38th IEEE Conference on Decision and Control, pp. 2655–2660 (1999)
15. Liu, S.: Schur Complement, Encyclopedia of Statistical Sciences (2008)

Design of a Combined Bioinspired Active Touch Mechanism for Surface Detection in High Turbidity Water by AHP Optimization

Lianli Zhu[1] and Jing Hu[2(✉)]

[1] Research Center of China Coast Guard, China Coast Guard Academy, Ningbo 315801, Zhejiang, China
[2] Department of Mechanical and Electrical Management, China Coast Guard Academy, Ningbo 315801, Zhejiang, China

Abstract. Traditional sensing and detecting technologies, such as sonar, laser Doppler imaging and optoelectronic vision systems, cannot work well in high turbidity water. More and more bio-sensors inspired by rat's or seal's whiskers appeared, mainly applicate in regular target recognizing, but still cannot solve the arbitrary surface measuring problem well. This paper extends biological species to animals with tentacles, for example, octopus and nautilus, and proposed a new active touching mechanism for complex surface detecting by combined biological prototype candidates and AHP (Analytic Hierarchy Process) optimization, combining a whisker-like sensor and active tentacle-like mechanisms together. This new mechanism can be equipped on underwater or amphibious vehicles to detect targets with arbitrary surfaces. Experiment result shows that it is able to measure the rigid target with complex surfaces within 3 mm error range. Compared with the only whisker-inspired touch biosensors, the combined biomimetic design with whisker and tentacle can give a clear 3D point cloud data for irregular shape surface instead of regular 2D profile result by pattern recognition. The method shows a new programmable way to design bioinspired mechanism: biology structure analysis-structure combination-AHP optimization-new design, instead of scientist's inspirations.

Keywords: Design · Bio-sensor · Combined biomimetic · Active touch · High turbidity water · AHP

1 Introduction

Robots in amphibious or underwater environments always face crucial problems, when they are applied in resource exploration in off-shore zones, surveillance on reservoir dikes or river banks, disaster rescue in flooded zones, border patrolling and reconnaissance. One of the essential problems is the difficulty in perceiving the environment where a robot is located and what the nature of the object in front of its. In some extreme environments, for example, darkness, turbid water, the sensing system always does not work well as it is expected.

© Springer Nature Switzerland AG 2021
X.-J. Liu et al. (Eds.): ICIRA 2021, LNAI 13013, pp. 487–497, 2021.
https://doi.org/10.1007/978-3-030-89095-7_47

In such extreme environments, traditional detecting and sensing technologies for survey mainly involve optoelectronic vision systems and acoustic sonar systems. Scientists have been studying 3D reconstruction for underwater targets via multi-way [1–4]. Water or air penetrability is in the first place blocking the application of optoelectronic imaging, especially in turbid water or smoky air. Laser imaging is a useful way to capture information in such environment. However, the cost is very huge and laser systems still cannot solve the similar problem in water or air with high turbidity. In more than 200 NTU (Nephelometric Turbidity Unit) water, the scattering of particles like sands and jellies limits laser's ability to measure the geometric information of an object. Furthermore, sonar system is a good choice for object identification, even in high turbidity water. But sonar is used to detect large underwater objects in a distance and not good for nearby targets taking into consideration that the sonar blind area ranges from 0.5 m to 1 m. Bottom reverberation also hinders the sonar application in area near the sea floor. Thus, designing new low cost kind of detector measuring in nearby object underwater while offering good results is urgent.

Bioinspired touch sensor is a good choice to solve the problem mentioned above. After the first bio-whisker sensor came into being, a lot of bio-whiskers appeared [5, 6]. Biologists and scientists tried to figure out the exact mechanism about how the animals with whiskers get information around the nearby environment, or apply the artificial whiskers to capture enough information in real world [7–9]. Some studies focus on the problem of identification and measurement of target with bio-whiskers [10]. However, active sensors with arrays of whiskers can only supply qualitative results instead of quantitative ones, based on pattern recognition [11]. While in real applications, it is of great significance to know the exact geometrical information of the target. On land, the active sensors with whisker arrays could not solve the problem until now, not to mention its application is in under water environments, only few studies can give some result on regular geometries [12].

A few studies try to apply bio-whisker sensor to locate identify and classify underwater targets [13]. However, the fluidic loading on the sensor shaft can increase bending and potentially change the perception of contacted object [14]. That leads to inaccurate and unacceptable results. And the bio-whiskers array can only tell the difference between objects with regular geometric surfaces [15], the main reason being that the whisker may flip around the arbitrary surface, making it difficult to confirm the touching point along the whisker correctly.

Above all, the bio-whisker sensors can give some information of the target location, but cannot clearly supply the exact position of the touching point on the target surface. A more reasonable explanation is that to identify the touching point position in a certain coordinate frame, 3D information should be shown. However, if the bio-whisker sensing system only supply 2D data, so it is impossible to affirm the exact position of the touching point in 3D world. Beyond the bio-whisker itself, one more mechanism corresponding to the 3rd dimensional information should be added.

In this paper, inspired by the tentacles of cephalopods and the whiskers of pinnipeds, we mixed the two kinds of biological mechanisms together, considering the tentacle as the active mechanism, and the whisker as the passive receptor. For one thing, the distance towards the target can be measured, for another, the soft whisker as a switch can help to locate the exact touch point in a small error range. We designed a new mechanism for active touch sensing in a combined way. The steps of our methodology is shown in Fig. 1. Firstly, we chose 4 biological prototypes: rat, seal, octopus and nautilus. Secondly, after analyzing and classifying their mechanisms for touch sensing, 2 passive ones and 3 active ones are divided. Thirdly, 6 kinds of new designs are combined by the 2 different mechanism sets. Fourthly, the 6 new combined designs are evaluated by AHP method based on requirements in high turbidity water, then an optimized design is derived in the end.

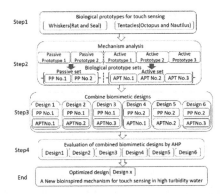

Fig. 1. The steps of combined biomimetic methodology.

The following are the sections explaining this paper. Firstly, the bio-inspiration theory is introduced. Secondly, the model of the touch sensing mechanism is derived. Thirdly, the design of the combined biosensor is described. Fourthly, the target surface identification and measurement algorithm is shown. Fifthly, the experiment of applying the combined biosensor on a complex surface testing is carried out on land and underwater. A discussion about this bioinspired active sensing mechanism is at the end.

2 Method

2.1 Bio-inspiration

For special environment sensing, nature always gives us a lot of inspirations. Animals that live in extreme environments always have amazing ability in sensing. In darkness or turbid water, touch sensing is almost the only way for animals except for acoustic perception. Tactile perception mainly contains two types: passive and active, while, the latter plays a leading role for surface detection [16]. Typical active touch sensing mechanisms involve vibrissal system which rodents and pinnipeds have, and tentacular systems which cephalopods have, as is shown in Fig. 2.

Active vibrissal systems lead to whisking movement which is described as motor strategies for gathering tactile information about the location, texture of objects [17]. The movement is controlled by facial muscles that have been identified in rats and other rodent species.

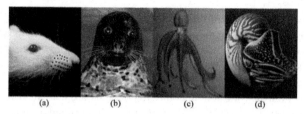

Fig. 2. Typical vibrissal animals and tentacular animals (a) Rat (b) Seal (c) Octopus (d) Nautilus.

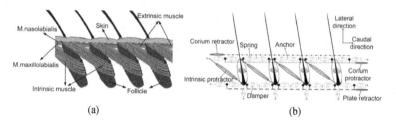

(a)   (b)

Fig. 3. Active vibrissal mechanism

As is shown in Fig. 3(a) and (b), Whisker dynamics mainly depends on the combination of muscles involved in each movement. Each whisker is associated with an intrinsic muscle and extrinsic muscles involving the m.maxillolabialis and m.nasolabialis that work in whisker retraction. And the m.nasolabialis profundis (MNP) including the mediosuperior (PMS) and the medioinferior (PMI), are involved in whisker protraction [18]. The rat mystical pad is linked to two kinds of superficial muscles involving the m.nasolabialis superficialis and the m.buccinatorius. The superficial muscles can cause deviation by muscle contraction, from the main caudal trajectory. The single whisker trajectory can be described as occupying an expanded 2D space [19].

Nautilus, octopus are typical animals among cephalopods. They all live in deep water and having a lot of tentacles. The tentacles have special ability to identify and grasp targets with arbitrary surface. They do not have good vision. Instead of a vision system, these animals can locate preys by tentacles' elongation and shortening. By the tactile sensors along the tentacle or at the tip, they can touch, discriminate and grasp the object. Since the tentacles can also bend, they can fit the target with arbitrary surface by stretching their tentacles [20, 21]. The sensors along the tentacle can underestimate the distance of the prey [22].

The obvious character except the shell is the digital tentacles. Each nautilus tentacle is composed of a long, soft, flexible cirrus and is retractable into a corresponding hardened sheath. Nautilus typically has more tentacles than other cephalopods—up to ninety. Furthermore, nautilus tentacles differ from those of other cephalopods. Lacking pads, the tentacles stick to preys by virtue of their ridged surface. Nautilus has a powerful grip. Attempts to take an object already seized by a nautilus may tear away the creature's tentacles, which will remain firmly attached to the surface of the object [23].

The tentacle's elongation is just like a linear motor. Along the tentacle, including the outer and inner part, there distribution has a lot of nerve fibers that can sense the distance

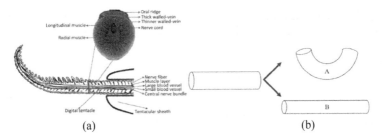

Fig. 4. Typical mechanisms of tentacular animals.

of the elongation and the touching signal on the target surface, just like displacement transducer and touching switch.

It's difficult to tell which plays key role in touch sensing among the active or passive mechanism. Passive touch sensing is always working together with the active one. In animals with whisking, the whisker is as a key passive receptor, with a complicated mechanism, the detail described in [5]. While in cephalopods, the receptors along the tentacle are considered to be tactile switches.

2.2   Combined Biomimetic Design

The key biomimetic elements are as follows: whisker-like sensors and tactile switches to be passive receptors, as is shown in Fig. 5(a) and (b) correspondingly. Parallel array, bending and elongation mechanisms as are shown in Fig. 5(c) (d) (e) to be active ones.

In Fig. 5(a), the long yellow part expresses whisker, the green part means the follicle, the two parts together represent the whisker model. In Fig. 5(b), the short yellow part shows the tactile switch receptor, and the green part indicates the base of the receptor, both of them form a switch model. The longer yellow shaft in 5 (a) represents the whisker, while the shorter one in Fig. 5(b) indicates a receptor like tactile cells on the tentacle. "Passive" here means to be a receptor. While "Active" in Fig. 5(c)–(e) means to be an activator.

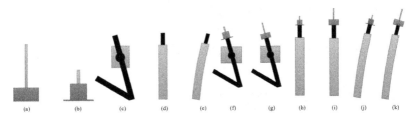

Fig. 5. Original models and combined models (a)–(b) Passive mechanism, (c)–(e) Active models, (f)–(k) Combined models (a) Whisker model (b) Switch model, (c) Parallel (d) Elongation and shortening (e) Bending, (f) **P+S** (g) **P+W** (h) **E+S** (i) **E+W** (j) **B+S** (k) **B+W**. (Color figure online)

In Fig. 5(c)–(e), three types of biological active mechanisms, the Parallel Fig. 5(c) represents the rat's whisker system, as is shown in Fig. 3(b), the Elongation and shortening (d) means tentacle elongation as is shown in Fig. 4(b) B, the Bending (c) implies tentacle flexible bending as in Fig. 4(b) A.

Thus, the 2 passive models and 3 active mechanisms are combined in 6 types, as is shown in Fig. 5, **P**, **E**, and **B** indicate parallel, elongation and bending mechanisms, **S** and **W** indicate tactile switch and whisker-like sensor. Figure 5(f)–(k) represent combinations "**P+S**", "**P+W**", "**E+S**", "**E+W**", "**B+S**" and "**B+W**" sequentially.

2.3 Evaluation of Combined Designs

Different design has different merits and drawbacks. For target surface detection, it is necessary to analyze and evaluate each mechanism so as to find an optimized one. For such a mechanism, the following items should be considered: mechanism complexity, effective space, detection accuracy, detection efficiency, information processing difficulty, environmental applicability, process difficulty and cost. Among these items, mechanism complexity, effective space, detection accuracy, detection efficiency and cost can be analyzed qualitatively, but information processing difficulty, environmental applicability and process difficulty can be analyzed quantitatively instead of qualitatively. All the candidate designs could be compared according to the items above, for the evaluation requirements of a mixed problem with quantitative and qualitative items, a good choice is AHP (Analytic Hierarchy Process).

AHP is a multi-criteria decision making method with factors being arranged in a hierarchical structure [24]. AHP always uses pairwise comparisons to measure, and it relies on the experts' judgments to give priority scales. AHP becomes a mathematical science nowadays [25] and one of the most widely used multi-criteria decision making system tools. In biomimetic studies, AHP has served as a useful decision tool [26, 27].

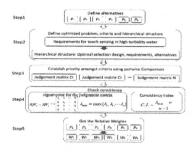

Fig. 6. AHP process for design candidates' optimization.

As is shown in Fig. 6, there are 5 steps to use AHP: Step1, the AHP process begins by defining the alternatives that need to be evaluated, 6 design candidates from "P+S" to "B+W" are defined. Step2, define the optimized problem, construct a hierarchical structure with an optimization goal in 3 classes: Goal, Requirements and Alternatives. Step3, establish priority using pairwise comparison, and a series of judgement matrices are derived. Step4, check the consistency index of the judgement matrices, so as to evaluate the reliable of judgement matrices. Step5, calculate all the alternatives' weights, and it's easy to get the best candidate design relatively among the 6 alternatives.

Based on the analysis above and the AHP method, the evaluation indexes system of bio-inspired active touch mechanisms is established. The system includes object hierarchy, rule hierarchy, and candidate hierarchy, as in shown in Fig. 7. G indicates the optimal selection design result, C_1, C_2, $\cdots C_8$ indicates the 8 items mentioned above correspondingly, and P_1, P_2, $\cdots$, P_6 indicates the design candidates "**P+S**", "**P+W**", "**E+S**", "**E+W**", "**B+S**" and "**B+W**".

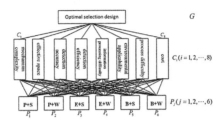

Fig. 7. Hierarchical structure for AHP method.

With the AHP calculation process, the final weight results for 6 design candidates are: 0.0972, 0.0861, 0.2708, 0.2714, 0.1389, 0.1357. Thus, according to the AHP method, the optimal selection design for active touch sensing mechanism is "**E+W**".

The detail for "**E+W**" is as follows:

The "**E**" part is the elongated and shortened one, implemented by the Firgelli linear actuator L12-30-P. And the "**W**" part is the whisker sensor, a Whisker-like sensor with a fiber glass rod as the shaft and a Hall position sensor (MLX90333), with a magnet as the sensing sensitive pair, involving shaft, hull, silicone rubber, magnetic cylinder, Hall effect position sensor and base, as is shown in Fig. 8.

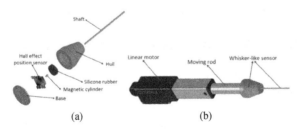

(a)   (b)

Fig. 8. Sensor design. (a) The Explosion diagram of whisker-like sensor (b) The combined design

The whole design is shown in Fig. 8. The linear motor has a moving rod which can elongate and shorten in a range of L mm (For L12-30-P, $L = 30$). At the end of the rod, the whisker-like sensor is located where its central axis of the shaft coincides with the one of the motor rod.

2.4   Analysis of Sensing Mechanism

The linear motion of motor can lead to the whisker-like sensor covering a range of L mm distance, so as to touch any point of surface within the range. The length of the whisker-like rod L_w determines the position of the potential touch point relative to the motor base, and L_x indicates the current length. For the linear Firgelli motor L12–30-P used here, its range is 30 mm, so it covers 30 mm distance, $L_w = 30$ mm.

3   Result and Conclusion

3.1   Measuring Experiment

As is shown in Fig. 9, 4 units are fixed together. According to the analysis above, the array can cover 4 line segments with 30 mm length in a surface measuring application.

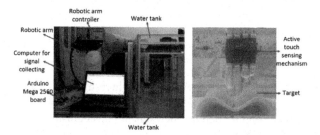

Fig. 9. Underwater surface measuring experiment setup

3.2   Experiment Results and Analysis

With the measuring process presented above, 362 points are gained, as is shown in Fig. 10(a). Figure 10(b) shows a combination with two data groups, the pink surface is the original model file "huaping007.stl", the other is the tested touch points measured by the active sensing array. The result shows that blue points preserve the pink surface tested. That means the active sensing array works. However, there're some points that seems with a little error, because the mechanism has system error and after a lot of times testing, the error may increase.

Figure 11(a)–(b) are the random cutting planes parallel with the yoz plane, $x = 25.2$ and $x = 44.1$. Figure 11(c)–(d) are the ones parallel with the xoy plane, $z = 15$ and $z = 45$. The comparision shows that the touch points tested by the active touch mechanism array are well fitted with the original surface. And can give a good result for surface measurement in underwater environments.

According to the tested results, the following conclusions are made:

a.   The new bioinspired sensing mechanism, designed by combined biomimetic methodology including whiskers and tentacles, is able to detect irregular target's surfaces in high turbidity water, and the measuring error is within 3 mm.

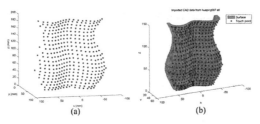

Fig. 10. Experiment results. (a) Touch points tested (362 points) (b) Combination of transformed experiment result and original STL file huaping007.stl (Color figure online)

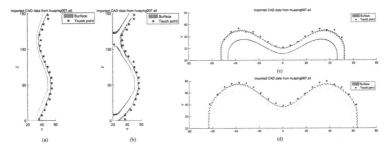

Fig. 11. Experiment analysis. (a) Sectional view on x = 25.2 (b) Sectional view on x = 44.1 (c) Sectional view on z = 15 (d) Sectional view on z = 45

b. Compared with the only whisker-inspired touch biosensors, the combined biomimetic design with whisker and tentacle can give a clear 3D point cloud data for irregular shape surface instead of regular 2D profile result by pattern recognition.

4 Discussion

The new combined bio-sensor can be applicable to targets with arbitrary surface and gain the geometric information of the target in an underwater environment. But now limited to rigid object with hard surface, soft ones maybe damaged. Because of the fluid shock, hard whisker rod is the first choice. How to reduce the surface damages is our future work. Obviously, this paper only considered limited kinds of animals with whiskers or tentacles, and derived to touch switch and active tentacle as the two models referring to active touch sensing, even though, the combined designs are close to these two kinds of models. If a more biological model could be considered, there could appear more and more combined designs by editing different effective items. The combination method of the combined design and AHP selection model maybe an applicable way to create new bionic designs. This should be studied and tested in near future.

Comparing the typical existed whisker sensors for detecting, [12, 13], our new design has significant advantages as are shown in the following Table 1:

Table 1. Performance of detecting sensors with typical artificial whiskers

No	Name of artificial sensor	Detect distance	Detect regular surface	Detect irregular surface	3D surface result
1	Rooney, T [13]	No	No	No	No
2	Hannah M. E [12]	Yes	Yes	No	No
3	Lianli Zhu	Yes	Yes	Yes	Yes

Acknowledgement. This work of the paper was partially supported by The National Key Research and Development Program of China (grant number 2017YFC0821206), the Research Plan of Ministry of State Security of China (grant number 2017JSYJC09), the Natural Science Foundation of Ningbo (grant number 2018A610072).

References

1. Cai, L., Sun, Q., Xu, T., Ma, Y., Chen, Z.: Multi-AUV collaborative target recognition based on transfer-reinforcement learning. IEEE Access **8**, 39273–39284 (2020)
2. Negahdaripour, S.: Application of forward-scan sonar stereo for 3-D scene reconstruction. IEEE J. Oceanic Eng. **45**(2), 547–562 (2020)
3. Negahdaripour, S.: Analyzing epipolar geometry of 2-D forward-scan sonar stereo for matching and 3-D reconstruction. In: 2018 OCEANS 2018 MTS/IEEE Charleston, Charleston, USA, pp. 1–10 (2018)
4. Lee, S., Park, B., Kim, A.: A deep learning based submerged body classification using underwater imaging sonar. In: 2019 16th International Conference on Ubiquitous Robots, Jeju, Korea, pp. 106–112 (2019)
5. Zhu, L., Zeng, L., Chen, X., Luo, X., Li, X.: A bioinspired touching sensor for amphibious mobile robots. Adv. Robot. **29**(22), 1437–1452 (2015)
6. Eberhardt, W.C., et al.: Development of an artificial sensor for hydrodynamic detection inspired by a seal's whisker array. Bioinspiration Biomimetics **11**(5), 056011 (2016)
7. Welker, W.I.: Analysis of sniffing of the albino rat. Behaviour **22**(3–4), 223–244 (1964)
8. Zucker, E., Welker, W.I.: Coding of somatic sensory input by vibrissae neurons in the rat's trigeminal ganglion. Brain Res. **12**(1), 138–156 (1969)
9. Moore, J.D., Deschenes, M., Furuta, T., Huber, D., Smear, M.C., Demers, M., Kleinfeld, D.: Hierarchy of orofacial rhythms revealed through whisking and breathing. Nature **497**(7448), 205–210 (2013)
10. Dehnhardt, G., Sinder, M., Sachser, N.: Tactual discrimination of size by means of mystacial vibrissae in harbour seals: in air versus underwater. Zeitschrift fü Saugetierkunde **62**, 40–43 (1997)
11. Hallam, B., Floreano, D., Meyer, J., Hayes, G.: Whisking: an unexplored sensory modality. In: 2002 From animals to animats 7: Proceedings of the Seventh International Conference on Simulation of Adaptive Behavior, London, England, pp. 58–69 (2002)
12. Emnett, H.M., Graff, M.M., Hartmann, M.J.Z.: A novel whisker sensor used for 3D contact point determination and contour extraction. In: 2018 Robotics: Science and Systems XIV, Pittsburgh, Pennsylvania, USA (2018)

13. Rooney, T., Pipe, A.G., Dogramadzi, S., Pearson, M.: Towards tactile sensing applied to underwater autonomous vehicles for near shore survey and de-mining. In: Herrmann, G., et al. (eds.) TAROS 2012. LNCS (LNAI), vol. 7429, pp. 463–464. Springer, Heidelberg (2012). https://doi.org/10.1007/978-3-642-32527-4_60

14. Kahn, J.C., Tangorra, J.L.: The effects of fluidic loading on underwater contact sensing with robotic fins and beams. IEEE Trans. Haptics 9(2), 184–195 (2016)

15. Schultz, A.E., Solomon, J.H., Peshkin, M.A., Hartmann, M.J.: Multifunctional whisker arrays for distance detection, terrain mapping, and object feature extraction. In: 2005 IEEE International Conference on Robotics & Automation, Berlin, Germany, pp. 2588–2593 (2005)

16. Prescott, T.J., Diamond, M.E., Wing, A.M.: Active touch sensing. Philos. Trans. R. Soc. B Biol. Sci. 366(1581), 2989–2995 (2011)

17. Haidarliu, S., Kleinfeld, D., Deschênes, M., Ahissar, E.: The musculature that drives active touch by vibrissae and nose in mice. Anat. Rec.-Adv. Integr. Anat. Evol. Biol. 298(7), 1347–1358 (2015)

18. Bosman, L.W.J., et al.: Anatomical pathways involved in generating and sensing rhythmic whisker movements. Front. Integr. Neurosci. 5, 53 (2011)

19. Herfst, L.J., Brecht, M.: Whisker movements evoked by stimulation of single motor neurons in the facial nucleus of the rat. J. Neurophysiol. 99(6), 2821–2832 (2008)

20. Cianchetti, M., Calisti, M., Margheri, L., Kuba, M., Laschi, C.: Bioinspired locomotion and grasping in water: the soft eight-arm octopus robot. Bioinspiration Biomimetics 10(3), 035003 (2015)

21. Kier, W.M.: The musculature of coleoid cephalopod arms and tentacles. Front. Cell Dev. Biol. 4, 10 (2016)

22. Nixon, M., Young, J.Z.: The Brains and Lives of Cephalopods. Oxford University Press, Oxford (2004)

23. Willey, A.: Memoirs: the pre-ocular and post-ocular tentacles and osphradia of nautilus. Q. J. Microscopical Sci. 40(1), 197–201 (1897)

24. Saaty, T.L.: How to make a decision: the analytic hierarchy process. Eur. J. Oper. Res. 48(1), 9–26 (1990)

25. Greco, S., Ehrgott, M., Figueira, J.R.: Multiple criteria decision analysis: state of the art surveys. International Series in Operations Research & Management Science, vol. 78. Springer, New York (2016). https://doi.org/10.1007/978-1-4939-3094-4

26. Moore, D., Janneh, A., Philen, M.: Development of a biologically inspired hydrobot tail. Active Passive Smart Struct. Integr. Syst. 9057, 90573D (2014)

27. Liu, S., Weng, S., Liao, Y., Zhu, D.: Structural bionic design for digging shovel of cassava harvester considering soil mechanics. Appl. Bionics Biomech. 11(1–2), 1–11 (2014)

Design and Simulation Analysis of Bionic Jellyfish AUV Driven by SMA Flexible Driver

Jianfeng Yu$^{(\boxtimes)}$ ⓘ, Chao Zhang ⓘ, and Shaoping Wang

School of Automation Science and Electrical Engineering, Beihang University, Beijing 100191, China

Abstract. In this paper, the structure and movement of sea moon jellyfish were analyzed. For the purpose of better synthesis, a novel bionic actuator was designed using SMA, and its mathematical modeling and simulation were carried out. On this basis, a new bionic jellyfish AUV was designed, and the fluid-structure coupling simulation of the model was carried out.

Keywords: Soft robotics · Biomimetic robotics · Bionic tendon · CFD simulation

1 Introduction

Jellyfish, as an important plankton in the aquatic environment, has a very low metabolic rate and can maintain normal movement while consuming a small amount of energy [1]. In addition, their diameters range from a few millimeters to a few meters, and they can survive in various water environments, whether in shallow waters of tens of centimeters or in deep seas of more than 7000 m, whether it is high temperature or low temperature, or different salinity. Jellyfish is one of the most diverse and widely distributed aquatic organisms in the ocean [2,3]. Moreover, jellyfish has a series of excellent features such as a symmetrical and flexible anatomical structure, simple propulsion, and noise-free swimming, all of which arouse the interest of scientific researchers in its research.

The development of biomimetic jellyfish robots can have important applications in many directions. Compared with traditional underwater robots, it also has many advantages, such as low cost, strong endurance, and low noise. Bionic jellyfish can be widely used in: (1) Underwater monitoring that requires strong endurance and complete functions. (2) The direction of military reconnaissance that requires robots to have good concealment and can carry some equipment for reconnaissance. (3) The direction of the recreational bionic robot that requires the motion form to highly simulate the real jellyfish.

When developing a jellyfish AUV, the first thing to consider is the driving method. At present, the research on the driving method of jellyfish robots at

Supported by Beihang University.

home and abroad mainly starts from the following five methods: motor drive (Fig. 1a), EAP (electroactive polymer) drive (Fig. 1b), SMA (shape memory alloy) drive (Fig. 1c), fluid drive (Fig. 1d), EMA (electromagnetic) drive (Fig. 1e) and biosynthetic composite material drive (Fig. 1f).

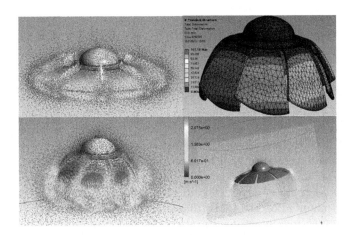

Fig. 1. (a) The Biomimetic Materials and Equipment Laboratory of Virginia Tech, USA, designed a jellyfish robot named "Cyro" by imitating the shape and swimming mechanism of jellyfish [4]; (b) The Intelligent Material System and Structure Center of Virginia Institute of Technology in the United States led the development of a bionic jellyfish robot based on IPMC drive [5]; (c) The SMA-driven bionic jellyfish robot developed by the University of Science and Technology of China; (d) The fluid-driven AUV developed by Atlantic University in the United States [6]; (e) Hyunchul Choi and others at Chonnam National University in South Korea used the EMA system to develop a miniature jellyfish robot [7]; (f) The biohybrid robot jellyfish developed by the Stanford University School of Engineering and the Department of Bioengineering of the School of Medicine [8]

SMA is one of the earliest and most widely used smart materials. At present, more than 50 alloys with shape memory effect have been discovered. The driver made by SMA has the advantages of small structure, large deformation and force output, strong explosive force, simple driving mode and relatively high controllability, making it has successful examples in the fields of aerospace, clinical medicine, bionic robotics and other fields, which also makes SMA considered as the smart material closest to artificial muscles. With the improvement of SMA production process, the performance of SMA is getting better and better. When SMA is combined with silica gel and spring steel, it can convert a shape memory alloy wire with a standard shrinkage rate of 4% into a beam-shaped driver with large deflection deformation, or SMA made of shape memory spring can greatly increase the deformation and shrinkage rate of SMA. These new processes have accelerated the application of SMA-based drives in the field of bionic robots. The bionic jellyfish robot based on SMA is one of the most representative applications. In this paper, the structure and movement mode of jellyfish were simulated. After summarizing the advantages and disadvantages of the existing bionic jellyfish robot, a novel flexible bionic tendon driver was designed using shape memory alloy (SMA) flexible drive module, and a novel bionic jellyfish AUV was designed according to it.

2   Design and Simulation Analysis of SMA Flexible Tendon

2.1   Mathematical Modeling of Bionic Tendon Module

Since the SMA wire itself has a limitation on the driving range of its maximum strain (approximately 7%), in order to improve the driving amplitude, the unilateral SMA artificial muscle driver in this article embeds the SMA wire into a flexible composite structure, and we named the flexible drive SMS, as shown in Fig. 2. The SMS adopts a three-layer hierarchical structure, namely: drive layer, filling layer and recovery layer. The driving layer consists of two sets of SMA wires fixedly mounted on the PCB (diameter of 0.15 mm, phase transition temperature of 90 °C, maximum denaturation shrinkage rate of 4.5%); the recovery layer is a spring steel plate with a thickness of 0.1mm as the bias plate. The spring steel stores elastic potential energy when the drive module is heated and deformed, and the stored elastic potential energy is used to restore the original position when the drive module is cooled; the filling layer adopts PDMS to fit SMA wire and PCB. The good ductility of PDMS reduces the influence of reverse compressive stress when the drive module is bent and deformed.

In order to build a model of SMA artificial muscle driver (referred to as SMS), the driving schematic diagram is shown in Fig. 3. First of all, this article makes the following assumptions:

1) It is assumed that the stress and strain distribution of the SMA wire is uniform, the instantaneous curvature of the SMA driving block is constant, and the SMA driving module is standard arc. (arc assumption).
2) The spring steel plate embedded in the driver is the neutral surface of the driver, and the distance d between the SMA wire and the spring steel plate remains unchanged during the bending process.
3) Since PDMS is a highly elastic silicone material, its elastic modulus is much smaller than spring steel, so the moment generated by the reverse tensile stress of PDMS is ignored.

When the SMS is bent by the contraction force F_{SMA} of the SMA wire, the bending deformation of the driver is characterized by the angle φ. According to the bending moment equation of Euler beam, we can get:

$$\frac{F_{\text{SMA}}d}{E_{\text{SMS}}I_{\text{SMS}}} = \frac{1}{\rho} \tag{1}$$

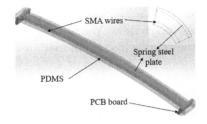

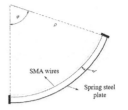

Fig. 2. The composite structure of the SMS

Fig. 3. SMS deformation diagram

E_{SMS} is the effective modulus of elasticity of SMS, I_{SMS} is the area moment of inertia of SMS, and ρ is the radius of curvature of SMS. Since the curved shape of the single-sided actuator is approximately a circular arc, the expression for the radius of curvature is as follows:

$$\rho = \frac{L_{\text{SMS}}}{\varphi} \tag{2}$$

L_{SMS} is the length of SMS. The bending deformation angle can be approximated by the strain of SMA wire:

$$\varphi = \frac{(\varepsilon_{\text{ini}} - \varepsilon) L_{\text{SMS}}}{d} \tag{3}$$

ε_{ini} is the initial strain of the SMA wire. When the prestress of the SMA wire is large enough, it can be considered as the maximum residual strain ε_{L}.

According to Formula (1) (2) (3), the shrinkage force of SMA wire is:

$$F_{\text{SMA}} = \frac{E_{\text{SMS}} I_{\text{SMS}}}{d^2} (\varepsilon_{\text{ini}} - \varepsilon) \tag{4}$$

The force balance equation of SMS is:

$$F_{\text{SMA}} = \sigma A_{\text{SMA}} - F_{\text{ini}} \tag{5}$$

A_{SMA} is the cross-sectional area of the SMA wire, and F_{ini} is the initial tension of the SMA wire. Therefore, the stress of the SMA wire is:

$$\sigma = k (\varepsilon_{\text{ini}} - \varepsilon) + \sigma_{\text{inj}} \tag{6}$$

Among them, k is the equivalent stiffness of SMS, and
$k = (E_{\text{SMS}} I_{\text{SMS}}) / d^2 A_{\text{SMA}}, \sigma_{\text{inj}} = F_{\text{ini}} / A_{\text{SMA}}$
Derivation on both sides of the Formula (6), we get:

$$\dot{\sigma} = -k\dot{\varepsilon} \tag{7}$$

According to Liang's model [9], the constitutive model of SMA wire can be expressed as:

$$\dot{\sigma} = E(\xi) \left(\dot{\varepsilon} - \varepsilon_L \dot{\xi}\right) \tag{8}$$

$E(\xi)$ is the Young's modulus of SMA wire. The relationship between $E(\xi)$ and Young's modulus (E_M) when SMA is completely martensite, Young's modulus (E_A) when SMA is completely austenite, and the volume fraction of martensite (ξ) is shown in the following formula:

$$E(\xi) = (1 - \xi)E_A + \xi E_M \tag{9}$$

From Formula (7) (8) (9), we can get:

$$\dot{\varepsilon} = \frac{E(\xi)\varepsilon_L}{E(\xi) + k}\dot{\xi} \tag{10}$$

When the SMA wire is energized and heated, the thermodynamic equilibrium equation of the SMA wire is:

$$mc_{\mathrm{SMA}}\dot{T} = -\frac{(T - T_{\mathrm{amb}})}{R_\lambda} + g_T u + mH\dot{\xi} \tag{11}$$

Among them, m is the quality of SMA, and $m = \rho_{\mathrm{SMA}}$, $V_{\mathrm{SMA}} = \rho_{\mathrm{SMA}}\pi\frac{d_{\mathrm{SMA}}^2}{4}l_{\mathrm{SMA}}$, ρ_{SMA} is the density of SMA, d_{SMA} is the diameter of SMA, l_{SMA} is the length of SMA, and c_{SMA} is the specific heat capacity of SMA, R_λ is the thermal resistance of PDMS, and $R_\lambda = \frac{1}{2\pi\lambda l_{\mathrm{SMA}}}\ln\left(\frac{d_{\mathrm{SMA}}+d_{\mathrm{PDMS}}}{d_{\mathrm{SMA}}}\right)$, S_{SMA} is the surface area of SMA, and $S_{\mathrm{SMA}} = \pi d_{\mathrm{SMA}}l_{\mathrm{SMA}}$, T_{amb} is room temperature, $g_T u = i^2 R(\xi)$, i is the energizing current, $R(\zeta)$ is the resistance of SMA, H is the latent heat of phase change of SMA.

The volume fraction of martensite in SMA wire ξ is divided into two situations, namely, the transformation of martensite into austenite during heating (M $\rightarrow$ A) and the recovery of austenite into martensite during cooling (A $\rightarrow$ M), the change trend of ξ is as follows:

$$\xi = \begin{cases} \frac{\xi_M}{2}\cos\left[a_A\left(T - A_S\right) + b_A\sigma\right] + \frac{\xi_M}{2} & \mathrm{M} \rightarrow \mathrm{A} \\ \frac{1-\xi_A}{2}\cos\left[a_M\left(T - M_f\right) + b_M\sigma\right] + \frac{1+\xi_A}{2} & \mathrm{A} \rightarrow \mathrm{M} \end{cases} \tag{12}$$

Among them: a_A, a_M are the material properties related to the four different phase transition temperatures (M_f, M_s, A_s, A_f), $a_A = \pi/(A_f - A_s)$, $a_M = \pi/(M_s - M_f)$. $b_A = -a_A/C_A$, $b_M = -a_M/C_M$, C_A and C_M represent the influence coefficient of stress on the temperature of austenite and martensite. ξ_M and ξ_A represent the percentage of martensite content in the initial state and in the austenite state. Taking the derivative of the above equation and expanding the equation in the form of a bit matrix can be obtained:

$$\dot{\xi} = \eta_\sigma(\sigma, T)\dot{\sigma} + \eta_T(\sigma, T)\dot{T} \tag{13}$$

Among them:

$$\eta_\sigma = \begin{cases} -b_M\frac{1-\xi_A}{2}\sin\left[a_M\left(T - M_f\right) + b_M\sigma\right] & \mathrm{A} \rightarrow \mathrm{M} \\ -b_A\frac{\xi_M}{2}\sin\left[a_A\left(T - A_s\right) + b_A\sigma\right] & \mathrm{M} \rightarrow \mathrm{A} \\ 0 & \mathrm{otherwise} \end{cases} \tag{14}$$

$$\eta_T = \begin{cases} -a_M \frac{1-\xi_A}{2} \sin\left[a_M\left(T-M_f\right)+b_M\sigma\right] & A \to M \\ -a_A \frac{\xi_M}{2} \sin\left[a_A\left(T-A_s\right)+b_A\sigma\right] & M \to A \\ 0 & \text{otherwise} \end{cases} \tag{15}$$

Combining Formulas (10) (11) (13) can be obtained:

$$\begin{aligned}
\dot{\xi} &= \eta_\sigma(\sigma,T)\dot{\sigma} + \eta_T(\sigma,T)\dot{T} \\
&= -\eta_\sigma k \frac{E(\xi)\varepsilon_L}{E(\xi)+k}\dot{\xi} + \eta_T \frac{1}{mc_{SMA}}\left[g_T u - \frac{(T-T_{amb})}{R_\lambda} + mH\dot{\xi}\right] \\
&= \frac{1}{mc_{SMA}} \frac{\eta_T\left[g_T u - \frac{(T-T_{amb})}{R_\lambda}\right]}{1+\eta_\sigma k \frac{E(\xi)\varepsilon_L}{E(\xi)+k} - \eta_T \frac{H}{c_{SMA}}} \\
&= f(\sigma,T)
\end{aligned} \tag{16}$$

Define the state variable of the SMS system as $x = \begin{bmatrix} \xi & T & \varepsilon \end{bmatrix}^T$, and the input variable is the energized current i, then the state equation of the SMS system is:

$$\dot{x} = \begin{bmatrix} \dot{\xi} \\ \dot{T} \\ \dot{\varepsilon} \end{bmatrix} = \begin{bmatrix} f(\sigma,T) \\ \dfrac{-\frac{(T-T_{amb})}{R_\lambda} + g_T u + mH f(\sigma,T)}{mc_{SMA}} \\ \dfrac{E(\xi)\varepsilon_L}{E(\xi)+k} f(\sigma,T) \end{bmatrix} \tag{17}$$

The output equation is:

$$\varphi = \frac{(\varepsilon_{ini} - \varepsilon) L_{SMS}}{d} \tag{18}$$

2.2   SMS Thermodynamic Simulation

According to Formulas (16) (17) (18), we can use MATLAB/Simulink to establish a simulation model of the flexible drive module. Adding a negative feedback control to the signal input can get better simulation results and save energy. Figure 4 shows the control block diagram of SMS, where thetar is the expected bending amplitude of SMS.

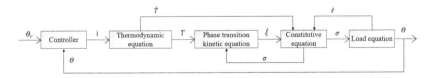

Fig. 4. Schematic diagram of SMS control block diagram

The control rate:

$$u = \zeta\left(k_p e\right) \tag{19}$$

Among them, k_p is the proportional coefficient of P control, and e is the difference between the expected bending amplitude and the actual bending amplitude.

$$\zeta(i) = \begin{cases} i_{max} & i \geq i_{max} \\ i & 0 < i < i_{max} \\ 0 & i \leq 0 \end{cases} \tag{20}$$

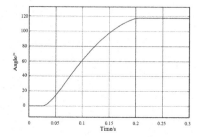

Fig. 5. The bending angle of the SMS changes with time during heating

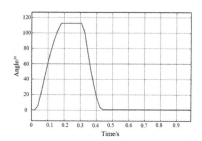

Fig. 6. SMS complete response

Matlab/Simulink was used for simulation calculation, and all parameters in the model were shown in Table 1.

The change in the bending amplitude of the SMS with time during the heating process of the SMA wire is shown in Fig. 5. It can be seen from the figure that the bending amplitude of SMS is approximately linear with time. The simulation results are in good agreement with the experimental results.

The step response of SMS after adding control optimization is shown in Fig. 6. It can be seen from Fig. 6 that the step response of a single SMS has a certain time lag at the initial stage. This is due to the austenite transformation of the SMA wire when the temperature is higher than the non-temperature point, and then the bending amplitude of the SMS changes. It can be seen from the figure that the SMS starts braking at about 18 milliseconds after the current is loaded, and the bending angle of the braking process changes approximately linearly with time. After maintaining the maximum angle for a period of time, the SMS bending angle decreases rapidly and returns to the initial position in about 400 ms. It can be seen that the SMS braking is very rapid, and the bending angle is linear with time in the bending and recovery phases, indicating that the braking process is stable and reliable.

Table 1. Structural parameters in the simulation model.

Structure attributes	Value	Structure attributes	Value
SMS Effective length (mm)	87	SMA wire resistivity	55 (Ω/m)
SMS width (mm)	10	Load current (I)	1.5 (A)
SMS thickness (mm)	2.5	Density of SMA wire (ρ)	6.45 g/cm^3
Length of spring steel (mm)	100	Specific heat capacity of SMA wire (c)	837 J (kg · °C)
Width of spring steel (mm)	10	Latent heat coefficient of SMA wire (h)	24.2 × 10^3 J/kg
Thickness of spring steel (mm)	0.1	Initial strain of SMA wire $(\varepsilon_{\text{ini}})$	0.04
SMA wire diameter (mm)	0.15	Austenite initial temperature (A_S)	80 °C
Distance between SMA wire and spring steel (mm)	1.5	Austenite end temperature (A_f)	108 °C
PDMS equivalent diameter (mm)	1	Martensite end temperature (M_f)	60 °C
Ambient temperature (°C)	10	Martensite initial temperature (M_s)	78 °C

3 Bionic Jellyfish AUV Overall Design and CFD Simulation

3.1 Bionic Jellyfish AUV Overall Design

Jellyfish, as an important plankton in the ocean, are different from marine life such as algae, corals, and sea anemones, they can migrate freely in the ocean. They are "dancers" in the ocean, and human beings admire their graceful steps and graceful postures. After millions of years of evolution, jellyfish have a wide variety of different shapes, colorful colors, and a complete movement system, which can achieve high-efficiency (The COT (COT: cost of transport, unit: $J/(kg * m)$) index of sea moon jellyfish is 0.49, and the COT index of fish of the same quality is 1.29) and noise-free underwater movement. The simple, soft

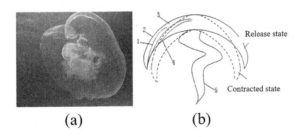

Fig. 7. Jellyfish structure: (a) Physical map; (b) Topology

and symmetrical anatomical structure makes the jellyfish have the ability to get food from any direction and avoid hazards.

As shown in Fig. 7 (take moon jellies as an example), it usually has a transparent or translucent umbrella-shaped structure. The umbrella-shaped structure is divided into three layers: upper umbrella surface, middle gel and lower umbrella surface. Their diameters vary from a few millimeters to a few meters. The action cycle of Aurelia aurita is divided into two steps. First, the water inside the jellyfish structure is discharged in a jet manner by the contraction of the under umbrella muscles, thereby generating thrust, and the elastic fibers distributed in the middle gel layer are stretched for energy storage. Then the umbrella body is restored to the released state by the elastic energy stored in the elastic fiber (Fig. 8).

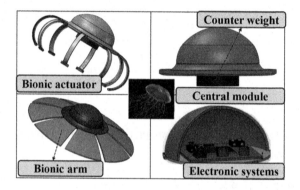

Fig. 8. Jellyfish AUV prototype design

The simplest way to obtain many movement advantages of jellyfish is to imitate its morphological structure and movement mode. In this paper, moon jellyfish is taken as the bionics model. Following the principles of bionic form and bionic movement, a bionic jellyfish AUV is designed by using the bionic actuator designed above. In this scheme, four teams of SMA drive modules are distributed symmetrically and installed on the mounting seat of the central cabin, which is installed at 15° from the level. Large swing Angle tentacles are adopted to obtain more powerful thrust, and PCB board is added in the central cabin and ring mounting seat as support material to accommodate the internal electronic system. The AUV body uses dragon-skin bionic silica gel as the outer Skin, which has the bionic characteristics of soft muscle.

3.2 CFD Simulation

Next, we carried out bidirectional fluid-structure coupling simulation of the prototype model, using the large commercial software ANSYS, which is the most widely used in the market at present. It mainly in two-way fluid-structure coupling simulation USES is sequential solution, as shown, first to solve the calculation in the fluid, speak to calculate the displacement data is passed to the solid, and then calculated in a solid, the calculation results of displacement and stress data passed to the computation of the flow field, in order to solve. Ansys fluid-structure coupling first requires model processing, then mesh generation, solution setup in Fluent and Structural, and finally coupling setup in System Coupling. The unstructured meshing method is adopted for mesh conversion. Because the displacement of fluid-structure interaction surface is relatively large, the tetrahedral mesh must be used as the slip and smooth mesh.

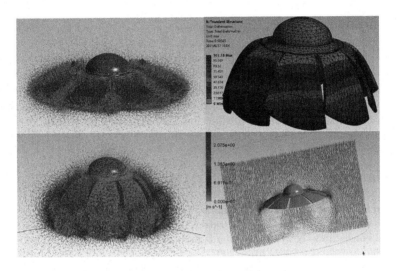

Fig. 9. Deformation of Jellyfish AUV

Figure 9 is a simple simulation result of fluid-structure interaction done in this paper. As can be seen from the simulation results, the maximum strain generated by jellyfish AUV is 0.00984737 < 0.1(maximum material strain), and the maximum stress is 0.011816 mpa < 0.152 mpa (maximum material strain). Therefore, we can think that the process of changing motion is safe and reliable. At the same time, we can also see the phenomenon of eddy currents in the flow field when AUV moves. In the future, we will model and analyze the generation and influence of eddy currents to improve the control scheme.

At the same time, we can also derive the velocity, acceleration and thrust characteristic curves of jellyfish AUV (Fig. 10). It can be seen that the thrust received by the JELLYFISH AUV is relatively stable and changes periodically, and the maximum velocity can reach 5.28 cm/s, and no residual strain will be generated.

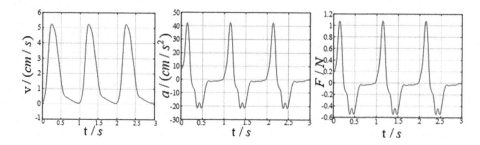

Fig. 10. Some characteristic curves

4   Conclusions

In this paper, the research status of bionic jellyfish AUV at home and abroad is summarized. On this basis, a new bionic actuator based on SMA is designed, and the modeling and simulation of the actuator are carried out. Then a bionic jellyfish robot was designed and the fluid-structure interaction simulation was carried out with the model. Prototype production and experiments will be carried out later.

References

1. Drazen SJC: Environmental constraints upon locomotion and predator: prey interactions in aquatic organisms || the rate of metabolism in marine animals: environmental constraints, ecological demands and energetic opportunities. Philos. Trans. Biol. Sci. **362**(1487), 2061–2078 (2007)
2. Omori, M., Kitamura, M.: Taxonomic review of three Japanese species of edible jellyfish (Scyphozoa: Rhizostomeae). Plankton Biol. Ecol. **51**(1), 36–51 (2004)
3. Purcell, J.E.: Climate effects on formation of jellyfish and ctenophore blooms: a review. J. Mar. Biol. Ass. Uk **85**(3), 461–476 (2005)
4. Villanueva, A.A., Marut, K.J., Michael, T., Priya, S.: Biomimetic autonomous robot inspired by the Cyanea capillata (Cyro). Bioinspiration Biomimetics **8**(4), 046005 (2013)
5. Yeom, S.W., Jeon, J., Kim, H., Youn, B.D., Oh, I.K.: Bio-inspired Jellyfish Robots based on Ionic-type Artificial Muscles (2011)
6. Frame, J., Lopez, N., Curet, O., Engeberg, E.D.: Thrust force characterization of free-swimming soft robotic jellyfish. Bioinspiration Biomimetics **13**(6), 064001 (2018)
7. Ko, Y., et al.: A jellyfish-like swimming mini-robot actuated by an electromagnetic actuation system. Smart Mater. Struct. **21**(5), 057001 (2012)
8. Xu, N.W., Townsend, J.P., Costello, J.H., Colin, S.P., Dabiri, J.O.: Field testing of biohybrid robotic jellyfish to demonstrate enhanced swimming speeds. Biomimetics **5**(4), 64 (2020)
9. Tanaka, K., Sato, Y.: Phenomenological Description of the Mechanical Behavior of Shape Memory Alloys. Tran. Jpn. Soc. Mech. Eng. Ser. A (1987)

Adaptive Grasping Without Damage System with Pneumatic Muscle as End-Effector of Robot

He Chuang-Chuang[1]([⊠]), Yan Hong-Wei[1], Shang Ya-Qi[1], Wang Qing-Dong[1], Cao Te-Te[2], and Li Zhe[3]

[1] School of Transportation, Lu-dong University, Yantai 264025, Shandong, China
[2] School of Mechanical Engineering,
Dalian University of Technology, Dalian 116024, Liaoning, China
[3] Harbin Institute of Technology, Weihai 264209, China

Abstract. In this paper, the mechanical gripper driven by pneumatic artificial muscle is taken as the research object, through theoretical analysis and experimental verification, the feasibility of force feedback control and incremental PID control applied to the mechanical gripper driven by pneumatic muscle is deeply studied, and the results of nondestructive and flexible grasping are obtained. The adaptive control process and deviation comparison link are designed to determine the expected output force of different items. Subsequently, the incremental PID control algorithm is used to eliminate the steady-state error, so as to achieve the self-adaptability of the control system to determine the expected force according to different items.

Keywords: Pneumatic muscle · Adaptability · Force feedback control · PID control

1 Introduction

Today's society has entered the era of Industry 4.0, modern industry for industrial robots, the degree of artificial intelligence, bionic degree is also increasing. The traditional end-effectors of industrial robots are driven by motors or cylinders, which have many shortcomings, such as high cost and lack of market competitiveness. In order to solve the above problems, the new pneumatic component of pneumatic muscles is derived. The pneumatic muscle is composed of rubber cylinder embedded with double helix fiber braiding network, which can achieve radial expansion and axial expansion can be realized, and the force can be output accurately. Different from cylinder, the adjustment of the middle position can be realized.

In today's field of control engineering, pneumatic position servos are primarily regulated by displacement sensors or pressure sensors. This study introduces pull sensors, directly connected with pneumatic muscles, real-time detection of the output force of pneumatic muscles, while using force as feedback control, and determine whether the current force value is the output force expectations of pneumatic muscles, and then implement PID algorithm, eliminate steady-state error, achieve lossless grasping of different items, verify the feasibility and accuracy of this control process.

© Springer Nature Switzerland AG 2021
X.-J. Liu et al. (Eds.): ICIRA 2021, LNAI 13013, pp. 509–518, 2021.
https://doi.org/10.1007/978-3-030-89095-7_49

In present research, we need to grab different items, and the study needs to judge the output force expectations have a certain degree of difficulty, so a set of control process is designed. First of all, a reference model of pneumatic muscle output force is established, the function relationship between the model and time is semi-elliptical law. Under the influence of the semi-elliptical law, the decrease of slope will cause the cumulative value to decrease, so the crawled item will not be damaged, will still retain the integrity of the item. Then the controller needs to eliminate the steady-state error caused by the cumulative action and achieve adaptive lossless grasping.

Therefore, based on the natural passive softness of pneumatic muscles and the high power/mass ratio, this study designs pneumatic muscle-driven mechanical grippers, including mechanical systems, pneumatic systems and sensor control systems. The results show that the mechanical grippers driven by pneumatic muscles can determine the desired output force of pneumatic muscles needed to grab different items, and then control by PID, and can achieve adaptive non-destructive grasping.

2   Design of Gas System and Control Algorithm

2.1   The Design of Mechanical Grippers

In order to verify the adaptability and non-destructive grasping of this control system, a mechanical gripper driven by pneumatic muscles is designed. The 3D model and physical diagram are shown in Fig. 1:

a)   3D model   b) physical prototype

Fig. 1. Pneumatic muscle-driven mechanical grippers

When the pneumatic muscle rushes into the gas, it shrinks to the center, and the pneumatic muscle pulls the slider to do linear motion on the guide rail. The slider drives the arc clip at both ends to move around the rotating pair at both ends through the guiding component, so as to realize the clamping claw closure. When deflated, the elastic force of the pneumatic muscle rubber layer restores it to its original length and releases the claws. Pneumatic muscle external fiber braiding net and its own structural characteristics determine that pneumatic muscles will automatically brake when the push and pull limit is reached, will not break through the predetermined range, making it more conducive to the protection of the clamped object, so as to achieve lossless crawl. The whole claw-in-one motion is combined with the telescopic movement of the pneumatic muscles to form the entire mechanical system.

2.2 Design of Circuit and Gas Circuit System

System Design of Circuit Part. The electrical system is mainly composed of STM32 controller, voltage-to-current module, force sensor and transmitter.

Force Sensor. The pull sensor used in this force feedback control, which is small in size, light in mass, high in sensitivity and good in repeatability, can convert the pull signal output from the pneumatic muscle into an electrical signal, convert it to a digital signal by the transmitter.

System Design of Gas Part. In this research, the pneumatic muscles are filled and exhausted by controlling the electrical proportional valve. When the proportional valve receives the control signal, the compressed gas enters the proportional valve body, and the built-in pressure sensor provides real-time feedback on the gas pressure in the valve body, forming a pressure closed-loop control. The pneumatic system is designed as shown in Fig. 2, and the core pneumatic element of the system is the Electro-pneumatic valve (proportional valve), which regulates the inflatable pressure of the pneumatic muscles for the scaling of the pneumatic muscles.

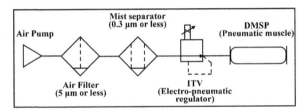

Fig. 2. Pneumatic circuit diagram

When the above air path and electrical control system are connected, the pull sensor collects the force signal in real time and converts the force signal into an electrical signal through the internal bridge circuit. This signal is still an analog signal and needs to be converted into a digital signal by a transmitter to communicate with the microcontroller. The microcontroller transmits the control signal to the proportional valve via the D/A module, which controls the pressure in the pneumatic muscle cavity. Pneumatic muscles can stretch the braided mesh according to the size of the internal air pressure to produce an output pull, which is combined with the mechanical grippers to achieve the grip action.

2.3 Control Algorithm Design

PID control algorithm. The control system uses an incremental PID algorithm.

$$\Delta u(t) = K_p[e(t) - e(t-1) + \frac{1}{T_i}e(t) + T_d(e(t) - 2e(t-1) + e(t-2))] \quad (1)$$

It can be concluded from the above equation that the algorithm adopts the weighted processing without accumulation, and the control increment $\triangle u(t)$ is only related to the sampling value of nearly three times. Each time the controller is adjusted by PID, it will only output the control increment $\triangle u(t)$, that is, the tension change of the actuator, which can be switched without disturbance. Compared with the position PID algorithm, the incremental PID algorithm can avoid the integral saturation phenomenon, only need to limit the output, without integral limit.

In the PID control algorithm, the proportional component reduces the steady-state error. When the controller detects this deviation signal, it immediately takes this force value as the expected value for a non-destructive grab and saves it in an array inside the program, where there is a steady-state error as the pneumatic muscles continue to output forces. Then the proportional component of the incremental PID program is carried out inside the controller to reduce the steady-state error. The adaptive nature of this control system is demonstrated by grasping different items to determine the output force expectations of different pneumatic muscles.

The existence of steady-state error will affect the effect of claw-free grabbing items, so the steady-state error should be eliminated with the integral link to improve the system's non-difference. In this control system, the differential link is added to speed up the action speed of the system and reduce the adjustment time, so as to improve the dynamic performance of the system.

In summary, the application of PID control, it is necessary to improve the proportional coefficient, integral time constant and differential time constant, so that the whole system can get good performance.

The establishment of reference models. In order to make the pneumatic muscle output force value output in a flexible law output, and the mechanical claws without loss to grasp the item can produce a deviation signal, trigger the controller to perform an incremental PID program to eliminate steady-state errors, so establish a reference model of the pressure size and time relationship in the pneumatic muscle cavity, as shown in Fig. 3:

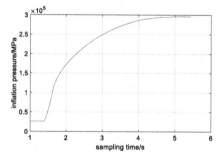

Fig. 3. Refers to the pressure curve in the pneumatic muscle cavity of the model

After this study, it is proved that the pneumatic muscle inflatable pressure is positively correlated with the output force, and the greater the inflatable pressure, the greater its output force value. In the function law shown in Fig. 3, the inflatable pressure and the time variable constitute the elliptical function relationship, that is, the pneumatic muscle output force and time become the elliptical function law. The function expression is: value $= \sqrt{(400t - t^2)}$, and this function is written to the controller in program form, and when the mechanical gripper grabs the item, the current force value feedback from the force sensor is biased from the theoretical force value of the reference model at the same time, stored in the array inside the program, and the judgment basis is established for subsequent implementation to eliminate steady-state error. As time increases, the increment of pneumatic muscle output force in unit time will decrease, the slope will decrease, and the output force value will gradually stabilize.

Control the Establishment of the Process. Adaptive control systems based on pneumatic muscle force feedback are shown in Fig. 4:

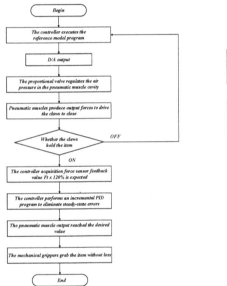

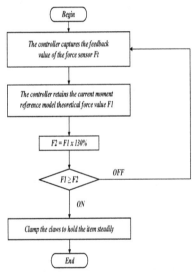

Fig. 4. Adaptive control system block diagram

Fig. 5. A flowchart of deviation comparison links

As shown in Fig. 4, the program process begins, the controller executes the reference model program, the control board integrated D/A module will be the value of the force in the form of an analog output, and then through the proportional valve to control the size of the air pressure in the pneumatic muscle cavity, the greater the pressure, the greater the pneumatic muscle output force. The claws are opened and closed by pneumatic muscle drive, while the controller collects the output force value of the pneumatic muscles through the pull sensor and feeds them back to the controller to form a closed-loop control system. The pressure in the pneumatic muscle cavity of the whole execution process is output according to the law given by the reference model.

Once the gripper grabs the item, the force sensor feedback force value will produce a large deviation from the theoretical force value of the reference model and enter the deviation comparison link, as shown in Fig. 5.

The sensor detection force value is fed back to the controller throughout the process, which retains it and records it as Ft. At the same time, the controller retains the theoretical force value of the reference model at the current moment, recorded as F1, and the controller expands the force value by 1.3 times, and records it as F2. When Ft is greater than or equal to F2, the control system determines that the non-destructive grab item, the deviation comparison link ends, when Ft is less than F2, the controller continues to carry out the reference model program, the pressure in the pneumatic muscle cavity continues to increase, and then the output force continues to increase, while continuing the judgment process.

When the above deviation comparison is completed, the controller immediately expands the force sensor feedback force value Ft by 1.2 times as expected. The controller then performs an incremental PID program to eliminate steady-state errors, as shown in Fig. 6:

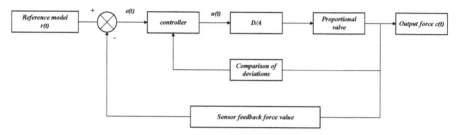

Fig. 6. A flowchart of a dual closed-loop adaptive control system

Further explanation from adaptive control system flow chart: Fig. 6 can be seen that the pneumatic muscle-driven adaptive control system is a double closed-loop automatic control system, wherein the inner ring deviation comparison link of the priority is higher than the outer ring steady-state error elimination link. After the inner ring deviation comparison link, the output force expectation of grabbing the current item is generated. The controller continues to perform outer ring control, triggering an internal incremental PID program that eliminates steady-state error e(t), keeps the pneumatic muscle output near the desired value, and drives the mechanical grippers to grab the item without loss. When the above process grabs different items, the output force expectations produced by the deviation comparison link are different, so this control system can determine for itself the desired force value required to grab different items without loss, indicating the adaptability of this control system.

3 Experiments

3.1 Specific Studies

Research objectives: Comprehensive above thinking, this study designed the following three schemes, to verify that the non-destructive grip force value by the pneumatic muscles to judge the output, drive the mechanical claws to achieve non-destructive grabbing items.

Research platform: The research platform is shown in Fig. 7, and the element is shown in Table 1.

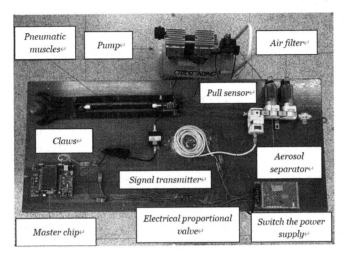

Fig. 7. Research platform

Table 1. Components and parameter.

Name	Manufacturers and models	Technical parameter
Pneumatic muscle	FESTO: DMSP-10-250N-RM-CM	250 mm 0–0.8 MPa
Electropneumatic proportional valve	SMC: ITV2050-012N	4-20 mA 0–0.9 MPa
Force transducer	Zhong Nuo: ZNLBS-V1-30 kg	Rated load: 1-30 kg Sensitivity: 1.0–1.5 mV/V Composite precision: 0.05%
Mechanical grip	Homemade	——
Switching power supply	Tong Hua: HS-150–24	Rated voltage:24 V 24 V/12 V/5 V/GND power
Microcontrollers	STM: STM32F103ZET6	Maximum frequency:72 MHz 3*12-bit A/D converters

3.2 Research Process

Grab the orange as shown in Fig. 8 (a) and the pneumatic muscle output force value as shown in Fig. 8 (b):

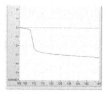

(a)   Physical maps   (b) Pneumatic muscle output force value

Fig. 8. Grab the oranges

The control system implements the reference model program, with the increasing output voltage of the D/A module of the microcontroller, the proportional valve controls the pressure in the pneumatic muscle cavity is increasing, the pneumatic muscle output force is also increasing until the mechanical gripper is undamaged grasping the orange, the output force is maintained near the steady state, the pneumatic muscle output force value is shown in Fig. 8 (b), the ordinate is kg, the expansion is 10 times the force value, the pull is positive, the pressure is negative.

In 105-110 ms, the pneumatic muscle output force is constantly increasing, indicating that the system in accordance with the reference model output force value, in the trend of 110 ms, pneumatic muscle-driven mechanical claws come into contact with oranges, and then implement the control system steady-state error elimination link, pneumatic muscle output to a steady state. As can be seen from the figure, the steady state value of the output force is about 34 N.

Grab the apple, ping-pong ball and eggs as shown in Fig. 9 (a), and the pneumatic muscle output force value is shown in Fig. 9 (b):

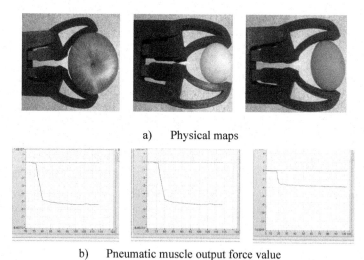

a)   Physical maps

b)   Pneumatic muscle output force value

Fig. 9. Grab the apple, ping-pong ball and eggs (form left to right)

4 Conclusions and Outlook

4.1 Conclusions

After the above research, this control model passed the test, pneumatic muscle-driven mechanical grippers can according to different sizes, mass of items, self-judge the size of the output force expectations, and the desired force values can grasp the items without loss. With force feedback, the control system enables closed-loop control of the entire system, ideally clamping oranges, apples, ping-pong balls and eggs. It is worth noting that this study designed a reference model inside the controller in advance, that is, in the case of mechanical grippers have not yet grasped the item, the pneumatic muscle output force value is output according to the law given by the reference model. The force value of this reference model is related to the elliptical function of time in half. Then the controller internal implementation of incremental PID program, play the role of proportion, integral and differential links, reduce and eliminate steady-state errors, and finally achieve pneumatic muscle output force to maintain near the steady state, and drive the mechanical claws adaptively and without loss to grab different items, the implementation of the entire control process, to complete the objectives of this experiment. At the same time, the controller can determine the expected force value of grabbing different items, showing the adaptability of this control system, and the pneumatic muscle output force can gradually stabilize and grab the item without loss.

After the above control and test, this study demonstrates three conclusions: first, the mechanical gripper driven by pneumatic muscle can grab the item without loss, and second, the control system with force as feedback can judge different output force expectations according to different volume and mass items, and have certain adaptability. Thirdly, the adaptive control system designed in this study can conform to the purpose of the study and verify the feasibility of PID regulation and force feedback as closed-loop control, which the coefficient 1.2 set in the control algorithm is the empirical value of the previous experimental study.

4.2 Outlook

Pneumatic muscle is a high-tech product of pneumatic technology in recent years, which adapts to the needs of industrial robot informatization and intelligence in Industry 4.0. It has the advantages of low cost, high power/mass ratio, and similar mechanics to biological muscles, which can replace the end actuator of industrial robot mainly driven by motor to some extent. Robotic bionics is the trend of future development, robots are not only close to human thought in the field of artificial intelligence, but also closer to human bones, muscles and so on in form. Pneumatic muscles are similar to the principle of human tendons, through the telescopic of their rubber braided mesh, to produce output force, mimicking human tendons to drive bones around the joint rotation. In this study, the force feedback control system driven by pneumatic muscles is verified from the field of control engineering and robotic bionics, and the adaptability of non-destructive grabbing items and this control system is realized.

Acknowledgment. This work was supported by the Shandong Natural Science Foundation of China (NO. ZR2017PEE025). We would like to thank anonymous reviewers for their useful comments, which have greatly improved the manuscript.

References

1. Wu, Y.: Research on Control Strategy of Pneumatic Artificial Muscle Flexible Manipulator. Nanjing University of Aeronautics and Astronautics (2019)
2. Ni, Z.-G., Mai, Y.-F., Yan, H.-W.: Research on static characteristics of pneumatic muscle based on MATLAB simulation. China Water Trans. (2020)
3. Bo, G.-J., Chen, Z.-P., Cai, S.-B.: A full-drive bionic dexterous hand based on pneumatic muscles: CN111390892A [P]. (2020)
4. Zhang, Y., Lu, D.-Y., Zhao, W.-C.: Design and implementation of pneumatic flexible massage manipulator claw. Mach. Tool Hydraul. (9)(2020)
5. Wang, L., Zhou, Z.-Y., Li, G.-L..: A pneumatic muscle: CN110840713A [P]. (2020)
6. Zhou, B.-B., Zou, R.-L.: Design and research of bionic hand driven by pneumatic muscle. Biomed. Eng. Res. (2020)
7. Gong, D.-X., He, R., Yu, J.-J.: A humanoid motion control method for pneumatic muscle antagonism driving robot joints. Robot (2019)
8. Shu, J., Tian, Y., Guo, Y.: Design of a soft pneumatic robotic gripper based on fiber reinforced actuator. J. Mech. Eng. **53**(13), 29–38 (2017)
9. Gong, Y., Ren, C., Wang, X., et al.: Development and performance analysis of the flexible pneumatic artificial muscle. In: International Conference on Mechatronics & Machine Vision in Practice. (2017)

Design of Strain Gauge Torque Sensor Used in the Modular Joint of Collaborative Robot

Peng Li[1], Fugui Xie[1,2], Yanlei Ye[1], Zihao Li[1], Yingzheng Liu[3], and Xin-Jun Liu[1,2(✉)]

[1] The State Key Laboratory of Tribology, Department of Mechanical Engineering, Tsinghua University, Beijing 100084, China
xinjunliu@mail.tsinghua.edu.cn
[2] Beijing Key Lab of Precision/Ultra-Precision Manufacturing Equipments and Control, Tsinghua University, Beijing 100084, China
[3] Yantai Tsingke+ Robot Joint Research Institute Co., Ltd., Yantai 264006, China

Abstract. With the characteristics of simple structure, good fabrication performance and stability, the disc strain gauge torque sensor is widely equipped in the collaborative robot to measure the modular joint output torque. The sensitivity and the stiffness are two important parameters of the torque sensor which influence robot torque control. However, the stiffness is paid less attention than the sensitivity during the robot design process. What is worse, some sensor design process improving the sensitivity weaken the stiffness unconsciously. In order to consider the sensitivity and the stiffness of the torque sensor during the design process simultaneously, the conflicting relationship between sensor sensitivity and the sensor stiffness about the measurement area thickness is established. With the guidance of the relationship the measurement area thickness is determined not only ensuring the sensitivity meet the safety demand but also improving the torque sensor has a higher stiffness. After designed a torque sensor model is made to detect the parameters. The experiment shows that the sensor has a good accuracy and the sensitivity is in accordance with the design.

Keywords: Design and test · Torque sensor · Modular joint · Collaborative robot

1 Introduction

Along with the development of the collaborative robot, the torque sensor become a basic configuration device realizing the interaction safety between human and robot. As the sensors based on resistance strain gauge has good process and good accuracy, many kinds of torque/force sensors use strain gauge as the detection unit [1–3]. The sensitivity is a vital parameter as higher sensitivity smaller torque detected which means the sensor has a nice detection ability. So many works have been carried out on the sensor body to improve the sensitivity. In Refs. [4, 5], the maximum strain area is searched to mount the strain gauge by the FEA method which is cost saving. Recently, some scholars explore the special structure to increase the amount of the strain [6, 7].

As more attention is paid to the sensitivity improving, there is rarely spotlight projected on the stiffness design of the sensor. However, the stiffness of sensor body has a

© Springer Nature Switzerland AG 2021
X.-J. Liu et al. (Eds.): ICIRA 2021, LNAI 13013, pp. 519–527, 2021.
https://doi.org/10.1007/978-3-030-89095-7_50

huge impact on the joint control bandwidth, as the sensor body is connected between the reducer and the output link in series which weakens the joint stiffness. For the collaborative robot, the high stiffness is more desirable as the harmonic reducer has a low stiffness which limits the robot control performance. So, the stiffness improving should be considered in the sensor design process.

In order to improve the sensitivity and stiffness simultaneously, the relationship among the measurement area thickness, the sensitivity and the stiffness of the torque sensor is revealed in this work. Based on the interaction condition, the sensitivity is determined and the stiffness is calculated by the relationship model. Meanwhile, the experiment is carried out to get the data of the torque sensor. The organization of this work is as follows. In the second part, the acquisition circuit, conditioning circuit and the sensor body are designed. The experiment and the data analysis are presented in the third part, and the conclusion is presented in the end.

2   Design of the Torque Sensor

The actuator is the essence of the joint which includes motor, motor driver, gear box and the output link. The joint is often in a cylindrical shape. In order to detect the accurate torque, the torque sensor is mounted on the output terminal of the joint. The torque sensor adopts disc shape conventionally which can improve the joint integration, and Fig. 1 is a side view of the joint.

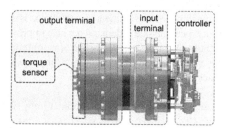

Fig. 1. A side view of the joint in this work

2.1   Design of the Signal Acquisition Circuit

The circuit of torque sensor usually consists of two parts which are the deformation acquisition circuit and the signal processing circuit. The deformation acquisition circuit generates the measurement signal and the signal processing circuit is designed for signal processing and transmission. There is a wide variety of signal processing circuit. For example, Kim design the special capacitance on the sensor body and obtain the deformation by measuring the change of the capacitance value in Refs. [8, 9]. An acoustic device is designed to detect the deformation by [10] and it is similar to the piezoelectric devices which is used to measure the torque of the machine tool spindle [11]. Recently an optical device is studied by Al-Mai to measure the torque/force in Ref. [12]. Compared with the above methods of torque/force measurement, the resistance strain gauge is more widely used for torque measurement in the modular joint of the collaborative robot because of its high precision, small size, simple process and low-cost characteristics [7, 13, 14]. So as to improve the integration of the joint, the resistance stain gauge is chosen as the deformation acquisition unit in this work.

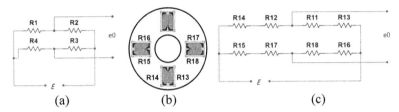

Fig. 2. The acquisition circuit: (a) The full-bridge Wheatstone circuit; (b) The configuration of strain gauges; (c) The mix-join full-bridge circuit consist of eight strain gauges

As shown in Fig. 2(a), the normal design, full-bridge Wheatstone circuit, is adopted which has higher sensitivity compared with the half-bridge, and the output voltage e_0 of full-bridge is given in the Eq. (1). E is the input voltage and R_1, R_2, R_3, R_4 are the four arms of the bridge whose corresponding small change are ΔR_1, ΔR_2, ΔR_3, ΔR_4. When the arm resistance value is equal, the output voltage can be expressed with the Eq. (2) in which R is the resistance value and the ΔR is the small change of the resistance value.

$$e_0 = E(\frac{\Delta R_1 + R_1}{\Delta R_1 + R_1 + R_2 - \Delta R_2} - \frac{-\Delta R_4 + R_4}{\Delta R_3 + R_3 + R_4 - \Delta R_4}) \tag{1}$$

$$e_0 = E\frac{\Delta R}{R} \tag{2}$$

Theoretically, the full-bridge has no nonlinear error and could eliminate the temperature interference. But it is disturbed by the harmonic reducer flexspline deformation due to that the flexspline deforms periodically and the inner senor flange is mounted on it which is introduced in Ref. [15]. In order to weaken the crosstalk of the flexspline deformation, in Ref. [16], the full-bridge is established with a mix-join method by eight strain gauges which is shown in Figs. 2(b) and (c). So, the acquisition circuit adopts the mix-join circuit. By calculation, the sensitivity of the mix-join circuit is same with the full-bridge formed by four strain gauges.

2.2 Design of the Sensor Body

In order to make the joint have a higher integration, the disc shape is adopted to design the sensor body. As shown in Fig. 3, the disc shape sensor body should have the inner and the outer flange to transfer torque. Based on the acquisition circuit, four measurement areas are reserved to fix the strain gauges and other parts are removed to place the circuit boards. In addition, the stiffeners are design on the two flanks of the measurement areas to strengthen the axial stiffness.

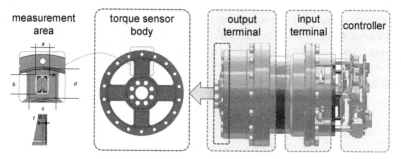

Fig. 3. The joint of the cooperative robot and the torque sensor body

The size of the measurement area is vital for the torque sensor design, as it affects the stiffness and the sensitivity of the torque which are the important parameters for the robot torque control. In this work, a parametric model is established with measurement width c, length d, thickness t, strain gauge width a and length b. The parameters meet same restrictions considering the production technology which is shown in Eqs. (3), (4) and (5).

$$d \geq 2b \tag{3}$$

$$c \geq 2a \tag{4}$$

$$t \geq 0.2 \tag{5}$$

Fig. 4. The FEA of the sensor body when t is 1 mm

The parameters are determined by the strain gauge. In this work, b is 9.6 mm and a is 6.4 mm. In order to have more space to mount the circuit on the material removed region, d is set $2b$ and c is set $2a$. So, the thickness t becomes the design central issue and it has to establish the relationship of t with the sensitivity and stiffness. The FEA method is used to deal with the issue which has a high accuracy and could obtain a large number of data in a short time. The parameters set in the FEA are that 7075 aluminum alloy material, 60 Nm rated torque on the inner flange and fixed outer flange. The Fig. 4

is the FEA of the sensor body and results of the FEA are display in the Table1 in which micro-stain amount $\mu\varepsilon$ is the mean value under the strain gauge area and the stiffness K is calculated by the deformation and the rated torque.

Table 1. The micro-stain data and stiffness data of the torque sensor corresponding to different thickness t.

The thickness t (mm)	0.1	0.2	0.4	0.6	0.8	1	1.2	1.4
Micro-stain $\mu\varepsilon$	4530	3360	2250	1720	1390	1180	1020	900
Stiffness of torque sensor K (10^4Nm/rad)	1.35	1.67	2.28	2.78	3.19	3.55	3.90	4.19

The two relationships are established by curve fitting of the data in Table 1 and shown in Eqs. (6) and (7). The Fig. 4 is more intuitive to show the relationship.

$$\mu\varepsilon = 3983e^{-5.8t} + 2469e^{-0.74t} \tag{6}$$

$$K = 3.559t^{0.46} \tag{7}$$

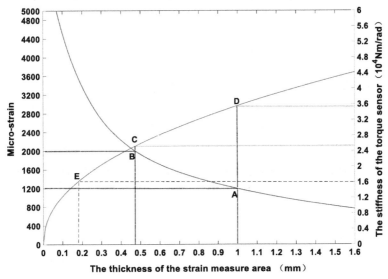

Fig. 5. The relationship of micro strain and the stiffness of torque sensor with the thickness of the strain measure area

Figure 5 shows that measurement area thickness is negatively related with mean strain and positively related with the body stiffness. The sensitivity of the torque sensor is $\Delta R/R$ shown in the Eq. (2) and its relationship with strain of the sensor body is shown in Eq. (8). The α is the strain coefficient of the strain gauge which is 2 provided by the manufacture.

$$\frac{\Delta R}{R} = \alpha \cdot \mu \varepsilon \tag{8}$$

As the torque sensor is equipped in the collaborative robot, it must ensure the physical safety when interacting with human. In Ref. [17], Suita takes the physical pain tolerance experiment which shows the minimal pain feeling when device impacts on experiment physical is 10 N. The experiment device used by Suita is a disc with 10 mm diameter which is harsh compared with collaborative robot surface, but this work still uses the experiment data as it makes more safety margin. So, it is supposed that the collision point is 10 mm far from the joint axis, and the resolution of the joint is 0.1 Nm at least which allows robot to protect the human.

According to the assembly process experience and the performance of the circuit, the resolution of the torque sensor is 0.2 micro-strains, but the resolution is set to two micro-strains to make the sensor have a better filtering effect. So, the number of micro-strains required for the range of 60 Nm are 1200 calculated by $2 \times 60/0.1$. Based on the value, the measurement area thickness value could be obtained approximated to 1 mm by the Eqs. (6) and (7) or the Fig. 6 and the stiffness is 3.56×10^4 Nm/rad. As the stiffness of the harmonic reducer is 0.84×10^4 Nm/rad, the composite stiffness is 0.68×10^4 Nm/rad which is equivalent to 81% of the reducer stiffness. From the result of the calculation, the introduction of the torque sensor weakens the joint stiffness which is the reason improving the stiffness of the torque sensor and the significance carrying out this work.

So, the sensitivity of the torque sensor is 2.4 mV/V which is calculated by Eq. (8).

2.3 Design of the Conditioning Circuit

The working principle of torque is that sensor body deforms with applied torque as well as the strain gauges, because the strain gauges are pasted on the sensor body. The deformation of strain gauge will lead to the change of the resistance value which is the reason of the output voltage. Limited by the strain amount of the strain gauges the output voltage of the acquisition circuit is millivolt level, but the voltage interface of the controller is volt level. It needs a conditioning circuit to deal with the signal conversion and transmission.

The joint needs to use a controller to process the information measured by the torque sensor. In this work the controller reserves an analog voltage input interface for the torque sensor whose input voltage ranges from 0 V to + 10 V and the resolution is 12 bits. Based on the interface feature of the controller, the conditioning circuit needs to amplify and filter the signal voltage as the analogy signal includes noise. At last, the controller reads the voltage information and converts it to torque. Of course, the digital filtering is needed to improve the stability of the torque signal. The process is shown in Fig. 6.

For the reason ensuring the sensor overload capability, the no load output voltage is set at 5 V and the voltage ranges from 1 V to 9 V. So the magnification of the conditioning circuit is 333 calculated by $(9–5) \times 1000/2.4$.

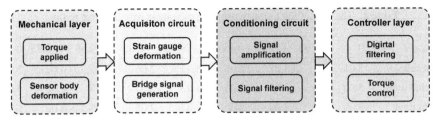

Fig. 6. The work principle of the torque sensor

3 Experiment and Data Processing

The experiment device is shown in Fig. 7, and its principle is dividing the weight's gravity G_p into two equal parts by the pulley block and applying them on the terminals of the lever in opposite direction. There are two groups pulley blocks being used to simulate the positive torque and the negative torque. The first step is setting the output voltage of the torque sensor at 5 V by adjusting the resistance on the conditioning circuit board. Secondly, it should put the weight on left (or right) tray up to the rated load intermittently and record the value of the load and the sensor output voltage. Thirdly, remove the weight and record the value of the load and the output voltage. Fourth step is repeating the second and third steps on the right (or left) tray. The steps from second to fourth should repeat three times to measure the repeatability of the sensor.

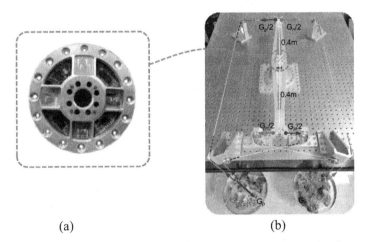

(a)   (b)

Fig. 7. The experiment of the torque sensor: (a) The torque sensor picture; (b) The experimental device picture

The results are listed in Table 2 and Table 3. Table 2 is the negative torque applied to the torque sensor and Table 3 is the positive torque applied to the torque sensor. The difference of the output voltage between the positive and the negative torque is caused by the voltage bias which meets the need of the joint controller.

Table 2. The data of the torque sensor output voltage with negative torque.

Torque T (Nm)	0	−14.95	−29.68	−45.07	−59.43	−45.07	−29.68	−14.95	0
First time	5.01	4.03	3.07	2.06	1.13	2.06	3.06	4.02	5.00
Second time	5.00	4.03	3.06	2.06	1.13	2.05	3.05	4.02	5.00
Third time	5.00	4.03	3.06	2.06	1.12	2.05	3.05	4.02	5.00

Table 3. The data of the torque sensor output voltage with positive rorque.

Torque T (Nm)	0	14.98	29.68	45.07	59.43	45.07	29.68	14.98	0
First time	5.00	5.96	6.94	7.94	8.90	7.97	6.96	5.99	5.00
Second time	5.00	5.97	6.94	7.94	8.89	7.96	6.96	5.99	5.00
Third time	5.00	5.97	6.93	7.95	8.88	7.96	6.96	5.99	5.00

By fitting the data in Table 2 and Table 3, the relationship between applied torque and sensor output voltage is shown by Eq. (9).

$$U_{out} = 0.063T + 5.00 \tag{9}$$

By the calculation, the nonlinearity of the torque sensor is 0.28% and the hysteresis characteristic is 0.38%. The synthetic sensitivity is 0.063 V/Nm.

4 Conclusions and Further Work

In this work, a torque sensor used in the collaborative robot modular joint is designed. To eliminate the crosstalk from the reduce flexspline, a mix-join circuit consisting of eight strain gauges is adopted to set up the acquisition circuit, and its matching conditioning circuit is designed to meet the requirement for the sensor. It becomes the focus of the design to establish the conflicting relationship between the sensor sensitivity and the sensor stiffness about the measurement area thickness. With the guidance of the relationship, the measurement area thickness is determined which makes the sensor have feasible sensitivity and optimal stiffness. Additionally, an experiment is conducted to detect the sensor parameters. The experiment result shows that the sensor accuracy is good and the sensitivity is consistent with the design. In the future, the torque stiffness will be tested to verify the design.

Acknowledgement. This work is supported by the National Key Research and Development Program of China (Grant No. 2019YFB1309900), a grant from the Key Research and Development Program of Shandong Province (Grant No. 2019JZZY010432), a grant from the Institute for Guo Qiang, Tsinghua University (Grant No.2019GQG0007).

References

1. Aghili, F., Buehler, M., et al.: Design of a hollow hexaform torque sensor for robot joints. Int. J. Robotics Res. **20**, 967 (2001)
2. Liang, Q.K., Zhang, D. et al: A novel miniature four-dimensional force/torque sensor with overload protection mechanism. IEEE Sens. J. **9**(12), December 2009
3. Wang, Y.J., Zuo, G.K. et al: Strain analysis of six-axis force/torque sensors based on analytical method. IEEE Sens. J. **17**(14), 15 July 2017
4. Shu, R., Chu, Z.G. et al.: A lever-type method of strain exposure for diskf-shaped torque sensor design. https://www.mdpi.com/1424-8220/20/2/541/xml. Accessed 30 April 2021
5. Ubeda, R.P., Gutiérrez Rubert, C.S. et al.: Design and manufacturing of an ultra-low-cost custom torque sensor for robotics. https://www.mdpi.com/1424-8220/18/6/1786. Accessed 30 April 2021
6. Zhang, H.X., Ryoo, Y.-J. et al.: Development of torque sensor with high sensitivity for joint of robot manipulator using 4-bar linkage shape. https://www.ncbi.nlm.nih.gov/pmc/articles/PMC4970042/. Accessed 30 April 2021
7. Hirzinger, G., Sporer, N. et al: Torque-controlled light weight arms and articulated hands-do we reach technological limits now?. http://www.robotic.de. Accessed 2 April 2021
8. Kim, U., Lee, D.-H. et al.: A novel six-axis force/torque sensor for robotic applications. IEEE/ASME Trans. Mech. **22**(3), June 2017
9. Kim, J.-I., Jeon, H.-S. et al.: High stiffness capacitive type torque sensor with flexure structure for cooperative industrial robots. In: 14th International Conference on Ubiquitous Robots and Ambient Intelligence (URAI), 28 June 2017 – 1 July 2017
10. Ji, X.J., Fan, Y.P. et al.: Passive wireless torque sensor based on surface transverse wave. IEEE Sens. J. **16**(4), 15 February 2016
11. Qin, Y.F., Zhao, Y.L., Li, Y.X. et al: A high performance torque sensor for milling based on a piezoresistive mems strain gauge. Sensor. https://www.mdpi.com/. Accessed 29 April 2021
12. Al-Mai, O., Ahmadi, M. et al: Design, development and calibration of a lightweight, compliant six-axis optical force/torque sensor. IEEE Sens. J. **18**(17), 1 September 2018
13. Huang, J., Zhang, X.H. et al.: A high-integrated and high-precision robot manipulator joint servo system. In: Proceeding of the 11th World Congress on Intelligent Control and Automation, Shenyang, China, 29 June 2014 – 4 July 2014
14. Kim, T.-K., Kim, D.Y. et al.: Development of joint torque sensor and calibration method for robot finger. In: 2013 10th International Conference on Ubiquitous Robots and Ambient Intelligence (URAI, Jeju, Korea), 31 October 2013 - 2 November 2013
15. Kim, I.-M., Kim, H.-S. et al.: Embedded joint torque sensor with reduced torque ripple of harmonic drive. In: Lee, S., et al. (eds.) Intelligent Autonomous Systems, vol. 12, AISC 194, pp. 633–640
16. Kashiri, N., Malzahn, J. et al.: On the sensor design of torque-controlled actuators: a comparison study of strain gauge and encoder-based principles. IEEE Robot. Autom. Lett. **2**(2), April 2017
17. Suita, K., Yamada, Y. et al.: A failure-to-safety "kyozon" system with simple contact detection and stop capabilities for safe human-autonomous robot coexistence. In: IEEE International Conference on robotics and automation 1995, Nagoya, Japan

ROS-Based Control Implementation of an Soft Gripper with Force Feedback

Yue Qiu, Xianmin Zhang, Hai Li$^{(\boxtimes)}$, and Rixin Wang

Guangdong Key Laboratory of Precision Engineering and Manufacturing Technology,
South China University of Technology, Guangzhou 510640, China
lihai@scut.edu.cn

Abstract. This paper demonstrates the use of Robot Operating System (ROS) to control an adaptive soft gripper. Firstly, the adaptive soft gripper used in this paper is introduced, including the main body, driving scheme and force sensors. Then, detailed control schemes including the ROS-based control framework and the force feedback based grasping strategy are presented. Finally, gripping experiments on different objects are performed to verify the performance of the proposed method. The results show that by adopting the proposed control scheme, objects of multi-shape objects can be grasped by the gripper safely and stably.

Keywords: ROS · Soft gripper · Multi-shape objects · Grasping

1 Introduction

As robotics become more complex in their operational tasks and are used more frequently in life scenarios, there is an increasing focus on the flexibility and safety of their grippers to enable human-robot cooperation [11]. This has given rise to the development of soft robotic hands. Inspiration from nature, combined with bionics, new materials and intelligent control methods, has given rise to the development of bionic soft manipulators. Current soft manipulators are typically made of silicone and driven by pneumatics, cables and functional materials, which can withstand large deformations [9]. Their fingers have greater flexibility and can adapt to different contours and sizes of objects without causing damage to the soft and fragile manipulated objects [10]. As a robotic end manipulator, it is safe and reliable, has good environmental adaptability and can be widely used to manipulate diverse objects with complex shapes and varying physical properties.

Currently, for the research topic of soft gripping, researchers have conducted research on soft and active materials, gripper structure and processing methods, adding distributed sensors to grippers for local information processing, and gripper control methods [9]. In general, soft gripping can be divided into three main categories, which are (i) gripping by external motors [4,7], shape memory alloys [8] and other actuators; (ii) gripping by variable stiffness; (iii) gripping by

© Springer Nature Switzerland AG 2021
X.-J. Liu et al. (Eds.): ICIRA 2021, LNAI 13013, pp. 528–538, 2021.
https://doi.org/10.1007/978-3-030-89095-7_51

adhesion [9]. For the second category, someone designed the gripper fingers to be rigid in order to increase the gripping force, coupled with variable stiffness joints made of shape memory alloys can have their stiffness changed by varying the temperature [5]. Variable stiffness can be achieved by means of particle blocking, low melting point alloys, galvanic variation [6] and magnetorheological fluids [9]. For the third category, there are two general ways of gripping by adhesion, namely electrical bonding and gecko bonding [1,3]. However, as the material of the gripper body are relatively soft, it is not easy to accurately model its complex deformation [2,12], thereby increasing the difficulty of design and control.

In our previous research, a mechanical soft gripper designed by topology optimization is presented in Fig. 1. Though a serial of grasp experiments are implemented, the control implementation of the gripper and the robot arm are separated, i.e., the robot are controlled under ROS, while the gripper is controlled by a micro-controller. To improve the control convenience, it important to control the two under the same framework. In this paper, we demonstrate the use of Robot Operating System (ROS) to control an adaptive soft gripper considering force feedback.

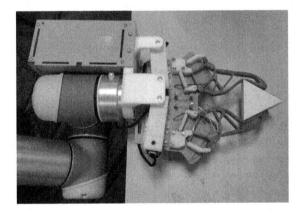

Fig. 1. Soft gripper mounted on the UR robot arm

The rest of this article is organized as follows. The Sect. 2 briefly introduces the research objects of this article. Section 3 describes the control method and grasping strategy of the soft gripper based on ROS. In Sect. 4, the proposed gripper control method is experimentally verified. Section 5 gives the conclusion.

2   Brief Description of the Adaptive Soft Gripper

In our previous work, a cable-driven soft gripper using a topology optimization method considering geometric nonlinearity is developed. Figure 1 shows the collaborative work of the gripper and the UR robot. The gripper adopts a two-input two-output configuration design scheme, and considers the adaptive grasping of various shapes of objects. It can not only realize finger closing movement, but also can cooperate with two fingers to realize the rotation of the object. The soft gripper is manufactured using 3D printing technology. In order to achieve independent control of multiple motion conditions, a cable-driven scheme is employed, and each finger is assigned two servo motors with a maximum torque of 15 kg-cm via rigid cords. The driving system layout of the gripper is shown in the Fig. 2.

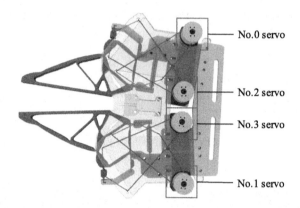

Fig. 2. View of the back of the gripper and arrangement of the four servos

3   ROS-Based Control Schemes

The communication of the servos is based on the UART serial protocol and there are two command packet formats, a long protocol and a short protocol. The command package is close to machine language, which is not conducive to writing and reading control programs. So we use Serial, a library of functions packaged in Python, to implement communication between serial ports by calling servo functions to change the state of the servo and read its state, which greatly simplifies the control program.

This paper focuses on the control method and gripping strategy of this soft manipulator, simplifying its control algorithm under the conditions of ensuring the safety of human-machine cooperation and the diversity of operating objects. A brief schematic flow diagram of the compliant gripper control system is shown in Fig. 3.

3.1   ROS-Based Control Framework

ROS stands for Robot Operating System, which enables the robot's "brain" mainframe, "hand" robot, "upper limb" robot arm, "lower limb" mobile platform, "eye" camera and other organs to communicate, just like the human nervous system, linking all parts and making the robot a complete distributed operating system.

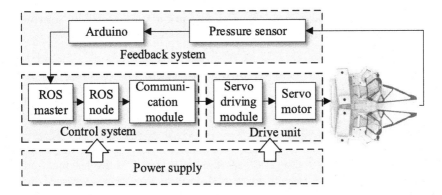

Fig. 3. Principle and composition of the gripper control system

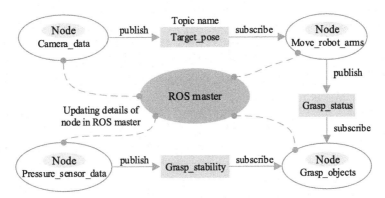

Fig. 4. Schematic diagram of ROS communication with individual components

There are four nodes in the Fig. 4 called camera_data, pressure_sensor_data, moving_robot_arm, and grasping_object. The camera_data collects environmental data from the depth vision sensor, move_robot_arms moves the robot arm to the target position, grasp_objects controls the gripper to grasp the object and pressure_sensor_data collects data from the thin film pressure sensor.

Taking the example of communication between the robot arm and the gripper. move_robot_arms wants to publish a topic with string message to inform the other party of its location and ask it to take the next action, it will first communicate to the ROS master node that it will publish a topic with string message called grasp_status and share its details. When another node, such as grasp_objects, tells the ROS master node that it wishes to subscribe to the grasp_status topic of string message, the master node will share the information about move_robot_arms and allocate a port to initiate communication directly between move_robot_arms and grasp_objects. In this way, direct communication can be established between multiple nodes, allowing the robot to complete a series of actions from acquiring visual information to successfully grasping a target, enabling closed-loop control of the entire robot.

3.2   Force Feedback Based Gripping Strategy

Based on the application scenarios of the soft gripper, four functions have been designed for it: gripping, releasing, rotating the target counterclockwise and rotating the target clockwise.

As shown in Fig. 2, the two servos 0 and 1 control the gripper in the Y-axis direction, corresponding to the two functions of grasping and releasing, and the two servos 2 and 3 control the gripper in the X-axis direction, corresponding to rotating the target clockwise and anti-clockwise. This paper will focus on the two functions of grasping and releasing for further research. The key point in implementing the above functions is that when the gripper receives the command to be executed, it is resolved into the corresponding servo action. And after the servo action is completed, the servo state is returned to check whether it is consistent with the target state. The specific flow of grasping the target object is shown in Fig. 5.

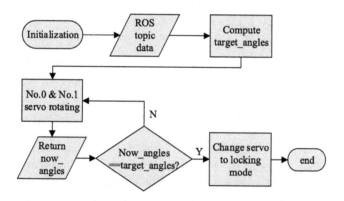

Fig. 5. Flowchart of grasp objects in detail.

For the soft gripper, the process of gripping a target goes from point to surface contact with the object as shown in Fig. 6, so it is a question of how to judge whether the gripping process is complete, or whether the gripper has reached just the right state of surface contact with the object surface (the gripping force is not too small to cause unstable gripping, nor too large to be destructive to the gripped target). A schematic showing the gripper in contact with the object surface is shown in Fig. 7.

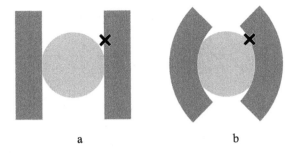

a   b

Fig. 6. Schematic diagram of the gripping process. The simplified model of the gripper fingers is shown in blue, the gripping target in grey and the location of the proposed arrangement of pressure sensors in black. **a** The gripper in the unclamped state, where the contact with the object is close to point contact; **b** The gripper in the clamped state, where the contact between the gripper and the object is surface contact.

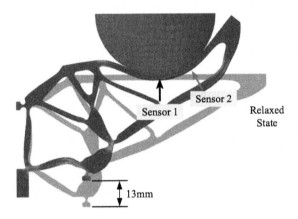

Fig. 7. More stable gripping when the gripper is in contact with the surface of the gripping object. The black arrow is the position at which the gripper first makes contact with the object, the red arrow is the position at which to determine whether the gripper is in face contact with the object [12]. (Color figure online)

To solve this problem, a thin-film pressure sensor is placed 1/3 of the way above the gripper fingers to measure the pressure between the object and the gripper, and the measured pressure value is transmitted back to the host computer in real time. When the pressure between the sensor and the object surface is too low, the gripping force is increased to improve gripping stability; when the pressure is too high, the gripping force is reduced to avoid damage to the gripping target. The closed-loop control, as shown in Fig. 8, allows the gripper to operate on the target using the appropriate gripping force.

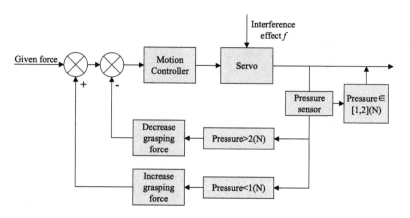

Fig. 8. Closed-loop control chart. The diagram actually contains two closed-loop controls. One represented by the entire schematic and the other contained in the motion controller flow, details of which are given in the Fig. 5.

4   Experiment

This section tests and evaluates the performance of the communication between host and gripper by ROS, and the stability of control algorithm.

4.1   Experimental Setup

The experiments were carried out using an Ubuntu computer with an soft gripper, a thin film pressure sensor and an Arduino development board to verify the safety of the adaptive gripper in terms of human-machine cooperation, gripping stability and the feasibility of coordinating the operation of the robot with the ROS. The two thin-film pressure sensors used in the experiments are RFP-601-500G, manufactured by Yubo Intelligent Technology Co.

The thin film pressure sensor is connected to the host computer via a conversion module and the Arduino NANO development board. Its resistance changes are represented by the output voltage, which is mapped to a value of $[0,1024]$ by the Arduino development board. The relationship between the input pressure, the resistance, the output voltage and the data obtained by the host can be described by the following relational equation:

$$R = \frac{a_1 P + b_1}{a_2 P + b_2} \tag{1}$$

$$U = \frac{uR}{R + 10} \tag{2}$$

$$O = \frac{1024U}{u} \tag{3}$$

Where R refers to the resistance of the sensor, P refers to the pressure on the sensor, U refers to the voltage output from the sensor and O refers to the

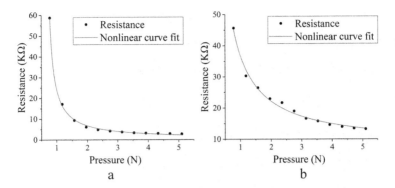

Fig. 9. Pressure-resistance curve of the sensor. **a** Fitted curve graph for sensor 1, **b** Fitted curve graph for sensor 2

data read by the host computer.a_1, b_1, a_2, b_2 is obtained by fitting a curve with a different set of values for different sensors as shown in Fig. 9. u measured by a multimeter, under the conditions set in this experiment, $u = 4.7$.

The above equation allows the raw input pressure to be solved from the data read by the host computer. In this experiment, due to the limited range of the pressure sensors, the raw input pressure was solved for in the range [0,5] (N).

4.2   Experimental Process

Based on the above theoretical basis, a control algorithm for the ros-based adaptive gripper was written, and the following is the experimental procedure for testing this control algorithm.

First, the safety of the human-machine cooperation of the gripper was tested. A pressure sensor was placed at the fingertip on the right side of the gripper, which opens when the finger is under pressure to prevent the human hand from being pinched by the gripper. Secondly, the gripper's gripping stability and safety when handling objects is tested. A thin-film pressure sensor is placed in the middle of the gripper and another sensor is placed 1/3 of the way from the fingertip. The sensor in the middle is the first to come into contact with the object, so it is affected by the pressure change before the other sensor. When the pressure on the object is too low, the gripping force is increased to prevent the object from falling, while when the pressure on the object is too high, the gripping force is reduced to avoid damage to the object. In summary, the pressure sensor monitors the pressure between the gripper and the object and fine-tunes the gripping force to keep it within the right range to ensure a stable grip without damaging the object. The experimental procedure and results are shown in Fig. 10.

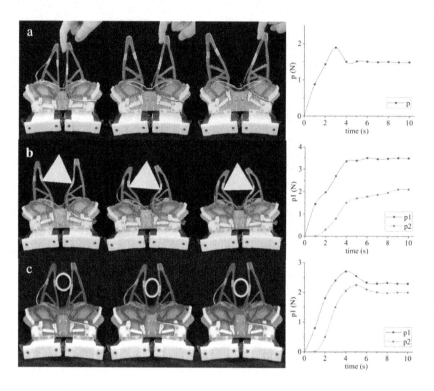

Fig. 10. The experimental process. **a** corresponds to the human-machine safety experiment, **b** to the experiment in which the gripping force is too small to hold the object, and **c** to the experiment in which the gripper is too large to crush the object; from left to right, the initial state, the intermediate process state, the end state and the change in pressure on the sensor. **p** indicates the sensor data placed at the fingertip, **p1** indicates the sensor data placed at the middle of the finger, **p2** indicates the sensor data placed 1/3 of the way from the fingertip.

Finally, regarding the load range of the soft gripper, a simple experiment was did. Although the drive of this gripper is provided by four high-torque servos, its load range is actually affected by some other factors, so the relationship between the driving force and the gripper is non-linear. The factors that affect the load range of the gripper include the gripping angle, the shape of the gripping target and its surface roughness. In this experiment, the weight of the object to be measured is 500 g, and the diameter of the grasping position is 6 cm. This experiment shows that this soft gripper can grip objects weighing up to 500 g and has good gripping stability (Fig. 11).

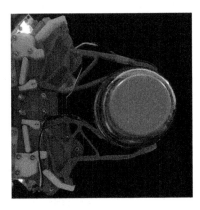

Fig. 11. The object is a bottle filled with water, with a total weight of 500 g.

5   Conclusion

In this paper, ROS-based communication is used to enable the establishment of communication channels between the host computer, the soft gripper and the sensors; by studying the gripping strategy of the gripper, thin-film pressure sensors are arranged at different locations of the gripper to establish a channel for the return transmission of gripping information. The establishment of these communication channels opens up possibilities for experiments in this paper as well as for subsequent developments, such as the application of the present soft gripper to an interactive robot, where the distributed operating system ROS is used to control the robot's hands, arms, eyes and brain to achieve coordinated operation of the whole machine.

Experiments have shown that the control method designed for the gripper allows for greater safety and flexibility in terms of human-machine cooperation. Rather than operating the target with a given uniform gripping force in an indiscriminate manner, it can be operated differently depending on the state of the object being operated. Making the gripper more widely adaptable to different targets based on a multi-degree-of-freedom.

There are still some issues that need to be addressed in future work. For example, environmental information such as vision is not currently used for assistance, which makes the gripper lack judgement of the physical characteristics of the object being manipulated. Therefore, in the future we will investigate the development of vision-assisted sorting robot systems, etc.

Acknowledgement. This work has been funded by National Natural Science of China (No. 518201050-07, 51905176), the Guangdong Basic and Applied Basic Research Foundation (2021A1515012418), Dongguan Postgraduate Joint Training (Practice) Workstation Project (2019707122025).

References

1. Alizadehyazdi, V., Bonthron, M., Spenko, M.: An electrostatic/gecko-inspired adhesives soft robotic gripper. IEEE Robot. Autom. Lett. **5**(3), 4679–4686 (2020)
2. Deimel, R., Brock, O.: A novel type of compliant and underactuated robotic hand for dexterous grasping. Int. J. Robot. Res. **35**(1–3), 161–185 (2016)
3. Glick, P., Suresh, S.A., Ruffatto, D., Cutkosky, M., Tolley, M.T., Parness, A.: A soft robotic gripper with gecko-inspired adhesive. IEEE Robot. Autom. Lett. **3**(2), 903–910 (2018)
4. Ilievski, F., Mazzeo, A.D., Shepherd, R.F., Chen, X., Whitesides, G.M.: Titelbild: Soft robotics for chemists (angew. chem. 8/2011). Angewandte Chemie **123**(8), 1765–1765 (2011)
5. Liu, M., Hao, L., Zhang, W., Zhao, Z.: A novel design of shape-memory alloy-based soft robotic gripper with variable stiffness. Int. J. Adv. Robot. Syst. **17**(1), 1729881420907813 (2020)
6. Mavroidis, C.: Development of advanced actuators using shape memory alloys and electrorheological fluids. J. Res. Nondestr. Eval. **14**(1), 1–32 (2002)
7. Renda, F., Giorelli, M., Calisti, M., Cianchetti, M., Laschi, C.: Dynamic model of a multibending soft robot arm driven by cables. IEEE Trans. Robot. **30**(5), 1109–1122 (2014)
8. She, Y., Li, C., Cleary, J., Su, H.J.: Design and fabrication of a soft robotic hand with embedded actuators and sensors. J. Mech. Robot. **7**(2), 021007 (2015)
9. Shintake, J., Cacucciolo, V., Floreano, D., Shea, H.: Soft robotic grippers. Adv. Mater. **30**(29), 1707035 (2018)
10. Sinatra, N.R., Teeple, C.B., Vogt, D.M., Parker, K.K., Gruber, D.F., Wood, R.J.: Ultragentle manipulation of delicate structures using a soft robotic gripper. Sci. Robot. **4**(33) (2019)
11. Trivedi, D., Rahn, C.D., Kier, W.M., Walker, I.D.: Soft robotics: biological inspiration, state of the art, and future research. Appl. Bionics Biomech. **5**(3), 99–117 (2008)
12. Wang, R., Zhang, X., Zhu, B., Zhang, H., Chen, B., Wang, H.: Topology optimization of a cable-driven soft robotic gripper. Struct. Multi. Optim. **62**(5), 2749–2763 (2020). https://doi.org/10.1007/s00158-020-02619-y

Design and Motion Analysis of a Pneumatic Soft Active Structure to Imitate Neck Muscle

Jianfeng Wang, Wangshu Xu, Xin Zhao, Yuting Yan, Chun Zhao, Yanjie Wang[✉],
and Minzhou Luo

Jiangsu Provincial Key Laboratory of Special Robot Technology, School of Mechanical and
Electrical Engineering, Hohai University, Changzhou Campus, Changzhou 213022, China
yjwang@hhu.edu.cn

Abstract. In this work, inspired by the human neck muscle, we proposed a soft active structure by controlling three pneumatic linear actuators to achieve the abilities of multi-DOF bending motion. To establish the motion model of the proposed active structure, the length of each linear actuator can be inversely calculated according to the pose of the upper motion platform. We utilized MATLAB to simulate the motion space of the center point of the upper motion platform. The accuracy of the model is verified through a series of experiments, and the results show that the proposed structure has excellent motion performance.

Keywords: Soft active structure · Pneumatic linear actuators · Motion model

1 Introduction

As one kind of emerging robots, soft robot provides adaptable structure in response to environmental changes, which has a wide application prospect in military detection, medical examination and other fields [1–4]. Currently, soft robots are made of soft frame materials and soft actuating and sensing materials, such as Shape Memory Alloy (SMA), Electroactive Polymers (EAP), thermoplastic polyurethane (TPU), silicone elastomers, hydro-gels, and so on. The soft actuating and sensing abilities can be achieved by a variety of stimuli, including electrical voltage, chemical reactions and hydraulic and pneumatic device [5–11].

According to the soft material characteristics, the active structure usually has low operating accuracy and limited workspace [12, 13]. Relevant researchers tried to employ cross-disciplines such as machinery and materials to solve the defects of current soft active structure. LASCHI C et al. [14] designed a bionic robot octopus arm using coupling structure design to achieve variable stiffness. TANIGUCHI H et al. [15] proposed a soft actuator using magnetic fluids for flexible walking robot, achieving variable stiffness through phase change of material. The evenly distributed structure of the three groups of OctArm pneumatic muscles has high stability [16]. Additionally, to simulate soft structure, cosserat beam theory can be used to establish a high-precision dynamic model, but the modeling process is very complex [17, 18].

© Springer Nature Switzerland AG 2021
X.-J. Liu et al. (Eds.): ICIRA 2021, LNAI 13013, pp. 539–551, 2021.
https://doi.org/10.1007/978-3-030-89095-7_52

To solve the problems of soft active device from the aspects of material stiffness adjustment, structure design and kinematics modeling, a soft active structure consisted of fixed base and three soft linear actuators driven by compressed air are designed in this work by studying the muscle distribution of human neck. And then we established a kinematic model of the proposed structure and predicted its working space. Through ABAQUS finite element analysis, we obtained structural design optimization parameters and improved the manufacturing process. Finally, the performance evaluation of the proposed structure was verified by a series of experiments.

2   Structural Design

Muscles are connected to specific parts of bones through tendons, which drive the bones to move. According to human anatomy, the neck muscle groups and back muscle groups are related to neck movement.

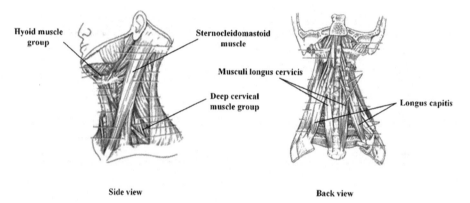

Fig. 1. Distribution map of neck muscle group

The main distribution of neck muscles is shown in Fig. 1. When we imitate the movement of human neck to create a soft active structure, we mainly consider the movement state of the sternocleidomastoid muscle, the muscle longus cervicis and the Longus capitis. The simplified model of neck muscles is showed in Fig. 2.

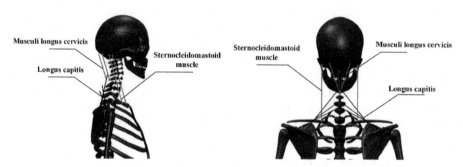

Fig. 2. Simplified model of neck muscles

Based on the model of human neck muscles, a soft active structure is designed to improve the bearing capacity of tangential force and transverse force of soft active structure (as shown in Fig. 3). The principle of the structure is that the expansions of the three pneumatic linear actuators cause the upper base to deflect in space. When a certain air pressure is applied to one or multiple of the air chambers, the pneumatic linear actuator will be elongated. Due to the antagonistic effect of the other actuators, the upper base will produce a turning and bending motion in the space. The structure can realize almost omni-directional rotation in space, which is simple and easy to assemble.

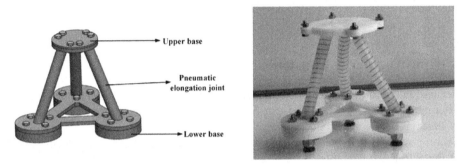

Fig. 3. Soft active structure (left: model, right: prototype)

The soft active structure consists of three parts: the upper and lower base and three pneumatic linear actuators, as shown in Fig. 4.

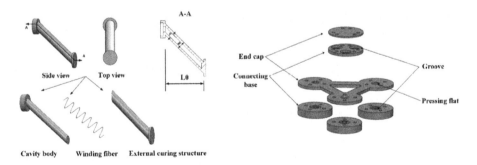

Fig. 4. Pneumatic linear actuators (left) and the base structure (right)

Taking the bending angle as the evaluation parameter, the size of the structure is optimized by finite element software, and the optimized size is shown in Table 1. So the angle during the three air chambers (linear actuator) is set to 120° to get good bending performance for this structure.

Table 1. Optimum size of soft active structure

Distance between upper and lower base/mm	Upper base diameter/mm	Lower base diameter/mm	Air cavity wall thickness/mm
80	25	75	3
Air cavity length/mm		Tilt angle/°	
89		66.5	
The distance from the center of the linear actuators on the upper base/mm		The distance from the center of the actuators on the lower base/mm	
10		50	

3 Construction of Kinematic Model

Because the deformation of elastic materials changes nonlinearly under the action of external force. The Yeoh model can fit this form of deformation based on the data of uniaxial tensile experiments, which is suitable for simulating large deformations. Therefore, the Yeoh model is used to establish the relationship between stress and strain of the soft active structure. Ecoflex-0050 was used to the elastic material of the soft actuators.The Yeoh model is simplified as following, the first two items are retained, and the parameter is determined by the following Eq. (1).

$$W = C_1(I_1 - 3) + C_2(I_2 - 3)^2 \tag{1}$$

The material factor can be texted by uniaxial tension and compression tests. For Ecoflex-0050, the parameters in the formula are: $C_1 = 0.11$, $C_2 = 0.02$. Through the virtual work theorem, the relationship between the air pressure and the elongation of a single air chamber can be obtained (Fig. 5).

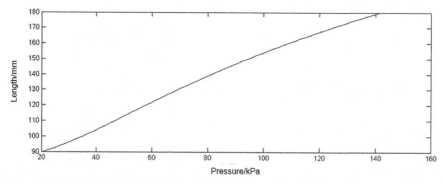

Fig. 5. Relation diagram of single air chamber pressure and elongation length

The pneumatic actuators can rotate in a large range at the connection with bases, so it is considered that the connections between the pneumatic actuators and the upper or lower bases are a ball pair. the pneumatic actuators can change the length.

3.1 Establish the Positional Relationship of the Overall Structure

In order to explore the motion space of the structure, the lower base of the structure is fixed to the XOY plane, and the spatial angle coordinate system (as shown in Fig. 6 (a)) is established. The O_1 point is the center point of the upper base.

Among them, the arrangement position of the three soft linear actuators are shown as Fig. 7, where A_0A_1, B_0B_1, and C_0C_1 are respectively the center lines of the three actuators. A_0A_1 is coplanar with the x-axis. The length and position of the actuators are represented by the center line of the pneumatic linear actuators. In this state of motion, the selected air chamber A_0A_1 does not change the length, while the air chamber B_0B_1 and C_0C_1 change lengths.

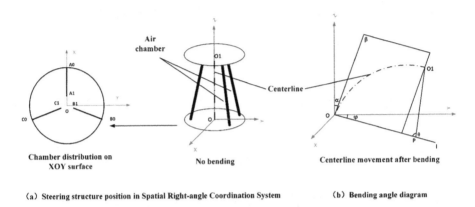

(a) Steering structure position in Spatial Right-angle Coordination System   (b) Bending angle diagram

Fig. 6. Location of the overall structure

If the structure is not bent, its state is shown in Fig. 6(a). But when the chambers B_0B_1 and C_0C_1 are simultaneously infused with air of different pressures, the different elongation states of the three air chambers lead to spatial movement of the overall structure. In order to define the spatial movement state of the upper base, the angles (as shown in Fig. 6(b)) are defined for expression. Make plane β through curve OO_1, the intersection line of plane β and XOY plane is l, the angle between the line l and the Y axis is φ; the angle between the plane β and the Z axis is α; Taking a point P on line l satisfies $PO = PO_1$, the angle between OP and O_1P is θ, and the length of $\overset{\frown}{OO_1}$ is L.

3.2 Establish the Position Coordinates of the Center Point O_1

In order to define the motion state of the upper base, it is necessary to determine the spatial position of the point OO_1, so the position coordinates of the point O_1 are established first. Let the coordinate of point O_1 be P (m, n, p), Make a straight line O_1D through O_1, satisfying O_1D and OD in vertical direction, and the intersection point is D. Make a straight line O_1Q perpendicular to the plane XOY, intersection plane XOY to point Q, and connect QD, to establish the coordinate system as shown in Fig. 7, where (b) is the projected coordinate system on the XOY plane.

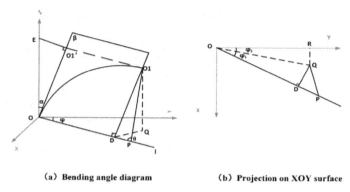

(a) Bending angle diagram   (b) Projection on XOY surface

Fig. 7. Schematic diagram of the position coordinates of point O1.

In summary, the coordinate of point O_1 are as follows.

$$P = \begin{bmatrix} m \\ n \\ p \end{bmatrix} = \begin{bmatrix} \cos\varphi_2\sqrt{(1-\cos\theta)^2 + (\sin\theta\sin\alpha)^2} \\ \sin\varphi_2\sqrt{(1-\cos\theta)^2 + (\sin\theta\sin\alpha)^2} \\ \sin\theta\cos\alpha \end{bmatrix} \cdot \frac{L}{\theta} \qquad (2)$$

3.3 Establishing a Motion Relationship

The position coordinates of the upper base center point are established by the geometric relationship. The solution of the Eq. (2) is multi-group, and the appropriate solution of the central point coordinates can be screened by position conditions. The length of the three air chambers will be calculated when the coordinate point O_1 is known.

Most of the current flexible structures do not have kinematic model, and are generally established with reference to the model of rigid mechanisms, which cannot be bent due to its high rigidity. There are often one or more singularities in the entire space, restricting movement. The flexible mechanism can move freely and unimpeded due to its high flexibility. Therefore, when the flexible pneumatic actuators replace the rigid actuators, the degree of freedom is higher, the deformation range is larger, realizing large-deformation elongation and bending movement modes. The angle and range of motion are far beyond the rigid parallel structure of the same size, and there is no singularity in the entire motion space.

In order to determine the pose of the upper base, the orthogonal coordinate system $O_1X_1Y_1Z_1$ based on the above base is established, which has 6 degrees of freedom relative to the base coordinate system OXYZ of the base. Among them (m, n, p) defines the translational displacement of the moving platform relative to the base. In addition, there are three rotational degrees of freedom, which can be defined by the offset angle between the $X_1Y_1Z_1$ axis of the movable platform and the XYZ axis of the base. As shown in Fig. 6, the projection of air chambers A_0A_1 is arranged on the X axis, and the length does not change. So the rotation angle on the X axis is 0, the rotation angle on the Y axis is φ, and the rotation angle on the Z axis is α.

the rotation matrix of the upper platform relative to the base is:

$$R_B = R_X \cdot R_Y \cdot R_Z = \begin{bmatrix} \cos\alpha\cos\varphi & -\sin\alpha & \cos\alpha\sin\varphi \\ \sin\alpha\cos\varphi & \cos\alpha & \sin\alpha\sin\varphi \\ -\sin\varphi & 0 & \cos\varphi \end{bmatrix} \tag{3}$$

The pose matrix of point O_1 relative to the base is:

$$T_B^U = \begin{bmatrix} R_B & P \\ 0 & 1 \end{bmatrix} \tag{4}$$

The vector expression of the centerline of the pneumatic linear actuator is:

$$\begin{cases} \overrightarrow{A_0 A_1} = \overrightarrow{OO_1} + \overrightarrow{O_1 A_1} \cdot \overrightarrow{R_B} - \overrightarrow{OA_0} \\ \overrightarrow{B_0 B_1} = \overrightarrow{OO_1} + \overrightarrow{O_1 B_1} \cdot \overrightarrow{R_B} - \overrightarrow{OB_0} \\ \overrightarrow{C_0 C_1} = \overrightarrow{OO_1} + \overrightarrow{O_1 C_1} \cdot \overrightarrow{R_B} - \overrightarrow{OC_0} \end{cases} \tag{5}$$

In Eq. (5), $\overrightarrow{O_1 A_1}$, $\overrightarrow{O_1 B_1}$, $\overrightarrow{O_1 C_1}$ refers to the vector in the moving platform of coordinate system $O_1 X_1 Y_1 Z_1$. $\overrightarrow{OA_0}$, $\overrightarrow{OB_0}$, $\overrightarrow{OC_0}$ is the vector in the pedestal coordinate system OXYZ. $\overrightarrow{OO_1} = [m, n, p]$, $\overrightarrow{R_B}$ is the rotation matrix of the moving platform.

When the coordinates of the center point of the upper platform are known, the actual length of the three chambers can be solved by formula (5). The model is reversely solved, knowing the bending angle and pressure of each chamber. In this section, the length of two pneumatic actuators changes, and one pneumatic linear actuator does not deform. But also applicable for the three pneumatic actuators pass into different air pressure.

3.4 Motion Space Analysis

The working space of the mechanism refers to all the positions that the end effector can reach under the conditions allowed by the driving part and the connecting joint. The movement space in this work refers to the center point of the upper base can reach in the space. Here, each angle is discretized based on formula (2) and (3) to simulate the movement space of the center point of the upper base.

Three angles are first discretized, select N values uniformly within $[0, 20°]$ as the α angle, select M values uniformly within $[0, 20°]$ as the φ angle, select P values uniformly within $[0, 360°]$ as the θ angle.so take a total of N*M*P center point positions. In this sports space model, assuming that the length of the center line $\overrightarrow{OO_1}$ remains unchanged at 80mm.

The final movement position of the center point on the upper base in the whole space is shown in Fig. 8. Before deformation, the coordinate of the center point on the upper base in the coordinate system O-XYZ is (0, 0, 80). After deformation, the spatial location distribution map was shown in Fig. 8.

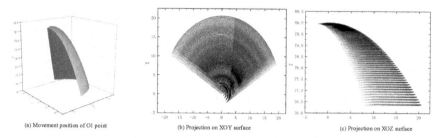

(a) Movement position of O1 point   (b) Projection on XOY surface   (c) Projection on XOZ surface

Fig. 8. Mathematical model calculation spatial location distribution

4 Experimental Verification

The accuracy of the model needed to be verified. First of all, the model of inflating to single chamber was used to prove the accuracy of the model built by the virtual work theorem used in unidirectional bending; Secondly, we confirmed that multi-DOF bending model has good applicability through the experiment of inflating to double chambers; Finally, we tested the model of inflating to three chambers and compared with the actual sports space model. A test platform was built and the images of the camera were used to analyze the value of the measurement angle (as shown in Fig. 9).

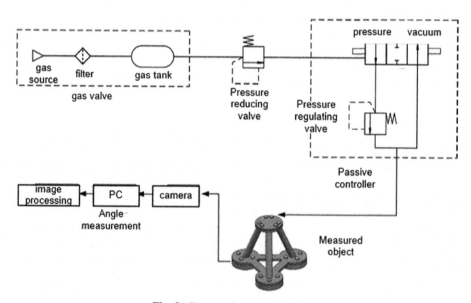

Fig. 9. Pneumatic control platform

4.1 Single- Directional Deformation Experiment

Single- directional deformation experiment is used to verify the relationship between the air pressure and the bending angle. The bending deformation state of the structure is shown in Fig. 10. Single air chamber is injected with the air pressure from 0 kPa to 40 kPa by the internal of 5 kPa, defining the bending angle of the structure is θ. The experimental data, mathematical model data and finite element model data of the bending angle are shown in Fig. 10 and 11.

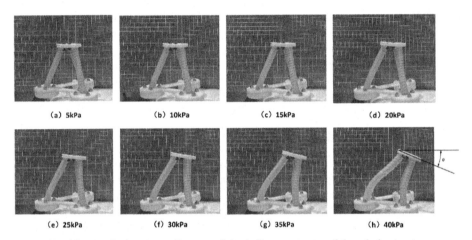

(a) 5kPa   (b) 10kPa   (c) 15kPa   (d) 20kPa

(e) 25kPa   (f) 30kPa   (g) 35kPa   (h) 40kPa

Fig. 10. Ventilation curve diagram of single linear actuator of the whole structure

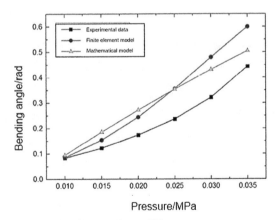

Fig. 11. Angles at different pressures

For actual bending angle, because the silica gel material needs to absorb energy, the bending angle changes little under low pressure. Once the energy is sufficient, actual bending angle will have a sudden change when the pressure reaches 30 kPa. In order to verify the accuracy of the mathematical model, the error between the theoretical bending angle and the actual bending angle is calculated through the mean square error formula by Eq. (6).

$$e = \sqrt{\frac{\sum\limits_{i=1}^{n} (\alpha_i - \beta_i)^2}{n}} \tag{6}$$

Where α_i is the bending angle of each test point in the mathematical model, β_i is the bending angle of each test point in the experimental test, and n is the number of test points. This paper tested the bending angles under 9 different air pressures, so n = 9. The root mean square error between the mathematical model and the experimental measurement value is 0.03971rad (6.9% of the overall bending angle), the error is less than 10%, and the root mean square error of the finite element model is 0.05671rad (10% of the overall bending angle)), the mathematical model proposed in this work can approximate simulate the actual bending deformation state.

4.2 Multi-directional Bending Verification

The deformation of the three-chamber inflating compared with the deformation of the two-chamber inflating is mainly manifested in the effect of elongation on the Z axis, and has little effect on rotation and bending. So the experiment that inflating to double chambers was used to observe the change of bending angle in the multi-DOF soft active structure. One pneumatic linear actuator was not inflated to make it at its original length, the other two actuators were injected with the pressure from 0 kPa to 40 kPa by the internal of 5 kPa, the relationship between pressure and structural deformation parameters can be obtained.

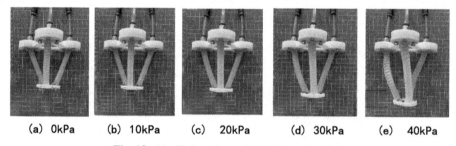

(a) 0kPa   (b) 10kPa   (c) 20kPa   (d) 30kPa   (e) 40kPa

Fig. 12. Ventilation elongation of three chambers

We measured the parameter α, θ, φ, and L (As shown in Fig. 7), a total of 64 sets of data. According to mathematical modeling, the bending angle was converted to the coordinate of the upper base center point O_1 in the coordinate system OXYZ, as shown in Fig. 12. The picture was the distribution map of the spatial position, where the intersection of the line on the surface and the line was the discrete position point under different air pressure.

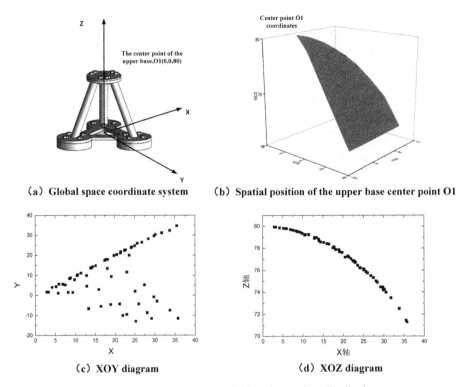

(a) Global space coordinate system   (b) Spatial position of the upper base center point O1

(c) XOY diagram   (d) XOZ diagram

Fig. 13. Actual measurement spatial location surface distribution map

By comparing the actual coordinate of O_1 in Fig. 13 with the mathematical model in Fig. 8, it is found that the motion trajectories of the two are similar, and have the same movement characteristics. Therefore, it can be preliminarily determined that the built kinematics model has certain accuracy.

When the lengths of the three air chambers are known, the position of the upper base center point can be obtained by using the mathematical model. Likewise, if the actual bending angle α, θ, φ, and L are known, the length of three pneumatic linear actuators can be derived from the mathematical model. As shown in Table 2, actual measurement data of the actuators is compared with the mathematical model Simulation data.

Table 2. Comparison of actual length and mathematical model

Bending angle	$\alpha/\circ$	$\theta/\circ$	$\varphi/\circ$	L/mm
Actual measurement data	4.8	6.87	63.4	91.2
The length of the three pneumatic linear actuators	A_0A_1/mm	B_0B_1/mm	C_0C_1/mm
Actual measurement data	85	91.5	92
Mathematical model calculation	84.7	94.1	94.3

The error of the result is 2.7 mm (3.0% of the total length). There are a few reasons for the above errors. First, the spiral springs are used in the pneumatic linear actuators, and the torsional deformation occurs during the pneumatic deformation process, which affects the bending angle. Secondly, when establishing the hypothetical mathematical model, there may be certain errors because the ideal situation is conceived. Finally, during the test, the constraints of the upper and lower base and the action of gravity may cause the measurement errors.

4.3 Conclusions

In this work, a soft active structure with multi-DOF bending is proposed inspired by the human neck muscle. The structure is consisted of three soft pneumatic linear actuators with the tilting arrangement. Then the kinematics model between the pose of the upper platform center point and the length of pneumatic linear actuators is established, by which the parameters of the structure were optimized. Based on the optimized structure, the pneumatic measured platform was built. Through testing the performance of the pneumatic soft active structure, and comparing actual measurement with the theoretical model, we proved the rationality of the designed structure. The error was also analyzed to prove the accuracy of theoretical model within 5%. Meanwhile, it is confirmed that the soft active structure has the advantages of low manufacturing cost, simple control, and lower requirements for operation, which is suitable for potential applications in future.

References

1. Li, T., Li, G., Liang, Y., et al.: Summary of research on the structure mechanism and driving materials of soft robots. Chin. J. Theor. Appl. Mech. **48**(4) (2016)
2. Calista, M., Armenta, A., Guanacline, M.E., et al.: Study and fabrication of bioinspired Octopus arm mockups tested on a multipurpose platform. In: IEEE Ras & Embs International Conference on Biomedical Robotics & Biomechatronics. IEEE (2010)
3. Marchese, A.D., Opal, C.D., Rus, D.: Autonomous soft robotic fish capable of escape maneuvers using fluidic elastomer actuators. Soft Rob. **1**(1), 75–87 (2014)
4. Wang, Hao, Y., Yang, X., et al.: Soft robot: structure, drive, sensing and control. Chin. J. Mech. Eng. (13) (2017)
5. Cao, Y., Shang, J., Liang, K., et al.: Overview of the research status of soft robots. Chin. J. Mech. Eng. **48**(3), 25–33 (2012)
6. Rus, D., Tolley, M.T.: Design, fabrication and control of soft robots. Nature **521**(7553), 467–475 (2015)
7. Seok, S., Opal, C.D., Cho, K.J., et al.: Meshwork: a peristaltic soft robot with antagonistic nickel titanium coil actuators. IEEE/ASME Trans. Mechatron. **18**(5), 1485–1497 (2013)
8. Leschi, C., Mazzola, B., Mattioli, V., et al.: Design of a biomimetic robotic octopi's arm. Bioinspiration & Biomimetics **4**(1), 015006 (2009)
9. Hubbard, J.J., Fleming, M., Palmer, V., et al.: Monolithic IPMC fins for propulsion and maneuvering in bioinspired underwater robotics. IEEE J. Oceanic Eng. **39**(3), 540–551 (2014)
10. Hao, Y., Gong, Z., Xin, Z., et al.: Universal soft pneumatic robotic gripper with variable effective length. In: Control Conference. IEEE (2016)
11. Wang, Z., Zhu, M., Kawamura, S., et al.: Comparison of different soft grippers for lunch box packaging. Robot. Biomimetics **4**(1), 10 (2017)

12. Martinez, R.V., Branch, J.L., Fish, C.R., et al.: Robotic tentacles with three-dimensional mobility based on flexible elastomers. Adv. Mater. **25**(2), 205–212 (2013)
13. Matz, V., Peronei, M.: the superficial musculo-aponeurotic system (SMAS) in the parotid and cheek area. Plast. Reconstr. Surg. **58**(1), 80–88 (1976)
14. Li, F., Lavelle, A., Bonneau, D., et al.: Study on cervical muscle volume by means of three-dimensional reconstruction. J. Magn. Resonan. Imag **39**(6), 1411–1416 (2014)
15. Yang, J.: Brain injury biomechanics in real world vehicle accident using mathematical models. Chin. J. Mech. Eng. **21**(4), 81–86 (2008)
16. Yan, J., Shi, P., Zhang, X.,et al.: Review of biomimetic mechanism, actuation, modeling and control in soft manipulators. J. Mech. Eng. **54**(15), 1–14 (2018)
17. Cao, Y., Shang, J., Liang, K., et al.: A review on the soft robotics. J. Mech. Eng. **48**(3), 25–33 (2012)
18. Renda, F., Cacucciolo, V., Dias, J., et al.: Discrete Cosserat approach for soft robot dynamics: a new piece-wise constant strain model with torsion and shears. In: IEEE/RSJ International Conference on Intelligent Robots and Systems (IROS), 5495–5502 (2016)

Cable-Driven Parallel Robot

Smooth Trajectory Planning for a Cable-Driven Waist Rehabilitation Robot Using Quintic NURBS

Meng Jiang, Zhengmeng Yang[✉], Yuan Li, Zhi Sun, and Bin Zi

Hefei University of Technology, Hefei 230000, China

Abstract. In response to a cable-driven waist rehabilitation robot (CDWRR), a smooth trajectory planning algorithm is proposed in this paper by employing an improved quintic Non-Uniform Rational B-Splines (NURBS). The aim is to enhance the smoothness of the trajectory when used in rehabilitation training. The model of CDWRR is constructed, and kinematics and dynamics analyses are performed to obtain the constraint conditions for the trajectory since the cable can only exert pulling axial forces. The trajectory is dominated by two key variables, which can be determined by maximizing the multi-objective function. The improved NURBS (IN) exhibits superior kinematics parameters performance than those with the conventional NURBS (CN) by simulations. A prototype is built for experiments. By comparing with the conventional NURBS trajectory (CN), both the simulations and experimental results prove the validity of the algorithm.

Keywords: Smooth trajectory planning · Cable-driven waist rehabilitation robot · Quintic NURBS · Multi-objective optimization

1 Introduction

In recent years, many scholars have set their sights on the cable-driven rehabilitation mechanism, which is safer and more reliable for patients due to outstanding advantages such as small inertia, large workspace, high payload, simple structure, et al. [1, 2]. The patient regains the waist performance with the aid of the rehabilitation robot. At present, when using rehabilitation robots for treatment, researchers mainly plan the motion trajectory in advance [3]. Moreover, the work quality of the robot is closely related to the trajectory [4]. For this reason, trajectory planning should be the prerequisite and basis for rehabilitation treatment. Various algorithms for trajectory planning in rehabilitation training have been proposed in the last decades.

A cubic polynomial interpolation algorithm was employed by Feng, Z. et al. [5] for trajectory planning of a gait rehabilitation robot. Ghobadi et al. [6] introduced the minimum jerk as the objective optimization to coordinate the coefficients of the quintic polynomial used in the trajectory planning of an upper limb exoskeleton rehabilitation robot. The trajectory will get smoother as the degree of the polynomial increases, but on the other hand, the high computational costs are indispensable. In some cases, Runge's phenomenon may even appear. Therefore, scholars gradually focus on the B-splines and

© Springer Nature Switzerland AG 2021
X.-J. Liu et al. (Eds.): ICIRA 2021, LNAI 13013, pp. 555–563, 2021.
https://doi.org/10.1007/978-3-030-89095-7_53

Non-Uniform Rational B-Splines (NURBS). In contrast to polynomial interpolation curves, they can guarantee continuity in velocity and acceleration with a lower order. Jaka Ziherl [7] presented B-splines for trajectory planning of a haptic robot which aims to assist arms with movement from pick to place point. A trajectory planning method is proposed by Javad Jahanpour [4] for parallel robots based on NURBS which is more comprehensive compared to the B-spline.

The methods of trajectory planning for the robot with rigid links are introduced above. However, due to the fact that cables can only exert pulling axial forces, this brings new challenges to the trajectory planning of the cable-driven rehabilitation robots, which has to satisfy the cable tension constraints [8, 9]. In order to improve the smooth performance of the trajectory subject to the constraints mentioned above for a cable-driven robot, this paper presents an approach for smooth trajectory planning of a cable-driven waist rehabilitation robot (CDWRR) using an improved quintic NURBS. The improved NURBS (IN) is generated by substituting the optimal solution of the multi-objective function. We conclude that the IN exhibits superior performance with respect to the specific kinematic parameters than the conventional NURBS (CN) by simulations and experiments.

2 Kinematics and Dynamics Analysis of CDWRR

The model of the CDWRR is shown in Fig. 1, which mainly consists of an end-effector, six cable groups, six driving units, and a static external frame. The safety line through the drum supports the upper part of the weight of the body.

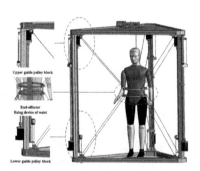
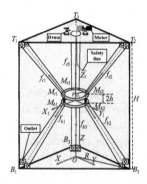

Fig. 1. 3D model of the CDWRR   **Fig. 2.** Schematic sketch of the CDWRR

The schematic sketch of the CDWRR is shown in Fig. 2. A global coordinate frame $O - XYZ$ is attached to the center of the bottom whose triangle circumcircle radius is R taken as 811 mm. The auxiliary coordinate frame $O_1 - X_1Y_1Z_1$ is set at the reference point $P = [x, y, z]^T$ at the center of the end-effector, whose radius is r taken as 175 mm. The height of the static external frame H is set to 1788 mm. The vertical distance 2 h of the end-effector is taken as 200 mm.

The inverse kinematics equation of the CDWRR can be expressed as Eq. (1).

$$l_{ti} = \|M_{ti} - T_i\| \qquad l_{bi} = \|M_{bi} - B_i\| \qquad i = 1, 2, 3 \tag{1}$$

where l_{ti} and l_{bi} represent the lengths of the top and bottom cables, respectively. $T_i = \begin{bmatrix} R\cos\theta_i\ R\sin\theta_i\ H \end{bmatrix}^T$ and $B_i = \begin{bmatrix} R\cos\theta_i\ R\sin\theta_i\ 0 \end{bmatrix}^T$ indicate the coordinates of cable exit points of the pulley anchored on the frame, respectively. $M_{ti} = \begin{bmatrix} x + r\cos\theta_i\ y + r\sin\theta_i\ z + h \end{bmatrix}^T$ and $M_{bi} = \begin{bmatrix} x + r\cos\theta_i\ y + r\sin\theta_i\ z - h \end{bmatrix}^T$ denote the coordinates of the cable attachment points at the top and bottom of the end-effector.

By deriving formula (1), the linear mapping relationship between the cable velocity and the end-effector velocity can be written in matrix form as Eq. (2).

$$\dot{L} = J_0\dot{P} \tag{2}$$

where $\dot{L} = \begin{bmatrix} \dot{l}_{t1}, \dot{l}_{t2}, \dot{l}_{t3}, \dot{l}_{b1}, \dot{l}_{b2}, \dot{l}_{b3} \end{bmatrix}^T$, $\dot{P} = \begin{bmatrix} \dot{x}, \dot{y}, \dot{z} \end{bmatrix}^T$ indicates the velocity of the end-effector. J_0 represents a Jacobian velocity matrix.

The dynamic analysis of the top and bottom parts of the end-effector can be expressed as Eq. (3)

$$\begin{cases} \sum\limits_{i=1}^{3} f_{ti}e_{ti} + m\,G + m\ddot{P} + F_{kt} = 0 \\ \sum\limits_{i=1}^{3} f_{bi}e_{bi} + m\,G + m\ddot{P} + F_{kb} = 0 \end{cases} \tag{3}$$

where $e_{ti} = l_{ti}/\|l_{ti}\|$ and $e_{bi} = l_{bi}/\|l_{bi}\|$ denote the corresponding cable unit vectors, respectively. f_{ti} and f_{bi} indicate the tension of cables exerted to the top and bottom of the end-effector, respectively. $G = \begin{bmatrix} 0, 0, -g \end{bmatrix}^T$ is the acceleration of gravity g takes $9.8\text{m}/\text{s}^2$. $F_{kt} = F_{kb} = \begin{bmatrix} 0, 0, -f_k \end{bmatrix}^T$, f_k denotes the total tension of the three springs exerted to the end-effector.

Equation (4) can be deduced by Eq. (3), the tension constraints of cables can be expressed by the position and the acceleration of the end-effector as follows:

$$\begin{cases} (\ddot{z} - A_t - g)(R + 2x - r) + 2\ddot{x}(H - h - z) \leq 0 \\ (\ddot{z} - A_t - g)\left(R \pm \sqrt{3}y - x - r\right) - \left(\ddot{x} \mp \sqrt{3}\ddot{y}\right)(H - h - z) \leq 0 \\ (\ddot{z} + A_t - g)(R + 2x - r) + 2\ddot{x}(h - z) \geq 0 \\ (\ddot{z} + A_t - g)\left(R \pm \sqrt{3}y - x - r\right) - \left(\ddot{x} \mp \sqrt{3}\ddot{y}\right)(h - z) \geq 0 \end{cases} \tag{4}$$

where $A_t = f_k/m$.

3 Smooth Trajectory Planning

3.1 Waist Trajectory Generation

The NURBS [4] of degree p can be defined as a piecewise polynomial vector function shown in Eq. (5).

$$S(u) = \frac{\sum\limits_{i=1}^{n} N_{i,p}(u)\omega_i \cdot Q_i}{\sum\limits_{i=1}^{n} N_{i,p}(u)\omega_i} \tag{5}$$

where Q_i is the control point, and ω_i is the corresponding weights. $N_{i,p}(u)$ is the basis function which can be determined by the De Boor formula.

The path parameters of the NURBS are refined as a quintic polynomial of time in this paper as follows.

$$u = a\tau^5 + b\tau^4 + c\tau^3 + d\tau^2 + e\tau + f \tag{6}$$

where $a = 1/2T_{total}^5$, $b = 3/4T_{total}^4$, $c = 5/4T_{total}^3$, $d = 1/3T_{total}^2$, $e = 2/3T_{total}$, $f = 0$, T_{total} represents the time for the CDWRR to pass through the entire trajectory.

The control points are obtained by constructing the corresponding constraint equations, which can be expressed by substituting the sequence of nodes to Eq. (5) as follows:

$$\begin{cases} S(0) = S_1 = p_1 \,,\, S(1) = S_f = p_n \\[2mm] S(u_{p+k+1}) = S_k = p_k = \dfrac{\sum\limits_{i=1}^{n} N_{i,p}(u_{p+k+1})\omega_i Q_i}{\sum\limits_{i=1}^{n} N_{i,p}(u_{p+k+1})\omega_i} \quad k = 2, 3, \cdots, f-1 \end{cases} \tag{7}$$

where p_k are the via-points. Furthermore, it is indispensable to increase six boundary conditions of zero velocity, acceleration, and jerk that should be satisfied at both ends.

The control points of the quintic NURBS can be obtained by calculating the equations above, which can be rewritten in matrix form as Eq. (8).

$$Q = W^{-1}P \tag{8}$$

where $W = \begin{bmatrix} W_1 \\ W_2 \end{bmatrix}_{n \times n}$, $P = \begin{bmatrix} p_1 & p_2 & p_3 & \cdots & p_f & 0 & 0 & 0 & 0 & 0 & 0 \end{bmatrix}_{(f+6) \times 1}^{\mathrm{T}}$.

In this paper, nine via-points are selected for interpolation, i.e., $f = 9$. The number of control points is 15, i.e., $n = f + 6 = 15$. The node vector length $m = f + 12 = 21$. The variable k_1 is introduced at the two virtual nodes [10] inserted at the second and penultimate points, and the sequence of nodes can be shown as Eq. (9).

$$u = \begin{bmatrix} u_1, u_2, \cdots u_6 = 0, \ u_7 = 0.1 \cdot k_1, \\ u_8 = 0.2, u_9 = 0.3, u_{10} = 0.4, u_{11} = 0.5, u_{12} = 0.6, \\ u_{13} = 0.7, u_{14} = 0.7, u_{15} = 1 - 0.1 \cdot k_1, u_{16}, u_{17}, \cdots u_{21} = 1 \end{bmatrix} \tag{9}$$

3.2 Optimization Analysis

In this section, the maximum value of the jerk [11] and the standard deviation of the cable force [12] are defined as evaluate indexes using k_1 and T_{total} as optimization variables, subject to certain constraints detailed in Sect. 2.

The two functions mentioned above can be described by formulas (10) and (11).

$$j_{max}(k_1, T_{total}) = \max_{0 \leq u \leq 1} |j(t)| \tag{10}$$

where j_{max} represent the maximum value of jerk over the trajectory.

$$std_i(k_1, T_{total}) = \sqrt{\frac{1}{N-1} \sum_{m=1}^{N} \left(f_{i,m}(t) - F_i(t)\right)^2} \quad i = 1, 2, 3, 4, 5, 6 \tag{11}$$

where $f_i(t)$ denotes the i-th group of cables' force, $F_i(t)$ denotes the mean force of the i-th group of cables, and N indicates the number of via-points of the trajectory.

It can be observed in Fig. 3 that the minimum value of j_{max} is obtained when $k_1 = 0.57$ and $T_{total} = 56$ s. When the minimum of j_{max} is acquired, it is not that the standard deviation of cable force obtains the most appropriate value, as can be seen in Table 1. So further optimization is desired to search for the most prominent value.

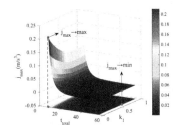

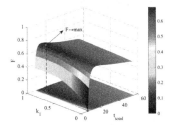

Fig. 3. Distribution of j_{max} versus k_1 and T_{total}

Fig. 4. Distribution of F versus k_1 and T_{total}

Table 1. The value of (k_1, T_{total}) when $std(f_i)$ takes the extreme value

	f_{b1}	f_{b2}	f_{b3}	f_{t1}	f_{t2}	f_{t3}
$std(f_i) \rightarrow$ max	(0.01,8)	(0.01,8)	(0.01,8)	(0.01,56)	(0.01,56)	(0.01,56)
$std(f_i) \rightarrow$ min	(0.99,56)	(0.99,56)	(0.99,56) 15.2010	(0.01,8)	(0.99,8)	(0.99,8)

Two evaluation indexes mentioned above are normalized to get the functions, e.i., F_f and F_j, which are briefly presented as the formulas below:

$$F_f = \frac{\min\limits_{0<k_1<1} \min\limits_{T_{min}<T_{total}<T_{max}} F_f(k_1, T_{total})}{F_f(k_1, T_{total})} \qquad F_j = \frac{\min\limits_{0<k_1<1} \min\limits_{T_{min}<T_{total}<T_{max}} j_{max}(k_1, T_{total})}{j_{max}(k_1, T_{total})} \tag{12}$$

where $F_f(k_1, T_{total}) = \sqrt{\prod_{m=1}^{6} std_m(k_1, T_{total})}$

The smooth optimization problem of thsse waist trajectory can be formulated as a multi-objective optimization problem by introducing weight coefficients, i.e., ω_j and ω_f, which is given in formula (13).

$$
\begin{aligned}
&\text{Find}: \ k_1, T_{total} \\
&\max F = \omega_j F_j + \omega_f F_f \\
&\text{Subject to}: \ \omega_j + \omega_f = 1, 0 < \omega_j < 1, 0 < \omega_f < 1
\end{aligned}
\tag{13}
$$

Similarly, F takes the maximum value of 0.69036 when $k_1 = 0.89$ and $T_{total} = 14$s, which is shown in Fig. 4. This set of values will be adopted throughout the simulations and experiments in this paper.

4 Simulations and Experiments

4.1 Simulations

Figures 5, 6 and 7 show the kinematics parameters of the trajectories generated by the two algorithms, respectively. Generally speaking, the improved NURBS (IN) exhibits superior kinematics parameters performance. The peak values of the velocity, acceleration and jerk of the end-effector along x axis are decreased by 9.1%, 20% and 4.5% than the conventional NURBS (CN).

It can be observed in Table 2 that the standard deviations of the norms in terms of velocity and acceleration of the IN are 8.5% and 22.4% less than those of CN. Meanwhile, the standard deviation of the jerk of IN is 79.3% of the CN.

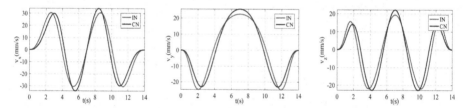

Fig. 5. The velocity of the end-effector along x axis, y axis and z axis

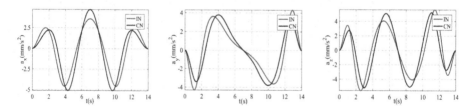

Fig. 6. The acceleration of the end-effector along x axis, y axis and z axis

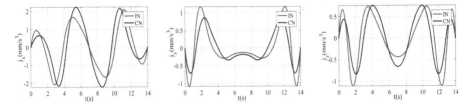

Fig. 7. The jerk of the end-effector along x axis, y axis and z axis

Table 2. Standard deviation of the norms in terms of velocity, acceleration, jerk

	$|v|std$	$|a|std$	$|j|std$
CN	16.4049	5.1555	3.0042
IN	14.9816	4.0011	2.3828

Fig. 8. Experiment platform

4.2 Experiments

A CDWRR prototype is built for the experiment to verify the correctness of the simulation results. The experimental tests are conducted on the platform consisting of the cable drive modules, the end-effector, the force sensors, and the related servo drivers shown in Fig. 8. The experiment was conducted under no-load conditions. Figures 9 and 10 show the velocity and acceleration of the end-effector along the x, y and z axis. One can obtain is that these figures are approximately consistent with the simulation mentioned above. The peak values of the velocity in Fig. 9 are 5.3%–21.7% less than those generated by the CN, while Fig. 10 shows the peak values of acceleration are reduced by 3.2%–7.8% compared to the CN.

The standard deviations of the end-effector velocity and acceleration along the x, y and z axis are decreased, as indicated in Table 3. In general, both the peak values and standard deviations in terms of kinematics parameters are reduced. In addition, as shown in Table 4, the mean of the cable force from $l1$ to $l6$ has a certain degree of reduction, which indicates the lower energy consumption can be obtained by employing the IN.

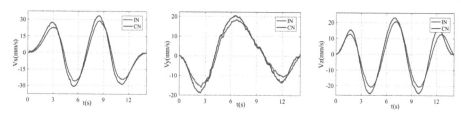

Fig. 9. The velocity of the end-effector along x axis, y axis and z axis

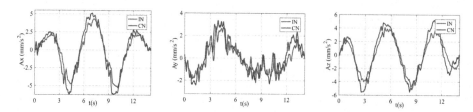

Fig. 10. The acceleration of the end-effector along x axis, y axis and z axis

Table 3. Standard deviations of end-effector velocity and acceleration along x, y and z axis

	$Std(v_x)$	$Std(v_y)$	$Std(v_z)$	$Std(a_x)$	$Std(a_y)$	$Std(a_z)$
CN	32.9685	25.2692	17.3341	7.0531	4.7265	4.5323
IN	31.1468	24.6429	16.3244	6.0531	3.8949	4.0788

Table 4. Mean values of six groups of cable forces

	$mean(l_{t1})$	$mean(l_{t2})$	$mean(l_{t3})$	$mean(l_{b1})$	$mean(l_{b2})$	$mean(l_{b3})$
CN	17.4058	15.9341	15..2934	10.2228	9.3341	9.4159
IN	17.2013	15.6847	15.2010	10.0915	9.1933	9.2717

5 Conclusion

In this paper, an algorithm is presented for smooth trajectory planning of a CDWRR by employing an improved quintic NURBS. The model of CDWRR is constructed. Based on kinematics and dynamics analysis, the constraints for trajectory can be expressed by the position and acceleration of the end-effector. The trajectory is dominated by two key variables. The optimal solution, i.e., $k_1 = 0.89$ and $T_{total} = 14$s, is derived by maximizing the multi-objective function. The IN exhibits superior kinematics parameters performance than the CN by simulations. A CDWRR prototype is built to verify the simulation results. One can obtain is that both the peak values and standard deviations in terms of kinematics parameters are decreased. Therefore, the algorithm proposed in this paper improves the smoothness of the rehabilitation trajectory, with energy consumption and wear of the robot reduced.

Acknowledgment. This work was supported by the National Natural Science Foundation of China (91748109 and 51925502).

References

1. Li, Y., Zi, B., Yang, Z., Ge, J.: Combined kinematic and static analysis of an articulated lower limb traction device for a rehabilitation robotic system. Sci. China Technol. Sci. **64**(6), 1189–1202 (2021). https://doi.org/10.1007/s11431-020-1719-5
2. Chen, Q., Zi, B., Sun, Z., Li, Y., Xu, Q.: Design and development of a new cable-driven parallel robot for waist rehabilitation. IEEE/ASME Trans. Mechatron. **24**(4), 1497–1507 (2019)
3. Tao, T.F., et al.: Trajectory planning of upper limb rehabilitation robot based on human pose estimation. In: 2020 17th International Conference on Ubiquitous Robots, pp. 333–338. IEEE, Kyoto, Japan (2020)
4. Jahanpour, J., Motallebi, M., Porghoveh, M.: A novel trajectory planning scheme for parallel machining robots enhanced with NURBS curves. J. Intell. Rob. Syst. **82**(2), 257–275 (2015). https://doi.org/10.1007/s10846-015-0239-6
5. Feng, Z., Qian, J., Zhang, Y., Shen, L., Zhang, Z., Wang, Q.: Dynamic walking planning for gait rehabilitation robot. In: 2008 2nd International Conference on Bioinformatics and Biomedical Engineering, pp. 1280–1283. IEEE, Shanghai, China (2008)
6. Ghobadi, M., Sosnoff, J., Kesavadas, T., Esfahani, E.T.: Using mini minimum jerk model for human activity classification in home-based monitoring. In: 2015 IEEE International Conference on Rehabilitation Robotics (ICORR), pp. 909–912. IEEE, Singapore (2015)
7. Ziherl, J., Podobnik, J., Sikic, M., Munih, M.: Pick to place trajectories in human arm training environment. Technol. Health Care. **17**(4), 323–335 (2009)
8. Hwang, S.W., Bak, J.-H., Yoon, J., Park, J.H., Park, J.-O.: Trajectory generation to suppress oscillations in under-constrained cable-driven parallel robots. J. Mech. Sci. Technol. **30**(12), 5689–5697 (2016). https://doi.org/10.1007/s12206-016-1139-9
9. Zhang, N., Shang, W.W., Cong, S.: Geometry-based trajectory planning of a 3–3 cable-suspended parallel robot. IEEE Trans. Rob. **33**(2), 484–491 (2017)
10. Gasparetto, A., Zanotto, V.: A new method for smooth trajectory planning of robot manipulators. Mech. Mach. Theory **42**(4), 455–547 (2007)
11. Li, Y.H., Huang, T., Derek, G., Chetwynd: An approach for smooth trajectory planning of high-speed pick-and-place parallel robots using quintic B-splines. Mech. Mach. Theor. **126**, 479–490 (2018)
12. Qian, S., Bao, K., Zi, B., Zhu, W.D.: Dynamic trajectory planning for a 3-DOF cable-driven parallel robot using quintic b-splines. J. Mech. Des. **142**(7) (2019)

Configuration Selection and Vibration Analysis of Double Layer Suspended Cable-Driven Parallel Robot for Intelligent Storage System

Yao Wang, Fujie Yu, Qingzhong Li, and Yuan Chen[✉]

School of Mechanical, Electrical and Information Engineering, Shandong University,
Weihai, China
cyzghysy@sdu.edu.cn

Abstract. Warehousing system plays an increasingly important role in the development of industry. However, the traditional warehousing system has the disadvantages of low efficiency, large space occupation and high maintenance difficulty, which has been unable to meet the needs of economic and social development. The demand for high efficiency and high stability intelligent storage system is more and more urgent. With the characteristics of large workspace and strong flexibility, suspended cable-driven parallel robot has great application potential in the field of intelligent storage. In this paper, the foundation of a two-layer suspended cable-driven parallel robot was proposed to meet the requirements of intelligent storage. Based on this foundation, a double layer suspended cable-driven parallel robot was established. The kinematics model of the double layer suspended cable-driven parallel robot was established, and the cable length curve in a motion period was obtained. Based on Hamilton's principle, the vibration model of the double layer suspended cable-driven parallel robot was established. The motion and vibration characteristics of the robot were analyzed in ADAMS, and the vibration law of the system was obtained.

Keywords: Intelligent storage · Suspended cable-driven parallel robot · Bilayer configuration · Vibration characteristics

1 Introduction

With the rapid development of national modernization, all kinds of factories, large-scale warehousing and logistics centers urgently need an intelligent warehousing system with high utilization rate and strong stability. In particular, the warehousing system has occupied a major position in the logistics link, which is related to the storage, distribution and information circulation of products, and has an increasingly important impact on the cost and efficiency of the entire industrial ecosystem. At the same time, the cost of human and land resources is rising, and the traditional storage system gradually shows the defects of low space utilization and low operation efficiency, which is difficult to meet the needs of economic and social development.

© Springer Nature Switzerland AG 2021
X.-J. Liu et al. (Eds.): ICIRA 2021, LNAI 13013, pp. 564–574, 2021.
https://doi.org/10.1007/978-3-030-89095-7_54

Therefore, the unmanned intelligent storage system has become a research hotspot, and the performance of the storage robot is directly related to the function realization of the storage system. In other words, in a warehouse center of the same scale, the more shelves there are, the stronger the ability of the storage system to store goods; the less storage robots are used, the higher the stability of the storage system. This requires the storage robot to have the characteristics of small size, no space occupation, multi-purpose and so on.

At present, the most widely used is the automatic guided vehicle (AGV) to carry goods [1, 2]. The guided vehicle to work normally, there should stick a magnetic stripe or two-dimensional code on the ground to form a preset path, and the robot will drive according to the preset path to complete the task. However, these two navigation methods not only have the problem of poor flexibility in path transformation, but also have the disadvantages of magnetic stripe and two-dimensional code easy to break, glue opening, pollution and so on [3]. And the storage center has the characteristics of large space and many kind of goods. Using a large number of automatic guided vehicles to carry goods, there will be problems such as difficult control, high cost, difficult maintenance and so on.

Compared with AGV, cable-driven parallel robot is suitable for working in large space, because the cable driven parallel mechanism has the characteristics of larger workspace and higher efficiency [4]. Cable-driven parallel mechanism is divided into full cable-driven parallel mechanism and suspended cable-driven Parallel mechanism [5]. Cable-driving parallel robot has be applied to the storage system [6, 7], but it only transfer goods to two shelves at most. For large storage centers, there are many robots needed, which still cannot meet the actual needs. Therefore, a double layer suspended cable-driven parallel robot is proposed in this paper, which has the characteristics of compact structure, strong flexibility and multi-function.

The double layer suspended cable-driven parallel robot is coupling superposition of flexible cables. Due to the characteristics of cables, the double layer system may have forced vibration, which affects the normal transportation of goods. Therefore, in view of the long-distance transportation of goods, it is necessary to analyze the vibration of the upper and lower layers respectively. The analysis method is similar to elevator transportation, they have similar vibration characteristics [9, 10], the partial differential equation of vibration of the double layer suspended cable-driven parallel robot is established based on Hamilton principle [11–13]. The simulation analysis is carried out by comparing the vibration process, which provides a theoretical support for the practical application of the double layer suspended cable-driven parallel robot.

2 Configuration Selection

For a large storage center, as shown in Fig. 1, the inbound robot places the goods carried by the inbound truck on the inbound conveyor belt, and the double layer suspended cable-driven parallel robot is responsible for the inbound operation; similarly, the double layer suspended cable-driven parallel robot places the goods to be outbound on the outbound conveyor belt, and the outbound robot places the goods on the outbound truck.

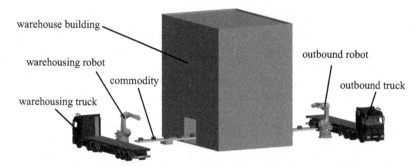

Fig. 1. Intelligent storage system

According to the design criteria of cable-driven parallel mechanism, the workspace of its moving platform is affected by the position of cable installation point [8]. However, the double layer suspended cable-driven parallel mechanism is quite special, because its gravity is equivalent to a cable moving in the same direction with the lower platform, so it is necessary to fully consider the accessibility of the lower platform position and the force on the cable during the task.

Based on the above analysis, this paper proposes the configuration basis of the double layer suspended cable-driven parallel robot for intelligent warehouse, as shown in Fig. 2a. The basic configuration of the double layer suspended cable-driven parallel robot is mainly composed of translation module and lifting module. The translation module controls the position of the lifting module in the X direction through the extension and shortening of the cable. However, since the translational module at any position has three attitudes, as shown in Fig. 2b, and the force and vibration of the cable in the translational module, it is necessary to add a stable cable based on this configuration to realize the translational function.

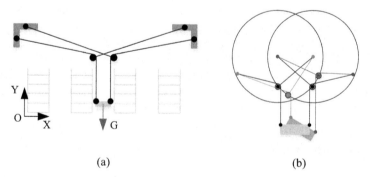

(a)   (b)

Fig. 2. Configuration basis of double layer suspended cable-driven parallel robot

According to the configuration foundation of the double layer suspended cable-driven parallel robot, two cables and a rigid beam are added to the translational module to realize stable translational function, as shown in Fig. 3a. At this time, the translational module consists of four cables and a rigid beam, which is a stable and controllable configuration. According to the configuration of the double layer suspended cable-driven parallel robot, a double layer suspended cable-driven parallel robot for intelligent storage is designed, as shown in Fig. 3b. The robot consists of two groups of parallel module and lifting module, which ensures the balance of force on the platform, and reduces the deflection and vibration.

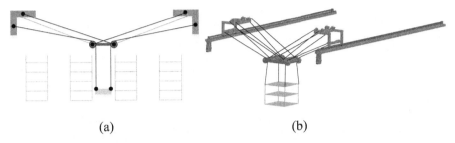

(a)   (b)

Fig. 3. Double layer suspended cable-driven parallel robot

3 Kinematic Analysis

The fixed coordinate system OXY of the robot is established in the middle of the cable connection point on the upper side of the translation module, as shown in Fig. 4. In the center of the moving platform of the translational module, the dynamic coordinate system oxy of the robot is established.

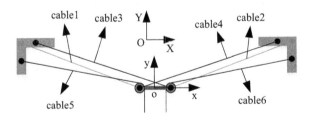

Fig. 4. Coordinate system of double layer suspended cable-driven parallel robot

Although the translational module is a redundant three degree of freedom mechanism, only one translational degree of freedom is used in this application, so the rotation matrix from the dynamic coordinate system to the static coordinate system of the double layer suspended cable-driven parallel robot is the identity matrix E.

$$\mathbf{P}_i = \mathbf{E}\mathbf{n}_i + \mathbf{T} \tag{1}$$

$$L_i = \|\mathbf{E}\mathbf{n}_i + \mathbf{T} - \mathbf{m}\| \tag{2}$$

Where, P_i is the vector from the connection point of the cable of the moving platform of the translational module to the fixed coordinate system. n_i is the vector from the cable connection point of the translational module moving platform to the moving coordinate system. T is the vector from the moving coordinate system to the fixed coordinate system. m is the vector from the beam cable connection point to the fixed coordinate system. L_i is the length of the cable.

In order to facilitate the kinematic analysis, the following assumptions are put forward: in the kinematic analysis of the system, the elastic deformation of the cable is ignored, the sag caused by the dead weight of the cable is ignored, and the connection points of the cable are ideal spherical hinges.

The simulation content is a inbound delivery cycle, and the outbound delivery cycle is similar to it, which will not repeated. At the initial time, the lifting module is above the warehousing conveyor belt; from 0 s to 10 s, the lifting module descends; from 10 s to 20 s, the lifting module grabs and fixes the goods; from 20 s to 30 s, the lifting module rises to the translational track position; from 30 s to 40 s, the lifting module reaches the translational track position, The translation module moves the lifting module to the top of the gap between the two designated shelves; from 40 s to 50 s, the lifting module descends to the designated container of the designated shelf; from 50 s to 60 s, the lifting module pushes the goods out to the designated position; from 60 s to 70 s, the lifting module rises to the translation track; from 70 s to 80 s, the lifting module moves to the top of the warehousing conveyor belt. In this paper, cubic spline interpolation is used to fit the path to simulate the length of the cable, and the graph of the cable length with time is obtained, as shown in Fig. 5. Because the front and rear two groups of translation module and lifting module are the same, only one group of cable data can be used to represent.

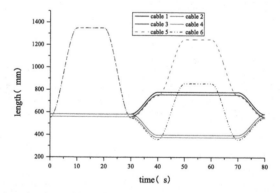

Fig. 5. The changing law of double layer suspended cable-driven parallel robot cable

4 Vibration Characteristics

Regardless of the resonance caused by the natural frequency, this paper studies the mechanical vibration caused by the change of the state of the cable itself. According to the research, the longer the length of the flexible cable is, the smaller the stiffness is; The smaller the load, the smaller the stiffness [14]. The lifting module needs to provide a long-distance cargo displacement.

In the process of moving, the coupling of complex factors such as posture error of translational module moving platform, mutual influence between double layer cables, elastic deformation of cables and winding error will cause complex vibration of double layer cables cargo. In addition, there are transverse vibration and axial vibration in the cable, and the transverse vibration is ignored because the kinetic energy of transverse modal vibration accounts for only 0.01% [15].

However, in this paper, the cables are parallel and long, so the lateral vibration of the end load cannot be ignored. The vibration system will affect the cargo transportation function and the service life of the cable, so the research on the vibration of the double layer cable system is the premise to ensure the normal operation of the double-layer cable system. The system model of double-layer suspended cable traction parallel robot is established, as shown in Fig. 6.

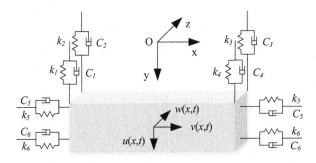

Fig. 6. Model of double layer suspended cable-driven parallel robot lifting system

The lifting module platform and the translational module platform are connected by springs with stiffness K_1, K_2, K_3 and K_4 and dampers with damping C_1, C_2, C_3 and C_4 respectively. The two sides of the loading platform and the shelf are connected by springs with stiffness of K_5 and K_6 and dampers with damping of C_5 and C_6 respectively to simulate the external excitation caused by the position and attitude error of translational module in the lifting state. The height of the lifting module loading platform is $2h$, the mass is m_c, the moment of inertia is J_c, the displacements in X, Y and Z directions are v_c, u_c, w_c, respectively, and the angular displacements are θ_c, respectively. The lateral displacements at the upper and lower ends of the loading platform are, v_5, v_6, respectively. The mass per unit length of each cable is ρ, the cross-sectional area is A, and the elastic modulus is E. During the movement of the loading platform, the length of the cable is $l_i(t)$, the longitudinal vibration on the cable $x(t)$ is $u_i(x, t)$, and the transverse vibration is $v_i(x, t)$. $\gamma(t) = \dot{l}(t)$ is the operating speed of the loading platform.

The geometric relationship between the lateral vibration displacement of the platform and the lateral displacement of the mass center can be equivalent to

$$\begin{cases} v_5 = v_c - h\theta_c \\ v_6 = v_c + h\theta_c \end{cases} \tag{3}$$

The kinetic energy of the system during the lifting process of the lifting module is

$$T = \sum \frac{1}{2}\rho \int_0^{l(t)} (\frac{Du}{Dt} + \gamma)^2 dx + \sum \frac{1}{2}\rho \int_0^{l(t)} (\frac{Dv}{Dt})^2 dx + \sum \frac{1}{2}\rho \int_0^{l(t)} (\frac{Dw}{Dt})^2 dx$$
$$+ \frac{1}{2}m_c(\dot{u}_c + \gamma)^2 + \frac{1}{2}m_c\dot{v}_c^2 + \frac{1}{2}J_c\dot{\theta}_c^2 \tag{4}$$

Where, differential operator $\frac{D}{Dt} = \frac{\partial}{\partial t} + v\frac{\partial}{\partial x}$.

The elastic potential energy of the system during the lifting process of the lifting module can be written as:

$$V_e = \sum \frac{1}{2} \int_0^{l(t)} EA\varepsilon(x,t)^2 dx + \sum \frac{1}{2}k_i[u_c - u(l,t)]^2 + \frac{1}{2}(k_5 v_5^2 + k_6 v_6^2) \tag{5}$$

$$\varepsilon(x,t) = \sqrt{(1+u_x)^2 + v_x^2} - 1 \approx u_x + \frac{1}{2}v_x^2 \tag{6}$$

During the lifting process of lifting module, the gravity potential energy of the system is defined as:

$$V_g = \int_0^{l(t)} \rho g[u(x,t) + x] dx + m_c g[u_c + h + l(t)] \tag{7}$$

The virtual work of the system damping force during the lifting process of the lifting module is

$$\delta W = \sum \int_0^{l(t)} (c_u \frac{Du}{Dt} \delta u + c_v \frac{Dv}{Dt} \delta v) dx + \sum C_i[\dot{u}_c - \frac{Du(l,t)}{Dt}][\delta u_c - \delta u(l,t)]$$
$$+ C_5 \dot{v}_5 \delta v_5 + C_6 \dot{v}_6 \delta v_6 \tag{8}$$

According to the generalized Hamilton principle, the system satisfies the equation

$$\int_{t_1}^{t_2} \delta(T - V_e + V_g - W) dt = 0 \tag{9}$$

The vibration equation of the loading platform during the lifting process of the lifting module is

$$\begin{cases} m_c\ddot{u}_c + \sum C_i(\dot{u}_c - \frac{Du(l,t)}{Dt}) + \sum k_i(u_c - u(l,t)) = m_c(g - \dot{\gamma}) \\ \frac{m_c h^2 + J_c}{l_c^2}\ddot{v}_5 + \frac{m_c h^2 - J_c}{l_c^2}\ddot{v}_6 + \sum EA\varepsilon(l,t)v_x(l,t) + C_5\dot{v}_5 + k_5 v_5 = 0 \\ \frac{m_c h^2 - J_c}{l_c^2}\ddot{v}_5 + \frac{m_c h^2 + J_c}{l_c^2}\ddot{v}_6 + C_6\dot{v}_6 + k_6 v_6 = 0 \end{cases} \tag{10}$$

According to the vibration equation and geometric relationship of the system, the transverse vibration of the platform is

$$
\begin{cases}
\sum \rho \frac{D^2 v}{Dt^2} - (\bar{p}(x,t)v_x)_x - \sum EA[(\tilde{u}_x + \frac{1}{2}v_x^2)v_x]_x + c_v \frac{Dv}{Dt} = 0 \\
\frac{m_c h^2 + J_c}{l_c^2}\ddot{v}_5 - \frac{m_c h^2 - J_c}{l_c^2}\ddot{v}_6 + [\bar{p}(l,t) + \sum EA(\tilde{u}_x + \frac{1}{2}v_x^2)]v_x(l,t) + C_5\dot{v}_5 + k_5 v_1 = 0 \\
\frac{m_c h^2 - J_c}{l_c^2}\ddot{v}_5 - \frac{m_c h^2 + J_c}{l_c^2}\ddot{v}_6 + C_6\dot{v}_6 + k_6 v_6 = 0
\end{cases}
$$

$$(11)$$

$\bar{p}(x,t)$ is the static tension of the cable due to gravity at t.

According to the above analysis, the simulation model is established in ADAMS, as shown in Fig. 7. The kinematics results of the double layer suspended cable-driven parallel robot are used for simulation analysis. Taking 20 kg and 50 kg rectangular containers as an example, 1 kg high-strength lightweight engineering plastics is used for the translational module platform. The weight of the lifting module platform is 12 times that of the translational module platform, and the weight of the goods is 20 times and 50 times that of the translational module platform. Measure the position of the cable connection point of the moving platform of the translation module and the cable connection point of the loading platform of the lifting module.

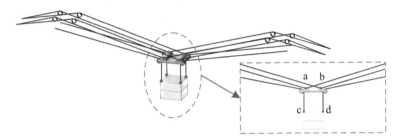

Fig. 7. ADAMS simulation model

To determine the vibration of the system, the motion of the measuring points of the translational module and the lifting module shall be measured, as shown in Fig. 8. In the figure, the attitude error of the moving platform of translational module exists in the process of cargo transportation, but there is no obvious vibration in the X direction; the lifting module loading platform has obvious vibration during the cargo transportation, starting from the movement of the 40 s translational module, and the vibration gradually increases. The main reason of vibration is the position error of the moving platform of the translational module.

In order to determine the pose change of the moving platform of the translational module, the measurement points a and b are measured, and the difference curve of a and b is obtained, as shown in Fig. 9. In the figure, the X-direction and Y-direction vibration of the translational module appears after the translational movement starts in 30 s; the vibration amplitude is the largest in the process of loading and unloading, that is, 30 s to 60 s. At the same time, the goods with 20 times moving platform mass have high frequency vibration in Z direction after 40 s, on the contrary, the goods with 50 times moving platform mass have no vibration in Z direction.

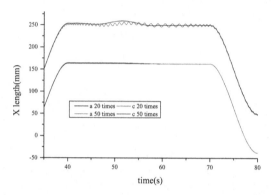

Fig. 8. Measure the displacement of points a and c in the X direction

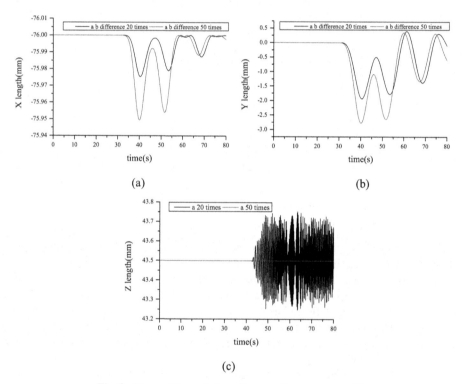

Fig. 9. The position relation of measuring points a and b

In order to determine the position and posture change of the lifting module loading platform, the measurement points c and d are measured, and the difference curve of c and d is obtained, as shown in Fig. 10.

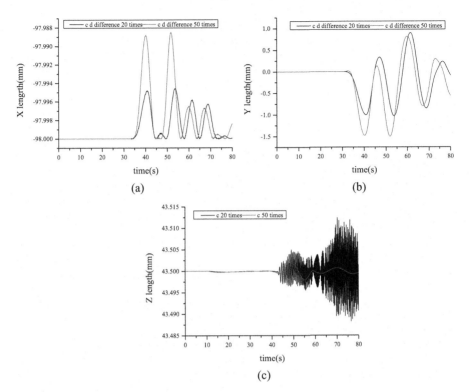

Fig. 10. The position relation of measuring points c and d

The vibration law of the lifting module in Fig. 10 is similar to that of the translational module above, and there is no significant difference in the amplitude. High frequency vibration also occurs in the process of 20 times the weight of the moving platform. The difference is that the Z direction of the cargo with 50 times the mass of the moving platform also vibrates.

5 Conclusion

The double layer suspended cable-driven parallel robot has good cargo transportation performance, which can meet the needs of large-scale intelligent storage center. Among them, the upper translation module of the double layer suspended cable-driven parallel robot has good stability and can provide accurate translation displacement. However, due to the different elastic deformation of the cable during the movement of the translational module, the pose error of the translational module platform is caused, which affects the normal operation of the lifting module. This problem can be solved by the follow-up force control strategy. Due to the long-distance displacement of goods provided by the lower lifting module of the double layer suspended cable-driven parallel robot, the vibration of the loading platform is difficult to avoid. However, appropriate control strategy can meet the requirements of keeping the vibration in a controllable range.

Acknowledgments. Grateful acknowledgement is given to the National Natural Science Foundation of China with Grant No. 52075293, Natural Science Foundation of Shandong Province with Grant No. ZR2019MEE019 and the Fundamental Research Funds for the Central University with Grant No. 2019ZRJC006.

References

1. Setiawan, Y.D., Nguyen, T.H., Pratama, P.S., Kim, H.K., Kim, S.B.: Path tracking controller design of four wheel independent steering automatic guided vehicle. Int. J. Control Autom. Syst. **14**(6), 1550–1560 (2016). https://doi.org/10.1007/s12555-015-0216-7

2. Zou, W., Pan, Q., Tasgetiren, M.F.: An effective discrete artificial bee colony algorithm for scheduling an automatic-guided-vehicle in a linear manufacturing workshop. IEEE Access **99**, 1–1 (2020)

3. Olmi, R., Secchi, C., Fantuzzi, C.: Coordination of industrial AGVs. Int. J. Veh. Auton. Syst. **9**(1/2), 5–25 (2011)

4. Izard, J.B., et al.: A Reconfigurable Robot for Cable-Driven Parallel Robotic and Industrial Scenario Proofing (2012)

5. Seriani, S., Gallina, P., Wedler, A.: A modular cable robot for inspection and light manipulation on celestial bodies. Acta Astronaut. **123**, 145–153 (2016)

6. Saber, O.: A spatial translational cable robot. J. Mech. Robot. Trans. Asme (2015)

7. Torres-Mendez, S.J., et al.: Analytical workspace delineation of a translational undercon-strained cable-based robot. In: 2017 International Conference on Electronics, Communications and Computers (CONIELECOMP) IEEE (2017)

8. Alikhani, A., et al.: Design of a large-scale cable-driven robot with translational motion. Robot. Comput. Int. Manuf. **27**(2), 357–366 (2011)

9. Thuan, et al.: Analysis and control of vibration of cables in a high-rise elevator under earthquake excitation. Earthquake Eng. Eng. Vibr. **18**(02), 214–227 (2019)

10. Jing-Wei, L.I., et al.: Horizontal vibration of elevator car based on experimental system. J. Mech. Electr. Eng. (2019)

11. Ma, Y., et al.: Pattern recognition of rigid hoist guides based on support vector machine. Adv. Mech. Eng. **10**(12) (2018)

12. Ma, Y., Xiao, X.: Dynamic analyses of hoisting cables in a multi-cable friction mine hoist and determination of pcabler hoisting parameters. J. Vibroengineering **18**(5), 2801–2817 (2016)

13. Zi-Gui, L.I., Wang, Z.Y., Ji-Zheng, L.V.: Analysis and calculation of emergency braking antiskid check of multiple-cable friction mine hoist. Coal Mine Mach. (2006)

14. Dagalakis, N.G., et al.: Stiffness study of a parallel link robot crane for shipbuilding applications. J. Offshore Mech. Arct. Eng. **111**(3), 183 (1989)

15. Diao, X., Ou, M.: Vibration analysis of cable-driven parallel manipulators. Multibody Sys.Dyn. **21**(4), 347–360 (2009)

Workspace Quality Evaluation and Optimal Design of a Redundantly Constrained 6-Dof Cable-Driven Parallel Manipulator

Jinshan Yu[1] , Xiao Li[2], Jianguo Tao[1(✉)], Hao Sun[3], and Haowei Wang[2]

[1] School of Mechatronic Engineering, Harbin Institute of Technology, Harbin 150001, China
jgtao@hit.edu.cn
[2] Institute of Spacecraft System Engineering, China Academy of Space Technology,
Beijing 100094, China
[3] Department of Mechanical Engineering and Automation,
Fuzhou University, Fuzhou 350108, China

Abstract. Cable-driven parallel manipulator (CDPM) has the characteristics of simple structure, light weight, large workspace and strong carrying capacity, so it is applied to many fields. In this paper, we proposed the tension distribution index (TDI) to evaluate the tension distribution performance of the CDPMs and improved the original stiffness index (SI) considering the influence of cable tension. Comprehensively considering TDI, SI and dexterity index (DI), the global quality workspace (GQWS) is proposed. A redundantly constrained 6-Dof CDPM is studied in this paper as an example. We optimized the geometrical parameters of the CDPM with the goal of maximizing the global quality workspace (GQWS). The simulation results show that the optimized CDPM has better performance than before, which demonstrate that the evaluation approach proposed in this paper is of effectiveness and value for the design and analysis of CDPMs. This approach can also be used in other kinds of CDPMs.

Keywords: Cable-driven parallel manipulator · Workspace quality · Tension distribution · Dexterity

1 Introduction

Cable-driven parallel manipulator(CDPM) has the characteristics of simple structure, light weight, large workspace and low energy consumption. These advantages make it can be applied in many fields [1]. In this paper, a redundantly constrained six-Dof CDPM driven by eight cables is studied as shown in Fig. 1. Compared with the conventional eight-cable six-Dof redundantly constrained CDPM (as shown in Fig. 2), this configuration has a larger rotational motion range and a stronger carrying capacity.

Based on the application conditions of CDPM, scholars have respectively defined different kinds of workspace [3–5]. When the workspace of the CDPM is determined, how to evaluate the quality of it becomes an important research content. Verhoeven proposed quality index to measure the distance between the position of the moving

© Springer Nature Switzerland AG 2021
X.-J. Liu et al. (Eds.): ICIRA 2021, LNAI 13013, pp. 575–585, 2021.
https://doi.org/10.1007/978-3-030-89095-7_55

platform and the boundary of the workspace [2]. This evaluation method is relatively simple and lacks pertinence, and needs to be further studied. Pham proposed tension factor(TF) and global tension index(GTI) to evaluated the quality of workspace [6]. TF reflects the tension distribution property by the minimum tension over maximum tension, but does not reflect the uniformity of tension distribution. Xiaoqiang Tang evaluated the workspace quality of a planar CDPM by analyzing the cable tension distribution difference and the stiffness performance [7]. In addition, dexterity is also an important index for evaluating the quality of workspace, which reflects the force and velocity transmission performance of CDPM at a certain posture [8]. Until now, many studies mainly analyzed the size and shape of the workspace or use a single index to evaluate the quality of the workspace of CDPMs [9–11]. Therefore, it is valuable and interesting to analyze the workspace of CDPM comprehensively considering multiple indexes. Some original evaluation indexes also need to be further improved, which is of great significance to the design and performance analysis of the CDPMs.

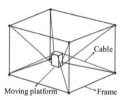

Fig. 1. The 8–6-CDPM studied in this paper.   **Fig. 2.** The conventional 8–6-CDPM.

In this paper, the kinematic and static models of the CDPM are established, and the workspace considering the cables tension conditions is calculated in Sect. 2. The tension distribution index(TDI) is proposed and the stiffness index(SI) is improved in Sect. 3. Comprehensively considering TDI, SI and dexterity index(DI), the global quality workspace(GQWS) is defined. The geometric parameters are optimized based on the maximum GQWS in Sect. 4. and the performance of the CDPM after optimization is discussed in Sect. 5. Finally, the conclusions are summarized in Sect. 6.

2 Workspace Calculation Considering Tension Conditions

2.1 Modeling of CDPM

The kinematic model of the CDPM is shown in Fig. 3. b_i is the position vector of the outlet point in the global coordinate system, p is a translation vector between the origin of the global coordinate system and the origin of the local coordinate system, p_i is the vector from the origin P to the moving platform joints P_i in the local coordinate., system, $^{O}R_P$ is the rotation matrix. The cable vector l_i can be described as.

$$l_i = b_i - p - {}^{O}R_P p_i (i = 1, 2, ..., 8) \tag{1}$$

Let t_i represent the cable tension vector, $t_i = t_i u_i$, t_i is the tension of cable i, u_i is the unit direction vector of cable i, $u_i = l_i / \|l_i\|$. Let f_p be the external force on the

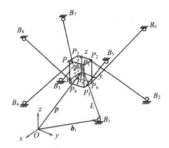

Fig. 3. Kinematic model of the CDPM.

moving platform and $\boldsymbol{\tau}_p$ be the external torque on the moving platform. From the static equilibrium condition, we have

$$J^{\mathrm{T}}T + F = 0 \tag{2}$$

where $J^{\mathrm{T}} = \begin{bmatrix} \boldsymbol{u}_1 & \cdots & \boldsymbol{u}_8 \\ \boldsymbol{p}_1 \times \boldsymbol{u}_1 & \cdots & \boldsymbol{p}_8 \times \boldsymbol{u}_8 \end{bmatrix}$ is the structure matrix, $T = \begin{bmatrix} t_1 & \cdots & t_8 \end{bmatrix}^{\mathrm{T}}$ is the cable tension vector, $F = \begin{bmatrix} f_p & \boldsymbol{\tau}_p \end{bmatrix}^{\mathrm{T}}$ is the external wrench.

2.2 Calculation of Cable Tension Distribution

In practical applications, there is a safety upper limit $t_{\max}$ for the cable tension due to the limitation of the driving torque of the driver. In addition, in order to avoid looseness during the movement of cable, the cable tension should not be lower than the minimum tension $t_{\min}$. The constraint condition of the cable tension is

$$0 < t_{\min} \le t_i \le t_{\max} (i = 1, ..., m) \tag{3}$$

A reasonable cable tension distribution can effectively improve the performance of CDPM. Linear programming methods, p-norm methods, polyhedra centroid calculation methods, etc. [12, 13] have been proposed to calculate the cable tension distribution. These methods have a relatively large amount of calculations, and some methods have the disadvantage of discontinuous tension distribution. Pott A proposed a closed-form tension distribution algorithm [14]. This algorithm has continuous.

tension distribution, no iteration, and the computational efficiency is extremely high. The calculation process is as follows.

$$T = T_m - J^{\mathrm{T}+}(F + J^{\mathrm{T}}T_m) \tag{4}$$

where T_m is the mean feasible tension distribution, $T_m = (T_{\min} + T_{\max})/2$, $T_{\min} = \begin{bmatrix} t_{\min} & \cdots & t_{\min} \end{bmatrix}^{\mathrm{T}}$, $T_{\max} = \begin{bmatrix} t_{\max} & \cdots & t_{\max} \end{bmatrix}^{\mathrm{T}}$, $J^{\mathrm{T}+}$ is the pseudo-inverse of J^{T}.

For a CDPM with n-Dof, a posture belonging to the workspace should satisfy the following conditions:

$$rank(J^{\mathrm{T}}) = n \cap J^{\mathrm{T}}T + F = 0, T_{\min} \le T \le T_{\max} \tag{5}$$

where $\text{rank}(\boldsymbol{J}^{\mathrm{T}})$ is the rank of the structure matrix $\boldsymbol{J}^{\mathrm{T}}$, the value is the degree of freedom of the CDPM.

The CDPM frame is a cuboid structure with the length and width of 2 m and the height of 1 m. The moving platform is a cuboid with the volume of 0.003 m^3, and the length, width and height of the moving platform are L4, L5 and L6, as shown in Fig. 4, In order to be universal, we randomly set the geometric dimensions of the CDPM as shown in Table 1.

Regardless of the external force on the moving platform, the workspace for two different attitude angles of the CDPM is calculated as shown in Fig. 5 and Fig. 6.

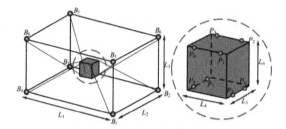

Fig. 4. Dimensional parameters of CDPM.

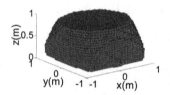

Fig. 5. Workspace for CDPM with $\alpha = \beta = \gamma = 0$.

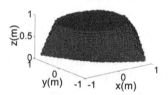

Fig. 6. Workspace for CDPM with $\alpha = 4, \beta = 0, \gamma = 2$.

Table 1. Dimensions of CDPM.

L_1	L_2	L_3	L_4	L_5	L_6	$\|P_1P_4\|/\|P_2P_3\|$	$\|P_5P_6\|/\|P_7P_8\|$
2 m	2 m	1 m	0.15 m	0.1 m	0.2 m	0.1 m	0.08 m

3   Evaluation of Workspace Quality

3.1   Tension Distribution Index(TDI)

When the moving platform moves in workspace, the smaller the difference in the tension of different cables, the better the quality of the workspace. Cong Bang Pham proposed the tension factor (TF) [6] as the performance index to evaluate the quality of the workspace of CDPM, that is the ratio of minimum tension to maximum tension. But it can't reflect the uniformity of tension distribution. Xiaoqiang Tang defined all cable tension distribution index (e_t), that is, the variance of all tensions over the minimum tension [7]:

$$e_t = \frac{\sqrt{\sum_{i=1}^{m}(t_i - \bar{t})^2/(m-1)}}{\min(t_i)} (i = 1, 2, ...m) \tag{6}$$

However, when the difference between the maximum allowable tension and the minimum allowable tension of cable is large, the variation range of e_t is large, which is not universal and effective for the evaluation of the cables tension distribution. Based on the idea of mean feasible tension distribution in the closed-form tension distribution algorithm, we proposed the tension distribution index (TDI):

$$\text{TDI} = \frac{\sqrt{\sum_{i=1}^{m}(t_i - \bar{t})^2/m}}{t_m} (i = 1, 2, ...m) \tag{7}$$

where $\bar{t}$ is the average value of tensions, t_m is the mean feasible tension, $t_m = (t_{\min} + t_{\max})/2$.

The TDI of the two workspace are shown in Fig. 7 and Fig. 8. The cable tension distribution is more uniform at the center of the work space. Increasing the attitude angle of the moving platform will increase the difference in cable tension distribution.

3.2   Stiffness Index (SI)

The stiffness matrix of the CDPM can be expressed as:

$$K = \frac{dF}{dX} = -\frac{dJ^{\mathrm{T}}}{dX}T - J^{\mathrm{T}}\frac{dT}{dX} = \sum_{i=1}^{8}\left[-\frac{d}{dX}\begin{pmatrix} u_i \\ p_i \times u_i \end{pmatrix}T_i\right] + J^{\mathrm{T}}K_{diag}J = K_1 + K_2 \tag{8}$$

In Eq. (9), K_{diag} is the cable stiffness matrix, $K_{diag} = diag(\frac{E_1 A_1}{l_{o1}} \cdots \frac{E_8 A_8}{l_{o8}})$, E_i, A_i and l_{oi} represent the elastic modulus, cross-sectional area and elastic modulus, cross-sectional area and original cable length, respectively.

It can be seen from Eq. (8) that the stiffness matrix of CDPM is composed of K_1 and K_2. K_1 is related to the cable tension, and K_2 is related the stiffness of cables. In [7] and [8], only the second part K_2 is considered when analyzing the quality of workspace while

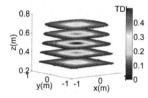

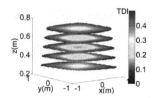

Fig. 7. TDI quality workspace with $\alpha = \beta = \gamma = 0$

Fig. 8. TDI quality workspace with $\alpha = 4, \beta = 0, \gamma = 2$.

ignoring the influence of cable tension. In fact, the cable tension has a very important effect on the stiffness of CDPM. Therefore, it is more feasible to study the stiffness of CDPM considering whole stiffness matrix including K_1 and K_2.

The stiffness index (SI) is an important index for evaluating the stiffness performance of CDPM, and its expression is the inverse of the condition number of the stiffness matrix K, that is:

$$SI = \frac{1}{\kappa(K)} \tag{9}$$

The condition number of K ranges from one to infinity and thus the stiffness index (SI) is limited between 0 and 1. The closer it is to 1, the more isotropic the CDPM's stiffness at this point.

In Eq. (8), dF contains force and moment, and dx contains length and angle. Therefore, the stiffness matrix K is inhomogeneous. To homogenize the stiffness matrix K, we make the following transformation:

$$dF_H = S^{-1}dF \tag{10}$$

$$dX_H = SdX \tag{11}$$

where $S = \begin{bmatrix} I_{3\times3} \\ & LC \end{bmatrix}$, $LC = diag(Lc, Lc, Lc)$, Lc is the characteristic length. The value of it is generally taken as the average value of the distance from the moving platform joints to the origin of the local coordinate system. LC is used to convert torque into force and angle into length.

Substituting Eq. (10) and Eq. (11) into Eq. (8), we get

$$dF_H = S^{-1}KS^{-1}dX_H \tag{12}$$

And the stiffness matrix K can be homogenized as:

$$K_H = S^{-1}KS^{-1} \tag{13}$$

In this paper, we use Dyneema as the cable material, and the cable section radius is set to 1 mm. The SI distribution in the workspace of the CDPM is shown in Fig. 9 and Fig. 10. The value of SI is largest in the center, which means that at the center position, the stiffness of CDPM is most isotropic, and this is helpful for the smooth movement of the moving platform.

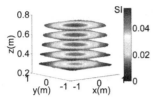 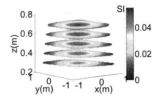

Fig. 9. SI quality workspace with $\alpha = \beta = \gamma = 0$

Fig. 10. SI quality workspace with $\alpha = 4, \beta = 0, \gamma = 2$.

3.3 Dexterity Index (DI)

The condition number of the Jacobian matrix of the CDPM reflects the distance between the posture and the isotropic point. The smaller the condition number value, the higher the degree of isotropy of CDPM, and the better the force and velocity transmission performance of the CDPM at this position. The dexterity index (DI) is defined [8] as:

$$DI = \frac{1}{\kappa(\boldsymbol{J})} \tag{14}$$

Likewise, the Jacobian matrix is inhomogeneous. In order to let the condition number of Jacobian matrix make sense, we make the following transformation:

$$\boldsymbol{J}_H = \boldsymbol{J}\boldsymbol{S}^{-1} \tag{15}$$

DI varies between $(0, 1]$ and the closer it gets to 1, the better the force and velocity transmission performance of the CDPM at this position.

The calculated DI of two different workspaces is shown in Fig. 11 and Fig. 12. It can be seen from the figures that at the same height, DI is largest in the center position, indicating that at the center position, the CDPM has the best force and speed transmission performance. The closer to the edge of the workspace, the smaller the value of DI and the worse the force and velocity transmission performance of CDPM.

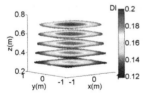 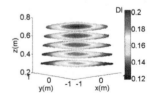

Fig. 11. DI quality workspace with $\alpha = \beta = \gamma = 0$.

Fig. 12. DI quality workspace with $\alpha = 4, \beta = 0, \gamma = 2$.

3.4 Global Quality Workspace (GQWS)

Let V_{TDI} be the volume of workspace with TDI less than or equal to the allowable value.

$$V_{TDI} \approx \frac{n_{TDI}}{n_{WS}} V_{WS} \tag{16}$$

where n_{TDI} is the number of points whose TDI value is less than or equal to the allowable value, n_{WS} is the number of all discrete points in the workspace, and V_{WS} is the volume of the workspace.

V_{SI} and V_{DI} are defined similarly to V_{TDI}. Considering TDI, SI and DI comprehensively, the global quality workspace (GQWS) is proposed. Let V_{GQWS} be the volume of GQWS.

$$V_{GQWS} = V_{TDI} \cap V_{SI} \cap V_{DI} \tag{17}$$

4   Analysis and Optimization of the Geometric Parameters Based on the Maximum GQWS

For the CDPM we studied, the moving platform is a cuboid with the fixed volume of $0.003\ m^3$, and the length, width and height of the moving platform are L_4, L_5 and L_6. If L_4 and L_5 are determined, then L_6 will also be determined. We set TDI $= 0.4$, SI $= 0.03$ and DI $= 0.2$ (these values can be varied according to practical requirements) and analyze the changes in the values of V_{TDI}, V_{SI} and V_{DI} when L_4 and L_5 are of different size. The influence of changes in L_4 and L_5 on V_{TDI}, V_{SI} and V_{DI} are shown in Table 2. In this process, we set the connection points of the cables and the motion platform to be located at the eight vertexes respectively and the attitude angle $\alpha = \beta = \gamma = 0$. The position parameters of the connection points will be optimized later.

As shown in Table 2, the smaller L_4 and L_5, the larger V_{TDI}, which means the slender moving platform is conducive to improving tension distribution for this configuration. However, the changes in L_4 and L_5 do not have a particularly regular effect on V_{SI} and V_{DI}. The optimum $L_4 = 0.2$ m and $L_5 = 0.1$ m can be obtained based on maximum GQWS through analyzing V_{GQWS} with various L_4 and L_5. The maximum V_{GQWS} is $0.61\ m^3$. It is worth noting that the values of L_4 and L_5 cannot be equal. If they are equivalent, the structure matrix J^T will be singular and the CDPM will be uncontrollable.

In order to further improve the workspace quality of the CDPM, we optimize the position of the connection points between cables and the moving platform. Set the length of P_1P_4 and P_2P_3 to a, P_5P_6 and P_7P_8 to b. The optimization problem can be.

Table 2. V_{TDI}, V_{SI} and V_{DI} with various L_4 and L_5.

$V_{TDI}/V_{SI}/V_{SI}(m^3)$		$L_4(m)$		
		0.15	0.25	0.3
$L_5(m)$	0.1	0.66/0.54/0.14	0.59/1.69/1.69	0.56/1.63/1.63
	0.2	0.57/0.75/0.36	0.52/0.42/0	0.51/1.24/1.48
	0.3	0.53/1.56/1.56	0.49/0.14/0	0/0/0

described as

$$\max F(a, b)$$

$$s.t. \begin{cases} 0 \le a \le 0.2 \\ 0 \le b \le 0.1 \end{cases} \tag{18}$$

Since there's no closed-form expression for the objective function, we use the grouped coordinate descent(GCD) method to solve the optimization problem [10]. This method has the advantage of simple calculation and does not require a derivative process. However, the optimization result is locally convergent. This problem can be addressed through changing the iterative step. The iteration process is as follows

$$\begin{cases} b^{r+1} = \arg \max_{b} F(a^r, b) \\ a^{r+1} = \arg \max_{a} F(a, b^{r+1}) \end{cases} \tag{19}$$

The optimum $a = 0.1$ and $b = 0$ can be obtained through the GCD method. And $V_{GQWS} = 0.6381$ m^3.

5   Results of Simulation

In order to compare the performance of the CDPM before and after optimization, we planned the trajectory of the moving platform as shown in Fig. 13.

The changes of TDI, SI and DI are shown in Fig. 14. The average value of TDI, SI and DI(expressed as $\overline{TDI}$, $\overline{SI}$ and $\overline{DI}$) of the CDPM during the movement are shown in Table 3.

It can be observed that there is no distinct difference of TDI between before and after optimization. While the value of SI and DI after optimization is much larger than before optimization. The data in Table 3 presents in more detail the performance improvement of the optimized CDPM. Since the GQWS takes TDI, SI and DI into account, the overall performance of the CDPM is improved after optimizing for the maximum V_{GQWS}. This also indicates that the global quality workspace (GQWS) is effective and valuable in designing and evaluating CDPM.

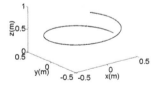

Fig. 13. The planned trajectory.

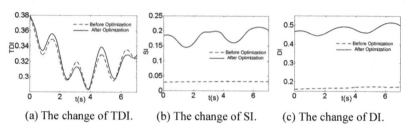

(a) The change of TDI.   (b) The change of SI.   (c) The change of DI.

Fig. 14. The changes of TDI, SI and DI.

Table 3. The average value of TDI, SI and DI of the CDPM before and after optimization during the movement.

Indicator	Before optimization	After optimization	Relative change%
$\overline{TDI}$	0.3207	0.3226	+0.59
$\overline{SI}$	0.0306	0.1884	+515.69
$\overline{DI}$	0.1683	0.4777	+183.83

6 Conclusions

In this paper, several new indexes are proposed to evaluate the quality of the workspace of CDPM. The dimension parameters of a 8-6-CDPM are optimized based on the maximum GQWS. The conclusions can be drawn are as follows:

(1) To evaluate the uniformity of cable tension distribution, the tension distribution index (TDI) is proposed. And the stiffness index (SI) is improved considering the effect of cable tension on the stiffness of CDPM.
(2) Considering TDI, SI and DI comprehensively, the global quality workspace (GQWS) is further proposed. This index is more effective and valuable in evaluating the quality of the workspace and designing the CDPM.
(3) The dimension parameters of the CDPM are optimized based on the maximum GQWS. Simulation results indicate that the optimized CDPM has better overall performance than before.

Actually, for various configurations of CDPM, the shape and quality of the workspace are different. And this will be discussed in our further work.

Acknowledgments. This research is funded by Higher Education Disciplinary Innovation Program (also known as the "111 Program", No. B07018) and the General Department of China Academy of Space Technology.

References

1. Tang, X.Q.: An overview of the development for cable-driven parallel manipulator. Adv. Mech. Eng. **2014**(1), 1–9 (2014)

2. Verhoeven, R.: Analysis of the workspace of tendon-based Stewart platforms, Ph.D.dissertation, University Duisburg-Essen, Duisburg, Germany (2004)
3. Diao, X., Ma, O.: Force-closure analysis of 6-DOF cable manipulators with seven or more cables. Robotica **27**(2), 209–215 (2009)
4. Loloei, A.Z., Taghirad, H.D.: Controllable workspace of cable driven redundant parallel manipulator with more than one degree of redundancy. In: International Conference on Control. IEEE (2011)
5. Barrette, G., Gosselin, C.M.: Determination of the dynamic workspace of cable-driven planar parallel mechanisms. J. Mech. Des. **127**(2), 242–248 (2005)
6. Pham, C.B., Yeo, S.H., Yang, G.L., Chen, I.-M.: Workspace analysis of fully restrained cable-driven manipulators. Robot. Auton. Syst. **57**, 901–912 (2009)
7. Tang, X., Tang, L., Wang, J., Sun, D.: Workspace quality analysis and application for a completely restrained 3-Dof planar cable-driven parallel manipulator. J. Mech. Sci. Technol. **27**(8), 2391–2399 (2013). https://doi.org/10.1007/s12206-013-0624-7
8. Li, Y., Xu, Q.: GA-based multi-objective optimal design of a planar 3-dof cable-driven parallel manipulator. In: IEEE International Conference on Robotics and Biomimetics, Kunming, 17–20 December 2006, pp. 1360–1365 (2006)
9. Zhang, Z., Shao, Z., Wang, L., et al.: Optimal design of a high-speed pick-and-place cable-driven parallel robot. In: 3rd International Conference on Cable-Driven Parallel Robots, vol. 53, pp. 340–352 (2018)
10. Zhang, B., Shang, W.W., Cong, S., et al.: Size optimization of the moving platform for cable-driven parallel manipulators based on stiffness characteristics. Proc. Inst. Mech. Eng. C J. Mech. Eng. Sci. **232**(11), 2057–2066 (2018)
11. Pott, A., Miermeister, P.: Workspace and interference analysis of cable-driven parallel robots with an unlimited rotation axis. In: Advances in Robot Kinematics 2016, pp. 341–350. Springer, Cham (2018)
12. Borgstrom, P.H., Jordan, B.L., Sukhatme, G.S.: Rapid computation of optimally safe tension distributions for parallel cable-driven robots. IEEE Trans. Robot. **25**(6), 1271–1281 (2009)
13. Gosselin, C., Grenier, M.: On the determination of the force distribution in overconstrained cable-driven parallel mechanisms. Meccanica **46**(1), 3–15 (2011)
14. Pott, A., Bruckmann, T., Mikelsons, L.: Closed-form force distribution for parallel wire robots. In: Kecskeméthy, A., Müller, A. (eds.) Computational Kinematics, pp. 25–34. Springer, Heidelberg (2009). https://doi.org/10.1007/978-3-642-01947-0_4

Design and Experimental Research of Cable-Driven Upper-Limb Rehabilitation Robot

Xiangshu Wu, Yupeng Zou[(✉)], Qiang Zhang, Baolong Zhang, Xuebin Gu, and Jiping Zhang

China University of Petroleum, Qingdao 266580, China
zouyupeng@upc.edu.cn

Abstract. To help patients with upper-limb dysfunction in rehabilitation training, a parallel cable-driven upper-limb rehabilitation robot was proposed. The robot has advantages in modular design, simple mechanism, low cost, lightweight and good human-machine compatibility. The robot can help patients with upper-limb dysfunction to carry out various forms of rehabilitation training. Trajectory planning, kinematics analysis, workspace verification and human-machine experimental research were also carried out for shoulder joint flexion/extension. The results show that the parallel flexible cable-driven upper-limb rehabilitation robot in this paper has certain significance for patients to carry out rehabilitation training.

Keywords: Upper-limb rehabilitation · Cable-driven · Kinematics analysis · Human-machine experiment

1 Introduction

As the global aging of the population is becoming increasingly serious, stroke has become the second leading cause of death in people over 60 years old [1]. In addition, the number of patients with upper-limb dysfunction caused by natural disasters, emergencies and other acquired causes is also increasing. How to maximize the recovery of normal motor ability of patients with upper-limb dysfunction is a difficult problem in the field of rehabilitation medicine. Compared with the artificial rehabilitation, the upper-limb rehabilitation robot has the advantages in precise rehabilitation training, low cost and high efficiency. Therefore, it has unique advantages to realize the functional recovery of the affected limb through the upper-limb rehabilitation robot [2].

According to the different structure forms, upper-limb rehabilitation robot can be divided into two types: the exoskeleton rehabilitation robot and the end traction rehabilitation robot [3]. The exoskeleton upper-limb rehabilitation robot realizes rehabilitation training by controlling the exoskeleton to drive the coordinated movement of the affected limb. The Chicago Institute of Rehabilitation and the University of California had jointly developed a 3-DOF upper-limb rehabilitation robot ARM Guide. The robot has an active degree of freedom, the linear guide is driven by the motor to realize the flexion/extension

© Springer Nature Switzerland AG 2021
X.-J. Liu et al. (Eds.): ICIRA 2021, LNAI 13013, pp. 586–596, 2021.
https://doi.org/10.1007/978-3-030-89095-7_56

movement of the upper-limb [4, 5]. A 5-DOF SAIL upper-limb rehabilitation robot was designed by the University of Southampton in the United Kingdom. The torsion spring elastic auxiliary support mechanism was installed at the shoulder and elbow joints. VR technology was combined with electrical signal stimulation of upper-limb muscles. The robot realizes upper-limb rehabilitation through the above measures [6]. The main mechanism of the end traction upper-limb rehabilitation robot is an ordinary linkage mechanism or a tandem robot mechanism. Through the mechanism at the end of the robot to pull the affected limb to complete the rehabilitation. Hogan proposed a robot system with gravity compensation—the 2-DOF arm planar rehabilitation robot system MIT-MANUS [7]. Subsequently, a 2-DOF wrist rehabilitation robot was also proposed [8, 9]. The two rehabilitation robots formed a complete upper-limb 4-DOF rehabilitation system. The GENTLE/S upper-limb rehabilitation robot developed by the University of Reading used cable to reduce the weight of the affected limb. Based on the drive of Haptic MASTER industrial robot, the shoulder and elbow joint were trained [10, 11]. Many institutions have conducted in-depth research on upper-limb rehabilitation robot. However, the research on the size, structure, human-machine compatibility and secondary injury prevention of the upper-limb rehabilitation robot can still be carried out in-depth [12].

The cable-driven robot is a new type of robot. It uses cable to replace traditional rigid connectors. By controlling the motor to drive the pulley to change the length of cable, the pose control of the end effector is completed. British Jensen designed a 9-cable drive parallel robot SACSO. The literature detailed the kinematics, cable tension and dynamic characteristics of the object under the redundant constraint state driven by 9 cables. The wind tunnel model test was carried out [13]. Williams of Ohio State University designed a simulation dynamics and control system of the planar translational cable-oriented robot (CDDR). It improved the cable interference problem of the existing CDDRs, and avoided applying negative cable tension to the environment during dynamic movement [14]. The cable-driven robot has the advantages in large workspace, high inertia ratio, fast response of load speed, and easy reorganization of robot mechanism [15, 16].

To solve the problems of the upper-limb rehabilitation robot mentioned above, a cable-driven upper-limb rehabilitation robot (CULR) with features of modular design, simple structure, and good human-machine compatibility was presented in this paper. Through the shoulder flexion/extension, trajectory planning, kinematics analysis, workspace verification and human-machine experiment research were carried out. Based on these, the robot assisted patients in different rehabilitation stages to develop a variety of task-oriented rehabilitation.

2   Cable-Driven Upper-Limb Rehabilitation Robot

2.1   Composition of CULR

As shown in Fig. 1, CULR is composed of frame, seven groups of cable-driven units, rotating seat, cable and movable platform. Movable platform is shown in Fig. 2. By controlling the angle change of the rollers in the seven groups of cable-drive units, the structure of the cable-drive units is shown in Fig. 3, the coordinated variation of the seven cables are realized. Therefore, the platform can be pulled to drive the affected limb

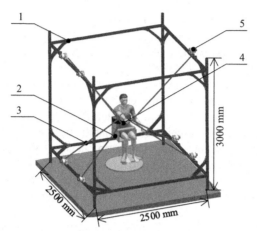

1. Frame; 2. Rotating seat; 3. Cable; 4.Movable platform;5. Cable-driven unit.

Fig. 1. The composition of CULR.

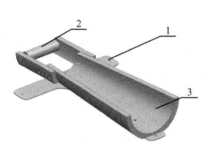

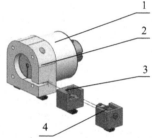

1. Traction point; 2. Armrest;
3.Movable platform.

1. Permanent magnet DC torque motor;
2. Motor bracket 3. Guide wheel;
4. Tension sensor.

Fig. 2. The structure of movable platform

Fig. 3. The structure of the cable-drive unit

according to the planned trajectory to perform rehabilitation. The contact part between the patient and robot is small, and the human-machine compatibility is good.

2.2 Shoulder Flexion and Extension

This paper has planned a trajectory that simulated the flexion / extension movement of the shoulder joint in the xOz plane (as shown in Fig. 4). The law of forearm center of mass movement is as formula (1), where the shoulder joint rotation angle θ_s ranges from $-30°$ to $30°$ (anti-clockwise rotation is positive, clockwise rotation is negative).

$$\begin{cases} x = -430(\cos(u) - 1) \\ z = 430\sin(u) \qquad (-\pi/6 \leq u \leq \pi/6) \\ \theta_y = u \end{cases} \tag{1}$$

Fig. 4. Shoulder flexion and extension

3 Robot Kinematics Analysis

3.1 Inverse Kinematics

Figure 5 shows the 3R3T (three rotation and three translation) parallel cable-drive mechanism (PCDM). The seven driving points M_i (X_{Mi}, Y_{Mi}) $(i = 1, 2,..., 7)$ of mechanism are M_1 $(-a, -b, -e)$, M_2 $(a, -b, -e)$, M_3 $(a, b, -e)$, M_4 $(-a, b, -e)$, M_5 $(-a,-b, e)$, M_6 (a, b, e), M_7 $(-a, b, e)$ $(a, b$ and e are greater than 0), the global rectangular coordinate system $Oxyz$ is located at the center of the cube composed of seven driving points. The seven (three) traction points of the movable platform (some traction points coincide) are shown in Fig. 5. The seven cables P_iM_i $(i = 1, 2, ..., 7)$ are connected to the seven (three) traction points of the movable platform by the output of seven driving points. The local coordinate system of the movable platform is $Px_py_pz_p$, the pose of the center of movable platform in the global rectangular coordinate system is expressed as P $(x, y, z, \theta_x, \theta_y, \theta_z)$. P_i (X_{Pi}, Y_{Pi}, Z_{Pi}) represents the traction point in the local coordinate system, then

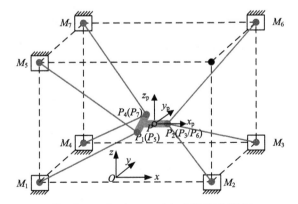

Fig. 5. Mechanism model of 3R3T PCDM

the point P_i $(i = 1, 2,..., 7)$ in the global coordinate system can be expressed as:

$$\begin{bmatrix} x_{P_i} \\ y_{P_i} \\ z_{P_i} \end{bmatrix} = \begin{bmatrix} x \\ y \\ z \end{bmatrix} + D \begin{bmatrix} X_{P_i} \\ Y_{P_i} \\ Z_{P_i} \end{bmatrix} \tag{2}$$

Among them, D is the direction cosine vector.

$r_i = PP_i$ $(i = 1, 2,..., 7)$ is the vector from the center point P of the movable platform to the traction point P_i. $L_i = P_i M_i$ is the vector from the traction point P_i to the driving point M_i, then the length of the cable can be expressed as $l_i = \|L_i\|$. $u_i = L_i / l_i$ is the unit vector of the ith cable, t_i is the force value of the ith cable, then the tension vector of the ith cable acting on the movable platform is $t_i = u_i t_i$. According to the principle of robot mechanism and mathematics vector closure, the length of the cable is:

$$l = \begin{bmatrix} l_1 & l_2 & l_3 & l_4 & l_5 & l_6 & l_7 \end{bmatrix}^T \tag{3}$$

3.2   Forward Kinematics

The variation of the cable has been calculated during the movement of the movable platform, the next step is to control the length of the cable in real time to pull the movable platform to complete the expected action. Because there is no root formula for solving the nonlinear equations of the cable length, so the approximate solution of cable length is solved by numerical calculation, that is, the Newton-Raphson iterative method is used to solve the Eq. (3). The principle of this method is to substitute the guessed solution, iterate layer by layer, and produce an ideal solution within the allowable error range after a finite iteration step. The specific solution process is as follows:

According to formula 3, construct the following formula:

$$F_i(X) = \|L_i\|^2 - l_i^2, i = 1, 2, \dots, 7 \tag{4}$$

$$J_i = \begin{bmatrix} \frac{\partial F_i}{\partial x} & \frac{\partial F_i}{\partial y} & \frac{\partial F_i}{\partial z} & \frac{\partial F_i}{\partial \alpha} & \frac{\partial F_i}{\partial \beta} & \frac{\partial F_i}{\partial \gamma} \end{bmatrix}_{1 \times 6}, i = 1, 2, \dots, 7 \tag{5}$$

$$J = \begin{bmatrix} J_1 & J_2 & J_3 & J_4 & J_5 & J_6 & J_7 \end{bmatrix}_{7 \times 6}^T, i = 1, 2, \dots, 7 \tag{6}$$

$$F(X) = [F_1(X)\ F_2(X)\ F_3(X)\ F_4(X)F_5(X)\ F_6(X)\ F_7(X)]^T \tag{7}$$

$$X = \begin{bmatrix} x & y & z & \alpha & \beta & \gamma \end{bmatrix}^T \tag{8}$$

$$J\delta X_K = -F(X) \text{ or } \delta X_K = -J^+ F(X) \tag{9}$$

$$X_{K+1} = X_K + \delta X_K \tag{10}$$

$$\|\delta X_K\| < \varepsilon \tag{11}$$

According to matrix theory, the pseudo-inverse of Newton-Raphson Jacobian matrix $\boldsymbol{J}$ is $\boldsymbol{J}^{+} = \left(\boldsymbol{J}^{\mathrm{T}}\boldsymbol{J}\right)^{-1}\boldsymbol{J}^{\mathrm{T}}$.

Through the above method, the forward kinematics analysis is carried out on the 3R3T PCDM. The center pose of movable platform can be obtained according to the length of the cable for subsequent motion control.

3.3 Workspace Analysis

The 3R3T PCDM in this paper is a fully constrained mechanism. Considering the general situation, when solving the workspace of the 3R3T PCDM, the DOF of the mechanism is n. Assuming that the pose of the movable platform in the global Cartesian coordinate system is $\boldsymbol{X}^{n}$, $\boldsymbol{T} \in \boldsymbol{R}^{m}(\boldsymbol{T} \geq 0)$ is the tension of each cable, $\boldsymbol{F} \in \boldsymbol{R}^{n}$ is a force spiral vector acting on the movable platform. If $\boldsymbol{J}^{\mathrm{T}}\boldsymbol{T} = \boldsymbol{F}$ holds, $\boldsymbol{X}^{n}$ is the controllable workspace of the movable platform [17]. The tension matrix is $\boldsymbol{T} = \begin{bmatrix} t_1 & \dots & t_m \end{bmatrix}^{\mathrm{T}}$, and the $\boldsymbol{J}^{\mathrm{T}}$ is the

structure matrix, $\boldsymbol{J}^{\mathrm{T}} = \begin{bmatrix} u_1 & \dots & u_m \\ r_1 \times u_1 & \dots & r_m \times u_m \end{bmatrix}$.

Figure 6 shows the n-DOF mechanism model of PCDM. Assuming that the force and torque acting on the movable platform by the cable are removed, f_{P} and τ_{P} are the external force and torque.

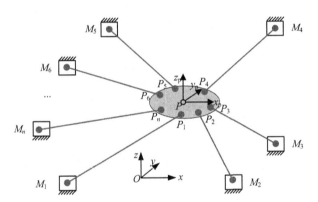

Fig. 6. n-DOF mechanism model of PCDM.

According to the D'Alembert principle, the force spiral balance equations of the movable platform are:

$$\sum_{i=1}^{m} t_i + f_{\mathrm{p}} = 0 \tag{12}$$

$$\sum_{i=1}^{m} r_i \times t_i + \tau_{\mathrm{P}} = 0 \tag{13}$$

According to (12) and (13),

$$\boldsymbol{J}^{\mathrm{T}}\boldsymbol{T} = \begin{bmatrix} u_1 & \dots & u_m \\ r_1 \times u_1 & \dots & r_m \times u_m \end{bmatrix} \boldsymbol{T} = \boldsymbol{F} \tag{14}$$

In the formula, F is the external force spiral matrix acting on the movable platform, $F = \left[-f_P \; -\tau_P\right]^T$.

If the workspace has practical significance, the pose of movable platform of the PCDM must meet the following conditions:

(a) The movable platform is controllable, that is $J^T T = F$;
(b) The tension value of the cable is greater than 0, that is, $t_i > 0$ $(i = 1, 2, ..., m)$, and it is within the allowable tension range;
(c) There is no singular position in the movement of the movable platform, that is rank $(J^T) = n$;
(d) The PCDM has sufficient strength.

In addition, based on the tension t_i of each cable must be greater than 0, that is $T = (I - J^{T+}J) > 0$ (J^{T+} is the pseudo-inverse matrix of the cable structure matrix J^T), Kawamura and Verhoeven obtained the necessary and sufficient condition for judging whether the movable platform pose X^n in the PCDM is in the controllable workspace: the zero space structure matrix J^T is greater than $\mathbf{0}$, which is $N(J^T) > 0$ [18].

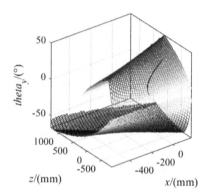

Fig. 7. Relationship between shoulder joint flexion/extension movement trajectory and workspace

Therefore, for the n-DOF PCDM, only rank $(J^T) = n$ and $N(J^T) > 0$ are satisfied at the same time, the pose of the movable platform is within the controllable workspace.

When the upper-limb is driven by the movable platform to conduct shoulder joint flexion/extension, the relationship between the motion trajectory of the center of mass of forearm and the workspace is shown in Fig. 7. It can be seen from the figure that the trajectory of the center of the movable platform (the center of mass of forearm) is completely enclosed in the robot's workspace. Therefore, the 3R3T parallel CULR can meet the requirements of upper-limb basic rehabilitation. At this time the length changes of each cable under the two motion trajectories are shown in Fig. 8, it will pave the way for the subsequent experimental verification.

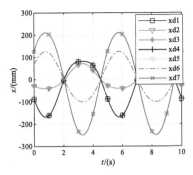

Fig. 8. Cable variation of shoulder joint flexion/extension movement

4   Experimental Research on CULR

This experimental research was carried out based on the LINKS real-time semi-physical simulation system. In the experiment, a healthy adult male with a height of 178 cm and a weight of 63 kg was selected as the experimental object. The robot drove the experimental object to move the upper-limb to simulate the shoulder flexion/extension. The movable platform drove the subject's upper-limb to make a circular motion with a rotation angle θ of 60° and a period T of 5 s. The experimental process is shown in Fig. 9, and the experimental results are shown in Fig. 10.

Fig. 9. Shoulder joint flexion/extension exercise experiment

From the experimental results in Fig. 10(a) to 10(g), in the experimental research of shoulder joint flexion/extension rehabilitation exercise, the actual length change of the seven cables basically is coincide with the given amount. It can be seen from Fig. 10(h) that the maximum error of the cable length change amount is about 10 mm. The extremely small error is caused by the cable-drive unit mechanism itself. But the experimental effect reached the expected goal and met the requirements. It can be seen from Fig. 10(i) and 10(j) that the change range of tension and linear velocity of each cable is small, and in a controllable range, without large mutation. The effectiveness and safety of the upper-limb rehabilitation robot are verified.

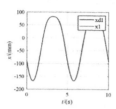

(a) Length changes of cable 1

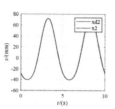

(b) Length changes of cable 2

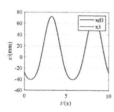

(c) Length changes of cable 3

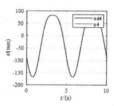

(d) Length changes of cable 4

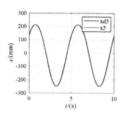

(e) Length changes of cable 5

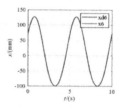

(f) Length changes of cable 6

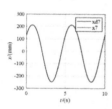

(g) Length changes of cable 7

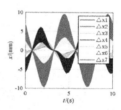

(h) Error of each cable length change amount

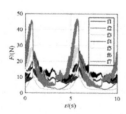

(i) Tension of each cable

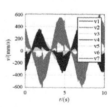

(j) Linear velocity of each cable

Fig. 10. Experimental curve of shoulder joint flexion/extension exercise

By analyzing the experimental results, the following conclusions can be drawn:

(a) By analyzing the relationship between the actual length change of the flexible cable and the given amount, the effectiveness of the designed position servo controller isSS verified.
(b) The human-machine experiment has completed the simulation of the flexion/extension movement of the shoulder joint, the experimental effect is good. The feasibility of the upper-limb rehabilitation robot is verified, and the rehabilitation has high efficiency and diversified forms.
(c) By interviewing the subject's feelings and analyzing the feedback data during the experiment, the CULR drives the upper-limb for rehabilitation with less human-machine interference and high comfort.

5   Conclusion

In this paper, a cable-driven upper-limb rehabilitation robot was proposed based on 3R3T PCDM. The shoulder joint flexion/extension movement trajectory was planned, and the kinematics analysis of the 3R3T PCDM was carried out, the method of controllable workspace analysis was proposed, finally, the change law of cable was obtained. The human-machine experiment that simulated the rehabilitation of shoulder joint flexion/extension exercise has been completed and the experimental effect is good. This paper has laid a strong foundation for the research of parallel cable-driven upper-limb rehabilitation robot.

Based on this work, the kinematic characteristics will be analyzed further, and the control strategies of different rehabilitation modes will also be studied. The results were prepared for the following prototype experiment and human-machine experiment.

References

1. Jiang, X.Z.: Servo Control of Joint Driven by Two Pneumatic Muscles in Opposing Pair Configuration for Rehabilitation Robot. Huazhong University of Science and Technology, Wuhan (2011)
2. Yang, Q., Cao, D., Zhao, J.: Analysis on state of the art of upper limb rehabilitation robots. Robot **35**(5), 630–640 (2013)
3. Yang, Z., Zi, B., Chen, B.: Mechanism design and kinematic analysis of a waist and lower limbs cable-driven parallel rehabilitation robot. In: 2019 IEEE 3rd Advanced Information Management, Communicates, Electronic and Automation Control Conference (IMCEC), pp. 723–727 (2019)
4. Kahn, L.E., Zygman, M.L., Rymer, W.Z., et al.: Robot-assisted reaching exercise promotes arm movement recovery in chronic hemiparetic stroke: a randomized controlled pilot study. J. Neuro Eng. Rehab. **3**(12), 1–13 (2006)
5. Reinkensmeyer, D.J., Kahn, L.E., Averbuch, M., et al.: Understanding and treating arm movement impairment after chronic brain injury: progress with the ARM guide. J. Rehabil. Res. Dev. **37**(6), 653–662 (2000)
6. Cai, Z., Tong, D., Meadmore, K.L., et al.: Design & control of a 3D stroke rehabilitation platform. In: IEEE International Conference on Rehabilitation Robotics. Piscataway. IEEE (2011)

7. Fasoli, S., Krebs, H., Stein, J., Frontera, W., Hogan, N.: Effects of robotic therapy on motor impairment and recovery in chronic stroke. Arch. Phys. Med. Rehab. **84**(4), 477–482 (2003)
8. Charles, S.K., Krebs, H.I., Volpe, B.T., et al.: Wrist rehabilitation following stroke: Initial clinical results. In: IEEE International Conference on Rehabilitation Robotics, Piscataway, pp. 13–16. IEEE (2005)
9. Krebs, H.I., Dipietro, L., Levy-Tzedek, S., et al.: A paradigm shift for rehabilitation robotics. IEEE Eng. Med. Biol. Mag. **27**(4), 61–70 (2008)
10. Amirabdollahian, F., Gradwell, E., Loureiro, R., et al.: Effects of the GENTLE/S robot mediated therapy on the outcome of upper limb rehabilitation post-stroke: Analysis of the battle hospital data. In: 8th International Conference on Rehabilitation Robotics, pp. 55–58 (2003)
11. Harwin, W., Loureiro, R., Amirabdollahian, F., et al.: The GENTLE/S project: a new method of delivering neuro rehabilitation. In: 6th European Conference for the Advancement of Assistive Technology, Amsterdam, Netherlands, pp. 36–41. IOS Press (2001)
12. Guo, S., Gao, J., Guo, J., Zhang, W., Hu, Y.: Design of the structural optimization for the upper limb rehabilitation robot. In: 2016 IEEE International Conference on Mechatronics and Automation, pp. 1185–1190 (2016)
13. Jensen, F.V., et al.: The SACSO methodology for troubleshooting complex systems. AI EDAM **15**(4), 321–333 (2001)
14. Williams, R.L., Gallina, P., Vadia, J.: Planar translational cable-direct-driven robots. J. Robot. Syst. **20**(3), 107–120 (2003)
15. Laribi, M., Carbone, G., Zeghloul, S.: On the optimal design of cable driven parallel robot with a prescribed workspace for upper limb rehabilitation tasks. J. Bionic Eng. **16**(3), 503–513 (2019)
16. Chen, Z.Y., Zhang, T.T., Li, Z.H.: Hybrid control scheme consisting of adaptive and optimal controllers for flexible base flexible-joint space manipulator with uncertain parameters. In: Proceedings of the 9th International Conference on Intelligent Human-Machine Systems and Cybernetics, pp. 341–345. IEEE, Hangzhou (2017)
17. Zhang, C., Zhang, L.: Kinematics analysis and workspace investigation of a novel 2-DOF parallel manipulator applied in vehicle driving simulator. Robot. Comput.-Integr. Manuf. **29**(4), 113–120 (2013)
18. Ferravante, V., Riva, E., Taghavi, M., Braghin, F., Bock, T.: Dynamic analysis of high precision construction cable-driven parallel robots. Mech. Mach. Theory **135**, 54–64 (2019)

Design and Optimization of the New Cable-Driven Ankle Rehabilitation Equipment

Ye Huo[1,2,3], Jinhao Duan[1,2,3], Zhufeng Shao[1,2,3]([✉]), Hanqing Liu[1,2,3],
and Chunjiao Liu[4]

[1] State Key Laboratory of Tribology and Institute of Manufacturing Engineering,
Tsinghua University, Beijing 100084, China
shaozf@mail.tsinghua.edu.cn
[2] Beijing Key Lab of Precision/Ultra-Precision Manufacturing Equipments and Control,
Tsinghua University, Beijing 100084, China
[3] Department of Mechanical Engineering, Tsinghua University, Beijing 100084, China
[4] Beijing Soft Robot Tech Company, Beijing 100070, China

Abstract. Ankle injuries are common in daily life, and the recovery process requires rehabilitation training. Manual rehabilitation training relies on doctors, which is inefficient, labor intensive, difficult to popularize and evaluate the rehabilitation effect objectively and accurately. Rehabilitation equipment overcomes above shortcomings and can achieve precise treatment, which has become an important part of the public health and health protection system. In this paper, a new cable-driven rehabilitation device is proposed for the ankle rehabilitation. The cable-driven technology reduces the weight and volume of the mechanical structure and mitigates the rigid impact with the cable flexibility. Besides, it improves the integration of sensing, driving and control. According to the movement requirements of human ankle joints, the configuration of the rehabilitation device was proposed. On this basis, a multi-parameter-oriented stepwise optimization method was established to minimize the maximum cable force, considering the constraints of volume and scale. The optimal dimension was deduced on the basis of the performance trend analysis. Finally, a virtual prototype of the rehabilitation mechanism was designed to form the new ankle joint rehabilitation equipment.

Keywords: Cable-driven · Parallel mechanism · Rehabilitation · Optimization design

1 Introduction

Rehabilitation training is an important means to rebuild patients' motion function, which is mainly relies on the manual treatment of doctors with problems such as high labor intensity, low efficiency, difficult to accurately control training process and evaluate training effects. Rehabilitation equipment can replace doctors to carry out rehabilitation training, which not only reduces the work intensity of doctors and relieves the shortage of medical resources, but also accurately records rehabilitation training data to achieve

© Springer Nature Switzerland AG 2021
X.-J. Liu et al. (Eds.): ICIRA 2021, LNAI 13013, pp. 597–607, 2021.
https://doi.org/10.1007/978-3-030-89095-7_57

precise evaluation. Rehabilitation equipment has become an important part of the public health and health protection system.

Rehabilitation equipment can be divided into two categories: end effector type and exoskeleton type, as shown in Fig. 1. The end effector type rehabilitant equipment usually adopts multi-link mechanism, which contacts and drags the patient's limb ends for movement. The exoskeleton type can completely restrain the movement of the patient's limbs to control the movement of each joint. It is simple in structure and easy to control. It is suitable for the rehabilitation training of extremity joints of the limbs, such as wrist and ankle [1–3]. The exoskeleton type can achieve more precise motion control of multiple joints at the same time [4–7], and is particularly suitable for rehabilitation training of non-terminal joints such as elbow and knee joints. However, it faces the following problems: First, it is difficult to achieve the consistency of the kinematic characteristics of the exoskeleton with the complex human joints, which causes additional loads on the joints. Secondly, the exoskeleton type will increase the movement inertia of the limbs and change the dynamic characteristics of the limbs. Finally, there is a lack of reliable connection between the exoskeleton and the limbs.

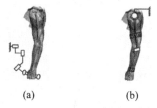

(a)   (b)

Fig. 1. Types of rehabilitation mechanism: (a) end effector type; (b) exoskeleton type.

Fig. 2. End effector type ankle rehabilitation mechanism.

Ankle joint has three DoFs with large rotation range, which plays an important role in human movement. At the same time, the ankle joint is also vulnerable to injury. Rehabilitation training is required to accelerate and improve recovery. Since the ankle joint is a terminal joint, most ankle rehabilitation mechanisms use the end effector type, as shown in Fig. 2 [8–10]. Existing ankle rehabilitation devices mostly adopt rigid parallel mechanisms to achieve 3 DoFs rotations with compact structure. As an excellent transmission medium, the cable has the advantages of light weight and high energy efficiency. It can also improve the portability and flexibility. The cable can transmit the force from one end to the other, which feedback tension while driving. The feature is favorable improving the integration of sensor, drive and control. Cable-driven mechanism has become a new direction and hot spot in the research of rehabilitation robots [11–13], as shown in Fig. 3.

However, the current research on cable-driven rehabilitation robots for the ankle joint is limited. The feasibility and advantages of using cable-driven rehabilitation for the ankle joint is discussed in [11], without specific design or scheme. The ankle rehabilitation platform named IK is proposed [12], which adopts an unconstrained four-cable suspension configuration. Exoskeleton type ankle rehabilitation device named CABLEankle is designed, which will produce a large additional force on the human joints during the rehabilitation process. This article proposes a novel cable-driven mechanism with rigid constraint branch, which provides full constraint without additional force.

(a)   (b)

Fig. 3. Cable-driven ankle rehabilitation mechanism: (a) IK; (b) CABLEankle.

Scale optimization needs the support of performance indicators and optimization methods. The performance indicators mainly include: workspace, stiffness, dexterity and cable force [14–16]. Workspace mainly describes the size of the set of poses that the terminal can reach. Stiffness describes the ability of the mechanism to resist external interference. The dexterity is used to measure the transmission accuracy between the input and output motion (force), which is usually evaluated by the condition number of Jacobian matrix. The closer the condition number is to 1, the better the dexterity is. Cable force indicators include: maximum cable force and cable force factor etc. The maximum cable force reflects the maximum tension of the cable during the movement. The smaller the value is, the smaller the rated torque of the drive device is, which can effectively reduce the requirements for driving and improve the lightweight design. Rehabilitation robots do not require high rigidity and move slowly, and indicators such as static workspace, dexterity, and maximum cable force are considered in this paper.

The optimization methods mainly include atlas method and objective function method [17–19]. The atlas method displays the mapping between design parameters and performance indicators intuitively, which reflects the trend of performance change and facilitate the understanding of new configurations. However, the parameters should not exceed 3. The objective function method adopts nonlinear optimization algorithms to solve problems within the design constraints. It can optimize multiple parameters. However, it lacks configuration performance analysis. Due to many parameters of the proposed rehabilitation equipment, a stepwise optimization method will be adopted, and the general performance trend is analyzed.

This paper proposes a new cable-driven parallel ankle rehabilitation device. Unnecessary translational DoFs are constrained by the rigid branch. A four-cable CDPM with cross layout is adopted to increase the range of motion and reduce the volume of the mechanism. The content is arranged as follows: Sect. 2 analyzes the motion requirements of the ankle joint. And a new type of cable-driven parallel ankle rehabilitation mechanism is proposed. In Sect. 3, kinematics and dynamics models are established. The 2-norm minimum method is used to solve the cable tension. In Sect. 4, the stepwise optimization method is used to minimize the maximum cable force. The simulation analysis and verification of the optimized cable tension and dexterity is conducted. Section 5 illustrates the detailed structural design of the mechanism and the conclusion is given finally.

2   Motion Analysis and Mechanism Design

The function of ankle joint can be simplified as a spherical joint, and its complex motion can be approximated by three rotational motions, as illustrated in Fig. 4: plantarflexion and dorsiflexion in the sagittal plane (α), abduction and adduction in the transverse plane (β), inversion and eversion in the frontal plane (γ).

Due to the difference in physiological structure, the ranges of above three rotations may slightly varies from person to person. The motion range is determined based on the reference [20], as shown in Fig. 4. Considering the torques of rehabilitation training, 10 N · m is adopted as the rated rehabilitation torque.

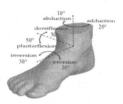

Fig. 4. Morphological motions of the human ankle joint.

According to the vector closed-loop principle, four cables are required to realize the 3 DoFs rotation considering fully constrained. At the same time, a rigid branch is used to restrict the translational DoFs. Among the rotations, the range of α is large, a cross arrangement of cables is adopted to achieve the 80 degrees rotation. The cable-driven parallel ankle rehabilitation mechanism is proposed as shown in Fig. 5. The end effector is labeled as B_1, B_2, B_3, B_4. The base is labeled as A_1, A_2, A_3, A_4. O and O_1 are the two end points of the rigid restraint branch. The four cables move together to realize the rotation of the end effector.

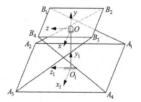

Fig. 5. Cable-driven parallel ankle rehabilitation mechanism.

3   Kinematics and Dynamics

3.1   Kinematics Analysis

The symbols are defined as follows: the fixed coordinate system $O_1 - x_1 y_1 z_1$ and the moving coordinate system $O - xyz$ are attached to the center of the base and the end effector respectively, as shown in Fig. 5. a_i is the position vector of point A_i in the fixed coordinate system. b_i is the position vector of point B_i in the moving coordinate system. $l_i = \overline{B_i A_i}$ ($i = 1, 2, 3, 4$) is the cable vector. $p = \overline{O_1 O}$ represents the vector pointing from O_1 to O. Using static Euler angle description, the moving coordinate system rotates by α angle around the x_1 axis, rotates by the β angle around the y_1 axis, and rotates by the γ angle around the z_1 axis. The rotation matrix R is

$$R = R(z_1, \gamma)R(y_1, \beta)R(x_1, \alpha) \tag{1}$$

The vector chain for the mechanism can be expressed as

$$l_i = a_i - p - Rb_i, \ i = 1, 2, 3, 4 \tag{2}$$

The length of the ith cable can be deduced as

$$l_i = \|l_i\| = \left\|\overline{A_i B_i}\right\|, \ i = 1, 2, 3, 4 \tag{3}$$

Dot product with l_i at both sides and take the derivative of Eq. (3) with respect to time. The velocity of the ith cable can be written as

$$\dot{l}_i = -l_i^T \dot{R} b_i / l_i \tag{4}$$

where $\dot{R} = \omega \times R$ is the derivatives of R. Substitute $\dot{R} = \omega \times R$ into Eq. (4) and organize it into matrix form as.

$$\dot{l} = J\omega \tag{5}$$

where $\dot{l}, J, \omega$ are defined as

$$\dot{l} = \begin{bmatrix} \dot{l}_1 & \dot{l}_2 & \dot{l}_3 & \dot{l}_4 \end{bmatrix}^T, \ \omega = \begin{bmatrix} \omega_x & \omega_y & \omega_z \end{bmatrix}^T = \begin{bmatrix} \dot{\alpha} & \dot{\beta} & \dot{\gamma} \end{bmatrix}^T,$$
$$J = \begin{bmatrix} (-Rb_1 \times l_1)^T/l_1 & (-Rb_2 \times l_2)^T/l_2 & (-Rb_3 \times l_3)^T/l_3 & (-Rb_4 \times l_4)^T/l_4 \end{bmatrix}^T \tag{6}$$

In Eq. (5), ω is the speed vector of the end effector, and J is the Jacobian matrix. According to Eq. (5), we can analyze the change of cable length.

3.2   Dynamics Analysis

Dynamics is the basis of drive matching and detailed design. The end effector is subjected to the pulling force F_i of the four cables, the gravity G, the supporting force N, and the external moment M_e. The moment balance equation can be expressed as

$$\sum_{i=1}^{4} (Rb_i \times F_i) + M_e - I\dot{\omega} - \omega \times (I\omega) = 0 \tag{7}$$

where the $F_i = f_i \cdot l_i/l_i$ is the tension vector of the ith cable. f_i represents the scalar of the cable tension. I is the inertia tensor of the end effector at point O, and ω is the angular velocity of the end effector.

Arranging Eq. (7) into the form of a matrix gives

$$QT = W \tag{8}$$

where $Q = \begin{bmatrix} Rb_1 \times l_1/l_1 & Rb_2 \times l_2/l_2 & Rb_3 \times l_3/l_3 & Rb_4 \times l_4/l_4 \end{bmatrix}$ is the structure matrix. $T = \begin{bmatrix} f_1 & f_2 & f_3 & f_4 \end{bmatrix}^T$ is the cable force vector. $W = -M_e + I\dot{\omega} + \omega \times (I\omega)$ is the external force matrix.

Because this mechanism is redundant in drive, there will be an infinite number of cable force solutions. This problem is usually transformed into the tension optimization. In this article, the minimum 2-norm of cable forces are adopted, which can be summarized as the following optimization problem with $T_{\min} = 5$ N and $T_{\max} = 300$ N:

Objective function:

$$\min_{T} \|T\|_2 \tag{9}$$

Constraints:

$$\begin{cases} QT = W \\ 0 \le T_{\min} \le T \le T_{\max} \end{cases} \tag{10}$$

4 Optimization

4.1 Parameters and Methods

The parameters that need to be optimized are: $c = \|\overline{B_1B_4}\|$, $c' = \|\overline{B_1B_2}\|$, $p = \|\overline{A_2A_3}\|$, $q = \|\overline{A_1A_2}\|$ and $e = \|\overline{O_1O}\|$. Based on c, all the parameters that need to be optimized are transformed into dimensionless parameters: c_w, k_1, k_2 and e_w. Value ranges of the parameters and the discrete step length ε are shown in Table 1.

$$c_w = c'/c, \ k_1 = p/c, \ k_2 = q/c, \ e_w = e/c \tag{11}$$

Table 1. Value range of parameters and discretization step ε.

	c_w	k_1	k_2	e_w
Lower bound	1.50	0.45	0.75	1.00
Upper bound	2.25	2.00	3.00	2.00
ε	0.075	0.155	0.225	0.020

The parameters can be divided into two groups and optimized by group. The parameters c_w, k_1 and k_2 determine the specific position of the cable connection points on the end effector plane and the base plane and belong to the group 1, while e_w determines the relative distance between these two planes and belongs to the group 2. First use the atlas method to optimize the parameter c_w, k_1 and k_2, and then optimize e_w.

4.2   Results and Analysis

The maximum cable force simulation result is shown in Fig. 6 when the initial value of e_w is 1.25. Three coordinate axes represent the parameters to be optimized c_w, k_1 and k_2. The color of the points represents the maximum cable force F_{max} during the three independent rotations. It can be seen from Fig. 6(a) that the maximum cable force value is also reduced with the decrease of k_1 and k_2, while the influence of c_w is not obvious. Figure 6(b) shows the candidate region where the maximum cable force below 100 N. We select the point where the maximum cable force index achieves the minimum value. The corresponding parameter value is: $c_w = 1.65$, $k_1 = 0.765$, $k_2 = 0.75$.

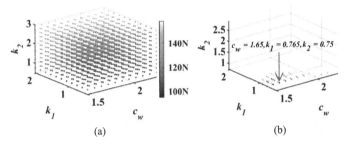

(a)   (b)

Fig. 6. Optimization results: (a) maximum cable force; (b) candidate region.

After above parameters are determined, the optimal value of e_w is analyzed. As shown in Fig. 7, the maximum cable force curve has an inflection point when $e_w = 1.35$, so it is chosen. After obtaining dimensionless values of these parameters, we can determine the specific size of each parameter of the mechanism by giving c a value. Considering that the overall size should not be too large, we give $c = 0.2$ m and the other parameters can be calculated accordingly as:

$$c' = 0.33\,\text{m}, p = 0.153\,\text{m}, q = 0.15\,\text{m}, e = 0.27\,\text{m}$$

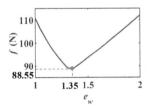

Fig. 7. Influence of parameter e_w on the maximum cable force.

4.3   Cable Force Simulation

In order to verify the optimized mechanism, the cable force is simulated. Cable forces are deduced and shown in Fig. 8. It can be seen that the cable forces during the adduction/abduction and inversion/eversion movement are relatively larger than the cable forces during the plantarflexion/dorsiflexion movement. Considering all three motions, the cable tension was maintained below 90N.

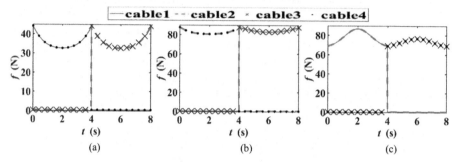

Fig. 8. Cable force of optimized mechanism: (a) cable force in dorsiflexion/plantarflexion; (b) cable force in abduction/adduction; (c) cable force in inversion/eversion.

4.4 Dexterity Simulation

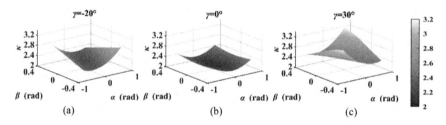

Fig. 9. Dexterity analysis results: (a) $\gamma = -20°$; (b) $\gamma=0°$; (c) $\gamma=30°$.

The dexterity is measured by the condition number of the Jacobian matrix, which is defined as

$$\kappa = \sigma_{max}/\sigma_{min} \tag{12}$$

where σ_{max} and σ_{min} are the largest and smallest singular values of the Jacobian matrix $\boldsymbol{J}$. They can be calculated as

$$\sigma_i = \sqrt{\lambda_i \boldsymbol{J}^T \boldsymbol{J}} \tag{13}$$

where λ_i is the eigenvalue of the matrix $\boldsymbol{J}^T \boldsymbol{J}$. The closer the condition number κ is to 1, the better the dexterity of the mechanism is. Figure 9 shows the condition number distribution of $\boldsymbol{J}$ when $\gamma = -20°, 0°, 30°$. It can be seen that the value of the condition number is small, and gradually increases with the increase of the rotation angle of the mechanism without drastic changes.

5 Detailed Design

Based on the above analysis, detailed mechanism design is implemented.

Servo motors are selected depending on the required torque, which can be calculated as

$$\tau = F_{max}r \tag{14}$$

where F_{max} is the maximum required cable force and r is the radius of winch.

In this research, the maximum cable force after optimization is 88 N and the radius of winch is designed as 25 mm. The safety factor is selected as 2. Therefore, the rated output torque of the motor need to be larger than 4.4 N · m. The eBob70I servo motor from ZeroErr is selected. Its rated torque is 7.8 N · m. The actuating component consists of motors and winches. Spiral grooves are machined on the winches for better spooling of cables. As is shown in Fig. 10, pulley component is composed of the fixed pulleys for guiding cables and the combined V-groove pulleys to achieve large swing angle of cables and avoid detachment.

Combined V-groove pulley   Hooke

Rotation shaft

Fixed pulley   Strut

Fig. 10. Pulley component.   **Fig. 11.** Rigid branch component.

Inclined plane   Rigid restraint component

End effector

Motor

Pulley

Winch   Pedestal

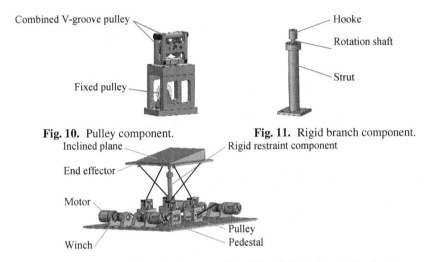

Fig. 12. Detailed design of cable-driven parallel ankle rehabilitation mechanism.

The rigid restraint branch component consists of the hooke joint, the rotation joint and the strut, as is shown in Fig. 11. The hooke joint realizes Pitch and Roll, and the rotation joint realizes Yaw. The two joints form an equivalent spherical joint with larger rotation ranges. The rigid restraint branch component restricts the translational DoFs of the ankle and solves the problem of incomplete restraint in [12]. At the same time, the combination of hooke joint and rotation joint is easier to manufacture and assemble than traditional spherical joint.

The pedal is an inclined plane with an angle of 10°, which is attached on the end effector. The incline is designed to make α symmetrical. Figure 12 shows the virtual prototype of the cable-driven parallel ankle rehabilitation mechanism, which can realize the three rotational DoFs rehabilitation.

6 Conclusion

In this paper, a new cable-driven parallel mechanism is proposed for the ankle rehabilitation exercise to improve the performance of existing devices. In order to achieve an interpretable optimization based on the performance analysis of the new mechanism, design parameters are divided into two groups. A stepwise optimization design method is established, and the maximum cable force is minimized.

The effectiveness of the optimization is verified by simulation, and the virtual prototype design of the ankle rehabilitation device is completed. The optimization method established in this paper provides an effective path for the design of other cable-driven parallel robots. At the same time, a new rehabilitation device is proposed with good performance. Researches on prototype development and control of the device will be carried out in the future.

Acknowledgement. This work was supported by the National Natural Science Foundation of China (grant number U19A20101).

References

1. Schmidt, H., Werner, C., Bernhardt, R., Hesse, S., Kruger, J.: Gait rehabilitation machines based on programmable footplates. J. NeuroEng. Rehabil. **4**, 1–7 (2007)
2. Hesse, S., Tomelleri CzBardeleben, A., Werner, C., Waldner, A.: Robot-assisted practice of gait and stair climbing in nonambulatory stroke patients. J. Rehabil. Res. Dev. **49**, 613–622 (2012)
3. Wang, Z., Cui, L., et al.: Modeling analysis and structural design of human lower limb rehabilitation robot (2018)
4. Duschau-Wicke, A., Caprez, A., Riener, R.: Patient-cooperative control increases active participation of individuals with SCI during robot-aided gait training. J. NeuroEng. Rehabil. **7**, 13 (2010)
5. Veneman, J., Kruidhof, R., Hekman, E., Ekkelenkamp, R., Van Asseldonk, E., van der Kooij, H.: Design and evaluation of the LOPES exoskeleton robot for interactive gait rehabilitation. IEEE Trans. Neural Syst. Rehabil. Eng. **15**(3), 379–386 (2007)
6. Van Asseldonk, E.H.F., Ekkelenkamp, R., Veneman, J.F.Z., Van der Helm, F.C.T., van der Kooij, H.: Selective control of a subtask of walking in a robotic gait trainer(LOPES). In: 2007 IEEE 10th International Conference on Rehabilitation Robotics, vols. 1 and 2, pp. 841–848 (2007)
7. Kazerooni, H., Steger, R., Huang, L.: Hybrid control of the Berkeley Lower Extremity Exoskeleton (BLEEX). Int. J. Robot. Res. **25**(5–6), 561–573 (2006)
8. Schmidt, H.: Hapticwalker-a novel haptic device for walking simulation. In: Proceedings of EuroHaptics, Tokyo, Japan, pp. 66–67 (2004)
9. Saglia, J.A., Tsagarakis, N.G., Dai, J.S., Caldwell, D.G.: A high-performance redundantly actuated parallel mechanism for ankle rehabilitation. Int. J. Robot. Res. **28**(9), 1216–1227 (2009)
10. Wang, C., Fang, Y., Guo. S., et al.: Design and kinematical performance analysis of a 3-rus/rrr redundantly actuated parallel mechanism for ankle rehabilitation. J. Mech. Robot. **5**, 041003 (2013)

11. Jamwal, P.K., Aw, K.C., Xie, S.Q., Tsoi, Y.H.: Multi-criteria optimal design of cable driven ankle rehabilitation robot. In: Mobile Robots-State of the Art in Land, Sea, Air, and Collaborative Missions. INTECH Open Access Publisher, London (2009)

12. Shahrol, M.N., Basah, S.N., Basaruddin, K.S., Ahmad, W.K.W., Ahmad, S.A.: Modelling of a Cable-driven ankle rehabilitation robot. J. Telecommun. Electron. Comput. Eng. **10**, 53–59 (2018)

13. Russo, M., Ceccarelli, M.: Analysis of a wearable robotic system for ankle rehabilitation. Machines **8**(3), 48 (2020)

14. Gouttefarde, M., Gosselin, C.: Analysis of the wrench-closure workspace of planar parallel cable-driven mechanisms. IEEE Trans. Rob. **22**(3), 434–445 (2006)

15. Quintero-Riaza, H., Mejía-Calderón, L., Díaz-Rodríguez, M.: Synthesis of planar parallel manipulators including dexterity, force transmission and stiffness index. Mech. Based Design Struct. Mach. **47**(6), 680–702 (2019)

16. Lamine, H., Laribi, M., Bennour, S., Romdhane, L., Zeghloul, S.: Structure optimization of the cable driven legs trainer. In: Ferraresi, C., Quaglia, G. (eds.) Advances in Service and Industrial Robotics, pp. 691–698. Springer International Publishing, Cham (2018). https://doi.org/10.1007/978-3-319-61276-8_73

17. Gao, Z., Zhang, D., Ge, Y.: Design optimization of a spatial six degree-of-freedom parallel manipulator based on artificial intelligence approaches. Robot. Comput.-Integr. Manuf. **26**(2), 180–189 (2010)

18. Liu, X.J., Wang, J.S.: A new methodology for optimal kinematic design of parallel mechanisms. Mech. Mach. Theory **42**(9), 1210–1224 (2007)

19. Shao, Z.F., Tamg, X.Q., Wang, L.P., et al.: Atlas based kinematic optimum design of the stewart parallel manipulator. Chin. J. Mech. Eng. **28**(1), 20–28 (2015)

20. Brockett, C.L., Chapman, G.J.: Biomechanics of the ankle. Orthop. Trauma **30**, 232–238 (2016)

Human-Centered Wearable Robotics

Flexible Non-contact Capacitive Sensing for Hand Gesture Recognition

Tiantong Wang[1,3], Yunbiao Zhao[1,3], and Qining Wang[1,2,3(✉)]

[1] Department of Advanced Manufacturing and Robotics, College of Engineering, Peking University, Beijing 100871, China
qiningwang@pku.edu.cn
[2] Institute for Artificial Intelligence, Peking University, Beijing 100871, China
[3] Beijing Engineering Research Center of Intelligent Rehabilitation Engineering, Beijing 100871, China

Abstract. Hand gesture recognition has become a popular research topic of human machine interface (HMI), and effective wearable sensor is an important component in the loop of hand gesture recognition system. In this paper, we introduce a flexible non-contact capacitive wristband that can be used to detect both wrist and finger gestures. To demonstrate the effectiveness and performance of the designed prototype, nine wrist gestures and ten finger gestures were selected. Five subjects participated in the experiment. To validate the importance of considering spacial relationship among channels, especially when discriminating intricate finger gestures, CNN was implemented and compared with LDA. In the wrist gesture recognition task, LDA achieved the average accuracy of 98.38%, and CNN achieved the average accuracy of 99.81%. In the finger gesture recognition task, LDA achieved the average accuracy of 90.04%, and CNN achieved the average accuracy of 95.54%. This study suggested that the designed flexible non-contact capacitive wristband could be used as an alternative for hand gesture recognition, and considering spacial relationship among channels on different measuring location yields better recognition result.

Keywords: Capacitive sensing · Hand gesture recognition · Pattern recognition

1 Introduction

Hand gesture recognition has become a popular research topic in the realm of human machine interface (HMI), it can be used in the areas of upper extremity rehabilitation, virtual reality/augmented reality, human machine interaction and

This work was supported by the National Key R & D Program of China (No. 2018YFB1307302), the National Natural Science Foundation of China (No. 51922015, No. 91948302), PKU-Baidu Fund (No. 2020BD008) and the Beijing Natural Science Foundation (No. L182001).

X.-J. Liu et al. (Eds.): ICIRA 2021, LNAI 13013, pp. 611–621, 2021.
https://doi.org/10.1007/978-3-030-89095-7_58

so on. Comparing to the vision-based hand gesture recognition system, system based on wearable electronic devices is not limited by the source of light, location of space, and is less intrusive to the users, thus is a promising approach for long-term hand gesture detection.

Inertial measurement unit (IMU) is widely used in hand gesture recognition tasks [1]. However, it only measures kinetic characteristic of movements, thus mostly it is used for recognizing dynamic hand gestures, which involve large-scale arm/wrist movement during the gesture. In the purpose of recognizing static hand gestures, sEMG signal is integrated together with 3D accelerometer to recognize complex hand gestures and is applied in virtual game control [2]. sEMG signal may suffer from electrode shift after re-wearing or long-time use. When the electrode shifts, it will severely affect the recognition result of the classifier, because the obtained signal will become so different from the original one [3]. This shortcoming could be alleviated by the usage of high density sEMG (HD-sEMG) sensors [4]. Because HD-sEMG sensors are able to cover a large area of the target skin, it may be invariant to the shift of the electrodes. Since HD-sEMG sensor records myoelectric activity from a specific muscle or muscle group, it has specific placement location requirement, therefore could be inconvenient for daily use.

Finger angles could directly reflect the type of hand gestures which are being performed, measuring the degree of bending of fingers provides rich information for gesture recognition tasks. Based on this idea, various data gloves are designed [5,6]. These gloves are able to distinguish multiple finger gestures and even are able to accomplish complex sign language translation. In spite of the powerful functions of the data gloves, they prevent the fingers from free movement. Therefore, data gloves are not the best choice for gesture recognition systems.

Subtle muscle and tendon movements of different gestures could be reflected by the fluctuation detected by pressure sensors placed around the wrist, and the wristband around the wrist is less cumbersome for daily use. Therefore, pressure sensors based on capacitor [7] and resister [8] are deeply researched. Even though the pressure sensor wristbands are easy to wear, most of them use rigid capacitive/resistive sensors, which are not comfortable for the wearers. A novel non-contact capacitive sensing method is proposed [9] and used in upper limb gesture recognition [10], nine wrist gestures are recognized by the armband. Non-contact capacitive sensors are sensitive, and can detect very slight muscle movements. However, the armband in [10] is made by rigid copper films and is placed on upper part of forearm, thus it is not able to detect finger movements.

To recognize both wrist and finger gestures, a flexible non-contact capacitive sensing front-end was designed, and two classification strategies were implemented and analyzed. Five subjects participated in the experiment. The designed prototype was wrapped around subject's wrist to measure the tendon deformation when performing gestures. Nine wrist gestures and ten finger gestures were selected to validate the effectiveness of the prototype. The vanilla LDA was firstly used as the classification tool. Being enlightened by the idea of HD-sEMG, which considers the spacial correlation between channels on different measurement locations, we also formed the signals from five channels into signal images, then used CNN as an automatic spacial feature extractor and classifier. The classification results of the two strategies were compared.

2   Method

2.1   Flexible Non-contact Capacitive Sensing System

This study designed a flexible capacitive sensing system to detect tendon deformation when performing different types of wrist and hand gestures, as shown in Fig. 1.

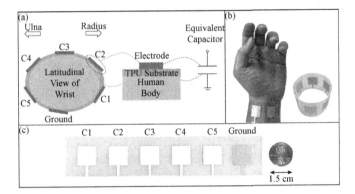

Fig. 1. Overview of the flexible capacitive sensing system: (a) The sensing principle of the flexible capacitive sensing system. (b) the sensing system is placed on the wrist of one subject and (c) the optical image of the sensing system.

As described in [9] and Fig. 1(a), the human skin is considered as a large conductor and can be perceived as one electrode of the capacitive sensor, the space between skin and electrodes is separated by a combination of air and substrate, which serves as dielectric of the capacitor, and the conductive ink printed on the other side of the substrate serves as the other electrode of the capacitor. When hand gestures are performed, the deformation of surface of the wrist causes the thickness change of the dielectric, which immediately causes capacitance change of the capacitive sensor. The fluctuation of the capacitance measurement directly reflects the features of various wrist/finger gestures. Figure 1(b) shows the placement of the flexible capacitive sensor on human wrist.

The optical image of the sensor is shown in Fig. 1(c). The overall size of the prototype is 15.5 cm × 3 cm. The electrodes were screen-printed on 100 μm-thick thermoplastic polyurethanes (TPU) substrate using conductive ink, and cured in oven at 80 °C for 4 h. There are 6 printed electrodes in total, five (which are sensing channels) on the same side of the TPU substrate and one (which is connected to ground) on the other side of the TPU substrate. Each electrode has the size of 1.5 cm × 1.5 cm, and is 1 cm apart from each other. The ground channel is placed directly onto human skin, while the other five channels form five capacitors with human skin.

The capacitance signal was measured by PCAP01AD, and all sensor data were sampled 100 Hz and transmitted to a computer through a 2.4-GHz wireless module.

2.2   Experimental Procedure

Five healthy subjects (3 males, 2 females) with an average age of 25.2 participated in the study. All subjects were provided informed written consents and the experiments had been approved by the Local Ethics Committee of Peking University.

Due to the obvious deformation of the tendons around the wrist when conducting wrist and finger gestures, we placed the flexible sensing system around participants' wrist to detect and recognize wrist/finger gestures as shown in Fig. 1(b). Each participant was given thorough guidance to understand the experimental process.

In order to give more comprehensive evaluation of the sensing system, we selected nine wrist gestures (gesture set 1) and ten finger gestures (gesture set 2) as our gesture sets. Nine wrist gestures were studied and recognized in [10] and shown in Fig. 2 (a): relax (R), wrist flexion/extension (WF/WE), wrist pronation/supination (WP/WS), wrist radius/ulna deviation (RD/UD), fist (F) and palm (P).

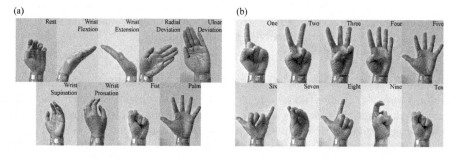

Fig. 2. Wrist and finger gestures: (a) Nine wrist gestures, which contains relax (R), wrist flexion/extension (WF/WE), wrist pronation/supination (WP/WS), wrist radius/ulna deviation (RD/UD), fist (F) and palm (P), and (b) Ten finger gestures, which contains Chinese number gestures from one to ten.

Ten finger gestures are Chinese number gestures, which were studied in [11] and shown in Fig. 2 (b).

For both gesture sets, five trials were conducted. In each trial, the subjects were asked to stay in the relax state (R) for 3–4 s, and performed the corresponding gesture to their maximum extent following the instructions. After maintaining the gesture for a few seconds (about 4 s), the subject returned to the relax state and remained still for a further 3–4 s, then performed the next instructed gesture. The procedure was repeated until all the gestures in this gesture set were performed. To avoid muscle fatigue, the participants took a rest of 1 min between each trial if they wanted to.

2.3 Data Processing Framework

The data preprocessing and gesture recognition framework is depicted in Fig. 3. The framework contains two parts: training process and testing process. In the training process, the raw data is preprocessed and fed into the classifier for training, while in the testing process, the raw data is preprocessed and fed into the already-trained classifier for recognition.

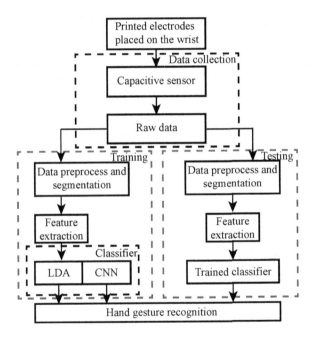

Fig. 3. Data preprocessing and gesture recognition framework.

For the classifier, we firstly considered LDA, which is easy to implement and train. However, the spacial relationship between each channel is not considered in the LDA classifier, thus we further explored CNN classifier, which extracts spacial features automatically.

Data Preprocessing. In the data preprocessing step, all the collected data was labelled manually and passed through a 4th order Butterworth low pass filter with the cut-off frequency at 0.5 Hz to filter out noise. Then the data was segmented by a sliding window with window length of 200 ms and step size of 1 ms. Since the signal was sampled 100 Hz, each window contained 20 data samples.

Feature Extraction. For the LDA classifier, we extracted 4 time-domain features for each channel in each window: $ave(\mathbf{x})$, $std(\mathbf{x})$, $tan(\mathbf{x})$ and $max(\mathbf{x})$, in which $\mathbf{x}$ is the data vector in each sliding window of one channel. $ave(\mathbf{x})$ is the average value, $std(\mathbf{x})$ is the standard deviation, $max(\mathbf{x})$ is the maximum value, and $tan(x) = [\mathbf{x}(end)\text{-}\mathbf{x}(1)]/WinLen$, where WinLen is the length of the sliding window, $\mathbf{x}(end)$ and $\mathbf{x}(1)$ denote the last and the first value of the sliding window, respectively [10]. After the feature extraction procedure, each data vector was transformed to a feature vector with the size of $(1, 20)$.

For the CNN classifier, in order to take the spacial relationship between each channel into consideration, we used the signal image formation algorithm proposed in [12] to make every channel have a chance to be adjacent to every other channel, which enables CNN to extract hidden correlations between neighboring channels. Since there are 5 channels in total, according to the algorithm in [12], each output signal image has the size of $(20, 11)$. After that, the signal image was normalized by the maximum pixel in each image.

Classification. The processed data samples were divided into a training set and a testing set by 5-fold cross-validation. Before being fed into LDA classifier for training, the feature vectors were subtracted by the average value of the training data and divided by the standard deviation of the training data.

The CNN architecture consists of two convolutional layers, one spacial dropout layer, one max pooling layer, one fully connected layer, and one output layer. The first convolutional layer has 32 kernels with the size of 3×3 and uses relu as the activation function, The second convolutional layer has 64 kernels with the size of 3×3 and also uses relu as the activation function, the spacial dropout layer has the dropout rate of 0.3, the max pooling layer uses the kernel with the size of 2×2, after that, the output of the max pooling layer is flattened and input to the fully connected layer with 50 neurons, then the fully connected layer is connected to the final output layer.

3 Results

3.1 Time Domain Waveforms of Two Gesture Sets

The time domain waveforms of gesture set 1 (wrist gestures) and gesture set 2 (finger gestures) are shown in Fig. 4(a) and Fig. 4(b), respectively.

As we can see in both figures, the capacitance between each channel and human skin is roughly around 100–200 pF, and the sharp change of the signal can be observed when switching from one gesture to another. Because each channel covers different spots around the wrist, the thickness of the dielectric

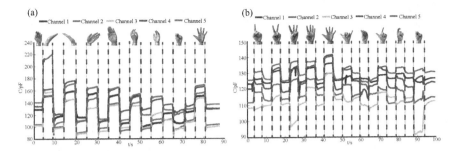

Fig. 4. Time domain waveform of: (a) gesture set 1 (wrist gestures) and (b) gesture set 2 (finger gestures).

of the equivalent capacitor changes differently, which results in different shape and magnitude of the waveform during one particular gesture. Due to different tendon shapes of different gestures, the waveform differences between gestures are easily observed, which lays a solid foundation for us to discriminate various gestures.

3.2   Classification Result on Gesture Set 1

The confusion matrix was constructed to evaluate the recognition ability of the classifier. The labels in each row of the confusion matrix denote the ground truth, and the labels in each column of the confusion matrix denote the predicted gestures. The diagonal elements represent the percentage of correctly classified samples, while the off-diagonal elements represent the percentage of mis-classified samples. The confusion matrix was averaged out among five subjects for each gesture set and each classifier.

The confusion matrix of gesture set 1 using LDA classifier is shown in Fig. 5(a). The recognition accuracies of R, WF, WE, RD, UD, WS, WP, F, P are 100.00%, 92.76%, 99.94%, 99.64%, 93.19%, 99.91%, 100.00%, 99.96%, 100.00%, respectively, with an average accuracy of 98.38%. It is clear to observe that the highest recognition accuracy can reach 100.00%, with the corresponding gestures R, WP, P. The recognition accuracies of WF and UD are relatively low, which do not reach 95%. Since the wrist gestures are easy to distinguish, the classification accuracy of each gesture is above 90%.

The confusion matrix of gesture set 1 using CNN classifier is shown in Fig. 5(b). The recognition accuracies of R, WF, WE, RD, UD, WS, WP, F, P are 100.00%, 100.00%, 99.81%, 99.74%, 99.30%, 99.98%, 100.00%, 99.41%, 100.00%, respectively, with an average accuracy of 99.81%. Taking the advantage of the excellent spacial feature extraction ability of CNN classifier, the classification accuracy of each gesture is above 99%.

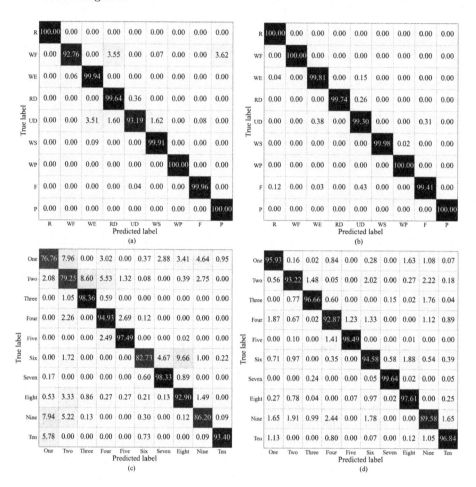

Fig. 5. The confusion matrix (%) of: (a) gesture set 1 using LDA classifier, (b) gesture set 1 using CNN classifier, (c) gesture set 2 using LDA classifier and (d) gesture set 2 using CNN classifier.

3.3   Classification Result on Gesture Set 2

The confusion matrix of gesture set 2 using LDA classifier is shown in Fig. 5(c). The recognition accuracies of one, two, three, four, five, six, seven, eight, nine, ten are 76.76%, 79.25%, 98.36%, 94.93%, 97.49%, 82.73%, 98.33%, 92.90%, 86.20%, 93.40%, respectively, with an average accuracy of 90.04%. It is clear to observe that with the increase of complexity of the hand gestures, the classification accuracy of each gesture decreases correspondingly, and the low classification accuracy is achieved by gesture one and two, with the accuracy of 76.76% and 79.25%.

The confusion matrix of gesture set 2 using CNN classifier is shown in Fig. 5(d). The recognition accuracies of one, two, three, four, five, six, seven, eight, nine, ten are 95.93%, 93.22%, 96.66%, 92.87%, 98.49%, 94.58%, 99.64%, 97.61%, 89.58%, 96.84%, respectively, with an average accuracy of 95.54%. The overall accuracy increases sharply comparing to LDA classifier for gesture set 2. Most of the classification accuracies are above 90%, except from gesture nine, which has the accuracy of 89.58%.

3.4   Comparison of Classification Result Between LDA and CNN

In order to directly compare the classification result between LDA classifier and CNN classifier, the average classification accuracies for each subject based on gesture set 1, gesture set 2, LDA, and CNN are plotted in Fig. 6.

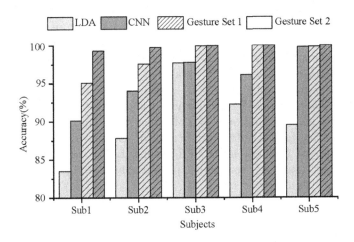

Fig. 6. The average classification result comparison between LDA and CNN of all subjects.

For subject 1, the average accuracies of LDA on gesture set 1 and 2 are 95.08% ± 0.40% and 83.50% ± 0.58% respectively, the average accuracies of CNN on gesture set 1 and 2 are 99.30% ± 0.42% and 90.12% ± 2.81% respectively. For subject 2, the average accuracies of LDA on gesture set 1 and 2 are 97.60% ± 0.55% and 87.81% ± 1.40% respectively, the average accuracies of CNN on gesture set 1 and 2 are 99.76% ± 0.26% and 94.02% ± 1.77% respectively. For subject 3, the average accuracies of LDA on gesture set 1 and 2 are 99.95% ± 0.04% and 97.72% ± 0.30% respectively, the average accuracies of CNN on gesture set 1 and 2 are 99.98% ± 0.03% and 97.82% ± 1.12% respectively. For subject 4, the average accuracies of LDA on gesture set 1 and 2 are 100.00% ± 0.00% and 92.30% ± 0.40% respectively, the average accuracies of CNN on gesture set 1 and 2 are 100.00% ± 0.00% and 96.16% ± 1.52% respectively. For subject 5, the average accuracies of LDA on gesture set 1 and 2 are 99.83% ± 0.05% and 89.52% ± 1.01% respectively, the average accuracies of CNN on gesture set 1 and 2 are 99.99% ± 0.02% and 99.79% ± 0.25% respectively.

4   Discussion

The purpose of the experiments is to evaluate the wrist/finger gesture recognition ability of the designed sensing prototype, and to compare two classification strategies.

In order to evaluate the hand gesture recognition ability of the prototype, nine wrist gestures and ten finger gestures were selected as target gestures, and 5 subjects were recruited. The classification result of gesture set 1 achieves the accuracy over 98% using both LDA and CNN. However, when switching to gesture set 2, which involves more complex finger gestures, the classification accuracy of CNN clearly outperforms that of LDA.

As we can see from the classification result in Fig. 6, when considering the spacial relationship between channels using CNN classifier, the classification accuracy achieves comparable performance in some cases (gesture set 1 for subject 3, 4, and 5) and rises notably in rest of the cases comparing with the vanilla LDA classifier for both gesture set 1 and gesture set 2. We notice that most cases where LDA classifier and CNN classifier achieve similar average accuracy occur in the recognition of gesture set 1, which consists of easily distinguishable wrist tendon deformation. However, when it comes to the finger gestures with slight wrist tendon deformation, CNN classifier gives much better classification performance. This indicates the importance of the consideration of the signal distribution among different measure locations. If the sensor is manufactured with high density and high sensitivity, presumably more intricate gestures will be recognized with higher accuracy.

5   Conclusion

In this study, a flexible non-contact capacitive sensing system is proposed and two sets of hand gestures are recognized. The study shows that our sensing prototype is able to realize the recognition task of both wrist gestures and finger gestures with high classification accuracy. Also, two classification algorithms (LDA and CNN) are implemented and compared. We find that in the finger gestures recognition task, in which the wrist tendon deformation is slight, CNN classifier can achieve much higher average classification accuracy than LDA classifier. In the future, we will consider designing the capacitive sensor with large density and high sensitivity, and apply it to the accurate control of upper limb prosthesis.

References

1. Xie, R., Cao, J.: Accelerometer-based hand gesture recognition by neural network and similarity matching. IEEE Sens. J. **16**(11), 4537–4545 (2016). https://doi.org/10.1109/JSEN.2016.2546942

2. Xu, Z., Xiang, C., Wang, W.H., Yang, J., Wang, K.: Hand gesture recognition and virtual game control based on 3d accelerometer and EMG sensors. In: Proceedings of the 2009 International Conference on Intelligent User Interfaces, pp. 401–406. Association for Computing Machinery, Sanibel Island, Florida, USA (2009). https://doi.org/10.1145/1502650.1502708

3. Vidovic, M.M., Hwang, H., Amsuss, S., Hahne, J.M., Farina, D., Muller, K.: Improving the robustness of myoelectric pattern recognition for upper limb prostheses by covariate shift adaptation. IEEE Trans. Neural Syst. Rehabil. Eng. **24**(9), 961–970 (2016). https://doi.org/10.1109/TNSRE.2015.2492619

4. Wu, L., Zhang, X., Wang, K., Chen, X., Chen, X.: Improved high-density myoelectric pattern recognition control against electrode shift using data augmentation and dilated convolutional neural network. IEEE Trans. Neural Syst. Rehab. Eng. **28**(12), 2637–2646 (2020). https://doi.org/10.1109/TNSRE.2020.3030931

5. Yuan, G., Liu, X., Yan, Q., Qiao, S., Wang, Z., Yuan, L.: Hand gesture recognition using deep feature fusion network based on wearable sensors. IEEE Sens. J. **21**(1), 539–547 (2021). https://doi.org/10.1109/JSEN.2020.3014276

6. Chen, X., et al.: A wearable hand rehabilitation system with soft gloves. IEEE Trans. Ind. Inf. **17**(2), 943–952 (2021). https://doi.org/10.1109/TII.2020.3010369

7. Liang, X., Heidari, H., Dahiya, R.: Wearable capacitive-based wrist-worn gesture sensing system. In: 2017 New Generation of CAS (NGCAS), pp. 181–184. IEEE, Genova, Italy (2017). https://doi.org/10.1109/NGCAS.2017.80

8. Zhang, Y., Liu, B., Liu, Z.: Recognizing hand gestures with pressure-sensor-based motion sensing. IEEE Trans. Biomed. Circuits Syst. **13**(6), 1425–1436 (2019)

9. Zheng, E., Wang, L., Wei, K., Wang, Q.: A noncontact capacitive sensing system for recognizing locomotion modes of transtibial amputees. IEEE Trans. Biomed. Eng. **61**(12), 2911–2920 (2014). https://doi.org/10.1109/TBME.2014.2334316

10. Zheng, E., Mai, J., Liu, Y., Wang, Q.: Forearm motion recognition with noncontact capacitive sensing. Front. Neurorobotics **12**, 47 (2018). https://doi.org/10.3389/fnbot.2018.00047

11. Zhu, Y., Jiang, S., Shull, P.B.: Wrist-worn hand gesture recognition based on barometric pressure sensing. In: 2018 IEEE 15th International Conference on Wearable and Implantable Body Sensor Networks (BSN), pp. 181–184. IEEE, Las Vegas, NV, USA (2018). https://doi.org/10.1109/BSN.2018.8329688

12. Jiang, W., Yin, Z.: Human activity recognition using wearable sensors by deep convolutional neural networks. In: ACM International Conference on Multimedia, pp. 1307–1310. Association for Computing Machinery, New York (2015). https://doi.org/10.1145/2733373.2806333

A Novel Design of Electro-hydraulic Driven Active Powered Ankle-Foot Prosthesis

Qitao Huang[✉], Bowen Li, Fei Jia, and Peng Wang

Harbin Institute of Technology, Harbin 150000, China
19s108212@stu.hit.edu.cn

Abstract. This paper presents the design and control architecture of a full active powered ankle prosthesis driven by electro-hydrostatic actuator (EHA) to improve amputee gait during the level-ground walking in full-time gait cycle. A 100 W brushless DC motor driving a 0.92 cc/rev bi-directional gear pump serves as the power kernel. An elastic element is configured in series connection with the hydraulic cylinder as energy store unit. With this architecture, better power characteristic, ability of energy storage and passive compliance were obtained to revive sound human characteristic as much as possible. To smooth the gait pattern, a neuromuscular model with Hill-type muscle tendon structure is introduced into the control system scheduled by finite state machine which was designed to carry on different control strategy during individual gait phase. The overall simulation was established utilizing MATLAB/Simulink platform to validate its feasibility.

Keywords: Ankle-foot prosthesis · EHA · Hill-type muscle model

1 Introduction

Millions of people are suffering from lower limb amputations worldwide, including 1.6 million in China alone, while the number is continuously growing due to illness and accidental injury. Wearing prosthesis is the most effective way to restore basic daily activities under the current medical level. Conventional passive prosthesis is designed utilizing a series of composite materials which can storage and release energy during locomotion [1]. This kind of prosthesis duplicate the function of human tendon having advantages of small size and light weight, but obviously, has shortcoming of lacking the ability of provide motivation. This results in amputees with passive ankle-foot prosthesis having lower walking speed, more energy consumption and distinctly asymmetric gait pattern especially for unilateral transtibial amputees [2].

To overcome the defects of the passive prosthesis, powered prosthesis, putting forward by researchers a few decades ago, is enjoying rapid development in recent years which have the able to duplicate the kinematic and kinetic characteristics of the human body one step further [3].

When it comes to active or rather powered domain, power to mass/volume ratio turns into the maximal limitation. According to research [4], the below-knee complex of a medium weight (75 kg) person weighs approximately 2 kg which meanwhile can

© Springer Nature Switzerland AG 2021
X.-J. Liu et al. (Eds.): ICIRA 2021, LNAI 13013, pp. 622–630, 2021.
https://doi.org/10.1007/978-3-030-89095-7_59

produce up to 350 W and 140 Nm peak power and torque. Under current research level, it is arduous to match both weight and drive capability, thus powered ankle prostheses are significantly less commercial. A variety of kernels has been attempted by researchers to provide net power output, including pneumatic actuation [5], pneumatic artificial muscles [5] and series-elastic actuator (SEA) [6]. Electro-hydrostatic actuator is a power-by-wire (PBW) servo system widely used in aerospace industry which is appropriate for a powered ankle prosthesis due to its high output power to mass ratio, good controllability and robustness [7].

To provide sufficient power output and duplicate the dynamic characteristics of sound body, this paper proposes a novel EHA based full-time active prosthesis. The hydraulic system is streamlined and an elastic element is introduced into to form the series elastic actuator (SEA) to change the energy output pattern. Furthermore, Neuromuscular model is introduced into the control system serving as a feedforward element to duplicate the nonlinear impedance and active power output characteristics of human ankle joint.

2 Overall Design and Control

2.1 Ankle Foot Prosthesis

The EHA powered ankle prosthesis used in this study is an improved successor to the throttle-based MK-I tethered prototype developed by our group. As shown in Fig. 1(a), the sole is designed referring to the Flex-Foot [8], a passive carbon fiber made structure absorbing the ground contact shock to the amputee while storing part of the energy like traditional ankle-foot prostheses do. The ankle joint is a simple rolling bearing-based unit joining the sole to upper shank structure then providing a limited range of fixed-axis rotation.

To get rid of the throttling valves to avoid unnecessary high-pressure loss, a brushless DC motor (Maxon ECi-40 operating at 48 V) and a bi-directional gear pump (VIVOLO XV-0R/0.98) were used to deliver hydraulic oil directly to either side of the ankle cylinder via a very short pipeline integrated inside the manifold block. The hydraulic circuit is shown in Fig. 1(b), a pneumatic source supplies the oil tank working as an accumulator to charge the low-pressure side through the check valve of the loop to avoid cavitation. The prosthesis system will operate in full-active mode during the whole gait cycle and a relatively complex low-level controller was designed to drive (or back-drive against the flow) the motor-pump unit in stance phase generating desired impedance which covers both damping and stiffness.

A National Instruments (NI) CompactRIO was selected as the control platform handling signal acquisition, overall control and communications for the ankle-foot prosthesis. The motor is controlled by an Escon 50/5 servo controller which is able to record the motor speed in the meantime. Design specifications and parameters of components can be seen in our previous work [9].

There is a series spring configured in series with the cylinder. We combine the EHA system and the series spring to form the Series-Elastic Actuator (SEA). The combination of actuators and springs is a biological substitute for muscle and Achilles tendon respectively. The SEA provides force control by controlling the extent to which the series spring is compressed. Using pressure sensors configured on each port of hydraulic cylinder, we get the force output by multiply the pressure difference and the cylinder area. The design of the spring parameters will be developed in the following chapter.

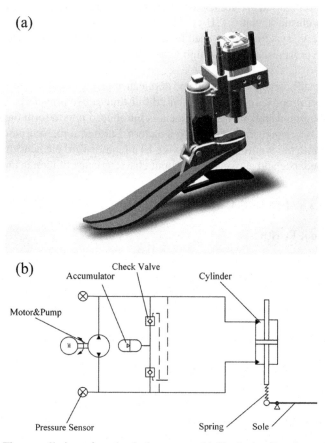

Fig. 1. (a) The overall view of mechanical structure, (b) The hydraulic schematic diagram

2.2 Energy Store Series Spring

According to the biomechanics, the dynamics of the ankle are mainly nonlinear elastic characteristics during the controlled dorsiflexion which has the proportion of time in stance phase [10]. During the controlled dorsiflexion (CD) phase, some of the gravitational potential energy is stored in the Achilles tendon and released during the powered plantarflexion (PP) phase, reducing the burden on the muscle's force output. Obviously, with the same joint torque, lower stiffness allows the spring to store more energy. Nevertheless, too low stiffness will result in insufficient force bandwidth, a widely accepted measure of an actuator's ability to achieve a desired performance [11], thus cannot meet the needs of amputees to walk at a specific speed. Research [12] had pointed out that, the goal of the force bandwidth is 2–4 Hz at 50–140 Nm torque during human level-ground walking.

To determine the spring stiffness by force bandwidth requirement, the EHA model is analyzed. Firstly, the motor is not an ideal torque source. The torque output of the motor decreases with the increase of the motor speed due to the influence of the back electromotive force. The motor speed can be described as (1):

$$\omega(s) = \omega_0 - K_m T_f(s) \tag{1}$$

where ω_0 is the maximum speed of the motor, K_m is the velocity-torque coefficient, T_f is the load torque.

Because the motor and gear pump are directly connected through the coupling, the gear pump load torque is the motor by the load torque. The load of gear pump is given by Formula (2), while (3) is the force equation of the hydraulic cylinder.

$$T_f(s) = \Delta p(s)(D + K_f) \tag{2}$$

$$F_L(s) = \Delta p(s)A \tag{3}$$

Where Δp is the pressure difference across the pump; D is the pump displacement; K_f is pressure-based friction coefficient; F_L is the load of hydraulic cylinder; A is the working area of the cylinder.

Because the hydraulic cylinder volume is small and the working pressure is low, the change of the liquid volume due to the pressure is ignored.

$$D\omega(s) = (C_{ic} + C_{ip})\Delta p(s) + As \cdot x(s) \tag{4}$$

Where C_{ic} is the cylinder leakage coefficient, C_{ip} is the pump leakage coefficient, x is the displacement of cylinder piston.

According to the force equation of the spring (5), we get the force output of the cylinder under motor saturation (6)

$$F_L = k_s \cdot x(s) \tag{5}$$

$$F_L = \frac{k_s A \omega_0 D}{A^2 s + k_s(k_m D(D + k_f) + C_{ic} + C_{ip})} \tag{6}$$

In the same way, we can get the maximum output (7) of the hydraulic cylinder in the saturation of the motor, with considering the leakage and friction of hydraulic element. Finally, we have the normalized bandwidth Eq. (8).

$$F_{sat} = \frac{A\omega_0 D}{k_m D(D + k_f) + C_{ic} + C_{ip}} \tag{7}$$

$$\frac{F_l}{F_{sat}} = \frac{1}{s\frac{A^2}{k_s(k_m D(D+k_f)+C_{ic}+C_{ip})} + 1} \tag{8}$$

Table 1. Main parameters of the driven system

Symbol	Specification	Value
ω_0	Motor maximum speed	5000 rpm
D	Pump displacement	0.92 cm³/rev
C_{ic}	Cylinder Internal Leakage Coefficient	2×10^{-12} m³/(Pa·s)
C_{ip}	Pump Internal Leakage Coefficient	1.46×10m³/(Pa·s)
K_m	Motor velocity-torque coefficient	1160 rpm/Nm
K_f	Pump Pressure-based Friction Coefficient	1.07×10^{-3} Nm/bar
A	Cylinder Working Area	6.5 cm²

Through the above analysis and calculation, we had got that the stiffness of 2000 KN/m is a relatively appropriate stiffness value. The result is shown in the Fig. 2, the bandwidth of which is about 9.9 Hz at 110 Nm torque output (Table 1).

To save space and not attach too much extra weight and guarantee the power density of the prosthetic system, this paper selects the cantilever structure to design a spring as shown in Fig. 3. The design adopts the cantilever beam with rectangular cross section, the stiffness of which is determined by the deflection formula (9).

$$K_{sp} = \frac{3EI}{l_s^3} = \frac{Eh^2 w_s}{4l_s^3} \tag{9}$$

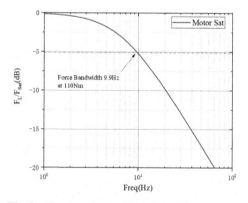

Fig. 2. The force bandwidth of the driven system.

2.3 Simulation Model of the Ankle-Foot Prosthesis

Before clinical evaluation, a simulation experiment is carried out in Matlab/Simulink to verify its feasibility. The spring part was not added in the previous model of prosthetic

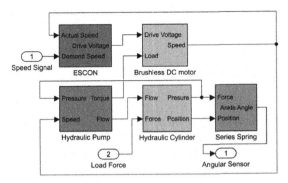

Fig. 3. The Simulink model of the ankle-foot prosthesis.

ankle [9], while it was added in the simulation of this paper. Meanwhile, pressure loss is ignored, for the hydraulic circuit are greatly simplified compared with the those in MK-I. The simulation block diagram is shown in Fig. 4.

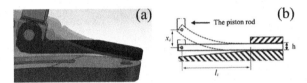

Fig. 4. (a) Structural view of the spring (b) Mechanical schematic diagram of the spring.

2.4 Control System

The design concept of the control system is restoring the dynamic characteristics of a sound ankle in level ground walking and small gradient adaption, in a word, constructing a real-time relationship between ankle angle measured and ankle torque produced by the prosthesis. As aforementioned, the controller designed is able to determine the corresponding torque using feed forward with neuromuscular model as kernel. A finite-state machine (FSM) is used as high-level controller to estimate the gait phase of the amputee on the basis of sensor signals. Since the EHA is force controllable [13], the physical torque at the ankle joint produced by the prosthesis will follow the command torque. Neuromuscular model is a Hill-type MTS with positive force reflex scheme, which is of the most importance in the control system since it is the base of the non-linear impedance characteristics. The MTS consists of two major parts: an active element called contractile element (CE) models the muscular tissue and a series element (SE) models the tendon. The unidirectional force generated by the CE is a function of the CE length l_{CE}, velocity v_{CE} and active state A[14]. The resulting force F_{CE}, referring [15], can be described by

$$F_{CE}(l_{CE}, v_{CE}, A) = F_{\max} f_L(l_{CE}) f_v(v_{CE}) A \tag{10}$$

The SE can be simply characterized by a non-linear elastic force–length relationship [16]described by

$$F_{SE}(\varepsilon) = \begin{cases} F_{\max}(\varepsilon/\varepsilon_{ref})^2, & \varepsilon > 0 \\ 0, & \varepsilon \leq 0 \end{cases} \qquad (11)$$

Where ε is tendon strain defined by $\varepsilon = (l_{SE} - l_{slack})/l_{slack}$, l_{slack} is the SE's rest length and ε_{ref} is the reference strain obtained by $F_{SE}(\varepsilon_{ref}) = F_{\max}$.

Since the CE and SE are in series, ignoring the effect of their negligible mass, they have equal force defined as F_{MTS}.Combining the equations aforementioned, the FMTS can be uniquely determined for a specific given MTS length $l_{MTS}(t)$ and real-time active state $A(t)$.

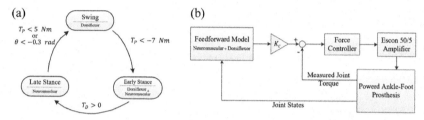

Fig. 5. (a) The State Machine, (b) The diagram of The control system

As aforementioned, the synergy as well as the working mode of the two virtual actuators are controlled by a finite-state machine based decisive controller. A gait cycle is divided into three phases based on the variational environment interaction of the prosthesis: early stance (controlled dorsiflexion), late stance and swing. The detection and switch between phases are triggered by the decisive controller as shown in Fig. 5(a). In addition, the torque command is multiplied by a gain coefficient K_C to compensate the attenuation in force margin of the prosthesis before sent into the force controller. Combining the feedforward model, the compensation gain and the force controller, the architecture of the control system is shown in Fig. 5(b).

3 Results and Discussion

The simulation experiment model consists of the two parts mentioned above. The pre-sampled biological ankle torque from [9]is adopted as the input of the ankle prosthesis system model simulating the interaction among the upper-limb, the prosthesis and the ground in form of moment. The simulation result of ankle angle is shown in Fig. 6(a) with matched groups, where dotted line refers to the angular displacement of the actuator, the full line refers to the angular displacement of the ankle prosthesis and the dash line is the angle profile of sound body. Due to the introduction of the spring, the actual dorsiflexion angle of the actuator is reduced by about 5°, which significantly reduced the velocity of the actuator during the power plantar-flexion phase. And this result in a 35 w drop in peak power, as shown in Fig. 6 where full line refers to the ankle power output without elastic element, dotted line refers to ones with spring.

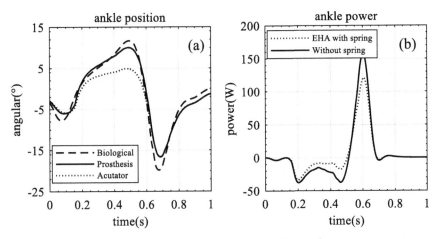

Fig. 6. Comparison of ankle prosthesis angle and power.

4 Conclusions

According to the simulation result, the novel design of EHA is able to duplicate the dynamic characteristics of sound human body during level walking. Comparing to the design without elastic element, prosthesis with SEA can change the displacement of actuator, and reduce the required flow rate significantly, which can reduce the peak power produced by the motor. To ensure that the ability of power output isn't affected by the plastic element, evaluation of the force bandwidth is needed. The actual situation may be different from the simulation result, while adjust may need when constructing the prototype.

The future work will continue focus on optimizing the drive system. Hugh Her and his team proposed an optimization method for motor driven lower limb prosthesis combining motor selection, transmission ratio optimization, and spring design, so as to improve the performance of the prosthesis system in terms of energy consumption [11]. Similarly, our team will explore specific optimization schemes for EHA-based ankle-foot prosthesis.

Acknowledgment. This research was supported by National Key R&D Program of China, Research and application of key technology of intelligent powered lower-limb prosthesis system project (2018YFB1307303).

References

1. Seymour, R.: Prosthetics and Orthotics: Lower Limb and Spinal. Lippincott Williams & Wilkins, Philadelphia (2002)
2. Breakey, J.: Gait of unilateral below-knee amputees. Orthot. Prosthet. **30**(3), 17–24 (1976)
3. Jimenez-Fabian, R., Verlinden, O.: Review of control algorithms for robotic ankle systems in lower-limb orthoses, prostheses, and exoskeletons. Med. Eng. Phys. **34**(4), 397–408 (2012)

4. Au, S.K., Dilworth, P., Herr, H.: An ankle-foot emulation system for the study of human walking biomechanics. In: Proceedings 2006 IEEE International Conference on Robotics and Automation, 2006, ICRA 2006, pp. 2939–2945 IEEE (2006)

5. Versluys, R., Desomer, A., Lenaerts, G., et al.: A pneumatically powered below-knee prosthesis: Design specifications and first experiments with an amputee. In: 2008 2nd IEEE RAS & EMBS International Conference on Biomedical Robotics and Biomechatronics, pp. 372–377. IEEE (2008)

6. Hitt, J.K., Sugar, T.G., Holgate, M., et al.: An active foot-ankle prosthesis with biomechanical energy regeneration. J. Med. Dev. 4(1), 01100 (2010)

7. Yu, T., Plummer, A., Iravani, P., et al.: The design of a powered ankle prosthesis with electro-hydrostatic actuation. In: Fluid Power Systems Technology. American Society of Mechanical Engineers, vol. 57236, p. V001T01A041 (2015)

8. Ossur (2020). Accessed 27 Dec 2020, Össur http://www.ossur.com

9. Liu, H., Huang, Q., Tong, Z.: Simulation and analysis of a full-active electro-hydrostatic powered ankle prosthesis. In: 2019 19th International Conference on Advanced Robotics (ICAR), pp. 81–86. IEEE (2019)

10. Palmer, M.L.: Sagittal plane characterization of normal human ankle function across a range of walking gait speeds. Massachusetts Institute of Technology (2002)

11. Carney, M., Herr, H.M.: Energetic consequences of series and parallel springs in lower-extremity powered prostheses (2019)

12. Au, S.K., Weber, J., Herr, H.: Biomechanical design of a powered ankle-foot prosthesis. In: 2007 IEEE 10th International Conference on Rehabilitation Robotics, pp. 298–303. IEEE (2007)

13. Yongling, F.U., Xu, H.A.N., Sepehri, N., et al.: Design and performance analysis of position-based impedance control for an electrohydrostatic actuation system. Chin. J. Aeronaut. 31(3), 584–596 (2018)

14. van Soest, A.J., Bobbert, M.F.: The contribution of muscle properties in the control of explosive movements. Biol. Cybern. 69(3), 195–204 (1993)

15. Geyer, H., Seyfarth, A., Blickhan, R.: Positive force feedback in bouncing gaits? Proc. Roy. Soc. Lond. Ser. B Biol. Sci. 270(1529), 2173–2183 (2003)

16. van Ingen Schenau, G.J.: An alternative view of the concept of utilisation of elastic energy in human movement. Hum. Mov. Sci. 3(4), 301–336 (1984)

Simulation of Human Posture Sway Based on Reference Control

Qiuyan Zeng$^{(\boxtimes)}$, Muye Pang, Biwei Tang, and Kui Xiang

School of Automation, Wuhan University of Technology, Wuhan, Hubei, China

Abstract. Investigating human movement mechanism is meaningful since it can provide clues to controller designs of bionic robots. However, the complicated interactions between human neural and musculoskeletal cause this issue to be challenging. Fortunately, the reference control has recently shown its potential and reliability to deal with this issue. In order to evaluate the roles of this control mechanism in the simulation of human upright swing, this paper firstly builds a simulation platform of musculoskeletal model augmented with reference controller via leveraging OpenSim. Then, the muscle-driven simulations of anti-disturbance and intentional swing in sagittal plane are conducted by using the established platform. During this process, the parameters contained in the reference controller and the reference point trajectory in swing are optimized using the fminsearch optimizer. Lastly, the established platform is verified by computer simulation and experimental test. The results between comparison of the simulation results and experimental data confirm that the established method can simulate the actual human upright standing motion.

Keywords: OpenSim · Musculoskeletal model · Reference control · Reference point trajectory

1 Introduction

Studying the mechanism of human movement control not only helps to clarify the relationship between posture and movement stability, but also promotes the development of robots. However, the complicated transformations between neural control and purposeful movement poses a significant barrier to the development of these fields [1]. One thorn to this issue could be that measuring important variables, such as muscle and joint forces, remains difficult in real-world applications. Computer simulation complements experiments and plays an increasingly important role in solving complex engineering problems, such as physiology, clinical medicine and robotics.

With the maturity of musculoskeletal modeling technology, different types of simulation software have been applied to the dynamic simulation and calculation of human musculoskeletal system. As an open-source biomechanical simulation software, OpenSim allows users to custom musculoskeletal models, analyses, contacts, actuators, controllers and other components to build and expand its available functions by using application programming interface (API) [2]. Previous studies have used OpenSim and controller

© Springer Nature Switzerland AG 2021
X.-J. Liu et al. (Eds.): ICIRA 2021, LNAI 13013, pp. 631–641, 2021.
https://doi.org/10.1007/978-3-030-89095-7_60

driven simulations to study muscle functions [3], predict human movements [4] and investigate human balance mechanisms [5]. However, the works considering the generation mechanism and stability analysis of purposeful movements are rare.

Universally, human movement is produced by complex interactions of nervous, muscular and skeletal systems. According to the traditional view of motor control, the nervous system preprograms kinematic and kinetic characteristics, and directly specifies the requisite motor commands to muscles (i.e., electromyogram [EMG] activity, forces or torque) to plan and execute body movements. Yet, the intention movements and posture stability are resisted under this mechanism and the simulation based on these measured characteristics from the devices is hard to build correctly.

In recent years, more and more researchers from the community of sensorimotor control proposed to apply the reference control to handle the challenge noted above. This could be interpreted by the fact that the mechanism of reference control indicates that the CNS does not give specific instructions to the muscle, such as muscle force or joint angle [6]. Instead, the reference control merely regulates the internal balance posture by changing the reference point (threshold) of muscle activation, which is similar to the balance point in impedance control.

Due to the aforementioned advantages, the reference control has been recently aroused increasing attentions in the field of human biomechanics and bionic robotics [7, 8]. Nonetheless, the most of those terrific studies concentrates on analyzing the effective of reference control by the experimental data, which may only provide important but limited suggestions in revealing kinematic dynamics. In order to reveal the human kinematic dynamics as fully as possible, there exists heavy demands to develop other technologies which can combined with reference control.

To this end, this paper has been devoted to integrating the optimization technology, the musculoskeletal model in OpenSim with reference control to reveal human movement mechanism under the task of human posture sway. Firstly, this paper designs a computer simulation platform of musculoskeletal model based on a simplified lower-limb model. Subsequently, a reference controller is established in the musculoskeletal model simulation platform to investigate the relationship between postural and movement stability in swing of human. Moreover, the key parameters of the controller and the reference point trajectory of the built model swing are optimized in the built platform. Finally, the developed platform is verified by comparing the computer simulation results with the experimental results. The results between comparison of the simulation results and experimental data confirm that the established method can simulate the actual human upright standing motion.

2   Methods

2.1   Statement of Reference Control Strategy for Human Posture Sway

Currently, it has been discovered that human neural system may exercise a specific form of reference control by defining the reference point of body segments where muscles begin to be activated to generate the needed active torque [7]. In this way, the nervous system can predetermine the places where the muscle elements work, rather than the manners they need to work. Human nervous system adopts the reference control strategy to regulate the internal reference position by changing the reference point and indirectly adjusts the degree of muscle activation to obtain the desired movement. Human nervous system adopts the reference control strategy to regulate the internal reference position by changing the reference point and indirectly adjusts the degree of muscle activation to obtain the desired movement.

In terms of modeling the reference control strategy contained in the human neural system, one can assume that the neural system regards the distance of the center-of-mass in the x direction (COM_x) as the reference variable. Human muscle is activated if the following condition is satisfied:

$$x - \lambda^* \geq 0 \tag{1}$$

where x is the current COM_x. λ^* is the dynamic muscle activation threshold, that is, the reference point of COM_x, and can be approximately expressed as:

$$\lambda^* = \lambda - \mu v \tag{2}$$

where λ is the central component of the threshold. v stands for the velocity of COM_x. μ represents the dynamic sensitivity of the threshold.

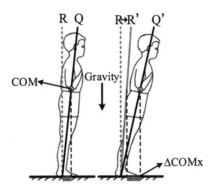

Fig. 1. The forward leaning of human body under reference control. COM is the center of mass. R and R' is the reference position at which muscles reach their activation thresholds. Q and Q' is the actual position at which body balance is achieved. ΔCOM_x is the deviation of COM_x between the reference and actual body position.

As displayed in Fig. 1, assuming that during vertical stance on the horizontal plane, the human ankle muscles reach their activation thresholds at R which aligns with the vertical direction of the ground. Since the center of mass (COM) of body locates in front of the ankle joint [8], there is a torque of gravity tilts the body slightly forward from R to Q. The deviation between R and Q, which is reflected by COM_x, activates the muscles and the extensor ankle torque is just in balance with the gravitational torque. In order to intentionally lean the body forward, nervous system adjust the reference orientation form R to R'. This leads to a drop in the muscle activation. Unbalanced gravitational torque leans the body until re-stretched muscles to balance the increased gravitational torques at a more learned position Q'. Similarly, body leans backwards by decreasing the reference point after the posture is stabilized.

2.2   Design of Simulation Platform Based on Reference Controller

In order to reveal the reference control mechanism of human posture sway as fully as possible, as visualized in Fig. 2, this paper first completes the design of a simulation platform for human musculoskeletal model based on gait10dof18 in OpenSim. Note that only one degree-of-freedom of the ankle joint and two main ankle muscles, that is, the soleus (SOL) and tibialis anterior (TA), are considered in the musculoskeletal model since this study mainly investigates the simulation effect of the reference control during human body swaying around the ankle joint. Then, a reference controller is developed in the musculoskeletal model. The established platform and controller are depicted in the herein contents in this section.

For representing the landing surface, a contact surface fixed on the platform to interact with human feet is added to the simulation platform. Six equally-sized elastic foundation contact models are added between each foot and the contact plane to simulate the reaction forces between the foot and the ground in reality. The contact properties of the foot-floor contact model are shown in Table 1. The parameters of SOL and TA are reported in Table 2.

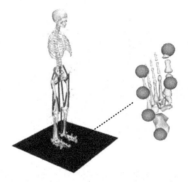

Fig. 2. Musculoskeletal model

Table 1. Parameters of muscle

Parameters	SOL	TA
Maximum tension /N	5137.0	3000.0
Muscle fiber length /m	0.1	0.1
Muscle-tendon length /m	0.2514	0.2228

Table 2. Parameters of contact properties

Parameters	Rigidity	Dispersion	Static friction	Dynamic friction	Viscous friction
Value	10^8	0.5	0.9	0.9	0.6

As illustrated in Fig. 1, the COM_x of the model is considered as the reference variable to reflect the variations of the reference positions R and Q in the controller. The reference controller developed in this paper can be mathematically defined as follows:

$$u(t) = K_P\big(x(t) - \lambda^*(t)\big) + K_v \frac{dx(t)}{dt})$$ (3)

where K_P is the position deviation coefficient of COM_x. K_v is the velocity gain of COM_x. $u(t), x(t)$ and $\lambda^*(t)$ are, respectively, the degree of muscle activation, the current position of COM_x and the reference point at time t.

2.3 Parameter Optimization for the Developed Reference Controller

It can be easily observed from Eq. (3) that performance of the developed controller heavily relies on its parameters K_P and K_v, as well as the reference point $\lambda^*(t)$. In order to enhance the controller's performance, there exists necessity to optimize these parameters. Thanks to its simplicity and promising robustness to highly-dimensional nonlinear issues, the fminsearch optimizer is implemented to optimize the three parameters stated above in our developed simulation platform [9].

We first use fminsearch to optimize K_P and K_v, and then refer to the reference point trajectory $\lambda^*(t)$. When optimizing the coefficients of K_P and K_v, suppose the reference points of SOL and TA are adjusted by the nervous system individually. As shown in Fig. 1 above, the reference position of body in static standing is R. In simulation, R is the upright position of the model which is invariable during standing stability and anti-disturbance, and its COM_x is -0.07 m. K_P and K_v can be obtained by specifying the angle of ankle measured by human experiment in static standing. During the optimization process of K_P and K_v, the objective function is given as follows:

$$\min_{K_P, K_v} J = \omega_1 \int_{T_0}^{T} (q_m(t) - q_0)^2 dt + \omega_2 \int_{0}^{T} u(t)^2 dt$$ (4)

where q_0 is the stable angle of ankle joint in static standing and can be obtained by experimental test. $q_m(t)$ is the ankle angle of the model which can be computed by the dynamic equation built in OpenSim. ω_1 and ω_2, respectively, are predefined weights of angle and muscle activation in the objective function. T is the simulation duration. T_0 is the longest time for the model to reach stability.

After the establishment of the objective function, K_P and K_v are optimized according to the following steps.

*Step*1: Initialize values of K_P, K_v, T, T_0, q_0, λ^*, ω_1 and ω_2.
*Step*2: Start the fminsearch optimization operation.
*Step*3: Carry out the simulation of static standing under the developed reference controller in the established simulation platform and return the state variables of the whole process, including the degree of muscle activation $u(t)$ and the ankle angle $q_m(t)$, from the simulation platform.
*Step*4: Calculate the objective function according to Eq. (4) and check whether or not the termination condition of the fminsearch optimizer is satisfied. If yes, output the optimized values of K_P and K_v. Otherwise, return to *Step*2.

Substitute the optimized values of K_P and K_v into Eq. (3) and then optimize the trajectory of reference point $\lambda^*(t)$ in swing using fminsearch optimizer to track the angle of ankle joint in human experiment. The tracking optimization problem of reference point trajectory can be described as finding the reference points $\lambda^*(t)$ to minimize the objective function as follows:

$$\min_{\lambda^*(t)} J = \omega_1 \int_{T_1}^{T} (q_m(t) - q_e(t))^2 dt + \omega_2 \int_{T_1}^{T} u(t)^2 dt \tag{5}$$

where $q_e(t)$ is the ankle angle in human body swing. T_1 is the time to start tracking.

The implementation steps of reference points in swing based on fminsearch is described:

*Step*1: Set the optimal node density of reference points and initialize their values.
*Step*2: Start the fminsearch optimization operation.
*Step*3: Carry out the simulation of swing and get the ankle joint and the degree of muscle activation. In the simulation process, the unset reference points between two collocation reference points takes the previous values.
*Step*4: Calculate the objective function value shown in Eq. (5) and check if the end condition of the fminsearch is met. If yes, output the optimized value of $\lambda^*(t)$. Otherwise, go back to *Step*2.

3   Experimental Setup and Protocol

The developed method is verified by comparing the simulation results obtained by our designed simulation platform with the experimental results. Prior to conducting experimental tests, a healthy volunteer without neuromusculoskeletal problems participate in two motor tasks in this study. The kinematics of the recruited volunteer are recorded in a Nokov optical three-dimensional motion capture system (Beijing NOKOV Science & Technology, 50 Hz) with eight high-definition cameras. Six reflective markers are placed on the medial and lateral shank and toes of the right leg to calculate the angle of the ankle. The muscle EMG signals of SOL and TA are measured by electromyography (ELONXI EMG 100-Ch-Y-RA). In the preparation of the experiment, the leg hairs of the subjects are removed and the skin is cleaned with alcohol. After that, EMG activity levels during maximal isometric voluntary contractions (MVC) are measured in standard muscle testing position for the subject before the experiment and used to normalize the EMG signals. The sampling frequencies of Nokov and EMG are 50 Hz and 1000 Hz, respectively. Moreover, we implement the real-time simulator to achieve the synchronous reception of experimental data.

The first task executed in the experimental test is human upright anti-disturbance experiment. As visualized in Fig. 3 the subject is asked to stand on a horizontal plane. Around 5 s later, a sandbag weighing 750 g and pulled by a rope is released from a given height (2.5 m) to hit the back of the subject. For this task, we need to repeat it three times with an interval of about 5 s between each sandbag experiment.

Task 2 is referred to human upright swing experiment. As illustrated in Fig. 4, the subject is informed to stand quietly for about 5 s to collect ankle joint angles under the static posture. Note that then, the subject is notified to lean forward at a self-paced

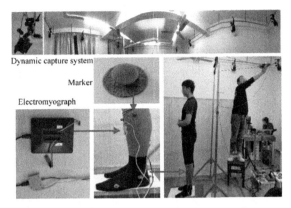

Fig. 3. Human upright anti-disturbance experiment

speed, avoiding leaving his toes and heels off the ground. After reaching the maximum lean-forward angle of the subject, the subject needs to return to the initial position and stay for 3 s. During the entire experiment, the subject crosses his arms in front of his chest, and the feet are with the same width as his shoulder. Without losing stability, the subject is asked to try to keep his body straight and move the body by using ankle strategy as much as possible. Each experiment is repeated 3 trials.

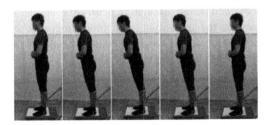

Fig. 4. Human upright swing experiment

4 Results and Analysis

4.1 Upright Standing Anti-disturbance

To verify the effectiveness of the developed simulation platform in resisting disturbance on human upright standing anti-disturbance mission, we simulate the anti-disturbance task via the platform and compare the obtained numerical results with the anti-disturbance experimental data. The initial values of needed simulation parameters are given in Table 3. The initial guess of K_P and K_v generated by manual testing and their optimized results are reported in Table 4. During the platform simulation, a given instantaneous disturbance force is applied to the pelvis of the model at $t = 5$ s to carry out the simulation of upright standing anti-disturbance. It linearly increases to 200 N in the first 100 ms and decreases to 0 N in the second 100 ms.

Table 3. Parameter settings for the optimization

Parameters	$T(s)$	$T_0(s)$	$q_0(°)$	$\lambda^*(m)$	ω_1	ω_2
Value	5	2	4.5	−0.07	100	1

Table 4. Initial guess and results

Muscle	SOL		TA	
Parameters	K_P	K_v	K_P	K_v
Initial guess	3.5	0.8	1	0.1
Optimized results	3.2	0.9	0.97	0.2

Figure 5(a) and Fig. 5(b) show the angle changes of the ankle joint of the subject by the platform simulation and experimental test under the anti-disturbance task, respective. It can be seen from Fig. 5(a) that under the control of reference controller, the model is statically stable in 2 s and the ankle angle is 4.5°. It is consistent with the actual human body in Fig. 5(b), which verifies the effectiveness of the parameter optimization. Then, the model is forced to tilt forward under the impact of disturbance and finally reaches stability at a new balance position with the action of controller. Furthermore, it can be observed from Fig. 5 that the variation tendency after being disturbed with respective to the ankle joint angle obtained by our simulation platform is similar to that gained by the experimental test. However, the ankle joint of the model recovers to stability faster than that of the human body. The main reason may be that simulation is superior to human body in signal detection and calculation.

Figure 6 shows the muscle activation levels of SOL and TA by the simulation platform and experimental test, respectively. We can make an observation from Fig. 6 that the changes of muscle activation levels after interference in the simulation are similar to that in the experiment. To summarize, under the reference control, the model basically simulates the process of upright anti-disturbance, and can achieve the effect of vertical balance of the actual human body.

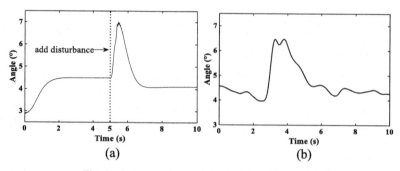

Fig. 5. Ankle angle of the model(a) and human(b)

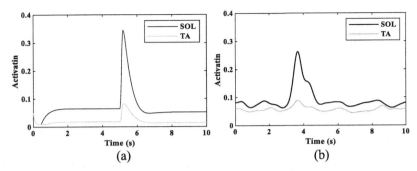

Fig. 6. Muscle activation levels of the model(a) and human(b)

4.2 Upright Swing

To evaluate the roles of reference control in the simulation of upright swing, another experimental test is conducted to track human ankle joint angle and get the reference point trajectory in swing. The parameters of ω_1 and ω_2 are 100 and 1, respectively. The tracking starts at $T_1 = 3$ s, where the model is in a standing stable. The optimal node density of the optimized reference point is set as 1. The initial guesses of all of the nodes are set to -0.07 m.

The reference point trajectory curve of SOL and TA in swing is depicted in Fig. 7. The comparison diagram of ankle joint angle and muscle activation levels between the experiment test and the platform simulation in upright swing are illustrated in Fig. 8 and Fig. 9, respectively. Because the activation level of SOL is much greater than TA in swing, subsequent analysis is based on the SOL. Combined with the ankle joint angle in Fig. 7, it can be seen that in the process of the forward (3–5 s), the reference point of SOL generally shows a rising variation tendency, whereas the backward (5–8 s) overall shows a falling trend. This could verify that the reference control performs the specified motion by shifting the reference point.

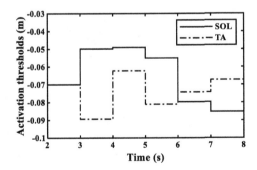

Fig. 7. Reference point trajectories of SOL and TA

Also, as can be seen from Fig. 8, the angle error between the experiment data and that of the simulation in upright swing is not large. The optimized reference point trajectory makes the simulation action of the model basically tend to the experimental action. Figure 9(a) shows that after the model is stable, the reference point of SOL increases at $t = 3$ s and there is a short-lasting decrease in SOL EMG activity at the beginning of leaning forward with a subsequent gradual increase in EMG activity during leaning. This result shows that the narrowing of the gap between the current COM_x and new reference point leads to the decrease of muscle activity and the unbalanced gravitational torque leans the body forward. Similarly, muscle activity drops in lean backward as the distance between the current COM_x and reference point decreasing until the model is stable. Moreover, the activation levels of SOL in experiment also have a similar short-lasting decline and overall change which is consistent with the referent control theory. It is suggested that human movement may be controlled in combination with the reference control.

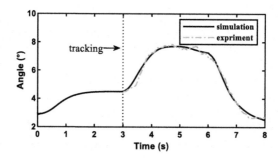

Fig. 8. Comparison of ankle angle between experiment and simulation

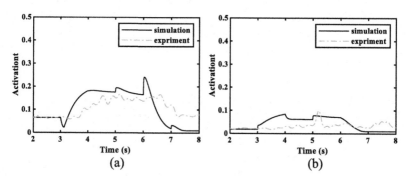

Fig. 9. The muscle activation level of SOL and TA in simulation and experiment. (a) is the muscle of SOL, and (b) is TA.

Here, it is important to note that the angle tracking error reduces with the increasing of the node density of reference point. The larger the node density setting is, the longer the optimization time consumes. Therefore, the node density set in this paper is relatively small and the experimental results show that the tracking error is acceptable. Moreover, due to the synergy of other muscles and the influence of external environment in the process of human movement, the muscle activation obtained by simulation and experiment are different in absolute values. Therefore, this paper only makes a comparison on the changing trend rather than numerical comparison.

5 Conclusion

This paper builds a simulation platform using OpenSim and carries out the simulation of model upright anti-disturbance and swing based on the reference control. Under the control of this strategy, the movement of human swing is reproduced in the simulation platform. When the reference point is fixed, the model can resist the disturbance quickly to reach a new stability. Similarly, the model can lean forward by increasing the reference point and lean back by decreasing it after stabilization. Analyzing the data of angle and muscle activation levels, the simulation data are basically consistent with experiments, which verifies the effectiveness of the simulation platform.

The human body is simplified as an ankle inverted pendulum model in the study. Thus, the comparative analysis of simulation data and experimental data only makes a reference on the changing trend rather than absolute values. In the future, we will further study the multi joint motion problem based on the reference control, enrich the simulation action of the model, and improve the structure and parameters of the controller.

Acknowledgment. This work was supported by the National Natural Science Foundation of China under Grant 61603284 and 61903286.

References

1. Reinbolt, J.A., Seth, A., Delp, S.L.: Simulation of human movement: applications using OpenSim. Procedia IUTAM **2**, 186–198 (2011)
2. Seth, A., Hicks, J.L., Uchida, T.K.: OpenSim: simulating musculoskeletal dynamics and neuromuscular control to study human and animal movement. PLOS Comput. Biol. **14**(7), e1006223 (2018)
3. DeMers, M.S., Hicks, J.L., Delp, S.L.: Preparatory co-activation of the ankle muscles may prevent ankle inversion injuries. J. Biomech. Eng. **52**, 17–23 (2017)
4. Ong, C.F., Hicks, J.L., Delp, S.L.: Simulation-based design for wearable robotic systems: an optimization framework for enhancing a standing long jump. IEEE Trans. Biomed. Eng. **63**(5), 894–903 (2016)
5. Xiao, T., Tang, B., Pang, M., Xiang, K.: Simulation of human upright standing anti-disturbance based on openSim. In: The 14th International Conference on Intelligent Robotics and Applications (ICIRA 2020), pp. 308–319. IEEE (2020)
6. Feldman, A.G.: Referent Control of Action and Perception. Springer, New York (2015)
7. Mullick, A.A., Turpin, N.A., Hsu, S.-C., Subramanian, S.K., Feldman, A.G., Levin, M.F.: Referent control of the orientation of posture and movement in the gravitational field. Exp. Brain Res. **236**(2), 381–398 (2017). https://doi.org/10.1007/s00221-017-5133-y
8. Feldman, A.G.: The relationship between postural and movement stability. Adv. Exp. Med Biol. **957**, 105–120 (2016)
9. Lagarias, J.C., Reeds, J.A., Wright, M.H.: Convergence properties of the Nelder-Mead simplex method in low dimensions. SIAM. J. Opt. **9**(1), 112–147 (1998)

Human Control Intent Inference Using ESNs and Input-Tracking Based Inverse Model Predictive Control

Peili Gong[✉], Muye Pang, Kui Xiang, Liyan Zhang, and Biwei Tang

School of Automation, Wuhan University of Technology, Wuhan, Hubei, China
307289@whut.edu.cn

Abstract. Acquiring human motor control strategies or intents is helpful for clinical research, wearable robotic device design and human-robot cooperation control. The state-of-art method is to construct an optimal control framework which is capable to predict the target motion and take the cost function as the potential control intents. Aimed to solve this problem, an echo state networks based state space model (SSM) extraction method and input-tracking inverse MPC algorithm are proposed in this paper. By applying Taylor expansion around an operating point, it is convenient to acquire the SSM via the SSM extraction method and more detailed information about human musculoskeletal system is preserved. Setting the target of the upper level optimization as input-tracking is more rational than conventional output-tracking structure, given the consideration that human motion control is a multiple-solution problem. The effectiveness of the proposed method is verified in both simulation and real-world experiments.

Keywords: Movement intent inference · Model predictive control · Echo state networks

1 Introduction

Estimating human motor control strategies or control intents is strongly required in clinical or robotic fields.

However to acquire the control intent is of a great challenge. One of the promising and widely accepted methods is to implement optimal control framework to obtain the potential control intent [1]. Kuo verified the possibility of applying optimal control and state estimation to explain the selection of control strategies in response of small perturbations to upright stance [2]. Dorn et al. predicted human adaptations during loaded and inclined walking in simulation using dynamic optimal control combined with force feedback and muscle reflex control [3]. The cost function of the optimal control framework is assumed to represent the control intents. It is always a great problem to obtain a proper cost function as human movement control is proved to be multiple objects optimization.

© Springer Nature Switzerland AG 2021
X.-J. Liu et al. (Eds.): ICIRA 2021, LNAI 13013, pp. 642–653, 2021.
https://doi.org/10.1007/978-3-030-89095-7_61

The state of art method for acquiring the desired cost function is to imply the inverse optimal control(IOC) [4]. IOC is a bilevel optimal structure in which the upper level is a tracking problem to guarantee a match between optimal solution and measurements, and the lower level is the optimal control problem as mentioned above. Rebula et al. inferred the cost function of bipedal walking by IOC and a 5 link planar walking model [5].

As there is a hypothesis that human use internal model to control the movement and consider the physiological constraints, it is prefer to implement the model predictive control (MPC) to represent human control strategy and take the cost function of MPC to state the control intents [6].

Users who want to imply the inverse-MPC method to infer the control intents have to deal with two problems: 1) how to get the state space model (SSM) of human dynamic movement and 2) how to construct the cost function of upper level. To obtain the SSM, the widely used approach is to build the human body dynamic differential equations and extract the SSM from these equations. Assumptions of linearity and reductions of the degree of freedoms (DoFs) have to be applied to simplify the process of obtaining SSM. For the second problem, the usual process is setting movement tracking as the upper level cost function.

An alternative approach to model the dynamic system is using the neural networks, specifically the recurrent neural networks (RNNs) which are more suitable for nonlinear dynamics modeling whereas feed-forward neural networks are more competitive in static mapping. Among RNNs, echo state networks (ESNs) are introduced with properties of being conceptually simple and computationally inexpensive. It is convenient to extract the SSM from ESNs by applying Taylor expansion around an operating point. Some attentions have been paid on implementation of ESNs on MPC problems in recent years [7–9]. Furthermore it should be noticed that more and more advanced methods of obtaining human dynamic movement data are available, such as OpenSim, which have the ability to provide reliable training data for ESNs.

In this paper, a human movement control intents inference method based on ESNs and MPC is introduced. Our contributions are as two points. First, to simplify SSM development process and preserve more dynamic properties, we proposed a SSM extraction method from a complex human body dynamic computational environment, i.e. OpenSim, based on ESNs and ridge regression. Second, we constructed a tracking-input based inverse-MPC (TIB-iMPC) structure where the upper level is designed to minimize the difference between prediction inputs and real inputs. The validity of the proposed method is tested by simulation and real-world experiments.

2   Methods

2.1   The SSM Extraction Method

In our proposed method, the basic ideas of extracting SSM of human dynamic movement can be abstracted as three steps. First, obtaining the kinetics inputs, such as joint torques or muscle forces, and kinematics outputs, such as joint angles and angular velocities, of a target movement through OpenSim environment. Second, training ESNs via the obtained inputs and outputs and convert the networks into a standard SSM through Taylor expansion. Third, operating the TIB-MPC process on experimental data and seeking for the optimal parameters to infer the movement control intents.

It is important to acquire the accurate inputs and outputs data for ESNs train-ing.Normally, the proper inputs of a human movement control are muscle activations, muscle tendon force or joint torques. The open source program of OpenSim provides an alternative indirect approach to obtain these inputs. In order to calculate the joint torques or muscle tendon forces, kinematics data and, if available, the external forces are required. These required inputs can be easily accessed via motion capture system (Nokov, Duliang Technology Co. Ltd., CHN) and 6-axis force platform (BMS400600-1K, AMTI, USA). In this paper, ankle,knee, hip and lumbar joint torques are obtained through OpenSim inverse dynamic function and calibrated by Residual Reduction Algorithm function.

The neural network selected to extract SSM is a plain ESN. Equations to model the ESN are described as:

$$
\begin{cases}
\mathbf{x}(k+1) = f\left(s^{in}\mathbf{W}^{in}\mathbf{u}(k+1) + \rho\mathbf{W}\mathbf{x}(k) + s^{fb}s^{out}\mathbf{W}^{fb}\mathbf{y}(k)\right) \\
\mathbf{y}(k+1) = 1/s^{out}\mathbf{W}^{out}\mathbf{x}(k+1)
\end{cases}
\tag{1}
$$

where $f(\cdot)$ is an activation function, which is selected as tanh in this study, $\mathbf{u}(k)$ denotes the input vector, $\mathbf{x}(k)$ is the internal state matrix, and $\mathbf{y}(k)$ is the output vector. In this study, $\mathbf{y}(k)$ is fed back to $\mathbf{x}(k+1)$ as shown in the last item of the upper equation. All weighting matrices $\mathbf{W}^*$, except $\mathbf{W}^{out}$, are randomly generated and normalized before supervised training. All the scalar parameters (ρ, s^{in}, s^{out}, and s^{fb}) in Eq. (1) are subject to manual settings, whereas ρ should be smaller than 1. The superscripts are added to discriminate the weighting matrices, where "in," "out," and "fb" denote the input, output, and feedback loop, respectively.

Readout coefficients (matrix $\mathbf{W}^{out}$) needs to be learned from teaching data by parameter estimation algorithm such as ordinary least square (OLS) estimation:

$$
\hat{\mathbf{W}}^{out} = \mathbf{y}^{tchr}\mathbf{x}^{T}\left(\mathbf{x}\mathbf{x}^{T}\right)^{-1}
\tag{2}
$$

With respect to the colinearity in the data collected from a partially observed dynamic system, the matrix $\mathbf{x}\mathbf{x}^{T}$ is singular such that computing $(\mathbf{x}\mathbf{x}^{T})^{-1}$ by using Eq. (2) would result in numerical instability. In this study, ridge regression is implemented to improve the stability of the matrix inversion. As a consequence, Eq. 2 is rewritten as shown in Eq. 3 by adding a small constant term after $\mathbf{x}\mathbf{x}^{T}$ to remove the singularity.

$$
\hat{\mathbf{W}}^{out} = \mathbf{y}^{tchr}\mathbf{x}^{T}\left(\mathbf{x}\mathbf{x}^{T} + \beta\mathbf{I}\right)^{-1}
\tag{3}
$$

β is a manually selected parameter for ridge regression. It is possible to convert Eq. (3) into a minimizing problem of root mean square errors under the L_2 norm penalty:

$$\hat{\mathbf{W}}^{\text{out}} = \arg\min\left(\left(\mathbf{y} - \mathbf{y}^{\text{tchr}}\right)^{\text{T}}\left(\mathbf{y} - \mathbf{y}^{\text{tchr}}\right) + \lambda\left\|\mathbf{W}^{\text{out}}\right\|_2\right) \tag{4}$$

Equation 1 can be linearized by first-order Taylor expansion near a setpoint of χ_0:

$$\mathbf{x}(k+1) = f(\chi_0) + \nabla f(\chi_0)(\chi(k) - \chi_0) + e(\chi(k) - \chi_0) \tag{5}$$

where

$$\chi(k) = \rho\mathbf{W}\mathbf{x}(k) + s^{\text{in}}\mathbf{W}^{\text{in}}\mathbf{u}(k+1) + s^{\text{fb}}s^{\text{out}}\mathbf{W}^{\text{fb}}\mathbf{y}(k) \tag{6}$$

$\nabla f(\chi_0)$ is a Jacobian matrix, and $e(\cdot)$ denotes all other high-order terms. Equation (1) can then be converted into a standard state space:

$$\begin{cases} \mathbf{x}(k+1) = \mathbf{A}\mathbf{x}(k) + \mathbf{B}\mathbf{u}(k+1) + \mathbf{C}\mathbf{y}(k) + \mathbf{c} \\ \mathbf{y}(k+1) = \mathbf{D}\mathbf{x}(k+1) \end{cases} \tag{7}$$

where

$$\begin{cases} \mathbf{A} = \rho\nabla f(\chi_0)\mathbf{W} \\ \mathbf{B} = s^{\text{in}}\nabla f(\chi_0)\mathbf{W}^{\text{in}} \\ \mathbf{C} = s^{\text{fb}}s^{\text{out}}\nabla f(\chi_0)\mathbf{W}^{\text{fb}} \\ \mathbf{D} = 1/s^{\text{out}}\mathbf{W}^{\text{out}} \end{cases} \tag{8}$$

Equation 7 can be further processed in an incremental format in order to eliminate the constant term $\mathbf{c}$:

$$\begin{cases} \Delta\mathbf{x}(k+1) = \mathbf{A}\Delta\mathbf{x}(k) + \mathbf{B}\Delta\mathbf{u}(k+1) + \mathbf{C}\Delta\mathbf{y}(k) \\ \Delta\mathbf{y}(k+1) = \mathbf{D}\Delta\mathbf{x}(k+1) \end{cases} \tag{9}$$

The MPC problem can then be converted into a constrained quadratic programming:

$$\begin{cases} \min_{\Delta u} J = \Delta\mathbf{U}^T\mathbf{H}\Delta\mathbf{U} - \Delta\mathbf{U}^T\mathbf{S}_u^T\mathbf{T}_y^T\mathbf{T}_y\mathbf{E}_p(k+1) - \mathbf{E}_p(k+1)^T\mathbf{T}_y^T\mathbf{T}_y\mathbf{S}_u\Delta\mathbf{U} \\ s.t. \quad \Psi\Delta\mathbf{U} \geq \mathbf{b} \end{cases} \tag{10}$$

The definition of $\Delta\mathbf{U}$, H, Su, Ty, Ep(k + 1) can be found in [9].

In this study, we select ankle, knee, hip, and lumbar flexion/extension torques as the model inputs and the corresponding joint angles as the outputs.

2.2   The Tracking-Input Based Bilevel MPC Structure

The lower level of the control intent estimation algorithm is the ESN-MPC method in the purpose of achieving the predefined movement. The cost function of ESN-MPC are addition of weighted summations of square inputs and square differences between prediction and measured outputs:

$$J = \sum_{i=1}^{m} \left\| \mathbf{W}_{u,i} \Delta \mathbf{u}(k+i-1) \right\|^2 + \sum_{i=1}^{p} \left\| \mathbf{W}_{y,i}(\mathbf{y}_c(k+i|k) - \mathbf{r}(k+i)) \right\|^2 \quad (11)$$

where $\mathbf{W}_{u,i}$ and $\mathbf{W}_{y,i}$ are the penalty parameters or cost function parameters. For simplicity we assume that parameters are the same among different time steps, which means $\mathbf{W}_i = \mathbf{W}_j$ if $i \neq j$. It can be easily noted that the linear proportion of an optimized parameter set is also an optimized set. In order to eliminate this problem of equivalent replicates, normalization is adopted in this paper. We fit the parameter of $\mathbf{W}_{y,i}$ as **1**, and left only the parameters of $\mathbf{W}_u$ to be optimized.

The upper level of the algorithm is an optimization problem of minimizing deviation of prediction results from measurement ones by adjusting parameters of the lower level cost functions. Specifically, the prediction results are control inputs in our proposed method, which are usually kinematics outputs in other literatures. By this reason, it is called tracking-input based bilevel optimal structure. The particle swarm optimization algorithm (PSO) is adopted to solve the upper level optimization problem. Each individual in the PSO file is referred to be a particle and assigned a velocity which is dynamically updated based on its own flight memory, as well as those of its companions. From the current iteration k to the next iteration k þ 1, particles update their velocities and positions in the conventional PSO as follows:

$$\mathbf{V}_m^{k+1} = \omega \mathbf{V}_m^k + c_1 r_1 (\mathbf{pbest}_m^k - \mathbf{W}_m^k) + c_2 r_2 (\mathbf{gbest}^k - \mathbf{W}_m^k) \quad (12)$$

$$\mathbf{W}_m^{k+1} = \mathbf{W}_m^k + \mathbf{V}_m^{k+1} \quad (13)$$

where $\mathbf{V}_m^k$ and $\mathbf{W}_m^k$ denote the velocity and position of the mth particle at iteration k, respectively. In this paper, position $\mathbf{W}$ is exactly the cost function weights $\mathbf{W}_u$ of the lower-level MPC problem. ω is the inertia weight parameter, c_1 and c_2 are the cognitive and social acceleration parameters, r_1 and r_2 are two random numbers uniformly distributed in [0, 1]. **pbest** and **gbest** denote the personal best position of the mth particle and global best position of the swarm at iteration k, respectively (Table 1).

The detailed main process of the proposed bilevel ESN-MPC for human control intent inference can be found in Algorithm I:

Table 1. Algorithm I

ALGORITHM 1 Bilevel ESN-MPC

Initialization:
- Initialize k, $\Delta\mathbf{x}(0)$, $\Delta\mathbf{y}(0)$, $\mathbf{u}(0)$, $\mathbf{x}(0)$, and $\mathbf{y}(0)$, usually set as 0.
- Calculate the desired joint torques of target movement by inverse dynamic tools of OpenSim with the collected kinematics and kinetics data from experiment.
- Prepare the training data and establish the ESN.
- Linearize the ESN model with Taylor expansion, and obtain SSM matrices $\mathbf{A}$, $\mathbf{B}$, $\mathbf{C}$, and $\mathbf{D}$.
- Set the expected input $\mathbf{x}_r$ which is for upper level and expected output $\mathbf{y}_r$ for lower level,
- Set the prediction horizon N_p, the control horizon N_c, and initialize the weighting matrices $\mathbf{P}$ and $\mathbf{Q}$.
- Obtain g_{best} of the swarm and p_{best} of each particle at the first iteration

while not exit condition **do**:
- Initialize the velocity and position information of each particle in the swarm
- Calculate the fitness value and the personal best fitness value of each particle

  for i = 1 : N **do**
  - o Update the velocity and position of particle i using (12) and (13)
  - o Calculate the fitness value of particle i
  - o Update the personal best solution **pbest** of particle i

  end for
- Update the global best solution **gbest** of the swarm

end while

Fitness value calculation by ESN-MPC:

while not converge **do**
- Compute the coefficient matrices $\mathbf{E}_p(k+1)$, $\mathbf{G}(k+1)$, and $\mathbf{H}$.
- Obtain $\Delta\mathbf{U}$ by solving the quadratic programming problem (15) subject to the constraint condition (17).
- Select the first component of $\Delta\mathbf{U}$ and compute $\mathbf{u}(k+1)=\mathbf{u}(k)+\Delta\mathbf{u}(k+1)$
- Excite the real system and the ESN model with $\mathbf{u}(k+1)$ so as to obtain the new system output $\mathbf{y}(k+1)$ and state $\mathbf{x}(k+1)$;
- Compute $\Delta\mathbf{x}(k+1)$, $\Delta\mathbf{y}(k+1)$;
- $k=k+1$;

end

---

3 Experiment Setup

To investigate the validity of the proposed method, both simulation and real-world test experiment are designed. In simulation environment, a non-linear time-delay system, which has been used to test the performance of ESN-based MPC before, is applied to demonstrate the ability of seeking for the proper potential cost function parameters. The equation of the non-linear system is given as:

$$
\begin{aligned}
\mathbf{y}(k) &= 0.2\sin(0.5\mathbf{y}(k-1) + 0.5\mathbf{y}(k-2)) \\
&+ 0.2\sin(0.5\mathbf{y}(k-2) + 0.5\mathbf{y}(k-3) + 2\mathbf{u}(k-1) + \mathbf{u}(k-2)) \\
&+ \frac{4\mathbf{u}(k-1) + \mathbf{u}(k-2)}{1 + 0.2\cos(0.4\mathbf{y}(k-1) + 0.2\mathbf{y}(k-2))}
\end{aligned}
\tag{14}
$$

where input $\mathbf{u}$ and output $\mathbf{y}$ are 4 element vectors. As the possibility of ESN-based MPC to perform predicted control on this system has been proved in [7], we skip the MPC process here and just show the results of bilevel ESN-MPC part. First we apply ESN-based MPC to this system with predefined reference output trajectories on a manual set of cost function parameters. Then we take the MPC calculated control inputs as the reference trajectory of the upper level to perform the bilevel ESN-MPC with random initial cost function parameters for the lower level. The results of optimized cost function parameters of the bilevel MPC are compared with the original manual set after the PSO algorithm is executed.

The purposes of real-world experiment are twofold: 1) to test the possibility of extracting SSM from a complex human body dynamic computational environment by ESNs and 2) to infer the control intents from the experimental data by applying the proposed bilevel ESN-MPC structure.

The motions are bodyweight squat with three different depths and stoop with three different hip joint bending angles (as illustrated in Fig. 1). In other words, there are 6 groups (3×2) of experiments for one subject to perform. Two subjects (age: 23 and 26 years, weight: 55 and 65 kg, height: 1.68 and 1.72 m) participated in the experiment. Each motion is repeated continuously five times at a time and a five-minute break is provided after one group of experiment is finished. The kinematics data were recorded by motion capture system, with Helen Hayes Hospital marker set and 50 Hz sampling frequency. Subjects stood on a 6-axis force plate to record the ground reaction forces and center of position data. The sampling frequency of force plate is 1000 Hz and the kinematics data are resampled up to 1000 Hz using polyphase filter. All of these data were imported into OpenSim to calculate the joint torques driving the motions. We assume that movement dynamic of left and right side of subject are symmetrical and the force plate data were divided equally into both sides. The human dynamic model loaded in OpenSim is gait2392 and scaled individually by physical marker set. The joint torque data was obtained by invers dynamics and adjusted by residual reduction algorithm provided by OpenSim. There are totally 23 actuators or DoFs in the model and ankle, knee, hip and lumbar joint torques are selected as inputs of the SSM. Outputs of the SSM are the corresponding joint angles.

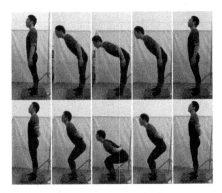

Fig. 1. Experiment of stoop and bodyweight squat movement

The essential first step of establishing a ESN is to warm up or wash the zero state of x(0) = [0,...,0] to an initial state. The data used to wash ESN state are composed by the first 1000 sequence of each group data and these data are discarded after warming. Training data are composed by the first 60% of the rest data of each group and the last 40% ones are used for testing. All of the data are removed mean value and normalized between 0 and 1. The size and spectral radius of the reservoir are set to 100 and 0.6, respectively in this study. The penalty of ridge regression is set to 0.01. Too small penalty value may cause regression unstable and induce impulse-like saltation in prediction results. This phenomenon will be illustrated in experimental results. The number of particle and iteration time of PSO is set as 40 and 8, respectively.

The goodness of prediction was quantified by normalized root mean square error (NRMSE) given by:

$$\text{NRMSE} = \sqrt{\sum\nolimits_i (y_i^r - y_i^p)^2/n/\text{var}(y^r)} \tag{15}$$

where superscript r and p represent reference and prediction result, respectively. var is the variance function. The program was tested on a computer with an Intel Core i7-6700K CPU and a 16 GB memory chip (DDR3 SDRAM).

4 Experimental Results and Discussion

4.1 Simulation Results

The inputs of the simulated non-linear system are three sinusoidal functions with different amplitude and frequency. The prediction result of the ESN with ridge regression is shown in Fig. 2 where blue line is the reference output and the red line is the prediction one. The NRMSE of this prediction result is 0.06, indicating that ESN has a good ability of modeling non-linear system.

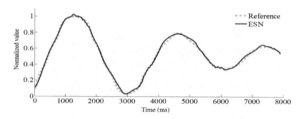

Fig. 2. Prediction results for a simulated nonlinear system by ESNs

In simulation environment the aimed cost function parameters of ESN-based MPC are set as [0.4, 0.2, 0.4, 1] while the solved result of input-tracking bilevel ESN-MPC is [0.39, 0.18, 0.38, 1]. It can be found (as shown in Fig. 3) that the predicted control inputs are consistent with the original control inputs with the proper cost function parameters, indicating that the proposed bilevel ESN-MPC structure is able to find out the potential cost function parameter set or the control intent.

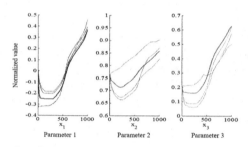

Fig. 3. Cost function adjustment results via proposed TIB-iMPC method

4.2   Real-World Experimental Results

The measured kinematics data and calculated kinetics data of ankle, knee, hip and lumbar joint of one subject are depicted in Fig. 4. The left side shows the results of bodyweight squat while the right side shows the results of stoop.

There are 117266 sampling points in the data sequence and the sequence is then separated into wash part, training part and test part as mentioned in the experiment setup section. Inputs of ESN are joint torques and outputs are joint angles. The dynamic of human body, which is intended to be learned by ESN, is the compositive exhibition of musculoskeletal system and is supposed to be identical under the two movements. Thus only one ESN is used to extract the SSM of body dynamics from the experimental data of the two movements.

The effectiveness of using ESN to model bodyweight squat and stoop is shown in Fig. 5. The dash lines are the measured joint angles and the solid lines are the prediction results. The NRMSEs of ESN predicted results for ankle, knee, hip and lumbar joint are 0.12, 0.18, 0.18 and 0.22, respectively. The time consumption of training and prediction is 5.7 s. It should be mentioned that the depicted results are combination of the six groups

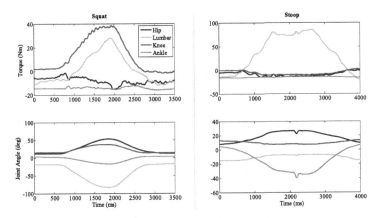

Fig. 4. Kinematics and kinetics data of squat and stoop movement

of motions and some abrupt changes can be found in the figures which are the connection points of different groups of data, not caused by calculation instability. Because only one ESN is applied in this study, the experimental results indicate that ESN is capable to model the dynamic of human movement no matter what kind of movements it is learned.

The size of the reservoir (n) and the spectral radius (ρ) of the reservoir connection matrix are the two important parameters involved the performance of ESN. They are usually adjusted manually according to the experience of the designer. We tested various combination of these two parameters to evaluate their effect on the experimental data. The results are shown in Fig. 6. Values are summation of NRMSEs of the four joints. It can be seen that there is no significant difference (T-Test, $p < 0.05$) among combinations of the two parameters except for the first column which represents the prediction results via reservoir size of 10. Considering that it takes more time to compute with a larger reservoir size, it is reasonable to choose the smallest size, which is 20 in our case, for SSM extraction.

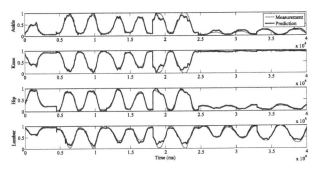

Fig. 5. Squat and stoop movement prediction results via ESNs. The results are normalized by maximum value.

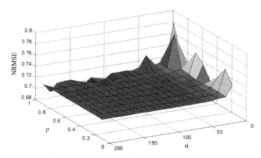

Fig. 6. ESNs parameter adjustment result for size of the reservoir (n) and the spectral radius (ρ)

The TIB-iMPC optimization results of MPC cost function parameter set of subject A are [0.89, 0.34, 0.01, 0.99] for bodyweight squat and [0.16, 0.35, 0.01, 0.99] for stoop. The parameters respectively represent the importance in the motion control process for hip, knee, ankle and lumbar joint. It can be indicated that weight for lumbar joint is the heaviest in both motions while hip joint weight is bigger in squat movement than in stoop movement. The weights for knee and ankle joint are almost the same in both motions and ankle joint weight is the smallest in both motions.

5 Conclusion and Future Work

In this paper, an ESN and input-tracking based inverse MPC method is proposed to extract human motion control intent in squat and stoop movement. The implementation of ESN simplifies the modeling process and preserves more modeling details for SSM of human dynamic movement. The input-tracking based bilevel optimization structure is capable to reveal the potential weights of cost function or control intent for various movements. The proposed method is verified by simulation and real-world experiments.

In the present study it is hard to implement OpenSim musculoskeletal model for forward dynamic prediction driven by physics engine. In the future we are intending to embed OpenSim model into MPC to increase movement prediction accuracy and reliance.

Acknowledgment. This work was supported by the National Natural Science Foundation of China under Grant 61603284 and 61903286.

References

1. Todorov, E.: Optimality principles in sensorimotor control. Nat. Neurosci. **7**, 907–915 (2004)
2. Kuo, A.D.: An optimal control model for analyzing human postural balance. IEEE Trans. Biomed. Eng. **42**, 87–101 (1995)
3. Dorn, T.W., Wang, J.M., Hicks, J.L., Delp, S.L.: Predictive simulation generates human adaptations during loaded and inclined walking. PLoS One **10**, e0121407 (2015)
4. Mombaur, K., Truong, A., Laumond, J.-P.: From human to humanoid locomotion—an inverse optimal control approach. Auton. Robot. **28**, 369–383 (2010)

5. Rebula, J.R., Schaal, S., Finley, J., Righetti, L.: A robustness analysis of inverse optimal control of bipedal walking. IEEE Robot. Autom. Lett. **4**, 4531–4538 (2019)
6. Ramadan, A., Choi, J., Radcliffe, C.J., Popovich, J.M., Reeves, N.P.: Inferring control intent during seated balance using inverse model predictive control. IEEE Robot. Autom. Lett. **4**, 224–230 (2019)
7. Pan, Y., Wang, J.: Model predictive control of unknown nonlinear dynamical systems based on recurrent neural networks. IEEE Trans. Industr. Electron. **59**, 3089–3101 (2012)
8. Armenio, L.B., Terzi, E., Farina, M., Scattolini, R.: Model predictive control design for dynamical systems learned by echo state networks. IEEE Control Syst. Lett. **3**, 1044–1049 (2019)
9. Xiang, K., Li, B.N., Zhang, L., Pang, M., Wang, M., Li, X.: Regularized Taylor echo state networks for predictive control of partially observed systems. IEEE Access **4**, 3300–3309 (2016)

EEG Characteristic Investigation
of the Sixth-Finger Motor Imagery

Yuan Liu[1]($\boxtimes$), Zhuang Wang[1], Shuaifei Huang[1], Jinze Wei[1], Xiaoqi Li[2],
and Dong Ming[1]

[1] Tianjin University, Tianjin 300072, China
ryanliu@tju.edu.cn
[2] No.208 Research Institute of China Ordnance Industries, Beijing 102202, China

Abstract. Supernumerary Robotic Limbs (SRL) are body augmentation robotic devices by adding extra limbs or fingers to the human body different from the traditional wearable robotic devices such as prosthesis and exoskeleton. We proposed a novel MI-based BCI paradigm based on the sixth-finger which imagines controlling the extra finger movements. The goal of this work was to investigate the EEG characteristics and the application potential of MI-based BCI systems based on the new imagination paradigm (sixth-finger MI). 14 subjects participated in the experiment involving the sixth-finger MI tasks and rest state. Event-related spectral perturbation (ERSP) was adopted to analyze EEG spatial and time-frequency features. Common spatial patterns (CSP) were used for feature extraction and classification was implemented by support vector machine (SVM). ERD (event-related desynchronization) was found in the supplementary motor area (SMA) and primary motor area (M1) with a faint contralateral dominance. Unlike traditional human hand MI, ERD was also found in frontal lobe. The highest accuracy of 80% and mean accuracy of 70%. This work provided a novel paradigm for MI-based MI system, widened the control bandwidth of the BCI system. In addition, we discussed the application potential of the sixth-finger MI.

Keywords: Supernumerary robotic limbs · Brain–Computer interface · Motor imagery · Wearable robotic · EEG characteristic

1 Introduction

SRL (Supernumerary Robotic Limbs) is an emerging wearable robot that supplements and augments the capability of existing biological limbs by adding extra limbs or fingers to the normal human body [1]. Compared with traditional wearable robotic devices such as prosthesis and exoskeleton which replace or attached to the human body, SRL exist independently of the human limbs, and will never restrict the movement of the human body [2, 3]. Therefore, the extra limbs have the following two advantages: 1) Innovated the morphological existence of human body, showing great potential to augment the motor function of healthy people [4]; and 2) for stroke patients with hemiplegia of the hand but intact limbs, the extra limbs can assist the patient to supplements for the lost hand motor function [5].

© Springer Nature Switzerland AG 2021
X.-J. Liu et al. (Eds.): ICIRA 2021, LNAI 13013, pp. 654–663, 2021.
https://doi.org/10.1007/978-3-030-89095-7_62

With the emergence and development of SRL, how to reasonably control the extra limbs is an active topic of discussion in the scientific community, and has received extensive attention from scholars [6–8]. At present, there are not only researches focusing on the enhancement of motor function of healthy human body by extra limbs, but also a few studies mentioning its important role in compensating for impaired motor function of patients with hemiplegia: In 2015, Faye Y. Wu proposed a SRF (Supernumerary Robotic Fingers) control strategy based on the Bio-Artificial Synergy [9]: mapping the posture of SPF through the body hand posture, and demonstrate that the extra fingers have the potential to provide those with impaired hands the opportunity to live with more independence and work more productively. However, this control strategy requires the user to wear data glove, which restricts the movement of human hands; moreover, most patients with upper limb hemiplegia do not have the hand movement function and cannot capture their hand movement posture. In 2016, Irfan Hussain propose a novel electromyographic (EMG) control interface to control SRF [10]. They use a commercial EMG armband for gesture recognition to control the robotic device and surface one channel EMG electrodes interface to regulate the compliance of the robotic device. And they have validated that the device can compensate and augment for the hand movement function with two sets of experiments. However, using this strategy to control SRF while occupying the freedom of the body limbs. In the same year, Irfan Hussain proposed a solution for this problem: an electromyographic (EMG) control interface E-Cap [11], through the forehead EMG signal (contracting the frontalis muscle) to control the flexion/extension of SRF. However, E-Cap will lead to an inconsistency between the intention of movement and the action of the end effector, which is called cognitive disconnection [12]; in addition, it lacks the participation of the central nervous system, so active training of the central nervous system for improving the stroke patients with hemiplegia motor function is not be fully mobilized.

Recently, BCI (Brain-computer interface) has become an important technical field for the transformation of brain science research into applications. It can provide a direct information exchange and control pathway for the brain directly interact with the external environment or external devices [13]; and it is also an applicable technology that helps patients with neurological and muscular disease establish contact with the outside [14]. Compared with EMG control interface and Bio-Artificial Synergy, the advantages of BCI are 1) expressing ideas or manipulating the device without the need of action, bypassing the brain's normal output pathways of peripheral nerves and muscles [15]; 2) the MI-based BCI system is of great significance to the motor rehabilitation for the stroke patients [16], because previous studies have shown that MI possesses the same activation of the brain area during the task movement execution and task movement imagination [17]. But at present, most of the studies about MI takes the motion of the body limbs as the imagination paradigm, this greatly limits the movement execution of the body limbs that is imagined to be in movement [18]. Only in 2018, Christian I. Penaloza proposed a BCI system in which healthy participants control the human-like robotic arm by imagining the movement of the robotic arm [19]. It is the first proof about the feasibility of controlling SRF through MI-based BCI under the multi-task conditions. However, this study only tried to recognize the movement intention of users, and not to further explore the response characteristics of the brain when imagining the movement of the robotic arm. And the classification accuracy has large individual differences, so if it is used as a universal control strategy, further exploration is needed.

The main contributions of this paper are 1) to propose a novel paradigm based on the sixth-finger for MI-based BCI; 2) to explore EEG patterns based on the sixth-finger MI tasks; 3) to discuss the application potential of the sixth-finger MI.

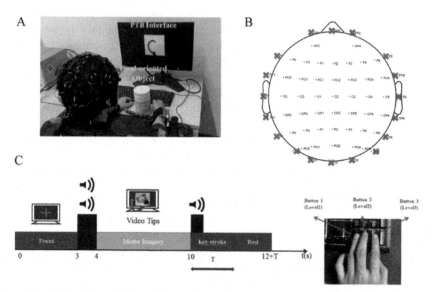

Fig. 1. Experimental paradigm and electrode positions. (a) Scene diagram of the experiment. (b) 42-electrode positions. (c) Experimental paradigm of one trial.

2   Methods

2.1   Experimental Procedure

14 right-handed healthy subjects (2 females and 12 males, 22–25 years old) participated in this experiment. All of the subjects have no prior experience with MI-based BCI before. As shown in Fig. 1(A), the subjects were sitting in a chair at one-meter distance in front of a computer screen, wearing SRF on the right wrist, and a cylindrical object is placed in front of the subjects. The evidence presented by Yong and Menon indicated that goal-oriented MI tasks lead to a better classification performance compared with simple MI tasks [20]. Figure 1(C) illustrates the experimental paradigm, each trial began with a green cross at the center of the monitor for 3 s. At second 3, a sound lasting for 1 s (beep sound, preparation cue) appeared to remind subjects of being prepared for MI task. At second 4 a video tip (SRF bended) appeared, and in the next 6 s, subjects are asked to perform MI tasks (grasping an object with SRF). At second 10, a text and a beep sound appeared to remind subjects to score the completion quality of their MI task within Ts (max 0.5 s) based on subjective judgment, there are three levels,

corresponding to three buttons. At last, the screen became blank for 2 s and subjects remained at rest to prepare for the next trial. Experiments are divided into three sessions, 1) Training session: subjects completed the MI tasks (40 trails) according to the tips, and the experimenter controlled the bending of SRF through Bluetooth at second 6–7 s; 2) MI tasks signal acquisition session: subjects completed the same MI tasks (100 trails) as the training session, but in this session SRF remain still; 3) Rest signal acquisition session: subjects kept rest (80 trails). The subjects were asked to concentrate mind on performing the indicated motor imagery task kinesthetically rather than a visual type of imagery while avoiding any motion during imagination. As shown above, SRF were worn on the subject's right wrist. This is because that the human likeness of the robot may raise the illusion of body ownership transfer (BOT) in subjects [21]. And through the movement feedback of SRF during the training session, the subjects can raise the sensation of owning the robot's body [22]. Finally, we take the second (MI tasks signal acquisition) and third session (Rest signal acquisition) EEG data for analysis.

The EEG signals were acquired by a Neuroscan SynAmps2 amplifier whose sampling rate is 1000 Hz and band-pass filtering range is 0.5–100 Hz. Besides, an additional 50-Hz notch filter was used during signal acquisition. EEG data was recorded from 42 Ag/AgCl scalp electrodes placed according to the International 10/20 System referenced to nose and grounded prefrontal lobe from Fig. 1(B). Peripheral channels along frontal and temporal sites were rejected. These channels were removed because they were most likely to be strongly influenced by artifacts such as visual interference, eye movements, or muscular activity. Thereafter, the original EEG signals were common average referenced, band-pass filtered between 8 and 30 Hz, and downsampled at 250 Hz. Before further analysis, ICA was adopted here in the pre-processing to remove eye movement artifacts.

The study was approved by the ethical committee of Tianjin University. All subjects signed informed consent in advance.

2.2 Time–frequency and Topographical Analysis of ERD/ERS

MI produces significant ERD over the contralateral central area during imagination of right and left hands movement. The event-related spectral perturbation (ERSP) allows us to observe the spectral power changes of the induced EEG relative to the stimulus from the views of time-frequency domain [23], which could supply more details about ERD/ERS patterns of MI tasks [24]. ERSP defined as follows:

$$ERSP(f,t) = \frac{1}{n}\sum\nolimits_{k=1}^{n}(F_k(f,t)^2) \qquad (1)$$

where n is the number of trails, and $F_k(f,t)^2$ is the spectral estimation of kth trial at frequency f and time t. Topographical distribution is a method for us to figure out which areas of the brain are involved when ERD occurs during the different tasks [25], mean ERSP values of 42-electrode Mu (8–13 Hz) and central Beta rhythm (20–25 Hz) were calculated from 2000 to 5000 ms after the MI task onset (at second 4). And, in order to explore the differences of energy changes over time in specific brain regions between the rest tasks and the MI tasks, mean ERSP values of single-channel were calculated from −1000 to 5000 ms after the MI task onset (at second 4) in Mu and central Beta rhythm for two types tasks. In this study, the time-frequency maps from three key electrodes C3, Cz, C4, and the ERSP wave maps from C3 were presented for analysis.

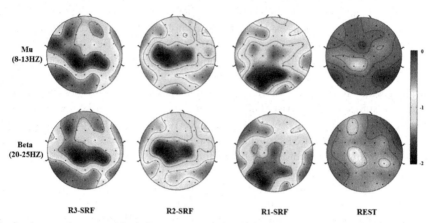

Fig. 2. Averaged topographical distribution of all subjects in the Mu band (8–13Hz) and central Beta band (20–25Hz). Blue indicates ERD.

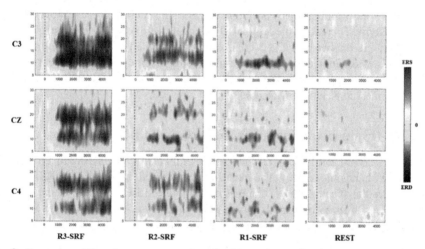

Fig. 3. Examples of time-frequency maps for all subjects,4 mental tasks, and 3 electrodes locations. R3-SRF represents the best performance on the MI task. R1-SRF represents the worst performance on the MI task. Blue means ERD. The red dashed lines indicate the onset of the MI task-related period.

2.3 EEG Signal Classification

Common spatial patterns (CSP) algorithm is a method to extract features of two classes based on multi-channel EEG information [26]. And SVM was used as the classifier. Firstly, the original 42-channel EEG data was preprocessed (downsampled at 250 Hz, common average referenced, band-pass filtered between 8 Hz and 13 Hz, total 4000 ms from 1000 to 5000 ms after the MI task onset). Then whole dataset of one subject was divided into a training set and a testing set. The training set served as the input of 2-class CSP algorithms in order to achieve CSP filters which were used to extract features. The classifier calculated based on the training set was used to classify the testing set. The estimation of the classification accuracy was executed by a 10-fold cross-validation strategy, and the final classification accuracy was calculated by averaging over all results of testing sets.

3 Results

3.1 EEG Topographical Distribution Maps

Figure 2 shows the average EEG topographical distribution maps of all subjects based on the 3 levels of MI tasks and rest state. R3/R2/R1-SRF respectively correspond to the best/ normally/ worst completing the MI tasks. The results show that ERD was found in the supplementary motor area (SMA) and primary motor area (M1) especially near C3 and C4 electrodes. With the improvement of the MI task quality, the more concentrated ERD occurs in the parietal lobe. When the level is R1-SRF, ERD in the parietal lobe will be weakened and will occur near the occipital lobe. This may be due to subjects applied incorrect mental strategy of MI tasks (imagining the scene of squeezing an object in the mind, but not its haptic sensation, force or position) [27]. Different from other studies about MI based on human hand, ERD was also found in frontal lobe in this work [12].

3.2 Time–frequency and ERSP Wave Maps

Figure 3 shows the averaged time-frequency maps of C3, C4 and Cz electrodes for MI tasks (R3/R2/R1-SRF) and rest state. The maps present a long-lasting Mu-ERD (8–13 Hz) and central beta-ERD (20–25 Hz) from MI task onset, especially clear for R3-SRF. It shows that the ERD in the key electrodes was more obvious with the increase of the quality of the MI tasks. A faint contralateral dominance could be observed for MI tasks, which have an obviously enhancement for R3-SRF. The averaged ERSP waves of Mu-ERD for R3-SRF are proposed, as shown in Fig. 4. From "All Subject", a long-lasting Mu-ERD occurs from MI task onset with −1000 to 0 ms as the baseline. For individual, the difference of the ERSP wave for bad subjects (in the red dashed frame) between the MI tasks (R3-SRF) and the rest state are significantly smaller than that for good subjects.

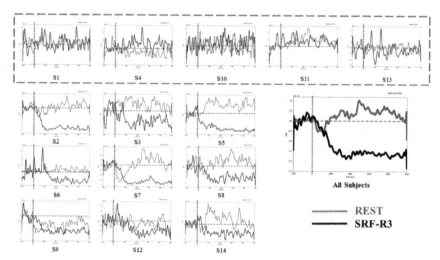

Fig. 4. The comparison of power (in dB) changes with time (in s) during MI tasks (SRF-R3), and resting state (REST) for electrode C3,in the Mu band (8–13Hz) .The red dotted line represents the start time of the task. S1-S14 represent the ERSP waves of 14 subjects, and All Subjects represents the average ERSP waves of all subjects. The ERSP wave maps of bad subjects are placed in the red dashed frame in the first row.

3.3 Classification Performance

To validate the separability of two task types, we analyzed the classification accuracy by CSP and SVM. As Fig. 5(A) shows, there are differences between each subject, but 8 subjects were 70% accurate or better, only 2 subjects have the classification accuracy of less than 60%. For some bad subjects (S4, S13), the classification accuracy is more than 70% but the difference of ERSP value in C3 between the MI tasks and rest state is small, this may because subjects applied incorrect mental strategy of MI tasks which caused ERD in the occipital lobe instead of the parietal lobe.

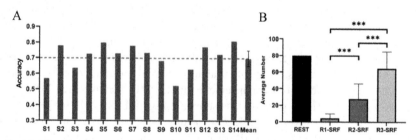

Fig. 5. (a) Classification accuracy obtained with CSP+SVM method. The error bar represents the STD. (b) The mean value of the number of 4 labels in 14 subjects. One-way ANOVA was conducted. *** represents P<0.001.

4 Discussion

4.1 EEG Characteristics of the sixth-finger Motor Imagery

The sixth-finger motor imagery activates neural networks in the motor area of Mu rhythm and Beta rhythm [28]. Such Mu-ERD and Beta-ERD was found during sixth-finger motor imagery with a faint contralateral dominance which is similar to the ERD spatial features of the human right-hand MI [25]. This may be due to the extra finger being worn on the right wrist of subjects.

Different from the human hand MI, ERD also was found in the frontal lobe during sixth-finger motor imagery. The reasons for this outcome may be that 1) in order to better regard the extra finger as their real finger when performing MI tasks, the subjects mobilized a lot of cognitive and attention resources on the sixth-finger; 2) for a better MI performance, subjects were explicitly asked to do a goal-oriented MI tasks, as shown in Fig. 1(A). There is evidence that frontal cortical areas are important in the control of goal-oriented behaviors and mediating cognition, abstraction, and attention [29]. Similarly, Christian I. Penaloza proposed that the extra limbs MI were able to modulate other brain areas which different from common motor imagery, such as the left and right frontal lobe [19].

As shown in Fig. 2, there is a difference between the best and worst completing the MI tasks. Different from R3-SRF level, in R1-SRF level (worst MI performance), ERD was weakened in the motor cortex, and more obvious ERD was found near the occipital lobe. It may be possible that, the subjects applied a visual type of MI rather than kinesthetic MI. In previous studies about MI, electrodes in occipital areas were not used due to their commonly known sensitivity to visual stimuli [19, 30].

4.2 The Sixth-Finger MI Application Potential

To the best of our knowledge, only one study [19] focused on the extra limb control by the third limb MI. The power spectral density (PSD) of an electrode was calculated and used to control the third arm. The classification accuracy for the MI tasks was 68.8% (mean). Besides, their aim is the application rather than the mechanism investigation. Different from them, we provide a systematic investigation of EEG characteristics to the extra finger MI. A more precision paradigm (sixth-finger MI) is implemented, and the classification accuracy were improved up to 70% (mean), which can meet the requirement of BCI recommended minimum accuracy level (70%) for controlling an external device [31]. Moreover, according to the higher number of R3-SRF (best MI performance) in Fig. 5(B), the novel paradigm is easy to be accepted by subjects. It indicates that the proposed novel imagination paradigm is feasible.

As MI-based BCI has been widely applied in the motor rehabilitation domains, the novel six-finger MI paradigm has the great application potentials in neural rehabilitation. It can recruit a larger range of neural activity in parietal lobe, and produces the ERD in frontal lobe which can't be activated by traditional human hand MI [25]. However, several limitations still exist. The classification accuracy of the sixth-finger MI is lower than that of the human inherent hand MI. The reasons may be: 1) short time using experience of the sixth-finger; 2) second (MI tasks signal acquisition) session without feedback leading to the weak body ownership. Although the application potential of the novel paradigm is discussed in this work, the actual clinical performance should be further verified in future work.

5   Conclusions

In our work, a novel imagination paradigm was proposed based on the sixth-finger. ERD was found in the supplementary motor area (SMA) and primary motor area (M1) with a faint contralateral dominance. Unlike traditional human hand MI, ERD was also found in frontal lobe. The highest accuracy of 80% and mean accuracy of 70%. These findings verified the feasibility of the sixth-finger MI, widened the control bandwidth of the MI-based BCI. In addition, the application potential of the sixth-finger MI is discussed, and we will conduct the clinical experiments to prove it in future work.

Acknowledgments. This work was supported in part by the National Natural Science Foundation of China (51905375), the China Post-doctoral Science Foundation Funded Project (2019M651033), Foundation of State Key Laboratory of Robotics and System (HIT) (SKLRS-2019-KF-06), and Peiyang Elite Scholar Program of Tianjin University (2020XRG-0023).

References

1. Prattichizzo, D., et al.: The sixth-finger: a modular extra-finger to enhance human hand capabilities. In: 2014 23rd IEEE International Symposium on Robot and Human Interactive Communication, pp. 993–998 (2014)
2. Carrozza, M.C., et al.: The SPRING hand: development of a self-adaptive prosthesis for restoring natural grasping. Auton. Robot. **16**(2), 125–141 (2004)
3. Rathee, D., et al.: Brain-machine interface-driven post-stroke upper-limb function-al recovery correlates with beta-band mediated cortical networks. IEEE Trans. Neural Syst. Rehabil. Eng. **27**(5), 1020–1031 (2019)
4. Wu, F.Y., Asada, H.H.: Decoupled motion control of wearable robot for rejecting human induced disturbances. In: 2018 IEEE International Conference on Robotics and Automation, pp. 4103–4110. IEEE (2018)
5. Salvietti, G., et al.: Compensating hand function in chronic stroke patients through the robotic sixth finger. IEEE Trans. Neural Syst. Rehabil. Eng. **25**(2), 142–150 (2017)
6. Shin, C.-Y., et al.: Ceiling work scenario based hardware design and control algorithm of supernumerary robotic limbs. In: 2015 15th International Conference on Control, Automation and Systems, pp. 1228–1230 (2015)
7. Hussain, I., et al.: Vibrotactile haptic feedback for intuitive control of robotic extra fingers. In: Colgate, J.E. et al. (eds.) 2015 IEEE World Haptics Conference, pp. 394–399 (2015)
8. Llorens-Bonilla, B., Asada, H.H.: A robot on the shoulder: coordinated human-wearable robot control using coloured petri nets and partial least squares predictions. In: 2014 IEEE International Conference on Robotics and Automation, pp. 119–125 (2014)
9. Wu, F.Y., Asada, H.H.: Implicit and intuitive grasp posture control for wearable robotic fingers: a data-driven method using partial least squares. IEEE Trans. Robot. **32**(1), 176–186 (2016)
10. Hussain, I., et al.: An EMG interface for the control of motion and compliance of a supernumerary robotic finger. Front. Neurorobot. **10**, 18 (2016)

11. Hussain, I., et al.: The soft-sixthfinger: a wearable EMG controlled robotic extra-finger for grasp compensation in chronic stroke patients. IEEE Robot. Autom. Lett. **1**(2), 1000–1006 (2016)
12. Ma, X., Qiu, S., He, H.: Multi-channel EEG recording during motor imagery of different joints from the same limb. Sci. Data **7**(1) (2020)
13. Bandara, D.S.V., Arata, J., Kiguchi, K.: A noninvasive brain-computer interface approach for predicting motion intention of activities of daily living tasks for an upper-limb wearable robot. Int. J. Adv. Robot. Syst. **15**(2) (2018)
14. Daly, J.J., et al.: Feasibility of a new application of noninvasive brain computer interface (BCI): a case study of training for recovery of volitional motor control after stroke. J. Neurol. Phys. Ther. **33**(4), 203–211 (2009)
15. Hochberg, L.R., et al.: Reach and grasp by people with tetraplegia using a neurally controlled robotic arm. Nature **485**(7398), 372-U121 (2012)
16. Wang, X., et al.: Differentiated effects of robot hand training with and without neural guidance on neuroplasticity patterns in chronic stroke. Front. Neurol. **9**, 810 (2018)
17. Bai, Z., et al.: Immediate and long-term effects of BCI-based rehabilitation of the upper extremity after stroke: a systematic review and meta-analysis. J. Neuroeng. Rehabil. **17**(1) (2020)
18. Penaloza, C., Hernandez-Carmona, D., Nishio, S.: Towards intelligent brain-controlled body augmentation robotic limbs. In: 2018 IEEE International Conference on Systems, Man, and Cybernetics (SMC), pp. 1011–1015 (2018)
19. Penaloza, C.I., Nishio, S.: BMI control of a third arm for multitasking. Sci. Robot. **3**(20) (2018)
20. Yong, X., Menon, C.: EEG classification of different imaginary movements within the same limb. PLoS One **10**(4) (2015)
21. Botvinick, M., Cohen, J.: Rubber hands 'feel' touch that eyes see. Nature **391**(6669), 756 (1998)
22. Alimardani, M., Nishio, S., Ishiguro, H.: Effect of biased feedback on motor imagery learning in BCI-teleoperation system. Front. Syst. Neurosci. **8**, 52 (2014)
23. Yi, W., et al.: EEG feature comparison and classification of simple and compound limb motor imagery. J. Neuroeng. Rehabil. **10** (2013)
24. Pfurtscheller, G., et al.: EEG-based discrimination between imagination of right and left hand movement. Electroencephalogr. Clin. Neurophysiol. **103**(6), 642–651 (1997)
25. Pfurtscheller, G., et al.: Mu rhythm (de)synchronization and EEG single-trial classification of different motor imagery tasks. Neuroimage **31**(1), 153–159 (2006)
26. Ben Hamed, S., Schieber, M.H., Pouget, A.: Decoding M1 neurons during multiple finger movements. J. Neurophysiol. **98**(1), 327–333 (2007)
27. Wang, Z., et al.: A BCI based visual-haptic neurofeedback training improves cortical activations and classification performance during motor imagery. J. Neural. Eng. **16**(6), 066012 (2019)
28. Asif, Z.U., et al.: Classification of non-discriminant ERD/ERS comprising motor imagery electroencephalography signals with novel REP-based approach. Int. J. Adv. Comput. Sci. Appl. **11**(1), 364–375 (2020)
29. Medendorp, W.P., et al.: Parietofrontal circuits in goal-oriented behaviour. Eur. J. Neurosci. **33**(11), 2017–2027 (2011)
30. Paek, A.Y., Agashe, H.A., Contreras-Vidal, J.L.: Decoding repetitive finger movements with brain activity acquired via non-invasive electroencephalography. Front. Neuroeng. **7**, 3 (2014)
31. Vidaurre, C., Blankertz, B.: Towards a cure for BCI Illiteracy. Brain Topogr. **23**(2), 194–198 (2010)

Performance Analysis of a Suspended Backpack Minimizing the Vertical Acceleration for Human Load Carriage

Bowen Zhang, Songyuan Zhang$^{(\boxtimes)}$, Xuanqi Zeng, and Yili Fu

State Key Laboratory of Robotics and System,
Harbin Institute of Technology, Harbin 150001, China
zhangsy@hit.edu.cn

Abstract. Backpacks are our commonly used tools to transport materials. However, when people are walking, the center of gravity of the human body will vibrate up and down with a certain amplitude and frequency. The traditional backpack vibrates vertically at the same amplitude and frequency as the human's COM movement, which will have a huge impact on the human body and increase energy consumption. In this paper, the model of human-backpack is analyzed and an active and passive mixing suspended backpack is designed, which had the ideal effect of reducing acceleration force, amplitude and improving energy efficiency. Through the prototype experiment and the walking test, it is verified that low damping and low stiffness can improve the damping performance of the backpack, and the effect of decreasing amplitude and acceleration force reduction of the backpack under the optimal parameters are obtained.

Keywords: Human walking · Load carriage · Energetic cost · Suspended backpack

1 Introduction

Backpacks are very common tools which have been used to carry a load. It is easy to find that the center of gravity (CoM) of human will move up and down as a different amplitude and frequency when humans with different height are walking at different speeds. However, due to tradition backpack's stiff connection to the human, it will vibrate in vertical direction as a same amplitude and frequency as the movement of CoM of human, which can cause extra force and make users less comfortable.

In recent years, there are several researches which aim to augment human capacity of bearing heavy load. Gonzalez et al. [1] designed a novel device, Extra Robotic Legs, which used two robotic legs to help operator bear heavy load. Park et al. [2] studied a wearable upper body suit with an actuator and springs to transfer a part of load from the shoulder to the waist and reduce dynamic load. And Rome et al. [3] used suspended backpack to achieve very desirable vibration reduction and accelerative force reduction.

© Springer Nature Switzerland AG 2021
X.-J. Liu et al. (Eds.): ICIRA 2021, LNAI 13013, pp. 664–675, 2021.
https://doi.org/10.1007/978-3-030-89095-7_63

Above all, we regard the suspended backpacks as most economic-friendly and practical device to replace the traditional backpack. Compared with traditional stiff backpack, these backpacks are designed as a suitable stiffness and damping to reduce the vertical vibration of load when people are walking. There are several researches about backpack with elastic elements which achieve different effect of reducing accelerative force and amplitude. For instance, Rome's suspended backpack [3] could achieve 82% decrease in peak accelerative vertical force and reduce 61.31% vertical oscillation while walking at 5.6 km/h with 27 kg load, whereas Foissac's backpack [4] only achieved 22% decrease in peak accelerative force with 3.7 km/h walking. According to the analysis by Ackerman et al. [5] and Hoover et al. [6], this is due to the fact the natural frequency of systems is different. However, although the benefit of the suspended backpack can be maximized by reducing the stiffness and damping to as close to zero as possible, the challenge is that the reduction of the spring coefficient is limited by the static deformation [6] which is so large that it cannot be used in practical backpack.

In this paper, we will analysis the human-backpack model and design a novel suspended backpack with most desirable effect in peak impact reduction, decreasing amplitude and improving energic efficiency with a more practical weight of load and in a large range of walking speed. This suspended backpack was designed as novel mechanical structure to achieve lowest stiffness and damping as well as solve the problem brought by large static deformation of springs. Besides, we also designed experimental platform to prove the desirable effect of this suspended backpack and proved that the lowest value of stiffness and damping really could make a great contribution to high performance of suspended backpack. In the end, we obtained the effect of decreasing amplitude and acceleration force reduction of the backpack under the optimal parameters through the walking test.

2   The Movement of CoM During Human Walking

According to the research conducted by Saunders et al. [7], the movement of center of gravity can be simplified as a sinusoidal vibration in the vertical direction as shown in Eq. (1):

$$y_1 = Y_1 sin(\omega t) \tag{1}$$

where, y_1 represents the vibration of CoM of human walking in the vertical direction, Y_1 represents the amplitude, ω represents the radial frequency and t represents the time.

According to the research conducted by Grieve et al. [8], the relationship between walking frequency f and walking velocity v can be described as Eq. (2):

$$f = 2 \times 64.8(\frac{v}{S})^{0.57} \tag{2}$$

where, S is the stature of human. Hence, the relationship between radial frequency ω and walking velocity v can be presented in Eq. (3):

$$\omega = \frac{4\pi \times 64.8(\frac{v}{S})^{0.57}}{60} \tag{3}$$

In order to simplify the human walking model, the leg length l_0 can be approximately described as 53% of stature according to anthropometry data in research of Roebuck et al. [9]. Then, the radial frequency ω can be written as Eq. (4):

$$\omega = 2\pi \times 1.504(\frac{v}{l_0})^{0.57} \tag{4}$$

Xu [10] described the human leg as an inverse pendulum model to analyze the movement of CoM of human in the vertical plane while walking. According to the analysis, the amplitude of CoM of human can be described as Eq. (5):

$$Y_1 = \frac{1}{2}l_0(1 - \sqrt{1 - (\frac{0.963v}{l_0 \times 2 \times 1.504(\frac{v}{l_0})^{0.57}})^2}) - 0.0157l_0 \tag{5}$$

According to the Eq. (1)–(5), the amplitude of CoM Y_1 and radial frequency ω when a person with 1.8 m height is walking as a different speed varying from 0.6 m/s to 2 m/s can be shown in Fig. 1. As shown in Fig. 1, the relationship between Y_1 and v is approximate linear. And with the increase of v, both Y_1 and ω rise.

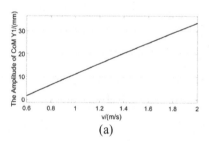
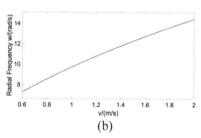

(a)   (b)

Fig. 1. The amplitude of CoM and radial frequency change with different walking speed: (a)The curve of the amplitude of CoM, (b)The curve of radial frequency.

3 Human-Backpack Model

According the analysis above, the movement of CoM during human walking can be simplified as a sine curve. Besides, the connection between human and backpack can be described as a spring K and a damper B. Hence, the human-backpack model can be built as Fig. 2. The vertical position of CoM of body is given as y_1 and the vertical position of backpack is given as y_2.

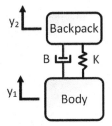

Fig. 2. Human-backpack model

As for a traditional backpack, the value of stiffness K and damping B are very high, where the load is fixed to the human body ($y_1 = y_2$). With regard to suspended backpack, the stiffness K and damping B can be designed as a suitable value to reduce the vertical movement of backpack ($y_1 > y_2$). Considering the model of Fig. 2, the motion of the backpack can be described as Eq. (6):

$$y_2 = Y_2 sin(\omega t - \phi) \tag{6}$$

where, Y_2 is the amplitude of vibration of backpack and φ is phase difference between the body and backpack.

Because there is an initial deformation of spring to support the backpack, the gravity of backpack can be eliminated from equilibrium equation. Equilibrium equation in the human-backpack model can be described as Eq. (7):

$$K(y_1 - y_2) + B\left(\dot{y}_1 - \dot{y}_2\right) = m\ddot{y}_2 \tag{7}$$

where m is the mass of the backpack.

Bringing Eq. (1) and Eq. (6) into Eq. (7), we can find that:

$$Y_2 = \sqrt{\frac{K^2 + \omega^2 B^2}{(K - m\omega^2)^2 + \omega^2 B^2}} Y_1 \tag{8}$$

$$\phi = a\ tan(\frac{m\omega^3 B}{K^2 - m\omega^2 K + B^2\omega^2}) \tag{9}$$

Because the spring and damper are the only connection between body and backpack, the force which the backpack exerts to the body can be described as Eq. (10):

$$F_{backpack\ to\ body} = K(y_1 - y_2) + B\left(\dot{y}_1 - \dot{y}_2\right) + mg$$

$$= mg + m\ddot{y}_2 = mg - m\omega^2 Y_2 \sin(\omega t - \phi) \tag{10}$$

Hence, the maximum impact which backpack exert to the body can be presented as Eq. (11):

$$F_{impact} = m\omega^2 Y_2 = m\omega^2 Y_1 \sqrt{\frac{K^2 + \omega^2 B^2}{(K - m\omega^2)^2 + \omega^2 B^2}} \tag{11}$$

According to the Eq. (8) and Eq. (11), there is no trade-off between reducing amplitude and reducing impact. we define β as amplitude reduction and impact reduction coefficient:

$$\beta = \sqrt{\frac{K^2 + \omega^2 B^2}{(K - m\omega^2)^2 + \omega^2 B^2}} \tag{12}$$

Figure 3(a) shows the change of β with stiffness K and damping B when m = 11 kg, v = 1.5 m/s. It can be found that when the B and K close to zero β also close to zero, which means that the system can achieve the most desirable effect of reducing amplitude and impact. However, whenever the stiffness K or damping B reaches a high value, the β will close to 1, which means that there is not any amplitude reduction and impact reduction effect.

Except that, the frequency ratio $\lambda = \frac{\omega}{\omega_n}$, natural radial frequency $\omega_n = \sqrt{\frac{K}{m}}$, damping ratio $\xi = \frac{B}{2m\omega_n}$, and β can also be expressed as below:

$$\beta = \sqrt{\frac{1 + (2\xi\lambda)^2}{(1 - \lambda^2)^2 + (2\xi\lambda)^2}} \tag{13}$$

And the amplitude-frequency characteristics curve of the human-backpack system is shown in Fig. 3(b). We can conclude that in order to achieve a desirable effect of reducing impact and amplitude, the human-backpack system should be in the suspended area. Under this situation, λ should be larger than 1.4.

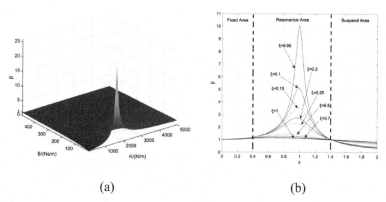

(a)   (b)

Fig. 3. The value of β under different stiffness K and damping B (a) and amplitude-frequency characteristics curve (b)

4 Mechanical Design

According to the above calculation and analysis, under the condition of low stiffness and damping, the natural radial frequency ω_n of the suspended backpack is very low. At this time, when people walk at normal or high speed, the walking redial frequency ω is much higher than the natural radial frequency ω_n of the suspended backpack and the effect of the backpack is very ideal. Besides, although low stiffness and damping will cause resonance of the system when the walking speed is slow, which will further increase the vibration and impact force, the vibration of human or backpack is very small due to the low speed.

However, in practice, there are two challenges to achieve low stiffness and low damping. Firstly, the stiffness and damping cannot be infinitely small and the bearing capacity of the spring with low stiffness is relatively poor. Secondly, once the suspended backpack bears a large load, the static displacement of spring will be very large due to the low stiffness of the system, which will lose its practical value.

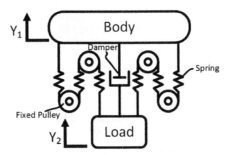

Fig. 4. Schematic diagram of structure

In order to solve the above two problems, we designed suspended backpack with a new mechanism as shown in Fig. 4. The system is designed by connecting two group springs and each group had three springs in series to reduce the stiffness and damping of the three springs in series to 1/3 of the single spring without reducing the bearing capacity. In order to solve the problem of static deformation of spring, the designed scheme adopts the structure of fixed pulleys to make the space needed in the vertical direction becomes one third of the original.

At the same time, in order to study effect of damping exerting to the system, a magnetic fluid damper FMR-70s-403 was also designed on the mechanism to adjust the damping. The prototype platform of suspended backpack is shown in Fig. 5(left). What's more, there is a locking mechanism used to evaluate whether the suspended backpack can outperform its traditional counterpart. There is a motor driving vibration behind the prototype of suspended backpack to simulate the vibration of CoM of different people at different walking speeds.

In addition, in order to test the damping effect of suspended backpack carried by human, we designed a wearable suspended backpack for walking test as shown in Fig. 5 (right). Based on the experimental prototype, we installed a DC motor for the wearable suspended backpack in order to control the backpack actively and optimized the mechanical mechanism to make the backpack more comfortable to carry.

Fig. 5. The Experimental platform of prototype and the wearable suspended backpack

5   Prototype Experiment

In order to verify theoretical analysis that low damping and low stiffness can achieve better effect of impact reduction and amplitude reduction the experimental environment was built as shown in Fig. 6. The NDI Optotrak Certus is used to capture movement of the vibration source and the suspended load. And there are a battery and a switching power supply which are used to supply the controller and motor respectively. Besides, the driver (Elmo) and controller are used to drive motor to rotate as a sinusoidal motion with different amplitude and frequency to simulate human walking at different speeds. During the experiment, the stature S was set to 1.8 m.

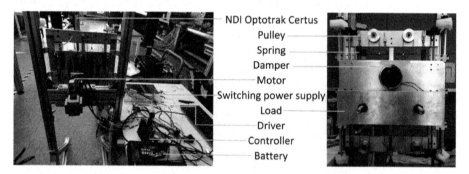

Fig. 6. The experimental environment of prototype experiment

In order to evaluate the performance of the suspended backpack under different spring stiffness, six different stiffness spring combinations from 238.67 N/m to 928.00 N/m are prepared by selecting springs with different pitch diameters and lengths.

5.1 Damping Measurement

For the sake of obtaining the actual damping value of the system, we exerted the suspended load(11.01 kg) with an initial disturbing force. By such means, the spring generates an initial deformation. The actual measured oscillation curve is shown in Fig. 7.

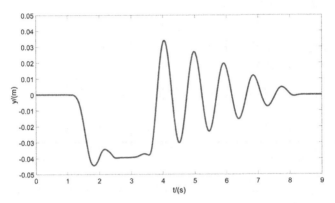

Fig. 7. The oscillation curve after being exerted an extra force

According to the energy conservation law, the energy conservation formula of system can be shown as below:

$$E_{spring1} + E_{p1} = E_{spring2} + E_{p2} + E_{damp} \tag{14}$$

where, $E_{spring1}$ and $E_{spring2}$ are the stored energy of the spring while E_{p1} and E_{p2} are the gravitational potential energy before and after the disturbance respectively. E_{damp} is the energy expended by the damping force. Then, it can be calculated that the damping of the system B is approximate 9 Ns/m.

5.2 Actual β Under Different Stiffness Value

We tested the actual performance of prototype of suspend backpack with different values of stiffness under a variety of walking speeds and compared them with theoretical results to prove the theoretical analysis. By changing the vibration amplitude and frequency of the motor to simulate the vibration movement of CoM of human with different walking speeds and real-time detecting the amplitude Y_1 of the vibration source and the amplitude Y_2 of the suspended load under different stiffness, we got actual β under different walking speed and stiffness as shown in Fig. 8.

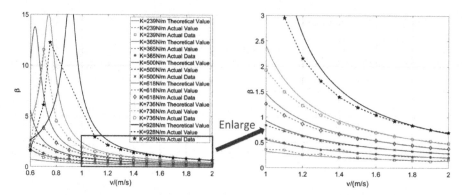

Fig. 8. The value of β under different stiffness

According to the Fig. 8, we can find that the theoretical curve and actual curve of β are similar basically and the lower stiffness of system can cause the lower value of β, which means that the effect of reducing amplitude is greater. Especially, when the value of stiffness is 238.67 N/m which is the lowest stiffness the system can achieve, the amplitude can be reduced to 26% or even lower at the walking speed varying from 1.2 m/s to 2 m/s. The amplitude of suspended load with 5.6 km/h walking speed with 11 kg load was shown in Fig. 9, which can achieve 81.74% amplitude reduction. Through the data from experiment, the peak acceleration force decreases from 40.87 N to 6.81 N, which achieves 83.33% reduction of acceleration force.

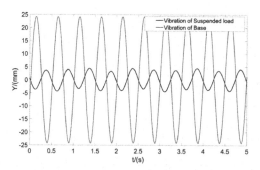

Fig. 9. Vibration under $K = 238.67$ N/m and walking speed $= 5.6$ km/h

Due to the travel limitation of the mechanical structure during the test, it is impossible to measure the amplitude of some resonance points. But it can be concluded that although it will have resonance when the damping is only about 9 Ns/m and the walking speed is less than 0.6 m/s, the active vibration amplitude Y_1 is only 1.7 mm and the vibration amplitude Y_2 of the suspended load is about 2.57 mm, which is acceptable.

6   Walking Test

In the walking test, the NDI Optotrak Certus tracked the marked points on the suspended platform and back frame. The computer received the coordinate data recorded and connected the controller to record the acceleration data of IMU on the suspended platform. The experimental environment is shown in Fig. 10.

Fig. 10. The experimental environment of walking test

The volunteer (age: 23, height: 1.82 m, weight: 72 kg) moved at a constant speed of 5, 6 and 7 km/h on the treadmill, respectively with 16 kg load (excluding the weight of the backpack). Three experimental groups were designed: 1) The load moved passively relative to the back frame, 2) The load moved relative to the back frame with active control, and 3) The load was locked on the back frame. When the gait was stable, the acceleration data of the load and the displacement data of the volunteer and the load in the vertical direction were recorded. After data processing, we calculated the ratio of the load amplitudes of the active/ passive backpack to the amplitudes of CoM of the human body as well as the ratio of the acceleration force of active/passive backpack to the acceleration force of the lock backpack as shown in Table 1.

Table 1. The performance of wearable suspended backpack

Backpack status	Walking speed	The ratio of the load amplitudes	The ratio of the acceleration force
passive	5 km/h	22.32%	6.55%
passive	6 km/h	22.17%	6.30%
passive	7 km/h	20.03%	5.63%
active	5 km/h	18.44%	6.71%
active	6 km/h	16.84%	5.98%
active	7 km/h	18.87%	5.39%

According to the Table 1, we can find that the amplitude can be reduced to as much as 20.03% and acceleration force can be reduced to 5.63% with the passive backpack at 7 km/h while the amplitude can be reduced to as much as 16.84% and acceleration

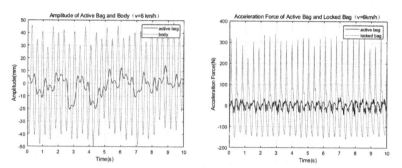

Fig. 11. The amplitude and acceleration force of active backpack at 6 km/h with 16 kg load

force can be reduced to 5.98% with the active backpack at 6 km/h. The best damping performance of backpack is at 6 km/h with active control as shown in Fig. 11.

Through the walking test as shown in Fig. 11, it is also verified that the movement of the human body in the vertical direction tends to be sinusoidal and the motion frequency increases with the increase of speed. While although the load movement of the passive/active backpack is not a sinusoidal motion, it can be seen that its motion has a certain regularity. When the average position of CoM of the human body is stable at a certain height, the suspended platform will fluctuate slightly near a certain position. However, due to the uneven force exerted by the legs, when the average height of CoM of the human body fluctuates constantly up and down, the average position of the suspended platform will move up and down greatly. In addition, we find that the suspended backpack has a certain influence on the movement of the human, and the backpack will have a better damping effect when human adapts to the suspended backpack.

7   Conclusion

According to the experiments and analysis, there is the better effect of amplitude reduction and acceleration force reduction with higher walking frequency. At the same time, under the low stiffness, the human frequency will be far greater than the natural frequency of the backpack when people walk at normal speed, which can effectively reduce the amplitude of the load. As for the damping, the lower damping can cause the larger vibration difference between the load and the CoM of the human body result in the vibration of the load is very small. And for the suspended backpack with low stiffness, although the resonance phenomenon will occur when the walking speed of people is very low, the amplitude of the suspended load is still very small after certain amplification due to the vibration of CoM of people is also very small at low speed, which will not be much extra burden. Moreover, the walking speed of people is generally about 1.5 m/s, under which the walking frequency is far larger than the natural frequency of low stiffness backpack. So, the suspended backpack with low stiffness and low damping has great practical value.

Acknowledgement. This research was funded by the National Natural Science Foundation of China (61703124), and the Self-Planned Task (NO. SKLRS201714A) of State Key Laboratory of Robotics and System (HIT).

References

1. Gonzalez, D.J., Asada, H.H.: Design of extra robotic legs for augmenting human payload capabilities by exploiting singularity and torque redistribution. In: Maciejewski, A. (ed.) 2018 IEEE/RSJ International Conference on Intelligent Robots and Systems (IROS), pp. 4348–4354. IEEE, Madrid (2018)
2. Park, J.-H., Stegall, P., Zhang, H., Agrawal, S.: Walking with a backpack using load distribution and dynamic load compensation reduces metabolic cost and adaptations to loads. IEEE Trans. Neural Syst. Rehabil. Eng. **25**(9), 1419–1430 (2017)
3. Rome, L.C., Flynn, L., Yoo, T.D.: Biomechanics: rubber bands reduce the cost of carrying loads. Nature **444**(7122), 1023–1024 (2006)
4. Foissac, M., Millet, G.Y., Geyssant, A., Freychat, P., Belli, A.: Characterization of the mechanical properties of backpacks and their influence on the energetics of walking. J. Biomech. **42**(2), 125–130 (2009)
5. Ackerman, J., Seipel, J.: A model of human walking energetics with an elastically-suspended load. J. Biomech. **47**(8), 1922–1927 (2014)
6. Hoover, J., Meguid, S.A.: Performance assessment of the suspended backpack. Int. J. Mech. Mater. Des. **7**(2), 111–121 (2011)
7. Saunders, J.B., Inman, V.T., Eberhart, H.D.: The major determinants in normal and pathological gait. J. Bone Joint Surg. **35**(3), 543–558 (1953)
8. Grieve, D.W., Gear, R.J.: The relationships between length of stride, step frequency, time of swing and speed of walking for children and adults. Ergonomics **9**(5), 379–399 (1966)
9. Roebuck, J.A., Kroemer, K.H.E., Thomson, W.G.: Engineering Anthropometry Methods. Wiley-Interscience, New York (1975)
10. Xu, X.: An investigation on the interactivity between suspended backpack and human gait. Graduate dissertation, Faculty of North Carolina State University, Raleighc (2008)

The Design Principle and Method of Load-Carrying Lower Limb Exoskeleton Based on Passive Variable Stiffness Joint

Huaqing Fan, Wenbin Chen[✉], Jingming Che, and Zhijie Zhou

Huazhong University of Science and Technology, Wuhan 430074, Hubei, China
wbchen@hust.edu.cn

Abstract. In human daily life, walking with load is a very common activity, it can significantly increase the pressure on the body's musculoskeletal system even lead to injury when human walking with excessive load. Several exoskeleton devices have been developed to assist the body with load carriage in recent years, though these devices still have some limitations. In this paper, we propose a passive variable stiffness joint based on a Shear-Thickening Gel (STG) with shear-thickening properties, which rapidly increases in stiffness upon impact. Based on such feature of the joint, we propose a new design method of a passive load-carrying lower-limb exoskeleton that can passively induce the joint to vary stiffness during the walking phase. The joints of the exoskeleton show high stiffness in the support phase and weak stiffness in the swing phase during assisted walking. In addition, the motion simulation of the exoskeleton is carried out in ADAMS software in this paper, the simulated joint movement and plantar force data show that the exoskeleton can move freely with the human body without interference, and it can transfer the partial load to the ground during human walking with the loaded carriage. The work in this paper provides a new idea and method for the research related to assisted human load-carrying walk, and also has a certain guidance and reference role for the design of lower limb exoskeleton devices.

Keywords: Shear-thickening gel · Variable stiffness joint · Passive exoskeleton

1 Introduction

Walking with load is a common activity in military operations, with the modernization of military equipment, soldiers are required to carry 20 kg or heavier backpacks for various operations during military missions, which greatly increases the burden on themselves [1–3]. In order to reduce the burden on soldiers, researchers have developed several exoskeleton devices to assist the body in load-carrying movements.

Lower limb exoskeletons can be divided into active and passive exoskeletons according to the presence or absence of the external power source [4, 5]. Active exoskeletons have many limitations due to the excessive mass and lack of power and other factors. Therefore, researchers have turned their attention to passive exoskeletons to circumvent the limitations of active exoskeletons,for example: researchers at MIT proposed a

© Springer Nature Switzerland AG 2021
X.-J. Liu et al. (Eds.): ICIRA 2021, LNAI 13013, pp. 676–686, 2021.
https://doi.org/10.1007/978-3-030-89095-7_64

quasi-passive load-carrying lower limb exoskeleton in 2007 [6]; W. Van Diik proposed a non-anthropomorphic quasi-passive lower limb exoskeleton called Exobuddy which can transfer the load of backpack to the ground in 2018 [7]; and researchers at the University of Ottawa in Canada proposed a seated passive lower limb exoskeleton to assist body's own mass in 2019 [8]. Combined with the above studies, we can find that the devices that can assist walking with load mostly are quasi-passive exoskeletons, which still need additional power source to control the device's work, purely passive exoskeletons are mostly designed to assist the body's own movement, can't directly transfer the load to the ground. The purely passive exoskeleton which can assist walking with load is still need to be developed.

Inspired by the special properties of a new smart material: Shear-Thickening Gel (STG) [9], we propose a design method of passive variable stiffness joints in this paper. STG is a smart material widely used in the field of protection, its nature is a long-chain polymer, which subjected to shear, compression or other external forces will exhibit shear thickening characteristics. In the normal state, STG is rubbery, showing the characteristics as fluid; and when subjected to impact, its stiffness will increase rapidly, showing the characteristics as rigid body, and will gradually return to its original state after the impact disappears [10].

According to the movement pattern of lower limbs, we know that during the walking phase, the joints overall show a law that high stiffness in the support phase to transmit the load, and weak stiffness in the swing phase to swing freely [11–15]. In order to make the variable stiffness feature of the vs-joints fit better with the motion law of human body, we clarify the working process of the vs-joints in the exoskeleton: the stiffness of the vs-joints increases with impact during the support phase, so as to transfer the load to the ground as a rigid structure; during the swing phase, the stiffness of the vs-joints returns to normal, so as to move freely with the human lower limb. Therefore, we propose a design method to embed the vs-joints into the whole exoskeleton and induce its variable stiffness characteristics reasonably by human motion. Then, we develop a passive load-carrying lower limb exoskeleton device to assist the human walking with load.

For lower limb exoskeleton devices, their effectiveness usually requires both kinematics and kinetics to be verified: kinematic data can verify if the human body can wear the device to move freely without interference, and through the dynamics data we can evaluate the effect of the exoskeleton device to assist walking with load [16–18]. The device was simulated and analyzed by the dynamic simulation software ADAMS in order to verify the effectiveness of the exoskeleton device design method [19]. And the result shows that the exoskeleton device can freely follow the body movement without interference, and the exoskeleton device can transfer part of the load to the ground.

In this paper, we design a passive variable stiffness joint based on a new material-STG, and combined with the law of human lower limb movement, we propose a variable stiffness joint embedding mechanism that uses human motion to passively trigger changing of joint stiffness. Through the regulator mechanism ensures that the variable stiffness joints undergo a regular sudden change in stiffness to support the load periodically. On this basis, this paper proposes a new design method of passive load-carrying lower limb exoskeleton, and verifies the effectiveness of the device design principle by simulation.

The research content of this paper has some guiding significance and reference value for the design of load-carrying devices and the application of intelligent materials STG.

2 Method

2.1 Human Movement Gait and Principles of Exoskeleton Design

As an anthropomorphic exoskeleton [7, 20], the exoskeleton should simulate the movement pattern of human lower limbs, and the law of variable stiffness of the vs-joint should also be matched with human joints.

According to the movement law of human joints, we propose the design principle of the lower limb exoskeleton, as shown in Fig. 1B, since the space at the ankle joint is less and the movement is complicated, the vs-joints are arranged at the hip and knee joints respectively. As shown in Fig. 1A, we know that the hip joint is continuously extended during the support phase, the vs-joint also continues to be compressed and leads to the increase of stiffness; and during the swing phase, the hip joint starts to flex, the vs-joint is stretched and the stiffness returns to normal. However, the motion law of the knee joint is more complicated than the hip joint, the knee joint performs the reciprocal motion of extension and flexion during both the support phase and the swing phase, which causes compression and tension to the vs-joint reciprocally. Therefore, we set a clutch at the knee joint as a regulating device to convert the reciprocal oscillation of the knee joint into one-way linear motion, which ensures that the vs-joint will only be compressed in the support phase and will return to its original state in the swing phase. And in thus way, the vs-joint can be matched with the motion pattern of the human lower limb knee joint.

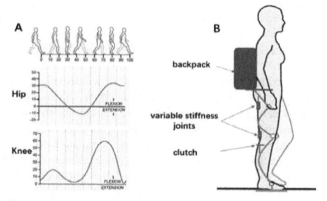

Fig. 1. Lower limb movement law and exoskeleton model. A: Hip and knee joint motion angle; B: The principle model of exoskeleton.

2.2 The Variable Stiffness Joint

Based on the above analysis of STG material properties and the working principle of lower limb exoskeleton, we propose the design method of the variable stiffness joint, as shown in Fig. 2A. The vs-joint consists of components such as shell, compression stick, STG material, material capsule, and spring. The material capsule is made of an elastic soft rubber, which is filled with STG material. A gap exists between the material capsule and the shell so that the material capsule can expand when STG is compressed. The compression stick is connected to the material capsule and the exoskeleton respectively, whose main purpose is to transmit the motion of the exoskeleton and to compress or stretch the STG material. And the main function of the spring is to accelerate the recovery of the STG, the restoration process of the STG material can be adjusted by choosing springs with different stiffness.

Since the motion law of the hip joint is relatively simple, we take the hip joint as an example to introduce the arrangement and design of the variable stiffness joint. It is essential to comprehend the connection between the lower limb joint stiffness and the variation pattern of vs-joint during the gait cycle [21–23]. Joint stiffness is usually defined as the ratio of the variation of the joint moment to the variation of the joint angle, and the equation is as follows:

$$K_{JOINT} = \Delta M / \Delta \theta \tag{1}$$

In the equation, K_{JOINT} represents the joint stiffness, ΔM represents the variation value of joint torque, and $\Delta \theta$ represents the variation value of joint angle.

As shown in Fig. 2B, the vs-joint is in a triangular shape with two rods in the center of rotation of the hip joint. The stiffness of the vs-joint can be described approximately by a variable stiffness spring, and the equation is as follows:

$$K_{VSJ} = \Delta F / \Delta L \tag{2}$$

In the equation, K_{VSJ} represents the stiffness of the vs-joint, ΔF represents the value of the variation of the pressure on the vs-joint, ΔL represents the value of the variation of the length of the vs-joint, which is the compressed length.

If the hip joint torque is supplied entirely by the variable stiffness joint in the theoretical case, we can obtain:

$$M = F * h \tag{3}$$

In the equation, M represents the joint torque of hip, F represents the pressure on the vs-joint, h is the vertical distance from the vs-joint to the center of rotation of the hip joint.

By the cosine theorem in the triangular structure formed by the two rods at the center of rotation and the vs-joint, we can obtain:

$$L^2 = a^2 + b^2 - 2ab\cos\theta \tag{4}$$

In the equation, L represents the length of the rod which the vs-joint is located, a, b are the two rod lengths at the center of hip rotation, θ is the angle of the center of hip rotation.

The maximum stiffness of the vs-joint is mainly determined by the maximum pressure to be imposed and the maximum compressed length. From Eq. (3), we can obtain:

$$F_{max} = M_{max}/h \tag{5}$$

That means that the maximum pressure is determined by the maximum value of the joint torque and the distance from the vs-joint to the center of rotation of the hip joint.

In the triangular structure, the compressed length of the variable stiffness joint is determined by the rotation angle of the center of rotation of the hip joint, and according to Eq. (4), we can obtain:

$$\Delta L = \sqrt{a^2 + b^2 - 2ab\cos(\theta_0 + \Delta\theta)} - \sqrt{a^2 + b^2 - 2ab\cos\theta_0} \qquad (6)$$

In the equation, θ_0 is the initial angle of the rotation center of the hip joint, $\Delta\theta$ is the maximum variation of the rotation angle of the center of rotation.

According to the size limitation of the exoskeleton to fit the body, we initially set a $= 50$ mm, b $= 100$ mm, $\theta_0=130°$, and according to the law of human gait walking, we know that the human body in the process of walking, the hip joint maximum rotation angle range $\Delta\theta \approx 40°$, the maximum joint torque of hip $M_{max} \approx 1000$ N mm/kg the mass of backpack is 20 kg [12]. By substituting the above data into Eqs. (5) and (6), we can initially obtain the maximum pressure and maximum compressed length of the vs-joint as: $F_{max} = 400$ N, $\Delta L = 15$ mm, and based on these two parameters, the overall dimensions of the variable stiffness joint and the specific parameters of the STG material can be determined.

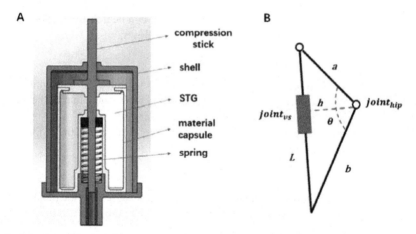

Fig. 2. Principle of the vs-joint structure and arrangement. A: Structure of the vs-joint; B: Principle of the vs-joint arrangement

2.3 Design Method and Working Process of Exoskeleton

Based on the above analysis of the human walking motion law and exoskeleton design principles, combined with the design of vs-joint, we propose the design method of passive lower limb exoskeleton based on the vs-joint to assist human walking with load. As shown in Fig. 3A, the exoskeleton is mainly consist of load carrying mechanism, load supporting mechanism, variable stiffness joint mechanism and clutch regulating mechanism. The load carrying mechanism mainly includes a width adjustable belt and the corresponding connection device, which mainly plays the role of fixing and loading the load backpack, and due to the relatively complex curve of human waist, considering the comfort and compactness of the device, we adopted the inverse modeling method, and designed a load carrying mechanism that fits the curve of human waist by extracting the data of human waist curve; the load supporting mechanism mainly includes thigh and shank connecting rods, ankle device and corresponding connections for transferring the load of the belt and the weighted backpack to the ground, where the thigh and shank connecting rods are connected to the lower limbs of the human body through flexible straps to freely follow the motion of the human body, and their length is designed according to the size of the lower limbs of an adult of 170 cm in height, the ankle device is directly connected to the ground for finally transferring the load to the ground; the vs-joints are arranged at the hip and knee joints respectively, and their stiffness can be changed passively with the movement of the lower limbs during human movement to transfer the load. As the control device of knee joint, The main function of the clutch is to convert the reciprocal oscillation at the human knee joint into a straight line motion in one direction, thus ensuring that the vs-joint at the knee joint will only be compressed in the support phase and stretched in the swing phase.

As shown in Fig. 3B, the clutch device mainly consists of two rack and gear rotating pairs, and each rotating pair consists of a rack and two gears, all four gears are connected to the drive shaft through unidirectional bearings with a maximum damping of 2.5 N/mm, The rack 1 engages with two unidirectional gears 1, 2 and is connected to the exoskeletal calf rod by a connecting rod that slides in a slide groove in the clutch shell, and the rack 2 engages with the unidirectional gears 3 and 4 and is connected to the compression rod of the vs-joint.

The working process of the clutch is shown in Fig. 4. During the support phase, the exoskeleton shank rod drives the rack 1 through a crank slider mechanism, and the reciprocating oscillation of the shank rod is converted into a one-way linear motion and transmitted to the rack 2 due to the one-way bearing, which is converted into compression of the vs-joint. And the rack 1 is disengaged from the gear when it is about to enter the swing phase by the designing of the engagement length of the gear and rack 1, and the variable stiffness joint can return to original state by gravity.

As shown in Fig. 5, we introduce the working process of the exoskeleton device by introducing the hip joint in one gait cycle of human walking: at the beginning of the gait cycle, the human foot begins contact the ground, the lower limb enters the support phase, and the human hip joint gradually begins to extend. The human thigh drives the thigh rod of the exoskeleton to extend and compress the stiffness of the vs-joint, which leading to a rapid increase in stiffness, and the triangle formed by the vs-joint becomes a rigid structure and transfers the load to the knee joint. And when entering the swing phase, the human hip joint begins to flex, the human thigh drives the exoskeleton thigh rod movement, the variable stiffness joint is stretched and its stiffness returns to normal, at which time the exoskeleton can swing freely with the human body. At this point, the exoskeleton completes a whole gait cycle of movement for the next gait cycle of human walking.

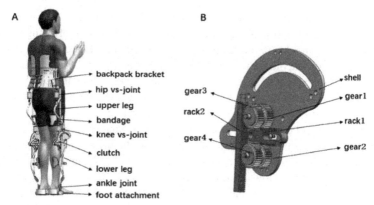

Fig. 3. Structure design of the exoskeleton. A: Sketch of the overall structure of the exoskeleton; B: Structure of the clutch.

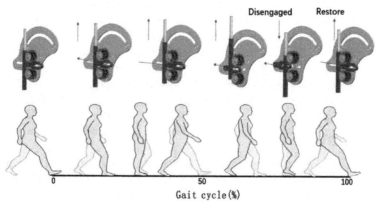

Fig.4. Working process of the clutch. In gait cycle, the rack and gear in the clutch continuously engages and disengages with the exoskeleton, and acting on the vs-joint through the rack 2. And the red arrow represents the direction of movement of the rack.

2.4 Simulation

In order to verify the effectiveness of the exoskeleton device, we use the multi-body dynamics software-ADAMS to simulate the kinematics and dynamics of the exoskeleton.As shown in Fig. 6A, in order to facilitate the simulation calculation, we simplified the human body and the lower limb exoskeleton device in the process of importing the exoskeleton model into ADAMS. The vs-joints are replaced by vs-springs, and the variable stiffness curve of the vs-joints is used as the stiffness curve of the springs, which can approximate simulate the variable stiffness characteristics of the vs-joints.

In the simulation process, we input the joint motion data of human walking to make the human walk on the ground in two states with or without the exoskeleton device. The exoskeleton joint motion data and ground support force were measured to verify whether the exoskeleton can assist in load-carrying without interfering with the human body.

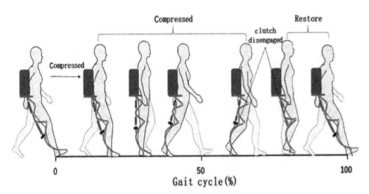

Fig. 5. Working process of the exoskeleton. During the gait cycle, the stiffness of the vs-joints at hip and knee increase in support phase to transmit the load; the stiffness returns to original state in swing phase to move freely. The green color in the figure represents the initial state of the vs-joints; red represents the vs-joints being compressed; and yellow represents the vs-joints being stretched or restoring. (Color figure online)

3 Result

3.1 Joint Motion Angle

As shown in Fig. 6B, the joint motion angle curves of the hip and knee of the human model and the exoskeleton device during one walking gait cycle are shown. It can be seen that the hip and knee joint motion angle curves of the exoskeleton are basically coincident with the human model under the neglect of errors, which indicates that the exoskeleton device can freely follow the human motion during the motion without interference.

3.2 Ground Reaction Force

We can verify the ability of the exoskeleton device to assist the body in load-carrying movement by measuring the ground reaction force of the body with or without the exoskeleton. As shown in Fig. 6C, the ground reaction force has a somewhat reduced with exoskeleton compared to without exoskeleton (about 45% of the pack load on average). This means that a part of load is transferred directly to the ground through the exoskeleton device, and the exoskeleton has the function of assisting the body to walk with load.

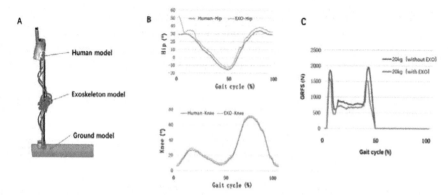

Fig. 6. Result of the simulation. A: the model of human and exoskeleton in simulation. During the simulation, the exoskeleton is driven on the ground model by inputting motion to the human body. B: The curve of the motion of hip and knee. In the figure, the above is the hip curve and the below is the knee joint, the orange curve represents the human joint angle and the light green curve represents the exoskeleton. C: Ground reaction force with or without Exo. The blue curve represents the grfs without Exo and the orange represents the grfs with Exo. In the support phase, the grfs curve with Exo is significantly compared to without Exo. (Color figure online)

4   Conclusion

This paper presents a lower limb exoskeleton device designed to assist the human body walking with load. Different from previous load-carrying exoskeleton devices, the working mechanism of this exoskeleton is completely passive, whose central part is a variable stiffness joint designed based on STG material. The working process of the exoskeleton device is completely triggered by human motion passively without additional power source, which greatly simplifies the complexity and mass of the exoskeleton device.

It is also necessary to study the characteristics of STG materials and variable stiffness joints. The assistive effect of exoskeleton is determined by the variable stiffness characteristics of the vs-joints. If the stiffness of the STG material varies too widely, it will interfere with human movement and bring discomfort; and if the stiffness of the STG material varies too short, the effect of the exoskeleton will be limited. The choice of STG materials with different variable stiffness properties and vs-joints within the range of effective assistance can be adapted to the requirements of different subjects and experiments.

In this paper, the effectiveness of the exoskeleton device is verified through simulation. The analysis of the simulation results show that the exoskeleton can move freely with the human body without interference, and the exoskeleton can transfer a part (about 45% on average) of the backpack load to the ground in the support phase of the gait cycle. However, this paper has not yet developed wearable experiments for the exoskeleton device, and the actual effect assistance of the exoskeleton is still left to verify.

In conclusion, this paper proposes a design method of a passive lower limb exoskeleton for load-carrying. The exoskeleton is designed based on a vs-joint with shear-thickening properties of STG material as the centerpiece. And through simulation analysis, it is initially verified that the exoskeleton can assist the human body in load-carrying without interference. In view of the fact that there are few purely passive lower limb exoskeletons for load-carrying, the exoskeleton device proposed in this paper has certain significance for the design of lower limb load-carrying equipment.

5 Future Work

Although this paper proposes the design method of the load-carrying lower limb exoskeleton and verify the effectiveness of the exoskeleton through simulation analysis, the human experiments have not yet been developed. Whether the exoskeleton is truly effective in assisting the human body in load-carrying and reducing metabolic energy expenditure is still unproven. Therefore, the future work needs to focus on human experiments and verification of the effectiveness of the exoskeleton device.

Acknowledgment. This work was partially supported by the National Key R&D Program (Grant No. 2018YFB1307201, 2020YFC2007802), the National Natural Science Foundation of China (Grant No. U1913205, 52075191), and the Program for HUST Academic Frontier Youth Team.

References

1. Westerterp, K.R.: Physical activity and physical activity induced energy expenditure in humans: measurement, determinants, and effects. Front. Physiol. **4** (2013)
2. Knapik, J.J., Reynolds, K.L., Harman, E.: Soldier load carriage: historical, physiological, biomechanical, and medical aspects, Mil. Med. **169**(1), 45–56 (2004)
3. Orr, R.M., Pope, R.R.: Load carriage: an integrated risk management approach. J. Strength Cond. Res. **29**, S119–S128 (2015)
4. Cornwall, W.: In pursuit of the perfect power suit. Science **350**(6258), 270–273 (2015)
5. Young, A.J., Ferris, D.P.: State of the art and future directions for lower limb robotic exoskeletons. IEEE Trans. Neural Syst. Rehabil. Eng. **25**(2), 171–182 (2017)
6. Walsh, C.J., Endo, K., Herr, H.: A quasi-passive leg exoskeleton for load-carrying augmentation. Int. J. Humanoid Robot. **4**(3), 487–506 (2007)
7. Van Diik, W., Van De Wijdeven, T., Hölscher, M.M.: Exobuddy-a non-anthropomorphic quasi-passive exoskeleton for load carrying assistance. In: Proceedings of the IEEE RAS and EMBS International Conference on Biomedical Robotics and Biomechatronics, pp. 336–341 (2018)
8. Lovrenovic, Z., Doumit, M.: Development and testing of a passive walking assist exoskeleton. Biocybern. Biomed. Eng. **39**(4), 992–1004 (2019).
9. Bing, L., Chengbin, D., Yankai, F.: The preparation process of shear thickening materials and the application in hydraulic shock absorber. In: IOP Conference Series: Earth and Environmental Science, pp. 639(1) (2021)
10. Zhao, C., Xu, C., Cao, S.: Anti-impact behavior of a novel soft body armor based on shear thickening gel (STG) impregnated Kevlar fabrics. Smart Mater. Struct. **28**(7) (2019)
11. Yang, X., Zhao, G., Liu, D.: Biomechanics analysis of human walking with load carriage. Technol. Health Care **23**, S567–S575 (2015)
12. Neumann, D.: Kinesiology of the Musculoskeletal System. Foundation for Rehabilitation (2010)
13. Farley, C.T., Houdijk, H.H.P., Van Strien, C., Louie, M.: Mechanism of leg stiffness adjustment for hopping on surfaces of different stiffnesses. J. Appl. Physiol. **85**(3), 1044–1055 (1998)

14. Tilbury-Davis, D.C., Hooper, R.H.: The kinetic and kinematic effects of increasing load carriage upon the lower limb. Hum. Move. Sci. **18**(5), 693–700 (1999)
15. Sartori, M., Maculan, M., Pizzolato, C., Reggiani, M., Farina, D.: Modeling and simulating the neuromuscular mechanisms regulating ankle and knee joint stiffness during human locomotion. J. Neurophysiol. **114**(4), 2509–2527(2015)
16. Hwang, J., Kumar Yerriboina, V.N., Ari, H., Kim, J.H.: Effects of passive back-support exoskeletons on physical demands and usability during patient transfer tasks. Appl. Ergon. **93** (2021)
17. Chen, Q., Cheng, H., Shen, W., Huang, R., Chen, X.: Hybrid control for human-powered augmentation exoskeleton. In: 8th Annual IEEE International Conference on Cyber Technology in Automation. Control and Intelligent Systems, pp. 682–687 (2018, 2019)
18. Simon, A.A., Alemi, M.M., Asbeck, A.T.: Kinematic effects of a passive lift assistive exoskeleton. J. Biomech. **120** (2021)
19. Yu, Z.W., Wang, L.Q., Wang, P., Dai, Z.D.: Dynamic humanoid gait simulation of biped robot based on ADAMS. Appl. Mech. Mater. **2850** (2014)
20. Suzuki, K., Mito, G., Kawamoto, H., Hasegawa, Y., Sankai, Y.: Intention-based walking support for paraplegia patients with Robot Suit HAL. Adv. Robot. **21**(12), 1441–1469 (2007)
21. Latash, M.L., Zatsiorsky, V.M.: Joint stiffness: myth or reality?. Hum. Move. Sci. **12**(6), 653–692 (1993)
22. Farley, C.T., González, O.: Leg stiffness and stride frequency in human running. J. Biomech. **29**(2), 181–186 (1996)
23. Morin, J.-B., Samozino, P. (eds.): Biomechanics of Training and Testing. Springer, Cham (2018). https://doi.org/10.1007/978-3-319-05633-3

Design of a Dynamic Waist Strap for Reducing Migration of Knee Exoskeletons

Ming Xu[1,3], Zhihao Zhou[1,2,3], Jinyan Shao[1,2], and Qining Wang[1,2,3(✉)]

[1] Department of Advanced Manufacturing and Robotics, College of Engineering,
Peking University, Beijing 100871, China
qiningwang@pku.edu.cn
[2] Institute for Artificial Intelligence, Peking University, Beijing 100871, China
[3] The Beijing Engineering Research Center of Intelligent Rehabilitation Engineering,
Beijing 100871, China

Abstract. As a key element of knee exoskeleton, the stability of thigh cuff is essential to ensure the force acting on the motion of knee without failure. The challenge of its design is preventing the cuff downward sliding when external downward force exists. Generally, it is in virtue of the friction force between the cuff and skin, so the cuff being tighter means more reliable. However, for the thigh with the large cross area in the proximal part and the small cross area in the distal part, only depend on the tightness is not feasible, meanwhile it will limit the muscle activation and cause discomfort and pain. To address this problem, we propose a dynamic waist strap (DWS) where thigh cuff is connected to a waist belt though ropes dynamically. To verify the effectiveness of proposed DWS, a serious of contrast experiments based on a textile waist belt for rock climbing and a custom thigh cuff made of thermoplastic polyurethanes (TPU) are implemented. The results indicate this design can prevent the knee exoskeleton from downward sliding more effectively compared with three existing knee exoskeleton wearing forms. The thigh cuff supported by proposed DWS only slides down by 0.505 mm after the whole experimental process is finished, far less than the data in other conditions (10.525 mm, 19.234 mm and 30.538 mm respectively), when the interaction force between thigh cuff and waist belt is not large. This research highlights the importance of waist belt when attaching a knee exoskeleton to human and introduces a new dynamic interaction interface to improve the coupling from an exoskeleton to an individual.

Keywords: Dynamic waist strap · Downward sliding · Thigh cuff · Knee exoskeleton

This work was supported by the National Key R&D Program of China (No. 2020YFC2008803, 2018YFC2001503), the National Natural Science Foundation of China (No. 51922015, No. 91948302, No. 52005011), PKU-Baidu Fund (No. 2020BD008) and the Beijing Natural Science Foundation (No. L182001).

X.-J. Liu et al. (Eds.): ICIRA 2021, LNAI 13013, pp. 687–697, 2021.
https://doi.org/10.1007/978-3-030-89095-7_65

1   Introduction

The concept of exoskeleton is an extension of the exoskeleton in biology, referring to a kind of mechanical system which covers and supports the body of the creature [1]. From the initial military use to clinical sports rehabilitation, elderly sports assistance and other fields, it has been widely concerned by researchers all around the world [2,3]. For knee exoskeleton, it can be divided into two types according to their main structure: rigid exoskeleton and flexible exoskeleton, the research interest of the latter has gradually risen in recent ten years [4]. The robotics research group of Peking University proposed a rigid knee exoskeleton, Bionic Knee Exoskeleton (BioKEX), which weighs 2.1kg, and utilizes gear meshing instead of the traditional single-axis hinge [5,6]. It can achieve a maximum knee flexion of 135° and provide a maximum boost of 64Nm. Conor et al. designed a soft exoskeleton for knee extension assistance during walking, the total on-body mass of which is 1.72 kg [7]. This exoskeleton can apply a wide range of assistance profiles using a flexible multi-point reference trajectory generator.

As far, knee exoskeleton should be attached closely to human leg through thigh cuff and calf cuff aiming at transmitting assistance force effectively. However, the cuff strapping on thigh always tends to slide down during motion since the thigh of human is tapered, which is still a major barrier to a wider adoption of knee exoskeleton technology [8]. Traditionally, both rigid and soft exoskeletons are attached to the surface of human leg by the fricton force between cuff and skin, so the cuff being tighter means more reliable. However, only depend on the tightness to keep knee exoskeleton stable is not feasible, meanwhile it will limit the muscle activation and cause discomfort and pain. In order to solve this problem, Conor et al. attached the thigh cuff of knee exoskeleton to the girdle of human through a connecting belt located outside the thigh [7], as the girdle is limited by the hip bone and the thigh strap is tightened through the connecting belt. Furthermore, Fu et al. applied two connecting belts arranged both outside and inside the thigh to solve this problem [9]. Besides, Robert et al. also proposed a connecting scheme which set one connecting belt in front of the thigh while the other located in the back [10–13].

Compared to traditional method as reducing migration of knee exoskeleton by tightening the cuff, the above three connection forms have achieved some beneficial effects, but there are still some problems need to be solved. All the existing connection forms adopt fixed connection belts, which cannot move by themselves or have no movement relationship with each other. During hip flexion, the distance between the front side of thigh cuff and waistband is shortened, while the distance between the back side and waistband is prolonged, leading to the connecting belt on the front side/outside/inside of thigh relax and causing the front side of thigh cuff to slide down. Meantime, the connecting belt at the back of the thigh is tensioned, so it must deform itself to allow the hip joint to move, which will limit the hip flexion angle.

To address these problems, we propose a novel dynamic waist strap for reducing the migration of knee exoskeleton during movement in order to improving stability and comfortableness. In this design, two dynamic rope loops are used to strap the thigh cuff of knee exoskeleton instead of fixed connecting belts. Applying dynamic rope loops in this case can not only tension the thigh cuff of knee exoskeleton effectively, but also prevent it from sliding down without affecting the movement of the hip joint during the whole movement cycle. To verify the effectiveness of the design, the optical capture experiment of cuff location monitoring and the evaluation experiment of interactive force between girdle and thigh cuff are carried out.

2   Method

In this section, the mechanical design of dynamic waist strap is explained. The protocol of experiment and the evaluation methods which were carried out are described.

2.1   Design of Dynamic Waist Strap

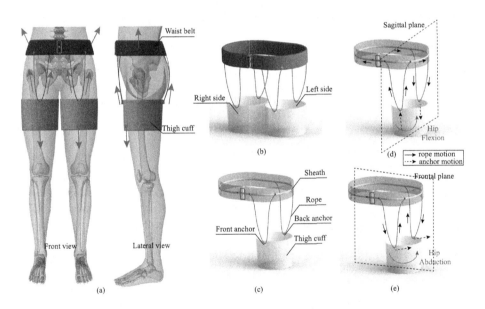

Fig. 1. The prototype of proposed dynamic waist strap (DWS). The red arrows in (a) represent the external forces applied to thigh cuff and waist belt. The black arrows in (d) and (e) represent the movement direction of rope and anchor.

The proposed DWS consists mainly of a textile waist belt for rock climbing and two wire loops. It can be seen from Fig. 1.b and Fig. 1.c that the wire loops are surrounded by the sheaths embedded in the waist belt. In front of thigh of human, the wire stretches out from the sheath and hold the upper front edge of thigh cuff, when the same wire stretches out from the sheath in the back to pull the upper back edge of thigh cuff. Two wire loops are symmetrically arranged with respect to the sagittal plane. The force which causes thigh cuff downward sliding can be transmitted to the waist, as shown in Fig. 1.a. To guarantee the natural motion of the hip joint, the connection of ropes is moving while the hip rotates. The process is adaptive and automatic for our connection and arrangement. The displacement and direction when hip rotates in sagittal plane (flexion/extension) and in frontal plane (abduction/adduction) are depicted in Fig. 1.d and Fig. 1.e.

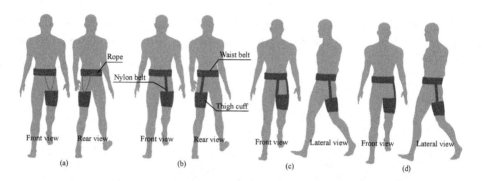

Fig. 2. Four connection forms to prevent thigh cuff of knee exoskeleton downward sliding. (a) The proposed DWS. (b) The connection form designed in [10]. (c) The connection form illustrated by [9]. (d) The connection form used in [7].

2.2   Experimental Protocol

A healthy volunteer from Peking University participated in this study (age 22 years old, weight 65 kg, height 170 cm, male). The participant wore a DWS around his waist and a custom thigh cuff made of thermoplastic polyurethanes (TPU) on his left leg during experiments. Two sandbags with a total weight of 2.5 kg were fixed on the TPU thigh cuff to simulate the external downward force generated by knee exoskeleton.

In order to verify the effectiveness of proposed DWS compared to three existing connection forms illustrated by [7,9,10], several comparative experiments under four different conditions were set up:

Condition 1: As can be seen from Fig. 2.a, the volunteer wore the proposed DWS and TPU thigh cuff on his left leg.
Condition 2: The participant wore the same textile waist belt constituting the proposed DWS and TPU thigh cuff on his left leg, when two nylon belts are used to link the upper front edge and upper back edge of the thigh cuff to the mentioned textile waist belt, as shown in Fig. 2.b.

Condition 3: Figure 2.c shows the third connection form. Unlike condition 2, two nylon belts are arranged on the upper left edge and upper right edge of the TPU thigh cuff.

Condition 4: Only one nylon belt is used to hold the thigh cuff, lying between upper left edge of the TPU thigh cuff and the textile waist belt, as described by Fig. 2.d.

The experimental process of four conditions illustrated by Fig. 2 is shown in Fig. 3. Under each condition, firstly, the volunteer stands upright on the treadmill for 10 s, which followed by a one-minute-walk with the speed of 0.7 m/s. After that, the volunteer stops and stands for 10 s again, before a one-minute-walk with the speed of 0.9 m/s on the treadmill. Subsequently, he walks at a speed of 1.1 m/s for a minute after standing upright for another 10 s. The experiments under one condition will be finished after he stands for the fourth 10 s.

Before each group of experiments, the thigh cuff will be re-worn and adjusted, ensuring it lying right on the uppermost edge of participant's crotch.

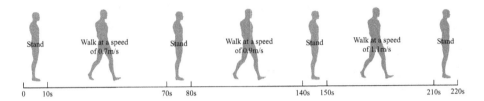

Fig. 3. Experimental process in four cases.

2.3   Evaluation Method

Before the start of experiments, 8 reflective markers are posted on the body of the volunteer, the locations of which can be seen from Fig. 4.a. The tracking of the reflective markers' position is achieved using a motion capture environment comprising 12 cameras (Mars4H, NOKOV, Beijing, China) with a sampling frequency 100 Hz. In order to evaluate the interaction force between thigh cuff and waist belt, two loadcells (LSB 205, FUTEK, CA, USA) are applied, both of which are installed between the anchor point of thigh cuff and the rope/nylon belt (only one loadcell is used in condition 4). Besides, four custom diaphragm pressure sensors are used aiming at quantifying the strapping pressure of thigh cuff, of which arrangement is described in Fig. 4.b. Above all, all the experimental data are collected synchronously by an acquisition card (USB-6218, National Instruments, TX, USA) with a sampling frequency 100 Hz and then stored on a personal computer.

Relative Motion: As shown in Fig. 4.a, at first, the line connecting Marker 3 (A') with Marker 4 (B') is chosen to represent the position of volunteer's thigh in space, and the midpoint (C') between Marker 6 and Marker 8 is selected to

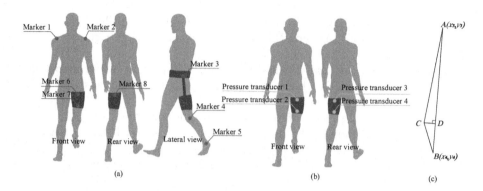

Fig. 4. Evaluation scheme. (a) The distribution of reflective markers. (b) The arrangement of pressure transducers. (c) The definition of distance between thigh cuff and hip joint.

represent the position of the thigh cuff. Then, A', B' and C' are projected to the sagittal plane shown in Fig. 1.d, with the projected points defined as A, B and C respectively. It can be seen in Fig. 4.c, the distance between C and A along the line connecting A with B (the length of line connecting A with D) indicates the position of thigh cuff relative to volunteer's thigh, so the downward sliding distance (DSD) of thigh cuff can be characterized by the change of the length of line connecting A with D.

Interaction Force: The force data measured by loadcells is used to express the interaction force (IF) between waist belt and thigh cuff. It is necessary to ensure that the IF between waist belt and thigh cuff is roughly equal before each group of experiments starts, so as to eliminate the influence of IF on thigh cuff downward sliding.

Strapping Pressure: The digital quantity measured by four pressure sensors is used to characterize the strapping pressure of thigh cuff. In order to eliminate the effect of initial strapping pressure on thigh cuff migration, ensuring the initial strapping pressure of thigh cuff is roughly equal before the start of each group of experiments is of great importance.

The raw IF data and raw strapping pressure data are first filtered with a zero-lag 1st order Butterworth filter with a cut-off frequency 10 Hz.

Hip Flexion Angle: The midpoint of the line connecting Marker 1 with Marker 2 is defined as E'. Then, A', B' and E' mentioned before are projected to the sagittal plane, with the projected points defined as A, B and E respectively. Finally, we apply the included angle between the line linking E with A and the line connecting A with B to represent hip flexion angle (HFA) of the participant.

3 Experimental Results

3.1 Relative Motion

After zeroing the initial relative distance between thigh cuff and volunteer's hip joint, only the fluctuation of cuff position is considered, the experimental results can be seen from Fig. 5. It is obvious that the variation tendency of DSD curve under condition 1 is similar to that of DSD curve under condition 2, and the shape of DSD curve under condition 3 resembles that of DSD curve under condition 4. Table 1 illustrates the DSD before and after experiments in four cases, among which the DSD of condition 1 is the smallest (only 0.505 mm), while that of condition 4 is the largest (30.538 mm). Besides, the DSD of condition 2 and condition 3 are 10.525 mm and 19.234 mm respectively. Above all, the maximal mean square error (MSE, not shown in Fig. 5 and Fig. 7 for clarity) of DSD cross the gait cycle under condition 1 is smaller than that under condition 3, condition 4, and even condition 2, which indicates that the gait of the volunteer is most stable when wearing proposed DWS. What's more, both the maximum of the mean DSD cross different gait cycles and the maximal fluctuation of the mean DSD under condition 1 are smaller than those under condition 2, while which are far smaller than those under condition 3 and condition 4, no matter the volunteer walks slowly (0.7 m/s), moderate (0.9 m/s) or fast (1.1 m/s).

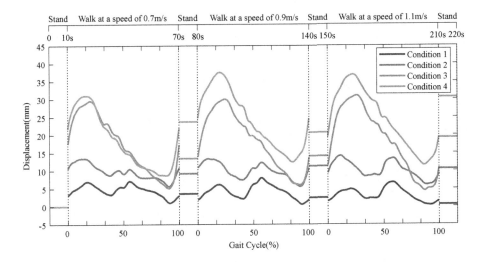

Fig. 5. The DSD of thigh cuff relative to hip joint. The curves represent the mean DSD cross different gait cycles when walking in various speed under different conditions, while the straight lines symbolize the mean DSD when stance.

Table 1. The DSD of thigh cuff after walking in various speed

	First-stance*(mm)	Second-stance*(mm)	Third-stance*(mm)	Fourth-stance*(mm)	Start-end Change*(mm)
Condition 1	0	3.641	2.453	0.505	0.505
Condition 2	0	9.238	11.256	10.525	10.525
Condition 3	0	13.471	14.092	19.234	19.234
Condition 4	0	23.745	20.688	30.538	30.538

Note: (1) First-stance*: The DSD of thigh cuff before walking in 0.7 m/s. (2) Second-stance*: The DSD of thigh cuff after walking in 0.7 m/s. (3) Third-stance*: The DSD of thigh cuff after walking in 0.9 m/s. (4) Fourth-stance*: The DSD of thigh cuff after walking in 1.1 m/s. (5) Start-end Change*: The change of DSD between start time and end time of a group of experiments under one condition.

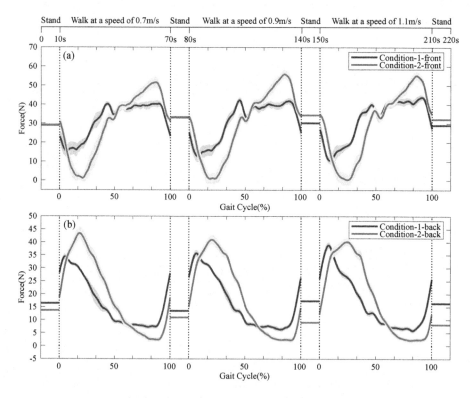

Fig. 6. The IF between thigh cuff and waist belt. The solid curves represent the mean IF cross different gait cycles when walking in various speed under different conditions, while the straight lines symbolize the mean IF when stance, and the shaded areas show the MSE of IF cross the gait cycle. (a) The IF between upper front edge of thigh cuff and waist belt. (b) The IF between upper back edge of thigh cuff and waist belt.

3.2   Interaction Force

Under each condition, the initial IF between thigh cuff and waist belt measured by loadcells is 39.624 ± 5.789N. The difference among four conditions is not significant. Therefore, the DSD caused by the difference of initial IF are ignored. Figure 6 demonstrates the changes of IF between condition 1 and condition 2. Under the circumstance that there is no significant difference between the initial IF of condition 1 (45.413N) and that of condition 2 (42.861N), the fluctuation of IF in condition 1 is obviously smaller than that of condition 2 during walking in 0.7 m/s, 0.9 m/s and 1.1 m/s. What's more, the maximal MSE of the IF cross the gait cycle under condition 2 is larger than that of condition 1, except the IF at the back of thigh when walking in 0.9 m/s.

3.3   Hip Flexion Angle

The variation of hip flexion (HFA) angle during walking in four cases is shown in Fig. 7. It should be stated that the volunteer walks on the treadmill without wearing any device under condition 5. Generally speaking, the influence of four wearing forms on human gait is not significant, but compared to natural gait cycle, the HFA under four conditions is obviously larger. It can be seen from Fig. 7 that the changes of HFA between four cases are similar when walking with a speed of 0.9 m/s, but the MSE under condition 3 is obviously smaller than that of other conditions during walking in 0.7 m/s and 1.1 m/s. For instance, when walking slowly (0.7 m/s), the maximal MSE in condition 3 is only 0.572 rad, while that of condition 4 is 0.632 rad, the maximal MSE in condition 1 and condition 2 are 0.614 rad and 0.625 rad respectively.

As the thigh cuff is not soft enough to fit perfectly with volunteer's thigh all the time during walking, the data measured by four pressure sensors is not convincing. But what can be guaranteed is that the initial strapping pressure under condition 1 is smaller than other conditions.

Finishing all the planed experiments in four cases, the volunteer tries to walk without the support of the waist belt with a speed of 0.7 m/s, but the thigh cuff slides down to treadmill after several gait cycles.

4   Discussion

In terms of reducing migration of thigh cuff of knee exoskeletons, the proposed DWS has a remarkable effect. The thigh cuff supported by proposed DWS only slides down by 0.505 mm after the whole experimental process is finished, far less than the data in other conditions (10.525 mm, 19.234 mm and 30.538 mm respectively). The beneficial effects of proposed dynamic waist belt are not only reflected at the start time or end time, but also in every stage of the whole gait cycle. It can be obviously seen from Fig. 5 that the fluctuation of the DSD under condition 1 is the smallest. Specifically, for instance, the maximal MSE of the DSD under condition 1 (6.132 mm) is smaller than that of condition 2 (7.839

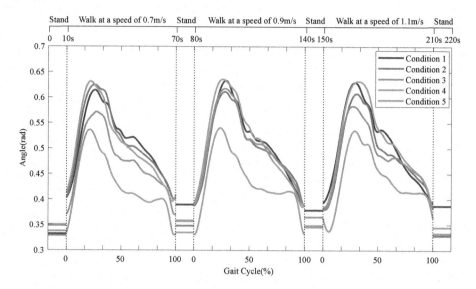

Fig. 7. The changes of HFA when walking in four situations. The curves represent the mean HFA of different gait cycles when walking in various speed under different conditions, while the straight lines symbolize the mean HFA when stance.

mm), while which are far smaller than that of condition 3 (24.458 mm) and condition 4 (22.358 mm) when the volunteer walks slowly (0.7 m/s), showing the stableness and reliability of proposed dynamic waist belt.

Although the IF between thigh cuff and waist belt under condition 1 is smaller than that of condition 2, as demonstrated by Fig. 6, the thigh cuff supported by condition 1 migrates along the thigh more slightly, which indicates the effectiveness of proposed dynamic waist belt adequately. Besides, the volunteer wearing proposed DWS can achieve larger HFA than natural gait cycle, illustrating that the DWS does not limit the muscle activation and affect the gait of human.

Overall, the advantage of the proposed dynamic waist belt is that the rope pulling thigh cuff can move along the sheath embedded in the textile waist belt. For this reason, the cuff can be tightened along the surface of thigh during the whole gait cycle.

5   Conclusion and Future Work

In this paper, we proposed a DWS for reducing the DSD of thigh cuff of knee exoskeletons. Compared with the existing wearing forms of knee exoskeletons, the proposed DWS can prevent the knee exoskeleton from sliding down more effectively and improve the wearing comfortableness and power transmission efficiency of knee exoskeleton under the condition that the strapping pressure and IF between thigh cuff and waist belt without extra increase. The verification experiments of optical motion capture and IF measurement during walking in various speed are completed, aiming at testing and verifying the effectiveness of proposed DWS. The experimental results are great and convincing, but more extensive movement tasks, for instance, running, sloped walking, stair ascending and stair descending are not included. In the future, we will apply a real knee exoskeleton to test and complete more comprehensive verification experiments.

References

1. Yang, C.J., Zhang, J.F., Chen, Y., Dong, Y.M., Zhang, Y.: A review of exoskeleton-type systems and their key technologies. In: Proceedings of the Institution of Mechanical Engineers, Part C: Journal of Mechanical Engineering Science, vol. 222, no. 8, pp. 1599–1612 (2008)
2. Dollar, A.M., Herr, H.: Lower extremity exoskeletons and active orthoses: challenges and state-of-the-art. IEEE Trans. Robot. **24**(1), 144–158 (2008)
3. Young, A.J., Ferris, D.P.: State of the art and future directions for lower limb robotic exoskeletons. IEEE Trans. Neural Syst. Rehabil. Eng. **25**(2), 171–182 (2016)
4. Asbeck, A.T., De Rossi, S.M., Galiana, I., Ding, Y., Walsh, C.J.: Stronger, smarter, softer: next-generation wearable robots. IEEE Robot. Autom. Mag. **21**(4), 22–33 (2014)
5. Liu, X., Zhou, Z., Mai, J., Wang, Q.: Real-time mode recognition based assistive torque control of bionic knee exoskeleton for sit-to-stand and stand-to-sit transitions. Robot. Auton. Syst. **119**, 209–220 (2019)
6. Liu, X., Wang, Q.: Real-time locomotion mode recognition and assistive torque control for unilateral knee exoskeleton on different terrains. IEEE/ASME Trans. Mech. **25**(6), 2722–2732 (2020)
7. Park, E.J., et al.: A hinge-free, non-restrictive, lightweight tethered exosuit for knee extension assistance during walking. IEEE Trans. Med. Robot. Bionics **2**(2), 165–175 (2020)
8. Langlois, K., et al.: Investigating the effects of strapping pressure on human-robot interface dynamics using a soft robotic cuff. IEEE Trans. Med. Robot. Bionics **3**(1), 146–155 (2021)
9. Huang, G., Ma, L., Zhu, H., Qian, Y., Leng, Y., Fu, C.: A biologically-inspired soft Exosuit for knee extension assistance during stair ascent. In: 2020 5th International Conference on Advanced Robotics and Mechatronics (ICARM), pp. 570–575. IEEE (2020)
10. Haufe, F.L., et al.: User-driven walking assistance: first experimental results using the MyoSuit. In: 2019 IEEE 16th International Conference on Rehabilitation Robotics (ICORR), pp. 944–949. IEEE (2019)
11. Duarte, J.E., Schmidt, K., Riener, R.: The myosuit: textile-powered mobility. IFAC-PapersOnLine **51**(34), 242–243 (2019)
12. Schmidt, K., et al.: The Myosuit: bi-articular anti-gravity exosuit that reduces hip extensor activity in sitting transfers. Front. Neurorobot. **11**, 57 (2017)
13. Haufe, F.L., Schmidt, K., Duarte, J.E., Wolf, P., Riener, R., Xiloyannis, M.: Activity-based training with the myosuit: a safety and feasibility study across diverse gait disorders. J. Neuroeng. Rehabil. **17**(1), 135 (2020)

Research on Trajectory Tracking of Lower Limb Exoskeleton Rehabilitation Robot Based on Sliding Mode Control

Jing Wang, Jian Li$^{(\boxtimes)}$, Weixuan Zhang, and Fuxin Zhou

School of Mechanical and Transportation Engineering, GuangXi University of Science and Technology, No.19, Guantang Avenue, Yufeng, Liuzhou, Guangxi, China
`lijian@gxust.edu.cn`

Abstract. The patient number of lower limb motor dysfunction, such as stroke and spinal cord injury, was increasing every year. For the early rehabilitation, repeated high-intensity exercise was very important for the recovery of limb motor function and the reduction of amyotrophy. Therefore, this paper was proposed a lower limb exoskeleton robots (LERs) for rehabilitation training. Based on the input-output stability theory, we established the mathematical model of sliding mode controller (SMC) and built the control hardware system. From the simulation, we found the tracking error of SMC was smaller and the response was faster than PD controller. So it was proved that SMC was more suitable for exoskeleton trajectory tracking than classical PD controller. According to the simulation and walking experiments, the chattering of SMC was decreased by using the saturation function as the switching function. Therefore, the reaching law of the gait trajectory tracking error would approach to zero at different rates inside and outside of the boundary layer (δ), and thus the SMC could be adaptive. The simulation and experiments results indicate that SMC was a suitable choice for controlling a physical exoskeleton robot.

Keywords: Exoskeleton · Gait trajectory tracking · Sliding mode control

1 Introduction

According to the NBSPRC, China's population aged 65 or older stood at 176.03 million at the end of 2019, accounting for 12.6% of the total population. [1] It was expected to rise to 33.3% by 2050. And with the intensification of aging, there would be more than 400 million elderly patients over 60 years old and more than 500 million chronic disease patients in the next 20–30 years who need rehabilitation training [2]. The LERs was a wearable device that combined human kinematics and mechanical characteristics. It involved many fields such as rehabilitation medicine, biomechanics, robotics, and artificial intelligence and other fields. With the emergence of rehabilitation robots such as LOKOMAT [3] BLEEX [4], HAL [5], and several clinical applications, LERs have become an important tool to assist patients with rehabilitation training. It had the advantages of saving labor cost, high efficiency, as well as stable and evaluable rehabilitation training effect.

© Springer Nature Switzerland AG 2021
X.-J. Liu et al. (Eds.): ICIRA 2021, LNAI 13013, pp. 698–708, 2021.
https://doi.org/10.1007/978-3-030-89095-7_66

Because of the body movement requirement, most LERs could not install large sensors at the hip and knee joints. At present, LERs could use position control for robot movement. However, it was hard to achieve the desired control by using general control algorithms because of large loading problem from the walking exoskeleton robots. The SMC had the advantages of fast response, insensitive to disturbances, and simple physical implementation. However, when the order of the system was large and the structural parameters were uncertain, SMC was difficult to directly obtain the control law and it would lead to chattering. Therefore, experts and scholars had proposed several solutions for these problems, such as convergence rate method, observer method and combination with intelligent algorithms. Hu Fei et al. [6] used self-designed fuzzy PID SMC to solve the problems of nonlinearity and extraneous interference in electro-hydraulic servo system during the movement of lower limb exoskeleton. Song Shengli et al. [7] proposed a fast second-order terminal SMC to improve the global convergence of conventional second-order terminal SMC by hiding the absolute value function in the integral term. Juan C et al. [8] designed a control algorithm using the interaction forces between the patient's ankle joint and the exoskeleton and applied it to the ankle joint to control the exoskeleton. It can be seen from these works that the SMC is a very effective method in dealing with time-varying calculation and control problems.

In this paper, based on the gait tracking error problem of LERs, we proposed a SMC according to the input-output stability principle and the estimation model of exoskeleton. Our design of the sliding surface was to minimizes chattering meanwhile the system state point could be quickly approaching the sliding surface. Therefore, the error of the trajectory tracking control of the exoskeleton robots could be decreased.

2 Methodology

2.1 Mechanical Subsystem

Structural Design of Lower Limb Exoskeleton Robot. In this paper, a LERs based on disc motors was designed. According to "GB-10000–88 Chinese adult body size" and the data from American Academy of Orthopedic Surgeons [9], the parameters could be seen from the Table 1.

Table 1. Exoskeleton robot joint design

Joint	Active/Passive	Driving torque	Sagittal flexion angle	Sagittal extension angle
Hip	Active	0–45 N·m	0–120°	0–30°
Knee	Active	0–38 N·m	0–135°	–
Ankle	Passive	–	0–20°	0–50°

According to the research results in the laboratory, it was found that the sheet metal exoskeleton has poor rigidity performance. The lateral force would cause large deformation to the end of the ankle joint. So the tube exoskeleton was designed to improve the rigidity. The mechanism of the exoskeleton was shown in Fig. 1. As hemiplegic patients were prone to outward and inward hooking of the foot during rehabilitation, foot pedals were set at the ankle joint. MAXON EC90(0.46 N·m) disk motor was connected to harmonic reducer (LHD-20–100-C-I) at the drive joint to increase the torque and reduce the rotational speed. Then the power was transmitted to the thigh and calf linkages of exoskeleton.

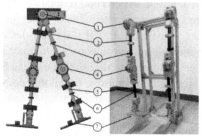

1. Hip joint disc motor 2. Thigh linkage 3. Thigh linkage quick lock 4. Knee joint disc motor 5. Calf linkage 6. Calf linkage quick lock 7. Foot pedal

Fig. 1. Exoskeleton models and prototypes

Kinematics Modeling. In order to achieve accurate and reliable control of the LERs, it was necessary to analyze the motion relationship and motion change pattern of the exoskeleton. The unilateral human lower limb exoskeleton was simplified into a planar system composed of rigid links and rotating pairs.

The end position of each linkage of the exoskeleton in generalized coordinates $q_i = [x_i\ y_i\ \theta_i]$ $(i = 1,2,3)$, where (x_i, y_i) was the coordinate of the projection of the end point of the connecting rod in the sagittal plane. θ_i was the relative rotation angle of the connecting rod. The Danevit-Hartenberg method was used to express the relative positions between the connecting rods. The coordinate system was established as shown in Fig. 2 and the D-H parameters are shown in Table 2.

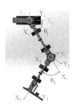

Fig. 2. D-H coordinate system

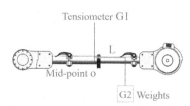

Fig. 3. Schematic diagram of center-of-mass solution

Table 2. D-H parameter table

i	α_{i-1}	a_{i-1}	d_i	θ_i
1	0	0	0	θ_1
2	0	l_1	d_1	θ_2
3	0	l_2	d_2	0

The transformation matrix T was identified by Eq. 1. The end position of hip and knee was determined by Eq. 2 and Eq. 3.

$$^0_3T = {}^0_1T \cdot {}^1_2T \cdot {}^2_3T = \begin{bmatrix} c_{12} & s_{12} & 0 & l_2c_{12}+l_1c_1 \\ -s_{12} & c_{12} & 0 & -l_2s_{12}-l_1s_1 \\ 0 & 0 & 1 & d_1+d_2 \\ 0 & 0 & 0 & 1 \end{bmatrix} \tag{1}$$

Expressed in generalized coordinates as:

$$q_1 = \begin{bmatrix} l_1c_1 & l_1s_1 & \theta_1 \end{bmatrix}^T \tag{2}$$

$$q_2 = \begin{bmatrix} l_2c_{12}+l_1c_1 & l_2s_{12}+l_1s_1 & \theta_2 \end{bmatrix}^T \tag{3}$$

where c_1 denoted $\cos\theta_1$; s_1 denoted $\sin\theta_1$; c_{12} denoted $\cos(\theta_1+\theta_2)$; s_{12} denoted $\sin(\theta_1+\theta_2)$, the same expressions were used in the following text.

Dynamics Modeling. For the exoskeleton multi-joint tandem rigid linkage system, the dynamics model of LERs designed in this paper was obtained from the Lagrange equations, which could be expressed by a second-order nonlinear differential equation as:

$$M(\theta)\ddot{\theta} + V(\theta,\dot{\theta})\dot{\theta} + G(\theta) = \tau + \tau_d \tag{4}$$

τ was the control moment of each joint and $\tau_d \in R^n$ denoted the disturbance term of the system. $M_{(\theta)} = \begin{bmatrix} M_{11(\theta)} & M_{12(\theta)} \\ M_{21(\theta)} & M_{22(\theta)} \end{bmatrix}$, $V_{(\theta,\dot{\theta})} = \begin{bmatrix} V_{11(\theta,\dot{\theta})} & V_{12(\theta,\dot{\theta})} \\ V_{21(\theta,\dot{\theta})} & V_{22(\theta,\dot{\theta})} \end{bmatrix}$, $G_{(\theta)} = \begin{bmatrix} G_{1(\theta)} \\ G_{2(\theta)} \end{bmatrix}$, the mass matrix $M(\theta)$ was expressed as $M_{11(\theta)} = A_1 + A_2 + 2A_3c_2$, $M_{12(\theta)} = M_{12(\theta)} = A_2 + A_3c_2$, $M_{22(\theta)} = A_2$; the centrifugal and Coriolis force matrices $V(\theta,\dot{\theta})$ was expressed as $V_{11(\theta,\dot{\theta})} = -A_3 \sin\theta_2 \cdot \dot{\theta}_2$, $V_{12(\theta,\dot{\theta})} = -A_3s_2 \cdot (\dot{\theta}_1 + \dot{\theta}_2)$, $V_{21(\theta,\dot{\theta})} = A_3s_2 \cdot \dot{\theta}_1$, $V_{22(\theta,\dot{\theta})} = 0$; while the gravity term $G(\theta)$ was $G_{1(\theta)} = A_4gc_1 + A_5gc_{12}$, $G_{2(\theta)} = A_5gc_{12}$. Above all, $A_1 = m_1d_1^2 + m_2l_1^2 + I_1$, $A_2 = m_2d_2^2 + I_2$, $A_3 = m_2l_1d_2$, $A_4 = m_1d_1 + m_2l_1$, $A_5 = m_2d_2$.

The length and the quality of the exoskeleton thigh and calf linkage with the motor would be measured. A schematic diagram to get the center of mass was shown in Fig. 3. We could find the position d of exoskeleton barycenter by using the equation $d = G_2 \times L/G_1$ and the inertia of leg linkage could be identified by $I = ML^2/3$. The specific parameters of the exoskeleton were shown in following Table 3.

Table 3. Mechanism model parameters

Parameters	Parameter Name	Value	Unit
m_1	Thigh quality	3.191	Kg
l_1	Thigh length	0.509	M
d_1	Thigh center of mass position	0.463	M
I_1	Thigh rod rotational inertia	0.197	kg·m
m_2	Calf quality	3.223	Kg
l_2	Calf length	0.491	m
d_2	Calf rod center of mass position	0.381	m
I_2	Lower leg rod rotational inertia	0.156	kg·m

2.2 Control Subsystem

Sliding Mode Control Strategy Based on Input-Output Stability. A control strategy was developed for LERs to "drive" the patient's lower limbs on a reference trajectory for ultra-early walking rehabilitation. During the dynamic calculation, the exoskeleton robot model inevitably had uncertainties, such as structural and non-structural factors. Therefore, for the nonlinearity of the LERs system and the uncertainty of the model, a SMC was designed using the input-output stability theory and the estimation model, which would be provided with good robustness and anti-disturbance.

The main purpose of the exoskeleton trajectory tracking control was to track the time-varying desired trajectory $\dot{\theta}_d(t)$. The position tracking error was calculated by the following Eq. 5.

$$e = \theta_d - \theta \tag{5}$$

Defined:

$$\dot{\theta}_r = \dot{\theta}_d + \Lambda(\theta_d - \theta) \tag{6}$$

The sliding (or switching) surface s was selected according to the tracking error to ensure the ideal sliding mode:

$$s = \dot{\theta}_r - \dot{\theta} = \left(\dot{\theta}_d - \dot{\theta}\right) + \Lambda(\theta_d - \theta) = \dot{e} + \Lambda e \tag{7}$$

s was the sliding surface of a single degree of freedom. Λ was a positive diagonal matrix. If the error vector stayed on the sliding surface, a first-order differential equation (Eq. 7) was used to indicate the tracking error could converge to zero. According to the literature [11], the kinetic equations could be linearly parameterized. The lower extremity exoskeleton kinetic system had the following kinetic properties:

$$M(\theta)\ddot{\theta}_r + V\left(\theta, \dot{\theta}\right)\dot{\theta}_r + G(\theta) = Y\left(\theta, \dot{\theta}, \dot{\theta}_r, \ddot{\theta}_r\right)p \tag{8}$$

$$\tilde{M}(\theta)\ddot{\theta}_r + \tilde{V}\left(\theta, \dot{\theta}\right)\dot{\theta}_r + \tilde{G}(\theta) = Y\left(\theta, \dot{\theta}, \dot{\theta}_r, \ddot{\theta}_r\right)\tilde{p} \tag{9}$$

P was the minimum vector of parameter sets. Y was the coefficient matrix of the minimum parameter set. The elements of the matrix were functions of the joint variables θ, $\dot{\theta}$, $\ddot{\theta}$. The SMC law based on the estimation model was proposed as:

$$\tau = \hat{M}(\theta)\ddot{\theta}_r + \hat{C}(\theta,\dot{\theta})\dot{\theta}_r + \hat{G}(\theta) + \tau_d \tag{10}$$

The Lyapunov function was determined by the following equation:

$$V(t) = \frac{1}{2}s^T M(\theta)s \tag{11}$$

Then:

$$\dot{V}(t) = s^T\left(\tilde{M}(\theta)\ddot{\theta}_r + \tilde{C}(\theta,\dot{\theta})\dot{\theta}_r + \tilde{G}(\theta) - \tau_d\right) = s^T\left(Y(\theta,\dot{\theta},\dot{\theta}_r,\ddot{\theta}_r)\tilde{p} - \tau_s\right) \tag{12}$$

Among them $\tilde{p} = [\tilde{p}_1,\cdots,\tilde{p}_j]^T$, $|\tilde{p}_j| \le a_j$, $Y(\theta,\dot{\theta},\dot{\theta}_r,\ddot{\theta}_r) = Y[Y_{ij}^r]$, $\left|Y_{ij}^r\right| \le \overline{Y}_{ij}^r$, $i = 1,2$; $j = 1,2$. In order to maintain the stability of the slipform system and keep the state of the controlled object moving within the sliding surface, the product value of $s \cdot \dot{s}$ was not larger than zero. Therefore, the control law of switching term was identified by Eq. 13.

$$\tau_d = ksgn(s) + s \tag{13}$$

Where $k = [\lambda_1,\lambda_2]^T$, λ_1, λ_2 was the switching control gain coefficient, $\lambda_i = \sum_{j=1}^{m}\overline{Y}_{ij}^r a_j$, $i = 1,2$, $\lambda_1, \lambda_2 > 0$. The above values would be calculated by Eq. 12, and then the following Eq. 14 could be deduced as:

$$\dot{V}(t) = -\sum_{i=1}^{n}s_i^2 \le 0 \tag{14}$$

The value of $\dot{V}$ was zero when the value s was zero. Therefore, the Lyapunov function designed based on the input-output stability control law could satisfy the stability condition. And from the stability criterion of Lyapunov's second method, it could be inferred that the motion state of the controlled object would reach the sliding mode surface. Convergence to a large scale asymptotically stable equilibrium will occur over a period of time.

According to the symbolic function, the characteristic of the SMC1 was that when the state point moved near the sliding surface, the sign function was sharply changed. Meanwhile, the output control torque would also be sharply changed. The whole system of the controlled object would produce chattering and have a significant effect on the tracking result. This paper replaced the sign function by the saturation function to design SMC2 as shown in Eq. 17, where $\delta \ge 0$ [11]. Therefore, in the range of the boundary layer (δ), the linear switching function was used to control the exoskeleton robot. The saturation function changed slowly as s tended to 0, and thus the chattering caused by the dramatic change in the sign function at the zero [10] would be weakened. The control law was shown in Eq. 18.

$$sat(s) = \begin{cases} \frac{s}{\delta} & |s| \leq \delta \\ sgn(s) & |s| \geq \delta \end{cases} \tag{15}$$

$$\tau = \hat{M}(\theta)\ddot{\theta}_r + \hat{C}(\theta, \dot{\theta})\dot{\theta}_r + \hat{G}(\theta) + k \cdot sat(s) \tag{16}$$

Simulation Platform Construction. Figure 4 showed the control schematic. In the system, the function of the SMC was divided into two parts: controlling the exoskeleton robot and decoupling the nonlinear system by removing the Coriolis force term and the gravity term from the dynamics equations [10]. The desired angular trajectory of the active joint of the exoskeleton was defined as input, and then the error vector $(e, \dot{e})$ was rapidly approached to the sliding surface when the value of s was zero. After that, it converted to the sliding mode, where the error vector slides on the slide surface until it reached the equilibrium point.

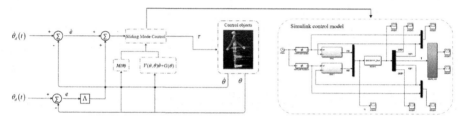

Fig. 4. Control schematic and Simulink control model

Based on the control schematic, MATLAB simulation S-functions was proposed to describe the control algorithm. The Simulink control model of the SMC was shown in Fig. 5 and it would be used for simulation analysis. In order to accurately simulate the operation of the actual exoskeleton, a certain degree of noise $f(t) = 2sin(\pi t)$ was considered in the programming of the control body of the exoskeleton robot.

With the comparison by MATLAB curve fitting tool, the continuous curves of the hip and knee joints in the same walking cycle were obtained by fitting the 4th order sine approximation (Eq. 17 and 18). After that, the softness of the exoskeleton gait and the control of the drive joint motors could be improved.

$$\theta_{d\_hip}(t) = 10.95 \times sin(1.53 \times t + 1.94) + 9.19 \times sin(0.70 \times t - 0.75)$$
$$+ 1.36 \times sin(3.62 \times t - 2.71) + 1.26 \times sin(5.06 \times t + 0.83) \tag{17}$$

$$\theta_{d\_knee}(t) = 30.89 \times sin(0.65 \times t - 0.28) + 5.28 \times sin(4.17 \times t - 3.80)$$
$$+ 0.85 \times sin(6.21 \times t - 2.62) + 14.64 \times sin(2.37 \times t - 5.15) \tag{18}$$

Exoskeleton Control System. Figure 5 showed the exoskeleton hardware platform schematic. 4 angle sensors were installed on the center of 3D printed turnplate which was located in the center of the joint. In order to help patients conduct effective rehabilitation training, the SMC was used to realize real-time and accurate trajectory tracking control of the LERs. To ensure real-time control algorithms, the node controller was connected with the main controller via CAN bus to control the motors (Maxon, EC90) on the hip and knee joints. The angle data from the encoders at the hip and knee joints was immediately transmitted to the main control board through the SPI bus. Therefore, the rotation angle curve of the motor was obtained when the exoskeleton was moved, and then it would be the feedback in the control algorithm to achieve closed-loop control.

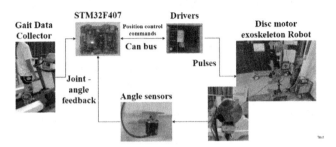

Fig. 5. Exoskeleton hardware platform

The walking experiments were conducted to verify the whole system. The rehabilitation robot was equipped with the mobility and weight reduction functions, shown as Fig. 6. The experimental subject was selected as a medical mannequin (Dummy) with a height of 1.75 m and a leg length of 1.0 m. Rehabilitation robot gravity support suspension system (BWS) could provide 0–25 kg of gravity support for the human body. During the experiment, the Dummy was put on the weight-loss suit for getting a reasonable weight-loss value, so that the dummy was in a standing state by the suspension system. The goniometer from the MiniSun IDEEA®3 motion posture system was installed on the hip and knee joints, shown in Fig. 6. The hip and knee joint angle values were recorded when the Dummy was walking. With the drive of the exoskeleton, the gait tracking experiments were carried out. During the experiment, Dummy's hip and knee gait data was measured by the goniometer in order to compare and analyze with the gait curve.

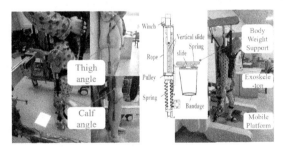

Fig. 6. Lower extremity exoskeleton rehabilitation robot

3   Analysis and Discussion

3.1   Analysis and Discussion of Simulation

In order to compare the performance of PD controller and SMC, we have also built a simulation model of PD controller. The tracking results of SMC1 and classical PD controller was shown in Fig. 7 in which the tracking error of SMC was smaller than PD controller. Also, it was difficult to adjust the parameters of PD controller.

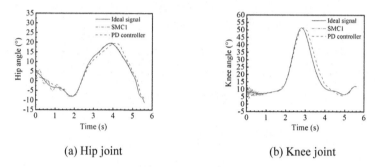

(a) Hip joint   (b) Knee joint

Fig. 7.   Joint angle tracking

From Fig. 7, due to the interference terms, the hip and knee curves deviated significantly from the reference curves in 0–1.5 s. The maximum tracking angle errors were 2.8° and 5.6° of hip and knee. However, the system stabilized after 1.5 s and the curve tracked more closely to the desired curve. The maximum errors of hip and knee curves were 4.6% and 5.2% and the average errors were 2.5% and 3.6%, respectively. The error angle of the hip joint was 0.1–0.8° and the knee was 0.5–1.2°. The results of SMC were acceptable but there still existed a small chattering.

The simulation analysis effect of SMC2 was shown in Fig. 8, where Ref1 was the simulation trajectory curve under symbolic function switching and Ref2 was the simulation curve under saturation function switching. Before the system stabilizes at 0–1.2 s, the tracking curve still fluctuated above and below the desired trajectory curve. However, after the system was stabilized, the tracking angle error of hip and knee trajectory was reduced to 0.1–0.5° and the maximum tracking error was 3.2%, which showed that the chattering was significantly decreased.

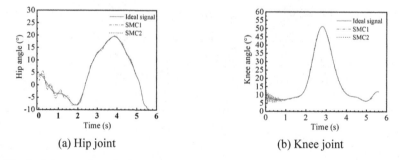

(a) Hip joint   (b) Knee joint

Fig. 8.   Joint angular velocity tracking curve under saturation function switching law

3.2   Analysis and Discussion of Experiment

The results of the walking test were showed in Fig. 9. In the start-up phase of the motor, the certain amount of vibration was existed, and thus the angle error was appeared in the 0 to 2 s. Meanwhile, the experimental curve was unsmooth. When the entire system was stable, due to the delay in the response of the hardware system, there was a small time-domain lag in the band after 2 s. The maximum error of the hip joint experimental curve was 6.1%, the average error was 4.8%, and the error angle was 0.5–1.2°. The variation of the angle range of the knee joint was large and the stability of the fixed connection of the mechanical system was relatively poor. Therefore, the maximum error of the experimental curve was 8.6%. The average error was 6.5% and the error angle was 0.5–1.8°. Overall, an effective tracking of the reference curve was achieved.

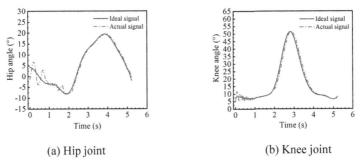

(a) Hip joint   (b) Knee joint

Fig. 9. Trajectory tracking experimental curve

4   Conclusion

In this paper, we designed a LERs to establish mathematical model of SMC and build the control hardware system. Based on the results of the laboratory study, we obtained the following conclusions: (1)A SMC was designed using the input-output stability theory and the estimation model to achieve trajectory tracking control. With the comparison of the joint angle tracking curves according to different switching functions, it was found that the saturation function as the switching function could be effectively weaken the chattering. Also, comparison with classical PD controller, the tracking error of SMC was smaller while the response was faster. The proposed SMC could be applied to the exoskeleton robot control, and thus it could improve active joint trajectory tracking. (2) Based on the results of the walking tests, the mechanical structure and the correctness of the control algorithm were reasonably proved. It showed that the sliding mode control based on the saturation function was feasible. In sum up, this paper provided theoretical and experimental basis for realizing compliance control.

Acknowledgment. This study was supported by the National Natural Science Foundation of China (No. 81960332) and the Guangxi innovation-driven development special (No. AA172204062).

References

1. NBSPRC Homepage. http://www.stats.gov.cn/. Accessed 21 Apr 2021
2. Sun, Z.K.J.M., Zhang, B., Wang, H., et al.: Current situation and thinking of nursing talent training in medical and nursing care institutions for the aged. J. Nurs. **23**(23), 31–34 (2016)
3. Swift, E.C., Williams, T.M., Stephenson, C.: Practical recommendations for robot-assisted treadmill therapy (Lokomat) in children with cerebral palsy: indications, goal setting, and clinical implementation within the WHO-ICF framework. Neuropediatrics **46**(4), 248–260 (2015)
4. Zoss, A.B., Kazerooni, H., Chu, A.: Biomechanical design of the Berkeley lower extremity exoskeleton (BLEEX). IEEE/ASME Trans. Mechatron. **11**(2), 128–138 (2006)
5. Sankai, Y.: HAL: hybrid assistive limb based on cybernics. In: Robotics Research - The 13th International Symposium, ISRR 2007, 26–29 Nov 2007, DBLP, Hiroshima, Japan (2010)
6. Hu Fei, X., Dezhang, W.Y.: Design of exoskeleton control system based on fuzzy PID sliding mode control. J. Anhui Univ. Eng. **32**(4), 56–61 (2017)
7. Shengli, S., Wenhao, C., Xinglong, Z., Yuxuan, C.: Fast second-order terminal sliding mode control and its application in lower limb exoskeleton. Control Decis. Making **34**(1), 162–166 (2019)
8. Pérez-Ibarra, J.C., Siqueira, A.A.G., Silva-Couto, M.A., de Russo, T.L., Krebs, H.I.: Adaptive impedance control applied to robot-aided neuro-rehabilitation of the ankle. IEEE Robot. Autom. Lett. **4**(2), 185–192 (2019). https://doi.org/10.1109/LRA.2018.2885165
9. Haitao, Z.: Research on structural design and control method of lower limb exoskeleton rehabilitation robot. Harbin Institute of Technology (2015)
10. Livingstone, E., Livingstone, S.: Joint motion: method of measuring and recording. Br. J. Surg. **53**, 562 (1966)
11. Hasan, S.K., Dhingra, A.K.: 8 Degrees of freedom human lower extremity kinematic and dynamic model development and control for exoskeleton robot based physical therapy. Int. J. Dyn. Control **8**(8) (2020)

A Performance Evaluating Platform for Variable Stiffness Exoskeleton Joint

Zhuo Ma, Baojun Chen, Jianbin Liu[✉], and Siyang Zuo

Key Laboratory of Mechanism Theory and Equipment Design, Ministry of Education,
Tianjin University, Tianjin, China
jianbin_liu@tju.edu.cn

Abstract. This paper presents a torque testing platform for variable stiffness evaluation of knee joint exoskeleton, a testing platform was designed based on the body size of a normal adult. It includes mechanical structure, control system and data acquisition. The mechanical structure is mainly composed of a stepper motor, a guide screw, a displacement sensor, a force sensor as well as thigh and calf models. A controller and Data Acquisition Board (firmware NI USB-6009) were used to control stepper motor and collect data. According to the equation of static equilibrium, a mechanical model of the platform was built to calculate disturbance torque and angle of exoskeleton joints. The joint angle measurement range of the platform is from 42° to 180° and the maximum tested torque value is 40 Nm. Finally, a test about tension spring was conducted illustrating that variable stiffness performance of joints can be evaluated by this device.

Keywords: Torque testing platform · Variable stiffness · Exoskeleton

1 Introduction

The close cooperation of humans, machine and environment puts high demands on the performance of human interactive robots. Robots must be gentle to humans and the environment and they need to be powerful enough to achieve pre-set goals [1]. Therefore, robots must have the property to change stiffness. The reason why variable stiffness exoskeleton is widely used in the fields of medical rehabilitation, military and industrial production is because of its good compliance and human-machine interaction [2, 3]. However, how to evaluate the variable stiffness performance of exoskeleton robots has always been difficult.

The traditional method of measuring stiffness is based on three-point bending tests [4–6] and the stiffness is calculated based on experimental data [7]. However, this only applies to small and soft continuum structures, not to rotary joints. The torsion tester can be applied to measure the torque of rotary joints, nevertheless, it is not applicable for variable stiffness exoskeleton joints. That is because exoskeleton joints are designed to fit human limbs. More importantly, torsion tester cannot measure torque and rotation angle of joints at the same time. Various testing platforms were fabricated by researchers

© Springer Nature Switzerland AG 2021
X.-J. Liu et al. (Eds.): ICIRA 2021, LNAI 13013, pp. 709–716, 2021.
https://doi.org/10.1007/978-3-030-89095-7_67

to verify variable stiffness performance of robots [3, 8]. Clearly, these platforms, only designed for special occasions, are hard to be popularized.

At this point, a performance evaluation platform for variable stiffness exoskeleton joint is presented in this paper. Compared with torsion tester, it can record the torque and rotation angle of the joints at the same time, which relies on displacement sensor and force sensor. The platform is designed to imitate the structure of human lower limbs, which is conducive to the wearable ability design of lower limb exoskeleton. The imitated hip joint of the platform moves up and down on the ball screw, causing the imitated knee joint to bend and extend. With joint angle measurements ranging from 42° to 180° and torque measurements ranging from 0 to 40 Nm, the platform is capable of testing not only exoskeleton joints but also other types of robotic joints.

2   System Design of the Testing Platform

2.1   Modeling and Mechanical Analysis

In order to calculate torque value and rotation angle of variable stiffness joint on the platform, it is necessary to make force analysis on thigh and calf models. Following hypotheses are employed: firstly, the thigh and calf models are simplified to mass rods, with the center of mass in the middle of the rod; secondly, weight of the exoskeleton is very small compared to thigh and calf models, which can be ignored; at last, errors caused by sensor measurement and part assembly are ignored. When the sliding block down slowly at a uniform speed, the platform is in a dynamic equilibrium state, as shown in Fig. 1.

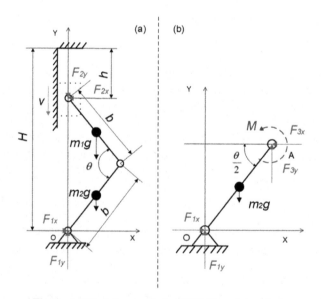

Fig. 1. (a) Modeling analysis. (b) Calf model analysis.

As shown in Fig. 1(a), thigh and calf models were regarded as a whole to analyze force. Based on the equation of static equilibrium, the value of resultant force in the horizontal direction and sum of all torques around O point both are zero. Thus, following equations can be listed:

$$F_{2X} = F_{1X} \tag{1}$$

$$F_{2X}(H - h) = \frac{1}{2}(m_1 + m_2)gb\cos(\frac{\theta}{2}) \tag{2}$$

where F_{2X} and F_{1X} are horizontal forces, H is the length of guide crew, h is a measured value by displacement sensor, m_1 and m_2 are qualities of thigh and calf models, b is the length of rods and θ is the rotation angle of imitated knee joint.

According to the geometric axiom, a relationship between the measured value of displacement sensor and rotation angle of imitated knee joint could be deduced, as follows:

$$\theta = \arccos(\frac{2b^2 - (H - h)^2}{2b^2}) \tag{3}$$

As shown in Fig. 1(b), force analysis for only calf model was done. It should be noted that variable stiffness exoskeleton joint produces disturbance torque M at point A. The sum of all torques around A point is zero.

$$F_{1X}b\sin(\frac{\theta}{2}) + m_2g\frac{1}{2}b\sin(\frac{\theta}{2}) + M = F_{1y}b\cos(\frac{\theta}{2}) \tag{4}$$

where F_{1y} is vertical force measured by force sensor. Rearranging these equations, the following can be obtained:

$$M = F_{1y}b\cos(\frac{\theta}{2}) - \frac{1}{2}m_2gb\sin(\frac{\theta}{2}) - \frac{(m_1 + m_2)gb\sin\theta}{4\sqrt{2 - 2\cos\theta}} \tag{5}$$

All parameters are defined as shown in Table 1.

Table 1. Values of all parameters.

B	m_1	m_2	G
370 mm	2.3 kg	1.7 kg	9.8 N/kg

2.2 Mechanical Structure Design

The movement forms of human lower limb are very rich. The joints, as connecting parts between the bones, determine movement forms of the bone movement chain. For example, human knee joint mainly performs flexion and extension movement. According to the corresponding investigation, the length range of human thigh is from 337 to

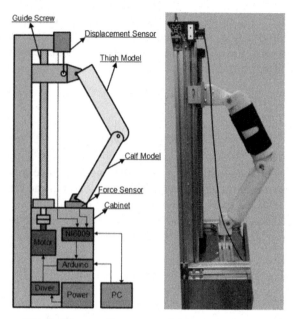

Fig. 2. The overall structure of the testing platform.

523 mm, and the length range of calf is from 300 to 419 mm [9]. In order to simplify the structure design and subsequent solution, the same length of thigh and calf models was defined as 370 mm. The overall structure of this platform is shown in Fig. 2

In Fig. 2, testing platform mainly consists of mechanical structure, data collection system and control part. Thigh model was connected by imitated hip joint to a sliding block of guide screw. Calf model was connected by imitated ankle joint to force sensor fixed on the cabinet. Thigh and calf models were joined by imitated knee joint. A displacement sensor was mounted on top of the cabinet, where the front end of the wire was fixed on the sliding block to record motion distance. A Stepper motor was utilized to drive the guide screw to make imitated knee joint rotated. A motor, driver, power, and firmware were positioned in the cabinet.

2.3 Strength Check

In whole structure, thigh and calf models made of Somos 8000 nylon materials are the main force-bearing parts, hence it is necessary to utilize finite element analysis (FEA) to check strength in ANSYS Workbench software (Ansys Inc., USA). The allowable strength equation of the material is as follows:

$$[\sigma] = \frac{\sigma}{S_H} \tag{6}$$

where σ is bending strength, S_H is the factor of safety and $[\sigma]$ is allowable strength. As the values of bending strength and factor of safety respectively were defined as 67 MPa and 2.0, the calculated value of allowable strength was 33.5 MPa.

When a normal human walks, the knee joint torque does not exceed 40 Nm [10] and lengths of thigh and calf models both are 0.37 m. Consequently, the calculated force should not exceed 108 N. In Workbench, a downward force of 108 N was placed on an upper supported area of thigh model, and the lower supported area of calf model was constrained. According to material attribute, density was defined as 1.16 g/cm^3; Poisson's ratio was defined as 0.41; Elastic modulus was defined as 2500 MPa. Analysis results are shown in Fig. 3.

Fig. 3. Equivalent stress results in Workbench.

As shown in Fig. 3, select three representative joint angles during motion process for respectively static analysis, namely 50°, 100°, and 150°. The largest equivalent stress of the three is about 5.2 MPa, which is less than the value of allowable strength (33.5 MPa). Therefore, testing platform meets the strength requirement.

2.4 Control System and Data Collection

As an important part of testing platform, a control and data collection system must be designed. Control system includes the firmware Arduino Uno R3, stepper motor, driver, and power supply. One end of the driver was connected to the stepper motor, and the other end was connected to Arduino. The program was compiled in the Arduino IDE software and downloaded to the firmware. Pulse width modulation (PWM) signals are sent by Arduino to the driver to realize motor rotation. Modifying the frequency of PWM signals could change the rotating speed of the stepper motor. Force and angle values from sensors were collected to the computer through firmware NI USB-6009. Specific details are shown in Fig. 4.

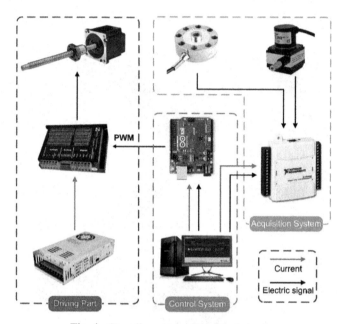

Fig. 4. Overall control principle schematic.

In Fig. 4, with the laptop as the upper-level computer and Arduino as the lower-level computer, overall control system was built. The upper-level refers to the computer on which people could directly issue operation commands. LabVIEW software was chosen to provide a man-machine interface to control the lower-level. It's important to observe that a Data Acquisition Board (firmware NI USB-6009) was chosen to transmit data to a PC. At the same time, it could also display the collected sensor data in the front panel. In a broad sense, the lower-level can directly control the equipment and obtain the status of the equipment, generally Microprogrammed Control Unit (MCU). Obviously, the firmware Arduino is the lower-level computer, which can directly control the rotation of the motor.

In the control process, commands issued by the upper-level are first sent to the lower-level that interprets these commands into the corresponding timing signals to control the equipment to produce actions. In fact, the sensor data can be read at the lower-level computer and directly fed back to the upper-level during the test. However, the sampling frequency of the controller Arduino is limited. Thus, Data Acquisition Board (firmware NI USB-6009) was chosen to transmit data to the PC, and the sampling frequency was set as 1 kHz.

3   Experimental Verification

Because variable stiffness exoskeleton joint was not found, to verify a measured performance of the platform, an experiment about tension spring was designed in Fig. 5

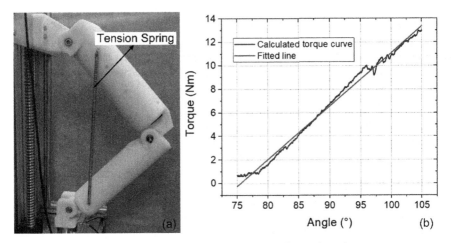

Fig. 5. (a) Tension spring test. (b) Experimental results.

As shown in Fig. 5(a), one end of tension spring was fixed on the thigh model and the other end was fixed on the calf model. Even if this spring has a steady stiffness value, it can replay the exoskeleton joint to provide a disturbance torque, when the sliding block of testing platform is upwardly moving. As tension spring starts to get stretched, the angle value of imitated knee joint is about 75°, and as this spring is stretched by 60%, the angle value is about 105°.

As shown in Fig. 5(b), the vertical ordinate represents disturbance torque calculated by Eq. 6 and the horizontal ordinate represents joint angle calculated by Eq. 4. The blue curve represents torque measured by testing platform, which has been smoothed by a mean filter in LabVIEW. It can be seen that the disturbance torque varies almost linearly. When the joint angle is about 105°, the disturbance torque reaches a maximum value of 13 Nm. The red line is a result of linear regression fitting. Its slope is about 0.45 Nm/deg, which is also stiffness value from tension spring working on thigh and calf models.

4   Conclusion

This paper presents a performance evaluation platform for variable stiffness exoskeleton or other types of robotic joints. During the tests, it is enabled to obtain torque and rotation angle of the tested joints at the same time. Next, according to the torque-angle curve, the stiffness of joints can be calculated. The mechanical structure of the platform was designed and strength check results in Workbench software showed usability. A human-machine interface was built by LabVIEW to control the rotation of imitated knee joint and this interface could show the calculated angle and torque of joints. Finally, a tension spring, replacing variable stiffness robotic joints, was mounted on the testing platform. Torque value from 75° to 105° rotation angle could be obtained and this stiffness acting on the platform was calculated as 0.45 Nm/deg. As there is the design of humanoid lower limb, this platform can be adopted to testing complicated exoskeletons. In the future, a deep study will be done to eliminate slight vibration resulting from the slow-moving platform. In addition, the control and data collection system must be improved for testing precision.

Acknowledgements. This work was supported in part by National Key R&D Program of China under Grant No. 2019YFB1311501, in part by National Natural Science Foundation of China under Grant No. 51905374 & 61773280.

References

1. Wolf, S., Hirzinger, G.: A new variable stiffness design: matching requirements of the next robot generation, 2008, pp. 1741–1746. IEEE (2008)
2. Moltedo, M., et al.: Variable stiffness ankle actuator for use in robotic-assisted walking: control strategy and experimental characterization. Mech. Mach. Theor. **134**, 604–624 (2019). https://doi.org/10.1016/j.mechmachtheory.2019.01.017
3. Liu, Y., Guo, S., Hirata, H., Ishihara, H., Tamiya, T.: Development of a powered variable-stiffness exoskeleton device for elbow rehabilitation. Biomed. Microdevice **20**(3), 1–13 (2018). https://doi.org/10.1007/s10544-018-0312-6
4. Huang, J., Zhang, Q., Scarpa, F., Liu, Y., Leng, J.: Shape memory polymer-based hybrid honeycomb structures with zero Poisson's ratio and variable stiffness. Compos. Struct. **179**, 437–443 (2017). https://doi.org/10.1016/j.compstruct.2017.07.091
5. Miller-Jackson, T., Sun, Y., Natividad, R., Yeow, C.H.: Tubular jamming: a variable stiffening method toward high-force applications with soft robotic components. Soft Robot. **6**(4), 468–482 (2019). https://doi.org/10.1089/soro.2018.0084
6. Chenal, T.P., Case, J.C., Paik, J., Kramer, R.K.: Variable stiffness fabrics with embedded shape memory materials for wearable applications. Paper presented at the 2014 IEEE/RSJ International Conference on Intelligent Robots and System
7. Sun, T., Chen, Y., Han, T., Jiao, C., Lian, B., Song, Y.: A soft gripper with variable stiffness inspired by pangolin scales, toothed pneumatic actuator and autonomous controller. Robot. CIM-Int. Manuf. **61**, 101848 (2020). https://doi.org/10.1016/j.rcim.2019.101848
8. Li, Z., Bai, S.: A novel revolute joint of variable stiffness with reconfigurability. Mech. Mach. Theor. **133**, 720–736 (2019). https://doi.org/10.1016/j.mechmachtheory.2018.12.011
9. Coding, C.I.O.S.: Human dimensions of Chinese adults. The State Bureau of Quality and Technical Supervision (2009)
10. Yang, L.: Research on the cable-pulley underactuated lower limb exoskeleton. Master of Engineering, Harbin Institute of Technology (2018)

Self Adjusting Exosuit for Shoulder

Weijie He[1], Wuxiang Zhang[1,2(✉)], and Xilun Ding[1,2]

[1] School of Mechanical Engineering and Automation at Beihang
University in Beijing, Beijing 100191, China
zhangwuxiang@buaa.edu.cn
[2] Beijing Advanced Innovation Center for Biomedical Engineering,
Beihang University, Beijing 100191, China

Abstract. To help the shoulder lift the arm against gravity, this paper proposes a soft cable-driven exoskeleton system. The shoulder posture is measured in real time by the heading and attitude reference systems distributed on the forearm and torso, and the ideal output tension of the two rope systems is calculated based on this. The flexible actuator realizes the tension tracking to assist the frontal flexion and lateral abduction of the user's shoulder. The difference of the EMG signal of anterior deltoid and middle deltoid was analyzed in static/dynamic test, with/without exoskeleton, shoulder joint muscles The results show that the exoskeleton is compliant with the movement, and there is a significant decrease of the EMG signal of the anterior deltoid and middle deltoid wearing the exoskeleton, meaning a reduction of the muscle load.

Keywords: Exoskeleton · Compliant · sEMG

1 Introduction

The upper limb exoskeleton is a wearable intelligent device that provides auxiliary power for human movement. The majority of the current upper limb exoskeleton are rigid structures with large volume and weight, which are difficult for daily use, and are lack of compliance. Therefore, with intrinsic compliance and rather small weight and volume, the upper limb exoskeleton with a flexible structure has become a current research hotspot.

Upper limb exoskeleton with a rigid structure can ensure sufficient stiffness and strength to achieve high-precision motion control and large force output [1–4], but the large structural weight and volume and the lack of flexibility make it difficult to adapt to the actual movement of the joint.

As the development of the compliance actuators and flexible structure, exoskeletons with a soft structure (or exosuit) has emerged. The overall structure is light and the additional mass on the arm is small, which can minimize the

National Natural Science Foundation of China (Grant No. 91848104) and Beijing Natural Science Foundation-Haidian Foundation (Grant No. 2018YFB1307000).

© Springer Nature Switzerland AG 2021
X.-J. Liu et al. (Eds.): ICIRA 2021, LNAI 13013, pp. 717–727, 2021.
https://doi.org/10.1007/978-3-030-89095-7_68

impact on human joint movement. At present, most studies focus on the lower limbs [5–7], while few studies focus on the soft exoskeleton of shoulder joint.

Compared with the rigid structure, the exosuit system introduces more uncertainties, so researches on exosuits for the shoulder joint mostly assist a single degree of freedom of the shoulder joint [8, 9]. In 2017 Gaponov et al. adopted twisted string actuator(TSA) technic to develop a wearable robot called Auxilio, which can assist the motion of the abduction and the flexion of the shoulder joint and the flexion of the elbow joint [10]. These studies mainly focus on the a single degree of freedom of the shoulder or mechanically combine multiple single-degree-of-freedom motions neglecting the coupling effect between different degrees of freedom of shoulder joint. However, rather than just a simple constant axis rotation, the motion of shoulder joint is the coupling of every degree of freedom from different joints. Based on industrial application, Yongtae G. Kim et al. develop an flexible exoskeleton system, which places the pulley that lifts the shoulder on a curved guide to passively adapt the internal/external rotation of shoulder joint [11]. The passive adaptation to the internal/external rotation of the joint add uncertainties to the system leading to a decrease of the control accuracy.

This paper proposes a soft cable-driven exoskeleton system, which assists the abduction and the flexion of the shoulder joint and adapt to internal/external rotation. Motor-driven series elastic actuator is adopted to assist the motion of abduction and flexion of shoulder joint. Through AHRS module, the posture of shoulder joint is monitored to dynamically adjust the output force of the two cable system and compensate for the internal/external rotation of shoulder joint to meet the requirement of activities of daily living (ADL).

In the following chapters, the structure of shoulder joint was analyzed to clarify the design parameters. Then we introduce the mechanical design, control design and experiment result in detail. Finally, we conclude the function and effectiveness of the exosuit system and point out the direction of the future research.

2   Structure of Shoulder

The shoulder joint has multiple degrees of freedom coupled to each other [12] and the motion of shoulder joint can be simplified as the combination of the three-degree-of-freedom rotation and the shift of the center of glenohumeral joint [13]. During the design process of the exosuit, the translation of glenohumeral joint can be neglected and the motion of shoulder joint can be simplified as a three-degree-of-freedom rotation around a fixed axis, including abduction/adduction, flexion/extension and internal/external rotation. The range of motion, average torque [14] and the motion bandwidth [15] of every degree of freedom of shoulder joint are shown in Table 1. In the motion of abduction and horizontal flexion, muscles has a relatively higher level of activation. While in other motion, the function of muscles are to maintain the stability of shoulder joint and control the speed of the motion, leading to a lower activation level. The designed exosuit system are able to assist the shoulder joint in abduction and flexion against gravity.

Table 1. Kinematic and dynamic parameters of shoulder joint in ADL.

Joints	Flexion/extension	Abduction/adduction	Internal/external rotation
ROM (°)	110	100	135
Average torque (Nm)	3.5	1.0	−0.3
Bandwidth	4–8 Hz		

3 Flexible Mechanism Subsystem

The flexible mechanism subsystem include wearing part, transmission mechanism and actuator (Fig. 1). Wearing part is the interaction part between human and exoskeleton, therefore it is necessary to ensure comfort and safety. The transmission mechanism is responsible for power transmission from the motor to the anchor point. This article adopts the structure of the Bodwen cable. Actuator refers to 2 motor actuated series elastic actuator.

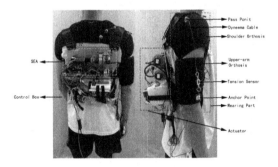

Fig. 1. Flexible mechanism subsystem.

3.1 Overall Composition

The flexible mechanism subsystem is the basic mechanism of the exoskeleton (Fig. 1). The wearing part is directly worn on the human body, including shoulder part and upper arm part, with only 300 g. Transmission mechanism is able to transmit the power from the actuator on the back of the user to the anchor point. Bodwen cable is adopted to transmit power through a long distance. The rope starts from the reel, and the position of the guiding point is set reasonably. The Bodwen cable is fixed relatively to the guiding point. The rope passes through the Bodwen cable and is finally fixed on the anchor point of the upper arm orthosis.

Transmission Mechanism. In order to ensure the assist function and reduce the power consumption of the system in the largest possible workspace, it is necessary to adjust the cable distribution, check the tension solution in the workspace, and reduce the peak value of the required output tension.

As shown in Fig. 2, the coordinate system O with the center of glenohumeral joint as the origin and the coordinate system P with the center of elbow joint as the origin are respectively established [16]. The arms shown are in the initial position, that is, the arms hang down naturally with the palms pressed to the sides of the body (N pose). Points a, c are the fixed points at the end of each cable (or anchor points) while points d, f are the pass points of the cables. The position of a, c and d, f are relatively constant to the coordinate system O and the coordinate system P. Position of every point can be solved by the transformation of coordinates $\vec{r}_{oa}$ and $\vec{r}_{oc}$ are the radius vector of points a, c to the center of the glenohumeral joint. $\vec{F}_{ad}$ and $\vec{F}_{cf}$ represent the force vector of the two cable systems. In the coordinate system P, the torque at the center of the glenohumeral joint generated by the two cable force are

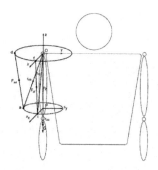

Fig. 2. Build the coordinate system on shoulder joint and the big arm.

$$^{P}\vec{T}_{ad} = {}^{P}\vec{r}_{oa} \times {}^{P}\vec{F}_{ad} \tag{1}$$

$$^{P}\vec{T}_{cf} = {}^{P}\vec{r}_{oc} \times {}^{P}\vec{F}_{cf} \tag{2}$$

Point g is the center of gravity of one arm and is the gravity vector of an arm. If the movement of the elbow joint is ignored and the unilateral arm is treated as a single rigid body, then in frame P, the torque generated by the gravity of the unilateral arm at the center of the glenohumeral joint is

$$^{P}\vec{T}_{G} = {}^{P}\vec{r}_{og} \times {}^{P}\vec{G} \tag{3}$$

In order for the exoskeleton to partially or fully assist the upper limb in lifting against gravity, the following formula shall be satisfied:

$$^{P}\vec{T}_{ad} + {}^{P}\vec{T}_{cf} = \varepsilon^{P}\vec{T}_{G} \tag{4}$$

We call ε the assist proportionality coefficient. By adjusting ε, different level of assist can be realized to achieve personalized and differentiated wearing experience and assist effect. Because cable can not sustain pressure, the force of cables should

$$
\begin{aligned}
{}^{P}\overrightarrow{F}_{ad} &> 0 \\
{}^{P}\overrightarrow{F}_{cf} &> 0
\end{aligned}
\tag{5}
$$

To simplify the model, we assume points a, c and points d, f remain constant during movement. In initial position, $\overrightarrow{r}_{of}$ and $\overrightarrow{r}_{pc}$ are in line with axis x and axis ${}^{P}x$ while $\overrightarrow{r}_{od}$ and $\overrightarrow{r}_{pa}$ are in line with axis$y$ and axis ${}^{P}y$ separately. α_1 is the rotation angle of $\overrightarrow{r}_{of}$ and $\overrightarrow{r}_{pc}$ about the axis z. α_2 is the rotation angle of $\overrightarrow{r}_{od}$ and $\overrightarrow{r}_{pa}$ about the axis z. Adjust the cable distribution by modifying the rotation angle of the point around the z-axis α_1 and α_2 to maximize the assist range.

Fixing $\alpha_2 = 0$, the assist range is calculated on different α_1 in MATLAB. The evaluation of the exosuit in the predefined workspace(abduction/adduction angle $[-90, 0]$, flexion/extension angle $[-180, 0]$, internal/external rotation angle $[-30, 90]$) is conducted to search qualified points. The result of the optimization indicated that the best angle for α_1 is 0.502(28.8) where 2955 possible points can be found (Fig. 3(a)). Then fixing α_1 to 0.502, the optimization of α_2 is conducted. The results show that the effective assist range decreases monotonically as α_2 increases, so α_2 remain 0 (Fig. 3(b)). At this point, the output tension of the two rope systems respectively peaks at: $F_{ad} = F_{cf} = 218N$.

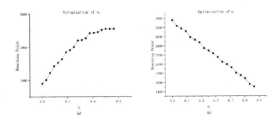

Fig. 3. (a) Number of reaching points of different α_1. (b) Number of reaching points of different α_2.

Actuator. Each cable system is driven by a series elastic actuator to achieve the output of the specified torque. Each series elastic actuator is composed of a motor (Maxon, EC-4pole 22), a torsional spring and a reel (Fig. 4). Two encoders separately at the end of motor and on the other end of the reel are used to measure the conformation angle as the feedback of the force control. In order to avoid cable overlapping or looseness, the reel is machined with spiral grooves where cable slides.

Fig. 4. SEA structure.

4   Control Design

The control system of the exosuit adopts a hierarchical control framework based on shoulder joint posture (Fig. 5). The ground layer control the SEA(series elastic actuator) to pull the rope to output ideal force. Top layer, or model calculation layer, measures the shoulder posture through AHRS and calculates the joint moment of shoulder combined with the human kinetic model. The joint moment is mapped to the ideal output force through the rope layout.

Fig. 5. Control system structure.

Posture Evaluation of Shoulder Joint. Each attitude of shoulder joint corresponds to a set of tension solutions, so accurate measurement of shoulder joint attitude is crucial to the control system. An AHRS module is arranged at the arm and shoulder joint respectively. The modified quaternion from the AHRS module is considered with sufficient accuracy. By determining the attitude of shoulder and elbow relative to the earth coordinate system and comparing the attitude of adjacent joints, the attitude of shoulder joint can be determined [17]. The following formula can be used to determine the attitude of human joints relative to the coordinates of the earth,

$$\,_J^E q = \,_S^E q \otimes \,_J^S q \tag{6}$$

$\,_J^E q$ is the attitude of the human body joints relative to the earth coordinate system, $\,_S^E q$ is the attitude of the AHRS module coordinate system relative to the earth coordinate system, and $\,_J^S q$ is the attitude of the human body joint coordinate system relative to the AHRS module coordinate system. $\,_S^E q$ can be accessed by AHRS module in real time. During movement, the position of the AHRS module relative to the human joint is fixed, so $\,_J^S q$ is measured by a predefined posture. N pose, that is two arms naturally droop, palm close to the body side, is adopted to determine $_J^S q$. At N pose, the attitude of the human body joint relative to the earth coordinate system and the attitude of the AHRS module coordinate system relative to the earth coordinate system are known so that the attitude of the human joint coordinate system relative to the reference system coordinate system $_J^S q$ is

$$_J^S q = (_S^E q)^{-1} \otimes _J^E q \tag{7}$$

When the attitude of the human joint coordinate system relative to the AHRS module coordinate system attitude is calculated, the attitude of the big arm and shoulder joint relative to the earth coordinate system can be determined by Eq. (6). Then the attitude of frame P with respect to frame O is

$$_P^O q = _{J_S}^E q \otimes _{J_U}^E q \tag{8}$$

$_{J_S}^E q$ and $_{J_U}^E q$ are the attitude of the shoulder joint coordinate system and the big arm coordinate system relative to the earth coordinate system respectively. Through $_P^O q$, the position of points a, c, d, f can be determined and the ideal force of the two cable system can be solved.

Ideal Force Source. In order to achieve comfortable human-machine interaction, the control system not only needs to be able to output an ideal force, but also exhibit a specific spring damping characteristic [18]. It is assumed that the series elastic actuator exhibits the spring damping characteristics shown in Fig. 6 is the preload torque at the equilibrium position. k_v is the stiffness of the virtual spring and B_v is the damping coefficient of the virtual spring.

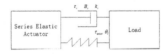

Fig. 6. SEA spring-damping system.

From Fig. 6, we have,

$$\tau_{inter} = \tau_v - k_v \theta_l - B_v \dot{\theta}_l \tag{9}$$

According Hooke's law,

$$\tau_{inter} = k_s (\theta_m - \theta_l) \tag{10}$$

Combined with (9), this is:

$$\tau_{inter} = \tau_v - k_v \theta_{md} + \frac{k_v}{k_s} \tau_{inter} - B_v \dot{\theta}_{md} - \frac{B_v}{k_s} \dot{\tau}_{inter} \tag{11}$$

Stiffness of the real spring $k_s = 0.03$ is much larger than the damping coefficient of the virtual spring

$$B_v = 0.003,$$

therefore the final term in the above equation becomes a small contributor to the overall control law. Thus, we ignore the fmal term in the above equation, arriving at:

$$\tau_{inter} = \tau_v - k_v\theta_{md} + \frac{k_v}{k_s}\tau_{inter} - B_v\dot{\theta}_{md} \tag{12}$$

The motors are considered as the ideal velocity source. And the position of the motors can be measured by the encoder at the end of the motor. The ideal velocity is shown as:

$$\dot{\theta}_{md} = \frac{\tau_v - k_v\theta_m + \frac{k_v-k_s}{k_s}\tau_d}{B_v} \tag{13}$$

We design a control architecture shown below (Fig. 7).

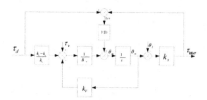

Fig. 7. SEA PID control structure.

As a human interaction device, exoskeleton need to consider the stiffness of the end effector. The end stiffness is defined as the ratio between the torque on the end and the end rotation angle:

$$Z(s) = \frac{\tau_L}{-\theta_L} \tag{14}$$

According to the control diagram above, neglecting the preload torque τ_v, we have:

$$Z(s) = \frac{K_sK_vs + B_vK_s}{B_vs^2 + (1 - K_pB_v)K_ss - K_IK_sB_v} \tag{15}$$

Replacing the s with $j\omega$, the frequency domain response of the end stiffness can be achieved [19]. As shown in Fig. 8, for low frequency, the end stiffness approximate to ideal stiffness Kv, whereas for frequencies above the bandwidth, the system behaves like the mechanical spring.

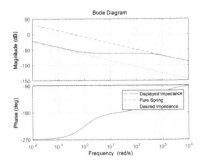

Fig. 8. Frequency domain response of end stiffness.

5 Experiment and Analysis

In order to verify the effectiveness of the exosuit, RMS values of EMG signals of the shoulder joint muscles were measured to compare the metabolic level of the muscles under the same action with and without the exosuit.

In lateral raise and frontal raise, the EMG signals of the lateral deltoid and the anterior deltoid was measured by a wireless sEMG capture system egree (Delsys USA) to evaluate the efficiency of the exosuit.

The experiment subject is a 24-year-old healthy male. With and without exosuits, the dynamic and static experiments of lateral raise and frontal raise were performed respectively, and each group was repeated 5 times. In the dynamic experiment, each group of experiments lasted for 30 s, with a stable movement rate. In the static experiment, the experiment subject tries to keep the arm position as stable as possible for 10 s. During dynamic experiment, the subjects were instructed to frontally or laterally raise their arms to 90°, and then drop naturally beside thigh. During static experiment, the subjects were asked to horizontally flex and extend their arm while maintaining 90° of abduction or flexion. During the experiment, the subject should keep the elbow straight, and the shoulder does not rotate internally or externally. Between each group, the subject must rest for 5 min to avoid muscle fatigue.

The raw EMG signal contains a lot of noise so burst RMS value of the raw signal was used for analysis. The result show that, with exosuit, the activation level of the anterior deltoid and the middle deltoid respectively drop 32.3% and 35.2% during static lateral raise, 44.7% and 30.8% during dynamic lateral raise, 27.6% and 20.2% during static frontal raise, and 12.2% and 71.8% during dynamic forntal raise (Fig. 9).

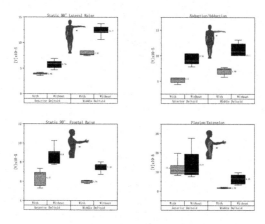

Fig. 9. Experiment result.

6   Conclusion

In order to help the user overcome gravity to lift the arm, an exosuit system was proposed to control the abduction and forward flexion of the shoulder joint by means of two cables, which could adapt to the influence of the internal/external rotation of the shoulder joint. By optimization and simulation of the tension distribution, the work space of the exosuit is maximized. The control system monitors the posture of shoulder joint in real time through the two AHRS module and therefore adjusts the rope tension. The results showed that the designed exosuit can effectively reduce the activation level of shoulder joint muscles in daily life, demonstrating the potential of exosuit to assist human movement with high portability and lightweight.

However, there are some problems left to be solved: 1. When the tension is too large, the anchor point and the pass point will produce the displacement, and there exists a relative large error between the expected layout and the actual one. 2. If the tension is too large, the rope will be tight so that the cable will press the shoulder joint and cause discomfort. 3. Exoskeleton suits are not responsive enough to accommodate excessive frequency.

References

1. Sugar, T.G., et al.: Design and control of RUPERT: a device for robotic upper extremity repetitive therapy. IEEE Trans. Neural Syst. Rehabilitation Eng. **15**(3), 336–346 (2007)
2. Cai, Z., et al.: Design & control of a 3D stroke rehabilitation platform. In: 2011 IEEE International Conference on Rehabilitation Robotics. IEEE, pp. 1–6 (2011)
3. Ren, Y., Park, H.-S., Zhang, L-Q.: Developing a whole-arm exoskeleton robot with hand opening and closing mechanism for upper limb stroke rehabilitation. In: 2009 IEEE International Conference on Rehabilitation Robotics. IEEE, pp. 761–765 (2009)

4. Mihelj, M., Nef, T., Riener, R.: ARMin II-7 DoF rehabilitation robot: mechanics and kinematics. In: Proceedings 2007 IEEE International Conference on Robotics and Automation. IEEE, pp. 4120–4125 (2007)
5. De Rossi, S., et al.: Gait improvements in stroke patients with a soft exosuit. In: The Proceedings of the Gait and Clinical Movement Analysis Society (GCMAS) Meeting. Portland, OR (2015)
6. Asbeck, A.T., et al.: Biologically-inspired soft exosuit. In: 2013 IEEE 13th International Conference on Rehabilitation Robotics (ICORR). IEEE, pp. 1–8 (2013)
7. Asbeck, A.T., et al.: A biologically inspired soft exosuit for walking assistance. Int. J. Robot. Res. **34**(6), 744–762 (2015)
8. Galiana, I., et al.: Wearable soft robotic device for post-stroke shoulder rehabilitation: Identifying misalignments. In: 2012 IEEE/RSJ International Conference on Intelligent Robots and Systems. IEEE, pp. 317–322 (2012)
9. O'neill, C.T., et al.: A soft wearable robot for the shoulder: design, characterization, and preliminary testing. In: 2017 International Conference on Rehabilitation Robotics (ICORR). IEEE, pp. 1672–1678 (2017)
10. Gaponov, I., Popov, D., Lee, S.J., Ryu, J.-H.: Auxilio: a portable cable-driven exosuit for upper extremity assistance. Int. J. Control, Autom. Syst.**15**(1), 73–84 (2016). https://doi.org/10.1007/s12555-016-0487-7
11. Kim, Y.G., et al.: Development of a soft exosuit for industrial applications. In: 2018 7th IEEE International Conference on Biomedical Robotics and Biomechatronics (Biorob). IEEE, pp. 324–329 (2018)
12. Charalambous, C.P., Eastwood, S.: Normal and abnormal motion of the shoulder. In: Classic Papers in Orthopaedics, pp. 331–333. Springer, London (2014)
13. Lenarcic, J., Stanisic, M.: A humanoid shoulder complex and the humeral pointing kinematics. IEEE Trans. Robot. Autom. **19**(3), 499–506 (2003)
14. Rosen, J., et al.: The human arm kinematics and dynamics during daily activities-toward a 7 DOF upper limb powered exoskeleton. In: ICAR'05. Proceedings., 12th International Conference on Advanced Robotics, pp. 532–539. IEEE (2005)
15. Winter, D.A.: Biomechanics and motor control of human movement. Wiley (2009)
16. Prayudi, I., Kim, D.: Design and implementation of IMU-based human arm motion capture system. In: IEEE International Conference on Mechatronics and Automation. IEEE 2012, pp. 670–675 (2012)
17. Roetenberg, D., Luinge, H., Slycke, P.: Xsens MVN: Full 6DOF human motion tracking using miniature inertial sensors. Xsens Motion Technologies BV, Technical report, 1 (2009)
18. Pratt, G.A., Williamson, M.M.: Series elastic actuators. In: Proceedings 1995 IEEE/RSJ International Conference on Intelligent Robots and Systems. Human Robot Interaction and Cooperative Robots. IEEE, pp. 399–406 (1995)
19. Veneman, J.F., et al.: Design of a series elastic-and Bowden cable-based actuation system for use as torque-actuator in exoskeleton-type training. In: 9th International Conference on Rehabilitation Robotics, 2005. ICORR 2005. IEEE, pp. 496–499 (2005)

Design of a 6 DOF Cable-Driven Upper Limb Exoskeleton

Letian Ai, Tianlin Zhou, Lei Wu, Wei Qian, Xiaohui Xiao, and Zhao Guo[✉]

School of Power and Mechanical Engineering, Wuhan University, Wuhan, China
guozhao@whu.edu.cn

Abstract. To provide post-stroke patients with rehabilitation training, this paper presents a six degrees of freedom (DOF) cable-driven upper limb exoskeleton, where 3 active DOF, 1 active DOF, and 2 passive DOF are given to the shoulder, elbow, and wrist, respectively. Carbon fiber materials are mainly used to consist of the frame of the prototype, achieving the lightness and compactness design. Cable-driven series elastic actuators are used to minimize the inertia and complexity of the exoskeleton's joints and provide compliant actuation, resulting in better human-robot interaction. A double parallelogram mechanism is designed to transfer rotation from a remote center to the glenohumeral joint. To evaluate the performance of the prototype, PID controllers are designed to conduct position tracking and torque tracking experiments in the elbow joint. The experimental results show that the prototype has a good tracking performance and is capable to assist patients in rehabilitation training.

Keywords: Upper limb exoskeleton · Carbon fiber materials · Cable-driven SEA · Double parallelogram mechanism

1 Introduction

Post-stroke patients suffering from motor dysfunction caused by neurological diseases usually face inconvenience in activities of daily living (ADL) [1], and need rehabilitation training to regain proper muscular functions. Because robots can substitute therapists to provide patients with diversified, repeatable, and intensive rehabilitation training [2, 3], adopting robots to assist recovery therapy has gained momentum in recent decades. Various types of upper limb exoskeletons have been developed [4–9].

Wearability and reliability are important for upper limb exoskeletons that aim at assisting patients with effective and safe rehabilitation training. On the one hand, the complex and bulky structure will introduce unwanted interference and increase control difficulty; on the other hand, misalignment and impact between robots and wearers can result in impairment and danger to patients. Therefore, making upper limb exoskeletons lightweight, compact, and compliant is significant.

A direct approach to achieve lightweight is to minimize the mass of materials. Most exoskeletons adopt metal materials to ensure the stiffness and strength of their structure, whereas it will greatly increase the mass. For example, Emilio Trigili et al. developed

© Springer Nature Switzerland AG 2021
X.-J. Liu et al. (Eds.): ICIRA 2021, LNAI 13013, pp. 728–736, 2021.
https://doi.org/10.1007/978-3-030-89095-7_69

a four (DOF) shoulder exoskeleton robot NESM weighing 12.017 kg; Urs Keller et al. proposed a four DOF upper limb exoskeleton robot ChARMin weighing 5.7 kg. Heavy metal parts make exoskeletons cumbersome and increase the burden of the actuator, leading to misalignment between exoskeletons and patients. With the development of material technology, carbon fiber materials provide solutions. Carbon fiber materials have a high strength-weight ratio that is strong enough to substitute metal materials and make the exoskeleton lighter. In view of this, carbon fiber materials are mainly used to construct the frame of the proposed exoskeleton. Other parts of the exoskeleton that sustain relatively small force are made of 3D printing materials to further reduce the weight.

Another approach to decrease the inertial of the exoskeleton and increase its compactness is adopting the cable-driven method. Traditional exoskeleton robots often integrate motors and reducers into joints, which makes the joints complex and bulky, while cable-driven exoskeletons can mount actuators away from joints. Cable-driven exoskeletons are well researched, such as CABXLexo-7 designed by Feiyun Xiao et al., which adopts a cable-conduit mechanism to transmit the power of motors [6]; Xiang Cui et al. proposed a 7 DOF arm exoskeleton (CAREX-7) which mounts 8 cables to drive the whole-arm motion [10]. Though their designs successfully detach motors from joints, the cable-guided mechanism is complex. To address the deficiency, a compact cable-driven exoskeleton is proposed in this paper. In addition, the exoskeleton adopts the series elastic actuator (SEA) to enhance control compliancy, for the SEA that integrates elastic elements and motor can achieve compliancy and low impedance without violating the requirement of lightness and compactness [11–16].

The glenohumeral joint (GHJ) has 3 DOF, engendering the main range of motion (ROM) of the shoulder. Since parallel linkage systems are superior to serial linkage systems especially in minimizing collision between the exoskeleton and the trunk of wearers [17, 18], a double parallelogram mechanism (DPM) was designed to transmit the inner/outer rotation center to the GHJ in the previous work [错误!未找到引用源。]. In this paper, a modified DPM is proposed to ensure the exoskeleton compatible with wears' ROM to further increase the safety and comfort of the rehabilitation.

The main contributions of this paper are as follows: 1) The exoskeleton's structure is mainly made of carbon fiber materials to achieve the low-weight design and improve the wearability; 2) The cable-driven SEAs render the exoskeleton compact and compliant, which increases the safety and comfort of the rehabilitation training; 3) The renewed DPM helps to ensure patients' ROM and minimize the risk of collision. To verify the performance of the exoskeleton, position control and impedance control experiments based on PID controllers were conducted.

The rest of this paper is organized as follows: Sect. 2 introduces the mechanical design of the exoskeleton. In Sect. 3, experimental characterizations of the exoskeleton are presented. Section 4 draws the conclusion and discusses the future work.

2   Mechanical Design

2.1   Overall Design of the Exoskeleton

Figure 1 presents the CAD model of the 6-DOF upper limb exoskeleton which includes two parts: backboard and upper limb. The backboard integrates control electronics and SEAs, which are illustrated in Sect. 2.2. The shoulder mechanism of the upper limb is detailed in Sect. 2.3, while the elbow mechanism and wrist mechanism are discussed in Sect. 2.4.

As shown in Fig. 1 and Fig. 2, carbon fiber materials and 3D printing materials are used to construct the frame of the exoskeleton where the backboard, upper arm, and forearm are made of carbon plates and arm bracers are made of PLA. Relying on the low density and high strength of the carbon fiber, the exoskeleton can be lightweight without sacrificing its strength. Though the strength of PLA is lower than that of carbon fiber, light PLA that does not have to withstand large torque is capable to support the wearer's arm. The adoption of light materials reduces the weight of the exoskeleton's upper limb to 3.15 kg.

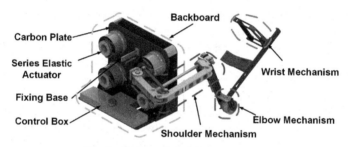

Fig. 1. CAD model of the exoskeleton

The multiple views of the exoskeleton are illustrated in Fig. 2. The exoskeleton is mounted on a wheeled working platform that has mobility and lifting function, by which patients with different physiques can wear the exoskeleton easily. It contains four active DOF, corresponding to three shoulder DOF (flexion/extension, ab-/adduction, in-/external rotation) and one elbow DOF (flexion/extension). Because the exoskeleton focuses on the rehabilitation of shoulder and elbow joints, the forearm supination/pronation is not considered. The wrist mechanism has two passive DOF (flexion/extension, radial/ulnar deviation) to enable patients to grasp the handle comfortably and avoid wrist sprain. As shown in Table 1, the exoskeleton meets the main requirement of wearers' ROM.

Table 1. The ROM of humans and the exoskeleton.

DOF	ROM of humans	ROM of the exoskeleton
Shoulder flexion / extension	150°–180°/40°–50°	180°/40°
Shoulder abduction/ adduction	180°/40°	120°/60°
Shoulder internal/ external rotation	60°–90°/40°–70°	60°/60°
Elbow flexion/ extension	135°–140°/0°	140°/140°
Forearm supination / pronation	85°–90°/70°–90°	0°/0°
Wrist flexion / extension	73°/70°	70°/70°
Wrist radial / ulnar deviation	27°/27°	30°/30°

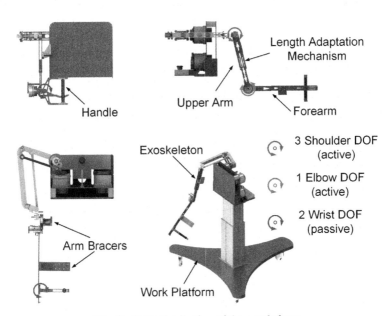

Fig. 2. DOF distribution of the exoskeleton

2.2 Design of Cable-Driven SEA

Figure 3 shows the schematic diagram of the cable-drive SEA that adopts torsion spring as the elastic element. Compared with traditional linear spring, integrating torsion spring into SEA can reduce the size of the actuator and render it smaller mechanical friction and backlash, which is beneficial to improve the resolution of the actuator. The stiffness of the torsion spring is 37.5 N/rad obtained by the simulation of finite element analysis software ANSYS. The relative deflection angle between the torsion spring and reducer can be detected by the built-in encoder, so as to calculate the output torque of the SEA, which can be used in torque control.

The force and motion of the actuator are transmitted to the joint through the relative motion of the tendon and sheath of the Bowden cable. To decrease the rotational inertia of the joints, cable pulleys mounted in joints are made of nylon which is lower density than metal and strong enough to sustain the torque transmitted via cable. Compactness and lightweight design of joints are achieved by cable-driven SEA.

2.3 Design of Shoulder Mechanism

The shoulder complex consists of two parts, namely, the shoulder girdle and the GHJ. The shoulder girdle has two DOF (elevation/depression, pro-/retraction) to ensure slight vertical and horizontal translation of the GHJ. Several mechanisms were designed to compensate for the movements of the GHJ and thus to minimize the misalignment between the robotic center and the biological center, such as NESM [4], clever arm [8], and the previous work [错误!未找到引用源。]. It is more practical, however, to focus on three rotational DOF of the GHJ [17], for the self-alignment mechanical for shoulder joint is complex and redundant which fails to achieve the desired function. In this regard, the renewed shoulder mechanism removes the mechanism for GHJ translation.

As shown in Fig. 4(a), a virtual inner/outer rotation center is constructed by the DPM, transferring the rotation of center A to the GHJ. Relying on the characterization of the parallel mechanism, the transferred virtual rotation center is fixed in the plane decided by the DPM. Considering that the GHJ equals a socket ball which converges three rotation DOF of the shoulder, each rotation axis is required to intersect at one point, namely, the GHJ. To achieve it, the rotation axis of ab- / adduction has a fixed angle α_1 with the AB extension line, and the rotation axis of extension/flexion has a fixed angle α_2 with the GF extension line. Figure 4(b) represents 3 rotation axes of the shoulder mechanism that intersect with each other at GHJ. Each joint is equipped with a corresponding encoder to feedback the rotation angle.

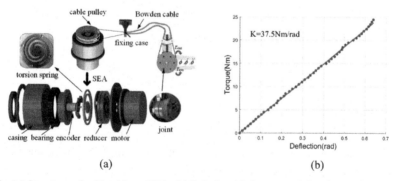

(a)   (b)

Fig. 3. (a) Structure of cable-driven SEA, (b) Relationship between deflection angle and torque

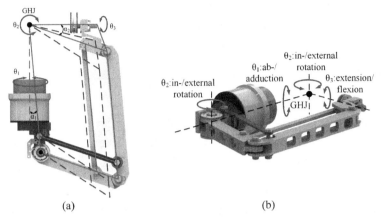

Fig. 4. (a) Presentation of the shoulder mechanism, (b) Intersection of the 3 rotation axes.

2.4 Design of Elbow and Wrist

As shown in Fig. 1, the elbow mechanism that integrates a torque sensor and an encoder is mounted on the end of the upper arm, while the wrist mechanism is positioned in the forearm. Since high wearability can improve the alignment between patients and the exoskeleton, and patients differentiate in arms' length, the adjustability of fixing wearers' arms is significant. Therefore, several methods are adopted to make the wearing more convenient and comfortable. The length of the upper arm can be adjusted by the length adaptation mechanism, and the wrist mechanism can be mounted in different positions of the forearm through its sliding slot. In addition, the installation position of the arm cuffs can be adjusted for patients accordingly.

3 Controller Design and Experiments

3.1 Controller Design

Robot-in-charge control and patient-in-charge control are two main training programs for rehabilitation [4]. In the robot-in-charge program, position control is adopted to facilitate patients in moving along the planned trajectory. The patient-in-charge program uses force control to keep the exoskeleton transparent or provide certain impedance for patients with limited movement capabilities. To evaluate the effectiveness of the system, PID controllers are designed to carry out position tracking and torque tracking experiments on the exoskeleton. The control diagrams are shown in Fig. 5.

In the position tracking mode, the input signal of the PID controller is the error value θ_{err} between the target joint angle θ_{id} and the measured joint angle θ_{ij} (i represents the serial number of the joints). The input signal of the PID controller in torque tracking mode is the error between target torque τ_{id} and SEA feedback torque τ_{ij}. In Fig. 5(b) K is the stiffness of the torsion spring and has the following relation:

$$\tau_{ij} = K \cdot \theta_{is} \tag{1}$$

where θ is the deflection angle of the torsion spring.

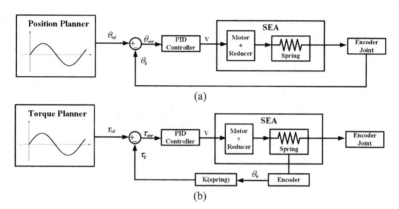

Fig. 5. (a) Position tracking control diagram, (b) Force tracking control diagram.

3.2 Experimental Characterizations

Experimental Platform

The motor (EC flat60, Maxon) has a rated torque of 0.298 Nm, a locked-rotor torque of 4.18 Nm; the harmonic reducer (XB3-2-50, HBDI, China) has a reduction ratio of 125; the encoder (LQ_ECM141803, Beijing Long Qiu Sci, China) has a maximum resolution of 0.18; the servo driver (joint servo driver, Anhui Hedong Intelligent Technology Co., Ltd., China) has 20–60VDC input voltage and supports CANopen protocol.

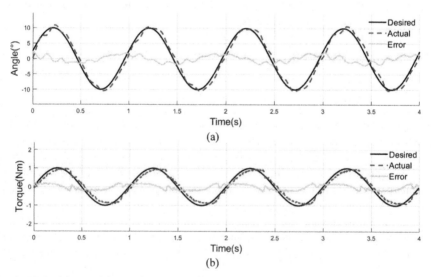

Fig. 6. (a) Position tracking performance with a frequency of 1 Hz and a desired deflection angle of 10°, (b) torque tracking performance with a frequency of 1 Hz and a desired torque of 1 Nm

Experimental Results

The sinusoidal tracking parameters are set to a frequency of 1 Hz, matching the human motion frequency which is about 0.5–1 Hz. In Fig. 6(a), when the desired angle is 10°, the max error is 2.3566°, the root mean square error (RMSE) is 1.1107°; in Fig. 6(b), when the desired torque is 1 Nm, the max error is 0.2668 Nm and the RMSE is 0.1146 Nm.

4 Conclusions

This paper details the design and features of the lightweight, compact and compliant 6 DOF upper limb exoskeleton. The low weight principle is realized by constructing the exoskeleton with low-density carbon fiber materials and 3D printing materials. The compliancy of the exoskeleton is enhanced by cable-driven SEAs, assuring reliability and appropriate human-robot interaction. The DPM is developed to implement a reasonable arrangement of 3 shoulder rotation DOF. In addition, position tracking experiments and torque tracking experiments are conducted in the elbow joint, the results of which show that the exoskeleton is capable to assist patients in rehabilitation training. However, the tracking performance also indicates that the time lag effect possibly caused by the friction in the Bowden cable is non-negligible. Future studies aim at modifying the exoskeleton's structure and developing more advanced control algorithms to improve the exoskeleton's performance and developing its effectiveness and practicability in clinical therapy.

Acknowledgements. This work was supported by the Experimental Technology Project of Wuhan University in 2020 under the research project number WHU-2020-SYJS-10.

References

1. Kim, J., et al.: Global stroke statistics 2019. Int. J. Stroke **15**(8), 819–838 (2020)
2. Brewer, B.R., McDowell, S.K., Worthen-Chaudhari, L.C.: Poststroke upper extremity rehabilitation: a review of robotic systems and clinical results. Top Stroke Rehabil. **14**(6), 22–44 (2007)
3. Asl, H.J., Yamashita, M., Narikiyo, T., Kawanishi, M.: Field-based assist-as-needed control schemes for rehabilitation robots. IEEE/ASME Trans. Mechatron. **25**(4), 2100–2111 (2020)
4. Trigili, E., et al.: Design and experimental characterization of a shoulder-elbow exoskeleton with compliant joints for post-stroke rehabilitation. IEEE/ASME Trans. Mechatron. **24**(4), 1485–1496 (2019)
5. Keller, U., van Hedel, H.J., Klamroth-Marganska, V., Riener, R.: ChARMin: The first actuated exoskeleton robot for pediatric arm rehabilitation. IEEE/ASME Trans. Mechatron. **21**(5), 2201–2213 (2016)
6. Xiao, F., Gao, Y., Wang, Y., Zhu, Y., Zhao, J.: Design and evaluation of a 7-DOF cable-driven upper limb exoskeleton. J. Mech. Sci. Technol. **32**(2), 855–864 (2018). https://doi.org/10.1007/s12206-018-0136-y
7. Keller, U., Riener, R.: Design of the pediatric arm rehabilitation robot ChARMin5th. In: IEEE RAS/EMBS International Conference on Biomedical Robotics and Biomechatronics, 2014, pp. 530–535. IEEE (2014)

8. Zeiaee, A., Soltani-Zarrin, R., Langari, R., Tafreshi, R.: Design and kinematic analysis of a novel upper limb exoskeleton for rehabilitation of stroke patients2017 International Conference on Rehabilitation Robotics (ICORR), 2017, pp, 759–764. IEEE (2017)

9. Oguntosin, V.W., Mori, Y., Kim, H., Nasuto, S.J., Kawamura, S., Hayashi, Y.: Design and validation of exoskeleton actuated by soft modules toward neurorehabilitation—vision-based control for precise reaching motion of upper limb. Front. Neurosci.-Switz. **11**, 352 (2017)

10. Cui, X., Chen, W., Jin, X., Agrawal, S.K.: Design of a 7-DOF cable-driven arm exoskeleton (CAREX-7) and a controller for dexterous motion training or assistance. IEEE/ASME Trans. Mechatron. **22**(1), 161–172 (2016)

11. Zhang, Q., Xu, B., Guo, Z., Xiao, X.: Design and modeling of a compact rotary series elastic actuator for an elbow rehabilitation robot. In: Huang, YongAn, Wu, H., Liu, H., Yin, Z. (eds.) ICIRA 2017. LNCS (LNAI), vol. 10464, pp. 44–56. Springer, Cham (2017). https://doi.org/10.1007/978-3-319-65298-6_5

12. Chen, B., Zhao, X., Ma, H., Qin, L., Liao, W.: Design and characterization of a magneto-rheological series elastic actuator for a lower extremity exoskeleton. Smart Mater. Struct. **26**(10), 105008 (2017)

13. Sun, J., Guo, Z., Zhang, Y., Xiao, X., Tan, J.: A novel design of serial variable stiffness actuator based on an archimedean spiral relocation mechanism. IEEE/ASME Trans. Mechatron. **23**(5), 2121–2131 (2018)

14. Cummings, J.P., Ruiken, D., Wilkinson, E.L., Lanighan, M.W., Grupen, R.A., Sup, F.C.: A compact, modular series elastic actuator. J. Mech. Robot. **8**(4) (2016)

15. Pan, Y., Guo, Z., Gu, D.: Bioinspired design and control of robots with intrinsic compliance. Front Neurorobotics **14** (2020)

16. Sun, J., Zhang, Y., Zhang, C., Guo, Z., Xiao, X.: Mechanical design of a compact serial variable stiffness actuator (SVSA) based on lever mechanism. In: 2017 IEEE International Conference on Robotics and Automation (ICRA), 2017, pp. 33–38. IEEE (2017)

17. Bai, S., Christensen, S., Islam, M.R.U.: An upper-body exoskeleton with a novel shoulder mechanism for assistive applications. In: 2017 IEEE International Conference on Advanced Intelligent Mechatronics (AIM), 2017, pp. 1041–1046. IEEE (2017)

18. Christensen, S., Bai, S.: Kinematic analysis and design of a novel shoulder exoskeleton using a double parallelogram linkage. J. Mech. Robot. **10**(4) (2018)

A Current-Based Surface Electromyography (sEMG) System for Human Motion Recognition: Preliminary Study

Cheng Zeng[1,2], Enhao Zheng[1(✉)], Qining Wang[3], and Hong Qiao[1]

[1] The State Key Laboratory of Management and Control for Complex Systems, Institute of Automation, Chinese Academy of Sciences, Beijing 100190, China
enhao.zheng@ia.ac.cn
[2] School of Information Engineering, China University of Geosciences (Beijing), Beijing 100083, China
[3] Department of Advanced Manufacturing and Robotics, College of Engineering, Peking University, Beijing 100871, China

Abstract. The myoelectric interface acts as an important role in the field of wearable robotics. This study explores the current-based sEMG technology for upper-limb motion recognition. Different from the voltage-based sEMG system, the current-based sampling approach can directly extract the current signals and be free from the cross talks. The technology facilitate the myoelectric sampling in a non-ideal environment such as underwater. We designed the sensing circuit with a feedback-loop current amplification module, and analyzed the stability. After development of the system, three healthy subjects participated in the experiment. Six basic wrist joint motions were investigated. With the selected feature set and the designed classification method, The average recognition accuracies across the subjects were 96.3%, 94.2%, and 95.8% respectively. The preliminary results demonstrate that the current-based sEMG technology is a promising solution to upper-limb motion recognition in a rigorous environment.

Keywords: Current-based sEMG · Stability · Human upper limb · Motion recognition

1 Introduction

Wearable robotic is a hot research branch in the field of robotics. The rapid development of the wearable robots in recent 20 years greatly benefit the people in the area of human strength augmentation [1,2], motion disorder rehabilitation [3] and missing-limb function restoration [4,5]. With the development of human demanding in practical applications, the wearable robotics are studied with more abundant forms. For instance, the researchers of study [6] proposed a soft

© Springer Nature Switzerland AG 2021
X.-J. Liu et al. (Eds.): ICIRA 2021, LNAI 13013, pp. 737–747, 2021.
https://doi.org/10.1007/978-3-030-89095-7_70

exoskeleton to provide forces in parallel with the dominant muscles, reducing the metabolic cost in long-term ambulation. The researchers of study [7] proposed an exoskeleton for underwater motion assistance. The water-proof structure can provide extra forces on the ankle joint during the breaststroke, increasing the propelling efficiency during the stroke phases. In wearable robot control, human-machine interface for human motion intent recognition/decoding/esitmation is a key part [8,9].

In state-of-the-art, most of the human-machine interfaces are designed by extracting the muscular electric activities from the skin, i.e., the sEMG signals. The sEMG-based interfaces (or myoelectric interfaces) comprises the sensing system and processing algorithms. The sensing system is the primary part as it directly connects (in cognitive connection) the human body with the robot system. The sEMG sensing system is usually designed with the electrodes and the signal processing circuit. The preferred material for the electrodes of sEMG is AgCl [10]. There are several types of electrode structures, including the unipolar, bipolar and arrays [11]. Existing EMG acquisition systems are mainly divided into three categories, including high-end data acquisition platforms for medical and prosthetics applications, embedded data acquisition platforms for research purposes, and low cost wearable device for interactive applications [12]. For the recognition tasks, the sEMG-based interfaces address the issues of discrete human motion recognition and continuous motion estimation/decoding [13]. In human discrete motion recognition, the main procedure is signal sampling → data segmentation → feature calculation → motion classification/recognition. The tasks include gesture recognition and locomotion mode/transition recognition. The crucial metric to evaluate the performance is recognition accuracy. In state-of-the-art, the average recognition accuracies ranged from 90% to 98% in tasks of upper-limb motion recognition [14] and ≥90% in lower-limb tasks [15]. The other types of tasks is human motion estimation/decoding, which often involves continuous motion parameters such as joint angles, joint torques and motion phases (gait phases). The processing methods are focused on the data regression and biologically-inspired models. The performances are usually quantified with coefficients of determination (R^2) and root-mean-square errors (RMSEs). The current studies produced an average R^2 values ranging from 0.79 to 0.88 [16,17], in the tasks of Joint angle and position prediction, Acceleration prediction and velocity prediction.

Although the sEMG-based interfaces produced extremely high accuracies in laboratory environment, it is still challenging to meet the requirement of reliable, accurate and timely decoding/estimation/recognition in practical applications. Most current sEMG systems sampled voltages from the skin by recording the potential difference between the electrodes. With the voltage-based sensing method, the impedance on the skin will brings about extra currents between the electrodes due to the potential differences, leading to signal cross-talk between different channels [18]. The issue of cross-talk negatively impacts on the EMG signal quality and further decrease the recognition performances if the skin is covered with sweats and water. High expense of water-proof preparation has to be made before the sEMG measurement underwater. One way to alleviate the problem is to convert the EMG sampling from voltages to currents. In the study [18], the authors designed the current-based sEMG technology, and they verified the performance of the technology by conducting comparative experiment with the voltage-based sEMG technology. On the other side, only the ability of the current-based sEMG technology to suppress cross-talk was evaluated and the application of this technology to motion intention recognition have yet to be addressed.

In our study, we proposed a current-based sEMG system for human-machine interfaces. In our preliminary study, we designed the circuit, analyzed the stability for parameter setting, and compared the signal with the commercial system. We also carried out experiment with the sensing position immersed in the water. The discrete forearm motion recognition method with the current-based EMG was designed and performances were preliminarily evaluated.

2 Current-Based EMG System

2.1 System Design

The EMG originated from the human central nervous system. The generated electrical impulses (motor potential units) by the motor neurons are transmitted along the axons (via the spinal cord) down to the neural-muscle junctions on the muscle fibers. With a series of activation and muscle fiber cells' motions, the muscle belly contracts and generates forces. The spatial and temporal superposition of the motor potential units of the muscle fibers form the EMG signals[19]. The electric signals (part) are transmitted to the surface of the skin and can be measured. According to the principle of circuits, the sEMG generation can be modeled as a voltage source or a current source. Z denotes the impedance caused by the skin and other soft tissues. In our study, we treated the EMG signal as a current source with an internal impedance Z.

The system was composed of the electrodes and the sensing circuit. The electrodes were made up of with AgCl. As shown in Fig. 1, the sensing circuit (of each EMG channel) was designed with a current amplification module, a band-pass filter module (it consists of a first-order low-pass and a first-order high-pass filter circuit), a secondary amplifier module and an adder module. The current amplification module was designed to amplify and convert the current EMG signals to the voltage signals. It was a trans-impedance (current-to-voltage converting) circuit. Due to the large gain, we designed a negative feedback module in the circuit to remove the baseline drift. The feedback module consists of a second-stage low-band-pass filter, a voltage follower and a feedback resistor. The feedback resistor was used to adjust the feedback gain. The band-pass filter module was designed to intercept signals that fit the theoretical frequency range (10–500 Hz). The secondary amplifier module is an in-phase proportional amplifier circuit for amplifying the voltage further. The adder module was designed to convert the signals to positive values by adding a suitable positive voltage. The voltages were sampled by an analog-to-digital converter (ADC) with a resolution of 12 bit and a sampling frequency of 1 kHz. The ADC was embedded in a micro-control-unit (STM32). The sampled data were packaged in the MCU and transmitted to the computer in each 1 ms. We designed a graphic user interface (GUI) based on MATLAB R2016b on the computer to store and process the data.

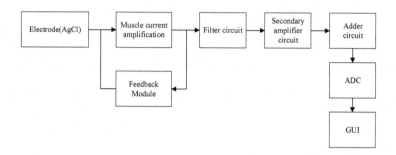

Fig. 1. The system block diagram.

2.2   Stability Analysis

The EMG signals are weak and full of noises. We designed the closed-loop current feedback to remove the baseline drifting and amplify the tiny current signals. The feedback gain of the circuit should be carefully tuned to guarantee the stability. In our designed system the feedback gain was determined by the feedback resistor in the feedback module. We constructed the dynamic models of the current amplification module and the feedback module, and the control block chart with laplace transformation was shown in Fig. 2(b). In the control block, $I(s)$ was the input current, and $U(s)$ was the output voltage. $G(s)$ was the transfer function, modeled from the current-to-voltage circuit, $H_1(s)$ and $H_3(s)$ were the transfer functions low-band-pass filters of the two stages, and H_2 was the transfer function of a voltage division circuit, $H_4(s)$ was the transfer function of the feedback resistor. According to the control theory, the stability of the closed-loop system can be represented indirectly by calculating the open-loop transfer function $G_o(s)$ of the closed-loop system, which is the product of all the transfer functions in the ring. The calculation formula of $G_o(s)$ was expressed as:

$$G_o(s) = G(s)H(s), \tag{1}$$

$$H(s) = H_1(s)H_2(s)H_3(s)H_4(s). \tag{2}$$

We placed the corresponding parameters in the transfer functions and we obtained the open-loop transfer function as:

$$G_o(s) = \frac{2200000000}{0.33R_x s^2 + (47R_x + 330000)s + 1400R_x + 14000000} \tag{3}$$

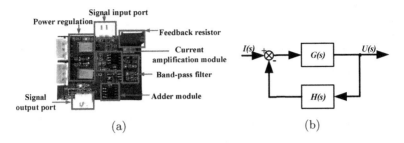

Fig. 2. (a) The picture of the sensing circuit. (b) Transfer function model of closed-loop circuits.

where R_x is the value of feedback resistance. So the characteristic equation of the closed-loop system is:

$$1 + G_o(s) = 0 \tag{4}$$

Substitute Eq. 3 into Eq. 4:

$$0.33R_x s^2 + (47R_x + 330000)s + 1400R_x + 2214000000 = 0 \tag{5}$$

The stability of the closed-loop system can be judged by calculating the roots of the characteristic equation. It can be derived that the locus of the 2 poles of the close-loop transfer function for different values we choosed of R_x are located in the left half of the S plane, which means that the closed-loop system has no poles located in the right half of the S plane, so the system is stable. In this paper, the value of R_x is 0.5 $M\Omega$, where the close-loop transfer function can maintain stability and has poles with a small imaginary part that does not cause violent oscillations.

3   Methods

3.1   Signal Quality Analysis

The quality of EMG signals is easily affected by the interference factors of the external environment. After receiving the EMG data, the analysis of the signal quality is essential. We compared the EMG signals of the proposed system with that of a commercial EMG acquisition system (Delsys, Trigno, Wireless Biofeedback System). One male subject participated in the test. Written and informed consent were provided by the subject before the experiment. During the measurement, the subject firstly wore the current-based EMG sensing system (AgCl unipolar electrodes) on his right forearm. We measured four muscles (The Palmaris Longus (PL), The Extensor Carpi Ulnaris (ECU), The Extensor Digitorum (ED) and The Brachioradialis). The sensing spots were at the middle of the muscles and the positions were determined based on palpation. A reference electrode (signal ground) was fixed on the position of radius. We measured two trials for the subject with the current-based EMG system, one was on the ground and the other was in the water. In each trial, the subject kept his hand clenched with his maximum voluntary muscle contraction for 20 s. The data were recorded by the system and stored. The measurement procedure with the Delsys system was the same as that of the current-based EMG system. The sampling frequency of the Delsys system was set 2148 Hz. We only measured one trial on the ground as the system cannot work underwater. We calculated the power spectrum (0–500 Hz) of the EMG signals.

3.2   Underwater Forearm Motion Recognition

Experimental Protocol. Three male subjects were employed in the underwater motion recognition experiment. They had an average age of 24, an average weight of 65 kg, and an average heigh of 170 cm. They all proved written informed consent before the measurement. As mentioned above, we used an unipolar AgCl-made electrode for each channel. For each subject, we measured four forearm muscles from the right forearm (according to the subjects' handness), i.e., PL, ECU, ED and The Brachioradialis. The sensing positions were determined by the palpation, which located at the middle (muscle belly) of the measured muscle. A reference electrode (signal ground) was fixed on the position of radius. During the experiment, each subject placed the measured forearm in the basin with all the electrodes immersed inside the water. We measured 6 forearm motion patterns for each subject, including relax (R), wrist flexion/extension (WF/WE), ulna deviation (UD), radius deviation (RD), and fist. Each motion pattern was measured for 10 trials. During the experiment, subjects put his arms in the water and get ready. In each trial, the subject started from the neutral position (palm vertical to the ground) to motion pattern at his maximum extent. The EMG data were simultaneously recorded by the experimenter. After keeping the posture for 20 s, the subject moved back to the neutral position and relaxed for 5 s. The motion patterns were alternatively measured. The experiment was separated in 10 groups, and in each group, all the motion patterns were measured for one trial (Fig. 3).

Data Segmentation. We firstly preprocessed the raw EMG data with a band-stop filter to remove the 50-Hz noises. The parameters of the band-stop filter were set as 49 51 Hz. We used sliding windows to segment the EMG data. The sliding window length was 350 ms, which was 350 samples. The step length of the window was 50 ms. We measured four channels of EMG signals. Therefore, each siding window was a matrix with 4×350 elements.

Feature Calculation. On each sliding window, we calculated time-domain features to extract the motion information from the current-based EMG signals. The features were Mean Absolute Value (MAV), Root Mean Square (RMS), Zero Crossings (ZC), and Variance (VAR). The features were expressed as:

$$MAV = \frac{1}{N} \sum_{i=1}^{N} |x_i| \tag{6}$$

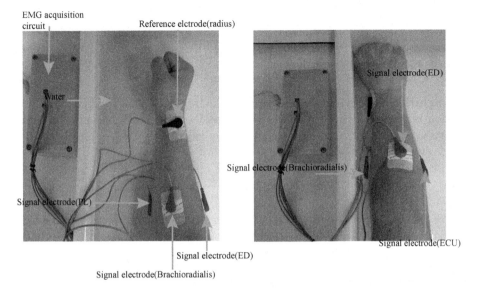

Fig. 3. The placement of the electrodes on the forearm during the experiment.

$$RMS = \sqrt{\frac{1}{N}\sum_{i=1}^{N}|x_i^2|} \tag{7}$$

$$ZC = \sum_{i=1}^{N-1} sgn[(x_i > 0 \land x_{i+1} < 0) \lor (x_i < 0 \land x_{i+1} > 0) \land |x_i - x_{i+1}| \geq \varepsilon] \tag{8}$$

$$VAR = \sqrt{\frac{1}{N}\sum_{i=1}^{N}(x_i - x)^2} \tag{9}$$

where N was the total number of data in each sliding window, x_i was concrete voltage data, x was the mean of data in each sliding window, and ε was a threshold. sgn was the function with output of 0 and 1, where $sgn[true] = 1$. We measured four EMG channels. Therefore for each sliding window, the feature vector was a 1×16 vector.

Classifier. After EMG data preprocessing and feature extraction were completed, the next step was to recognize different motions. In our study, we used quadratic discriminant analysis (QDA) to classify the forearm motion patterns.

3.3   Evaluation Method

Cross-Validation. In our study, we used 1 vs. 1 cross-validation (CV) to evaluate the recognition results. The data of one subject were divided into two groups based on the trials (5 vs. 5). The first 5-trial data were used for training and the other data for testing. The procedure repeated again with the latter 5-trial data for training and the former data for testing. The two recognition results were averaged as the final result of the subject.

Recognition Accuracy and Confusion Matrix. A specific label for each motion is specified when using the QDA classifier. In the classification results, the recognition accuracy can be obtained by calculating the proportion of the labels successfully identified in the group.

$$Accuracy = \frac{N_{success}}{N_{total}} \times 100\% \tag{10}$$

where $N_{success}$ is the number of labels successfully classified for each motion in their groups, N_{total} is the total number of labels for each motion. Confusion matrix is a $n \times n$ matrix (n motions in this paper). Elements on the diagonal of the matrix represent the recognition accuracy of each motion and other elements in the same row represent classification error rate.

4   Results

4.1   Signal Quality Analysis

As shown in Fig. 4, the EMG signal spectrum under the three conditions are distributed in the range of 0–500 Hz and the main power are concentrated in the part 150 Hz. It can be determined from the comparison of the EMG signals spectra of the Delsys sEMG acquisition system and the current-based sEMG acquisition system on the land that the signal of the current-based sEMG acquisition system is the EMG signal that fits the theory. In addition, there is no significant difference in the spectrum between the land and underwater environments. The current-based sEMG acquisition system has strong stability in the harsh environment.

4.2   Recognition Results

Table 1 consists of the confusion matrixs of three subjects. The average recognition accuracy for all the six motion patterns of three subjects were 96.3%, 94.2%, and 95.8% respectively. For all the motion patterns of subject 1 except RD, the approach could achieve ≥94% recognition accuracy. The lowest accuracy was 91.8% for RD and 6.4%, 1.8% of them were misclassified as fist, UD respectively. For all the motion patterns of subject 2, the approach could achieve ≥90% recognition accuracy. The lowest accuracy was 90.3% for WE and 0.4%, 2.6%, and 6.7% of them were misclassified as fist, UD, RD respectively. For all the motion patterns of subject 3 except fist, the approach could achieve ≥93% recognition accuracy. The lowest accuracy was 90.3% for fist and 6.0% and 1.8% of them were misclassified as WF, RD respectively.

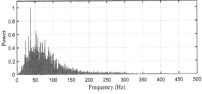

(a) Results of Delsys

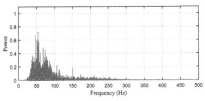

(b) Results of current-based EMG on the land

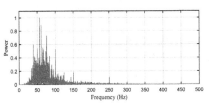

(c) Results of current-based EMG in the water

Fig. 4. Spectrum of EMG signals under three different measurement methods. (a) Spectrum of EMG signals from Delsys sEMG acquisition system; (b) Spectrum of EMG signals from the current-based sEMG acquisition system on the land; (c) Spectrum of EMG signals from the current-based sEMG acquisition system underwater.

Table 1. Confusion matrix (mean) of 3 subjects for 6 motion patterns with QDA classifier (%)

Targets	subject1						subject2						subject3					
	R	fist	WF	WE	UD	RD	R	fist	WF	WE	UD	RD	R	fist	WF	WE	UD	RD
R	100.0	0.0	0.0	0.0	0.0	0.0	100.0	0.0	0.0	0.0	0.0	0.0	100.0	0.0	0.0	0.0	0.0	0.0
fist	0.0	94.1	0.9	0.0	1.0	4.0	0.0	93.0	0.0	0.0	4.2	2.8	0.0	92.2	6.0	0.0	0.0	1.8
WF	0.0	0.0	96.4	0.0	3.6	0.0	0.0	0.8	91.1	0.0	8.1	0.0	0.0	4.8	94.1	0.0	0.2	0.9
WE	0.0	0.0	0.0	99.1	0.0	0.9	0.0	0.4	0.0	90.3	2.6	6.7	0.0	1.4	0.0	93.8	1.2	3.6
UD	0.0	0.0	2.4	0.0	96.3	1.3	0.0	0.6	7.5	0.0	91.1	0.8	0.0	0.8	0.3	0.0	98.4	0.5
RD	0.0	6.4	0.0	0.0	1.8	91.8	0.0	0.0	0.0	0.0	0.4	99.6	0.0	1.5	0.0	2.1	0.4	96.0

5 Concluding Remarks

In this study, we addressed the problems of current-based sEMG technology on upper-limb motion recognition in the water. The designed sEMG acquisition system could effectively record the forearm muscle contractions in different motion patterns. With the selected feature set and a simple classifier, the system produced accurate results in motion recognition for six forearm motions. Compared with other studies based on sEMG for upper limb discrete motion recognition in controlled laboratory environments [14], the current-based sEMG system in the water have similar results and its performance did not degrade significantly.

The study involved with 3 able-bodied subjects and several simple forearm motion patterns. There are three main limitations in this study. Firstly, variations on arm shape and muscle contraction patterns exist among different individuals. The repeatability of the current-based sEMG system and the recognition have yet to be evaluated. Secondly, only 6 basic wrist joint motion patterns were investigated in the experiment. More motion combinations have not been studied. Thirdly, the recognition of continuous motion patterns was not analyzed.

Nevertheless, the current-based sEMG technology is a promising issue which worth being exploited. Future works will be carried out on the following aspects. Firstly, the existing circuit system is susceptible to external electromagnetic interference, so the circuit system needs further improvement. Secondly, we will design a wearable front-end with good performance for acquiring sEMG. Thirdly, the experiments on more complicated motions such as swimming experiment will be carried out.

Above all, the preliminary study broaden the application environment of sEMG. The experiment results proved the feasibility of the current-based sEMG technology in the harsh environment. Future endeavors will be made on more extensive experiments and more complex motion tasks.

Acknowledgments. This work was supported by the National Natural Science Foundation of China (No. 62073318).

References

1. Kazerooni, H., Racine, J.L., Huang, L., Steger, R.: On the Control of the Berkeley Lower Extremity Exoskeleton (BLEEX). IEEE Int. Conf. Robot. Autom. **14**(3), 4353–4360 (2006). https://doi.org/10.1109/ROBOT.2005.1570790
2. Kawamoto, H., Sankai, Y.: Power assist method based on Phase Sequence and muscle force condition for HAL. Adv. Robot. **19**(7), 717–734 (2005). https://doi.org/10.1163/1568553054455103
3. Talaty, M., Esquenazi, A., Jorge E. Briceño.: Differentiating ability in users of the ReWalk(TM) powered exoskeleton: an analysis of walking kinematics. IEEE Int. Conf. Rehabil. Robot., 1–5 (2013). https://doi.org/10.1109/ICORR.2013.6650469
4. Gao, S., Mai, J., Zhu, J., Wang, Q.: Mechanism and controller design of a transfemoral prosthesis with electrohydraulic knee and motor-driven ankle. IEEE ASME Trans. Mechatron., (on-line) (2020). https://doi.org/10.1109/TMECH.2020.3040369
5. Rogers, E.A., Carney, M.E., Yeon, S.H., Clites, T.R., Herr, H.M.: An ankle-foot prosthesis for rock climbing augmentation. IEEE Trans. Neural Syst. Rehabil. Eng. **29**, 41–51 (2021). https://doi.org/10.1109/TNSRE.2020.3033474

6. Wehner, M., et al.: A lightweight soft exosuit for gait assistance. In: IEEE International Conference on Robotics and Automation, pp. 3347–3354 (2013). https://doi.org/10.1109/ICRA.2013.6631046

7. Wang, Q., Zhou, Z., Zhang, Z., Lou, Y., Mai, J.: An underwater lower-extremity soft exoskeleton for breaststroke assistance. IEEE Trans. Med. Robot. Bionics **2**(3), 447–462 (2020). https://doi.org/10.1109/TMRB.2020.2993360

8. Wu, Y., Jiang, D., Liu, X., Bayford, R., Demosthenous, A.: A human-machine interface using electrical impedance tomography for hand prosthesis control. IEEE Trans. Biomed. Circuits Syst. **12**(6), 1322–1333 (2018). https://doi.org/10.1109/TBCAS.2018.2878395

9. Delpreto, J., Rus, D.: Sharing the load: human-robot team lifting using muscle activity. In: IEEE International Conference on Robotics and Automation, pp. 7906–7912 (2019). https://doi.org/10.1109/ICRA.2019.8794414

10. Merletti, R., Botter, A., Troiano, A., Merlo, E., Minetto, M.A.: Technology and instrumentation for detection and conditioning of the surface electromyographic signal: state of the art. Clin. Biomech. **24**(2), 122–134 (2009). https://doi.org/10.1016/j.clinbiomech.2008.08.006

11. Hermens, H.J., Freriks, B., Disselhorst-Klug, C., Rau, G.: Development of recommendations for SEMG sensors and sensor placement procedures. J. Electromyogr. Kinesiol. **10**(5), 361–374 (2000). https://doi.org/10.1016/S1050-6411(00)00027-4

12. B Rodríguez-Tapia, Soto, I., DM Martínez, Arballo, N. C.: Myoelectric interfaces and related applications: current state of EMG signal processing-A systematic review. IEEE Access, 7792–7805 (2020). https://doi.org/10.1109/ACCESS.2019.2963881

13. Bi, L., Feleke, A.G., Guan, C.: A review on EMG-based motor intention prediction of continuous human upper limb motion for human-robot collaboration. Biomed. Signal Process. Control **51**(5), 113–127 (2019). https://doi.org/10.1016/j.bspc.2019.02.011

14. Rechy-Ramirez, E.J., Hu, H.: Bio-signal based control in assistive robots: a survey. Digit. Commun. Netw. **1**(2), 85–101 (2015). https://doi.org/10.1016/j.dcan.2015.02.004

15. Huang, H., Zhang, F., Hargrove, L.J., Dou, Z., Rogers, D.R., Englehart, K.B.: Continuous locomotion-mode identification for prosthetic legs based on neuromuscular-mechanical fusion. IEEE Trans. Biomed. Eng. **58**(10), 2867–2875 (2011). https://doi.org/10.1109/TBME.2011.2161671

16. Tang, Z., Zhang, K., Sun, S., Gao, Z., Zhang, L., Yang, Z.: An upper-limb power-assist exoskeleton using proportional myoelectric control. Sensors **14**(4), 6677–6694 (2014). https://doi.org/10.3390/s140406677

17. Zhang, Q., Liu, R., Chen, W., Xiong, C.: Simultaneous and continuous estimation of shoulder and elbow kinematics from surface EMG signals. Front. Neurosci. **11**, 280–291 (2017). https://doi.org/10.3389/fnins.2017.00280

18. Tscharner, V.V., Maurer, C., Ruf, F., Nigg, B.M.: Comparison of electromyographic signals from monopolar current and potential amplifiers derived from a penniform muscle, the gastrocnemius medialis. J. Electromyogr. Kinesiol. **23**(5), 1044–1051 (2013). https://doi.org/10.1016/j.jelekin.2013.07.011

19. Vigotsky, A. D., Halperin, I., Lehman, G. J., Trajano, G. S., Vieira, T.: Interpreting signal amplitudes in surface electromyography studies in sport and rehabilitation sciences. Front. Physiol. **8** (2018). https://doi.org/10.3389/fphys.2017.00985

A Novel Modular and Wearable Supernumerary Robotic Finger via EEG-EMG Control with 4-week Training Assessment

Yuan Liu[✉], Shuaifei Huang, Zhuang Wang, Fengrui Ji, and Dong Ming

Tianjin University, Tianjin 300072, China
ryanliu@tju.edu.cn

Abstract. The Supernumerary Robotic Limbs (SRL) is an emerging kind of wearable robot to help reconstruct and enhance human movement functionality by adding extra limbs, such as arms, legs, or fingers. For the control, EEG can transmit human intentions to control external devices independently, hence it has the particular advantages to control the SRL naturally especially when human limbs are occupied. However, the classification accuracy of EEG is very limited. In this paper, we proposed a novel EEG-EMG strategy to improve the classification accuracy. In addition, a novel supernumerary robotic finger (SRF) system is built with a modular design consideration. The whole system contained seven modules: EEG acquisition, EEG control, EMG acquisition, SRF control, SRF finger, TENS feedback and status information Module. To the best of our knowledge, this is the first wearable brain control SRL system. Meanwhile, as the SRF is a soft finger, the system is compliance, affordable, wearability, modularity, and lightweight, named CAWML-SRF. The finger weight is less than 195 g, and the whole system weight is less than 1 kg. The experiments show that the CAWML-SRF can enhance the grasp functionality for helping the single hand to accomplish the bimanual grasp task (such as opening the bottle and grasping the larger objects), and assist the remaining functionality to accomplish the grasp task. A 4-week EEG triggering training experiment is conducted to further evaluate the rehabilitation application potentials: the high control accuracy rate (94.53% ± 0.044) and fine learning performance of human brain to the system are verified.

Keywords: Wearable robot · Supernumerary Robotic Finger (SRF) · Brain-Computer Interface · EEG-EMG control

1 Introduction

Human hand is an important medium for humans to interact with the outside world [1–4]. However, hand motor function impairment which caused by natural disasters, accidents, diseases, etc., greatly influence the patient activities of daily life (ADL). Prosthetic hand [5] and hand exoskeleton [6] are two kinds of common equipment for rehabilitation and enhancement of hand motor function. However, the prosthetic hand is only suitable for amputees, hence the scope of suitable users is limited. For the exoskeleton, it is necessary

© Springer Nature Switzerland AG 2021
X.-J. Liu et al. (Eds.): ICIRA 2021, LNAI 13013, pp. 748–758, 2021.
https://doi.org/10.1007/978-3-030-89095-7_71

to be attached to the human body to provide the power assistance. The use safety should be fully considered [7].

Different from the prosthesis and exoskeleton, supernumerary robotic limbs (SRL) are an emerging kind of wearable robot to help reconstruct and enhance human movement functionality by adding extra limbs, such as arms, legs, or fingers. Supernumerary robotic finger (SRF) is used to enhance hand grasp functionality and has attracted roboticists particular attentions in recent years. For the mechanical implementation, current SRF can be mainly divided into rigidity and flexibility structure. For the rigid SRF, the controllability is relatively better as the motors are used to actuate the rigid finger knuckle by link or tendon-pulley mechanism [7–11]. However, the weights of most systems are too heavy. Wu et al. [8] designed a SRF with two fingers. Two servos are employed and the tendon-pulley mechanism is applied to actuate the finger link. Each finger has one independent DOF actuated by one servo. The extension is accomplished by embedding the torsional springs into the finger joint. Some bimanual collaboration tasks are performed by wearing SRF with one hand, such as fixing a bottle with one hand while opening the bottle cap, fixing a bowl with one hand while mixing salad, etc. Domenico et al. [7] designed a SRF employing 4 servomotor to directly provide the rotation torque to each finger link. One servomotor is used to accomplish the finger abduction/adduction motion and the other three are used to realize the flexion/extension motion of three joints.

The soft manufacturing method provides a novel solution to build the robotic system with the lightweight, compliance, safety and affordable advantages [12–14]. A soft SRF [12, 13, 15, 16] was designed and single actuator is employed in order to decrease the finger weight. A soft 3D printed thermoplastic polyurethane part acts as the flexible joint and 3D printed ABS (Acrylonitrile Butadiene Styrene) is selected as the stiff finger phalange. The polyurethane material has the high elongation feature allowing for repeated movement and impact without wear or cracking. The flexible wire acting like a loaded spring, brings the SRF back when extension is commanded. The soft SRF was used to assist the patient of hand motor function impairment to grasp the daily object by cooperating with the patient inherent finger or wrist, such as grasp a cylinder and pick up a glass.

For the control, SRF as an extra finger independent to human inherent body, is difficult for users to control naturally without any disturbs of human inherent limb movement. Therefore, different from the prosthesis and exoskeleton control by using the corresponding limb muscle, the control intensions should be imparted independently. EEG has the great advantages to transmit human intentions to control external devices independently, which has been verified in a third arm control research [17]. The third arm is independently controlled when human two hands are occupied. However, to the best of our knowledge, few studies focus on the brain control of SRF. Previous studies mainly investigated the postural synergy control [8, 17, 18], [19] and EMG control [9, 15]. The posture synergy control method is simple and reliable, but can't control SRF independently. For controlling the SRF, human inherent limb must move for mapping the move ratio characteristic to SRF joint. The EMG signal from the human limb is also correlated with the limb motion, hence the independent control is also difficult to be accomplished. Hussain [12] utilized the EMG of frontalis muscle on their forehead to control the SRF. The independent control is partly accomplished by moving the eyebrows upwards, but the control is not natural and the great advantages of EEG-based motor imagery to neural rehabilitation is not involved. Besides, if using the EEG to control SRF, a big problem should be solved that the classification accuracy of EEG is very limited.

In this paper, we proposed a novel EEG-EMG strategy to accomplish the SRF independent control and improve the task success completion rate. On this basis, a novel supernumerary robotic finger (SRF) system is built with a modular design consideration. The whole system contained seven modules: EEG acquisition, EEG control, EMG acquisition, SRF control, SRF finger, TENS feedback and status information Module. To the best of our knowledge, this is the first wearable brain control SRL system. Meanwhile, as the SRF is a soft finger, the system is compliance, affordable, wearability, modularity, and lightweight, named CAWML-SRF. The finger weight is less than 195 g, and the whole system weight is less than 1 kg. The experiments show that the CAWML-SRF can enhance the grasp functionality for helping the single hand to accomplish the bimanual grasp task (such as opening the bottle and grasping the larger objects), and assist the remaining functionality to accomplish the grasp task.

This paper is organized as follows. The structure and control system design of the SRF are presented in Sect. 2. Section 3 presents an experimental evaluation and its results. A conclusion is given in Sect. 4, respectively.

2 SRF System Design

2.1 SRF Biomechtronic Framework

The biomechtronic framework of the SRF includes the acquisition and processing of EEG-EMG signal, the transmission of the control commands, the realization of the overall hardware architecture, etc. The hardware architecture consists of EEG control module which based the RaspberryPi chip (BroadcomBCM2711, China) and other modules like EEG acquisition, EMG acquisition, SRF control, TENS feedback and status information Module which based the STM32 chip (STM32F070F6P6, China), as shown in Fig. 1.

The communication between each module using bluetooth and the serial communication was used between the SRF control and the SRF finger module. The system embedded in the SRF was designed to be powered by a customized lithium battery (2,500 mAh, rated voltage of 8.4 V, peak current of 5 A).

2.2 Mechanical Design

The mechanical design of the SRF mainly use tendon-pulley mechanism. Previous studies have shown that when the SRF was used as a separate finger for grasping assistance, it only needs to bend to complete the movement while satisfying the grasping force and speed [7]. A previous study on the fingers found that the fingertip force of the thumb and index finger is in the range of 11–25 N, and the joint angular velocity should be at least

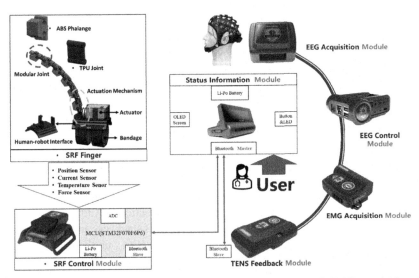

Fig. 1. The Embedded System include EEG acquisition, EEG control, EMG acquisition, SRF control, SRF finger, TENS feedback and status information Module. Bluetooth communication was used in the whole system and the serial communication was used between the SRF control and the SRF finger module.

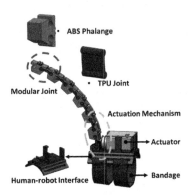

Fig. 2. 3D printed SRF having flexible thermoplastic polyurethane (TPU) as flexible joints and stiff ABS material acting as phalange. The actuator is a servomotor.

4 rad/s [18]. Taking into account the fingertip force and speed, as well as the characteristics of lightweight and adaptability, we design the SRF finger has one independent DOF actuated by one actuator.

The SRF finger is driven by a single actuator and has one DOF. The overall structure consists of ABS phalange, TPU joint, Human-robot interface, actuator, bandage, as shown in Fig. 2. Each phalange is polymerized by 3D printing ABS (Acrylonitrile Butadiene Styrene, Rainbow CeGo, China) to form a rigid part and a 3D printed thermoplastic polyurethane (TPU, Rainbow CeGo, China) part that realizes the flexible joint. By sliding the TPU joints in the phalange parts, the two parts are alternately connected to form a flexible finger. The finger length is changed by adjusting the number of ABS phalange and TPU joint modules to adapt to people with different hand lengths. The Human-robot interface is polymerized by 3D printing ABS (Acrylonitrile Butadiene Styrene, Rainbow CeGo, China) to form a rigid part that supports the flexible fingers and embeds the actuator. The radian design with ergonomics consideration is adopted to facilitate the perfect fit with the hand; and the bandage channel is reserved to be wearable on the forearm. The structure of the human-robot interface is symmetrical which allows the robot fingers to be worn on both the left or right hand without any modification in the device.

The actuator is a servomotor (HP8-U45, Fashion Star, China) which can provide 45 kg-cm torque. The hole under the rigid phalange allows the cable (polyethylene dyneema fiber, China) to pass through in sequence. The tendon wire is attached on one side to the fingertip and on the other to the pulley of the actuator. Adding elastic passive elements behind the phalange can avoid the flexible joints slackness and provide the pre-tightness force to ensure the passive extension. Specifications on the actuator features and the size of the SRF are reported in Table 1.

Table 1. Specifications of the SRF.

The SRF module	Dimensions	Weight
ABS Phalange	$20 \times 28 \times 15$ mm^3	5.1 g
TPU Joint	$20 \times 24 \times 6$ mm^3	4 g
Human-robot Interface	$60 \times 80 \times 50$ mm^3	43.6 g
Actuator	$40 \times 20 \times 40$ mm^3	62 g
Total finger	$220 \times 80 \times 50$ mm^3	194.5 g
Actuator	Technical target	Parameter
	Nominal Voltage	7.4 V
	Runaway Velocity	0.098 s/60°
	Locked-rotor Torque	45 kg-cm
	Processor	32-bit MCU

2.3 Control System

The status information module is the core component and the master part of the whole system, as shown in Fig. 1. The finite state machine is embedded in status information module as the top-layer control algorithm. The status information module is responsible for receiving information from the EEG control module and the EMG acquisition module, combining EEG-EMG signals to discriminate movement intention by finite state machine, communicating with SRF control module, sending signals to TENS feedback module according to the SRF finger feedback status. A LED screen as a human-machine interaction interface, is embedded for users to switch machine, build the connection network with slave modules, and accomplish the slave system self-check. The main tasks of EEG acquisition module are to acquire 8 channels of the EEG signals, and communicate with the EEG control module that is used to decode the EEG signals. The function of the EMG acquisition module is to acquire single-channel EMG signals and communicate with status information module.

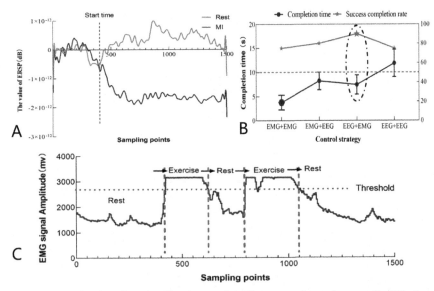

Fig. 3. (A) Signal processing classification results. The comparison of power (in dB) changes with time (in sampling points) during MI tasks and resting state (REST) for electrode C3, in the Mu band (8–13 Hz). The red dotted line represents the start time of the task. (B) EEG/EMG trigger or release time and success completion rate. The abscissa represents the combination of trigger and release signal methods, for example EMG+EEG represent using the EMG as the trigger signal and the EEG as the release signal. The blue line measures the time of different control mode (EMG+EMG, EMG+EEG, EEG+EMG, EEG+EEG). The red line measures the success completion rate of different control mode. (C) EMG classification results: the transition from the resting state to the exercise state can be clearly observed. The red dotted line represents the start time of the task. (Color figure online)

EEG Pattern Recognition Classifier. The EEG acquisition module uses the module OPENBCI to collect the 8 channels EEG signals of FC1, FC2, FCZ, etc., with a sampling frequency of 250 Hz. Then the EEG signal is resampled, filtered (8–13 Hz bandpass, 50 Hz notch), re-referenced, ICA, and time-frequency features extracted. Finally, the preprocessed EEG signal is imported into the Convolutional Neural Network (CNN) to obtain the training model. The CNN was formed by two convolutional layers: a pooling layer and two completely connected layers. A novel "sixth-finger" motor imaginary (MI) paradigm is performed to provide the SRF natural control. The detailed mechanism analysis is investigated in another paper of our team. Based on the developed "sixth-finger" MI decoding algorithm, the difference between the MI and resting (Rest) state of EEG signal can be classified, and the training model of MI state is used for online classification. Finally, the difference between MI and Rest state can be clearly seen and classified based on the Event-related spectralperturbation (ERSP) of C3 EEG channel.

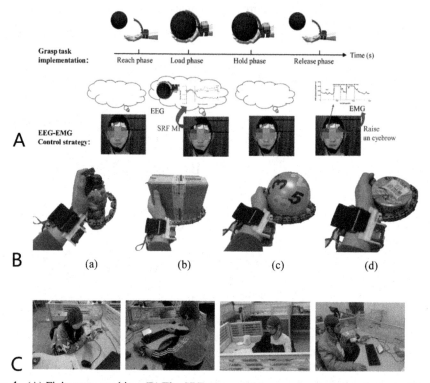

Fig. 4. (A) Finite state machine. (B) The SRF grasps: (a) grasp enhancement to fix the bottle and open it with one hand, (b) grasp enhancement to fix the large box, (c) grasp assistance to fix the large ball, (d) grasp assistance to fix the cylinder. (C) Scene of subjects wearing SRF training.

EMG Pattern Recognition Classifier. Three electrodes (one for reference and the other two for acquiring EMG signal) were used to collect frontal muscle myoelectric signals. The analog EMG signals were sampled by an STM32 chip of EMG acquisition module with a 200 Hz sampling frequency. The EMG signals were then smoothly filtered and normalized, and an appropriate threshold is selected by the pre-experiment through muscle extension and contraction. After comparing the EMG signal value with threshold value, the decoding result is imparted. As shown in Fig. 3 C after the EMG signal pre-processing, the obvious transition of the EMG signal amplitude from the resting state to the exercise state can be clearly observed.

The Control Strategy. A novel EEG-EMG control strategy is proposed. The EEG is used to provide an independent and natural control of SRF, and the great advantages of EEG MI for neural rehabilitation is involved. The EMG is used to improve the task success completion rate. In order to realize the higher success completion rate and shorter decoding time, an evaluation experiment was performed. In experiments, we com-pared the combination of using EEG and EMG as trigger(T) and release(R) sig-nals: T(EMG) + R(EMG), T(EMG) + R(EEG), T(EEG) + R(EMG), T(EEG) + R(EEG), as shown in Fig. 3B. In Fig. 3B, the trigger time means the time from planned movement to the actual movement, and the release time means the time from planned release movement to the actual release movement. At the same time, we also counted the success completion rate of 20 consecutive trigger and release movement. In experiments, the trigger and release movement completed within 10 s is considered as a success completion trial, and the trial completed in more than 10 s or wrongly trigger or release is considered a failure. As shown in the ellipse of Fig. 3C, using EEG as trigger signal and EMG as release signal, which has not only the relative shorter completion time (7.46 $\pm$ 1.97s), but also the highest success completion rate (90%). It was also found that EEG + EEG mode has the longest time (more than 10 s, as shown in completion time of EEG + EEG in Fig. 3B) in the 4 control strategies. Although the EMG + EMG mode completion time is shortest but is hard to be triggered after long time training (completion success rate is 75%). The EMG + EEG mode has a lower success completion rate (80% as shown in Fig. 3C) because the EEG signal is disturbed as the hand moves cooperatively with the SRF during the release time.

Finite-State Machine for the Reach-Load-Hold-Release Task.
The reach-load-hold-release task is divided into four discrete phases of the SRF: reach, load, hold and release, as shown in Fig. 4A.

Reach: Human hand wears the SRF and reaches to the right position relative to the target object. In this phase, EEG/EMG triggering is not needed.

Load: In this phase, human hand has been moved to the right position relative to the target object. People triggered the SRF into the flexion mode by the EEG signal of the sixth-finger MI, and the SRF begins to flex.

Hold: The SRF begins to contact the target object until the object is held stably. In this phase, EEG/EMG triggering is not needed.

Release: After finishing the detailed task, people triggered the SRF into the release mode by identifying the EMG of raising an eyebrow. The SRF begins to release until returning to the full extension.

3   Evaluation of the SRF Performance

3.1   Pinch Force and Velocity

To evaluate SRF performance, several tests were performed. A load cell (FSR, China) was used to measure the fingertip force. Fingertip forces were measured by applying the maximum power of the motor for 3 s. The maximum output fingertip force, using the load cell, was approximately 10 N. The maximum speed was measured using the actuator encoder of the finger during automatic grasps performed in free space. The measured speeds were 70°/s for finger flexion and 80°/s extension.

3.2 Power Consumption

To evaluate the SRF power consumption, an endurance test was performed to determine how long the SRF could operate by a single battery (2,500 mAh, rated voltage of 8.4 V, peak current of 5 A). The SRF were preprogramed to sequentially perform the flexion/extension motion at 80% of the maximum velocity. Under these continuous-operation conditions, our SRF could be operated for approximately 4 h and stopped when the battery voltage dropped to 4.4 V from the initial 8.5 V.

3.3 SRF Grasps

Our SRF can achieve the goal of grasp enhancement and grasp assistance. Some preliminary experiments have been implemented, as shown in Fig. 4B. As two examples, two bimanual tasks are performed to evaluate the grasp enhancement function: people can wear SRF to fix and open the bottle with one hand (Fig. 4B a) and fix the large box with one hand (Fig. 4B b). As two examples, two grasp assistance tasks are performed to evaluate the grasp assistance function: for the hand movement impairing patients, they can fix the large ball (Fig. 4B c) and cylinder (Fig. 4B d) by using the SRF to provide the opposite support with the impaired hand.

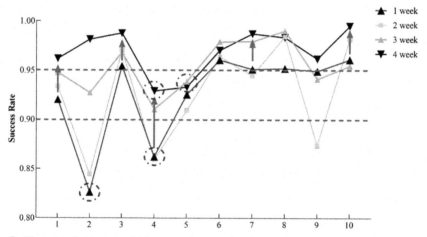

Fig. 5. The control accuracy of this system by counting the number of success rate of 10 subjects in 4 weeks of training. The red arrow means the significantly improved of the success rate after 4 weeks. (Color figure online)

3.4 Control Accuracy Assessment in 4-week EEG Triggering Training

In order to reveal the neural plastic mechanism of brain control SRF, we conducted a longitudinal 4-week EEG triggering training experiment. Ten subjects (as shown in Fig. 4C) are involved. Each participant train one hour per day, and five days in one week. The number of success (ST) and failure completion times (FT) is recorded. The control accuracy (CA) of each subject for each week is calculated by ST/(FT + ST). The success completion means the successful MI and completing the finger to finger contact between SRF and user finger. In contrary, the failure completion means the failed MI and the finger to finger contact motion cannot be triggered.

The results were shown in Fig. 5. Three obvious observations are obtained: (1) the simple six-finger MI control algorithm can be easily accepted and the system can be relatively simply controlled. In the first week of training, except for two subjects success rate below 90%, the CA of the other subjects can reached more than 90%; (2) all subjects performed a fine learning performance to the EEG MI control of SRF. After four weeks of training, the success rate in all subjects in the fourth week was significantly improved compared to the first week, as shown by the red arrow in the Fig. 5; (3) After a longitudinal EEG triggering training, SRF control system has a good reliability. The average control accuracy rate of 10 subjects in 4 weeks is 94.53% ±0.044.

Consequently, after simultaneously considering the high CA and fine learning performance of human brain by using six-finger MI control, the rehabilitation application potentials should be further investigated. This is also our future work.

4   Conclusion

In this paper, we proposed a novel EEG-EMG strategy to improve the classification accuracy. In addition, a novel supernumerary robotic finger (SRF) system is built with a modular design consideration. The whole system contained seven modules: EEG acquisition, EEG control, EMG acquisition, SRF control, SRF finger, TENS feedback and status information Module. To the best of our knowledge, this is the first wearable brain control SRL system which is compliance, affordable, wearability, modularity, and lightweight, named CAWML-SRF. The finger weight is less than 195 g, and the whole system weight is less than 1 kg. The experiments show that the CAWML-SRF can enhance the grasp functionality for helping the single hand to accomplish the bimanual grasp task (such as opening the bottle and grasping the larger objects), and assist the remaining functionality to accomplish the grasp task. A 4-week EEG triggering training experiment is conducted to further evaluate the rehabilitation application potentials: the high control accuracy rate (94.53% ± 0.044) and fine learning performance of human brain to the system are verified.

Several limitations of the finger structure and control method should be improved Now, the fine learning performance of human brain by using six-finger MI control has been proved. In the future, the neuroplasticity study of the SRF training will be further explored based on the MRI data we have already collected.

Acknowledgments. This work was supported in part by the National Natural Science Foundation of China (51905375), the China Post-doctoral Science Foundation Funded Project (2019M651033), Foundation of State Key Laboratory of Robotics and System (HIT) (SKLRS-2019-KF-06), and Peiyang Elite Scholar Program of Tianjin University (2020XRG-0023).

References

1. Cartmill, M.: Rethinking primate origins. Science **184**(4135), 436–443 (1974)

2. Napier, J.R.J.J.o.Z.: Studies of the hand of living primates. **134**(4), 647–657 (2009)
3. Napier, J.J.S.A.: The evolution of the hand. **207**(6), 56–62 (1963)
4. Jones, L., Lederman, S.: Human hand function. 2006: Oxford University Press (2006)
5. Belter, J.T., et al.: Mechanical design and performance specifications of anthropomorphic prosthetic hands: a review. J. Rehabil. Res. Dev. **50**(5), 599–617 (2013)
6. Heo, P., et al.: Current hand exoskeleton technologies for rehabilitation and assistive engineering. **13**(5), 807–824 (2012)
7. Prattichizzo, D., et al.: The sixth-finger: a modular extra-finger to enhance human hand capabilities. In: 2014 23rd IEEE International Symposium on Robot and Human Interactive Communication, pp. 993–998. IEEE, New York (2014)
8. Wu, F.Y., Asada, H.H.J.P.-I.I.C.o.R.: Automation, 'hold-and-manipulate' with a single hand being assisted by wearable extra fingers. **2015**, 6205–6212 (2015)
9. Leigh, S.W., Maes, P.: Body integrated programmable joints interface. In: The 2016 CHI Conference (2016)
10. Prattichizzo, D., et al.: The sixth-finger: a modular extra-finger to enhance human hand capabilities. In: ROMAN 14 (2014)
11. Salvietti, G., et al.: Compensating hand function in chronic stroke patients through the robotic sixth finger. **25**(2), 142–150 (2016)
12. Hussain, I., et al.: A magnetic compatible supernumerary robotic finger for functional magnetic resonance imaging (fMRI) acquisitions: device description and preliminary results. **2017**, 1177–1182 (2017)
13. Hussain, I., et al.: Toward wearable supernumerary robotic fingers to compensate missing grasping abilities in hemiparetic upper limb (2017)
14. Hu, Y., Leigh, S.W., Maes, P.: Hand development kit: soft robotic fingers as prosthetic augmentation of the hand. In: Adjunct Publication of the 30th Annual ACM Symposium (2017)
15. Hussain, I., et al.: A soft supernumerary robotic finger and mobile arm support for grasping compensation and hemiparetic upper limb rehabilitation. **93**, 1–12 (2017)
16. Irfan, H., et al.: An EMG Interface for the control of motion and compliance of a supernumerary robotic finger. **10** (2016)
17. Penaloza, C.I., Nishio, S.: BMI control of a third arm for multitasking. Sci. Robot. **3**(20), 6 (2018)
18. Bennett, D.A., et al.: A multigrasp hand prosthesis for providing precision and conformal grasps. IEEE-ASME Trans. Mechatron. **20**(4), 1697–1704 (2015)

Compliance Control Method of Exoskeleton Robot Assisted by Lower Limb Knee Joint Based on Gait Recognition

Dingan Song[1][(✉)], Ligang Qiang[1], Yali Liu[2], Yangyang Li[1], and Lin Li[1]

[1] Guizhou Aerospace Control Technolgy CO. LTD., Guiyang 550001, Guizhou, China
[2] Beijing Institute of Technology School of Mechatronical Engineering, Haidian, Beijing 100081, China

Abstract. To realize compliance control of lower limb-assisted exoskeleton robot, a control method based on human gait recognition is adopted to design the controller. In this paper, force control strategy and position control strategy are adopted respectively in stance phase and swing phase of human walking. Walking experiment shows that, in the stance phase, force output can quickly track the force command and realize the rapid response output of force. And in the swing phase, position control can make the system position output appropriate. In sum, the system has good assistance response characteristics and adaptive cable release control, which meets the expected requirements of the design.

Keywords: Exoskeleton · Compliance control · Gait recognition

1 Introduction

Exoskeleton robot is wearable man-machine integration equipment in which man plays a dominant role. It combines human intelligence and machine power effectively to enhance man's body function and endurance [1]. It can be applied in the fields of walking assistance, load carrying and disaster relief [3, 4], and can be extended to high-end industries such as advanced manufacturing and rehabilitation training [5–8]. The core of exoskeleton technology is to realize man-machine integrated cooperative movement. Therefore, the compliance control technology becomes crucial, which directly determines the coordination and flexibility of exoskeleton movement.

At present, based on bioelectrical signal and motion characteristic information are two main control methods for exoskeleton [9]. The former is based on biometric sensors signal to predict the motion intention and motion state, which further control the exoskeleton accordingly [10]. This control method can predict human motion in advance, so it is no control delay. Japan's hybrid assisted prosthesis (HAL) is one of the most successful representatives [11–14]. However, EMG and EEG sensor is complicated to wear and easy to be disturbed. Therefore, it has been greatly limited. The latter method controls exoskeleton robot through man-machine interaction force and human posture, so as to realize follow-up control of the exoskeleton [15]. For example, Long [16] proposed

© Springer Nature Switzerland AG 2021
X.-J. Liu et al. (Eds.): ICIRA 2021, LNAI 13013, pp. 759–768, 2021.
https://doi.org/10.1007/978-3-030-89095-7_72

an exoskeleton robot control method based on kalman filter to predict human motion intention. Chen [17] analyzed and divided human gaits based on lower limb exoskeleton gait prediction method of SAE and LSTM. But this method relies on large quantity of data information and complicated algorithm.

In view of these problems, this paper designs controller based on exoskeleton's gait recognition. Control strategies are designed respectively according to the results of gait recognition: force tracking control is adopted in stance phase of walking, and position follow-up control is employed in swing phase, so that coordination between exoskeleton movement and human motion is consistent, and compliant assistance of exoskeleton joint can be realized.

2 System Structure of the Exoskeleton Robot Powered by Knee Joint at Lower Limb

2.1 System Structure

The system structure of the exoskeleton is shown in Fig. 1. Upper limb structure, mainly consisting of bionic back-structure. It is to transfer the load of the upper limb down to the ground through lower limb support structure. Lower limb supporting structure, mainly consisting of hip joint structure, knee joint structure, and upper and lower leg adjustment structures, upper and lower leg support structures, lower limb man-machine binding interface and sensing shoes. It is to reduce the load that man is carrying. Series elastic driving system, including integrated driving system which integrates driving motor, deceleration mechanism, cable driving mechanism, control circuit and feedback sensor as a whole and series elastic device.

The integrated driving system is fixed at the waist of the exoskeleton, assisting man's body movement by controlling the cable driving mechanism. It includes two symmetrical driving modules with the same structure. Each driving module includes: driving motor, deceleration mechanism, cable retracting device and battery.

The series elastic device is installed on the lower leg near the knee joint and the cable sleeve is fixed on the upper leg near the knee joint. It includes connecting rod, spring, tension sensor, press plate and sleeve. The take-up of the cable drives the connecting rod, tension sensor and press plate to compress the spring in the sleeve.

There are two sensors in each sensor shoe as shown in Fig. 1. Inner part of the sensor shoe is designed with wire slot to protect the sensor. The signal acquisition circuit board is installed on the outside of the heel. In normal walking process wearing exoskeleton, the sensor 2 first collects the man-ground interaction force, and then the sensor 1 starts to collect man-ground interaction force when the palm touches the ground. The man-ground interaction force direct present the gait phase.

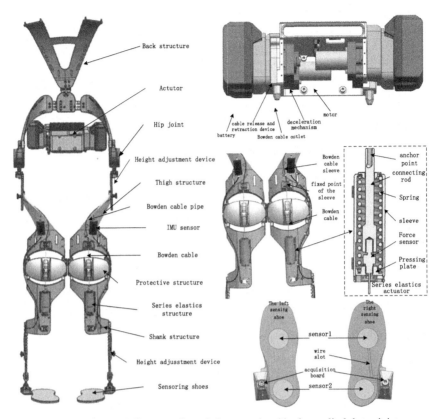

Fig. 1. Structural diagram of exoskeleton assisted by lower limb knee joint

3   Controller Design and Experimental Results

The lower limb exoskeleton adopts control strategy based on gait recognition. The control structure includes four main parts, as is shown in Fig. 2. Motion recognition part, which judges the gait phase in the process of human movement according to the signal recognition of sensing shoes. Control system part, include two control methods: force feedback control mode is used in stance phase, and position feedback control mode in the swing phase; The man-machine part: the human-machine system is formed by the coordinated movement of man and machine; The sensor system, which includes position sensors, force feedback sensors, human posture sensors and sensing shoes, is used for exoskeleton control and motion recognition respectively.

3.1   Gait Recognition of Human Motion

Human motion gait, which refers to the behavior characteristics of human walking, is the general name of walking state. Gait recognition is one of the key technologies of exoskeleton. According to the requirements of exoskeleton control application, this paper divides it into three phases: stance phase, swing phase and transition phase.

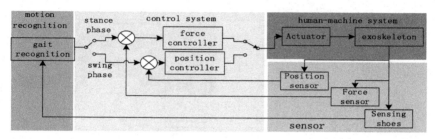

Fig. 2. Control structure the exoskeleton system

Stance phase: start with foot touching ground to the other foot touching ground;

Transition phase: start with the other foot touching ground to the foot completely lift off the ground;

Swing phase: start with the foot lift off the ground to the foot touching the ground again.

The plantar pressure profile and gait division during walking are shown in Fig. 3, in which *sensor1_l* and *sensor1_r are* the pressure signal detected by the left and right palm pressure sensor respectively, *sensor2_l* and *sensor2_r are* the pressure signal detected by the left and right heel pressure sensor respectively, *footforce_l* and footforce_r are the left and right foot pressure respectively.

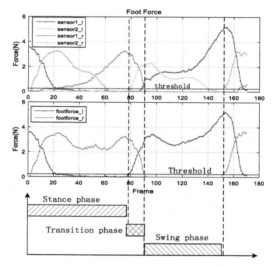

Fig. 3. Gait Phase

The recognition of gait phase is based on threshold method. The gait judgment expression is shown in Eq. 1,

$$gait(i) = \begin{cases} 1, & gait(i) = 3\&\&F_r(i) >= F_T \\ 2, & gait(i) = 1\&\&F_r(i) >= F_T\&\&F_l(i) >= F_T \\ 3, & F_r(i) < F_T \\ gait(i-1), & else \end{cases} \quad (1)$$

Where, i means i moment, $gait(i)$ is the result of gait phase, $F_r(i)$ is the plantar pressure of the right foot, and F_T is the threshold of plantar pressure. The expression of plantar pressure $F_r(i)$ of the right foot is

$$F_r(i) = F_{r1}(i) + F_{r2}(i) \quad (2)$$

Where $F_{r1}(i)$ and $F_{r2}(i)$ is the pressure signal value detected by the right foot pressure sensor and the right heel pressure sensor at the i moment respectively.

Gait recognition result profile of the exoskeleton can be obtained, as shown in Fig. 4. The *lgait* is the left foot gait phase, *rgait* is the right foot gait phase, 1 means stance phase, 2 means transition phase, and 3 means swing phase.

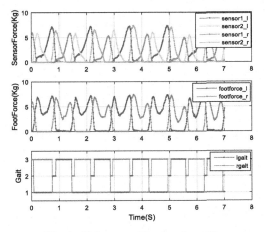

Fig. 4. Gait recognition result profile

3.2 Exoskeleton Control

In the process of human walking, the musculoskeletal system has different work states in stance phase and swing phase. The exoskeleton robot adopts two different control strategies: force feedback and position feedback.

3.2.1 Force Tracking Model in Stance Phase

Exoskeleton robot supports the load for human body in stance phase. In this phase, force feedback control strategy is adopted for its more flexibility and compliance. This control strategy needs build a force tracking command model. This paper constructing force tracking command based on the change of knee joint angle in stance phase.

In the stance phase, the change trend of knee flexion angle first increases, and then gradually decreases to knee extension. When the knee flexion angle becomes large, the load transfer efficiency of exoskeleton is decreases. So the exoskeleton's driving system needed to provide higher torque to enhance the stiffness of the knee joint, thus increasing the external load transfer efficiency on the exoskeleton, and vice versa. That is to say, the stiffness of the knee joint is closely related to the joint angle, which can be used to build the force tracking command model of the knee joint.

The model of knee joint force tracking command and joint angle can used the first-order linear model to approximate, and add the saturation characteristic to constrain the force tracking command. The expression is shown in Eq. 3,

$$
F_r(i) = \begin{cases} \overline{F}, & \theta_{knee}(i) > \overline{\theta} \\ k\theta_{knee}(i) + b, & \underline{\theta} < \theta_{knee}(i) < \overline{\theta} \\ \underline{F}, & \theta_{knee}(i) < \underline{\theta} \end{cases} \tag{3}
$$

Where, i means i moment, $F_r(i)$ denotes the force tracking command, $\overline{F}$ and $\underline{F}$ denotes the upper and lower bounds of the force tracking command respectively, $\overline{\theta}$ and $\underline{\theta}$ denotes the upper and lower bounds of the linear correlation interval of the knee joint angle, $\theta_{knee}(i)$ denotes the knee joint angle, k, b denote the linear coefficients, parameters k, b, $\overline{F}, \underline{F}, \overline{\theta}$ and $\underline{\theta}$ can be adjusted according to the practical application to adapt to different individuals and motion states.

3.2.2   Position Prediction Model in Swing Phase

In the swing phase, the series elastic driving system of exoskeleton needs to release the cable to eliminate the resistance of knee flexion, and then take up the cable to reduce the response time of assistance control in stance phase. Therefore, position predictive control is used in the swing process of human walking to make the exoskeleton motion match the human motion position.

The basic idea of prediction control of exoskeleton swing phase position is as follows: firstly, establish the mathematical model of knee joint angle and driver output angle; secondly, establish the prediction model of the swing state angle during walking, and estimate the output angle of the driver by the predicted knee joint angle, which is used as the position tracking command of the exoskeleton driving system; and finally, conduct servo tracking of the position command.

The profile of knee joint angle (*kneeAngle*) and driver output angle (*potention-meter*) is shown in Fig. 5(left). It can be concluded from the figure that the knee joint angle has a positive correlation with the driver output angle. Therefore, the first-order linear polynomial can be used to fit the mathematical model of knee joint angle and driver output angle. It is shown in Eq. 4.

$$
\theta_p = k_m \theta_{knee} + p_m \tag{4}
$$

Where, θ_p represents the output angle of the driver, θ_{knee} represents the knee joint angle, k_m and p_m represents the coefficients of the model to be fitted respectively.

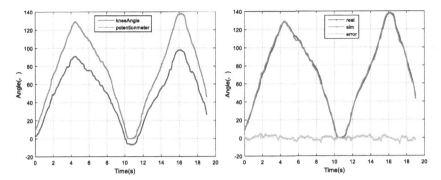

Fig. 5. Knee joint angle and driver output angle (left) and fitting model results (right)

The fitting model results of knee joint angle and driver output angle are shown in Fig. 5(right). It test the fitting model can well describe the linear relationship between knee joint angle and driving output angle.

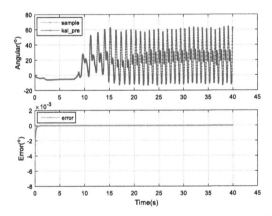

Fig. 6. Estimation results of knee joint angle by Kalman prediction

The estimation of knee joint angle is calculated by *kalman* prediction algorithm. Signal acquisition period of the exoskeleton system is 10 ms. Therefore, it can be assumed that the angle, angular velocity and angular acceleration of knee joint are fixed in a sampling interval.

The results of Kalman prediction of knee joint angle is shown in Fig. 6. As can be seen from the figure, the knee joint angle of exoskeleton can be well predicted through the Kalman prediction algorithm, and the angle prediction residual converges rapidly close to 0. That is to say, the expected output angle can be predicted.

3.3 Experimental Results

The servo tracking of the exoskeleton adopts PID control. Different PID control parameters are set for force feedback control and position feedback control, which can achieve good tracking performance.

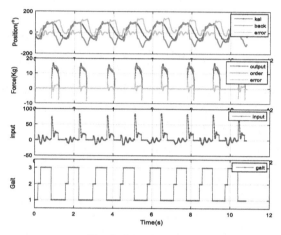

Fig. 7. Control results

Test results of man wearing the exoskeleton are shown in Fig. 7. In stance state, we need force output quickly. It can be seen from the figure that, the system can quickly track the force command and realize quick response output of the force.

In swing state, kalman prediction is used to estimate the output position, and the position tracking control is adopted to make the system position output appropriate. That is, making the output resistance to 0 and meanwhile keep the cable is released appropriately. It can be seen from Fig. 7 that the force output is basically 0 and the position output can quickly track and predict the expected command, and meanwhile the position residual converges. Therefore, the system can not only realize fast assistance response output in stance state but also release cable with the desired length in swing state, achieving good matching of the force output and position output of the exoskeleton driving system with the human motion, so as to meet the expected requirements of the design.

4 Conclusion

Aiming at the problem of compliance control of exoskeleton assisted by lower limb knee joint, this paper adopts the control method based on human gait recognition. Force control strategy and position control strategy are employed in stance phase and swing phase respectively. For the stance phase, a force tracking command model based on knee joint angle is proposed. For the swing phase, the kalman prediction is used to estimate the desired position and realize the appropriate output of the position angle.

Walking experiment shows that, in the stance phase, force output can quickly track the force command and realize the rapid response output of force. And in the swing phase, position control can make the system position output appropriate. In sum, the system has good assistance response characteristics and adaptive cable release control, which meets the expected requirements of the design.

Acknowledgments. This work was support by grants from the Ministry of Science and Technology's national key R&D program (grant Number: 2017YFB1300500).

References

1. Yang, C., Chen, Y., Lu, Y.: Study on the humachine intelligent system and its application. Chin. J. Mech. Eng. **36**(6), 42–47 (2000)
2. Yan, T., Cempini, M., Oddo, C.: Review of assistive strategies in powered lower-limb orthoses and exoskeletons. Robot. Auton. Syst. **64**, 120–136 (2015)
3. Song, Q., Wang, X., Wang, X.: Development of multi-joint exoskeleton-assisted robot and its key technology analysis: an overview. Acta Armamentarii **37**(1), 172–185 (2016)
4. Li, J., Zhu, L., Gou, X.: Survey on exoskeleton lower limbs rehabilitation robot and key technologies. Chin. Med. Equip. J. **38**(8), 95–100 (2018)
5. Zanotto, D., Akiyama, Y., Stegall, P.: Knee joint misalignment in exoskeletons for the lower extremities: Effects on user's gait. IEEE Trans. Robot. **31**(4), 978–987 (2015)
6. Li, J., Deng, C., Zhang, Z.: Design and kinematics analysis of the exoskeleton mechanism for detecting motion information of lower-limb arthosis. J. Beijing Univ. Technol. **8**, 1127–1133 (2013)
7. Schiele, A., Helm, F.: Kinematic design to improve ergonomics in human machine interaction. IEEE Trans. Neural Syst. Rehabil. Eng. **14**(4), 456–469 (2006)
8. Dollar, A., Herr, H.: Lower extremity exoskeletons and activeorthoses: Challenges and state-of-the-art. IEEE Trans. Robot. **24**(1), 144–158 (2008)
9. Zhao, X., Tan, X.: Development of soft lower extremity exoskeleton and its key technologies: a survey. Robots **42**(3), 365–384 (2020)
10. Yin, Y., Fan, Y., Xu, L.: EMG and EPP-integrated human-machine interface between the paralyzed and rehabilitation exoskeleton. IEEE Trans. Inf Technol. Biomed. **16**(4), 542–549 (2012)
11. George, T., Shalu, G., Sivanandan, K.: Sensing, processing and application of EMG signals for HAL (hybrid assistive limb). In: International Conference on Sustainable Energy and Intelligent Systems, Stevenage, UK, pp. 749–753 (2011)
12. Kasaoka, K., Sankai, Y.: Predictive control estimating operator's intention for stepping-up motion by exo-skeleton type power assist system HAL. In: IEEE/RSJ International Conference on Intelligent Robots and Systems, Piscataway, USA, pp. 1578–1583 (2001)
13. Kawamoto, H., Lee, S., Kanbe, S.: Power assist method for HAL-3 using EMG-based feedback controller. In: IEEE International Conference on Systems, Man and Cybernetics, Piscataway, USA, pp. 1648–1653 (2003)
14. Lee, S., Sankai, Y.: Power assist control for walking aid with HAL-3 based on EMG and impedance adjustment around knee joint. In: IEEE/RSJ International Conference on Intelligent Robots and Systems, Piscataway, USA, pp. 1499–1504 (2002)
15. Liu, H., Wang, T., Fan, W.: Self anti-interference control of pneumatic muscle joint. Robot **33**(4), 461–466 (2011)

16. Long, Y., Du, Z., Wang, W.: Control and experiment for exoskeleton robot based on kalman prediction of Human motion Intent. Robot **37**(3), 304–309 (2015)
17. Chen, C., Jiang, L., Wang, H.: Gait prediction method of lower extremity exoskeleton based on SAE and LSTM neural network. Comput. Eng. Appl. **55**(12), 110–116 (2019)

Human Action Recognition Using Skeleton Data from Two-Stage Pose Estimation Model

Ruiqi Sun[1], Qin Zhang[1,2(✉)], Jiamin Guo[2], Hui Chai[2], and Yueyang Li[1]

[1] School of Electrical Engineering, University of Jinan, Jinan, China
cse_zhangq@ujn.edu.cn
[2] School of Control Science and Engineering, Shandong University, Jinan, China

Abstract. This paper presents a method of human action recognition based on the key points of skeleton, aiming to guide the robot to follow a leader in complex environments. We propose a two-stage human pose estimation model which combines the Single Shot Detector (SSD) algorithm based on ResNet with Convolutional Pose Machines (CPMs) to obtain the key points positions of the human skeleton in 2D images. Based on the position information, we construct structure vectors. Feature models consisting of eight angle features and four modulus ratio features are then extracted as the representation of actions. Finally, multiclassification SVM is used to classify the feature models for action recognition. The experimental results demonstrate the validity of the two-stage human pose estimation model to accomplish the task of human action recognition. Our method achieves 97% recognition accuracy on the self-collected dataset composed of six command actions.

Keywords: Human action recognition · Key points position of skeleton · Convolutional pose machines · Multi-classification SVM

1 Introduction

Human action recognition is one of the most important areas of computer vision research. It is widely used in video surveillance, human-computer interaction and medical care. Autonomous movement of robots usually adopts the strategy of "leader-following" in complex outdoor environment, which can reduce operation burden of the joystick to the operator and the difficulty of autonomous movement of robots. Therefore, it is crucial for robots to identify the leader's command actions accurately.

Feature extraction is a key step of human action recognition. Johansson's experiment indicates that human motion can be described by major joints [1]. At present, there are two main ways to get joints information: Motion Capture System (MoCap) [2–4] and depth camera [6–10]. MoCap can only be used in a specific environment and it is expensive. Depth cameras are widely used because of their simplicity and unmarked properties. Shotton et al. used depth images provided by Kinect to estimate the human skeleton accurately [5]. Xia Lu et al. extracted 3D skeletal joint locations based on [5] to construct histogram features [6]. Li Wanqing et al. used a bag of 3D points feature

© Springer Nature Switzerland AG 2021
X.-J. Liu et al. (Eds.): ICIRA 2021, LNAI 13013, pp. 769–779, 2021.
https://doi.org/10.1007/978-3-030-89095-7_73

to obtain more semantic information [7]. Some scholars described an action sequence by calculating the position differences of joints in both temporal and spatial domains [8–10].

Deep learning can autonomously learn features with strong discrimination and representation ability from data. Many researchers designed convolutional neural networks for skeleton-based action recognition [11, 12]. With the development of computer vision technology, a variety of human pose estimation models based on deep learning appeared. CPMs used intermediate supervision to addresses vanishing gradients [13]. Chen Yilun et al. presented the cascaded pyramid network to solve the problem of inconsistent detection difficulty of different parts [14]. Xiao Bin et al. added deconvolution layers to the backbone network to find a simpler pose estimation method [15]. These methods reduce the noise of joint data effectively and are suitable for ordinary monocular cameras. However, the detection accuracy of above methods is limited by the integrity of human detection. Therefore, we present a two-stage human pose estimation model which combines the SSD [16] and CPMs to obtain the key points of skeleton. Based on the position information of the key points, we construct a feature model. Then the human actions are classified by Support Vector Machine (SVM). The overall framework of our system is shown in Fig. 1.

2   Two-Stage Human Pose Estimation

Two-stage human pose estimation model is proposed to detect human skeleton points. Firstly, we establish the SSD algorithm based on ResNet to obtain the locations of the human in images. CPMs locate the person in images through position information and detect skeleton key points. Based on the joint positions, we use the method in Sect. 3.1 to extract action features.

2.1   Introduction of Network Structure

A human detection network as shown in Fig. 2 is proposed to acquire the human position in the scene. We select ResNet-50 as the backbone (blue part) for extracting rich features and avoiding model degradation. The conv5_x, average pool, fully connected and softmax layers are removed from the original ResNet-50 model. Five groups of feature extraction modules (green part) are connected in series behind ResNet-50 so as to

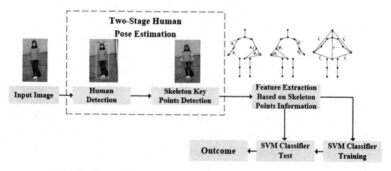

Fig. 1. Overall framework of the action recognition system

perform detection at multiple scales. The different feature maps labeled as ①②③④⑤⑥ are extracted respectively to predict both location and confidences. The feature extraction modules use the structure in [16], however, they are enhanced by additional Batch Normalization layers between each convolution and ReLu layer in order to accelerate the model training.

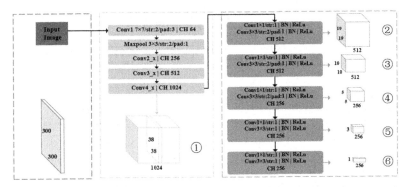

Fig. 2. Human detection network (Color figure online)

A skeleton key points detection network based on [13] is established to extract skeleton key points, as shown in Fig. 3. The first stage of CPMs is a convolutional neural network, i.e., the first 13 layers of VGG-19 and 7 convolution layers. The network structure of stage ≥ 2 is completely consistent, including 7 convolution layers. Three types of data (image features, spatial context and center constraints) are fused by the concat layer as input. The final output is a feature map of $w \times h \times c$, where $w \times h$ is the width and height of the feature map, and c is the depth of the feature map. Each stage has a part of the intermediate supervision which avoids vanishing gradients in the deep network [17].

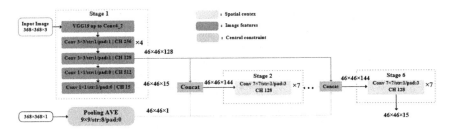

Fig. 3. Skeleton key points detection network

2.2 Two-Stage Detection of Skeleton Key Points

Two-stage detection is divided into human detection and skeleton key points detection. The process is displayed in Fig. 4. The human detection network (Fig. 2) takes a single picture X_0 as input. Prediction feature layers of different scales $[F_1, F_2, \cdots, F_k]$ are respectively convolved using 3×3 convolution kernels to calculate confidence and position of objects in each default box. According to the category score, it is determined whether the object is a person. We apply Non-Maximum Suppression (NMS) to filter out redundant boxes and obtain the bounding box we need.

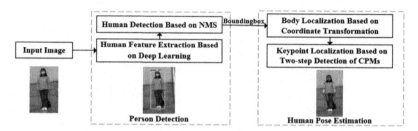

Fig. 4. Two-stage detection

Position information of the human is transmitted to skeleton key points detection model. In this way, the human can be accurately selected in original image. Then the image is input into the network (Fig. 3) and the belief map corresponding to i key points is output. The (x, y) coordinates of maximum values in the belief map is the 2D coordinate of the key points.

3   Human Action Recognition

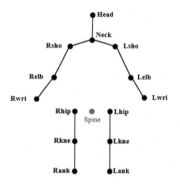

Fig. 5. Human skeleton model. (Color figure online)

In the previous section, 14 key points (black points in Fig. 5) and their position coordinates are obtained by two-stage human pose estimation model. The center point of the link between left hip and right hip is selected as spine (red point in Fig. 5). Human pose can be reflected by the connection between skeleton key points in the image. However, we need to analyze and extract the relationship between key points to recognize human actions. Therefore, we propose a feature extraction method based on the geometric relationship of key points and use SVM to classify the extracted action features.

3.1 Feature Extraction

Considering that simple actions are more convenient for human-computer interaction, we choose six command actions shown in Fig. 6. It is found that the changes of key points of different actions mainly focus on the arms and torso. We construct structure vectors with the key points of the two parts respectively. In this way, human feature extraction is specific to the two parts so as to increase the accuracy of action recognition.

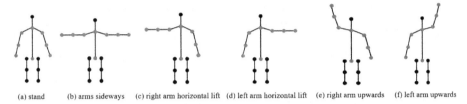

(a) stand   (b) arms sideways   (c) right arm horizontal lift   (d) left arm horizontal lift   (e) right arm upwards   (f) left arm upwards

Fig. 6. Command actions

We connect two skeleton key points to form a structure vector and construct 13 structure vectors totally, as shown in Fig. 7. Taking the vector $\overrightarrow{a_1}$ for instance, $\overrightarrow{a_1}$ is the vector from the neck to the right shoulder. Similarly, the remaining 12 vectors are connected in a similar way. Since the trunk will not move significantly in human motion, we select the vector from the spine to the head as the reference vector $\vec{r}$.

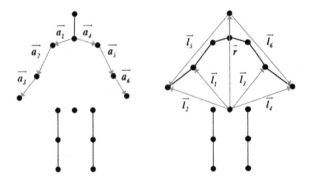

Fig. 7. The definition of the 13 structure vectors

When different people execute different actions, each structure vector has different position and angle information. Therefore, we select the angle and modulus ratio between structure vectors as action features. The swing amplitude of the two arms is reflected by the angle feature. The position change of two arms relative to the trunk is reflected by the modulus ratio. The feature selection is shown in Fig. 8.

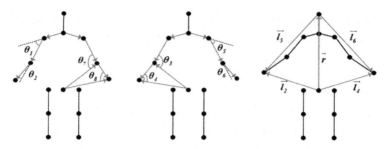

Fig. 8. Angle and modulus ratio characteristics

Eight angle features and four modulus ratio features are selected to construct the feature model. The characteristic parameters and their meanings are shown in Table 1. Taking the angle feature θ_1 as an example, $\langle \overrightarrow{a_1}, \overrightarrow{a_2} \rangle$ represents the angle between vector $\overrightarrow{a_1}$ and $\overrightarrow{a_2}$. The calculation formula is as follows:

$$\theta_1 = \cos^{-1} \frac{\overrightarrow{a_1} \cdot \overrightarrow{a_2}}{\|\overrightarrow{a_1}\| \|\overrightarrow{a_2}\|} \tag{1}$$

Taking mod_1 as an example, $\overrightarrow{l_5}\_\overrightarrow{r}$ represents the modulus ratio of the vector $\overrightarrow{l_5}$ and the reference vector $\overrightarrow{r}$, and the calculation formula is as follows:

$$mod_1 = \frac{\left|\overrightarrow{l_5}\right|}{|\overrightarrow{r}|} \tag{2}$$

Table 1. Action characteristic parameters

Feature	Attribute	Feature	Attribute
θ_1	$\langle \overrightarrow{a_1}, \overrightarrow{a_2} \rangle$	θ_7	$\langle \overrightarrow{a_5}, \overrightarrow{l_3} \rangle$
θ_2	$\langle \overrightarrow{a_2}, \overrightarrow{a_3} \rangle$	θ_8	$\langle \overrightarrow{a_6}, \overrightarrow{l_4} \rangle$
θ_3	$\langle \overrightarrow{a_2}, \overrightarrow{l_1} \rangle$	mod_1	$\overrightarrow{l_5}\_\overrightarrow{r}$
θ_4	$\langle \overrightarrow{a_3}, \overrightarrow{l_2} \rangle$	mod_2	$\overrightarrow{l_2}\_\overrightarrow{r}$
θ_5	$\langle \overrightarrow{a_4}, \overrightarrow{a_5} \rangle$	mod_3	$\overrightarrow{l_6}\_\overrightarrow{r}$
θ_6	$\langle \overrightarrow{a_5}, \overrightarrow{a_6} \rangle$	mod_4	$\overrightarrow{l_4}\_\overrightarrow{r}$

3.2   Action Recognition

We use SVM to classify the action features extracted from Sect. 3.1. SVM is a supervised learning model used for binary classification calculating the optimal hyperplane that separates two classes in the feature space. For classification problems that can't be linear separated, SVM uses kernel function $K(x)$ to transform it into a higher-dimensional space to make the sample linearly separable in this feature space.

In this paper, we adopt "one-to-one" strategy to extend SVM to a multi-classification to classify six instruction actions. Since the action feature parameters are nonlinear and noisy, we choose Radial Basis Function (RBF):

$$K(x_i, x) = exp\left(-\gamma \|x - x_i\|^2\right) \tag{3}$$

where γ is the kernel function parameter to be determined. We use the grid search method to optimize γ and penalty factor C.

4 Experiments

4.1 Experimental Environment and Datasets

The computer used in the experiment is configured with Intel Core i7–8700 processor and Nvidia GTX1660 graphics card. We select the Ubuntu 16.04 operating system, Pytorch and CPMs-release as the development environment.

Three benchmark datasets and one self-collected dataset are used in this paper. Human detection experiments are conducted on Pascal VOC 2007/2012 [18], in which VOC 2012 train dataset and validation dataset (11540 images) are used for training and VOC 2007 test dataset (4952 images) is used for testing. We use MPII Human Pose dataset [19] and Leeds Sports Pose (LSP) dataset [20] for human pose estimation. The CPMs-Stage 6 model is trained based on 28000 human samples from MPII dataset and verified based on 2000 samples from LSP dataset.

We made a self-collected dataset containing 6 types of actions which were collected by RealSense D435i depth camera in the indoor and outdoor environment. The subjects faced the camera and located 1–2 m in front of the camera during the performance. Each action was collected 500 samples from 5 different persons (4 males and 1 female) in two environments. Altogether, the dataset contains 3000 action samples. Sample images from the dataset are shown in Fig. 9.

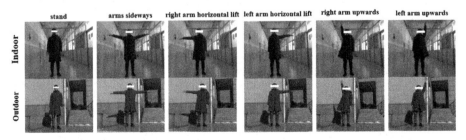

Fig. 9. Examples of six command actions collected in two different environments

4.2 Human Detection Results

We train the model using Stochastic Gradient Descent (SGD) and set the initial learning rate as 10^{-3}. We use a momentum of 0.9 and a weight decay of 0.0005. The batch size is set to 16. The mean Average Precision (mAP) is used as the evaluation metric. The SSD based on ResNet-50 (SSD_ResNet50) achieved 75.6%. When the training set contains only "person", the detection accuracy of SSD_Person model is 9% higher than SSD_ResNet50 model, reaching 84.6%.

Figure 10 displays the comparison of the detection accuracy of SSD_Person (the green box) and SSD_ ResNet50 (the yellow box) for the different scenes of dim light or sufficient light respectively. It can be seen that no matter in which condition, SSD_Person has a higher accuracy for human detection, so we select SSD_Person for human detection.

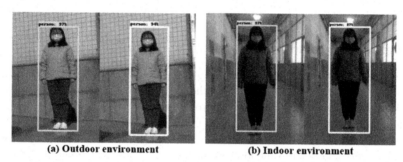

(a) Outdoor environment   (b) Indoor environment

Fig. 10. Comparison of detection accuracy of two models. (Color figure online)

4.3 Skeleton Key Points Detection Results

For model training, we set the maximum iterations as 320000 with batch size of 16. The learning rate is initialized as 8e−4 and learning strategy is "step". We use a momentum of 0.9 and a weight decay of 0.0005. The evaluation is based on PCK@0.2 metric. When the distance between the prediction and ground truth is less than 20% of the pixel length of the human trunk in the image, it is considered to be correct.

Our results on the LSP dataset are shown in Fig. 11. The PCK@0.2 reaches 87.4%. The detection effect of the CPMs-Stage 6 model on self-collected dataset is shown in Fig. 12.

4.4 Human Action Recognition Results

Firstly, the Z-score standardization method is used to standardize the self-collected dataset to reduce the impact of data anomalies on the classification accuracy. The self-collected dataset is divided into training set and test set according to the ratio of 3:2. Based on the training set, the grid search method is used to optimize the parameters (C, g), that is, $C = 8.00; g = 0.25$. The optimal parameters (C, g) are utilized to train the model, and the trained model is used to test. The confusion matrix of the output result is shown in Fig. 13. The ordinate is the real label and the abscissa is the prediction label.

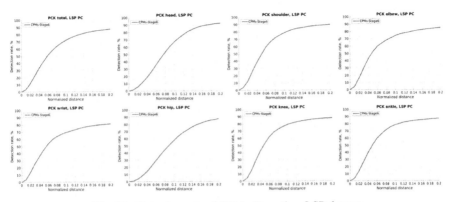

Fig. 11. Detection rate of CPMs-Stage 6 on LSP dataset

Fig. 12. Effect of skeleton key points detection based on self-collected dataset

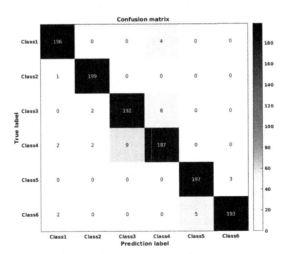

Fig. 13. Confusion matrix of six actions

The accuracy of action classification is shown in Table 2. The recognition accuracy of six command actions is more than 90% and the overall mean accuracy is 97.0%. Combining Fig. 13 and Table 2, it can be seen that the main classification error is the confusion between left-hand and right-hand actions. This is mainly caused by the error detection in CPMs-Stage 6 model.

Table 2. Recognition rate of each action type

Command actions	Accuracy	Command actions	Accuracy
Stand	98%	Left arm horizontal lift	93.5%
Arms sideways	99.5%	Right arm upwards	98.5%
Right arm horizontal lift	96.0%	Left arm upwards	96.5%
Overall		97.0%	

5 Conclusion

In this paper, we presented a method of action recognition based on human skeleton information obtained by the two-stage human pose estimation model. Action features were generated by calculating angles and modulus ratios between structure vectors and classified by SVM. The two-stage human pose estimation model combined with improved SSD algorithm and CPMs solved the problem that the detection accuracy of CPMs depends on the integrity of human detection. According to the characteristics of linearly inseparable, multi-class and noisy of feature space, we designed a multi-class SVM based on RBF kernel function. Our method achieved 97% accuracy on the self-collected dataset. The result showed that our method can effectively recognize human action and realize the more natural interaction between humans and robots in the future. The following research will be focused on how to improve the detection rate of CPMs so as to avoid confusing left and right skeleton key points when the light is insufficient.

Acknowledgments. This study was supported by the National Natural Science Foundation of China (Grants No. 91948201 and 61973135), and the Fundamental Research Funds of Shandong University (Grant No. 2019GN017).

References

1. Johansson, G.: Visual perception of biological motion and a model for its analysis. Percept. Psychophys. **14**(2), 201–211 (1973)
2. Vieira, A.W., Schwartz, W.R., Campos, M., et al.: Distance matrices as invariant features for classifying MoCap data. In: International Conference on Pattern Recognition, pp. 2934–2937. IEEE (2012)
3. Barnachon, M., Bouakaz, S., Boufama, B., et al.: Human actions recognition from streamed Motion Capture. In: International Conference on Pattern Recognition, pp. 3807–3810. IEEE (2012)

4. Ma, H.T., Zhang, X., Yang, H., et al.: SVM-based approach for human daily motion recognition. In: TENCON 2015–2015 IEEE Region 10 Conference, pp. 1–4. IEEE (2015)
5. Shotton, J., Fitzgibbon, A., Cook, M., et al.: Real-time human pose recognition in parts from single depth images. In: 24th Computer Vision and Pattern Recognition, pp. 1297–1304. IEEE, Piscataway (2011)
6. Lu, X., Chen, C.-C., Aggarwal, J.K.: View invariant human action recognition using histograms of 3D joints. In: Computer Vision and Pattern Recognition Workshops, pp. 20–27. IEEE (2012)
7. Li, W., Zhang, Z., Liu, Z.: Action recognition based on a bag of 3D points. In: Computer Vision and Pattern Recognition Workshops, pp. 9–14. IEEE (2010)
8. Yang, X., Tian Y.: EigenJoints-based action recognition using naïve bayes nearest neighbor. In: Computer Vision and Pattern Recognition Workshops, pp. 14–19. IEEE (2010)
9. Yang, X., Tian, Y.: Effective 3D action recognition using EigenJoints. J. Vis. Commun. Image Represent. **25**(1), 2–11 (2014)
10. Lu, G., Zhou, Y., Li, X., et al.: Efficient action recognition via local position offset of 3d skeletal body joints. Multimedia Tools Appl. **75**(6), 3479–3494 (2016)
11. Liu, J., Shahroudy, A., Dong, X., Wang, G.: Spatio-temporal LSTM with trust gates for 3D human action recognition. In: Leibe, B., Matas, J., Sebe, N., Welling, M. (eds.) ECCV 2016. LNCS, vol. 9907, pp. 816–833. Springer, Cham (2016). https://doi.org/10.1007/978-3-319-46487-9_50
12. Li, C., Zhong, X., Xie, D., et al.: Co-occurrence feature learning from skeleton data for action recognition and detection with hierarchical aggregation. In: 27th International Joint Conference on Artificial Intelligence, pp. 3807–3810. IEEE (2018)
13. Wei, S.E., Ramakrishna, V., Kanade, T., et al.: Convolutional pose machines. In: Conference on Computer Vision and Pattern Recognition, pp. 4727–4732. IEEE (2016)
14. Chen, Y., Wang, Z., Peng, Y., et al.: Cascaded pyramid network for multi-person pose estimation. In: Conference on Pattern Recognition, pp. 7103–7112. IEEE (2018)
15. Bin, X., Wu, H., Wei, Y.: Simple baselines for human pose estimation and tracking. In: European Conference on Computer Vision, pp. 472–487. IEEE (2018)
16. Liu, W., Anguelov, D., Erhan, D., et al.: SSD: single shot multibox detector. In: European Conference on Computer Vision, pp. 21–37. IEEE (2016)
17. Bengio, Y., Glorot, X.: Understanding the difficulty of training deep feed forward neural networks. In: 13th International Conference on Artificial Intelligence and Statistics, pp. 249–256. IEEE (2010)
18. Everingham, M., Gool, L.V., Williams, C., et al.: The pascal visual object classes (VOC) challenge. Int. J. Comput. Vision **88**(2), 303–338 (2010)
19. Andriluka, M., Pishchulin, L., Gehler, P., et al.: 2D human pose estimation: new benchmark and state of the art analysis. In: Computer Vision and Pattern Recognition, pp. 3686–3693. IEEE(2014)
20. Johnson, S., Everingham, M.: Learning effective human pose estimation from inaccurate annotation. In: Computer Vision and Pattern Recognition, pp. 1465–1472. IEEE (2016)

Assistive Torque of Ankle Exoskeleton Based on a Simple Biomechanical Model and a Genetic Algorithm

Nianfeng Wang[✉], Zitian Li, Yihong Zhong, and Xianmin Zhang

Guangdong Provincial Key Laboratory of Precision Equipment and Manufacturing Technology, School of Mechanical and Automotive Engineering, South China University of Technology, Guangzhou 510640, China
menfwang@scut.edu.cn

Abstract. To better study how the ankle exoskeleton reduces the metabolic consumption of human body during walking, a simple biomechanical model is built to study the effect of ankle exoskeleton on the metabolism of plantar flexor muscle. Two types of exoskeleton assistive torque are brought into the model simulation, one is the proportional assistive torque, and the other is the optimal torque generated from the biomechanical model by a genetic algorithm. Compared with the former, the optimal torque has two counter-intuitive features: the amplitude peak delays and its amplitude during the main gait phase is less than that of the proportional torque. In further research, it is found that their internal mechanism is better to adapt to the changes in muscle efficiency caused by changes in muscle length and speed.

Keywords: Ankle exoskeleton · Human walking · Muscle-tendon dynamics · Metabolic consumption · Genetic algorithm

1 Introduction

Research on exoskeleton is getting more and more popular and the ability of walking exoskeleton to reduce metabolism is constantly improving. The exoskeleton developed in the early stage not only failed to reduce human metabolic consumption but also increased their burden [1]. Nowadays, some exoskeletons have achieved a 14.88% reduction in human body's metabolic consumption [2]. A crucial reason for it is the innovation of exoskeleton configuration, such as pneumatic exoskeleton [3], passive exoskeleton [4], wire drive soft exosuit [5,6], etc. These configuration innovations have greatly lightened the weight of the exoskeleton. Moreover, most of the weight is arranged at the proximal end of human body, which reduces the increase in human metabolic consumption caused by wearing exoskeleton. Another important reason is the research progress on assistive torque forms [7–9]. These studies have conducted experiments to explore which

© Springer Nature Switzerland AG 2021
X.-J. Liu et al. (Eds.): ICIRA 2021, LNAI 13013, pp. 780–790, 2021.
https://doi.org/10.1007/978-3-030-89095-7_74

assistive torque form is more effective for reducing metabolism. However, it is difficult to exhaust all cases based on experimental studies. Model-based guidance is necessary.

Model-based studies have given a lot of useful enlightenments [10,11], but these studies are more based on mechanical energy of human body during walking and seldom pay attention to biological aspects. Therefore, the research in this article intends to use muscle-tendon dynamics to study how the assistive torque of ankle exoskeleton can reduce human metabolic energy consumption, and generate the optimal exoskeleton assistive torque through genetic algorithms, and explore the internal mechanism.

2   Biomechanical Model

2.1   Muscle-Tendon Unit Contraction Dynamics

The Hill-type model is applied to the modeling of muscle [12], which is represented by a simplified muscle-tendon unit (MTU). An MTU comprises a series elastic element (SEE), a contractile element (CE), and a parallel elastic element (PEE) [see Fig. 1(a)]. The elements satisfy the formulas (1) and (2) [13] in terms of force and length.

$$F_{MTU} = F_{CE} + F_{PEE} = F_{SEE} \tag{1}$$

where F_{MTU} is MTU force, F_{CE} is CE force, F_{PEE} is PEE force, and F_{SEE} is SEE force.

$$L_{MTU} = L_{CE} + L_{SEE} \tag{2}$$

where L_{MTU} is the MTU length, L_{CE} is the CE length, and L_{SEE} is the SEE length.

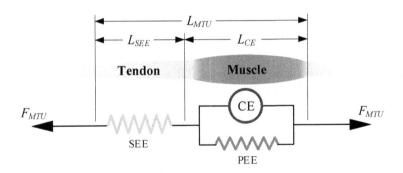

Fig. 1. The structure and elements of MTU

CE dynamics: Muscle is composed of CE and PEE, of which CE is the actuator generating muscle contractility. The calculation of muscle contraction force is based on the following formula:

$$F_{CE} = F_{MAX} \times a \times \tilde{f}^a_{CE}(\tilde{L}_{CE}) \times \tilde{f}_{CE}(\tilde{V}_{CE}) + F_{MAX} \times \tilde{f}^p_{PEE}(\tilde{L}_{CE}) \tag{3}$$

where F_{MAX} is the maximum isometric muscle force, a is muscle activation, $\tilde{L}_{CE}$ is the muscle length normalized by the optimal muscle length L_{CE_0}, $\tilde{V}_{CE}$ is the speed of the muscle normalized by the maximum speed $V_{CE_{MAX}}$ that the muscle can reach. The details of the empirical functions $\tilde{F}_{CE}^a(\tilde{L}_{CE})$, $\tilde{F}_{CE}(\tilde{V}_{CE})$ and $\tilde{F}_{PEE}^p(\tilde{L}_{CE})$ are given in [13].

SEE dynamics: The calculation of tendon force is based on the following formula:

$$F_{SEE} = F_{MAX} \times \tilde{F}_{SEE}(\tilde{L}_{SEE}) \tag{4}$$

where $\tilde{L}_{SEE}$ is the tendon length normalized by its original length without stretching L_{SEE_0}, which can be simply obtained by L_{MTU_0} minus L_{CE_0}. The details of function $\tilde{F}_{SEE}(\tilde{L}_{SEE})$ is given in [13].

CE energetics: In MTU, only CE consumes energy. A model for predicting muscle metabolic consumption [14] is used to estimate the metabolic consumption of CE. The calculation of metabolic power is shown in the formula (5).

$$P_{Met} = a \times F_{MAX} \times V_{CE_{MAX}} \times f_{Met}(\tilde{V}_{CE}) \tag{5}$$

where P_{Met} is the muscle metabolic power, and the function $f_{Met}(\tilde{V}_{CE})$ is the coefficient of muscle speed on metabolism whose details are given in [14]. The metabolic cost can be calculated by integrating the metabolic power over time.

2.2   Ankle Musculoskeletal Model with Double MTUs

An improved sagittal musculoskeletal model of the ankle joint have been established in [13,15] to analyze the changes in the muscles of the ankle joint while receiving assistive torque. Since plantarflexion is much greater than dorsiflexion in amplitude and the effect on pushing human body forward, most exoskeletons apply plantarflexion torque as the main assistance. Therefore, the model is aimed at the exoskeleton assistive torque in the plantarflexion direction. The model mainly comprises two MTUs. One is the plantarflexor (PF), which is a synthetic muscle that contains the soleus, medial gastrocnemius and lateral gastrocnemius. The other is the dorsiflexor (DF). The tibialis anterior is the most important dorsiflexor of the ankle joint, used here to represent DF. Both PF and DF are modeled with the Hill-type model. The model schematic is shown in Fig. 2(a) and its geometry is shown in Fig. 2(b).

The geometric parameters of the model are shown in Table 1, and the MTU contraction dynamics parameters are shown in Table 2. All the parameters come from the data of several adult men who are close to 170 cm in height and 70 kg in weight.

2.3   Metabolic Cost Calculation

The calculation framework for solving muscle metabolic consumption is shown in Fig. 3. First, calculate the muscle moment of PF and DF with the exoskeleton. Since only the case where the exoskeleton does not hinder ankle movement

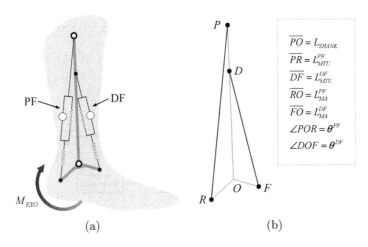

Fig. 2. The schematic (a) and geometry (b) of the ankle musculoskeletal model with double MTUs.

Table 1. Musculoskeletal Geometric Parameters

Parameter Type	Parameter value	Source
thigh length L_{SHANK}	40 cm	[13]
length of PF insertion point from knee joint	0.125 L_{SHANK}	[13]
length of DF insertion point from knee joint	0.25 L_{SHANK}	[14]
PF moment-arm length L_{MA}^{PF}	56 mm	[15]
DF moment-arm length L_{MA}^{DF}	42 mm	[15]
PF moment-arm angle θ^{PF}	106°	[15]
DF moment-arm angle θ^{DF}	100°	[15]

Table 2. MTU Contraction dynamics parameters

Parameter type	Parameter value	Source
PF maximum muscle force F_{MAX}^{PF}	6420 N	[15]
DF maximum muscle force F_{MAX}^{DF}	1000 N	[14]
PF MTU slack length $L_{MTU_0}^{PF}$	366 mm	[15]
DF MTU slack length $L_{MTU_0}^{DF}$	304 mm	[15]
PF optimal CE length $L_{CE_0}^{PF}$	$0.108 L_{MTU_0}^{PF}$	[13]
DF optimal CE length $L_{CE_0}^{DF}$	$0.217 L_{MTU_0}^{DF}$	[14]
PF CE maximum velocity V_{CEMAX}^{PF}	$8.24\ L_{CE_0}^{PF}$	[14]
DF CE maximum velocity V_{CEMAX}^{DF}	$12\ L_{CE_0}^{DF}$	[14]
PF SEE linear stiffness $K_{SEE_0}^{PF}$	169 N/mm	[15]
DF SEE linear stiffness $K_{SEE_0}^{DF}$	32 N/mm	[15]

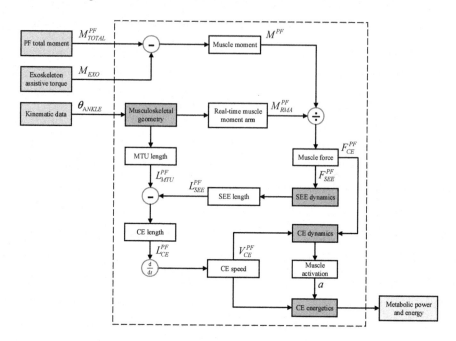

Fig. 3. The calculation framework for solving muscle metabolic cost

is discussed here, that is, where DF does not generate antagonistic force, the metabolic cost of DF is the same as when not wearing the exoskeleton. At this time, Eq. (6) is satisfied, and the PF muscle moment M^{PF} can be calculated by Eq. (7).

$$M_{EXO}(t) \leq M_{TOTAL}^{PF}(t) - M_{MIN}(t) \tag{6}$$

$$M^{PF}(t) = M_{TOTAL}^{PF}(t) - M_{EXO}(t) \tag{7}$$

where $M_{EXO}(t)$ is the assistive torque of exoskeleton at time t, $M_{MIN}(t)$ is the passive moment generated by MTU stretching as a passive elastomer when CE is not activated. Equations (1), (2) and (3) form an equation set, set $a = 0$ in Eq. (3) to get the PF muscle force, and then multiply it by the real-time muscle moment arm $L_{RMA}^{PF}(t)$ to obtain $M_{MIN}(t)$.

Then, import the ankle kinematics data within a gait cycle during normal walking [4] and calculate the other parameters according to the calculation framework. Finally metabolic power $P_{Met}(t)$ and metabolic cost W_{Met} can be obtained.

The effect of the exoskeleton assistive torque can be analyzed based on the above calculation results. Two types of assistive torque are used for comparison. One is based on a certain proportion of the original ankle moment, and the other is a optimal torque obtained by a genetic algorithm (GA).

3   Construction of the Genetic Algorithm

A standard GA is applied whose objective function is set to minimize W_{Met} of PF in the gait cycle. Import a certain type of exoskeleton assistive torque into the biomechanics model to obtain the corresponding metabolic cost of PF. DF is not involved in the GA because its metabolic cost is constant and will not cause overall changes.

The GA sets a total of four constraints. The first constraint is to ensure that the muscle moment is between 0 and the total PF muscle moment. The second constraint is to keep the exoskeleton output less than a certain ratio k of the peak amplitude of the total PF muscle moment. The third constraint is to ensure that the exoskeleton torque is not too large for DF to produce antagonistic torque increments and additional metabolic consumption. According to the simulation results of the proportional assistive torque, the assistance from the exoskeleton provides little metabolic benefits in the non-main gait phase (not the main phase of the muscle applying force, including the time before 10% and after 65% of gait cycle); hence the fourth constraint is to limit the exoskeleton to apply assistance in the non-main gait phase. The four constraints are shown in Eqs. (9), (10), (11), (12) and the optimization problem is as follows.

$$\min \quad W_{Met} = \int_{tp=0\%}^{tp=100\%} P_{Met}(t)dt \tag{8}$$

$$\text{s.t.} \quad 0 \le M^{PF}(t) \le M_{TOTAL}^{PF}(t) \tag{9}$$

$$M^{PF}(t) \ge M_{TOTAL}^{PF}(t) - \max_t(M_{TOTAL}^{PF}(t)) \times k \tag{10}$$

$$M^{PF}(t) \ge M_{MIN}(t) \tag{11}$$

$$M^{PF}(t) = M_{TOTAL}^{PF}(t), tp < 10\% \text{ or } tp > 65\% \tag{12}$$

The last three constraints have been transformed into a more uniform form by Eq. 7 so that all the constraints are about muscle moment. These constraints constitute the upper bound Ub and the lower bound Lb of $M^{PF}(t)$. By setting a coefficient $x(t)$ with values from 0 to 1, $M^{PF}(t)$ can be expressed as follow:

$$M^{PF}(t) = Lb + (Ub - Lb)x(t), 0 \le x(t) \le 1 \tag{13}$$

A set of $x(t)$ of the gait cycle represents a muscle moment profile as well as an individual in the GA. Each individual can find the corresponding metabolic cost under the current assistance condition by the biomechanical model. The GA can make the population composed of individuals continue to iterate, to obtain the muscle moment profile satisfying the objective function. Then, by subtracting $M^{PF}(t)$ from the total moment of the ankle joint, the optimal theoretical exoskeleton assistive torque can be obtained.

The time in the gait cycle is divided by 1% from 0% to 100% discretely, so every $x(t)$ has a total of 101 values. With such a considerable number of values, the convergence speed of $x(t)$ is too slow and the optimization results can easily fall into the local optimum. Experimentally, it is found that smoother profiles have better performance in convergence and result values, inspiring that the randomly generated torque profile itself should have a certain degree of smoothness. It helps reduce the possibility of amplitude oscillation to avoid meaningless local optimum. Therefore, the algorithm is improved on this idea: part of the value of $x(t)$ is still randomly generated from 0 to 1, and the other part is obtained by interpolation based on these values. In actual operation, only every third value of $x(t)$ is random. It smooths the profile initially. Then after computing $M^{PF}(t)$, a least square filter smoothing is performed to smooth the profile further.

4   Results

Three corresponding optimal exoskeleton assistive torques are obtained by using the GA under the conditions of setting different upper limit ratios, that is,

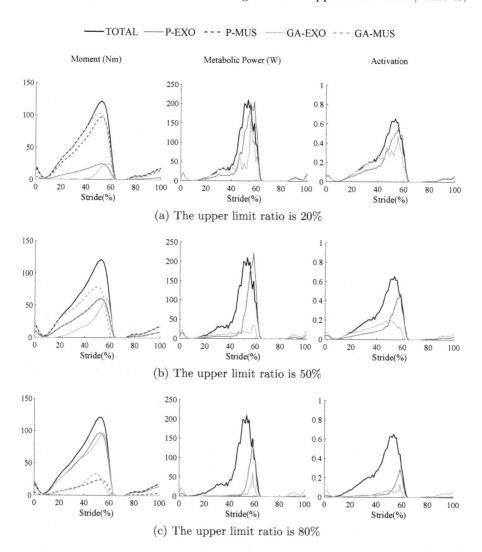

Fig. 4. Exoskeleton assistive torque, muscle activation and metabolic power

whose maximum amplitude are 20%, 50%, and 80% of the total PF moment's. The optimal torques are compared with the proportional torques equal to 20%, 50%, and 80% of the total PF moment. The results are as follows.

4.1   Exoskeleton Assistive Torque and Muscle Moment

The exoskeleton assistive torque and the muscle moment is shown in Fig. 4. Compared with the proportional torque, the optimal torque obtained by GA has some counter-intuitive features: first, the maximum torque values does not appear at the same time as the total moment's, but slightly delayed; second, in the rising phase of the torque profile (approximately from 10% to 53% of the gait cycle), the amplitude of optimal torque is smaller than the amplitude of proportional torque, while in the decreasing phase (approximately from 53% to 65% of the gait cycle) the optimal torque amplitude is larger. These features of the optimal torque are particularly evident when the upper limit ratio is small.

4.2   Muscle Activation, Metabolic Power and Metabolic Cost

The results of muscle activation and metabolic power are shown in Fig. 4. They present the following characteristics after applying the optimal torque: first, both of their peak amplitude are reduced and their phase are advanced; second, the muscle activation is higher in the rising phase of the torque profile and lower in the decreasing phase compared to applying the proportional torque; third, the decrease rate of metabolic power is larger than that of activation, which means PF works relatively inefficiently during 50% to 65% of the gait cycle, so a relatively small increase in activation level results in a large difference in metabolic power.

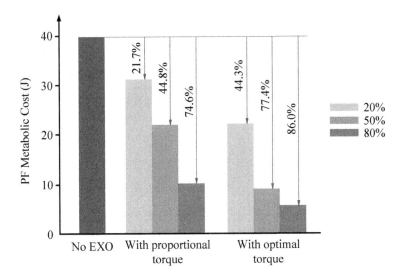

Fig. 5. The metabolic cost under different conditions of upper limit ratio

The metabolic cost under different conditions are shown in the Fig. 5. It can be seen that the optimal torque has the better potential to reduce metabolism.

4.3   Effects of Muscle Length and Speed on Active Muscle Force

The active muscle force coefficient of muscle length $\tilde{f}^a_{CE}(\tilde{L}_{CE})$ and active muscle force coefficient of muscle speed $\tilde{f}_{CE}(\tilde{V}_{CE})$ reflect the difficulty of active muscle force generation at different muscle lengths and muscle speeds. A larger coefficient value means it is easier to generate muscle force while it requires less muscle activation. $\tilde{f}^a_{CE}(\tilde{L}_{CE})$ and $\tilde{f}_{CE}(\tilde{V}_{CE})$, and Their independent variables $\tilde{L}_{CE}$ and $\tilde{V}_{CE}$ are shown in Fig. 6.

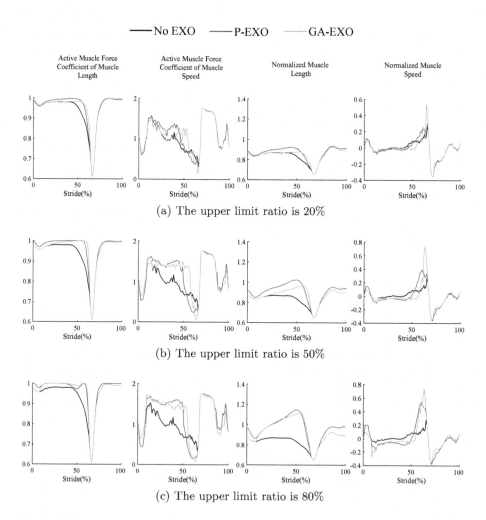

Fig. 6. Active muscle force coefficient of muscle length, active muscle force coefficient of muscle speed, normalized muscle length and normalized muscle speed

The main difference between the effects of the proportional torque and the optimal torque is the improvement of muscle speed. During most of the 50% to 60% of the gait cycle, $\tilde{V}_{CE}$ when applying the optimal torque is smaller than that when applying the proportional torque, indicating that the muscle contracts more slowly and thus leading to larger $\tilde{f}_{CE}(\tilde{V}_{CE})$ values. At the end of the main gait phase, there is an explosive increase in muscle speed, which is greater when the optimal torque is applied. It would greatly aggravate the difficulty of muscle exerting force, but as can be seen from Fig. 4, the muscle no longer needs to generate muscle torque at this time. The muscle is just passively shortened and hardly generates muscle force or consumes energy.

5   Discussion

From the above analysis of the results, it can be seen that at the latter part of the main gait phase, the muscle efficiency of PF decreases sharply. It is worth noting that this symptom exists in the original state of the human body, and it is more apparent when wearing exoskeleton.

The reasons for the counter-intuitive features of optimal torque may be inferred. Due to the decrease of the muscle efficiency, applying as much assistance as possible can minimize the additional metabolic consumption caused by inefficiency. Therefore, the optimal torque presents the characteristics of peak amplitude delayed so that it can match the timing of the muscle efficiency decrease. Although the muscle is more inefficient after the assistance completed, the muscle no longer needs to work, so it does not cause any adverse effects. In the same way, the changes in muscle length and speed in the earlier phase should be as small as possible to keep the muscle efficiency, which is the reason why the amplitude of the optimal torque is less than that of the proportional torque during this phase: the changes in muscle length and speed can be inhibited better.

These two special characteristics of the optimal torque make it more in line with the requirement to reduce the metabolic consumption of ankle during walking, thus two essential principles of ankle exoskeleton development can be drawn: the first is to minimize the workload of the ankle muscles during the main gait phase, especially when it is close to the toe-off time; the second is to adjust the muscle contraction reasonably to make changes in length and speed smoother.

Predictably, it will not be the best exoskeleton assistive torque for practical applications in quantitative terms, because the kinematics and dynamics of the human body in actual situations will change to a certain extent, and the muscle activation has memory and is not as intelligent as the theoretical model in receiving external assistance. However, it does not mean that the simulation conclusions should not be used in practice. The property of optimal torque has a key guiding significance for tuning the exoskeleton. The changes in kinematics and dynamics as well as the adaptability of the human body to external load or assistance should be fully considered.

Acknowledgment. The authors would like to gratefully acknowledge the reviewers' comments. This work is supported by the National Natural Science Foundation of

China (Grant Nos. U1713207), Science and Technology Planning Project of Guangdong Province (2017A010102005), Key Program of Guangzhou Technology Plan (Grant No. 201904020020).

References

1. Cornwall, W.: In pursuit of the perfect power suit. Science **350**(6258), 270–273 (2015)
2. Lee, S., et al.: Autonomous multi-joint soft exosuit for assistance with walking overground. In: 2018 IEEE International Conference on Robotics and Automation (ICRA), pp. 2812–2819. IEEE (2018)
3. Wehner, M., et al.: A lightweight soft exosuit for gait assistance. In: 2013 IEEE International Conference on Robotics and Automation, pp. 3362–3369. IEEE (2013)
4. Collins, S.H., Wiggin, M.B., Sawicki, G.S.: Reducing the energy cost of human walking using an unpowered exoskeleton. Nature **522**(7555), 212 (2015)
5. Asbeck, A.T., Dyer, R.J., Larusson, A.F., Walsh, C.J.: Biologically-inspired soft exosuit. In: 2013 IEEE 13th International Conference on Rehabilitation Robotics (ICORR), pp. 1–8. IEEE (2013)
6. Mooney, L.M., Rouse, E.J., Herr, H.M.: Autonomous exoskeleton reduces metabolic cost of human walking during load carriage. J. Neuroeng. Rehabil. **11**(1), 80 (2014)
7. Lee, S., Crea, S., Malcolm, P., Galiana, I., Asbeck, A., Walsh, C.: Controlling negative and positive power at the ankle with a soft exosuit. In: 2016 IEEE International Conference on Robotics and Automation (ICRA), pp. 3509–3515. IEEE (2016)
8. Quinlivan, B., Lee, S., Malcolm, P., Rossi, D., Grimmer, M., Siviy, C., Karavas, N., Wagner, D., Asbeck, A., Galiana, I., et al.: Assistance magnitude versus metabolic cost reductions for a tethered multiarticular soft exosuit. Sci. Robot. **2**(2), 1–10 (2017)
9. Zhang, J., Fiers, P., Witte, K.A., Jackson, R.W., Poggensee, K.L., Atkeson, C.G., Collins, S.H.: Human-in-the-loop optimization of exoskeleton assistance during walking. Science **356**(6344), 1280–1284 (2017)
10. Kuo, A.D.: Energetics of actively powered locomotion using the simplest walking model. J. Biomech. Eng. **124**(1), 113–120 (2002)
11. Zelik, K.E., Huang, T.W.P., Adamczyk, P.G., Kuo, A.D.: The role of series ankle elasticity in bipedal walking. J. Theor. Biol. **346**, 75–85 (2014)
12. Zajac, F.E.: Muscle and tendon: properties, models, scaling, and application to biomechanics and motor control. Crit. Rev. Biomed. Eng. **17**(4), 359–411 (1989)
13. Sawicki, G.S., Khan, N.S.: A simple model to estimate plantarflexor muscle-tendon mechanics and energetics during walking with elastic ankle exoskeletons. IEEE Trans. Biomed. Eng. **63**(5), 914–923 (2016)
14. Minetti, A., Alexander, R.M.: A theory of metabolic costs for bipedal gaits. J. Theor. Biol. **186**(4), 467–476 (1997)
15. Wang, N., Zhong, Y., Zhang, X.: An improved model to estimate muscle-tendon mechanics and energetics during walking with a passive ankle exoskeleton. In: Yu, H., Liu, J., Liu, L., Ju, Z., Liu, Y., Zhou, D. (eds.) ICIRA 2019. LNCS (LNAI), vol. 11740, pp. 83–96. Springer, Cham (2019). https://doi.org/10.1007/978-3-030-27526-6_8

Hybrid System Modeling
and Human-Machine Interface

Augmented Assembly Work Instruction Knowledge Graph for Adaptive Presentation

Wang Li, Junfeng Wang$^{(\boxtimes)}$, Sichen Jiao, and Maoding Liu

School of Mechanical Science and Engineering, Huazhong
University of Science and Technology, Wuhan, China
wangjf@hust.edu.cn

Abstract. The application of Augmented Reality (AR) that present work instruction through visual elements for assembly operation can effectively reduce the cognitive load of operators. Among challenges that prevent AR systems from being widely used in complex assembly operations, the lack of augmented work instruction (AWI) adaptive presentation is an important aspect. This paper propose an augmented assembly work instruction knowledge graph (AWI-KG) for adaptive presentation to solve the problem. The characteristics of AWI are analyzed to abstract the concepts and relationships for domain ontology constructing. And using the domain ontology to extract the entities in assembly manual to establish the AWI-KG. Then, a collaborative filtering method based on AWI-KG is proposed. The multidimensional vectors are used to calculate the adaptive presentation mode for AWI according to the operator's capabilities. The proposed method was applied in an AR system. The results show that the recommended visual elements can effectively adapt to the operator's capabilities.

Keywords: Augmented assembly · Work instruction · Knowledge graph · Adaptive presentation

1 Introduction

With the development of intelligent manufacturing technology of Industry 4.0, automated production has significantly reduced the demand of human assembly. However, for complex and small amount products, human still occupies an important position [1]. In the process of manual assembly, the operator often undertakes the multiple processes assembly task which contains complex assembly work instructions. Traditional human operation adopts technical manual for assembly guidance, and the operator have to understand the content by information extraction and transform. The whole process requires higher memory and cognitive ability of people, and the understanding levels is greatly affected by subjective factors [2]. Augmented Reality (AR) uses computers to superimpose virtual information and model into real scenes for human. The usage of AR to guide assembly operation can effectively reduce the operator's cognitive load and improve their work efficiency [3].

In the past decades, more and more scholars begin to study the augmented assembly, and have achieved positive research results. For instance, Wang et al. [4] presented

© Springer Nature Switzerland AG 2021
X.-J. Liu et al. (Eds.): ICIRA 2021, LNAI 13013, pp. 793–803, 2021.
https://doi.org/10.1007/978-3-030-89095-7_75

an AR system for assembly planning and simulation. By using interaction with both real and virtual components in AR environment, the user can assess the difficulty level of assembly operation. Cardoso et al. [5] developed a markless augmented system for mobile devices, and the AR system is applied in aeronautical structural brackets assembly for outlines calibration. Compared with traditional manual operation, the AR system can simplify the operation process and reduce the assembly difficulty.

Despite the recently advance, visual elements adaptive presentation still prevent AR systems from being widely used. Adaptive presentation refers to the dynamic adjustment of visual elements according to operator's capability and operation state for AWIs during augmented assembly process. Perhaps, adaptive presentation also known as context-relevant presentation, scalability, applicability, context-aware, flexibility in literature [6].

2   Related Work

KG is a structured semantic network which is used to symbolically describe the concepts and the relationships in the real world. Due to the ability of efficient organization, presentation and knowledge reasoning for massive and heterogeneous data, KGs have been widely used in intelligent search, intelligent question and answer, personalized recommendation, intelligent manufacturing, etc. In terms of the coverage, KGs are divided into two categories, generalized KGs and dedicated KGs [7]. Generalized KGs contain a broad range of knowledge in the open world and provide the user with common-sense knowledge, such as Freebase [8], and DBkWik [9]. The knowledge of dedicated KGs covers a limited area and is used to provide precise guidance in the professional domain. The AWI-KG is one of the dedicated KG.

The research on assembly work instruction KG starts from the construction of ontology model [10], which is used to normalize the concepts and relationships for knowledge. Barbau et al. [11] translated work instruction information in product lifecycle to Ontology Web Language (OWL), and established OntoSTEP ontology model with rich semantic expression. Huang et al. [12] modeled the domain knowledge in assembly process and proposed an assembly work instruction knowledge ontology model which contain assembly requirement, spatial information, assembly operation and assembly resource. On the basis of the ontology, He et al. [13] constructed an ontology-based Manufacturing Knowledge Graph (MKG) to integrate the complex work instruction in production processes. The MKG is used to answer production problems and recommend the most relevant knowledge and tools driven by the problem. Kwon et al. [14] proposed a fusion design and inspection data KG. They use semantic web technologies to represent different work instruction data in a homogeneous manner for making better decisions. Chen et al. [15] proposed an assembly information model based on knowledge graph (KGAM) to improve the information interaction efficiency in the development phase of assembly process.

3   Augmented Assembly Work Instruction Knowledge Graph

3.1   Knowledge Structure for Augmented Assembly

Assembly manual express the assembly process information by text and chart description. The operator have to transform the description information into action for assembly operation through the cognitive process which is time-consuming. Augmented assembly can express the information in digital 3D space and real physical space by fusing virtual models with real scenes, which can improve the guidance efficiency for assembly operations. In augmented assembly, the knowledge structure is shown in Fig. 1.

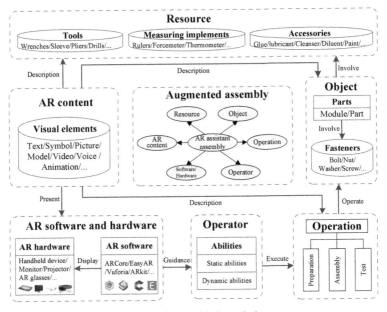

Fig. 1. Augmented assembly knowledge structure.

The knowledge elements in augmented assembly mainly include AR content, assembly object, assembly resource, operation, operator and AR software/hardware. During augmented assembly process, AR contents are used to describe the assembly object, operation category and the requirement resources. Operator finished the assembly operation according to the AR contents that presented in AR display device. For AWI design, we mainly considered the interrelationship among operation, object and resource in virtual and real fusion environment to express the assembly work instruction information. Operation refers to the assembly operation which is divided according to different action sequences. Object refers to physical and virtual parts for assembly operation in augmented assembly. Resource refers to other resources information which is involved in the assembly process.

3.2 AWI Ontology

Ontology belongs to the conceptual layer of KGs, and it can be used to define the concepts to constrain and describe various elements in KGs. By defining different categories ontology concepts for AWI, the correctness of inherent logic for AWI-KG can be guaranteed. The basic goal of AWI domain ontology construction is to implement a standardized description of the concepts and relationships for operation, object and resource in a formal language. AWI domain ontology will serve as the basis for knowledge extraction and AWI-KG establishment. The definition of AWI domain ontology in this paper is as follows:

Definition 3.1 AWI domain ontology. The AWI domain ontology can be expressed as: AWIO = {OP, OB, RE, RL}. Where OP is the concept of operation ontology, OB is the concept of object ontology, RE is the concept of resource ontology, RL is the relationship set of different ontology concept.

Operation ontology is the most important part of AWI. The action sequence of assembly operation should to be abstracted and redefined for AR expression, so that the operator can easily understand them. The operation ontology is defined as follows:

Definition 3.2 Operation ontology. AR operation ontology can be expressed as: OP = {COP, ROP, AOP}. Where COP is the set of ontology concepts for OP, ROP is the relationship set of different OP, AOP represents the attributes set of OP.

OP is divided by the action sequence in assembly operation for easily understanding. Each individual action sequence is regarded as an ontology concept in OP. The concepts in OP are classified according to the stages in assembly process. The assembly process are divided into preparation, assembly and test. And the class information is stored in AOP as the attribute information for ontology. The ontology concepts in the preparation stage mainly includes deburring, wiping, scribing, coating, locking, lubricating, heating, cooling, etc. Assembly stage mainly includes screwing, pressing, inserting, repairing, aligning, placeing, knocking, etc. Test stage mainly includes removing, cleaning, checking, calibrating, etc. Protégé is used to construct the OP model with OWL language, and the concepts relationship of OP are obtained as shown in Fig. 2.

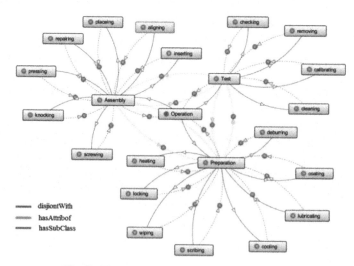

Fig. 2. The relationship between concepts in OP.

Object is physical and virtual parts for assembly operation. In the process of augmented assembly, the object ontology concepts needs to be standardized and managed to explicit AWI operation object. The object ontology is defined as follows:

Definition 3.3 Object ontology. Object ontology can be expressed as: OB = {COB, ROB, AOB}. Where COB is the set of ontology concepts for OB, ROB is the relationship set of different OB, AOB represents the attributes set of OB.

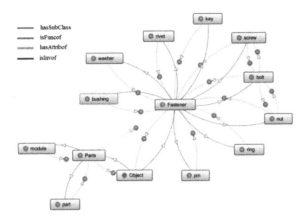

Fig. 3. The relationship between concepts in OB.

For operator easily understanding, only single part or module with connecting pieces is considered in single operation step during augmented assembly process. According to the dependency of the current operating object, the concepts in OB are divided into parts and fastener, and the class information is stored in AOB. Parts refers to the assembly object that mainly include part and module. The fastener refers to the connecting pieces for direct part, such as bolts, nuts, washers, etc. The concepts relationship of OB are shown in Fig. 3.

In order to complete an assembly operation, a series of assembly resources are needed to ensure the successful implementation of the operation process. There are many kinds of assembly resources involved in the augmented assembly. The normative definition and management of resource ontology concepts are conducive to clarifying the logical relationship between different resources. The resource ontology is defined as follows:

Definition 3.4 Resource ontology. resource ontology can be expressed as: RE = {CRE, RRE, ARE}. Where CRE is the set of ontology concepts for RE, RRE is the relationship set of different RE, ARE represents the attributes set of RE.

RE is used to assist the assembly objects installation. According to the function of resource, the ontology concepts in RE are divided as four categories: assembling tool, measuring tool, assembly accessories and technical knowledge. The ontology concept in assembling tool mainly includes: wrenches, sleeve, pliers, drills, hammer, rope, saw, etc. Measuring tool mainly includes: rulers, forcemeter, thermometer, thickness meter, inclinometer, noise meter, etc. Assembly accessories mainly includes: glue, lubricant, welding material, cleanser, diluent, paint, etc. Technical knowledge mainly includes: quality requirements, technical requirements, technological parameter, detecting parameter, etc. The concepts relationship of RE are shown in Fig. 4.

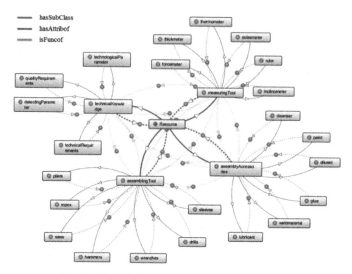

Fig. 4. The relationship between concepts in RE.

There are many kinds of concepts in AWI domain ontology with complex association relationships. Normalized definition of relationships between different ontology concepts can combine different ontology for knowledge expression. The concept relationships in AWI domain ontology are defined as follows:

Definition 3.5 Concept relationship. The concept relationships in AWI domain ontology can be expressed as: RL = {ID, ATP, ADS}, Where ID is the identifier of the relationship, ATP represents the semantic definition symbol of the relationship, and ADS is the description of the relationship.

By extracting the relationships from concepts in AWI, the relationships in AWI domain ontology can be established. The commonly used relationships in AWI domain ontology are shown in Table 1. For more complex relationships, the relationship types can be added in practical applications.

Table 1. The commonly used relationships in AWI domain ontology

ID	ATP	ADS	Examples
1	hasSubClass	A have subclass B	directpart<hasSubClass>nut
2	hasAttribof	A has attribute of B	part<hasAttribof>directpart
3	disjiontWith	AB mutual repulsion	heating<disjiontWith>knocking
4	isFuncof	AB simultaneously appear	nut<isFuncof>wrenches
5	isInvof	A involved with B	directpart<isInvof>indirectpart

3.3 AWI-KG Information Extractions

A complete KG is consisted by conceptual layer and data layer. Through the construction of AWI domain ontology in the previous section, the conceptual layer of AWI-KG was built. To complete the AWI-KG, it is necessary to extract knowledge from data sources to fill the AWI domain ontology as KG data layer.

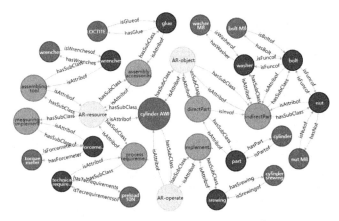

Fig. 5. AWI-KG local entities relationships diagram.

AWI-KG has a large number of entities. And the relationships between different entities are complex and changeable. When there are new entities and relationships, AWI-KG needs to be updated. To meet the above requirements, Neo4j graph database is adopted to store the data in AWI-KG. According to the AWI ontology, all entities data obtained from assembly manual are filled in the Neo4j to complete the AWI-KG. Taking cylinder assembly as an example, different entities and relationships in AWI-KG are shown in Fig. 5.

4   AWI Adaptive Presentation

In augmented assembly, AWI data come from the assembly manual. And the AWIs are presented by AR visual elements to guide operators for assembly operations. We define the combination of different visual elements categories as presentation mode. For AWI adaptive presentation according to the operator's capabilities, the presentation mode recommendation method is proposed in this paper. The method consists of two stages: offline and online as show in Fig. 6.

In offline stage, data collection and processing are completed. There are AWI-KG data and history operation data. For AWI-KG data collection, the augmented assembly domain ontology should be built. Knowledge extraction is carried out by the domain ontology to extract the entity data in assembly manual. The extracted entity data are stored in the Neo4j as knowledge triple to establish the AWI-KG.

In online stage, it mainly realized presentation mode adaptive recommendation according to current operator information. The operator similarity matrix is used to

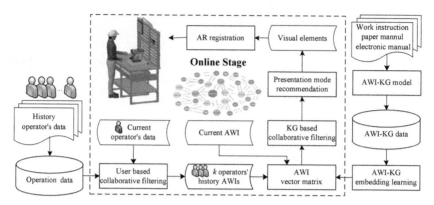

Fig. 6. Framework of AWI adaptive presentation.

find the adjacent k operators. The presentation modes of k operators for history AWIs in operation data set are chosen as the potential options for current operator. Then, the AWI similarity matrix is used to calculate the similarity between current AWI and history AWIs to find the best presentation mode in potential options as the recommendation result.

5 Case Study

The proposed method is applied in an augmented assembly work station and the assembly of engine is taken as an example. The work station is shown in the left of Fig. 7. The workbench can be rotated around the intermediate axis to facilitate the assembly of parts in different directions. Four different artificial markers are set at the four corners of the workbench for the AR registration.

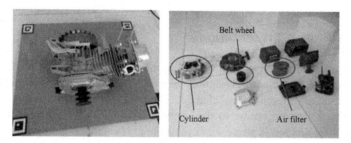

Fig. 7. Engine augmented assembly scene.

The AWIs for cylinder was chosen as the test case. The assembly object is shown in the right of Fig. 7. The AWI is screwing in OP ontology; parts, bolt, nut and washer entities in OB ontology; glue and technical requirements entities in RE ontology. These entities are representative for AWI domain ontology. The capabilities information of operators for the test case are show in Table 2. Before the start of augmented assembly, operator is required to input their capability information into the AR system. The presentation modes are recommended according to the capabilities information of the three operators.

Table 2. The capability information of operators for test case.

Operator	Gender	Age	Background	Operation quantity	Assembly error
Operator A	Male	32	Mechanical	10	0%
Operator B	Male	24	Mechanical	2	20%
Operator C	Femal	20	Industrial design	0	100%

1) Cylinder screwing.

The AWI of cylinder screwing is used to guide operator for cylinder assembly on the engine. The objects involved in this assembly operation mainly include Cylinder, Bolt M8, Washer M8, Open-end Wrench 14, and threadlocker LOC-TITE234. Using CylinderA1 as the AWI's entity symbols, the triples in AWI-KG mainly include: <CylinderA1, hasScrewing, cylinderScrewing>, <CylinderA1, hasPart, Cylinder>, <CylinderA1, hasBolt, Bolt M8>, <CylinderA1, hasWasher, Washer M8>, <CylinderA1, hasWrench, Open-end Wrench 14>, <CylinderA1, hasGlue, LOCTITE234>, <CylinderA1, hasTecrequirements, preload 10N>.

During augmented assembly process, the assembly task CylinderA1 and operators' capabilities information are put into the AR system. The adaptive presentation modes that recommended by the proposed method are shown in Fig. 8. The recommended presentation mode for operator A is show in Fig. 8(a). And for operator B and C are Fig. 8(b) and Fig. 8(c). The presentation mode in Fig. 8(a) only contains text to remind the cylinder screwing operation. The presentation mode in Fig. 8(b) is composed by text and symbols. The symbol is used to remind the operator for the assembly object and assembly location. The presentation mode in Fig. 8(c) contains text, picture and animation. The information of threadlocker LOCTITE234 is express by picture. The assembly information of Cylinder, Bolt, Washer and Open-end Wrench is present by animation.

Fig. 8. Cylinder screwing AR guidance.

6 Conclusion

In this paper, a visual elements adaptive presentation method for augmented assembly systems based on KG is proposed. AWI-KG for work instructions in augmented assembly was built. The AWI domain ontology was established as the conceptual layer of AWI-KG by using ontology to extract concepts and relationships in assembly work instructions. Using AWI domain ontology, the entities were extracted from the traditional assembly manuals as the data layer of AWI-KG. Adaptive presentation recommendations for different operators and AWIs were realized by fusing collaborative filtering and KG.In the future, a more adaptable operation data can be established, and more factors for operators can be considered to further improve the adaptability and accuracy of the adaptive presentation.

Acknowledgments. This research is supported by the Defense Industrial Technology Development Program of China (JCKY2016204A502).

References

1. Zubizarreta, J., Aguinaga, I., Amundarain, A.: A framework for augmented reality guidance in industry. Int. J. Adv. Manuf. Technol. **102**, 4095–4108 (2019). https://doi.org/10.1007/s00 170-019-03527-2
2. Danielsson, O., Syberfeldt, A., Holm, M., et al.: Operators perspective on augmented reality as a support tool in engine assembly. Procedia CIRP **72**(1), 45–50 (2018)
3. Tani, E., Vignali, G.: Augmented reality technology in the manufacturing industry: a review of the last decade. IISE Trans. **51**, 284–310 (2019)
4. Wang, X., Ong, S.K., Nee, A.Y.C.: Real-virtual components interaction for assembly simulation and planning. Robot. Comput.-Integr. Manuf. **41**, 102–114 (2016)
5. Cardoso, L.F.D., Mariano, F.C.M.Q., Zorzal, E.R.: Mobile augmented reality to support fuselage assembly. Comput. Ind. Eng. **148**, 106712 (2020)
6. Gattullo, M., Evangelista, A., Manghisi, V.M.: Towards next generation technical documentation in augmented reality using a context-aware information manager. Appl. Sci.-Basel **10**(3), 780 (2020)
7. Yan, H., Yang, J., Wan, J.: KnowIME: a system to construct a knowledge graph for intelligent manufacturing equipment. IEEE Access **8**, 41805–41813 (2020)
8. Bollacker, K., Cook, R., Tufts, P.: Freebase: a shared database of structured general human knowledge. In: AAAI Conference on Artificial Intelligence. DBLP (2007)
9. Hertling, S., Paulheim, H.: DBkWik: extracting and integrating knowledge from thousands of Wikis. Knowl. Inf. Syst. **62**, 2169–2190 (2020)
10. Imran, M., Young, B.: The application of common logic based formal ontologies to assembly knowledge sharing. J. Intell. Manuf. **26**(1), 139–158 (2015)
11. Barbau, R., Krima, S., Rachuri, S., et al.: OntoSTEP: enriching product model data using ontologies. Comput. Aided Des. **44**(6), 575–590 (2012)
12. Huang, Z., Qiao, L., Answer, N., et al.: Ontology model for assembly process planning knowledge. In: Proceedings of the 21st International Conference on Industrial Engineering and Engineering Management (2014)
13. He, L., Jiang, P.: Manufacturing knowledge graph: a connectivism to answer production problems query with knowledge reuse. IEEE Access **99**, 1 (2019)

14. Kwon, S., Monnier, L.V., Barbau, R., et al.: Enriching standards-based digital thread by fusing as-designed and as-inspected data using knowledge graphs. Adv. Eng. Inform. **46**, 101102 (2020)
15. Chen, Z., Bao, J., Zheng, X., et al.: An assembly information model based on knowledge graph. J. Shanghai Jiaotong Univ. (Sci.) **5**, 578–588 (2020)

Study of Muscular Fatigue Effect on Human-Machine Interface Using Electromyography and Near-Infrared Spectroscopy

Weichao Guo, Xinjun Sheng$^{(\boxtimes)}$, and Xiangyang Zhu

State Key Laboratory of Mechanical System and Vibration, School of Mechanical Engineering, Shanghai Jiao Tong University, Shanghai 200240, People's Republic of China
xjsheng@sjtu.edu.cn

Abstract. It is evident that surface electromyography (EMG) based human-machine interface (HMI) is limited by muscle fatigue. This paper investigated the effect of muscular fatigue on HMI performance using hybrid EMG and near-infrared spectroscopy (NIRS). Muscle fatigue inducing experiments were performed with eight subjects via sustained isometric contraction. Four fatigue metrics extracted from EMG and NIRS signals were evaluated during fatigue process. Utilizing the time-varying characteristic of fatigue metrics and their relations, modified features were proposed to dampen the effect of muscle fatigue. The experimental results showed that modified features extracted from combined EMG and NIRS could overcome the impact of muscle fatigue on classification performance to a certain extent, although this slight compensation was still inadequate. It thus suggested that, to minimize the muscle fatigue effect on HMI, high-intensitive sustained muscle contraction should be avoided in HMI usage.

Keywords: Surface EMG · NIRS · Human-machine interface · Muscle fatigue

1 Introduction

Human-machine interface (HMI) attracting extensive attention is an effective technique to enhance the capability of human beings, especially improving the life quality of the elderly and disabled. Surface electromyography (EMG) is widely used as intuitive HMI to control prostheses [1], rehabilitation robots [2], wheelchairs [3] and powered exoskeletons [4,5]. However, myoelectric control is limited by muscle fatigue, which mainly manifests performance degeneration due to signal variations resulting from sustained muscle contraction [6–9].

To overcome the weakness of EMG based approach caused by muscle fatigue, D. Tkach *et al.* [6] enhanced the pattern classification performance by selecting

© Springer Nature Switzerland AG 2021
X.-J. Liu et al. (Eds.): ICIRA 2021, LNAI 13013, pp. 804–812, 2021.
https://doi.org/10.1007/978-3-030-89095-7_76

appropriate feature combinations although the fatigue influence could not be fully solved. J.-H. Song *et al.* [10] proposed a robust classifier using adaptive learning algorithm of Fuzzy Min-Max Neural Network (FMMNN). This method was able to improve the pattern classification accuracy for wheelchair control during sustained muscle contraction. However, the supervised adaptive learning of FMMNN needed a long time for re-adjustment and was grounded on specific assumptions, its generalization ability was thus restricted. Up to present, it was still an open issue to overcome fatigue impact on myoelectric interface. Moreover, the effect mechanism of muscular fatigue on HMI performance has rarely been evaluated. It is widely accepted that near-infrared spectroscopy (NIRS) can measure muscle oxidative metabolism and hemodynamics, providing insightful muscle fatigue information [11,12]. The purpose of this study is to investigate the fatigue effect on HMI using hybrid EMG and NIRS, and to compensate the influence of muscle fatigue as much as possible.

In this paper, muscle fatigue inducing experiments were performed, during which EMG and NIRS signals were acquired by using hybrid sensors. The fatigue process was evaluated with four fatigue metrics extracted from simultaneous EMG and NIRS signals. Based on the correlation analysis among fatigue metrics, features for pattern classification were modified to compensate the impact of muscular fatigue. The relation analysis between the variation of fatigue metrics and the deterioration of classification accuracy indicated the effect mechanism of muscle fatigue on HMI performance.

2   Experiment and Signal Processing

2.1   Experimental Paradigm

Eight male able-bodied subjects were recruited to take part in the fatigue inducing experiments. This study was approved by the Ethics Committee of Shanghai Jiao Tong University. Before the experiment, all the subjects had signed the informed consents. The experimental procedure was in accord with the declaration of Helsinki. For every subject, two hybrid EMG/NIRS sensors [13] were attached on Flexor Digitorum Superficialis (FDS) and Extensor Digitorum (ED) muscles respectively (Fig. 1 (a)), after skin cleaning with alcohol. These two muscles were anatomically associated with finger movements. The subjects were asked to relax their arms naturally during the experiment, and maximal voluntary contraction (MVC) force of four hand movements was measured and defined for each subject. The four hand movements were power grasp, tip prehension, lateral prehension and four-finger prehension grip, as shown in Fig. 1 (b). The contraction force was measured with dynamometers (Biometrics Ltd, UK). The contraction force value was real-timely displayed on a computer screen in front of the subject to provide visual feedback.

The experiment included three sequential sessions: unfatigued session, fatigue inducing session and fatigued session. During the unfatigued session, the subjects were instructed to perform five movements (Fig. 1 (b)) under 50% MVC for eight trials, each movement was asked to hold for 5 s in each trial. Subsequently, the

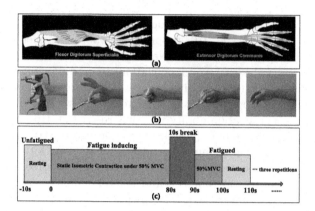

Fig. 1. Experiment setup: (a) sensor locations on targeted muscles; (b) involved hand movements, they are power grasp, tip prehension, lateral prehension, four-finger prehension grip and rest, respectively; (c) protocol of fatigue inducing session and fatigued session via sustained isometric contraction at 50% of MVC force.

fatigue inducing session was begun with 10 s rest to record baseline data, and then the subjects performed 50% MVC of one randomly selected hand movement for 80 s to induce short-term muscular fatigue. After 10 s rest, fatigued session was performed immediately. The subject was asked to perform 50% MVC of the same movement for four repetitions with the short-term fatigued muscle (Fig. 1 (c)). The protocol in Fig. 1 (c) was defined as a trial, and two trials were carried out for each movement. There was 5–10 min' break between two adjacent trials to recover from the short-term fatigue. During the whole experiment, EMG and NIRS signals were acquired simultaneously using a hybrid sensor system [13]. The EMG signal was band-pass filtered at $20-450\,Hz$ and the NIRS signal was low-pass filtered $300\,Hz$. The sampling rate of EMG and NIRS signals was set $1000\,Hz$. The wavelength of three near-infrared light emitted by the NIRS sensor was $730\,nm$, $805\,nm$ and $850\,nm$, respectively.

2.2   Signal Processing

To comprehensively assess muscle fatigue, four fatigue metrics were derived from raw EMG and NIRS signals: root mean square (RMS) and median frequency (MDF) of EMG, blood volume (BV) and muscle oxygenation ($\triangle HbO_2$) extracted from NIRS, as reported by our previous study [14]. The four fatigue metrics were calculated every 5 s during the fatigue inducing and fatigued sessions. To evaluate the variations of fatigue metrics, one way ANOVA was performed between the first 5 s and the remaining sustained muscle contraction, and statistical significance level was set at $p < 0.05$. Furthermore, correlation and linear regression analysis among fatigue metrics were performed to gain a better understanding and interpretation of muscle fatigue. Note that, the typical data used for analysis were from the ED muscle of power grasp movement.

Subsequently, the EMG and NIRS signals were segmented into a series of 300 ms windows with an increment of 100 ms. Four feature sets were extracted from these sliding windows for pattern recognition to evaluated the HMI performance, namely, time domain (TD) information, modified time domain (MOD-TD) information, concatenation of TD and MDF (TFD), modified TFD (MOD-TFD). The TD feature set included mean absolute value (MAV), zero crossings (ZC), slope sign changes (SSC) and waveform length (WL) of EMG signal [15]. The MOD-TD feature set was derived from TD set by multiplying its feature vectors with MDF. Additionally, the MOD-TFD feature set was the concatenation of MOD-TFD and MDF multiplied by BV. Linear discriminant analysis (LDA) classifier was used to measure the classification accuracy of different feature sets. Half of the data from unfatigued session were used to train the LDA classifier and the remaining data were used as unseen testing set.

3 Experiment Results and Analysis

3.1 Variations of Fatigue Metrics During and After Fatigue

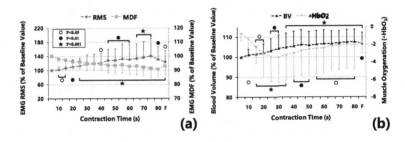

Fig. 2. Variations of the fatigue metrics during and after muscular fatigue: (a) RMS and MDF of EMG; (c) blood volume (BV) and concentration change of HbO$_2$ derived from NIRS. The reported values are averaged [mean±std] across all subjects. Note that, different significant levels are marked with specific symbols.

The fatigue metrics variations of fatigue inducing session and fatigued session across all subjects were illustrated as Fig. 2. During the fatigue inducing session, the RMS of EMG manifested a increasing trend, which was consistent with previous reports [11,16,17]. It was observed that the RMS was significantly increased after 40 s in the fatigue inducing session, and the RMS value of the fatigued muscle was higher than that of the first 5 s sustained contraction (Fig. 2 (a)). The increment of RMS was likely attributed to the recruitment of fresh motor units, which were used to compensate the reduced motor unit performance within fatigue inducing muscle [11,16,17]. The MDF of EMG signal showed a decrease trend and significant change was found from 10 s later during sustained muscle contraction. The decline in MDF indicated the compression of frequency spectrum. This phenomenon might be caused by the decreased conduction velocity of action potential [18], the signal power spectrum was thus shifted toward lower frequencies.

During the muscle fatigue process, the BV was increased because of blood accumulation and significant changes were appeared from 15 s during fatigue inducing session (Fig. 2 (b)). It was reasonable that blood flow was partially restricted during sustained muscle contraction [19], thus it was the accumulation of blood that increased the BV during the fatigue process. The concentration change of HbO_2 ($\triangle HbO_2$) showed a fast decline phase at the beginning of sustained muscle contraction and then reached a plateau in the fatigue inducing session. These phenomena indicated a rapidly decrease in muscle oxygen haemoglobin saturation due to oxygen consumption. Subsequently, anaerobic metabolism might occur because of inadequate oxygen supply.

3.2   Correlation Analysis Among Fatigue Metrics

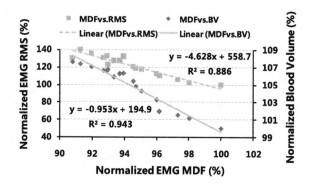

Fig. 3. The correlation and linear regression among fatigue metrics. The MDF is measured on the horizontal axis, the RMS is on the left side of the vertical axis, and the BV is displayed on the right side.

Correlation and regression analysis were performed to investigate the relationship between RMS, MDF and BV, which were extracted from the fatigue inducing and fatigued sessions, as shown in Fig. 3. A linear negative correlation was found between BV and MDF ($R^2 = 0.943$), as well as between RMS and MDF ($R^2 = 0.886$). It was known that BV was highly related to muscular blood flow and $\triangle HbO_2$ reflected muscle oxidative metabolism. The slow fluctuation phase of $\triangle HbO_2$ (Fig. 2 (b)) might result from the restriction of blood flow and inadequate oxygen supply, which led to anaerobic metabolism. Physiologically, the anaerobic metabolism and blood flow restriction caused the accumulation of lactic acid. Thus, the intracellular PH and conduction velocity of action potential were decreased, which was correlated to the decline of EMG MDF [16,18]. Therefore, the variation of BV provided a supportive interpretation for the compression of EMG frequency spectrum.

RMS and MDF represented muscular fatigue in the time domain and frequency domain of EMG, respectively. The relation between the changes of RMS and MDF during the fatigue process could explain the fatigue mechanism with EMG more comprehensively. Furthermore, EMG and NIRS applied together provided much more reliable and detailed information about muscle fatigue, gaining a insightful understanding of fatigue mechanisms: from the perspective of electrophysiology, hemodynamic (blood flow) and oxidative metabolic. Based on the relations of fatigue metrics, modified features would have potential to compensate the deteriorated HMI performance under muscle fatigue scenario.

3.3   Classification Performance Under Different Fatigue Scenario

The classification performance within unfatigued session and fatigued session using four different feature sets was given in Fig. 4. Generally, under unfatigued condition, the pattern recognition accuracy to classify five hand movements was above 90% regardless of feature set selection. Additionally, although the muscle was fatigued, the classification accuracy was not influenced when both the training data and testing data were from fatigued session. This result indicated that the EMG and NIRS signals of fatigued muscles were stable for pattern classification.

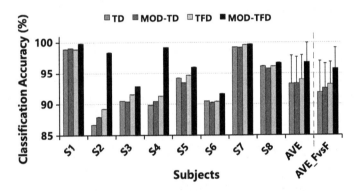

Fig. 4. The classification accuracy (CA) within unfatigued session and fatigued session using four feature sets. Note that the AVE_FvsF is the average CA of fatigued session, with both the training data and testing data from fatigued muscles.

However, using the LDA model trained by unfatigued muscles, the classification accuracy was significantly decreased in fatigue inducing and fatigued sessions, as shown in Fig. 5. Based on EMG TD features, the MOD-TD and TFD feature sets that combined MDF could not improve the accuracy. Since the MDF also fluctuated during muscle fatigue, adding MDF to TD feature set directly (TFD) provided worthless information for pattern classification. In spite of the correlation between MDF and RMS, modifying TD by multiplying MDF

(MOD-TD) was invalid to improve the classification performance. The classification performance was partially compensated using MOD-TFD feature set, although this slight accuracy improvement was still inadequate. The effectiveness of MOD-TFD was attributed to the modified term using MDF multiplied by BV.

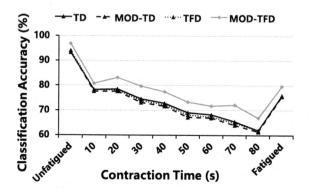

Fig. 5. The classification accuracy of sustained contraction muscles and fatigued muscles. Note that the classifier is trained using the data from unfatigued session, and is tested by unfatigued session, fatigue inducing session and fatigued session, respectively. During the fatigue inducing session, the CA is calculated and averaged every 10 s.

3.4 Correlation Analysis Between Fatigue Metrics and Classification Performance

The results of correlation and linear regression analysis between classification accuracy and fatigue metrics were shown in Fig. 6. All the variations of three fatigue metrics had strong linear correlation ($R^2 \geq 0.9$) with the degeneration of classification performance during muscular fatigue. The fatigue metrics comprehensively explained the deterioration mechanism of CA due to muscle fatigue. Specifically, the RMS represented the time domain information of EMG, and a increasing trend was found during fatigue inducing process. The MDF reflected the frequency information of EMG, manifesting a decline along with the sustained muscle contraction. On the other hand, BV related to muscular blood flow showed increase due to restriction. It was likely that the fluctuation of fatigue metrics led to the degeneration of classification accuracy. Thus, the fatigue metrics extracted from hybrid EMG and NIRS indicated the effect mechanism of muscle fatigue on HMI performance.

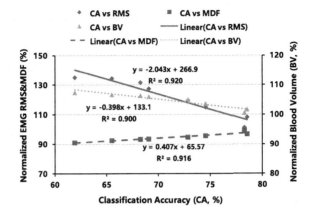

Fig. 6. The correlation and linear regression between CA and fatigue metrics. The CA is measured on the horizontal axis, the RMS and MDF of EMG are on the left side of the vertical axis, and the BV is displayed on the right side. Note that the CA is calculated with the TD feature set of EMG.

4 Conclusion

This paper presents the research study of muscular fatigue effect on HMI performance through the fusion of EMG and NIRS. The four fatigue metrics extracted from EMG and NIRS provide more detailed and reliable physiological interpretation about muscle fatigue. The fatigue metrics variations uncover the deterioration mechanism of pattern classification performance during fatigue process. Modified features from hybrid EMG and NIRS can partially compensate fatigue effect, but it is still a challenge to adopt HMI under muscle fatigue scenario. Therefore, high-level sustained muscle contraction should be avoided in HMI usage.

Acknowledgment. The authors would like to thank all the subjects for participating in the experiments. This work is supported in part by the China National Key R&D Program (Grant No. 2018YFB1307200), the National Natural Science Foundation of China (Grant No. 51905339, 91948302).

References

1. Farina, D., et al.: The extraction of neural information from the surface EMG for the control of upper-limb prostheses: emerging avenues and challenges. IEEE Trans. Neural Syst. Rehabil. Eng. **22**(4), 797–809 (2014)
2. Dipietro, L., Ferraro, M., Palazzolo, J.J., Krebs, H.I., Volpe, B.T., Hogan, N.: Customized interactive robotic treatment for stroke: emg-triggered therapy. IEEE Trans. Neural Syst. Rehabil. Eng. **13**(3), 325–334 (2005)
3. Ferreira, A., Silva, R., Celeste, W., Bastos Filho, T.F., Sarcinelli Filho, M.: Human-machine interface based on muscular and brain signals applied to a robotic wheelchair. J. Phys. Conf. Ser. **90**, 012094–012101 (2007)

4. Rosen, J., Brand, M., Fuchs, M.B., Arcan, M.: A myosignal-based powered exoskeleton system. IEEE Trans. Syst. Man Cybern. A **31**(3), 210–222 (2001)
5. Lee, S., Sankai, Y.: Power assist control for walking aid with HAL-3 based on EMG and impedance adjustment around knee joint. In: IEEE/RSJ International Conference on Intelligent Robots and Systems, vol. 2, pp. 1499–1504. IEEE (2002)
6. Tkach, D., Huang, H., Kuiken, T.A.: Research study of stability of time-domain features for electromyographic pattern recognition. J. NeuroEng. Rehabil. **7**, 21 (2010)
7. Cifrek, M., Medved, V., Tonković, S., Ostojić, S.: Surface EMG based muscle fatigue evaluation in biomechanics. Clin. Biomech. **24**(4), 327–340 (2009)
8. Artemiadis, P.K., Kyriakopoulos, K.J.: An EMG-based robot control scheme robust to time-varying EMG signal features. IEEE Trans. Inf. Technol. Biomed. **14**(3), 582–588 (2010)
9. Lalitharatne, T.D., Hayashi, Y., Teramoto, K., Kiguchi, K.: Compensation of the effects of muscle fatigue on EMG-based control using fuzzy rules based scheme. In: Engineering in Medicine and Biology Society (EMBC), 2013 35th Annual International Conference of the IEEE, pp. 6949–6952. IEEE (2013)
10. Song, J.H., Jung, J.W., Lee, S.W., Bien, Z.: Robust EMG pattern recognition to muscular fatigue effect for powered wheelchair control. J. Intell. Fuzzy Syst. **20**(1), 3–12 (2009)
11. Felici, F., Quaresima, V., Fattorini, L., Sbriccoli, P., Filligoi, G.C., Ferrari, M.: Biceps brachii myoelectric and oxygenation changes during static and sinusoidal isometric exercises. J. Electromyogr. Kines. **19**(2), e1–e11 (2009)
12. Ito, K., Hotta, Y.: EMG-based detection of muscle fatigue during low-level isometric contraction by recurrence quantification analysis and monopolar configuration. In: Engineering in Medicine and Biology Society (EMBC), 2012 Annual International Conference of the IEEE, pp. 4237–4241. IEEE (2012)
13. Guo, W., Sheng, X., Liu, H., Zhu, X.: Development of a multi-channel compact-size wireless hybrid sEMG/NIRS sensor system for prosthetic manipulation. IEEE Sens. J. **16**(2), 447–456 (2016)
14. Guo, W., Sheng, X., Zhu, X.: Assessment of muscle fatigue by simultaneous sEMG and NIRS: from the perspective of electrophysiology and hemodynamics. In: International IEEE EMBS Conference on Neural Engineering (NER) (2017)
15. Englehart, K., Hudgins, B.: A robust, real-time control scheme for multifunction myoelectric control. IEEE Trans. Biomed. Eng. **50**(7), 848 (2003)
16. Yoshitake, Y., Ue, H., Miyazaki, M., Moritani, T.: Assessment of lower-back muscle fatigue using electromyography, mechanomyography, and near-infrared spectroscopy. Eur. J. Appl. Physiol. **84**(3), 174–179 (2001)
17. Shi, J., Zheng, Y.P., Chen, X., Huang, Q.H.: Assessment of muscle fatigue using sonomyography: muscle thickness change detected from ultrasound images. Med. Eng. Phys. **29**(4), 472–479 (2007)
18. Farina, D., Pozzo, M., Merlo, E., Bottin, A., Merletti, R.: Assessment of average muscle fiber conduction velocity from surface EMG signals during fatiguing dynamic contractions. IEEE Trans. Biomed. Eng. **51**(8), 1383–1393 (2004)
19. Shadgan, B., Reid, W.D., Gharakhanlou, R., Stothers, L., Macnab, A.J.: Wireless near-infrared spectroscopy of skeletal muscle oxygenation and hemodynamics during exercise and ischemia. Spectroscopy **23**(5–6), 233–241 (2009)

A Wearable Multi-channel Sensor System Combined with Video Image Synchronization for Skiing Training

Shufan Gao[1,2] and Jingeng Mai[1(✉)]

[1] College of Engineering, Peking University, Beijing 100871, China
jingengmai@pku.edu.cn
[2] School of Telecommunication Engineering, Xidian University, Xian 710071, China

Abstract. This paper presents the design and implementation of a wearable multi-channel sensor system for skiing training. The hardware consists of several wearable sensors including inertial measurement units, foot pressure sensors and positioning module. This system also includes a visualization software platform for video image synchronization and 3D skeleton visualization. This system was implemented for collecting angle data with seven posture sensor modules, foot-bottom interaction data with pressure sensors, position data with global positioning sensor. The software was designed for data collecting, store, replay and visualization. Posture data and foot pressure data were sampled synchronously by hardware, and transmitted to the computer with data package. And posture data was combined with video image replay with time aligning operation on the software platform. The proposed hardware and software system were tested and verified preliminarily with a snowboarder volunteer.

Keywords: Wearable sensor · Posture sensor · Foot pressure sensor · Skiing

1 Introduction

Wearable sensors play an important role in scientific trainings of many sport competitions. Small size, light weight and little influence on movement are the advantages of wearable sensor in sports application. For example, inertial measurement unit (IMU) was applied for ski skating [1] and for fencing [2] analysis also. Besides, IMU was also used to collect data for analyzing jump load of youth basketball players [3], or quantification of motion in judo [4]. And for some sports with repetitive movements, such as paddling, IMU sensor maybe also a useful tool [5].

Foot-bottom pressure has been used for motion analysis and injury analysis and recover [6]. In aspect of video and other virtual analysis technology, both training and competition were proposed for analyzing athletes' motion and reaction [7]. Besides, GPS has also been used for some long-range sports, such as orienteering and marathon [8].

Skiing is a sport that requires a combination of physical strength and skill, and it is very important to get scientific analysis in training. There were some attempts combing

© Springer Nature Switzerland AG 2021
X.-J. Liu et al. (Eds.): ICIRA 2021, LNAI 13013, pp. 813–821, 2021.
https://doi.org/10.1007/978-3-030-89095-7_77

IMUs and plantar pressure distribution sensors for analyzing ski skills [9–11], but lack of considering positioning sensor and video image synchronization method.

In this paper, we proposed a wearable multi-sensor system combing IMUs, foot pressure sensors, positioning module. This system also includes a visualization software platform for video image synchronization and 3D skeleton visualization.

2   Hardware Design

2.1   Structure of the System

Hardware system consists of several modules, including seven posture sensor modules, two foot-bottom pressure sensors, one positioning module, one video module and one data collection module. The motion attitude sensor modules are designed for collecting attitude angle and acceleration by fastened to athletes' legs and waists with belts or ski suits and sending data to the data collection module through Bluetooth. The foot-bottom pressure sensors are designed to be in ski boots to collect multi-channel pressure data to the data collection module with Bluetooth. Positioning module is designed for collecting locating and speed information to the data collection module (Fig. 1).

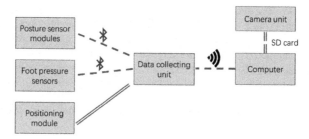

Fig. 1. Hardware system structure.

2.2   Posture Sensor Module

Posture sensor module is designed for body posture measurement based on real-time calculation of human body's three-axis attitude angles and accelerations by using triaxial accelerometer and gyroscope. This hardware module includes a power source management circuit, a communication circuit and a IMU collection and processing circuit. Power source management circuit which is powered by 3.7 V lithium battery provides voltage, charge-discharge protection, voltage monitoring and switch control functions. IMU collection and processing circuit is used to gather 3-dimension motion attitude data (sampling frequency of 100 Hz) from strap-down mode IMU chip, process data analytically through micro-control unit and transmit data scheduled. This circuit uses acquisition chip for IMU specially, it joints three-axis accelerometer, three-axis gyroscope, three-axis magnetometer, and some other sensors. Through its unique algorithm correction and data fusion calculations, this circuit could provide accurate data includes

Eulerian angles and accelerations. Micro-control unit uses new ultra-low power consumption micro controller of ST Microelectronics company's STM32L series. With frequency of 80 MHz, 100DMIPS is attainable for the CPU. Besides, its low power consumption peripheral devices (LPUART, LP timer), safety and secrecy could satisfy the requirement completely (Fig. 2).

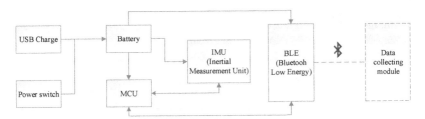

Fig. 2. Posture sensor module scheme.

2.3 Foot-Bottom Pressure Sensor Module

Foot-bottom pressure sensor module is designed to measure athletes' gait symmetry and pressure distribution while walking. This module is consisted of a pressure shoe-pad, a power source management circuit, a signal collection and processing circuit and a communication circuit. Pressure shoe-pad is a shoe-pad with thin film pressure sensor covered, its theory is that when the pressure sensor coating be pressed, coating's resistance will change with ambient pressure, after conditioning and collecting to electrical signals, pressure and pressure distribution can be gotten. Power source management circuit uses 3.7 V lithium battery to provide voltage, charge-discharge protection, voltage monitoring and switch control functions. Signal collection and processing circuit uses op-amp chip AD8618 with low noseband low bias to realize signal conditioning so that suitable voltage that used on micro controller collection can be gotten. Micro-control unit uses new ultra-low power consumption micro controller of ST company's STM32L series (Fig. 3).

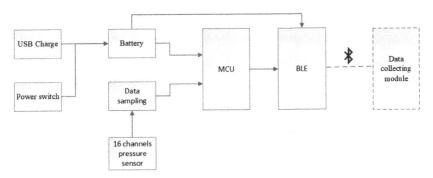

Fig. 3. Hardware system structure.

For software, row and column scan is used to gather pressure data from sixteen channels in total circularly. Adding software lowpass filter to get rid of signal noise so that pressure data from sixteen channels can be output timely with the update rate of 10 mS.

2.4 Positioning Module

Positioning module uses high accuracy GNSS unit based on ZED-F9P chip which support signals from GPS, GLONASS, Galileo and Bei Dou navigation system simultaneously. This module includes one mobile station and one base station. Mobile station works as a sensor powered by battery on human body which could collect body's velocity and position while base station works as providing reference coordinates. The connection between mobile station and base station is wireless so that differential positioning can be realized.

2.5 Video Module

Shooting the whole process by camera, and stores in the SD card to form film files. The recommend video velocity is 100 Hz at least. This file could be used to guide into the software. After calibration based on real time data from sensors, synchronous playback will be available.

2.6 Data Collection Module

This module includes power source management circuit, Bluetooth receiver circuit, data analysis and store circuit and WIFI wireless communication circuit. Power source

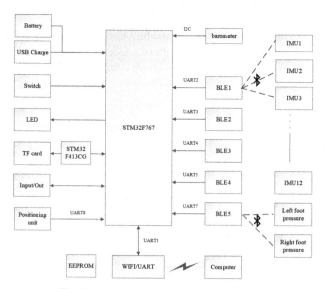

Fig. 4. Structure of data collection module.

management circuit change the battery (3.7 V lithium battery) voltage to the direct voltage (5 V and 3.3 V) that follow-up circuits need. Bluetooth receiver circuit has five Bluetooth units, and can receive twelve groups of data from motion attitude sensor modules and two groups of data from foot-bottom pressure sensor modules, with 10 mS data transmission interval. Data analysis and store circuit receives data groups about motion attitude, foot-bottom pressure and position which come from 110 channels in total. It also packages real time data and stores data through UART transmission and TF card so that later analysis will be convenient. WIFI wireless communication circuit transmits packaged data reliably and stably to the display interface of upper computer to reach high-level human-computer interaction. Micro-control chooses high-level ARM chip of STI company's STM32F7 series. This chip is based on Cortex-M7 core with 216 MHz dominant frequency, eight interface resources like UART, SDMMC, FMC, SPI, I2C and so on. So, it can satisfy multiple channel synchronously collecting and storing requirement (Fig. 4).

3   Software Design

3.1   Structure of the Software System

In order to realizing the data collecting and visualization analysis of wearable posture sensors, foot-bottom pressure sensors, positioning sensors and videos, a visualization software platform was designed.

The main functions of the platform include data receive, data store, 3D skeleton model visualization and arthrosis angle analysis. This platform could align posture data and video timely so that synchronous playback function was realized, and motion posture data was mapped into a 3D skeleton model for real-time or historic data 3D visualization of the motion. And this 3D visualization function was based on OpenGL engine (Fig. 5).

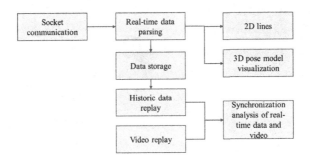

Fig. 5. Function block diagram

3.2   Motion Data and Video Image Aligning Method

Motion posture data acquisition supports two sampling forms: Socket and COM, with sampling frequency of 100 Hz. Data format is a hexadecimal data frame. Data packet is in set-long form, and data includes waist angles, left and right thigh angles, left and right crus angles, each angle data is in Float form. Making an appointment with athlete that waist angle (fore rake) should be about ninety degrees and rise right arm at the beginning of the whole race when sampling. Besides, video shooting will be started and this specific action will be captured to correspond with the time of posture sensors' data. When video being displayed, synchronization parameter setting can be accomplished through this specific action. And in the later display, the display will be synchronized according to the frequency of video collection (obtained by software) and the sampling frequency of motion data (100 Hz).

3.3   Three-Dimension Visualization Driven By Real Time Data

Three-dimension visualization was implemented with 3D skeleton model loading with SMD file, with Cartesian coordinates pitch, yaw and roll standardized inside. Pitch rotates around x-axis; yaw rotates around y-axis and roll rotates around z-axis. The procedure of initializing posture calibration is athlete needs to stand erectly, and then collecting data of pitch, yaw and roll angles at this time as calibration values. After calibration, the software platform can collect real time data of pitch, yaw and roll angles for 3D skeleton visualization. Finally, the three-dimension model of human body's bones was synchronize mapped with athlete's posture.

4   Implementation of the System

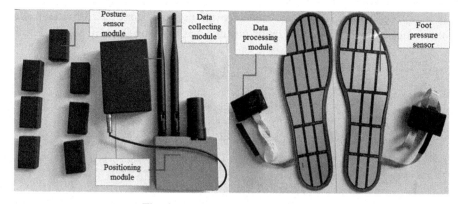

Fig. 6. Customized wearable sensors

As Fig. 6 shown above, sensor units and Bluetooth transmission units are integrated in a single PCB, and encapsulated in a nylon box which is xx * xx * xx cm with batteries inside and batteries' lives are x hours. Positioning module and data collection module are fastened on the waist. Foot-bottom pressure sensor's thickness is xx mm and connected with pressure collection module through FPC wire to provide different size of sensors for athletes with different foot size.

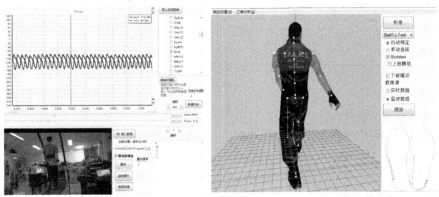

(a) Real time data synchronizing with video   (b) Human posture visualization

Fig. 7. Data collection and visualization platform

Figure 7 shows the data collection and visual software system designed. Real time data includes attitude angle, acceleration, position and foot-bottom pressure with 110 channels in total. Real time data and video's synchronous operation is available so that any time of the video and the time of the real-time data are uniformly equivalent within the error range. Besides, human posture visual module also supports synchronous actions for real time or history data.

5   Preliminary Result

The proposed system was tested preliminarily by a volunteer. He is 22-year-old, 86 kg weight and 175 cm height, and with amputation of right thigh. Seven posture sensors are fastened on ski boots, cruses, thighs and back for both sane leg and handicapped leg. Figure 8(a) shows method on fixing sensors, Fig. 8(b) shows number of posture sensors and meanings of angles. Foot-bottom pressure sensors are out inside boots and positing module and data collection box are fixed on back through braids.

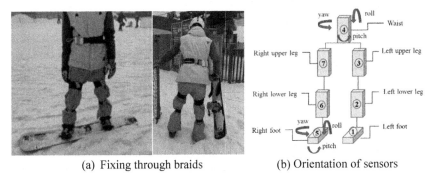

(a) Fixing through braids   (b) Orientation of sensors

Fig. 8. Binding of posture sensors

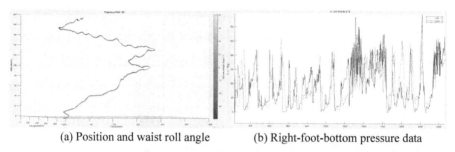

(a) Position and waist roll angle   (b) Right-foot-bottom pressure data

Fig. 9. Data of posture sensors and foot pressure sensors

Figure 9(a) shows roll angle data from waist posture sensor, and Fig. 9(b) shows pressure data of left-foot-bottom. Because of collecting sixteen channels of foot-bottom pressure from right foot, we sum up data from nine sensors in the front as forefoot data and six sensors as heel data in order to getting intuitive data.

6   Conclusion

We designed a wearable hardware sensor system for sampling motion posture data, position, and foot-bottom data. And software system for real time data collection, store, payback, and three-dimension visual human posture was also designed. A prototype of hardware and software was proposed to use in athletes, and shows that synchronous visual analysis of multiple sensors' data is feasible.

7   Future Work

In the future, more data and deeper analyses would be available based on this system. Such as collecting data from different athletes to analysis connection between individual posture characteristics and grades, collecting data from one athlete in different phases of training to analysis training effects and collecting data that athletes using different artificial limbs or artificial limbs with different parameters to analysis whether there are potential differences between different artificial limbs and grades.

Acknowledgments. This work was supported by the National Key Research and Development Program of China (No. 2018YFF0300606).

References

1. Myklebust, H., Gløersen, Ø., Hallén, J.: Validity of ski skating center-of-mass displacement measured by a single inertial measurement unit. J. Appl. Biomech. **31**(6), 492–498 (2015)
2. Malawski, F.: Depth versus inertial sensors in real-time sports analysis: a case study on fencing. IEEE Sens. J. **4**, 5133–5142 (2021)

3. Benson, L., Tait, T., Befus, K., et al.: Validation of a commercially available inertial measurement unit for recording jump load in youth basketball players. J. Sports Sci. **38**(8), 928–936 (2020)
4. Frassinelli, S., Niccolai, A., Zich, R.E., et al.: Quantification of motor abilities during the execution of Judo techniques. Acta Bioeng. Biomech. **21**(3), 3–12 (2019)
5. Udagawa, Y., Hashimoto, T., Kikuchi, N.: Development of motion sensor system for kayak paddlers. In: The Proceedings of JSME Annual Conference on Robotics and Mechatronics (Robomec) 2018, 2P2-F07 (2018)
6. Qi, C., Wang, L., Li, C.: Synchronizel study on IEMG and foot pressure of jump shoot for young basketball athletes. J. Tianjin Univ. Sport **5**, 422–424, 429 (2010)
7. Singh, P., Aggarwal, R., Tahir, M., Pucher, P.H., Darzi, A.: A randomized controlled study to evaluate the role of video-based coaching in training laparoscopic skills. Ann. Surg. **261**(5), 862–869 (2015)
8. Hodun, M., Clarke, R., De Ste Croix, M.B., Hughes, J.D.: Global positioning system analysis of running performance in female field sports. Strength Conditioning J. **38**(2), 49–56 (2016)
9. Matsumura, S., Ohta, K., Yamamoto, S.-I., Koike, Y., Kimura, T.: Comfortable and convenient turning skill assessment for Alpine Skiers using IMU and plantar pressure distribution sensors. (Basel Switzerland) **21**(3), 834 (2021)
10. Yu, G., et al.: Potential of IMU sensors in performance analysis of professional Alpine Skiers. Sensors **16**, 463 (2016)
11. Martínez, A., Jahnel, R., Buchecker, M., Snyder, C., Brunauer, R., Stöggl, T.: Development of an automatic Alpine Skiing turn detection algorithm based on a simple sensor setup. Sensors **19**(4), 902 (2019)

Author Index